Readers as well as television and radio audiences are constantly being bombarded with names of places, people and things. No one can be familiar with all these references—ancient and modern. But now in this one volume, we have a carefully selected, handy guide to those proper names which are most frequently encountered.

The Merriam-Webster Pocket Dictionary of Proper Names was originally published under the title **Webster's Dictionary of Proper Names** by G. & C. Merriam Company.

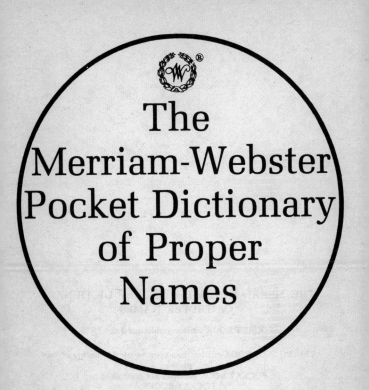

The Merriam-Webster Pocket Dictionary of Proper Names

compiled by

Geoffrey Payton

PUBLISHED BY POCKET BOOKS NEW YORK

THE MERRIAM-WEBSTER POCKET DICTIONARY OF PROPER NAMES

POCKET BOOK edition published July, 1972

This POCKET BOOK edition has been printed from brand-new plates.
POCKET BOOK editions are published by
POCKET BOOKS,
a division of Simon & Schuster, Inc.,
A GULF+WESTERN COMPANY
630 Fifth Avenue,
New York, N.Y. 10020.
Trademarks registered in the United States
and other countries.

Printed in the U.S.A.

To Mary,
without whose constant encouragement
and advice this book would have been
finished in half the time

PREFACE

The purpose of this book, which is believed to be unique, is to help readers through the barrage of proper names with which we are daily bombarded by journalists, broadcasters, novelists and even the man next door. We are expected to know the difference, for instance, between the DRS. NO, STRANGE LOVE, ZHIVAGO and JEKYLL; between FANNY MAE and FANNIE FARMER; DIAMOND JIM and DIAMOND LIL; BILLY THE KID, BILLY BUDD and BILLY MITCHELL; BLUEBEARD, BLUE BIRD, BLUE EAGLE and the BLUE TAIL FLY. How can we keep up with the JONESES if we are not on first-name terms with BUSTER and CHARLIE BROWN; or with the Joneses' children if we don't know BRER RABBIT from UNCLE WIGGILY, MISS BIANCA from THE MOUSE THAT ROARED?

Then again there are, alas, all those things which, unlike MACAULAY'S SCHOOLBOY, we don't know about, although we feel we ought to: the Battle of ACTIUM, the CONGRESS OF VIENNA, the BASTILLE, or the BOXER MOVEMENT. Who dare admit to an Irishman with three BOILERMAKERS in him that he can't remember a thing about the BOYNE; to a Scot awash with GLENLIVET that he thought BLUIDIE CLAVERS and BONNY DUNDEE met in single combat at CULLODEN? The Britisher who takes BULL RUN for a baseball term can be matched with the American who thinks that LORD'S is reserved for peers of the realm. And many a housewife must wish she knew what the Brooklyn DODGERS are doing in LA, whether a SOLING is an underprivileged DOVER SOLE, and can she make PEACH MELBA with GEORGIA PEACH. As for the aspiring Congressman who cannot pick up a reference to the Jack Acid Society (see POGO)—he will never get nominated.

The list is endless; the dictionaries don't help; only a roomful of reference books could save us from embarrassment. Hence this book. It is aimed at all ages and all walks of life: the child who has missed the joys of the WIZARD OF OZ; the professor at home in the PARTHENON, but all at sea with POSEIDON missiles; JOE DOAKES, who knows more of BABE RUTH than of RUTH DRAPER or RUTH amid the alien corn; the browser, the journalist, the librarian—the lot.

The critical will not fail to notice that the author, in ranging from prehistory to 1984—and even 2001: A SPACE ODYSSEY—has stretched the term "proper names" to its furthest limits (and indeed far beyond). Others may ask: why all the Greek mythology? (answer: because it crops up in so many plays and operas, and even on the psychiatrist's couch); why the foreign names? (because vacationing abroad has become so popular); why the Biblical names? (because Biblical allusions remain embedded in our language long after compulsory Bible-study has been abandoned; and there are, after all, quite a lot of people who speak or read English but are not Christians).

The book is selective. It has to be; there is no reason why a book on these lines should not extend to several volumes, but selection according to rigid rules would have compelled the inclusion of boring or trivial entries for the sake of consistency alone. The author has therefore been forced to make a *highly personal choice* of names which he thinks are likely to be useful or interesting. It must be stressed that this is in no way a dictionary of potted biographies, nor is it a gazetteer of place-names.

The preparation for press of a work of this scope calls for omniscient readers, and in this connection the author wishes to thank, among others, Miss Ervina E. Foss and Mrs. Doris N. Sherwood of Springfield, Mass., Donald van Eman of Arcadia, Calif., John Lucas and Patrice Charvet of Gloucestershire, Eng., whose combined wisdom proved invaluable.

As a further guide, to give the reader a general idea of what he may hope to find in this book, a list of some of the main subject categories, with a few examples, follows.

Geoffrey Payton
South Zeal

A SELECTION OF THE
SUBJECT CATEGORIES

AIRCRAFT: MiG, Galaxy, Concorde, F-111, Jumbo jet, Ling-Temco-Vought.

ANIMALS: Boston Terrier, Palomino horse, Dan Patch, Charbray, Lipizzaners, Cheshire Cat, Suffolk Punch.

ANTIQUES and ANTIQUITIES: Mary Gregory glass, Bennington ware, Meissen, Empire style, Duncan Phyfe, Parke-Bernet, Terry, T'ang dynasty, Montezuma Castle, Cardiff Giant.

ARMED FORCES: Thunderbirds, VMI, Pinkville massacre, Rand Corporation, Van Doos, OSS, USO, Seabees.

ARTS: "Watson and the Shark," Sistine Madonna, "Guernica," Grandma Moses, Rube Goldberg, "Broadway Boogie-Woogie," Currier & Ives, Les Fauves, Bauhaus, "The Twittering Machine."

ASTRONOMY: Big Bang theory, Mount Palomar Observatory, Betelgeuse, Jodrell Bank.

BALLET: *Appalachian Spring, Petrushka, Coppélia, Rodeo.*

BIBLE: Balaam's Ass, Susanna and the Elders, Dead Sea Scrolls, Tophet, Septuagint.

BIG BUSINESS: Dun & Bradstreet, Procter & Gamble, The Thundering Herd, Sumitomo group, Alcan, IG Farben, Seven Sisters.

BROADCASTING: Huntley-Brinkley Report, Allen's Alley, CATV, PTV, PBL, TW3, Voice of America.

CLUBS: Friars, Drones', Crockford's, Hellfire, Royal and Ancient.

COMICS: *Gasoline Alley,* Milquetoast, Dagwood, Jiggs, Popeye, Krazy Kat, Snoopy, *Alphonse and Gaston,* Fearless Fosdick.

CRIME and PUNISHMENT: Sharon Tate murders, Boston Strangler, Murder Inc., Charlie Chan, Pinkerton's, Brink's robbery, Lizzie Borden, Burgess and Maclean, Jack the Ripper, Lucky Luciano.

ECONOMICS: Eurobond, Kennedy Round, Dow Jones averages, Faceless Gnomes of Zurich, Phillips curve, EFTA, Parkinson's law.

EDUCATION: Chautauqua, Cooper Union, Dotheboys Hall, Cal. Tech., Pestalozzi system, Atlantic College, Dewey educational system.

FEASTS and FESTIVALS: Sadie Hawkins Day, Groundhog Day, Mardi Gras, Fasching, Oberammergau, Edinburgh and Aldeburgh festivals, Tanglewood.

FICTION: Walter Mitty, Miss Matty, Leopold Bloom, Raskolnikov, Frodo Baggins, Hopalong Cassidy, Sam Slick, *Candida, Candide, Ship of Fools,* "The Devil and Daniel Webster," Studs Lonigan trilogy, *Saratoga Trunk, The Lady or the Tiger?,* "The Legend of Sleepy Hollow," *The Thin Man, The Maltese Falcon, Fahrenheit 451.*

FOOD and DRINK: Canadian bacon, Manhattan clam chowder,

Baked Alaska, Wimpy, Eggs Benedict, Oysters Rockefeller, Stroganoff, Antoine's, Top of the Sixes, VSOP, Daiquiri, Slivovitz, Calvados.

HISTORY: Six-day War, *Pueblo* incident, Bay of Pigs, Munich, Massey Report, Dachau, Comintern, Tontons Macoute, French and Indian War, Whiskey Rebellion, Trail of Tears, Gadsden Purchase, The Defenestration, Diaspora, Battle of Shiloh, Sitting Bull, Chicago fire, Golden Spike.

INITIALS: TGIF, MIK, UFO, FFV, FHA, FHB, TLC, VX, K of C, PDQ.

INSTITUTIONS: Interpol, CIA, World Bank, Unicef, KGB, Cinque Ports.

LEGEND: Babe the Blue Ox, Valkyries, "The Arkansas Traveller," Guinevere, Mike Fink, Deirdre, Daphnis and Chloe, Pecos Bill, Prometheus, Wandering Jew, Febold Feboldson.

LITERARY ALLUSIONS: Yoknapatawpha County, 007, Horatio Alger, Grand Fenwick, Time-style, One-Upmanship, *Bardell v. Pickwick*, Big- and Little-endians, Mr. Dooley, Admass.

LOCAL NAMES: Haight-Ashbury, Seventh Avenue, Golden Triangle, Back Bay, Beekman Place, Metro Centre, Ponte Vecchio, Petit Trianon, Street Called Straight, Tokaido Line, Metroliner, Ho Chi Minh trail, Carnaby Street, Boul' Mich', Watts, Lombard Street Curlicue, Fisherman's Wharf, Neiman-Marcus, Fraunces Tavern, The Block, Marina City, Sunset Strip.

LONDON: Big Ben, Downing Street, Old Lady of Threadneedle Street, The City, Burlington House, Marble Arch, Inns of Court, Pall Mall.

MEDICAL: Salk vaccine, Chinese restaurant syndrome, ACTH, The Pill, Phaedra complex, Freudian slip, Medex, MSG.

MISSILES: ICBM, Minuteman, ABM, BMEWS, SS9.

MOVIES: *Bonnie and Clyde*, Rin-Tin-Tin, *The Graduate*, Battleship Potemkin, Cinerama, *The Four Horsemen of the Apocalypse*, Cannes Film Festival.

MUSEUMS, LIBRARIES, GALLERIES: Guggenheim Museum, Huntington Library, Bodleian, Uffizi, Prado.

MUSIC: *The Choral Symphony*, Moog, *Siegfried Idyll*, Dixieland jazz, Brandenburg Concertos, Boston Pops, 'Boléro', *Louisiana Story*, Julliard School, Leventritt Award, Satchmo.

NICKNAMES: Main Liner, Vinegar Joe, Swedish Nightingale, Papa Doc, Hell's Angels, The Law West of the Pecos, Jax, Typhoid Mary, Axis Sally, Arkie, Camille, Praise-God Barebones, Jersey Lily, Blood and Guts, Welsh Wizard, Sultan of Swat, Copperhead, Rail Splitter, Der Alte, "Stonewall" Jackson.

NUMBERS: "54-40 or Fight!," Forty and Eight, 49th Parallel, 49ers, 19th Amendment, Sixth Commandment, Fourth of July, Four Freedoms, Fourteen Points.

OPERA: Carmen, Carmen Jones, Götterdämmerung, Figaro, The Bartered Bride, Duke of Plaza-Toro, The Met, La Scala.

PEN NAMES etc.: Ellery Queen, Boz, Herblock, Elia, Leclerc.

PHILOSOPHY: Existentialism, Behaviorism, Hobbes's *Leviathan*, Neoplatonism.

PLACES: Evangeline country, Silesia, Badlands, Bessarabia, Colter's Hell, The Roaring Forties, Costa Blanca, Colonial Williamsburg, Bondi Beach, Corn Belt, Bible Belt, Natchez Trace, Baedeker.

POETRY and VERSE: "The Face Upon the Floor," "Annabel Lee," Xanadu, *archy and mehitabel*, *The Waste Land*, 'Casey Jones', 'Casey at the Bat', 'The Purple Cow', 'Quantrell', *Howl*, *The Courtship of Miles Standish*.

POLITICAL PHRASES: 'Tippecanoe and Tyler Too', Silent Majority, Manifest Destiny, Brinkmanship, Popular Front, Cliveden set, New Frontier, Clear Grit Reformers, Red Power, Tammany Hall.

POLITICS: El Fatah, New Left, Maoism, McCarthyism, Dawk, Christian Democrats, Social Democrats, Quai d'Orsay, Bleus, Duma, The Grange, Storting.

PREHISTORY: Hohokam culture, Tutankhamen's Tomb, Peking Man, Carbon-14 dating, Abu Simbel, Altamira, Sumerians, Stonehenge, Cro-Magnon Man.

PRESS: AP, UPI, *Christian Science Monitor*, Tass, Beaverbrook Press, Pyle Memorial Award.

PRIZES and MEDALS: Obie, Coty, Emmy, Eddie, Grammy, Pulitzer prizes, Purple Heart, Laetare Medal.

RACES and LANGUAGES: Ojibwa, Slavs, Slovak and Slovenian, Volapük, Tamil, Cape Coloureds.

REFERENCE BOOKS: DAB, DNB, *Interpreter's Bible*, *Almanach de Gotha*, Fowler.

RELIGION: Gideons, Fisherman's Ring, Little Church around the Corner, Rig-Veda, Christian Endeavor, *Pacem in terris*, Billy Sunday revivals, Cistercians, MRA, Papal Infallibility, Exclusive Brethren, Pentecostalism, Epworth League.

SCIENCE: Hudson Institute, Pugwash movement, Lamarckism, Appleton layer, Planck's constant, CERN, Boyle's law, Mendelism, Michelson-Morley experiment, Sealab, Cobol, $E = mc^2$, Lysenkoism, Scopes Trial.

SHIPS: *Mary Celeste, Nautilus, Merrimac* and *Monitor, Savannah, Cutty Sark, Discovery, Dreadnought,* Big Mo.

SLANG etc.: The real McCoy, The Harlot's Romp, Mickey Finn, Siwash, John Hancock, John Q. Public, John Law.

SOCIETIES etc.: Americans for Democratic Action, SDS, John Birch Society, Cosa Nostra, Black Muslims, B'nai B'rith, Lions clubs, Daughters of the American Revolution, KKK, Junior Achievement, Junior League.

SONGS: "Sweet Adeline!," "Frankie and Johnny," "Alexander's Ragtime Band," "Waltzing Matilda," "Lilliburlero," "Lilli Marlene."

SPACE AGE: Apollo space program, Comsat, *Soyuz, Early Bird,*

Mariner, Lunik, Telstar 1, Cosmos, Essa.

SPORTS and GAMES: Stanley Cup Playoffs, Ryder Cup, All-Star game, Big Ten, The Cresta, Dad Vail Regatta, Vail Cup, Fenway Park, NASCAR racing, Helms World Trophy, Heisman Trophy, Cy Young Award, Indy, Dan, Chisox, Soap Box Derby, House that Ruth Built, Acol system, Monopoly.

STATELY HOMES: Monticello, Hyde Park, The Enchanted Hill, The Hermitage, The Breakers, Fort Belvedere, Woburn Abbey.

THEATER: *The Lion in Winter, Marat/Sade, Hair,* Theater of the Absurd, Mr. Bones, *Hello, Dolly!,* Angry Young Man, *The Sound of Music, West Side Story,* Method acting, Lincoln Center, *Pal Joey, The Man Who Came to Dinner.*

TOWNS: Los Alamos, Tarsus, Brasilia, Chandigarh, Little Rock, Aldermaston.

TRADE UNIONS: AFL/CIO, Teamsters Union, Equity.

TRUE OR FALSE?: ESP, Cheiro, Tarot, Sister Aimee, Psi force, Gurdjieff's teachings, Borley Rectory, Mother Shipton.

UNIVERSITY TERMS: Whiffenpoof song, Ivy League, Seven Sisters, Phi Beta Kappa, Mayweek.

NOTES TO THE READER

Alphabetical order: Entry words are treated as if spelled out in full, e.g. VC-10 as vcten; 007 as ooseven; 18th amendment as eighteenth amendment; Mr. Bones as Mister Bones, etc.

Cross-references: Words in SMALL CAPITALS indicate references to main entries which appear in their appropriate alphabetical place.

Trademarks: The inclusion of a term in this dictionary is not to be taken as an expression of the publishers' opinion as to whether or not it is subject to proprietary rights, but only as an expression of their belief that such a term is of sufficiently general use and interest to warrant its inclusion in a work of this kind. No entry in this dictionary is to be regarded as affecting the validity of any trademark.

The
Merriam-Webster
Pocket Dictionary
of Proper
Names

A

AA (1) See ALCOHOLICS ANONYMOUS. (2) (UK) Automobile Association.

AAA (1) See AGRICULTURAL ADJUSTMENT ADMINISTRATION. (2) American Automobile Association. (3) (UK) Amateur Athletic Association, which controls all athletic (in the UK sense, track-and-field events only) events in England and Wales, including the AAA Championships at the White City, London, in July.

Aachen German name of Aix-la-Chapelle, Rhine-Westphalia.

Aaron Son of Levi and elder brother of Moses; he made the GOLDEN CALF (*Exodus* xxxii, 4), and in some traditions is the founder of the Jewish priesthood.

Aaron's rod Name given to various garden plants, including the goldenrod and mullein (*Numbers* xvii, 8).

Aase The mother of PEER GYNT, whose death is an important episode in Ibsen's play and in Grieg's incidental music.

AAU See AMATEUR ATHLETIC UNION.

AAUP Initials used for American Association of University Professors, an organization of university (and college) professors.

AAUW Initials used for American Association of University Women.

ABA See (1) AMERICAN BAR ASSOCIATION; (2) AMERICAN BASKETBALL ASSOCIATION.

Abadan crisis (1951) Caused by the nationalization of the Persian oil industry by Dr Mosadeq and the replacement of the ANGLO-IRANIAN OIL CO. by an international consortium. (Site of a large oil refinery in the Persian Gulf.)

Abbasids (750-1258) The dynasty of Caliphs who ruled at Baghdad after the massacre of the OMAYYADS.

Abbevillean culture Earliest of the PALEOLITHIC cultures, lasting perhaps from 500,000 to 400,000 BC, during which early forms of apelike creatures learned to make crude flint hand axes. (Abbeville, France; also called the Chellean culture.)

Abbey Theatre The Irish national theater, Dublin, founded in 1901. It was burned down in 1951 and re-opened in 1966.

Abbots Bromley Horn Dance (UK) A festival held in September at Abbots Bromley, west of Burton-on-Trent, with an elaborate and sinister dance by 6 men in Tudor costume carrying reindeer antlers, accompanied by Robin Hood and his men, and a hobbyhorse.

Abbotsbury Swannery (UK) Situated near the coast between Weymouth and Bridport, in the grounds of a 12th-century Benedictine abbey with subtropical gardens, open to the public.

Abbotsford Home of Sir Walter Scott, near Melrose, Roxburghshire.

ABC The American Broadcasting Company, one of the 3 coast-to-coast TV networks.

ABC Powers Sometimes used of the 3 leading South American states, Argentina, Brazil, Chile.

ABC-TV (UK) Until 1968 the commercial TV company that served Lancashire, Yorkshire and the Midlands at weekends; wholly owned by EMI's Associated British Pictures Corporation, which has several hundred (ABC) cinemas, and in which Warner Bros. has a large holding. In 1968 it merged with Associated Rediffusion as THAMES TV.

Abd Arabic for 'slave of', 'servant of', as in Abdallah (Abdullah), 'servant of God'; Abdulkadir, 'servant of the great one' (i.e. God).

Abderite, The Democritus, Greek philosopher of the 5th and 4th centuries BC. (Born at Abdera, Thrace.)

Abdication Crisis (1936) Caused by the decision of King Edward VIII (later Duke of Windsor) to abdicate rather than renounce his intention to marry the twice-divorced Mrs Simpson.

Abdul the Damned Abdul Hamid II, the Sultan of Turkey (1876-1909), a despotic ruler deposed by the YOUNG TURKS.

Abel The son of Adam and Eve, a shepherd killed by his elder brother, CAIN (*Genesis* iv, 8).

Abélard See HÉLOÏSE AND ABELARD

Abel spy case The Russian KGB colonel, Rudolf Abel, an expert on nuclear physics and missiles, was given a 30-year prison sentence for spying in the US (1957) but exchanged in 1962 for Garry Powers, the pilot in the U-2 INCIDENT, partly in order to discover whether the latter was, as the Russians claimed, shot down from 65,000 ft by a new type of rocket (he was).

Abercrombie & Fitch A store on Madison Avenue, NYC, particularly famous for its gun room, facilities for practicing fly-fishing, and for all kinds of sporting goods and attire. It helped to equip Byrd's and Theodore Roosevelt's expeditions and has been known to supply exigent customers with live reindeer and camel saddles. Another distinction was the introduction of mah-jongg to the Western world.

Aberdeen Angus The finest breed of beef cattle, black and polled.

Aberfan disaster (1966) (Wales) The death of nearly 150 persons, mostly children, caused when a slag heap, which had been built up to a dangerous height, slipped and overwhelmed part of the village of Aberfan, Glamorgan, including the school.

Abernethy A hard biscuit, flavored with caraway seed.

'Abide with Me' (1861) A famous hymn written by an English clergyman, H. F. Lyte; music by W. H. Monk.

Abie's Irish Rose (1922) A record-breaking play by Anne Nichols, her only famous work, a tears-and-laughter comedy about the tribulations of a young Jew and an Irish Catholic who get secretly married by a Methodist minister. Later the story was used for a novel, a movie and a radio series.

Abigail (1) 'Handmaid' and wife of David (I *Samuel* xxv); (2) a name given to maidservants in various plays and novels; (3) hence, a synonym for maidservant.

Abinger Harvest (1936) E. M. Forster's first collection of essays, on a variety of topics.

Abitur German equivalent of the GCE or French Baccalauréat. (Abbreviation of German *Abiturientenexamen*, 'examination of those about to depart', i.e. to the university; from Latin *abituri* 'those about to go'.)

ABM system Initials used for anti-ballistic missile system, e.g. the NIKE-X SYSTEM.

Abnaki A group of Algonquian tribes in Maine, who fought for the French against the English. About 2000 survive in Quebec and New Brunswick.

Abo Australian abbreviation for 'Aboriginal'.

ABO blood groups The 4 groups A, B, AB and O, to one of which everyone belongs. This is important (1) in blood transfusion, some groups being incompatible with others; (2) in ethnological research as the incidence of the groups varies from race to race; (3) in eliminating suspects in criminal cases where bloodstains are present. See RH FACTOR.

Abominable Snowman An unknown creature said to have been seen by Sherpas high up in the Himalayas; its presumed tracks have been described by several mountaineers. Also called Yeti. See SASQUATCH.

Aboukir Bay Scene of the Battle of the NILE in 1798.

Abraham The first Hebrew patriarch, who migrated with his wife Sarah and Lot from Ur of the Chaldees in Mesopotamia to the Promised Land of Canaan. Their son was ISAAC.

Abraham Lincoln (1) A biography by the poet Carl Sandburg, comprising 2 volumes subtitled *The Prairie Years* (1926) and 4 subtitled *The*

War Years (1939). (2) A play by John Drinkwater (1918).

Abraham-men See TOM O'BEDLAM.

Absalom Son of David, killed in a revolt against his father (II *Samuel* xv – xviii).

Absalom, Absalom! William Faulkner's chronicle (1936) of the rise and fall of the poor white Sutpen family in Mississippi, as seen through the eyes of 3 of the characters. (Title from David's lament in II *Samuel* xviii, 33.)

'Absalom and Achitophel' Dryden's satire, in which Absalom is the Duke of Monmouth. See MONMOUTH'S REBELLION.

'Absent-minded Beggar, The' Kipling's ballad of the soldiers who fought in the BOER WAR.

'Absinthe Drinkers, The' (1876) A study by Degas of a man and woman in a bistro, a picture of deep despair. (Louvre.)

Absolute, Sir Anthony In Sheridan's play *The Rivals*, the testy father of the young man who loves Lydia LANGUISH.

Abstract art A nonrepresentational form of art which, reacting against naturalism, stresses the aesthetic values of form, color and texture; leading exponents: Kandinski, Mondrian, Ben Nicholson.

Abstract Expressionism (Action Painting, Tachisme) An extreme form of ABSTRACT ART associated with the name of the American, Jackson Pollock, who covered vast canvases with splashes of paint.

Absurd, Theater of the (1950) A movement born in Paris, numbering Ionesco, Beckett and Pinter among its chief exponents. They stress the ludicrous irrationality of human conduct and beliefs.

Abu Simbel The Nile site in the Sudan near Wadi Halfa of rock temples built by Rameses II (1250 BC); the temples were moved in the 1960s to prevent submersion by the lake formed behind the ASWAN HIGH DAM.

Abydos (1) See SESTOS. (2) Ancient Egyptian city north of Thebes, with temples dating back to 3000 BC, including the Great Temple of Osiris of the 14th century BC.

Abyssinia Older name for the ancient African kingdom of Ethiopia. Derived from Arabic *Habashah*.

Academgorodok The 'Science City', site of the Academy of Sciences near Novosibirsk, Siberia.

Academic Festival Overture (1881) An overture composed by Brahms after he had received an honorary doctorate at Breslau University; it makes use of student songs, including GAUDEAMUS IGITUR.

Académie française (1635) The French Academy, restricted to 40 members ('The Immortals') chosen from distinguished men of letters, formed to preserve the purity of the French language, in particular by the compilation of a dictionary.

Academy awards Awards (principally OSCARS) made by the Academy of Motion Picture Arts and Sciences. See also EDDIE.

Acadia Early name for Nova Scotia, still preserved in the form Acadian for Nova Scotian. See FRENCH AND INDIAN WAR. (From name of local river.)

Acadia National Park (1919) A scenic, rugged coastal area on Mount Desert Island, Maine, the highest land (up to 1530 ft) on the Atlantic coast north of Rio; it also includes the picturesque Schoodic Point on the mainland, which is linked to the island by bridge.

Acapulco The chief center of the Mexican Riviera on the Pacific coast, a favorite winter resort for Americans.

Aceldama Name of the field of blood or potter's field bought with Judas's 30 pieces of silver, and used to bury strangers in (*Matthew* xxvii, 3-8 and *Acts* i, 19). (Hebrew, 'field of blood'.)

'A' certificate Granted by the British Board of Film Censors to films which until 1970 could be seen by children under 16 only if accompanied by an adult.

Achaeans A Bronze Age Greek race; the earliest references to them are in Hittite records from *c.* 1350 BC. They introduced chariots, bronze spears, helmets and armor. Homer used the name for Greeks in general.

Achaemenids (6th-4th centuries BC) A dynasty of Persian kings founded by Cyrus the Great, which extended Persian rule to the Indus and to Egypt; they included Darius and Xerxes. Defeated by Alexander the Great and succeeded by the SELEU-CIDS.

Achates In Virgil's *Aeneid* the companion of AENEAS, always called *fidus Achates*, faithful Achates.

Acheron In Greek legend the 'river of woe', one of the rivers of the Underworld.

Acheulean culture Second of the main PALEOLITHIC cultures, perhaps lasting from 400,000 to 150,000 BC, during which PITHECANTHROPINES in the Far East and in Africa learned to use fire and to make improved flint hand axes. (St Acheul, near Amiens, France.)

Achillea The genus name of yarrow. (Supposed, like Achilles' spear, to have curative powers.)

Achilles The Greek hero without whom Troy could not be taken. In the last year of the war his cousin Patroclus was killed by Hector, and this roused Achilles, who had retired sulking to his tent in a quarrel with Agamemnon about who should have the girl prisoner Briseis, to return to the fight and take his revenge on Hector, whose body he dragged round the walls of Troy. But Paris found his one vulnerable spot (see ACHILLES' HEEL) and killed him.

Achilles and the tortoise The 4th-century BC Greek philosopher Zeno's paradox: if Achilles runs 10 times faster than a tortoise which has a 100-yd start, then while Achilles runs 100 yd the tortoise runs 10; while Achilles runs these 10 yd the tortoise adds another yard, and so on. Thus, theoretically, Achilles can never catch up with it.

Achilles' heel A phrase derived from the Greek myth that his mother dipped ACHILLES in the Styx to make him invulnerable, but the heel she held him by was not immersed and remained his one vulnerable spot.

To it Apollo unsportingly guided an arrow shot by Paris.

Achilles statue A statue in Hyde Park, London, made from guns taken by the Duke of Wellington. It is in fact a copy of an Italian sculpture of some other hero.

Achilles tendon The tendon connecting the heel (see ACHILLES' HEEL) to the calf.

Achitophel Dryden's name, in AB-SALOM AND ACHITOPHEL, for the Earl of Shaftesbury, leader of the Whig (Country Party) opposition to the succession of the Catholic James II. See AHITHOPHEL.

Acis and Galatea In Greek mythology a Sicilian shepherd and his lass. POLYPHEMUS killed Acis as he wanted Galatea. The story is told by Ovid.

Acol system A calling system at Bridge, developed from the old Culbertson and Lederer systems. The only opening bid forcing to game is 2 Clubs. Hand valuation is by both point counts and quick tricks, and additions are made for suit length.

'Acres of Diamonds' A famous lecture on the theme: Everyone can and should get rich and use his riches for the good of his fellows. Russell Conwell (1843-1925), soldier, lawyer, editor, Baptist minister and most famous CHAUTAUQUA lecturer, toured the US delivering this lecture over 6000 times, and netted $8 million which he devoted to the education of young men.

Acropolis The fortified hill round which many ancient Greek cities were built; specifically, that at Athens; see PARTHENON.

Across the River and into the Trees (1950) Ernest Hemingway's novel in which, in the guise of a battered old warrior, Col. Cantwell, the author tried to sum up all he had learned in life. Its failure to impress his public was a major shock in his career. (Title based on last words of 'STONE-WALL' JACKSON.)

Actaeon In Greek mythology a hunter who chanced upon the huntress-goddess ARTEMIS bathing in a pool. Being an untypically prudish goddess, she turned him into a stag and set her hounds upon him, who tore him to shreds.

ACTH (1933) A synthetic hormone used in treating rheumatoid arthritis.

Action Painting See ABSTRACT EXPRESSIONISM.

Actium (31 BC) The decisive naval battle in which Mark Antony, left in the lurch by CLEOPATRA, was defeated by Octavian (the future Augustus). Egypt became a Roman province and Antony and Cleopatra committed suicide. (A cape on the west coast of Greece.)

Act of Settlement (1701) An Act vesting the succession to the English throne, after William and Anne, in the Protestant House of Hanover; it led to the accession of George I in 1714.

Act of Supremacy The Act (1534) appointing the King of England supreme head of the Church of England, repealed by Mary and reenacted by Elizabeth (1559).

Act of Uniformity (1559) An Act which made the Prayer Book the only legal form of worship in England; reenacted in 1662 at the Restoration (see CLARENDON CODE).

Acton (UK) A former Middlesex borough, since 1965 part of the borough of EALING.

Actors' Studio The New York school where METHOD ACTING was taught from 1947.

Acts of the Apostles A book of the New Testament ascribed to St Luke; it begins with Christ's Ascension, tells of the missions of Peter, Paul and Stephen, and ends with Peter's return to Rome, where he was placed under house arrest but still allowed to preach.

Acts of Union (1) In 1536, uniting England and Wales; (2) in 1707, uniting Scotland and England, thus creating Great Britain; (3) in 1800, uniting Ireland and Great Britain, thus creating the United Kingdom from 1 Jan. 1801.

ADA See AMERICANS FOR DEMOCRATIC ACTION.

Adam The name of the first man, not mentioned until Genesis ii, 19, although his creation is described in Genesis i, 27 and ii, 7.

Adam Bede (1859) George Eliot's novel of Adam's love for Hetty Sorrel, who however sets her cap at the local squire, gets seduced by him, murders her child and is sentenced to transportation. Adam is said to have been based on the author's father.

Adams, Parson The kind, unsophisticated parson in JOSEPH ANDREWS.

Adams Memorial (1891) One of the finest sculptures by Saint-Gaudens, in Rock Creek Cemetery, Washington, D.C., depicting a mysterious hooded figure, sometimes called 'Grief'.

Adam style (1758) A Neoclassical (see NEOCLASSICISM) style introduced in England from Italy by Robert Adam, characterized by ornamentation with urns, festoons etc., applied especially to fireplaces, ceilings and doorways, and influencing HEPPLEWHITE and SHERATON. It yielded place to the more severe style of the REGENCY PERIOD. See ADELPHI.

ADC (UK) Abbreviation used when a telephone operator is asked to ring back after a long-distance call and tell the subscriber its cost. ('Advise Duration and Charge'.)

Addison's disease A condition caused by the malfunction of certain endocrine glands, resulting in undue loss of salt from the body, lassitude, and a bronze pigmentation of the skin. Formerly fatal, it is now treated by cortisone.

Addled Parliament (1614) Summoned by James I and lasted 2 months before he had the members arrested for refusing to grant him funds. (So called because it passed no laws.)

Adele Simpson A New York fashion house.

Adelphi, The (1768) A group of buildings between the Thames and the Strand in London, designed by the Adam brothers (see ADAM STYLE), and largely rebuilt in the 1930s. (Greek adelphoi, 'brothers', i.e. Robert Adam and his 3 brothers, architects and interior decorators.)

Adieux, Les A Beethoven piano sonata suggested by the Archduke Rudolph's departure from Vienna in the face of Napoleon's advance.

Adler school of psychology See IN-DIVIDUAL PSYCHOLOGY.

Admass J. B. Priestley's name for those who are oversusceptible to the pressures of mass advertising and modern publicity methods.

Admetus In Greek legend the king of Thessaly whom Apollo served for a year as shepherd. His wife was AL-CESTIS.

Admirable Crichton, The (1902) J. M. Barrie's play about a party of aristocrats shipwrecked on a desert island; the butler, Crichton, demonstrates his innate superiority to the rest, and takes command, only to revert to the previous social hierarchy after the party has been rescued and returned to England. (Name taken from the nickname of a historical character.)

Admirable Doctor, The A name for the 13th-century English philosopher and scientist Roger Bacon. (Translation of *Doctor Admirabilis*, referring to posthumous legends of his achievements in alchemy and astrology.)

Admiral's Cup (1957) An international trophy for teams of 3 boats from each country who compete in the FASTNET, BRITANNIA CUP, New York Yacht Club Cup, and the Channel Race; the unofficial championship of handicap offshore racing. (Presented by the Admiral and other members of the RORC.)

Admiralty Arch (1910) In London a triple arch at the Trafalgar Square entrance to the MALL, designed by Sir Aston Webb as part of a memorial to Queen Victoria. It houses part of the library of the Admiralty, which adjoins it.

Admission Day The date of admission of a state into the Union, kept in some states as a legal holiday; e.g. Sept. 9th in California.

Adolf Beck case (1896 and 1904) (UK) An outstanding case of mistaken identity. Beck was twice arrested as having, under the name of Smith, defrauded several women; while serving his second sentence he learned that the real culprit was known to be a Jew, whereas he was uncircumcized. He was released and compensated, and the real Smith was arrested. This mistake led to the establishment of the court of criminal appeal.

Adonai Another name for Jehovah, used by the Jews. (Hebrew plural of *adon*, 'lord'.)

Adonais (1821) Shelley's elegy on the death of Keats.

Adonis In Greek legend the beautiful youth whom APHRODITE loved, and who was gored to death by a boar; the anemone sprang from his blood. Another legend links him with TAMMUZ: Aphrodite gave him as an infant in charge to PERSEPHONE in the Underworld; the latter fell in love with him and refused to return him. Zeus then reconciled the two by arranging that Adonis (i.e. vegetation) should spend 8 months on earth with Aphrodite and 4 below with Persephone. This repeats the myth about Persephone herself.

Adonis An aperitif of sherry, Italian vermouth and bitters.

Adoration of the Kings, The The visit of the MAGI, often depicted in art, notably by Mabuse (1500) and Pieter Brueghel (1525); both these paintings are in the London National Gallery. See next entry.

'Adoration of the Magi' A Rubens picture which was sold at SOTHEBY'S (1959) at the then world record price of £275,000

Adrianople A Turkish city now called Edirne.

ADT Initials used for American Detective Telegraph, a burglar-alarm system.

Adullamite A man at odds with his party, from John Bright's description (1866) of a disaffected Liberal as having retired to a 'political Cave of Adullam' and 'called about him everyone that was in distress and . . . discontented'. (Quotation from 1 *Samuel* xxii, 1-2, where David fled from Saul to the cave Adullam.)

Adventists Generic term for various American sects who originally expected the Second Coming of Christ in 1843 (see SEVENTH-DAY ADVENTISTS). In general, they hold that only members of their particular sect will be saved.

Advocates' Library, The (1689) The Scottish National Library, at Edinburgh.

Æ Nom de plume of George William Russell (1867-1935), Irish poet and mystic, friend of W. B. Yeats.

AEC See ATOMIC ENERGY COMMISSION.

Aëdes mosquito Generic name of a kind of mosquito, of which the species Aëdes aegypti is the only carrier of yellow fever; formerly known as Stegomyia.

AEF Initials used in World War I for the American Expeditionary Force sent to Europe in 1917.

A-effect Abbreviation for Alienation effect, chief feature of Brecht's theory of how his plays should be produced and acted so as to make audiences think rather than feel. The actor must not become too emotionally involved in his part but adopt an attitude of critical detachment towards it. The audience, similarly, should be discouraged from emotional identification with the characters, and encouraged to pass intellectual judgment on the social issues raised by the play. He tried to ensure that this judgment would inevitably accord with Marxist views. (German, V-Effekt, for Verfremdung-Effekt.)

Aegisthus See AGAMEMNON.

Aegospotami (405 BC) The last battle of the PELOPONNESIAN WAR, in which the Spartans destroyed the Athenian fleet in the HELLESPONT.

AEI Initials used for what was Britain's largest electrical manufacturer, Associated Electrical Industries, which absorbed British Thomson-Houston, Ediswan, Siemens, and Metropolitan-Vickers, and was associated with C. A. Parsons etc. Its interests covered power generators, transformers, electric traction, switchgear, electronics, telecommunications and domestic appliances. In 1967 it was absorbed by GEC.

Aeneas The Trojan hero of the AENEID, son of Anchises and Aphrodite, who set out after the fall of Troy to found a new race in Italy, from which the Romans claimed their origin.

Aeneid (19 BC) Virgil's patriotic epic poem, left unfinished, in which he describes the adventures of AENEAS on his voyage from Troy to Italy, including his sojourn at Carthage (see DIDO) and his visit to the Underworld.

Aeolus The Greek god of winds.

Aer Lingus The Irish Republic's airline.

Aeroflot Soviet government (and only) airline, run by the Chief Administrator of the Civil Air Fleet.

Aesculapius The Roman and better-known name of the Greek god of medicine, Asclepius.

Aesop's Fables A collection of didactic tales in which talking animals illustrate human foibles; attributed to a slave who lived in Samos in the 6th century BC. In the form in which they are now known they date only from 15th-century Italy.

Affluent Society, The The phrase coined by Professor Galbraith, in his book (1958) of that name, for the social conditions resulting from the high average standard of living now prevailing in Western countries. He argues that economists need to recast their theories, born in an era of poverty, to fit the vast new opportunities of today.

Afghan hound A breed introduced into Europe from Afghanistan, where it had been used as a hunting dog for at least 4000 years. It has a long silky coat and a long narrow head; colors vary.

Afghan rugs Rugs resembling coarse BOKHARA RUGS, normally red and characterized by large octagonal patterns, made by Afghan tribes.

AFL See AMERICAN FOOTBALL LEAGUE.

AFL/CIO (1955) Initials used for the US federation of trade unions, the American Federation of Labor and Congress of Industrial Organizations.

African lily The Agapanthus, a non-bulbous border plant with heads composed of many bright blue flowers.

African National Congress (1912) Formed in South Africa to fight for African rights, it denounced the PASS LAWS as early as 1919. From 1952 until it was banned in 1960 it was led by the Nobel Peace prize winner, Albert Luthuli. In 1959 the more militant members broke away to form the PAN-AFRICANIST CONGRESS.

African Queen, The (1951) John Huston's movie famous for its box-office success, based on C. S. Forester's novel (1935) in which the owner of an ancient launch of that name rescues a woman from a mission station during the German East African campaign of World War I and joins battle with a German gunboat.

African violet A popular house plant with violet, pink or white flowers and fleshy, hairy leaves; it is sensitive to drafts, temperature changes and overdoses of sunlight.

Afrikaans A simplified form of Dutch with borrowings from European and African languages, spoken by AFRIKANERS; became an official language in South Africa in 1925.

Afrika Korps Rommel's German army which arrived in North Africa in Feb. 1941 to reinforce the Italians against the British.

Afrikander A humped breed of beef cattle, dark red in color, developed in South Africa from the ZEBU.

Afrikaners Boers; the Afrikaans-speaking people in South Africa, of Dutch, German or Huguenot descent.

Afrit In Muslim mythology, a type of gigantic malicious devil.

AFS See AMERICAN FIELD SERVICE.

Afternoon of a Faun, The (1895) English title of a ballet choreographed by Nijinsky to the music of *Prélude à l'* APRÈS-MIDI D'UN FAUNE.

'After the Hunt' A famous example of the *trompe l'oeil* paintings of William Harnett (1848-92).

Agadir Crisis (1911) The tension created in Europe when the German Kaiser sent the gunboat *Panther* to Agadir as a demonstration against French expansion in Morocco.

Agag The King of the AMALEKITES, spared by Saul and slain by Samuel (1 *Samuel* xv, 32-33). When summoned before Samuel he 'came unto

him delicately', i.e. with tottering footsteps.

Aga Khan Title given by the British to the leader of the ISMAILI SECT when he settled in Bombay after his flight from Persia. (Turkish, 'master ruler'.)

Aga Khan Cup A show jumping competition at the Royal Dublin Horse Show, which attracts a very high quality international entry.

Agamemnon King of Argos, leader of the Greek army at Troy, and brother-in-law of the Helen who caused the Trojan War. On his return from Troy he was murdered by his wife CLYTEMNESTRA and her lover Aegisthus. His murder was avenged by his son ORESTES. See ATREUS, HOUSE OF.

AGB Initials used for Audits of Great Britain, a firm which in 1968 took over from TAM-RATINGS the assessment of audiences for ITV programs. They introduced a new system whereby meters record the viewing habits in 2650 homes, and the data are then computerized.

Agena US Air Force unmanned reconnaissance satellite, used in the first docking operation in space (see GEMINI).

Agency for International Development (1961) The US government body which administers and co-ordinates US schemes of economic aid abroad. It absorbed the functions of the INTERNATIONAL COOPERATION ADMINISTRATION and the Development Loan Fund (1958).

Age of Innocence, The (1920) Edith Wharton's novel drawing on her childhood memories for a satirical picture of New York society in the 1870s, with a plot about a man's love for his wife's freethinking cousin, frustrated by the conventions.

Age of Reason, The (1) Another name for the ENLIGHTENMENT. (2) The title of Thomas Paine's treatise (1795), in which he rejected supernatural revelation and advocated deism.

Agfa-Gevaert, The (UK) A golf stroke-play tournament open to members of the PGA, and to amateurs with a handicap of scratch or better, played in May at Stoke Poges, near

Slough. The prize money totals $10,000.

Agincourt (1415) The battle in the HUNDRED YEARS WAR where Henry V's longbowmen defeated a superior French force on St Crispin's Day. (Village in the Pas-de-Calais.)

Agitprop The Soviet organization for disseminating the views of the Communist Party to all parts of the country through a large staff of full-time workers, kept continually briefed with all changes in the Party line, and directed by the Central Committee from Moscow. (Abbreviation of Agitation and Propaganda.)

Agnus Dei (1) Part of the Mass beginning with these words. (2) Figure of a lamb bearing a banner with a cross, as emblem of Christ. (Latin, 'Lamb of God'.)

Agricultural Adjustment Administration A NEW DEAL measure (1933) to stop overproduction of major crops by paying farmers to reduce acreage.

Aguecheek, Sir Andrew The silly man in Shakespeare's *Twelfth Night* who joins Sir Toby BELCH in playing tricks on MALVOLIO.

Ahab A 9th-century BC King of Israel who married JEZEBEL.

Ahab, Captain See MOBY DICK.

Ahasuerus (1) Xerxes, see ESTHER. (2) One of the names of the WANDERING JEW.

Ahithophel David's trusted counsellor who deserted him to support ABSALOM's rebellion.

Ahriman In the Zoroastrian religion the spirit of evil and enemy of man; see AHURA MAZDA.

Ahura Mazda (Ormuzd, Ormazd) In the Zoroastrian religion, the spirit of good, creator of all things, destined eventually to defeat AHRIMAN.

Ah, Wilderness! (1933) Eugene O'Neill's popular and uncomplicated play about an innocent young boy growing up in a small town.

AID (1) See AGENCY FOR INTERNATIONAL DEVELOPMENT. (2) Initials used for Artificial Insemination by a Donor (i.e. by a human donor unknown to the prospective parents).

Aïda (1871) Verdi's opera, written to celebrate the opening of the Suez Canal. Aïda, the King of Ethiopia's daughter, is slave to the Pharaoh's daughter and in love with the latter's betrothed, the conquering hero Radames; accused of betraying his country, Radames is condemned to be buried alive, and Aïda dies with him.

Ailanthus A genus of trees native to the Far East; the best-known is the Chinese Tree of Heaven, much planted in parks and gardens of Europe and America. It is tall and handsome and thrives in the smoky atmosphere of cities, but the small greenish flowers have an unpleasant smell.

Aintree (UK) A racecourse 5 miles north of Liverpool, famous as the scene of the chief steeplechase of the year, the GRAND NATIONAL.

Ainu The aborigines of Japan, who may have lived in the northern island of Hokkaido for 7000 years. Tall, strong, hairy and comparatively fair in complexion, they are not Mongoloid in appearance; their language has no known affinities. Some 300 of pure blood and another 15,-000 identifiable as Ainu are scattered about Hokkaido and include groups that once lived in Sakhalin and the Kurils; they are in process of complete absorption by the Japanese.

Air Canada (1964) Formerly TCA, Trans-Canada Airlines, established by government (1937) and operating to Europe. Canadian Pacific Airlines operate on the South American and Pacific routes.

Air Force Academy, US (1954) Situated at the foot of the Rockies near Colorado Springs, Col. Cadets, mostly Congressional nominees, take a 4-year course in science, the liberal arts and military training before graduating with a BS degree and an Air Force commission; most then train as pilots or navigators, others for technical appointments.

Air Force Cross (1) USAF equivalent to the DISTINGUISHED SERVICE CROSS and the Navy Cross. (2) UK award to officers (1918) for valor or devotion to duty while flying, but not in combat, or for distinguished service to aviation.

Air Medal An award equivalent to the US Army's SOLDIER'S MEDAL.

Aix-la-Chapelle French name of the German city of Aachen.

Ajanta caves Cave-temples near Bombay, richly carved and decorated by Buddhist monks who lived there from 200 BC to AD 600.

Ajax The Greek hero of the Trojan War who goes mad when the armor of Achilles is awarded to Ulysses instead of to him.

A-K See ARLBERG-KANDAHAR.

AKC See AMERICAN KENNEL CLUB.

Akhenaten The name taken by the Egyptian Pharaoh Amenhotep IV in the 14th century BC, when he introduced the monotheistic worship of the Solar Disk at AMARNA.

Akkadians A Semitic race which under Sargon I conquered SUMER about 2370 BC and founded an empire stretching from Elam to the Mediterranean; it lasted for some 200 years. Their capital, Akkad, has not been identified.

ALA (1) American Library Association. (2) Automobile Legal Association.

Alabama arbitration (1871) The award of heavy damages against the British government by an international tribunal of arbitration for allowing the Confederate ship *Alabama* to sail in 1862 from Birkenhead, where she was built, to take part in the American Civil War.

Aladdin The poor Chinese boy of the *Arabian Nights* who comes into possession of a magic lamp which, when rubbed, calls up two Slaves of the Lamp to do his bidding; he acquires a palace and the King of China's daughter.

Alamein, Battles of (El) (1) 'First Alamein' (30 June-25 July 1942), fought by Gen. Auchinleck, who took over direct command of the British 8th Army and halted Rommel's advance on the Nile. (2) 'Second Alamein' (23 Oct.-4 Nov. 1942), the more famous opening engagement of Gen. Montgomery's offensive in the Western Desert, after Gen. Alexander had replaced Auchinleck. (An Egyptian village 40 miles west of Alexandria.)

Alamo, The A fort in San Antonio, Texas, besieged in 1836 by Mexicans, who killed all its defenders.

Alamogordo Scene in New Mexico of the test detonation of the prototype atomic bomb (July 1945).

Alaska Highway A road built in 1942, linking Fairbanks, Alaska, to the railhead at Dawson Creek, British Columbia.

Alaskan Malamute See ESKIMO DOG.

Alaska standard time The civil time of the 150th meridian, 5 hours slower than Eastern standard time; observed in most of Alaska, and in Hawaii.

Alastor In Greek legend an avenging deity who drives the sinner to fresh crimes. Shelley's Alastor is, however, the Spirit of Solitude.

Al-Azhar An ancient university at Cairo, founded 988, a center of Muslim learning ever since; modernized in the 1960s. (Arabic, 'the brightest', one of Fatima's titles.)

Albacore (1954) A popular national class dinghy; overall length 15 feet; cost around $800.

Albany Ancient poetic name for the Scottish Highlands; also Alba, Albania, Albin etc. (Perhaps from Gaelic *alp,* 'cliff'.)

Albany A London Georgian mansion on the north side of Piccadilly, built round a secluded central court; from 1802 converted into 'residential chambers', originally for bachelors only, and still one of the most fashionable London addresses. (Albany Chambers, once occupied by the Duke of York and Albany, son of George III.)

Alberich (1) In Scandinavian mythology the dwarf who guards the NIBELUNGS' gold. (2) In Wagner's RING OF THE NIBELUNGS cycle, he steals the Rhine Gold from the RHINE MAIDENS and makes a magic ring from it which he is forced by the gods to yield up to them, but not before he has placed a curse on it.

Albert In Stanley Holloway's best-loved monologue, a little boy who inadvisedly prodded a lion at the Zoo with his stick (with a 'orse's 'ead 'andle). His parents' outrage at the carelessness of the Zoo officials is skillfully exploited.

Albert Herring (1947) Benjamin Britten's comic opera in which the lady of the manor decides that as no village girl is morally qualified to be Queen of the May, there shall be a King instead. The greengrocer's virtuous boy, Albert, is selected and succumbs to the temptation of spending his prize money on his first binge.

Albertine (1909) A favorite rambler rose, producing fragrant medium-sized orange-salmon flowers in abundance.

Albertine (Simonet) · One of the chief characters in Proust's REMEMBRANCE OF THINGS PAST. The narrator meets her as a girl at Balbec and she eventually becomes his mistress. Tired of his jealousy of her Lesbian relationships, she escapes from him, but is killed when thrown from a horse. Marcel (the narrator) is surprised to find how quickly he forgets her.

Albert the Good The Prince Consort, Queen Victoria's husband.

Albigensians Adherents of a form of MANICHAEISM widespread in southern Europe in the 11th-13th centuries and savagely suppressed by the Pope's Albigensian crusade under Simon de Montfort (father of the Simon de Montfort of English history) and by the Inquisition then set up to put down such heresies. The Albigensians were supported by the Counts of Toulouse, and in the crusade the aristocracy of Provence was virtually exterminated. (Albi, French town near Toulouse.)

Albion An ancient and poetical name for England. (Traditionally from Latin *albus*, 'white', in reference to the chalk cliffs of Dover.)

ALBM Initials used for air-launched ballistic missile.

Alcalá The main street of Madrid.

Alcan Short name for Aluminium of Canada, a $1.7 billion firm which created the ambitious smelter at Kitimat on the coast of British Columbia opposite Queen Charlotte Islands, but then faced problems of overproduction.

Alcan championships Two stroke-play golf championships played in the fall, at various venues: (1) The Alcan Golfer of the Year for leading professionals chosen by qualification and invitation; the prize money totals about $130,000. (2) The International Championship, for players not qualified for (1); prize money, $30,000. (Sponsored by ALCAN.)

Alcan Highway Unofficial name for the ALASKA HIGHWAY, originally called the Alaska-Canada military highway.

Alcatraz The Federal prison on the island of that name in San Francisco Bay; closed in 1963.

Alcazar A Moorish palace in Spain; specifically that at Seville which became a royal palace famous for its architecture and gardens. The Alcazar at Toledo was famous for its prolonged and successful defense by the Nationalists against the Republicans in 1936 during the Spanish Civil War. (Arabic, 'castle'.)

Alceste See MISANTHROPE.

Alcestis The wife of ADMETUS who, to save his life, surrendered herself to Hades, but was rescued from the Underworld by Heracles (Hercules).

Alcmene Mother of Heracles by Zeus; see AMPHITRYON.

Alcoa (1888) Normal abbreviation of the Aluminum Company of America, the largest US aluminum producer, financed from the beginning by Andrew W. Mellon and his family. Its other interests include mining, shipping, railroads, hydroelectric power etc. One of the 30 industrials that make up the DOW JONES Industrial Average.

Alcoholics Anonymous An organization which encourages alcoholics to meet others who have cured themselves, to obtain advice; addresses of branches are in local telephone directories.

Aldebaran An orange-red star, the brightest in TAURUS, and one of the HYADES. (Arabic, 'the following', as following the Pleiades.)

Aldeburgh Music Festival (1948) (UK) An annual festival of music and other arts founded by Benjamin Britten (who lives at Aldeburgh) and the British tenor Peter Pears. It presents Britten's own compositions and other contemporary music chosen by him. (Coastal town of Suffolk, northeast of Ipswich.)

Aldermaston A village near Reading, Berkshire, the site of the UK Atomic Energy Authority's atomic weapons research establishment. See next entry.

Aldermaston march The CND's protest march from London to ALDERMASTON, first made on 4 Apr. 1958 and until recently repeated each Easter in the reverse direction.

Aldershot A name associated since 1855 with the largest army camp in Britain. (Hampshire town near Farnham and Farnborough.)

Aldershot Tattoo See SEARCHLIGHT TATTOO.

Aldine Press (1490-1597) The Venetian press which printed editions of the Greek and Latin Classics, popularized the smaller octavo format which replaced the folio, and introduced italic type. (Aldus Manutius, Latinized name of the printer.)

Aldwych farce One of a series of farces at the Aldwych Theatre, London, in the 1920s and 1930s, starting with *Cuckoo in the Nest* (1925) and including *Tons of Money, Rookery Nook* etc. They were written by Ben Travers, produced by Tom Walls, and featured Robertson Hare and Ralph Lynn in various riotous roles.

Aleuts An Eskimo people inhabiting the Aleutian Islands and speaking a language similar to Eskimo but not intelligible to mainland Eskimos.

Alexander A cocktail of gin or brandy, with crème de cacao and sweet cream. (Presumably so named for reasons suggested under ROB ROY.)

'Alexander's Ragtime Band' (1911) Irving Berlin's slow march, one of TIN PAN ALLEY's earliest and most successful breaks with the tradition of sentimentality. Mistakenly regarded as a landmark in ragtime's history, it has almost no syncopation in it, despite the title.

Alexandra Palace The building on Muswell Hill, London, which was the first home of the BBC TV service and of experimental color TV; there

is also an adjacent recreation park with a racetrack.

Alexandra Rose Day (1912) (UK) A day in June when rose emblems are sold in aid of a fund to assist hospitals. (Inaugurated by Queen Alexandra.)

Alexandria Quartet Novels (*Justine, Mountolive, Balthazar, Clea*) by Lawrence Durrell (1957-60) set against a background of sophisticated decadence in modern Alexandria.

Al Fatah See EL FATAH.

Algeciras Conference (1906) The conference that ended the first MOROCCAN CRISIS by regulating international commercial relations in Morocco.

Algol (1) The best-known of the eclipsing variable stars, in PERSEUS (beta-Persei), normally of 2nd magnitude but eclipsed by its companion star every 69 hours. (Arabic, 'destruction'.) (2) An algebraic and logical language for programming a computer, using the principles of Boolean algebra. (For Algorithmic Language.)

Algonquin A nomadic Indian race which once roamed over much of the eastern half of North America but was pushed westward in the 17th century by the Iroquois. There are now 1-2000 survivors ('Ottawa Indians') in Quebec and Ontario. Their name is given to the Algonquian family of languages spoken by Arapaho, Blackfoot, Cree, Micmac, Narraganset, Ojibwa, Sauk and Shawnee.

Algonquin Hotel See ROUND TABLE (2).

Alhambra A huge 13th-century fortified palace built by the Moors at Granada, Spain, with encircling walls of red sun-dried brick. (Arabic, 'the red'.)

'Ali Baba and the Forty Thieves' Traditionally, an *Arabian Nights* story, though not found in any manuscript edition of them. Overhearing the magic password 'Open Sesame' Ali Baba gains access to the thieves' cave and treasure; they swear vengeance, but his slave Morgiana pours boiling oil on them as they lie in wait for him.

Alice blue US name for a shade of greenish-blue admired by Alice, daughter of Theodore Roosevelt (President, 1901-09); rendered familiar by the song 'Alice Blue Gown'.

Alice in Wonderland (1865) The best-known book in English for children of all ages, by Lewis Carroll (Charles L. Dodgson), most of the characters of which have become household names; the keynote is sustained mad logic.

'Alice's Restaurant' A half-hour-long part-sung autobiography by Arlo Guthrie, who joined a hippie community established (1966) in an old church in Stockbridge, Mass., by Alice Brock; she also ran a restaurant there. The experiment was abandoned in 1967, but its story was expanded into a movie in which Guthrie and other hippies acted.

Alids Descendants of Ali, husband of Fatima and thus Mohammed's son-in-law, and fourth Caliph (first according to the SHI'ITES). The FA-TIMITES and the sharifs of Morocco are among those who claimed descent from him.

Aligarh University (1920) A famous Muslim university in Uttar Pradesh, India, opened to non-Muslims in 1956.

Alitalia The chief Italian airline.

Alitalia Airlines Trophy The prize for the outright winner of the SE-BRING 12-hour car race.

Alken prints Sporting prints by several members of the Alken family, of whom Henry (1784-1851) was the best, depicting foxhunting, steeplechasing and other English sports. Henry illustrated NIMROD and Surtees.

All-Africa Peoples' Conference (1958) The first of a series of conferences, held at Accra, which led to the foundation of the Organization of African Unity.

All-American Quarter Horse Futurity The world's richest horse race, run over a 400-yd course at Ruidoso Downs, N.M.; prize money, $430,600.

Allan-a-Dale The minstrel of ROBIN HOOD's band.

Allegro, L' and **Il Penseroso** Companion poems (1632), gay and grave, by Milton. (Italian, 'the gay', 'the thoughtful'.)

Allemande A savory white sauce made with egg yolk and cream.

All England Lawn Tennis and Croquet Club A private club which owns the WIMBLEDON lawn-tennis courts, where the annual championships are held by joint arrangement with the Lawn Tennis Association.

All England Plate A lawn-tennis competition for men and women players defeated in the first 2 rounds of the WIMBLEDON singles championships.

Allen's Alley (1940-49) The comedian Fred Allen's contribution to the Texaco Star Theater radio program; he peopled his alley with memorable characters such as Senator Claghorn and Mrs. Nussbaum.

All for Love (1678) Dryden's blank verse tragedy, with the sub-title *or the World Well Lost*, about the last days of Antony and Cleopatra.

All God's Chillun Got Wings (1924) Eugene O'Neill's tragedy about a mixed marriage.

All Hallows (Day) An older name for ALL SAINTS. (Old English *halig*, 'holy'.)

All Hallows Eve Another name for HALLOWEEN.

Alliance for Progress (1961) A US-sponsored movement to coordinate the economic and social development of the Latin American countries as a defense against Communist infiltration; it is largely financed by the AGENCY FOR INTERNATIONAL DE-VELOPMENT. Results have been disappointing. (Spanish title, *Alianza para el progreso*.)

Allied Breweries A group of British brewers, including Ind Coope, Ansells, Friary Meux, and Tetley, Walker. It controls one-eighth of Britain's public houses, and makes Double Diamond, Long Life canned beer, Skol lager etc. In 1968 it acquired the Showerings group which market cider, Babycham, Harvey's sherries and Britvic soft drinks.

Allied Chemical (1920) A leading US chemicals group, with headquar-

ters in New York; one of the 30 industrials that make up the DOW JONES
Industrial Average.

Allium The genus name of garlic.

Alloway A hamlet 2 miles south of
Ayr, Scotland, the birthplace of
Robert Burns, where his cottage is
preserved as a museum, with a
memorial nearby.

'All quiet along the Potomac' (1) A
phrase now in general use for 'all is
calm'. It originated with Gen. Mc-
Clellan who, having allowed Robert E. Lee's forces to withdraw across
the river after Antietam (1862) and
while continuing to procrastinate,
used it repeatedly in his reports,
thus exasperating a public eager for
an advance on Richmond. Lincoln
dismissed him for this excessive
caution. (2) Ethel Beers's poem
(1861), her only famous work, about
the Civil War, on the theme: 'Tis
nothing—a private or two now and
then / Will not count in the news of
the battle.

All Quiet on the Western Front
(1927) One of the most famous novels about World War I, on the note
'war is hell'; written by a German,
Erich Maria Remarque (German title,
Im Westen nichts Neues.)

All Saints (Day) Nov. 1st. set aside
in the Anglican, Roman Catholic
and other Church calendars for a
general celebration of the saints who
have no day of their own; formerly
called All Hallows.

All Souls (Day) Nov. 2nd, a day set
aside in the Roman Catholic calendar for prayers to mitigate the sufferings of souls in purgatory ('all the
faithful deceased').

All Souls, Oxford (1438) Until recently the only British college with
no undergraduates. Election to the
54 Fellowships of the college is an
honor reserved for distinguished
scholars. Some Honorary Fellowships for men distinguished in other
fields and some Junior Research Fellowships are also given.

All-Star game (1933) A baseball
game played annually in July by
teams composed of outstanding
players from the teams of the American and National Leagues; they play

one game, league against league;
75% of the proceeds go to the players' pension fund.

All's Well that Ends Well (about
1600) Shakespeare's late, disillusioned comedy recounting the wiles
of Helena in forcing Bertrand to accept her as his wife; the happy ending is quite artificial.

All the Talents, Ministry of (1806-
07) The coalition government
formed by the Whig leader, Lord
Grenville, after the death of his
cousin, the Younger Pitt. Charles
James Fox was Foreign Minister. It
did nothing to justify its title except
abolish the slave trade.

Allworthy, Squire The upright and
benevolent foster father and, as it
transpires, uncle of the hero of
Fielding's novel, TOM JONES.

Almack's (1765-1890) Fashionable
assembly rooms in St James's, London, started by the founder of
BROOKS'S CLUB, used for dancing,
matchmaking, and backbiting.

Alma Mater (1) Roman title for Cybele, Ceres, and other goddesses. (2)
Used, with reference to its students,
of a school or university. (3) A
school or college song (US usage). (Latin, 'nourishing, bountiful,
mother'.)

Almanach de Gotha (1763) A German publication, in French and
German, giving statistical and historical information regarding the
countries of the world, but chiefly
famous for its detailed genealogies
of European royal and princely families. (Originally published in
Gotha.)

Almansur A title given to various
Muslim heroes, specifically to a
10th-century Moorish King of Andalusia. (Arabic, 'the victorious'.)

Almaviva, Count See BARBER OF SE-
VILLE; MARRIAGE OF FIGARO.

Almayer's Folly (1895) Conrad's
first novel, about an ambitious trader in the Malayan Archipelago and
his beloved half-caste daughter; the
'folly' is the pretentious house he
builds for himself.

Almoravids (11th-12th centuries)
A BERBER dynasty which conquered
Morocco and OLD GHANA, and then

took over Moorish Spain from the successors to the OMAYYADS.

Alnwick Castle Originally a 12th-century border fortress, in Northumberland, in Percy hands since Norman times and still the home of the Dukes of Northumberland.

Aloha State Nickname for Hawaii. (Hawaiian, 'greetings', also 'farewell'.)

Alph The river of Coleridge's KUBLA KHAN at XANADU: Where Alph, the sacred river, ran / Through caverns measureless to man. . . . A wicked man once printed this as: Where, Alf, the sacred river ran.

Alpha and Omega The first and last letters of the Greek alphabet (*a* and long *o*), used in *Revelation* i, 8: I am Alpha and Omega, the beginning and the ending, saith the Lord.

Alpha, Bravo, Charlie The phonetic ABC of the English-speaking armed forces and police, also used in civil telecommunications. It runs: Alpha, Bravo, Charlie, Delta, Echo, Foxtrot, Golf, Hotel, India, Juliet, Kilo, Lima, Mike, November, Oscar, Papa, Quebec, Romeo, Sierra, Tango, Uniform, Victory, Whiskey, Xray, Yankee, Zulu.

Alphonse and Gaston A comic strip for the Hearst press by Frederick Burr Opper, first published in book form in 1902. Ill-drawn, it is remembered for the phrases 'You first, my dear Alphonse' and 'After you, my dear Gaston', constantly interchanged by a couple of stage Frenchmen as they flounder through absurd vicissitudes.

Alpine events (Skiing) Downhill and slalom races; see NORDIC EVENTS.

Alpine race A roundheaded race thought to have inhabited the Alpine regions between the areas occupied by the 2 longheaded races of Europe, the Nordic and Mediterranean; no longer a separate entity.

Alps express A morning train from Copenhagen via Hamburg, Munich, Innsbruck, the Brenner Pass, Genoa, Venice and Florence to Rome, reached in 36½ hours.

Alsace-Lorraine Two French provinces (capitals, Strasbourg and Nancy respectively) seized by Germany after the FRANCO-PRUSSIAN WAR, regained in 1919 and once more lost to Germany from 1940 to 1945; now comprising the *départements* of Haut-Rhin, Bas-Rhin and Moselle.

Alsacienne (Cooking) With a garnish of sauerkraut, ham and Strasbourg sausage.

Alsatia Until the end of the 17th century a sanctuary for debtors and criminals at Whitefriars, London. (Named after Alsace.)

Altaic languages A division of the URAL-ALTAIC LANGUAGES which includes MANCHU, Mongolian, Turkish and a Western Turkish group spoken in the southern republics of the USSR east of the Caspian, i.e. Kazakh, Turkmen, Uzbek, Kirghiz and Tadzhik. Japanese and Korean were once, but are no longer, considered to be distantly related. (From the Altaic mountains of west Mongolia.)

Altamira The site where the first examples of Old Stone Age cave art were discovered (1879) — strikingly naturalistic color paintings of bison and other animals, perhaps 30,000 years old. See AURIGNACIAN CULTURE. (Village near Santander, Spain.)

Altmark incident (Feb. 1940) A British destroyer's rescue of 300 prisoners of war from the German ship *Altmark* in neutral Norwegian territorial waters.

Alto Adige A name for the Italian province of Bolzano (German Bozen), in 1969 officially named South Tirol; for many years an area disputed with Austria, which complained of the Italianization of the German-speaking inhabitants who form two-thirds of the population. (Italian, 'upper Adige', the river which drains it.)

Altona (1959) Sartre's play about a German family racked by guilt feelings regarding its Nazi past, and especially the use of torture; it refers obliquely to contemporary French conduct in Algeria. (French title, *Les Séquestrés d'Altona*.)

Aluminum War (1958-59) A bitter struggle between the US firm Reynolds Metals, allied with (British) Tube Investments, and a rival US firm, ALCOA, for control of British

Aluminium. Reynolds, advised by Warburgs, won against strong opposition by British Aluminium, advised by Lazards and other merchant bankers.

Alving, Mrs See GHOSTS.

AMA The American Medical Association (1847), a physicians' organization to promote medicine and public health; it publishes the weekly *Journal of the AMA*, *Today's Health* (for the public) and other periodicals. It has no legal powers; the headquarters are in Chicago. Compare BMA.

Amadis de Gaul A 16th-century Spanish romance of chivalry, in which the knight Amadis de Gaul (Wales) falls in love with Oriana, the king of England's daughter.

Amalekites A nomadic Arab tribe to the south of Judah with whom the Israelites fought from the time of Joshua until David 'smote' them finally (1 *Samuel* xxx, 17); they are generally represented as notably treacherous.

Amalthea The nymph in Greek legend who fed the infant Zeus in a Cretan cave with the milk of a goat (also named Amalthea in some versions). Zeus gave her a horn of the goat, which he had magically transformed into a horn of plenty or cornucopia.

Amarna Ancient Egyptian city between Memphis and Thebes, founded by AKHENATEN as his capital; also called Tell el'Amarna.

Amaryllis A shepherdess in the pastoral poems of Theocritus; hence the name was widely used in later poetry for any rustic beauty.

Amaryllis belladonna The species name of the Belladonna lily.

Amateur Athletic Union (1888) Founded during a controversy over professionalism, this Union took over responsibility for certifying athletes as amateurs, claiming jurisdiction in 17 sports. Its rules sometimes differ from those laid down by the NATIONAL COLLEGIATE ATHLETIC ASSOCIATION, and cooperation between these 2 bodies is often minimal.

Amazons In Greek legend, a race of female warriors of Scythia who burned off their right breasts the better to shoot off their arrows. The River Amazon got its name from a local tale of a similar race. (The legend explains the probably false derivation from Greek *a-*, 'without'; *mazos*, 'breast'.)

Ambassadors, The (1903) Henry James's novel, which tells of a New England widow who sends an 'ambassador' to recall her son from Paris; her envoy is converted to the view that the young man is better where he is.

Amber roads European trade routes used from Neolithic times to transport Baltic amber to the Mediterranean ports.

Amboina massacre (1623) The Dutch massacre of English merchants in the Spice Islands (Moluccas), after which the EAST INDIA COMPANY turned its attention to India.

Amboise conspiracy (1560) A Huguenot plot to seize the King of France and Catherine de Medici; it was discovered and foiled. Three years later, after the King's death, a reversal of policy brought the Huguenots considerable religious freedom. (Town on the Loire.)

'America' (1831) A national hymn with words (beginning 'My Country 'tis of Thee') by the Rev. Samuel Francis Smith of Boston, set to the tune of 'God Save the King' which was also used in 'God Bless Our Noble Land' (1844). This tune perhaps dates back to the 17th century and may have originally been a folk melody; it appears in several old European national anthems and in works by Beethoven and Weber. See OF THEE I SING.

American One of the bigger US domestic airlines.

American Academy in Rome Prize Fellowships Grants to young Americans for research or creative work in architecture, music, painting, sculpture, history of art, or classics; recipients live at the Academy (established in Rome, 1894) and are given $3650 per annum, initially for one year.

American Academy of Arts and Letters (1904) An honorary organization restricted to 50 distinguished members of the National Institute of Arts and Letters (1898); it promotes literature, art and music by exhibitions, publications, awards, grants and international exchanges. The headquarters are in New York. Compare BRITISH ACADEMY.

American Alps A nickname for the North Cascades in Washington State, in which lies the highest peak, Mt. Rainier.

American Bar Association (1878) The leading national association of its kind, claiming about 40% of the profession as members. It has no disciplinary powers but exercises considerable influence on professional standards, on legislation, and on law schools, which are subject to its approval.

American Basketball Association One of the 2 major professional basketball associations (BUCCANEERS, CHAPPARALS, COLONELS, CONDORS, COUGARS, FLORIDIANS, NETS, PACERS, ROCKETS, SQUIRES, STARS).

American beauty (1875) A hybrid perpetual rose, with large crimson flowers; vigorous, free-flowering, rather thin in petals.

American Bible Society (1816) A nondenominational organization founded in New York 'to encourage a wider circulation of the Holy Scriptures, without note or comment'. It has sponsored translations into many languages and cooperates with the British and Foreign Bible Society in distributing them.

American Brands Formerly American Tobacco, which manufactures Lucky Strikes, Lucky Filters, Pall Mall and other cigarettes and has big interests in food and drinks. It is one of the 30 industrials that make up the DOW JONES Industrial Average.

American Can A New York firm, one of the 30 industrials that make up the DOW JONES Industrial Average.

American Civil Liberties Union (1920) A society dedicated to restraining governmental interference with personal freedom.

American Civil War (1861-65) The war between the CONFEDERATE STATES and the Union government, caused partly by the election of Abraham Lincoln as President after

he had denounced slavery, and partly by a continued dispute on states' rights, i.e. the power to be delegated by the Union (or Federal) government to the individual states.

American Conference (1970) One of the 2 conferences of the NATIONAL FOOTBALL LEAGUE (BENGALS, BILLS, BRONCOS, BROWNS, CHARGERS, CHIEFS, COLTS, DOLPHINS, JETS, OILERS, PATRIOTS, RAIDERS, STEELERS).

American Dream, The (1961) Edward Albee's Theater of the ABSURD play in which a woman seeks happiness by adopting a son, who turns out to be an unscrupulous self-seeker; she symbolizes an American society divorced from reality by false ideals.

American Express Co. (1850) A worldwide travel agency; originally a carrying firm. As there was no US parcel post until 1913 and the railroads did not like handling small consignments, private companies arose which ran express services from door to door, COD (the origin of the banking side of the modern firm). This firm was closely connected with WELLS FARGO.

American Federation of Labor See AFL/CIO.

American Field Service (1914) A privately sponsored nonpolitical and nonsectarian organization which operates an international scholarship program (1946) for the exchange of high-school students between the US and foreign countries. (Originally a volunteer ambulance service.)

American Football League (1959) One of the 2 major professional football leagues through 1969 (BENGALS, BILLS, BRONCOS, CHARGERS, CHIEFS, DOLPHINS, JETS, OILERS, PATRIOTS, RAIDERS). Merged with the NFL in 1970 and became the AMERICAN CONFERENCE of the NATIONAL FOOTBALL LEAGUE.

American Fur Company (1808) The first of the fur-trading companies established by John Jacob Astor; it extended its operations from the Great Lakes and the Mississippi-Missouri basin to the far West, where it established trading posts (e.g. Astoria in Oregon, 1811) and eventually took the lead over the rival ROCKY MOUNTAIN FUR COMPANY.

'American Gothic' (1930) An unforgettable painting by Grant Wood of a pioneer farmer-preacher holding a pitchfork and standing with his wife before a 19th-century Gothic Revival farmhouse. Its relentlessly bleak realism was intended to typify the sober, industrious farming community of the Midwest, but nevertheless aroused the ire of the Iowa section of it. (Art Institute of Chicago.)

American Indian languages A group distantly related to Mongolian languages. They include MAYAN LANGUAGE, KECHUAN, ARAUCANIAN and TUPI-GUARANI, among very many others.

American in Paris, An (1928) An orchestral tone poem written and orchestrated by George Gershwin, and inspired by his homesick boyhood in Paris. It also supplied the theme for a movie (1951).

American Kennel Club (1884) An organization with headquarters in New York and over 360 clubs elsewhere, founded a few years after the WESTMINSTER KENNEL CLUB.

American Language, The H. L. Mencken's comparative study (1919-48, with 2 supplements) of the development of the English language in England and America, including vocabulary, spelling and dialects. He came to believe that America had attained a dominant influence on the language of the English-speaking peoples.

American League (1901) One of the 2 major professional baseball leagues. Originally the Western League of Midwest cities, formed in 1893, it became a major league under its present name in 1901. (ANGELS, ATHLETICS, BREWERS, INDIANS, ORIOLES, RED SOX, ROYALS, SENATORS, TIGERS, TWINS, WHITE SOX, YANKEES).

American Legion (1919) US veteran organization, now including veterans of both world wars and the Korean War.

American Pillar (1902) A favorite rambler rose, with clusters of large single carmine-pink flowers, white at the center.

American plan US term for en *pension* hotel rates, i.e. inclusive of meals; see EUROPEAN PLAN.

American Savoyards, The Dorothy Raedler's company, responsible for excellent revivals of GILBERT & SULLIVAN OPERAS; see SAVOYARD.

'American School, The' (1765) Mathew Pratt's conversation piece depicting a group of young artists working in Benjamin West's studio; West is seen criticizing one of Pratt's own paintings. (Metropolitan Museum of Art, NYC.)

Americans for Democratic Action (ADA) (1947) An active liberal group, composed mostly of Democrats. Hubert Humphrey was one of the founders, and John Kenneth Galbraith a strong supporter.

American Shakespeare Festival Theatre (1954) A replica, at Stratford, Conn., of the Elizabethan GLOBE THEATRE, modified by being roofed in and air-conditioned. Shakespearean actors appear there in a cycle of plays each season (June—September).

American Songbag, The (1927) A compilation of folk songs and ballads by Carl Sandburg, who used to sing them to banjo or guitar.

American Standard Version (1901) A revision of the Bible by a committee, also known as the American Revised Version; it differs little from the REVISED VERSION.

American Tobacco See AMERICAN BRANDS.

American Tragedy, An (1925) Theodore Dreiser's novel, based on a famous trial, of a young man from a poor home who, obsessed with dreams of luxury, causes the death of the girl he has made pregnant so that he can make a rich marriage. He is executed, but Dreiser indicts the materialist society into which he was born.

American War of Independence (1775-83) The revolt of the 13 American colonies on the issue of 'no taxation without representation' (i.e. at Westminster), ending in the recognition of their independence by the

Treaty of Paris. See BOSTON TEA PARTY.

America's Cup An international 12-meter yacht race, sailed at Newport, R.I. Originally presented by the Royal Yacht Squadron for the 1851 race around the Isle of Wight, it was won by the schooner America. The US, challenged from time to time by Britain (see SHAMROCK) and later by Australia, has never lost possession of the cup, named after the first winner.

America's Tragedy (1933) A history of the Civil War by James Truslow Adams.

'America the Beautiful' (1895) A national hymn with words by Katherine Lee Bates, set to Samuel A. Ward's hymn-tune 'Materna' (1888); regarded by many as superior in words and music to 'The Star-Spangled Banner'.

Amerindian Ethnologists' term for American Indian.

Amersham Site of the British Atomic Energy Authority's radiochemical center where radioactive material produced in atomic reactors is prepared for medical, industrial and scientific use. (Town in Buckinghamshire.)

Amethyst, HMS (1949) A gunboat which during the Chinese Civil War ran the gauntlet between Chinese shore batteries and made her escape down the Yangtse River by night with lights out, a remarkable feat of navigation.

Amgot (1943) Initials standing for Allied Military Government of Occupied Territory, formed to take over the civil administration as countries were retrieved from Nazi and Fascist hands; first came into operation in Sicily.

Amharic The Semitic language of the dominant minority, the Amharas, of Abyssinia.

Amiens, Peace of (1802) After the British and French had reached a stalemate in the Napoleonic wars, and Addington had replaced Pitt, a peace was made by which Britain restored French colonies but kept Ceylon (formerly Dutch) and Trinidad (formerly Spanish). War was resumed the following year.

Amish, Old Order One of the strictest sects of the MENNONITES; they settled in Pennsylvania and shun electricity, automobiles, and other things not mentioned in the Bible.

Amnesty (1961) An organization founded by the British lawyer, Peter Benenson, which campaigns for the release of persons in any part of the world who have been detained in prison for their religious or political beliefs, provided they have not advocated or been guilty of violence, racialism or espionage, and are serving a sentence of not less than 6 months.

Amon (Ammon, Amun) Ancient Egyptian ram-headed god, originally local to Thebes, who became the state god of all Egypt under the 18th Dynasty (16th century BC) and was later linked with RA, the sun-god, as Amon-Ra. The Greeks identified him with Zeus (see JUPITER AMMON).

Amontillado A FINO sherry, darker, less dry and fuller-bodied than MANZANILLA.

Amor brujo, El (Ballet) See LOVE THE MAGICIAN.

Amoroso sherry See OLOROSO.

Amos n' Andy A famous radio and television series beginning in the 1930s. Starring Freeman Gosden and Charles Correll, it was one of the first Negro situation comedies.

Amphion In Greek legend the son of Zeus whose magic lyre caused the stones to leap into place in building the walls of Thebes. He married NIOBE.

Amphitrite In Greek legend the wife of POSEIDON, mother of TRITON.

Amphitryon In Greek legend a king of Thebes who married Alcmene; she became the mother of Heracles (HERCULES) by ZEUS when he invited himself to the house disguised as her husband, and gave a banquet, interrupted ineffectively by the arrival of the real Amphitryon. See next entry.

Amphitryon 38 (1929) A play in which the French dramatist Giraudoux brings a wicked modernist eye to bear on the legend of AMPHITRYON. (The title implied that this was about the 38th version of a theme already treated by Plautus, Molière,

Dryden and many others.)

Amritsar massacre (1919) The killing of 379 Indian rioters who had assembled in a square called the Jallianwala Bagh, during widespread disturbances in the Punjab. Gen. Dyer's action in ordering his troops to fire on the crowd was condemned by a committee of inquiry.

AMSA Initials standing for Advanced Manned Strategic Aircraft, a VG model proposed as a replacement for the STRATOFORTRESS in about 1976.

Amu Darya Modern name of the great Russian river which flows into the Aral Sea; formerly known as the OXUS.

AMVETS (1944) Initials used for the American Veterans of World War II and Korea.

Amy Vanderbilt, According to According to the rules of etiquette as laid down since 1952 by Miss Vanderbilt in a syndicated newspaper column and various books. Compare EMILY POST, ACCORDING TO.

Anabaptists (1) Extremists of the Reformation movement, so called because they rejected infant baptism; (2) at one time a derogatory term for English Baptists.

Anabasis (about 370 BC) The account by Xenophon, commanding a Greek mercenary force assisting Cyrus against his brother Artaxerxes in a Persian civil war, of his retreat from Mesopotamia to the Black Sea, which his soldiers greeted with the famous cry: *Thalassa! thalassa!*, 'the sea!'. (Greek, 'the walk up', i.e. 'the march to the north'.)

Anaconda Company (1895) A large copper and silver mining group based on the Anaconda copper mine at Butte, Mont.; it now has mines in other US states, as well as in Chile, Mexico, Canada and other countries. One of the 30 industrials that make up the DOW JONES Industrial Average.

Anadama bread Yeast-raised bread made with cornmeal, molasses etc. (Picturesquely but unconvincingly derived from 'Anna, damn her!', the expostulation of a New England fisherman as, satiated with his lazy wife's eternal cornmeal mush, he mixed it with flour and yeast and made bread of it.)

Anadyomene See APHRODITE ANADYOMENE.

Analects (of Confucius) A collection of random musings attributed to Confucius, which carried great authority in pre-Communist China. (From Greek, 'gleanings'.)

Ananias (1) The husband of Sapphira; both were struck dead for giving only part of what they had to the Apostles and pretending that it was the whole or, as Peter called it, 'lying to the Holy Ghost' (*Acts* v, 1-11). (2) The high priest who ordered his men to smite St Paul on the mouth (*Acts* xxiii, 2).

Anasazi culture A term covering the prehistoric BASKET MAKERS and their successors, the CLIFF DWELLERS; they formed communities in the region where Arizona, New Mexico, Colorado and Utah adjoin. To their west were the peoples of the HOHOKAM CULTURE. (*Anasazi* is Navajo for 'ancient ones'.)

Anastasia Title of a movie and a play on the subject of Anna Anderson's claim to be the Russian Tsar's daughter and to have escaped from the EKATERINBURG massacre in 1918.

Anatolia Another name for Asia Minor, virtually equivalent to modern Turkey-in-Asia.

Anatolian rugs The earliest oriental rugs to be imported into Europe, made from the 12th century in what is now Turkey, and showing strong Persian influence from the 15th century. Coarsely knotted and with bold colors, mostly red and blue, with the sacred green reserved for prayer rugs, their manufacture came to be largely monopolized by Greeks living in Turkey and ceased with their expulsion by Mustapha Kemal in the 1920s.

Anatomist, The (1930) James Bridie's first successful play, based on the story of BURKE AND HARE.

'Anatomy Lesson, The' (1632) Rembrandt's first important work after he moved from Leyden to Amsterdam, commissioned by the Guild of

Surgeons and portraying its members surrounding an opened cadaver. (Mauritshuis, The Hague.)

Anatomy of a Murder A novel and movie (1959) by Robert Traver (pen name of J. Voelker).

Anatomy of Melancholy, The (1621) Robert Burton's mammoth essay on mental maladies ranging from depression to extremes of insanity, enriched by copious quotations from Classical sources on the afflictions of mankind.

Anchises A Trojan prince, father of AENEAS who visits him in the Underworld.

Ancien Régime The old order, especially in reference to pre-Revolution France, where absolute monarchy prevailed.

Ancient Mariner, Rime of the (1798) Coleridge's hypnotic poem, written in his youth, of the spell cast on a sailor who broke an old tabu by killing an albatross. It contains many oft-quoted lines, such as: Alone, alone, all, all alone, / Alone on a wide wide sea.

Ancient of Days, The God, a phrase used in *Daniel* vii, 9. It merely means 'the old man'.

Ancona A light breed of domestic fowl kept as an egg-producer and used for crossing. (Italian port.)

Andalouse (1) Mayonnaise with tomatoes and pimento. (2) Of fish, meat or poultry, served with eggplant or rice pilaf, and tomato. (Andalusia, Spain.)

Anderson shelter The family air-raid shelter distributed in Britain at the beginning of World War II. (Sir John Anderson, Home Secretary; later Lord Waverley.)

Andersonville The site of a Confederate prisoner-of-war camp in southwest Georgia, notorious during the Civil War and the setting of MacKinlay Kantor's horrifyingly realistic novel *Andersonville* (1955), awarded a Pulitzer prize. Conditions there were so bad that the commandant was executed after the war.

Andhra Pradesh (1956) A state of India comprising the Telugu-speaking region (Andhra) of northeast

Madras established as a separate unit in 1953, and the Telangana area of the former Hyderabad state; capital Hyderabad.

Andover The military version of the HAWKER SIDDELEY HS-748 airliner.

Andrea Chenier (1896) Umberto Giordano's best-known opera, a drama of the French Revolution.

Androcles A runaway Roman slave sent into the arena to fight a lion, which recognized him as the man who had once removed a thorn from its paw, and licked him affectionately. Bernard Shaw wrote a play on the theme, *Androcles and the Lion* (1912).

Andromache In Greek legend HECTOR's beautiful wife. In Euripides' play named after her she is carried off by Achilles' son and cruelly treated by the Spartans. Racine also wrote a play of that name (1667).

Andromeda In Greek legend the daughter of CASSIOPEIA; she was chained to a rock exposed to a sea monster to placate Poseidon. PERSEUS rescued and married her.

Andromeda A northern constellation below CASSIOPEIA; it contains the Great Spiral Nebula, one of the 3 galaxies visible to the naked eye, about 2 million light-years away from earth.

Andromeda Strain, The Michael Crichton's SF novel about the danger of unmanned spacecraft from other worlds landing on earth and introducing unknown lethal germs.

Andy Capp The aggressively working class creation of the British *Daily Mirror* cartoonist, Reg Smythe, with built-in cigarette butt and cap (or flat 'at).

ANF See ATLANTIC NUCLEAR FORCE.

Angeleno A nickname for a resident of Los Angeles.

Angel of the Battlefields Another nickname for Clara Barton; see MOTHER OF THE RED CROSS.

Angels The California Angels, American (Baseball) League, playing at Anaheim Stadium, Los Angeles.

Angels of Mons A widely believed legend that angels had been seen at the Battle of MONS, started by a short story written by Arthur Machen for the London *Evening News* in August 1914.

'Angelus, The' (1859) An untypically sentimental peasant scene painted by Millet. (Louvre.)

Angevin Of ANJOU; see PLANTAGENETS.

Angiosperms The flowering plants, a division subdivided into the monocotyledons and dicotyledons.

Angkor The ancient KHMER capital in Cambodia (8th-15th centuries), the ruins of which were discovered in the jungle in 1860. See next 2 entries. (*Angkor*, 'ruins'.)

Angkor Thom The walled city of ANGKOR itself.

Angkor Vat The largest temple in the world, covered with Buddhist and Hindu carvings and sculpture; 1 mile south of ANGKOR THOM. (*Vat*, also spelt *wat*, 'temple'.)

Angles The Teutonic invaders from Schleswig who, from the 5th century AD, settled in East Anglia, Mercia and Northumbria.

Anglican Church A communion of Protestant Churches, including the Church of England, Churches in Wales, Scotland, Ireland and the Commonwealth, and the Episcopal Church in USA. The Archbishop of Canterbury presides over the LAMBETH CONFERENCE at which their representatives meet.

Anglo Short for ANGLO-AMERICAN.

Anglo-American A US citizen of English origin or descent; abbreviated to 'Anglo', especially in the southwest, with a shift of meaning to 'not of Mexican or Latin American descent'.

Anglo American Corporation (1917) The late Sir Ernest Oppenheimer's mining group, with interests in South African gold, uranium, diamonds, and coal and, until 1969 when it had to cede them to the Zambian government, in the COPPERBELT.

Anglo-Catholicism The views and practice of the High Church party of the Church of England; see OXFORD MOVEMENT.

Anglo-Dutch Wars *First* (1652-54), the result of the NAVIGATION ACT passed by the RUMP PARLIAMENT. *Second* (1665-67), in which Charles II acquired New York and De Ruyter burned British ships in the Medway. *Third* (1672-74), declared by Charles II under the Secret Treaty of DOVER.

Anglo-Iranian Oil Co. Originally the Anglo-Persian Oil Co., formed in 1909 by the Burmah Oil Co. to exploit the petroleum found in the Persian Gulf area. The British government bought control of it in 1914 to ensure supplies for the Navy. After the 1951 nationalization (see ABADAN CRISIS) it joined the international consortium of 8 firms formed in 1954 to manage the Persian oil industry, and was renamed the British Petroleum Co. (see BP).

Anglo-Irish War (1918-21) The name sometimes given to the period when Irish nationalists resisted suppression by the RIC (including the BLACK AND TANS) and troops; part of the period called the TROUBLES.

Anglo-Persian Oil Co. See ANGLO-IRANIAN OIL CO.

Anglo-Saxon Attitudes (1956) Angus Wilson's novel about a medievalist who starts to inquire into an apparent academic fraud, with surprising results.

Anglo-Saxon Chronicle An Old English collection of sagas and annals covering English history to 1154, compiled by clergy from the time of King Alfred onwards.

Anglo-Saxon language See OLD ENGLISH.

Anglo-Saxons Name given to the Teutonic ANGLES, SAXONS and JUTES who invaded England in the 5th century AD.

Angola An overseas province of Portugal, in West Africa.

Angora Older name of Ankara, now the Turkish capital. It survives in current use as the name of species of cat, goat and rabbit with long silky hair, and of a wool mixture made of Angora rabbit hair and sheep's wool.

Angostura A kind of bitters, formerly made at Angostura (Ciudad Bolivar) in Venezuela by a French doctor in 1825 as a tonic for Bolivar's army of liberation; now made in Trinidad for use in gin cocktails. In the Victorian era Englishmen put it in sherry!

Angria and Gondal The settings of numerous melodramatic novels written by the Brontë family when they were young, Angria being an African and Gondal a northern country.

Angry Young Man A man who, like Jimmy PORTER, impotently and indiscriminately lashes out at modern society as he sees it.

Angus The Scottish county until 1928 known as Forfarshire.

Animal Farm George Orwell's satire (1946) on Stalinist Russia. Napoleon the boar is dictator of the farm animals; he keeps changing the party line as it suits him, even the basic slogan '4 legs good, 2 legs bad'.

Anisette An aniseed-flavored liqueur or cordial.

Anitra An Arab girl whom PEER GYNT meets on his travels; her dance was set to music by Grieg.

Anjou A former French province (capital, Angers) west of Touraine, inherited by the Angevin (PLANTAGENET) kings of England but lost by King John. It occupied the modern département of Maine-et-Loire and adjacent districts. The name is applied to wines of this region.

Anjou A late-ripening dessert pear of European origin (where it is called Beurre d'Anjou), one of the chief varieties grown in California.

Ankara The capital of Turkey, formerly called ANGORA.

'Annabel Lee' A poem by Edgar Allan Poe, containing among many other haunting lines: I was a child and she was a child, / In this kingdom by the sea; / And we loved with a love that was more than love—/ I and my Annabel Lee.

Anna Christie (1921) Eugene O'-Neill's early play about an old barge captain and a woman redeemed by love.

Anna Held Girls The ensemble of 50 'of the most beautiful girls ever presented on the stage', who appeared in the first edition of the ZIEGFELD FOLLIES (1907).

Anna Karénina (1877) One of Leo Tolstoy's 2 greatest novels, in which the happy life of Squire Lévin, married to Kitty and busy with schemes of improvement on his estate, is sharply contrasted by the puritanical author with the miseries of Anna, who deserts her husband for the handsome young army officer, Vronski, and commits suicide under a train when he abandons her.

Anna Livia Plurabelle Earwicker's wife in James Joyce's FINNEGAN'S WAKE, said to represent Eve, the River Liffey etc.

Annam A former Indo-Chinese state, now divided between North and South Vietnam.

Annapolis The US Naval Academy at Annapolis, Md. (Seaport and state capital, near Chesapeake Bay.)

Ann Arbor Michigan city to which the University of Michigan (1817) was moved in 1841 from Detroit.

Anne Hathaway's Cottage The cottage at Shottery, near Stratford-on-Avon, where Shakespeare's wife lived as a girl.

Annelids A phylum of segmented worms (including the common earthworm) and leeches.

Anne of Green Gables (1908) A story for girls by the Canadian novelist Lucy Maude Montgomery, who drew on memories of her youth in Prince Edward Island; it scored a worldwide success and was made into a play which had a long run in London. There were many sequels.

Annie Get Your Gun (1946) A Rodgers and Hammerstein musical with music by Irving Berlin and based on the story of the American markswoman ANNIE OAKLEY, presented as a naïve backwoods girl. The hits included 'Doin' What Comes Natur'ly', 'Anything You Can Do (I can do better)' and the eternal ensemble 'There's No Business Like Show Business'.

'Annie Laurie' A poem by Sir William Douglas (about 1700) concerning the daughter of Sir Robert Laurie of Maxwelton, who had jilted him; it was not set to music until 1855.

Annie Oakley A free ticket to a performance. (From the resemblance of a punched pass to a playing card with bullet holes through the spots, one of the parlor tricks of a noted markswoman of that name, who died in 1926.)

'Anniversary, The' A painting by Marc Chagall in the Museum of Modern Art, NYC.

Annual Register A record of the chief events of the year, published in England annually since 1759.

Annunciation, The Gabriel's announcement to the Virgin Mary that she would bear a son, Jesus (*Luke* i, 26-38), a scene often depicted in art, notably by Fra Angelico, Fra Filippo Lippi and D. G. Rossetti.

Annus Mirabilis Name given by Dryden, in his poem, to the year (1666) of the Great Fire of London and the Dutch fleet's raid up the Medway. (Latin, 'year of wonders'.)

Anopheles mosquito The generic name of the type of mosquito of which many species carry malaria.

Another Country (1961) A novel by the American Negro writer, James Baldwin, on the theme of race relations.

Anschluss (March 1938) The union with Nazi Germany imposed on Austria by Hitler, with considerable assistance from the Austrians. (German, 'union'.)

ANTA The American National Theater and Academy, a federally chartered theatrical organization with local chapters that is devoted to furthering the development of new talent, stimulating community interest in theater, and contributing to the international exchange of acting companies.

Antakya A Turkish city, formerly called Antioch.

Antarctic Treaty (1959) A 30-year 12-nation treaty of agreement to suspend political claims to Antarctic territory and to cooperate in research.

Anthony Adverse (1933) The first of the mammoth best-selling historical novels, written by Hervey Allen and set in Napoleonic times.

Anthony Eden A black felt hat much in vogue in Whitehall before World War II, when Sir Anthony Eden (Lord Avon), Foreign Secretary (1935-38), set the trend.

Anthropologie structurale, L' (1958) The most massive and, in France, influential of Lévi-Strauss's works on anthropology.

Anthropophagi A name for cannibals, taken from the Greek by Shakespeare in the lines in *Othello*: The Anthropophagi, and men whose heads / Do grow beneath their shoulders. (Greek, 'man-eaters'.)

Anthroposophical Society (1913) A society founded by an Austrian Theosophist, Rudolf Steiner, to propagate his eclectic mystical religion of which Goethe was the Messiah. He built the Goetheanum, a spectacularly novel building near Basle, but it was burned down.

Antic Hay (1923) Aldous Huxley's early satirical novel about rootless aimless intellectuals in London. (*Hay* in sense 'country dance'; phrase from Marlowe's *Edward II*: shall with their goat feet dance the antic hay.)

Antichrist (1) Christ's final adversary who was expected to appear before the SECOND COMING; identified with the Beast of the Apocalypse; the word is also used in the New Testament of an apostate. Later the name was applied to various obnoxious figures in history, from Caligula, who wanted to put a statue of himself in the Jewish Temple, to Napoleon. (2) Title of a book by Nietzsche.

Anti-Comintern Pact (Nov. 1936) An agreement between Germany and Japan to cooperate in opposing Communism (see COMINTERN) made about the same time as the ROME-BERLIN AXIS came into being. It was joined by Italy a year later. In return Germany recognized Japan's puppet government of MANCHUKUO. See also TRIPARTITE PACT.

Anti-Corn-Law League (1839) A movement founded at Manchester, the home of Free Trade, which successfully campaigned under the leadership of Cobden and John Bright for the repeal of the CORN LAWS.

Antigone In Greek legend the daughter of Oedipus who defies King Creon of Thebes by sprinkling earth

on the corpse of her brother Poly-
neices. Creon condemns her to
death but relents after a protest by
TIRESIAS; too late, as Antigone and
Creon's son, whom she was to marry, had both committed suicide.
Also the title of Anouilh's play
(1942) on the same subject with contemporary implications.

Antioch Older name of the city of
Antakya, Turkey.

Anti-Party group (USSR, 1956-57)
The opposition to Khrushchev's policies, particularly on decentralizing
industry and on Hungary, formed by
Molotov, Malenkov, Kaganovich,
and (later) Bulganin. Khrushchev,
assisted by Zhukov and Mikoyan,
outmaneuvered them and dismissed
them from office, posting Molotov to
Outer Mongolia and Malenkov to
Kazakhstan.

Antique Automobile Club of America
(1935) A VETERAN CAR club, with
headquarters at Hershey, Pa.

Antirent War (1840-46) A revolt
against the almost feudal land tenure system unique to New York
State. Farmers disguised as Indians
and using the slogan 'Down with the
rent' harried sheriffs trying to serve
warrants, and the militia had to turn
out. New land legislation ended the
trouble.

Antoine's The most famous (and
expensive) restaurant in New Or-
leans, in the VIEUX CARRÉ. It inspired
Frances Parkinson Keyes's novel
Dinner at Antoine's (1948), a New
Orleans murder story. See also OYS-
TERS ROCKEFELLER.

Anton Nom de plume of the British
cartoonists Antonia Yeoman and H.
Underwood Thompson, whose cartoons mildly satirizing the social
scene are all joint efforts.

Antonines, Age of the (AD 96-180)
The Golden Age of the Roman Empire, during which the dynasty
founded by Nerva ruled, including
Trajan, Hadrian, Antoninus Pius,
and Marcus Aurelius.

Antonine Wall The wall built in
Scotland by the Romans about AD
150, from Carriden on the Forth to
Old Kilpatrick on the Clyde. (Antoninus Pius, Roman Emperor.)

Antonio (1) The name of the Merchant of Venice in Shakespeare's
play. (2) The character in Shakespeare's *The Tempest* who usurps
the dukedom of his brother PROS-
PERO.

Antony and Cleopatra (1606) (1)
One of Shakespeare's greatest plays,
on the theme of the relationship
between Mark Antony and CLEOPA-
TRA, the disaster of ACTIUM, and the
suicide of the 2 protagonists. (2)
Samuel Barber's opera (1966) writ-
ten for the opening of the new MET-
ROPOLITAN OPERA HOUSE in Lincoln
Center.

Anual (1921) The battle in which
the RIFF leader, Abd-el-Krim, defeated the Spanish forces in Morocco;
the consequent feeling of national
humiliation led to the dictatorship
of Primo de Rivera (1923-30).

Anubis Ancient Egyptian jackal-
headed god of the Underworld, local
to ABYDOS, and later regarded as a
son of OSIRIS. The Greeks identified
him with HERMES.

Anvil Code name for the Allied
landings in the south of France,
1944 (later called Dragoon).

Anyang The Chinese archeological
site in Honan Province, discovered
in 1934. It revealed that the earliest
(SHANG) Chinese Dynasty had already reached a high stage of civilization, with sculpture, bronzes,
carved jade, and pottery comparable
with those of its successors.

Anzac Name formed from the initial
letters of the Australian and New
Zealand Army Corps in World War
I, and applied to troops from those
countries in both world wars.

Anzac Cove The Dardanelles beach
where the ANZACS landed on Anzac
Day (Apr. 25, 1915).

Anzam (1949) A term used to denote
arrangements to coordinate defense
policies made by Britain, Australia,
and New Zealand. (Initials of Australia, New Zealand, and Malaysia.)

Anzio bridgehead (Jan. 1944)
Formed by an Allied landing behind
the German lines, south of Rome,
hotly contested.

Anzus (1951) The Pacific Security
Treaty signed in San Francisco by

Australia, New Zealand, and USA; Britain was excluded from it by USA. (From the initials of the 3 countries.)

AP (Associated Press) The oldest and largest of the US news agencies, founded 1848.

Apache (1) An American Indian tribe of the southwestern states. (2) A name given to Parisian gangsters.

Apache State Nickname of Arizona.

Apache Wars (1871-86) The result of unsuccessful attempts to keep the various Apache tribes to their reserves, and ended only by the capture of CERONIMO, their leader. The Apaches were settled in various parts of Arizona, New Mexico and Oklahoma, where about 10,000 survive today.

Apartheid The racial policy, adopted (1948) by South Africa's AFRIKANER Nationalist Party, of segregating Africans, CAPE COLOUREDS, Asians and whites, in theory so that each community can develop separately, e.g. in BANTUSTANS such as TRANSKEI. It involves separate transport, schools, residential areas etc., and even the prohibition of mixed marriages. One of the most controversial of postwar policies, it led to South Africa's leaving the Commonwealth in 1961. (Afrikaans, literally 'apart-hood', officially called 'Separate Development'.)

Aphrodite The Greek goddess of love, who was born of the sea foam and stepped ashore on the isle of Cythera. She was the wife of HEPHAESTUS, who trapped her in bed with ARES by throwing a net over them, then calling the other gods to mock them. In later legend she is the mother of EROS. She derives from ISHTAR, and is the Roman Venus. See also ADONIS; PARIS.

'Aphrodite Anadyomene' A painting of APHRODITE rising from the foam, painted by the 4th-century artist Apelles at the court of Alexander the Great; it was renowned in ancient times, but not even a copy has survived. See BIRTH OF VENUS. (Greek, 'rising up'.)

Apis Ancient Egyptian bull-god of Memphis, later identified with Osiris. Under the Ptolemies Osiris-Apis

became the Serapis of SAKKARA, god of the Underworld.

APO Initials for Army Post Office.

Apocalypse Name given to any of several religious works (but applied specifically to the *Book of Revelation* in the New Testament) on the theme of the final triumph of God at the end of the world, after a period of extreme tribulation. Their purpose was to strengthen faith in times of distress. (Greek, 'revelation'.)

Apocrypha, The An ill-defined collection of books found in the SEPTUAGINT and VULGATE versions attached to the Old Testament, not accepted by the Jews (the Hebrew originals having been lost), and accepted only with reservations by Protestants and Catholics. They include *The Wisdom of Solomon, Ecclesiasticus, Tobit, Judith, Maccabees, Esdras, Bel and the Dragon, the History of Susanna*. (Greek, 'hidden things', i.e. withheld from general circulation as being of doubtful authenticity.)

Apollo An essentially Greek god; he has no Roman counterpart. The son of ZEUS and brother of ARTEMIS, he had very varied functions illustrated by numerous legends: he was god of prophecy (taking over the Delphic Oracle); of healing (father of AESCULAPIUS); of flocks (shepherd to ADMETUS); of light (as Phoebus—'shining'—Apollo), and leader of the Muses. Statues depicted him as the ideal of male beauty, and to him are ascribed the famous counsels of moderation: Know thyself; Nothing too much.

'Apollo Belvedere' (4th century BC) The best-known Greek sculpture of a male figure, artist unknown. The bronze original is lost, but there is an inferior Roman copy in the Vatican Museum. (Belvedere is the name of the art gallery it is in.)

Apollonian Nietzche's adjective for all he despised, the negative attitude to life which he saw in the 'slave religion' born of failure, resentment and vengefulness, as taught by St Paul, Roman Catholics and Protestants (but not by Jesus himself), haunted by guilt feelings inspired by a false belief in original sin. In a wider sense he applied it to all that individualizes and defines, to structure and form in art, to rational thought. See DIONYSIAN. (APOLLO as the god of light, which clarifies and defines.)

Apollo space program US project to land a man on the moon, using a SATURN 5 rocket. In November 1967 the unmanned *Apollo 4* spacecraft simulated a moon flight with a LEM module, which was successfully parachuted into the ocean on target. *Apollo 7* was the first US 3-man flight (Oct. 1968) and *Apollo 8* the first manned flight (December) to leave the influence of earth gravity, orbit the moon and send back live TV pictures. *Apollo 9* tested a LEM in earth orbit and on *Apollo 10* (May 1969) the LEM *Snoopy* with a crew of 2 descended to within 9 miles of the moon. *Apollo 11* was the historic space flight on which Neil Armstrong and Edwin Aldrin became the first men on the moon (20 July 1969); Michael Collins was command pilot. *Apollo 12* was the space flight on which Charles Conrad and Alan Bean made the second landing on the moon (18 Nov. 1969), and visited SURVEYOR 3 (which had landed in 1967); Richard Gordon was command pilot. *Apollo 13* (April 1970) was the flight to the moon frustrated by an explosion which the 3-man crew (James Lovell, Fred Haise, Jack Swigert) miraculously survived, managing through incredibly skillful improvization by all concerned to make a safe return, though half-frozen and short of oxygen, water, and power. See also LUNAR ORBITER.

Apostles' Creed The oldest Christian creed, used only in Western Churches; attributed to the Apostles but in its present form it goes back only to AD 750; date of origin unknown.

Apostolic Fathers, The Those FATHERS OF THE CHURCH who were born in the 1st century AD and were thus approximately contemporaries of the Apostles, e.g. Clement of Rome.

Appalachia The hilly region, formerly CHEROKEE country, on the borders of Tennessee and North Carolina together with adjoining parts of Georgia, in the southern Appalachians. It is predominantly a wilderness of poor whites.

Appalachian Spring (1945) A musical work, with frontier life as its inspiration, composed by Aaron Copland for Martha Graham; an exceptionally beautiful and distinctively American score for full symphony, from which an effective ballet version was taken.

Appalachian Trail A foot trail extending 2000 miles through the Appalachians from Maine to Georgia.

Appassionata, The Name given to a famous Beethoven piano sonata written in a mood of passionate despair. Op. 57.

Appian Way (4th century BC) The first great Roman road, from Rome to Capua and Brindisi. (Named after Appius Claudius.)

Apple Cart, The (1929) Bernard Shaw's play in which he pillories Ramsay MacDonald for deserting the Labour Party in 1931. He represents him as Proteus, Prime Minister of a 'Socialist' government which is under the hidden control of industrialists. See King MAGNUS.

Apple Corps Ltd. (1968) The successor to Beatles Ltd. (1963) formed by the Beatles pop group; it had several divisions and subsidiary companies handling motion-picture production, music, electronics etc.

Appleton layer The 2 upper layers (F-1 and F-2) of the ionosphere which, being electrically charged by the sun's ultraviolet rays (ionized), reflect shortwave radio signals. F-1 lies at a height of about 100 miles, F-2 200 miles above the earth. See HEAVISIDE LAYER. (Sir Edward Appleton, Cambridge physicist.)

Appomattox Court House The place where the Confederate general, Robert E. Lee, surrendered to Gen. Grant (Apr. 1865), the virtual end of the American Civil War. (Town of central Virginia.)

Après-midi d'un faune, Prélude à l' (1894) Debussy's sun-drenched symphonic poem based on a SYMBOLIST poem by Mallarmé.

April Fools' Day April 1st; by ancient tradition of unknown origin a day for playing practical jokes on the unsuspecting, particularly by sending them on a fool's errand. It is observed in English-speaking countries, France (where the joke is called *poisson d'avril*), Germany and elsewhere.

Apsley House   149 Piccadilly, Hyde Park Corner, bought by the 1st Duke of Wellington and now the Wellington Museum.

Aquarius   The Water-Bearer, 11th constellation of the Zodiac, between Pisces and Capricornus; the sun enters it about Jan. 21st. Astrologers claim that those born under this sign may be strong-willed individualists, sincere and imaginative. (So named as representing a man pouring water from a vessel in his right hand.)

Aqueduct racetrack robbery   (1969) The second largest in US history, netting $1.37 million in cash for 3 armed men who in Brooklyn ambushed a Wells Fargo truck in which were the racetrack's takings for the day.

Aquila   A northern constellation above CAPRICORNUS and AQUARIUS. (Latin, 'eagle'.)

Aquitaine   A province of Roman Gaul which became a duchy and, with GASCONY, was inherited by the PLANTAGENETS but lost by Henry VI. At one time it stretched from the Loire to the Pyrenees; the capital was Bordeaux.

Arab   (horse) Originally a Bedouin breed from what is now Saudi Arabia, used with effect against the Crusaders. Small (14.2 hands), handsome, sturdy rather than fast, and ideal for polo, it is the chief strain in the THOROUGHBRED; see DARLEY ARABIAN.

Arabia Deserta, Travels in   (1888) C. M. Doughty's classic of Arabian travel, a sensitive description of his sojourn with the Bedouin and of the antiquities he found in the desert, written in stately Elizabethan prose.

Arabian Nights, The   Short title for *The Arabian Nights' Entertainments* or the *Thousand and One Nights*, a collection of oriental (Indian, Persian, Arab) tales going back to the 9th century, supposed to have been told by SCHEHERAZADE. They include stories of ALADDIN, ALI BABA, SINBAD,

the BARMECIDE FEAST etc., many set in the time of HARUN AL-RASHID, 8th-century Caliph of Baghdad.

Arab League   (1945) An uneasy association of Arab states for the promotion of common interests and opposition to Israel.

Arab Legion   The elite camel corps built up in Jordan between the wars by 2 British officers, Peake Pasha and Glubb Pasha; the latter was dismissed in 1956 during a xenophobic spasm.

Arab Revolt   (1916) The revolt that freed Arabia from Turkish rule, led by Hussein (Hashemite Sherif of Mecca and later King of Hejaz) and his son Feisal (later King of Iraq), with Allied support (including the secondment of Lawrence of Arabia). After their wartime successes, they were driven out of Arabia by the WAHABIS, implacable enemies of the HASHEMITES.

Arab Union   (1958) A federation of Iraq and Jordan to counter the formation of the United Arab Republic by Egypt and Syria. It survived 2 months.

Arachne   In Greek legend a girl who challenged ATHENE to a contest in weaving and defeated her. She was turned into a spider. (Greek, 'spider'.)

Arachnids   See ARTHROPODS.

Aragon   A kingdom of northeast Spain, capital Saragossa, taken from the Moors (1131) and joined to CASTILE (1479) by the marriage of Isabella of Castile and Ferdinand of Aragon. See NAVARRE.

Aramaic   A SEMITIC LANGUAGE, once the lingua franca of the western Persian Empire. From about the 7th century BC it displaced Hebrew, which became a learned language; the Jews, including Jesus and the Apostles, conversed in Aramaic and the Gospels were probably originally written in it. Later, Greek replaced it in cities, but in the countryside a dialect of Aramaic, Syriac, was spoken over a wide area. (*Aram*, 'Syria'.)

Aramco   Abbreviated name of the Arabian-American Oil Co. which exploits the petroleum of Saudi Arabia.

Arapaho An Algonquian-speaking nomadic tribe of northern PLAINS INDIANS, courageous fighters who, after the wars of 1861-64, were settled in Wyoming and Oklahoma, where about 4000 survive.

Ararat Traditionally the mountain on which Noah's Ark came to rest. It is in Turkey near the borders of the Armenian Republic of the USSR.

Araucanian The American Indian language of Chile.

Arbela Alternative name for the battle of GAUGAMELA; it was where Darius encamped before the battle.

Arbor Day An annual date, varying from state to state, dedicated to the planting of trees; a custom which originated in Nebraska.

Arbor Low A Neolithic stone circle and double-entrance tomb, near Bakewell, Derbyshire, England.

Arcadia The mountainous center of the Greek Peloponnese, an Ancient Greek SHANGRI LA. *Et in Arcadia ego* is a tomb inscription, quoted now (probably incorrectly) as meaning 'I too (once lived) in Arcady', i.e. knew perfect happiness. *Arcades ambo* ('Arcadians both') was used by Virgil of 2 shepherd-poets, but is now quoted with the meaning given it by Byron – 'blackguards both'.

Arcadia Code name for the Washington Conference (Dec. 1941-Jan. 1942) at which Roosevelt and Churchill decided to set up a combined chiefs of staff committee.

Arc de Triomphe (Paris) The triumphal arch in the center of the ÉTOILE, planned by Napoleon but not finished until 1836. It bears huge sculptures depicting the triumphs of Napoleon. The Tomb of the Unknown Warrior now lies under it. There is another Arc de Triomphe (1808) by the Louvre.

Archangels In the apocryphal *Book of Enoch* xxi there are 7, including Michael and Gabriel (who are also mentioned as chief angels in the Koran), and Raphael. See also PRINCIPALITIES.

Archduke Trio, The (1811) Beethoven's piano trio (No. 7), dedicated to Archduke Rudolph of Austria, his patron.

Archean (1) Geological term for the earliest PRECAMBRIAN crystalline rocks in any given region. (2) Sometimes used as a synonym of PRECAMBRIAN. (Greek *archaios*, 'ancient'.)

Archeozoic Period Term sometimes used as a subdivision of the PRECAMBRIAN ERA, between the PROTEROZOIC and EOZOIC periods. (Greek *archaios*, 'ancient', *zoé*, 'life'.)

Archer-Shee case See WINSLOW BOY.

Archibald Bell-the-cat Archibald Douglas, a 16th-century Earl of Angus who, when his fellow nobles agreed that James III's favorites should be put to death, undertook to do this, and in the presence of the King. (From an old fable of mice agreeing that a bell should be hung round a cat's neck to give them warning of its approach; a wise mouse asked: But *who* will bell the cat?)

Archimedean screw A spiral device for raising water through a tube. (See next entry.)

Archimedes, Principle of The loss of weight of a body immersed in water is equivalent to the weight of the water which it displaces. (Archimedes, Greek mathematician of the 3rd century BC.)

Archpoet The mythical leader of the Goliards of 12th-13th century Europe who wrote light satiric Latin verse. To him was attributed the famous medieval drinking song: Meum est propositum in taberna mori ('It is my firm intention to die in a tavern').

archy and mehitabel (1927) A book of ingenious blank verse by the US journalist Don Marquis. It was allegedly composed at night on Marquis' typewriter by a cockroach (archy) who could not reach the shift key (hence there are no capital letters). Archy recounts the adventures of mehitabel the cat, whose battle cry was 'toujours gai, archy, toujours gai'. There were several sequels.

Arcos raid (1927) A police raid ordered by the British Home Secretary, Joynson-Hicks, on the Soviet Trade Mission in London, thought to be engaged in subversive activities; Russia severed all relations with Britain.

Arctic Current Another name for the LABRADOR CURRENT.

Arcturus The brightest star in BOÖTES and the second brightest in the northern sky. (Greek, 'bear-guard', as found in a line with the tail of the Great Bear; in the Bible it is the NORTH STAR.)

Ardabil carpet (1540) One of the most famous antique rugs, now in the Victoria and Albert Museum, London. It was made for a mosque at Ardabil in northern Persia.

Ardagh Chalice A unique Celtic Christian silver chalice, possibly of the 9th century, decorated with enamel, mica, glass and amber; now in the National Museum, Dublin. (Village in Co. Limerick, Ireland, where found.)

Arden, Forest of A forest covering the English Midlands long ago, the remnants of which account for the name 'leafy Warwickshire'; chiefly remembered as the setting of AS YOU LIKE IT.

Ardennes Offensive (Dec. 1944-Jan. 1945) Von Rundstedt's sudden counterattack in the Ardennes, which took the Allies by surprise, creating a large salient and coming near to success. Also called the Battle of the Bulge.

Arden Shakespeare, The A standard annotated edition of Shakespeare's works, one volume for each play.

Areopagitica (1644) Milton's famous attack on a new law imposing censorship of books.

Areopagus A hill in Athens near the Acropolis, in ancient times the seat of a judicial council which also had administrative functions; called Mars' Hill in Acts xvii, 22.

Ares The Greek god of war (Roman Mars), a son of ZEUS and HERA. He was remarkably unsuccessful in his own wars and the Greeks liked to make fun of him (see APHRODITE).

Arethusa In Greek legend a NEREID whom ARTEMIS changed into a spring in Sicily so that she could escape from the river-god Alpheus.

Argenteuil (1) The finest French asparagus; (2) garnished with this.

(A district in Seine-et-Oise.)

Argive Of Argos, a town and kingdom of southern Greece. As AGAMEMNON, its king, was leader of the Greeks at Troy, Homer used the word as a synonym for Greek.

Argo The ship of the ARGONAUTS.

Argonauts In Greek legend, JASON and his companions, who included HERCULES, THESEUS, ORPHEUS and many other well-known heroes. They sailed in the *Argo* to capture the GOLDEN FLEECE, and MEDEA helped Jason to accomplish this task.

Argos See ARGIVE.

Argus In Greek legend the 100-eyed giant sent by HERA to watch IO, and slain by HERMES on behalf of ZEUS; hence *Argus-eyed*, vigilant.

Ariadne In Greek legend the daughter of King MINOS who gave THESEUS a ball of thread to help him to find his way back out of the Labyrinth (see MINOTAUR). They escaped together but Theseus later deserted her, and she married DIONYSUS.

Arian heresy That Jesus was of similar, but not of the same, substance as the Father, nor coeternal with him; it was condemned by the Council of NICAEA. The UNITARIANS hold similar views. (Arius, Alexandrian priest, 256-336.)

Ariel (1) An angel, in Cabbalistic literature. (2) A rebel angel in *Paradise Lost*. (3) The fairy in Shakespeare's *Tempest* whom PROSPERO rescued from CALIBAN's victimization.

Ariel Name given to Anglo-American research satellites, launched from California, including *Ariel-1* (1962) and *2* (1964), carrying British instrumentation, and *Ariel-3* (1967), made in Britain by BAC and GEC.

Ariel (1923) André Maurois' imaginative biography of Shelley.

Aries The Ram, 1st of the constellations of the Zodiac, between Pisces and Taurus; the sun enters it at the spring equinox about March 21st. Astrologers claim that those born under this sign may be outspoken and aggressive.

Aristotelian method A priori reasoning, from general to particular; see NOVUM ORGANUM.

'Aristotle Contemplating the Bust of Homer' (1653) Rembrandt's painting, in which Aristotle is shown in contemporary clothes with his hand resting on the bust. It is the chief treasure of the Metropolitan Museum of Art, NYC, which bought it for $2.3 million in 1961.

Arita ware Japanese ceramics; see IMARI PATTERN.

Arkansas toothpick Another name for BOWIE KNIFE, in the Arkansas Traveller tradition.

'Arkansas Traveller, The' (1840) A folk dialogue and tune (printed 1847), the former embodying the distrust of the squatter for the stranger, and probably first told by Col. Sandy Faulkner, who came to a lonely cabin in the Ozarks seeking accommodation. The squatter fends him off with deliberate 'misunderstandings' of the type: 'Where does this road go to?' 'It's never gone anywhar since I've lived here; it's always thar when I git up.' The lively tune, played on the fiddle by both of them, according to the story, became one of the most popular in the US; it may be the work of José Tasso of Cincinnati.

Arkie Nickname for an itinerant agricultural worker, especially one from Arkansas; compare OKIE.

Arkle One of the greatest horses in the history of English steeplechasing. In a 10-year career interrupted by injury in 1967, he won almost every important race except the Grand National, for which he was never entered.

Ark of the Covenant A wooden chest carried by the Israelites in their wanderings (Numbers x, 33), symbolizing Jehovah's presence and containing the tablets of the law.

Arlberg-Kandahar (1928) One of the most important events in Alpine (downhill and slalom racing) skiing, held at various centers in the Alps. (First held at St Anton in Arlberg, Austria; named after Lord Roberts of Kandahar.)

Arlecchino Italian name of HARLEQUIN.

Arles An ancient Roman town in Provence, associated particularly with the painter Van Gogh, who went there in 1888 and was joined there for a brief unhappy period by Gauguin.

Arlésienne (Cooking) With tomatoes, onion and, sometimes, eggplant. (ARLES, in Provence.)

Arlésienne, L' (1872) Bizet's incidental music for Daudet's play of hopeless love and tragic death. (French, 'the woman of Arles'.)

Arlington National Cemetery (1864) The site in Virginia facing Washington across the river, on the estate which once belonged to Robert E. Lee and then to Washington's adopted son, where US soldiers from every war, including a few from the Revolution, lie buried. The chief features are vast rows of plain gravestones in the Fields of the Dead, the Tomb of the UNKNOWN SOLDIER, an amphitheater for Memorial Day services, and the tombs of President J. F. Kennedy and his brother, Senator Robert F. Kennedy.

ARLP In France, initials of the Alliance Républicaine pour la Liberté et le Progrès, a group of extreme rightwing opponents of de Gaulle formed by Maître Tixier-Vignancourt.

Armada, The (1588) The Spanish fleet which sailed to invade England and was defeated by Lord Howard of Effingham and his captains, Drake, Hawkins and Frobisher; the surviving ships were wrecked while trying to get home via the north of Scotland.

Armageddon The last battle of the kings of the earth before the end of the world; name often applied to World War I. (Revelation xvi,16.)

Armagnac A darker, more pungent brandy than Cognac, made in the Gers département of Gascony.

Armenia Originally a large region on the borders of Turkey, Persia and Russia, inhabited by Christian peoples of very mixed origin who nevertheless preserved a sense of racial solidarity akin to that of the Jews, and were persecuted for it (see next entry). The name Armenia is now only used of the small Armenian republic of the USSR.

Armenian massacres (1896) The worst of several massacres to which

the Armenians have been subjected.
They began in Constantinople after
Armenian nationalists, as a demonstration to world opinion, had
seized the Ottoman Bank, and they
spread to the provinces, lasting till
the end of the year. There were other
such massacres in Turkey in 1909
and 1915.

Arminianism   The view, adopted
later by the Wesleyan Methodists,
that God is not responsible for evil,
and which rejected Calvin's doctrine of predestination. (Arminius,
Latin name of a Dutch theologian,
died 1609.)

Armistice Day   11 Nov. 1918, i.e. the
last day of World War I; in the US
now called Veterans Day.

Armorica   The name of Brittany before the Celts from southwest England took refuge there in the 4th
century AD. See BRETON.

Armoricaine   (Cooking) With a
white wine sauce, peppers, tomatoes and brandy. (ARMORICA.)

Arms and the Man   (1894) Bernard
Shaw's play satirizing heroics about
war. See also CHOCOLATE SOLDIER.
(Title taken from the first words of
Virgil's AENEID: 'Arms and the man I
sing . . .')

Arnhem   (Sept. 1944) A Dutch town
on the Rhine where Montgomery
tried unsuccessfully to establish a
bridgehead across the river by a
major parachute drop.

'Arnolfini and his Wife'   (1434) Jan
van Eyck's painting of a wedding
ceremony, in which the artist is seen
reflected in a mirror; now in the
National Gallery, London.

Artemis   The Greek huntress-goddess, who became identified with
the Asian mother-goddess (see DI-
ANA OF THE EPHESIANS) and later with
SELENE.

Artful Dodger, The   The young pick-
pocket trained by FAGIN in Dickens's
OLIVER TWIST.

Arthropods   A very large phylum of
creatures with hard bodies and
jointed limbs, including the In-
secta, with 3 pairs of legs (HEMIP-
TERA, DIPTERA, LEPIDOPTERA, COLEOP-
TERA, HYMENOPTERA, ORTHOPTERA);

the arachnids, with 4 pairs of legs
(spiders, scorpions, mites); crusta-
ceans, with many pairs of legs and
mostly aquatic (crabs, lobsters,
prawns, barnacles, woodlice); centi-
pedes and millipedes, among many
others.

Arthur   (1) Historically, perhaps a
West Country chieftain and leader of
the Romanized Britons in one of
their last stands against Anglo-Saxon invaders in the 6th century; (2) in
legend, the chivalrous king of all
England, leader of the Knights of the
ROUND TABLE. See ARTHURIAN LEG-
END.

Arthurian legend   A collection of
stories about King ARTHUR and his
knights, first mentioned some 300
years after his death; it absorbed
other originally unconnected folktales and was transformed by medieval Church chroniclers and court
bards in England and France, and by
later poets.

Articles of Confederation   (1781-89)
The constitution of the 13 American
colonies, replaced by the CONSTITU-
TION OF THE UNITED STATES.

Artiodactyla   An order of 2-toed
(cloven-hoofed) or 4-toed hoofed
mammals, including sheep, goats,
cattle, pigs, antelopes, camels, hip-
popotamuses, giraffes.

'Artist's Mother, The'   Whistler's
portrait of his aged mother; now
in the Luxembourg, Paris.

Art nouveau   (1890-1910) A style,
mainly of interior decoration, with
long curves and writhing asymmetrical shapes inspired by vegetational
forms, regarded with abhorrence
until recently but now again being
collected, ugly though most of it is,
especially when rendered in cast
iron. In Germany called Jugendstil
after a magazine *Jugend*. (Named after a shop opened in Paris in 1895.)

Arts Council of Great Britain   (1946)
A body partly subsidized by government which aims to develop a greater knowledge, understanding and
practice of the fine arts (including
drama, music and the visual arts), to
increase their accessibility to the
people as a whole, and to improve

their standards.

Arundel Castle An ancient Sussex castle rebuilt in the 18th century, the seat of the Dukes of Norfolk.

Aryan myth, The The view, adopted by the German Nazis from Houston Stewart Chamberlain and others, that the Germans were the purest ('NORDIC') descendants of the ancient and noble ARYANS, and therefore entitled to massacre those who were not, such as Jews and Slavs, to preserve their racial purity. In Nazi jargon 'Aryan' was used of a German who had no Jewish blood in his pedigree.

Aryans A term once used for the people who spoke INDO-EUROPEAN LANGUAGES. It fell into disrepute, especially after Nazi misuse of it (see last entry), but is still convenient in distinguishing between the pre-Aryan, and non-Aryan peoples of India. (Sanskrit *arya*, 'noble'.)

ASCAP (1914) Initials used for the American Society of Composers, Authors and Publishers.

Ascendancy, The The Anglo-Irish Protestants who dominated Ireland, especially after the Protestant succession of William III.

Ascension Day Holy Thursday, the 40th day after the Resurrection, on which the Ascension of Christ is commemorated.

Ascent of F6, The (1936) W. H. Auden and Christopher Isherwood's verse play satirizing modern values.

Asclepius See AESCULAPIUS.

Ascot Gold Cup (1807) The chief event of GOLD CUP DAY at ROYAL ASCOT, a race over a distance of 2½ miles. The original cup was stolen in 1907.

ASE Signifies the American Stock Exchange on WALL STREET; it originated antebellum as a Curb Exchange, which ceased at one time to function at all hours in streets and hotels; gradually organized as a voluntary association it was given its present title in 1953, and is the second largest stock exchange in the US after the NYSE.

ASEAN (1968) Initials used for Association of South-East Asian Nations: Philippines, Indonesia, Siam, Malaysia, Singapore. It began as a nonmilitary pact of cooperation from which, at the insistence of Malaysia and Indonesia, USA was excluded; it was subsequently proposed to convert it into a defense pact to replace SEATO.

ASG (1965) Initials used for the Association of Student Governments, which claims 2 million members in 300 colleges. It aims to coordinate moves to persuade college administrations to relax social restrictions and modernize curricula, but appears to be relatively conservative in tone.

Asgard The Scandinavian Olympus, at the center of the universe; VALHALLA is one region of it.

Ashanti Wars (1807-1900) Four British expeditions against the Ashanti people of the northern Gold Coast (Ghana), which ended in the annexation of their country.

Ashburton glass Glass fashioned in perhaps the earliest general pressed-glass patterns, a form of molding in large curvate thumbprint panels. This pattern, at the turn of the century, was often called Colonial.

Ashcan School Nickname of an early 20th-century group of American Realist painters led by Robert Henri (1865-1929), and sometimes called the Henri Group, and originally 'The Eight'. The nickname derived from their preoccupation with slum scenes, especially in the case of George Bellows, one of the best-known members. Another, George Luks, specialized in child studies. See SOCIAL REALISM.

Ashdown Traditional site, west of Lambourne, Berkshire, of the defeat of the Danes in 871 by King Ethelred and the future King Alfred.

Ashenden (1928) One of Somerset Maugham's novels, based on his experiences in the secret service in World War I. Ashenden reappears in *Cakes and Ale*.

Ashes, The Symbol of victory in England v. Australia Test cricket series. When in 1882 Australia won, the *Sporting Chronicle* published an obituary on English cricket, adding 'the remains will be cremated and the ashes taken to Australia'. The ashes of a cricket stump in an urn were given to the English team when it won the next year.

Ashkenazim The Jews of northern and central Europe, especially Germany and Poland. See SEPHARDIM. (Ashkenaz, *Genesis* x, 3 and *Jeremiah* li, 27; the name given to Germany by medieval rabbis.)

Ashmolean Oxford University museum and library of ancient history, the fine arts and archeology, housed in separate buildings, the Old (1683) and New (1897). (Founded by Elias Ashmole.)

Ashtoreth Biblical name of ISHTAR.

Ash Wednesday The first day of Lent. (From the custom of sprinkling penitents with ashes on that day.)

Ash Wednesday (1930) T. S. Eliot's first poem after he became an Anglo-Catholic, and the first to speak of the consolation and joy to be found in Christianity.

Asian flu (1957-58) A world epidemic of influenza, milder in type than the SPANISH FLU of 1918; it originated in China.

Asian Highway project A UN plan to improve existing roads and so provide 2 all-season arterial routes through Asia: (A1) from the Turco-Persian border via Teheran, Kabul, the Khyber Pass, Delhi, Calcutta, Mandalay to Saigon; (A2) from the Iraqi-Persian border via Teheran, Kerman, Lahore, Delhi, Nepal, Dacca, Rangoon, Bangkok to Singapore.

Asiento, The (1713) A 30-year contract made at the end of the War of the SPANISH SUCCESSION whereby Britain was to ship a specified number of slaves to Spanish America. (Spanish, 'contract'.)

'As Maine goes, so goes the country' A US political maxim based on the fact that Maine held presidential balloting earlier than the rest of the country, and the Maine results corresponded with all but one of the national results during 1860–88, and with all but 3 during 1888–

1928. With Franklin Roosevelt's victory in 1932 and his reelection in 1936 by all states but 2, his campaign manager sardonically amended the phrase to 'As Maine goes, so goes Vermont'.

Asmodeus A devil in the Talmud and the Apocrypha, possibly derived from Persian mythology. His speciality was killing bridegrooms on their wedding day.

Aspasia The cultured mistress of the Athenian statesman Pericles; hence applied to any highly educated courtesan.

Aspen Award A tax-free award of $30,000 to the person anywhere in the world judged to have made the greatest contribution to the advancement of the humanities.

Asphalt Jungle A colloquial term for a big city or a specified part of one.

Asquithian Liberals Those who remained loyal to Asquith after Lloyd George overthrew him in 1916 to form a Coalition government with the Conservatives.

Assassins The Persian Muslim secret sect of fanatics founded by the OLD MAN OF THE MOUNTAIN; its members, for rewards of opium (not hashish, despite the name), carried out widespread assassinations not only of Crusaders but of the leaders of rival Muslim sects. (Arabic, 'hashish-eaters'.)

Assassins Oxford University club of those who have fought for the university in 3 fencing matches.

Assizes (UK) Courts held in at least one town per county at least 3 times a year by judges (usually 2) of the High Court on circuit. They have unlimited criminal jurisdiction and also hear civil, especially divorce, cases. The London Assize Court is the Central Criminal Court (Old Bailey).

Associated British Foods The group built up by the Canadian, Garfield Weston, on a foundation of cracker firms, which has absorbed Allied Bakeries, ABC Teashops and Fortnum & Mason, with subsidiaries in South Africa, Australia etc. Products include a wide range of groceries, and bread.

Associated Newspapers (UK) The Rothermere press, which includes the *Daily Mail*, *Daily Sketch* and *Evening News*.

Associated Television See ATV.

Assumption, The Bodily The dogma of the physical transfer to heaven of the Virgin Mary, proclaimed an article of Catholic faith (1950), and celebrated at the Feast of the Assumption on Aug. 15th.

Assyria Originally a city-state of SUMER, became Babylon's chief rival; from the 9th century BC it came to dominate Mesopotamia, and conquered Syria, Palestine and Egypt. Assyrian rule ended when the Medes and Babylonians destroyed the capital, Nineveh, in 612 BC.

AST See ATLANTIC STANDARD TIME.

Astarte Syrian name of ISHTAR.

Astbury ware A label for a type of glazed earthenware made in Staffordshire from about 1730, some of it by John Astbury, of whom little is known. Typically it was a red (sometimes white or brown) clay covered with a yellowish transparent lead glaze, used to make quaintly naïve figures of pop-eyed musicians, horsemen and the delightful 'pew groups'. Models with colored glazes are sometimes classified as Astbury-WHIELDON.

Astérix le Gaulois (1959) A French cartoonist's creation, of growing international fame; a fiery little man with a drooping moustache who, with his pugnacious companion Obélix, a menhir deliveryman, lives in the village of Petitbonum, which alone of all 3 parts of Gaul has held out against the Roman conqueror. The first French satellite was named Astérix.

Asti Spumante A sparkling Italian wine produced at Asti, Piedmont; there are also still wines of Asti, less famous.

Astolat See LADY OF SHALOTT.

Aston University A new university at Birmingham, formerly a CAT.

Astor Place riots (1849) Demonstrations in NYC by the fans of the first great American-born actor, Edwin Forrest (said to have been badly treated in London a few years earlier), against those of the English actor Macready. In clashes near the Opera House in Astor Place, 22 people were killed.

Astrodome, The See HOUSTON ASTRODOME.

Astrophel A name, based on an elaborate Greek pun, for the Elizabethan poet Sir Philip Sidney, used in poetry by him and about him.

Astros The Houston Astros, NATIONAL (Baseball) LEAGUE, playing at the HOUSTON ASTRODOME.

Asturias, The An old province on the Biscayan coast of Spain; the heir to the throne used to be called the Prince of the Asturias. This region, the modern Oviedo, is noted for its coal and anthracite mines, and for unrest among the miners.

ASV Initials standing for the AMERICAN STANDARD VERSION of the Bible.

Aswan High Dam A new dam a few miles upstream from the Aswan Dam (1902) at the First Cataract of the Nile near the Sudan border. The height is 350 ft to impound a lake 300 miles long, providing water for irrigation and hydroelectricity. Withdrawal in 1956 of an Anglo-American offer of finance led to the SUEZ CRISIS and the advent of Russian finance and technicians who began construction in 1960.

As You Like It (about 1600) Shakespeare's comedy of an exiled duke living in the Forest of ARDEN with his daughter Rosalind, who is disguised as a boy. Other characters are TOUCHSTONE and the 'melancholy' JAQUES.

At (UK) Colloquial abbreviation for a member of the ATS.

Atalanta In Greek legend a swift-footed girl of ARCADIA who would only marry the man who could outrun her. Aphrodite gave one suitor, Melanion, 3 golden apples to drop on the course. Atalanta stopped to pick them up, and he won the race and her. See also CALYDONIAN BOAR.

Atalanta in Calydon (1865) Swinburne's dramatic poem in which he weds Romantic atheism to Classical

Greek tragedy in a version of the legend of Atalanta and the Calydonian boar-hunt. See last entry.

Atalide, Princess See BAJAZET.

AT & T (1885) American Telephone & Telegraph Co., originally a subsidiary of the old American Bell Co., which it took over in 1900. It runs the BELL SYSTEM; has many subsidiaries, e.g. Western Electric (which makes its equipment) and the Bell Telephone Laboratories; developed the GEMINI program, TELSTAR and early warning systems; and is one of the 30 industrials that make up the DOW JONES Industrial Average.

Atatürk The name given to Mustapha Kemal in 1934 after he had become dictator of the new Turkey. (Turkish, 'father of the Turks'.)

Ate Greek goddess of discord, retribution and hate.

Aten The Solar Disk god whom AKHENATEN tried unsuccessfully to establish as the sole god of Ancient Egypt.

Athalie (1691) Racine's play about Athaliah, daughter of Ahab and Jezebel and wife of the King of Judah. She killed all the house of David except one, who survived to become king and take his revenge (2 Kings xi).

Athanasian Creed A hymn on the Trinity incorporating the views of Athanasius (died 373) and dating from not earlier than the 5th century, possibly much later. It stresses that the 3 Persons of the TRINITY are coequal and coeternal.

Athenaeum Club (1824) A London club in Waterloo Place with a learned and distinguished membership of scientists, bishops, vice-chancellors, professors etc. Its particular cachet is summed up in the old story of its hall porter venturing the opinion that 2 of the 3 taxis which a departing member claimed to see were 'purely subjective phenomena.'

Athene The patron goddess of Athens, to whom the PARTHENON was dedicated. She sprang fully armed from the head of ZEUS, and was the Greek goddess of war, wisdom, arts and crafts; frequently called PALLAS Athene. Athene is the Homeric spelling, Athena the later local Athenian form. The Roman equivalent is Minerva.

Athens of the North, The A name for Edinburgh.

Athinganoi Byzantine name for Gypsies, from which are derived their names in German (Zigeuner), Italian (Zingari) and Spanish (Gitanos). (Greek, 'untouchables'.)

Athletics The Oakland Athletics, AMERICAN (Baseball) LEAGUE playing at the Oakland-Alameda County Coliseum.

Athos, Porthos and Aramis The THREE MUSKETEERS.

Atlantic, Battle of the The campaign waged by the Royal Navy, Coastal Command and the Merchant Navy throughout World War II against German sea and air forces in the Atlantic.

Atlantic Charter (Aug. 1941) A declaration of long-term aims issued by Churchill and Roosevelt (President of a still-neutral state) after their conference at sea off Newfoundland, affirming belief in self-determination, freer trade, freedom of the seas, and disarmament 'after the final destruction of the Nazi tyranny'.

Atlantic College (1962) A school at St Donat's Castle, near Cardiff, first of a projected series of international colleges giving a 2-year preuniversity course. The ultimate aim is that anyone who passes out of an Atlantic College can enter any university of any country participating in the scheme, which was conceived by Kurt Hahn of GORDONSTOUN and the OUTWARD BOUND SCHOOLS.

Atlantic Community The community of NATO Powers.

Atlantic Monthly (1857) A distinguished magazine published in Boston, Mass., with articles on literature, politics, science and art, as well as short stories from new writers.

Atlantic Nuclear Force (ANF; 1964) A British compromise proposal to replace the MULTILATERAL FORCE project, combining the MLF with a British-manned force of V-bombers and Polaris submarines. It came to nothing.

Atlantic Pact (1949) The treaty which set up NATO, signed in Washington by USA, Canada and most of the countries of Western Europe (except Spain and Sweden), and later joined by Greece, Turkey and Western Germany.

Atlantic standard time The civil time of the 60th meridian, 1 hour faster than Eastern standard time; observed in Puerto Rico and Nova Scotia.

Atlantic Wall The coastal defenses of France built by the Germans during their occupation (1940-45).

Atlantis A land submerged by the sea about 9500 BC according to a legend recorded by Plato, who attributed it to Solon (6th century BC) and ultimately to Egyptian sources; Plato assumed that it lay beyond the Pillars of Hercules in the Atlantic. See THIRA; LEMURIA.

Atlas In Greek legend a Titan condemned to stand on the Atlas Mountains in North Africa and hold up the heavens; Atlantic and ATLANTIS are derived from his name. Mercator used the figure of Atlas with the world on his back as an emblem on his volumes of maps.

Atlas (1958) The first American ICBM, made by Convair for the Air Force; liquid-fueled, range 6300 miles, 5-megaton warhead. When tested it landed within 30 miles of the target at full range.

Atomic Energy Authority (1954) The body which controls nuclear research and development in Britain; see ALDERMASTON; CULHAM LABORATORY; RISLEY.

Atomic Energy Commission (1) A UN body set up (1946-52) to consider measures for the international control of the production of nuclear energy. While the USSR wanted stockpiles destroyed before control was instituted, the US wanted control first. It was replaced by the DISARMAMENT COMMISSION. (2) The body which supervises the US nuclear

energy program. It also monitors nuclear tests abroad.

Atomic Weapons Research Establishment See ALDERMASTON.

Atoms for Peace A program of international cooperation in the development of nuclear power for peaceful uses, launched by President Eisenhower (1953), implemented by the establishment of the INTERNATIONAL ATOMIC ENERGY AGENCY.

Atonement, Day of See YOM KIPPUR.

ATP A compound occurring throughout the body which, particularly in muscle, produces energy; in doing so, it is converted to ADP, which is reconverted to ATP by the action of breathed-in oxygen on the sugar in the body. Hence the connection between heavy exertion and panting for breath. (Initials of adenosin tri- and di-phosphate, respectively.)

Atreus, House of A family (in Greek the Atreidae, sons of Atreus) that includes many of the most familiar figures of Greek tragedy. Thyestes placed an effective curse on it after his brother Atreus had induced him unwittingly to eat a stew made from his own sons' flesh; this crime was not expiated until the time of ORESTES, AGAMEMNON'S SON.

Atropos One of the 3 FATES.

ATS (1938) Initials of the British Auxiliary Territorial Service which replaced the WAAC (Women's Army Auxiliary Corps) of World War I and was replaced in 1949 by the WRAC (Women's Royal Army Corps).

At Swim-Two-Birds (1939) A novel (if that is the word) by Flann O'Brien, strongly influenced by James Joyce. The less incomprehensible parts are uproariously funny.

Attic Greek The Ancient Athenian dialect, used by most of the great Greek writers; on the analogy of 'Standard English', it might be called Standard Ancient Greek. (Athens was the capital of Attica.)

Attic salt The delicate wit characteristic of the Ancient Athenians. (In Latin, *sal* meant both 'salt' and 'wit'.)

Atticus The friend to whom Cicero wrote many letters, which were collected and published; also used by Pope as a pseudonym for Addison. (T. Pomponius, surnamed Atticus because of his long sojourn in Athens; see ATTIC GREEK.)

Attis A Phrygian god of the spring, who was driven mad by the jealous CYBELE, and castrated himself.

Attwood Group A group of British market research companies which provide classified data on household consumption collected through a Consumer Panel; and, in Britain until 1968, TAM-RATINGS (see NEILSENS). It also operates in most countries of Western Europe.

ATV (UK) Initials standing for Associated Television, the program contractors for the Midlands (and until 1968 for London at weekends). It was the first commercial service to go on the air in Britain. The company was formed by the principal lobbyists for commercial TV, led by Norman Collins, and was originally financed by Moss Empires (Lew Grade, Val Parnell), the *Daily Mirror*, Pye Radio and Warburgs. Their programs were generally regarded as being notably easy on the mind. The headquarters are in Birmingham.

Aubrey's Brief Lives Delightful short biographical notes on the leading figures of Tudor and Jacobean times, liberally spiced with gossip and anecdotes, written by John Aubrey (1690) but not published under his name until 1813.

Aubusson carpets French carpets of supreme quality in the 18th century, made at Aubusson where, traditionally, tapestry was made from the 8th century, and Savonnerie carpets and GOBELINS and Beauvais tapestries are woven on handlooms to this day, also at Felletin nearby. (Town in central France, east of Limoges.)

Auchinleck James Boswell's family estate in Ayrshire.

Audley End House A Jacobean palace built near Saffron Walden, Essex, by the 1st Earl of Suffolk, and now owned by the Ministry of Works.

Audubon prints Color prints of American birds and animals made from excellent paintings by J. J. Audubon, American ornithologist and artist (1785-1851), who was born of French and Creole parents.

Audubon Society, National (1905) A society for the preservation of wildlife (especially birds) founded at the height of the craze for bird feathers to decorate women's hats. (Named for J. J. Audubon, see last entry.)

Aufklärung The ENLIGHTENMENT in Germany.

Augean stables In Greek legend the stables where Augeus, King of Elis, had kept 3000 oxen for 30 years. It was one of Heracles' labors to cleanse them.

Augsburg, League of (1685) A secret alliance of Holland, Spain, Sweden, the Empire and the Papacy, to prevent Louis XIV from gaining control of the Spanish Empire; joined by England in 1689. See next entry.

Augsburg, War of the League of (1689-97) A war (see last entry) which, after destroying French sea power, ended in the Treaty of Ryswick, by which France gave up its earlier conquests, and (temporarily) recognized William III as King of England.

Augsburg Confession (1530) A declaration of Protestant tenets drawn up by Luther and presented to the Emperor Charles V at the Diet of Augsburg. It is still accepted as authoritative by the LUTHERAN CHURCH.

Augustan Age (1) The golden age of Latin literature when Virgil, Horace and Ovid flourished, corresponding with the era of Augustus (27 BC-AD 14). (2) A golden age of English literature variously defined as that of Pope, Addison and Swift (and Queen Anne) or extended to include the earlier Dryden. (3) In France the era of Racine, Corneille and Molière.

Auguste The professional term for a circus clown of the silent, baggy-trousered buffoon type who gets in everyone's way. (The clown proper is a dignified white-faced figure in a conical hat.)

Augustinians A name covering various religious communities which followed the Rule of St Augustine of Hippo (not a formal Rule, but one compiled from his writings), such as the AUSTIN CANONS and AUSTIN FRIARS.

Augustus See OCTAVIAN.

Auld Alliance, The Name given to the traditional defensive alliance of Scotland and France against England, dating from the 13th century and still a force during the Jacobite rebellions. The royal families often intermarried, and French influences on Scottish language, law and customs still survive.

'Auld Lang Syne' A Scottish song of uncertain origin, partly rewritten by Robert Burns, and beginning: Should auld acquaintance be forgot,/ And never brought to mind? (Syne, 'since'; auld lang syne, 'times of long ago'.)

Auld Reekie A Scottish nickname for Edinburgh, meaning 'Old Smoky'.

Auld Robin Gray (1771) A Scottish ballad written by Lady Anne Lindsay about her father's cowherd, set to a traditional air.

Aunt Edna plays Plays for people who go to the theater to be entertained, to get away from the kitchen sink rather than to have their noses rubbed in it. (Phrase coined by Terence Rattigan.)

Auriga A northern constellation between PERSEUS and GEMINI, also called the Wagoner (as is BOÖTES). Alpha-Aurigae is Capella, the 5th brightest star. (Latin, 'charioteer'; see CHARLES'S WAIN.)

Aurignacian culture A phase of the PALEOLITHIC AGE, perhaps lasting from 70,000-18,000 BC, during which CRO-MAGNON MAN appeared in a comparatively warm interglacial period, and began to produce the remarkable cave paintings of ALTAMIRA and elsewhere. (Aurignac rock shelter in the Pyrenees, France.)

Aurora Latin name for the goddess of dawn (Greek EOS).

Aurora Borealis A vivid glow in the northern night sky, predominantly greenish yellow, often seen in high latitudes and sometimes much further south, particularly when sunspot activity is at its maximum. It is caused by charged solar particles attracted to the magnetic pole meeting the atmosphere at heights of 60-500 miles, but the process is not fully understood. The corresponding Antarctic phenomenon is called the Aurora Australis.

Aurora Leigh (1857) Elizabeth Browning's rather pedestrian blank-verse novel. When Mrs Browning died, Edward Fitzgerald commented 'No more Aurora Leighs, thank God!' and got trounced by Browning in a vituperative poem.

Aurora's Wedding In ballet, a one-act divertissement originally performed as part of The Sleeping Beauty ballet by Tchaikovsky.

Aurore (Cooking) With a thick tomato sauce. (Named from the resultant color.)

AUS Initials used for Army of the United States.

Auschwitz (1939) Site near Katowice, Poland, of the first Nazi concentration camp to be equipped with gas chambers for mass genocide. (German form of Polish name Oswiecim.)

Ausgleich (1867) See DUAL MONARCHY.

Austerlitz (Dec. 1805) The battle in which Napoleon defeated the Austrians and Russians and brought the HOLY ROMAN EMPIRE to an end. See THIRD COALITION. (Now Slavkov, Czechoslovakia, east of Brno.)

Austin Canons (12th century) A religious order of clergy following the Rule of St Augustine (see AUGUSTINIANS). They were not monks, but clergy living in communities though performing normal pastoral duties. Also called Augustinian Canons, Black Canons, and Canons Regular.

Austin Friars (13th century) An order of mendicant friars (originally hermits) who followed the Rule of St Augustine (see AUGUSTINIANS). Several communities still exist, especially in Ireland.

Australasia Australia, New Zealand and the islands of the southwest Pacific.

Australopithecines ('southern apes') PLIOCENE apes living in South and East Africa from about 3 million years ago; the earliest to walk upright, and therefore classed as hominids (manlike). The earliest fossil specimen is thought to be an armbone found in Kenya by Professor Patterson of Harvard; it was announced in 1967 that this was 2½ million years old.

Austrian Succession, War of the (1740-48) A war precipitated by Frederick the Great's seizure of Austrian Silesia after Maria Theresa's succession under the PRAGMATIC SANCTION. France joined in the attack on Austria but was defeated at Dettingen by the Austrians, Hanoverians and English under George II; the position was reversed 2 years later at Fontenoy. Under the inconclusive Treaty of Aix-la-Chapelle Prussia retained Silesia.

Auteuil Paris racetrack adjoining the LONGCHAMP course in the Bois de Boulogne.

Authentics Oxford University cricket club of the 60 best players in residence (elected for life); it has no ground of its own and mostly plays against schools.

Authorized Version (1611) The English Bible published by command of King James I and still in general use; largely based on TYNDALE'S BIBLE.

Autobiography of a Super-Tramp (1908) An account by the Welsh poet W. H. Davies of his life as a hobo in America.

Autocrat of the Breakfast Table, The (1858) The first of Oliver Wendell Holmes's series of 'Breakfast Table' collections of essays, in which he represents himself as expatiating on a wide range of themes to a largely silent company gathered at his table.

Autolycus (1) In Greek legend a crafty thief, son of Mercury. (2) In Shakespeare's *Winter's Tale* the name of a thieving pedlar, 'a snapper-up of unconsidered trifles'.

Autostrada del Sole The motorway from Milan to Naples and on to the toe of Italy. (Italian, 'motorway of the sun'.)

Autumn Double (UK) A bet on the CESAREWITCH and CAMBRIDGESHIRE races, both run in October.

Auxis Nickname for the Auxiliary Division recruited in 1920 to fight the Irish rebels; a quite separate body from the BLACK AND TANS, and notorious for brutality.

Avalon In Arthurian legend an Island of the Blessed ruled by MORGAN LE FAY; mistakenly identified with GLASTONBURY. (Celtic, 'island of apples'.)

Avalon Foundation (1940) A foundation established by Mrs. Ailsa M. Bruce, NYC, which makes grants to tax-exempt organizations working on medical, cultural, educational, civic or youth programs.

Avare, L' (1668) Molière's comedy of the rich miser Harpagon, whose children get their own way by impounding his money box.

Avebury The site in southern England of one of the world's largest stone circles. There were originally 3 circles, with an outer diameter of a quarter of a mile, and a long avenue of stones leading to a neighboring 'sanctuary'. (Village near Marlborough.)

Ave Maria A salutation to the Virgin Mary, combined in the Roman Catholic Church with a prayer to her as Mother of God.

'Avenue, Mittelharnis, The' (1689) Hobbema's best-known painting, now in the National Gallery, London.

Avernus Latin name for the Underworld, of which Virgil said: 'The descent to Avernus is easy, but the return journey — that is the difficulty', a passage applied to the picking up of evil ways.

Avesta See ZEND-AVESTA.

Avianca The Colombian airline which, as SCADTA (1919), was the first in Latin America.

Avignonese Captivity (1305-78) The period during which 7 Popes reigned at Avignon, subservient to the King of France, while Italy was in a state of anarchy. See GREAT SCHISM.

Avogadro's hypothesis (1811) That equal volumes of all gases contain the same number of molecules, if under the same conditions of pressure and temperature. (Italian physicist.)

Avon, 1st Earl of Formerly Sir Anthony EDEN.

Avro (1910) An aircraft firm founded by Sir A. V. Roe which produced many famous planes before it was absorbed by the HAWKER SIDDELEY GROUP in 1936.

AVS project A projected V/STOL swing-wing supersonic (Mach 2) fighter-bomber, intended to be developed by USA and Western Germany in partnership as a replacement for the STARFIGHTER in the late 1970s. (Initials standing for Advanced V/STOL Study.)

AWG Initials for American Wire Gauge, a classification of the thickness of wire and rods; the highest numbers are the thinnest, as in BWG.

AWOL (Army term) Absent without leave.

Axel Paulsen An ice-skating jump, of which there are various types.

Axel's Castle (1931) Edmund Wilson's best-known work of literary criticism.

Axis See ROME-BERLIN AXIS.

Axis powers See TRIPARTITE PACT.

Axis Sally Nickname of Mildred E. Gillars, convicted (1949) in New York City by a Federal jury of treason in broadcasting Nazi propaganda; released 1961.

Axminister carpets (1) Carpets inspired by Persian models, made in England at Axminster (1755-1835) and thereafter at Wilton. (2) Trade term for a process of weaving carpets which economizes in materials as all the pile yarn is on the surface, with none hidden in the fabric. Multicolored patterns are common, there is always a cut-pile surface, and the back is less smooth than in WILTON CARPETS.

Ayesha (1) The favorite wife of Mohammed. (2) Title of a novel (1905) by Rider Haggard, a sequel to *She* (1887). Ayesha ('She') is here an African sorceress.

Aylesbury duck The most popular breed of English domestic duck for the table.

Ayot St Lawrence See SHAW'S CORNER.

Ayrshire cattle A widespread dairy breed producing milk often used in cheese-making; colored red, brown and white in varying proportions.

Azad Kashmir 'Free' Kashmir, the northwest part of Kashmir occupied by Pakistan. See KASHMIR DISPUTE.

Azerbaijan A region bordering on the southwest shore of the Caspian Sea, now divided between the USSR constituent republic of that name (capital, Baku) and 2 adjoining Iranian provinces: Eastern (capital, Tabriz) and Western Azerbaijan (capital, Rizayeh).

Aztecs The American Indian race which flourished in Mexico in the 15th century and was conquered by the Spanish in the 16th. They had absorbed the Mayan culture passed on to them by their predecessors, the TOLTECS, exaggerating its feature of human sacrifice to insane extremes.

B

Baal The Phoenician form of the Assyrian name Bel. Originally it meant 'owner', 'lord', and then a local god (each town had its own); hence, in the Bible, a false god. The word appears in many names, as in Beelzebub, Hannibal.

Baalbek The site in Lebanon, 36 miles northeast of Beirut, of an ancient center of Syrian BAAL-worship. The Greeks renamed it Heliopolis and the Romans built several temples there, that dedicated to BACCHUS (2nd century AD) being one of the largest and best preserved of the Greco-Roman temples.

Baathists Members of a radical pan-Arab movement, strong in Syria and Iraq but less so in Jordan and elsewhere; standing for democratic freedom, they are opposed to the Nasser regime in Egypt, which they fear. (Arabic, 'revival'.)

Babar the Elephant (1931) Chief character in a series of witty children's books written and illustrated by the Frenchman, Jean de Brunhoff (died 1937) and then by his son Laurent; they proved immensely popular and were translated into English.

Bab Ballads (1869) A collection of light verse by W. S. Gilbert, of which the best known is 'The Yarn of the *Nancy Bell*'.

Babbitt (1922) Sinclair Lewis's novel of a parochial realtor who tries unsuccessfully to struggle free from the conformities of business life in the small Middle West town of Zenith. See next entry.

Babbittry The smug unimaginative conformity and worship of business success which characterized the hero of BABBITT.

Babel Biblical name for Babylonia.

Babe Ruth The commonest form of the greatest name in US baseball. Born George Herman Ruth, he played (1914-35) successively for the Boston RED SOX, New York YANKEES and Boston Braves, hit 714 home runs in regular season play and 15 in WORLD SERIES competition.

Babes in the Wood A story which originated from a 16th-century ballad of a man who hires 2 thugs to kill his infant nephew and niece in order to seize their inheritance. One of the thugs kills the other and abandons the children in a wood. They die, the birds cover them with leaves, and the uncle is suitably punished.

Babe the Blue Ox The constant companion of Paul BUNYAN; he measured 42 axe handles and a plug of Star tobacco between the eyes.

Babington's plot (1586) The last of a series of Roman Catholic plots against the English Queen Elizabeth I, which led to the execution of Mary Queen of Scots.

Babu (1) The Hindu equivalent of 'Mr'. (2) Used by the British of a Hindu, especially Bengali, clerk whose English had characteristic Indianisms (e.g. 'I am having' for 'I have').

Baby Austin (1921) The Austin Seven, a 7 h.p. car which was the first small mass-produced car to be made in Britain.

Babylonian Captivity (1) The period 586-538 BC when leading Jewish families were in enforced exile at Babylon, deported there by Nebuchadnezzar. When the Persian Cyrus took Babylon and freed them, most of them chose to stay (see DIASPORA). Also called the Exile. (2) Another name for the AVIGNONESE CAPTIVITY.

Babylonian Empire (1) The first or Old Empire (1900-1600 BC) which flourished under Hammurabi in the 18th century. (2) The New or Chaldean Empire (625-538 BC) which reached its height under Nebuchadnezzar II, who carried off the Palestinian Jews into captivity in Babylon. It fell to the Persian king, Cyrus the Great.

BAC (1960) Initials of the British Aircraft Corporation, which merged the fixed-wing aircraft and guided weapon interests of the English Electric Co. (40%), Bristol Aeroplane Co. (20%) and Vickers (40%); with aircraft divisions at Filton, Preston and Weybridge making the Concorde, One-Eleven, VC-10 and Lightning, and guided weapons centers at Filton, Cardiff and Stevenage making BLOODHOUND and THUNDERBIRD ballistic missiles and Vigilant antitank missiles.

Baccalauréat French equivalent to the GCE or German ABITUR. (French, 'bachelor's degree' but not in the English sense; the equivalent to the English bachelor's degree is the *diplôme*.)

Baccarat paperweights The best-known of the 19th-century French paperweights, mostly of the millefiori type with tiny silhouettes of animals etc. on the ends of some of the rods and often a date (usually 1848). The firm still produces high-quality weights (now marked 'Baccarat'), and is located in the Vosges town of Baccarat.

Bacchanalia The Roman festival (Greek Dionysia) in honor of BACCHUS, orgiastic, licentious, and drunken.

Bacchants The followers (also called Maenads or Bacchae) of DIONYSUS (Bacchus), who danced in the mountain forests, and tore animals and human beings to pieces.

Bacchus The Roman name of DIONYSUS, taken from one of his Greek epithets (Bakchos).

'Bacchus and Ariadne' (1514) Titian's painting of Bacchus leaping from his chariot to console ARIADNE, whom THESEUS had deserted; now in the National Gallery, London.

Back Bay An area of Boston, Mass., reclaimed from mud flats from 1856. Commonwealth Avenue and Beacon Street run through it from BOSTON COMMON and for nearly a century it was the city's most desirable residential quarter.

Backs, The The attractive grounds laid out on either side of the River Cam at the backs of Trinity and neighboring colleges in Cambridge, England.

Back to Methuselah (1922) A cycle of 5 plays by Bernard Shaw in which he returns to the theme of CREATIVE EVOLUTION (see MAN AND SUPERMAN) and adds the LAMARCKIAN theory of evolution through adaptation to environment. The first play starts in the Garden of Eden and the last ends in the far future, by which time man has by willpower evolved himself into a being almost wholly intellectual and able to live for hundreds of years.

Baconian method See NOVUM ORGANUM.

Baconian theory The theory that Francis Bacon wrote Shakespeare's plays; of 18th-century origin, it relied chiefly on the supposition that Shakespeare was too ignorant to have been their author. Ignatius Donnelly, in *The Great Cryptogram* (1888), 'discovered' that the plays were one vast code message from Bacon to posterity; this he solved by making up a complicated code as he went along, and altering it as convenient. The results were hilarious.

Bactria Ancient name of a town and district of Persia, now in Afghanistan and named Balkh.

Bad Child's Book of Beasts, A. (1896) An illustrated book of light verse by Hilaire Belloc, of which the following is typical: I shoot the Hippopotamus / With bullets made of platinum, / Because if I use leaden ones / His hide is sure to flatten 'em.

Badger State Nickname of Wisconsin.

Badlands Specifically, a region of western South Dakota and northwest Nebraska, arid, barren and eroded into deep gullies; similar regions elsewhere.

Badminton Horse Trials (1952) (UK) A 3-day event including dressage, a speed and endurance test over a varied and difficult course of 17 miles, and show jumping; the rider with the highest total score is the winner. Held in the Duke of Beaufort's park at Badminton, Gloucestershire, in April, and instituted by him to raise the standards of British horsemanship.

Badminton House The 17th-century home of the Dukes of Beaufort, near Chipping Sodbury, Gloucestershire.

Baedeker The name of a series of detailed and authoritative tourist guides, using the star system to distinguish points of particular interest, started in the early 19th century. (Name of German publishing firm of Leipzig, now moved to Hamburg.)

Baedeker raids (April 1942) A series of air raids on the cathedral towns of Canterbury, York, Bath and Exeter, in retaliation for the bombing of Lübeck, Rostock and Cologne. (Named after the BAEDEKER guides.)

Bagdad-on-the-Subway O. Henry's name for Manhattan, the setting of many of his best-known short stories and where he lived after coming out of prison.

Baghdad Pact (1955) A mutual security pact signed by Turkey and Iraq and joined by Pakistan, Persia and Britain; renamed CENTO in 1959.

Bahai faith An international eclectic mystical religion which tries to unite people of all religions and races in a crusade for universal peace; it won many converts among retired British officers. (Persian *baha-ullah*, 'splendqr of God', title of the founder.)

Bahasa Indonesia A modernized form of the Malay language, with Dutch and other loanwords, which has become the lingua franca of Indonesia since World War II.

Bahrein Petroleum Co. An oil company, owned by STANDARD OIL OF CALIFORNIA and TEXACO on a 50:50 basis, which discovered oil at Bahrein in 1932.

'Baignade, La' (1884) Seurat's painting of youngsters bathing and resting on the banks of the Seine at Asnières, in which he tried to combine Impressionist technique with clarity of form in a method known as 'pointillisme'. Now in the Tate Gallery, London.

Baikonur A town in Kazakhstan, USSR, near where there is a huge 'cosmodrome' in the desert, the chief Soviet launching point for spacecraft and rockets.

Bailey bridge A temporary bridge much used in World War II, made of portable prefabricated interchangeable steel sections. (Sir Donald Bailey, inventor, of the Ministry of Supply.)

Baily's Hunting Directory (1897) An annual British publication giving full details of hunts of all kinds in all parts of the world.

Bairam The name given to 2 major Muslim festivals: the Lesser Bairam (or Id al-Fitr) at the end of RAMADAN; and the Greater (or Id al-Kabir) 70 days later, when a ram or other animal is sacrificed at the final ceremony of the pilgrimage at Mecca, and throughout Islam. (Persian and Turkish name, better known to the non-Muslim world than the Arabic forms.)

Bajazet, Bajazeth (1) Ottoman Turkish sultan conquered by TAMBURLAINE (1403), who was fabled to have carried him about in an iron cage; a character in Marlowe's play. (2) In Racine's play (1672) of the name, Bajazet is imprisoned in Constantinople in 1638; he pretends to fall in love with the Sultana Roxane, who plans to put him on her husband's throne until she finds out that his true love is Princess Atalide. The Sultan discovers the plot, executes both of them, and Atalide commits suicide.

Baked Alaska Sponge cake topped with ice cream, covered with meringue and baked briefly in a hot oven.

Baker Street Irregulars (1) The gang of street arabs used by SHERLOCK HOLMES to glean intelligence from London's underworld. (2) A society of Holmes *aficionados* formed in 1934. (3) Also applied to the SOE, which had its headquarters in Baker Street. (In Conan Doyle's stories, the great Holmes had rooms at 221b Baker Street.)

Bakewell Tart A baked covered tart filled with strawberry jam. (Bakewell, near Buxton, Derbyshire.)

Bakhtiari rugs Hard-wearing rugs in bold red, blue or cream, with floral decoration divided into small compartments; made by Persian nomads south of Isfahan.

Bakongo The African people who in the 14th century predominated in what later became Belgian and French CONGO, and ANGOLA.

Balaam's Ass The ass on which the prophet Balaam rode when sent by the Moabites to curse the Israelites; the ass stopped in her tracks, having seen the angel of the Lord barring the way (Numbers xxii, 23) and, given the power of speech, reproached her master for beating her; then Balaam saw the angel, and changed his curse to a blessing.

Balaclava (1854) A battle of the CRIMEAN WAR immortalized in Tennyson's 'CHARGE OF THE LIGHT BRIGADE'. (Town near Sebastopol.)

Balbec A fictitious French coastal resort on the shores of the English Channel, a setting for early scenes in Proust's REMEMBRANCE OF THINGS PAST.

Balcony, The (1957) Jean Genet's play about the habitués of a French brothel who amuse themselves by acting the parts of judge, general and bishop. When a revolution comes they find themselves playing these parts in real life.

Balder (Baldur) 'The beautiful', in Scandinavian mythology son of ODIN and FRIGG, the sun-god whose death, contrived by Loki, led to the GOTTERDÄMMERUNG, or Twilight of the Gods.

Baldwin war-debt settlement (1923) An agreement made by Stanley Baldwin, then Chancellor of the Exchequer, on terms for Britain's repayment of war debts to USA, then nearly $2½ billion. Britain was owed twice this sum by its Allies and by Germany, but recovered little from either. The onerous terms were sharply criticized and the debt repudiated after the HOOVER MORATORIUM.

Balenciaga A Paris fashion house.

Balfour, David Hero of R. L. Stevenson's novel KIDNAPPED and its sequel Catriona.

Balfour declaration (1917) A promise of British support, provided Arab rights were safeguarded, for a Jewish National Home in Palestine, made by the Foreign Secretary, A. J. Balfour, to Lord Rothschild, a Zionist leader.

Balkan League (1912-13) An alliance of Bulgaria, Serbia, Greece and Montenegro, which declared war on Turkey; see BALKAN WAR, FIRST.

Balkan Pact (1954) A military alliance between Greece, Yugoslavia and Turkey, which has not however prevented considerable tensions between its members over Cyprus and other matters.

Balkan War, First (Oct. 1912-May 1913) A war fought by the BALKAN LEAGUE to wrest MACEDONIA from Turkey. See next entry.

Balkan War, Second (June-Aug. 1913) A war in which Bulgaria turned against all her allies of the BALKAN LEAGUE, who were joined by Rumania and even by Turkey. Turkey lost almost all its remaining European territory, Greece gained Salonika, Albania was created, and Serbia and Montenegro divided the rest of the spoils.

Ballad of Peckham Rye, The (1960) A witty novel by Muriel Spark in which a Mephistophelean Dougal Douglas upsets the lives of all he comes into contact with, against a background of London textile factories.

Ballad of Reading Gaol, The (1898) Oscar Wilde's poem, based on his own experiences in that jail.

Ballet Rambert (1930) Founded in London by Polish-born (Dame) Marie Rambert and her husband Ashley Dukes, for the presentation of minor ballets; the company toured widely abroad and won a great reputation.

Balmain A Paris fashion house.

Balmoral A royal castle near Braemar, Aberdeenshire; the estate was bought in 1852 by Queen Victoria, who built a Scottish-baronial type granite castle there among the lonely grouse moors.

Balthazar One of the THREE KINGS, traditionally the King of Chaldea. ('Owner of treasure'.)

Baltic, The (1903) The London market for the chartering of cargo vessels of all nationalities; it also deals with marine insurance, air charters, purchase and sale of ships and of grains etc. It is in St Mary Axe. (Abbreviation of the Baltic Mercantile and Shipping Exchange, named after the Baltic Coffee House in Threadneedle Street where they first met.)

Balts The Letts (Latvians), Lithuanians and the Prussians (before they became Germanized), who for many centuries withstood the onslaughts of the Teutonic Knights (see TANNENBERG) but in the 18th century came mainly under Russian rule.

Baluba A tribe of the Kasai Province which tried to secede from Congo (Kinshasa) after Independence.

Baluchi Inhabitant, and Iranian language, of Baluchistan, formerly a province of India, now in Pakistan.

Baluchi rugs Attractively primitive Turkoman rugs in somber red, brown and blue, with a sparing use of white lines on flower heads, and designs of stylized geometrical flowers. They are made by the Baluchi nomads of the Afghanistani-Persian borders and marketed for export at Meshed, northeast Persia. They were not exported until this century.

Balzan Foundation (1956) An Italian fund which makes awards of up to $250,000 for work contributing to international progress or world peace, or in the fields of biology, mathematics, music etc. Recipients include Pope John XXIII, the UN and the NOBEL Foundation. The fund is administered by Father Zucca, Mussolini's reputed confessor, imprisoned in 1946 for hiding Mussolini's body and implicated in attempts in 1957 and 1967 to sell forged diaries attributed to Mussolini. Rumors that Father Zucca was connected with the 'treasure of DONGO' were denied. (Named after the founder, editor of the *Corriere della Sera*; died 1953).

Bambi (1942) A Walt Disney cartoon film of the life of a deer.

Bambino, The Another nickname for BABE RUTH.

Bambi project Code name for a US project to put into orbit satellite interceptors which would fire small highly explosive missiles at ICBMS

while they presented a slow-moving target, i.e. at takeoff. High costs caused suspension of the program in 1964, but it came up for reconsideration in 1967.

Bamboo Curtain The barrier between Communist and non-Communist countries in Southeast Asia. (On the analogy of IRON CURTAIN.)

Bampton Fair (UK) An October fair at which a major feature is the sale of Exmoor ponies. (Village north of Tiverton, Devon.)

Banana Republics Derisive name for the banana-producing republics of Central America, especially Honduras, Panama, Guatemala, Costa Rica and Nicaragua; connoting economic dependence on the United and Standard Fruit Cos., which had a monopoly of the trade, and political dependence on the US.

Banbury cake Slashed puff pastry filled with currants, spice, mixed peel etc., oval in shape; made for at least 400 years at Banbury, Oxfordshire. See ECCLES CAKE.

Banbury Cross In the nursery rhyme, the cross destroyed in 1646 by the PURITAN bigots for which Banbury, Oxfordshire, was notorious.

Bancroft Prizes Awarded by COLUMBIA UNIVERSITY for the best books on American history, diplomacy or international relations, and valued at $4000 each. (Named for George Bancroft, diplomat and historian, died 1891.)

B and B Initials used for a potent combination of brandy and Benedictine.

Band of Hope A temperance society, now named the UK Band of Hope Union, with headquarters in London.

B and S Colloquial abbreviation for brandy and soda.

Bandung Conference (1955) An important meeting of 29 Afro-Asian states convened by Indonesia; it was steered by the Indian Prime Minister, Nehru, into a policy of nonalignment, i.e. of neutrality as between the Western and Communist blocs, and condemned colonialism in terms that clearly included Russian interference. Chou En-lai stated that

China was ready to examine ways of easing tension with the USA. (Town of Java.)

Banff National Park (1885) The oldest and second largest of Canada's National Parks, in the Rocky Mountain area of western Alberta adjacent to British Columbia's YOHO NATIONAL PARK. The TRANS-CANADA HIGHWAY runs through it.

Bank for International Settlements (1930) Originally set up under the YOUNG PLAN to facilitate German payment of reparations; it now fosters cooperation between the central banks that own it (the US did not join and only sends observers). A unique institution, international yet closely linked to the Swiss banking system (the headquarters are in Basel), it covers the whole field of the European capital market, particularly EURODOLLARS, and manages the EUROPEAN MONETARY AGREEMENT. Its policies sometimes diverge from those of the INTERNATIONAL MONETARY FUND which took over some of its functions.

Bank of Canada (1934) A government-owned institution for carrying out governmental fiscal policy. It does not operate on a commercial basis or in competition with chartered (commercial) banks.

Bank of England (1694) Britain's central bank, nationalized in 1946, which is the note-issuing authority and acts as bankers to government, the commercial banks and to overseas central banks; see STERLING AREA.

Bannockburn (1314) The battle in which Robert the Bruce decisively defeated Edward II and secured Scottish independence of England for another 300 years. (Village south of Stirling.)

Banqueting House (1622) The only surviving part of the old Whitehall Palace in London, designed by Inigo Jones; the site of Charles I's execution. Until recently it housed the United Services Museum.

Banquo The fellow-general whose ghost haunts MACBETH in Shakespeare's play. Macbeth had had him murdered because the witches prophesied that his descendants would rule Scotland.

Bantam (1) Diminutive breed of domestic fowl with feathered legs, perhaps originating in Java. (2) One of a number of small, chiefly ornamental, domestic fowls, often miniatures of standard breeds. (Name of an old Dutch Residency in Java.)

Bantu (1) A term applied to the numerous peoples and languages of Africa south of the Equator, including SWAHILI, the Kikuyu of Kenya, XHOSA, ZULU, the Basuto of LESOTHO and the Barotse. (2) In South Africa, applied to Black Africans in distinction from Whites, Coloureds and 'Asiatics'. (Invented name of Bantu type, meaning 'people'.)

Bantustans In South Africa, areas set aside for Black Africans to run their affairs in accordance with the apartheid policy of equal but separate opportunities for development for whites and blacks. TRANSKEI was the first; 5 others were proposed for the Zulu and other races. (Coined from Bantu+Pakistan, the latter an example of a state formed for a separate community—the Muslims of India.)

Baptists Protestants who believe in adult baptism (by total immersion) after confession of faith and sins.

Barabbas A rebel who had committed murder and whom the Jews asked Pilate to release in preference to Jesus (*Luke* xv, 7-15).

Barataria, Isle of The imaginary island of which Sancho Panza is appointed governor in DON QUIXOTE.

'Bar at the Folies-Bergère, A' (1882) Manet's last major painting, a detailed study of a crowded bar, as seen reflected in a large mirror, in the famous Paris music hall; the center of the picture is dominated by a barmaid. Now in the Courtauld Institute Galleries, London.

Barbara Allen A ballad of a young man dying of love for the cruel Barbara, who taunted him but bitterly repented it when he died.

'Barbara Frietchie' (1863) Whittier's poem about a Civil War episode at Frederick, Md. Barbara, 96 years old, displayed the Union flag as 'Up the street came the rebel tread, / Stonewall Jackson riding ahead', and cried from her window: 'Shoot, if you must, this old gray head, / But spare your country's flag', she said. Whereupon Jackson commanded: 'Who touches a hair of yon gray head/Dies like a dog! March on!' he said. In fact, the flag was shown by a much younger woman, and the Confederate officers raised not their weapons but their hats ('to you, madam, not your flag'). Barbara displayed the flag later, and to Federal troops. But let not truth prevail!

Barbarians   (1890) A rugger touring club with no ground of its own; players are drawn from the home countries (England, Scotland, Ireland, Wales), France and Commonwealth teams, and are noted for spectacular open football. By tradition they play certain home teams and, since 1948, overseas teams touring Britain, and now also tour abroad.

Barbarossa   Nickname of the 12th-century Holy Roman Emperor, Frederick I. (Italian, 'red beard'.)

Barbarossa   German code name for the invasion of Russia (1941).

Barbary Coast   Nickname of the vice and gambling quarter on the waterfront at San Francisco, particularly notorious in the 1850s.

Barbary Pirates   Moorish CORSAIRS who plagued Mediterranean shipping from the 16th century until France occupied Algeria in 1830. (Barbary, old name for northwest Africa, inhabited by BERBERS.)

Barber of Seville, The   (1816) Rossini's opera dealing with the first of Beaumarchais's trilogy of plays, the second of which is the source of the MARRIAGE OF FIGARO. Count Almaviva, with the aid of the barber FIGARO, wins Rosina, ward of the sly Dr Bartolo.

Barbershop   The impromptu unaccompanied vocal harmonizing of popular songs by a male quartet (or any informal group) in the style traditionally associated with barbershops of yore.

Barbican development   (1959) A scheme to rebuild 40 bombed-out acres of the City of London (see CITY, THE), with skyscrapers not only for offices but for residential use, shops and schools, so that the City should no longer become virtually uninhabited every evening and weekend. The blocks are connected by raised footways. (Name of a London street on the site of a watchtower ('barbican') in the City walls.)

Barbizon School   A colony of French painters who settled in the 1850s outside Paris in the village of Barbizon to paint unromanticized pictures of peasant life and rural landscapes; they included Corot, Millet and Théodore Rousseau.

Barchester novels (or **Chronicles of Barsetshire**)   Six novels (1855-67) by Anthony Trollope set in the imaginary town of Barchester (based on Salisbury and/or Wells) in 'Barsetshire', exploiting the humors of ecclesiastical intrigue and ambition. The most famous are *The Warden*, *Barchester Towers* and *The Last Chronicle of Barset*. The many memorable characters are headed by Mrs PROUDIE.

Bardell v. Pickwick   A fictional breach-of-promise case in Dickens's *Pickwick Papers*, in which Mrs Bardell is awarded damages against her lodger, Mr Pickwick, who, since he will pay 'not one halfpenny'. is consigned to the FLEET.

Bardolph   With PISTOL, a swaggering follower of FALSTAFF in Shakespeare's *Merry Wives* and *Henry IV*, who also appears in *Henry V*; his face is 'all bubukles, knobs . . . and flames o' fire'.

Barebones Parliament   (July-Dec. 1653) (English history) The Little Parliament, of 140 Puritan members elected by Cromwell's suggestion soon dissolved itself after proving its incompetence. (Named after PRAISE-GOD BAREBONES.)

Barefoot in the Park   (1963) Neil Simon's satirical comedy, turned into a movie by Gene Saks (1967).

Baring Bros   (1763) A London merchant bank and acceptance house, which played a major part in developing South America, and has more recently taken an interest in breweries.

Barking London borough since 1965 consisting of the former borough of Barking and part of that of Dagenham; headquarters at Dagenham.

Barkis The carrier in Dickens's DAVID COPPERFIELD who conducted a long-range courtship of David's nurse, Clara PEGGOTTY, by sending messages that 'Barkis is willin'.

Barlow report (1940) A Royal Commission report on the geographical distribution of the industrial population of Britain. It made recommendations regarding remedial measures for the overcongested cities of London and the North which led to the NEW TOWNS Act of 1946.

Barlow report (1946) (UK) A report on scientific manpower which recommended doubling the output of university graduates in science and technology.

Barmecide feast An imaginary feast such as in the *Arabian Nights* a jesting Barmecide prince of Baghdad serves to a beggar, who pretends to enjoy the nonexistent food but draws the line at imaginary wine, pretends to get drunk and fells the prince; the latter takes the joke in good part and gives him a real meal.

Barnaby Bright Old English name for June 11th (OLD STYLE), St Barnabas' Day, the longest day of the year.

Barnaby Rudge (1841) Dickens's novel set in the times of the GORDON RIOTS, with a lurid plot about Barnaby, a half-wit, and his father, a murderer on the run.

Barnacle Bill the Sailor A polite form of the name of the virile hero in the 19th-century ballad.

Barnard (1889) One of the SEVEN SISTERS, in NYC.

Barnes A former borough of Surrey, England, since 1965 part of the borough of RICHMOND UPON THAMES.

Barnet London borough since 1965 consisting of the former borough of Finchley and Hendon and the urban districts of East Barnet and Friern Barnet; headquarters at Hendon.

Barney Google (1919) A boisterous comic strip started by Billy DeBeck and continued by Fred Lasswell. The diminutive Barney is one of nature's archetypal suckers, with a blob nose and poached-egg eyes, devoted to Spark Plug, a horse enveloped in a huge blanket even when racing. The wisecracking Snuffy Smith was later added to the cast and to the title.

Barnum & Bailey Show An American traveling circus, the 'Greatest Show on Earth', developed from P. T. Barnum's circus (started in 1871) by James A. Bailey in the 1890s; notable for sensational sideshows and JUMBO the Elephant.

Baroque (1620-1720) An exaggeration of the trends in MANNERISM which flourished in the Roman Catholic countries of Italy, Spain, Bavaria and Austria, where it served the purpose of emotional religious propaganda reflecting the spirit of the Counter-Reformation. Painting (Rubens, Caravaggio, Murillo), sculpture (Bernini), architecture (Borromini) were all influenced. In France it took a more sober form. ROCOCO was its final phase.

Barotseland The region occupied by the Barotse, cattle owners and fishermen, now a province of ZAMBIA.

Barrack-room Ballads (1892) A collection of Kipling's verse about British soldiers serving overseas; it includes 'GUNGA DIN', 'Tommy Atkins', 'Mandalay' and 'When 'Omer smote 'is bloomin' lyre'.

Barretts of Wimpole Street, The (1930) Rudolf Besier's play on Robert Browning's struggle to rescue his future wife, Elizabeth Barrett, from the clutches of her possessive and formidable father.

Barsac A sweet white wine, sold under its own name but sometimes classed with the SAUTERNES wines.

Barsetshire See BARCHESTER NOVELS.

Bartered Bride, The (1866) Smetana's opera, based on Czech folk music and dance, about a village girl who rejects an arranged marriage and, in spite of the intrigues of a marriage broker, is able in the end to marry the man of her choice.

Bartholomew Fair (1133) (1) England's chief cloth fair, held in the priory of St Bartholomew, Smithfield, London, at Bartholomew tide; later it developed into a riotous pleasure-fair, closed in 1840. (2) Title of a play by Ben Jonson (1614).

Bartholomew Massacre See ST BARTHOLOMEW MASSACRE.

Bartimaeus The blind beggar at Jericho whose sight Jesus restored, saying: thy faith hath made thee whole. (*Mark* x, 46-52.)

Bartlett A large yellow juicy pear widely used by the US canning industry. It is a variety of the early-maturing European William (or William's Bon Chrètien), grown also in Australia and South America.

Bartolozzi prints Colored prints made from plates lightly etched in with dots (stipple engraving), all the colors being on one plate. The subjects included shepherdesses, dandies, children, sentimental mythological scenes, reproductions of paintings by Angelica Kauffmann, and some excellent portraits. Genuine Bartolozzis are rare, fakes plentiful. (Francesco Bartolozzi, 1728-1813, Italian settled in London.)

Baruch (AD 70) A book of the APOCRYPHA, apparently meant to be used in religious services, containing a form of confession, a sermon on wisdom, and a song of consolation. (Attributed in the text to the Baruch mentioned in *Jeremiah* xxxvi, 4.)

Baruch plan (1946) The offer by USA to destroy its stock of atomic bombs and the fissionable material for them, provided that an international body was set up to see that no other nation produced such bombs (of which USA then had the monopoly) and to control all development of nuclear power for peaceful purposes. Russia rejected the plan, which was inspired by Dr Robert Oppenheimer (see OPPENHEIMER CASE). (Bernard Baruch, member of the UN ATOMIC ENERGY COMMISSION.)

Baseball Hall of Fame and Museum, National (1939) The shrine of organized baseball, in Cooperstown, N.Y., near the Abner Doubleday field where the American version of this old English game traditionally originated in 1839. It contains bronze plaques in the Hall of Fame, photographic records, and a museum of relics (bats, uniforms etc.). This is the nation's oldest sports Hall of Fame.

Bashan (Basan), Bulls of The fat bulls of Bashan (a land beyond the Jordan) are mentioned in *Psalms* xxii, 12, and are thought to be the now extinct European wild oxen, or aurochs.

Basildon (1949) (UK) A NEW TOWN in Essex, incorporating parts of the urban districts of Billericay and Thurrock, designed to take 106,000 inhabitants.

Basket Makers Peoples of the ANASAZI CULTURE (c. AD 100-700) in southwestern USA. They were skilled weavers of baskets and later learned to make pottery.

Basques A people of the western Pyrenees now found in a small coastal area facing the Bay of Biscay, from Bilbao in Spain to Bayonne in France. They are possibly the remnants of a Neolithic race displaced by the Indo-Europeans. Their language has no established affinity, and differs in every way from INDO-EUROPEAN LANGUAGES.

Bass, Sam (1851-78) The Texas ROBIN HOOD, who robbed and gave away with equal abandon — 'a better hearted fellow you scarce could hope to see' — but was shot dead by rangers; people have been searching for his alleged caches of golden dollars ever since, while every tenth Texan has an 'authentic' relic of his.

Bass, Charrington (1968) Britain's largest brewers, formed by merging Bass, Worthington, Mitchells & Butlers and Charrington United Breweries. Like the rival ALLIED BREWERIES, it has its headquarters at Burton-on-Trent.

Bassanio The character in Shakespeare's *Merchant of Venice* who wins PORTIA in the trial of the 3 caskets (with some help from Portia).

Bast Egyptian goddess; see BUBASTIS.

Bastille, Storming of the (14th July 1789) The event which marked the beginning of the FRENCH REVOLUTION; the Paris mob regarded the fortress-prison of the Bastille as the symbol of despotic rule. Although all they found there were 6 common criminals and a lunatic nobleman, the anniversary of its capture is still kept as a national holiday commemorating the Revolution.

Basutoland A former British protectorate in South Africa, renamed LESOTHO when it became independent in 1966.

Bat, The (1920) A mystery drama by Mary Roberts Rinehart and Avery Hopwood, frequently revived; it is an adaptation of the former's novel *The Circular Staircase* (1908), an amusingly ingenious example of her 'had I but known' theme.

Batavia Former Dutch name of Jakarta, capital of Indonesia.

Bateman's The 17th-century house where Kipling lived, at Burwash, Sussex, preserved by the NATIONAL TRUST as a Kipling museum.

Bates, Miss The kind-hearted chatterbox of Jane Austen's EMMA; Emma gets into trouble for snubbing her.

Bathsheba The wife of Uriah the Hittite, seduced by David, who brought about her husband's death in battle so that he could marry her (II *Samuel* xi).

Bathtub hoax (1917) H.L. Mencken's article, 'A Neglected Anniversary', in the New York *Evening Mail* which purported to give the historical facts about the first bathtub in America; although pure fiction, it was often cited as fact.

Bath University of Technology (1966) (UK) Formerly the Bristol College of Science and Technology, which became a CAT only in 1960; moved to Claverton Down, Bath, on attaining university status.

Bathurst Cup A tennis contest between Britain and the USA.

Battelle Memorial Institute (1929) A private industrial research organization with headquarters at Columbus,

Ohio, and branches at Geneva and Frankfurt; it carries out research for governments and industry on minerals, metallurgy, electronics etc.

Battenberg The original name of the Mountbattens, the British branch of the family founded by Prince Alexander of Hesse and a Polish countess who, after her morganatic marriage, was created Princess of Battenberg (in Hesse); they changed their name in 1917 in deference to current popular prejudice against German names.

Battersea A former London metropolitan borough, since 1965 part of the borough of WANDSWORTH.

Battersea Dogs' Home (UK) A home for lost and starving dogs and cats, where unclaimed animals can be bought. It is in the Battersea Park Road, south of the Thames in London.

Battersea enamels (1) Snuffboxes, watchcases, plaques, wine labels etc. of copper covered with opaque glass and hand painted or transfer-printed with landscapes, lovers' messages, greetings from a spa etc.; made at York House, Battersea, London, for the few years from about 1750 to 1756, and therefore extremely rare. (2) Similar articles made at Bilston, Staffordshire, and later in many other places, including countless deliberate fakes of (1).

Battery, The A park at the southern tip of Manhattan Island, NYC.

Battle Abbey Roll, The A 14th-century list, the earliest extant copy of which dates from the 16th century, of the families supposed to have come to England with William the Conqueror. It is spurious in part, if not altogether. (Found at Battle Abbey, Battle, near Hastings.)

Battleaxe (June 1941) Code name for a British attack on Rommel's forces on the Egyptian-Libyan border, using newly arrived Crusader tanks. These proved no match for the German tanks. After this failure, Wavell was relieved by Auchinleck; see CRUSADER.

Battle Born State A nickname for Nevada, as having become US territory after the Mexican War (1848).

'Battle Hymn, The' A patriotic hymn, see 'JOHN BROWN'S BODY'.

Battle of Britain (1940) Hitler's daylight air attacks on Britain, intended as a prelude to invasion, defeated by 'the Few' (RAF Fighter Command). It opened on July 10th, the successive targets being Channel shipping and ports, the airfields of southeast England, and London; and ended (officially) on Oct. 31st, overlapping the LONDON BLITZ.

Battle of Flowers A feature of the carnival festival, particularly associated with Nice, in the last days before Lent; see MARDI GRAS; ROSE BOWL.

Battle of the Books (1704) Jonathan Swift's pamphlet ridiculing contemporary scholarship in mock-heroic prose.

Battle of the Nations (1813) See LEIPZIG.

Bauhaus A school of architecture and industrial design founded by Walter Gropius at Weimar, Germany, after World War I to coordinate the skills of architects, artists and technologists; closed by Hitler.

Bavarian cream A flavored gelatine and custard pudding into which whipped cream is folded; served with macaroons.

Baxter prints (1836) Color prints made by superimposing on an engraving (which combined aquatint, etching and stipple) up to 20-30 color blocks in a process invented by George Baxter (died 1867). The result was a 'poor man's oil painting', varying in quality from excellent to poor; many of the poorer ones were made by persons licensed by Baxter to use his process.

Bayard (1) Names of RINALDO's horse. (French, 'bay-colored'.) (2) See CHEVALIER BAYARD.

Bayer (1863) A West German firm with headquarters at Leverkusen, north of Cologne, which manufactures drugs, dyestuffs, plastics, man-made fibers, chemicals and synthetic rubber. See IG FARBEN.

Bayer letters Letters of the Greek alphabet used to identify the chief stars of a constellation, generally in approximate order of brightness, but sometimes in sequence of position. Although superseded by FLAMSTEED NUMBERS, the Bayer nomenclature is often used for the better-known stars, e.g. alpha-Centauri, the brightest star in CENTAURUS.

Bayeux Tapestry, The A piece of needlework made for Bayeux Cathedral, France, 230 ft long, depicting the life of Harold, including the Battle of Hastings. Traditionally it was supposed to be the work of William the Conqueror's wife, Matilda. The original is still at Bayeux, and a copy is in the Victoria and Albert Museum, London.

Bay of Pigs (April 1961) The landing on Cuba, with the support of the American CIA, of anti-Castro forces which were killed or captured within 3 days.

Bay Psalm Book, The (1640) A metrical version of the *Book of Psalms* made by Richard Mather, John Eliot and 28 other Ministers, published in Cambridge, Massachusetts Bay Colony. It was the first bound book printed in English in America, and had reached 27 editions before 1750.

Bayreuth Festival (1876) A festival of Wagner's operas staged at the Wagner Theater in July and August. (Town of Bavaria.)

Bay State A nickname of Massachusetts. The Plymouth Settlement was absorbed into the Massachusetts Bay Colony (1691) — hence the alternative nickname, the Old Colony State.

BBC-2 (1964) (UK) The alternative TV program put out by the BBC with, on average, a higher artistic and intellectual standard than BBC-1; also used from 1967 as a vehicle for the first regular color transmission.

BCG A vaccine against tuberculosis, usually given in childhood. (Initials of French *Bacille* Calmette-Guérin.)

Beachcomber A zany column in the London *Daily Express* started by D. B. Wyndham Lewis and continued from 1924 by J. B. Morton; it introduced a gallery of characters such as Dr Strabismus, Major Foulenough etc.

Beacon Hill Once the central peak of the Trimountain which dominated Boston, Mass., and now its only surviving remnant, shorn of its top 60 ft to form the site of the Statehouse (1798) overlooking BOSTON COMMON. Its steep narrow streets and old brownstone houses form a most attractive residential area, once the summit of SILAS LAPHAM'S ambition and still the hideout of the last of the Boston aristocracy but increasingly invaded by apartment houses, the richer students and artists etc.

Beaconsfield, Earl of The title of Benjamin Disraeli from 1876.

Beagle, HMS See VOYAGE OF THE BEAGLE.

Beaker People An early BRONZE AGE people who infiltrated northwest Europe and Britain from Spain about 1800 BC; they had gold ornaments, bows and arrows, and buried their dead under barrows (tumuli). They are named after the finely decorated beakers which they made.

Beale and Buss, The Misses (UK) Two 19th century headmistresses (one of Cheltenham Ladies' College), the targets of an anonymous but famous little verse by their pupils: Miss Buss and Miss Beale / Cupid's darts do not feel. / How different from us, / Miss Beale and Miss Buss.

Béarnaise sauce A BÉCHAMEL-type sauce with egg yolk, vinegar and herbs, served with steaks.

Bears The Chicago Bears, NATIONAL FOOTBALL LEAGUE. Became member of the National Conference, National Football League in 1970.

Beast of Belsen A name for Josef Kramer, commandant at BELSEN.

Beat generation (1950s) Those of the young generation who rejected the values of modern civilization and lived from day to day and from hand to mouth; they were characterized by contempt for the 'oldies' (i.e. anyone over about 26) who were all squares, and by sexual promiscuity, drug taking and sartorial anarchy. The movement spread from Los Angeles, California, to Britain and elsewhere. Among their spokesmen were Jack Kerouac and Ginsberg. (Term used by Kerouac in the 1950s; see BEATNIKS.)

Beatitudes, The A section of the Sermon on the Mount declaring the qualities required in the Kingdom of Heaven. The version in *Matthew* v, 3-11 gives 9 Beatitudes, in the form: 'Blessed are the poor in spirit', the meek, merciful, pure in heart, peacemakers etc.

Beatniks Members of the BEAT GENERATION. ('Beat', variously interpreted as 'defeated by life' or referring to addiction to pop music with a strong rhythmic beat; plus a Russian or Yiddish suffix, -nik.)

Beatrice (1) Dante's beloved, a historic person who also appears in the DIVINE COMEDY as his guide in Paradise. (2) The heroine of Shakespeare's *Much Ado about Nothing* who carries on a running battle of words with BENEDICK.

Beau Brummell George Brummell, the arbiter of London fashion and friend of the PRINCE REGENT, with whom he later quarreled. He exiled himself to France, where he died in poverty, 1840.

Beauchamp's Career (1876) George Meredith's novel in which the gallant Nevil Beauchamp of the Royal Navy is frustrated in love and by his uncle's disapproval of his radical views and friends. All seems to have been brought to a happy ending, when he is drowned while rescuing a child.

Beaufort scale A scale of wind-strength on which Force 0 is calm; 1 light air (1-3 m.p.h.); 2 slight breeze (4-7 m.p.h.); 3 gentle breeze (8-12); 4 moderate breeze (13-18); 5 fresh breeze (19-24); 6 strong breeze (25-31); 7 high wind (32-38); 8 gale (39-46); 9 strong gale (47-54); 10 whole gale (55-63); 11 storm (64-72); 12 hurricane (73-82) and so on up to Force 17 (120-136 m.p.h.). (Admiral Sir F. Beaufort; adopted 1838.)

Beau Geste (1924) P. C. Wren's best-selling novel of the rigors suffered by the high-minded expatriate Englishman who served under the name of Beau Geste in the French Foreign Legion in the Sahara.

Beaujolais A light, red, French wine, preferably drunk when it is

young; grown in the hills between Lyons and Mâcon; the best bear the name of the village of origin, but most are blended.

Beaulieu The home near Lyndhurst, Hampshire, of Lord Montagu of Beaulieu and the Montagu Motor Museum.

Beau Nash Richard Nash, a gambler and at one time the arbiter of fashion at Bath. He outstayed his welcome and died poor in 1762.

Beaune See CÔTE DE BEAUNE.

Beautiful and Damned, The (1921) Scott Fitzgerald's second novel, written after his marriage to Zelda and, despite the glamorous life they were leading, increasingly critical of the rich young things who had acclaimed *This Side of Paradise*, his first novel.

Beautiful People, The See JET SET.

Beauty and the Beast (1) A fairy tale dating back to at least the 16th century. Beauty, daughter of a merchant, goes to the palace of the Beast to save her father's life. She begins to feel quite sorry for the ugly monster and agrees to marry him, whereupon he is transformed into a handsome prince. (2) A ballet (1912) with music by Ravel from his suite *Ma Mère l'Oye* ('My Mother Goose'), and choreography by John Cranko.

Beaux' Stratagem, The (1707) Farquhar's comedy about 2 fortune-hunting friends (the beaux), Aimwell who pretends to be an invalid, and Archer who poses as his servant. They arrive at a Lichfield inn and get themselves invited to the home of Lady Bountiful, whose daughter and daughter-in-law they manage to win.

Beaver, The A nickname for the dynamic Lord Beaverbrook, newspaper proprietor and wartime Cabinet Minister. See BEAVERBROOK PRESS.

Beaver, Tony The Paul BUNYAN of West Virginia, although his exploits in the Cumberland Mountains accompanied by Big Henry are pitched in a lower key. Best known among them was his discovery of peanut brittle when he dammed a river with molasses and peanuts.

Beaverbrook Press The newspapers owned by Max Aitken, 1st Baron Beaverbrook (died 1964) — the *Daily Express* (from 1919), *Sunday Express* (which he founded) and the London *Evening Standard*. He used them to campaign for EMPIRE FREE TRADE and, in the last years of his life, against British entry into the Common Market.

Beaver State Nickname of Oregon.

Béchamel (Cooking) A basic sauce, nowadays made by pouring boiling milk on a white roux (butter and flour mixture). (Named after Louis XIV's steward; but in those days it was a rich cream sauce.)

Bechuanaland A former British protectorate in South Africa, renamed BOTSWANA when it became independent in 1966.

Beckenham (UK) A former municipal borough of Kent, since 1965 part of the borough of BROMLEY.

Becky Sharp The first 3-color feature film (1935), in Technicolor; the story was based on Thackeray's VANITY FAIR.

Bed Bug, The (1929) Vladimir Mayakovsky's Socialist-realist play attacking vestigial bourgeois attitudes in Russia. (Russian title, *Klop*.)

Beddington and Wallington (UK) A former borough of Surrey, since 1965 part of the borough of SUTTON.

Bedford College for Women (1849) A college in Regent's Park, now a unit of London University.

Bedlam Corrupted abbreviation for the Hospital of St Mary of Bethlehem, Bishopsgate, London, which by the 15th century had become a lunatic asylum, moved to various sites later and now in Beckenham. It became notorious in the 17th century for the ignorant treatment of the inmates and as a public peep show.

Bedlington A curly-haired terrier with a distinctive sheeplike head, bred in various colors. (Town in Northumberland, England.)

Beecham Group A group of British firms which manufactures a wide variety of drugs, toilet requisites, soft drinks and foods under such well-known brand names as Eno's, Phensic, Phosferrine, Germolene,

Scott's Emulsion, Maclean's, Yeast-Vite, Brylcreem, Lucozade, Horlick's, but first became famous for BEECHAM'S PILLS.

Beecham's pills (1847) A patent medicine first launched in Lancashire; 'worth a guinea a box' and curing 'All Nervous Affections', Scurvy and Maladies of Indiscretion (i.e. VD), according to the advertisements, they were sold by Thomas Beecham (died 1907) at 1/1½d (cost of production, half a farthing); the ingredients were the same as for HOLLOWAY'S PILLS—aloes, ginger and soap.

Beecher's Brook The most formidable fence in the GRAND NATIONAL.

Beefeaters Popular name for (1) YEOMEN OF THE GUARD; (2) YEOMAN WARDERS of the Tower of London. (Apparently referring to their well-fed look; no connection with French *buffetiers du roi*, a derivation once favored.)

Beef State A nickname for Nebraska, where livestock, and particularly cattle, dominate the economy.

Beefsteak Club (1876) A London club in Irving Street, Leicester Square, which makes a point of informality despite the distinction of its members, who eat at one long table, sitting where the waiters put them. There were several earlier clubs of the name.

Beehive State Nickname of Utah.

Beekman Place One of the most exclusive residential areas of New York City, adjoining SUTTON PLACE, lying east of First Avenue between East 49th and 51st Streets and overlooking the East River. Most of the old homes have yielded to apartment houses; the UN Building dominates the scene.

Beelzebub A BAAL worshiped in Palestine, apparently as a healer (II *Kings*, i, 2); in *Matthew* xii, 24 he is the prince of devils; in *Paradise Lost* he is promoted next in rank to Satan. (Said to mean 'Lord of Flies', interpreted as 'preserver from fly-borne disease'.)

Beerage, The A collective nickname for the many brewers and distillers

raised to the peerage (e.g. Viscount Younger and several of the Guinness family).

Beer-hall Putsch Another name for Hitler's MUNICH PUTSCH (1923).

Beetle Nickname, later adopted as a trade name, for the beetle-shaped VOLKSWAGEN car.

Beggar's Opera (1728) John Gay's opera, a parody of contemporary Italian opera, with a highwayman, Capt. Macheath, as hero. The plot was used in Brecht's THREEPENNY OPERA.

Behaviorism A school of psychology which restricts itself to the objective study of behavior. The American, J. B. Watson, rejected Freudian introspection into the workings of the unconscious, minimized the importance of heredity and 'original sin', and borrowed the Russian Pavlov's theories of the conditioned reflex to explain all behavior, the pattern of which derives ultimately from emotions of fear, anger (at restraint) and content (e.g. on being caressed).

Behistun incription (5th century BC) An account of the reign of the Persian King, Darius the Great, inscribed on a mountainside in cuneiform writing in Persian, Babylonian and the language of Elam. (Site near Ardelan, between Kermanshah and Hamadan, Persia.)

Bel The Assyrian and Babylonian form of the Hebrew and Phoenician BAAL.

Bel Ami (1885) Maupassant's novel of a penniless Parisian journalist, Georges Duroy, who uses women (including his employer's wife and daughter) unscrupulously as stepping stones to power and wealth.

Bel and the Dragon A book of the APOCRYPHA which tells how the prophet Daniel exposed the trickery of the priest of BEL in Babylon and convinced the king that Bel was only an image, not a living god.

Belch, Sir Toby The convivial uncle of Olivia in Shakespeare's TWELFTH NIGHT, who plays tricks on MALVOLIO.

Belém A Brazilian seaport, now more usually called Pará.

Belfort gap   A wide valley around Belfort between the Vosges and Jura mountains near the Franco-Swiss-German frontier, strategically a weak point in the natural defenses of France, and from early times a main trade and communications route.

Belgian Congo   See CONGO, REPUBLIC OF.

Belgrade Theatre   (1958) The first new British theater to be opened after World War II, at Coventry; it produced Wesker's earlier successes.

Belial   The Devil; the expression 'sons of Belial' appears in *Deuteronomy* xiii, 13 and elsewhere. In *Paradise Lost* he is a fallen angel who 'could make the worse appear the better reason'. (Hebrew, 'worthlessness'.)

Belisha beacon   The flashing amber light used in Britain to indicate a pedestrian crossing. (Idea adopted by the Minister of Transport, Leslie Hore-Belisha, 1934-37, an ex-journalist with a flair for publicity.)

Bell, Acton, Currer and Ellis   Pen names of the Brontë sisters, Anne, Charlotte and Emily.

Bellamy's veal pies   It was the Younger Pitt whose last words (1806) were said to have been: 'I think I could eat one of Bellamy's veal pies'. A less unromantic tradition substitutes: My country! oh, my country!

Bellarmine jugs   Brown salt-glaze stoneware jugs with narrow neck and the mask of a bearded man. (Traditionally made by Flemish Protestants to caricature their Jesuit persecutor, Cardinal Bellarmine, 1542-1621; but apparently made in England before his time. They are still reproduced.)

Belle Dame sans Merci, La   (1819) Keats's version of a medieval ballad of a 'knight-at-arms, alone and palely loitering' who has woken from a dream of meeting a 'faerie's child' to find himself on the cold hill side, where 'no birds sing'.

Belleek ware   (1857) A form of PARIAN WARE with an imitation mother-of-pearl glaze, used in various marine fantasies involving mermaids, dolphins, shells, etc. made up into all kinds of tableware. (Village in Co. Fermanagh, Northern Ireland, where the factory still functions.)

Belle Hélène, La   (1864) Offenbach's operetta in which the heroes of the TROJAN WAR appear in comic roles.

Bellerophon   In Greek legend a hero who spurned the advances of his queen and, unjustly accused by her, was set to do many hazardous tasks (e.g. killing the CHIMAERA). He tried to reach heaven on PEGASUS but was thrown.

Bellerophon, HMS   The ship where Napoleon made his formal surrender after defeat at WATERLOO, and which took him to ST HELENA.

Belle Sauvage, The   A famous 15th-century London inn on Ludgate Hill. (The original name may have been Savage's Bell Inn, romanticized into the French for 'the beautiful wild woman'.)

Bell for Adano, A   (1944) John Hersey's novel, later made into a play, derived from his experiences as a war correspondent, about an American officer's efforts to find a new bell for an Italian village church damaged in the war.

Bellman, The   The captain of the crew in Lewis Carroll's *The Hunting of the* SNARK. His motto was: What I tell you three times is true.

Bellona   The Roman goddess of war, wife or sister of Mars. See also ARES.

Bell Rock   (1844) A lighthouse and rock some 20 miles off the Firth of Tay, east Scotland. Also known as Inchcape.

Bells, The   (1871) A famous English melodrama adapted from a French story of a Polish burgomaster, Mathias, haunted by guilt for an undiscovered murder. It was in this play that Henry Irving had his first great popular success, at the Lyceum.

Bell Song, The   (1883) A famous coloratura song from Delibes' opera *Lakmé*, the real title of which is 'Où va la jeune hindoue'. The opera is about a white man who falls deeply in love with an Indian girl and it is characterized by oriental exoticisms inspired by Pierre Loti's works.

Bell System   The US telephone system that operates 85% of the country's telephones through a federation of AT & T and 15 large regional operating subsidiaries, together with other companies which it partly controls. The first Bell Telephone Co. (1877) became the National Bell Telephone Co. in 1879. (Alexander Graham Bell, who patented the telephone in 1876.)

Bell X-1, 2 etc. US research rocket planes, launched at high altitudes from a parent plane, used in research on the behavior of alloys at ultrahigh speeds, and similar problems. One of the series was the first aircraft to break the sound barrier; the X-15 reached 4104 m.p.h. (1962) and an altitude of 67 miles (1963).

Belmont Park The oldest and largest US racetrack, in New York. It is the scene of the American Grand National and of the oldest of the 3 American classic flat races, the Belmont Stakes for 3-year-olds run in June over a distance of 1½ miles.

Bel Paese A mild semihard Italian cheese with, at its best, a delicate flavor.

Belsen A Nazi concentration camp, north of Hanover, Germany, the second to be liberated, by the British in April 1945.

Belshazzar's feast (539 BC) (1) The feast given by the last King of Babylon, Belshazzar, son of Nebuchadnezzar, at which he saw the 'writing on the wall', interpreted by Daniel as meaning that his kingdom would be divided between the Medes and Persians, as happened the same night when Babylon fell to Cyrus (*Daniel* v). (2) A choral work by Sir William Walton (1931).

Beltane The Celtic feast on May 1st, celebrated by the lighting of bonfires and, possibly, Maypole dancing.

Belter Name given to a rococo Victorian style of furniture made (1844-63) by a German-born New York craftsman, John Belter, who destroyed his molds and patterns when he closed down. Derived from Louis XV, the style was characterized by elaborate carving in high relief, and by balloon-shaped chair backs.

Belvoir Castle The seat, between Grantham and MELTON MOWBRAY, of the Dukes of Rutland since

Henry VIII's time, rebuilt by Wyatt in 1816.

Benares (Banaras) The Hindu holy city on the Ganges, now spelled Varanasi.

Benares ware Chased brassware in the form of trays, bowls, vases etc., brought to Europe in vast quantities by all who served in India. In the early years it was attractively decorated, but it deteriorated as the export trade grew.

Ben Barka case (1965-67) The disappearance in Paris of the Moroccan opposition leader, Ben Barka, last seen being driven away in a police car. Leading figures in France and Morocco were suspected of complicity, but the prolonged proceedings in a French court were stopped in 1967, the mystery remaining unsolved.

Bencher (UK) A Master of the Bench, i.e. a senior member of an INN OF COURT, one of the governors responsible for its administration and for the discipline of its students and barristers.

Ben Day process (1879) A method of adding tints made up of dots, lines or other patterns to original copy, negatives or plates, for reproduction as line engravings.

Benedick The sworn bachelor, and sparring partner of BEATRICE in Shakespeare's *Much Ado*, whom in the end he marries; hence any confirmed bachelor trapped into matrimony. (The spelling Benedict in the latter sense appears to arise from confusion with ideas of Benedictine celibacy.)

Benedictine The oldest liqueur, still made on the site of the Abbey of Fécamp, Normandy, where it originated in the 16th century. The D.O.M. on the label stands for Deo Optimo Maximo, 'to God, most good, most great'.

Benedictines (about AD 530) The oldest order of monks, founded by St Benedict in Italy, where MONTE CASSINO became the headquarters. It was supremely influential in Europe; in England it owned all the cathedral priories and most of the big abbeys, and founded several university colleges. Today it has abbeys at Downside, Ampleforth and elsewhere, as well as the recently rebuilt Buckfast Abbey in Devon. The CISTERCIANS and CLUNIACS were reformed Benedictine orders.

Benelux (1948) The customs union of Belgium, the Netherlands and Luxembourg. (Name coined from the initial letters of those countries.)

Benevolent and Protective Order of Elks See ELKS.

Bengal A former Indian province, now divided between West Bengal in India, and East Pakistan.

Bengali An inhabitant, or the Indo-European language, of the Ganges delta area now divided between India and East Pakistan.

Bengals The Cincinnati Bengals, AMERICAN FOOTBALL LEAGUE. Became member of AMERICAN CONFERENCE, NATIONAL FOOTBALL LEAGUE in 1970.

Ben Hur (1880) A novel by the American writer, Lew Wallace. Ben Hur is a Jewish aristocrat in the time of Christ, charged with trying to assassinate the Roman governor. Sent to the galleys, he escapes, joins the Roman army, defeats in a famous chariot race the man who had betrayed him, and becomes a Christian. There have been several movie versions.

Benin, Bight of The bay stretching westwards from the Niger delta. In the days before malaria and yellow fever had been conquered it was described as the place 'where few come out, though many go in'. See WHITE MAN'S GRAVE.

Benin bronzes Sculptures made at Benin in southern Nigeria, in the 17th century, by the *cire-perdue* process of bronze casting learned from Ife (see IFE HEADS).

Benjamin The youngest and favorite son of Jacob (*Genesis* xxxv, 18); hence any youngest (and favorite) son.

Benjamin, Tribe of The smallest of the 10 tribes of Israel, who claimed descent from Jacob's youngest son. King Saul and St Peter belonged to it.

Bennet family In Jane Austen's PRIDE AND PREJUDICE, consists of the sardonic Mr Bennet who keeps as far in the background as he can, and his harebrained wife, distracted by the burden of 5 unmarried daughters. Her frantic efforts to marry them off do much to delay the marriage of Elizabeth to Darcy, and of Jane to Bingley, as well as to promote Lydia's foolish elopement with Wickham. See also Mr COLLINS; Lady Catherine DE BOURGH.

Bennington ware American ROCKINGHAM ware was made at Bennington, Vt., and elsewhere, characterized by lustrous brown glaze, mottled or streaked. Julius Norton made the first 'Rockingham' (1841) at Bennington, including Toby jugs and lions; Fenton (later the US Pottery Co.), a much larger firm at Bennington, made 'Flint Enamel' (an improved version); but most American Rockingham was made (c. 1840-1900) at East Liverpool, Ohio, and at other factories far from Vermont.

Benz (1885) The first gasoline-driven automobile to be made on a commercial scale (first marketed in 1887); it was a 3-wheel 'horseless carriage' with a single-cylinder engine. Benz continued to make horseless carriages while DAIMLER was inventing more modern types. (Carl Benz, German inventor.)

Beowulf Scandinavian hero of an Old English alliterative epic of that name which combines memories of real events with trivial tales of fabulous monsters; the earliest poem in a Teutonic language, probably 8th century.

Bepo See HARWELL.

Berbers The non-Semitic fair-skinned brown-eyed people of North Africa (see HAMITES), called by the Romans Numidians (Greek *nomades*, 'nomads'), Gaetuli or Mauri (Hebrew *mahur*, 'western', compare MAGHREB).

Berchtesgaden The village on the Austrian border, near Salzburg, where Hitler had his heavily fortified lair, the Berghof or Eagle's Nest, built into the mountainside 6000 ft up, with another house at its foot.

Bercy sauce A sauce prepared with shallots and white wine, served with fish.

Berenice The name of several women and cities from the days of the PTOLEMIES onwards. (1) The Bérénice of Racine's and Corneille's plays was the widowed Queen of Chalcis with whom the Emperor Titus fell in love but, in deference to Roman public opinion, did not marry. (2) The Berenice who dedicated her hair to the gods for the safe return of her husband from a Syrian campaign was sister and wife of a 3rd-century BC Ptolemy king of Egypt. Her hair was wafted to heaven and became the constellation Coma Berenices. (Macedonian form of Greek *Pherenike*, 'victorious', Latin form *Veronica*.)

Berger (Meyer) Award A grant of $500 made by Columbia University Graduate School of Journalism for distinguished local reporting by a staff member of a New York daily.

Bergère (Cooking) With mushrooms and parsley. (French, 'shepherdess'.)

Berghof Hitler's 'Eagle's Nest' at BERCHTESGADEN.

Bergsonian philosophy See CREATIVE EVOLUTION. (Henri Bergson. French philosopher, died 1941.)

Bering standard time The civil time of the 165th meridian, 6 hours slower than Eastern standard time; observed in the extreme west of Alaska (Nome) and the Aleutians.

Berkeleian philosophy Subjective Idealism; see PRINCIPLES OF HUMAN KNOWLEDGE. (George Berkeley, Irish bishop, died 1753.)

Berkeley (1962) (UK) One of the earlier series of nuclear power stations. (Village near the Severn, south of Sharpness, Gloucestershire.)

Berkeley Castle The oldest inhabited castle in England, home of the Berkeley family for over 800 years, near Bristol.

Berkshire Festival See TANGLEWOOD.

Berlin, Congress of (1878) A conference of the Great Powers under Bismarck's chairmanship which redrew the map of the Balkans. Rumania, Serbia and Montenegro were finally freed from Turkish rule, Bosnia and Herzegovina were given to Austria, Cyprus to Britain, and many other changes were made, most of which lasted until World War I.

Berlin airlift (June 1948-Oct. 1949) The Anglo-US operation that kept West Berlin supplied by air during the BERLIN BLOCKADE.

Berlin-Baghdad Railway (1899) German name for what was in fact a projected line from Constantinople to the Persian Gulf, opposed by Russia and Britain, and, though never constructed, a source of diplomatic tension up to World War I.

Berlin blockade (1948-49) An unsuccessful Russo-East German attempt to deter the West from recognizing a free West German state by cutting off ground access to Berlin from the west. It followed the merging of the 3 Western Allied zones of Berlin, and led directly to the establishment of NATO. See BERLIN AIRLIFT.

Berlin Colonial Conference (1884) A conference of 15 nations called by Bismarck to settle disputes arising from the 'scramble for Africa'.

Berliner Ensemble (1949) Brecht's own theatrical company, in East Berlin; later a State theater, run after his death by his widow. It confines itself mainly to producing Brecht's plays.

Berlin porcelain (1740) The products of the factory sponsored by Frederick the Great; it produced high-quality Meissen-inspired figures and other wares in its earlier years, and is still operating.

Berlin Wall (Aug. 1961) A wall built by the East Germans to separate East (Communist) and West Berlin. Unauthorized people trying to cross the wall are shot at sight by East Germans. It follows a serpentine course through the heart of the city, with the BRANDENBURGER TOR as the main feature. See also CHECKPOINT CHARLIE.

Bermondsey A former London metropolitan borough, since 1965 part of the borough of SOUTHWARK.

Bermuda race (1923) A race from New York to Bermuda jointly sponsored by the Cruising Club of America and the Royal Bermuda Yacht Club; held in alternation with the FASTNET, i.e. in even-numbered years.

Bermudian rig A rig for a sailing boat, characterized by a tall triangular mainsail tapering directly from the top of the mainmast, there being no gaff or topmast. Also spelled Bermudan.

Bernadotte dynasty The ruling house of Sweden since 1818, founded by one of Napoleon's Marshals.

Bernese Oberland The Bernese Alps overlooking Berne in Switzerland, of which the most famous peak is the Jungfrau, and the chief resorts Grindelwald, Mürren and Wengen.

Bertram family In Jane Austen's MANSFIELD PARK, Sir Thomas Bertram, his wife and 4 children; the heroine, Fanny Price, is Sir Bertram's niece and is brought up with the family; she eventually marries the eldest son.

Bessarabia A former Rumanian province, now part of the Moldavian and Ukrainian SSRs, Soviet Russia.

Bessemer process (1856) A cheap method of purifying pig iron and converting it into molten steel; its invention revolutionized the steel industry. (Sir Henry Bessemer, died 1898.)

Bess of Hardwick Elizabeth Talbot, Countess of Shrewsbury, who died aged 90 in 1608 after a career which included 4 marriages, court intrigues and the building of HARDWICK HALL.

Beste-Chetwynd, Mrs The extremely wealthy, and odd, lady who appears in several of Evelyn Waugh's novels; she became Lady METROLAND.

Betelgeuse A red giant star in the east shoulder of ORION, of which it is the second brightest star; it is a cool irregular variable, and has a diameter of at least 200 million miles. See RED GIANT.

Bethel The name, meaning 'House of God', given by Jacob to the place where he had the vision of JACOB'S LADDER (Genesis xxviii, 19); applied to a NONCONFORMIST chapel.

Bethlehem Steel (1904) A large US corporation with interests in iron, steel, shipbuilding, coke and coke by-products, with headquarters at Bethlehem, Penn. It has subsidiaries in Chile, Brazil, Venezuela and elsewhere.

Bethnal Green A former London metropolitan borough, since 1965 part of the new borough of TOWER HAMLETS.

Betsey Ross legend The story that Betsey Ross made the first STARS AND STRIPES (1777) at the request of a committee headed by George Washington. It appears to date from 1870 and there is no evidence for it.

Betty lamp A Dutch type of iron oil-and-wick lamp, with a hook to hang it up by, of the kind brought with them by the PILGRIM FATHERS and used until c. 1790.

Beulah Virtually a synonym for 'Promised Land'. Isaiah lxii, 4, prophesies a brighter future for Israel and says: Thou shalt be called Hephzibah ('my delight is in her') and thy land Beulah ('married'). In Pilgrim's Progress Beulah is the land where the pilgrims await their summons to the Celestial City.

Bevanities (UK) Name for Labour MPs in sympathy with Aneurin Bevan when he resigned office (1951) in protest against charges for NATIONAL HEALTH SERVICE spectacles and false teeth imposed by Hugh Gaitskell; they also opposed their government's defense policy and its support for West German rearmament. They were never a united group, and Bevan rejoined the fold later.

Bevercotes (1965) The world's first fully automated coal mine, in Nottinghamshire, England; it is equipped with ROLF and other advanced mechanization devices.

Beveridge reports (UK) The 1942 report on which the WELFARE STATE legislation is based. (2) The 1951 report on broadcasting which opposed the introduction of commercial broadcasting and supported the existing BBC monopoly.

Beverly Hills An exceptionally attractive district of Los Angeles near

Hollywood, famous for bizarre houses built by film stars.

Bevin Boys (UK) Name given in 1940 to young men directed to work in coal mines as an alternative to service with the forces, under an Act sponsored by Ernest Bevin, then Minister of Labour and National Service.

Bewick wood engravings Accurate illustrations of animals, birds and rural scenes, produced by Thomas Bewick (1753-1828), using on wood a technique similar to that in engraving on copper.

Bexley London borough since 1965 consisting of the former boroughs of Bexley and Erith, and the urban districts of Crayford and part of Chislehurst-Sidcup; headquarters at Erith.

Beyond the Fringe (1961) A London revue with a cast of 4 talented young men who wittily satirized current attitudes to war, civil defense, religion, advertising etc.

Bezonian A beggar or rascal; used by PISTOL in Shakespeare's *Henry IV Part II:* Under which king, Bezonian? speak, or die! (Italian *bisogno*, 'need'.)

Bhagavad-Gita A section of the MAHABHARATA in which KRISHNA preaches compassion and the duties of the caste system; also called the Gospel of Krishna. (Sanskrit, 'song of the blessed one'.)

BHC An insecticide for plant and soil pests, which has to be used with care as it can make fruit and vegetables poisonous.

Bhoodan campaign (1951) A campaign started by Gandhi's disciple, Vinobha Bhave, in Hyderabad. He traveled about on foot from village to village begging for land to give to the landless; these gifts totaled over 5 million acres.

BIA See BUREAU OF INDIAN AFFAIRS.

Biafra Republic (1967) The name adopted by Eastern Nigeria when it decided to secede from the Federation of Nigeria, capitulating after a long civil war in January 1970. (Bight of Biafra, the bay between the Niger delta and Cape Lopez in Gabon.)

Bible Belt A name for the states (Arkansas, Mississippi and, until 1967, Tennessee) which prohibited the teaching of the Darwinian theory of evolution, as it conflicts with the account of the creation given in *Genesis.* See SCOPES TRIAL.

Bible box Plain or carved box used to hold a Bible and/or the very few books the average householder could afford in olden days. It had no lock; similar boxes with locks are not Bible boxes.

Bible in Spain, The (1843) George Borrow's fictionalized account of his travels in Spain distributing Bibles for the British and Foreign Bible Society during the CARLIST WARS and against Catholic opposition.

BICC British Insulated Callender's Cables, the world's largest cablemaking company.

Bickerstaff, Isaac The fictional astrologer in Jonathan Swift's attack (1708) on a contemporary publisher of almanacs.

Bicycle Thief, The (1946) De Sica's charming Italian movie about the adventures of a small boy searching for his father's stolen bicycle in the streets of Rome.

Biedermeier style (1815-48) An Austro-German version of the French EMPIRE and ADAM STYLES in furniture, using lighter wood (but ebony for pilasters and columns), dispensing with brass and ormolu, and adding painted pictures in the local cottage tradition. (Named after a magazine cartoon character, Papa Biedermeier, satirizing the unimaginative German middle class of the period, for whom such furniture was designed.)

Biennale, The An exhibition of modern painting and sculpture held in Venice from May to October in even-numbered years.

Big Bang theory (1957) Prof. Martin Ryle's hypothesis that the universe is evolving from a gigantic explosion of superdense matter about 5 billion years ago, and will eventually die. Like the STEADY STATE THEORY with which it is contrasted, it was suggested by the EXPANDING UNIVERSE THEORY.

Big Ben Nickname of the 13½-ton bell in the Clock Tower of the British Houses of Parliament which strikes the hours; it became particularly widely known during World War II when its sound continued to herald the 9 p.m. radio news nightly, despite the Blitz. (Named for Sir Benjamin Hall, Chief Commissioner of Works when it was installed in 1856; he happened to have a deep booming voice.)

Big Bend National Park (1944) A park in southwest Texas enclosed in the big bend of the Rio Grande, with spectacular mountain and desert scenery and a variety of unusual geological structures.

Big Berthas Nickname for the German long-range guns that shelled back areas of the Western Front in 1917 and Paris, at a range of 70 miles, in 1918. (German name, after Bertha KRUPP.)

Big Bill Thompson Nickname of William Hale Thompson, the pro-German Mayor of Chicago (1915-23 and 1927-31), during whose terms of office flourished the notorious gangsters led by SCARFACE AL CAPONE and others.

Big Board, The A nickname for the New York Stock Exchange.

Big Brother The Head of State in Orwell's novel 1984 (q.v.).

Big Brothers of America (1946) A federation of local agencies composed of volunteer laymen who work under the supervision of trained social workers to give guidance and companionship on an individual basis to fatherless boys.

Big D A nickname for Dallas, Texas, as one of the world's oil centers.

Big Dipper The 7 bright stars in the GREAT BEAR; also called the Plow, Charles's Wain and the Wagon. (Dipper in the sense of a can used to ladle liquid, referring to the pattern they, and the LITTLE DIPPER, form.)

Big Eight A College Athletic Conference, comprising Missouri, Nebraska, Colorado, Oklahoma, Oklahoma State, Kansas State, Kansas, Iowa State.

Big-endian and Little-endian The Lilliputian equivalents of Catholic and Protestant in GULLIVER'S TRAVELS, to whom it was of supreme importance whether one broke one's egg at the big or the little end; hence used of any petty doctrinal disputation.

Big Five, The (1) Old name for the principal British joint-stock banks: National Provincial, Westminster, Midland, Lloyds and Barclays. In 1968 the first two merged as the National Westminster, and the last merged with Martins. (2) The heads of the 5 main departments of SCOTLAND YEAR. (3) At the PARIS PEACE CONFERENCE in 1919, USA, Britain, France, Italy, Japan.

Big Mo Nickname of the US battleship *Missouri*, the scene of the Japanese formal surrender in Tokyo Bay, Sept. 2, 1945.

Big Sur A spectacular sector of the Californian coastline, south of Monterey. Orson Welles bought it for a song for Rita Hayworth and sold it at a slight profit; it is now a State Park.

Big Ten The College Athletic Conference, comprising Ohio State, Indiana, Illinois, Purdue, Iowa, Minnesota, Wisconsin, Michigan State, Northwestern, Michigan. One team plays each year in the ROSE BOWL against a team of the PACIFIC EIGHT Conference. See BOWL GAMES.

Bikini A Pacific atoll in the Marshall Islands, the scene (1946) of the first postwar tests of atomic bombs, which left it as bare as a bikini swimsuit leaves the body. Tests ended in 1958 and inhabitants were able to return in 1969.

Bildungsroman Literary term for a particularly German type of novel which is devoted to describing the development of one young person. An English example is DAVID COPPERFIELD. (German, 'novel of education'; sometimes called *Entwicklungsroman*, 'novel of development'.)

Bill Blass A New York fashion house.

Billings, Josh Pen name of the American humorist Henry Wheeler Shaw (1818-85), who wrote phonetically, like Artemus WARD.

Billingsgate A fish market (1699) just below London Bridge, and earlier a coal and corn market; bargees and fishwives made it notorious for foul language.

Billingsley flowers (1) Floral decorations on porcelain, much more naturalistic than those by his contemporaries, painted by William Billingsley (1760-1828) at DERBY, NANTGARW, COALPORT and other factories; his roses were especially famous. (2) Name applied indiscriminately to almost any cabbage rose painted on porcelain.

Bill of Divorcement, A (1921) A play by Clemence Dane on the hardship caused by the fact that insanity was not in Britain a ground for divorce; the law was subsequently changed.

Bill of Rights (1) The Act (1689) which embodied the provisions of the DECLARATION OF RIGHTS, barred Catholic succession to the British throne, and gave Scotland religious freedom. (2) Designation popularly applied to the first 10 Amendments to the CONSTITUTION OF THE UNITED STATES in force from 15 Dec. 1791.

Bills The Buffalo Bills, AMERICAN FOOTBALL LEAGUE. Became member of the AMERICAN CONFERENCE, NATIONAL FOOTBALL LEAGUE in 1970.

Billy Budd (1951) Benjamin Britten's opera, based on a tale by Herman Melville. Billy, the innocent crew-hand, is falsely accused by the master-at-arms, Claggart, of incitement to mutiny (the action takes place in 1797, the year of the NORE MUTINY). He is goaded into hitting Claggart, who dies. The captain reluctantly condemns Billy to death.

Billy Graham crusades The US evangelist Billy Graham's campaigns in the USA, Britain (first in 1954) and elsewhere, held in large arenas with maximum publicity and theatrical display; the audience are invited to come forward and rededicate themselves publicly to their religion.

Billy Liar (1959) A novel by Keith Waterhouse of a Yorkshire working-class boy who gets into trouble with his lies and fantasies, which are especially about success with the girls; the plot was used by Willis Hall for a play (1960).

Billy Mitchell trial (1925) The court-martial of an officer who until 1924 had been Assistant Chief of the Army Air Service, and had constantly preached the supremacy of air power over capital ships; in despair at the refusal of military and naval authorities to accept his views, he accused them of 'incompetency . . . and almost treasonable administration'. He was suspended, resigned, and died (1936) before the events of World War II vindicated him; he was posthumously restored to the rank of major general (1942).

Billy Sunday revivals A series of sensational revivalist meetings held from 1896 until his death in 1935 by one of the most widely known American evangelists, William Ashley Sunday, born in Ames, Ind.; over a million people were converted by his fundamentalist preaching.

Billy the Kid (1) Nickname of William Bonney, a bandit and bank robber in the Wild West days of 19th-century USA. (2) A ballet (1938), music by Aaron Copland, choreography by Eugene Loring, book by Lincoln Kirstein. See LINCOLN COUNTY WAR.

Biography for Beginners See CLERIHEW.

BIOT Initials used for BRITISH INDIAN OCEAN TERRITORY.

BIPO Initials used for BRITISH INSTITUTE OF PUBLIC OPINION.

Bird Man of Alcatraz, The A movie about Robert Franklin Stroud, a prisoner for 53 years (42 in solitary confinement), mostly in ALCATRAZ, but latterly in Springfield (Mo.) prison, where he died in 1963 aged 73, having attained world fame for his remarkable devotion to and sympathy with birdlife.

Birds, The (414 BC) Aristophanes' fantastical comedy, satirizing Athenian politics, but notable for its poetic lyrics. See CLOUDCUCKOOLAND.

Birds' Christmas Carol, The (1887) A best-selling children's book by Kate Douglas Wiggin in the contemporary taste of sweet innocence, about Carol Bird and her family, and their poor neighbors.

Birdseye Frozen Food process (1925) A method of preserving fresh vegetables discovered by the American, Clarence Birdseye.

Birds of America, The See AUDUBON PRINTS.

Birkbeck College (1920) A unit of London University, originally the London Mechanics' Institution (1823), founded by a Yorkshire doctor, George Birkbeck. It is noted for part-time tuition given to mature students.

Birkin, Rupert A character in D. H. Lawrence's WOMEN IN LOVE who marries URSULA BRANGWEN, and is the mouthpiece of the author's views.

Birmingham, George A. Pseudonym of Canon J. O. Hannay, Irish author of *Spanish Gold* (1908) and other humorous tales.

Birnam Wood An allusion to a line of Shakespeare's *Macbeth*. The witches prophesy that MACBETH will not be vanquished 'till Birnam wood do come to Dunsinane'; Malcolm's army arrives under cover of branches felled from this wood, and overthrows him. (A former royal forest near Perth.)

Birth of a Nation, The (1915) One of the earliest and most famous spectacular films, produced by D. W. Griffith, and dealing with the American Civil War.

'Birth of Venus, The' (late 15th century) Botticelli's version of the theme of APHRODITE ANADYOMENE; now in the UFFIZI, Florence.

Bishop A hot spiced wine drink, usually with port as a base.

Bishop Blougram's Apology (1855) Robert Browning's dramatic monologue in which the Bishop justifies his retention of office after he has lost faith in the doctrines he has to preach. Cardinal Wiseman is avowedly the model for Blougram.

Bishop Rock (1858) (UK) A lighthouse and rock west of the Scilly Isles. Built of granite, the lighthouse is one of the most exposed in the world.

Bishops' Wars (1) A bloodless victory for the Scottish COVENANTERS who

obtained Charles I's agreement to submit their disputes to a new Scottish Parliament and Church Assembly (1638). (2) A second victory for the Covenanters (1640), whom Charles I allowed to occupy the 6 northern counties of England and dictate their own terms.

Bismarck (1) German name for the mixed drink called in England BLACK VELVET. (2) A raised doughnut shaped like a ball, with filling usually of jelly. (For Prince Otto von Bismarck; see BLOOD AND IRON.)

Bismarck German battleship sunk in May 1941, 3 days after sinking the HOOD.

Bismarckhering Rolled or filleted pickled herring.

Bismarck Sea, Battle of the (March 1943) An action in which US carrier-borne aircraft sank the whole of a Japanese troop transport convoy bound for New Guinea, together with its escorts. (Bismarck Archipelago, north of New Guinea.)

Bitter Sweet (1929) An operetta by Noël Coward.

Black and Tan (1) A mixed drink of beer and stout. (2) Name given, for its color, to the Manchester terrier and the very similar English toy terrier.

Black and Tans (1920) (1) British recruits who filled vacancies in the Royal Irish Constabulary caused by the killing or intimidation of its Irish-born members during the TROUBLES. They gained a reputation for terrorist tactics. See also AUXIS. (From their khaki uniforms and black belts.) (2) Name given to those who favored increased participation by Negroes in politics, and advocated PR (proportional representation) for white and black. Compare LILY-WHITES.

Black and Tans (Scarteen) See SCARTEEN BLACK AND TANS.

Black Arrow (1967) A British 3-stage satellite-launching rocket developed from BLACK KNIGHT and designed to put a series of research satellites into orbit from WOOMERA at yearly intervals in the 1970s.

Black Arrow, The (1888) A story of the Two Roses written for the young by R. L. Stevenson in the WARDOUR

STREET or (to use his own term for it) 'tushery' style.

Blackbeard Nickname of an English privateer, Captain Edward Teach, who turned pirate (c. 1714), converted a captured French merchantman into a 40-gun warship and terrorized the Spanish Main. He wintered in North Carolina, whose governor shared the loot, but with the help of the governor of Virginia the Royal Navy cornered Teach and shot him dead (1718).

Black Beauty (1877) Anna Sewell's 'autobiography' of a horse, a long-lasting favorite with the young.

Black Belt (1) In judo, a member of one of the 5 lower DAN grades. (2) A narrow region of dark calcareous soil in central Alabama and Mississippi, especially suitable for cotton cultivation. See also BLACK EARTH BELT.

Black Bess Dick TURPIN'S mare on which, in Harrison Ainsworth's novel *Rookwood* (1834), he rides from London to York in a night, to establish an alibi.

Blackboard Jungle, The (1954) The first novel (made into a movie) of Evan Hunter (who also writes crime stories as Edward McBain). Written from personal experience, it is a sensational account of a city high school where the boys are ruffians, the headmaster a bully and the overworked teachers have additional problems in their private lives.

Black Boy (1945) A moving autobiography dealing with the early life of the Negro writer Richard Wright (1908-60).

Black Country The industrial Midlands of England, including Birmingham and Wolverhampton, blackened by factory smoke.

Black Death (14th century) An outbreak of bubonic plague which killed many millions of people in Europe, Asia and Africa. See GREAT PLAGUE.

Black Douglas Nickname give to (1) the Earls of Douglas, in distinction from the Earls of Angus (see RED DOUGLAS); (2) specifically, their earlier kinsman, Sir James Douglas, who ravaged northern England in the 14th century. (The name Doug-

las itself means 'black water', which may account for the origin of the nickname.)

Black Earth belt A belt of exceptionally fertile black or dark-brown soil formed under natural grassland, which covers much of southern Russia (especially the Ukraine), Rumania and Hungary. In Russia it is known as chernozem. A similar belt stretches from Saskatchewan in Canada to Texas.

Blackfoot An Algonquian-speaking tribe, once one of the largest and most warlike of the northern PLAINS INDIANS; some 7000 survive in Montana and Saskatchewan. (Wore black mocassins.)

Black Friars See DOMINICANS.

Blackfriars A Thames-side section of London south of FLEET STREET, named after the DOMINICANS who moved there in 1276. The elder Burbage built the first roofed theater there in 1596 (see also MERMAID THEATRE). UNILEVER House overlooks Blackfriars Bridge.

Black Friday (1) 24 Sept. 1869, culmination of a panic on the American Stock Exchange after an attempt to corner the gold supply; the price rose from 133 to 162½ and then fell sharply back again. (2) 19 Sept. 1873, culmination of another Wall Street panic caused by overexpansion and railroad speculation, leading to bank failures. (3) In the history of British trade unions, the day (15th Apr. 1921) the railway and transport unions canceled a strike in sympathy with the miners, thus breaking up the 'triple alliance' of these 3 major unions.

Black Hand (1911) A secret society which aimed at the unification of the southern Slavs, formed by 'Apis' (Col. Dimitriević) the man behind the SARAJEVO assassination.

Black Hawk A SAUK Indian chief who fought against the US in the WAR OF 1812 and was finally defeated in the Black Hawk war of 1832.

Black Hawks The Chicago Black Hawks, NATIONAL HOCKEY LEAGUE.

Black Hole of Calcutta (1756) The cell at Fort William, Calcutta, where the Nawab of Bengal, Suraj ud Dowlah, placed 146 British East India Co. prisoners, of whom only 23 survived the night. Recently doubts have been cast on this tradition, apparently based on the account of one unreliable witness.

Black Hundreds (1905-09) Russian terrorists who carried out pogroms, murdering some 50,000 Jews.

Black Jack Nickname for (1) General John A. Logan, who fought in the Union Army in the AMERICAN CIVIL WAR and (2) General John J. Pershing, who commanded the AEF in Europe in World War I. (Refers to swarthy complexion.)

Black (James Tait) Memorial Prize An annual prize awarded for the best novel and the best biography (or similar work), on the advice of the Professor of Literature, Edinburgh University. (In memory of a partner of the publishing firm, A. & C. Black.)

Black Knight The first British rocket, built by WESTLAND to put a 300-lb payload into space; fired at WOOMERA in 1958, it was later used for research into reentry problems during the development of BLUE STREAK. See also BLACK ARROW.

Black Knight, The The mysterious knight in Scott's IVANHOE who turns out to be Richard Coeur-de-Lion.

Black Madonna, The (Poland) See JASNA GORA.

Black Maria Nickname for the black-pointed police van used for the transport of arrested persons and criminals.

Black Militant A comprehensive term covering members of such movements as the BLACK PANTHERS.

Black Muslims A Negro sect founded in USA in the 1930s by Elijah Muhammed, based on a corruption of Islamic beliefs and the view that the white man is the devil. See MALCOLM X.

Black Panthers (1966) A US Marxist Negro party with the slogan BLACK POWER, which the STUDENT NONVIOLENT COORDINATING COMMITTEE founded under the leadership of Stokely Carmichael in Alabama.

Black Pope A name for the General of the Society of Jesus (i.e. the head of the JESUITS).

Black Power The slogan of Stokely Carmichael (see STUDENT NONVIOLENT COORDINATING COMMITTEE; BLACK PANTHERS). It sums up the views of those Negroes who feel that integration with whites is no longer possible or even desirable and that the only practical course to attain Negro equality in positions of power is to oppose the evils of white authority by every means possible, including violence. Not yet clearly formulated, this policy appears to verge on advocacy either of a Negro separatist movement in the USA or of a Negro-dictated form of APARTHEID.

Black Prince Edward Prince of Wales, son of Edward III; he died before his father, thus opening up the rivalry between descendants of his 2 younger brothers which led to the WARS OF THE ROSES. (Traditionally so called because he wore black armor.)

Black Rod The Gentleman Usher of the Black Rod, an official of the Lord Chamberlain's department who maintains order in the House of Lords and has the special duty of summoning the Commons thither to hear the Address from the Throne. (Carries an ebony wand of office.)

Blackshirts Another name for (1) the Nazi ss; (2) the BRITISH UNION OF FASCISTS.

Blackstone Short title of Blackstone's *Commentaries on the Laws of England* (1769), a standard popular, but not very accurate, exposition of the subject.

Blackstone An aperitif of sherry, gin and bitters.

Black Stripe Hot rum, molasses and lemon.

Black Tom explosion (1916) An explosion at the munition docks on Black Tom Island, N. J., which an official investigation attributed to German sabotage; probably organized by two minor German diplomats, Franz von Papen (the future Chancellor) and Boy-Ed, who were expelled later that year.

Black Tuesday 29 Oct. 1929, the day of the WALL STREET CRASH.

Black Velvet A mixed drink of champagne and stout, known in Germany as a Bismarck, and said to ease hangovers.

Black Watch (Royal Highland Regiment), The A regiment of the HIGHLAND BRIGADE, an amalgamation of the 42nd and 73rd Foot. (So called from the dark colors of their tartan; 'watch' in the old sense 'guard'.)

Blackwood convention At Bridge, a bid of 4 No-Trumps asking partner to indicate his Aces, and 5 No-Trumps to indicate Kings.

Blackwood's Magazine (1817) An Edinburgh monthly (often called Maga) which began as a literary magazine, with contributors such as Walter Scott and De Quincey. Later it tended to specialize in stories written by Empire-builders. It now takes articles and stories of all kinds, with the emphasis still on adventure overseas.

Blair Castle Home of the Dukes of Atholl at Blair Atholl, near Pitlochry, dating back to the 13th century.

Blair House (1824) The President's Guest House near the White House, the official residence for visiting heads of state since 1964.

Blake case (1961) The trial *in camera* of George Blake, an MI-6 agent who betrayed his comrades to the East Germans. He was given the longest sentence in British history (42 years) but escaped in 1966. His father was an Egyptian-born Sephardic Jew named Behar who fought in the British Army in World War I. Blake was born in Holland and worked for the Dutch Resistance. The story that he was 'brain-washed' while a prisoner in the Korean War has been disproved.

Blake, Nicholas Pen name assumed by the poet C. Day Lewis when writing detective stories.

Blake, Sexton The detective in a series of cheap novelettes published in Britain first in the *Marvel* and then as the Sexton Blake Library. He was invented by Hal Meredith in 1873, but when the copyright ran out Blake was taken over by numerous other writers, including Peter Cheyney. See Nick CARTER.

Blakeney, Sir Percy See SCARLET PIMPERNEL.

Blandford, Marquess of Courtesy title of the Duke of Marlborough's heir.

Blandings, Empress of The immense sow who is the center of attention at Blandings Castle, seat of the P. G. Wodehouse character, the 9th Earl of Emsworth.

Blast A literary and artistic magazine produced by Wyndham Lewis and Ezra Pound to propagate their aggressive modernist views ('vorticism') and the ideology which landed them both eventually in the Fascist camp.

Blatant Beast, The In Spenser's FAERIE QUEENE, the spirit of slander, offspring of Envy and Detraction. It is chained up by a knight, but breaks loose again to plague the world.

Blaue Reiter, Der See BLUE RIDERS.

'Blaydon Races' (England) The 'Tyneside anthem', written in the mid-19th century. (Blaydon, near Newcastle.)

Blaze (1932) A vigorous repeat-flowering pillar rose with large bright scarlet flowers.

Bleak House (1853) Dickens's novel, notable for its attack on the old Court of CHANCERY in an account of the JARNDYCE V. JARNDYCE case. At Mr Jarndyce's home, Bleak House, live his 3 wards, one of whom is, unknown to all, the illegitimate daughter of Lady Dedlock. Tulkinghorne, lawyer to the latter's husband, discovers her guilty secret, and this leads to Lady Dedlock's death and his own.

Bleep See HARWELL.

Blenheim (1704) First major battle of the War of the SPANISH SUCCESSION, in which Marlborough in command of Anglo-German forces defeated a Franco-Bavarian army under Tallard which threatened Vienna. See KASPAR. (English corruption of Blindheim, north of Nuremberg; known on the Continent as the Battle of Höchstadt, a town nearby.)

Blenheim Orange A dual-purpose apple, with yellow and red fruit ripening in November. (Pips first taken, 1818, from a Woodstock garden; see next entry.)

Blenheim Palace Vanbrugh's classical masterpiece in Woodstock, Oxfordshire, built for the 1st Duke of Marlborough; Sir Winston Churchill's birthplace.

'Blessed Damozel, The' (1850) D. G. Rossetti's poem in which a 'damozel' in heaven yearns for her lover on earth.

Bleus (1850) Nickname of the French-Canadian Conservatives who supported Louis H. Lafontaine; compare ROUGES.

Blifil The malevolent and treacherous half brother of TOM JONES in Fielding's novel.

Blimp, Colonel The Australian cartoonist Low's choleric character in the London *Evening Standard* whose *ex cathedra* pronouncements from a Turkish bath conveyed Low's left-wing sentiments under a die-hard cover ('Bayonets bring the best out of a man — and it stays out.').

Blind Earl pattern A WORCESTER PORCELAIN pattern of which the main feature is a large sprig of leaves impressed on the plate; often copied by other factories. (Traditionally first made for a blind Earl of Coventry so that he could feel the pattern; actually made before his time.)

Blind Harry (15th century) The only known name of a Scottish poet who told the story of Wallace in heroic couplets.

Blithe Spirit (1941) A Noël Coward comedy in which a man has to cohabit with his second wife and the ghost of his first, audible only to him.

Blitzkrieg The German strategy of sudden all-out onslaught, using every available new device, such as reckless thrust by small groups of tanks far ahead of the main force, STUKA dive-bombing, parachute drops on strongpoints etc.; used successfully in overrunning Poland, the Low Countries and France in 1939-40. (German, 'lightning war'.)

Blizzard of '88 A blizzard in March 1888, possibly the worst known, which swept from the northwest to obliterate the eastern states, cutting communication between New York,

Philadelphia and Boston, raising food prices to famine level, and causing some 400 deaths.

Block, The A name given to a notorious street of bars, striptease shows etc., in east Baltimore, Md.

Blondel The French minstrel who, according to tradition, discovered where Richard I had been imprisoned (in Dürrenstein, Austria) by singing one of their favorite songs under his prison window.

Blondie See DAGWOOD.

Blondin The stage name of a French tightrope walker who crossed the Niagara Falls on a rope in 1859 and subsequently repeated the feat blindfold.

Blood and Guts Nickname of US Gen. G. S. Patton, a man of violent habit and language who played a prominent part in Africa and Europe in World War II.

Blood and Iron The basis of Prussian policy, according to Bismarck (1886). (Translation of German *Blut and Eisen*.)

Bloodhound (1957) A British guided missile, ramjet-propelled, built by BAC for army and navy use as a surface-to-air weapon. See FERRANTI.

Bloodless Revolution, The (1688) Another name for the GLORIOUS REVOLUTION.

Bloody Assize (1685) The name given to the trials by the brutal Judge Jeffreys of those implicated in MONMOUTH'S REBELLION.

Bloody Butcher, The The Duke of Cumberland, son of George II, so named for his savage treatment of the Highlanders after the FORTY-FIVE and his victory at CULLODEN.

Bloody Mary Protestant name for Queen Mary I, the Roman Catholic queen who intervened between Edward VI and Elizabeth I, and was responsible for the MARIAN PERSECUTION.

Bloody Mary A mixed drink of vodka and tomato juice.

Bloody Sunday (22 Jan. 1905) The day when troops fired on the St Petersburg workers at the beginning of the 1905 RUSSIAN REVOLUTION.

Bloom, Leopold A Jewish advertising canvasser, chief character of

Joyce's ULYSSES. He is humiliatingly aware of his wife's unfaithfulness (see next entry).

Bloom, Molly The unfaithful Penelope of Joyce's ULYSSES, wife of Leopold (see last entry), remembered especially for her 60-page unpunctuated 'interior monologue' which ends the book.

Bloomer Girl (1944) An undistinguished musical by Harold Arlen and E. Y. Harburg. (Bloomers were trousers worn with or without a skirt by women for cycling and games; named after Mrs Amelia Bloomer of New York who in 1849 designed a masculine dress for women comprising jacket, short skirt and Turkish trousers.)

Bloomsbury group A coterie of the British intelligentsia who met and worked in Bloomsbury, London (about 1904-39); they included Virginia and Leonard Woolf (of the Hogarth Press), Bertrand Russell, J. M. Keynes, E. M. Forster, David Garnett and Lytton Strachey.

Bloor Derby (1811-48) The products of the DERBY PORCELAIN factory after it was bought by Robert Bloor. In this period it lost its high reputation, wares being made for the cheaper markets, with gaudy IMARI PATTERNS and Rococo designs and, on the figures, elaborate gilding. The firm sold out to COPELAND & GARRETT.

Blowpipe British man-portable, short-range antiaircraft weapon.

BLT Initials used for Bacon, Lettuce and Tomato sandwich.

Blue Angel, The The movie in which the director Josef von Sternberg launched Marlene Dietrich as a star in the 1930s.

Blue Angels US Navy precision exhibition flying team. Compare THUNDERBIRDS.

Blue-Backed Speller (1783) Noah Webster's book, later known as *Webster's Spelling Book* or *Blue-Backed Speller*, which had sold 70 million copies by 1883, and being used in all schools helped to standardize American spelling. Mr Webster was presumably responsible for spreading dismay among international printers and publishers by decreeing, e.g., that there should be one more l in *skilful* and one less in *traveller*, and that while *dialog* is OK, *leag* is not.

Bluebeard One of the MOTHER GOOSE'S TALES, with an eastern setting. Bluebeard's latest wife discovers a room full of the skeletons of her predecessors, and is rescued from his wrath by her brothers. See SISTER ANNE.

'Bluebeard' Nickname of Henri Landru, a Frenchman executed in 1922 for the murder of 10 women. (See previous entry.)

Bluebell line (1960) (UK) A branch railway line from Haywards Heath to Horsted Keynes in Sussex, closed by British Railways, then bought up and run by a society interested in preserving this particularly picturesque line. (So called because in the old days the conductor was alleged to stop trains to let passengers pick the bluebells en route.)

Bluebird (1935-67) The name of a series of racing cars, speedboats and hydroplanes used by Sir Malcolm Campbell and his son Donald in establishing various world speed records.

Blue Bird, The (1905) Maurice Maeterlinck's allegorical children's play, a theatrical fairy tale first produced in Russia by Stanislavsky (see STANISLAVSKY SYSTEM). (French title, *L'Oiseau bleu*.)

'Blue Boy, The' Gainsborough's portrait, painted partly to confound Reynolds, who held that masses of blue spoiled a picture; now at San Marino, Calif.

Blue-coat School Another name for CHRIST'S HOSPITAL. (From the uniform worn by the boys.)

Blue Cross (1) (USA; 1929) A nonprofit health insurance scheme. (2) A London organization engaged in animal welfare, which provides veterinary treatment for the pets of those who cannot afford to pay fees. It has absorbed Our Dumb Friends League.

'Blue Danube, The' (1867) The most famous of the Strauss waltzes. The German title is 'An der schönen blauen Donau'; the 'blue' must be taken as poetic or patriotic license.

Blue Devils   Nickname of the Chasseurs Alpins, an elite corps of the French Army, originally raised and trained to guard the Alpine frontiers, skilled mountaineers and skiers.

Blue Eagle   The symbol of the NATIONAL RECOVERY ADMINISTRATION.

Bluegrass, The   A region of Kentucky around Lexington where there is a luxuriant growth of bluegrass especially suitable for pasturing horses; it thus became the center of US racehorse breeding.

Bluegrass State   Nickname of Kentucky. See BLUEGRASS, THE

Blue Hen's Chickens   The people of Delaware. (From a story that the best fighting cocks are bred from blue hens; a Delaware regiment in the Revolutionary War, already bearing the nickname Caldwell's Gamecocks, changed it to this.)

Blue Hen State   Delaware; see last entry.

Bluemantle   A Pursuivant of the COLLEGE OF ARMS.

Blue Max   See POUR LE MÉRITE.

Blue Monday   The first day of the work week; compare TGIF.

Blue Norther   A cold wind from the north which brings rapidly falling temperatures to the Kansas-Oklahoma-Texas region. (From the color of the accompanying cloud bank.)

Blue Nose   Nickname for an inhabitant of the Maritime Provinces of Canada, especially Nova Scotia and New Brunswick. (Probably from the most easily observable result of their bitterly cold winters; SAM SLICK said it was the name of a potato grown there.)

Blue Point oyster   A small oyster, esteemed by gourmets, farmed on the shores of Long Island, N.Y. (Name of a headland.)

Blue Ribbon of the Atlantic   A title (later reinforced by a trophy) given to the liner which holds the speed record for transatlantic crossings in both directions. It was held in succession by the *Mauretania, Bremen, Queen Mary* (1938) and *United States* (1952). See CORDON BLEU. (Also spelled *riband*, an obsolete synonym.)

Blue Ribbon of the Turf   A name for the Epsom DERBY.

Blue Riders   A school of German Expressionist art founded 1911 by Kandinsky and Marc, and joined by Klee. (Kandinsky explained: 'We both liked blue and Marc liked painting horses.')

Blue Ridge Parkway   (1933) A scenic route following the Blue Ridge Mountains in Virginia, North Carolina and Georgia, linking the SHENANDOAH and the Great Smoky Mountains National Parks (see GREAT SMOKIES) at an average height of 3000 ft above sea level.

Blues   The St. Louis Blues, NATIONAL HOCKEY LEAGUE.

Blues and Greens, Factions of the   Rival street gangs in Byzantium whose nightly brawlings rose to a climax in the 6th century. (Originally the colors of rival teams of charioteers from different quarters of the city.)

Blues and Royals, The   (1661) Formerly The Royal Horse Guards (The Blues), one of the 2 regiments of the HOUSEHOLD CAVALRY, in origin a ROUNDHEAD regiment. They wear blue tunics and red plumes.

Blue Shield   (1917) US nonprofit health insurance scheme.

Blueshirts   (1933) General O'Duffy's Fascist National Guard, formed in the IRISH FREE STATE.

Blue Steel   (1962) British long-range air-to-surface missile for use by V-BOMBERS; it was to be replaced by the US SKYBOLT (which was canceled).

Bluestockings   (18th century) A literary coterie founded by a Mrs Montagu, so named because the men attended its meetings in informal dress, typified by blue worsted stockings.

Blue Streak   A British IRBM the development of which as a military weapon was abandoned in 1960 as too costly (having already cost $240 million) and as obsolete since it could be fired only from fixed launching pads. It was then developed as a first-stage rocket for ELDO.

'Blue Tail Fly' (1846) A famous song, in the CHRISTY MINSTRELS tradition, also called 'Jim Crack Corn'; attributed to Dan Emmett.

Blue Train, The See TRAIN BLEU.

Blue Water A British guided missile, development of which was abandoned in 1962.

Blue Water school Nickname for those in the Admiralty who successfully maintained between the world wars that the British Navy should continue to concentrate on capital ships for strategic use in distant parts of the world; as a consequence Britain entered World War II with no landing craft and an insufficiency of escort vessels.

Bluff King Hal A name for Henry VIII.

Bluidie Clavers Scottish nickname of John Graham of Claverhouse, Viscount Dundee, notorious for his brutal persecution of COVENANTERS (1679-88); and also victor at KILLIECRANKIE.

Blundell's An English 'Public' School at Tiverton, Devon; mentioned in LORNA DOONE. (Founded in 1604 by Peter Blundell, a local man.)

BMA (1832) Initials used for the British Medical Association, the largest of various associations of medical practitioners. The profession is controlled by the General Medical Council.

BMC (1952) Initials standing for British Motor Corporation, founded by William Morris (Lord Nuffield), and manufacturing vehicles under the names of Morris, Morris Commercial, MG, Austin, Austin-Healey, Wolseley, Princess and Vanden Plas, and Fisher and Ludlow components, as well as SU carburetors. BMC was merged with Jaguar in 1966 to form British Motor Holdings, and then with Leyland to form the BRITISH LEYLAND MOTOR CORPORATION.

BMEWS Initials of Ballistic Missile Early Warning System, a US system of giant radar stations at Thule (Greenland), Fylingdales (Yorkshire) and Clear (Alaska).

BMJ (1840) Initials commonly used for the *British Medical Journal*, the BMA's weekly paper which publishes authoritative articles on discoveries in, and theories about, medicine in all its branches.

B'nai B'rith (1843) The oldest and largest Jewish service organization, founded in New York and now established in over 30 countries. See HILLEL FOUNDATION LECTURES. ('Sons of the Covenant'.)

Boabdil The last Moorish King of Granada, died 1492. (Corruption of Abu Abdullah.)

BOADICEA (1967) Initials used for British Overseas Airways Digital Information Computer for Electronic Automation, a unique computerized system for handling all aspects of airline bookings.

Boanerges Sons of Thunder, Jesus' name for James and John, the sons of Zebedee (*Mark* iii, 17); hence a mighty orator. (The name has come down in corrupt form.)

Boar's Head, The FALSTAFF's favorite tavern, kept by Mistress QUICKLY in Eastcheap, London.

Boar's Hill (UK) A much favored residential area near Oxford. The late Poet Laureate, John Masefield, made his home there and had a private theater there.

Boat Race, The (1829) An annual race between Oxford and Cambridge University eights, rowed in March or April on the Thames, originally at Henley and later from Putney to Mortlake over a course of $4\frac{1}{4}$ miles.

Bobbsey Twins, The Characters in a series of children's books begun in 1904 by Laura Lee Hope. They became a household name, given for example to the 2-man crew of New York police cars (alternatively called Dolly Sisters).

'Bobby Shafto' An 18th-century song about a man said to have lived in Co. Wicklow, Ireland; given wider currency through application to a parliamentary candidate of that name.

Boche World War I name for a German. (From French *Alboche*, of uncertain origin, used in the same sense.)

Bodensee German name of Lake Constance, between Germany and Switzerland.

Bodhisattvas In MAHAYANA Buddhism, beings who attain Enlightenment in order to become Buddhas in future ages; they are worshiped as intercessors for mankind with the existing Buddha.

Bodiam Castle (UK) A well-preserved 14th-century moated castle near Hawkhurst, Sussex, owned by the National Trust.

Bodleian The OXFORD UNIVERSITY library founded by Duke Humphrey (1455), refounded by Sir Thomas Bodley (1597) and extended (1940) with ROCKEFELLER FOUNDATION funds.

Bodnant Gardens One of the finest gardens in Britain, at Tal-y-Cafn, near Conway, Denbighshire; given by Lord Aberconway to the NATIONAL TRUST.

Boeing US aircraft and missile firm, with headquarters at Seattle; it produced the FLYING FORTRESS, SUPERFORTRESS (B-29) and STRATOFORTRESS (B-52); the first big 4-jet airliner, (B-707 in 1958), carrying 179 passengers at 550 m.p.h.; the JUMBO JET (B-747 in 1970); to be followed by the supersonic (SST) rival to CONCORDE. Boeings also made MINUTEMAN, SATURN and LUNAR ORBITER.

Boeotian Boorish. (Boeotia, a comparatively isolated district of central Greece, capital Thebes, whose inhabitants in Classical times were famed for stupidity.)

Boers See AFRIKANERS.

Boer War (1899-1902) Name in common use for what historians call the Second SOUTH AFRICAN WAR, started by President Kruger of the Transvaal aided by the other Boer Republic, the Orange Free State, and supplied with German arms. The Boers besieged MAFEKING, KIMBERLEY and LADYSMITH, all of which were relieved by Gen. Roberts in 1900. Kitchener then combated the guerrilla tactics of the Boer commandos by a system of blockhouses combined with concentration camps for civilian sympathizers. The war ended with the Treaty of Vereeniging.

Bofors Swedish light antiaircraft gun firing 120 shells a minute, used in World War II. (Name of town where made.)

Boghazköy Site in Turkey of the 17th-century BC Hittite capital, Hattusas, where tablets inscribed with cuneiform writing were found, which threw new light on Hittite history. (Village 90 miles east of Ankara.)

Bogomils A Balkan religious community of MANICHAEISTIC views, which regarded the EASTERN ORTHODOX CHURCH as the work of Satan and was the source of many heresies in Russia. It was pacifist, egalitarian, and had no church or priest; it rejected most Christian dogma, but held that every individual could by intense effort and asceticism attain to the perfection of Christ. (Traditionally founded by Bogomil, a 10th-century Bulgarian Manichean.)

Bohème, La (1896) Puccini's opera of Bohemian life in Paris. Rudolph, in one of the best-known love duets ('Your tiny hand is frozen'), falls in love with the frail consumptive Mimi: later they quarrel and part, but Mimi is brought back at the end of the last act for a famous death scene.

Bohemian Club A San Francisco social club.

Bohemian glass A generic term for richly colored decorated glass made in or near the mountains on the Bohemia-Silesia borders, the best between the 16th century and the 1730s, especially the ruby and emerald glass of the 1670s. Wares were engraved, etched or enameled. Bohemian styles were extensively and successfully copied in the early 19th century, notably by the New England Glass Co. of East Cambridge, Boston, Mass.

Bohn A name familiar to generations of schoolboys for literal translations of Greek and Latin classics, used as 'ponies'. (H. G. Bohn, 1796-1884, English publisher.)

Boilermaker Whiskey with a beer chaser, popular in North America.

Bokhara rugs Small rugs made by Turkoman nomads over a wide area of Central Asia and collected for export at Bokhara (where none were made). Predominantly rich red or brown, they have retained since the 18th century the same traditional motifs of complicated designs of octagonal shape. They are now mostly made in the USSR, but the design is also copied in Pakistan and Afghanistan.

Bolero The wartime code name for the preliminary administrative work for opening up a SECOND FRONT in 1943, initiated when Harry Hopkins and General George Marshall came to London (April 1942).

'Boléro' (1928) A popular orchestral work composed by Ravel for the dancer Ida Rubinstein; a single melody is taken up by more and more instruments until the climactic finale is reached.

Bollingen Prize (1949) An annual award for achievement in American poetry, first presented by the Bollingen Foundation (created by Paul Mellon), under the auspices of the LIBRARY OF CONGRESS, to Ezra Pound. This created a political furore and subsequent prizes were awarded by the YALE University Library.

Bolsheviks Name given to the opportunist majority group, led by Lenin, after the MENSHEVIKS had seceded from the SOCIAL DEMOCRATS in 1903. The name was officially used as a synonym for Russian Communists until just before the end of the Stalin era. (Russian, 'majority group'.)

Bolshoi Theater (1824) One of the principal theaters in Moscow, famous since 1939 as the home of the Bolshoi Theater Ballet. (Russian, 'big'.)

Bomarc US ground-to-air defense missile with homing radar guidance and a range of 460 miles, designed to protect cities or a fleet.

Bomba, King Name given to Ferdinand II, Bourbon King of the TWO SICILIES, on account of his ruthless

bombardment of rebellious towns during the REVOLUTION OF 1848.

Bomb Alley Wry nickname for the parts of Kent and Sussex under the route taken by German flying-bombs in 1944; they suffered severe damage from the many which fell short of their London target.

Bombay duck Dried salted fish used as a relish with curried dishes; also called Bummalo and, deservedly, stink-fish. (Corruption of Mahratti *bombila*, a kind of small fish.)

Bombay State A former Indian state, now divided into the 2 states of MAHARASHTRA and GUJARAT.

Bomber Command See STRIKE COMMAND.

Bond, James The British secret agent, created by Ian Fleming, who as 007 (q.v.) battled with the dark forces of SMERSH. Gourmet, cad, womanizer and sadist, he became the *idéal laid* of the world.

Bondi Beach Australia's best-known surfing beach, at Waverley, a suburb of Sydney.

Boniface The jovial innkeeper of Farquhar's play *Beaux' Stratagem* (1707); a generic term for innkeepers.

Bonn The Federal capital of Western Germany; the name is used as a synonym for the West German government.

Bonn Convention (1952) The agreement to end the occupation of Western Germany and make it a free partner in Western alliances, provided the projected EUROPEAN DEFENCE COMMUNITY came into force. This proviso was canceled when the EDC plan failed.

Bonneville salt flats A natural racetrack in Utah, where world landspeed records were set up from 1937 onwards by racing motorists.

Bonnie and Clyde (1968) A highly successful movie produced by Warren Beatty based on documentary evidence about the less than competent Barrow gang that operated in the southwestern US in the Al Capone era. Clyde Barrow egged on by his girl, Bonnie Parker, and joined by 3 others take to robbery with violence. They are ambushed and shot by police just after they have decided to go straight. In general an amusing film, it is marred for some by the prolonged scene of carnage at the end.

Bonnie Prince Charlie See YOUNG PRETENDER.

Bonny Dundee A kinder nickname for BLUIDIE CLAVERS.

Bonus Army (1932) World War I veterans who marched on Washington demanding full payment, under a 1924 Act, of compensation covering the difference between wartime service pay and wages of civilian war workers. Four persons were killed, and Hoover called out tanks, cavalry etc. to disperse them. The claims were not met till 1936.

Boodle's Club (1762) A London club in St James's Street, with a membership drawn from country houses, banking families and the higher echelons of the Army and Navy; identifiable by its famous bow window from which the masses (i.e. nonmembers) may be quizzed.

Boojum A very special kind of SNARK; anyone sighting it will softly and suddenly vanish away.

Book of Hours The Roman Catholic breviary of psalms, lessons etc. for every day of the year (originally psalms for every hour of the day), used by priests rather than laymen.

Book of the Dead The Ancient Egyptian guide for the dead in the next world, consisting of hymns, spells etc., placed in the tomb.

Boone, Daniel (1734-1820) A brave and resourceful frontiersman, a hunter and trapper for most of his life, in Kentucky (1767-88), West Virginia and the Ozarks (then Spanish). The legend that he discovered Kentucky grew from his trip over the WILDERNESS ROAD (1767), his establishment of a fort (1775) at what now Boonesboro, and a fictional 'autobiography' by John Filson (1784); he also appears in Byron's *Don Juan* and James Fenimore Cooper's novels.

Boötes A constellation at the tail of the GREAT BEAR, also called the Wag-

oner (as is AURIGA). It contains the most distant galaxy known, perhaps 6000 million light-years away; alpha-Boötis is ARCTURUS. (Greek, 'plowman'.)

Boot Hill A Wild West name for a burial ground, as being full of men killed in gunfights 'who had their boots on when they fell' — a necessary precondition for canonization in the days of DEADWOOD DICK et al.

Bor, General The underground name of Tadeusz Komorowski, leader of the WARSAW RISING (1944) crushed by the Germans; the Russians failed to come to his assistance as he was not a Communist.

Bordeaux mixture A fungicide of lime and copper sulfate, first used in the vineyards of Bordeaux.

Bordeaux wines Red (claret) and white wines from vineyards on either side of the River Garonne near Bordeaux, including MÉDOC, POMEROL, ST ÉMILION, SAUTERNES and GRAVES.

Bordelaise (Cooking) A rich brown sauce made with Bordeaux wine. (French, 'of Bordeaux'.)

Boreas In Greek legend, the personification of the north wind; the adjectival form is Borealis.

Borehamwood Studios The MGM motion-picture studios near Elstree, east of Watford in Hertfordshire; the only American-owned major studio in England.

Borgias, The A Spanish family who settled in Italy and won a reputation as poisoners. They produced 2 Popes, the second of whom was the infamous Alexander VI (1492-1503). He had many illegitimate children, among them Cesare and Lucrezia, both patrons of art, the former guilty of many crimes which clouded the reputation of his sister, apparently unjustly.

Boris Godunov Title of Pushkin's blank-verse play (1825), and of Mussorgsky's opera (1869), about a historical character of that name who usurped the Russian throne in 1598 after murdering the rightful heir Dmitri. In the play a false Dmitri raises a revolt, in quelling which

Boris falls ill and dies.

Borley Rectory (UK) A famous haunted house, investigated by the Society for Psychical Research, and burned down in 1929. (Village near Sudbury, Essex.)

Born Free Joy Adamson's classic story of Elsa the Lioness, which had 2 sequels (published in an omnibus volume, 1966) and was made into a movie. She reared Elsa at her home in northeast Kenya, gradually trained her to fend for herself and then let her go free. She tried the same experiment with a cheetah and a leopard. (Title from Acts xxii, 28: and Paul said, But I was born free.)

Borodino (1812) A battle during Napoleon's invasion of Russia in which the Russian commander Kutuzov inflicted considerable loss on the French before continuing his withdrawal. (Village 70 miles west of Moscow.)

Borstal system (1902) (UK) A system for the detention of criminals aged 15-23 in either closed or open prisons where the emphasis is on education, training and rehabilitation. (Named after the first such prison, at Borstal, Kent.)

Bosc A large greenish yellow pear of European origin. (Shortened from Beurre Bosc.)

Boscobel House The farm near Shifnal, Shropshire, famous as the place where Charles II hid in an oak (the Royal Oak) in Sept. 1651 after his defeat at WORCESTER. See OAK-APPLE DAY.

Bosox Short for Boston RED SOX.

Boss Tweed See TWEED RING.

Boston baked beans Beans (as navy beans) seasoned with molasses and salt pork (or bacon) and baked for a long time at a low temperature.

Boston Common The heart of Boston, Mass., and still preserved as a pleasant park. See BEACON HILL; BACK BAY.

Boston lettuce Any of several butterhead lettuces.

Boston Marathon (1897) An annual international event run each April at Boston, Mass., over a distance of 26 miles, 385 yds (see MARATHON, 2),

under the auspices of the Boston Athletic Association.

Boston Pops Popular concerts of light music given in May and June by members of the Boston Symphony Orchestra, in Boston, Mass.

Boston rocker A rocking chair with the seat curved up at the back and down at the front, curved arms, tall spindle back and painted or gilded designs. It proved so popular that it was later mass-produced.

Boston Strangler, The A man who murdered at least 13 women, and put Boston, Mass., in a state of terror in 1962-64; he was later identified as Albert DeSalvo, who had been arrested for a separate series of several hundred sexual assaults from 1955 on. On the latter charges he was given a life sentence in 1967.

Boston Stump, The (UK) The tower of the very large parish church of Boston, Lincolnshire. Standing high above the flat countryside, it is a useful landmark for ships.

Boston Tea Party (1773) One of the incidents leading to the AMERICAN WAR OF INDEPENDENCE; disguised as American Indians, American colonists threw a cargo of tea into Boston harbor as a protest against the new British tax on tea.

Boston Terrier An American breed developed in Boston, Mass., in the 1850s from the English bulldog and the bull terrier; smooth-coated, brindle or black with white markings, less than half the weight of a bulldog.

Bosworth Field (1485) The final battle in the WARS OF THE ROSES, in which the Welsh Henry Tudor, Earl of Richmond, defeated and killed Richard III, and became the first TUDOR king, Henry VII. (Market Bosworth, near Leicester.)

Botany Bay The traditional name of the first convict settlement in Australia (1788), although on arrival the leaders of the expedition preferred Port Jackson, a few miles to the north. The city of Sydney now lies between these 2 points.

Botany wool A fine grade of wool obtained chiefly from Australia.

See BOTANY BAY.

Bo tree A species of Indian fig tree, under one of which, according to tradition, GAUTAMA attained enlightenment and thus became the Buddha; hence it is sacred to Buddhists. Pilgrims visit a descendant of this tree at a village south of the holy city of Gaya, in Bihar, India. (From *bodhi*, 'enlightenment'.)

Botswana The name adopted by BECHUANALAND on gaining independence in 1966.

Bottom, Nick The weaver in Shakespeare's MIDSUMMER NIGHT'S DREAM. Even though PUCK crowns him with an ass's head, TITANIA, under a spell, falls in love with him. In the play within the play, PYRAMUS AND THISBE, Bottom wants to play all the parts, and gets the lead.

Boulangist crisis (1889) The attempt by the popular French general and War Minister, Boulanger, to organize a right-wing coup d'état. His courage failed him, and he fled abroad, committing suicide 2 years later.

Boulder Dam See HOOVER DAM.

Boule de Suif (1880) Generally regarded as one of Maupassant's best short stories, about a group of respectable French citizens caught up in the FRANCO-PRUSSIAN WAR of 1870 and their changing attitudes to the little prostitute whom they had hoped to use to soften the hearts of their German captors.

Boul' Mich' Students' abbreviation for the Boulevard St-Michel which runs through the university quarter of Paris and where the cafés are thronged with students.

Boulter's Lock (UK) A Thames lock near Maidenhead where, in Edwardian days, crowds gathered to quiz the fashionable as they passed through in their boats.

Bounty, HMS Captain Bligh's ship, the crew of which mutinied under Fletcher Christian (1789); they landed at Tahiti, and some went on to Pitcairn Island. Bligh survived a 4000-mile voyage in an open boat to land at Timor.

Bourbon An ultra-Conservative who lives in the past, 'learning nothing, forgetting nothing', as was said of the BOURBONS; (US) 19th-century nickname for Southern Democrats.

Bourbons A French dynasty, descended from the Capets, which reigned in France from the time of Henry IV of Navarre and, restored after the FRENCH REVOLUTION, till 1830 (and through a cadet branch till 1848); in Spain (1700-1931); in the TWO SICILIES, and elsewhere.

Bourbon whiskey A grain whiskey, named after Bourbon county, Kentucky. It must by law contain 51% corn.

Bourgeois Gentilhomme, Le (1670) Molière's comedy of the nouveau riche M Jourdain who, in his determination to make a gentleman of himself, tries to master dancing, fencing and philosophy, to the financial gain of his unscrupulous tutors.

Bourguignonne (Cooking) With onions, mushrooms and red wine sauce. (French, 'of Burgundy'.)

Boutique fantasque, La (1919) Respighi's ballet written for Diaghilev using occasional music composed by Rossini in the last years of his life. (French, 'the fantastic toyshop'.)

Bow (1750-75) Possibly the earliest English soft-paste porcelain factory, but products made before 1750 have not been identified. Characteristic are figures in garish colors with crude bocages, charming but far less skillful than contemporary works from Chelsea. MEISSEN and Chinese influences were strong. The factory was bought up by Derby (see DERBY PORCELAIN).

Bow Bells The bells of St Mary-le-Bow, Cheapside, in the center of the CITY of London; hence 'born within the sound of Bow Bells' means 'a true COCKNEY'. The bells and most of the church were destroyed in a 1941 air raid, but the church has since been very well restored.

Bowdoin (1794) A college at Brunswick, Me.

Bowen, Marjorie The chief pen name of Margaret Campbell (later Mrs Long), the romantic historical novelist. She also used the names George R. Preedy, Joseph Shearing and many others.

Bowery, The   A street running diagonally through the east side of lower Manhattan, now a disreputable slum. (Dutch *bouwerij*, farm.)

Bow Group   (1951) (UK) A group of young conservative intellectuals of the left and right, who produce carefully documented pamphlets from time to time.

Bowie knife   A large hunting knife, especially one adapted for knife fighting; prominent in Westerns. (From James Bowie, US soldier, died 1836 at the ALAMO.)

Bowl games   (Football) Postseason matches, usually on Jan. 1st, between winning teams of the major conferences. (Named after the ROSE BOWL where the first such match was played in 1916, between the champion teams of the eastern and western US universities; other university stadiums subsequently being named 'bowls' also.)

Bowling, Tom   RODERICK RANDOM'S uncle in Smollett's novel of that name, a naval lieutenant at home only on a ship's deck.

Bow Street   The chief London Metropolitan police court, near Covent Garden.

Bow Street runners   The court police established in the 18th century by Henry Fielding (the novelist) when JP for Westminster; predecessors of Peel's London police. See BOW STREET; PEELER.

Box and Cox   (1847) J. M. Morton's farce, translated from the French and still played. A landlady lets the same room to 2 tenants, Box and Cox, one on day and one on night work, hoping that they will not get to know of each other. Hence the phrase is used of 2 people who do something turn and turn about.

Boxer Movement   A rebellion begun in China in the late 1890s by a peasant secret society and diverted by xenophobic Chinese officials against the imperialist powers, Christian missionaries and converts; see PEKING LEGATIONS, SIEGE OF. (From Chinese name, 'Society of Harmoni-

ous Fists'.)

'Boyhood of Raleigh, The'   (1870) The popular painting by Millais, in the TATE Gallery, London.

Boyle's Law   (1662) That at constant temperature the volume of a gas varies inversely with its pressure. (Robert Boyle, son of the 1st Earl of Cork.)

Boyne, Battle of the   (1 July 1690) An engagement in which James II's Catholic army of French and Irish fled before William III's Protestant army of European mercenaries; see TWELFTH OF JULY. (Boyne, a river in Meath, Ireland.)

Boys' Clubs of America   (1906) A national organization formed to coordinate the movement (started in 1860) to turn urban youngsters into productive citizens, providing facilities for practicing arts, crafts, sports, etc.

Boy Scouts of America   (1910) Founded by William D. Boyce of Chicago after he had visited with Baden-Powell in England. There are now over $5\frac{1}{2}$ million members; the headquarters are in New Brunswick, N. J.

Boys' Town   An institution for homeless boys near Omaha, Neb., run mainly by the boys themselves; it is open to visitors.

Boz   Pen name of Charles Dickens used, in particular, in writing PICKWICK PAPERS. (Childhood corruption of Moses, nickname of his young brother.)

Bozzy   Nickname for James Boswell, Dr Johnson's biographer, and the author of several autobiographical journals.

BP   Initials standing for British Petroleum, of which the government has 56% control; it owns 50% of Kuwait oil, has a 40% interest in the Iran oil consortium, 24% in Iraq Petroleum, and other interests in Alaska, Libya, Nigeria and Trinidad. It has linked up with Standard Oil of Ohio and has also expanded into plastics and chemicals. Formerly British Petroleum was known as the ANGLO-IRANIAN CO.

BPOE   See Benevolent and Protective Order of ELKS.

BPW Initials used for (1) Board of Public Works; (2) Business and Professional Women's Club.

Brabançon A Belgian breed of farm horse. ('Of Brabant'.)

'Brabançonne' (1830) The Belgian national anthem. ('Woman of Brabant', the district in which Brussels lies.)

Bracknell, Lady See IMPORTANCE OF BEING EARNEST.

Bracknell (1949) (UK) A NEW TOWN in Berkshire, north and west of the old village of the same name, and some 10 miles south of Windsor. It was designed for a population of 60,000.

Bradshaw (1839-1961) Short title of *Bradshaw's Railway Guide*, a British railroad timetable that is at once comprehensive and complex. (Named after George Bradshaw, a printer.)

Braemar Castle The 17th-century home of the Earls of Mar, in Aberdeenshire.

Braemar Gathering, The The Royal Highland Gathering held at Braemar Aberdeen, Scotland in September, and usually attended by the British Royal Family.

Brahamanas (700 BC) The second stage of Hindu religious literature in which, in contrast to the VEDAS and under contamination from the beliefs of the conquered Dravidians, prominence is given to ritual and sacrifices, caste and the sacred cow, and the BRAHMINS are exalted as the only repositories of true knowledge. The UPANISHADS were a reaction from these writings.

Brahma Originally the supreme god of the Hindu Trinity (the other members being VISHNU and SIVA), but now held in less veneration than they.

Brahman Brahmahood, a complex concept of philosophical HINDUISM. It is the true reality, of which the visible universe is only a manifestation; and also the Atman (breath, or the Self) in which all selves can merge through asceticism and meditation.

Brahman US name for humped Zebu cattle derived from the *Bos indicus* of India, used for crossing

with beef breeds to produce a type able to stand the hot humid climate of the Gulf states.

Brahma Samaj (1818) A Hindu religious reformist movement, founded in Bengal, which preached belief in one God; it subsequently broke up into several sects. ('Church of God'.)

Brahmins (1) The Hindu priesthood. (2) The highest Hindu caste, of priests and scholars. (3) (USA) Applied ironically, first by Oliver Wendell Holmes, to the pundits of NEW ENGLAND, especially of Boston. (4) Nickname for devotees of the music of Brahms.

Brains Trust (1941-56) A BBC radio program extremely popular during wartime; a panel of Sir Julian Huxley, Prof. C. E. M. Joad and Cmdr Campbell, under the chairmanship of Donald McCullough, answered questions put to them by the public. (Name originally given, in singular, to the team of experts who advised Roosevelt on NEW DEAL measures.)

Bramble, Col. The central figure of André Maurois' *The Silence of Colonel Bramble* (1918), an amusing study of the British officer at war as seen through French eyes by the author, who had served as a liaison officer with the British Expeditionary Force.

Bramley Seedling A first-class cooking apple, ripening in October and keeping well.

Brand (1865) Ibsen's symbolic verse play about a stern pastor who fights compromise in religion. In a distant town he sacrifices his wife and child to his ideals and is finally rejected by his parishioners. Ibsen felt strongly that unreasoning sacrifice to ideals of goodness was pernicious.

Brandenburg A former Baltic province of Prussia, capital Potsdam, now divided between Poland and Eastern Germany.

Brandenburg Concertos J. S. Bach's 6 concertos for various combinations of instruments, dedicated to the Margrave of Brandenburg.

Brandenburger Tor An 18th-century gateway in Berlin, built in imitation of the PROPYLAEA, at the end of UNTER DEN LINDEN. It now marks the entrance to East (Communist) Berlin. (German, Brandenburg Gate.)

Brandt, Isabella Rubens's first wife, whom he married in 1609 and who died in 1627. She sat for some of his finest portraits.

Brandywine, Battle of (Sept. 1777) The engagement in the AMERICAN WAR OF INDEPENDENCE in which Howe defeated Washington. (Brandywine Creek, a stream in Pennsylvania.)

Brangwen, Gudrun In D. H. Lawrence's WOMEN IN LOVE, a sculptor who falls in love with an industrialist; said to be based on the writer, Katherine Mansfield. She is a sister of Ursula. See BRANGWEN, URSULA.

Brangwen, Ursula The rebellious daughter of a Nottinghamshire wood-carver, heroine of D. H. Lawrence's The RAINBOW and Women in Love; in the latter said to represent the author's wife, Frieda. See BRANGWEN, GUDRUN.

Brasilia The ambitiously designed capital of Brazil, several hundred miles northwest of Rio, inaugurated 1960 but still building.

Bratislava A city of Czechoslovakia, formerly known by its German name, Pressburg.

Brave New World (1932) Aldous Huxley's preview of what is in store for the world. Human embryos are cultivated in laboratory bottles and there conditioned to perform the tasks to which they will be allotted. Any trace of individuality is a crime. In Brave New World Revisited (1958) Huxley commented that the world seemed to be approaching this state faster than he had expected. (Title from lines in The TEMPEST: O brave new world, / That has such people in 't.)

Braves (1) The Atlanta Braves, NATIONAL (Baseball) LEAGUE, playing at the Atlanta Stadium. (2) The Buffalo (N.Y.) Braves, NATIONAL BASKETBALL ASSOCIATION.

Brazzaville group (1960) A conservative, pro-Western association of former territories of French West and Equatorial Africa (except Guinea and Mali), and the Malagasy Republic, which wished to maintain friendly relations with France;

nucleus of the MONROVIA GROUP. (First met at Brazzaville, CONGO REPUBLIC.)

Brazzaville Manifesto (Oct. 1940) The Charter of the Free French, proclaimed by de Gaulle on a visit to rally French Africa to his cause.

Breakers, The The most splendid of the Newport (Rhode Island) 'cottages' (i.e. huge summer residences), built for Cornelius Vanderbilt by Richard M. Hunt (see MARBLE HOUSE); it is open to the public.

Brébeuf and His Brethren (1940) A narrative poem by the Newfoundlander, E. J. Pratt, about the martyrdom of St Jean de Brébeuf, a French Jesuit who worked in Canada among the Huron Indians and was, with another Jesuit, tortured to death by the Iroquois in 1649.

Brechtian An adjective with meanings as varied as Bertolt Brecht's plays and theories; it could refer to the A-EFFECT, EPIC THEATRE, absence of stage props, Communist intensity etc., and is in fact used with little discrimination.

Brecht on Brecht George Tabori's play based on Brecht's works.

Breck, Alan The young Jacobite of R. L. Stevenson's KIDNAPPED and its sequel Catriona.

Breda, Declaration of (1660) Issued by Charles, Prince of Wales, in exile, promising religious toleration and amnesty, and resulting in the RESTORATION. (Town in North Brabant, Holland, where Charles had his headquarters.)

Bredon Hill (UK) A hill by the Worcestershire Avon northeast of Tewkesbury, especially remembered from A. E. Housman's poem in A Shropshire Lad beginning: In summertime on Bredon / The bells they sound so clear. This was set to music by George Butterworth, Vaughan Williams and others.

Breeches Bible A nickname for the GENEVA BIBLE, so called because the word breeches is used instead of aprons in Genesis iii, 7.

Brehon law The tribal law of Gaelic Ireland, from the 3rd century BC, part of which has survived in manuscript copies. (English corruption of Gaelic breiteamh, 'judge'.)

Breitmann, Hans A character in Charles Leland's light verses; he is a German immigrant in the USA, remembered in the verse: Hans Breitmann gife a barty— / Vhere ish dat barty now? / All goned afay mit de lager-beer— / Afay in de ewigkeit.

Bren gun An automatic rifle used in World War II. (Compounded from Brno, Czechoslovakia, where originally made, and Enfield, England, where the British version was made by BSA.)

Brenner express A night train from Munich via Innsbruck, the Brenner Pass and Milan, reaching Rome in the afternoon.

Brensham The fictitious village which is the setting for John Moore's stories of Gloucestershire rural life. (The name seems to have been concocted from Bredon and Strensham, villages near Tewkesbury, England.)

Brent (1965) New London borough consisting of the former boroughs of Wembley and Willesden; headquarters at Wembley.

Brentford and Chiswick (UK) A former Middlesex borough, since 1965 part of the borough of HOUNSLOW.

Brer Rabbit With Brer Fox, one of the chief characters of the UNCLE REMUS series of books. See also TAR BABY. (Brer, Negro corruption of 'brother'.)

Breslau German name of Wroclaw, now a Polish city.

Brest-Litovsk, Treaty of (Mar. 1918) The treaty imposed by Germany on Bolshevist Russia, by which it lost the Ukraine, Poland, Finland and the Baltic provinces, representing a third of the population of Imperial Russia and much of its industry. (Town now called Brest, on the Polish frontier.)

Breton A CELTIC LANGUAGE brought to Brittany by emigrants driven out of Cornwall by the Saxons (4th century AD) and still spoken there. See ARMORICA.

Bretonne (Cooking) With white haricot beans.

Bretton Woods Conference (1944) The UN Monetary and Financial Conference which set up the INTERNATIONAL MONETARY FUND and the WORLD BANK. (Bretton Woods, N.H.).

Brewer (1870) Short title for *Brewer's Dictionary of Phrase and Fable* (and of words and phrases from archeology, history, religion, the arts and science), first compiled by the Rev. Ebenezer Brewer, whose AMDG (*Ad majorem Dei gloriam*) still appears at the end of even the latest of the many revised editions.

Brewers The Milwaukee Brewers, AMERICAN (Baseball) LEAGUE, playing at County Stadium, Milwaukee.

Brewster chair A 17th-century chair resembling the CARVER CHAIR but having 2 tiers of vertical spindles in the back, with other tiers below the seat in front and under the arms. (One belonging to William Brewster is preserved at Pilgrim Hall, Plymouth.)

Briareus In Greek legend, one of several hundred-handed giants born to GE (Earth) and URANUS (Heaven).

Bride of Lammermoor, The (1819) Walter Scott's historical novel of tragic love, on which is based Donizetti's opera, *Lucia di Lammermoor* (1835).

Bride of the Sea Venice. (Refers to an 11th-century ceremony in which the Doge dropped a ring in the Adriatic to symbolize his city's marriage to the sea, i.e. its sea power.)

Brideshead Revisited (1945) Evelyn Waugh's novel of a man billeted during the war in a house he had visited in peacetime; he recalls the alcoholic son and adulterous daughter who shattered the tranquillity of the Roman Catholic family that had lived there.

Brides in the Bath case (1915) (UK) The trial of G. J. Smith, charged with murdering 3 'brides' whom he had bigamously married. He was brought to justice through evidence of systematic conduct—all his victims were found dead in their bath after an alleged fit.

Bridewell (UK) Successively a palace, hospital and 'house of correction' in BLACKFRIARS, London; hence a generic name for other such institutions, where the unemployed, those who refused to work, and disobedient apprentices were herded under harsh discipline. The London Bridewell was closed in 1863.

Bridge Club, The Nickname for the 4 main participants in the KENNEDY ROUND—USA, UK, EEC, Japan.

Bridge of San Luis Rey, The (1927) Thornton Wilder's exploration of the theme whether chance or divine pupose brought together the 5 Peruvians who were killed when the bridge of the title collapsed.

Bridge of Sighs (1) The bridge at Venice connecting the Doge's Palace with the city's prison. (2) A bridge resembling it, at St John's College, Cambridge, over the Cam in the BACKS.

Bridge over the River Kwai, The (1952) A French novel by Pierre Boulle about British prisoners-of-war in Japanese hands, made by David Lean into a movie (1957).

Brie A soft white cheese similar to CAMEMBERT but saltier. (Originally made in the district so named, just east of Paris.)

Brief Encounter (1945) A film scripted by Noël Coward and produced by David Lean.

Brigade of Guards In order of rank: GRENADIER, COLDSTREAM, Scots, Irish and Welsh Guards.

Brigadoon (1947) A popular Lerner and Loewe musical comedy, with a plot apparently derived from a German classic, about Americans in a magical Scottish village which materializes only once in a century.

'Bright College Years' (1913) The alma mater of YALE University, written by Cole Porter, who was at Yale.

Brighton Rock (1938) Graham Greene's sleazy novel of teen-age criminals in unkempt bed-sitters, with a typically sadistic ending in which the gang leader, Pinkie, shatters, from beyond the grave, the illusions of the girl he had used to further his crimes.

Brighton trunk murders (1934) (UK) A case in which the police found a body in a trunk deposited in a baggage checkroom at Brighton, and in the course of their investigations found a second trunk with a body in it at the lodgings of a man living under the alias of Tony Mancini. He was acquitted on the ground that although he admitted to concealing the corpse, the murders might have been committed by another. See also MANCINI CASE.

Brillat-Savarin The type of the supreme chef and authority on cooking, being the name of a French lawyer and gastronome, author *inter alia* of the classic book on the art of good eating: *La Physiologie du goût* (1825).

Bring 'Em Back Alive (1930) A breezy account written (with Edward Anthony) by Frank Buck, the American motion-picture producer, about his adventures while capturing wild animals in various parts of the world; it was made into a movie, and there was a sequel, *Wild Cargo* (1932).

Bringing Up Father See JIGGS.

Brinkmanship The art of using world fear of a third world war as an instrument of policy, invented by the Secretary of State John Foster Dulles.

Brink's robbery (1950) The largest robbery in US history at the time. Masked men took $2.7 million (1.2 million in cash) from Brink's express office, Boston, Mass. In 1956 8 men were given life sentences for it.

Bristol Boy, The Thomas Chatterton, an 18th-century Bristol boy who at the age of 15 wrote poems he attributed to an imaginary 15th-century monk, Thomas Rowley. These 'Rowley poems' deceived many experts and showed that the boy had the makings of a genius, but he committed suicide at 17.

Bristol delft (1650-1770) A buff-colored DELFT decorated with purple or blue spots.

Bristol fashion Shipshape and tidy. (Bristol was at one time the second greatest port of England.)

Bristol glass (1) Rare opaque glass which looks like porcelain, made at Bristol, England, in the 18th century. (2) Colored glass, made at Bristol and many other places from the 18th century. In particular 'Bristol blue' is a term used of almost any blue glass, wherever made.

Bristol milk (1640) Sherry, later adopted as a trade name by Bristol shippers; also Bristol cream, for a richer type. (Bristol, the English port for Spanish trade.)

Bristol porcelain (1) Very rare soft-paste wares made 1748-52, after which the firm amalgamated with Worcester. (2) Hard-paste wares (1773-81) the making of which was taken over from Plymouth for a brief, brilliant period, influenced by LOUIS SEIZE Sèvres styles. After this the patents were sold to NEW HALL.

Britannia (1957) Bristol turboprop long-range airliner, the largest of its type; its success was marred by competition from pure-jet aircraft such as the BOEING 707 and from its twin rival, the VANGUARD.

Britannia Cup (1951) An international race for boats not less than 32 ft waterline length, held at Cowes in August. (Presented by King George VI to commemorate the centenary of the AMERICA'S CUP.)

Britannia metal (1769) An alloy like pewter but 90% tin with only a trace of copper, which resembled silver when new and pewter when aged. From 1840 some of it was 'restored' by electroplating.

Britannia Royal Naval College (1905) The college for officer cadets of the Royal Navy, at Dartmouth, Devon. Formerly known as the Royal Naval College, Dartmouth, and as HMS *Britannia*. See also OSBORNE HOUSE.

British Academy (1901) A learned society which promotes archeological and oriental research and arranges numerous periodical lectures on literature, philosophy, art, history, law etc.

British Antarctic Territory (1962) The land south of latitude 60° claimed by Britain; it includes Graham Land, the South Shetland Islands and the South Orkney Islands.

British Council (1934) A nonpolitical government-sponsored organization for disseminating overseas an understanding of the British way of life, through libraries, lectures etc.; it also provides educational and other facilities for overseas students in Britain.

British Hovercraft Corporation A government-sponsored group formed by WESTLAND AIRCRAFT and VICKERS to develop the HOVERCRAFT.

British Indian Ocean Territory (1965) Various small islands in the western Indian Ocean, organized, after the transfer of the very sparse population, as 'stationary aircraft-carriers' for British and US long-range bombers.

British Institute of Public Opinion (1938) The British organization which holds GALLUP POLLS; in 1952 it was renamed Social Surveys (Gallup Polls) Ltd.

British Israelites Members of the British Israel World Federation (1919), who believe that the British are descended from the LOST TRIBES OF ISRAEL.

British Legion (1920) An organization founded by Earl Haig for the welfare of men and women who served in World War I and subsequent wars.

British Leyland Motor Corporation (1968) A merger of British Motor Holdings and Leyland Motors. In addition to the BMC models, it makes Leyland, AEC and Guy commercial vehicles, Jaguar, Daimler, Triumph and Rover cars, and the Alvis military vehicles, such as STALWART.

British Lion A firm of motion-picture producers and distributors which owns the SHEPPERTON STUDIOS.

British Lions A rugger team selected for overseas tours from the England, Wales, Scotland and Ireland teams.

British North America Act (1867) The British Act which established the Dominion of Canada under a federal government covering Upper (Ontario) and Lower (Quebec) Canada, New Brunswick and Nova Scotia, but not Prince Edward Island or Newfoundland. Fear of US aggression helped to unite the rival racial and religious communities.

British Oxygen A firm which manufactures gases for industrial and medical use, chemicals and precision engineering components.

British Standards Institution (1901) A body, given a Royal Charter in 1929, which in consultation with manufacturers and consumers sets standards of quality and encourages standardization in patterns and sizes. The results of its work are published in a numbered series of *British Standards* (see KITEMARK). It is financed by government and by professional, industrial and trade organizations.

British Steel Corporation (1967) A nationalized corporation, one of the biggest industrial undertakings in Europe, set up under the Iron and Steel Act of 1967. Its interests include engineering and mining, besides iron and steel.

British Union of Fascists (1932) Oswald Mosley's black-shirted organization, founded after he had left the Labour Party and failed to form a NEW PARTY. From the original program of setting the country to rights, they descended to rowdy marches in the East End of London, rabble-rousing and Jew-baiting. They spent World War II in an Isle of Man concentration camp.

BRM (1950) Name given to a series of British Grand Prix racing cars, including a gas turbine model (1963). (Designed by P. Berthon and R. Mays; see ERA.)

Broadway A main street of New York City which runs 18 miles through Manhattan and the Bronx; the cinema, nightclub, theater and restaurant sector (the 'Great White Way') lies between 41st and 53rd Streets.

'Broadway Boogie-Woogie' (1942-43) Piet Mondrian's response to New York's night life and popular music, by which he was fascinated. It is a rectangular design of bright colors in the style of many of his other paintings. See MONDRIAN. (Museum of Modern Art, NYC.)

Brobdingnag An imaginary land in GULLIVER'S TRAVELS inhabited by high-minded giants, whose king commented that, from Gulliver's description of them, his countrymen must be 'the most pernicious race of little odious vermin that nature ever suffered to crawl upon the surface of the earth'.

Brocken The highest peak of the Harz Mountains in Saxony, on the boundary between East and West Germany; the most famous of the

traditional sites of the Witches' Sabbaths held on WALPURGIS NIGHT.

Brocken, Specter of the The magnified shadow of an observer on a mountaintop, thrown onto a bank of clouds or mist when the sun is low. (Observed on the BROCKEN.)

Brodick Castle The historic home, dating back to the 14th century, of the Dukes of Hamilton, on the Isle of Arran.

Brodie A dive, suicidal leap or, more metaphorically, a catastrophic failure or boner, as in the phrase 'do a Brodie'. (From Steve Brodie, a newsboy, who claimed to have dived off Brooklyn Bridge in 1886 but made the mistake of not having laid on any witness to prove it.)

Broederbond A nationalistic society in South Africa which still wields immense power behind the scenes among AFRIKANERS.

Bromley London borough since 1965 consisting of the former boroughs of Bromley and Beckenham, and the urban districts of Orpington, Penge and part of Chislehurst-Sidcup.

Brompton Oratory Common name for the Church of the London Oratory of St Philip Neri (1880) in Brompton Road, London, a fashionable Roman Catholic church with an Italian Renaissance interior, famed for its music.

Broncho Billy (1908-15) The hero of several hundred short Western films.

Broncos The Denver Broncos, AMERICAN FOOTBALL LEAGUE. Became member of the AMERICAN CONFERENCE, NATIONAL FOOTBALL LEAGUE in 1970.

Bronx, The The only mainland borough of New York City, separated from Manhattan, to the south, by the Harlem River; it contains numerous parks, the Zoo, and university and college buildings; it is primarily residential. (After J. Bronck, who bought the area in 1639.)

Bronx cheer A 'raspberry'.

Bronze Age The period following the NEOLITHIC AGE, when bronze (an alloy of copper and tin) replaced flint and stone in making tools and weapons. This culture began to spread from the Middle East about

4000 BC, reaching Western Europe via Troy and the Danube valley about 2000 BC; it was succeeded by the IRON AGE.

Bronze Star US military award for heroic or meritorious service, not involving participation in aerial flight, against an armed enemy; it ranks below the SILVER STAR.

Brooke, Dorothea (Mrs Casaubon, Mrs Ladislaw) The heroine of George Eliot's MIDDLEMARCH, who longs to espouse some great cause but is disillusioned in turn by her pedant husband CASAUBON and by Dr LYDGATE.

Brooke case Gerald Brooke, an English university lecturer, was given a 5-year sentence in 1962 for introducing anti-Soviet literature into Russia; in 1969, in what seemed a remarkably unequal bargain, he was exchanged for the Krogers of the KROGER SPY CASE.

Brook Farm (1841-46) An unsuccessful communistic utopia set up near West Roxbury, Mass., by the Transcendentalists George Ripley and C. A. Dana. Hawthorne tried living there and wrote a novel about it, *The Blithesdale Romance* (1852), but liked it little. A disastrous fire ended the experiment.

Brookhaven National Laboratory A nuclear research laboratory at Upton, Long Island, N. Y., with a famous proton accelerator (1960), producing particles of some 33 GeV (33 billion electron volts).

Brookings report (1968) A report on Britain's economic prospects by 11 US economists commissioned by the Brookings Institution, Washington, D. C. It severely criticized British management for its amateurism, distrust of skilled specialists, and reluctance to use new techniques.

Brook Kerith, The (1916) George Moore's story of a Jesus who did not die at the Crucifixion but lived on for 30 years with the ESSENES by the Brook Kerith, no longer believing in his own divinity. When he hears Paul preaching Christ Crucified, he wants to proclaim the true facts, but is persuaded that it is too late for him to be believed. (Name of the brook where the ravens fed ELIJAH, I Kings xvii, 5, there spelled Cherith.)

Brooklands (1907-46) Formerly Britain's chief car-racing and testing circuit, with a banked track, near Weybridge, Surrey; now closed.

Brooklyn A borough of New York City at the west end of Long Island.

Brooklyn Bridge (1884) A suspension bridge nearly 1½ miles long spanning the East River between MANHATTAN and BROOKLYN.

Brooks's Club (1764) A London club, opposite BOODLE'S in St James's Street, originally a Regency WHIGS' gambling den, but now mainly Conservative, though retaining a faint flavor from the past.

Broomielaw, The Glasgow harbor.

Brother Jonathan A nickname for a US citizen, possibly deriving from the English colonists' penchant for Christian names taken from the Old Testament.

Brothers and Sisters (1929) A typical sample of Ivy Compton-Burnett's numerous witty *sui-generis* novels set in anonymous country houses where everyone over the age of 3, whether above or below stairs, discourses endlessly in polite and polished English, and continues to do so even after the inevitable family skeleton has fallen noiselessly out of the cupboard.

Brothers Karamazov, The (1880) Dostoevsky's greatest novel. Karamazov père, a wild old sensualist, is murdered. His impulsive son Mitya (Dmitri) is charged with the crime; the tortured skeptic, Ivan, feels guilty since he wished the old man dead; the saintly Alyosha is an onlooker; the degenerate bastard half brother, Smerdyakov, is in fact the murderer. Most of the book is taken up with discussions of the problems of good and evil, of Russia's relationship to Western Europe, and above all with religious belief. See GRAND INQUISITOR.

Broun (Heywood) Memorial award A prize of $1000 for reporting done in the spirit of Heywood Broun (died 1939), a New York liberal journalist who was one of the founders of the American Newspaper

Guild which makes the award.

Brown (1764) An IVY LEAGUE university at Providence, R. I.

Brown Betty A Pennsylvania Dutch baked pudding of sliced apples layered with bread crumbs, flavored with molasses, cinnamon etc., and served with lemon sauce.

Brown Bomber Nickname of Joe Louis, world heavyweight champion 1937-48.

Brown Derby, The A Hollywood restaurant once frequented by the elite of the motion-picture industry.

Brownian motion (1827) The apparently erratic movement of tiny particles suspended in a fluid. In 1905 Einstein showed that these movements satisfied a statistical law which confirmed finally that they were due to bombardment of the particles by the molecules of the fluid.

Browning automatic rifle The BAR, a .30 shoulder-fired gas-operated rifle weighing 20 lb with the bipod support, used by the US Army for 40 years after World War I. (John Moses Browning, 1855-1926, designer of many automatic weapons.)

Browning Version, The (1948) Terence Rattigan's notable one-act play about the decline of a well-meaning schoolmaster with a detestable wife, whose life had collapsed about him.

Brownists A 16th-century NONCON-FORMIST sect formed at Norwich and in Holland, and regarded as the parent group of modern CONGREGATION-ALISTS. See also INDEPENDENTS. (Founded by Robert Browne, who came to terms with the Church later and held a benefice for 40 years.)

Browns The Cleveland Browns, NA-TIONAL FOOTBALL LEAGUE. Became member of the AMERICAN CONFER-ENCE, NATIONAL FOOTBALL LEAGUE in 1970.

Brownshirts Another name for the Nazi SA.

Brown's Hotel A London hotel in Mayfair, once known as a favorite retreat for exiled kings.

Brown Swiss One of the oldest cattle breeds, native to Switzerland; usually regarded as dual-purpose but in USA primarily as a good yielder of average quality milk.

Brücke, Die (1905-13) A group of German Expressionists who painted emotional protest pictures in bright colors. (German, 'the bridge'.)

Bruins The Boston Bruins, NATIONAL HOCKEY LEAGUE.

Brumaire In the FRENCH REVOLUTION calendar, the month from Oct. 22nd to Nov. 21st; 19 Brumaire (1799) is the date of Napoleon's coup which destroyed the DIRECTORY and led to the CONSULATE. ('Fog-month'.)

Brummagem Adjective applied to cheap and nasty goods of the kind made in Birmingham, England, in the early days of the Industrial Revolution. (Corruption of the old name of Birmingham; the abbreviation of this, Brum, is still used of the city itself.)

Brunel University (1966) A technological university, formerly a CAT at Acton, London, now moved to Hillingdon near Uxbridge.

Brunhild, Brünhilde In Scandinavian mythology a VALKYRIE; in the NIBELUNGENLIED the Queen of Iceland won by SIEGFRIED for GUNTHER, and the instigator of Siegfried's death.

Brunswick stew (1) A hunter's stew of rabbit and onion. (2) A stew of 2 or more meats with vegetables (e.g. game and chicken with corn, okra, tomatoes), sometimes with red wine added. (Named for Brunswick County, Va.)

Brussels carpet A type of hard-wearing carpet with uncut wool pile looped through a warp and weft of heavy linen thread.

Brussels sprouts The edible buds that sprout on the stalk of a kind of cabbage.

Brussels Treaty (1948) The mutual defense pact signed by Britain, France and the BENELUX countries; it set up the BRUSSELS TREATY ORGANI-ZATION.

Brussels Treaty Organization (1948) The organization set up under the BRUSSELS TREATY, which in 1955 was renamed the WESTERN EUROPEAN UNION.

Bryce Canyon National Park (1928) A park in southwest Utah, with a canyonlike series of amphitheaters and grotesque pinnacles of colored limestone and sandstone.

Bryn Mawr (1885) One of the SEVEN SISTERS, at Bryn Mawr, Pa.

Bryophyta A division of plants comprising the mosses and liverworts.

Brythons The Celts who invaded England in the Iron Age and became the ancestors of the Welsh, Cornish and Bretons; see CELTIC LANGUAGES. (Origin of the names Briton, Britain and Brittany.)

B-707 etc. See BOEING.

BSI Initials used for BRITISH STANDARDS INSTITUTION; BS is used for *British Standard*.

BTH Initials of British Thomson-Houston; see AEI.

Btu, BThU Abbreviations for British Thermal Unit, the amount of heat required to raise the temperature of 1 lb of water by 1°F; equivalent to 252 calories.

BUA (1960) Initials used for British United Airways, formed by merging Airwork (1928) and Hunting-Clan; now the largest independent airline in Europe.

Bubastis The Greek name for Bast or Pasht, the Ancient Egyptian cat-goddess of love and femininity, daughter of ISIS. The Greeks identified her with ARTEMIS. (Name of the chief center of her worship.)

'Bubbles' (1886) Millais' sentimental portrait of a child blowing bubbles, which became famous through its use in advertizing Lever Brothers' soap. The child-model overcame this handicap to become Admiral Sir William James.

Buccaneer (1962) A HAWKER SIDDELEY low-level strike-reconnaissance aircraft, with a designed speed of Mach 0.98 and a range of over 500 miles carrying a nuclear load; alternatively it can carry four 1000-lb bombs. It is in service with the RAF and the Royal Navy.

Buccaneers The New Orleans Buccaneers, AMERICAN BASKETBALL ASSOCIATION.

Bucephalus Alexander the Great's favorite charger.

Buchan periods (1867) Periods of relatively cold (6) or relatively warm (3) weather likely to occur at certain times of the year, as determined by Dr Alexander Buchan from meteorological records in Scotland.

Buchenwald (1934) The first of the Nazi concentration camps to be liberated by the Allies (1945). It was near Weimar and the inmates were mostly men and boys, used for various medical experiments. Ilse Koch, wife of the commandant, was sentenced to life imprisonment (1951) for her activities there, but committed suicide in 1967.

Buchmanism An early name for the movement for long misnamed the OXFORD GROUP and later rechristened MORAL REARMAMENT. (From its American founder, Dr Frank Buchman.)

Buckeye State Nickname of Ohio. (Dominant tree.)

Buckingham Palace Since Victoria's accession, the British Sovereign's London residence, at the western end of St James's Park and The Mall. Buckingham House was built for the Duke of Buckingham (1703), bought by George III, rebuilt (partly by Nash) for George IV, and refaced with Portland stone in 1913. There is an outstanding picture gallery and a huge ballroom. The daily ceremony of changing the Queen's Guard (usually provided by the Brigade of Guards) draws large crowds of tourists each summer. There are extensive grounds, where the Garden Parties are held; helicopters take off from the lawn behind the palace.

Buckinghamshire train robbery (1963) A mail train from Scotland to London was ambushed near Cheddington, Buckinghamshire, and over £2½ million in paper money was stolen from it. For their part in this crime 12 men were sentenced to a total of 307 years imprisonment.

Buckley's chance Australian expression for 'little or no chance'. (From a 19th-century convict who escaped from prison, and lived for 32 years among the aborigines of Victoria, where he was regarded as the reincarnation of a former chief.)

Buck Rogers (1929) A team-produced comic strip of an SF hero who, though lacking the physical advantages of SUPERMAN, is able to make out with atom bombs, death rays and other conveniences which, when first mentioned, seemed wildly improbable.

Bucks The Milwaukee Bucks, NATIONAL BASKETBALL ASSOCIATION.

Bucolics Alternative name for Virgil's ECLOGUES.

Budd, Lanny The wealthy hero of a series of popular novels by Upton Sinclair, beginning with *World's End* (1940). His ambition to put the world to rights brings him to the fore in international politics.

Buddenbrooks (1900) Thomas Mann's saga of a prosperous North German family whose fortunes decline with the decreasing interest in, and ability for, commerce of successive generations.

Buddha 'The Enlightened One', the name given to Gautama, a Hindu born in Nepal in the 6th century BC, after the revelation that came to him under the BO TREE. See BUDDHISM.

Buddhism The religion founded by BUDDHA, at one time the religion of all India (under Asoka); it died out there but spread elsewhere in the MAHAYANA and HINAYANA forms. It took over the Hindu concepts of *karma* (that all acts are rewarded or punished in the present life or some future reincarnation) and transmigration of souls to a higher or lower form of life. The Four Truths and the Eightfold Way taught the means of attaining NIRVANA.

Buffalo Bill The American cowboy, 'Colonel' Cody, who founded a Wild West show (1883) which he brought to Earls Court, London, in 1903. (So named by Ned BUNTLINE.)

Buffalo Bill Historical Center The site at Cody, east of Yellowstone, Wyo., of the BUFFALO BILL Museum (1927) and the Whitney Gallery of Western Art (1959).

Bug A nickname (like BEETLE) for the VOLKSWAGEN car.

Bugatti Type 13 (1910) The first successful small sports car, capable of 60 m.p.h.; built by an Italian firm.

Buggins's turn A phrase referring to promotion on long service rather than on merit.

Bulgarian atrocities (1875) The brutal massacre of their subject Bulgarian men, women and children by the Turks under ABDUL THE DAMNED, after a nationalist agitation which had the support of Russia and the EASTERN ORTHODOX CHURCH.

Bulge, Battle of the See ARDENNES OFFENSIVE.

Bulldog Drummond The vintage English tough patriotic hero, little to modern taste, who manages to outwit the vintage German villain, Carl Petersen, in Sapper's novel of that name (1920) and its many sequels.

Bullets The Baltimore Bullets, NATIONAL BASKETBALL ASSOCIATION.

Bull Moose (1912) A member of the Progressive Party founded by ex-President Theodore Roosevelt to oppose his own former nominee, W. H. Taft. It split the REPUBLICAN PARTY and let in the DEMOCRATIC PARTY'S Presidential candidate, Woodrow Wilson, with a huge majority. (From Roosevelt's remark to reporters: I feel as fit as a bull moose.)

Bull Run A small river in northeast Virginia, near Washington, scene of the first major battle (July 1861) of the AMERICAN CIVIL WAR, in which the Confederate general, 'STONEWALL' JACKSON, won his nickname by keeping the Union forces at bay. Confederates won another victory there a year later, but on both occasions failed to press home an attack on the capital.

Bulls The Chicago Bulls, NATIONAL BASKETBALL ASSOCIATION.

Bumble The pompous workhouse beadle in Dickens's *Oliver Twist*, immortalized in the word 'Bumbledom' (petty officiousness). It was he who was so distressed when Oliver asked for more, and who said 'the law is a ass'. He becomes a henpecked husband, and himself ends up in the workhouse.

Bumppo, Natty   See LEATHERSTOCK-
ING TALES.

Bundesrepublik   German name of
the GERMAN FEDERAL REPUBLIC, i.e.
West Germany.

Bundestag   The West German Federal Assembly.

Bundeswehr   The West German
Army. (German, 'federal defense'.)

Bunker Hill, Battle of   (June 1775)
The first battle of the AMERICAN WAR
OF INDEPENDENCE. (Near Charles-
town, now part of Boston, Mass.)

Bunthorne, Reginald   The 'fleshly
poet' of Gilbert and Sullivan's PA-
TIENCE. He is supposed to be based
on Oscar Wilde. 'Twenty love-sick
maidens' pursue him through most
of the opera.

Buntline, Ned   The pen name of
E.Z.C. Judson (1823-86), first of the
dime novelists. A founder of the
KNOW-NOTHING PARTY, imprisoned
for starting the ASTOR PLACE RIOTS,
nearly lynched when charged with
killing his mistress's husband, discharged from the Union army for
drunkenness, he had plenty of material to work on. BUFFALO BILL was the
hero of several of his novels, of
which he wrote some 400.

Bunyan, Paul   The mythical master
lumberjack of (mainly) northwestern folklore, a comic proto-'SUPER-
MAN' who created Puget Sound, dug
out the Grand Canyon and freed
logjams by diverting rivers. His
many famous companions included
BABE THE BLUE OX, Sourdough Slim
the cook and Johnny Inkslinger the
clerk. The first stories about him
were not published until 1910; his
legend was then used as an advertising gimmick by a lumber company,
and promoted into literature through
poems by Frost and Sandburg. Paintings, sculptures, an operetta (by Auden and Britten, 1941) and even a
ballet introduced him to circles
which would not have known a
hawk from a handsaw. There is no
foundation for the theory that a real
Paul Bunyan fought in the Quebec
rebellion of 1837.

Buraimi oasis   An area of long-
standing dispute between the Sul-
tanate of Muscat and Oman, the
TRUCIAL STATES, and Saudi Arabia.

Bureau of Indian Affairs   (1836) A
US government agency formed to
improve the lot of the 400,000
American Indians in the US, in the
fields of education (including vocational training), agriculture, health,
loans for specific purposes and aid
to depressed communities.

Bureau of Narcotics   A US Federal
agency that controls the import and
manufacture of narcotic drugs.

Bureau of the Mint   (1873) A section
of the Department of the Treasury
responsible for the minting of coins,
at PHILADELPHIA and DENVER MINTS
and at the SAN FRANCISCO ASSAY OF-
FICE; it also receives and disburses
gold and silver bullion (see FORT
KNOX).

Burge   The character in G. B. Shaw's
BACK TO METHUSELAH said to be
based on Lloyd George.

Burger, Die   (1915) A leading AFRI-
KAANS daily, published in Cape
Town.

Bürgerbräukeller   The Munich tavern where Hitler was wounded by a
bomb, Nov. 1939.

Burgess and Maclean case   (1951)
The case of 2 Foreign Office officials, Guy Burgess and Donald Maclean, recruited by H.A.R. PHILBY to
spy for Russia. Maclean held posts
in Washington and London which
enabled him to supply much information on US policy and nuclear
secrets. They escaped to Moscow
just in time to avoid arrest, having
been warned by Philby, who joined
them there in 1963.

'Burghers of Calais, The'   (1895)
Rodin's bronze group at Calais, of
which there is a copy outside the
Houses of Parliament in VICTORIA
TOWER Gardens. It depicts the 6
burghers who, with ropes round
their necks and the keys of the town
in their hands, pleaded with Edward
III in 1347 to spare the town's inhabitants.

Burghley House   Elizabethan mansion at Stamford, Lincolnshire, built
by William Cecil, 1st Lord Burghley,
and the home of the elder line of
Cecils (Marquesses of Exeter) ever
since.

Burgos government The rebel government set up by Gen. Franco in July 1936 at the beginning of the SPANISH CIVIL WAR. (Former capital of Castile, in northern Spain.)

Burgundy (1) A Germanic 5th-century kingdom (capital, Lyons) of the Rhône valley and neighboring districts; (2) a smaller Frankish kingdom; (3) an independent duchy (capital, Dijon) united to France in 1477; (4) today, the region of the Saône valley, including Dijon, Mâcon and Chalon-sur-Saône.

Burgundy wines (1) Red full-bodied wines made from the Pinot Noir grape grown in a defined area of the Côte d'Or between Dijon and Chagny; see CÔTE DE BEAUNE, CÔTE DE NUITS. (2) White wines, usually dry, made from the Chardonnay grape grown in 3 separate districts in the Côte d'Or (notably Meursault and the Montrachets), Saône-et-Loire (Pouilly-Fuissé) and Yonne (CHABLIS).

'Burial of Sir John Moore, The' (1817) The only famous poem by Charles Wolfe, on Gen. Moore's death at Corunna in the Peninsular War: Not a drum was heard, not a funeral note, / As his corse to the rampart we hurried.

Buridan's ass An ass placed between equidistant and equidelicious bundles of hay, having no reason to eat one rather than the other first, would die of starvation, according to an ingenious suggestion attributed to the 14th-century French philosopher, Jean Buridan; hence used of an indecisive person.

Burke and Hare An Irish laborer, William Burke, and his accomplice William Hare, who smothered people to provide bodies to sell to the Edinburgh School of Anatomy; Burke was executed in 1829, Hare having turned King's (i.e. state's) evidence. See The ANATOMIST. Hence 'to burke' came to be used for 'to smother', 'hush up', an issue.

Burke's Landed Gentry (1837) Short title of The Genealogical and Heraldic History of the Landed Gentry, published by Burke's Peerage Ltd., who also publish Burke's Peerage,

Baronetage and Knightage (1826).

Burlington House A building in Piccadilly, London, which houses the ROYAL ACADEMY, the Royal Academy Schools, the ROYAL SOCIETY (until 1967), the Society of Antiquaries and other learned societies. It is the scene of the Royal Academy's annual summer exhibition of contemporary works.

Burma road A road from Lashio, Burma railhead from Rangoon, to Kunming in southwest China, built just before World War II, which was the chief supply route to Chiang Kai-shek's forces after the Japanese had gained control of China's ports. Closed by Britain in 1940 as a gesture of appeasement to Japan, captured by the Japanese in 1941, reopened in 1945.

Burney, Fanny Maiden name of Mme d'Arblay (1752-1840), diarist and novelist, author of EVELINA.

Burnham Beeches A stretch of woodland near Slough, Buckinghamshire, with heavily pollarded grotesque stunted beeches, the property of the GREATER LONDON Council.

Burns's Cottage See ALLOWAY.

Burton, Gone for a A British forces' expression for 'missing' or 'dead'. The Army, Navy and RAF supply differing derivations, but it is an old nautical phrase. A 'burton' is a form of tackle and the phrase perhaps began life as a standard excuse for the absence of a shipmate from his post. The RAF undoubtedly assumed the word to refer to Burton ale; hence the capital initial usual today.

Burundi One of the 2 independent states formed from the Belgian Trust Territory of RUANDA-URUNDI, Central Africa.

Bushido The code of honor and conduct of the Japanese SAMURAI, involving fanatical self-sacrifice in the service of the Emperor, and the practice of hara-kiri. (Japanese, 'way of the warrior'.)

Bushmen An African tribe of the Kalahari Desert in BOTSWANA and neighboring districts who, unlike the related HOTTENTOTS, have kept to a primitive hunting life. They are short in stature and the women often have a characteristic overdevelopment of the buttocks (steatopygia; also found in some Hottentots). Only some 26,000 now survive.

Buss and Beale, the Misses See BEALE AND BUSS.

Bussy d'Ambois A 16th-century French courtier (a historical figure) who, given away by the King or the King's brother, is killed by the man he has cuckolded. The story is treated by George Chapman and Dumas.

Buster Brown (1902-09) A comic-strip character created by R. F. Outcault; an unpleasant little boy with a taste for violent mischief, he wore a wide-brimmed sailor hat and a LITTLE LORD FAUNTLEROY suit. The name was used adjectivally of the type of collar he wore and of his pageboy hairstyle.

Butler's Analogy (1736) Short title of Bishop Butler's *The Analogy of Religion*, in which he argued that if mankind with its known faults was created by God, then by analogy the Scriptures, with their imperfections, could well also be of God; faith is based on probability.

Butterfield 8 (1935) John O'Hara's hard-boiled novel, set in New York, whose heroine is the promiscuous alcoholic juvenile delinquent, Gloria Wandrous. The book was made into a movie (1960).

Buzfuz, Serjeant The comic counsel who appears for the plaintiff in BARDELL V. PICKWICK; having no case he resorts to the traditional tactics of abusing the defendant ('a Being erect on two legs and bearing all the outward semblance of a man'). (Serjeant in the old sense of 'senior barrister'.)

BVM Initials used for the Blessed Virgin Mary.

BWG Initials for Birmingham Wire Gauge, a British classification of the

thickness of wire and rods; the highest numbers are thinnest.

Byelorussia Russian name of White Russia.

Byerly Turk One of the 3 sires imported into England about 1700 from which all racehorses are descended. See THOROUGHBRED.

By-pass Variegated A self-explanatory name, one of many coined by Osbert Lancaster for various 20th-century styles of 'architecture'.

Byronic Characteristic of Lord Byron's poetry, outlook, dress, appearance, or romantic heroes; defying the conventions or fate.

Byzantine architecture (5th century) A style based on Greek, oriental and, later, Islamic models. It is characterized by domes over square or polygonal plans, often in clusters; the round arch; rich mosaics, frescoes and icons, in which gold is prominently used. Santa Sophia, Istanbul (537), is typical of the early phase; St Mark's, Venice (1085), of the later. (See BYZANTINE EMPIRE.)

Byzantine Church Another name for the EASTERN ORTHODOX CHURCH.

Byzantine Empire (395-1453) The eastern part of the ROMAN EMPIRE, consisting approximately of the Balkans, Greece and western Anatolia, of which the capital Byzantium (Istanbul) was founded by Constantine in AD 330; the formal division did not take place until 395, when 2 sons of Emperor Theodosius (both minors) became emperors of east and west. The Byzantine (Eastern) Empire, Christian in religion, part Greek and part oriental in spirit, quickly gained ascendancy over the Western, which it ruled from 476 until Charlemagne's time.

BZ A nerve gas which incapacitates without doing permanent harm; the US Army has carried out experiments with it, using volunteers as guinea pigs.

C

'C' Code name for the head of the British SIS (Secret Intelligence Service) (MI-6). (Possibly from the name of its founder — Mansfield Cumming — or standing for Control or Chief.)

Caaba See KAABA.

CAB See CIVIL AERONAUTICS BOARD.

Cabal (1667-73) Name given to the Committee of Foreign Affairs which replaced Clarendon as chief adviser to Charles II. Two members with Catholic sympathies alone knew of Charles's reversal of policy by the Secret Treaty of DOVER; another member, the Earl of Shaftesbury (Ashley Cooper), turned against Charles to lead the WHIG opposition. (Traditionally from the initials of Clifford, Arlington, Buckingham, Ashley Cooper, Lauderdale; actually from CABBALA in the sense 'secret doctrine', hence 'intrigue'.)

Cabaret (1966) A musical play depicting the decadence of Germany just before the rise of Nazism, based on Christopher Isherwood's *Berlin Stories* (1937-39), which was also the source of John van Druten's play (1951) and movie, *I Am a Camera*.

Cabbala (1) Traditions ascribed to Moses and transmitted orally by generations of rabbis. (2) In 9th–13th-century Spain and Provence, applied to mystical doctrines derived from the Old Testament.

Cabin in the Sky (1940) A musical comedy by Lynn Root and John La Touche, with outstanding music by Vernon Duke (Vladimir Dukelsky) and an all-Negro cast. It was made into a movie in 1942.

Cable and Wireless Ltd A company, nationalized in 1947, which operates Britain's telecommunication services, in conjunction with the Post Office.

Cable TV See CATV.

Cabots The aristocratic Boston, (Mass.) family of whom it was written: The Lowells talk to the Cabots / And the Cabots talk only to God.

Cabot Trail A 185-mile scenic coastal highway in northern Nova Scotia encircling the Cape Breton Highlands National Park.

Cactus Flower A farce adapted by Abe Burrows from a French play and later made into a movie (1969) directed by Gene Saks. A playboy dentist invents a wife and 3 children to protect himself from falling into matrimony with a girl he eventually decides he must marry, and then has to produce a bogus wife to prove that he was not lying.

Cadarache (1960) French nuclear research center which designs and tests reactors used in power stations and ships. (Site near Aix-en-Provence.)

Cadbury Castle (UK) A pre-Roman hill-fort southeast of GLASTONBURY, Somerset; pottery remains show that the site had been reoccupied by the 6th century AD by people of wealth. Excavations were begun in 1967 to seek evidence in support of local tradition that the hill is the site of CAMELOT.

Cadogan teapot (1790) A lidless teapot filled from a hole in the bottom, the interior being made on the inkwell principle so that the hole need not be stoppered. Traditionally made by a predecessor of the ROCKINGHAM factory for a Lady Cadogan, and usually covered with the typical Rockingham purple-brown glaze.

Ca' d'Oro (1440) An old Gothic palace in Venice on the Grand Canal, housing the Franchetti collection of paintings by Titian, Tintoretto, Tiepolo etc. (Italian, 'house of gold'.)

Caernarvon Castle (1284) A fortress built on the Menai Straits, North Wales, by Edward I, whose son was created the first Prince of Wales.

One of the best preserved British castles, it was the scene of the formal investiture as Prince of Wales of the future Edward VIII (1911) and of Prince Charles (1969).

Caesarian section An operation performed when normal birth would be dangerous, the child being removed through an incision in the abdomen. (Traditionally the way Julius Caesar was born.)

Caesar salad A green salad that may include anchovies and croutons. The dressing consists of lemon juice, olive oil, garlic, cheese, and raw or coddled egg.

Caesar's wife The remark that 'Caesar's wife must be above suspicion' was, according to Plutarch, made by Julius Caesar to justify his decision to divorce his wife even though he did not believe accusations made against her.

Café Royal A London restaurant in REGENT STREET, a meeting place for artists in the earlier part of the century, and later for BBC staff, journalists etc.

Cagoulards (1935) French Fascists who, after various outrages, were suppressed in 1938. (French, 'hooded men'.)

Caillaux scandal (1914) The shooting in Paris of the editor of *Le Figaro*, Gaston Calmette, by the wife of Joseph Caillaux, Minister of Finance. The editor had threatened to publish incriminating personal letters; the wife was acquitted.

Cain The eldest son of ADAM and Eve, the farmer who killed his brother ABEL; God made him a fugitive in the earth and set a mark on him lest any should kill him. (*Genesis* iv, 8-15). The story may refer to the eternal quarrel between nomads and farmers, whose crops are damaged by the nomads' herds.

Cain, To raise To create a tremendous disturbance, make a great fuss. (From CAIN, the first recorded murderer.)

Caine Mutiny, The (1951) A novel by Herman Wouk about a mutiny in a US minesweeper, the *Caine*, during World War II.

Cainozoic Alternative spelling of CENOZOIC.

'Ça ira' A French revolutionary song with the refrain: Ah! ça ira, ça ira! / Les aristocrates à la lanterne ('Things are going to be OK! String up the aristocrats!').

Cairo Conference (Nov. 1943) A meeting of Roosevelt, Churchill, and Chiang Kai-shek, after which the Cairo Declaration of Allied war aims in the Far East was issued.

Cakes and Ale (1930) Somerset Maugham's novel which satirizes the novelists Hugh Walpole ('Alroy Kear') and Thomas Hardy ('Edward Driffield'); Edward's first wife, Rosie, an uninhibited barmaid, is said to be based on Maugham's great and only love, 'Nan', who has not been identified.

Calamity Jane (1) Nickname of Jane Burke, a famous frontierswoman, quick on the draw, who was buried at Deadwood (see DEADWOOD DICK) in 1903. (2) The heroine of a series of dime novels (1884) based on her career. (3) Synonym for a person who is always prophesying calamity, like Jane Burke.

Caldecott medal (1938) An annual award by the American Library Association for the best American picture book.

Calder Hall (1956) The UK ATOMIC ENERGY AUTHORITY's nuclear power station, the first in the world to produce electricity for commercial use, but principally engaged in the production of plutonium.

Caledonia A Roman name for north Britain, used in poetical contexts for Scotland.

Caledonian Ball, Royal (1849) A charity ball, held since 1930 at Grosvenor House, Park Lane; the largest of the London season, attended by Scots from all over the world, and noted for its set reels and display of Highland dress.

Caledonian Market (New Caledonian Market) A Friday street market in London for antique dealers, held since the last war in BERMONDSEY.

Calgary Stampede Canada's most famous rodeo meeting, held in July at Calgary, Alberta.

Caliban The ill-disposed misshapen monster, son of the witch Sycorax, who appears in Shakespeare's THE

TEMPEST as PROSPERO'S servant. He is a composite picture of the aborigines of then recently discovered lands drawn from travelers' tales.

Caligula's horse The horse appointed Consul by the half-mad Roman Emperor Caligula (AD 37-41); a particularly unsuitable promotion is often derided with the words: There has been nothing like it since Caligula made his horse First Consul of Rome.

Caliphate The rule of the Caliphs (see OMAYYADS, ABBASIDS, FATIMITES), the supreme civil and religious rulers of Islam; the Sultans of the OTTOMAN TURKS and the Grand Sharifs of Morocco were also called Caliphs. (Arabic *khalifah*, 'successor', a title adopted by Abu Bakr on Mohammed's death.)

Calliope In Greek legend, the muse of epic poetry.

Call of the Wild, The (1903) Jack London's novel about Buck, a dog translated from a good home to the Klondike as a sledge dog. His only protector, John Thornton, is murdered and Buck becomes the leader of a wolf pack.

Cal. Tech. Abbreviation for the California Institute of Technology, Pasadena, the West Coast counterpart of MIT.

Calvados Cider brandy made in the Calvados *département* of Normandy.

Calvary (1) The hill at Jerusalem which is the traditional site of the Crucifixion; Golgotha. (2) A representation of the Crucifixion. (Latin *calvaria*, 'skull', a translation of GOLGOTHA.)

Calvinists An extreme Protestant sect, strong in Switzerland and Holland, who believe that souls are predestined to salvation or to eternal hell fire, and that human nature is totally depraved; a view recast by Karl Barth, professor of theology in Germany and Switzerland, 1921-68. (John Calvin, 16th-century French theologian.)

Calydonian boar In Greek legend a ferocious boar sent by ARTEMIS to ravage the land of Calydon (Aetolia). The Greek heroes hunted it down, ATALANTA wounded it, and Meleager killed it.

Calypso In the ODYSSEY, a nymph who falls in love with Ulysses, detaining him on her island of Ogygia for 7 years until Zeus ordered her to release him.

Camargo Society (1930) The London ballet club formed to keep British interest in ballet alive after Diaghilev's death, by giving performances to members. Its work done, it handed over its properties to the SADLER'S WELLS Ballet. (Named after a celebrated 18th-century dancer.)

Camargue, La A desolate marshy area of the Rhône delta, southern France, famous for its flamingoes and other birdlife, its white horses, and its small black bulls, used in a form of bullfight at Nîmes and ARLES, in which the aim is to place a cockade (*cocarde*) on the bull's forehead.

Camberley Sometimes used as a synonym for the British Army STAFF COLLEGE, situated at Camberley, Surrey.

Camberwell A former London metropolitan borough, since 1965 part of the borough of SOUTHWARK.

Camberwell Beauty A purely English name for a European and American butterfly known in the US as the Mourning Cloak but rare in Britain, which was occasionally found in the 19th century in what was then the village of Camberwell, now in London.

Cambrian Period The earliest period of the PALEOZOIC ERA, lasting from about 600 to 500 million years ago. In the later stages there are fossils of a great variety of marine creatures, but no vertebrates. (Latin *Cambria*, 'Wales', where rocks of this period were first studied, e.g. the Llanberis slates.)

Cambridge Complex, The A network of research establishments at HARVARD University and the Massachusetts Institute of Technology (MIT), forming one of the 'think factories' which, like the RAND CORPORATION, advise the government on strategic policy.

Cambridge Platonists A group of 17th-century Cambridge men, led by Henry More and Ralph Cudworth, who, using the concepts of Plato and the Neoplatonists, tried to reconcile Christian beliefs with the new findings of science and to oppose with humanism the excesses of Calvinism on the one hand, and the materialism of Hobbes and Descartes on the other.

Cambridgeshire, The (UK) The last major flat race of the season, run over 9 furlongs at the Newmarket (Houghton) meeting in October.

Cambridge University One of the 2 leading English universities, a center of learning since c. 1231, now consisting of 24 separately administered residential colleges (including 3 for women), the oldest being Peterhouse (1284), Clare (1326) and Pembroke (1347). A Senate administers the university's affairs. There are some 11,000 students in residence.

Cambulic Marco Polo's name for Peking. (From Mongol *Khanbalik*, 'Khan's city'.)

Camden (1965) New inner London borough consisting of the former metropolitan boroughs of Holborn, St Pancras and Hampstead; headquarters at Euston Road.

Camden Passage A passageway in Camden Town, North London, with several permanent antique shops, supplemented on Saturdays by stalls in a neighboring arcade.

Camden Town group (1911) A short-lived group of Postimpressionist artists, led by Sickert. See LONDON GROUP, POSTIMPRESSIONISM.

Camelot (1) King Arthur's capital, identified in local tradition with the hill fort of CADBURY CASTLE, near GLASTONBURY; also with Caerleon, Winchester, Camelford (Tintagel) etc. (2) A Lerner and Loewe musical (1960) based on T. H. White's Arthurian novels, collected as *The Once and Future King* (1958).

Camembert A rich yellowish cheese with a thick rind; it turns almost liquid when ready to eat and has a flavor nearly as strong as LIMBURGER. (Village of Normandy where originally made.)

Cameroun Republic (1960) The former French Cameroons with the addition (1961) of the southern part of the former British Cameroons.

Camford An alternative to OXBRIDGE as an abbreviation for Cambridge and Oxford universities.

Camille (1969) A hurricane which killed over 400 people when it swept across the Mississippi Gulf, August 17–25th; probably one of the most severe to hit the US.

Camorra A Neapolitan secret society founded in the early 19th century and dissolved by Mussolini; originally a prisoners' protection society, it developed into a Mafia-type smuggling, blackmail and robbery club which gained political power by assisting in the expulsion of the Bourbons.

Campagna, The The mosquito-infested plains round Rome which, according to a historian nicknamed 'Malaria' Jones, contributed largely to the decline of the Roman Empire. They were drained by Mussolini.

Campaign for Nuclear Disarmament Better known by the initials CND.

Campanula The genus that includes the Canterbury bell and also the harebell of summer and autumn. In Scotland and northern England the latter is called the bluebell, which in the south is the name of the spring-flowering wild hyacinth.

Campari An Italian bitters, drunk by Italians with or without soda.

'Campbells are Coming, The' A song of the 1715 Jacobite revolt, later the regimental march of the Argyll and Sutherland Highlanders. In 1857 Highland Jessie, wife of Corporal Brown, was the first to hear the pipes playing it as the regiment came to the relief of Lucknow; a favorite subject of popular art at the time.

Camp David meeting (1959) A meeting between President Eisenhower and Khrushchev at Camp David in Maryland, near Washington, at which they discussed plans for the PARIS SUMMIT CONFERENCE.

Campeador, El Another name for El CID. (Spanish, 'champion'.)

Camperdown (1797) Duncan's victory over the Dutch fleet. See FIRST COALITION. (Named after a village in north Holland off which it was fought.)

Camp Fire Girl A member of a national organization for girls, founded in 1910 and similar in objectives to the GIRL SCOUTS founded 2 years later. Camp Fire Girls proper are in the 10-15 age group but the movement also includes the Blue Birds (7-10) and the Horizon Club (15-18). Health, character and the ideals of the home and of citizenship are developed through camping and practical instruction in creative arts, sports, science etc.

Campobello A Canadian island in southwest New Brunswick, less than a mile from the Maine coast; it is a summer resort and was for many years Franklin Roosevelt's summer home.

Campo Formio, Treaty of (1797) The treaty under which France and Austria divided up the ancient Venetian Republic, Napoleon securing possession of the Venetian fleet.

'Camptown Races, De' (1850) A well-known song by Stephen Foster, containing the words: I'll bet my money on de bob-tail nag.

Canaan Western Palestine, the PROMISED LAND of the children of Israel.

Canaanites The pre-Jewish inhabitants of CANAAN, i.e. the Phoenicians.

Canada Council (1957) A Council for the Arts, Humanities and Social Sciences set up by the government as one result of the MASSEY REPORT. Half its funds go to grants for capital construction by universities and colleges; interest on the other half finances scholarships.

Canada Cup (1953) International professional golf tournament between teams of 2 from each country.

Canadian bacon Bacon cut from the loin of a pig.

Canadian National Railways (1923) The nationalized railroad system formed by merging the Canadian Northern, GRAND TRUNK, Grand Trunk Pacific and other railroads bankrupted during World War I. It includes 2 transcontinental routes joining Prince Rupert and Vancouver to Saint John, NB, and Halifax, NS, and lines to Chicago, Portland, Me., and Churchill (on Hudson Bay).

Canadian Pacific Airlines See AIR CANADA.

Canadian Pacific Railway (1881) A privately owned company whose main line is the transcontinental 3367-mile link between Vancouver and Saint John, NB, opened in 1887. It also operates steamship lines and airlines.

Canadian Shield The region of exposed rocks of the PRECAMBRIAN ERA found over most of Canada east of the Rockies, characterized by low relief and numerous lakes; it is the source of most of Canada's minerals as well as much of its timber and hydroelectric power.

Canadiens The Montreal Canadiens, NATIONAL HOCKEY LEAGUE, one of the 3 Canadian teams in the League.

Canal du Rhône au Rhin, Le Grand An important link in the West European canal system, designed to enable barges of over 1000 tons to navigate from Rotterdam to Marseilles.

Cana marriage feast The scene of the first miracle performed by Jesus, who turned water into wine (*John* ii, 1-11). Its best-known representation is a picture by Paolo Veronese in the Louvre. (A village said to have been near Nazareth.)

Canard enchaîné, Le (1916) A Paris satirical weekly, famous for its witty cartoons and its bold stand against governmental interference.

Canasta A card game for 4, developed from Rummy. (Spanish, 'basket'; name in the original Uruguayan version for the highest ranking combination of cards.)

Canberra RAF twin-jet bomber, in service since the early 1950s in the Far East, NATO and CENTO theaters as a nuclear strike aircraft; it was to have been replaced by the F-111, but the order was canceled.

Cancer The Crab, 4th constellation of the Zodiac, between GEMINI and LEO; the sun enters it at the summer solstice about June 21st. Astrologers claim that those born under this sign may be home-loving, possessive, moody.

Candace (1) Title of Ethiopian queens in Roman times. (2) A legendary Queen of Tarsus who held Alexander the Great in thrall.

Candia Italian name for Crete and for its capital, Iráklion (Heraklion).

Candida (1903) Bernard Shaw's play in which Candida Morell, realizing that her sensible Christian Socialist parson husband needs her continued support, resists the temptation to leave him for an idealist, unpractical poet.

Candide (1759) Voltaire's satire on Leibniz; see Dr PANGLOSS. Its last words ('We must cultivate our garden', i.e. attend to our own affairs) are often quoted.

Candleford See LARK RISE TO CANDLEFORD.

Candlemas Feb. 2nd, the feast of the Purification of the Virgin Mary, and a Scottish quarter-day. See GROUNDHOG DAY. (The year's supply of candles was consecrated on this day.)

Candy Striper A young woman assisting in a hospital, so called because she wears a striped uniform.

Canis Major A southern constellation, below ORION, and called Orion's Dog; its chief star is SIRIUS (the Dog Star). (Latin, 'great dog'.)

Canis Minor A southern constellation north of CANIS MAJOR; its chief star is Procyon. (Latin, 'small dog'.)

Cannae (216 BC) The crushing defeat of the Romans by Hannibal; see PUNIC WARS. (Village in Apulia.)

Cannes International Film Festival The most important of the film festivals, held in May.

Canopus The second brightest star in the sky (after SIRIUS), in the southern constellation Argo. (Name of Menelaus' helmsman.)

Canossa The castle where in 1077 the Holy Roman Emperor Henry IV who, in a struggle over the right to appoint clergy had declared the pope deposed and had been himself excommunicated, made his submission to Pope Gregory VII, after being made to wait 3 days in the snow in a penitent's shirt; hence 'to go to Canossa' is a phrase meaning 'to climb down'. (Village near Modena, northern Italy.)

Cantabrigian See TABS.

Cantabs See TABS.

Canterbury Tales Chaucer's poem (begun 1386, left unfinished), which gives a vivid picture of contemporary life through tales told by a group of pilgrims making their way from London to Becket's shrine at Canterbury.

Cantharides (1) Dried SPANISH FLY. (2) Also used of the live beetle of that name.

Canton Chinese city, officially Kuang-chou (Kwangchow).

Canton china (1) Early 19th-century Chinese porcelain painted in enamel colors, typically with flowers and butterflies on a green ground. (2) US name, confusingly, for NANKING CHINA.

Cantos (1917) Ezra Pound's life work, an open-ended epic poem dealing with just about everything.

Canucks The Vancouver (BC) Canucks, NATIONAL HOCKEY LEAGUE, one of the 3 Canadian teams in the League.

Canyonlands National Park (1964) A park in southeast Utah at the junction of the Colorado and Green rivers.

Caodaist sect In Vietnam, the adherents of a synthetic religion with elements of Christianity, BUDDHISM, TAOISM, Mormonism, etc.; its saints include the Duke of Wellington and Victor Hugo.

CAP (1) Initials used for the Common Agricultural Policy of the COMMON MARKET, on which members had the greatest difficulty in reaching agreement. (2) CIVIL AIR PATROL.

Capability Brown Lancelot Brown (1715-83), an English landscape gardener who laid out the grounds of Blenheim, Harewood and other great houses. (From his favorite comment: 'This land has capabilities'.)

Cape Canaveral Now renamed CAPE KENNEDY.

Cape Cod A style of domestic architecture characterized by oblong ground plan, 1 or 1½ stories, a steep gabled roof, central chimney, and the front door in one of the long sides.

Cape Cod lighter A lump of porous material fixed on a handle and soaked with kerosene, used to light fires.

Cape Cod turkey A name for codfish.

Cape Cod Yesterdays A novel by the Massachusetts author Joseph C. Lincoln (1870-1944), who was born on Cape Cod.

Cape Coloureds In South Africa, a long-established community, mainly in western Cape Province, of mixed African or Asian and European descent, who are Christians, and speak AFRIKAANS or English as their mother tongue; they are regarded, and regard themselves, as separate from and superior to the BANTU.

Cape Kennedy Formerly Cape Canaveral, Florida, America's chief launching site for satellites and space probes.

Capella (Astronomy) See AURIGA.

Capenhurst Site of one of the UK ATOMIC ENERGY AUTHORITY Production Group's factories for producing uranium and plutonium. (Cheshire village, northwest of Chester.)

Cape St Vincent (1797) Victory won by Admiral Jervis (later Lord St Vincent) and Capt. Nelson over the Spanish fleet. See FIRST COALITION. (In southwest Portugal.)

Capetians The dynasty which ruled France from the 10th century to the Revolution and for a short period thereafter, the VALOIS (1328) and BOURBON (1589) dynasties being branches of the Capet family. (It was Hugh Capet, who seized the French throne from the CAROLINGIANS.)

Cape-to-Cairo railway Cecil Rhodes's dream of a railroad spanning Africa from north to south, not destined to be realized.

Cape Triangle (1853-64) The first nonrectangular postage stamp, issued in the Cape of Good Hope Colony, South Africa.

Capistrano, San Juan A Spanish mission founded in the 1770s by Father Junipero Serra, 56 miles south of Los Angeles. It is famous for the tradition that swallows arrive from the south on St Joseph's Day (March 19th) and depart on St John's Day (October 23rd).

Capitol, The (1) The Ancient Roman national temple of Jupiter, on the CAPITOLINE, which contained the Sibylline Books. (2) (USA) The building in Washington, D.C., where Congress meets; also applied to the Statehouse or building where a US State legislature meets.

Capitoline The Roman hill on which the CAPITOL stood; earlier called the Tarpeian Hill.

Capodimonte (1743-1821) Soft-paste porcelain made at Naples, extremely rare, but faked in hard paste in great quantity from an early date. MEISSEN and Chinese influences were strong, and mythological subjects treated in a lively flamboyant style were typical. Cups and saucers with colored relief figures were for long erroneously thought to have been produced here.

Caporetto (Oct.-Nov. 1917) The disastrous defeat of the Italians in World War I by Austrian troops strengthened by German reinforcements. Allied forces had to be diverted to Italy to restore the situation. (Village north of Trieste on the ISONZO, then in Austria; now in Yugoslavia and renamed Kobarid.)

Capricornus The Goat, 10th of the constellations of the Zodiac, between SAGITTARIUS and AQUARIUS; the sun enters it at the winter solstice, about Dec. 21st. Astrologers claim that those born under this sign may be conventional, single-minded and stubborn. (Latin *caper*, goat; *cornu*, horn.)

Caprivi appendix A long, narrow strip of territory giving South-West Africa access to the Zambezi; formerly part of German South-West Africa, incorporated in BECHUANALAND (1922) and handed over to the Union of South Africa in 1939. (Named after a German Chancellor.)

Captain Kidd Almost a synonym for 'pirate'; Capt. William Kidd, Scottish sailor, was sent in 1696 to put down piracy in the Indian Ocean and there, it is alleged, turned pirate; he was hanged in 1701. Some think he was the innocent victim of political intrigue; nevertheless, the legend grew that he had left behind huge caches of loot, the inspiration of many treasure hunts, real and fictional (e.g. TREASURE ISLAND, The GOLD BUG).

Captains Courageous (1897) A Kipling story about the pampered son of an American millionaire; he falls overboard and is rescued by a trawler skipper who makes him work, to his lasting benefit. (Title taken from an old ballad.)

Captive European Nations, Assembly of An anti-Communist parliament-in-exile of representatives of the east-central European countries behind the Iron Curtain, which lobbies, especially in the USA where it controls so many votes, for the liberation of fellow countrymen from Communist rule.

Capuchins (1520) A reformed order of FRANCISCAN friars which returned to the strict observance of the Rule of St Francis. (French *capuche*, 'pointed hood', worn by them.)

Capulets In Shakespeare's ROMEO AND JULIET, the Verona family to which Juliet belonged, at feud with the Montagues, Romeo's family.

Caravelle (1959) The first clean-winged airliner (i.e. with jets mounted in the fuselage at the tail), and for many years the only medium-range pure-jet airliner; built in France.

Carbonari (1815) A secret society of Italian republicans, numbering Louis Bonaparte among its members, which after an ineffective career was absorbed by Mazzini's Young Italy movement, (Italian, 'charcoal-burners'.)

Carbon-14 dating The first of several new techniques for dating archeological finds. Carbon-14 is a radioactive isotope which decays very slowly at a known rate; thus the age of certain organic remains (e.g. timber) can be deduced from the amount left.

Carboniferous Period The latest but one of the periods of the PALEOZOIC ERA, lasting from about 350 to 275 million years ago. Fossils of the larger amphibians, and later of reptiles, appear, accompanied by many in-

sects (dragonfly, mayfly, cockroach), and a rich flora of ferns and evergreen trees, fungi etc. Rocks of great importance were formed, including the Coal Measures, Millstone Grits and Carboniferous Limestone. (Latin, 'coal-bearing'.)

CARD (1964) Initials used for the Campaign Against Racial Discrimination, founded in London after the passing of the Commonwealth Immigrants Act. When it passed under the control of extremists in 1967, the moderates formed an 'Equal Rights' splinter group.

Card, The The nickname of Denery Machin, the slick and successful young businessman in Arnold Bennett's novel of that name (1911). (Slang, = the 'character'.)

Cardiff Giant A bogus prehistoric relic now in Farmer's Museum, Cooperstown, N.Y. In 1868 George Hall transported a block of gypsum from Fort Dodge, Ia., to Chicago, had it carved into a statue of a man and buried it at Cardiff, N.Y. Discovered by well diggers the following year, it was exhibited as a 'petrified man' or prehistoric sculpture until, the hoax exposed, Hall told all. Compare PILTDOWN MAN.

Cardinal 500 The last, longest and richest ($28,000) race of the NASCAR season, held at the Martinsville speedway track, Va.

Cardinals The St. Louis Cardinals: (1) NATIONAL (Baseball) LEAGUE, playing at the Busch Memorial Stadium; (2) NATIONAL FOOTBALL LEAGUE. They moved from Chicago in 1960. Became members of the NATIONAL CONFERENCE, NATIONAL FOOTBALL LEAGUE in 1970.

Cardinal Virtues Defined by Plato as justice, prudence, temperance, fortitude; to these the SCHOOLMEN added the Christian theological virtues of faith, hope and charity.

CARE (1945) Initials standing for Cooperative for American Relief Everywhere Inc., an organization through which gift parcels of food and clothing were sent to Europe after World War II (until 1952 its name was Cooperative for American

Remittances to Europe) and later to any part of the world.

Caretaker, The (1959) Pinter's play of mutual incomprehension, in which Davies, a tramp, is too warped to be grateful for the accommodation given him by 2 brothers, and tries to play off one against the other until he is turned out.

Carfax The center of Oxford, England. (Latin *quadrifurcus*, crossroads.)

Caribs (1) The ferocious American Indians encountered by Columbus in the West Indies. They gave their name to the Caribbean Sea, and the word 'cannibal' is a corruption of the Spanish name for them. (2) A linguistic group of American Indians now scattered over the Guianas, Venezuela, Honduras and Nicaragua.

Carisbrooke Castle The medieval seat of government of the Isle of Wight, near Newport; it is still partly inhabited. Charles I was detained there for some time at the end of the English Civil War.

Carley float An emergency raft of copper tubing, cork and canvas for survivors of shipwrecks at sea; it floats either side up and is provided with paddles, drinking water and a signal light. It was used in World War I.

Carling tournament (1964) A world open golf tournament played alternately in North America and Britain, sponsored by the Charrington and Carling Breweries of USA, Canada and Britain. The total prize money is around $170,000.

Carlisle & Gregson The London firm of Army crammers, known as Jimmy's, whose greatest success was perhaps to get Winston Churchill into Sandhurst.

Carlists Supporters of Don Carlos, pretender (1833) to the Spanish throne, of his grandson (also Don Carlos), and of their descendants; see next entry.

Carlist Wars (1834-96) A series of sporadic civil wars in Spain between CARLISTS, supported by the Church, and Royalists; the latter accepted the succession of a woman

(Queen Isabella) to the throne, in spite of the SALIC LAW, which her father had declared invalid.

Carlovingians Alternative name of the CAROLINGIANS.

Carl Rosa Opera Company (1875) A London and touring company formed to present opera in English; in 1958 it was absorbed by the SADLER'S WELLS Opera Company. (Name of a German musician who settled in England.)

Carlsbad German name of Karlovy Vary, the Czechoslovakian spa.

Carlsbad Caverns A labyrinth of large limestone caves, with magnificent and curious formations; in Carlsbad Caverns National Park (1930), southeast New Mexico.

Carlsbad decrees (1819) Imposed by the German-born Austrian Foreign Minister, Metternich, on the newly formed confederation of German states to suppress manifestations of Liberalism in the universities and professions; they inaugurated 30 years of police repression.

Carlton Club (1832) A London club in St James's Street founded in the same year as the REFORM CLUB; it is the Tory club *par excellence*.

Carlton House Terrace The London street overlooking St James's Park, formerly associated with the German embassy (no longer there), particularly during the Nazi Ribbentrop's inglorious tenure of office.

Carmelites (12th century) A Roman Catholic order, originally of hermits, later mendicant friars (White Friars), founded in Palestine during the Crusades. In 1562 St Theresa formed a stricter sect of barefoot ('discalced') friars and nuns, which became dominant. They are active in missionary work. (Founded on Mt Carmel, traditionally in Biblical times; they wear a white cloak over a brown tunic.)

Carmen (1875) Bizet's last opera, based on a short story by Mérimée. The gypsy Carmen flirts with Corporal Don José, who allows her to evade arrest for stabbing a girl and is persuaded to desert his regiment to join the smugglers' band. But Carmen is now interested in a toreador, Escamillo, and is stabbed dead by the jealous Don Jose.

Carmen Jones A successful modernized movie version of CARMEN in which the smugglers become Negro soldiers, and the toreador Escamillo is renamed Husky Miller, the prizefighter.

Carnaby Street A shopping street east of Regent Street, London, which leapt into fame in the 1960s as the fashion center for modern youth.

Carnac A village in Brittany, site of tombs and a megalithic stone avenue dating back to about 2000 BC.

Carnatic, The Old European name for the part of Madras which lay between the Eastern Ghats and the Coromandel Coast; it was ruled by the Nawab of Arcot and acquired by the British in 1801 in their final struggle with the French for the domination of India.

Carnegie Hall (1890) A famous New York concert hall, acoustically perfect and long the headquarters of the New York Philharmonic; it lies on Seventh Avenue and 57th Street, and has music studios, a smaller hall for chamber music, and other ancillary buildings.

Carnegie Medal An annual award by the (British) Library Association for the best children's book written by a British subject.

Carnegie Trusts A series of trusts formed from 1896 onwards by Andrew Carnegie, the Scottish-born American millionaire steel magnate; most of them are designed to further the cause of education in USA and Britain. He is particularly remembered for the public libraries he endowed.

Carnival (1912) Compton Mackenzie's novel of the theater world into which he was born.

Carnival glass Pressed glass with an iridescent finish mass-produced in a variety of colors. (Frequently used as prizes at carnival booths.)

Carnival of the Animals, The (1886) Saint-Saens' 'zoological fantasy', a *jeu d'esprit* for small orchestra, not performed in his lifetime. The 'ani-

mals' include Pianists and Personages with Long Ears.

Carolingians (751-987) The Frankish dynasty founded by Pepin and succeeded by the CAPETIANS. (Named after Pepin's son Charlemagne, or Carolus Magnus.)

Carrhae (53 BC) The scene of the Parthian defeat of the Roman army under Crassus, in the first of several unsuccessful attempts by Rome to gain control of Mesopotamia. (Town east of the upper Euphrates, near Urfa in southern Turkey.)

Carroll, Lewis Pen name of the Rev. C. L. Dodgson, author of ALICE IN WONDERLAND.

Carroll International An Irish stroke-play golf tournament open to members of the British and Irish PGAS and invited Irish amateurs, played at Woodbrooke, near Dublin. Prize money totals $24,000. (Sponsored by P. J. Carroll Ltd.)

Carry Nation's hatchetations The exploits of a lady who, after brief marriage to an alcoholic, gathered a troupe of like-minded Furies and terrorized the tipplers of Kansas by what she called the 'hatchetation of joints' (i.e. wrecking saloons with hatchets), a campaign which reached its peak in the 1890s. Other targets of Mrs Nation's comprehensive disapproval were tobacco, short skirts, pinups and corsets.

Carson, Kit (1809-68) A latter-day Daniel Boone, explorer, guide and trapper who, after taking part in the conquest of California, was made Indian agent at Taos, N.M., rose to brigadier general in the Federal army and then resumed his work among the Indians, of whose languages and ways he had accumulated a deep knowledge invaluable to the government. Many legends gathered round his career; Joaquin Miller's poem 'Kit Carson's Ride' (1871) tells how he saved his Indian bride from a prairie fire.

Carter, Nick (1886-1920) The US counterpart of the English Sexton BLAKE; he was portrayed as a shrewd, tough detective in a series of dime novels written by various hands and also adapted for the screen and radio.

Carter's Little Liver pills A US patent medicine, the first to compete with BEECHAM'S PILLS in this lucrative trade.

Cartesian Adjective formed from Descartes, French mathematician and philosopher (1596-1650), who tried to argue from absolute certainties (*Cogito, ergo sum*, 'I think, therefore I must exist', was his starting point) reached by methodical doubt, arriving at the conclusion that mind and matter are quite separate entities which interact through the pineal gland; although his philosophy was purely materialistic, he placated the Church by saying that matter does not move of its own accord, the original impulse coming from God.

Carthaginian peace Very harsh terms imposed on the conquered, as by Rome on Carthage at the end of the 3rd PUNIC WAR.

Carthaginian Wars See PUNIC WARS.

'Carthago, Delenda est' 'Carthage must be destroyed', the phrase with which Cato the Censor ended every speech in the Roman Senate. He died just before his wish was fulfilled; see PUNIC WARS.

Carthusians (1084) (1) A Roman Catholic order of monks founded on the Chartreuse plateau near Grenoble, France (La Grande CHARTREUSE); the original austere regime has lasted unaltered for 9 centuries, monks living in separate hermitages, vowed to silence, eating one (meatless) meal a day, growing their own food, meeting only for prayer and on designated occasions. A 'Chartreuse' (anglicized to 'Charterhouse') was first founded in England in the 14th century. (2) Members of CHARTERHOUSE SCHOOL. (From Latinized form of *Chartreuse*.)

Carton, Sydney The dissolute character in Dickens's TALE OF TWO CITIES who during the French Revolution takes the place of Darnay, whom he closely resembles, at the guillotine, where he makes a famous last speech beginning: It is a far, far better thing that I do, than I have ever done.

Carver chair An early 17th-century Dutch-style armchair, distinguished from the BREWSTER CHAIR by having only one row of 3 vertical spindles in the back. Typically, it was of ash or maple with a rush seat. (John Carver, first governor of Plymouth Colony, is said to have brought one with him in the *Mayflower*.)

Casabianca The boy who stood on the burning deck in Mrs Hemans's poem, based on an incident aboard a French ship at the Battle of the Nile (1798).

Casablanca Conference (Jan. 1943) The meeting of Roosevelt and Churchill (joined later by de Gaulle), which decided on invasion of Sicily, and at which Roosevelt first mentioned the 'unconditional surrender' policy.

Casablanca Powers (1961) A group of neutralist, socialist African states (Ghana, Mali, Guinea, Morocco, UAR and Algeria), strongly pan-African in outlook. (First met at Casablanca, Morocco.)

Casanova A compulsive womanizer. (From the 18th-century Italian rake and rogue, Casanova, and his not always credible account of his amours, in 12 volumes.)

Casaubon, The Rev. Edward The uselessly pedantic but reputedly learned clergyman who disillusions his wife Dorothea BROOKE in MIDDLE-MARCH.

Casbah, The Specifically, the old quarter dominating the modern city of Algiers. (Arabic for a fortress-village or Moorish feudal settlement, corresponding to a medieval European castle.)

Casement diaries The diaries of Sir Roger Casement, who was executed (1916) for treason after a farcical German-assisted gun-running escapade in Ireland during World War I. They included the Black Diary which chronicled homosexual episodes, and were shown to the US government to forestall protests against his execution. In 1959 they were made available for public inspection to allay ill-founded suspicions that they were government forgeries.

'Casey at the Bat' (1888) The baseball fans' anthem, a mock-heroic poem by Ernest Thayer about a legendary hero of the Mudville team. 'There was ease in Casey's manner as he stepped into his place; / There was pride in Casey's bearing and a smile on Casey's face' — but alas! he struck out and lost the game. This story was also the theme of an operetta, *The Mighty Casey* (1953).

'Casey Jones' (1909) An American folksong about John Luther Jones (1864-1900), born in Cayce, Ky., — hence the name — the locomotive engineer hero who, reporting late for duty, decided: For I'm going to run till she leaves the rail — / Or make it on time with the southbound mail! The result was a collision in which he and others were killed. Published, and perhaps written, by 2 railroad men, Lawrence Seibert and Eddie Newton, the song is thought to be based on the wreck of the Cannonball Express in 1900.

Cash and Carry Act (Nov. 1939) The US Neutrality Act authorizing the export of arms to belligerents, but only on the basis that payment was to be made, and transport effected, by the purchaser.

Casket letters Love letters to Bothwell allegedly in the handwriting of Mary Queen of Scots, produced after Darnley's murder at KIRK O' FIELD, and held to implicate her in it; she maintained that they were forgeries. Copies of them were discovered at HATFIELD HOUSE in the 19th century.

Cassandra A prophet of woe; strictly, a prophetess who is not believed but is nevertheless right. (Daughter of King PRIAM of Troy, brought home captive by AGAMEMNON. She correctly foretold the death of both of them.)

'Cassandra' Sir William Connor, who over a long period of time contributed a column under that name in the London *Daily Mirror*. See CASSANDRA.

Casse-Noisette (1892) Tchaikovsky's ballet, now rarely performed; the music is familiar through the selections in the *Nutcracker Suite*, e.g. 'The Dance of the Sugar-Plum Fairy'.

Cassino (1944) See MONTE CASSINO.

Cassiopeia In Greek legend, a Queen of Ethiopia, mother of ANDROMEDA, who dared to say that her daughter was more beautiful than the NEREIDS.

Cassiopeia A northern W-shaped constellation close to the North Pole and CEPHEUS.

Cassiterides The 'Tin Islands', a name first used by the Greek historian Herodotus; they are usually identified as the Scilly Isles and Cornwall (or Britain as a whole), from which the Carthaginians had been the first to import tin to the Mediterranean countries.

Castel Gandolfo An ancient Roman castle overlooking Lake Albano, south of Rome; now the Pope's summer residence.

Casterbridge A town in Thomas Hardy's novels, said to represent Dorchester.

Castile A former kingdom of Spain, consisting in the 11th century of Old Castile, to the north and west of Madrid, to which Toledo, conquered from the Moors, was added in 1085, Leon in the 12th century, and Aragon in 1479. The capital was Toledo, with a royal palace also at Valladolid.

Castle, The (1926) Kafka's novel in which 'K' (the novelist, or Everyman) continually struggles through mists and fantastic bureaucratic obstruction to gain admittance to the right department of an unexplained castle to obtain something unspecified; it is a moving allegory of man's struggle to comprehend the incomprehensible, and his search for Grace. (German title, *Das Schloss*.)

Castleford ware (1790-1821) (UK) Best known for white stoneware teapots with 4 concave or convex corner panels, and decorated in relief; similar teapots were also made elsewhere. (Made at Castleford, Yorkshire, by Dunderdale & Co.)

Castle Howard (UK) A domed mansion near Malton, Yorkshire, which has been in the hands of the Howard family ever since Vanbrugh built it in the early 18th century. It contains fine art collections and from its earliest days has been open to the public.

Castle of Otranto (1764) The first major Gothic horror story, by Horace Walpole, in which various supernatural happenings lead to the destruction of the castle and its usurper, Manfred. See GOTHIC NOVELS.

Castle Rackrent (1800) Maria Edgeworth's novel of feckless Irish landlords and their equally feckless tenants.

Castle Walk, The A dance popularized in New York (with many others bearing their name) by the English dancer Vernon Castle and his American wife Irene just before World War I. It was a simple 'trot' and did not endure, but the Castles were the rage of New York, where they introduced the thé dansant, until he was killed when serving as a US army pilot in 1917.

Castor A double star, the brightest of the 2 stars in the heads of the GEMINI twins (the other being POLLUX). See CASTOR AND POLLUX.

Castor and Pollux In Greek legend, the twin sons of LEDA and a King of Lacedaemon (in later legend, of ZEUS), brothers of HELEN OF TROY. Castor was the tamer of horses, Pollux (also called Polydeuces) the boxer. Together they were known as the Dioscuri.

CAT (UK) Initials used for College of Advanced Technology, a state college, not under Local Education Authority control, for the education of technologists to university degree standard. Several CATs have been given university status in recent years.

Catacombs, The Galleries dug in the underground quarries of ancient Rome, used by the early Christians as chapels and hiding places; their dead were buried in the walls, which were decorated with symbolic scenes from biblical stories. (Name of unknown origin, originally given to the supposed burial place of Peter and Paul, under a church near Rome.)

Catalan The language of the people of CATALONIA, a dialect of Provençal, spoken also in Andorra, the Balearic Isles and in adjoining areas of France. It has its own literature, and there is also a distinctive type of Catalan music.

Catal Hüyük An important archeological site in central Turkey, where evidence has been found of settled town life going back to at least 6800 BC. If this is confirmed, the beginning of the NEOLITHIC AGE must be much earlier than previously supposed.

Catalonia An old Mediterranean province of northeast Spain, capital Barcelona, which has continually sought independence or at least some measure of autonomy. See CATALAN.

Cat and Fiddle An inn sign, probably derived from the nursery rhyme 'Hey diddle diddle / The cat and the fiddle', and indicating that tipcat could be played and that a fiddle was available for dances.

Cat and the Canary, The (1922) An evergreen comedy thriller by John Willard, which set a trend for murder plays about haunted houses; several movies were made from it.

Catawba A white, usually dry wine, still or sparkling, made from a grape grown in Ohio and New York state, and native to the Catawba River region of North and South Carolina.

Catch-as-Catch-Can (Wrestling) The Lancashire style, in which tripping is allowed and both shoulders must be forced on to the ground for a win.

Catcher in the Rye, The (1951) J. D. Salinger's first novel, about a runaway prep-school boy, Holden Caulfield, who explores New York and the antics of grown-ups.

Catch-22 (1961) An American novel about World War II by Joseph Heller which satirizes the ambitions and stupidities of senior air-force officers through the story of a madly undisciplined member of a bomber crew stationed on a Mediterranean island.

Cateau-Cambrésis, Peace of (1559) The treaty which ended the Hapsburg-Valois wars; France abandoned hopes of conquest in northern Italy, which was surrendered to the dead hand of Spanish Hapsburg rule; the most serious result was the eclipse of the Italian Renaissance. (Town near Cambrai.)

Caterpillar Club A club formed in World War II for airmen who survived baling out in action and who could supply the number of the parachute that saved them to the founding firm, the US Irvin Parachute Co.

Cathari (10th century) A widespread community of MANICHAEISTS of southern Europe, sometimes identified with the ALBIGENSIANS and the BOGOMILS. (Greek, 'pure ones'.)

Cathay Poetical name for China; see for example, LOCKSLEY HALL. (Name possibly of Tartar origin.)

Cathleen ni Houlihan Yeats's nationalist play (1904), in which an old beggar woman reveals herself as Cathleen ni Houlihan, the symbol of Ireland, struggling for freedom.

Catholic and Apostolic Church See IRVINGITES.

Catholic League (1587-98) A league of Catholic powers led by Spain and supported in France by the powerful GUISE family, which tried to prevent the succession of the Protestant Henry of Navarre as King Henry IV of France. After a brief success they collapsed when Henry nonchalantly declared himself a Roman Catholic, saying 'Paris is worth a mass'.

Catholic Revival Another name for the OXFORD MOVEMENT.

Cathy Come Home (1966) BBC TV semidocumentary drama of the homeless, particularly families where the husband is compulsorily separated from his wife and children, written by Jeremy Sandford, husband of Nell Dunn who wrote *Up the Junction*; both works shocked British conscience.

Cat on a Hot Tin Roof (1955) Tennessee Williams's play, set in Mississippi, in which 2 brothers and their wives maneuver for precedence in their dying father's will.

Catriona (1893) R. L. Stevenson's sequel to KIDNAPPED. (Gaelic, 'Catherine'.)

Cattle-raid of Cooley The best-known story of the Ulster cycle of

legends, a 7th-century account of an event at the beginning of the Christian era.

CATV (1950) Community Antenna TV, a service provided by private corporations using an elaborate and costly central antenna to get improved reception of distant stations and feeding subscribers' sets by underground cable. The Supreme Court's ruling (1968) that no royalties are payable for such retransmission was regarded as weakening the monopolies of local commercial TV companies.

Caucasian Chalk Circle (1954) Brecht's play, written 10 years before it was staged, based on an old Chinese play, in which Azdak, a rogue turned judge, decides the rival claims of 2 women to a baby by putting him in a chalked circle and telling them to pull him out. One hauls him out, the other is afraid of hurting him, and wins her case.

Caucasian languages A group including Georgian and CIRCASSIAN which, like Basque and Etruscan, may have been spoken in Europe long before the arrival of the Indo-Europeans. (Named after the mountain range between the Black Sea and the Caspian.)

Caucasian rugs Well-made long-lasting rugs from north and south of the Caucasus, formerly exported through Persia, now through USSR. The primary colors predominate and the designs, including stylized animals and flowers, are geometrical.

Caucasians An obsolescent term for the dominant white races, more commonly heard in USA than Britain. It derived from a fivefold classification of mankind by J. Blumenbach into Caucasian, Mongolian, Ethiopian, Amerindian and Malayan. He chose the name because his collection of skulls from the Caucasus were most typical of the group; he also thought that the 'Indo-Europeans' might have originated there.

Caudillo, El The title assumed by General Franco as supreme head of the Spanish state. (Spanish equivalent of *Der Führer* and *Il Duce*.)

Caudine Forks (321 BC) The crushing defeat of the Romans by the Samnites; the Romans surrendered and were humiliated by being made to 'pass under the yoke'. Hence used of any crushing military defeat. (A mountain pass near Capua.)

Caudle, Mrs The nagging wife of a series of *Punch* articles by Douglas Jerrold, published in book form as *Mrs Caudle's Curtain Lectures* (1846). (The title refers to the curtains surrounding four-poster beds.)

Caughley (1775-1814) An English factory making soft-paste porcelain, of which the best-known specimens are cabbage-leaf jugs with molded mask spouts. The WILLOW PATTERN was invented here. The factory was bought by COALPORT in 1799. Also called Salopian. (Village in Shropshire.)

Cauldron, Battle of the Heavy tank engagements in May 1942 south of Tobruk in Cyrenaica, prelude to the final battle at 'Knightsbridge'.

Caulfield, Holden See CATCHER IN THE RYE.

Caution, Lemmy Peter Cheyney's detective, an English version of the American tough guy, who appears in *Dames Don't Care* (1937) and its successors.

Cautionary Tales (1907) A book of light verse in rhymed couplets by Hilaire Belloc, such as the poem about the untruthful Matilda who was burned to death, since every time she shouted 'Fire!' her neighbours answered 'Little liar!'

Cavalcade (1931) Noël Coward's spectacular patriotic play dealing with the impact of historical events on a Victorian family; the author later hinted that in writing it he 'came to scoff, remained to pray'.

Cavalier Parliament The strongly Royalist assembly summoned by Charles II at his restoration, which attempted to crush Puritanism by the CLARENDON CODE.

Cavaliers (1) In the ENGLISH CIVIL WAR the name given to the Royalists who fought for Charles I, or less specifically for the retention of the monarchy or of the bishops, or of both; strong in the north and west, and in cathedral towns. (2) The Cleveland Cavaliers, NATIONAL BASKETBALL ASSOCIATION.

Cavalleria Rusticana (1890) Mascagni's one-act opera of jealousy and revenge in a Sicilian peasant setting. See CAV. AND PAG. (Italian, 'Rustic chivalry'.)

'Cavalry Charge on the Southern Plains' (1907) A realistic painting by Frederic Remington, outstanding painter of scenes on the western plains. (Metropolitan Museum of Art, NYC.)

Cav. and Pag. Opera-goers' shorthand for CAVALLERIA RUSTICANA and PAGLIACCI, which are always played together, the former being a one-act opera.

Cavell Memorial The memorial near TRAFALGAR SQUARE, London, to Nurse Edith Cavell, who during World War I (1915) was executed at Brussels by the Germans for helping prisoners-of-war to escape.

Cavendish Laboratory (1874) The CAMBRIDGE UNIVERSITY physics laboratory which Rutherford as director (1919-37) 'turned into the cradle of nuclear physics'. (Named after Henry Cavendish, the physicist.)

Cawnpore Older English spelling of Kanpur, on the Ganges, Uttar Pradesh, India; scene of a massacre in the Indian Mutiny (1857).

Cayuga A small group of Iroquois-speaking Indians in western New York, and one of the FIVE NATIONS; survivors live in Ontario.

CBC Signifies Canadian Broadcasting Corporation, a public body that controls all broadcasting in Canada but, unlike the BBC, carries advertising on many of its own programs and also grants licenses to private local stations and networks (e.g. the CTV), which operate commercially.

CBI (1965) The Confederation of British Industry, a merger of the Federation of British Industries (FBI), the British Employers' Confederation and the National Association of British Manufacturers, with associate members from the nationalized industries and other fields. It centralizes the guardianship of the interests of British industry, both in relation to government and internationally.

CBS (1927) Initials used for the independent Columbia Broadcasting System, one of the 3 coast-to-coast TV networks in USA.

CBW Initials used for Chemical and Bacteriological Warfare.

CCC (1) Civilian Conservation Corps, set up (1933) as a NEW DEAL measure to provide work and training for youths aged 18-25. (2) Commodity Credit Corporation, set up (1933) under the AGRICULTURAL ADJUSTMENT ADMINISTRATION to support farm prices by loans on crops; it also stores crops, finances new storage facilities and markets surplus crops. (3) Corpus Christi College, CAMBRIDGE UNIVERSITY.

CCTV Stands for Closed-Circuit TV in which picture and sound are not broadcast but transmitted over a closed channel to a limited number of interconnected receivers.

CD Stands for (1) Civil Defense; (2) Corps Diplomatique. (3) In France, Centre Démocratique, a center and right-of-center party of Liberal Catholics and Christian Democrats which, under Jean Lecanuet, succeeded to the MRP. It is anti-Communist, advocating a strong NATO and a united Europe.

CDU The Christian Democratic Party of West Germany, led for many years by Dr Adenauer.

CE Initials used for the International Society of CHRISTIAN ENDEAVOR.

Cecil Sharp House Headquarters of the English Folk Dance and Song Society (1932), near Regents Park, London. (Cecil Sharp, 1859-1924, collector of folk songs.)

Ceil Chapman A New York fashion house.

Celebes Older name of Sulawesi, a group of islands in Indonesia.

'Celebrated Frog of Calaveras County, The' (1865) The short story which launched Mark Twain into national fame, based on a real-life incident. An inveterate gambler ('If there was two birds sitting on a fence, he would bet you which one would fly first') backs his frog Dan'l Webster against all comers; a stranger wins by pouring quail shot into Dan'l, who fails under this unorthodox handicap.

Celestial City, The In PILGRIM'S PROGRESS, symbolizes Heaven.

Celestial Empire, The The Chinese Empire. (Translation of a Chinese name.)

Celsius scale Another name for the Centigrade temperature scale. (Swedish 18th-century astronomer.)

Celtic A Glasgow soccer team whose Roman Catholic supporters carry on a traditional feud with the Protestant supporters of RANGERS. (Celtic Park, home ground.)

Celtic fringe The Celtic-speaking peoples inhabiting the fringes of Britain, i.e. the Scots, Welsh and Cornish, together with their Irish cousins.

Celtic languages A branch of Indo-European languages, subdivided into: (1) the Goidelic, Gaelic or Q-Celtic group, which includes Scottish Gaelic, Irish Gaelic (Erse) and Manx; (2) the Brythonic or P-Celtic group, which includes Welsh, Cornish and Breton. The language of pre-Roman Gaul belongs to the latter, but survives only in place-names.

Celtics The Boston Celtics, NATIONAL BASKETBALL ASSOCIATION.

Celtic Twilight (1) The mystic fairyland background to Irish literature, prominent in the works of such writers as W. B. Yeats, Æ and Lord Dunsany. (2) The title of one of Yeats's books.

Celts A term commonly applied to the Celtic-speaking people of the British Isles (Scottish, Welsh, Irish etc.), who are probably non-Celtic in origin but adopted CELTIC LANGUAGES and culture. (Originally used by the Greeks of fair-haired peoples living north of the Alps.)

Cenci, The (1819) Shelley's tragedy about the historical Beatrice Cenci, who had her father murdered; her lawyer's false plea that attempted incest had provoked the murder was rejected, and Beatrice was executed in 1599.

Cenerentola, La See CINDERELLA.

Cenotaph (1920) Sir Edwin Lutyens's memorial in the middle of Whitehall, London, to the memory of men and women of the 3 services and the mercantile marine who died in World War I; later it became a memorial to the dead of both world wars. The REMEMBRANCE SUNDAY service is held there each November. (Greek, 'empty tomb'.)

Cenozoic Era The most recent geological era, covering the last 70 million years down to the present, and divided into the TERTIARY and QUATERNARY PERIODS; sometimes called the Age of Mammals. During this era man, mammals, trees and flowering shrubs evolved rapidly, but invertebrates changed little. The Alps, Himalayas, Andes and Rockies were formed. (Greek, 'modern life'.)

Centaurs The Greek legendary lustful creatures of Thessaly, with men's heads and horses' bodies; see CHIRON. Their battle with another Thessalian race, the Lapithae, is depicted on the PARTHENON frieze.

Centaurs OXFORD UNIVERSITY soccer club of the best 50 or so players in residence (elected for life).

Centaurus A southern constellation below VIRGO and LIBRA. Alpha-Centauri is the 3rd brightest star in the skies and one of the pointers to the SOUTHERN CROSS; Proxima Centauri is the nearest known star, except the sun; omega-Centauri is a globular cluster. (Named after CHIRON.)

Centennial State Nickname of Colorado. (Joined the Union 100 years after the Declaration of Independence.)

CENTO Initials used for the Central Treaty Organization, the new name adopted for the BAGHDAD PACT after the secession of Iraq and the transfer of headquarters from Baghdad to Ankara (1959).

Central African Republic The former French colony of Ubangi-Shari, which became independent in 1960.

Central Committee, The (USSR) Theoretically the supreme executive organ of the Communist Party in the USSR, consisting of some 360 members elected by the Party Congress. In fact its actions are dictated by its POLITBURO and Secretariat, which have only about 10 members each and are led by the General Secretary

of the Secretariat, who is also the senior member of the Politburo.

Central Criminal Court The Old Bailey, Greater London's ASSIZE Court.

Central Hall, Westminster (1912) The headquarters of the Methodist Church in Great Britain, opposite Westminster Abbey.

Central Intelligence Agency See CIA.

Central Office The headquarters of the Conservative Party in SMITH SQUARE.

Central Office (Scotland Yard) A department of the CRIMINAL INVESTIGATION DEPARTMENT which deals with serious crimes, including those outside London and, through INTERPOL, outside Britain. The FLYING SQUAD is a branch of it.

Central Park A large park in midtown Manhattan, containing the Metropolitan Museum of Art and CLEOPATRA'S NEEDLE.

Central standard time The civil time of the 90th meridian, 1 hour slower than Eastern standard time; observed in east-central USA and Manitoba.

Central Treaty Organization More usually referred to as CENTO.

Centurion (1946) A British medium tank which maintained its place for 20 years as the world's most efficient tank of its type: 49 tons, 600 h.p., 22 m.p.h. In 1960 a larger model with the same performance was produced.

Century Club A leading New York social club.

Century of Dishonor, A (1881) A tract by Helen Hunt Jackson which, with her novel *Ramona* (1884), aroused public conscience over the plight of American Indians. Unfortunately, resultant proposals were misconceived; see DAWES SEVERALTY ACT.

Century plant The American aloe, a plant that after some 60 years flowers on stems up to 20 feet high, and then dies.

Cephalopods See MOLLUSKS.

Cepheid variables Single stars which vary in light intensity over short periods (from a few hours to 50 days).

Cepheus A northern constellation between CASSIOPEIA, the GREAT BEAR and CYGNUS. (In Greek legend, husband of Cassiopeia.)

CEPT Initials used for the European Conference of Postal and Telecommunication Administrations, which works in conjunction with ELDO and ESRO on communications by satellite. (Initials from French title.)

Cerberus The 3-headed dog that guarded the entrance to HADES. The Sibyl who took AENEAS to the Underworld threw him a drugged cake, the first 'sop to Cerberus'.

Ceres See DEMETER.

Ceres The largest of the asteroids (or minor planets), about 400 miles across.

CERN (1954) An organization through which Western European countries cooperate in maintaining a nuclear research station at Meyrin near Geneva, equipped with a 28 GeV (28 billion electron-volt) proton synchrotron and a synchrocyclotron etc. (Initials of original name: Conseil — now Organisation — Européen pour la Recherche Nucléaire.)

Cerne Giant (UK) A figure of a man 180 ft high, with a club in his hand, cut in the downs above Cerne Abbas near Dorchester, Dorset. It may be a representation of HERCULES and date from the 2nd century AD.

Cesarewitch (UK) One of the last major races of the flat season, run at Newmarket over a distance of $2\frac{1}{4}$ miles.

Cestodes See PLATYHELMINTHS.

Cetaceans An order of aquatic mammals; the whales, dolphins, porpoises.

CETS The European Conference on Satellite Communications, which works in conjunction with ELDO and ESRO. (Initials of French title.)

Cetus The Whale, a large southern constellation below ARIES and PISCES; it contains Mira, a long-period (330-day) variable. (Latin, 'whale'; it represented the sea monster about to swallow ANDROMEDA.)

Ceylon tea There are 4 main types from different districts — Kandt, Uva, Dimbula and (the best) Nuwara Eliya; now that most teas are blend-ed, a heraldic lion appears on packages that contain a minimum of 51% Ceylon tea.

C-5A The technical designation of the Lockheed GALAXY.

Chablis A light wine, driest of the white Burgundies, traditionally drunk with oysters.

Chad, Mr A character who first appeared in a London *Daily Mirror* cartoon in 1937, his head peering over a wall, with a caption such as 'Wot — no beer?' Adopted by the troops, he appeared in wall scribblings the world over during the ensuing war years. Compare KILROY WAS HERE. (Developed from an elementary electrical circuit diagram; e.g. one eye was a + sign, the other a minus.)

Chadband, Rev. Mr The hypocritical and scarcely literate minister of an unspecified sect who, in Dickens's *Bleak House*, deploys the admired Chadband style of oratory, e.g.: What is peace? Is it war? No. Is it strife? No.

Chaeronea (338 BC) The defeat of the Athenians and their allies by Philip of Macedon, thus uniting Greece under Macedonian leadership.

Chairman Mao The usual Chinese designation for Mao Tse-tung, Chairman of the People's Government of China from 1949, and Chairman of the Central Committee of the Chinese Communist Party from 1959.

Chairman of the Council of Ministers Official designation of the Soviet Prime Minister.

Chairman of the Presidium of the Supreme Soviet Official designation of the President of USSR.

Chalcedon, Council of (451) The Ecumenical Council which condemned the MONOPHYSITE HERESY, and defined the nature of Christ as true man and true God, having 2 natures, perfectly distinct, perfectly joined, partaking of one divine substance. (Town of Bithynia, Asia Minor.)

Chaldea (1) A province of Babylonia at the head of the Persian Gulf; see CHALDEANS. (2) In the Old Testament, 'the land of the Chaldees' is used of all Babylonia.

Chaldeans (1) A Semitic race of unknown origin who settled at 'Ur of the Chaldees' (*Genesis* xi, 28) and later came to dominate the second BABYLONIAN EMPIRE. Thereafter Chaldean and Babylonian became synonymous. (2) In *Daniel* (ii, 2 and elsewhere) and in Greek writings, the Chaldeans are represented as magicians, astrologers, astronomers and mathematicians.

Chamberlain Worcester (1783-1840) Porcelain made by an English firm at Worcester founded by Robert Chamberlain, formerly employed at the main WORCESTER PORCELAIN factory. It made both soft paste and bone china and was famous for services painted with old castles on apple-green grounds. It amalgamated with FLIGHT & BARR and then traded as Chamberlain & Co.; in 1862 this firm was again named the ROYAL WORCESTER PORCELAIN CO.

Chamber of Commerce A businessmen's association formed to protect and promote the commercial interests of a city, state or country.

Chamber of Horrors A section of MADAME TUSSAUD'S, devoted to waxwork figures of famous criminals at their work.

Chambertin See CÔTE DE NUITS.

Champagne A former French province, capital Troyes, watered by the Marne. Rheims (Reims) is the center of the sparkling wine trade, famous from the 17th century onwards.

Champagne nature Nonsparkling wine from the Champagne country.

Chan, Charlie A fictional Chinese-American detective in the Honolulu police force, created by E. D. Biggers in *The House without a Key* (1925), who studied the characters of his criminal adversaries in order to predict their actions, and was much given to philosophical musings. He also appeared in a comic strip (1928) and on the screen.

Chanak crisis (Oct. 1922) Caused by Turkish entry into the Chanak neutral zone held by the British and French, just before the proclamation of the Turkish Republic by Mustapha Kemal; the Turks intended to wrest eastern Thrace from Greece. The Conservatives felt that Lloyd George acted rashly in sending reinforcements and withdrew from his coalition government at a famous Carlton Club meeting. (Chanak, the Asiatic side of the Dardanelles.)

Chance (1913) Joseph Conrad's sea story of Capt. Anthony's fidelity to Flora de Barral whose father, a fraudulent financier whom he had taken under his wing, tries to poison him.

Chancery Division (UK) The division of the High Court of Justice, nominally presided over by the Lord Chancellor, which deals, sometimes as a court of first instance, with such matters as wardship of infants, estates, real estate, partnerships and trusts. Most cases are taken in London by a judge sitting without jury. Until 1875 Chancery decisions constituted the law of Equity, as distinct from Common Law.

Chandigarh Formerly the capital of Punjab, India; claimed as capital by the 2 states of PUNJABI SUBA and HARYANA and awarded to the former in 1970. Designed by LE CORBUSIER.

Chanson de Roland (11th century) A troubadours' song of ROLAND's death at RONCESVALLES and Charlemagne's revenge on the Saracens and on Ganelon who betrayed him.

Chansons de Geste (11th-14th centuries) The epic poems of the troubadours of northern France, such as the CHANSON DE ROLAND, conforming to the traditions of courtly love and chivalry. (French, 'songs of heroic deeds'.)

'Chanticleer and Pertelote' Chaucer's version, in the *Nun's Priest's Tale*, of a theme from the REYNARD THE FOX cycle. (Pertelote, more familiar as Dame Partlet.)

Chantilly (Cooking) Served with rich cream. (French town noted for its cream.)

Chantilly porcelain (1725-1800) French soft-paste porcelain, at first covered with a tin-oxide glaze and decorated in KAKIEMON PATTERNS; from 1760 an orthodox glaze was used and MEISSEN-style decoration was introduced, in particular the

'Chantilly sprig' of cornflower and forget-me-nots (copied by DERBY PORCELAIN among others).

Chanucah, Chanukah See HANUKKAH.

'Chapeau de Poil, Le' Rubens's charming portrait of the sister of his second wife (Hélène Fourment); now in the National Gallery, London. (French, 'the beaver hat'.)

Chapel Royal (1) Clergy, musicians (now an organist) and choir, in attendance on the monarch; the institution goes back to the 12th century. (2) A similar institution at Holyrood which attends on the monarch there and at Balmoral. (3) The chapel (1532) attached to the original St James's Palace. (4) A second chapel nearby in Marlborough Gate, designed by Inigo Jones; also called the Queen's Chapel.

Chapman's Homer (1598-1615) A free translation into rhymed couplets of the *Iliad* and *Odyssey*, which inspired Keats's sonnet 'On First Looking into Chapman's Homer' (1816), where he compares the experience with that of 'Stout Cortez' staring at the Pacific, 'silent, upon a peak in Darien'.

Chapparals The Texas Chapparals, AMERICAN BASKETBALL ASSOCIATION.

Charbray A breed of cattle developed in southern US by intercrossing the CHAROLAIS with BRAHMANS.

'Charge of the Light Brigade, The' Tennyson's poem on the British cavalry charge at BALACLAVA when: Into the valley of Death / Rode the six hundred.

Chargers The San Diego Chargers, AMERICAN FOOTBALL LEAGUE. Became member of the AMERICAN CONFERENCE, NATIONAL FOOTBALL LEAGUE in 1970.

Charing Cross Road A London street traditionally associated with secondhand books and music publishing.

Charlemagne prize (1949) An annual prize awarded by citizens of Aachen to those who have contributed most to European cooperation and understanding, e.g. Churchill,

Hallstein, Spaak. (Aachen, formerly Aix-la-Chapelle, Charlemagne's capital.)

Charles's Wain Another name for the BIG DIPPER. (For 'Charlemagne's wagon', driven by neighboring AURIGA, the Wagoner.)

Charleston A peculiarly ungraceful and energetic dance, with side kicks from the knee as the chief feature, introduced in the Negro revue *Runnin' Wild* (1923). (For Charleston, S.C.)

Charley horse (1)Pain and stiffness from a bruise, usually of a thigh muscle; (2) muscular strain or soreness, especially in a leg. (Perhaps from Charley as a typical name for an old lame horse kept for family use.)

Charley's Aunt (1892) Brandon Thomas's apparently immortal farce, in which the 'aunt' is impersonated by a male undergraduate. It was the basis of George Abbott's musical, *Where's Charley?* (1949).

Charlie Brown (1) The manic-depressive chief character of PEANUTS whose self-confidence, frequently pricked, springs eternal. (2) Astronauts' name for the APOLLO 10 command module.

Charlus, Baron de In Proust's REMEMBRANCE OF THINGS PAST, a member of the GUERMANTES family, a secret homosexual who loses the violinist Morel to SAINT-LOUP.

Charmian Cleopatra's lively attendant in Shakespeare's ANTONY AND CLEOPATRA, who follows her mistress to her death.

Charolais A white breed of French cattle, imported from France in recent years to cross with US and British stock. See CHARBRAY.

Charon In Greek legend, the man who ferried the dead across the STYX to the Underworld, for one obol.

Charterhouse (1371) Originally a CARTHUSIAN monastery, near Smithfield, London; it then became a school (see CHARTERHOUSE SCHOOL). Now it is a home of rest for aged 'brethren', who must be members of the Church of England, bachelors or widowers over 60, and former officers, clergy or members of the professions.

Charterhouse School A boys' 'public' school, moved from London to Godalming, Surrey, in 1872; see CHARTERHOUSE.

Charter Oak The tree in what is now Charter Oak Place, Hartford, Conn., where the colony's royal charter of 1662 was hidden when the newly appointed high-handed governor of New England, Sir Edmund Andros, tried to seize it in 1687 as being far too liberal for his liking.

Chartists (1838-49) (English history) A group of left-wing intellectuals and workers who issued a People's Charter demanding the extension of the vote to the working classes, payment of MPs, and other reforms. There were riots at Birmingham, Newport and elsewhere, and a petition with over a million signatures was presented to the Commons.

Chartreuse A liqueur originally (and again, since 1940) made by monks at La Grande Chartreuse, the CARTHUSIAN headquarters near Grenoble; the recipe, discovered by a 16th-century alchemist, is a tight secret, but it is said to contain over 100 ingredients, of which angelica root is one. The green variety is much stronger (96% proof) than the yellow.

Chartreuse de Parme, La (1839) Stendhal's novel, a study of Italian life, which begins with a famous description of the Battle of Waterloo and ends in a Carthusian monastery.

Charybdis See SCYLLA AND CHARYBDIS.

Chateaubriand A thick tenderloin steak grilled and served with a butter-and-lemon sauce and Chateaubriand potatoes (parboiled and then broiled in butter). (From the French writer, the Vicomte de Chateaubriand, died 1848.)

Château du Prieuré A country house near Fontainebleau, where after World War I GURDJIEFF set up his Institute for the Harmonious Development of Man, which Katherine Mansfield and other intellec-

tuals attended. (French *prieuré*, 'priory'.)

Château d'Yquem See SAUTERNES.

Château Frontenac A lofty hotel and prominent landmark in the walled upper town of the City of Quebec, built in the French style by the CANADIAN PACIFIC RAILWAY. (Named for the Comte de Frontenac, governor of New France, 1672-82.)

Château Gaillard (1196) An almost impregnable fortress built by Richard I high above the Seine, to defend Normandy against the French; now in ruins. (Near Les Andelys, between Rouen and Paris.)

Château Thierry A French town associated with the first major action of US forces on the Western Front, in May 1918. (Town on the Marne, between Paris and Rheims.)

Chatsworth The 17th-century home of the Dukes of Devonshire, at Edensor, near Bakewell in Derbyshire, with many art treasures, fine gardens and parks.

Chattanooga (1863) A key point in Tennessee, won during the AMERICAN CIVIL WAR by the Union generals, Grant and Sherman, after bitter fighting.

Chautauqua A summer vacation school, sometimes combined with a course of home study, of the kind held at Chautauqua. (Village on Lake Chautauqua in southwest New York state.)

Chauvin, Nicolas A French soldier of the NAPOLEONIC WARS, an extremely bellicose patriot; he was lampooned in a number of French plays. Hence *chauvinism*, bellicose patriotism.

Chawton A village near Alton, Hampshire, where Jane Austen's home is preserved as a museum.

Cheapside A London street in the CITY, running east from St Paul's Cathedral to Poultry; once the town's principal marketplace (Anglo-Saxon *ceap*, 'barter'—which recurs in *Chipping* Camden etc.), with side streets called Bread, Milk, Wood etc. Street. The MERMAID TAVERN was there, but no buildings of note survive.

Chechen-Ingush A Russian ASSR in the north Caucasus inhabited by CIRCASSIAN Muslims, who were exiled en masse and scattered in 1944 as their loyalty was suspect. The republic was rehabilitated by Khrushchev in 1957, and survivors were free to return.

Checkpoint Charlie The most notorious of the checkpoints between East and West Berlin, at the junction of Friedrichstrasse and Zimmerstrasse, south of Leipzigerstrasse, and the only crossing point for foreigners. It was a barometer of East-West relations; when they deteriorated, the Russians would impose petty restrictions on through traffic.

Cheddar Gorge (UK) Limestone cliffs towering 400 ft over the road to Cheddar in the Somerset Mendips, with caves which were occupied by early man for tens of thousands of years.

Cheeryble brothers, The Two benevolent merchants in Dickens's NICHOLAS NICKLEBY.

Cheiro The pseudonym of Count Louis Hamon, a famous palmist who predicted the date of Edward VII's death; he was probably a clairvoyant rather than a palmist. (Name taken from cheiromancy, Greek word for palmistry, from *cheir*, 'hand'.)

Cheiron An alternative spelling of CHIRON.

Cheka (1917-22) Lenin's Secret police, formed to check counterrevolutionary activities in Communist Russia. It had full powers to arrest, try, sentence and execute. It was replaced by the OGPU. (Name formed from the initial letters of the Russian for 'Extraordinary Commission'; the full title added 'for Combating Counterrevolution, Sabotage and Speculation'.)

Chellean culture Older name for ABBEVILLEAN CULTURE.

Chelsea A former metropolitan borough of London, now part of the borough of KENSINGTON AND CHELSEA.

Chelsea-Derby (1770-83) Porcelain of the period when the CHELSEA PORCELAIN factory was made subsidiary to Derby, as indicated by the usual mark, which was a D.

Chelsea Flower Show Britain's major flower show, held in May in the gardens of CHELSEA HOSPITAL.

Chelsea Hospital (1682) Properly, Chelsea Royal Hospital, London, founded by Charles II and begun by Wren, with additions by Robert Adam; it accommodates 500 old and invalid soldier pensioners, who wear a distinctive uniform.

Chelsea porcelain (1743-69) English soft-paste wares, at first showing strong MEISSEN and Chinese influences. The red anchor period (1752-56) was the best, characterized by figures copied from Meissen, Watteau, Rubens etc.; followed by the gold anchor period (1758-69) with typical SÈVRES-type tableware. It was in this period that the characteristic elaborate bocages (leafy 'arbor' background to figures) were introduced. Early Chelsea has been extensively faked ever since 1830. See CHELSEA-DERBY.

Cheltenham Gold Cup (UK) A major steeplechase event over a course of 3¼ miles, run at Cheltenham in March.

Chemin des Dames An area between Rheims and Laon north of the Aisne, the scene of much heavy fighting in World War I from Apr. 1917 (see NIVELLE OFFENSIVE) to the end of the war.

Chequers (1921) The British Prime Minister's official country residence, presented to the state for that purpose by Lord Lee of Fareham. (Near Princes Risborough, Buckinghamshire.)

Chéri (1920) COLETTE's novel of an aging demimondaine, Léa, and her young lover, Chéri, who is torn between love for her and for his rich wife; in a sequel, *La Fin de Chéri* (1926), he kills himself.

Cherokee An Iroquois-speaking Indian race, one of the FIVE CIVILIZED NATIONS. From *c.* 1790 they assimilated the white man's skills to such effect that they made APPALACHIA into a prosperous region of farms and plantations, built churches and schools and eventually, thanks to SEQUOYA, had their own newspaper. In 1820 Georgia annexed some of their land, and in 1835 they were forced to cede the rest; they were, in accordance with Andrew Jackson's policy, sent over the TRAIL OF TEARS to Oklahoma and Tennessee, at least 4000 dying en route. Some 50,000 survive in Oklahoma and North Carolina, and regard themselves as the elite of their race.

Cherokee Strip or Outlet A vast Cherokee hunting preserve in northwest Oklahoma, at first leased to a livestock corporation, then reclaimed by the US government (1892) and thrown open to settlement.

Cherries Jubilee Cherries simmered in syrup, with KIRSCH poured on and set alight on serving.

Cherry Orchard, The (1904) Chekhov's play about an improvident landowning family who are forced to sell their estate and to hear at the end of the play the sound of their favorite orchard being cut down for a new housing estate; considering its early date, it is a remarkable preview of a major feature of life in the present century.

'Cherry Ripe' (1) One of Millais' most famous child portraits. (2) Title of a traditional song.

Cherry-Tree story See WASHINGTON AND THE CHERRY-TREE.

Cherubim First mentioned in Genesis iii, 24 as guarding the tree of life; later regarded as the second order of angels, grouped with Thrones. (Plural of *Cherub*.)

Cherwell, Viscount Professor Lindemann (died 1957), Churchill's personal adviser on scientific matters during World War II.

Cherwell, The A tributary which joins the Thames at Oxford.

Chesapeake Bay Bridge-Tunnel (1964) A toll bridge linking Cape Charles on Virginia's Eastern Shore with a point near Norfolk, Va., near the mouth of the Chesapeake Bay, thus providing a shorter route from coastal New Jersey to Florida. An engineering wonder of the US, it includes two bridges, two 1-mile tunnels and 4 artificial islands, the whole totaling, with approaches, over 17½ miles.

Cheshire Cat, The The Duchess's grinning cat in ALICE IN WONDERLAND, who has the disconcerting habit of vanishing by degrees, starting at the tail and ending with the grin. (The phrase 'to grin like a Cheshire cat' is of unknown origin, but used long before Lewis Carroll's time.)

Cheshire Cheese, The An ancient London inn (rebuilt in the 17th century) in Wine Office Court off Fleet Street, famous for old English fare, especially steak and kidney pudding, and for American tourists.

Chessie The well-known sleepy cat trade symbol of the Chesapeake and Ohio Railroad.

Chessman case (USA) An extreme example of delayed execution: Caryl Chessman was sentenced to death on a kidnaping and murder charge in 1948, but was not executed until 1960.

Chesterbelloc A composite nickname for G. K. Chesterton and Hilaire Belloc, who often collaborated in the production of books humorously illustrated by Chesterton and written by Belloc, and were likeminded Roman Catholics.

Chesterfield (1) An overcoat, originally for men but adapted for women, with velvet collar and no belt. (2) A davenport, usually with upright armrests at both ends. (Named for a 19th-century Earl.)

Chesterfield's letters (1774) Letters written by Philip Stanhope, 4th Earl of Chesterfield, to his illegitimate son, giving (disregarded) instruction in good breeding for a man of the world or, as Dr Johnson less kindly put it, teaching him the morals of a whore and the manners of a dancing master.

Chester Herald An officer of the COLLEGE OF ARMS.

Chestertonian Characterized by witty paradox, as were the writings of G. K. Chesterton.

'Chet Huntley Reporting' A national TV series on public affairs. See HUNTLEY-BRINKLEY REPORT.

Chetniks (1941) The guerrilla forces organized in Yugoslavia by Milhailović; the genuineness of their opposition to the German invaders became suspect, and Allied support was switched from them to Tito's PARTISANS.

Chevalier Bayard   A French hero of the 15th and early 16th century, known as the Chevalier sans peur et sans reproche.

Cheviot   (sheep) A breed of hill sheep, the wool of which is used in making tweeds. (Hills on the Scottish border.)

'Chevy Chase'   A ballad recounting an incident in the perennial Scottish border feud between the Percys and the Douglases.

Cheyenne   An American Indian tribe of the Great Plains, now found in Montana and Oklahoma.

Cheyenne Mountain   (1966) The site near the Warren Air Force ICBM base at Cheyenne, Wyoming, of NORAD underground headquarters, linked with the DEW-LINE and built primarily as the control center of an ABM system not yet in existence. Computers process data from early warning systems, permitting a minimum alert period of 15 minutes during which to prepare countermeasures and warn the population. It is manned by a self-contained community of about 900 men.

Cheynes-Stoke's respiration   The rhythmical waxing and waning of breathing characteristic of deep coma.

Cheyne Walk   A part of the Chelsea Embankment, London, associated with George Eliot, Rossetti, the artist Turner and many other famous people; in nearby Cheyne Row lived Thomas Carlyle. (Named after the former owner of the manor of Chelsea.)

Chi   Short for Chicago.

Chianti   An Italian wine produced in the mountainous area around Siena, Tuscany, and bottled in distinctive straw-covered bottles.

Chicago fire   (1871) A fire which, raging from October 8th to 11th, destroyed the heart of the city and caused damage estimated at $196 million. According to legend it was started by a cow kicking over a lantern in the barn of a Mrs O'Leary.

Chichen Itza   An 11th-century Maya city in Yucatan, Mexico, with splendid ruins excavated from 1924 onwards.

Chichester Theatre Festival   (1962) (England) A season of drama, old and new, staged annually from June to September at the Festival Theatre, Chichester, Sussex. The audience surrounds the stage on 3 sides.

Chichikov   The 'hero' of Gogol's DEAD SOULS.

Chicken à la Derby   Chicken served with rice and foie gras.

Chicken à la King   Creamed diced chicken spiced with pimento or green pepper.

Chicken Maryland   Chicken dipped in egg and bread crumbs, fried, and served with banana and sweet corn.

Chicken War   (1963) A dispute between the USA and the Common Market, in which America threatened retaliation for a prohibitive tariff on frozen poultry.

Chickasaw   A race of MUSKOGEAN INDIANS, originally of the Alabama-Mississippi region and one of the FIVE CIVILIZED NATIONS. They fought against the Spanish and with the English against the French. Their language is very similar to CHOCTAW. Some 5000 survive in northern Mississippi and Oklahoma, where they have benefited from mineral rights in coal. They are mostly Presbyterians.

Chicot the Jester   A French court jester who appears in several novels by Dumas.

Chiefs   The Kansas City (Mo.) Chiefs, AMERICAN FOOTBALL LEAGUE. Became member of the AMERICAN CONFERENCE, NATIONAL FOOTBALL LEAGUE in 1970.

Chief Whip   (UK) An MP responsible for the discipline of his party; his main task is, with his assistants, to secure the maximum necessary attendance of his party at a division (i.e. when a vote is taken) by written summons (also called a whip), on important occasions underlined 3 times ('3-line whip'). The government Chief Whip is salaried and holds the office of Parliamentary (Patronage) Secretary to the Treasury, responsible for recommending promotions and honors. (Abbreviation for 'whipper-in'.)

Chi'en Lung (1736-95) An emperor of the CH'ING DYNASTY during whose long reign artistic works became overelaborate and thereafter deteriorated, never to recover.

Childe Harold Romantic hero of Byron's autobiographical poem, who turns from revelry to make a European pilgrimage. (*Childe*, a medieval title for a youth of noble birth.)

Childermas Archaic name of the Feast of HOLY INNOCENTS.

Childe Roland The hero of a Scottish ballad ('Childe Roland to the dark tower came', *King Lear*, iii, 4) who rescued his sister from the fairies. Browning's poem of the same name has no connection with the ballad. (For *Childe*, see CHILDE HAROLD.)

Children's Hour, The (1) Longfellow's poem (1860) about the 3 daughters of his first marriage. (2) A play by Lillian Hellman (1934) about the results of a girl's starting a rumor that 2 of her teachers are Lesbians.

Childs Cup Regatta A race inaugurated in 1879, making it the second oldest intercollegiate fixture, as a contest between Columbia, Princeton and Pennsylvania universities. It lapsed in 1884 but was revived in 1912 as a duel between Princeton and Pennsylvania over a course of 1$\frac{7}{16}$ miles at various venues. (Trophy given by George W. Childs, publisher of the *Philadelphia Ledger*.)

Chillingham cattle Wild white cattle, reputed to be the survivors of the original wild ox of Britain, which still roam wild on Lord Tankerville's estate near Berwick, Northumberland.

Chiltern Hundreds (UK) The stewardship of the Chiltern Hundreds is a fictitious 'office of profit from the Crown', to which a member of Parliament is appointed if he wants to resign; this overcomes the difficulty that by law no MP may resign, since the appointment automatically disqualifies him from membership. See NORTHSTEAD, MANOR OF.

Chilton Club An exclusive women's club in Boston, Mass.

Chimaera In Greek legend a fire-breathing monster with a goat's body, dragon's tail and lion's head, killed by BELLEROPHON mounted on PEGASUS.

Chimène The wife of El CID. (French spelling of Ximena.)

China, The Republic of American euphemism for Formosa (Taiwan).

Chinaman's chance Marginally slimmer than BUCKLEY'S CHANCE.

Chinatown The Chinese quarter of a city, especially the crowded enclave in San Francisco, with the largest Chinese population outside Asia, which lies between the city's financial, hotel and apartment house districts, adjoining the BARBARY COAST on North Beach.

Chindits The British long-range penetration brigade which fought in Burma behind the Japanese lines under Brig. Orde Wingate, formed by Gen. Wavell in July 1942. (Burmese *Chinthay*, a mythical beast, the unit's badge.)

Ch'in dynasty (221-206 BC) A short but brilliant period of Chinese history, which saw the building of the GREAT WALL, the institution of the Mandarin civil-service system of orderly government, and the decline of the feudalism of the CHOU DYNASTY. The capital was near Sian (Shensi Province). The HAN DYNASTY followed.

Chinese checkers A form of checkers using a board in the form of a 6-pointed star; each of the 2-6 players starts with 10 colored marbles arranged in holes in one of the 6 sections, and tries to transfer them to the section opposite using the moves of the standard game.

Chinese Eastern Railroad (1904) A line built by the Russians from Chita through Manchuria to Vladivostok; until 1916 it served as the final stage of the TRANS-SIBERIAN RAILROAD. Its ownership became a bone of contention and Soviet Russia sold it to MANCHUKUO in 1935.

Chinese Lowestoft A term used commonly, but mistakenly, for Chinese porcelain made for the European market which happened to resemble in decoration, though not in shape, contemporary (English) LOWESTOFT PORCELAIN.

Chinese puzzle (1) The tangram (etymology unknown), a square of material cut into 5 triangles, a square and a lozenge; these can be arranged in over 300 figures. (2) Hence anything very complicated.

Chinese restaurant syndrome A set of symptoms, e.g. numbness of the neck and arms, dizziness, palpitations, that affects some people after eating Chinese food in a Chinese restaurant, caused by various agents including monosodium glutamate (MSG).

Ch'ing dynasty (1644-1912) The Manchu dynasty, last of the Chinese imperial dynasties; their capital was Peking. The MANCHUS forced the Chinese to wear the pigtail as a token of loyalty to the new regime. In art there were 2 main periods, the K'ANG HSI and the CHI'EN LUNG.

Chingford (UK) A former borough of Essex, since 1965 part of the new borough of WALTHAM FOREST.

Chinook (1) American Indians who once inhabited the Columbia valley from California to British Columbia. (2) Name given to the FÖHN wind that blows down the eastern slopes of the Rockies on to the western prairies. Being warm and dry, it may melt up to 2 ft of snow in 24 hours. A 'wet Chinook' is a warm moist southwester on the coasts of Washington and Oregon.

Chinook State A nickname for Washington.

Chippendale English furniture made by a generation of fine cabinetmakers, of whom Thomas Chippendale (1718-79) was but one, his name having come to represent them solely because he published a book of designs (1754 with later revisions) which were widely copied. The characteristics were a restrained Rococo style of flowing lines, plentiful carving, and strength combined with elegance. There were also Gothic and Chinese designs; and Chippendale himself in his later years produced furniture in the quite different ADAM STYLE. The furniture of later generations in these styles is also called 'Chippendale'.

Chippewa A corruption of the name OJIBWA.

Chips, Mr The schoolmaster of James Hilton's novel Goodbye, Mr Chips (1934).

Chips with Everything Wesker's play (1962) attacking the arrogance of the Establishment and the submissiveness to it of the sort of people who 'eat chips (i.e. French fries) with everything'.

Chiron The most famous of the CENTAURS and, untypically, represented as wise and learned in medicine and music. He taught many of the greatest legendary heroes, notably ACHILLES, and was accidentally killed by Heracles (HERCULES).

Chisholm Trail This once ran from San Antonio, Tex., to Montana and was the scene of the LONG DRIVE to Kansas and Nebraska; it is now part of the National Trail system. See 'OLD CHISHOLM TRAIL'.

Chislehurst and Sidcup (UK) A former urban district of Kent, now divided between the boroughs of BEXLEY and BROMLEY.

Chisox Short for Chicago WHITE SOX.

Chiuchuan The site in Kansu Province, China, of the missile-testing ground where China's first hydrogen bomb was tested in 1967. It lies in the Nan Shan mountain area 200 miles north of Lake KOKO NOR. (Also spelt Kiuchuan.)

Chloe See DAPHNIS AND CHLOE.

Chocolate Soldier, The (1908) Oscar Straus's comic opera based on Bernard Shaw's ARMS AND THE MAN.

Choctaw MUSKOGEAN INDIANS originally of the Alabama-Mississippi region, and one of the FIVE CIVILIZED NATIONS. Their language is very similar to CHICKASAW. They fought on the Confederate side in the Civil War and were then transported to Arkansas. Through intermarriage with white and black they have lost their racial identity to a great extent, but some survive in Oklahoma, where they have benefited from mineral rights on coal. They are mostly Presbyterians.

Choral Symphony, The (1823) Beethoven's 9th Symphony, in which the climax of the last movement is, uniquely, vocal – Schiller's 'Ode to Joy': Freude, schöner Götterfunke,/ Tochter aus Elysium ('Joy, spark of God, daughter of Elysium'.)

Chosen Name given to Korea after it was annexed by Japan in 1910.

Chou dynasty (1050-256 BC) An early Chinese dynasty during which a type of feudalism evolved.

Christadelphians (1848) An American sect of the ADVENTIST type, founded by an Englishman in New York.

Christian The hero of PILGRIM'S PROGRESS who makes the pilgrimage to the Celestial City.

Christian Action (UK) A movement founded (1946) by Canon Collins 'to put religion into politics'; it espoused postwar reconciliation with the Germans, opposition to apartheid, and the CND.

Christian Democrats A name widely adopted in Europe by political parties of the center, which usually draw their support from both Protestants and Catholics and from all social classes. Formerly they opposed liberals (in the continental sense of free-thinking anticlericals) and Socialists, but now often join with them in attacking antidemocratic parties of left or right.

Christian Endeavor (1881) An international society founded to promote spiritual life among the young, with the motto 'For Christ and the Church'. It grew from a society formed at a Congregational church in Portland, Me., and works principally in nonepiscopal fields.

Christian Science (1866) An American religion founded by Mary Baker Eddy, who believed that, since God is good, sin, disease and death exist only for those who are blinded by error. See NEW THOUGHT.

Christian Science Monitor (1908) A daily evening paper founded by Mrs Eddy (see last entry) to fight the YELLOW PRESS; published at Boston, Mass., it still has an international reputation for its coverage of world news.

Christian Socialism (1848) A movement started in England by F. D. Maurice and the novelist Charles Kingsley, advocating active participation in social reform by the Church. One of its more recent intellectual leaders was the American theologian, Reinhold Niebuhr. Protestant and Catholic clergy who take factory jobs and try to bring Christianity to the workshop are among the modern representatives of the movement.

Christie's London auction rooms, a close rival of SOTHEBY'S in international reputation, situated in St James's.

'Christina's World' (1948) A striking tempera painting by Andrew Wyeth showing a girl lying in a seemingly limitless field, looking back at a house; it has the typical Wyeth combination of realism and illusion. (Museum of Modern Art, NYC.)

Christmas Carol, A Dickens's story; see SCROOGE, EBENEZER.

Christmas club A savings account into which regular, usually weekly, deposits are made throughout the year to meet Christmas shopping needs.

Christmas Island The scene of the detonation in 1957 of the first British hydrogen bomb; a Pacific island halfway between Hawaii and Tahiti. (There is another Christmas Island in the Indian Ocean.)

Christmas tree Name given to the flashing red, yellow and green lights used to start drag races.

Christopher Robin The hero of A. A. Milne's children's books and many of his verses, e.g. WHEN WE WERE VERY YOUNG; he is the author's son.

Christ Scientist, First Church of The mother church of CHRISTIAN SCIENCE, in Boston, Mass.

Christ's Hospital (1552) Originally a 'hospital' for foundlings established by Edward VI on a London site now occupied by St Bartholomew's Hospital and the GPO; it soon became a school, which developed into the 'public' school moved to Horsham, Sussex, in 1902; also called the Blue-coat School (the boys wearing a uniform of blue coats and yellow stockings). A girls' school of the same foundation was moved to Hertford.

Christy Abbreviation for Christiania, a basic skiing turn with skis kept parallel.

Christy Minstrels One of the earliest blackface minstrel shows, who played in New York and London in the 1840s. (E. Christy, American impresario.)

Chronicles (4th century BC) A book of the Old Testament which repeats much of *Samuel* and *Kings*.

Chrysler (1925) A car-manufacturing corporation based in Detroit, which bought up Dodge Motors (1928) and later gained control of the Rootes Group in Britain and of Simca in France. Chrysler also makes boats, marine and industrial engines, refrigerators and space research equipment. One of the 30 industrials that make up the DOW JONES Industrial Average.

Chu Chin Chow (1916) A spectacular musical based on the ALI BABA story in the ARABIAN NIGHTS; starring Oscar Asche and Lily Brayton, it held the record for the longest London run until *The* MOUSETRAP surpassed it.

Chunnel Newspaper-headline name for the projected (English) Channel Tunnel.

Churchill College (1960) A new college of CAMBRIDGE UNIVERSITY, named in honor of Sir Winston Churchill.

Churchill Downs The racetrack at Louisville, Ky., scene of the KENTUCKY DERBY.

Churchill literary award (1967) A biennial prize of £5000 for a work in English by an author under 40 on any aspect of the history of the English-speaking peoples. (Named in honor of Sir Winston Churchill, author of a *History of the English-speaking Peoples*; administered by Cassels, Churchill's publishers.)

Chuzzlewit, Martin See MARTIN CHUZZLEWIT.

CIA (1947) Initials used for the US Central Intelligence Agency, with headquarters in the Washington suburb of McLean, Va.; it gathers political and military intelligence, conducts psychological warfare, supports anti-Communist groups abroad, and was responsible for the BAY OF PIGS fiasco.

Ciba (1884) A Swiss group with headquarters at Basle, which makes industrial chemicals, dyes, resins, adhesives and drugs. In 1969 it merged with Geigy, which makes agricultural chemicals, cosmetics and medical electronic equipment.

Ciba Foundation (1947) An international scientists' club established by Ciba Ltd (see last entry) in Portland Place, London, to promote international cooperation in medical and chemical research, including biochemistry, endocrinology and geriatrics. Symposia, study groups, an annual foundation lecture, and publications of proceedings are features of its work.

'Cicero' Nom de guerre of a spy in World War II who was valet to a British ambassador; he was falsely credited with handing over the full details of OVERLORD to the Germans.

CID CRIMINAL INVESTIGATION DEPARTMENT.

Cid, El The 11th-century Castilian hero Don Rodrigo, whose story is told in many medieval ballads and by later authors, including Corneille (1637); he won fame by his campaigns against (and, during a period of disgrace, for) the Moors. (Corruption of Arabic *Al-Sidi* or *As-sayyid*, 'lord'.)

Cider with Rosie (1959) The English poet Laurie Lee's delightful account of his childhood in a Cotswold village in the early 1920s, where he was brought up by his deserted, penniless but resourceful mother with 7 other children, 5 of them her stepchildren.

Cigar-store Indian The wooden figure of an Indian, placed at the door to advertise a cigar store.

Cimarron (1930) Edna Ferber's novel (made into a movie, 1960), in which the Oklahoma land rush of 1889 and the later oil boom are the setting for the story of the decline of a lawyer-editor and the rise of his capable wife, who eventually enters Congress. (A river of northwest Oklahoma.)

Cimmerians People who, according to Homer, lived in a land of eternal night; later applied to a coastal tribe of the Black Sea region, from whom the name Crimea is derived.

Cincinnatus A legendary Roman hero called 'from the plow' in the 5th century BC to save Rome from its enemies. Having succeeded in this, he declined office and honors, and returned to his plow 16 days later.

Cincy Colloquial abbreviation for Cincinnati, O.

Cinderella (1) Heroine of a fairy tale, probably of oriental origin. The story of the family drudge whose fairy godmother sends her to a ball at which a prince falls in love with her is used in Rossini's opera *La Cenerentola* (1817). (2) A ballet (1948), based on this story, created for the SADLER'S WELLS Ballet, with music by Prokofiev and choreography by Frederick Ashton.

CinemaScope (1953) The first widescreen cinema system, used for spectacular movies in color.

Cinerama (1952) A cinema system employing 3 cameras, 3 projectors, a wide curved screen and stereophonic sound, to produce an illusion of actuality.

Cinna The Roman leader of a conspiracy against Augustus. In Corneille's play, *Cinna* (1640), he is betrayed by the rejected suitor of Amélie, the woman who loves him, but is pardoned by Augustus.

Cinquecento Italian for '16th century', used of the style of architecture and art that followed the Renaissance; see MANNERISM. See QUATTROCENTO. (Italian, '500' for '1500', i.e. the 1500s.)

Cinque Ports An ancient confederation of Channel ports reconstituted by William the Conqueror and given special privileges in return for supplying ships and men. The original five were Dover, Hastings, Sandwich, Romney and Hythe, later joined by Winchelsea and Rye; there

are also associated towns or 'limbs' (Folkestone, Deal, Margate etc.). The Lord Warden is an honorary appointment, with an official residence at Walmer Castle, near Deal; there are also Barons of the Cinque Ports. (French *cinq*, 'five'.)

CIO (1935) John L. Lewis's trade union organization, see AFL/CIO.

Circassian A people, and CAUCASIAN LANGUAGE, of Georgia, USSR, whose womenfolk were from early times renowned for their beauty and highly prized as slaves and concubines. (Russian name.)

Circe In Greek legend, an enchantress who turns Ulysses' men into swine; Ulysses himself, protected from a like fate by the gods, compels her to restore them to human form. She then becomes more friendly, and gives Ulysses useful advice, and also a son. See also ODYSSEUS.

Circumlocution Office Dickens's caricature of a government department in LITTLE DORRIT, manned by such people as Barnacle Junior, author of the remark: Upon my soul you mustn't come into the place saying you want to know, you know.

Cirencester Park A polo ground reopened by Earl Bathurst in 1952, near Cirencester, Gloucestershire.

Cisalpine Gaul An ancient Roman province of northern Italy, consisting of the fertile Po valley region colonized by Gauls from over the Alps. See CISALPINE REPUBLIC.

Cisalpine Republic (1797) A union of the states of North Italy formed by Napoleon after his successful Italian campaign. (Latin, 'this side of the Alps'.)

Cistercians (1098) A reformed order of BENEDICTINES, further reformed by St Bernard of Clairvaux (12th century), and revived by the TRAPPISTS. (*Cistercium*, Latin name of Cîteaux, near Dijon, France, where founded.)

CIT Initials used for the Compagnia Italiana Turismo, an Italian travel agency with branches in most towns.

Citadel, The The historic center of Halifax, NS, built on a hill and once one of the strongest fortresses in the

British Empire; it is now a national historic park with a museum, forts and palisades.

Citadel, The (1842) A state college for men, in Charleston, S.C.

Cité radieuse See UNITÉS D'HABITATION.

Cities of the Plain Sodom and Gomorrah (*Genesis* xix, 29).

Citizen Kane (1940) A movie written and directed by Orson Welles, who also starred in it, about a journalist who tries to find out the real facts concerning the recently deceased Kane, who bears a striking resemblance to William Randolph Hearst, the newspaper proprietor.

Citizen King, The Another name for Louis Philippe, KING OF THE FRENCH.

City, The The SQUARE MILE that was the Roman town of Londinium, scene of the GREAT FIRE OF LONDON after which Wren rebuilt 52 of its churches (including St Paul's Cathedral), and, 3 centuries later, of the CITY OF LONDON BLITZ which destroyed many of them again. Long since the financial and commercial center of the UK, it contains the BANK OF ENGLAND (see OLD LADY OF THREADNEEDLE STREET), the Stock Exchange, MINCING LANE, BILLINGSGATE etc. Its independence, with its own Lord Mayor and Corporation, its GUILDHALL, LIVERYMEN, police etc., is symbolized by the tradition that the Sovereign may not enter the City without the Lord Mayor handing over the keys of the TEMPLE BAR (even though it is not there). See BARBICAN DEVELOPMENT.

City of Dreadful Night, The (1874) James Thomson's long pessimistic poem about an imaginary city, the product of the poet's nocturnal perambulations of London during bouts of insomnia.

City of London blitz (29 Dec. 1940) The heavy incendiary raid which destroyed the GUILDHALL and several Wren churches.

City University, The (1966) A new university in the CITY of London, with large engineering departments; formerly the Northampton CAT (named after the Marquess of Northampton).

Ciudad Trujillo (1936-61) Name of the capital of the Dominican Republic during the dictatorship of President Trujillo; on his assassination the old name of Santo Domingo was restored.

Civil Aeronautics Board (1940) A US Federal agency that regulates tariffs, fares, mail rates and other economic aspects of commercial air transport.

Civil Air Patrol A civilian organization of people interested in flying and space projects, since 1948 an auxiliary of the US Air Force. Over half the members are teen-agers and a fifth are girls; they are given instruction courses organized by the headquarters at Ellington AFB, Tex.

Civil Liberties Union See AMERICAN CIVIL LIBERTIES UNION.

Civil List (UK) The annual grant made by Parliament to the Monarch to cover the maintenance of the Royal Household, but not the upkeep of palaces, grants to other members of the Royal Family etc. See CROWN ESTATE COMMISSIONERS.

Civil Rights Commission (1964) The body set up under the Civil Rights Act to ensure the ending of segregation and of discrimination in voting qualifications between whites and Negroes, as well as the provision of equal opportunity for employment, pay and promotion.

Civil Service Commission (1883) A US government board of 3 bipartisan members, set up to substitute the merit system for President Jackson's spoils system in the appointment of Federal civil servants. Its success in converting 95% of appointments to full-time Federal executive posts to this system has induced 30 State governments to follow its lead.

Civil War See AMERICAN (ENGLISH, SPANISH) CIVIL WAR.

Clapham Common murder (1911) The murder on Clapham Common, London, of Léon Béron. Steinie Morrison, a burglar and pimp, was sentenced to death; reprieved by Winston Churchill, then Home Secretary, he starved himself to death in prison, vigorously protesting his innocence to the end.

Clapham Sect A politically powerful 18th-century coterie of evangelical humanitarians, led by the abolitionists William Wilberforce and Thomas Clarkson. Most of them lived at Clapham (then a village near London). Also called the Saints. The sect is mentioned in Gosse's FATHER AND SON.

Clapper (Raymond) Memorial Award (1944) An annual award of $1000 for exceptionally meritorious journalism; winners are selected by the American Society of Newspaper Editors.

Clarence House (1825) The house adjoining ST. JAMES'S PALACE, London, which was the home of Princess Elizabeth and the Duke of Edinburgh, and later of the Queen Mother. (Built for William IV when Duke of Clarence.)

Clarendon Code (1661-65) The 4 Statutes passed by the CAVALIER PARLIAMENT against the wishes of Charles II and, despite the name, of Lord Clarendon; they excluded Catholics and PURITANS from office (Corporation Act), expelled nonconforming clergy from the Church (ACT OF UNIFORMITY), banned nonconformist forms of worship (Conventicle Act) and teaching and preaching within 5 miles of a town (Five Mile Act).

Clarendon Laboratory The main physics laboratory at OXFORD UNIVERSITY.

Clarendon Press Another name for the Oxford University Press, now in London; more strictly applied to publications of that Press published in Oxford itself. (From Clarendon House, Oxford, built with profits from the publication in 1704 of Clarendon's history of the English Civil War.)

'Classical' Symphony Prokofiev's Symphony No. 1 in D minor, an early and amusing little work which became widely popular.

Claudine Heroine of 4 of COLETTE'S semiautobiographical novels of adolescence (1900-03).

Claudius In Shakespeare's play, the King of Denmark, uncle and stepfather of HAMLET, who married Hamlet's mother so precipitately as a form of thrift, Hamlet scornfully suggests, for: the funeral bak'd meats / Did coldly furnish forth the marriage tables.

Claudius the God See I, CLAUDIUS.

Clay, Cassius US Negro boxing champion who took the name of Muhammad Ali when he joined the BLACK MUSLIMS.

Clayhanger Family, The (1925) Arnold Bennett's trilogy of novels of the FIVE TOWNS. Clayhanger (1910) tells of Edwin Clayhanger's difficult courtship of Hilda; Hilda Lessways (1911) retells the story from her point of view; These Twain (1916) describes their life together. The work is notable for its many references to contemporary events.

Claymore mine A land mine that is shaped like a flattened brick slightly curved from end to end and that upon explosion sprays fragments into an arc.

Clearances, The Evictions of Scottish Highland crofters so that landowners could introduce sheep farming. They continued from 1750 on into the 19th century; many of the crofters emigrated to Canada and the USA.

Clear Grit Reformers (1850) A radical movement in Western Canada (compare ROUGES) reflecting agrarian discontent with the Dominion government and demanding US-style democracy. (From a leader's remark; 'We want only men who are clear grit'; also called Grits. The name is sometimes still applied to the Liberals.)

Cleon Athenian demagogue and general of the 5th century BC, son of a tanner and a favorite butt of Aristophanes.

Cleopatra Joint ruler of Egypt with her brother in the 1st century BC, deposed after his death; restored to her throne by Julius Caesar, by whom she had a son; aided against Augustus by Antony, by whom she had 3 children, but whom she deserted at ACTIUM. See next 2 entries.

Cleopatra's Needle Name given to 2 Ancient Egyptian inscribed obelisks

(1600 BC) erected at Heliopolis and later moved to Alexandria. One now stands on the Thames Embankment, London, and the other in CENTRAL PARK, New York. (No connection with Cleopatra.)

Cleopatra's nose An allusion to Pascal's famous note: 'Cleopatra's nose: had it been shorter, the whole face of the earth would have been changed'.

Clerihew A type of 4-line nonsense biography invented by E. Clerihew Bentley (author of TRENT'S LAST CASE), of which a typical example is: 'George the Third / Ought never to have occurred. / One can only wonder / At so grotesque a blunder'. They were published as *Biography for Beginners* (1919).

'Clerk Saunders' A Scottish border ballad telling how a brother slew his sister's lover as she lay in his arms.

Clerk's Tale, The In the CANTERBURY TALES, the story of the patient GRISELDA.

Clermont A twin-paddle-wheel riverboat powered by a Watt steam engine and designed by Robert Fulton which in 1807 pioneered commercial steamboat navigation by a voyage up the Hudson from New York to Albany.

Clichy paperweights Weights made in the Paris suburb of that name *c.* 1840-70, remarkable for their striking color effects. They are rarely marked and, unlike BACCARAT PAPERWEIGHTS, never dated but a distinctive 'Clichy' rose is usually part of the design; spiral designs ('swirls') are also typical.

Cliff Dwellers (1) The prehistoric ancestors of the PUEBLO INDIANS who built high rock dwellings in northwest Mexico and southwest USA, of which examples can be seen in the MESA VERDE NATIONAL PARK and at MONTEZUMA CASTLE. They made characteristic black-on-white pottery. See ANASAZI CULTURE. (2) Nickname for people who live in lofty apartment houses. (Perhaps from Henry Fuller's novel of that title, 1893.)

Clio In Greek legend, the muse of history.

Cliveden set The group of British political notabilities who gathered at Cliveden, the Buckinghamshire home of the 2nd Viscount Astor and his wife Nancy, thought to have influenced British foreign policy in the 1930s, especially towards German appeasement in order to contain Bolshevism. The Astors denied its existence; Claud Cockburn claims to have invented the term in his news sheet *The Week*.

Cloister and the Hearth, The (1861) Charles Reade's 15th-century historical novel, which gives a romantic version of the birth of Erasmus.

Cloisters, The A branch of the Metropolitan Museum of Art at Fort Tryon Park, NYC, on the Hudson; there are 5 reconstructed cloisters, with a collection of European medieval art, including paintings, sculpture, stained glass, tapestries, furniture and metalwork.

Clostridium A genus of bacteria which do not need oxygen (are anaerobic); some of them attack the nervous system, as in lockjaw and botulism.

Closure, The (1882) (Parliament) A device to bring unfruitful debate to an end, taking the form of a motion 'That the question be now put'. If carried, the matter under debate is then put to the vote. The US cloture.

Clotho One of the 3 FATES.

Cloudcuckooland An ideal city in the clouds, built in Aristophanes' *The* BIRDS by 2 young men, dissatisfied with Athenian political life, with the help of the birds. From this base they blackmail the gods into accepting their demands by intercepting the savory smells of sacrifices on earth so that they do not reach up to heaven.

Cloud of Unknowing (14th century) A famous mystical work of unknown authorship.

Clouds, The (423 BC) Aristophanes' comedy which attacks Socrates by grossly distorting his methods and confusing him with the worst of the Sophists, as a man who can make the worse appear the better cause.

CLU Initials used for (1) (AMERICAN) CIVIL LIBERTIES UNION (1920); (2) Chartered Life Underwriter.

Club Row market A London street market for animals, birds and aquarium fish, behind Bishopsgate station.

Cluniacs An order of monks which separated from the BENEDICTINES in the 11th century. It became very rich, with several opulent Romanesque daughter abbeys, and was frowned on by St Bernard and the CISTERCIANS. (Cluny Abbey, near Mâcon, France.)

Clyde Fortnight Scotland's premier regatta, held in July and catering particularly for keelboat classes, especially the DRAGON.

Clydesdale A farmhorse bred in Lanarkshire, Scotland, in color dark brown or black with white markings.

Clydesdale Colliery disaster (1960) South Africa's worst mining disaster, in which 435 miners were killed at Coalbrook, Orange Free State.

Clytemnestra In Greek legend, the half sister of Helen of Troy, whom AGAMEMNON forcibly married after killing her first husband. She murdered Agamemnon because he had sacrificed her daughter, IPHIGENEIA.

CND (1958) Initials used for the Campaign for Nuclear Disarmament, a movement launched by Bertrand Russell advocating the abolition of nuclear weapons. See ALDERMASTON MARCH; COMMITTEE OF 100.

Cnossus Latin spelling of KNOSSOS.

CNR See CANADIAN NATIONAL RAILWAYS.

Coalbrookdale porcelain See COALPORT.

Coalport (1796) An English porcelain factory founded by John Rose, who later bought up the CAUGHLEY, SWANSEA and NANTGARW factories; it made tableware in the style of CHELSEA, MEISSEN etc. and was fond of gaudy applied flowers. After changes of ownership it moved to the POTTERIES in 1926 and continued to make tablewares, with green and rose grounds. Sometimes called Coalbrookdale. (Village in Coalbrookdale, south of Wellington, Shropshire.)

Coastal Command A section of the RAF which during World War II operated with naval support against enemy submarines and surface craft, and was based on the British Isles, Gibraltar and Iceland.

Coast Guard Academy, US (1876) A military academy in New London, Conn., entered by competitive examination and offering a 4-year course in seamanship, engineering, military training etc. together with cultural education. Successful graduates receive a BS degree and are commissioned as Ensigns.

Cóbh The port for Cork, formerly known as Queenstown.

Cobol A business language for programming computers, consisting of common English words, phrases and sentences reduced to code form (as in a telegraph code). (For Common Business Oriented Language.)

Coca-Cola (1885) A soft drink, first marketed in Atlanta, Ga., as a brain tonic, by a purveyor of patent medicines. It now contains 14 ingredients, including coca, kola-nut extract, caffeine and a secret substance called 7X. (Often abbreviated to 'Coke'.)

Cocacolaization A term coined in France for the infiltration of European culture by the American way of life as a result of World War II, symbolized by the phenomenal sales of COCA-COLA, even in wine-drinking France.

Cochin China A former French colony, now part of South Vietnam.

Cockaigne, Land of In medieval legend, a land of luxury and idleness; the name has been applied, as a pun, to the land of the COCKNEYS, i.e. London.

Cocker, According to Correct, accurate. (Edward Cocker, author of a 17th-century arithmetic book.)

Cock Lane Ghost (1762) A hoax at Smithfield, London. A man invented a story about rappings in his house by the ghost of a murdered woman, actually by his daughter.

'Cockles and Mussels' A traditional Irish song: In Dublin's fair city, / where the girls are so pretty, / I first set my eyes on sweet Molly Malone . . . / Crying, Cockles and mussels! alive, alive, oh!

Cockney (1) A 'cockered' (i.e. pampered) child; (2) a soft townsman; (3) a Londoner, later defined as one

born within the sound of BOW BELLS;
(4) the dialect spoken by (3).

Cockney School Derisive name given in BLACKWOOD'S MAGAZINE to a group of writers living in London, including Keats, Shelley, Hazlitt and Leigh Hunt.

Cockpit of Europe, The Belgium, whose unhappy destiny it has been to provide the terrain for many a major battle between the Great Powers.

Cock Robin In the nursery rhyme 'Who killed Cock Robin?', perhaps BALDER or some other figure of Scandinavian myth; but the name gained wider currency when applied to Robert Walpole on his fall from power in 1742.

Cocktail Party, The (1949) T. S. Eliot's drama on the eternal Christian verities, written in conversational verse. At the party, a stranger (God, the psychiatrist) warns Edward that his decision to abandon his mistress Celia and return to his wife will have unforeseen consequences. Later the stranger lectures him on the 2 Christian ways of life — the acceptance of the humdrum obligations of everyday marriage, and the path of self-abnegation chosen by Celia, who goes as a missionary to the tropics, where she is murdered.

Cocoanut Grove fire, The (1942) A fire at a Boston (Mass.) nightclub, in which 491 people died.

Cocytus In Greek legend the river of wailing, one of the rivers of the Underworld.

COD Initials used for Cash (or Collect) on Delivery.

COD Initials used for the *Concise Oxford Dictionary.*

Code Napoléon (1803-04) The codification of French civil law carried out under the direction of Napoleon as First Consul, the basis of the *Code Civil* today.

Codlin and Short Two characters in *The* OLD CURIOSITY SHOP, who run a traveling Punch and Judy show. Short is a nice little man, but the evil-minded Codlin, eager to make money out of Little Nell's grandfather, assures her that: Codlin's the

friend, not Short.

Coelenterates A phylum of invertebrate, mostly marine animals, including jellyfish, sea anemones, corals and the Portuguese man-of-war.

Cognac Brandy made from grapes grown in the immediate vicinity of the town of Cognac, on the Charente west of Angoulême.

Cohen inquiry (1955) An investigation into the COMET air disasters of 1954; it found that they were due to metal fatigue.

Coinage Act (1) The act effected February 12, 1873 which temporarily discontinued the coinage of the US silver dollar. (2) The act of July 23, 1965 which authorized a change in the metallic composition of US half dollars, quarters and dimes to clad or composite-type coins.

Cointreau A white CURAÇAO liqueur.

Coke of Norfolk Thomas Coke, Earl of Leicester, of Holkham (1754-1842), who revolutionized English agriculture through his introduction of greatly improved methods at HOLKHAM HALL.

Colbert (Cooking) Fish egged and crumbed before frying; tarragon-flavored butter sauce served with it.

Cold Comfort Farm (1932) A riotous skit by Stella Gibbons on the gloomy rustic school of novelists (Hardy, PRECIOUS BANE etc.). Grandma when young had seen 'something nasty in the woodshed' which seemed to color her whole life, though she never explained what it was. The purple passages were marked with asterisks for the greater convenience of the reader.

Coldstream Guards (1650) The second oldest regiment in the British Army (after the Royal Scots), originally Gen. Monk's regiment. They wear their buttons in pairs, and a scarlet plume. See BRIGADE OF GUARDS. (Village on the Scots border where they were stationed at the Restoration.)

Coleoptera The beetles, an insect order with horny forewings, the grubs of some of which do great damage, e.g. the boll weevil to cotton, and the wireworm of click beetles, a garden pest.

Colette Maiden name, also pen name, of Gabrielle Colette, French novelist who wrote of CLAUDINE and CHÉRI. She also used the pen name Collette WILLY. (Died 1954.)

College of Arms (1483) A royal corporation under the Earl Marshal (the Duke of Norfolk), authorized to grant armorial bearings, and responsible for all matters concerning the armorial bearings and pedigrees of English, Irish and Commonwealth families. Scottish families are dealt with by LYON KING OF ARMS.

Collins, Mr The pompous snob of a country parson who has the effrontery to woo Elizabeth Bennet in Jane Austen's PRIDE AND PREJUDICE. See next entry.

Collins A bread-and-butter letter of thanks for hospitality received; named after Mr Collins (see last entry) who wrote one to Mr Bennet 'with all the solemnity of gratitude which a twelvemonth's abode in the family might have prompted'.

Collins A long iced drink of lemon juice with gin (JOHN COLLINS, TOM COLLINS), rum, whiskey or BOURBON WHISKEY and soda. (Said to be named after a New York barman.)

Colombo Plan (1950) The British Commonwealth's counterpart to the US POINT-FOUR PROGRAM, which provides technical assistance to former British territories in South and South-East Asia, and to Indochina, Indonesia, the Philippines and Siam. It also offers them facilities for technological training in Britain and the Dominions. (Proposed by a Commonwealth conference at Colombo, Ceylon.)

Colonels The Kentucky Colonels, AMERICAN BASKETBALL ASSOCIATION.

Colonial Dames of America (1890) A patriotic organization resembling the DAUGHTERS OF THE AMERICAN REVOLUTION.

Colony Club An exclusive women's club in New York City.

Colorado beetle A serious menace to potato crops which first appeared in England in 1933; its native habitat is Colorado. The grub is bright pink or red, and the beetle has longitudinal black and yellow stripes.

Colorado Springs A town in central Colorado; the site of the Air Force Academy and the headquarters of NORAD are nearby. See CHEYENNE MOUNTAIN.

Colosseum (AD 80) The huge amphitheater in Rome, impressive even as a ruin, completed in the reign of Titus. It held over 100,000 spectators, and was used for gladiatorial combats or, flooded with water, for naval displays.

Colossi of Memnon Greek name for 2 seated figures at THEBES, 64 ft high, all that remains of the mortuary temple of Amenhotep III (14th century BC). One of these was reputed to sing when touched by the rays of the morning sun, a fanciful description of the soughing of the wind.

Colossus of Rhodes (3rd century BC) A statue of HELIOS, said to be over 100 ft high, one of the SEVEN WONDERS OF THE WORLD, destroyed by earthquake some 50 years after completion. The story that it bestrode the entrance to Rhodes harbor was a much later invention.

Colt (1830) The first successful revolver, a 6-shooter designed by Samuel Colt of Connecticut. His firm also produced the .45 automatic pistol (1911) used by US forces in both world wars; and the Colt Commander, a much lighter model with an aluminum frame.

Colter's Hell An early name given to the Yellowstone region by fur traders, from the description of it by John Colter (c. 1775-1813), a pioneer fur trader who accompanied the Lewis and Clark expedition; see LEWIS AND CLARK TRAIL.

Colts The Baltimore Colts, NATIONAL FOOTBALL LEAGUE. Became member of the AMERICAN CONFERENCE, NATIONAL FOOTBALL LEAGUE in 1970.

Columbia The name of the APOLLO 11 Command Module.

Columbia Icefield The largest icefield in North America, alongside the scenic highway that connects BANFF and JASPER NATIONAL PARKS in Alberta.

Columbia University (1754) Oldest of the universities in New York City.

Columbine Daughter of PANTALOON and sweetheart of HARLEQUIN.

Columbus Day Properly, October 12th, commemorating Columbus's discovery of the New World on 12 Oct. 1492, when he landed on San Salvador (probably Watling Island, in the Bahamas). From 1971 kept as a legal holiday on the second Monday in October.

Comanche A group of Shoshonean PLAINS INDIANS (see SHOSHONI) originally living in the plains of western Texas, who took the lead in raiding the whites on the Mexico-Texas borders to get horses. Some 2500 survive in western Oklahoma.

Combray A fictitious village, based on childhood memories of Auteuil and Illiers, the setting of the earlier books of Proust's REMEMBRANCE OF THINGS PAST.

Comecon (1949) Abbreviated name of the Council for Mutual Economic Assistance, the Soviet counter to MARSHALL AID. Its policy took the form of cheap loans and credits for barter deals, and an attempt at economic coordination within the Communist bloc.

Comédie-Française (1680) The French National Theater, with a repertoire of tragedies and comedies that have won an established reputation. Recruitment to the company is an honor, but the rule which bound members to serve exclusively in it for long periods has now been abandoned. Choice of play and style of acting follow set traditions. The company has 2 theaters in Paris, the main one being known officially as the Salle Richelieu and colloquially as Le Français.

Comédie humaine (1829-50) The name Balzac gave to his works as a whole, indicating that he was trying to portray the whole French scene at all levels of society and in both Paris and the provinces. His chief characters mostly embody some single obsessive passion, and are set against a vividly detailed background.

Comet The world's first jet airliner, built by De Havilland. Comet-1 opened a service from London to Johannesburg (1952) but later developed trouble with metal fatigue (see COHEN INQUIRY). Comet-4 opened the first transatlantic jet service (BOAC) in 1958 and was highly successful.

Comice pear The best of pears, but not easy to cultivate; the fruit is pale yellow and of medium size. The full name is Doyenne de Comice.

Cominform (1947-56) Abbreviated name for the Communist Information Bureau, an international organization formed, in succession to the COMINTERN, to coordinate, under Russian leadership, the policies of all Communist countries and the Communist parties of other countries. Its first objective was to ensure the rejection of MARSHALL AID.

Comintern (1919-43) Short name of the Third International, a Soviet-controlled world organization of Communist parties.

'Comin' thro' the Rye' Robert Burns's song, with the refrain: Gin a body meet a body / Comin' thro' the rye; / Gin a body kiss a body, / Need a body cry?

Commedia dell' Arte (16th century) Italian theatrical entertainment in which actors improvised on a skeleton plot, with such stock characters as the Doctor, SCARAMOUCHE and PANTALOON. HARLEQUIN and PULCINELLA were added later. Several of the best MEISSEN and other early porcelain figures are representations of these characters. (Italian, 'comedy of skill', as testing the actors' skill in improvisation.)

Committee of 100 (1960) (UK) The militant vanguard of the protest movement that developed from the Direct Action Committee (1957) to take direct action, e.g. sit-down protests (which it pioneered), against nuclear armament. The moving spirits were prominent in show business, the arts or literature. When it took up other causes, Bertrand Russell (see CND) resigned from it (1962), and by 1968 it seemed a spent force.

Committee of Public Safety (6 Apr. 1793-1795) A small cabinet of JACOBINS set up by Danton, only theoretically subordinate to the CONVENTION, to control army and foreign affairs. In July 1793 Robespierre was elected to it, pushed Danton into the background, and presided over the Reign of TERROR until his assassination by moderates in July 1794 (THERMIDOR). The Committee was later superseded by the DIRECTORY.

Common Man, The Century of the A phrase coined by Vice-president Henry Wallace in 1942: 'The century on which we are entering can be and must be the Century of the Common Man'.

Common Market, The (1959) The name in common use for the European Economic Community of France, West Germany, Italy, Belgium, Holland and Luxemburg ('the Six'), set up by the Treaty of Rome (1957). Its main objectives were the abolition of customs tariffs within the area and the establishment of uniform tariffs for imports into it; the working out of a common agricultural policy; and eventually, the formation of a United States of Europe.

Common Sense (1776) Thomas Paine's pamphlet attacking George III and calling for America's immediate independence. Sales reached 100,000 in a few months, and it was an important factor in securing the DECLARATION OF INDEPENDENCE.

Commonwealth (1649-53) Name given to the period of Cromwell's republican government from the time of Charles I's execution to the creation of the PROTECTORATE; or, loosely, to the RESTORATION (1660).

Commonwealth Centre See MARL-BOROUGH HOUSE.

Commonwealth Day See EMPIRE DAY.

Commonwealth Fund (1918) A fund that finances Harkness fellowships for young graduates from Britain, Australia, New Zealand and Western Europe to study in the US, and also promotes medical education and health services in the US. Founded by the mother of E.S. Harkness (see PILGRIM TRUST), who added his own bequest in 1930.

Commonwealth Institute (UK) Exhibition galleries illustrating the histo-ry and geography of the countries of the Commonwealth, housed since 1962 in a building in Kensington High Street, London. There is also a library, art gallery, and a cinema showing documentary films. Formerly the Imperial Institute (1893).

Commonwealth Office (UK) The latest name for the Dominions, later Commonwealth Relations, Office, with which the Colonial Office was merged in 1966.

Communist Manifesto (1848) A detailed program for Communist revolution issued by Marx and Engels during the REVOLUTIONS OF 1848. It stated that history is a record of successive class struggles in which new classes replace the old; the final revolution would be of the proletariat against the capitalists, in which 'the workers have nothing to lose but their chains . . . Workers of the world, unite!'

Compiègne The French town west of Soissons near which, in a forest clearing, the Germans signed the armistice of 11 Nov. 1918; on the same spot, by Hitler's whim, the French had to sign the armistice of 22 June 1940.

Compleat Angler, The (1653) Izaak Walton's prose eclogue of English country life, in the form of a discursive dialogue between Piscator (the fisherman) and Venator (the hunter) on the joys of angling.

Compositae The largest plant family, the daisies, characterized by a flower head comprising many flowers clustered together. It includes dandelion, groundsel, thistle, aster, chrysanthemum, goldenrod, dahlia, artichoke, lettuce.

Compostela One of the most famous pilgrimage places in medieval Europe, the shrine where the patron saint of Spain, St James the Elder, is supposed to be buried, in the cathedral of Santiago de Compostela, Galicia, northwest Spain.

Comprehensive School (1) A secondary school offering comprehensive curricula, usually college preparatory, commercial and vocational courses. (2) A consolidated school formed by merging 2 or more public schools (usually rural elementary schools). (3) In Britain, a large school which brings the grammar, secondary modern and technical streams under one roof, facilitates the move of children from one stream to another after the age of 11, and enables the clever and the dull to mix outside class, as they do at 'public' schools. See 11 PLUS.

Compton Wynyates An exceptionally beautiful Tudor house near Banbury, Warwickshire, with the interior largely unchanged; home of the Marquesses of Northampton.

Comsat (1963) The Communications Satellite Corporation which launched EARLY BIRD and represents the US on INTELSAT, whose operations it manages on behalf of the consortium. The corporation, privately owned, also aims to organize domestic networks for braodcasting and to replace landline telephones etc.

Comstockery Misdirected zeal in censoring whatever is thought to be salacious. (Anthony Comstock, died 1915, a US crusader against 'vice'; word invented by Bernard Shaw when he heard that the New York Public Library had banned his MAN AND SUPERMAN under Comstock's influence.)

Comstock Lode, The (1859) The exceptionally rich silver deposits discovered at Virginia City. Nev From 1882 the Comstock Mine declined in importance because of flooding and a slump in the price of silver.

Comte Ory, Le Rossini's opera in which young men disguised as nuns invade a castle in pursuit of a beautiful widow whose kinsmen are away at the Crusades.

Comus (1634) Milton's masque, composed for the 1st Earl of Bridgewater at Ludlow; a girl is wooed by the monster Comus, but is saved by SABRINA, nymph of the River Severn. (Comus. Roman god of sensual pleasure.)

Concert of Europe (1815) The agreement of the Quadruple Alliance (Austria, Prussia, Russia and Britain), made after the CONGRESS OF VIENNA, to meet periodically in order to concert diplomatic moves to preserve Europe from a repetition of the chaos caused by the French Revolution and Napoleonic Wars. Castlereagh, and his successor Canning, gradually withdrew British support (completely in 1822) when Metternich imposed his policy of suppressing liberalism everywhere, even to the extent of interfering in the domestic affairs of other states. Also called the Congress System. See HOLY ALLIANCE.

Conchobar (Conor) The legendary King of Ulster at the beginning of the Christian era, who ruled at Emain Macha in Armagh (the ruins of which survive), with an army of RED BRANCH KNIGHTS. See CUCHULAIN; DEIRDRE; MAEVE.

Concorde The first supersonic airliner, an Anglo-French project on which BAC and Sud Aviation began work in 1963. Designed to carry 130 passengers at 1300 m.p.h., it was first tested in 1968.

Concord grape A large dark-blue grape, grown in eastern USA.

Concordia The Roman goddess of peace, represented in art as a veiled matron holding a horn of plenty in one hand and in the other a scepter.

Concord wagon A 19th-century stagecoach built for cross-country travel, with a body swung on braces; there was a similar Concord buggy. (Concord, N. H., where made.)

Concours de la Reine Elisabeth One of the most testing competitions for pianists and violinists, held in Brussels; see LEVENTRITT AWARD. (Named for the wife of King Albert I.)

Condé, House of A branch of the BOURBON family founded by the first prince of Condé in the 16th century. He and his son were Huguenot enemies of the GUISES. The fourth in the line, called the Great Condé, was a general of Louis XIV's reign (see FRONDE).

Condition humaine, La (1933) André Malraux' novel based on the struggle between Chinese Communists and KUOMINTANG forces in

Shanghai in 1927. (English title, *Storm over Shanghai*.)

Condors The Pittsburgh Condors, AMERICAN BASKETBALL ASSOCIATION.

Conestoga wagon A heavy covered freight wagon first used in the mid 18th century, and generally drawn by 6 horses; the body curved up toward the ends and suggested the shape of a boat (hence the name 'prairie schooner' for the smaller model developed from it). Both types were used by pioneers going West. (Conestoga Valley, Pa., where made.)

Coney Island A seaside resort and amusement center in New York.

Confederate States of America The 11 States who seceded from the Union and set up (Feb. 1861) a government at Richmond, Virginia, under Jefferson Davis as President. They were the original 7—South Carolina, Alabama, Georgia, Florida, Louisiana, Mississippi and Texas— joined later by Arkansas, Tennessee, Virginia and North Carolina. See AMERICAN CIVIL WAR.

Confederation of British Industry See CBI.

Confederation of the Rhine (1806-13) A Confederation of Bavaria, Baden, Württemberg and other German states, formed by Napoleon and subject to him.

Conference pear An excellently flavored variety of pear, easy to grow, with a characteristic long tapering russet fruit which ripens in late September.

Confessions of an English Opium-eater (1822) De Quincey's autobiographical account of how he took to opium to ease pain and how after much suffering he managed to cure himself of the habit.

Confidential Clerk, The (1954) A verse drama by T. S. Eliot who disguises its Classical origin and religious purpose by dressing it up as a conventional farce.

Confrontation (1963-66) The Indonesian challenge to the creation of Malaysia, regarded by President Sukarno as an imperialist device to maintain British influence in South-East Asia.

Confucianism (6th century BC) Down-to-earth conservative codes of personal morality, etiquette, and statesmanship, taught by the Chinese magistrate and philosopher Confucius. His sayings, which had little influence during his lifetime, were recorded by his followers and, much later, under the HAN DYNASTY, became the basis of the official code of behavior in China, continuing to guide the way of life of rulers and ruled until the coming of the Communists.

Congo, Republic of The name of 2 African republics, usually distinguished by adding the name of the capital town of each: (1) The former Belgian Congo, referred to as Congo (Kinshasa), the latter being the new name of Léopoldville, the capital. (2) The former French Congo (Moyen or Middle Congo), now known as Congo (Brazzaville).

Congo Free State The private property of King Leopold II of the Belgians (1885-1908) until it was annexed by the Belgian government as a colony (Congo Belge), after disclosures from 1903 onwards by Roger Casement, E. D. Morel and others of scandalous maladministration.

Congregationalists NONCONFORMIST descendants of the BROWNISTS and INDEPENDENTS, who hold that the only head of the Church is Jesus Christ. Each of their churches is, therefore, completely self-governing and recognizes no outside ecclesiastical authority.

Congressional Medal of Honor See MEDAL OF HONOR.

Congress of Vienna (1814-15) The assembly of European powers after the Napoleonic Wars which (though interrupted by the HUNDRED DAYS) redrew the map of Europe; it was dominated by Metternich, Castlereagh, the Tsar Alexander and Talleyrand. A loose confederation of 39 German states was formed; the Austrian Netherlands (Belgium) and Holland were united; Russia took Poland (the Duchy of Warsaw); Austria took much of northern Italy and

Dalmatia; and many other changes were made, bringing comparative peace for the next 40 years.

Congress Party (1885) The leading political party in India at Partition in 1947. Originally it was formed by Hindus and Muslims to improve relations between the 2 communities and with Britain. It developed into a Hindu nationalist party, with which the MUSLIM LEAGUE finally broke in 1935.

Congress System   See CONCERT OF EUROPE.

Conibear style American rowing style with a short swing and fast recovery. (Hiram Conibear, Washington University coach.)

Coningsby (1844) Disraeli's contemporary political novel, which traces the career of Harry Coningsby through Eton and Cambridge, his love for the daughter of a Lancashire industrialist, Millbank (said to represent Gladstone), his disinheritance for such unaristocratic behavior, and his rescue from drudgery at the Bar by Millbank, who gets him elected to the Commons. The story enabled the author to air his own views on TORY DEMOCRACY, and introduces SIDONIA and TADPOLE AND TAPER.

Connacht (Connaught) The western province of the Irish Republic, formerly a Celtic kingdom, now consisting of Galway, Leitrim, Mayo, Roscommon and Sligo.

Connaught The English spelling of CONNACHT.

Connecticut Yankee, A (1927) A Rodgers and Hart musical play with a libretto by Herbert Fields, based on Mark Twain's novel *A Connecticut Yankee in King Arthur's Court* (1889). The songs included 'My Heart Stood Still'. Hit on the head, the manager of an armaments factory finds himself transported back to Arthurian times. Unimpressed by what he finds, he establishes ascendancy by predicting an eclipse and sets about modernizing the knights, e.g. by remounting them on bicycles. MERLIN sends this unwelcome rival back to the 19th century. Several movies were made on this theme.

Connemara Carl Sandburg's home in Flat Rock, N.C., from 1945 until his death in 1967. A Confederate-era house, it is now a national historic site open to the public. There is a library and a manuscript collection.

Conscript Fathers (1) The Roman Senate; (2) the medieval Venetian Senate. (Latin *patres* (*et*) *conscripti*, 'heads of families and the newly elected'.)

Consistory (1) In the Church of England, a diocesan court now mainly concerned with authorizing alterations to a church or parsonage, but also having power to try clergy accused of immorality. (2) In the Church of Rome, a senate of all the cardinals, presided over by the Pope.

Consols (1751) The government securities of Britain consolidated into a single loan stock at 3% (from 1903 at 2½%), at one time forming a large part of the country's funded debt, but after 2 world wars accounting for only about 1% of the total national debt. (Abbreviation for 'consolidated annuities'.)

Constable country The Suffolk-Essex border country around the Stour where John Constable was born and which he loved to paint.

Constance, Lake See BODENSEE.

Constantia The best and most famous of South African wines. (Named after a vineyard near Cape Town.)

Constantinople Older name of Istanbul.

Constantinople, Fall of (1453) The OTTOMAN TURK conquest which ended the Byzantine Empire, and scattered Greek scholars to Western Europe, there to reinforce the REVIVAL OF LEARNING.

Constant Nymph, The (1924) Margaret Kennedy's best-selling romantic novel about an eccentric Bohemian musician, Albert Sanger, and his large family; a long-running play was made from it.

Constellation See LOCKHEED AIRCRAFT.

Constitutional Act (1791) A British Act giving Canada self-government in local affairs in recognition of its loyalty during the American Revolution. The colony was divided at the Ottawa River into Upper (mainly English) and Lower (mainly French) Canada, each with a representative assembly.

Constitution mirror   A mirror usually having a row of balls under the top cornice, side pilasters, and a painted panel above the looking glass.

Constitution of the United States, The   The supreme law of the Federal government; the final draft of the original 7 Articles was prepared for the Constitutional Convention by Gouverneur Morris, September 1787, in the Philadelphia State House (Independence Hall). They came into effect on 4 March 1789, and the first set of amendments followed 2 years later, see BILL OF RIGHTS (2).

Consulate   (1799-1804) In French history, the triumvirate set up after Napoleon had overthrown the DIRECTORY in the BRUMAIRE coup. Napoleon was made First Consul and in 1802 First Consul for life; the other two Consuls were mere figureheads.

Consumer Council   (1963) A body set up by the British Board of Trade to protect the shopper from the industrial and advertising forces ranged against her.

Consumers' Association   (UK) A private body to protect shoppers. It publishes a monthly periodical, *Which?*, where detailed reports are printed of tests on competing brands of goods or kinds of service, usually indicating which is best value for money.

Consumers Union of US   (1936) A nonprofit organization that provides consumers with impartial information and advice on consumer goods and services, and on all matters concerning family expenditure, through a monthly, *Consumer Reports*. The headquarters are at Mount Vernon, N.Y.

Contemptible Little Army   See OLD CONTEMPTIBLES.

Continental Army   The army of the American Revolution. ('Continental' came into general use about 1774 as an adjective for the colonies on the

eve of the Revolution.)

Continental Congress   Name given to 3 meetings of representatives of the American colonies; the first (1774) met in Philadelphia to discuss the grievances which led to the AMERICAN WAR OF INDEPENDENCE; the third proclaimed the DECLARATION OF INDEPENDENCE (1776) and thereafter carried on the government of the country.

Continental Divide   Another name for the GREAT DIVIDE.

Continental Divide Trail   A 3082-mile trail from the Montana-Canadian boundary in GLACIER NATIONAL PARK to Silver City, N.M., along the GREAT DIVIDE.

Continental Shelf   The submerged fringe of a continent, sloping gently downwards to a depth of up to 100 fathoms over a width of (usually) up to 100 miles, beyond which there is a sudden drop to 1000 fathoms or more.

Continental System   (1806) Napoleon's attempt by various decrees (the Berlin Decree being the first) to close European ports to English trade; it was ineffective, as even France itself found it necessary to import British goods. It led to the PENINSULAR WAR and to Napoleon's invasion of Russia.

Continental tea   Tea said to have been drunk during the Revolution after the boycott of taxed imported tea, made from the Labrador tea plant of eastern North America.

Contrat social, Le   (1762) See SOCIAL CONTRACT.

Convair   A division of the US aircraft firm, GENERAL DYNAMICS, with headquarters at Fort Worth, Tex. They made the HUSTLER, Delta Dart, and the Convair-880, which was a rival to the BOEING-720.

Conventicle Act   (1664) See CLARENDON CODE.

Convention, National   (21 Sept. 1792-26 Oct. 1795) The sovereign assembly of France, divided into the PLAIN and the MOUNTAIN. The latter gained complete control and was responsible for the execution of Louis XVI and the establishment of the TERROR.

Conventions, National (USA) Assemblies of party delegates from all the states, staged by Republicans and Democrats in the summer before the November presidential election to select their candidates for the presidency and vice-presidency, and to hammer out a 'platform' likely to win votes without splitting the party. This supreme exercise in 'wheeling and dealing' takes place in an atmosphere as hectic as an American football game.

Co-op, The Colloquial abbreviation for a cooperative store or society.

Cooper Union (1859) An institution 'for the advancement of science and art' in Cooper Square, NYC, where free degree courses are offered in many branches of engineering, art, architecture and the humanities, as well as adult education and, during winter, thrice-weekly Forum lectures open to the public. There is also a Museum for the Arts of Decoration, an important library and a branch on the Ringwood Manor estate, N.J. Lincoln and many other US Presidents have addressed audiences at the Copper Union. (Named for the founder, Peter Cooper.)

Co-optimists, The (1921-31) A highly successful London concert-party (a peculiarly English institution, a sort of white minstrel show), starring Phyllis Monkman, Stanley Holloway and Davy Burnaby.

Copacabana A town near Rio de Janeiro, Brazil, with famous bathing beaches.

Copeland & Garrett (1847) The successors to SPODE, owned by the Copeland family who first gained control of the older firm in 1829. The name was retained in many of their marks, e.g. 'Copeland late Spode'. They bought up the molds and models of DERBY, BOW, CHELSEA and LONGTON HALL.

Copernican theory (1543) That the sun, not the earth, is the center of our universe; not generally accepted until the 17th century. See PTOLEMAIC SYSTEM. (Copernicus, Polish astronomer.)

Cophetua A legendary African king of great wealth who married a beggar maid; mentioned by Shakespeare,

the story was also told in an old ballad, and a poem of Tennyson's; but is best known through a Pre-Raphaelite painting by Burne-Jones.

Copley Medal (1709) Royal Society medal awarded annually for philosophical research.

Coppélia (1870) A famous comedy ballet, music by Délibes (who introduced a Hungarian czardas), choreography by Arthur Saint-Léon (and others), and a story from E.T.A. Hoffmann about a young man who falls in love with a mechanical doll, Coppélia, made by the toymaker-magician Dr Coppélius.

Copperbelt, The The copper-mining area of northern ZAMBIA adjoining that of Katanga (Congo), and developed by Rhokana, Mufulira, Roan Antelope, and other mining companies.

Copperhead A person in the Northern states who sympathized with the South in the Civil War. (The name of a venomous snake.)

Coppins The Duke of Kent's home at Iver, Buckinghamshire.

Copts A Christian heretical sect established from the 5th century in Egypt and Abyssinia. (Ultimately derived from Greek *Aiguptios*, 'Egyptian'.)

Coq d'or, Le (1909) Rimsky-Korsakov's fairy-tale opera. An astrologer presents the king with a golden cockerel which will give warning of danger. The king refuses the reward demanded by the astrologer and is killed by the bird.

Coral Sea, Battle of the (May 1942) The first naval battle fought entirely by carrier-borne aircraft, with no contact between ships; the US Navy turned back a Japanese invasion fleet bound for New Guinea.

Corbillon Cup (1933) An international table tennis championship for teams of women.

Corble Cup (1947) (Fencing) An international individual saber championship.

Corby (1950) (UK) A NEW TOWN in Northamptonshire, 7 miles north of Kettering, designed for a population of 80,000.

Cordelia The youngest and favorite daughter of KING LEAR who, misconstruing her words, disinherits her. She marries the King of France and brings an army to England to rescue her father from the clutches of her sisters GONERIL and Regan, but is defeated and hanged.

Cordon Bleu (1) The blue ribbon of the highest Bourbon order of chivalry. (2) Applied to a first-class chef etc., in much the same spirit as BLUE RIBBON (of the Order of the Garter) is used in English.

CORE Initials used for the Congress on Racial Equality, one of several US movements for Negro rights.

Corfu incident (1923) Mussolini's occupation of the Greek island of Corfu in retaliation for the murder by Greeks of Italian soldiers delimiting the Greek-Albanian frontier. The LEAGUE OF NATIONS managed to restore Corfu to Greece under Anglo-French pressure.

Corinthian (UK) In the 19th century, a man-about-town; a profligate. (From ancient Corinth, notorious in Greek literature for its licentiousness and luxury.)

Corinthian Order The most ornate of the 3 Greek orders of architecture, with slender columns of which the capitals were embellished with acanthus leaves. The Order found more favor in Rome than in Greece.

Corinthians (New Testament) St Paul's 2 epistles to the Church at Corinth.

Coriolanus (1608) Shakespeare's play about a Roman general of the 5th century BC who, banished by the Romans after he had won them victory over the Volscians, joins the enemy in an attack on Rome, yields to his family's plea to make peace, and is killed by the Volscians for betraying their cause.

Corn Belt The midwestern region of USA, particularly Iowa, Illinois, Indiana and Nebraska, where the long summers and cool climate favor corn, which is the staple crop and used in feeding cattle.

Cornell (1865) University at Ithaca, N.Y.

Cornhusker State Nickname of NEBRASKA.

Corning glass Made by the Corning Glass Co. (1851) of STEUBEN County,

N.Y., which among other things made the reflector for the MOUNT PALOMAR OBSERVATORY telescope.

Cornish language A CELTIC LANGUAGE, the basis of BRETON and itself preserved after the Norman Conquest by Breton overlords.

Cornish style (Wrestling) An (English) West Country style, in which contestants wear canvas jackets on which all holds must be placed. For a win, both shoulders and a hip (or both hips and a shoulder) must touch the ground.

Corn Laws, The (1804-28) Acts imposing restrictions and levies on the import of grain into Britain, passed by parliaments dominated by landowners. They caused much distress among the poor, especially during the HUNGRY FORTIES, and were repealed in 1846 by Sir Robert Peel. See ANTI-CORN-LAW LEAGUE.

Coronation Cup A skiing competition held in April in the Cairngorms, Scotland.

Coronel (Nov. 1914) A naval engagement in World War I in which von Spee sank Cradock's cruisers *Monmouth* and *Good Hope*; see FALKLAND ISLANDS, BATTLE OF THE. (Chilean port.)

Corporal US Army's first ground-to-ground guided missile, with a range of up to 100 miles; superseded by SERGEANT.

Corporation Act (1661) See CLARENDON CODE.

Corporative State A state in which the electorate is organized not on a geographical basis but by trades and professions, delegates to the national assembly being elected by employers' and employees' federations. Originally a Syndicalist idea, it was adopted by Fascism, with support from the Roman Catholic Church. Deliberative bodies of this kind were set up in Italy, Spain and Portugal, but under dictatorial regimes have had no opportunity to demonstrate whether they could be effective.

Corpus Christi The Thursday after TRINITY SUNDAY, falling in May or June, appointed for the commemoration of the Feast of the Blessed Sacrament or Body of Christ. In Roman Catholic countries it is a major festival, observed with processions and pageantry.

Corridors of Power, The See STRANGERS AND BROTHERS.

Corsair US Air Force and Navy aircraft designed by the Dallas firm of Ling-Temco-Vought as a close-support 'counterinsurgency' transport, i.e. slow and relatively unarmed but able to drop large units where no antiaircraft defenses exist.

Corsair, Le The name of a ballet choreographed by Mazilier with music by Adolphe Adam.

Corsairs Another name for BARBARY PIRATES. (Latin-French word for 'raider'.)

Corsican ogre, The A name for Napoleon I, who was born in Corsica.

Cortes The Spanish CORPORATIVE legislative assembly.

Cortez, Stout A phrase from Keats's sonnet, see CHAPMAN'S HOMER. In fact it was Balboa, not Cortez, who first saw the Pacific.

Cortland A variety of apple.

Corunna (1809) A port in northwest Spain where Sir John Moore was killed in battle after his retreat before Napoleon's forces in the PENINSULAR WAR.

Corvo, Baron Pen name of the British writer, Frederick Rolfe (1861-1913); see QUEST FOR CORVO.

Corybants See CYBELE.

Corydon A shepherd in the pastoral poems of Theocritus and Virgil, and thereafter in general poetic use for any rustic.

Cosa Nostra The name (first revealed by VALACHI) adopted by the MAFIA in USA. There are said to be 30 groups ('families') under unified command (see JOE BANANAS); they have turned from bootlegging and prostitution to gambling, loans at astronomic rates of interest (e.g. 150% a week), and the wholesale import and retail trade in narcotics. See LUCKY LUCIANO. (Italian, 'our business'.)

Così fan tutte (1790) Mozart's comic opera in which the cynical Don Alfonso bets that the sisters with whom 2 of his friends are in love will be flirting with others the moment their backs are turned. On his instructions they disguise themselves as foreigners and lay siege to the girls with such success that Alfonso wins his bet. (Italian, 'thus do all women'.)

Cosmos Name given to a continuous and very numerous series of Russian reconnaissance satellites carrying high-definition cameras.

Cosmos Club A Washington, D.C., social club.

Cospar (1958) Abbreviated name for the international Committee on Space Research, a nongovernmental organization of scientists to promote exchange of information and cooperation in carrying out space projects.

Costa Blanca The coastal resorts of Valencia, in eastern Spain, lying between Alicante and Valencia.

Costa Brava The Catalonian resorts of the Spanish Mediterranean coast from the French frontier to Barcelona.

Costa de la Luz Tourist industry's name for the Atlantic seaboard resorts of Spain around the Gulf of Cadiz, northwest of Gibraltar. (Spanish, 'coast of light'.)

Costa del Sol The Spanish coastal resorts of southern Andalusia, around Malaga and as far west as Estepona, near Gibraltar. (Spanish, 'sunny coast'.)

Costa Dorada Tourist industry's name for the Catalonian coast resorts from Barcelona to Valencia, southwest of the COSTA BRAVA. (Spanish. 'golden coast'.)

Costa Smeralda The coastal resorts of northeastern Sardinia, developed by Aga Khan IV. (Italian, 'emerald coast'.)

Côte d'Azur Better known in English as 'the South of France' or the Riviera, i.e. the coastal resorts from the Italian frontier to Marseilles.

Côte de Beaune The southern part of the Côte d'Or, producing red (e.g. Beaune, Pommard) and most of the best white BURGUNDY WINES.

Côte de Nuits The northern part of the Côte d'Or, producing the best red BURGUNDY WINES, e.g. Chambertin, Vougeot, Nuits-St Georges,

Romanée-Conti.

Côte Vermeille A new coastal tourist area in the south of France, adjoining the Spanish frontier.

Cotter's Saturday Night, The (1786) Robert Burns's poem, famous for its description of the nobler side of Scottish rural life.

Cotton Bowl (1) Sports stadium at Dallas, Tex. (2) The invitational BOWL GAME played in the Cotton Bowl usually with one team from the SOUTHWEST CONFERENCE.

Cotton State Nickname of Alabama.

Coty Award An annual award to the American fashion designer whose work has had the most significant effect on the American woman's way of dressing. The winner is selected by a jury of fashion editors, in New York City.

Couéism A psychological panacea for the stresses of modern life which swept Europe in the 1920's; believers constantly assured themselves: Every day, in every way, I feel better and better. See NEW THOUGHT. (Professor Coué, French inventor.)

Cougars The (North) Carolina Cougars, AMERICAN BASKETBALL ASSOCIATION.

Coulport A village on Loch Long, near Glasgow, site of the Royal Navy's Polaris School and POLARIS missile storage depot.

Council for Mutual Economic Assistance See COMECON.

Council of Europe (1949) An organization of non-Communist countries of Western Europe (excluding Spain and Portugal) which Turkey and Cyprus, among others, joined later. There is a Committee of Foreign Ministers and a Consultative Assembly meeting at Strasbourg which makes recommendations to the Committee on matters other than Defense.

Council of Foreign Ministers See NATO.

Council of Foreign Relations US counterpart of the ROYAL INSTITUTE OF INTERNATIONAL AFFAIRS.

Council of Industrial Design (1944) (UK) A body established to provide courses of instruction to raise standards of industrial design. See DE-SIGN CENTRE; DESIGN INDEX.

Council of Ministers (USSR) The state executive, elected by the SU-PREME SOVIET. Its chairman is the equivalent of the premier in other countries.

Council of the European Communities A proposed single council of ministers, with a single executive commission under it, to direct the operations of the COMMON MARKET, EURATOM and the EUROPEAN COAL AND STEEL COMMUNITY. The proposal was debated from 1965 onwards, but its implementation was delayed by disagreements between the SIX.

Council of Trent (1545-63) The ecumenical council which, after the upheaval of the REFORMATION, laid down the main doctrines of the Roman Catholic Church in their final form and checked various abuses attacked by the Protestants. See COUNTER-REFORMATION. (Held at Trento, north Italy.)

Counterblast to Tobacco, A (1604) The first attempt to stop people smoking, written by that very odd man, King James I.

Counter-Reformation (16th century) The Catholic reaction to the REFOR-MATION, which began after the COUN-CIL OF TRENT and, working through the newly formed Order of JESUITS and (chiefly in Spain) the INQUISI-TION, tried to win back all Europe to the Mother Church, in the process all but extinguishing the RENAIS-SANCE.

Countess of Huntingdon's Connection (1748) A Calvinist Methodist sect, founded by a Countess of Huntingdon, at one time a follower of John Wesley, under the influence of her chaplain, George Whitefield (see METHODISM). Most of its chapels are affiliated with the Congregational Union, the consultative body of the CONGREGATIONALISTS.

Count of Luxembourg, The (1911) Franz Lehar's tuneful operetta set in the Paris of the 1890s, in which the Count falls in love with a woman he has married (but never seen) as part of a moneymaking bargain.

Count of Monte Cristo, The (1844) Alexandre Dumas' novel about

Edmond Dantès who, framed on a political charge, escapes to the island of Monte Cristo (a real island, near Elba). There he finds buried treasure which enables him to wreak his revenge on his persecutors.

Country Party (1673) See WHIGS.

Country Wife, The (1673) William Wycherley's comedy of an uxorious husband whose suspicions drive his wife into the arms of a lover who has set it about that he is a eunuch. David Garrick wrote a less licentious version, *The Country Girl*, which replaced it from 1764 until modern times, when the old play was revived.

County Palatine In England, the title still applied to Lancashire, Cheshire and Durham, and formerly to all countries under an Earl PALATINE.

Coupon election (Dec. 1918) (UK) The postwar election in which the Liberal Prime Minister Lloyd George and Conservative leader Bonar Law arranged the uncontested election of coalition candidates—a device to ensure the return of at least 150 Liberals although public opinion was swinging overwhelmingly to the Conservatives. (Asquith's name for the joint sponsoring letter given to such candidates. which he contemptuously compared with wartime ration coupons.)

Court, The (BANK OF ENGLAND) An advisory body under the chairmanship of the Governor of the Bank of England, comprising representatives of banks, industry, commerce and the trade unions, which meets weekly to decide whether Bank Rate should be changed, and to give general advice to the Treasury on the financial outlook.

Courtauld Institute Galleries A London art gallery in Woburn Square, with a fine collection of Impressionist and Postimpressionist paintings as well as other important sections.

Courtauld Institute of Art A unit of the University of London in Portman Square, where the history and appreciation of art is taught.

Courtaulds A group of companies which absorbed British Celanese, British Cellophane, Gossard, Lancashire Cotton Corporation, Bairns-Wear and Pinchin, Johnson; it manufactures three-quarters of the UK synthetic fiber output (mainly cellulose fibers), cotton and other textiles, chemicals, plastics, paint and packaging.

Courtship of Miles Standish, The (1858) Longfellow's long narrative poem telling how Standish, captain of the Plymouth Settlement, sends his friend John Alden to court Priscilla Mullins for him. She (who prefers John) makes the often quoted comment: Why don't you speak for yourself, John?

Cousine Bette, La (1846) One of the novels of Balzac's COMÉDIE HUMAINE, in which an aging spinster eaten away by concealed jealousy ruins the romance of a young couple.

Cousin Pons, Le (1847) One of the novels of Balzac's COMÉDIE HUMAINE, of a musician who sacrifices everything to his obsessive collecting of works of art.

Covenant In the Bible, the name given to various pacts between Jehovah and the Israelites, e.g. those of the PROMISED LAND, the establishment of David on the throne (2 *Samuel* vii), and the giving of the priesthood to the tribe of Levi (*Deuteronomy* xxxiii, 9); the New Covenant (later mistranslated as New Testament) is that of *Jeremiah* xxxi, 31-34, which indicated the rebirth of Jewish religion (interpreted as referring to Christianity).

Covenant, Day of the See DINGAAN'S DAY.

Covenanters (1) The Scottish Presbyterians who in 1638 signed the National Covenant to defend their religion against Popery and tyranny; see BISHOPS' WARS. (2) Those who signed the Solemn League and Covenant (1643) and by promising military aid to the ROUNDHEADS in the ENGLISH CIVIL WAR obtained assurances from the English Church and Parliament that Presbyterianism would be established in both countries and in Ireland.

Covenant of the League of Nations Its constitution, which was incorporated in the Versailles Treaty,

Covent Garden (1638) (1) A London residential area laid out by Inigo Jones. (2) Britain's largest market for fruit, flowers and vegetables, which now occupies most of (1). (3) Used for the Royal Opera House, situated on the northern side of (1).

Coventry, To send to To ostracize, refuse to speak to. (Phrase of uncertain origin, perhaps dating from the ENGLISH CIVIL WAR, when Coventry was held by the Parliamentarians.)

Coventry blitz (14–15 Nov. 1940) The air raid that destroyed Coventry Cathedral, made by German aircraft using X-apparatus, an improved beam-navigation system.

Coventry Stakes (UK) A 5-furlong flat race for 2-year-olds, run at Ascot in June.

Coverdale's Bible (1535) The first complete translation of the Bible into English, by Miles Coverdale. See GREAT BIBLE.

Covered Wagon, The (1923) A famous movie about the conquest of the Wild West.

Coverley, Sir Roger de The typical old Worcestershire squire created by Addison in the SPECTATOR. He was named after the country-dance, which Addison said was invented by his character's ancestor. (Coverley is an older spelling of Cowley, near Oxford.)

Cowboys The Dallas Cowboys, NATIONAL FOOTBALL LEAGUE. Became member of the NATIONAL CONFERENCE, NATIONAL FOOTBALL LEAGUE in 1970.

Cowdray Park One of England's 2 main polo grounds, on the estate of Viscount Cowdray, near Midhurst, Sussex.

Cowes Week (UK) Annual regatta held at the end of July and beginning of August under the auspices of the Royal Yacht Squadron and other local yacht clubs; the BRITANNIA CUP is one of the major events. Cowes Week is a great social occasion marking the end of the London SEASON. (Cowes, yachting center on the north coast of the Isle of Wight.)

Coxey's Army (1) One of the groups of unemployed who marched on Washington, D. C., in 1894, demanding public-works relief programs;

led by the Populist, Jacob Coxey (1854–1951), only 400 reached the capital, and 3 of their leaders were arrested. (2) Hence, a rabble.

Coyote State Nickname of South Dakota.

CP Signifies the Canadian Press, the leading national news service, with sole Canadian rights to the news services of AP and REUTER.

CPR See CANADIAN PACIFIC RAILWAY.

CPSU Initials used for the Communist Party of the Soviet Union.

Crabbe incident (1956) The disappearance of the British frogman, Commander Crabbe, who, apparently working independently, went exploring the underside of the Soviet cruiser in Portsmouth harbor which had brought Bulganin and Khrushchev to England; he was presumed drowned or killed, but occasionally rumors are revived that he is alive and behind the Iron Curtain.

Crab Nebula A bright nebula in TAURUS, the remains of the supernova observed by the Chinese in AD 1054; it is a strong source of radio noise.

Cracker State Nickname of Georgia.

Crack Up, The (1936) Scott Fitzgerald's essays on his own sad downfall, induced by his wife's mental breakdown and by financial troubles.

Cradle of Liberty, The Another name for FANEUIL HALL.

'Cradle Song' See 'WIEGENLIED'.

Crafts Centre of Great Britain The London headquarters and shopwindow in Mayfair of the leading crafts societies. Its organizers introduce craftsmen and designers to industry and the public, and work in cooperation with the COUNCIL OF INDUSTRIAL DESIGN, the ARTS COUNCIL and the Rural Industries Bureau.

Cramlington (1963) (UK) A NEW TOWN 8 miles north of Newcastle upon Tyne, designed for a population of 48,000.

Crane, Ichabod A character in 'The LEGEND OF SLEEPY HOLLOW'.

Cranford The idyllic village of Mrs Gaskell's novel of that name, based on recollections of Knutsford,

Cheshire, where she spent her child-hood.

Cranwell The SANDHURST of the RAF, near Lincoln.

Crater Lake A lake of purest blue, 1932 ft deep, in the heart of a volcano with multicolored lava walls 500-2000 ft high, and lying at a height of 6176 ft in the Cascades, southwest Oregon. It was discovered only in 1853 and is now part of the Crater Lake National Park (1902).

Craven Meeting (UK) The earliest of the Newmarket flat-race meetings, held in April.

Crawfie Nickname of Marion Crawford, one-time governess to the Queen and Princess Margaret; the publication of her sentimentalized account of the homelife of her charges (as *The Little Princesses* in *Woman's Own*) was regarded as a betrayal of trust. The phrase 'doing a Crawfie on' is used for similar indiscretions, especially if accompanied by cloying sentimentality.

Crawley, Rev. Josiah The perpetual curate of Hogglestock in Trollope's *Last Chronicles of Barset*, under suspicion of stealing a check though finally proved innocent despite all Mrs PROUDIE's efforts, aided by his own, to provide evidence of his guilt.

Crawley, Rawdon In Thackeray's VANITY FAIR a spendthrift heavy dragoon, trapped into marriage by Becky SHARP.

Crayon, Geoffrey A pen name of Washington Irving, under which he published The SKETCH BOOK and *The Crayon Miscellany* (1835).

Crazy Horse SITTING BULL's righthand man. See SIOUX WARS.

Creative Evolution (1907) Bergson's theory stressing the creative element in evolution and explaining everything that exists in terms of the continual thrust of the LIFE FORCE. These ideas were popularized in MAN AND SUPERMAN and BACK TO METHUSELAH by Bernard Shaw as the religion of the 20th century; Man can will the acceleration of his development into SUPERMAN, instead of sitting back and waiting for the 'chapter of accidents' postulated by Darwin's theory of NATURAL SELECTION to do it for him.

Crécy (Cooking) Served with carrots.

Crécy, Battle of (1346) The victory, early in the HUNDRED YEARS WAR, of Edward III over Philip VI, in which, according to a disputed tradition, gunpowder was used for the first time. (Town near Abbeville, France.)

Credit-Anstalt Austrian bank whose collapse in 1931 marked the beginning of the DEPRESSION in Europe.

Creditists Members of the SOCIAL CREDIT PARTY.

Cree Algonquian-speaking Indians who acted as guides and hunters for fur traders; some 10,000 survive in the Hudson Bay area.

Creek A confederacy of MUSKOGEAN INDIANS, originally centered in Alabama and Georgia, and one of the FIVE CIVILIZED NATIONS. After defeat by Andrew Jackson (1814), some 15,000 were ordered to Oklahoma, but 3500 died en route. About 13,-000 survive, mostly Baptists or Methodists. See SEMINOLE.

Creevey Papers (1903) The gossipy journals and letters of the English Whig politician, Thomas Creevey (1768-1838); they are of considerable interest for the insight they afford into the political life of his day.

Crêpe Suzette Thin pancake with an orange sauce, served burning in a liqueur.

Cressida See TROILUS AND CRESSIDA.

Cresta, The (1884) (1) A run for one-man 'skeleton' bobs at St Moritz, Switzerland; it has an average gradient of 1 in 7·7 over 1320 yd. (2) Used erroneously of a track parallel to (1), for 4- and 2-man bobs.

Cresta Run, The (1965) N. F. Simpson's Theatre of the ABSURD play about spying, set in suburbia.

Cretaceous Period The most recent subdivision of the MESOZOIC ERA, lasting from about 150 to 70 million years ago. Mammals predominated, the primitive reptiles became extinct, marsupials appeared, flowering plants predominated over others. The climate was mild. (Latin *creta*, 'chalk', deposited in shallow seas covering most of northwest Europe.)

Crime and Punishment (1866) Dostoevsky's novel; see RASKOLNIKOV.

Crimean War (1853-56) A war started by the Tsar's claim to be protector of the Balkan Christians against Turkey. Britain and Napoleon III, suspicious of Russian intentions, came to Turkey's assistance, landing in the Crimea and besieging Sebastopol (see BALACLAVA, INKERMAN). Russia was forced to withdraw its claims.

Crime de Sylvestre Bonnard, Le (1881) Anatole France's novel about an aged scholar who rescues from an unhappy school the daughter of his first love, now orphaned, whose guardian he eventually becomes.

Criminal Investigation Department The headquarters at SCOTLAND YARD of the London Metropolitan detective force and of various branches which also serve the rest of the country, e.g. the SPECIAL BRANCH, CENTRAL OFFICE, Criminal Record Office, Fingerprint Department, Scientific Laboratory and FRAUD SQUAD.

Crimond A famous tune to which the metrical psalm 'The Lord is my shepherd' is sung.

Crimson, The (1873) The HARVARD University daily newspaper, student owned and operated, more radical than The HARVARD INDEPENDENT.

Crippen murder case (1910) The murder of his wife by an American dentist and quack doctor living in Camden Town, London. He dissected the body and buried it in the cellar, then sailing for America with his lover, who was disguised as a boy. The ship's captain, suspicious of their conduct, sent a message to London by radio which resulted in their arrest—the first use of radio in crime detection. Crippen was executed; his mistress, defended by F. E. Smith (Lord Birkenhead) in his first big case, was acquitted.

Crippsian austerity A term referring to the period (1947-50) when the left-wing Socialist, Sir Stafford Cripps, was Chancellor of the Exchequer. Inflation and a serious balance of payments crisis (1949) led to the devaluation of the pound and to drastic economies.

Cripps mission (1942) A mission led by Sir Stafford Cripps, which offered India postwar Dominion status; the offer, described by Gandhi as a 'postdated cheque', was rejected by the Indian CONGRESS PARTY.

Crispin, Edmund Pen name used by Robert Bruce Montgomery when writing his humorous detective stories.

Crispin, St The patron saint of shoemakers. He and his brother Crispian are said to have come from Rome to convert the Gauls in the 4th century, supporting themselves by shoemaking. Agincourt was fought on St Crispin's Day (Shakespeare's 'Crispin Crispian'), Oct. 25th.

Criterion, The (1922-39) A literary quarterly edited by T. S. Eliot.

Croagh Patrick Pilgrimage An annual pilgrimage to the top of Ireland's Holy Mountain (Croagh Patrick, 2500 ft) near the coast of Co. Mayo; it starts on the eve of the last Sunday in July, from either Westport or Louisburgh. There is a small church on the summit, where Mass is said.

Crockford (1857) Short title of Crockford's *Clerical Directory*, an annual 'staff list' of the Church of England, famous for its anonymous prefaces on Church matters.

Crockford's (1827) A London gambling club. (William Crockford, fishmonger, its founder.)

Crock of Gold, The (1912) James Stephens's best-known work, a collection of original fairy stories.

Croesus (6th century BC) The last King of Lydia (in southwest Anatolia), of legendary wealth, and the first to issue gold and silver coins.

Cro-Magnon Man One of the earliest races of HOMO SAPIENS. He produced the ALTAMIRA cave paintings (see AURIGNACIAN CULTURE). (Name of cave in the Dordogne, France, where remains first found.)

Cromwellian chair A mid-17th century low-backed chair of simple design, with strips of leather for seat and back secured by brass tacks, and turned (sometimes spiral) legs.

Cromwellian Settlement, The (1649-52) After the great Irish rebellion of

1641 in which thousands of Protestants were masssacred, and after James Butler, Earl of Ormonde, had declared for Charles II in 1649, Cromwell quelled all revolt by massacring the garrisons at DROGHEDA and Wexford; he then left Ireton to complete the PLANTATIONS by evicting Catholic landowners east of the Shannon and replacing them by Protestants, including his own soldiers (who were soon absorbed into the native population).

Cronus In Greek mythology, a Titan who overthrew his father URANUS and was in turn overthrown by his son ZEUS. He was also the father of HERA, DEMETER, POSEIDON and HADES. The Romans identified him with Saturn.

Crotchet Castle (1831) Thomas Love Peacock's 'novel', on much the same lines as NIGHTMARE ABBEY.

Crouchback, Guy The hero of Evelyn Waugh's SWORD OF HONOUR, the wondering, disillusioned observer of events and people.

Crow A Sioux-speaking tribe of PLAINS INDIANS native to Montana, where about 2000 still survive.

Crown Derby (1786-1811) The name given to the products of the DERBY PORCELAIN factory in the period following its founder's death. Figures continued to predominate but, with the introduction of bone china, tablewares were made, often decorated with IMARI PATTERNS, figures and landscapes on pastel grounds in the SÈVRES style, or (until 1796) BILLINGSLEY FLOWERS. The name was revived by the unconnected Royal Crown Derby Porcelain Co., not founded until 1876. See BLOOR DERBY.

Crown Estate Commissioners (UK) The administrators of revenue from the Crown Estates (formerly called Crown Lands), next to the Forestry Commission the largest landowners in Britain. The Crown Lands were those which George III surrendered to government in return for the CIVIL LIST; they do not include the Duchies of Cornwall and Lancaster.

Croydon London borough since 1965 consisting of the former county borough of Croydon and the urban district of Coulsdon-Purley.

Crucible, The (1953) Arthur Miller's play based on the SALEM WITCH HUNT, constituting a telling attack on political persecution and in particular on MCCARTHYISM, the spirit of which was to lead to his own conviction for contempt of Congress 4 years later.

Cruciferae The cabbage and wallflower family, characterized by the 4 petals arranged in the form of a cross. The chief group is the Brassicas (cabbage, turnip, watercress etc.), but the family also includes nasturtium, aubretia, honesty, candytuft etc. (Latin, 'cross-bearing'.)

Cruden Short title for the *Concordance to the Bible* (1737) compiled by Alexander Cruden, for long the standard concordance.

Cruel Sea, The (1951) A long and lusty best-selling novel by Nicholas Monsarrat about naval life during World War II.

Cruelty, Theater of (1938) A type of play advocated by the French playwright Artaud, which should suppress reason and logic and use fantasies of torture, madness and perversion to act as a catharsis on actors and audience alike, bringing to the surface unavowable obsessions and desires. An outstanding example of the genre is MARAT/SADE.

Cruikshank cartoons Political cartoons, less coarse and a little less venomous than those of ROWLANDSON and GILLRAY, attacking in particular Napoleon and George IV; drawn by George Cruikshank (1792-1878), who later turned to attacks on the evils of gin, and then to illustrating the work of most of the great novelists of his time.

Crummles, Vincent An eccentric theatrical manager in Dickens's NICHOLAS NICKLEBY.

Cruncher, Jerry A minor character in Dickens's A TALE OF TWO CITIES; he works in a bank by day and at night is a body snatcher. His wife spends her time 'flopping' (as he calls it), i.e. on her knees in prayer.

Crusade in Europe, The (1948) General Dwight Eisenhower's account of the war in North Africa and Europe, published 4 years before he became President.

Crusader (Nov. 1941) The code name for the second British invasion of Libya, carried out by the newly formed 8th Army after Auchinleck had relieved Wavell. It reached the Tripolitanian border by the end of the year, but was flung back into Egypt by mid-1942. See BATTLEAXE.

Crusader (1941) (1) A British cruiser tank of World War II, first used in Operation BATTLEAXE: 18 tons, 340 h.p., 27 m.p.h. (2) US fighter made by the Dallas firm of Ling-Temco-Vought, makers of the CORSAIR.

Crusaders CAMBRIDGE UNIVERSITY cricket club of the best 75 players in residence (elected for life); the equivalent of the AUTHENTICS at Oxford.

Crusades (1095-1291) A series of campaigns to rescue the Holy Land from the Muslim SELJUK TURKS. The first was carried out by an unorganized rabble which was massacred, and then by an army which took Jerusalem. In the third (1189) Richard I and the French king failed to recapture the city from Saladin. The fourth (1202) was diverted by the Venetians into sacking Byzantium. In the end the Crusaders lost all their Near Eastern territories except Acre, and that fell in 1291.

Crustacea See ARTHROPODS.

Cry, the Beloved Country (1948) Alan Paton's moving novel of the degrading effects of city (in this case Johannesburg) life on Africans who migrate there from the veld.

Crystal Palace (1851) (London) Joseph Paxton's building, entirely of glass and iron, built to house the GREAT EXHIBITION in Hyde Park; it was then reerected at Penge in South London, but was burned down in 1936. The site, still named after it, is now used for the Greater London Council's National Recreation Centre.

CS Initials used for CHRISTIAN SCIENCE.

CSA Initials used for the Confederate States of America, i.e. the 11 which seceded from the Union in 1860-61.

CSC (1) Initials used as pen name by Charles Stuart Calverley, 19th-century parodist. (2) See CIVIL SERVICE COMMISSION.

CST See CENTRAL STANDARD TIME.

CT Central Time, i.e. CENTRAL STANDARD TIME.

CTV (1961) Signifies Canadian Television Network, a licensed private network which operates in the larger cities; see CBC.

Cuban crisis (Oct. 1962) The tension resulting from the discovery by US reconnaissance planes that Russia was installing rockets in Cuba directed against the USA. President Kennedy's sharp reaction led to Khrushchev's agreeing to dismantle them at once. See PENKOVSKY SPY CASE.

Cubism (1907-14) An art movement started by Picasso and Braque; they brought out the 3-dimensional structure of an object by combining several views of it in cubic or other geometric patterns. Picasso described it as painting 'what he knew was there' rather than what he saw.

Cubs The Chicago Cubs, NATIONAL (Baseball) LEAGUE, playing at WRIGLEY FIELD.

Cuchulain The ACHILLES of Ulster legend, nephew of CONCHOBAR, the boy warrior who, single-handed, defended Ulster against MAEVE (Medb), Queen of Connacht.

Culbertson system (1930) The most famous of the calling systems at Bridge; in hand valuation, points are now counted instead of quick tricks as in the earlier versions; additions are made for long suits. A forcing two call indicates 23 points. (Ely Culbertson, USA, died 1955.)

Culham Laboratory The UK ATOMIC ENERGY AUTHORITY's research center for fusion (thermonuclear) power for use in generating electricity; see ZETA. (Village south of Oxford, near HARWELL.)

Cullinan diamond (1905) A large diamond found in the Premier mine, Transvaal, and presented to Edward VII.

Culloden (1746) The final defeat of the YOUNG PRETENDER, with great loss of life, by Cumberland (the 'BLOODY BUTCHER') in the FORTY-FIVE. (Moor east of Inverness.)

Cultural Revolution, Chinese (1965-67) A campaign launched by Chairman Mao Tse-tung against 'revisionists', i.e. opponents of his policies; its agents were the RED GUARDS.

Cumberland, The A Federal wooden sloop, rammed and sunk by the Confederate ironclad *Merrimac* (1862) the day before the encounter of the MERRIMAC AND MONITOR. Her sinking ended the era of wooden battleships.

Cumberland Gap The pass (1650 ft) through the Cumberland Mountains near the junction of the Kentucky, Tennessee and Virginia state lines, first discovered in 1750; the WILDERNESS ROAD used this route, which was important strategically in the Civil War.

Cumberland Road (1818) A National Pike (also called the Old National Road) from Cumberland, Md., through a deep gorge in the Appalachian Mountains to Wheeling on the Ohio, later extended to Columbus and Vandalia, Ill. It was the first Federal-built road to the West and was used by the Western mails; after a period of neglect it was incorporated in Highway 40.

Cumberland style (Wrestling) A style popular in northwest England and in Scotland; the initial hold is all important and a win is scored simply by throwing an opponent to the ground.

Cumbernauld (1956) (UK) A NEW TOWN in Dunbartonshire, designed to take Glasgow overspill population up to 70,000.

Cunard (1878) A British shipping firm formed from the British and North American Royal Mail Steam Packet Co. founded in 1839 by a Canadian, Sir Samuel Cunard. It is now the Cunard Steam-Ship Co., which owns the Port Line, Brocklebanks, Cunard White Star etc., and made a brief excursion into the transatlantic airline field in the 1960s.

Cupid The Roman equivalent of EROS. See next entry.

Cupid and Psyche A story in the GOLDEN ASS, in which Cupid (Eros) falls in love with a king's daughter, PSYCHE, whom he visits nightly. She disobeys his command not to try to identify him, because he is one of the immortals, and he goes off in a huff; but in the end they are reunited and she too is made immortal.

Curaçao A liqueur, originally Dutch, made with the peel of bitter Curacao oranges. (One of the Netherlands Antilles in the West Indies.)

Curragh, The (Irish Republic) An extensive down east of the town of Kildare, from ancient times used as a racetrack, and now the scene of all the Irish classic races; also formerly used as a British military camp (see next entry). (Irish *cuirrech*, racetrack.)

Curragh 'mutiny' (Mar. 1914) The occasion (not a mutiny) when British cavalry officers at the CURRAGH declared that they would resign rather than fight against Carson's ULSTER VOLUNTEERS.

Currier & Ives A firm famous for its topical lithographs in the era before press photography began, founded by Nathaniel Currier of Roxbury, Mass., partnered later by James Ives. In 1835 Currier's lithograph, 'Ruins of the Merchants' Exchange', depicting a big New York fire only 4 days after the event, proved a best seller and was followed by one of a recent steamship fire. Thereafter the partners concentrated on illustrating events in the news, but also did sets of biblical, Wild West and other scenes, all highly prized today.

Curse of Scotland A name, since the 18th century, for the 9 of Diamonds; many explanations are suggested, e.g. the 9 lozenges in the arms of the Earl of Stair, blamed by some for the GLENCOE MASSACRE.

Curtis Cup (1930) Women's golf contest between USA and Britain, played annually in either country alternately.

Curzon Line A boundary between Poland and Russia first proposed by Lloyd George in 1920, when it was rejected, and imposed on Poland after the MOSCOW CONFERENCE ('Tolstoy') in 1944. It deprived Poland of areas where Russians, Ukrainians or Lithuanians are in the majority. (Lord Curzon, Foreign Secretary, who handled the negotiations in 1920.)

Cushites The non-Semitic people of northern Africa. See HAMITES.

Custer's last stand (1876) The last fight (the Battle of Little Big Horn) of General Custer, when surrounded by Sioux in Dakota Territory; he and his troops were all killed. See SIOUX WAR.

Cutty Sark (1896) The last of the tea clippers, now lying in the Thames at Greenwich Pier, and open to the public. (Scottish, 'short shirt'; used in Robert Burns's *Tam O'Shanter* of a witch.)

Cwmbran (1949) (UK) A NEW TOWN in Monmouthshire, 5 miles north of Newport, designed for a population of 55,000.

Cybele The Phrygian mother goddess who loved ATTIS; worshiped with orgiastic rites by eunuch Corybants. Identified with RHEA by the Greeks, and worshiped in Rome as the Great Mother.

Cyclopean masonry Ancient building works constructed without mortar of huge, perfectly fitting blocks of stone, examples of which can be seen at TIRYNS and MYCENAE in Greece, and in other parts of the world. (Traditionally built by the CYCLOPS giants.)

Cyclops In Greek legend, any of several one-eyed giants who helped HEPHAESTUS to forge thunderbolts; POLYPHEMUS was a Cyclops. (Greek, 'round-eyed'.)

Cygnus The Swan, a northern constellation between Pegasus and Dra-

co, with about 200 stars visible to the naked eye; it contains a dark nebula.

Cymbeline Shakespeare's name for Cunobelinus, a British king at the beginning of the Christian era, father of Caractacus. Shakespeare's play (1610) is about his daughter Imogen and her secret marriage. She is unjustly suspected of infidelity, but there is the final reconciliation scene characteristic of Shakespeare's last plays.

Cymric Welsh. (Welsh *Cymru*, 'Wales'.)

Cynthia A less common name for ARTEMIS. (Born on Mount Cynthus, on the island of Delos.)

CYO Initials used for the Catholic Youth Organization.

Cypripedium The genus name of the Lady's Slipper orchids.

Cyrano de Bergerac (1897) Rostand's play about a 17th-century French soldier and dramatist, famous for his long nose, his duels and his accounts of visits to the moon and sun rather in the style of *Gulliver's Travels*.

Cyrillic The Russian alphabet, based on the Greek. Serbo-Croat is sometimes written in a modernized and simplified form of it, but a Latin alphabet is also used. (Traditionally introduced by St Cyril, a 9th-century Greek missionary to the Slavs.)

Cy Young Award (1956) Made to the outstanding major league pitcher of the year. (Named for Cy ('Cyclone') Young, famous fast pitcher, retired 1911.)

Czestochowa Madonna See JASNA GORA.

Czernowitz Rumanian name of Chernovtsy, now a city of the Ukrainian SSR in Soviet Russia.

D

DAB Initials used for the standard *Dictionary of American Biography*, published in 20 volumes (1928-37).

Daboll Almanac Another name for the NEW ENGLAND ALMANAC.

Dachau (1933) Hitler's first concentration camp, near Munich.

Dacia A Roman province which fell to the GOTHS in the 3rd century; corresponding to modern Rumania and neighboring districts.

Dacron American form of TERYLENE made by DU PONT.

Dadaism (1915) The first of the really mad 'artistic' movements, started in unlikely Zurich. It took almost any form, from a lecture by 38 lecturers in unison to painting moustaches on MONA LISA.

Dad Vail Regatta (1939) A university race for 8-oared shells rowed on Schuylkill River, Philadelphia, over a course of 1 $\frac{5}{16}$ miles. Among the contestants are: Amherst, Boston University, Brown, Dartmouth, Florida Southern, Howard, La Salle, Marietta, Rollins, Rutgers, Tampa. (Named for a coach of Wisconsin.)

Daedalus In Greek legend a craftsman, symbolic of invention and creative activity, who built the Labyrinth at KNOSSOS, was imprisoned in it with his son Icarus, but escaped. He fastened wings on their shoulders with wax and flew away. Icarus flew too near the sun, which melted the wax, and he fell into the Icarian Sea; Daedalus landed safely at Naples. (Greek, 'skillful', 'variegated'.)

Dagenham (UK) A former Essex borough, since 1965 divided between the boroughs of REDBRIDGE and BARKING.

Dagwood An enormous sandwich, named for Dagwood Bumstead of Chic Young's comic strip *Blondie* (1930) who, cut off by his millionaire father for marrying the gaffe-prone Blondie, relieves the tensions of suburban life by frequent recourse to gargantuan icebox sandwiches.

Dáil Éireann The Irish Republic's parliament. It was first formed (illegally) in 1919 by the Sinn Fein MPs who had refused to take their seats at Westminster; it set up a parallel administration to the British, with its own courts and raising its own taxes. In 1921, at the Partition, it became the legal government of the Irish Free State. (Erse, 'assembly of Ireland'.)

Daily News (1846) A London Liberal newspaper, of which Charles Dickens was the founder and first editor; absorbed by the *News-Chronicle* in 1930.

Daimler (1885) One of the first gasoline-driven automobiles to be marketed, a 'horseless carriage' soon to be replaced by more modern types. A Daimler Co. was formed in 1891, and was later renamed MERCEDES. See BENZ. (Gottlieb Daimler, German inventor.)

Daiquiri An iced cocktail made with Cuban rum, lime juice and sugar. (A town near Santiago da Cuba.)

Dairen Chinese port built by Russia, also called Talien, and grouped with Port Arthur as the conurbation of Lü-ta.

Daisycutter A low-altitude version of the BLUE STEEL air-to-surface missile.

Dakar expedition (Sept. 1940) Gen. de Gaulle's expedition to Dakar, then the capital of French West Africa, in the expectation that Frenchmen there would rally to him; the VICHY GOVERNMENT elements were, however, in control and the expedition was repulsed.

Dakota (1) British name for the US DC-3 aircraft, virtually the first modern airliner, a twin-engined all-metal plane which had an immense worldwide success and was in service from 1935 to the 1960s. (DC = DOUGLAS Commercial.) (2) American Indians better known as the SIOUX.

Dalai Lama The chief priest of the Tibetan Buddhists; each is said to be a reincarnation of his predecessor, and is recognized while still an infant by certain traditional signs. With the Chinese Communist invasion of Tibet, the last Dalai Lama took refuge in India.

Dalcroze Institue of Eurhythmics (1910) An influential school founded in Bavaria and moved to Geneva, where children were taught to interpret the spirit of music in spontaneous dances. (Founded by Émile Jaques-Dalcroze, Swiss composer.)

Dall sheep Wild bighorn sheep, almost pure white, found in Alaska, especially in MT MCKINLEY NATIONAL PARK. (Named for W. H. Dall, US zoologist, 1845-1927.)

Dalmatian A medium-sized short-haired dog, white spotted with black or liver; it was originally trained to follow behind or under coaches, and kept in the stables. (Believed to have originated from Dalmatia.)

Dalriada (1) Ancient Gaelic kingdom of northern Antrim. (2) Kingdom of Argyll founded about AD 500 by emigrants from Irish Dalriada, the first Scots to arrive in Scotland.

Dalton plan Helen Parkhurst's educational system in which children's initiative is developed by giving them monthly assignments to complete in their own way and with self-imposed discipline. (Dalton, Mass., where first tried out in 1920.)

Daltons London Stock Exchange name for the issue (1946) of 2½% Irredeemable Treasury Stock, made when Hugh Dalton was the Labor Chancellor of the Exchequer; they became notorious when holders found that their value fell rapidly.

Damascus, The road to An allusion to the scene of St Paul's conversion after hearing a voice saying: Saul, why persecutest thou me? (*Acts* ix.)

Damascus steel Ornamental steel with a watered variegated pattern produced by welding iron and steel (damascening), used especially for sword blades. The craft flourished at Damascus and knowledge of it was brought to Europe by Crusaders.

Dame aux camélias, La (1848) The novel by Alexandre Dumas *fils* on which he based a play, Verdi an opera (*La* TRAVIATA), and Hollywood a movie (*Camille*, with Garbo). Marguerite Gautier, a fashionable courtesan, spurns a rich suitor, runs off with the penniless Armand Duval, gives him up at his father's request, and dies of consumption. See also LADY OF THE CAMELLIAS.

Dame Partlet Wife of Chanticleer; see CHANTICLEER AND PERTELOTE.

Damocles A courtier who envied the wealth and happiness of Dionysius the Elder, tyrant of Syracuse in the 5th century BC. To teach him that 'uneasy lies the head that wears a crown' Dionysius gave him a banquet, during which he noticed a sword suspended over his head by a single hair. Hence *sword of Damocles*, ever-present danger, especially when all seems well.

Damon and Pythias Two Greeks of Syracuse in the 5th century BC, whose friendship was proverbial. When Pythias was condemned to death, Damon stood security for him at the risk of his own life; moved by this, the tyrant of Syracuse pardoned Pythias.

Dan A grade of mastership of judo. Those placed in the 1st-5th Dan (the lowest) wear black belts; 6th-8th Dan, red and white; 9th-10th, red belts. Pupils are graded as 1st-6th Kyu.

Danaë In Greek legend, the daughter (symbolizing the earth dying of drought) of a King of Argos who locked her up because of a prophecy that her son would destroy him. ZEUS visited her in the guise of a shower of gold (i.e. as a rain god), and fathered PERSEUS by her.

Dance of Death (1) Strindberg's realistic play (1901) about the love-hate of a tyrannical husband and his submissive wife. (2) See DANSE MACABRE.

Dane, Clemence Pen name of Winifred Ashton (1888-1965), English novelist and playwright, best known for her play BILL OF DIVORCEMENT.

Danegeld A land tax imposed in 10th-century England, and used by

Ethelred the Unready to buy off the Danes.

Danelaw The area of England occupied by the Danes; Alfred the Great and Guthrum the Dane agreed on WATLING STREET as the boundary between it and Wessex in AD 878.

Danforth Foundation (1927) One of the largest US foundations, formed to promote education through its own programs and by grants to educational institutions. The headquarters are in St Louis, Mo.

Dangerous Corner (1932) J. B. Priestley's play in which a chance remark leads a happy group into highly embarrassing mutual revelations; the play starts again, with the remark left unspoken, and all ends happily.

Daniel (6th century BC) A major prophet (see next entry). See BELSHAZZAR'S FEAST; SUSANNA AND THE ELDERS. The story of Daniel's being cast into the lions' den and escaping miraculously unharmed is told in *Daniel* vi, 7-23.

Daniel (2nd century BC) The Old Testament book which tells the story of Daniel (see last entry), regarding whom there is no other source of information.

Daniel Deronda (1876) George Eliot's last novel. The eponymous hero, brought up as a Christian, discovers that he is a Jew, marries a Jewess and with her brother goes to Palestine fired with what would now be called Zionist ambitions (the Zionist movement started 20 years after the book was published.)

Danilo See MERRY WIDOW.

Danish A rich Danish pastry made of dough raised with yeast, and the shortening rolled in.

Danish Blue The ubiquitous soft blue cheese, strictly that made from cow's milk and ripened in caves in Denmark; it has a much harsher flavor than the older-established blue cheeses.

D'Annunzio raid (Sept. 1919) The seizure of Fiume from Yugoslavia by Italian irregular forces led by the swashbuckling poet Gabriele d'Annunzio. Defying the Allied

Council of Foreign Ministers, he proclaimed a government there and was not ejected until Jan. 1921.

Dan Patch A famous harness horse which in 1905 set up a record for pacing the mile which stood till 1938.

Danse macabre A mimed dance of death of medieval German origin, in which Death seizes representatives of every age and condition of life one by one. It has often been depicted in art and music.

Dan to Beersheba A phrase from *Judges* xx, 1, meaning from one end of Canaan (or, by extension, any country) to another.

Danzig The German name of the Polish port of Gdańsk.

Daphne In Greek legend a girl who escaped the advances of APOLLO by being turned into a laurel.

Daphnis and Chloe (1) Rustic lovers in a Greek pastoral romance of the 4th century AD. (2) A Diaghilev ballet (1912) with entrancing music by Ravel and choreography by Fokine.

DAR See DAUGHTERS OF THE AMERICAN REVOLUTION.

D'Arblay, Frances See BURNEY, FANNY.

Darby and Joan A couple who have been long and happily married. (Name taken from a ballad, said to be based on a historical couple of London or, in another version, of Yorkshire.)

Darcy A character in Jane Austen's *Pride and Prejudice* whose snobbishness and pride eventually yield to admiration for Elizabeth Bennet (see BENNET FAMILY), whom he marries.

Dardanelles campaign (Feb. 1915-Jan. 1916) A campaign sponsored in World War I by Winston Churchill as First Lord of the Admiralty, designed both to outflank Germany via Turkey and to open up communications with Russia. It failed owing to hesitant support from the Cabinet and weak command on the spot. The Anglo-French fleet failed to penetrate the Dardanelles, and British and ANZAC forces were landed on Gallipoli under Ian Hamilton at

ANZAC COVE and later at Suvla Bay, under withering fire from the Turks who had had overlong notice of Allied intentions. The whole force was evacuated in Dec./Jan., having achieved nothing at heavy cost.

Dare, Virginia The first English child born in America (1587). She was born on Roanoke Island during the stay of the fourth expedition there, which was led by her grandfather, John White. See ROANOKE ADVENTURE.

Daresbury Laboratory (1967) A British nuclear physics laboratory which has an accelerator for electrons (complementary to the proton accelerator at the RUTHERFORD LABORATORY), generating a powerful source of a type of X ray as a byproduct. (Daresbury, village near Warrington, Lancashire.)

Darjeeling tea The best-known of Indian teas, grown in the extreme north of West Bengal, near the Sikkim border.

Dark Ages A term formerly used for the MIDDLE AGES, abandoned when historians discovered that they were not so dark as they had been painted; now sometimes applied to the first 4 centuries of that period, from the fall of Rome to Charlemagne.

Dark Lady of the Sonnets, The The woman to whom Shakespeare addressed Sonnets 127-152, and whom the poet loves despite her unfaithfulness. Described as 'as dark as night', 'black wires grow on her head', she has never been identified; she may have been Elizabeth's maid of honor, Mary Fitton.

Darkness at Noon (1941) Arthur Koestler's novel based on the Russian purges of the 1930s, a study of a Communist idealist forced to make a false confession of treason against the State.

Darley Arabian See THOROUGHBRED.

Darling, Grace Daughter of an English lighthouse keeper who with her father rescued survivors from a wreck off the Farne Islands (1838).

'Darling Daisy' letters Written by Edward VII to Frances, Countess of Warwick, who threatened at one time to publish them; auctioned in 1967.

Darracq An early French car. In 1906 a 200-h.p. V-8 model reached 122 m.p.h.

D'Artagnan See THREE MUSKETEERS.

Dartington Hall (1926) (UK) An imaginatively planned economic and cultural community near Totnes, Devon, now a trust with agricultural and commercial enterprises (including a sawmill, textile mill, cattle breeding research center), and a coeducational boarding school where the children make their own rules and there are no compulsory lessons or games, no marks, punishments, prefects, bounds or religious services. (Founded by Leonard and Dorothy Elmhirst.)

Dartle, Miss Rosa The excitable spinster in Dickens's DAVID COPPERFIELD who falls inappropriately and violently in love with the cad Steerforth; her keynote line is: I only ask for information.

Dartmouth College (1769) A university at Hanover, N. H.

Dartmouth RNC Now named the BRITANNIA ROYAL NAVAL COLLEGE.

Darwin College (1963) The first graduate college at CAMBRIDGE UNIVERSITY, built on to an existing country house.

Darwinism See ORIGIN OF SPECIES; SCOPES TRIAL.

Darwin's finches The finches noted by Darwin on the Galapagos Islands during the VOYAGE OF THE BEAGLE. Isolated on the scattered islands of the archipelago, they had developed widely differing beaks to deal with the food locally available. He mentions this as among the main starting points for his theory of the ORIGIN OF SPECIES.

Dashwood family Characters in Jane Austen's *Sense and Sensibility* (1811). Elinor, the heroine, represents 'sense' and her sister Marianne 'sensibility'; John, their stepbrother, is persuaded by his wife not to fulfill his obligations to them.

Daughters of Isabella (1897) A Catholic women's organization, with headquarters in New Haven, Conn.

Daughters of the American Revolution (1890) A patriotic society of women descended from those who fought in the War of Independence, and are dedicated to the preservation of the ideals of that war.

Daughters of the Nile An order with membership limited to female relatives of Masons.

Dauphin, The The title of the French crown prince, from the 14th century until the ORLEANIST MONARCHY. His wife was the Dauphine.

DAV Signifies Disabled American Veterans, an organization founded in Cincinnati in 1920.

'Dave Brinkley's Journal' A national TV series on public affairs. See HUNTLEY-BRINKLEY REPORT.

Davenport (1793-1876) An English pottery and china firm at Longport, Staffordshire, particularly noted for high-class bone china with fruit and flower decorations in brilliant colors, and for lusterware tea services. It also made earthenware and stoneware.

David King of Israel (c. 1004-966 BC) who succeeded SAUL, slew the Philistine giant Goliath (1 *Samuel* xvii, 4-51), was the inseparable friend of Saul's son Jonathan (1 *Samuel* xviii, 1), fell in love with BATHSHEBA, and whose son ABSALOM rose in revolt against him. He is the traditional author of *Psalms*.

David Copperfield (1850) One of the best known of Dickens's novels, partly autobiographical. David, turned loose when young, leaves his nurse Clara PEGGOTTY, lodges with MICAWBER, is championed by his great-aunt Betsy TROTWOOD, works for a lawyer who is being blackmailed by Uriah HEEP, and marries the lawyer's daughter as his second wife.

Daviot, Gordon Pen name assumed by Elizabeth Mackintosh when she wrote the popular historical play *Richard of Bordeaux* (1933) and other plays. See also TEY, JOSEPHINE.

Davis apparatus A device to enable the crew to escape from a damaged submerged submarine.

Davis Cup (1900) Officially the International Lawn Tennis Championship, which began as a match between USA and Britain and grew into an international contest between teams playing 4 singles and 1 doubles; the winner in eliminating rounds (played in 3 zones — American, European and Eastern) challenges the holder. (Dwight Davis, US donor.)

Davy Crockett A US man-portable tactical nuclear weapon, with a range of 6-7 miles. (See next entry.)

Davy Crockett cap A coonskin cap, almost obligatory wear for small boys in the 1950s, in memory of an American hunter and trapper (died 1836) whose exploits against American Indians and Mexicans are recorded in numerous books, including his own.

Davy Jones's locker The grave of those who are buried at sea. (18th-century phrase; Davy Jones was the spirit of the sea, perhaps a name derived from Jonah.)

Davy Medal Royal Society medal awarded annually for the most important discovery in chemistry in Europe or Anglo-America. (Founded by Sir Humphry Davy's brother.)

Dawes Plan (1924) A scaling down of German reparations combined with a large German loan which produced a 5-year truce in the postwar wrangle over reparations. Superseded by the YOUNG PLAN. (C. G. Dawes, US statesman.)

Dawes Severalty Act (1887) An allotment Act which authorized the breakup of Indian reserves into individual holdings (160 acres for a householder, 80 for the unmarried). It was meant (but failed) to meet the criticism that life on the reserves fostered laziness and hampered acculturation. Unallotted land (over half the total) was confiscated, leaving future generations landless or land-hungry, detribalized but unassimilated.

Dawk One who is neither a HAWK nor a DOVE but takes the middle of the road.

Dawley (UK) A NEW TOWN in Shropshire, southeast of the Wrekin, designed for a population of 90,000.

Daylight Saving Act (1916) (UK) The law which first introduced British Summer Time, as a wartime economy measure.

Daylight Saving Time (1) Time one or more hours faster than standard time, introduced to lengthen daylight working hours in summer. (2) A uniform system introduced in the US from 1967 by the UNIFORM TIME ACT, providing for clocks to be advanced one hour from the last Sunday in April to the last Sunday in October. (See last entry.)

Day of the Triffids, The (1951) John Wyndham's outstanding science fiction novel, well-known outside the circle of SF addicts, about the survivors of a world struck down with blindness and a plague, and menaced by huge ambulatory lethally stinging vegetables evolved by man in the search for new sources of vegetable oil.

Daytona Beach A resort on the Atlantic coast of Florida with a 20-mile stretch of sandy beach on which many automobile speed records have been established from the 1920s onward.

Daytona Continental The first of the 8 annual auto-racing events counting towards the Sports-GT championships, run at Daytona Beach, Fla.

DB-6 Aston-Martin 4-liter 2-door sports sedan or convertible; twice the price of the E-TYPE Jaguar and presumably conferring twice the prestige.

D.C. (USA) Initials standing for District of Columbia, the federal unit, not part of any state, which is in fact the city of Washington, the US capital. The city is always referred to as Washington, D.C.

D-Day (6 June 1944) The first day of the Allied landings in Normandy.

DDT A powerful insecticide, the effectiveness of which was first observed in Switzerland in 1939. (Initials of its chemical name.)

Dead End Kids, The The young actors who appeared in Sidney Kingsley's play (1935) and movie (1937), *Dead End*, about New York slums during the DEPRESSION. They also played in several movie sequels,

e.g. *The Dead End Kids on Dress Parade* (1939).

Dead March in Saul, The The march from Handel's oratorio *Saul* (1739), often played at state funerals.

Dead Sea fruit The 'apple of Sodom', a legendary fruit of the desert which turned to ashes in the mouth; hence a symbol of frustrated hope. (Presumably a fanciful description of a desert fruit, still called by that name, which is quite uneatable.)

Dead Sea Scrolls Ancient manuscripts found (from 1947 onwards) in caves around Qumran, near the Dead Sea, possibly written by ESSENES (a Jewish sect) in the first century AD. They include the earliest extant manuscripts of the Old Testament and the APOCRYPHA. Their age and other crucial points are still debated.

Dead Souls (1842) Gogol's great comic novel about a rogue, Chichikov, who travels round the country buying the ownership of dead serfs in a complex scheme to mortgage them for land. The fun lies in the landowners' reactions to this extraordinary proposition.

Deadwood Dick (1) Sobriquet of several 19th-century cowboys, both white and Negro. (2) Hero of dime novels by E. L. Wheeler about the 1876 Gold Rush. The character was based on an English-born frontiersman, Richard Clarke (1845-1930), who made his name as a guard of gold consignments. (Deadwood, S.D.)

Deans, Jeanie The heroine of Walter Scott's *Heart of Midlothian*; she goes to London to obtain a pardon from the king for her half sister Effie, who has been found guilty of murdering her illegitimate child (who however turns out to be alive).

'Dear Abby' A column of advice by Abigail Van Buren, pen name of Pauline Friedman Phillips, syndicated since 1956.

Dear Brutus (1917) A play by James Barrie about lost opportunities and a chance to seize them in Lob's magic Wood of the Second Chance.

Dear John A letter (as to a soldier) in which a wife asks for a divorce or a girl friend breaks off an engagement or a friendship.

Death and the Maiden Quartet One of Schubert's string quartets, named after the song on which the variations in the second movement are based.

Death and Transfiguration (1891) A symphonic poem by Richard Strauss which begins with a powerful evocation of a dying man recalling his childhood.

Death Comes for the Archbishop (1927) Willa Cather's novel, based in part on historical incidents, in which Bishop Latour and the faithful Father Vaillant triumph over obstacles to found a cathedral in the wilds of New Mexico.

Death in the Afternoon (1932) Ernest Hemingway's novel about bullfighting, a subject which fascinated him and which he describes with a wealth of technical detail.

Death in the Family, A (1957) A partly autobiographical novel by James Agee, published after his death; on it was based Tad Mosel's play *All the Way Home* (1960); both won Pulitzer prizes.

Death of a Hero (1929) Richard Aldington's disillusioned novel about World War I.

Death of a President (1967) William Manchester's detailed account of events on the day that President John F. Kennedy was assassinated.

Death of a Salesman See LOMAN, WILLY.

Death Row A name for the 'death cells' where condemned prisoners await execution.

Death Valley A vast desert in eastern California and Nevada, up to 276 ft below sea level. It has varied birdlife but few plants, and was a serious hazard to the 49ERS. Now a National Monument (1933).

De Beers (1871) The corporation which, starting as a mining company near Kimberley, Cape Colony, South Africa, gained a virtual monopoly of African diamond mining and marketing, and from 1959 of the marketing of Russian diamonds outside the Communist bloc. (Name of its first mine.)

Deborah A prophetess and judge of Israel (*Judges* iv, 4) whose song of triumph after Barak's defeat of SISERA (*Judges* v) is possibly one of the oldest parts of the Bible.

De Bourgh, Lady Catherine The formidable female in PRIDE AND PREJUDICE who is outraged at the idea of Bingley and Darcy marrying into the despised BENNET FAMILY.

Debrett Common abbreviation for Debrett's *Peerage, Baronetage, Knightage and Companionage* (1802) and 2 other derivative annuals, now published by KELLY'S DIRECTORIES. (John Debrett, London publisher.)

Decalogue, The The Ten Commandments. (Greek, 'ten words'.)

Decameron (1353) A collection of tales supposed to have been told by a company of Florentines to while away their enforced confinement during an outbreak of plague, and compiled by Boccaccio. (Greek, 'ten days'.)

Decathlon An OLYMPIC GAMES or other contest in which individuals or teams compete in all of 10 events: long and high jump, pole vault, discus, putting the weight, javelin, hurdle race, 100,400 and 1500 meters. (Greek, '10 contests'.)

Deceased Wife's Sister Marriage Act (1907) A burning political issue in Britain over a long period, termed by W. S. Gilbert 'that annual blister— / Marriage of deceased wife's sister'. The Act authorized civil marriages of this kind but left it open to individual clergy to refuse to hold a church ceremony.

Decembrists (1825) In Russian history, revolutionaries, mostly Guards officers, who campaigned for the liberation of the serfs and the grant of a constitution. Their December revolt failed, and the ringleaders were hanged.

Declaration of Human Rights, Universal (1948) A declaration arising from the horrors of the Nazi regime, passed by the General Assembly of the UN, with USSR, South Africa and Saudi Arabia among those abstaining. The rights are those individual freedoms normally associated with Western democracy.

Declaration of Independence (1776) The document declaring the independence of the 11 North American colonies, which contains the words: We hold these truths to be self-evident, that all men are created equal . . . with certain unalienable rights . . . among these are life, liberty, and the pursuit of happiness. See FOURTH OF JULY.

'Declaration of Independence, The Signing of the' The best known of 4 paintings on Revolutionary themes by John Trumbull, commissioned by Congress in 1817 for the Rotunda of the Capitol in Washington.

Declaration of Indulgence (1672) Charles II's attempt to suspend discrimination against NONCONFORMISTS and Catholics under the CLARENDON CODE; he was forced by Parliament to rescind it a year later. Also similar declarations made by James II in 1687 and 1688.

Declaration of Rights (1688) Accepted by William and Mary at the GLORIOUS REVOLUTION; it established constitutional monarchy, with Parliament supreme; it was further strengthened by the ACT OF SETTLEMENT (1701). See BILL OF RIGHTS.

Declaration of the Rights of Man (1789) Drawn up by the French NATIONAL ASSEMBLY and reluctantly accepted by Louis XVI, it proclaimed the legal equality of man, their right to rule and make laws, and the freedom of the press; it condemned taxation without representation, and arbitrary imprisonment.

Decline and Fall (1928) Evelyn Waugh's first novel, famous for its opening chapters on the disreputable prep school at Llanabba Castle in Wales, which has on its staff the ineffable Capt. GRIMES.

Decline and Fall of the Roman Empire, The (1776-88) Edward Gibbon's monumental history covering the period from the reign of Antoninus Pius to the fall of Constantinople, i.e. AD 138-1453.

Decline of the West See SPENGLER.

Decorated (1290-1375) The middle period of English GOTHIC ARCHITECTURE, characterized by ornate window tracery, elaborate external decoration of the spires, and complex vaulting, exemplified in Exeter Cathedral.

Dedalus, Stephen The hero of James Joyce's PORTRAIT OF THE ARTIST AS A YOUNG MAN (and thus clearly meant to be a self-portrait), and one of the chief characters in his ULYSSES. He is an artist, at war with Irish Catholicism and nationalism, but cannot completely free himself from the shackles of his Irish upbringing. (For the name, see DAEDALUS.

Deep South, The (1) The southern, formerly slave and CONFEDERATE STATES OF AMERICA, traditionally anti-Civil Rights. (2) Iain Macleod's name for the safe right-wing Conservative constituencies of the south coast of England, where retired colonels and their like set the tone; e.g. Bournemouth, Eastbourne.

Deerslayer, The (1841) One of James Fenimore Cooper's LEATHERSTOCKING TALES, about the adventures of Natty Bumppo ('Deerslayer') as a young man when he lived and hunted with the Delaware Indians.

Defenestration, The (1618) The occasion at Prague when Protestants of the Bohemian National Council threw 2 Roman Catholic members out a window of Hradshin Castle; this provided an excuse to begin the THIRTY YEARS WAR. (Latin de fenestra, 'out of the window'.)

Defense Intelligence Agency A department of the PENTAGON which collects and analyzes military intelligence.

De Havilland (1920) The British aircraft firm which produced such famous types as the MOTH, MOSQUITO, VENOM and the first British plane to fly supersonic (1948). (Founded by Sir Geoffrey De Havilland, died 1965.)

Deianira See NESSUS.

Deirdre In Irish legend, the daughter of King CONCHOBAR's harpist, the intended bride of the king, who was brought up in seclusion because of a prophecy that she would be the most beautiful woman in Ireland but would bring death to the RED BRANCH KNIGHTS. She fell in love with the king's nephew, Noisi, who carried her off to Scotland, but was persuaded to return and treacherously killed. Deirdre killed herself. The legend was treated by Synge (DEIRDRE OF THE SORROWS), Yeats and others.

Deirdre of the Sorrows (1910) J. M. Synge's unfinished verse drama on the DEIRDRE legend.

'Déjeuner sur l'herbe' (1863) Manet's painting of a picnic, with one nude girl seated among dark-clad gentlemen; now in the Louvre.

Delaunay (Henri) Cup See EUROPEAN NATIONS CUP.

Delectable Mountains A place in PILGRIM'S PROGRESS whence the CELESTIAL CITY can be seen and where Christian and Hopeful talk with the shepherds Knowledge, Experience, Watchful and Sincere.

Delft Dutch and adopted English name for earthenware with a lead glaze made white and opaque by adding tin oxide; also called tin-enamelled ware. In France it is called faience (from Italian town Faenza), and in Italy MAIOLICA. The chief English producers were LAMBETH, LIVERPOOL and BRISTOL; wares decorated in blue often lack interest, but the polychrome examples with yellow, purple etc. are highly regarded. Dutch Delft of the 17th and 18th centuries was decorated in imitation of Chinese styles. (Town in Holland.)

Delgado murder (1965) The murder of Gen. Humberto Delgado, leading opponent of the Portuguese dictatorship, whose body was found near Badajoz in Spain; the circumstances of his death remained a mystery.

Delhi Pact (1950) An agreement signed by Nehru and Liaqat Ali Khan by which India and Pakistan undertook to protect each other's minorities and put an end to the communal massacres by Hindus and Muslims which had followed PARTITION.

Delilah The woman set by the Philistines to worm out of SAMSON the secret of his strength; eventually he told her that it lay in his hair, for 'there hath not come a rasor upon mine head'.(*Judges* xvi, 4-20.)

Della Robbia ware Brown terracotta bas-reliefs with a thick, colored lead glaze, typically representing white figures on a blue ground; made in Florence (1450-1528) by the great sculptor Luca della Robbia and his nephew, and later in France (1530-67).

Delmonico potatoes Hashed or sliced potato baked in cream sauce with butter, chives and sometimes grated cheese. (Named for DELMONICO's.)

Delmonico's A famous New York restaurant opened by Lorenzo Delmonico (died 1881).

Delphi The ancient Greek site on the foothills of Mount Parnassus, overlooking the Gulf of Corinth, of the temple of APOLLO whose priestess, Pythia, was his mouthpiece and oracle, consulted by the rulers of the ancient world before they made any important move. Her prophecies, couched in (deplorable) hexameters, were usually ambiguous enough to cover most eventualities, a lesson well learned by newspaper astrologers today.

Delta plan (Holland) The construction of 20 miles of dykes to connect the islands of the Rhine-Scheldt estuary and form freshwater lakes behind them; completion planned for 1978.

Demeter Greek goddess of grain (Roman Ceres), by ZEUS the mother of PERSEPHONE. Her major festival was the ELEUSINIAN MYSTERIES.

Demidov (Cooking) Term applied to various elaborate dishes, especially chicken cooked with truffles and port or Madeira. (Name of a Russian epicure.)

Democratic Center (French political party) See CD.

Democratic Party (1828) (USA) The main body of the old Republican Democratic Party after the REPUBLICAN PARTY seceded. They supported low tariffs and, in the AMERICAN CIVIL WAR, the maintenance of slavery. As 'trustbusters' and opponents of big business generally they swept into power under Woodrow Wilson, leading the country to abandon isolationism and to enter World War I; but Congress rejected their support of the League of Nations. They came back under F. D. Roosevelt to introduce the NEW DEAL and to enter World War II, and remained in power, except for the Eisenhower period, until 1968, advocating support of the United Nations, and domestic reform.

'Demoiselles d'Avignon' (1907) Picasso's semiabstract painting in which the influence of African sculpture and the signs of transition to Cubism first appear. In the Museum of Modern Art, New York.

DeMolay, Order of (1919) An order for boys who are sons of Freemasons; the headquarters are in Kansas City, Mo.

Dennis the Menace The *infant terrible* of the comic strips, drawn by Hank Ketcham. It was made into a TV series starring Jay North.

Denver Mint See BUREAU OF THE MINT.

Deposition, The The taking down of Christ from the Cross, a subject often treated by the Old Masters, e.g. Raphael and Memlinc.

Depression, The (1930s) Colloquial term for the worldwide effects of the WALL STREET CRASH, intensified by shortage of capital, agricultural overproduction and the collapse of the CREDIT ANSTALT from which France withdrew short-term credit. Sequels included the NEW DEAL, the raising of tariffs (see OTTAWA AGREEMENTS) and Hitler's rise to power.

De Profundis A letter written by Oscar Wilde from prison to Lord Alfred Douglas, not published in full until 1949. (Latin, 'from the depths'; taken from *Psalms* cxxx and the Roman Catholic burial service.)

Deptford A former metropolitan borough of London, now part of the borough of LEWISHAM.

Depth-bomb Whiskey in beer.

Der Alte Nickname of Dr Adenauer, who resigned the Chancellorship of Western Germany at the age of 87. (German, 'the Old Man'.)

Derby, The The premier British classic flatrace, for 3-year-olds over 1½ miles at Epsom, Surrey, in June.

Derby porcelain (1755-1848) The products of the English firm founded at Derby by William Duesbury, who also bought the Chelsea factory in 1770 (see CHELSEA-DERBY) and BOW in 1775. In its earliest period Derby was famous for its figures based on MEISSEN models, with elaborate bocage backgrounds derived from Chelsea. For later periods see CROWN DERBY; BLOOR DERBY.

Derby Scheme (UK) The system of voluntary registration for national service introduced by Lord Derby in 1915.

De rerum natura (1st century BC) A philosophical poem by Lucretius 'on the nature of things', in which he expounds the theory of Leucippus and his successors that the universe is composed of atoms come together fortuitously and not the creation of the gods. He wanted to rid men's minds of superstitious fear of the gods, for 'So great is the evil that superstition has persuaded man to do' (*Tantum religio potuit suadere malorum.)*

Der Spiegel case (1962) The resignation of 5 West German Ministers in protest against the arrest on the orders of the Defense Minister, Franz-Josef Strauss, of the editor of *Der Spiegel* for publishing secret information about technical faults which came to light during combined maneuvers. A month later, Chancellor Adenauer dropped Strauss from his Cabinet.

Desdemona Wife of Othello who, in Shakespeare's play, kills her when IAGO persuades him that she has been unfaithful.

Deseret The name given by the Mormons in 1849 to their settlement in what is now Utah. (A Book of Mormon word for 'honeybee', signifying 'industry'.)

Desert Fox, The Nickname of Field-Marshal Rommel, who commanded the German forces in North Africa during World War II.

Desert Rats The British 7th Armoured Division, a famous unit of the Eighth Army in the North African and European campaigns of World War II. (Named for the jerboa, prevalent in North Africa.

Des Grieux, Le Chevalier See MANON LESCAUT.

Design Centre (London) The head-quarters of the COUNCIL OF INDUSTRIAL DESIGN, in the Haymarket, with displays of the best-designed British goods. See next entry.

Design Index A photographic reference library of design, first formed for the FESTIVAL OF BRITAIN and now kept at the DESIGN CENTRE.

Desire under the Elms (1924) Eugene O'Neill's Freudian tragedy set on a New England farm, in which a young wife seduces her stepson and, threatened with exposure, kills their child.

Deucalion and Pyrrha Sole survivors in a Greek version of the flood legend. As instructed, they cast stones over their shoulders, from which men and women sprang. ZEUS and PROMETHEUS are fitted into the story, and the 'ark' grounded on Mount Parnassus.

Deuteronomy The last book of the PENTATEUCH, which repeats the Ten Commandments and other material from *Exodus*. (Greek, 'second law'.)

Deutsche mark (1948) Unit of currency (abbreviated DM) introduced in West Germany to replace the inflated Reichsmark (RM). This was regarded as the turning point in postwar reconstruction which began the ECONOMIC MIRACLE.

Deutsches Kreuz The highest German military order under the Nazi regime.

Deutschland (1931) German 'pocket battleship', small but fast, and well armed and armored, the first of her kind. In her construction electric welding was substituted for traditional riveting.

'Deutschland, Deutschland über alles' (1841) The German national anthem, sung to Haydn's tune for the old Austrian Imperial national anthem ('Gott erhalte unsern Kaiser'); as the words ('Germany over all') seemed . inappropriate the West German government in 1950 adopted the third verse beginning 'Einigkeit und Recht und Freiheit' ('Unity, Right and Freedom') as the official anthem.

Dev Abbreviation in common use for Éamon de Valera, President of the Republic of Ireland.

'Devil and Daniel Webster, The' (1937) A famous short story by Stephen Vincent Benét published in the SATURDAY EVENING POST and then in *Thirteen O'Clock*. Jabez Stone, a New England farmer, sells his soul to the Devil for worldly wealth. The great orator Daniel Webster (1782-1852) addresses an infernal jury and secures Stone's release from the obligation to keep his part of the bargain. The story was the basis of Douglas Moore's opera (1938) and of a play and a musical.

Devil's Island An island off French Guiana, notorious as the place to which French convicts were transported and kept under harsh conditions; closed down 1953. Dreyfus (see DREYFUS CASE) spent 5 years there.

Devils of Loudun, The (1952) Aldous Huxley's novel about a historical event in 17th-century France. A convent of nuns succumb to mass hysteria, attributed to demonic possession induced by a priest, who is burned at the stake. The story was used by John Whiting in his play *The Devils* (1961).

Devonian Period The fourth period of the PALEOZOIC ERA, lasting from about 410 to 350 million years ago. There are fossils of spiders, insects, tree ferns and the first land vertebrates (amphibians), while fishes are abundant. Northern Europe and America were inundated by a great flood. See OLD RED SANDSTONE.

Dewey decimal system The system of classifying books used in most public libraries, with 10 main divisions (000-099, 100-199 etc.) and open-ended finer subdivisions by decimal points. It was introduced in 1878 by Melvil Dewey, a US librarian. Many other libraries use a similar system, the Universal Decimal Classification (UDC).

Dewey educational system Based on theories advanced by the American. John Dewey (1859-1952), emphasizing that the primary purpose of education is not to impart knowledge for its own sake but to train children so that they will be able to make their maximum contribution to society according to their aptitudes and ability. Dewey held that too much weight was given to the arts, which were of interest mainly to the privileged few, and too little to the sciences which benefit all mankind.

DEW Line (1957) A line of radar stations at about the 70th parallel of latitude, from the Aleutian Islands through the Alaskan and Canadian Arctic to Greenland and Iceland, designed to give early warning of hostile planes or missiles. (Initials standing for Distant Early Warning.)

Dexter A breed of small dual-purpose cattle derived from the KERRY and common in Ireland; black, sometimes red, in color.

Dharma Bums, The (1959) One of Jack Kerouac's beatnik novels about Jack DULUOZ and ZEN. (*Dharma*, a Buddhist and Hindu term, 'that which is made firm', 'doctrine', 'conformity to doctrine'.)

Diadochi, The Alexander the Great's generals, who divided up his empire at his death, and fought among themselves. From them sprang the dynasties of the PTOLEMIES and the SELEUCIDS. (Greek, 'successors'.)

Dialectical Materialism Marx's explanation, using the logical method he adopted from HEGELIANISM (while discarding Hegel's philosophy), of historical development as arising solely from the conflict of social and economic forces generated by man's material needs, which operate in accordance with the dialectical laws of thesis, antithesis and synthesis. Thus, to Marx the fall of Capitalism, whether desirable or not, was simply an inevitably certain result of these laws, as was the end of slavery, feudalism etc. before it.

Diamond Horseshoe See GOLDEN HORSESHOE.

Diamond Jim The nickname of James Buchanan Brady, American rail magnate and financier, who liked wearing diamonds and other expensive jewelry.

Diamond Lil (1928) A hilarious play written by the film star Mae West;

she played the title role as the moll of a Bowery white slaver and saloon-keeper in the 1890s who showered her with diamonds. She then made it into a movie, *She Done Him Wrong* (1933) — a title borrowed from 'FRANKIE AND JOHNNY'. Her most famous line, 'Come up and see me some time', had its origin here.

Diamond Sculls, The Diamonds (1884) (UK) The premier international sculling event, open to all amateurs and rowed at HENLEY.

Diamond State Nickname of Delaware.

Diana An ancient Latin nature and fertility goddess, worshiped by women; identified with the Greek ARTEMIS.

Diana of the Crossways (1885) George Meredith's novel about political life, in which a high-spirited Irish girl, Diana Merion (said to be based on Sheridan's granddaughter), leaves her husband for a young politician.

Diana of the Ephesians The form of DIANA worshiped at Ephesus (south of modern Izmir) in Asia Minor; she had absorbed the characteristics of an earlier Asian multibreasted fertility goddess. *Acts* xix, 24-28, tells the story of the makers of silver images of Diana who, alarmed at the effect of Paul's preaching on their trade, staged a protest march, shouting 'Great is Diana of the Ephesians'.

Diary of a Nobody, The See POOTER.

Diaspora, The The dispersion of the Jews outside Palestine. When the BABYLONIAN CAPTIVITY ended, most of the Jews elected to remain in Babylon; they increased and multiplied until they far outnumbered those in Palestine, and gradually infiltrated into the main cities of the known world, although still regarding Jerusalem as their spiritual home. (Greek, 'scattering'.)

Dichterliebe Schumann's song cycle composed for songs by Heine. At first the singer voices his happiness, which turns to despair when he is jilted. (German, 'a poet's love'.)

Dick, Mr An amiable idiot in DAVID COPPERFIELD who lodges with Betsy TROTWOOD; he has spent 10 years trying in vain to write a 'Memorial' without bringing King Charles's head, his pet obsession, into it; but the King 'had been constantly getting into it, and was there now'.

Dick Tracy (1931) Chester Gould's comic strip, dating from PROHIBITION days, in which Tracy is a stylized square-jawed humorless cop who hunts down villains grotesque in face and name in unrealistic scenes of relentless violence, and later began to take on astrocrooks. The strip has over the years been the source of radio programs and movies and was parodied in the character FEARLESS FOSDICK.

Dido Queen of the Phoenician colony of Carthage, where AENEAS and the Trojans were wrecked. She fell in love with Aeneas and, when he obeyed a divine command to continue his journey to Italy, she committed suicide.

Didymus The Greek word for 'twin', applied to St Thomas (Thomas being derived from the Aramaic word for 'twin'); also used as a pen name.

Die-Hards (UK) Name given to the 600 Conservatives who demonstrated (July 1911) at the Hotel Cecil against the readiness of their leader, A. J. Balfour, to acquiesce in the VETO BILL; hence any right-wing Tories.

Dien Bien Phu A town in Tonking (now North Vietnam) where the last major French engagement of the INDO-CHINA WAR was fought. VIETMINH forces surrounded French paratroops and other units, who after a gallant defense were forced to capitulate on 7 May 1954.

Dieppe raid (Aug. 1942) A commando raid on the French coast by Canadian and British troops and US RANGERS, which met with heavy losses but afforded valuable experience in commando tactics.

Dieppoise (Cooking) Term applied to seafood cooked in white wine and served with mussels.

'Dies irae' A 13th-century hymn on the Last Judgment, sung in the Mass for the dead. (Latin, 'day of wrath', its first words; it continues, in translation, 'and doom impending, / Heaven and earth in ashes ending.)

Digger Colloquial term for an Australian. (Reference to the gold-digging era of 1857-60.)

Diggers A name given to Indians of the western and southwestern states who, when first discovered, subsisted to some extent on root crops; especially some of the SHOSHONI groups.

Digitalis The genus name of the foxgloves.

'Dignity and Impudence' A popular Landseer painting of a dignified bloodhound and a Scotch terrier who has pushed his way into the picture; see 'MONARCH OF THE GLEN'.

Diktat German word for 'dictation', 'arbitrary decree'; Hitler's favorite term for the VERSAILLES TREATY, implying the startling doctrine that an aggressor state, after defeat, should not be dictated to by its intended victims.

Dillinger era See PUBLIC ENEMY NO. 1.

Dingaan's Day (16 Dec. 1838) The day on which Boers defeated the Zulu chief, Dingaan, in Natal. Now renamed the Day of the Covenant, and kept by AFRIKANERS) as a day of thanksgiving for the spread of white civilization in Africa.

Dingley Dell In PICKWICK PAPERS, the place where Mr WARDLE lives at Manor Farm.

Dinmont, Dandie A farmer and dog breeder in Scott's Guy Mannering, whose name was given to a breed of hardy Border terriers. (Dandie for Andrew.)

Diocletian persecution, The (AD 303) A general persecution of Christians ordered by the Emperor Diocletian, which continued in the west until 306, in the east until 313.

Dionysian Nietzsche's adjective for all he admired and advocated, the freedom of the strong put to wise and creative use; the passionate enjoyment of life freed from all the inhibitions imposed by Christian religion; enthusiasm and ecstasy instead of pallid virtues inspired by a sense of original sin. See APOLLONIAN. (DIONYSUS.)

Dionysus The Thracian god of the vine and of fertility, adopted by the Greeks, who also called him Bakchos (see BACCHUS). Son of ZEUS, husband of ARIADNE, he was worshiped as a vegetation god at the Dionysian festivals held in December and March. See ORPHEUS.

Dior, Christian A Paris fashion house.

Dioscuri CASTOR AND POLLUX. (Greek, 'sons of Zeus'.)

Diploma in Technology (UK) A diploma with status equal to a degree, obtainable after 4-5 years of sandwich courses taken at a CAT (or certain other colleges) in between periods of work in an industry related to the subject being studied.

Dipper, The See BIG DIPPER; LITTLE DIPPER.

Diptera An order of insects with one pair of wings; the flies, including the housefly, mosquito and tsetse.

Directoire (1) Name given to a furniture style which during the DIRECTORY revived the NEOCLASSICISM of Louis XIV's reign; a typical example is the couch on which Mme RÉCAMIER reclines in David's painting. (2) A women's dress style with very high waistline; the trend was set by the future Empress Josephine.

Directory (Oct. 1795-Nov. 1799) The first post-Revolution government of France, an executive body of 5 Directors set up after the VENDÉMIAIRE coup, opposed to Jacobins, Girondins and Royalists alike. They became increasingly dictatorial and corrupt, and were superseded by the CONSULATE after the BRUMAIRE coup.

Dirty Dick's A pub in Chinatown, Limehouse, in London's dockland, famous in the 1920s when it was the smart thing to go 'slumming' there.

Dis A Roman name for HADES.

Disarmament Commission (1952) A UN organization which took over from the ATOMIC ENERGY COMMISSION and the Conventional Armaments Commission to prepare proposals for general disarmament. Its first success was the TEST-BAN TREATY.

Disarmament Conference (1932-34) See WORLD DISARMAMENT CONFERENCE.

'Discobolos, The' (5th century BC) The Discus Thrower, a sculpture by Myron. The original bronze is lost, but there is a marble copy in the National Museum, Rome.

Discoverer Name of a series of US satellites used from 1959 to test the feasibility of manned spacecraft. Unlike earlier types, they were stabilized instead of tumbling freely in space; some were successfully designed to eject a capsule for recovery after reentry through the earth's atmosphere.

Discovery, HMS (1901) Capt. Scott's ship, the first built for Polar research, now an RNR training ship moored in the Thames off the Victorian Embankment in the heart of London; it is open to the public, to view relics of Scott's Antarctic expeditions (including the last, which was made in the *Terra Nova*).

Disenchanted, The (1950) A novel by Budd Schulberg based on Scott Fitzgerald's life in Hollywood; also a play (1958) based on this.

Dismal Science, The Thomas Carlyle's name for Economics.

Disneyland (1955) A huge and fantastic amusement park opened at Anaheim near Los Angeles, by Walt Disney.

Dispersion, The Another name for the DIASPORA.

Disraeli's Two Nations See TWO NATIONS.

Dissenters (1) Puritans. (2) Earlier name for NONCONFORMISTS.

Dissolution of the Monasteries (1536-39) The suppression of the monasteries and confiscation of their property by Henry VIII on the advice of Thomas Cromwell during the English Reformation.

Distillers (1877) A merger of whiskey and gin distillers, with a near-monopoly in Scotch whiskey, including Buchanans (Black and White), Dewars (White Horse), Johnny Walker and Haig, together with Gordon's and Booth's gins; they also manufacture industrial alcohol and antibiotics.

Distinguished Flying Cross (1) USAF award for heroism or extraordinary achievement while participating in aerial flight; it ranks below the AIR FORCE CROSS. (2) UK award (1918) to officers for valor, courage or devo-

Distinguished Service Cross (1) US Army award (1918) for extraordinary heroism in connection with military operations in circumstances not justifying the award of the MEDAL OF HONOR; the equivalent of the Navy Cross and Air Force Cross. (2) UK award (1914) to naval officers below the rank of captain, for meritorious or distinguished service in action.

Distinguished Service Medal (1) US armed forces award (1918) for exceptionally meritorious service in a duty of great responsibility. (2) UK award to petty officers and men of the Royal Navy and Royal Marines for setting an example of bravery and resource under fire.

Dives Latin word for 'rich', which has come to be used for the rich man 'clothed in purple and fine linen' of the parable in *Luke* xvi, 19-31. See LAZARUS.

Divine Comedy, The (1320) Dante's major work, a poem in 3 parts: 'Inferno', in which Virgil guides the poet through the various circles of hell; 'Purgatory', describing the sufferings of the repentant as they await translation to Heaven; and 'Paradise', where the poet once more meets BEATRICE. (Italian title, *Divina Commedia*.)

Divine Sarah, The Sarah Bernhardt, the great French actress, who died in 1923.

Dix, Dorothy The pen name of Elizabeth Meriwether Gilmer (1870-1951) who wrote a syndicated column of advice to the lovelorn which first appeared in the New Orleans *Picayune*, 1896.

Dixie (1) The Southern, formerly slave, states of the USA. (Said to be from early Louisiana 10-dollar notes, marked *dix* for the benefit of French Creoles, and popularized by a song 'Dixie' [see (3)] apparently unconnected with the MASON AND DIXON LINE.) (2) Southwestern Utah, so called by early Mormons and still so called. (3) Dan Emmett's minstrel song (1860); although he was a Northerner, the song was adopted by the Confederates, but after the Civil War that President Lincoln suggested it as a song the whole reunited nation could sing. There were various versions and titles.

Dixiecrats (1948) Southern US Democrats who seceded to form the States' Rights Party which stood for white supremacy over the Negroes. They put up their own presidential candidate in 1948. (Formed from DIXIE and Democrats.)

Dixieland jazz style Pure New Orleans jazz, polyphonic and improvisational, played •by small groups and consisting chiefly of marches and foxtrots. Named after the Original Dixieland Jazz Band, perhaps the first to popularize jazz outside New Orleans, during World War I. They were a small group of Irish and Italian immigrants who went to New Orleans to study the Negro-Creole music there; they went to London in 1919.

Dizzy (1) Nickname of Benjamin Disraeli (Earl of Beaconsfield), Conservative Prime Minister (1874-80) and novelist. (2) Dizzy Gillespie, a jazz virtuoso of the trumpet, blamed by some for introducing the Bebop style into jazz in the 1940s.

DMZ Stands for the Demilitarized Zone, specifically that on the border between North and South Vietnam.

DNA Initials standing for deoxyribonucleic acid, an exceedingly complex molecule the structure of which was unraveled by Watson and Crick at Cambridge (England) in 1944. It forms the basis of the gene found in the cell nucleus and plays a vital part, with RNA, in the transmission of hereditary factors from one generation to another.

DNB (1881) Initials used for the British *Dictionary of National Biography*, a standard work of reference in many volumes, with later supplements.

DNOC A selective weed killer which also controls certain insect pests.

DOA Abbreviation used in hospitals for 'dead on arrival'.

Dobermann pinscher (1890) A medium-sized breed of terrier with long forelegs and short black and tan coat, developed as a watchdog. There is also a miniature breed. (*Dobermann*, name of breeder in Thuringia, Germany; German *Pinscher*, 'terrier'.)

Dobruja A fertile borderland, including the Black Sea port of Constanta, divided between Rumania and Bulgaria. The latter lost southern Dobruja to Rumania in the Balkan Wars but recovered it in World War II.

Dr Barnardo's Homes (1866) (UK) A voluntary organization with headquarters at Stepney Causeway, London, which runs homes for children throughout the UK, and 5 residential schools for the physically handicapped.

Dr Caligari, The Cabinet of (1919) A famous early German movie, Expressionist and heavily dramatic; directed by Wiene.

Dr Faustus, The Tragical History of (1588) Christopher Marlowe's play on the FAUST legend.

Doctor Fell The target of the rhyme (I do not like thee, Doctor Fell, / The reason why I cannot tell, etc.), a 17th-century Dean of Christ Church, Oxford; the verse is a free translation and adaptation of one of Martial's epigrams.

Dr Jekyll and Mr Hyde, The Strange Case of (1886) R. L. Stevenson's novel of the good Dr Jekyll who, as a research experiment into problems of good and evil, takes a drug which changes him into the evil Mr Hyde; although he has an antidote, the evil side takes increasing command and he, as Mr Hyde, commits murder. Unable to get back to his normal nature, he commits suicide.

Dr No (1959) The first of Ian Fleming's James BOND stories to appear as a movie (1962).

Doctor's Dilemma, The (1906) G. B. Shaw's satire on the medical profession; the dilemma is whether a distinguished surgeon should operate on the amoral artist Dubedat, or on an old colleague. The Preface to the play suggested, some 40 years before it was instituted, that what England needed was a National Health Service.

Doctors' Plot (Jan. 1953) An alleged plot by 9 Russian, mostly Jewish, doctors to poison the Soviet leaders they attended. Although completely baseless, Stalin chose to believe the story and had them arrested and 2 of them beaten to death; he was about to order the deportation of all Jews to Siberia when he died. According to one report, Stalin died of rage when rebuked by Marshal Voroshilov for his insane proposal.

Dr Strangelove (1963) Stanley Kubrick's film comedy about what happens when a madman acquires the final say in deciding whether to start a nuclear war.

Dr Syntax (1809-21) A ludicrous clergyman schoolmaster whose tours on his nag Grizzle were depicted in a series of plates by Rowlandson (see ROWLANDSON CARTOONS), with verses written by William Combe.

Dr Wall period (1751-83) The first period of WORCESTER PORCELAIN; also called First Period Worcester. Various styles of decoration were used, notably a fine underglaze blue, MEISSEN-style flower sprays, transfer printing, SÉVRES-type grounds including the characteristic shale blue, and 'Oriental Worcester'—a modification of the KAKIEMON PATTERNS. (Dr Wall was a founder member of the firm and took charge of it in 1772.)

Dr Zhivago (1957) Boris Pasternak's novel about a Russian Liberal doctor-poet's reaction to the Revolution; its implied criticism of Marxism as applied in Russia, its pervading religious tone, and the fact that Pasternak had it published abroad after the authorities had refused to publish it in Russia, all got the novelist into trouble, and he was forced to refuse the NOBEL PRIZE awarded him for it.

Dodgers The Los Angeles Dodgers, NATIONAL (Baseball) LEAGUE, playing at the Dodger Stadium, Chavez Ravine, LA. Until 1957 they were the Brooklyn (Trolley) Dodgers playing

at Ebbets Field. (The generic nickname for Brooklynites, as spending
much of their time dodging the trol-
leys, once a major feature of Brooklyn streets.)

Dodson and Fogg   The pettifogging
attorneys who acted for Mrs Bardell
in BARDELL V. PICKWICK.

DOFIC   Initials standing for Domain
Originated Functional Integrated
Circuit, a sensational new electronic
device developed at the Standard
Telecommunications Laboratories
(STL), Harlow, England, and in the
USA. It eliminates the conventional
components of radio and TV apparatus and substitutes minute crystals
of semiconductor material, compressing hundreds of components
into an area considerably smaller
than a pinhead.

Dogberry   The comic constable of
Shakespeare's MUCH ADO, whose
approach to constabulary duties and
the English language is eccentric.

Dogger Bank, Battle of the   (Jan.
1915) A naval engagement in which
the German cruiser *Blücher* was
sunk by Beatty's battle-cruiser
squadron.

Dogger Bank incident   (1904) An
extraordinary incident of the Russo-
Japanese War. The Russian Baltic
fleet, ordered to sail to Japan, fired
on some English fishing vessels off
the Dogger Bank under the inexpli-
cable delusion that they were Japanese torpedo boats.

Doggett's Coat and Badge   (1716)
The prize for a sculling race, also
called the Waterman's Derby, the
oldest annual race in the British
sporting calendar, rowed by Thames
watermen from London Bridge to
Chelsea, on or about Aug. 1st. (Endowed by Thomas Doggett, Drury
Lane actor-manager.)

Dogs of Fo   Favorite Chinese porcelain figures made since MING times,
mythical guardian animals, with
mouths drawn back in a horrific
snarl, playing with a ball or a puppy,
and usually green in color; also
called Lion Dogs of Fo.

Dolittle, Dr   The whimsical character
who appears in many children's
books written and illustrated by the
English-born American author,

Hugh Lofting, from 1920 onward.

Dollar Diplomacy   (1909-13) Name
given to the foreign policy of the US
Secretary of State, Philander C.
Knox; it was based on the search for
outlets for American capital in
China and Latin American countries.

Doll's House, The   (1879) Ibsen's
play about a spoiled daughter and
wife who resorts to fraud to save her
husband; his reaction opens her
eyes to her status as a mere doll, and
she leaves him to find her own personality.

Dolphins   The Miami Dolphins,
AMERICAN FOOTBALL LEAGUE. Became
member of the AMERICAN CONFER-
ENCE, NATIONAL FOOTBALL LEAGUE in
1970. (For the name see MARINE-
LAND.)

Dom.   Roman Catholic honorific prefix once given to the names of
church dignitaries, now to certain
Benedictine and Carthusian priests.
(Abbreviation of Latin *dominus*,
'master'.)

Dombey and Son   (1848) Dickens's
novel about a proud businessman
who concentrates his ambitions on
fitting his only son to be a partner in
his firm. When the son dies young,
he vents his disappointment on his
daughter, with whom he is reconciled only after the failure of his firm
and of his second marriage.

Domesday Book   (1086) A detailed
census of land, buildings and cattle
covering most of England, made for
taxation purposes in the reign of
William I. It is now kept at the PUB-
LIC RECORD OFFICE. (Anglo-Saxon
dom, 'judgment', as it was the final
authority in disputes.)

Dominican intervention   (1965) The
landing of US Marines in the Dominican Republic after a popular
revolution had aroused unfounded
fears of another Castro-style Communist take-over. The move was
badly received in Latin America and
elsewhere.

Dominicans   (1215) An order of
mendicant friars (Black Friars), of
whom St Thomas Aquinas (see
THOMISM) was one; now widespread,
with many mission stations.
(Founded by the Spaniard, St Dom-

inic, at Toulouse.)

Dominion Day July 1st, Canadian public holiday commemorating the coming into force of the BRITISH NORTH AMERICA ACT on that day in 1867.

Dominions and Powers Two orders of angels, grouped with Virtues; see also PRINCIPALITIES.

Dominion status (1926) Full political autonomy, equal status with Britain and common allegiance to the Crown; a status defined by the Balfour Commission and accepted by Canada, Australia, New Zealand and South Africa. It was redefined in the Statute of Westminster (1931).

Domini redemptoris (1937) Pope Pius XI's encyclical on Communist atheism.

Donald Duck The character, second in popularity only to Mickey Mouse, whose incoherent tantrums were long a feature of Walt Disney animated cartoons.

Donbas The 'Russian Ruhr', the coalfields and industrial area in the Donets Basin of the Ukraine. Donetsk (formerly Stalino) is the chief city, with iron, steel, chemical and engineering industries. The other major center is Lugansk (formerly Voroshilovgrad), which makes diesel locomotives and textiles.

Don Camillo The parish priest who battles good-humoredly with the Communist mayor in *The Little World of Don Camillo* and other books of short stories by the Italian writer Giovanni Guareschi.

Don Carlos (1867) Verdi's opera based on Schiller's play and extensively revised in 1884. The theme is Don Carlos's love for the bride of his father, the 16th-century Spanish King, Philip II.

Don Giovanni (1787) Mozart's opera on the story of DON JUAN.

'Dongo, Treasure of' A hoard of gold supposed to have been in Mussolini's possession in April 1945 when he was captured by Italian Partisans at Dongo, near Lake Como. See BALZAN FOUNDATION.

Don Juan In Spanish legend, the devil-may-care womanizer of Seville, who invited to dinner the statue of a man he had murdered.

The statue came, and dragged him down alive to hell. The legend has been treated by countless writers, artists and composers. See next entry; also DON GIOVANNI; MAN AND SUPERMAN.

Don Juan Byron's satirical poem which, he said, was 'meant to be a little quietly facetious about everything'.

Don Juan in Hell See John TANNER.

Donnithorne, Arthur The squire in George Eliot's ADAM BEDE who ruins Hetty Sorrel and rides up with her reprieve just as she is mounting the scaffold.

Donnybrook Fair A fair held near Dublin from the 13th century until banned in 1855, notorious for its rowdiness. (Former village, now a suburb of Dublin.)

Don Pasquale (1843) Donizetti's best comic opera, in which the old bachelor Don Pasquale is tricked into a bogus marriage with the girl his nephew loves, and loses her to him.

Don Quichotte (1910) Massenet's opera about DON QUIXOTE.

Don Quixote The scraggy old crackpot of La Mancha in Cervantes' romance (1605-15) who sallies forth in search of knightly adventure, mounted on ROSINANTE, accompanied by SANCHO PANZA, and having dedicated his deeds to the massive DULCINEA. He mistakes sheep for armies, windmills for giants, an inn for a castle. The book combines contemporary satire, and a parody of chivalric romance, and an oblique statement of Christian values.

'Don't give up the ship!' The words of the dying Capt. Lawrence of the US frigate *Chesapeake* as she was boarded during the War of 1812 by men from HMS *Shannon* to be taken as prize to Halifax (1813). He added: Sink her, blow her up! The words became a US naval slogan.

Doolittle raid (18 Apr. 1942) A low-level raid on Tokyo by US carrier-borne aircraft, led by Lt. Col. J. H. Doolittle.

Doorn A village near Utrecht, Holland, where the German ex-Kaiser, Wilhelm II, lived in exile (1918-41).

Doors of Perception, The (1954) Aldous Huxley's account of his experiences under the influence of mescaline; he followed it up with *Heaven and Hell* (1956).

Doppelgänger In German myth, a person's double, seen just before, and presaging, his death. (German, 'double-walker'.)

Doppler effect At very high speeds the color of a luminous body appears bluer as it approaches and redder as it recedes; in the former case it is catching up with its own light waves, compressing them and shortening the wavelength; in the latter, the process is reversed. This phenomenon is used e.g. in estimating the speed at which distant galaxies are receding. A similar phenomenon obtains with radio and sound waves, e.g. a train whistle appears to rise in pitch as it approaches an observer and to fall after it has passed. (Christian Doppler, 19th-century Austrian scientist.)

Dorian Gray, The Picture of (1891) Oscar Wilde's fantasy about a decadent dandy whose moral disintegration is symbolized by changes in a portrait of him painted when he was young and innocent. Finally he stabs the painter and the painting, and is found dead with a knife through his own heart at the foot of the picture, now restored to its original form.

Dorians Iron Age peoples of the Peloponnesus, Classical Crete and Rhodes, of whom the SPARTANS became the most important, and who emerged into history in the 8th century BC (see MYCENAEAN CIVILIZATION.

Doric Of the DORIANS; rustic; (of accent) broad.

Doric Order The most austere of the 3 Greek orders of architecture; unlike the others, the columns had no base.

Dorking A breed of white domestic fowl with distinctive long full body and short legs, kept for meat production. (Dorking, Surrey, England.)

Dorneywood (UK) A country house with extensive grounds near Burnham Beeches, Slough, presented to the nation by Lord Courtauld-Thomson as an official residence for a Minister of the Crown selected by the Prime Minister.

Dorothy Perkins (1901) A popular old rambling rose, producing masses of small rose-pink flowers from mid-July.

Dotheboys Hall The 'academy' in Dickens's NICHOLAS NICKLEBY where Nicholas serves as usher to the unspeakable SQUEERS.

Douai Bible The English version of the Bible authorized by the Roman Catholic Church, translated from the VULGATE. The New Testament was published at Rheims (1582) and the Old at Douai (1610).

Doubting Castle The place in PILGRIM'S PROGRESS where Christian and Hopeful are imprisoned by the Giant Despair. Christian unlocks his cell with a key called Promise and escapes.

Doubting Thomas A skeptic. (When the other Apostles told St Thomas that they had seen Christ after the Resurrection, he said: Except I shall see in his hands the print of the nails . . . I will not believe. See *John* xx, 25.)

Douglas aircraft A range of US civil and military transport planes made by Douglas Aircraft of Santa Monica, California. The DC-4 (1943) was a 4-engined version of the DAKOTA; DC-6 and 7 were popular 4-engined models; DC-8 resembled the BOEING 707 and appeared on the transatlantic route about the same time; the DC-9 (1965) is a short-range rival of the BAC ONE-ELEVEN. See MCDONNELL DOUGLAS CORPORATION. (DC = Douglas Commercial.)

Douglas fir A pine which flourishes in western North America, growing to over 250 ft in the northwestern states. It is one of the most important sources of timber and plywood. Also called Douglas spruce, Oregon pine etc. (Named for David Douglas, Scotch botanist, 1798-1834.)

Doulton pottery (1815) Pottery made by Doultons at Lambeth, London. Apart from industrial and utilitarian wares, there were brown salt-glaze mugs with relief decoration, stoneware spirit flasks and, from 1871, art pottery made specifically for the collector and decorated by Hannah Barlow, George Tinworth etc.

Dounreay The UK ATOMIC ENERGY AUTHORITY's experimental nuclear research station in Caithness, with the first fast breeder reactor in the world to produce electricity on a commercial scale (1959). A larger reactor was begun in 1969. Both are designed to produce from uranium more plutonium than they consume. (Coastal site west of Thurso in extreme north of Scotland.)

Dove Cottage The cottage at Grasmere in the Lake District where Wordsworth lived with his sister Dorothy (1799-1807) now preserved as a museum.

Dover, Secret Treaty of (1670) Signed by Charles II and Louis XIV at a time when the CABAL's official policy was anti-French and pro-Dutch. Charles, in return for financial help, promised to support France against Holland and to make England Catholic.

Dover sole Name given to the true sole to distinguish it from the lemon sole, which is a European flounder.

Doves Supporters of a policy of caution and conciliation in foreign affairs, as opposed to the HAWKS.

Dow Jones averages The best known of several US indexes of movements in price on Wall Street of representative groups of stocks. The Industrial Average is based on the prices of 30 industrials; there are also indexes of commodity prices, spot and future. (Dow Jones & Co.)

Down and Out in Paris and London (1933) The old Etonian George Orwell's bug-ridden account of his voluntary period of utter poverty in these 2 cities.

Down breeds Generic name for English lowland short-wool sheep, including the SOUTHDOWN, SUFFOLK, Hampshire, Dorset, Oxford and Shropshire breeds.

Downing Street (1) A short cul-de-sac off WHITEHALL, London, containing the official residence of the Prime Minister (at No. 10), Chancellor of the Exchequer (No. 11) and Government Chief Whip (No. 12).

(2) Used as a synonym for the British government, since the Cabinet meets at No. 10. (Named for Sir George Downing, an Englishman who, after joining his uncle, Governor John Winthrop, in New England, was in HARVARD's first graduating class (1642), returned home and served both Cromwell and Charles II, winning a reputation for treachery and meanness, but also a knighthood —the first Harvard man to be knighted.)

Doxology, The A liturgical form of praise to God. The Greater Doxology, *Gloria in excelsis Deo* ('Glory be to God on high'), is used in the communion service and mass; the Lesser, *Gloria patri* ('Glory be to the Father, and to the Son'), is used to conclude hymns etc.; a metrical form begins: Praise God from whom all blessings flow'. (From Greek for 'praise'.)

D'Oyly Carte Opera Co. The London company which produced the GILBERT AND SULLIVAN OPERAS at the Savoy, its own theater in the Strand. (Founded by Richard D'Oyly Carte; died 1901.)

DP Initials used for Displaced Person, i.e. (1) a citizen of German-occupied territory taken to Germany for forced labor under the Hitler regime; (2) a person who has fled or been expelled from Communist-occupied Europe.

DPA (1949) The West German news agency, which quickly became one of the largest in Europe. (Initials of Deutsche Presse-Agentur.)

Dracula (1897) Bram Stoker's blood-curdling tale of vampires and werewolves.

Dragon (1929) A Norwegian-designed keelboat of 18 ft 11 in waterline length, originally intended as an inexpensive cruiser-racer class. Given international status in 1949, it developed into an expensive but popular purely racing class, for which there are world and European championships. See DRAGON GOLD CUP; EDINBURGH CUP.

Dragon Gold Cup (1937) An international sailing championship for the DRAGON class, raced during the

CLYDE FORTNIGHT.

Dragon project A EURATOM project for a nuclear reactor to bridge the gap before fast breeder reactors come into operation in the late 1970s. See WINFRITH.

Dragoon (wartime code name) See ANVIL.

Dragoon Guards The surviving regiments, all in the ROYAL ARMOURED CORPS, are: 1st The Queen's Dragoon Guards; 3rd Carabiniers (Prince of Wales's Dragoon Guards); 4th/7th Royal Dragoon Guards; 5th Royal Inniskilling Dragoon Guards.

Dragoons The surviving regiments, all in the ROYAL ARMOURED CORPS, are: The Royal Dragoons (1st Dragoons); The Royal Scots Greys (2nd Dragoons).

Drag racing Automobile racing from a standing start over (usually) a ¼-mile course. The more sophisticated cars are of light tubular construction with the driver's seat behind the rear wheels. A 1200-h.p. dragster can reach over 200 m.p.h. in the quarter-mile. Sponsored by the National Hot Rod Association (1951).

Dramamine Proprietary name of a travel sickness preventive.

Drambuie A Scottish liqueur of whiskey, honey and herbs.

Drang nach Osten The German urge, from the 12th century onwards, to expand eastwards, at the expense of the Slavs whom they despised. (German, 'drive towards the east'.)

D ration An emergency ration (of concentrated chocolate) issued to US troops. (One of a series of such rations labeled by letters of the alphabet.)

Dravidian languages The non-Indo-European languages spoken in South India, of uncertain origin. They include TAMIL, TELUGU, MALAYALAM and KANARESE. (Sanskrit *Dravida*, 'Tamil'.)

Dreadnought, HMS (1) First all-big-gun battleship, launched 1906. (2) Britain's first nuclear submarine, built in the UK but powered by a US reactor; commissioned 1963. See VALIANT SUBMARINES.

Dream, The Common abbreviation of the title of Shakespeare's A MID-SUMMER NIGHT'S DREAM.

Dream of Gerontius (1865) Cardinal Newman's poem, inspired by Dante, on the experiences of the soul in Purgatory. Set to music by Elgar as an oratorio (1900).

Dream of the Red Chamber An 18th-century Chinese love story by Tsao Hsueh-chin. Autobiographical in form and colloquial in style, it describes the decline in fortune of his large family and in the process throws much light on contemporary social life and outlook.

Dred Scott decision (1857) A majority ruling by the Supreme Court that a slave is property and not a US citizen; that he did not become free when taken into a free state; and that the MISSOURI COMPROMISE was unconstitutional. Lincoln, and Northerners in general, sharply criticized the decision. (Scott was a house servant taken from Missouri to Wisconsin where, under the Missouri Compromise, slavery was not recognized.)

Dreigroschenoper See THREEPENNY OPERA.

Dreikaiserbund (1872) German name for the league of the 3 emperors (Germany, Austria-Hungary. Russia); they agreed to coordinate their foreign policy and to unite in opposition to Socialist revolution.

Dresden porcelain (1) See MEISSEN. (2) Imitations of Meissen made by factories in and around Dresden and in many other parts of Germany. (3) Sometimes applied to 19th-century genuine Meissen to distinguish it from the superb products of the 18th century.

Dreyfusards The campaigners for the rehabilitation of Dreyfus (see next entry), led by Clemenceau and Zola. They included liberal intellectuals and left-wing politicians, ranged against the army High Command, the Church and the right. The split went right through the nation, leaving a legacy of bitterness for decades.

Dreyfus case (1894-1906) A major French scandal. Capt. Dreyfus, a Jew, was sent to Devil's Island for selling military secrets to

Germany. In 1896 it transpired that the real culprit was a Major Esterhazy, but the frightened army High Command concealed this, even forging documents to bolster their case. The DREYFUSARDS pressed home their attacks and Dreyfus was pardoned in 1899 and restored to his commission in 1906. He served with distinction in World War I.

Drogheda (1649) In the last phase of the ENGLISH CIVIL WAR Cromwell's army besieged the forces under the Earl of Ormonde, who had declared Charles II king, and annihilated them at Drogheda. (Seaport in Co. Louth, Ireland.)

Drones' Club, The Bertie WOOSTER'S club in the P. G. Wodehouse books.

Drood, Edwin The chief character of *The Mystery of Edwin Drood*, Charles Dickens's only detective story, left unfinished; the orphan Edwin disappears and is presumed murdered; the author's intentions are unknown, and no satisfying solution to the mystery has been suggested.

'Dropping the Pilot' (1890) Most famous of Sir John Tenniel's political cartoons in *Punch*, depicting Kaiser Wilhelm II watching his dismissed Chancellor, Bismarck, leaving the ship of state.

Drosophila A genus of flies of which one species, the fruit fly, is used in genetic research because of its rapid multiplication.

Druids The Celtic priesthood of Gaul and Britain described by Julius Caesar. Their religion was associated with veneration of the oak and mistletoe, belief in immortality and reincarnation, and, probably, human sacrifice. STONEHENGE and other such monuments are much more ancient than the Druids, though coupled with them in popular belief.

Druids, The Order of A society which tries to keep alive the ancient Druid ceremonies at STONEHENGE etc. In 1963 there was a schism which resulted in there being 2 Chief Druids in England, heading respectively the British Circle of the Universal Bond and the Order of Bards, Ovates and Druids.

Druids, United Ancient Order of (1781) A friendly society founded in London, now with lodges, called 'groves', in USA and elsewhere; it has Masonic-type rites.

Drums Along the Mohawk (1936) A novel by Walter D. Edmonds which gives a well-authenticated account of the destruction wrought in the Mohawk Valley during the Revolution by Tory Loyalists and their Indian allies.

Druses (11th century) A religious sect of Syria, of Muslim origin but rejecting Mohammed as Prophet; there is said to be an inner doctrine, kept strictly secret. Fanatically independent, they rebelled against Turkish, Egyptian and French (1925-27) rule.

DST See DAYLIGHT SAVING TIME.

DT's Signifies delirium tremens.

Dual Alliance (1) The alliance of Germany and Austria-Hungary (1879); see TRIPLE ALLIANCE. (2) The alliance of France and Russia in the face of (1), consolidated in 1894.

Dual Monarchy, The (1867) Austria-Hungary as reorganized after SADOWA by the Ausgleich ('compromise') under which Hungary became self-governing in purely internal affiars.

Dubarry (Cooking) Served with cauliflower and MORNAY SAUCE.

Dublin Now officially known as BAILE ÁTHA CLIATH.

Dublin Bay prawns Rock lobsters about the size of prawns; the Italian scampi, French langoustines.

Dublin Castle The seat of British government in Ireland until the IRISH FREE STATE was established.

Dubliners (1914) A collection of short stories by James Joyce, written before he took to veiling his literary powers in linguistic obscurities.

Dubna A town in USSR west of Tula, site of the Russian equivalent to CERN.

Dubrovnik A medieval seaport, of which the Italian name was Ragusa; now in Yugoslavia.

Duce, Il Title taken by Mussolini; compare FÜHRER; CAUDILLO. (Italian, 'the leader'.)

Duchesse (Cooking, of potatoes) Creamed and blended with egg yolk, and baked in the oven.

Duchess of Malfi, The (about 1614) John Webster's grim tragedy of intrigue and crime, in which the widowed duchess marries her steward: they and her children are murdered by her outraged relations.

Duchy of Cornwall (1337) An estate established by Edward III for the BLACK PRINCE, inherited by his son and by the sovereign's eldest son ever since.

Duchy of Lancaster (1362) The estates and jurisdiction known as the Duchy and County Palatine of Lancaster, established by Edward III for his son John of Gaunt, and belonging to the Crown ever since. The Chancellorship of the Duchy is an honorary appointment held by a member of the government who has other, nondepartmental, duties.

Duffy's Tavern A radio series by Ed Gardner, and a movie (1945) adapted from it.

Dugway Proving Ground An area in Utah where chemical and biological warfare weapons and agents are tested. See VX.

Duke, The (1931) Philip Guedalla's biography of the Duke of Wellington.

Duke Endowment (1924) A large charitable trust whose interests center on North and South Carolina and the Methodist Church; it helps to finance DUKE UNIVERSITY, various colleges, hospitals, rural churches and retired Methodist ministers. (James B. Duke of the American Tobacco Co., died 1925.)

Duke Humphrey's Library The oldest part of the BODLEIAN, the library presented by the Duke of Gloucester (died 1447), son of Henry IV, who appears in Shakespeare's historical plays.

Duke of York The grand old Duke of York of the nursery rhyme was Frederick Augustus, son of George III; the implied inefficiency in the rhyme has no basis in fact.

Dukeries, The (UK) A district in northwest Nottinghamshire where the country seats of the dukes of Portland. Norfolk and Newcastle were once situated.

Duke University (1838) A Methodist university at Durham, N.C. See ESP.

Dukhobors A Russian religious sect, founded in the 18th century at Kharkov, which rejected the Orthodox Church. As a result of persecution, many emigrated (1899) to western Canada, where they caused much trouble by their resistance to taxation, education and conscription, their protests taking the form of arson, bombs and demonstrations in the nude. (Russian, 'wrestlers with the spirit'; also spelled Doukhobors.)

DUKW Code name of the US amphibious load carrier, first used in landings on Sicily in July 1943.

Dulcinea The simple, though rather massive, country girl to whom, though she does not know it, DON QUIXOTE has decided to dedicate his deeds of chivalry; hence an idealized mistress.

Dulles Airport (1962) An international airport at Chantilly, Va., 27 miles from Washington, D.C. (Named for John Foster Dulles.)

Duluoz, Jack The hero of a series of novels (1958 onward) by Jack Kerouac, the French-Canadian-American beatnik leader of California.

Duma (1906-17) Russian Imperial Parliament, the establishment of which was announced in the OCTOBER MANIFESTO. The first two Dumas were too radical for the Tsar and lasted only a few months before being disolved; the third (1907-12) was elected under a system which ensured the supremacy of the ruling classes; the fourth was swept away at the Revolution.

Dumbarton Oaks Conference (1914) A meeting of delegates from USA, Britain, Soviet Russia and China at which proposals for UN were discussed and arrangements made for the SAN FRANCISCO CONFERENCE. (Name of a country house near Washington, D.C.)

Dun & Bradstreet A credit-rating agency, with offices in New York and London; the most authoritative in that field in the US and UK business world.

Dunbar, Battle of (1650) An engagement in the last phase of the ENGLISH CIVIL WAR in which Cromwell routed the Scots under Leslie, who had declared Charles II their king, and went on to take Edinburgh.

Duncan Phyfe A distinctive American style of furniture derived from SHERATON, characterized by elegance, absence of moldings and extensive use of lyre motifs. (Name of Scottish-born designer who came to New York in 1790 and retired in 1847.)

Dunciad, The (1728) Alexander Pope's 'dunce epic', an astringent poem satirizing critics hostile to him.

Dundee University (1967) Formerly a unit of St Andrew's University, Aberdeen, and known as Queen's College, Dundee.

Dunedin A poetic name for Edinburgh. (Gaelic *dun*, 'fortress'; *Edin* for Edwin, King of Northumbria, who built it.)

Dungeness lighthouse The first fully automated lighthouse in Britain, still under development. (In Kent.)

Dunhill A name associated internationally with the best in tobacco pipes. (An old London firm.)

Dunkirk (May–June 1940) The miraculous evacuation of over 300,000 British and French troops from Dunkirk to Britain, using every available form of seacraft, rendered possible by Rundstedt, with Hitler's consent, halting the German advance and by the Luftwaffe's abstention from attack.

Dún Laoghaire The port of Dublin, formerly known as Kingstown.

Dunlop A rubber firm with headquarters in London and plantations in Malaya, manufacturing tires (including John Bull and India), foam rubber, and Slazenger tennis and golf equipment etc.

Dunmow Flitch (1111) (UK) A flitch of bacon given to any married couple who, at the church door of Little Dunmow, Essex, swore that they had not quarreled or wished themselves unmarried during the previous year and a day. The custom

has been revived many times, and persists today.

Dunne's theory of time See SERIALISM.

Dunster Force (1918) A detachment of the Mesopotamian Expeditionary Force under Major General Dunsterville (the Stalky of STALKY AND CO.), which took Baku.

Dunvegan Castle A castle in the Isle of Skye inhabited continuously by the Chiefs of Macleod since the 13th century.

Dupin, Chevalier Auguste The first fictional amateur detective, who appears in E. A. Poe's 'The MURDERS IN THE RUE MORGUE' (1841) and subsequent tales.

Du Pont (1802) A US combine, in full, E. I. Du Pont de Nemours, which started as an explosives firm founded by a French refugee of that name at Wilmington, Del. Its chemicals division first made nylon, DACRON and ORLON. One of the industrials that make up the DOW JONES Industrial Average.

Dupree, J. M. W. G. A character in A. A. Milne's WHEN WE WERE VERY YOUNG: 'James James/Morrison Morrison/Weatherby George Dupree/Took great/Care of his Mother/Though he was only three'. He insisted: You must never go down to the end of the town, if you don't go down with me.

Durham report (1839) A historic report, after disturbances in Canada, which first recommended responsible local self-government for a British possession. It also proposed the union of Upper and Lower Canada, which would put the French population in a minority; the encouragement of immigration; and the building of railroads. (1st Earl of Durham, 'Radical Jack', previously Governor-General.)

Dust Bowl A region where overcultivation, drought, and dust storms which carry off the topsoil combine to convert farmland into virtual desert; specifically, the area so created in 1932–37 around western Kansas, the Dakotas, Iowa, Nebraska and parts of Texas and Oklahoma.

Dutch auction An auction at which the asking price is gradually lowered until a buyer is found.

Dutch cheese Cottage cheese, soft and white, made of soured skim milk.

Dutch Colonial A style of architecture of Dutch and Flemish inspiration, found in the Hudson valley, western Long Island and northern New Jersey, and persisting until after the Revolution. It made more use of stone and brick than the NEW ENGLAND COLONIAL style.

Dutch courage Evanescent courage inspired by drink.

Dutch elm disease A highly destructive fungous disease of elms, first identified in Holland (1921), reached North America in 1930, transmitted by beetles. Leaves wilt and drop, and upper branches die; the disease spreads particularly rapidly on young trees.

Dutch oven A name given to various 'primitive' cooking devices: (1) a brick oven; (2) an open-ended tin box for roasting before an open fire; (3) in the US, a heavy kettle for pot roasts and stews; (4) a 3-legged iron pot with live coals on its lid, for cooking in a fireplace.

Dutch Reformed Church The chief Protestant church of the Netherlands and of the Boer population of South Africa; its government is presbyterian. In USA it was called the Reformed Church in America, which merged with the United Church of Christ (1957).

Dutch treat A meal or entertainment for which each pays his share; also called 'going Dutch'.

Dutch 200 (Bowling) A score of 200 in a game, obtained by scoring alternate strikes and spares.

Dutch uncle To talk like a Dutch uncle is to administer a stern lecture.

Dutch William A name for William III of England, WILLIAM OF ORANGE.

Dyaks (Dayaks) Malayan name for a group of non-Muslim races of Borneo, including the Land Dyaks and the headhunting Sea Dyaks, the latter so called because they used to raid the coastal areas, not because they are seafarers.

'D'Ye Ken John Peel' An English hunting song written by a friend of Peel, the master of his own pack of hounds in the Cumberland fells who died in 1854. It was set to an older tune.

'Dying Gaul, The' A Hellenistic sculpture commemorating the victory of Attalus I of Pergamum over the Gauls (241 BC), artist unknown; now in the Capitoline Museum, Rome.

'Dying Swan, The' The *pas seul* towards the end of Tchaikovsky's SWAN LAKE, rendered famous by Pavlova, among many.

Dynasts, The (1904-08) Thomas Hardy's ambitious verse drama (not intended for the stage) on Europe during the Napoleonic Wars.

Dzhugashvili The family name of Stalin, the latter being a revolutionary name ('man of steel') of the kind affected by the early revolutionaries.

E

EAEC See EURATOM.

Eagle The name of the APOLLO 11 LEM.

Eagle, Solomon (1) A lunatic who, during the Great Plague (1665), ran naked through the streets of London with a pan of burning coals on his head, crying 'Repent!' (2) Pen name used by (Sir) John Squire, the poet and critic, in the *New Statesman* (1913-19).

Eagles The Philadelphia Eagles, NATIONAL FOOTBALL LEAGUE. Became member of the NATIONAL CONFERENCE, NATIONAL FOOTBALL LEAGUE in 1970.

Eagles, Fraternal Order of (1898) A large US fraternal organization with Masonic-type rites.

Eagle's Nest, The A name for Hitler's Berghof at BERCHTESGADEN.

Eagle Squadron A squadron (later 3 squadrons) of US volunteer pilots manning SPITFIRES of the RAF, which shot down 73 German planes before the time of Pearl Harbor; eventually transferred to the US 8th Air Force.

Ealing London borough since 1965 consisting of the former boroughs of Ealing, Acton and Southall.

EAM The Greek, Communist-dominated National Liberation Front, an underground movement formed in German-occupied Greece in the autumn of 1941; see ELAS. (Initials of the Greek name.)

Éamon Irish name equivalent to Edmund.

Earlham (1922) Percy Lubbock's nostalgic re-creation of Earlham Hall, the Norfolk mansion of an old Quaker family, the Gurneys, as he knew it when a child.

Earl Marshal (UK) The officer of state who is governor of the COLLEGE OF ARMS and supervises arrangements for all state ceremonies. The office has been held by the Dukes of Norfolk since 1672.

Earl's Court (1937) The London exhibition hall at which are held the Royal Tournament, Royal Smithfield Show, Radio Show and Motor Show; it can also be converted into a large swimming pool.

Early American A style of furniture made in the Colonial and post-Revolutionary periods up to the 1820s, based on English styles but smaller, more informal and using local woods which offered better resistance to insects and heat.

Early Bird The first commercial communications satellite, launched from USA in 1965. It is a 'stationary' (or synchronous) type, see SYNCOM; COMSAT.

Early English (1200-90) The first period of English GOTHIC ARCHITECTURE, in which the pointed arch was introduced. It was also characterized by lancet windows with little or no decoration, and clusters of slender pillars (sometimes of PURBECK MARBLE around a stone center) instead of the massive columns of NORMAN ARCHITECTURE. Salisbury Cathedral is an outstanding example.

Earnshaw family, The In WUTHERING HEIGHTS, Catherine, who marries Edgar Linton and dies giving birth to Cathy; and her brother Hindley, whose son Hareton is, at the end of the novel, free to marry his cousin Cathy and thus to unite the Earnshaw and Linton families which HEATHCLIFF had sought to destroy.

Earp, Wyatt A historical character (1848-1929), marshal of the Old West, frontiersman and gunfighter, happily immortalized in a TV series based on his supposed exploits.

Earwicker, H. C. See FINNEGANS WAKE.

Easter The festival commemorating the Resurrection, celebrated on the Sunday following the first full moon after the spring equinox, i.e. between Mar. 22nd and Apr. 25th. (Named after the Teutonic pagan festival held in honor of the goddess Eostre at the spring equinox.)

Eastern Church   Another name for the EASTERN ORTHODOX CHURCH.

Eastern Empire   See BYZANTINE EMPIRE.

Eastern Orthodox Church   The Byzantine Church, which finally broke with the Western Church in 1054 (sometimes called the GREAT SCHISM) owing to the mutual antipathy of Greek and Roman cultures, but ostensibly on the minor theological point the word *filioque* in the NICENE CREED) of whether the Holy Ghost 'proceeded' from the Father *and* the Son or *through* the Son (if the Son is one with the Father, the Holy Ghost must proceed from both). It is the Church of Russia, Greece, the Balkans and elsewhere; distinguished from the Roman Catholic Church by: married clergy, icons instead of 'graven images', no instrumental music, elaborate ritual, services held in Old Slavonic, Hellenistic Greek or other dead languages. The acknowledged head is the Ecumenical Patriarch, the chief bishop of Constantinople.

Eastern Question   Historians' name for the problems created in the 19th century by Turkey's decline to the position of Sick Man of Europe. Manifestations included the Greek War of Independence, the CRIMEAN WAR, Balkan rivalries, and disputes about the status of the Dardanelles; they usually involved clashes between Russian and European aims.

Eastern Schism   (1054) The break between the (Greek) EASTERN ORTHODOX CHURCH of Byzantium and the Western Church of Rome. Also called the GREAT SCHISM.

Eastern standard time   The civil time of the 75th meridian, 5 hours slower than GMT (6 hours slower than New British Time, i.e. British Summer Time); observed in eastern USA and east mainland Canada.

Eastern Star   (1874) An international social organization with membership restricted to Master Masons, their wives, daughters and sisters.

Easter Parade   A promenade by thousands of people on FIFTH AVENUE, NYC, on Easter Sunday, celebrated in a revue song (1933) and a

Fred Astaire movie (1947).

Easter Rising   (24-29 Apr. 1916) The Irish rebellion in Dublin, rendered abortive through the secret leadership (the IRB) keeping their fighting forces (the IRISH NATIONAL VOLUNTEERS and the Citizen Army) in ignorance of their plans.

East Fulham by-election   (1933) (UK) Famous because a Labor candidate won a hitherto safe Conservative seat by a large majority, just after Germany had walked out of the Disarmament Conference and the LEAGUE OF NATIONS. The result was interpreted as a vote for pacifism (although later shown to be merely against the MEANS TEST), and provided Baldwin and Neville Chamberlain (then serving under Ramsay MacDonald) with a future excuse for not rearming in time against Nazi Germany.

East Germany   See GERMAN DEMOCRATIC REPUBLIC.

East Ham   A former Essex county borough, since 1965 part of the London borough of NEWHAM.

East India Company   (1600) English chartered company formed to trade with India and the East; it laid the foundations of British rule in India.

East Kilbride   (1947) (UK) A NEW TOWN in north Lanarkshire 7 miles southeast of Glasgow, designed to take 100,000 inhabitants.

Eastlake style   A style of sturdy neo-Gothic but machine-made furniture with rectangular lines. (Designs copied from *Hints on Household Tastes*, 1868, published in England but widely read in the US.)

Eastland   An excursion boat overturned in Chicago River by people rushing to one side of it, with the loss of 812 lives (1915).

East Lynne   (1861) A romantic novel by Mrs Henry Wood, dramatized by various hands from 1864 on. Lady Isabel leaves her husband for another but, disguised as a nursemaid, returns to him after his remarriage to look after their children. In the end the two are reconciled. The line 'Dead! . . . and never called me mother', inserted in one of the stage versions, released floods of tears from Victorian audiences, and then became a standard music-hall catch-phrase.

Eastman Kodak The leading manufacturers of photographic equipment and materials, founded at Rochester, N. Y., by George Eastman who in 1880 patented the first practicable dry plate and marketed the first Kodak camera in 1888. One of the 30 industrials that make up the DOW JONES Industrial Average.

East Prussia The part of PRUSSIA which, while remaining under German rule, was in 1919 isolated from the rest of Germany by a tongue of territory transferred to Poland. East Prussia was divided between USSR and Poland after World War II.

East Village An area in New York City, now the haunt of hippies and young revolutionaries.

East-West Center (Hawaii, 1961) An international university dedicated to East-West understanding, established by the US government on the University of Hawaii's campus, with students from USA and 26 Asian and Pacific countries.

Eatanswill The scene of a famous election visited by Mr Pickwick in Dickens's novel (PICKWICK PAPERS); it was on this occasion that he met the redoubtable Mrs Leo Hunter.

Eaton Hall A British Officer Cadet School for infantry officers until it was closed in 1958. See MONS OFFICER CADET SCHOOL. (Former seat of the Duke of Westminster, in Cheshire.)

Eblis In Muslim legend, the Devil, also called Shaitan (Satan). See also VATHEK. (Traditional English spelling; also spelled Iblis.)

E boat A high-speed unarmored motorboat equipped with torpedoes and guns, used by the Germans and Italians in World War II. Equivalent to the PT BOAT. (For 'Enemy-boat'.)

Eboracum Roman name of York.

Ebor Handicap (UK) A flat race run at York in August over a distance of 1¾ miles; now a £10,000 event sponsored by Johnnie Walker, the whiskey firm.

Ebury Street A street near Victoria Station, London, associated with George Moore (*Conversations in Ebury Street*) and with Noel Coward, both of whom lived there.

ECA (1958) (1) Initials used for the Economic Commission for Africa, set up by the ECONOMIC AND SOCIAL COUNCIL. (2) See ECONOMIC COOPERATION ADMINISTRATION.

ECAFE (1947) Initials used for the Economic Commission for Asia and the Far East, set up by the ECONOMIC AND SOCIAL COUNCIL.

Ecce Homo (1) Pilate's words (Latin, 'behold the man!') as Jesus appeared, wearing the crown of thorns and the purple robe after he had been scourged (*John* xix, 5). (2) A picture representing Jesus thus.

Ecclefechan The village where Carlyle was born, near Lockerbie, Dumfriesshire.

Eccles cake The Lancashire version of the BANBURY CAKE, having the same ingredients but round in shape. (Eccles, a Lancashire town.)

Ecclesiastes (3rd century BC) A short book of the Old Testament, once attributed to Solomon, on the theme 'Vanity of Vanities . . . all is Vanity'. (Greek from Hebrew, 'preacher'.)

Ecclesiasticus (2nd century BC) A book of the APOCRYPHA which gives a disjointed but full account of the Jewish faith before the Christian era. It was written by a Sadducee, Jesus (i.e. Joshua) ben Sirach, and is also called *The Wisdom of Jesus the Son of Sirach* or simply *Sirach*. ('Church book', i.e. to be read in church though not part of the Canon.)

ECCM Initials used for electronic counter-countermeasures; see ECM.

ECE See ECONOMIC COMMISSION FOR EUROPE.

ECG Initials used for electrocardiogram, a chart, produced by an electrocardiograph, showing the electrical impulses from the heart muscle. These, in health, have a characteristic pattern and abnormal rhythms are readily diagnosed.

Echinoderms A phylum of marine invertebrates, including sea urchins and starfish.

Echo 1 The first communications satellite, launched from USA in Aug. 1960. A metallized plastic balloon, some 1000 miles up, it relayed radio and television signals without amplification (see SYNCOM).

ECLA (1948) Initials used for the Economic Commission for Latin America, set up by the ECONOMIC AND SOCIAL COUNCIL.

Eclipse An 18th-century English racehorse, great-grandson of the Darley Arabian (see THOROUGHBRED), never beaten; hence: 'Eclipse first, the rest nowhere'.

Eclipse Stakes (UK) A flat race for 3- and 4-year-olds run at Sandown Park in July over a distance of 1¼ miles.

Eclogues (37 BC) Virgil's pastoral poems, also known as the *Bucolics*. The Fourth Eclogue, which refers to the birth of a child (probably to Augustus), was in early times taken to be a prophecy of Christ. (Greek, 'selections'.)

ECM Initials used for electronic countermeasures, i.e. electronic eavesdropping. They include detecting signals sent to guided missiles (so as to jam them); collecting code messages (so as to break the code by computer); jamming defense radar; jamming other agencies engaged on ECM (called ECCM — electronic counter-countermeasures); use of underwater listening devices; general monitoring of radio and radar. The Russians use 'trawlers' which dog NATO and other fleets on maneuver; the British use old V-bombers; the US NATIONAL SECURITY AGENCY uses specially equipped 'spy ships' such as the *Victory* (accidentally bombed by the Israelis in 1967) or the *Pueblo* (see PUEBLO INCIDENT); submarines, satellites and land-based posts are also used.

École Polytechnique See X, LES.

Economic and Social Council One of the principal organs of the UN, dealing with economic, social, cultural, educational, health and related fields. It keeps touch with the INTERNATIONAL AGENCIES and has established various specialist commissions (e.g. on narcotic drugs, human rights) and regional economic commissions (see ECA, ECAFE, ECLA and next entry).

Economic Commission for Europe (1947) A UN agency set up by the ECONOMIC AND SOCIAL COUNCIL to assist in the postwar economic rehabilitation of Europe.

Economic Consequences of the Peace, The (1919) J. M. Keynes's unorthodox analysis of the likely consequences of trying to exact huge reparations from Germany after World War I, and of other major problems of international economics. See KEYNSIAN ECONOMICS.

Economic Cooperation Administration (1948-51) The US body set up to administer ERP; it was replaced by the MUTUAL SECURITY AGENCY.

Economic Miracle, The The astonishing recovery of West Germany after World War II, under the 'social free enterprise' policy of Ludwig Erhard, Economics Minister (1949-57) and later Vice-Chancellor and Chancellor. See DEUTSCHE MARK.

ECOSOC See ECONOMIC AND SOCIAL COUNCIL.

ECSC See EUROPEAN COAL AND STEEL COMMUNITY.

ECT Initials used for electroconvulsive therapy. Electric shocks are applied to the head of a patient under anesthesia. For reasons still unknown, this can cure the depressive phase of manic-depressive insanity and similar conditions.

Ecumenical Council See VATICAN COUNCIL.

Ecumenical Patriarch The head of the EASTERN ORTHODOX CHURCH, the Bishop of Constantinople.

Edam A hard-pressed yellow cheese, originally made of whole, now usually of skimmed, milk. The whole cheese is round with a red rind. (Dutch town.)

EDC See EUROPEAN DEFENSE COMMUNITY.

Edda Name given to two 13th-century Icelandic collections of Scandinavian poems and myths, known as the Prose Edda and Poetic Edda.

Eddie (1951) An annual award by the American Cinema Editors for the best editing of feature-length and TV films; the film editors are nominated by the Academy of Motion Picture Arts and Sciences.

Eddystone (1882) (UK) A lighthouse on a rock 14 miles south of Plymouth, the fourth to be built there since 1698. The light is 133 ft above sea level.

Eden Family name of the Earl of Avon and of the Barons Auckland and Henley.

Edentates An order of New World mammals with no or only vestigial teeth, usually insect-eating; the sloths, armadilloes, anteaters, pangolins etc.

Edgar award (1945) A prize for the best detective story of the year, awarded by the Mystery Writers of America Inc., a body of crime fiction writers who seek to raise standards in this field. (Named after Edgar Allan Poe.)

Edgehill (1642) The first, and indecisive, battle of the ENGLISH CIVIL WAR; Charles I marching on London was stopped by the ROUNDHEADS under the Earl of Essex but went on to take Oxford, which he made his headquarters. (A ridge north of Banbury.)

Edgewood Arsenal A research establishment in Maryland were chemical warfare weapons are produced.

Edict of Nantes (1598) The grant by Henry IV of some degree of religious toleration to the HUGUENOTS of France; revoked by Louis XIV (1685).

Edinburgh Castle Located on a rock which dominates the center of Edinburgh, the castle dates back at least to the 11th century, when a chapel was built named for Queen (Saint) Margaret, who died there. Features of interest include the crown and the royal jewels (the 'Honours of Scotland'), the room where JAMES SIXT AND FIRST was born, the 15th-century 5-ton cannon called 'Mons Meg', and the fine views of the city and its surroundings.

Edinburgh Cup (1949) A sailing championship for the International DRAGON class, raced at the CLYDE REGATTA in June / July.

Edinburgh Festival (1947) An annual international festival of music (including opera), drama and ballet, held in August and September.

Edinburgh Festival Happening (1963) The parade of a naked woman on the stage at this august festival. (A 'Happening' is what used to be called a practical joke played on the public.)

Edinburgh Review, The (1802-1929) A Whig political and literary quarterly, which savagely attacked Wordsworth and Southey, and was counterattacked by Byron in *English Bards and Scotch Reviewers*. See QUARTERLY REVIEW.

Edirne A Turkish city, formerly known as Adrianople.

Edison-Bell records The cylindrical records used on the earliest form of phonograph. (Alexander Graham Bell and Thomas Edison, joint inventors.)

Edmonton (UK) A former Middlesex borough, since 1965 part of the borough of ENFIELD.

Edmund Ironside Edmund II, King of England for a few months in his last year (1016), defeated by Canute at Ashington in Essex, and possibly murdered by him. (A nickname alluding to his bravery.)

EDP Signifies Electronic Data Processing.

EDT Eastern Daylight Time, one hour faster than EASTERN STANDARD TIME. See DAYLIGHT SAVING TIME.

Edwardian cars Arbitrary name for automobiles which are neither VETERAN nor VINTAGE, i.e. made between 1906 and 1918.

Edwin Drood See DROOD, EDWIN.

EEC Initials used for the European Economic Community; see COMMON MARKET.

EEG Initials used for electroencephalogram, a chart showing electrical impulses arising from the brain ('brain waves'), used in diagnosing epilepsy, brain tumors and other abnormal conditions of the brain. The electroencephalograph records the changing voltages between pairs of electrodes applied to the scalp.

EEOC See EQUAL EMPLOYMENT OPPORTUNITY COMMISSION.

E=mc² The equation which summarizes Einstein's Special Theory of Relativity (1905), in which m = the mass of an object, c = the speed of light (3×10^{10} cm/sec.) and E = energy. It indicated that, since c is very great, the mass of any body is equivalent to an enormous quantity of energy; the truth of this was demonstrated by the first atomic bomb. See EINSTEIN'S THEORIES.

Eeyore The old gray donkey of WINNIE-THE-POOH who lives by himself in a thistly corner of the Forest, gloomily mistrustful of all friendly advances.

Effigy Mounds Prehistoric American Indian burial mounds in the shape of animals; see MOUND BUILDERS.

EFTA (1960) The European Free Trade Association of the UK, the Scandinavian countries, Switzerland, Austria and Portugal, with Finland an associate member; formed after their failure to join the Common Market. The headquarters are at Geneva.

Egdon Heath A stretch of heath described at the beginning of Thomas Hardy's The Return of the Native (1878) which plays a prominent part throughout the book. It is also mentioned in other novels and poems of Hardy's.

Egeria A woman who acts as guide and counselor, especially to a statesman. (In Roman legend a nymph who advised the lawgiver Numa Pompilius, King of Rome.)

Eggs Benedict A dish of poached eggs on fried ham on English muffins, the whole edifice topped with hollandaise sauce.

Egmont, Count The Flemish leader of a 16th-century revolt against Spanish rule, who was executed by the Duke of Alva; the hero of a play by Goethe for which Beethoven wrote a famous overture.

Egoist, The See PATTERNE, SIR WILLOUGHBY.

Egypt, Corn in Abundance, profits, available for the taking in a foreign country, a phrase taken from Genesis xlii, 2.

Egyptians, To spoil the To rob enemies or foreigners, a phrase taken from Exodus iii, 22, and xii, 36.

Eichmann trial (1961) The trial of Adolf Eichmann, Austrian Nazi head of the organization for the extermination of Jews; he was kidnapped in Argentina by Israeli agents, brought to trial at Tel Aviv,

and hanged in 1962.

18th Amendment (1919) The amendment to the US Constitution introducing Prohibition, which came into force in 1920 after the passing of the VOLSTEAD ACT.

18th Dynasty (1570-1370 BC) A great period in the history of ancient Egypt, the first dynasty of the NEW KINGDOM, which included Thothmes III, Amenhotep III, AKHENATEN and TUTANKHAMEN. It saw conflicts with the Assyrians and Hittites and the building of the great temples of AMON at KARNAK and LUXOR.

1812 Overture (1880) A popular work by Tchaikovsky, with realistic gunfire effects and themes based on the French and Russian national anthems representing the opposing armies at BORODINO.

Eighth Commandment 'Thou shalt not steal' (Exodus xx, 15). To Roman Catholics this is the Seventh Commandment.

Eights, The OXFORD UNIVERSITY summer college boat races.

Eights Week Celebration of the end of the academic year at Oxford University, with dances, tea parties on college barges etc.

Eilean Donan Castle A former Mackenzie stronghold, dating back to the 13th century, in the Kyle of Lochalsh, Wester Ross.

Einstein's theories The Special Theory of Relativity (1905) which dealt with the physics of particles moving at near the speed of light, and showed that mass and energy are 2 aspects of the same concept (see $E = MC^2$); the General Theory (1915) which explained gravitation in terms of a 4-dimensional geometry of space-time in which space is curved, finite but expanding; and the Unified Field Theory (1953), which was a step towards linking gravitation and electromagnetism.

Eire (1) In common usage, the name of southern Ireland from 1937 to 1949; (2) in official theory, the whole of Ireland, the Six Counties of Northern Ireland being only temporarily excluded from the operation of laws passed by the government in Dublin, pending reintegration of the whole country.

Eisenhower Cup (1958) A golf tournament for teams of 4 amateurs from each competing country, held every 2 years. (Presented by General Eisenhower.)

Eisenhower Doctrine (1957) The US policy of giving aid to Middle Eastern countries to contain Communism. (President Eisenhower; John Foster Dulles, Secretary of State.)

Eisenhower jacket A short jacket fitting snugly at the waist and cuffs, specifically as part of a military uniform. (As worn by General Dwight D. Eisenhower.)

Eisteddfod An annual meeting of Welsh bards at which there are contests in music and poetry. Compare FEIS CEOIL. (Welsh, 'assembly'.)

Ekaterinburg A town east of the Urals where the Russian Royal family were massacred in 1918; now renamed Sverdlovsk.

'EL', The New York City's elevated railway, closed down 1955 except in the BRONX, parts of QUEENS and BROOKLYN.

Elaine In ARTHURIAN LEGEND, the LADY OF SHALOTT who died for love of LANCELOT.

El Al The name of the Israeli airline.

ELAS People's National Army of Liberation, the armed forces organized in Greece by EAM in 1942, which devoted more energy to fighting non-Communist fellow citizens than to anti-German operations. (Initials of the Greek name.)

E layer (ionosphere) See HEAVISIDE LAYER.

Elba The island between Corsica and Italy where Napoleon was first exiled (1814-15); he was allowed to retain the title of Emperor and was nominally the ruler of the island. When he judged the time ripe, he embarked on the HUNDRED DAYS campaign.

Elder, The A character in Bernard Shaw's *Too True to be Good* said to be based on Dean Inge, the GLOOMY DEAN.

ELDO (1964) The European Launcher Development Organization, formed by the countries of Western Europe, the UK and Australia for the construction of launchers for heavy astronomical and communications satellites. In 1968 Britain announced a phased withdrawal. See ESRO; EUROPA.

El Dorado A tribal chief in Colombia, smeared with gold dust at an annual rite; rumors of this started the legend of El Dorado, a city paved with gold, sought by the Conquistadors, Raleigh and others. (Spanish, 'the gilded one'.)

Eleanor Crosses Nine crosses erected in the 13th century by Edward I to mark the places where the body of his Queen, Eleanor of Castile, rested en route from Nottinghamshire to Westminster Abbey. Three remain (Northampton, Geddington and Waltham Cross). That at Charing Cross (popularly derived from Chère Reine) is a modern replica.

Elector A German prince entitled to vote in the appointment of the Holy Roman Emperor (962-1803).

Elector Palatine The Count Palatine of the Rhine (PALATINATE).

Electra In Greek legend, the sister of ORESTES who conspires with him to murder their mother CLYTEMNESTRA. The story is treated by all 3 of the great Greek tragedians, and by numerous writers since, and in an opera by Richard Strauss; see also MOURNING BECOMES ELECTRA.

Electra complex Freud's term for the psychological effects of a girl's excessive attachment to her father and consequent (often unconscious) jealousy of and hostility to her mother. See OEDIPUS COMPLEX. (See ELECTRA.)

Elephant and Castle A London road junction and railroad depot in Newington, south of the Thames, which took its name from a public house there. (Variously derived from the Infanta of Castile, and the arms of the Cutlers' Company, which included an elephant with howdah.)

Eleusinian Mysteries The festival held each fall in honor of DEMETER and PERSEPHONE at Eleusis (near Athens), celebrating the sowing of wheat and barley (in Greece sown at the end of September and harvested in May). Although the Mysteries were celebrated until well on in the

Christian era, not much is known of their origin or nature.

11 Downing Street The official London residence of the Chancellor of the Exchequer, next door to the Prime Minister. See DOWNING STREET.

11 plus (UK) The examination taken at state schools at age 11 to determine whether a child should go on to grammar, secondary modern, or technical school. The target of much criticism, as sealing a child's fate at too tender an age, it is in process of abandonment (see COMPREHENSIVE SCHOOL; LEICESTERSHIRE PLAN).

Eleventh Commandment Cynically said to be: 'Thou shalt not be caught out'.

El Fatah (1957) An Arab guerrilla organization dedicated to the 'liberation' of Palestine, recruited from Palestinians in refugee camps etc. It absorbed the Palestine Liberation Organization in 1969 and became the largest group of FEDAYEEN. (Formed from initials of Arabic for Palestine National Liberation Movement; also spelled Al Fatah.)

Elginbrodde, Martin The subject of George Macdonald's epitaph: Here lie I, Martin Elginbrodde: / Hae mercy o' my soul, Lord God; / As I wad do, were I Lord God, / And ye were Martin Elginbrodde.

Elgin Marbles The collection of Greek antiquities which includes parts of the frieze from the Parthenon and many other ancient sculptures, together with plaster casts of yet more, brought from Athens by the Earl of Elgin in 1803 and now in the British Museum.

Elia The pen name under which Charles Lamb wrote his *Essays* (1820-25) for the *London Magazine*. He wrote on a wide range of topics, displaying a gentle, serene outlook which was not reflected in his personal life.

Elijah (9th century BC) A major prophet of Israel in the reign of Ahab. He went up by a whirlwind to Heaven (II *Kings* ii, 11) and Elisha took up his mantle as his successor. See also next entry.

Elijah and the ravens A biblical incident often treated in popular art, representing the prophet Elijah at the brook Cherith (Kerith) being brought 'flesh and bread' by the ravens. (I *Kings* xvii, 3-6.)

Eliot, George Pen name of Mary Ann Evans (1819-80), English novelist.

Eliot, Lewis See STRANGERS AND BROTHERS.

Eliot Memorial lectures (1967) Lectures on literature, endowed by the London publishers, Faber & Faber, in memory of T. S. Eliot, given 4 times a year at Eliot College, KENT UNIVERSITY.

Elis A nickname for athletes of YALE University. (From Elihu Yale.)

Elisir d'amore, L' (1832) Donizetti's tuneful comic opera about love-sick rustics and a quack doctor with his love potions. (Italian, 'elixir of love'.)

Elizabeth Pen name of Elizabeth Beauchamp, Countess Russell (1866-1941), author of *Elizabeth and her German Garden* (1898), an account of her life in Prussia with her first husband; her second was Bertrand Russell's brother.

Elks, Benevolent and Protective Order of (1868) A large US fraternal organization with Masonic-type rites.

Ellis Island The New York immigration station, notorious for the insolence and inhumanity of its staff; closed in 1954.

Elsie Dinsmore (1867) The first of 26 children's books with the same heroine, written by Martha Finley (pen name of Martha Farquharson). A female LITTLE LORD FAUNTLEROY, the unlikable Elsie is understandably persecuted by one and all.

Elsie Venner (1861) A novel by Oliver Wendell Holmes about a girl who, soon after her mother had been bitten by a snake, is born with a symbolic birthmark (permanently hidden by a gold necklace) and then develops a cold reptilian nature which repels the man with whom she falls in love, despite her efforts to make herself more human. Holmes is here attacking the Calvinistic doctrine of Original Sin and asking the reader to rely on psychology rather than religion in passing judgment on his heroine.

Elsinore Old English spelling of Helsingör, a seaport in Denmark the scene of Shakespeare's *Hamlet*.

Elstree Studios (UK) ABC's film studios, between Watford and Barnet, Hertfordshire, which specialize in TV series. See ABC-TV.

Elvira Wife of DON JUAN, whom he abandons.

Elvish The language of the Elves invented by Tolkien in *The LORD OF THE RINGS*; for example *orcs* are goblins, *ents* a treelike people, and *mathom* is an article one saves but never gets around to using. Elvish enjoys a vogue on the campuses of America, and some words are said to be passing into general circulation.

Élysée Palace The official residence of the French President, situated just north of the Avenue des Champs-Élysées.

Elysium The abode of heroes and the virtuous dead, in Greek legend separate from the Underworld of HADES, and located somewhere in the far west in a land without cold or snow. See FORTUNATE ISLES.

Emancipation Proclamation Lincoln's proclamation of 1 Jan. 1863 freeing all slaves in regions still in rebellion against the Union; hence his name of Great Emancipator.

Emanuel Quint (1910) Short title of Gerhart Hauptmann's novel *The Fool in Christ, Emanuel Quint*. The son of a village carpenter, Quint is Jesus in a modern setting; he is expelled by his outraged compatriots and is later found dead in the Alps.

'Embarkation for the Island of Cythera' (1717) The established title of a Watteau painting which in fact depicts the departure from Cythera, the island of Venus, of young couples preparing to leave it (i.e. love's young dream) forever. There are versions in the Louvre and at Berlin.

'Embarkation of the Queen of Sheba, The' (1648) Claude Lorraine's combination of Classical architecture and biblical story in a study of the play of sunlight on water; now in the National Gallery, London.

Ember Days Three days in each season of the year appointed by the Christian Churches for prayer and fasting. (Derivation unknown.)

Emden A German light cruiser in World War I which had a brief but successful career shelling ports and sinking ships in eastern waters until HMAS *Sydney* sank her off the Cocos-Keeling Islands in Nov. 1914.

Emergent Evolution (1920) A philosophical theory of an Australian, Samuel Alexander: matter emerged from space-time with an innate tendency to strive towards a higher state, life; life similarly to evolve into mind; and mind into deity.

EMI (1931) Initials used for Electrical and Musical Industries, the leading British phonograph and electrical goods company, with headquarters at Hayes, London. It makes HMV and Columbia records, Morphy-Richards domestic equipment, Ardente hearing aids etc., and has acquired the Grade Organization (Lew and Leslie Grade), a variety and theatrical agency, Associated British Pictures (see ABC-TV) and control of Capitol Industries (USA).

Emily Post, According to According to the rules of etiquette as laid down by Mrs Post (1873-1960) who ran a widely syndicated newspaper column and a radio program on the subject, and published a book on it (1922), since updated by Elizabeth Post. Compare AMY VANDERBILT, ACCORDING TO.

Eminent Victorians (1917) Lytton Strachey's collection of revealing ironic biographical sketches of Cardinal Manning, Dr Arnold of Rugby, Florence Nightingale and Gen. Gordon.

Emma (1816) Jane Austen's novel in which Emma Woodhouse, having little to do except run the house for her hypochondriac father, devotes her time to arranging other people's lives for them, with conspicuous nonsuccess. Finally she marries the eligible Mr Knightley whom she had at first destined for her protégée Harriet Smith.

Emmanuel, Immanuel The son of a virgin birth mentioned in the Old Testament prophecy (*Isaiah* vii, 14) referred to in *Matthew* i, 23. (Hebrew, 'God with us'; spelled with *I* in OT, with *E* in NT.)

Emmaus The village not far from Jerusalem where Jesus appeared after his death to Cleophas and Simon Peter (*Luke* xxiv, 15-31).

Emmentaler A fairly mild hard-pressed cheese with a sweetish flavor, characterized by holes larger than those in Gruyère. The whole cheese is very large, flat and round. (Originally made in the Emme valley, Switzerland.)

Emmy A statuette awarded by the Academy of Television Arts and Sciences for the year's outstanding TV performance and programming. (Named for Faye Emerson, American entertainer.)

Emperor Concerto, The An English name for Beethoven's last piano concerto, not used on the Continent.

Emperor Jones (1920) Eugene O'-Neill's play about a black Pullman porter who sets himself up as emperor of an island in the West Indies.

'Emperor's New Clothes, The' One of Hans Christian Andersen's original fairy tales. Two rogues persuade the Emperor that they can weave him clothes which will be invisible only to those who are idiots or unfit for office. His courtiers are afraid to lay themselves open to either charge, and it is left to a child to cry out, when the Emperor parades through the streets in his 'new clothes': why, he has nothing at all on!

Empire, The (1804-15) The period in French history, also called the First Empire, from the time when Napoleon ended the CONSULATE by crowning himself Emperor, to the Battle of WATERLOO.

Empire Day (1903) A day set aside throughout the British Empire for the celebration of Queen Victoria's birthday (May 24th); it was renamed Commonwealth Day in 1958 and from 1966 was celebrated on the official birthday of Queen Elizabeth II in June.

Empire flying boat (1936) A British airliner built by Short Bros. for service with Imperial Airways on routes to Australia and South Africa. It carried 16 passengers, for whom comfortable sleeping quarters were provided, and took 9½ days on the Southampton-Sydney trip.

Empire Free Trade A crusade launched by Lord Beaverbrook in 1929 for the conversion of the British Empire into a free-trade area; unrealistic, since the Dominions had no intention of allowing free entry to British manufactures, it was killed by the OTTAWA AGREEMENTS. See UNITED EMPIRE PARTY.

Empire Loyalists (UK) An extreme right-wing political group, known to the public for the frequency with which they have to be thrown out of political meetings for making a noise.

Empire State Nickname of New York State.

Empire State Building Standing in midtown New York, 102 stories and 1250 ft high, the tallest building in the world when completed in 1931.

Empire State of the South A 19th-century nickname for Georgia because of its size and its agricultural and industrial prominence. It is now more often called the PEACH STATE.

Empire style (1800-30) The French style influenced by Ancient Egyptian art (which became familiar through Napoleon's campaigns) and even more by Ancient Greek and Roman models (e.g. Greek vases, the PARTHENON), interest in which was stimulated by political sympathy with the revolutionary struggles of Greece and Italy. Furniture tended to be heavy and comfortless, embellished with brass and ormolu. The period corresponded with the reigns of Napoleon, Louis XVIII and Charles X, and with the English REGENCY PERIOD.

Emporia Gazette One of the best of the small-circulation American newspapers, liberal Republican in politics, owned and edited by William Allen White (1868-1944) of

Emporia, Kan.

Empress of Canada A liner which caught fire and capsized in a Liverpool dock in 1953.

Empress of Ireland A liner which sank in the St Lawrence in May 1914.

Ems telegram (1870) A telegram from the King of Prussia to the Chancellor of the new North German Confederation, Bismarck, reporting his acceptance of a French request not to support a Hohenzollern candidate for the Spanish throne; Bismarck altered it to convey a brusque refusal and published it, so causing France to declare war (see FRANCO-PRUSSIAN WAR).

Enchanted Hill, The William Randolph Hearst's princely San Simeon estate in California, inland from Monterey. The house, known as Hearst Castle, contained crates of antiques and paintings which he had not bothered to unpack before he died—as depicted in CITIZEN KANE.

Encyclopédistes The group of contributors (including Voltaire and Rousseau) to the *Encyclopédie* (1751) in 34 volumes edited by Diderot and D'Alembert, in which all contemporary institutions, ideas and superstitions were challenged in the light of Reason; a major influence on the French Revolution.

Endgame (1957) Beckett's play about the sole survivors of some world disaster, the blind and paralyzed Hamm, his legless parents who live in garbage cans, and his would-be rebel servant, Clov. They all hate each other; Hamm has the only food, Clov alone can run away (as he wants to do); but since they are mutually dependent he never does.

Endor, The Witch of The witch who at SAUL's request calls up the ghost of SAMUEL; he prophesies the destruction of Saul's army by the Philistines (I *Samuel* xxviii, 7-20).

Endymion (1818) Keats's long, overrich allegorical poem of a Greek shepherd's love for the Moon, apparently representing the poet's own

search for ideal beauty. It begins: A thing of beauty is a joy for ever.

Enemy of the People (1882) Ibsen's play in which Dr Stockman is regarded as an enemy by his fellow citizens when he tries to close down a spa because its waters are polluted.

Enfants terribles, Les (1930) Jean Cocteau's novel and play on the same kind of theme as HIGH WIND IN JAMAICA, i.e. the amorality of children.

Enfield London borough since 1965 consisting of the former boroughs of Enfield, Edmonton and Southgate.

Engadine A favorite tourist ground in southeast Switzerland, the valley of the Inn stretching from the Maloja Pass to the Austrian frontier.

English Bards and Scotch Reviewers See EDINBURGH REVIEW.

English Civil War (1642-51) The war between the CAVALIERS and ROUNDHEADS, and its aftermath. After the battles of EDGEHILL, MARSTON MOOR and NASEBY, Charles I surrendered to the Scottish army at Newark, ending the first phase (1646). Cromwell then (1648) crushed Royalist risings in Kent and Essex and a Scottish army at PRESTON, ending the second phase. Charles, Prince of Wales, then took the field and was defeated at DUNBAR and WORCESTER (1650-51), ending the third phase.

English horn A woodwind instrument similar to the oboe but a fifth lower in pitch, with a rich melancholy tone. Known also as the cor anglais, it is neither English nor a horn.

English muffin Bread dough rolled and cut into rounds and baked on a griddle, usually sliced and toasted before serving.

English Renaissance (16th century) The age of the Reformation; of Colet, More, Marlowe, Spenser, Shakespeare and Bacon; and of Tudor architecture. See RENAISSANCE.

English-Speaking Union (1918) Founded by (Sir) Evelyn Wrench to bring together Commonwealth and American people, and to help students and teachers of English throughout the world.

English Stage Company (1956) A London repertory company which opened at the Royal Court Theatre, Sloane Square, Chelsea, and gained early fame from LOOK BACK IN ANGER. It stages the work of new British and established foreign playwrights, as well as occasional classical revivals. The associated English Stage Society gives experimental productions on Sundays.

Enigma Variations (1899) Elgar's Variations on an Original Theme, each a sound-portrait of one of his friends, who have since been identified. Elgar never disclosed the nature of the 'enigma'.

Eniwetok A Pacific atoll, scene of the detonation of the first US hydrogen bomb on 1 Nov. 1952 (Operation Ivy), not announced until 1954. (In the Marshall Islands, near Bikini.)

Enlightenment, The The 18th century as the period when political, moral, religious, social and other beliefs were put to the test of reason by such thinkers as Rousseau, Voltaire, Kant, Newton, Adam Smith; and enlightened despots such as Frederick the Great and Catherine the Great tried to put the new theories into practice. Also called the Age of Reason. (Translation of German *Aufklärung*, used of this period in Germany.)

'Ennui' Sickert's vivid depiction of the deep boredom of a Sunday afternoon in a working-class home; now in the TATE Gallery, London.

Enoch Arden (1864) Tennyson's poem of a great renunciation. Enoch marries Annie but is shipwrecked and presumed dead. Annie marries another, Enoch returns and, watching their happiness from afar, decides not to ruin it by revealing himself.

Entente Cordiale (1904) The Anglo-French agreement which formed the basis of the TRIPLE ENTENTE; it defined spheres of influence in Egypt and Morocco.

Enterprise (1956) A national one-design class of dinghy, 13 feet 3 inches long, cheap but exciting to sail, and raced regularly almost everywhere in Britain; designed by Jack Holt and built in many places.

Enterprise, USS (1961) The first nuclear-powered aircraft carrier.

Enzian An incomparably foul liqueur made from gentian and drunk in Alpine regions presumably because of its bogus reputation as an aphrodisiac. (German, 'gentian'.)

Eocene Epoch The earliest subdivision of the TERTIARY PERIOD, lasting from about 70 to 50 million years ago. Carnivores, hoofed animals and the more primitive primates, e.g. the lemur, appeared. The London clay was deposited. (Greek, 'dawn of the modern', i.e. modern forms of life.)

Eos The Greek dawn-goddess, sister of SELENE and HELIOS; the Roman Aurora.

Eothen (1844) Kinglake's amiable description of the vicissitudes of travel in the Near East in the 19th century. (Greek, 'from the east'.)

Eozoic Period Term sometimes used for the earliest period of the PRECAMBRIAN ERA. (Greek *eos*, 'dawn', *zoé*, 'life'.)

EP Initials used for Extended-Play phonograph records, usually of 7-inch diameter and played at 45 rpm; with the LP, they replaced the old 78 rpm records in 1948.

Ephesus, Council of (431) The Ecumenical Council which condemned the NESTORIAN HERESY.

Epic Theatre (1920s) A type of play advocated by Brecht and other Germans, appealing rather to reason than to the emotions, and using the A-EFFECT (alienation) to put over political argument. The social and political background to a plot is presented by various devices, e.g. movies and placards shown during the course of the play, which is itself broken up into many self-contained episodes (hence the name Epic). Piscator applied this idea in dramatizing Tolstoy's *War and Peace* (1955).

Epicureanism The Greek philosophy which held that the highest good is happiness, to be sought through a virtuous life, avoidance of pain and the serenity that comes from the harmony of a healthy mind

in a healthy body. The use of 'epicure' for one who is fond of luxury
and comfort is due to a complete
misunderstanding of this. (Epicurus,
341-270 BC.)

Epigoni (1) The sons of the SEVEN
AGAINST THEBES who avenged their
fathers by destroying THEBES, and,
by extension, those of a succeeding
and less distinguished generation.
(2) The heirs to the DIADOCHI. (Greek,
'descendants'.)

Epiphany The manifestation of
Christ to the Gentiles, in the persons
of the MAGI, commemorated on Jan.
6th. (Greek, 'an appearance'.)

Episcopalians (1) (UK) Scottish
name for Anglicans; Presbyterians
are the official Church of Scotland;
Anglicans are thus technically 'non-
comformists' in Scotland. (2) Name
for members of Protestant Episcopal
Church. (Greek *episkopos*, bishop.)

Epithalamion (1595) Spenser's bridal hymn, perhaps written for his
own marriage. (Greek, 'at the door of
the bridal chamber'.)

Epsom Downs (UK) The downs
within the circle of Epsom racetrack
in Surrey, where the gypsy caravans
gather for the 4-day meeting in June
and, since entry is free, particularly
crowded on Derby day.

EPU (1950-58) The European Payments Union, an organization financed by US loans to cover im-
balances in payments between
European countries pending the
lifting of restrictions on currency
convertibility; replaced by the EU-
ROPEAN MONETARY AGREEMENT.

Epworth League (1889) The Methodist youth organization, formed to
promote fellowship, worship, Christian service and the study of the
Scriptures.

Epworth Old Rectory The Lincolnshire home of John and Charles Wesley, where poltergeist phenomena
were reported in 1716; now a Methodist center and museum.

**Equal Employment Opportunity
Commission** A US government
agency appointed to promote the
cause of equal opportunity for all
US citizens, though lacking powers
of enforcement.

Equality State Nickname of Wyoming. (First state to give votes to
women.)

Equal Opportunity Employer An
employer who hires both white and
Negro workers.

Equity (1929) Shortened title of the
US and British Actors' Equity Associations, the actors' trade unions.

ERA (1934) Name given to a series of
British racing cars designed by Peter
Berthon (who later helped to design
the BRM) and others. (Initials of English Racing Automobiles Ltd.)

Erastian Adjective applied to the
view that the Church should be subordinate to the State, then a shock-
ing heresy, now Anglican orthodoxy. (Erastus, Greek translation of
the German name of a 16th-century
writer, Lieber.)

Erebus In Greek legend, the personification of darkness, and a dark cav-
ern through which the dead passed
on their way to HADES.

Erebus (1) The ship in which Ross
sailed to Antarctica (1839-41), and
which was abandoned by Franklin,
with the *Terror*, north of Canada
during his search for the Northwest
Passage (1848). (2) The Antarctic
volcano named after (1).

Erewhon (1872) Samuel Butler's
UTOPIA in which Higgs, the narrator,
comes upon an odd community in
an unexplored part of New Zealand
whose institutions provide the author with material for satirical attacks on English ways (e.g. criminals
are sent to the doctor, the sick are
punished). Higgs escapes by balloon
(see next entry). (The title is 'nowhere' spelled, approximately, backwards.)

Erewhon Revisited (1901) In this
sequel to EREWHON Higgs returns to
find that, on account of his miraculous balloon ascent, he is worshiped
as 'Sunchild'. He tries to explain,
but is got quickly out of the country
by the vested interests of the new
religion.

Eric, or Little by Little (1858) A
moralizing school story about a
monumental little prig, by F. W. Farrar, later headmaster of Marlborough
and Dean of Canterbury.

Erie An Iroquoian Indian tribe who inhabited the Lake Erie region; they were defeated and absorbed by the Seneca.

Erie Canal The main canal of the New York State Barge Canal system, extending 352 miles from Albany on the Hudson to Buffalo on Lake Erie.

Erin go bragh! Erse for 'Ireland for ever', quoted in a poem of Thomas Campbell's.

Erinyes Older Greek name for the EUMENIDES.

Erith (UK) A former municipal borough of Kent, since 1965 part of the borough of BEXLEY.

Eritrea A former Italian colony, now part of Ethiopia.

Erlking A Black Forest elf who lures children to their doom; a legend used by Goethe in a poem made famous through Schubert's dramatic song based on it. A rider arrives at his destination to find that his child whom he was carrying lies dead in his arms, his spirit lured away by the soft-spoken elf. (German-*Erlkönig*, 'king of the alders' a mistranslation of the Danish for 'king of the elves'.)

Ermine Street A pre-Roman road from London through Lincoln to York, extended by the Romans to HADRIAN'S WALL.

Eroica, The Beethoven's 3rd Symphony, which contains the Funeral March (there is another Funeral March in a piano sonata of his). Beethoven gave it its present name after deleting the original dedication to Napoleon when he betrayed the democratic cause by accepting the title of Emperor.

Eros In Greek legend, the son of APHRODITE, identified with the Roman Cupid, represented in art as a golden-winged child with bow and arrows, and sometimes as blindfold. Those pierced by his arrows fall hopelessly in love. See CUPID AND PSYCHE, (Greek, 'love'.)

'Eros' (1893) Sir Alfred Gilbert's aluminum statue in the middle of Piccadilly Circus, London, part of a memorial to the 7th Lord Shaftesbury, philanthropist, and originally meant to represent the Angel of Christian Charity.

ERP (1948-52) The European Recovery Program or Marshall Plan, a program of US aid in the economic reconstruction of Western Europe and Turkey, which led to the formation of the OEEC.

Erse The Celtic (Gaelic) language spoken in Ireland, sometimes called Irish or Irish Gaelic. (Formerly used also of Scottish Gaelic.)

Erskine May Used as the short title of Sir Erskine May's *Treatise on the Law, Privileges, Proceedings and Usage of Parliament* (1844), still a standard work of reference.

Esau Son of Isaac and Rebecca and elder (twin) brother of JACOB; he was red and hairy at birth, and sold his birthright for a mess of pottage (*Genesis* xxv, 33-34).

Escorial (1584) A vast group of buildings 30 miles northwest of Madrid, comprising palaces, monastery, church, mausoleum, college and a famous library, built by Philip II in fulfillment of a vow. All subsequent kings (except the last) are buried there, and it has one of the finest art collections in the world. (From Spanish for 'refuse dump'.)

Esdras Two books of the APOCRYPHA, the first a compilation from old Hebrew texts of the Old Testament; the second an apocalyptic book written about AD 120 but using older material. (Esdras, Latin form of the name Ezra.)

Eskimo dog A sledge dog, longhaired, 50-85 lbs, of which there are several breeds. The Alaskan Malamute is particularly favored for Arctic expeditions. Like the SIBERIAN HUSKY, the Eskimo dog is also trainable for military use.

Eskimo roll A method of righting a capsized canoe while remaining seated in it.

Eskimos A Mongoloid people of the Arctic regions of Siberia, Alaska, Canada and Greenland.

Esmond, Beatrix The beautiful and headstrong character in Thackeray's HENRY ESMOND who rejects Henry, flirts with the Old Pretender, marries her mother's chaplain (who becomes a bishop) and reappears in

The VIRGINIANS as the sardonic old wife of Baron Bernstein.

ESP Initials used for Extrasensory Perception, a term covering telepathy, precognition, clairvoyance and other forms of perception not apparently derived from the 5 senses; the phrase is particularly associated with J. B. Rhine of DUKE UNIVERSITY, who set up a parapsychological laboratory there for scientific statistical study of such phenomena. See PSI FORCE.

Espadon Grill The Ritziest rendezvous of the Paris Ritz.

Espagnole (Cooking) The basic rich brown sauce.

Esperanto (1887) The most successful of the synthetic universal languages, based mainly on the RO-MANCE LANGUAGES. (Derived from Latin-type word for 'optimist'.)

ESRO (1964) The European Space Research Organization, set up in conjunction with ELDO to promote research by rocket and satellite.

Essa A series of weather satellites, first launched in 1966 and representing an improvement on TIROS. They are called 'environmental survey satellites' and named for the Environmental Science Services Administration, which is also responsible for the Tiros and NIMBUS series.

Essay on Man (1734) Pope's attempt to justify the ways of God to man, best known in quotation, e.g.: 'Hope springs eternal in the human breast; / Man never is, but always to be blessed'; 'All is but are parts of one stupendous whole, / Whose body nature is, and God the soul'; 'For forms of government let fools contest: / Whate'er is best administered is best'. Dr Johnson growled that it displayed vulgarity of sentiment and penury of knowledge, 'happily disguised'.

Essenes An ancient Jewish ascetic and mystical sect, founded about the 2nd century BC; the DEAD SEA SCROLLS have been attributed to them.

Essex rebellion (1601) A demonstration in London led by Robert Devereux, Earl of Essex, former favorite of Queen Elizabeth but by then in disgrace for mishandling the Ulster rebellion and for general insubordination. He was arrested, prosecuted by Lord Bacon among others, and executed for treason.

Essex University (UK) Founded 1964 at Wivenhoe Park, near Colchester.

Esso A subsidiary of STANDARD OIL OF NEW JERSEY, Shell's chief competitor; it built the FAWLEY refinery. The group includes Esso Chemical, with headquarters in Brussels, and Esso Europe, an oil company with headquarters in London.

Esso Tournament A British match-play golf tournament for the 10 leading players in the PGA ORDER OF MERIT and 5 invited players, held in July at Moor Park, Rickmansworth, Hertfordshire. Each competitor has to play all the others. The prize money totals $14,000. (Sponsored by Esso Petroleum Ltd.)

EST See EASTERN STANDARD TIME.

Establishment, The (1) A term (originally derogatory) which came into use in 1954 to designate the guardians of traditional British institutions such as the Church, the army, the 'public' schools and the City, regarded as reactionary or out-of-date. Hence (2) any group of social, economic and political leaders who form a ruling class and (3) the leaders or pundits of a section of society, e.g. the literary Establishment.

Esterházy family An ancient Hungarian family dating back to the 13th century which until recent years was always prominent in state affairs.

Esther In the Bible, a beautiful Jewess of the 5th century BC who keeps her nationality secret when chosen by the Persian king, Ahasuerus (Xerxes), as his queen. When his minister Haman plotted to exterminate the Jews of Persia, she and her uncle Mordecai foiled him and he was hanged. The story seems to have been invented to explain the Jewish festival of PURIM.

Esther Waters (1894) George Moore's novel of the love of a house-maid for her illegitimate son, whose father later returns to marry her. He is now a publican and bookmaker, and the plot turns on his success on the racetrack.

Estragon One of the 2 tramps in GODOT.

ESU Initials standing for the ENGLISH-SPEAKING UNION.

ET Eastern Time, i.e. EASTERN STANDARD TIME.

ETA Initials used, originally by air pilots, for Estimated Time of Arrival.

ETD Initials used, on the analogy of ETA, for Estimated Time of Departure.

Eternal City, The Rome; a name given to it from ancient times.

Etesian winds Strong dry northerly winds in the eastern Mediterranean which blow during the daytime from May to October, raising storms at sea and clouds of dust on land.

Ethan Frome (1911) Edith Wharton's grim short novel about an impoverished New England farmer who falls in love with his wife's cousin. Permanently crippled in a joint suicide attempt, the 2 lovers are devotedly cared for by the wife, while her cousin degenerates into the nagging hypochondria which had previously been her own chief characteristic.

Ethiopia See ABYSSINIA.

ETO Initials used in World War II for European Theater of Operations.

Étoile, L' The huge rotary in Paris at the top of the Champs-Élysées, site of the ARC DE TRIOMPHE and meeting place of 12 avenues.

ETO medal Medal given to all those who served in the ETO.

Eton jacket (1) Very short black jacket, as worn by the younger boys at Eton College; (2) similar short jacket worn by women.

ETOUSA Initials used in World War II for European Theater of Operations, US Army.

Être et le Néant, L' (1943) Sartre's chief exposition of EXISTENTIALISM. (French, 'being and nothingness'.)

Etruscans The non-Indo-European predecessors of the Ancient Romans who left their name to modern Tuscany; they dominated northwest Italy (Etruria) from the 7th century BC and ruled Rome under the TARQUINS.

Their numerous brief inscriptions are still largely undeciphered; their artistic remains, though impressive, indicate that they borrowed inspiration from all quarters. They bequeathed to the Romans the curious art of divination by inspection of entrails.

Ettrick Shepherd A name for James Hogg (1770-1835), the Scottish shepherd-poet born at Ettrick, Selkirkshire.

E-type Jaguar 4.2 liter 2-seater coupe, esteemed as a status symbol among young executives and the professional classes before shades of the prison house of paternity begin to close / Upon the growing boy. Much mentioned in James Bond-type novels. But see DB-6.

Eugene Onegin Title of a verse romance by Pushkin (1831) and an opera by Tchaikovsky (1879). The bored Byronic hero repulses the advances of the young Tatyana, who herself repulses Eugene's when, now married to a general, she meets him again years later.

Eugénie Grandet (1833) One of the novels of Balzac's COMÉDIE HUMAINE, a study of a rich miser mewed up in his country house with his unfortunate daughter Eugénie.

Eumenides Greek name for 3 winged avenging goddesses (the Furies), who relentlessly pursued those who had failed in duty to their parents or who had otherwise contravened the accepted code of conduct. Also called ERINYES. (Literally, 'the kindly ones', a euphemism meant to placate them.)

Euphorbiaceae The spurge or milkweed family, characterized by an acrid milky juice, often poisonous; it includes poinsettia, cassava, castor-oil plant, rubber trees.

Euphues (1578) John Lyly's romantic picture of polite society, remembered not for its content but for its florid rhetorical style, full of antitheses and other literary quirks, which for a time set a fashion called euphuism. (Greek, 'well cultivated'.)

EUR Initials of the Italian for 'Universal Exposition of Rome', still used as the sole name of a suburb of southwest Rome; originally the site for Mussolini's grandiose world fair planned for 1942 (which never took place). It has since been developed as a luxury suburb, with skyscrapers, government departments, and museums, all set in parklike surroundings.

Euratom (1958) The European Atomic Energy Community, one of the main COMMON MARKET organizations, set up to establish a powerful joint industry to develop the peaceful uses of nuclear energy; the headquarters are at Brussels. See CERN.

Eurobond A US corporation bond sold outside of the US but denominated and paid for in dollars and yielding interest in dollars.

Eurocontrol (1960) A supranational civil organization working for safe air navigation for high-flying aircraft in Europe, in coordination with the national military authorities; it has an experimental research center at Bretigny, near Chartres, France.

Eurodollars Privately owned freely convertible dollar balances which have accumulated in European commercial banks as a result of US loans to and expenditure in Europe.

Europa In Greek legend, the daughter of a Phoenician king whom Zeus, in the guise of a bull, carried off to Crete, where he sired MINOS, RHADA-MANTHUS and Sarpedon.

Europa A 3-stage space rocket planned by ELDO for ESRO. The first and second stages are French, the third German, and the satellite Italian.

Europastrasse Name given to a projected series of transcontinental highways, e.g. Europastrasse No. 1 from London to Sicily via Paris, Nice, Genoa, Rome; No. 4 from Helsinki to Lisbon via Bremen, Frankfurt and Basle; No.5 from London to Istanbul, via Frankfurt and Nuremberg. The completed sections lie mainly in West Germany.

European Assembly (1958) See EUROPEAN PARLIAMENTARY ASSEMBLY.

European Atomic Energy Community See EURATOM.

European Coal and Steel Community (1952) A Common Market organiza-

tion, based on the SCHUMAN PLAN, which pooled its resources, abolished all internal trade restrictions, and more than doubled steel production in the first 13 years. The headquarters are at Luxembourg.

European Defense Community A stillborn organization designed to integrate the West German army into a European defense force, in accordance with the Paris Treaty of 1952. France, however, never ratified the treaty. The WESTERN EUROPEAN UNION was adopted as a substitute.

European Economic Community See COMMON MARKET.

European Free Trade Association See EFTA.

European Monetary Agreement (1955) An agreement by OEEC members to restore currency convertibility through a European Fund which provides short-term loans to facilitate monthly settlements between central banks. The Fund began work when the EPU ceased to operate in 1958.

European Nations Cup (1960) A soccer tournament run on the same elimination system as the World Cup, held every 4 years in between World Cup contests. The trophy is officially called the Henri Delaunay Cup.

European Parliamentary Assembly (1958) An assembly of delegates from the parliaments of member states of the Common Market, Euratom and the European Coal and Steel Community. It meets at Strasbourg to consider the annual reports and budgets of those bodies, and has power to pass a vote of censure on their work and to compel the resignation of the highest executives concerned.

European Payments Union See EPU.

European plan US term for hotel rates that do not include meals; see AMERICAN PLAN.

European Recovery Program See ERP.

Europe des patries, L' The phrase attributed to President de Gaulle to describe the ultimate objective of the FOUCHET PLAN. De Gaulle, however, later claimed that his term was

L'Europe des états (i.e. a loose confederation of states), to distinguish it
from the supranational European
government envisaged by the COM-
MON MARKET.

Europort (1961) By far the biggest
and busiest port in the world, at
Rotterdam, opposite the Hook of
Holland, able to take vessels up to
250,000 tons. (In Dutch spelled Eu-
ropoort.)

Eurospace A nonprofit association
of the aerospace equipment manufacturers of Western Europe, formed
to cooperate in development and to
coordinate policies.

Eurydice In Greek legend the wife of
ORPHEUS. When she died, Orpheus
went to fetch her back from the
Underworld, and so charmed HADES
with his lyre that he was allowed to
take her away provided he did not
look at her until he had set foot on
earth. He broke this condition and
lost her forever.

Eustachian tube A tube connecting
the middle ear with the back of the
throat; it is the channel through
which infections reach the parts of
the ear lying on the inner side of the
eardrum.

Euxine Greek name for the Black
Sea. (Greek, 'welcoming', a euphemism to propitiate it, as it was a
stormy, treacherous sea.)

EVA Initials used by astronauts for
Extravehicular Activity, e.g. the
moon walks of *Apollo* 11 and 12,
and the 'space walks' on earlier
flights.

Evangelical Church (1) An American Church on Methodist lines,
founded in 1800. (2) A name for the
German Lutheran Church, now
called the Evangelical United Brethren Church. (From Greek for 'bringing good tidings'.)

Evangelicalism Emphasis on the
authority of the New Testament as
against that of a Church, as in the
Low Church doctrines of some Anglicans which are the opposite to
ANGLO-CATHOLICISM: salvation is by
faith in Christ as the redeemer of
mankind through his sacrifice, and
cannot be achieved through sacra-

ments and good works; elaborate
ritual is a distraction from true worship. See EVANGELICAL CHURCH.

Evangeline (1847) Longfellow's narrative poem, subtitled *A Tale of
Acadie*, about 2 lovers separated
when the British expelled the
Acadians from Nova Scotia and,
despite years of search, united only
at death. See next entry.

Evangeline country (1) The village
of Grand Pré near Wolfville, NS, the
setting of the early part of EVANGE-
LINE, and now a national historic
park. (2) The Longfellow-Evangeline
State Park in Louisiana near Bayou
Teche, where the hero of that poem
and other 'Cajuns' were moved in
1755.

Evangelist (1) Any of the authors of
the 4 Gospels. (2) A travelling missionary. (3) One who preaches the
need for a 'new birth' (conversion)
as an essential step to salvation. See
EVANGELICAL CHURCH.

Evelina (1778) A delicate social
comedy published anonymously by
Fanny Burney (Mme d'Arblay),
about 'a young lady's entrance into
the world' of London society.

Evelyn's Diary (1818) The interesting and amusing diary, covering the
whole life from the age of 20, of John
Evelyn (1620-1706), a Royalist who
went into exile during the ENGLISH
CIVIL WAR, returned to hold office
under Charles II, and was one of the
founders of the ROYAL SOCIETY.

Eve of St Agnes, The (1819) Keats's
narrative poem based on the superstition that girls dream of their future husbands on the night before St
Agnes's Day (Jan. 21st). (St Agnes,
child martyr in the DIOCLETIAN PER-
SECUTION, and patron saint of virgins.)

Everglades, The A wide area of
swamp and subtropical forest in
southern Florida, part of it a National Park, part reclaimed for agriculture.

Evergreen State Nickname of Washington State.

Everyman A 15th-century Dutch
morality play. Everyman, summoned by Death, is accompanied by

Good Deeds alone of all his friends, among whom were Beauty, Strength etc.

Evian agreement (1962) The agreement between France and the Algerian rebels which ended the Algerian revolt by the grant of independence. (French spa where secret talks were held from 1961; see next entry.)

Evian water An alkaline mineral water from Evian-les-Bains, a French spa on the south shore of the Lake of Geneva. (The spa took its name from the water, *evian* being formed from a local dialect word for 'water'.)

Excalibur The magic sword which ARTHUR alone was able to free from the stone or anvil in which it was embedded, thus proving his right to become king.

Exclusion Bill (1679) A Bill put forward by the Earl of Shaftesbury to exclude the Roman Catholic James, Duke of York, from succession to the throne. Charles II dissolved 3 Parliaments rather than let it pass.

Exclusive Brethren (1848) A subsect of PLYMOUTH BRETHREN, also called Darbyites, which itself split into several divisions. One, under 'Big Bill' Taylor in New York, attained notoriety by refusing to eat with members of other persuasions.

Exile, The (Biblical history) The BABYLONIAN CAPTIVITY; hence the adjectives *Exilic, Postexilic.*

Existentialism A blanket term for philosophies of lonely man, solely dependent on God (Kierkegaard), on Christian principles (Karl Jaspars), on himself in a meaningless godless world, with infinite potentialities for self-development (Sartre), or haunted by *Angst*, a general dread of nothingness (Heidegger).

Exit the King (1962) A play by Eugene Ionesco in which the Bérenger of the earlier RHINOCEROS reappears as the dying king of an imaginary country, sustained by fortitude alone.

Exodus The second book of the PENTATEUCH, telling the story of Moses, the Exodus of the Israelites from the Land of GOSHEN (at some time between the 15th and 13th centuries BC), their wanderings in the desert, and the giving of the Law.

Expanding Universe theory The hypothesis that all groups of galaxies are receding from all other groups at speeds proportionate to distance, which arose from Edwin Hubble's observations (1930) that distant spectra show 'red shifts' interpreted as Doppler shifts. It led to the BIG BANG THEORY and the STEADY STATE THEORY. See DOPPLER EFFECT; HUBBLE'S LAW.

Experiences of an Irish RM, Some (1899) A book by E. Oe. Somerville (1861-1949) and her cousin Martin ROSS which exploits the humors of Irish hunting and country life. They also wrote *Further Experiences* (1908). (RM, Resident Magistrate, title given in those days to a stipendiary magistrate in Ireland.)

Experiment with Time, An See SERIALISM.

Explorer The name given to a series of US research satellites. *Explorer 1*, launched 31 Jan. 1958, was America's first earth satellite, and sent back data which led to the discovery of the VAN ALLEN BELTS.

Expos The Montreal Expos, NATIONAL (Baseball) LEAGUE, playing at Jarry Park. They are the only major-league baseball team outside the US.

Eyeless in Gaza (1936) The first of Aldous Huxley's novels to show his growing preoccupation with oriental mysticism. A young profligate, Beavis, is converted in mid-life to the author's own views. (Title from Milton's *Samson Agonistes*.)

Ezekiel (6th century BC) A book of the Old Testament in which the major prophet, Ezekiel, an exile in Babylon, encourages his countrymen in Jerusalem not to despair.

F

F As a prefix to a number in aircraft designations, F = Fighter; formerly P (for 'patrol') was used.

FAA See FEDERAL AVIATION AGENCY.

Faber (Geoffrey) Memorial prize (1963) An annual award of £250 made alternately for a volume of verse and a novel, written by a British or Commonwealth author under 40 years of age.

Fabergé wares The products of the St Petersburg and Moscow workshops of the Russian-born jeweler and goldsmith, Carl Fabergé (1846-1920). He is especially famous for his Easter eggs made for the Imperial family. His work was of great delicacy, sometimes exquisite, sometimes overelaborate to suit the taste of his customers.

Fabian Society (1884) (UK) Founded by left-wing intellectuals such as Beatrice and Sidney Webb, Bernard Shaw, H. G. Wells and R. H. Tawney, who believed in 'the inevitability of gradualness' (Sidney Webb's phrase) in the spread of socialist attitudes. It publishes pamphlets, advises the Labour Party, and stimulates fresh ideas.

Fabian tactics Moving cautiously, as did Fabius Maximus Cunctator ('the delayer'), the Roman general who thwarted Hannibal by avoiding meeting him in pitched battle; of him it was written: *Unus homo nobis cunctando restituit rem* ('One man by delaying tactics restored our republic').

Fables in Slang (1899) The collected journalistic sketches of George Ade, written for the Chicago *Record* in lively colloquial style.

'Face Upon the Floor, The' (1887) Doggerel verse possibly by Hugh Antoine D'Arcy and based on John Henry Titus's earlier 'The Face Upon the Barroom Floor'. In a New York saloon a drunk draws 'a picture of the face that drove me mad'

— 'You shall see the lovely Madeleine upon the barroom floor' — and having completed this self-imposed task 'he fell across the picture — dead!'.

Fact, Theater of (1960s) A form of documentary play on recent history, e.g. on the Robert OPPENHEIMER CASE, Lee Harvey Oswald, or the AUSCHWITZ trial. See also *The* REPRESENTATIVE. Verbatim reports of trials are mixed with reconstructions of what probably occurred.

Faerie Queene, The (1590-95) A national heroic poem by Edmund Spenser, chronicling the romantic adventures of medieval knights, each of whom portrays one of the cardinal virtues.

Fafnir In Scandinavian mythology the dragon who seized the NIBELUNGS' gold and was slain by Siegfried.

Fagin The head of a school for pickpockets in Dickens's OLIVER TWIST; the Artful Dodger was the most promising of his pupils, but Oliver himself was a backward learner.

Fahrenheit 451 (1953) Ray Bradbury's science-fiction story about a future 'burning of the books' when the wisdom of the past comes to be regarded as inimical to future progress; a group memorizes their contents and thus saves civilized values for future generations.

Fairbairn style A rowing style which put more emphasis on arm pull than body swing and sacrificed appearance to speed. (Steve Fairbairn, an Australian at Jesus College, Cambridge, subsequently a leading coach.)

Fair Deal (1948) President Truman's NEW DEAL-type program announced in his presidential election campaign.

Fairey Delta 2 A British turbojet research aircraft which made history in 1956 as the first plane to exceed

1000 m.p.h.

'Fair Harvard' HARVARD's Alma Mater, set to a 17th-century English melody possibly composed by Matthew Locke for 'My Lodging is on the Cold Ground' and also used by Thomas Moore for his 'Believe Me, if All Those Endearing Young Charms' (1808). The words were written for Harvard's bicentenary (1836) by the Rev. Samuel Gilman.

Fair Maid of Perth (1828) Walter Scott's novel of the 15th century; the maid is Katie Glover, who marries the armorer, Hal o' the Wynd.

Fair Rosamond One of the Clifford family, mistress of Henry II, who according to legend built her a house in a labyrinth so that no one could get to her; but his Queen, Eleanor, did so and poisoned her. She was buried in Godstow nunnery.

Faithful Shepherd suite A suite constructed by Sir Thomas Beecham from material in Handel's unsuccessful opera (1712) of that name.

Fala A famous White House dog buried in the Rose Garden at HYDE PARK, N. Y., alongside his owners, Eleanor and Franklin Roosevelt.

Falaise Gap, Battle of the (13-20 Aug. 1944) A crucial battle of World War II, in which large German forces were nearly encircled south of Caen, Normandy; a high proportion of them fought their way out before the gap was closed.

Falangists (1933) Spanish Fascist Party founded by the dictator Primo de Rivera's son; although the only party permitted to exist, its relations with Franco are uneasy. (Falange española, 'Spanish phalanx'.)

Falcon (1955) US Air Force electronically controlled air-to-air missile with a range of several miles, mounted in fighter aircraft.

Falcons The Atlanta Falcons, NATIONAL FOOTBALL LEAGUE, Became member of the NATIONAL CONFERENCE, NATIONAL FOOTBALL LEAGUE in 1970.

Falkland Islands, Battle of the (Dec. 1914) The revenge for CORONEL in World War I, in which Sturdee's

squadron sank von Spee's *Scharnhörst, Gneisenau* and other ships.

Fall, The The Fall of Man, the state of continuing sin in which mankind lives owing to the disobedience of Adam; a doctrine propounded by St Paul, and not mentioned by Jesus.

Fallen Angels (1925) An early Noël Coward comedy in which 2 wives get steadily drunk while awaiting an undesired visit from their former lover.

Fall Line The line formed by joining points marking the limit of river navigation east of the Appalachians; it runs approximately through Philadelphia, Baltimore and Richmond.

Fallodon Papers (1926) The literary papers of the first Viscount Grey of Fallodon, who as Sir Edward Grey was Foreign Secretary at the outbreak of World War I. (Name of his ancestral home near Alnwick, Northumberland.)

'Fall of the House of Usher, The' (1839) One of Edgar Allan Poe's short Tales of Mystery and the Imagination, in which a man visits an old school friend, the last of the House of Usher, sees him and his twin sister die in the GOTHIC NOVEL style, and the house disintegrate and disappear.

Fallopian tube The tube from ovary to womb, down which ova pass.

Fall River Legend (1948) A ballet based on the LIZZIE BORDEN MURDER CASE, with music by Morton Gould and choreography by Agnes de Mille.

Falstaff, Sir John The fat knight who appears in Shakespeare's HENRY IV and the MERRY WIVES, created as a foolish, sensual, lying glutton, but often played as a gay harmless old rogue, rather shabbily treated by Prince Hal.

Fancy Free (1944) Leonard Bernstein's cheerful little ballet about sailors in a bar, with choreography by Jerome Robbins; it was the foundation of his refreshingly adult musical show, *On the Town*.

Faneuil Hall The old market hall in Dock Square marketplace, Boston, Mass. As a principal meeting place for Revolutionaries, it became known as 'The Cradle of Liberty'. There is a gallery with historic paintings. (Given to the town in 1742 by Peter Faneuil.)

Fannie Farmer   Short title of *The Fannie Merritt Farmer Boston Cooking School Cookbook*, first published in the days of 12-course dinners (1896) and since continuously revised, like MRS BEETON, to suit the contracting stomachs of later generations.

Fanny Mae   Nickname formed from the initials FNMA of the Federal National Mortgage Association, a government-sponsored corporation that helps private lenders to finance home building, and is thought to have kept the government-guaranteed housing market from collapse in 1969.

Fanny's First Play   (1911) Bernard Shaw's play about respectable parents whose son and daughter are sent to prison and make what their elders regard as unsuitable marriages.

Fantasticks, The   A popular, record-breaking off-Broadway musical by Tom Jones and Harvey Schmidt. By 1971, still running after 11 years, it had played over 4,500 performances.

FAO   (1945) Initials standing for the Food and Agriculture Organization, a UN agency to raise the standards of rural populations, increase production of wholesome food, and promote efficiency in its distribution; among its many fields of activity are campaigns against soil erosion, crop diseases and pests, and malnutrition; it also runs the FREEDOM FROM HUNGER CAMPAIGN. The headquarters are in Rome.

'Far above Cayuga's Waters'   Cornell University's Alma Mater, words by C. K. Urquhart; the tune, taken from H. S. Thompson's 'Annie Lisle', was also used in several other college songs. (Cayuga is one of the Finger Lakes, with Ithaca, site of Cornell, at its southern tip.)

Farewell to Arms, A   (1929) Ernest Hemingway's novel of World War I; a young American is caught up in

the CAPORETTO disaster in Italy in 1917, deserts, and eventually escapes with an English nurse into neutral Switzerland.

Far from the Madding Crowd   (1874) Thomas Hardy's Wessex novel (and a movie based on it) about Bathsheba Everdene, loved by 3 men. She marries one of them, who deserts her and is murdered by the second; the murderer is sent to an asylum, and Bathsheba eventually marries the third, the faithful Gabriel Oak.

Fario Club   An international troutfishers' club with headquarters in Paris.

Farm Credit Administration   A US Federal agency formed to supervise the Federal Land Banks, production credit associations etc. which finance the cooperative farm credit system.

Farmer George   King George III, so named because of his bucolic tastes.

Farm Street, Mayfair   Name in common use for the Jesuit Church of the Immaculate Conception (1849), one of the best-known Roman Catholic churches in London, and headquarters of the British Jesuits.

Fasching   German for 'Carnival', which in Bavaria takes the form of 6 weeks of masquerade balls and other uninhibited festivities, ending on Fastnacht (Shrove Tuesday, Mardi Gras).

FASE   For Fundamentally Analyzable Simplified English, an English for use with computers.

Fashoda incident   (1898) The encounter of British troops under Kitchener and a French force under Marchand in an area of the Sudan disputed by the two countries; the French yielded. (Village on the White Nile in southern Sudan, now renamed Kodok.)

Faslane   (UK) A village on the Gare Loch, 23 miles from Glasgow, site since 1967 of the British POLARIS SUBMARINE base.

Fastnet, The   (1925) The principal offshore race counting to the ADMIRAL'S CUP, but not confined to Cup teams. Sailed in August (in alternate years with the New York to Bermuda race) over a course of 605 miles from Cowes, Isle of Wight, to the Fastnet Rock (off Cape Clear, south-west Ireland) and back to Plymouth.

Fat Boy, The A boy named Joe in Dickens's PICKWICK PAPERS who spent in sleep any time he was not eating.

Fates, The In Greek legend the 3 daughters of ZEUS who decide man's span on earth. Lachesis assigns the individual lot, Clotho spins the thread of life, and Atropos, the inflexible, cuts it. Called in Greek Moirai, in Latin Parcae.

Father and Son (1907) Sir Edmund Gosse's biography of his father, Philip, a zoologist connected with the CLAPHAM SECT; it gives a vivid picture of Victorian times.

Father Brown stories G. K. Chesterton's crime stories, in which the detective is a Roman Catholic priest with an unorthodox approach. The author and his creation regarded crime as a sin rather than as material for police investigation. The detective-priest first appeared in *The Innocence of Father Brown* (1911).

Father of American Drama, The The title given to William Dunlap (1766-1839) who wrote plays, encouraged other Americans to do so, founded the Park Theater and wrote *A History of the American Theater*.

Father of His Country A name for George Washington; his portrait with the caption *Des Landes Vater* appeared in Francis Bailey's almanac for 1779. Bailey was official printer to the Continental Congress.

Fathers and Sons (1861) Turgenev's great novel on the rise of the Nihilists (a word he invented), represented by Bazarov.

Father's Day The third Sunday in June, founded in the spirit of sex equality to offset MOTHER'S DAY.

Fathers of the Church The influential among the orthodox Christian writers of the first 6 centuries AD, e.g. Augustine, Athanasius, Pope Gregory I, Chrysostom, Tertullian, Origen. See also APOSTOLIC FATHERS.

'Father William' A parody of a poem of Robert Southey's recited by Alice in ALICE IN WONDERLAND, beginning:

'You are old, Father William', the young man said . . ./'And yet you persistently stand on your head;/Do you think at your age it is right?'

Fatimites (908-1171) An independent dynasty of caliphs founded in North Africa when the ABBASID caliphate of Damascus became subservient to the Turks; they ruled Egypt, founding Cairo in 970. They were overthrown by Saladin. (The founder claimed descent from the Prophet's daughter, Fatima.)

Faubourg St Germain The quarter where the elite of 18th-century Parisian society used to live, on the Left Bank opposite the Tuileries. The large houses are now foreign embassies or in government hands. (Originally a village built round the Abbey of St Germain-des-Prés.)

Faulkner (William) Foundation award (1961) A bronze plaque awarded annually for a notable first novel selected by members of the University of Virginia English faculty. (Named for the famous novelist, died 1962.)

Faust In German legend, an astrologer who sells his soul to the devil in return for enjoyment of all the pleasures of the world. This is the theme of Marlowe's *Dr Faustus*, Goethe's *Faust* (see next entry), and operas by Berlioz (*The Damnation of Faust*) and Gounod.

Faust Goethe's poem, in Part I of which (1808) Faust (see last entry) is represented as having mastered all knowledge and yearning to taste all worldly experience, MEPHISTOPHELES grants his wish, and rejuvenates him; he seduces MARGARET (Gretchen) and the poem ends with the realization of the price he has to pay. Part II (1832) is a vehicle for Goethe's meditations on a very wide range of topics.

Fauves, Les (1905) Name given by hostile critics to a group of French painters, led by the young Matisse, Vlaminck and Rouault, who exhibited their works together. Though not a coherent school, they had in common the use of violent color, flat patterns and absence of perspective. By 1907 they had gone their separate ways. (French, 'wild beasts'.)

Fawcett Library A London library devoted to the interests and achievements of women of all periods in all countries.

FBI The Federal Bureau of Investigation, established (1908) as an agency of the Department of Justice, with powers of arrest, to handle counterespionage, treason, other internal security matters and all crimes that break Federal laws. The agency was reorganized under the direction of J. Edgar Hoover from 1924 onward, tackling such major criminal organizations as MURDER INC. and COSA NOSTRA. The FBI came under criticism in the 1970s with charges of excessive surveillance of private citizens.

FCA See FARM CREDIT ADMINISTRATION.

FCC See FEDERAL COMMUNICATIONS COMMISSION.

FDA See FOOD AND DRUG ADMINISTRATION.

F.D.R. Initials used as nickname for Franklin Delano Roosevelt, 32nd US President.

Fearless Fosdick A dutiful detective worshipped by LI'L ABNER; a parody of DICK TRACY.

Feboldson, Febold A folk hero of the Plains of the Middle West, counterpart to the mountain forest hero Paul BUNYAN; his legend was not widely publicized until the 1920s and his problems, arising chiefly from the harsh climate and political machinations, have a more modern ring than Bunyan's.

February Revolution (1917) (Russia) See OCTOBER REVOLUTION.

Fedayeen A convenient generic term to cover members of EL FATAH and of the smaller but fiercer Popular Front for the Liberation of Palestine. (Arabic, 'those who sacrifice all for a cause'.)

Federal Aviation Agency (1959) A US government agency which coordinates air-traffic management (civil and military), installs navigational aids, and licenses pilots and aircraft.

Federal Bureau of Investigation See FBI.

Federal Communications Commission A US government agency consisting of 7 members that regulates interstate broadcasting and telecommunications.

Federalist, The (1788) A collection of 85 remarkable essays on the practical implementation of political theory written, under the pen name Publius, by Alexander Hamilton, James Madison and John Jay. They successfully persuaded New Yorkers to approve the US Constitution.

Federal Mediation and Conciliation Service (1947) A US government agency set up under the TAFT-HARTLEY ACT to assist in settling labor disputes that threaten widespread distruption of the nation's economy. It is independent of the Department of Labor.

Federal Reserve System (1914) A system comprising a Federal Reserve Board and central banks in each of 12 districts, which controls and coordinates banking operations and policy throughout the US.

Federal States, The The northern states which fought the Confederates in the AMERICAN CIVIL WAR.

Federal style (1780-1825) The American version of NEOCLASSICISM, sometimes called the Republican style as mirroring the post-Revolutionary reaction from the Georgian styles of monarchist Britain to those of the French and Ancient Roman republics. It is associated particularly with the name of Thomas Jefferson (see MONTICELLO) and exemplified by early buildings in Washington, D.C.

Federal Trade Commission (1914) A US 5-man government agency formed to control monopolies, trusts and price-fixing, administer Federal laws covering interstate trade, and formulate trade practice rules and guides on such subjects as cigarette advertising, tire classification or consumers' guarantees.

Federation Cup A tennis championship for women's teams of all nations.

Feis Ceoil (1897) A competitive festival of traditional Irish music and folk dance held in Dublin and elsewhere in the Republic and in Northern Ireland; it resembles a Welsh EISTEDDFOD. Usually referred to as 'the Feis'. (Erse, 'festival of music') See FEIS OF TARA.

Feis of Tara (700 BC to AD 560) The assembly of the High Kings of Ireland, princes, priests and bards which met on TARA HILL every 3 years; after its political deliberations, it turned to festivity. (Erse, 'festival').

Felix Holt (1866) George Eliot's novel in which Felix, the radical hero, is the rival of Harold Transome in both love and politics.

Felix the Cat A cat with far more than 9 lives, who first appeared in Pat Sullivan's animated cartoons (1921), was celebrated in the song 'Felix Keeps on Walking' and then continued in a King Features Syndicate comic strip.

Fell, Dr Gideon The fat, shrewd detective in John Dickson Carr's crime mysteries, written under the pen name of Carter Dickson.

Fenians Members of a secret anti-British society formed in Ireland and the USA after the POTATO FAMINE, pledged to expel the British and found a republic; their activities were confined to random dynamite outrages and the PHOENIX PARK MURDERS. (Old Irish *Fene*, 'the Irish'; see FINN.)

Fenway Park The home of the RED SOX at Boston, Mass. – the baseball park with the shortest left-field fence.

Ferdinand the Bull A bull created by Munro Leaf in a book for children, and popularized in a Walt Disney animated cartoon (1939). Ferdinand loved to lie in the shade of a tree smelling the flowers, and did not care for bullfighting at all.

Fermi award (1954) A US annual award for work in nuclear physics. (Named after the first recipient, Enrico Fermi.)

Fernet Branca An Italian bitters, drunk like CAMPARI.

Ferranti A British electronics firm with headquarters in Manchester; it made the first commercial computer in Europe, and also makes missile guidance and control equipment. In 1966 Ferranti repaid to government $10 million excess profits made on BLOODHOUND contracts. See PYE GROUP.

Fertile Crescent A name given to the fertile lands north of the deserts of Arabia, stretching from the Mediterranean (Syria and Palestine) to the Persian Gulf (Mesopotamia), united politically until the 2nd century BC and forming an economic unit which ever since has been divided politically; it now consists of Syria, Lebanon, Israel, Jordan and Iraq.

Feste The clown in Shakespeare's TWELFTH NIGHT; his song 'O mistress mine! where are you roaming?' is particularly remembered.

Festival Gardens (UK) The pleasure garden and Fun Fair established in Battersea Park, representing the lighter side of life at the FESTIVAL OF BRITAIN, and now a permanent feature of London.

Festival of Britain (1951-52) An imaginative and successful commemoration of the centenary of the GREAT EXHIBITION, centered on the South Bank site around Waterloo Bridge, London, where the ROYAL FESTIVAL HALL was built, and linked with exhibitions and festivals of music elsewhere in the country. At once a demonstration of British achievements in the previous 100 years, and a celebration of emergence from postwar austerities, it also awakened the public to realization of the potentialities for development of the hitherto neglected South Bank.

Festung Europa Hitler's concept of a Europe under German leadership rendered inpregnable to outside interference from the Allies. (German, 'Fortress Europe'.)

FFV Initials signifying 'First Families of Virginia', and hence used as a synonym for 'distinguished'. The phrase echoes memories of Virginia as the MOTHER OF PRESIDENTS and of the 17th-century aristocratic planters in their colonnaded Colonial mansions staffed by white (not Negro) servants. These families, from the settlement of Jamestown (1607) onward, were predominantly of 'Anglo-Saxon' (in fact, mainly Scottish and Irish) ancestry.

FHA Initials used for the Federal Housing Administration, which operates insurance schemes to permit liberal mortgage terms for home buyers and to encourage owners to maintain property in good order.

FHB For Family Hold Back, a traditional nursery warning to the children not to eat up all the best things before their guests have had a fair chance.

Fianna Fáil A middle party formed in Ireland by De Valera (1923) when he turned from armed to political opposition to the FREE STATERS; it first formed a government in 1932. (Erse, 'soldiers of destiny'; see FINN.)

Fiat (1906) Italian motor vehicle manufacturers, with headquarters at Turin, who also make aircraft, steel, engineering equipment etc. In 1968 it formed an alliance with CITROEN and in 1969 acquired Lancia and Ferrari.

Fibber McGee and Molly A famous radio program that flourished in the mid 1930s and 1940s. The comic team of James Edward Jordan and Marion (Driscoll) Jordan played Fibber McGee, an amiable braggart, and Molly, his down-to-earth wife.

Fiddler on the Roof (1964) A musical play based on material from the Jewish stories of SHOLEM ALEICHEM, and containing the song-hit 'If I Were a Rich Man'.

Fidelio (1814) Beethoven's only opera, in which Leonora, disguised as a youth called Fidelio, saves her husband Florestan from murder at the hands of the political rival who has imprisoned him.

Fidgety Phil See STRUWWELPETER.

FIDO Initials forming wartime code name and standing for Fog Investigation and Dispersal Operation, a system used on airfield runways to disperse fog by burning jets of gasoline.

Field Enterprises American firm established by the grandson of the founder of MARSHALL FIELDS; it controls the Chicago Sun-Times and Daily News.

Fielding, Cyril The liberal, humanist English principal of a college, who tries to combat racial prejudice in Forster's A PASSAGE TO INDIA.

Field of the Cloth of Gold (1520) A meeting near Calais at which the King of France, Francis I, unsuccessfully tried to get Henry VIII and Cardinal Wolsey to desert the Holy League (the Empire, Spain and the Papacy) and come to his aid. (From the magnificence of the pageantry provided.)

FIFA The governing body of international soccer. (Initials of the French title: Fédération Internationale de Football Association.)

Fifteen, The The JACOBITE rebellion of 1715 led by the OLD PRETENDER and the Earl of Mar in Scotland and northern England; it was crushed at Sheriffmuir, north of Stirling.

5th Amendment (1791) The amendment to the US Constitution which enacted, inter alia, that no person should be compelled in a criminal case to be a witness against himself. It has been pleaded in self-defense by capitalists and Communists alike.

Fifth Avenue A New York street, famous for luxury shops.

Fifth Commandment 'Honor thy father and thy mother' (Exodus xx, 12). To Roman Catholics this is the Fourth Commandment.

Fifth Estate A useful phrase for any well-defined and influential group (e.g. scientists, trade unions) other than those covered by the traditional Estates; see THIRD ESTATE; FOURTH ESTATE.

Fifth Monarchy men (1657-61) Fanatical English PURITANS who decided that Christ was about to return and that they must therefore sever all allegiance to Cromwell, and later to the restored Charles II. (A reference to the fifth kingdom prophesied in *Daniel* ii, 44, read with verse 40.)

Fifth Republic The period of French history from the time of de Gaulle's return to power in 1958.

'54-40 or Fight!' (1844) A presidential campaign slogan referring to the territory, since 1818 under joint British and US occupation, known as Oregon, which then included Washington, Idaho and southern British Columbia, from 42° to 54°40' N. Britain was, through the Hudson's Bay Co., primarily interested in the fur trade of the Washington area, but American farmers had settled there in large numbers. Tension was relieved by the 1846 compromise fixing 49° as the border (except for Vancouver Island).

Figaro The scheming barber, later valet, of Count Almaviva, in Beaumarchais' plays *The Barber of Seville* (1775) and *The Marriage of Figaro* (1784), and of Mozart's *Figaro*, Rossini's *Barber of Seville* and other operas. It says much for his skill in intrigue that he is able to outwit everyone, even his master.

Figaro, Le (1826) A right-wing Paris daily newspaper.

Fighter Command See STRIKE COMMAND.

'Fighting Téméraire, The' (1839) One of J. M. W. Turner's masterpieces, now in the London National Gallery. It represents the veteran of Trafalgar being towed into port to be broken up.

'Final Solution, The' The extermination of Jews and Slavs, decreed by Hitler in April 1941.

Finchley (UK) A former Middlesex borough, since 1965 part of the borough of BARNET.

Fine Champagne A blend of Cognacs, usually of a single year, from the two best districts (named Grande Champagne and Petite Champagne; no connection with the wine of that name).

Fine Gael (1933) An Irish political party founded by W. J. Cosgrave when De Valera was elected President, in opposition to the latter's FIANNA FÁIL. From 1948 to 1957 it

formed a coalition government with MacBride's Clan na Poblachta, under a new leader, Costello, who declared a republic to forestall De Valera. (Erse, 'United Ireland'.)

Fingal See FINN.

Fingal's Cave (1) A large cave on the Isle of Staffa, in the Inner Hebrides of Scotland (see FINN). (2) The name given to Mendelssohn's *Hebridean Overture*, which was inspired by a Scottish tour.

Fings Ain't Wot They Used t'be (1961) A musical play about SOHO produced by the THEATRE WORKSHOP from an outline by Frank Norman.

Finian's Rainbow (1947) A musical with a happy-go-lucky Irish atmosphere and a mixed black and white cast; Yip Harburg supplied the book and Burton Lane the lyrics, which included 'How Are Things in Glocca Morra?'

Fink, Mike (?1770-1823) A frontier tough guy whose real life hardly needed the addition of legend, but got it. Of Scotch-Irish ancestry, after the usual frontier apprenticeship as scout, marksman and Indian fighter he became the 'king of the keelboatmen' on the Ohio and Mississippi. He had the traditional interests — drink, fistfights, women, bragging, sadistic practical jokes — and met a deservedly violent end (of which there are many conflicting versions) on the Yellowstone River while with a fur-trapping expedition. Stories, plays and verse have celebrated his exploits.

Finlandia (1901) Sibelius's well-known symphonic poem, inspired by the natural beauties of his native land.

Finn The chief hero of southern Irish legend (also called Fionn mac Cumhail), supposed to have lived in the 3rd century AD and to be the father of OSSIAN. He was leader of the Fianna, an army of muscular heroes whose name reappears in later history (see FENIANS; FIANNA FÁIL). In the OSSIANIC POEMS he becomes a Scotsman named Fingal.

Finn An international class of centerboard dinghies designed for single-handed sailing, 14 feet 9 inches in length, with a large single sail on a flexible unstayed mast. There is a Gold Cup championship.

Finnegans Wake (1939) James Joyce's last novel, which carries to extremes the tendencies mentioned under ULYSSES. It takes the form of the dreams of a Dublin publican, H. C. Earwicker, representing Everyman, and his wife ANNA LIVIA PLURABELLE. Many books have had to be written to explain what it is all about; the main theme is said to be the recurring cycles of world history.

Finno-Ugrian languages One of the 2 main divisions of the URAL-ALTAIC LANGUAGES; it includes Finnish, MAGYAR, Lapp and Estonian.

Fino One of the 2 main types of sherry (see OLOROSO), very dry and pale, drunk as an aperitif; includes AMONTILLADO and MANZANILLA.

Finsbury A former London metropolitan borough, since 1965 part of the borough of ISLINGTON.

Fir Bolg Legendary, perhaps Iberian, settlers in Ireland, driven later into the Western Isles of Scotland by CUCULAIN and the TUATHA DÉ DANANN. In Irish legend they are said to have come from Greece via Norway.

Firebird, The (1910) The first of Stravinsky's ballets written for Diaghilev, a fairy tale based on Russian folk tunes.

Fireflash (1953) The first British guided missile, used by the RAF and Navy.

Firefly (1946) A national one-design class of 12-foot dinghy, with molded plywood hull and metal mast; designed by Uffa Fox, built only at Hamble, Hampshire, and raced in most parts of England.

Fireside Chats The name given to a series of informal radio talks to the nation, instituted by President Roosevelt on 12 April 1933, only 8 days after his inauguration, and continued during the critical period of the NEW DEAL.

Firestreak An air-to-air missile made by HAWKER SIDDELEY for the LIGHTNING. It is an infrared-guided weapon for use against high- or low-flying attacks. Sea Vixen is a naval version; RED TOP a later development.

Fireworks Music (1749) Handel's 'Musick for the Royal Fireworks' written for a London celebration in Green Park of the Treaty of Aix (see AUSTRIAN SUCCESSION, WAR OF); the fireworks failed, but the music was a success.

First Coalition (1793-97) An alliance of Britain, Spain, Austria, Holland, Italian and German states, which drove the French out of the Netherlands but then began to disintegrate until finally Britain found itself fighting the Spanish and Dutch (CAPE ST VINCENT and CAMPERDOWN).

First Commandment 'Thou shalt have no other gods before me' (Exodus xx, 3). Jews regard this as part of the Second Commandment.

First Consul (Napoleon) See CONSULATE.

First Empire (1804-15) See EMPIRE, THE.

First International (1864-76) The earliest attempt, sponsored by Karl Marx, to form a world organization of the working classes.

First Lady, The The wife of the President of the US.

First Lord of the Admiralty Formerly the parliamentary chief of the Royal Navy, since 1964 styled Minister of Defence for the Royal Navy.

First Men in the Moon, The (1901) One of H. G. Wells's earliest novels, in the category now called science fiction.

First Reading (Parliament) The formal introduction of a Bill to the House, which does not debate it until the SECOND READING.

First Republic (1792-1804) (French history) The republic declared during the French Revolution and succeeded by the First Empire of Napoleon.

First Sea Lord The professional head of the Royal Navy, a post combined with that of Chief of the Naval Staff.

First State A nickname for Delaware as having been the first state to join the Union (1787).

Fisherman's Ring The signet ring placed on the Pope's finger at his election and broken up at his death.

It bears the device of St Peter in a boat hauling in a fishing net.

Fisherman's Wharf The picturesque fishing port of San Francisco, renowned for its seafood restaurants.

Fitzwilliam Museum (1837) (UK) An important Cambridge museum of pictures, antiquities, and medieval and Renaissance exhibits, together with a library; it was enlarged by a Courtauld bequest. (Founded by the 1st Viscount Fitzwilliam.)

Five Civilized Nations The Cherokee, Choctaw, Chickasaw, Creek and Seminole Indians, originally of the southeastern states, moved to Oklahoma (see TRAIL OF TEARS) where a reserve was established for them in 1867. (So called for their relatively high degree of acculturation.)

Five Little Peppers (1881) A series of moralistic children's books about the impoverished Pepper family, by Margaret Sidney (pen name of Harriet Lothrop), once best sellers.

Five Mile Act (1665) See CLARENDON CODE.

Five Nations A confederacy of Iroquois Indians: Mohawk, Oneida, Onondaga, Cayuga and Seneca, later joined by the Tuscarora.

Five Nights An under-the-counter Edwardian best seller by 'Victoria Cross', presumably written in competition with Elinor Glyn's THREE WEEKS and *Six Days*; the significance of this particularity as to duration is baffling.

Five-0-Five An international class of very fast sailing boat, length 16 feet 6 inches. (For 5.05 meters=16'6" approx.)

Five Pillars of Islam The essential obligations of the true believer, given in the Koran as: belief in one God; prayer 5 times daily facing Mecca; the giving of alms; keeping the RAMADAN fast; pilgrimage to Mecca at least once in a lifetime.

Five-star General A General of the Army, the highest rank in the US Army, next above General and equivalent to Fleet Admiral. (From the insignia worn.)

Five Towns Arnold Bennett's name for the (six) English towns of Burslem, Hanley, Stoke on Trent, Long-ton, Fenton and Tunstall—all now merged (1910) in the borough of Stoke on Trent. He used the term in his novel *Anna of the Five Towns* (1902) and elsewhere. See POTTERIES.

Flamboyant architecture (15th-16th centuries) The last period of French GOTHIC ARCHITECTURE, corresponding to English PERPENDICULAR. It is marked by elaborate flamelike tracery in the windows and other features, as in Rouen Cathedral. (French, 'flaming'.)

Flaminian Way (3rd century BC) The road from Rome to Rimini over the Apennines.

Flamsteed numbers Used to identify stars in a constellation; they increase from west to east and have largely superseded the BAYER LETTER system. (John Flamsteed, first Astronomer Royal.)

Flanders Name officially given only to 2 southwestern Belgian provinces (East Flanders, capital Ghent; West, capital Bruges); unofficially, the area where FLEMISH is spoken and Flemish architecture predominates; i.e. the Scheldt delta of Holland, most of north and west Belgium, and the adjoining Nord department of France. Brussels, Antwerp, Bruges, Ghent, Louvain and Tournai were the major towns of Flanders.

Flatbush The suburban region in the middle of BROOKLYN, with many small old homes and a growing number of apartment buildings.

Flatford Mill The mill near East Bergholt, between Ipswich and Colchester in southeastern England, which figures in many of the paintings of John Constable, whose father owned it.

Flatiron Building (1902) New York's first skyscraper, 20 stories high, between Broadway, Fifth Avenue and 23rd Street. (Named for its odd shape.)

Flavian Emperors (AD 69-96) The Emperors of Rome, Vespasian, Titus, and Domitian, all members of the Flavian family (gens).

F layer (ionosphere) See APPLETON LAYER.

Fléada Ceoil In Ireland, a festival of traditional music and dance, held

each June at Thurles, Co. Tipperary;
see FEIS CEOIL.

Flea Market (1) The vast street markets on the northern outskirts of Paris between the Portes de Clignancourt and St-Ouen, where ready-made clothes, antiques and junk are sold from Saturday to Monday each week. (French, Marche aux puces.) (2) An outdoor market in the US where mostly secondhand or antique articles are sold from parked vehicles.

Flèche d'Or, La A train; see GOLDEN ARROW.

Fledermaus, Die (1874) Johann Strauss's pearl of comic operettas, set in a 19th-century European spa. It is loved for its delightful music rather than for the complicated plot, in which all is misrepresentation, misunderstanding and mischief. (German, 'the bat'.)

Fleet, The A former prison in Farringdon Street, London, dating back to Norman times; it became notorious as a debtors' prison and is often mentioned in Dickens's novels etc.

Fleet Street The world of London journalism, a short street running from the Strand to Ludgate Circus; associated with printing since Caxton's day. (Named from the River Fleet, which still flows through the sewers there, into the Thames.)

Fleet submarines See VALIANT SUBMARINES.

Flemings The FLEMISH-speaking inhabitants of FLANDERS. They are less industrialized than the WALLOONS, whom they are beginning to outnumber and dominate, and more loyal to the monarchy and to the Roman Catholic Church.

Flemish The Dutch dialect spoken by the Flemings of FLANDERS; compare WALLOON.

Flemish School, The (1) The early school, which first perfected oil painting and, working in the 14th-16th centuries mainly at Bruges, painted religious pictures; the great names were the Van Eycks, Memling and Van der Weyden; (2) the unclassifiable painters of fantasies, Bosch and the Breughels; (3) the 17th-century portrait painters of Antwerp (Rubens and Van Dyck), together with Teniers and others.

Fleur (Forsyte) See MODERN COMEDY, A.

Fleurs du mal, Les (1857) A collection of poems by Charles Baudelaire, regarded by many critics and later poets as the greatest poet of the 19th century.

Flickertail State A nickname for North Dakota. (Name of a ground squirrel of north-central USA.)

Flight & Barr (1783-1840) The second period in the history of the WORCESTER PORCELAIN factory, during which it traded under this and similar names. It produced some very good wares, especially up to about 1800 when bone china was introduced. It amalgamated with the CHAMBERLAIN WORCESTER firm.

Flipper A porpoise who since 1962 has attained screen stardom in movies and TV programs.

Flodden (1513) The battle in which the English decisively defeated a Scottish army under James IV, Henry VIII's brother-in-law (who was killed), when they invaded Northumberland to help their French allies. France was under attack from the Holy League, to which England belonged. (Village near the Scots border.)

Flook (1949) Hero of a London *Daily Mail* strip cartoon by Trog (Wally Fawkes). An indeterminate animal, he has the useful ability to transform himself into any shape at will. In more recent years a considerable measure of political satire has been injected, together with recognizable caricatures of contemporary celebrities.

Florentine (Cooking) With spinach and MORNAY SAUCE.

Floridians The Miami Floridians, AMERICAN BASKETBALL ASSOCIATION.

Florizel (1) A character in Shakespeare's A WINTER'S TALE. (2) A nickname of the PRINCE REGENT, see PERDITA AND FLORIZEL. (3) Prince Florizel, the chief character in R. L. Stevenson's *New Arabian Nights*.

Florodora Girls A famous bevy of beauties in the English musical,

Florodora (1899), which enjoyed long runs on both sides of the Atlantic. The music by Leslie Stuart (composer of 'Lily of Laguna') included the outstandingly popular sextet "Tell me, pretty maiden, are there any more at home like you?'. Several of the girls married millionaires, but the stage could hardly have accommodated all the handsome middle-aged women who later claimed membership of the original chorus.

Flossa A Scandinavian handwoven rug; also the weave typical of this. (Swedish word, abbreviated, for 'long flock of wool'.)

Flowering Cherry, The (1958) Robert Bolt's tragi-comedy of a man who spent his life dreaming about retirement to a country cottage; when the time came he did not want to go.

Flowering of New England (1815-65), The (1936) Part of a 5-volume study of the development of American culture, by Van Wyck Brooks; it won a Pulitzer prize.

Flower People The name given in 1964 to the proto-hippies of San Francisco with their addiction to flower motifs as a symbol emphasizing the nonviolence of their protest against society. Also called Flower Children.

'Flowers of the Forest, The' The Scottish lament for those who fell at FLODDEN; two 18th-century ballads have been set to it, with the refrain: The flowers of the forest are withered away.

Fluellen The hot-tempered Welsh captain of Shakespeare's *Henry V.*

Flush The name of Elizabeth Barrett Browning's dog, which she took with her to Italy on her marriage; see *The* BARRETTS OF WIMPOLE STREET.

Flyers The Philadelphia Flyers, NATIONAL HOCKEY LEAGUE.

Flying Bedstead (1954) The first VTOL experimental vehicle, built by Rolls-Royce. It had no wings or rotors, and relied on 2 turbojets to lift it and 4 small jets for horizontal flight.

Flying Dutchman An international class of 2-man sailing boat, length 19 feet 10 inches, designed by a Dutchman; the fastest conventional dinghy afloat.

Flying Dutchman, The A legendary ghost ship whose captain is doomed to haunt the seas south of the Cape of Good Hope eternally; she brings bad luck to all who sight her. In Wagner's opera (*Der fliegende Holländer*, 1843) her captain is freed from the curse laid on him when he finds a woman willing to sacrifice herself for him.

Flying Fortress The BOEING B-17, a heavily armed US bomber used in raids on Germany from August 1942 onwards.

Flying Fox The Duke of Westminster's horse which in 1899 won the 2000 Guineas, Derby and St Leger.

Flying Saucers The name given in about 1947 to objects seen in the sky which some hoped were reconnaissance craft from outer space. Typically they are reported as round, illuminated, silent and flying erratically at high speed. Dignified with the official name of UFOs (Unidentified Flying Objects), they have usually been shown by expert investigation to be meteorological balloons or optical illusions, but some remain unexplained. Their importance may be psychological rather than cosmonautical.

Flying Scotsman See LNER.

Flying Squad A branch of the CENTRAL OFFICE of Scotland Yard, so called because it has a roving commission.

Flying Tigers A small air force manned by American volunteers, formed (Aug. 1941) in Kunming to fight for China against Japan; the nucleus of an air task force established in China after the USA entered the war.

FMCS See FEDERAL MEDIATION AND CONCILIATION SERVICE.

FM radio (1933) Abbreviation used for Frequency Modulation radio, a system of radio transmission which gives minimum background noise; the frequency of the wave is varied (modulated) but the amplitude remains constant.

FN 30 The Belgian rifle with which the British Army was equipped from

1954. Initials of Fabrique Nationale (d'Armes de Guerre), the Belgian armament firm.

FOA See FOREIGN OPERATIONS ADMINISTRATION.

FOBS Initials used for Fractional Orbital Bombardment System, by which space bombs are put into low (about 100 miles up) orbit round the earth; at a predetermined point, a retrorocket slows down the warhead, causing it to drop out of orbit onto the target. In 1967 it was announced that Soviet Russia appeared to be developing this system, which had already been abandoned by the USA.

Focke-Wulf Name of various German military aircraft, notably the Focke-Wulf 190 (1942), a night fighter with a very rapid rate of climb, prominent in World War II.

Fogg, Phileas The hero of Jules Verne's ROUND THE WORLD IN 80 DAYS, who performed this feat for a bet made in the Reform Club.

Foggy Bottom Former Washington, D.C. slum area; site of some State Department offices. An ironic term for political Washington.

Föhn A warm dry north wind from the Alps, which may raise temperatures by 20°F in a few hours. In spring it causes avalanches and uncovers mountain pastures; in autumn it ripens grapes.

Fokker The first aircraft to have a machine gun firing through the propeller, which gave the German air force temporary ascendancy on the Western Front in 1915; name also given to other aircraft designed by Anton Fokker, Dutch-born naturalized German.

Folger Shakespeare Library, The A fine collection of Shakespeariana and other Elizabethan relics, in Washington, D.C., made by Henry Clay Folger of Standard Oil (N.Y.), a Shakespeare scholar who financed the erection of the library building.

Folies-Bergère A Paris music hall famous for its opportunities for anatomical research, as also for its spectacular costume displays. The audience consists of the French bourgeoisie en famille and tourists, in about equal proportions.

Folkboat A BERMUDIAN 24-foot sloop designed by a group of Scandinavians as a people's cruiser, since became internationally popular; 5 tons (TM).

Folketing The Danish Diet or Parliament.

Folsom Man A North American form of early man which used a distinctive type of stone spearhead; the finding (1926) of one of these in the ribs of a species of bison extinct since Pleistocene times was unexpected, appearing to indicate a much earlier date for man on this continent than previously assumed — very tentatively put at 25,000 BC. Folsom remains were found as far north as Alaska, but the main center was probably the high plains of New Mexico-Colorado. (Named for a town in New Mexico where first found.)

F-111 (1968) US swing-wing (VG) fighter / bomber / reconnaissance aircraft, speed 1600 m.p.h., range 2000 miles; built by General Dynamics. The RAF was to have had it as a substitute for the cancelled TSR-2 and a replacement for the Canberra, but the order was withdrawn in 1968 as an economy measure.

F₁ hybrids The result of controlled fertilization of a selected female plant from a selected male plant and saving the seed, which may produce plants distinguished by vigor, size of flower or fruit, or early maturity etc. (F_1 for 'first filial' generation.)

'Fonthill' Beckford William Beckford (1760-1844), English author of VATHEK, so nicknamed for the extravagant fantasy he built — Fonthill 'Abbey' — at Fonthill Gifford, near Shaftesbury, Wiltshire, with a 260-foot tower which collapsed and destroyed the building.

Food and Agriculture Organization See FAO.

Food and Drug Administration A US agency of the Department of Health, Education and Welfare, formed to administer Federal laws which protect consumers by ensuring the maintenance of standards of purity, quality, safety, accurate labeling etc. of food, drugs and cosmetics.

Foot Guards   The BRIGADE OF GUARDS; compare HOUSEHOLD TROOPS; HOUSEHOLD CAVALRY.

Forbidden City, The   Lhasa, capital of Tibet, which foreigners were long forbidden to enter.

Ford Foundation   (1936) Formed by Henry Ford I and his son Edsel, this fund is chiefly devoted to educational schemes and to technical assistance programs in developing countries.

Ford Motor Co.   One of the world's largest manufacturers of consumer goods, with headquarters at Dearborn, Michigan. It was built up on the basis of the MODEL T car, the Ford V8 (1932) and models designed for particular countries, such as the Popular (see next entry). It now operates in most countries, selling Fords, Lincoln-Mercury cars, trucks, tractors, radio and TV, household appliances etc.

Ford Motors   (UK) Financially the largest motor and tractor manufacturers in Britain, wholly owned by the US parent company; headquarters Dagenham, Essex. It became important with the marketing in 1932 of the first Ford Popular, designed specially for the British market.

Ford's Peace Ship   (1915) A ship which sailed to Europe from USA with the pacifist car manufacturer, Henry Ford, and a mission of like-minded Americans in an effort to end World War I by negotiation.

Ford's Theater   The scene of the LINCOLN ASSASSINATION in Washington, D.C.; now restored as a museum, it is still also used to stage plays.

Foreign Legion   (1831) A French regiment formerly stationed in North Africa and recruited from foreigners, who were not required to reveal their identity, serving under French officers. It was disbanded (1940-45) but reformed, and took part in the Algerian crisis. It is now stationed in Corsica.

Foreign Operations Administration   (1953-55) The US body the func-

tions of which were eventually taken over by the AGENCY FOR INTERNATIONAL DEVELOPMENT.

Foresters, Ancient Order of   (1834) A large friendly society with lodges, called 'courts', in the USA and UK.

Forest Hills   The headquarters of the West Side Tennis Club since 1923, a private club which stages the American championship by arrangement with the US Lawn Tennis Association. (In QUEENS borough, NYC.)

Forest Lovers, The   (1898) Maurice Hewlett's romantic medieval novel.

Forever Amber   (1944) A long novel by the American Kathleen Winsor, about a RESTORATION PERIOD beauty whose amours raised it to best-selling status.

Formentor prize   (1960) A prize of $10,000 awarded for a novel selected by 13 publishers of 6 nations who meet annually at Formentor, Majorca, for the purpose and arrange simultaneous publication of the novel.

Former Naval Person   Wartime code name used for himself by Winston Churchill in messages to President Roosevelt. (Reference to his having been First Lord of the Admiralty.)

Formosa   European name for Taiwan, the Chinese island where Chiang Kai-shek set up a non-Communist republic in 1950.

Formula 1 cars   The cars which compete in GRAND PRIX RACES. The formula (specification) is often changed in order to keep ever-rising speeds within reasonably safe limits.

Formula 2 cars   A class of racing car less costly than FORMULA 1 CARS but like them raced by professional drivers in what are in effect prestige competitions between manufacturers. In 1957 a 'Junior' formula was introduced.

Formula 3 cars   Comparatively inexpensive single-seater cars with production engines of limited capacity, raced by amateurs.

Forsyte Saga, The   (1922) John Galsworthy's trilogy of novels, *The Man of Property* (1906), *In Chancery* (1920) and *To Let* (1921). Soames

Forsyte is a stern Victorian lawyer with a strong sense of property, in which category he includes his wife Irene, whom he divorces and who marries YOUNG JOLYON. See also *A MODERN COMEDY.*

Fort Belvedere The Prince of Wales's home near Sunningdale, Berkshire from 1929 until his abdication, as Edward VIII, in 1936.

Fort Detrick Site in Maryland of an Army microbiological research station which concentrates on potential biological warfare agents such as pneumonic plague, anthrax, dysentery and yellow fever. These are tested at DUGWAY PROVING GROUND.

Fort Hare (1916) The oldest Negro university college in South Africa, now the University College for the XHOSA group, TRANSKEI.

Fort Knox (1936) A US Army camp where lie bomb-proof vaults containing some $10 billions worth of US gold. Ian Fleming's GOLDFINGER had an elaborate plan to raid it, foiled, of course, by James Bond. (35 miles south of Louisville, Ky.)

Fortnums Abbreviated name for London's leading grocers, Fortnum & Mason of Piccadilly. See ASSOCIATED BRITISH FOODS.

Fortran An algebraic and logical language code for programming a computer to solve scientific problems. (For Formula Translation.)

Fort Sumter (12 Apr. 1861) The first incident in the AMERICAN CIVIL WAR, when Confederate troops fired on a Union garrison at Fort Sumter, S.C.

Fortunate Isles In Greek legend the Isles of the Blest beyond the Pillars of Hercules, another form of ELYSIUM; later the name was given to the Canaries and Madeira.

Fortunatus's purse An inexhaustible purse given by the goddess of Fortune to the hero of a medieval German legend; the gift proved the ruin of Fortunatus and his sons.

Fortune (1930) A monthly economic and financial tabloid magazine for businessmen, founded (like TIME and *Life*) by Henry Luce.

Fortune, Mr The character who brought his medical knowledge to

the aid of Scotland Yard in a series of crime stories by H. C. Bailey (died 1961).

Fortunes of Nigel, The (1822) Walter Scott's historical novel of young Nigel's efforts to recover money owed him by James I, in the face of the machinations of the Court and particularly of the villain, Lord Dalgarno.

Fortunes of Richard Mahoney, The (1930) A trilogy of novels by an Australian woman who used the pen name Henry Handel Richardson, which give a brilliant picture of Ballarat, Victoria, during the gold rush of the 1850s.

Forty and Eight (1920) A veterans organization founded in Indianapolis. (In World War I troops serving in France were sardonically amused to find themselves transported to the front in freight cars bleakly labeled 'Hommes 40, Chevaux 8'.)

48, The Common name for Johann Sebastian Bach's 2 books of preludes and fugues for the clavier (now usually played on the piano); each book contains 12 in each major, and 12 in each minor key. See WELL-TEMPERED CLAVIER.

Forty-Five, The The JACOBITE rebellion of 1745 in which the YOUNG PRETENDER, after a victory at Prestonpans near Edinburgh, led a Scottish invasion of England which reached Derby but was defeated at CULLODEN by the BLOODY BUTCHER.

49ers (1) Participants in the Californian gold rush of 1849, celebrated in the song 'O my darling Clementine'. (2) The San Francisco 49ers, NATIONAL FOOTBALL LEAGUE. Became member of the NATIONAL CONFERENCE, NATIONAL FOOTBALL LEAGUE in 1970.

49th Parallel The boundary between USA and Canada from the Pacific coast to a point south of Winnipeg.

'Forty Years On' Harrow's rousing school song, written by E. E. Bowen (died 1901), and beginning: Forty years on, when afar and asunder,/ Parted are those who are singing today.

For Whom the Bell Tolls (1939) Ernest Hemingway's novel of the SPANISH CIVIL WAR, in which he took part as a war correspondent. It tells of the blowing up of a vital bridge by guerrillas, and echoes the accounts of members of the INTERNATIONAL BRIGADE in stressing the untrustworthiness of the Republicans, ever ready to subordinate military necessities to sordid internecine political squabbles. (Title from John Donne's 'Any man's death diminishes me . . . therefore never send to know for whom the bell tolls; it tolls for thee'.)

Fosco, Count A character in Wilkie Collins's WOMAN IN WHITE.

Fosse Way A Roman road from Lincoln through Leicester, Cirencester and Bath to Exeter.

Fotheringhay Castle A castle built by William I at a village in Northamptonshire near Peterborough, where Mary Queen of Scots was executed. Only a mound and a moat remain to mark the site.

Fouchet plan (1961) A plan for the first step towards the political unification of Europe, consisting of a high council and periodical meetings of heads of states. See EUROPE DES PATRIES, L'.

Fougasse Pseudonym of Kenneth Bird, humorous artist and editor of *Punch*, who achieved fame during World War II for his posters warning against 'careless talk'. (French *fougasse*, a species of small landmine.)

Founder of the American Navy The proud title of John PAUL JONES, who was commissioned in the new Continental Navy (1775) and became the naval hero of the Revolutionary War.

Founding Fathers, The Another name for the PILGRIM FATHERS.

Foundling Hospital, London (1739) An institution for deserted children opened in Brunswick Square, Bloomsbury, but moved to Berkhamsted in 1929 as the Thomas Coram Foundation for Children; the old building now houses an art gallery.

Fountain of Youth A legendary spring with healing and rejuvenating properties which the Indians of Central America believed lay somewhere to their north. Ponce de León,

Narváez, De Soto and others sought it in Florida, the Bahamas and elsewhere.

Fountains Abbey (1132) A ruined abbey near Ripon, Yorkshire, formerly the largest in northern England, a Cistercian foundation in a beautiful setting; the ruins today are roofless but extensive.

Four Courts, The (1796) Dublin's central courts of justice, blown up in June 1922 during the TROUBLES but restored from the original designs.

Four Freedoms, The (1941) (1) Proclaimed by President Roosevelt during World War II; they are: freedom from fear and want, freedom of religion and speech. (2) Paintings illustrating the above, by Norman Rockwell (born 1894).

4-H movement A nationwide organization of rural youth clubs, encouraging initiative and cooperation, particularly in the field of agriculture. (Head, Heart, Hands, and Health, dedicated by members to the cause.)

Four Horsemen of the Apocalypse Conquest, Slaughter, Famine. Death, who symbolize the horrors of war in *Revelation* vi, 2-8.

Four Horsemen of the Apocalypse, The (1916) Blasco-Ibáñez' novel on World War I, from which a famous film was made (1921), starring Rudolf Valentino.

Four Hundred, The An expression used of the leading members of New York (later, US) society. (From a remark by the socialite, Ward McAllister, in the 1890s that there were only 400 people who really counted.)

Four Just Men, The (1906) Edgar Wallace's first novel, about a group of men who take it upon themselves to rid the world of various undesirables.

Four Last Things A theological term for death, judgment, heaven and hell. The doctrine of these is called eschatology.

Fourment, Hélène Rubens's second wife, whom he married in 1630 when she was 16, and of whom he painted many portraits. See BRANDT, ISABELLA.

Four Square Gospel (1915) A Fundamentalist sect founded at Belfast by George Jeffreys, now part of the Elim Four Square Gospel Alliance. They believe in healing by anointment with holy oil, total immersion at baptism, and the Second Coming. See also SISTER AIMEE.

Fourteen Points (Jan. 1918) President Wilson's formulation of the bases for a peace settlement with Germany; they included (omitting various qualifications): freedom of the seas, free trade, disarmament, respect for the interests of colonial peoples, aid to Communist Russia, Polish independence, self-determination for the peoples of the Turkish and Austro-Hungarian empires, restoration of Alsace-Lorraine, and an end to secret diplomacy.

14th Amendment (1868) The amendment to the US Constitution which enacted, *inter alia*, that no state shall make or enforce any law that shall abridge the privileges or immunities of citizens, nor deny to any person the equal protection of the law. Often quoted in disputes about racial segregation.

Fourteenth of July, The (France) Bastille Day, see BASTILLE, STORMING OF THE. (French *Quatorze juillet*.)

Fourth Commandment 'Remember the Sabbath' (*Exodus* xx, 8-11). To Roman Catholics this is the Third Commandment.

Fourth Estate The Press; a phrase attributed to Burke (and later used by Macaulay) and applied originally to the Reporters' Gallery in the House of Commons, said to be more important than the 3 other Estates (see THIRD ESTATE).

Fourth of July; The Fourth US holiday commemorating the adoption of the Declaration of Independence; also called Independence Day.

Fourth Republic (1946-58) The period of French history from the resignation of de Gaulle as provisional head of the government until he was recalled to deal with the Algerian crisis. The constitution differed little from that of the THIRD REPUBLIC, and the constantly changing governments were quite as ineffectual.

Four Winds of Love, The (1937-45) An enthralling 6-volume novel by Compton Mackenzie.

Fowler Short title for Fowler's *Modern English Usage* (see MEU).

Foxe's Martyrs (1559) Common title of John Foxe's *History of the Acts and Monuments of the Church*, which gave an inaccurate and highly colored account of the MARIAN PERSECUTION.

Foxy Grandpa (1900) A comic-strip character created by Bunny Schultze in the New York *Herald*; 2 boys plague their grandpa with their tricks but he always outfoxes them.

Foyle (William) Poetry Prize (1945) An annual prize of $600 for the best book of verse published in Britain.

F. P. A. Initials commonly used for Franklin Pierce Adams, American journalist who wrote a column, 'The Conning Tower' (1913-41), for several New York papers.

FPO Signifies Fleet Post Office.

Fra Diavolo Nickname of an 18th-century Italian brigand who led a revolt against French rule in Naples, and was shot in 1806. He is the hero of Auber's comic opera (1830) of that name. (Italian, 'Brother Devil'.)

Fra Lippo Lippi (1855) One of Robert Browning's dramatic monologues in which the painter-monk of the title (a historical character of 15th-century Florence) explains why he finds it necessary to break out of his monastery for a spree from time to time.

Fram (1893) Nansen's ship, specially designed for his Arctic explorations.

Framley Parsonage (1861) One of Trollope's BARCHESTER NOVELS.

Francesca da Rimini See PAOLO AND FRANCESCA.

Franchise Affair, The See TEY, JOSEPHINE.

Franciscans (1209) An order of friars founded by St Francis of Assisi, vowed to chastity, poverty and service; also called Grey Friars.

Franco-Prussian War (1870-71) A war caused by Napoleon III's fear of the new North German Confederation, brought to a head by the publication of the EMS TELEGRAM. After the French defeat at SEDAN, Paris withstood a 4-month siege; the war ended with its surrender. France lost Alsace-Lorraine and again became a republic; the King of Prussia became Emperor of a united Germany.

Frank, Anne A German Jewish girl who hid in Amsterdam (1942-44) until she, with her family, was betrayed to the Germans and sent to die at Belsen aged 16. She kept a diary, published in 1947 and made into a play, *The Diary of Anne Frank.*

Frankenstein (1818) A GOTHIC NOVEL by Mary Shelley, wife of the poet, in which a student creates out of corpses a monster whom he galvanizes into life, and by whom he is destroyed; sometimes regarded as the first science-fiction tale.

'Frankie and Johnny' (1850) An American folk song, with the refrain: 'He was her man / But he done her wrong'. There are about 100 versions.

Franklin Institute (1824) An institute in Philadelphia, Penn., founded for the study of the mechanical arts and applied science.

Franks A group of Germanic tribes which came to rule France under the MEROVINGIANS.

Franks report (1966) A report on OXFORD UNIVERSITY, which recommended increasing its size by a third, doubling the number of postgraduate places, increased attention to applied science and technology, diminution of college autonomy through the setting up of a Council of Colleges, and the institution of a single entrance examination. (Lord Franks, chairman.)

Fraud Squad A branch at SCOTLAND YARD which investigates company frauds.

Fraunces Tavern (1719) Situated at Broad and Pearl Streets, NYC, this mansion became a tavern in 1762 and there is still a restaurant there. The building also contains the Long Room where Washington bade farewell to officers of the Continental Army (1783), a Revolutionary War

Museum and art gallery, and the headquarters of the Sons of the Revolution (N. Y.).

Fraunhofer lines The dark lines in the solar spectrum caused by the absorption of specific wavelengths of radiation from the sun's inner core by the various gases making up its outer atmosphere, the chemical composition of which can thus be analyzed.

Freedom from Hunger Campaign (1960) A worldwide campaign organized by the FAO to bring home to the world the continuing gravity of the food and agricultural situation, and to rededicate the FAO to the elimination of hunger and malnutrition. The original 5-year period was extended to ten.

Freedom House (1960) The main building in Freedomland, an exhibition center formerly in the northeast of the BRONX, where scenes from America's past, such as the arrival of the PONY EXPRESS, were reenacted for the entertainment of the public.

Freedom March (1966) A march of Negro demonstrators under James Meredith to encourage the Negroes of Mississippi to overcome their apprehensions about what would happen to them if they exercised their right to register as voters.

Freedom Riders Demonstrators testing the desegregation of interstate bus terminals, as in the ride to Montgomery, Alabama, in May 1961.

Freedom 7 The name of the spacecraft in which the first American in space, Cmdr. Shepard, made one orbit of the earth, 5 May 1961, as part of the MERCURY PROJECT.

Freedom Statue The bronze statue on the dome of the Capitol, Washington, D. C.; it stands 19½ ft high, and was first modeled in plaster by Thomas Crawford in Rome.

Freedom Trail A tourists' walking tour around the historic sites of Boston, including the Old State House, FANEUIL HALL, PAUL REVERE'S House, BUNKER HILL and the site of the BOSTON TEA PARTY.

Free French, The (1940) The followers of Gen. de Gaulle, who opposed the VICHY GOVERNMENT. They formed the French Council of National Liberation (1943) which in 1944 was proclaimed the provisional government of France.

Freemasons (1) English medieval journeymen stonemasons who used secret signs to ensure that unqualified workmen were not employed in masonry; later they began to admit outsiders. (2) A fraternal society developed from (1), especially in the use of craft terms, secret signs and a 'history' of the craft going back to Solomon's Temple; it started with a London Lodge (1717), spread over the country and acquired great wealth, which enabled it to provide schools and hospitals for its members' families; it spread to the US, and also to the continent where it developed on quite different lines as a political anticlerical movement, condemned by the Roman Catholic Church. In the 1960s the British initiatory rites were exposed to BBC TV audiences as a quaint, unsmiling schoolboy charade.

Free State, The Nickname of Maryland.

Free Staters Irish followers of Michael Collins who were engaged in civil war with the Republicans under De Valera, from Partition (1921) until 1923 when the latter called for a cease-fire.

Free Trade The doctrine that international trade should be freed from restrictions such as import duties or quotas, export subsidies etc. It was held by the MANCHESTER SCHOOL and the British Liberal Party, and was adopted as British policy from 1860 to 1932. See EMPIRE FREE TRADE; PROTECTION.

Freikorps The German ex-officers' organization, used by the Ebert Socialist government to suppress the Communist SPARTACISTS in 1919, creating lasting bitterness between the 2 left-wing parties. Some units of it organized the KAPP PUTSCH.

Freikorps Deutschland A postwar neo-Nazi party in West Germany, banned in 1953.

Freischütz, Der In German legend, a man to whom the Devil gives 7 bullets guaranteed to find their mark, retaining control of one of them. In Weber's opera (1821) of that name, a forester uses them to win a shooting contest in order to gain a bride. The Devil tries to kill her with the last bullet, but it ricochets off her bridal wreath. (German, 'the free shooter'.)

French, Inspector The CID (see CRIMINAL INVESTIGATION DEPARTMENT) detective created by Freeman Wills Crofts in The Cask (1920).

French and Indian War (1754-63) The operations in the SEVEN YEARS WAR which ended the 150-year Anglo-French struggle for dominance in North America. After initial defeats by the French and their Indian allies, and the expulsion of the ACADIANS ('Cajuns') as a potential Fifth Column, the tide turned and Britain won Quebec on the PLAINS OF ABRAHAM (1759). By the Treaty of Paris (1763) Britain gained all Canada, the Ohio Valley and Florida (which the Spanish had given to France in exchange for Louisiana).

French Cameroons A former French colony, now the CAMEROUN REPUBLIC.

French Community (1958) A loose and voluntary association of former French colonies formed on De Gaulle's return to power, replacing the FRENCH UNION. The original rule that full independence disqualified membership was abandoned in 1960.

French dressing A salad dressing of which the basic ingredients are olive oil, wine vinegar, salt and pepper; sugar and mustard may be added.

French Equatorial Africa (1934) A grouping of the French colonies of Gabon, Middle Congo, UBANGI-SHARI and Chad, under a Governor-General at Brazzaville. These countries are now all independent.

French fries French-fried potatoes (English, 'chips'), i.e. triangular or rectangular strips of potato fried till brown in deep fat.

French horn A valved brass wind instrument of labyrinthine design, developed from the hunting horn; it has a particularly mellow tone (due to the flared mouthpiece) which blends with woodwind or with other brass instruments.

French Indo-China Now divided into North and South VIETNAM, Cambodia and Laos.

French leave Departure without permission or warning. (From the 18th-century French habit of leaving a party without saying thank-you to the hostess; yet the French dare to call it *filer à l'anglaise*.)

French pastry Fancy pastry made usually of puff paste baked in individual portions varying in shape and filled, e.g. with custard or preserved fruit.

French Provincial An 18th-century American style of furniture, architecture and fabric design, typically sturdy, plain and practical, derived from that originating in the French provinces.

French Quarter See VIEUX CARRE.

French Revolution (1789-95) Caused by Louis XVI's arbitrary, inefficient rule; new political theories and the influence of the American Revolution; antagonism to a wealthy Church; and peasant unrest under feudal conditions. Major events were: BASTILLE (July 1789); the SEPTEMBER MASSACRES (1792); Louis' execution (Jan. 1793); the setting up of the National CONVENTION and the COMMITTEE OF PUBLIC SAFETY (1792-93); the year of TERROR (1793-94) which ended after Robespierre's assassination in the THERMIDOR coup.

French Sudan Since 1960 the independent Republic of Mali, West Africa.

French Togoland Since 1960 the independent Republic of Togo, West Africa.

French Union (1946-58) An association of France and French overseas colonies, superseded by the FRENCH COMMUNITY.

French West Africa (1895) A grouping of the French colonies of Mauritania, Niger, Sudan, Senegal, Guinea, Ivory Coast, Upper Volta, and Dahomey, under a Governor-General originally at St Louis, from 1908

at Dakar. These countries are now all independent.

French window A glazed door, single or double, usually opening inward; it serves as door and window.

French without Tears (1936) Terence Rattigan's farce, which had a long run owing to the high quality of its humor, a memorable example being the labored translation of 'ideas above his station' into 'des idées au-dessus de sa gare'.

Frensham (1946) A floribunda rose with large clusters of deep crimson semidouble flowers.

Freudian psychology The earliest form of psychoanalytic theory; it emphasized the role of the libido (sexual instinct in a wide sense, including all the appetites) as a prime motive force. Freud introduced the idea of the unruly unconscious id which the conscious ego tries to adjust to the requirements of social life, and of the superego which acts as a censor of the mind. Other features were stress on the part played by sublimation (as when the sadist turns surgeon) and repression, and on diagnosis through analysis of a patient's dreams. (Sigmund Freud, Austrian psychologist, 1856-1939.)

Freudian slip A slip of the tongue (or pen) that reveals a half-repressed idea; as when a politician, in a speech after a rather spartan political dinner, said: 'You can always rely on X to give you a square meal' (for 'deal'), to the delight of the guests and the embarrassment of the host. (Freud developed the interpretation of many such slips, analyzing their causation and mechanism.)

Frey; Freyr In Scandinavian mythology, brother of FREYA and god of agriculture, peace and plenty.

Freya; Freyja The Scandinavian Venus, sister of FREY, and one of ODIN's wives. Friday is named after her.

Friars Club The most famous of New York's theatrical clubs; among other activities it nominates an 'entertainer of the year' etc.

Friar Tuck The fat and jovial chaplain to ROBIN HOOD's band.

Frick Collection An outstanding collection of 14th-19th-century paintings, bronzes and enamels bequeathed to New York City by Henry Clay Frick, an industrialist who died in 1919, and since added to. They are displayed together with appropriate antique furniture, paneling etc., in the rooms of a large house on East 70th Street.

Friendly Islands Capt. Cook's original name, still used, for the Tonga Islands.

Friends, Society of See QUAKERS.

Friendship 7 The name of the spacecraft in which the second American in space, Col. Glenn, orbited the earth 3 times (1962) as part of the MERCURY PROJECT.

Frigg; Frigga In Scandinavian mythology, the Mother of the Gods and one of ODIN's wives.

Frisco An abbreviation for San Francisco of which, it is said, its citizens do not approve.

Frisian (Friesian) A widespread breed of large black-and-white dairy cattle, yielding large quantities of milk of low butterfat content.

Frodo Baggins The chief HOBBIT character in The LORD OF THE RINGS.

Froebel Institute A training college for teachers at Roehampton, England, with branches elsewhere, which pioneered the 3-year course on lines now generally accepted (e.g. emphasis on active instead of passive learning). See next entry.

Froebel system A theory of education developed from the PESTALOZZI SYSTEM, with emphasis on social adjustment; it resulted in the institution of kindergarten schools for infants aged 4-6. (Friedrich Froebel, German educator, 1782-1852.)

Frogs, The (405 BC) Aristophanes' comedy in which DIONYSUS, made into a figure of fun, feels that dramatic talent on earth is running short, and goes to HADES to fetch back Euripides. After hearing a contest between Euripides and Aeschylus, he takes the latter instead. The plot enables Aristophanes to parody Euripides' style unmercifully.

From Here to Eternity (1951) James Jones's long novel about US Army life. (Title from Kipling's: Gentleman-rankers out on the spree,/ Damned from here to Eternity.)

Fronde, The (1648-52) A revolt against absolute monarchy in France, first by the Paris parlement and then by the nobles led by the Great CONDÉ and directed against Cardinal Mazarin during Louis XIV's minority. (French, 'sling', as stones were flung through the Cardinal's windows.)

FRS See FEDERAL RESERVE SYSTEM.

Fructidor In the French Revolution calendar, the month from Aug. 18th to Sept. 21st. ('Fruit-month'.)

Fruitlands (1842-43) A Utopian co-operative farming community in the village of Harvard, Mass., founded by the Transcendentalist, Bronson Alcott, whose daughter Louisa M. Alcott gave an amusing account of it in Transcendental Wild Oats (1876).

FTC See FEDERAL TRADE COMMISSION.

FT Indexes The London Financial Times Industrial Ordinary Index of the movements of 30 major stocks, and the Actuaries' Index of some 500 industrial stocks.

Fuchs spy case The trial of Klaus Fuchs, Communist German-born British subject, who confessed to handing to Russian agents the plans of the first atomic bomb; sentenced to 14 years imprisonment (1950), released (1959), and went to East Germany. See OTTAWA SPY RING; ROSENBERG SPY CASE.

Fudge Family, The A newly rich family invented by the Irish poet, Thomas Moore (1779-1852) in The Fudges in England and The Fudge Family in Paris.

Fugger family A German family of rich bankers who gained political power in the 16th-century through their loans to kings and emperors. The Fugger Newsletters (translated 1924-26) are an important source for the history of the period.

Führer, Der Title taken by Hitler; compare DUCE; CAUDILLO. (German, 'the leader'.)

Fujiwara period (7th-11th centuries) In Japanese history, the period when the country was virtually

ruled by the pleasure-loving Fujiwara family, who were eventually
swept from power by more militaristic dynasties.

Fulani A nomadic cattle-owning
people who roamed over much of
West Africa, many of whom since
the early 19th century have settled
to agriculture and even to urban life,
forming the ruling caste over much
of Northern Nigeria. When pure-
blooded they are fair-skinned
and fine-featured. Their origin and
the classification of their language
are disputed. The French called
them Peulhs; they call themselves
Fulbe.

Fulbright Committee inquiry (1966)
A televised inquiry into the VIETNAM
WAR and other aspects of US foreign
policy conducted by Senator Fulbright, Chairman of the Senate Foreign Relations Committee, and a
leading critic of his government's
conduct of the war.

Fulbright scholarships (1948)
Founded under the Fulbright Act of
1946 which provided for the inter-
change of US and foreign students
and the sending abroad of US professors and other teachers to give
assistance both in underdeveloped
and developed countries. (William
Fulbright, the Senator from Arkansas.)

Fulham A former London metropolitan borough, since 1965 part of the
borough of HAMMERSMITH.

Fulham by-election (1933) See EAST
FULHAM BY-ELECTION.

Fulham Palace The official residence of the Bishop of London, on
the south bank of the Thames at
Putney Bridge.

Fulton speech (1946) Churchill's
speech at Fulton, Mo., in which he
called for a drawing together of
English-speaking peoples in face of
growing Soviet imperialism, and
first publicly referred to the IRON
CURTAIN.

Fu Manchu, Dr The sinister Chinese
doctor of Sax Rohmer's novels (from
1913 on), who keeps a varied collection of poisonous animals at his
Wimbledon home and a gang of
thugs in Limehouse.

Fun City A name for New York City.

Funkia A plant genus now renamed
HOSTA.

Funny Girl (1964) A musical about
the career of the ZIEGFELD FOLLIES
singer Fannie Brice, who flourished
in the 1920s. The music was by Jule
Styne, the lyrics by Bob Merrill; a
movie version appeared in 1967.

Furies, The See EUMENIDES.

FX Provisional designation of the
US Air Force Mach 3 fighter, due
in service in the early 1970s. See
VFAX.

G

G (1) The film rating signifying 'for general audiences', under the Motion Picture Code of Self-Regulation. (2) Stands for 'grand' in the slang sense of $1000 ('a grand sum to have').

Gaberones Newly built capital of the BOTSWANA republic, on the South African border.

Gadarene swine The herd of swine which 'ran violently down a steep place into the sea' and were drowned, after Jesus had given permission for a legion of devils from a madman to pass into them. This man was then seen 'sitting, and clothed, and in his right mind' (*Mark* v, 1-20). The apparent indifference to the animals' fate is sometimes explained by Jewish abhorrence of pigs. (Of Gadara, a Greek settlement in Palestine; hence the presence of pigs.)

Gadsden Purchase (1853) A strip of land south of the Gila River, bought by the US after the MEXICAN WAR, partly in order to build a railroad to the Pacific through what is now southern Arizona and New Mexico.

Gads Hill Place Dickens's home for the last years of his life, at Gadshill, near Rochester, Kent. (Gadshill was also the scene of Prince Hal's plot to rob some travelers, in Shakespeare's *Henry IV, Part 1*.)

Gaelic football A type of football said to have been played in Ireland before the days of St Patrick, now, in a tamer form with established rules, played in Ireland and wherever the Irish have settled abroad. The ball is round and the goal a combination of rugger and soccer goals; a team has 15 players, and substitutes are allowed.

Gaelic language A term up to the 18th century applied to the CELTIC LANGUAGES spoken in Ireland and Scotland; now usually restricted to the latter, the former being called Erse.

Gaels A Celtic-speaking people who reached Ireland from France and Spain about 300 BC and subsequently colonized Scotland (see DALRIADA).

Gaiety girls Chorus girls at the London Gaiety Theatre in the Aldwych when it was under the management of George Edwardes in late Victorian and Edwardian times; they were famous for their beauty and their infiltration into the peerage.

Gainsborough hat A large very wide-brimmed hat such as the women who sat for Gainsborough's portraits often wore.

Gaité Parisienne (1938) Offenbach's one-act ballet, choreography by Massine, about flirtatious goings-on in the cafes of SECOND EMPIRE Paris.

Galahad In Arthurian legend the son of LANCELOT; a knight whose chastity was rewarded by the sight of the HOLY GRAIL and a seat at the ROUND TABLE.

Galatea (1) See ACIS. (2) See PYGMALION AND GALATEA.

Galaxy A US Lockheed troop transport, in service from 1969, described as the world's largest aircraft, weighing 320 tons and able to carry 100 tons.

Galéries Lafayette A large Paris department store near the Opéra.

Gal Friday Colloquialism for the feminine equivalent of a MAN FRIDAY.

Galicia (1) A former Austrian province north of the Carpathians; it was ceded to Poland after World War I, and the eastern half (including Lvov, formerly LEMBERG) was absorbed into Soviet Ukraine after World War II. The chief town in the Polish section is Krakow. (2) A former kingdom of northwest Spain.

Galilean Man of Galilee, i.e. Jesus. The last words of the Roman emperor, Julian the Apostate (AD 363), 'Thou hast conquered, Galilean', were echoed by Swinburne in his attack on Victorian religiosity in *Hymn to Proserpine*: Thou hast conquered, O pale Galilean; the world has grown grey from Thy breath.

Gallery of Modern Art (1964) The gallery at Columbus Circle, NYC, which housed the Huntington Hartford collection. Now the New York Cultural Center (20th-century works of art). The building was designed by Edward Durell Stone.

Gallipoli campaign See DARDA-NELLES CAMPAIGN.

Gallo-Romans The Romanized inhabitants of France before the FRANKS came.

Galloway A polled breed of beef cattle, bred chiefly in Scotland; it has a thick coat of curly black or dun hair.

Gallup Poll (1935) A method of testing public opinion, e.g. in election forecasts, by tabulating answers to key questions put to a cross section of a community. It accurately predicted the results of the US Presidential election in 1936. See BRITISH INSTITUTE OF PUBLIC OPINION. (Dr G. H. Gallup, founder of the American Institute of Public Opinion.)

Galosh NATO code name for the Russian antiballistic missile system (ABM) which is slowly being installed round Moscow; it is vulnerable to sophisticated 'penetration aids'.

Gamaliel A doctor of law and president of the SANHEDRIN who had taught Saul (Paul)—'brought up at the feet of Gamaliel' (*Acts* xxii, 3)—and who persuaded the Jews not to kill the Apostles (*Acts* v, 34-41).

Gamesmanship (1947) Stephen Potter's study of the art of winning games without actually cheating. To take an example from golf: excessive praise of an opponent's straight left arm just before he drives off, and asking him to demonstrate how he does it, should ruin his play for the rest of the game, and perhaps for life. The author applied similar principles to social situations in LIFEMANSHIP and ONE-UPMANSHIP.

Gammer Gurton's Needle (about 1560) A vigorous comedy in doggerel verse by an unknown author; the plot is of sublime simplicity—the

search for the needle; when Hodge sits down he literally jumps to the conclusion that it is in the seat of his breeches. (Gammer for 'godmother-grandmother', i.e. an old woman.)

Gamp, Sairey The bibulous monthly nurse in Dickens's MARTIN CHUZZLEWIT, whose baggy umbrella gave the word 'gamp' to the language she mishandled on so stupendous a scale. See also Mrs HARRIS.

Gandhism The policy pursued in India by followers of MAHATMA Gandhi, who preached Hindu-Muslim unity, abolition of caste, pacifism, equality of women, and humane ideals in politics, as well as the attainment of independence by the whole subcontinent, through non-cooperation, nonviolence, and the boycotting of British imports combined with the revival of cottage industries (including hand-spinning).

G and S Colloquial abbreviation for GILBERT AND SULLIVAN OPERAS.

Ganymede In Greek legend, a beautiful Phrygian youth who took ZEUS's fancy and was carried off to OLYMPUS to act as cupbearer to the gods.

GAO Signifies General Accounting Office, which watches over Federal spending.

GAR (1866) Initials used for the Grand Army of the Republic, a veterans society formed at Decatur, Ill., after the AMERICAN CIVIL WAR which for long had political as well as social importance.

Garand rifle (1936) US Army's semiautomatic gas-operated rifle firing 8 rounds, officially known as the M-1, which replaced the hand-operated SPRINGFIELD RIFLE. Used in World War II and the KOREAN WAR, it was replaced (1957) by the M-14 firing 20 rounds, made at the same armory. (J. C. Garand, of the Springfield Armory.)

Garcia, To carry a message to A phrase from an article in *The Philistine* (1900) by Elbert Hubbard, recounting the successful but hazardous mission of a US intelligence officer, Lt Rowan, sent to contact General Garcia, leader of the Cuban rebels in 1898. Hubbard turned it into a moral tale: It is not book learning young men need . . . but a stiffening of the vertebrae which will cause them to do a thing — 'carry a message to Garcia'.

Garden of the Gods A park between Colorado Springs and Manitou Springs, Col., with fantastic spires of bright-colored sandstone, resembling giant anthills.

Garden State Nickname of New Jersey.

Garden State Stakes (1953) An important horse-race, run at Garden State Park, Camden, N.J.

Garfield assassination (1881) The death of James Abram Garfield, Republican President of the US, shot in Washington railroad station by a disappointed office seeker.

Gargantua and Pantagruel (1532-64) Rabelais' great work in 5 books about 2 giants, father and son. Rabelais embroiders their adventures with riotous buffoonery, wild panegyrics on food and drink, bawdy humor, satire and philosophic wit all intermingled with long lists of incongruous objects and fantastic coined names. Sir Thomas Urquhart's translation (1653) is a work of art in its own right. (The names mean 'gullet' and 'all-thirsty'.)

Garibaldi biscuit A cracker better known in England as the squashed-fly biscuit, from the currants embedded in it. (Said to be a favorite of the Italian revolutionary; see next entry.)

Garibaldi's Thousand Redshirts The force, made up of various nationalities, with which Garibaldi drove King BOMBA out of Sicily and Naples in 1860.

Garrick Club (1831) A London club in Garrick Street, named after the actor, David Garrick. It is typically a theater and law club, with a sprinkling of editors and businessmen.

Garter ceremony The ceremonial gathering (in June) of Knights of the Garter at ST GEORGE'S CHAPEL, Windsor; the route is lined mainly by dismounted troopers of the Household Cavalry.

Garter King of Arms The principal King of Arms at the COLLEGE OF ARMS.

Gary Cooper Prize The CANNES INTERNATIONAL FILM FESTIVAL prize for the film which has contributed most to human understanding.

Gascony Originally a BASQUE province of France, later united with AQUITAINE. The Gascons were renowned for their pride, hot temper and boastfulness — hence *gasconnade*, 'a boastful tirade'.

Gas House Gang A nickname given in the 1930s to the St Louis CARDINALS, a colorful team which won the WORLD SERIES in 1934.

Gasoline Alley (1919) A comic strip by Frank King giving a sympathetic picture of life in a suburban business family, in which the characters develop and age realistically.

Gaspar One of the THREE KINGS, traditionally the Ethiopian King of Tarshish (perhaps a Phoenician colony in Spain).

Gaspé Peninsula The forested hilly peninsula in southeast Quebec north of New Brunswick, a vacation region offering hunting, fishing and rugged coastal scenery.

Gastropods See MOLLUSKS.

Gateway Arch The Gateway to the West, in St Louis, Mo., a 630-ft stainless steel catenary arch designed by Eero Saarinen. It is the tallest US monument.

Gath A Philistine city mentioned in DAVID's lament for SAUL and Jonathan (2 *Samuel* i, 19): 'How are the mighty fallen! Tell it not in Gath . . . lest the daughters of the Philistines rejoice'. 'Tell it not in Gath!' is properly used in the sense 'don't let our rivals hear of this setback'.

Gatling gun (1861) An early American machine gun used in the AMERICAN CIVIL WAR; it worked on the principle of the revolver, with up to 10 rifle barrels.

GATT (1947) The General Agreement on Tariffs and Trade, an international treaty to promote freer trade through the phased elimination of tariffs, preferences and quotas by its 60 signatories. See KENNE-

DY ROUND.

'Gaudeamus igitur' A rousing 13th-century student song adopted as a school song in many schools: *Gaudeamus igitur,/Juvenes dum sumus./Post jucundam juventutem,/Post molestam senectutem,/Nos habebit humus* ('Let us make merry therefore while still young; after happy youth and tiresome old age, the earth will claim us').

Gaudyware Popular US name for cheap gaily decorated pottery wares made in Britain mainly for the US market, with a characteristic formal floral design painted in much the same palette as MASON'S IRONSTONE jugs. Gaudy Dutch (c. 1810-30) was so called as mostly found in Pennsylvania, though it was made in Staffordshire; Gaudy Welsh (c. 1830-60) was probably made at SWANSEA, Wales.

Gaugamela (331 BC) The battle in which Alexander the Great finally defeated the Persians under Darius; also called Arbela. (Town on the Tigris in Iraq.)

Gauleiter Supreme governor of a *Gau* ('district') in Nazi Germany and German-occupied territory. ('Gauleader'.)

Gautama The family name of the BUDDHA.

Gautier, Marguerite See DAME AUX CAMÉLIAS.

Gawain King ARTHUR's nephew, a knight renowned for courtesy.

Gay Nineties, The The 1890s (also called the Naughty Nineties), the *fin-de-siécle* epoch when traditional Victorian religiosity and outward morality were flouted by such as Aubrey Beardsley (see YELLOW BOOK) and Oscar Wilde (see WILDE (OSCAR) CASE), while society, led by the Prince of Wales (the future Edward VII), took to new habits such as race-going, and weekend country-house parties (see TRANBY CROFT SCANDAL).

Gaza Strip A small coastal desert area on the borders of, and disputed by, Egypt and Israel, awarded in 1947 to Arab Palestine and seized by Egypt in 1949. It became an Egyptian district under UN supervision to control border incidents. It contained 200,000 Arab refugees from Palestine, from whom the Egyptians recruited forces to raid Israel. In 1967 the area was recaptured by Israeli forces.

GBS Initials commonly used for George Bernard Shaw, the playwright.

GCE (1950) (UK) Initials used for the General Certificate of Education which replaced the old School and Higher School Certificates. The O-LEVEL is taken at about age 16, the A-Level 2 years later. Papers are set and marked by various regional and national examining boards.

Gdańsk See DANZIG.

GE Common abbreviation for the GENERAL ELECTRIC Company (USA).

Ge In Greek legend, the Earth, personified as the wife of URANUS and mother of the TITANS.

GEC (1900) Initials of the General Electric Co., a British company making transformers, switchgear and nuclear plant, telephone, electronic and domestic equipment (e.g., Osram and McMichael products). It also operates in Canada, Africa and the Far East, including Japan. In 1967 it took over AEI, and in 1968 merged with English Electric.

Geffrye Museum (1914) A London museum at Shoreditch, with a series of rooms showing middle-class styles of furnishing for all periods after 1600; there are also photos of period costumes and a library.

Gehenna Another name for TOPHET, i.e. Hell.

Geiger counter (1928) A device for detecting and measuring radioactivity and other radiations. (Abbreviated from Geiger-Müller counter, named after its 2 German inventors.)

Geisha girls Highly trained girls hired out to amuse parties of tired Japanese businessmen with music and dance; they are mostly decorous and dull.

Gemini The Twins, third of the constellations of the Zodiac (also called CASTOR and POLLUX), between TAURUS and CANCER; the sun enters it about May 21st. Astrologers claim that those born under this sign may be superficial and smooth.

Gemini US space program to work out techniques for orbital rendezvous as a step to establishing a permanently orbiting space station, and also a step toward inspection of hostile satellites. The 2 occupants of Gemini 7 made the first space rendezvous (with Gemini 6) and spent 14 days in orbit (1965) without suffering ill effects from weightlessness (another problem studied in the program); Gemini 8 docked onto an unmanned AGENA satellite (1966).

Geminid meteors A shoal of meteors which orbit the sun and through which the earth passes each December, producing a display of shooting stars emanating from the direction of GEMINI.

Gem State Nickname of Idaho. (Mistranslation of Indian name.)

General Agreement on Tariffs and Trade See GATT.

General Assembly (UN) The assembly of (up to 5) delegates from each member state. A two-thirds majority is required for any major decision, and each state has one vote—e.g. the Maldive Islands and USA carry equal weight.

General Electric (1892) (USA) The world's largest electrical company, 3 times the size of its nearest rivals, WESTINGHOUSE ELECTRIC and ITT, and a leading manufacturer of aircraft engines. It resulted from a merger of the Edison and Thomson-Houston electrical companies and progressed from lamps to turbines, generators, transformers, household appliances (1920s), aircraft and radio equipment (World War II) and atomic energy. One of the 30 industrials that make up the DOW JONES Industrial Average. See also GEC.

General Foods (1929) One of the largest food-processing companies based at White Plains, N.Y.; one of the 30 industrials that make up the DOW JONES Industrial Average.

General Mills (1923) A large group of food-processing firms, with headquarters in Minneapolis.

General Motors Corporation (1908) The largest US automobile manufacturer. Based on the Buick Company, it successively absorbed OLDSMOBILE, Pontiac, Cadillac and Chevrolet; in addition to motor vehicles it makes aircraft engines, locomotives, household appliances etc. Vauxhall Motors is a British and Opel a West German subsidiary. One of the 30 industrials that make up the DOW JONES Industrial Average.

General Strike, The (1926) (UK) A 9-day strike, the only general strike that Britain has known. It began after government had abolished subsidies to the coal-mining industry, and mine owners had reduced wages. The miners, who continued on strike from May 1st to November, were supported by the Trade Union Congress which called out all the major unions in sympathy. Rail and road transport was paralyzed except for trucks run by the army and volunteers; and the only newssheet was Churchill's British Gazette.

Genesis The first book of the Old Testament, giving the stories of the Creation, ADAM and Eve, the Flood, ABRAHAM, ISAAC, JACOB and JOSEPH. (Greek, 'creation'.)

Geneva (1) Used as a synonym, during its existence, for the LEAGUE OF NATIONS, which had its headquarters there. (2) Dutch gin (HOLLANDS). (French genièvre, 'juniper'; no connection with Geneva.)

Geneva Agreements (1954) The terms agreed upon for the ending of the French INDO-CHINA WAR, at a conference under joint UK and USSR chairmanship, attended by the parties concerned, together with China and the USA. They included the temporary division of VIETNAM at the 17th parallel pending free elections. However the powers failed to back up the settlement and free elections were never held. SEATO was substituted for the agreement and it was under this treaty that the USA managed virtually singlehandedly to bog itself down for years after in Vietnam.

Geneva Bible (1560) An English translation compiled by exiles from the MARIAN PERSECUTION living in Geneva; the first to be printed in roman (not black letter) type, and to be divided into verses. See BREECHES BIBLE.

Geneva Conventions (1864) The international agreements under which the RED CROSS was established and regulations laid down for the more humane treatment of prisoners of war and the wounded. A further agreement in 1906 strengthened these.

Geneva Disarmament Conference (1932-34) See WORLD DISARMAMENT CONFERENCE.

Geneva Protocol (1924) A pact 'for the pacific settlement of international disputes', which provided for compulsory arbitration of disputes involving nonmembers of the LEAGUE OF NATIONS (e.g. Germany, Russia, USA), combined with disarmament and mutual defense agreements. Sponsored by the Labor Prime Minister, Ramsay MacDonald, it was repudiated by the Conservative government before ratification, and replaced by the LOCARNO PACTS.

Geneva Summit Conference (1955) The 4-power conference of heads of state (Eisenhower, Eden, Bulganin, Faure) called to discuss the reunification of Germany.

Genevoise Cooking term, usually indicating the presence of anchovies.

Genie US air-to-air missile designed to carry a nuclear warhead over a range of 6 miles.

Genji, Prince The hero of a long Japanese novel written in the 11th century by Lady Murasaki (translated by Arthur Waley as *The Tale of Genji*, 1933). In a realistic court setting, it tells of Prince Genji's many loves; scenes from it are often depicted in old scroll paintings.

Genoa Conference (1922) An abortive conference on world economic affairs attended by 29 nations; Soviet Russia made its first appearance at an international conference, and

Germany its first postwar appearance.

Genro Elder statesmen of Japan, who wielded very great power under the old imperial constitution.

Gentleman Jim Nickname of James Corbett, world heavyweight champion in the 1890s.

Gentlemen at Arms (UK) The Honourable Corps of Gentlemen at Arms is one of the 2 bodies forming the Queen's dismounted bodyguard (see YEOMEN OF THE GUARD); it consists of 40 retired officers of the Regular Army and the Marines. Their Captain is Chief WHIP in the Lords.

Gentlemen Prefer Blondes (1925) (1) Anita Loos' study of the world of the gold-digging blonde, Lorelei, whose girl friend, Dorothy, is the mouthpiece of the author's wit. (2) A musical (1949) by W. Leo Robin and Jule Styne based on (1), containing the famous number 'Diamonds Are a Girl's Best Friend'.

Gentlemen's Agreement An informal agreement between nations based on personal assurances only; specifically, that between Japan and USA (1908) restricting Japanese labor immigration.

Geoffrey Beene A New York fashion house.

Geordie (UK) Nickname for a Northumbrian, especially a Tynesider. (Local pronunciation of 'Georgie'.)

George Cross (1940) An award instituted by George VI which takes precedence over all decorations except the VICTORIA CROSS. Primarily for civilians, it is made for acts of the greatest heroism or the most conspicuous courage in circumstances of extreme danger. See MALTA GC.

Georgetown (1) A residential district of Washington, D.C. (2) (1789) A Roman Catholic university in Washington, D.C.

'George Washington, Portrait of' One of a series of 7 faithful and uncompromising portraits painted 1772-95 by Charles Willson Peale, now in the Metropolitan Museum of Art, NYC. He painted 60 portraits of Washington; his brother and 4 sons copied many of them.

George Washington, USS (1960) The first nuclear-powered submarine armed with 16 POLARIS missiles.

'George Washington at Yorktown' A painting by James Peale (see 'LAMPLIGHT PORTRAIT'). See also 'GEORGE WASHINGTON, PORTRAIT OF'. (Metropolitan Museum of Art, NYC.)

George White's Scandals The spectacular annual revue produced by George White from 1920 until the 1930s; during its first 4 years many of the songs were written by the young George Gershwin, and it specialized in introducing the latest eccentric dances.

Georgian period (1714-1800) A term applied to styles of decoration prevalent in England up to the REGENCY PERIOD. The reign of George I (1714-27) was influenced by BAROQUE; mahogany and gesso came into vogue and William Kent began to revive PALLADIAN ARCHITECTURE. The reign of George II (1727-60) was influenced by LOUIS QUINZE (ROCOCO) and was the age of CHIPPENDALE. In George III's reign HEPPLEWHITE and SHERATON introduced simpler styles.

Georgian poetry (1912-33) The poetry of a series of anthologies produced (and so named) by Sir Edward Marsh for the POETRY BOOK-SHOP, and continued later by Mrs Harold Monro. They were part of a successful movement to introduce poetry to a wider public, initiated by Rupert Brooke, Drinkwater, Harold Monro and others. Poets published included De La Mare, Masefield, Robert Graves, W. H. Davies, Housman, Blunden and Lascelles Abercrombie.

Georgia Peach, The Nickname for Ty (Tyrus) Cobb, one of the greatest names in baseball; he played 22 seasons with Detroit Tigers and managed them 1921-26. (Born in Georgia, the Peach State.)

Georgics (30BC) Virgil's 4 discursive poems on the delights of country life and the arts of agriculture. (Greek, 'farming topics'.)

Georgie Porgie (pudding and pie), of the nursery rhyme, variously and unconvincingly identified with Charles II, George I and George Villiers, Duke of Buckingham.

Geranium The genus of cranesbills; the pot or bedding plant called geranium is a Pelargonium.

German Democratic Republic (1949) The official name of East Germany, not recognized by non-Communist countries (see HALLSTEIN DOCTRINE). It consists of the former provinces of THURINGIA and MECKLENBURG, and parts of BRANDENBURG SAXONY and POMERANIA, names which have been officially obliterated by division into smaller districts. See GERMAN FEDERAL REPUBLIC.

German East Africa The German colony which became British-mandated TANGANYIKA Territory in 1920, and is now part of TANZANIA.

German Federal Republic (1949) The official name of West Germany (in German, the *Bundesrepublik*). The chief provinces are NORTH-RHINE WESTPHALIA, RHINELAND-PALATINATE, Bavaria, Baden-Württemberg, HESSEN and Lower Saxony. See GERMAN DEMOCRATIC REPUBLIC.

German silver (1836) An alloy of copper, zinc and nickel, used in making British plate, a cheaper substitute for SHEFFIELD PLATE which it replaced until the coming of electroplated nickel silver.

Germinal In the FRENCH REVOLUTION calendar, the month from Mar. 21st to Apr. 19th. ('Budding time'.)

Geronimo (1) An APACHE chief who surrendered in Arizona at the end of the APACHE WARS. (2) Used as a battle cry by paratroopers, usually at the moment of jumping.

'Gerontion' (1920) A pessimistic short poem by T. S. Eliot, a meditation on old age and decay.

Gestalt psychology An approach to psychology associated with the names of Koffka and Köhler, who held that analysis of psychological phenomena, especially perception, into separate elements is unrewarding; they must be studied as integrated wholes, which differ from the sum of the parts as a melody differs from a mere collection of the notes of which it is made up. This view has helped to a better understanding of the processes of learning and memory. (German, 'shape', 'pattern'.)

Gestapo Hitler's Secret State Police, merged with the ss in 1936. (From initial letters of *Geheime Staats-Polizei*.)

Gesta Romanorum (14th century) A collection of tales, each with a moral, about saints, knights and Roman emperors; though written in Latin, some of the tales are oriental. (Latin, 'deeds of the Romans'.)

Gethsemane, The Agony in The spiritual sufferings of Jesus in an olive grove of that name where he went to pray for his own death after the Last Supper (*Mark* xiv, 32-36), and where JUDAS betrayed him.

Gettysburg, Battle of (July 1863) The turning point of the AMERICAN CIVIL WAR; the Confederate army tried to invade northern territory across the Potomac, but was turned back. (Town in southern Pennsylvania.)

Gettysburg address (Nov. 1863) President Lincoln's speech during the AMERICAN CIVIL WAR at the dedication of the cemetery of those killed in the Battle of GETTYSBURG; it ended with the words: 'that we here highly resolve . . . that government of the people, by the people, and for the people, shall not perish from the earth'.

Gezira (1925) An area in the Sudan of about 1¾ million acres, between the Blue and White Nile south of Khartoum, irrigated from the Sennar dam on the Blue Nile for the cultivation of the main export crop, cotton.

Ghana Formerly the British colony of the Gold Coast, West Africa. See also OLD GHANA.

Ghent, Treaty of (1814) The treaty that restored the status quo at the end of the WAR OF 1812, but settled none of the issues that caused it. It was signed in December, but news of this did not reach Andrew Jackson until the following February, by which time he had gained the principal land victory of the war by foiling a British attempt to take New Orleans.

Ghiordes rugs Rugs made from the 17th century in northwest ANATOLIA, among the best of the Turkish family. They have a wine-colored or puce ground, and columns as part of the multicolored design. Prayer rugs are particularly numerous.

Ghost Goes West, The (1935) The first film made by René Clair after he went to Hollywood.

Ghosts (1881) Ibsen's play, in which Mrs Alving comes to realize that she had failed in love for her late husband from undue subservience to dead social conventions (the 'ghosts') which destroy happiness. The growing insanity of their son, who has inherited syphilis from his father, emphasizes the point.

Ghost Train, The Arnold Ridley's successful thriller play, of which 3 movie versions were made in the period 1928-41.

Giant Despair See DOUBTING CASTLE.

Giants (1) The San Francisco Giants, NATIONAL (Baseball) LEAGUE, playing at Candlestick Park. Until 1957 they were the New York Giants, playing at the Polo Grounds in Manhattan. (2) The New York Giants, NATIONAL FOOTBALL LEAGUE. Became member of the NATIONAL CONFERENCE, NATIONAL FOOTBALL LEAGUE in 1970.

Giants in the Earth (1925) Subtitled *A Saga of the Prairie*, the first of a trilogy of frontier novels by the Norwegian-born Ole Rölvaag, about a group of Norwegian immigrants who settle in virgin Dakota Territory in the 1870s; it deals both with the true farmer's enslavement by his land and with religious intolerance between denominations. Thomas Job used the book for a play (1928) and Douglas Moore for an opera (1951).

GI Bill of Rights Popular name for various Veterans' Readjustment Acts providing education, training, loans for homes and allowances to tide over the job-seeking period etc., for veterans of World War II (1944), the KOREAN WAR (1966; the 'New GI Bill') and VIETNAM WAR (1967).

Gibraltar, Capture of (1704) Effected by Admiral Rooke a few days before BLENHEIM; Britain retained it under the Peace of UTRECHT.

Gibson A dry martini with an onion replacing the customary olive.

Gibson girls Perhaps the first 'pin-ups', drawings of girls with hour-glass figures by the American cartoonist, Charles Dana Gibson (1867-1944), which had a great vogue in their time.

Gideon Commander George Gideon of SCOTLAND YARD, a character in a series of detective stories (e.g. *Gideon's Day*, 1955) by J. J. Marric, one of the many pen names of the English author John Creasey.

Gideons Members of the Gideon Society (1899), an interdenominational laymen's evangelical association founded at Janesville, Wis., as the Christian Commercial Men's Association, which distributes Bibles to hotels, hospitals, schools, prisons, barracks etc. (From the account in *Judges* vii of how Gideon smote the Midianites.)

'Gift of the Magi, The' (1906) One of O. Henry's stories, included in *The Four Million*, about an exchange of Christmas presents by a penniless couple. He sells his watch to buy her combs; she sells her hair to buy him a watch fob.

GI Jane A member of the US Women's Auxiliary Army Corps. (See GI JOE.)

GI Joe A soldier. (From the initials GI – 'general issue' – on his equipment.)

Gilbert and Sullivan operas The comic operas composed by Sir Arthur Sullivan with witty lyrics by W. S. Gilbert (produced 1875-96); also called Savoy operas (see D'OYLY CARTE OPERA CO.).

Gilberte In Proust's REMEMBRANCE OF THINGS PAST, the daughter of SWANN by ODETTE DE CRÉCY; socially ambitious, she eventually marries SAINT-LOUP. The narrator has a great affection for her.

Gilbertian Ludicrously topsy-turvy. (From W. S. Gilbert, see GILBERT AND SULLIVAN OPERAS.)

Gil Blas (1715-35) The first realistic picaresque novel, written by the Frenchman Lesage. The young Spaniard, Gil Blas, sets out to make his career and becomes pupil to the quack doctor, Sangrado. Although the setting is in Spain, the large gallery of characters are drawn, unsympathetically, from the author's own experiences in Paris.

Gilead, Balm in A phrase from *Jeremiah* viii, 22: 'Is there no balm in Gilead; is there no physician there?' JEREMIAH is bewailing the fate threatening JUDAH in troubled times, from which there seemed no escape. (Some now unknown medicinal herb for which Gilead was famous; the later antiseptic, balm of Gilead, was named after it.)

Gilgamesh epic A collection of SUMERIAN legends, some at least 4000 years old; the best-known is the story of the Flood, told to the hero Gilgamesh by Noah. The epic was first found, incomplete, on tablets written at NINEVEH in the 7th century BC and now in the British Museum; a version 1000 years older was found *c.* 1900.

Gillray cartoons Venomous political caricatures executed by James Gillray from 1780 onwards. His main victims were George III, Pitt, Fox and Burke and the chief figures of the period of the FRENCH REVOLUTION.

Gimbel's A New York department store in Herald Square almost as large as nearby MACY's; their rivalry was such that 'Does Gimbel's tell Macy's?' became a rebuke to the inquisitive. It sells groceries, toys, furniture, domestic wares, stamps and coins, *inter alia*. Adam Gimbel set up a trading post at Vincennes, Ind., in 1842; the New York store, still a family affair opened in 1910. See also SAKS FIFTH AVENUE.

Ginger Man, The A sprawling novel by J. P. Donleavy, notorious when published, about Sebastian Dangerfield, the manic-depressive antisocial hero who devotes his life to wine, women, stealing, lying and avoiding work.

Ginza A street in Tokyo of department stores and nightclubs.

Gioconda, La (1876) Ponchielli's best opera, set in 17th-century Venice. It is based on Victor Hugo's story of the tragic love of a singer, La

Gioconda, for a prince, but the libretto is a poor one.

'Gioconda, La' See 'MONA LISA'.

Gipsy Moth Name of 3 yachts owned by Sir Francis Chichester. In No. III he won the first single-handed transatlantic race in 1960, taking 40 days. In No. IV he circumnavigated the world in 226 sailing days in 1966-67, again sailing alone. (Named after the Gipsy MOTH aircraft in which he made a solo flight to Australia.)

Girl Guides (1) In Britain the female counterpart to the Boy Scouts. (2) The former name of the GIRL SCOUTS OF AMERICA.

Girl of the Golden West, The (1910) Puccini's Wild West opera set in a Californian mining camp during the 1849 Gold Rush. David Belasco's libretto tells the love story of the only woman in the camp, Minnie the bar owner.

Girl of the Limberlost, A (1909) Gene Stratton Porter's best-selling sentimental novel, set in the Limberlost Swamp of Indiana where she herself lived.

Girls Clubs of America (1945) A federation of clubs for girls aged 6-16. Their primary aim is to train girls to become good citizens, mothers and homemakers.

Girl Scouts of America (1912) A movement founded by Juliette Low as the counterpart to the BOY SCOUTS OF AMERICA, emphasizing the development of health, citizenship, character and homemaking ability.

Giro banking service (1968) (UK) A GPO service designed to provide a cheap credit transfer system for wage earners, available at every post office; all accounts are kept at the Giro center at Bootle, Lancashire. (Name and system adopted from the continent.)

Girondins (1791-93) The liberal middle-class republicans of the FRENCH REVOLUTION who broke away from the JACOBINS; in their enthusiasm they rushed France into a war, for which it was quite unprepared, against Austria and Prussia after the Declaration of PILLNITZ; the conse-

quent disasters swept them from power. (Named after the district of Gironde in southwest France, from which many of them came.)

Girton (1869) The oldest college for women at CAMBRIDGE UNIVERSITY.

Giselle (1841) A ballet about a village girl who falls in love with a nobleman disguised as a peasant. Her former lover gives him away and she goes mad. Act II is set in a haunted dreamworld where Giselle and others dance all night and lure to their doom all who come under their spell, including the 2 men in her life.

'Give 'em Watts, boys!' A phrase from Revolutionary days: in a battle (1780) at Springfield, N.J., the Rev. James Caldwell gathered an armful of Watts hymnbooks taken from the First Presbyterian Church and, with this cry, threw them to the soldiers, who had run out of gun wadding.

Givenchy A Paris fashion house.

Giverny A village northwest of Paris associated with Claude Monet, who lived and worked there for the last 43 years of his life, creating a famous garden and lily pond which appear in many of his paintings.

Giza (Gizeh etc.) A suburb of Cairo, north of SAKKARA; it is the site of 3 famous pyramids of the 4th Dynasty (26th century BC), including the Great Pyramid of Cheops (Khufu), and of the largest and best known of the many Sphinxes.

Glacier National Park (1910) A mountainous wilderness in northwest Montana, with spectacular scenery and wildlife; in 1932 the small WATERTON LAKES NATIONAL PARK over the Canadian border was merged with it to form the Waterton-Glacier International Peace Park.

Gladstonian Liberalism Free trade, retrenchment, political reform, a nonaggressive policy overseas, and HOME RULE for Ireland. (W. E. Gladstone, Prime Minister 1868-74, 1880-85, 1886 and 1892-94.)

Glamis Castle A mainly 17th-century château-style home of the Earls of Strathmore, near Kirriemuir, Angus, Scotland, scene of Duncan's murder in MACBETH. Birthplace of Queen Elizabeth the Queen Mother and her daughter Princess Margaret.

Glassboro meeting   (1967) See HOLLYBUSH SUMMIT.

Glass Menagerie, The   (1945) Tennessee Williams's first Broadway success, replete with symbolism. A homely crippled girl, Laura, retreats into an artificial private world collecting glass animals. Her mother, the author's typical faded southern belle, lives in a largely imaginary past; she persuades her son Tom to get a friend to court Laura out of her dreamworld. The experiment fails; Laura retreats further from reality and Tom alone achieves his ambition, by running away to sea.

Glastonbury   In ARTHURIAN LEGEND the place where JOSEPH OF ARIMATHEA planted his staff (which flowers each Christmas) and hid the HOLY GRAIL. See CAMELOT.

'Gleaners, The'   Millet's painting of 3 sturdy peasant women in the sunlit fields; now in the Louvre.

Glen Canyon Dam   (1963) A 710-ft concrete dam on the Arizona-Utah border, creating Lake Powell. It is part of the Colorado River Storage project and when built was second only to the HOOVER DAM in the US.

Glencoe Massacre   (1692) The massacre of 36 Roman Catholic Macdonalds in the pass above Loch Leven, Argyll, by soldiers (Campbells) of the Duke of Argyll's regiment who had accepted Macdonald hospitality for the previous 10 days.

Glenfinnan   Site at the head of Loch Shiel, Inverness-shire, of a monument to the YOUNG PRETENDER, who raised his standard there in 1745.

Glenlivet   A Scotch whiskey made (at first illicitly) in Banffshire, immortalized in the 19th-century parodist Sir Robert Aytoun's lines: Fhairson had a son, / Who married Noah's daughter, / And nearly spoiled ta Flood, / By trinking up ta water: / Which he would have done, / I at least pelieve it, / Had the mixture peen / Only half Glenlivet.

Glenrothes   (1948) (Scotland) A NEW TOWN in Fife, designed to take 55,-000 inhabitants.

Globe Theatre   (1599) One of the earliest London theaters, at SOUTHWARK, where many of Shakespeare's plays were produced.

Gloomy Dean, The   A nickname for the Right Rev. W. R. Inge, Dean of St Paul's, a theologian and philosopher, and a prolific journalist who in the interwar years contributed to the London *Evening Standard* many pessimistic articles on world affairs and the decay of Western civilization.

'Gloria in excelsis'   (1) The hymn 'Glory be to God on high', sung in Communion and other services. (2) A musical setting of this.

Gloriana   (1) A character in the FAERIE QUEENE, representing Queen Elizabeth. (2) Title of an opera by Benjamin Britten (1952).

Glorious First of June, The   (1794) Lord Howe's defeat of the French fleet off Ushant during the French Revolutionary Wars.

Glorious Revolution   (1688) The deposition of the Roman Catholic James II and his replacement by Protestant WILLIAM OF ORANGE and his wife Mary, 'to save the Protestant religion and the constitutional liberties of England'; William landed unopposed in Torbay, Devon, and James fled to Ireland (see BOYNE) and France.

Glorious 12th of July, The   See TWELFTH OF JULY.

'Glory Trail, The'   (1915) A cowboy ballad by Charles Badger Clark Jr; cowboys call it 'High Chin Bob', the name of the hero who ropes a mountain lion; since neither would give in, they continue together through all eternity.

Glossina   Generic name of the tsetse fly, carrier of the trypanosomes of human and animal sleeping sickness (trypanosomiasis).

Gloster aircraft   See METEOR; JAVELIN.

Gloucester cheese   Once a gourmet's delight, especially the double Gloucester (made from whole milk); it now seems to have suffered the same fate as WENSLEYDALE.

GL radar A British gunlaying radar device first used in an antiaircraft barrage in 1940.

Glyndebourne Festival (1934) An English festival of opera founded by John Christie (died 1962) and held each summer at his home near Lewes, Sussex. It is attended both by socialites and music lovers.

Glyptothek (Munich) A major museum of Greek and Roman art, rebuilt after World War II.

GM Initials standing for GENERAL MOTORS CORPORATION.

G-man An FBI detective. (For Government-man, i.e. Federal, not state, detective.)

Gnosticism A body of mystical beliefs derived from oriental religions, Pythagoras, Plato and Christianity; it flourished particularly in Egypt in the 2nd century AD. The main theme was the handing down of a body of esoteric knowledge attainable only from instruction by initiates, with strict self-discipline, contemplation and various physical drills, directed to individual salvation from the evil fate of the generality of mankind. The MUSLIM equivalent is SUFISM. (Greek *gnosis*, 'knowledge', specifically 'revelation'.)

GNP See GROSS NATIONAL PRODUCT.

Goat and Compasses An inn name corrupted from 'God encompasseth us', the usual sign in the Middle Ages for a pilgrims' hostel.

Gobbo, Lancelot The clown in Shakespeare's MERCHANT OF VENICE who deserts SHYLOCK for easier working conditions under Bassanio.

Gobelins, Les (1440) A French tapestry factory in Paris, bought by Louis XIV's minister, Colbert, and still run as a State factory, making carpets, upholstery and furniture; there is also a museum with interesting old carpets. (Jean Gobelin, dyer, head of the family who founded it.)

'God Bless America' (1939) A patriotic march chorus by Irving Berlin, written 22 years earlier but produced for Kate Smith to sing on the First Armistice (Veterans) Day after the outbreak of World War II. It is much easier to sing than the national anthem, which it has come near to displacing in popular esteem.

Goddard Space Flight Center The NASA research center at Greenbelt, Md. It is equiped to track and communicate with satellites, especially observatory satellites, such as LUNAR ORBITER.

Godey's Lady's Book (1830-98) The first women's periodical in the US, founded in Philadelphia by Louis Antoine Godey. It was famous for its stenciled colored fashion plates and art reproductions.

Godiva, Lady Wife of the 11th-century Earl of MERCIA, Leofric, who kept his promise to cancel certain taxes if she rode naked through Coventry.

Godolphin Arabian See THOROUGHBRED.

Godot The character in Samuel Beckett's play *Waiting for Godot* (1955) whom 2 tramps await; he appears to symbolize a revelation of the meaning of life which, like Godot, never comes.

God's country The land of opportunity in the West, one's home state or, usually in the form 'God's own country', the US.

God's Little Acre (1933) Erskine Caldwell's novel about the backward mountain dwellers of Georgia, which sold 9 million copies.

Gog and Magog (1) In *Ezekiel* xxxviii and xxxix Gog is the King of Magog, Israel's enemy. (2) In *Revelations* xx, 8 they are both persons, enemies of the Kingdom of God. (3) In English legend they are 2 giant offspring of daughters of the Emperor Diocletian brought captive to London. Their 15th-century effigies, placed outside GUILDHALL, were destroyed in the GREAT FIRE OF LONDON and their replicas destroyed in a 1940 air raid; new figures have again been made. (Gog may have meant 'darkness', 'the north'; and Magog 'land of darkness'.)

Gogmagogs, The Hills near Cambridge, England, named after a legendary giant who fell in love with GRANTA. (See GOG AND MAGOG.)

Goidelic languages   See CELTIC LAN-GUAGES. (Goidels, old Irish name for GAELS.)

Golconda   A source of wealth; a rich mine. (Ancient Indian Muslim city near Hyderabad, where diamonds were cut though not, as tradition used to have it, mined.)

'Gold Bug, The'   (1843) Edgar Allan Poe's short story describing the location of a vast treasure hidden by Capt. KIDD on Sullivan's Island off South Carolina; it was found by dropping a beetle (the gold bug) through the eye of a skull in accordance with remarkably complicated instructions in a cipher message, the solution of which is given at length.

Gold Coast   (1) The pre-independence name of Ghana, West Africa. (2) Nickname for various parts of the world frequented by the rich, e.g. The Florida Lido at Miami Beach; a residential area along Lake Shore Drive, Chicago; the Australian 'surfers' paradise' on the Pacific coast of Queensland.

Gold Cup   (1904) A race for power-boats under 40 ft over a 90-mile course, usually at Seattle or Detroit.

Gold Cup Day, Ascot   The Thursday of ROYAL ASCOT and the climax of the meeting; see ASCOT GOLD CUP.

Golden Arrow, The   The afternoon express train from London (Victoria) to Paris, which becomes La Flèche d'Or on the other side of the Channel.

Golden Ass, The   (2nd century AD) A satiric fantasy by Apuleius in which Lucian, accidentally transformed into an ass, comments on his various owners and their ways. He is eventually restored to human form by ISIS. The book, also called *The Meta-morphoses*, includes the earliest version of the story of CUPID AND PSYCHE.

Golden Bough, The   (1890-1915) Sir James Frazer's multivolume comparative study of the beliefs and institutions of primitive man. (Title from the bough broken by AENEAS before going down to the Underworld, an echo of an ancient priest-slaying ritual.)

Golden Boy   (1937) A play by Clifford Odets in which an Italian-American potential violinist finds fame as a boxer, but after killing an opponent commits suicide.

Golden Calf, The   The idol made by AARON (Exodus xxxii, 4) and worshiped by the Israelites while Moses was on Mount Sinai receiving the Ten Commandments. Moses destroyed it (verse 22). The phrase 'to worship the Golden Calf' came to mean 'to sacrifice principles in the pursuit of money'.

Golden Delicious   A hard sweet dessert apple of American origin, now the world's most widely grown variety.

Goldenes Dachl   (1500) A high balcony at Innsbruck, Austria, roofed with gilded copper plates, built for spectators at city festivals by the Emperor Maximilian. (Austrian, 'golden little roof'.)

Golden Fleece   In Greek legend the objective of the ARGONAUTS' expedition. It was the fleece of a ram hung on a tree in Colchis (the Black Sea coastal area of modern Georgia), guarded by a dragon. The legend may refer to a local method of collecting alluvial gold by putting sheepskins in rivers.

Golden Fleece, Knights of the   (1429) Members of a chivalric order founded for the protection of the Church by Philip the Good, Duke of Burgundy and the Netherlands; later divided into 2 separate orders for Spain and Austria. (Names variously explained.)

Golden Gate, The   The one-mile-wide entrance to San Francisco Bay, since 1937 spanned by the world's second longest single-span suspension bridge.

Golden Gloves   US amateur boxing tournament, sponsored by the press.

Golden Hind   The 100-ton ship in which Drake circumnavigated the world in 1577-80.

Golden Horde, The   (13th-15th centuries) The Mongol forces established in southeast Russia by Genghis Khan's grandson, Batu (Bator) Khan, which dominated east Russia and west-central Asia until overthrown by Ivan the Great, the first Russian Tsar. (Turkish *orda*, 'camp'; translation of the Mongol name for Batu's luxurious field headquarters; the word *horde* subsequently passed into the English language with the meaning of 'troop', 'rabble'.)

Golden Horn, The An arm of the Bosporus separating ISTANBUL proper from its northern suburbs of Galata and Pera.

Golden Horseshoe, The A nickname for the first 2 tiers of boxes in the old New York METROPOLITAN OPERA HOUSE. Later renamed The Diamond Horseshoe.

Golden Miller The Hon. Dorothy Paget's famous steeplechaser which won the CHELTENHAM GOLD CUP in 5 successive years (1932-36) and The GRAND NATIONAL in 1934.

Golden Rose, The (1961) An annual award at the Montreux International TV Light Entertainment Festival, held in April.

Golden Section The division of a line (or rectangle) so that the whole line bears the same ratio to the larger section as the larger to the smaller section. This aesthetically ideal proportion (equivalent approximately to 8:13) has been used extensively by artists and architects down the ages, consciously or unconsciously.

Golden Spike A national historic site at Promontory, northern Utah, where a gold spike was driven in 1869 to mark the linking of the tracks of the Central Pacific and Union Pacific railroads to form the first transcontinental railroad (San Francisco-New York).

Golden State Nickname of California. (Gold-producing state.)

Golden Stool, The The sacred symbol of the Ashanti of the Gold Coast (Ghana), ornamented with gold. After the ASHANTI WARS it was hidden from the British, but again displayed openly, with official approval, from 1935.

Golden Treasury, The (1861) Short title of Palgrave's anthology, *The Golden Treasury of the Best Songs and Lyrical Poems in the English Language*; a second volume was published in 1897.

Golden Triangle (1) Name given to the area in which the industries of northwest Europe are densely concentrated, in the triangle formed by Birmingham, Paris and the RUHR. (2) The business center of Pittsburgh, Pa., in the triangle formed by the Monongahela and Allegheny where they meet to become the Ohio River; it has a fine group of high-level office buildings and a small park, built on a site that was once a notorious slum.

Golden West A name for North Amerca given at the end of the 18th century when the limitless fields of (golden) grain there saved the Old World, which was suffering from an expansion of population unmatched by increase in food supplies.

Goldfine scandal (1958) The accusation that Sherman Adams, President Eisenhower's assistant, had accepted large sums from an industrialist. He denied that they were bribes, but resigned office.

Goldfinger, Auric A British-born SMERSH agent who, in Ian Fleming's *Goldfinger* (1959), organizes the leading US criminal gangs to loot FORT KNOX of all its gold.

Gold Glove Award An award for outstanding baseball fielding, made to 9 players in each major league on the basis of a poll among managers and coaches.

Gold Racquet The Martini & Rossi Tennis Player of the Year award to the lawn-tennis player adjudged the best in the world. See also MARTINI INTERNATIONAL CLUB.

Gold Record Award (1958) Awarded by the Record Industry Association of America to artists producing a record with sales topping $1 million (calculated at half the list price), or one selling over a million singles.

Gold Rush (1848) The rush which resulted from the discovery of gold at Sutter's sawmill in California (see SUTTER'S FEVER). By the end of 1849 the number of new prospectors (49ERS), from all over the world, reached 100,000 and continued to rise for the next 2 years.

Gold Rush, The (1924) A sentimental Chaplin silent film, chiefly remembered for the scene in which the comedian is reduced to cooking and eating a boot, the laces of which serve as *ersatz* spaghetti.

Gold Star Mother A member of the American Gold Star Mothers Inc. (1928), open to mothers of veterans who have died in service. They help disabled veterans and each other. (Mothers of those killed in war may display a gold star.)

Goldwater caper, The (1964) The phrase used in an American book for the unsuccessful candidacy in the Presidential elections of the Republican nominee, Barry Goldwater, in opposition to Lyndon Johnson. The phrase refers to the miscellaneous mutually contradictory but apparently extreme right-wing statements of policy he made which, coupled with his past voting record, were held to have damaged the Republican image.

Goldwynism A cross between an Irish bull and a Spoonerism, invented and exploited by the Hollywood producer Sam Goldwyn (e.g. 'include me out'; 'in two words: Impossible'.)

Golgotha CALVARY. (Aramaic word for 'skull', Latin *calvaria*.)

Goliards See ARCHPOET.

Goliath See DAVID.

Gollum A shapeless rubbery creature which trails the HOBBITS on their expeditions.

GOM Initials used for Grand Old Man, a name given by Lord Rosebery to Gladstone, who lived to be 89.

Gompelskirchner An Austrian semisweet light wine of fine quality.

Goncourt, The See PRIX GONCOURT.

Gondal See ANGRIA.

Gondoliere A summer express train from Munich to Venice (7½ hours).

Gondoliers, The (1889) A GILBERT AND SULLIVAN OPERA. One of 2 gondoliers is thought to be the rightful heir to the throne of Barataria who was betrothed in infancy to the Duke of PLAZA-TORO's daughter. As she does not want either of them, and as

they have just married, it is fortunate that a man she had already fallen in love with is finally identified as the true heir.

Gondwanaland Geologists' name for the southern supercontinent (once joined to LAURASIA) which, according to Wegener's continental drift theory (now generally accepted), split into South America, Africa, Australasia, India and Antarctica; they drifted in the SIMA to their present positions, piling up the Himalaya, Atlas and Andes mountains in the process.

Goneril One of the 2 evil daughters of KING LEAR, who poisons the other (Regan) and has her youngest sister, CORDELIA, hanged.

Gone with the Wind (1936) Margaret Michell's only work, a long historical novel of life in the southern states during and after the AMERICAN CIVIL WAR, made into a monumental movie (1939).

Goodbye to All That (1929) The poet Robert Graves's restrained autobiographical novel, generally regarded as the best British description of what life in the trenches during World War I was really like.

Good Companions, The (1929) J. B. Priestley's best-selling long novel in which various characters, led by Jess Oakroyd, break away from the increasingly somber world of mounting unemployment, tear up their National Insurance cards, and take to the road as a traveling concert party called The Good Companions.

Good Earth, The (1931) The most famous novel by the American NOBEL PRIZE winner, Pearl Buck. In the northern Chinese province of Anhwei, where the author had lived, the peasant Wang Lung, dedicated to farming, patiently invests his savings in land until he becomes a rich landowner and head of a great family. Success brings deterioration; Wang buys a second wife, which upsets his faithful first, and as he dies he overhears his sons planning to sell his land. There were 2 sequels.

Good Friday The Friday before Easter, commemorating the Crucifixion;

it is a legal holiday in some states of the US. ('Good' in the old sense of 'holy'.)

Good Joe   An obliging good-hearted person.

Good Neighbor Policy   In his first inaugural address in March 1933 President Roosevelt stated: In the field of world policy I would dedicate this nation to the policy of the good neighbor. Within a year he had recalled the US troops sent by Hoover to Nicaragua and Haiti and had made treaties with all Latin American republics renouncing further intervention.

Good Samaritan, The   The man of Samaria in the parable who succored the victim of thieves left half dead by the wayside, after a priest and a Levite had 'passed by on the other side'. (*Luke* x, 33.)

Good Soldier Schweik, The   (1923) A Czech 4-volume (unfinished) satire by Jaraslov Hasek recounting the misadventures of a simple Czech soldier serving in the Austrian army during World War I. The author had himself deserted to the Russians and then to the BOLSHEVIKS, so that Imperial Austria takes some hard knocks. See SCHWEIK IN THE SECOND WORLD WAR.

Good Templars   See TEMPLARS.

Good-time Charlie   Colloquialism for a happy-go-lucky person who regards having a good time as the prime object of life.

Goodwin, Archie   Nero WOLFE's likable assistant who in Rex Stout's detective stories does all the running about for his chair-bound chief.

Good Woman of Setzuan, The (1943) Brecht's play about the prostitute Shen Teh who opens a tobacco shop but is so generous that she soon fails. She then disguises herself as a man and, pretending to be a ruthless capitalist, does well.

Goodwood House   Home near Chichester of the dukes of Richmond and Gordon, designed by Wyatt in Sussex flint. In the grounds is the most attractive of English racetracks; there was also an auto racing circuit (1948-65).

Goodyear Tire & Rubber   The largest of the 3 rubber firms established at Akron, Ohio, in the 1890s; one of the 30 industrials that make up the DOW JONES Industrial Average.

Goonhilly   The British Post Office's satellite ground terminal station in Cornwall for receiving and transmitting signals by communications satellites. A second station (1968) made Goonhilly the center of Britain's TV and telephone traffic via satellites linking it to most parts of the world. (Goonhilly Downs, between Helston and the Lizard.)

Goop   An ill-behaved or disagreeable person, an epitome of horrid naughtiness; from the fantastic creatures invented by Gelett Burgess (1866-1951) and featured in his *Goops and How to Be Them* (1900). See PURPLE COW.

GOP   (1880) Initials for Grand Old Party, i.e. the REPUBLICAN PARTY.

Gopher State   A nickname of Minnesota, from the striped ground squirrel so called, still prevalent.

Gorbals, The   A formerly notorious slum area of Glasgow, now being rebuilt.

Gorboduc   (1562) A tragedy, written in blank verse by Thomas Sackville (Earl of Dorset) and Thomas Norton, based on a legend of fratricide and murder in the family of a British king.

Gordian knot   The intricate knot fastening yoke and pole of a wagon dedicated to ZEUS by Gordius, father of MIDAS. The legend grew that whoever untied it would inherit Asia. Alexander the Great cut it with his sword. Thus, to cut the Gordian knot came to mean to take a violent, drastic or unorthodox shortcut in resolving a problem or impasse.

Gordon Bennett Cup   (1899-1905) An international auto race for teams of 3 cars made entirely in the country entering them. The first races were won by PANHARD, NAPIER and MERCEDES. It was supplanted by the GRAND PRIX. (Presented by a US newspaper proprietor of that name.)

Gordon Riots   (1780) 'No Popery' riots in London fomented by a mad Protestant fanatic, Lord George Gordon, and suppressed by troops with considerable loss of life. Gordon was acquitted but other leaders were executed. The riots are described in Dickens's BARNABY RUDGE.

Gordonstoun   (1934) A boys' 'public' school near Elgin, Morayshire, Scotland, started by Kurt Hahn (see OUTWARD BOUND SCHOOLS), where the Duke of Edinburgh and the Prince of Wales were educated.

Goren system   A calling system at Bridge, with a forcing two bid as in the CULBERTSON SYSTEM. In hand valuation points are added for short suits and voids, instead of for length as in other systems.

Gorgons   In Greek legend, 3 sisters of horrific aspect, of whom the most famous was MEDUSA.

Gorgonzola   A semihard blue Lombardy cheese made from ewe's or whole cow's milk; the name is used also of inferior types resembling DANISH BLUE. (Once made at Gorgonzola, near Milan.)

Goschen   A name made familiar by Lord Randolph Churchill's note: 'All great men make mistakes. Napoleon forgot Blücher, I forgot Goschen'. Churchill resigned as Chancellor of the Exchequer in 1886, on the issue of the Defense Estimates, assuming that he would bring down the government; to his astonishment Goschen, though a Liberal, was appointed his successor in the Conservative Cabinet, and he himself faded from the political scene.

Goshen, Land of   Biblical name for Egypt east of the Nile, where the Israelites were allowed to settle, driven there by hunger (*Genesis* xlv, 10); a land of plenty and of light (*Exodus* x, 23), i.e. of tolerance.

Goss   Small porcelain ornaments made at Stoke on Trent by W. H. Goss from about 1860. They bore the arms of towns and were sold in thousands to Victorian holidaymakers.

Gotha   (1917) A German bomber used in air raids on England in World War I, the first purpose-built bombing plane.

Gotham   (1) A village near Nottingham, England, proverbial in the Middle Ages for the stupidity of its inhabitants; hence the 'three wise men of Gotham' in the nursery rhyme. (2) Washington Irving's name for New York, as a city of wiseacres.

Gothenburg   German name of the Swedish port of Göteborg.

Gothic architecture   (12th-16th centuries) The Western European style which succeeded ROMANESQUE ARCHITECTURE, characterized by the pointed arch (of Persian origin), soaring lines, loftiness and light rendered possible by cross-ribbed vaulting and the flying buttress. In England the successive phases were EARLY ENGLISH, DECORATED, and PERPENDICULAR; in France the final period was FLAMBOYANT. (Originally a term of disparagement, meaning non-Classical.)

Gothic Line   A German defensive line across Italy north of Florence; breached by the Allies, autumn 1944.

Gothic novels   Horror stories set in haunted Gothic castles, for which there was a craze in the 18th century. The genre was invented by Horace Walpole (see CASTLE OF OTRANTO) and parodied by Jane Austen in *Northanger Abbey*.

Gothic Revival, The   (1750) The revival of GOTHIC ARCHITECTURE in England, the fashion for which was started by STRAWBERRY HILL. Another example is the Houses of Parliament.

Goths   A Germanic race which, while in DACIA in the 4th century, split into OSTROGOTHS and VISIGOTHS.

Götterdämmerung   The Twilight of the Gods, the Ragnarok of Scandinavian mythology, when a struggle between the powers of good and evil (led by ODIN and LOKI) ends in universal destruction and chaos. A younger generation of gods survive to create a new universe and a new race of men.

Götterdämmerung   Title of the final opera in Wagner's RING OF THE NIBELUNGS.

Gouda A mild semi-hard cheese with a yellow rind; the whole cheese is round and flat. (Originally made at Gouda, Holland.)

Governor Winthrop desk A desk with an oxbow front and (usually) claw-and-ball feet. (Governor of Massachusetts Colony, died 1649.)

'Go West, young man, go West!' A phrase first used by J. B. L. Soule in the Terre Haute (Ind.) *Express* (1851) which was reprinted and given far wider currency by Horace Greeley in the New York *Tribune*.

GP (1) Initials standing for General Practitioner. (2) Film rating meaning 'all ages admitted – parental guidance suggested', under the Motion Picture Code for Self-Regulation.

GP 14 (1949) The *Yachting World* General Purpose 14-foot dinghy designed by Jack Holt and built in many places; a heavy one-design boat, not originally meant for racing, but now raced regularly almost everywhere in England.

GPU (1922-24) The Communist Russian secret police, formed primarily for state defense; successor to the CHEKA, and later renamed OGPU. (Initials of the Russian for 'State Political Organization'.)

Grace Abounding to the Chief of Sinners (1666) Bunyan's part fictional, part autobiographical confession, telling of a sinner's life and how he finds the 'miracle of precious Grace'.

Grace and Favour residences Houses and apartments in the gift of the Monarch, situated at WINDSOR CASTLE, the HAMPTON COURT, KENSINGTON and ST JAMES'S PALACES, and elsewhere.

Graces, The In Greek legend, Euphrosyne, Aglaia and THALIA, daughters of ZEUS, who lived with the Muses on Mount OLYMPUS, and bestowed the gifts of happiness, kindness and charm on mankind. With the increase in world population it has perhaps proved too heavy a task for a staff of three.

Gradgrind, Thomas The industrialist in Dickens's novel HARD TIMES, who is solely interested in Facts,

and the inadequacies of whose philosophy of life are pointed by the failure of his 2 children.

Graduate, The Charles Webb's novel from which a highly popular movie was made by Mike Nichols. It is a satirical comedy about Benjamin Braddock's experiences on leaving a leading US university.

Graduation Ball (1940) A ballet with music by Johann Strauss, choreography by David Lichine, set in a Viennese finishing school in the 1840s; the girls entertain the cadets from a neighboring academy, whose governor, the General, flirts with their headmistress.

Graf Spee German pocket battleship, blown up by her crew off Montevideo after the Battle of the RIVER PLATE.

Grafton Street Dublin's chief shopping street.

Graf Zeppelin (1) The first airship to operate on a transatlantic passenger service (1928-37). (2) A second airship, tested in 1938 but never put to commercial use because of World War II. (Named after Count Zeppelin, German airship pioneer, died 1917.)

Gramercy Park (1831) A very exclusive neighborhood in south-central Manhattan, between Fourth and Third Avenues, 20th and 22nd Streets. The houses surround the city's only surviving private park, the keys of which (originally golden!) are held by the residents. The PLAYERS CLUB is here.

Grammy A gold-plated miniature replica of an early gramophone awarded by the National Academy of Recording Arts and Sciences for the best efforts of recording artists and the recording industry.

Grampian (1961) (UK) The commercial TV company serving the eastern coastal regions of Scotland, financed by local shareholders.

Gram-positive, Gram-negative A classification of bacteria which aids in their identification. Gram's stain will stain some, e.g. *Staphylococcus* and *Streptococcus*, but not others, e.g. *Gonococcus*, typhus bacillus.

Gran Chaco War (1932-35) A war between Bolivia and Paraguay over a disputed boundary in the northern portion of the Gran Chaco region, settled by arbitration in 1938.

Gran Colombia (Greater Colombia) A short-lived union of Columbia, Venezuela and Ecuador formed by Simón Bolívar in 1819.

Grand, The (Henley) The GRAND CHALLENGE CUP.

Grand Alliance (1701) Formed by William III from members of the former League of AUGSBURG on the eve of the War of the SPANISH SUCCESSION and his own death. It included Britain, Austria, Holland, Denmark and Portugal, ranged against France, Spain and Bavaria.

Grand Banks The CONTINENTAL SHELF extending 350 miles off southeast Newfoundland, and the meeting place of the LABRADOR CURRENT and GULF STREAM, which together produce constant fogs but, more importantly, ideal conditions for plankton and hence for fish. These waters are therefore extensively fished by the trawler fleets of many nations, especially for cod.

Grand Canyon A gorge of the Colorado River in north Arizona, up to more than a mile deep, 4-18 miles wide, with fantastically eroded and colored rock masses giving a conspectus of geological time. Nearly half its length, which is well over 200 miles, lies in the Grand Canyon National Park (1919). PUEBLO INDIAN and CLIFF DWELLER ruins, motorboat trips along the river and mule rides down to it are among the attractions which make it the mecca of tourists from all over the world.

Grand Canyon State A nickname for Arizona.

Grand Canyon Suite A suite by the American composer Ferde Grofé, consisting of 5 movements: Sunrise, The Painted Desert, On the Trail, Sunset, Cloudburst.

Grand Central Station The terminal of the Penn Central (formerly the NY Central and the NY, New Haven and Hartford railroads), at Park Avenue and 42nd Street, NYC.

Grand Challenge Cup (1839) (Henley) The original HENLEY Regatta trophy, the open 8-oar event.

Grand Design (1962) President Kennedy's plan for an Atlantic association between the USA and some future United States of Europe, as 'partners of comparable magnitude'.

Grand Design, The (1947) The last of a trilogy of novels by John Dos Passos, published together as *District of Columbia*, the saga of the Spottswood family. It echoes the author's disillusion with Communism and attacks Roosevelt's policies, particularly his gift of Eastern Europe to Stalin after World War II.

Grande Armée, La Napoleon's army, particularly the force of some 400,000 with which he invaded Russia in 1812, two-thirds of them Germans, Austrians, Poles or Italians.

Grande Corniche The highest of the 3 mountain roads from Nice to Menton in the French Riviera. There are also a coastal Corniche and a Moyenne Corniche via Èze. (French, 'great cornice', which the mountain road resembles.)

Grand Fenwick A mythical duchy created by Leonard Wibberley in his rollicking satire The MOUSE THAT ROARED. It lies on the French border, and its size (15 square miles) and population (5808) are solemnly specified.

Grand Guignol What in the modern idiom might be termed the Theater of the Horror-comic—short eerie plays about ghosts, murder etc. The term was made familiar in Britain in the 1920s by a series of such plays starring Sybil Thorndike. (Guignol, chief character in a French version of the Punch and Judy show.)

Grand Inquisitor, The Legend of the The most famous chapter of The BROTHERS KARAMAZOV, reflecting Dostoievsky's own religious doubts. Ivan Karamazov tells his brother Alyosha of how Christ returns during the Inquisition at Seville and is arrested. The Grand Inquisitor tells him that the Church no longer wants him, that mankind needs leadership, not freedom which it is too weak and foolish to put to proper use. He opens the prison door; Christ, silent throughout, kisses his cheek and departs.

Grandma Moses Mrs Moses (1860-1961), American painter of Irish and Scottish descent, who did not begin to paint until she was nearly 70 and then produced famous 'primitives' of rural life in NEW ENGLAND, as she remembered it from her childhood days there.

Grand Marnier A French version of CURAÇAO.

Grand Monarque, Le Louis XIV.

Grand National, The (1839) The chief event of the British steeple-chasing year, run in March/April over a 4½-mile course with 30 fearsome fences, including BEECHER'S BROOK, which have to be jumped twice. Held at AINTREE, near Liverpool.

Grand Ole Opry The humorous title of a long-lived radio and television program of country and western music that is broadcast from Nashville, Tenn. It is famous for its colorful personalities and uninhibited performances.

Grand Prix de Paris The French equivalent of the DERBY, run at LONGCHAMP in June over a course one furlong longer (i.e. 13 furlongs).

Grand Prix races The 13 races for single-seater FORMULA 1 cars, held annually in 13 countries, in which points gained count towards the world championship for drivers.

Grand Remonstrance (1641) A resolution presented by John Pym condemning Charles I's policies and demanding Church reform, carried by a narrow majority in the LONG PARLIAMENT.

Grand Siècle, Le The reign of Louis XIV. (French, 'the great age'.)

Grandsire One of the principal methods of ringing changes on church bells.

Grand Tetons A range of mountains in northwest Wyoming, part included in the Grand Teton National Park (1929), with imposing peaks up to 13,766 ft (Grand Teton). (French té-

ton, 'teat'; once translated in politer days as 'Sweater-girl Mountains'.)

Grand Tour In the 18th century, part of the education of every young Englishman whose parents could afford it, a tour of the main artistic centers of Europe, especially France and Italy. Memorials to this custom remain in the names of hotels, e.g. Bristol, Carlton etc.

Grand Trianon (1687) A palace built at Versailles for Louis XIV by Mansart, allowed to go to ruin in the mid 19th century. Now rebuilt as a great new showplace, where visiting heads of state can reside.

Grand Trunk Railway A railroad linking Sarnia (Lake Huron) via Toronto and Montreal to Portland, Me., built in the 1850s. Faced with bankruptcy by CANADIAN PACIFIC RAILWAY competition, the company built the Grand Trunk Pacific (1914) over the ROCKY MOUNTAINS (Winnipeg-Prince Rupert); both lines were absorbed by the CANADIAN NATIONAL RAILWAYS.

Grand Trunk Road A highway across India, begun by the MOGULS and developed under the British regime to link the North-West Frontier Province with Calcutta via Delhi and Allahabad.

Grange, The (1867) An association, originally secret, formed to protect farmers' interests in the western states. Officially known as the National Grange, its campaigns to break monopolies, bypass middlemen by cooperative trading, force railroad and grain elevator owners to reduce charges etc., made it into a powerful national pressure group, and led to 'Granger' laws in the west regulating transportation rates (which the Supreme Court approved in 1877 and emasculated in 1886). The Grange was one element in the POPULIST PARTY.

Granicus (334 BC) The first of the 3 battles in which Alexander the Great defeated the Persians. (River of northwest ANATOLIA, near the Dardanelles.)

Granite State Nickname of New Hampshire.

Granny A mixture of old and mild beer.

Granny Smith A large, hard, green apple of excellent flavor imported into Britain from various parts of the world over much of the year. (Originated when Maria Ann Smith of New South Wales planted seeds from rotting apples found in a gin barrel, 1869.)

Granta (1889) A CAMBRIDGE UNIVERSITY undergraduate humorous magazine. (The name borne by the River Cam south of the town.)

Grantchester A village near Cambridge especially remembered for Rupert Brooke's poem, 'The Old Vicarage, Grantchester' (1912), written with nostalgic playfulness in a Berlin café. Its most famous lines are: Stands the Church clock at ten to three? / And is there honey still for tea?

Granth The sacred book of the SIKHS, the first part written by the founder of their religion.

Grantly, Archdeacon In Trollope's BARCHESTER NOVELS, the dynamic and not overtly spiritual Archdeacon of Barchester who marries the WARDEN'S daughter, and has no doubts about the Church's rightful place in the community.

Grant's Tomb A Roman-style mausoleum on RIVERSIDE DRIVE, NYC, where General Ulysses S. Grant, 18th US President, lies buried; now a national monument.

Grapes of Wrath, The (1939) John Steinbeck's saga of the Joad family, driven from the DUST BOWL of Oklahoma to California in search of work as fruit pickers. See OKIE.

Grasshopper A cocktail made with white crème de cacao, light cream, and green crème de menthe.

Grauman's Chinese Theater A Hollywood theater once famous for the footprints of movie stars imprinted in concrete in its forecourt, many now lost to view.

Graustark (1901) A romantic first novel by George Barr McCutcheon; subtitled *The Story of a Love Behind the Throne*, it is about a princess in a RURITANIA called Graustark who falls in love with an American.

There were 2 sequels.

Graves (1) Medium-sweet white BORDEAUX WINE, notably Château Carbonnieux; (2) claret, notably Château Haut-Brion.

Gray Lady A volunteer nonprofessional worker for the American RED CROSS. (From the uniform worn.)

Gray's Anatomy The standard textbook on human anatomy, by Henry Gray, now in its 30th edition.

Gray's Elegy (1750) Thomas Gray's *Elegy Written in a Country Church Yard*, traditionally written in a tree (still standing) by the church door at Stoke Poges (near Slough). Deliberately using the simplest, shortest words, not one of them otiose, he managed to pack into a brief poem a wealth of meditative reflection on mortality and a moving evocation of English peasant life; almost every line is quotable, and quoted, from the first (The Curfew tolls the knell of parting day) to the last (And Melancholy mark'd him for her own).

Gray's Inn (UK) The youngest of the INNS OF COURT, attended particularly by provincial barristers.

Great Assize The Day of Judgment.

Great Bear Ursa Major, the large northern constellation that contains the BIG DIPPER. The alpha and beta stars are the Pointers, pointing to the NORTH STAR.

Great Bible, The (1539) The revised edition of COVERDALE'S BIBLE commissioned by Thomas Cromwell, and reissued the following year with a preface by Archbishop Cranmer ('Cranmer's Bible').

Great Bonanza, The A name for the COMSTOCK LODE.

Great Britain See ACTS OF UNION.

Great Cham of Literature Nickname for Dr Samuel Johnson, coined by Smollett. (Cham, old French translation of Khan, i.e. ruler of the Tartars and Mongols, and emperor of China.)

Great Commoner, The The Elder Pitt, Earl of Chatham.

Great Depression, The See DEPRESSION, THE.

Great Divide (1) The watershed of the ROCKY MOUNTAINS in North America; (2) Death.

Great Eastern, The (1856) The largest steamship of its day, a 12,000-tonner designed by I. K. Brunel for the transatlantic run.

Great Elector Frederick William, Elector of Brandenburg (1620-88), who first made Brandenburg-Prussia a powerful state.

Great Emancipator, The A name for Abraham Lincoln, referring to his EMANCIPATION PROCLAMATION.

Greater East Asia Co-Prosperity Sphere The Japanese program announced (1940) by the prime minister, Prince Konoye, inspired by Hitler's NEW ORDER IN EUROPE and the TANAKA MEMORIAL. Under Japan's leadership the industrial areas of China, Manchuria and Korea (with Japan) were to be developed, fed with raw materials from the adjacent territories of Netherlands East Indies, FRENCH INDO-CHINA, Malaya, Burma and the Philippines, from which Japan would eject the Western Powers.

Greater London A local government area defined under the London Government Act (1963) and consisting of the former counties of London and Middlesex, and parts of metropolitan Essex, Kent, Surrey and Hertfordshire. It is divided into 32 London boroughs and the City of London; area 620 sq. m., population (1965) 8 million.

Great Exhibition, The (1851) (UK) The first industrial exhibition, promoted by Prince Albert and held in HYDE PARK in the CRYSTAL PALACE.

Great Expectations (1861) One of the best of Dickens's novels, in which the village boy Pip gets ideas above his station; cheated of his great expectations in London, he returns to his village friends and eventually marries the woman he loves.

Great Fire of London (1666) A fire which destroyed more than half the City of London, including Old St Paul's. See The CITY.

Great Gatsby, The (1925) Scott Fitzgerald's only great novel, a fable of the American JAZZ AGE. Jay Gatsby dreams only of winning back his early love, Daisy, now married to another. He has made a fortune dishonestly, solely to dazzle her with riches, but fails. He shields Daisy who, driving his car, unknowingly kills her husband's mistress, Myrtle. Myrtle's husband, wrongly supposing that Gatsby has seduced and killed her, shoots him. Of the hordes of people he had so lavishly entertained at his luxury home, only one turns up for his funeral, together with Gatsby's humble father (Gatz) and the narrator, Daisy's cousin.

Great George Street (London) The site of the 'New Public Offices' (1908) at the bottom of WHITEHALL, which house the Cabinet Office, the Treasury and part of the Ministry of Defense.

Great Harry (1540) The first battleship, a 3-master of 1000 tons re-equipped after a fire with 2 tiers of guns. (Her official name was *Henry Grâce à Dieu*, named after Henry VIII.)

Greatheart, Mr A character in Part II of PILGRIM'S PROGRESS who is appointed guide to Christian's wife and children on their pilgrimage.

Great Illusion, The (1910) Sir Norman Angell's book on the futility of war, for victor and vanquished.

Great Khan Title of the Mongol rulers of China.

Great Leap Forward (1958-59) Chinese name for Mao Tse-tung's program for a national effort to double China's productivity in agriculture and industry, and for the introduction of the commune system of self-contained rural units in which workers are housed and fed by the state. Its lack of success was attributed to 2 bad harvests and the withdrawal of Soviet technical assistance.

Great Mogul, The The MOGUL Emperor.

Great Mother See CYBELE.

Great Plague (1665) The last serious outbreak of bubonic plague in Britain, said to have killed one eighth of the population.

Great Plains The semiarid region in Canada and USA east of the ROCKY MOUNTAINS.

Great Pyramid of Cheops See GIZA.

Great Rebellion, The Another name for the ENGLISH CIVIL WAR.

Great Rift Valley A deep valley, caused by faults in the earth's crust. running from Syria through the Dead Sea and Red Sea to Lake Rudolf and there dividing into two, one valley continuing through Lake Albert to Lake Tanganyika, the other extending to Lake Nyasa.

Greats Final BA examination at OXFORD UNIVERSITY, especially for honors in LIT. HUM.; ses also MODERN GREATS.

Great Salt Lake The large but shallow lake in Utah, almost 25% salt, in which few things can live; this salinity is maintained by a high rate of evaporation in the face of the continued inflow of the large rivers that feed it.

Great Schism (1) The period 1378-1417 after the AVIGNONESE CAPTIVITY, when French efforts to maintain dominance over the Papacy led to a split in Western Christendom, with rival Popes ruling in Rome and in Avignon. (2) Less often used of the final break between the Western Church and the EASTERN ORTHODOX CHURCH (1054).

Great Smokies The highest range east of the Black Hills (Clingman's Dome, 6642 ft) and one of the oldest land areas on earth, partly in the Great Smoky Mountains National Park (1930) in western North Carolina and east Tennessee. Red spruce covers the summits and the flora is spectacular. The name comes from the blue smoky haze prevalent in the region. This was CHEROKEE country.

Great Society, The (1964) President Johnson's name for his proposed program of social reform and racial toleration, which was hampered by Congressional opposition and preoccupation with VIETNAM and the space race with Russia. Compare NEW FRONTIER.

Great Stone Face See OLD MAN OF THE MOUNTAIN (2).

Great Tom The bell of Christ Church, Oxford; see TOM TOWER.

Great Train Robbery (1963) See BUCKINGHAMSHIRE TRAIN ROBBERY.

Great Train Robbery, The (1903) The first successful one-reel narrative film, made by Edwin Porter, which marked the transformation of the cinema from a music-hall act to an entertainment in its own right.

Great Trek, The See VOORTREKKERS.

Great Wall of China A defensive wall along the old Chinese border with Manchuria and Mongolia; the first section was completed in the 3rd century BC, but later greatly extended until it was 1400 miles long. Restored under the Communist regime, it starts from the coast north of Tientsin, passes north of Peking and reaches almost to the border of Sinkiang.

Great Wen, The William Cobbett's name for London.

Great White Hope, The (1967) A powerful chronicle play by Howard Sackler based on the life of Jack Johnson, the first American Negro world heavyweight champion (1908-15).

Great White Way See BROADWAY.

Grecian Urn, Ode on a (1820) Keats's poem on the theme 'Beauty is truth, truth beauty' in which he contrasts, through the description of a Greek vase, the evanescence of mortal life and the timelessness of art.

Greco-Roman style (Wrestling) A style popular on the Continent, in which tripping and holds below the waist are barred.

Grecque Cooking term, usually indicating that the dish is fried in oil.

'Greek' Something not understandable, as in the phrase 'it's all Greek to me'. (From *Julius Caesar*, Act 1, ii, where Casca says: For mine own part, it was all Greek to me.)

Greek Anthology, The A collection of several thousand short poems covering about 17 centuries from the 7th century BC, which grew from earlier collections. The manuscript was not discovered until the 17th century.

Greek calends A phrase meaning 'never'. (Calends, first day of the month in the Roman calendar; there were no Greek calends.)

Greek Church Incorrect term for the EASTERN ORTHODOX CHURCH.

Greek fire An early form of flame-thrower used against the Arabs who attacked Byzantium in the 7th century AD.

Greek War of Independence (1821) A long struggle which began with revolts in the Peloponnese against the Turks, and in 1829 won the independence of mainland Greece south of Thessaly, thereafter ruled by a succession of foreign kings. The Ionian Islands, Thessaly, Crete, MACEDONIA and Thrace were all added by 1913.

Greenaway (Kate) Medal (UK) The Library Association's annual award for the most distinguished work in illustrating children's books. See KATE GREENAWAY.

Green Belt A device to contain urban sprawl; a wide belt of countryside round a city is designated as an area in which all building development is under strict control, although permission is often granted for 'infilling', i.e. putting up new buildings in among existing ones, a relaxation sometimes abused.

Green Berets (1952) Nickname of the US Special Forces trained to fight guerrillas, e.g. in VIETNAM, Bolivia. Their specialties include parachuting, radio, demolition and languages.

Green Mountain Boys (1) Vermonters who formed a militia in 1764 and played a prominent part in the early stages of the AMERICAN WAR OF INDEPENDENCE. (2) Any inhabitants of Vermont (see next entry).

Green Mountain State Nickname of Vermont. (After the Green Mountains, clothed with evergreen forest.)

Green Pastures, The (1930) A fantasy play for a Negro cast written by Marc Connelly from sketches in Roark Bradford's *Ol' Man Adam an' His Chillun* (1928), with Old Testament stories as amusingly adapted by a Negro preacher to the understanding of his congregation. The play won a PULITZER PRIZE.

Green Room Club (1877) A London club in Adam Street for stage professionals. (The Green Room was formerly the name given to a rest room for actors when not on stage; term now used for 'backstage' as in 'greenroom gossip'; the first such room, at Drury Lane, was decorated in green.)

'Greensleeves' (1584) An Elizabethan ballad and air, described as 'a new courtly sonnet of the Lady Greensleeves', which quickly became popular and is mentioned by Shakespeare.

Greenwich Inner London borough since 1965 consisting of those parts of the former metropolitan boroughs of Greenwich and Woolwich that lie south of the Thames.

Greenwich Village (The Village) An area of New York City west of WASHINGTON SQUARE, once the haunt of artists and writers.

Gregorian Calendar See NEW STYLE. (Introduced by Pope Gregory XIII in 1582.)

Gregorian chant A form of plainsong dating from the 6th century and still used in Roman Catholic and ANGLICAN (HIGH CHURCH) services. The music is sung in unison, unaccompanied, with the great freedom of rhythm also found in the Anglican chant used in singing psalms in English. (Named after Pope Gregory the Great.)

Grenadier Guards (1685) Ranks as the first regiment of the British Army, although the ROYAL SCOTS and the COLDSTREAM GUARDS are older units. They wear their buttons set singly, and a white plume. See BRIGADE OF GUARDS.

Gresham's Law (1558) That bad money tends to drive good out of circulation; e.g. if the gold content of the sovereign is reduced, the old coinage will be hoarded. (Attributed to Sir Thomas Gresham, but formulated first by Copernicus.)

Gretchen (In *Faust*) See MARGARET.

Gretna Green A village just over the Scottish border from Carlisle, favored by English runaway couples wanting to take advantage of the Scottish law that parental consent is not required after 16 and the form of legal marriage (made illegal in 1939) by simple declaration of intent before witnesses, without banns, clergy or special license. The village blacksmith used to augment his income by acting as witness, until 1939. Since 1856 it has been necessary for one party to have resided in Scotland for 21 days.

Gretna Green disaster (1915) One of the worst disasters in British railroad history, involving 2 passenger trains and a troop train during World War I; 227 people were killed. See GRETNA GREEN.

Greville Memoirs, The Three volumes of political memoirs covering the period 1817-60, written by Charles Greville and published posthumously at various dates but not in their complete form until 1938. They throw much light on the events and personalities of his times.

Grey Cup (Canada) A trophy fought for by professional football teams, a major sporting event in Canada.

Grey Friars See FRANCISCANS.

Greyhound buses Long-distance coaches providing swift, cheap travel over much of the US.

Greyhound Derby (1927) The culminating event of the dog-track season, held towards the end of June at the White City, London.

Gridiron Club The Press club in Washington, D.C.

Griffon Bruxellois A reddish-brown toy dog developed from a large terrier breed; also called the Brussels griffon.

Grimaldi, House of The ruling dynasty of the principality of Monaco since the Middle Ages; Prince Rainier III, who succeeded to the title in 1949, is the 30th of the line.

Grimalkin An old cat, especially a witch's familiar; a spiteful old woman. (From gray + Malkin, old diminutive of Matilda.)

Grimes, Capt. The seedy prep school master of Evelyn Waugh's DECLINE AND FALL who explains that he is always 'in the soup' but survives through the glamour conferred by a year or so at Harrow (before his expulsion), and his aritficial leg (he was run over by a Stoke on Trent

tram when drunk) which people assumed to be the reason for his brief war service (ended by court-martial).

Grime's Graves A 4000-year-old flint mine, still worked today, near Brandon, Norfolk, England.

Grimm's Law (1822) The law of regular consonantal changes from one INDO-EUROPEAN LANGUAGE to another. To take 2 examples: English brother (ten), in Sanskrit bhrator (dasa), Greek phrater (deka), Latin frater (decem), German Bruder (zehn). (Formulated by Jacob Grimm, one of the 2 brothers who wrote Grimm's Fairy Tales.)

Griselda (Grisel, Griseldis etc.) The patient, faithful wife in a tale told by Boccaccio and by Chaucer in the Clerk's Tale, among others.

Grock Stage name of the famous Swiss clown Adrien Wettach, who died in 1959.

'Gross Clinic, The' (1875) Probably the best of the paintings by Thomas Eakins, showing an operation in progress; Eakins had gone to the Jefferson Medical College, Philadelphia, to improve his knowledge of anatomy, and there the picture now hangs.

Gross National Product The market value of a nation's total output of goods and services in a given year and also comprising the total of expenditures by consumers and government plus gross private investment.

Grosvenor Square See LITTLE AMERICA.

Gros Ventre A name given to 2 Indian tribes, neither of them fat-bellied: (1) a Siouan tribe of Missouri, now settled in North Dakota; (2) a splinter group of ARAPAHO, in Montana. (Name apparently arose from a misunderstanding.)

Groundhog Day February 2nd, CANDLEMAS Day, from the tradition that if the groundhog (woodchuck) emerges from hibernation on that day and can see his shadow he will return to his burrow as another 6 weeks of winter is still to come. It derives from an English tradition that a fine Candlemas means more winter; in German lore the badger takes the place of the groundhog.

Group Areas Act (1950) The South African Act which provided for the residential segregation of Whites, Indians, CAPE COLOUREDS and BANTU, a major APARTHEID measure.

Group of Seven Canadian artists, a group chiefly in the sense that they held joint exhibitions (1920-33), who traveled into the heart of Canada to paint bold and distinctive landscapes; some of them were also commissioned to paint scenes of World War I. The leading members were J. E. H. MacDonald, A.Y. Jackson and Lawrens Harris.

Group of Ten USA, UK, Canada, France, West Germany, Holland, Belgium, Italy, Sweden and Japan who, after Britain's 1961 balance of payments crisis, agreed to pay extra quotas to the INTERNATIONAL MONETARY FUND as and when required, in order to increase its lending resources. Switzerland is an associate member. Also called the GAB (General Agreements to Borrow), the Club of Ten, and the Paris Club.

Grove Short title for Sir George Grove's *Dictionary of Music and Musicians* (1878-89, with subsequent revisions), still a standard work of reference on the subject.

GRS (1969) Initials standing for German Research Satellite, West Germany's first satellite, launched in California to study radiation belts and auroras.

GRU Chief Soviet army intelligence organization, working under the KGB. It carries out subversion abroad, the breaking down of foreign ciphers, and frontier operations.

Grub Street A term of disparagement applied to literary hackwork of poor quality. (Former name of Milton Street, Moorfields, London, where such work was produced in the 17th century.)

Gruyère A mild hard-pressed cheese characterized by holes smaller than those in EMMENTALER. (Originally made at Gruyères, Switzerland.)

G suit Jet pilot's tight-fitting inflatable suit designed to counteract the physical effects of acceleration due to gravity (G) in high-speed maneuvers, thus preventing blackouts.

GT car Abbreviation commonly used for Grand Touring Car, a production car (i.e. not designed primarily for racing) built in limited numbers with high standards of performance and/or comfort. Special races are held for cars of this category.

Guadalcanal, Battle of (Nov. 1942) A series of naval actions ending in US victory over the Japanese fleet in the Solomon Islands.

Guantánamo The US naval base in Cuba.

Guarnerius Name given to violins second only to the STRADIVARIUS and like them made in Cremona. They were the work of the last great Italian family of violin makers, led by Giuseppe (1698-1744), and were notable for sonority but less mellow and more crudely finished than Strads. Nevertheless, some virtuosi have preferred them.

Gudrun The counterpart in Scandinavian mythology to KRIEMHILD.

Guelph The family name of the Elector of Hanover who became George I of England, and of his successors of the House of Hanover. See next entry; see WETTIN.

Guelphs and Ghibellines (1) In 12th-century Germany the supporters respectively of the Dukes of Bavaria and the HOHENSTAUFENS in their struggle for the imperial throne. (2) In medieval Italy the name was adopted by those who supported the Pope and the Emperor, respectively. (Guelph was a family name; Ghibelline derives from the name of a Hohenstaufen estate.)

Guermantes The representatives of the highest Parisian society in Proust's REMEMBRANCE OF THINGS PAST, the duchess being related to several European royal families. In the course of the novel both the despised Mme VERDURIN and GILBERTE marry into the family.

Guernica (Apr. 1937) Ancient capital of the BASQUES in northern Spain, completely destroyed by German planes in the service of Franco dur-

ing the SPANISH CIVIL WAR; a quarter
of the population of this undefended
little township were killed.

'Guernica' (1937) Picasso's famous
painting, made immediately after
the event, symbolizing the horrors of
the purposeless destruction of GUER-
NICA. Now in the Museum of Modern
Art, NYC.

Guernsey cattle A dairy breed,
larger than the Jersey, producing
high-quality yellow milk; fawn,
sometimes with white markings.

Guernsey Lily The most beautiful
species of the Nerine lilies, a South
African bulbous plant which can be
cultivated out-of-doors in the Channel Islands but not in England.

**Guggenheim (John Simon) Memorial
Foundation** (1925) A foundation
that awards fellowships to assist
advanced workers in all fields (including art) to carry on research in
the freest possible conditions.

Guggenheim Museum New York
City's Museum of Nonobjective
Art, designed by Frank Lloyd Wright
on novel lines, access to exhibits
being by a continuous spiral ramp.

Guildenstern See ROSENCRANTZ AND
GUILDENSTERN.

Guildhall (1411) The "town hall' of
the CITY of London, off CHEAPSIDE.
Badly damaged in World War II, the
Great Hall where City banquets are
held has been restored. There is also
a large library and an art gallery.

Guild Socialism (1906) A form of
Socialism in which industries
would be run by their trade unions
reorganized on the lines of medieval
guilds; it rejected nationalization by
the State. The idea was first put forward by A. J. Penty, and then modified by S. G. Hobson and A. R. Orage.

Guillotine, The (1887) A Parliamentary device to expedite consideration of a long, complicated or hotly
disputed Bill; a time limit for debate
on each clause is enforced.

Guineas, The Common abbreviation
for the TWO THOUSAND GUINEAS.

Guinevere King ARTHUR's wife, who
fell in love with LANCELOT.

Guinness (1799) The Irish stout
firm, which also produces Harp la-

ger, Callard & Bowser butterscotch,
and tinned Irish salmon.

Guise, House of A French Catholic
family prominent in the 16th-centu-
ry religious wars and largely responsible for the ST BARTHOLOMEW MASSA-
CRE. See HOLY LEAGUE.

Gujarat (1960) An Indian State
formed from the northern districts of
BOMBAY STATE, with its capital
at Ahmadabad pending the building
of a new one at Gandhinagar.

Gujarati An INDO-EUROPEAN LAN-
GUAGE spoken by the majority of the
inhabitants of GUJARAT, India.

Gulbenkian Foundation (1955) An
international foundation which provides funds for charity and to
foster art, science and education. In
1969 it opened a large cultural center and headquarters in Lisbon. (Cal-
ouste Gulbenkian, Armenian financier.)

Gulf Stream A warm ocean current
which flows north from the Gulf of
Mexico up the east coast of North
America, meets the LABRADOR CUR-
RENT off Newfoundland and then
flows northeast to warm the climate
of Western Europe and especially of
the British Isles. See GRAND BANKS.

'Gulf Stream, The' (1899) Possibly
the greatest of the dramatic sea-
scapes painted by Winslow Homer
after he settled on the Maine coast.
(Metropolitan Museum of Art, NYC.)

Gullible's Travels (1917) Satiric
tales about the newly rich, by Ring
Lardner.

Gulliver's Travels (1726) Jonathan
Swift's great satire on mankind, in
the form of a journal kept by Lem-
uel Gulliver, a ship's doctor. See
LILLIPUT; LAPUTA; BROBDINGNAG;
HOUYHNHNMS; YAHOOS.

GUM Moscow's chief department
store, state-owned.

Gummidge, Mrs A self-pitying widow who keeps house for Daniel Peggotty in DAVID COPPERFIELD; 'every-
think goes contrariy with me'.

Gumps, The (1919) The first syndicated comic strip, begun by Sidney
Smith and continued (1947) by Gus
Edison, who raised the social status
of the jawless Andy Gump in a ma-

terialistic world where ideals are at a discount. Much use is made of soliloquy.

Gunbatsu The military caste of Japan which led it into World War II.

'Gunga Din' Kipling's poem in BARRACK-ROOM BALLADS about an Indian soldier, ending with the often quoted line: You're a better man than I am, Gunga Din!

Gunn, Martha A bathing attendant at Brighton said to have given the infant Prince of Wales (George IV) his first dip in the sea; her name is perpetuated in 'female TOBY' jugs.

Gunnar The counterpart in Scandinavian mythology to GUNTHER.

Gunpowder Plot (1605) A Roman Catholic plot to kill James I at the State Opening of Parliament on Nov. 5th by exploding barrels of gunpowder in the vaults. Guy Fawkes, found in the vaults, was tortured to betray the chief plotters, and executed with them.

Gunther In the NIBELUNGENLIED, King of Burgundy, husband of BRUNHILD and brother of KRIEMHILD.

Gupta dynasty (AD 320-647) Indian rulers who united northern India and revived HINDUISM, which in time absorbed the Buddhist religion; literature and the arts flourished under this patronage.

Gurdjieff's teachings A body of esoteric knowledge which, it is said, the Armenian Greek Gurdjieff was sent to the West by the SUFIS to impart as an experiment. Gurdjieff, a bizarre figure who wrote bizarre books, provided the mysticism, Ouspensky the brains, and intellectuals of Britain, France and USA the money. After his death the movement dissolved into dissentient sects. See CHÂTEAU DU PRIEURÉ.

Gurkhas The ruling race of Nepal, a MONGOLOID mountain people of Hindu religion who since 1815 have provided the British Army with soldiers renowned for loyalty and courage, now formed into the Brigade of Gurkhas.

GUS A shop and mail-order empire built up by Sir Isaac Wolfson, with headquarters in London and Man-

chester. It now includes Waring & Gillow, Global Tours and a merchant bank. (Initials of Great Universal Stores.)

Gussies Stock Exchange name for shares in GUS.

Gustav Line A German defense line across Italy, between Naples and Rome, with MONTE CASSINO as its central feature; breached May 1944.

Gutenberg Bible, The (1456) The first Bible printed from movable type, at Mainz, perhaps by Gutenberg. An edition of the VULGATE, it was discovered in 1760 in the Mazarin Library, Paris (and therefore sometimes called the Mazarin Bible); it is also known as the '42-line Bible', having 42 lines to the page. See HUNTINGTON LIBRARY.

Gutenberg Galaxy, The See MCLUHANISM.

Guy Fawkes plot See GUNPOWDER PLOT.

Guy Mannering (1815) Walter Scott's 18th-century novel about a child heir, Harry Bertram, smuggled out of the country by a lawyer who covets his estate. He joins the army in India, ignorant of his real name and parentage, but after many adventures returns to claim his inheritance. Meg MERRILIES and Dandy DINMONT appear in this book.

Guy's (1721) A teaching hospital near London Bridge station. (Founded by Thomas Guy, bookseller and a governor of St Thomas's Hospital.)

Guys and Dolls (1950) A long-run musical based on the most famous of Damon Runyon's books of short stories (1932), with music and lyrics by Frank Loesser and book by Jo Swerling and Abe Burrows. The characters are tough Broadway citizens cast in the celebrated Runyon mold.

GWR Initials of the Great Western Railway, with London headquarters at Paddington. It is now the Western Region of British Railways.

Gymnosperms The conifers, as opposed to the flowering ANGIOSPERMS.

Gypsies Nomadic people, probably from northwest India, who spread to ANATOLIA and North Africa (7th century BC) and from there into Europe; another stream went to Russia. Basically horse copers, tinkers and fortune-tellers (a craft they claim to have learned from the CHALDEANS). See ATHINGANOI. (English name, derived from *Egypt*, one of the many lands where they dwelt.)

Gypsy Moth   See GIPSY MOTH.

H

Habeas Corpus Act (1679) Shaftesbury's Act to abolish arbitrary imprisonment, which provided that every prisoner must be brought before a court within a specified time; passed in the reign of Charles II after the POPISH PLOT. From the first words of the writ: (I hear) that you have the body.

Habitation, The (1605) The first known settlement of white men north of the Gulf of Mexico, founded by De Monts and Samuel de Champlain, at Port Royal (renamed Annapolis Royal), NS. A replica has been reconstructed on its original site principally from Champlain's engravings and descriptions.

Habsburg More correct but less usual spelling of HAPSBURG.

Hackney Inner London borough since 1965 consisting of the former metropolitan boroughs of Hackney, Shoreditch and Stoke Newington.

Hadassah (1912) The Women's Zionist Organization of America, the world's largest Zionist group, founded in Baltimore, Md., by Henrietta Szoll. It made major contributions to the welfare of Palestine, and later of Israel.

Haddingtonshire Alternative name for East Lothian, Scotland.

Haddon Hall The best surviving example of a medieval manor house, situated near Bakewell, Derbyshire; it passed to the Earls (later Dukes) of Rutland through the elopement of Dorothy Vernon with Sir John Manners in the 16th century.

Hades (1) Greek god of the Underworld. The Latin name was Dis, but the Romans tended to prefer the alternative Greek name of Pluto. (2) The Underworld itself. (3) Hell (from its use to translate the Biblical Hebrew name *Sheol*, 'abode of the dead').

Hadith Oral traditions of the sayings and acts of the Prophet Muhammad, of varying authenticity, not committed to writing until 300 years after his death. Some of them are demonstrably spurious late additions.

Hadrian's Wall (AD 122-29) The Roman wall in northern England, built from Bowness to Wallsend across the isthmus between the Tyne and Solway Firth.

Haganah Jewish underground force in Palestine which from Turkish times protected Jewish settlers. It offered only passive resistance to British mandatory rule, and condemned terrorist tactics. It later became the nucleus of the Israeli army. (Hebrew, 'defense'.)

Hagar Sarah's servant, who bore ISHMAEL to ABRAHAM; after Sarah had given birth to Isaac, she persuaded Abraham to drive out Ishmael and his mother into the wilderness (*Genesis* xxi, 14).

Hagen In the NIBELUNGENLIED a henchman of GUNTHER who kills SIEGFRIED, seizes KRIEMHILD's gold and buries it in the Rhine. He refuses to reveal where it is hidden and is killed by KRIEMHILD.

Hagerstown Almanac One of the old American almanacs, published at Hagerstown, Md.

Hague Conferences First (1899), called by the Tsar, originally to discuss limitation of armaments; it set up a Permanent Court of Arbitration at The Hague (the Hague Tribunal). *Second* (1907), made rules against the use in war of dumdum (expanding) bullets, suffocating gases and missiles thrown from balloons.

Hague Court, The (1) The Permanent Court of International Justice of the LEAGUE OF NATIONS (1922-45). (2) The INTERNATIONAL COURT OF JUSTICE (1946), the principal judicial organ of the United Nations.

Hague Tribunal See HAGUE CONFERENCE (1899).

Haidée In Byron's DON JUAN, the lovely Greek girl who saves the hero from death. They are caught together by her pirate father, who sends him to slavery; she goes mad and dies.

Haigh murder case (1949) (UK) The trial of J. G. Haigh, executed after being found guilty of murdering a woman and disposing of her body by rendering it down in an acid bath. In the period 1944-49 he treated 5 other women in the same way.

Haight-Ashbury A sleazy section of San Francisco, long frequented by hippies and now a center for the underworld, where runaway youngsters take refuge.

Hail and Farewell (1911-14) George Moore's 3-volume autobiography.

'Hail Columbia!' (1798) The first national anthem of the USA, since superseded.

'Hail, Hail, the Gang's All Here!' (1917) A popular song with words by Teddy Morse (under his name spelled backwards—Esrom) to the tune of 'The Pirates' Chorus' in Gilbert and Sullivan's PIRATES OF PENZANCE—itself a parody of Verdi's 'Anvil Chorus'.

Hail Mary English for AVE MARIA.

Hair (1968) A rock musical, written by Gerome Ragni and James Rado, with music by Galt MacDermot. A staccato plotless gesture of youthful defiance, with the cast rampaging round the auditorium, it was chiefly noticed for the moment when, barely visible in the encircling gloom, they stripped to the buff and plunged under a communal blanket symbolic of racial and social equality.

Haj, Haji, Alhaji Title assumed by a MUSLIM who has made the pilgrimage to Mecca.

Hajji Baba The Persian rogue in 2 novels by James Morier (1824 and 1828) who turns a satirical eye first on Persian and then on English ways.

Hakluyt Society (1846) A society with a high reputation of scholarly editions, carefully edited and annotated, of old books of travel.

Hakluyt's Voyages In full The Principal Navigations, Voyages and Discoveries of the English Nation (1598-1600), compiled by an English clergyman, Richard Hakluyt, from English and foreign accounts of voyages made over the previous 1500 years.

Half Ton Cup An international sailing contest similar to the ONE TON CUP, for boats rating not more than 18 ft.

Halifax, 1st Earl of Edward Wood, Viceroy of India (as Baron Irwin), Foreign Secretary and Ambassador to USA (first as Lord Irwin, then as Lord Halifax).

Halifax (1941) A HANDLEY PAGE 4-engined heavy bomber used by the RAF in World War II.

Hallelujah Chorus By far the most widely known section of Handel's MESSIAH.

Halley's comet A comet observed in 1682, the return of which the astronomer Halley correctly predicted for 1759; last seen in 1910, due back in 1985.

Hall of Fame for Great Americans (1900) A colonnade on the campus of New York University, NYC, with busts and tablets commemorating famous Americans.

Halloween Oct. 31st, the 1st day of the old Celtic year, Christianized into the eve of All Hallows (see ALL SAINTS); celebrated particularly in Scotland and north England, and associated with witches, divination of future spouses, and various local customs.

Hallstatt The earliest IRON AGE culture of northern Europe, dating from the 7th century BC, and spread by CELTS to LA TÈNE. Named from a Celtic site in the Austrian Lake District.)

Hallstein doctrine (1955) That West Germany alone is competent to act on behalf of the whole German people (i.e. including East Germany), and that diplomatic recognition of Communist East Germany is an unfriendly act. (Dr Walter Hallstein, West German State Secretary.)

Halsbury report (1963) (UK) The report of a committee which recommended the adoption of decimal coinage, accepted in 1966 by the government, and coming into force

1 Feb. 1971 (Decimal Day, D-day).

Halsbury's Laws of England (1907-17) A 31-volume digest of English law in alphabetical order of subjects, edited by the first Earl of Halsbury, who had been Lord Chancellor.

Ham A son of Noah who offended by looking on his father when he was drunk and naked; according to the mutilated text of *Genesis* ix, 22-23, Noah thereupon cursed not Ham but Ham's son Canaan, to be a 'servant of servants'. In *Genesis* x, 6 Ham is also the father of Cush (Ethiopia), Mizraim (Egypt) and Phut (Babylon). See HAMITES.

Ham, Son of (1) A person accursed (see last entry). (2) A black man (according to one theory Ham was an ancient name for Egypt and meant 'black').

Hamadan rugs Hard-wearing Kurdish rugs (often in the form of long runners) with a heavy pile and bold designs in a limited range of good colors. They are named after the center in northwest Persia where they were collected for export.

Haman See ESTHER.

Hambledon Club (1750) The first cricket club, which ruled the game until the MCC took over control some 40 years later. It played on Windmill and Broadhalfpenny Downs in Hampshire. Its doings were chronicled by John Nyren (1764-1837), son of the founder.

Hambletonian The chief US trotting race for 3-year-olds, run at Goshen, New York. See STANDARDBRED. (Named after the ancestor of the best US trotting horses.)

Hambros (1839) A family merchant bank and acceptance house, founded by a Dane and still retaining its Scandinavian connections.

Ham House A Jacobean house at Petersham, below Richmond Hill, Surrey, with a collection of STUART PERIOD furniture; administered by the Victoria and Albert Museum.

Hamites The inhabitants of North Africa and the Horn of Africa, brown, slender, with fine features; they include the BERBERS of North Africa (still distinguishable from the Semitic Arabs there), the Ancient

Egyptians and the Cushites (Ethiopians, Somali, Eritreans etc.). See HAM; HAMITIC LANGUAGES.

Hamitic languages Those spoken by HAMITES, i.e., BERBERS (quite distinct from the SEMITIC LANGUAGES, and most common in North Africa and the Sahara), Ancient Egyptian, and Cushitic (i.e. the non-Semitic languages of Ethiopia, Somalia etc.). Roots of words tend to consist of 2 consonants instead of the 3 in Semitic languages.

Hamlet The introspective, vacillating Prince of Denmark of Shakespeare's play (1601), unable to steel himself to avenge the death of his father, whose ghost has accused CLAUDIUS, Hamlet's stepfather-uncle, of his murder; but the greatness of the play soars above the corpse-strewn plot.

Hamlet without the Prince A phrase used by Walter Scott (but of earlier origin) indicating that the most important person concerned has failed to appear or has not been mentioned etc. See HAMLET.

Hamm See ENDGAME.

Hammer, Mike The one-man police force and chief character in many of the novels of Mickey Spillane, America's Ian Fleming.

Hammer of the Scots A name for Edward I, earned by his attempts to subdue William Wallace and Robert the Bruce.

Hammersmith Inner London borough since 1965 consisting of the former metropolitan boroughs of Hammersmith and Fulham.

Hammond organ (1935) An electronic organ like the WURLITZER ORGAN but using rotating magnetic generators instead of vibrating reeds and electrostatic conversion.

Hammurabi's code (18th century BC) A codification of existing harsh Babylonian law made by King Hammurabi. There are several copies inscribed on partially defaced stelae; the most complete, from Susa, is in the LOUVRE.

Hampden, Village An allusion to lines of GRAY'S ELEGY (Some village Hampden, that with dauntless breast / The little tyrant of his fields withstood), referring to John Hampden, a Buckinghamshire squire who refused to pay ship money under Charles I in 1637, to force the issue of its legality.

Hampden Park The international soccer ground at Glasgow, also the ground of the amateur club, QUEEN'S PARK. See next entry.

Hampden roar, The The phenomenal noise which has become traditional at HAMPDEN PARK, generated by almost excessively partisan crowds, especially at the Scottish Cup Final.

Hampshire, HMS A cruiser, mined and sunk (June 1916) with all hands, while conveying Lord Kitchener, Secretary for War, to Russia.

Hampstead A former London metropolitan borough, since 1965 part of the borough of CAMDEN.

Hampstead Garden Suburb (1907) A privately developed estate on the edge of Hampstead Heath, London, now owned by Charles Clore. It is associated particularly with artists, economists and left-wing politicians.

Hampstead set A name given to the group of middle-class intellectual Labour MPs which formed at HAMPSTEAD around Hugh Gaitskell (Opposition Labour leader, 1955-63), determined to erase their party's proletarian image.

Hampton Court (1514) A palace built for Cardinal Wolsey but annexed by Henry VIII, now used in part for GRACE AND FAVOUR apartments. Famous for its Great Vine, Maze and the Fountain Court and Orangery by Wren. (Near KINGSTON UPON THAMES.)

Hampton Court Conference (1604) Summoned by James I in the first year of his reign, at which he rejected a petition by a thousand Puritan clergy for greater religious freedom with the words 'No Bishop, No King'. It sanctioned the publication of the AUTHORIZED VERSION of the Bible (1611).

Handley Page The British aircraft firm which made the first big twin-engine bomber (1917), many of the airliners used by IMPERIAL AIRWAYS,

the JETSTREAM and the HALIFAX bomber.

Handy Andy Nickname of Squire Egan's clumsy manservant in Samuel Lover's Irish novel of that name (1842); in the end he turns out to be an Irish peer.

Handy Man See 'HOMO HABILIS'.

Han Dynasty (206 BC–AD 221) A period during which all China came under one regime. Glazed pottery, lacquer work, silk weaving, calligraphy, portrait and other forms of painting were highly developed. The capital was Ch'ang-an, near Sian (Shensi Province). The next important dynasty was the T'ANG DYNASTY.

Hanging Gardens of Babylon One of the SEVEN WONDERS OF THE WORLD, a garden rising in terraces, said to have been built for his wife by Nebuchadnezzar.

Hannibalic War See PUNIC WARS.

Hanno's Periplous (5th century BC) An account of a Carthaginian coastal voyage down the west coast of Africa as far as Liberia or perhaps the Cameroons, during which trading stations were established. The account was inscribed on tablets in Phoenician, of which a Greek translation has survived. (Greek, 'sailing round'.)

Hanoi Capital of, and used as a synonym for the government of, North VIETNAM.

Hanover, House of (1714-1901) In Britain, the ruling house from the accession of George I (son of an ELECTOR of Hanover by James I's granddaughter) to the death of Queen Victoria. Hanover and Britain were united under one king until 1837, but on Queen Victoria's accession her uncle the Duke of Cumberland became King of Hanover.

Hanoverian Succession See ACT OF SETTLEMENT.

Hansard (1774) The official verbatim proceedings of the Houses of Parliament, since 1908 recorded by civil servants. (Luke Hansard, originator.)

Hans Brinker; or, The Silver Skates (1865) An evergreen juvenile classic by Mary Mapes Dodge. It describes the life in a Dutch village of 2 children, Hans and Gretel. The subtitle refers to a skating competition won by Gretel.

Hanseatic League A 13th-century association of North German cities which once monopolized Baltic trade, but lost influence in the 17th century; leading members were Lübeck, Hamburg and Bremen. (Old High German *Hansa*, 'association'.)

Hänsel and Gretel Children of a broommaker in Humperdinck's opera (1893) based on a fairy tale by the Grimm brothers.

Hanukkah, Chanukah The Jewish festival of the Dedication of the Temple, on a date at present falling near Christmas Day.

Happy Hooligan (1899) A cartoon character created by Frederick Opper (of ALPHONSE AND GASTON); he was a genial blundering hobo, who later appeared on the screen in animated cartoons (1917).

Happy Time, The A musical based on a play by Samuel Taylor derived from a book by Robert Fontaine which recalls memories of a home and family in a small Canadian town; also a movie (1952).

Happy Valley (Kashmir) The world-famous beauty spot in the Jhelum Valley of Indian-held Kashmir.

Happy Warrior, The Franklin Roosevelt's name for his friend Alfred E. Smith, whom he nominated for President in 1924 and 1928 and who was 4 times Governor of New York (1918-28). Nevertheless, Smith opposed Roosevelt's NEW DEAL. (Possibly from a Wordsworth poem.)

Hapsburg lip The protruding lower lip which was a marked characteristic of the HAPSBURGS for generations.

Hapsburgs A family dynasty founded by Emperor Rudolf I (1273) which ruled over the HOLY ROMAN EMPIRE with occasional interregna until it ended in 1806, and then as Emperors of Austria-Hungary until 1918. They gained the NETHERLANDS by marriage (1477) and in the 16th century, through Charles V, they inherited the Spanish dominions of Ferdinand V (Spain, Naples, Sicily, Sardinia, and the Spanish American colonies), but the Spanish branch died out in 1700 and was succeeded by the BOURBONS. (Castle Hapsburg, between Basle and Zurich, seat of the Counts of Hapsburg.)

Harambee A post-Independence slogan in Kenya, meaning 'let's get on with it'. Compare UHURU.

Harappa One of the sites of the IN-DUS VALLEY CIVILIZATION.

Harding, Rev. Septimus A character in Trollope's novels, see The WAR-DEN.

Hard Times (1845) Dickens's grim indictment of industrial England personified in Thomas GRADGRIND.

Hardwick Hall A country house near Chesterfield, Derbyshire, built by BESS OF HARDWICK, now owned by the NATIONAL TRUST.

Hardy Boys, The Characters in a series of boys mystery stories by Franklin W. Dixon, e.g. The Flickering Torch Mystery (1943), The Secret of Skull Mountain (1948). The boys, Frank and Joe, solved many mysteries using technique learned from their detective father.

Harewood House The house near Leeds built by Robert Adam for the Lascelles family (Earls of Harewood), in a park laid out by CAPABILITY BROWN. See also ADAM STYLE.

Haringey (1965) New London borough consisting of the former boroughs of Wood Green, Hornsey and Tottenham; headquarters at Wood Green.

Harlech TV (1968) The commercial program-contracting company which took over Wales and the West of England from TWW (TV Wales and the West). The headquarters are in Cardiff, the studios in Bristol. The company is financed by local, especially Welsh, interests. (Chairman, Lord Harlech.)

Harlem The Negro and Puerto Rican quarter in north MANHATTAN, NYC.

Harlem Globetrotters (1927) A famous team of highly skilled exhibition basketball players; 3 units annually appear on all 7 continents.

Harlequin The comic servant of the COMMEDIA DELL' ARTE, dressed in patchwork clothes of many colors, usually in love with COLUMBINE.

(Originally a jester in French mystery plays; Italian name, Arlecchino.)

Harley Street   A London street running north to Regent's Park, where some of the leading specialists have their consulting rooms, as also have psychiatrists, dentists etc.

Harlots' Romp, The   A nickname for QUEEN CHARLOTTE'S BALL.

Harlow   (1947) (UK) A NEW TOWN in Essex, southeast of the existing market town, designed to take 90,000 inhabitants.

Harmodius and Aristogeiton   Two Athenian tyrannicides of the 6th century BC; they killed one of the joint tyrants of Athens, but the other had them put to death; the motive was personal and not, as traditionally represented, political. There was a statue to them, of which a Roman copy survives in the National Museum, Naples.

'Harmonious Blacksmith, The'   A name given, not by the composer, to one of Handel's compositions, said to have been suggested by the sound of a blacksmith's anvil.

Harmsworth Professor   The holder of the chair of American History at OXFORD UNIVERSITY.

Harmsworth Trophy · (1903) The first international powerboat race, run over a distance of 135 miles, usually at Detroit or Picton, Ont., and often with several years between contests. (Given by Sir Alfred Harmsworth, later Lord Northcliffe.)

Harpagon   See AVARE, L'.

Harper's Bazaar   (1867) A monthly magazine for women, published in New York.

Harper's Ferry   (1859) A raid, 2 years before the AMERICAN CIVIL WAR, on an American government arsenal, led by the abolitionist John Brown (see 'JOHN BROWN'S BODY') to get weapons to arm a slave revolt in Virginia. No slaves joined him; he surrendered to Robert E. Lee (the future Confederate general) and was hanged. (Town in northeastern West Virginia.)

Harper's Magazine   (1850) An illustrated monthly magazine published in New York, with general articles, short stories etc.

Harp of David   Israeli movie and theater award comparable to the OSCAR. See I *Samuel* xvi, 23.

Harrier   HAWKER SIDDELEY (V/STOL) tactical strike-reconnaissance aircraft, a single-seat fighter able to fly close to Mach 1, developed from the KESTREL but more powerful; it replaced the HUNTER in 1969.

Harris, Mrs   The purely imaginary friend who is quoted in Sairey GAMP'S anecdotes as corroborating her opinions. As Betsey Prig remarks: I don't believe there's no sich a person!

Harrods   A leading London department store in fashionable Knightsbridge.

Harrow train disaster   (1952) A collision at Harrow and Wealdstone station, London, the worst in British history since GRETNA GREEN (1915).

Harry Price Library   A collection of books on occultism, spiritualism and conjuring, now at LONDON UNIVERSITY.

Harry Starkers   A slang phrase for 'stark naked'.

Harun al-Rashid   The Caliph in the *Arabian Nights* who wandered through the streets of Baghdad at night seeking adventure; based on a historical person of that name, Caliph from AD 786.

Harvard   (1636) Oldest US university, at Cambridge, Mass. Students from all over the world are sent to the graduate school of business administration (the 'Harvard Business School'), added in 1908 and housed in Boston.

Harvard beets   Diced or sliced cooked beets served in a vinegar sauce thickened with cornstarch.

Harvard Independent, The   (1969) A HARVARD University weekly newspaper, student owned and operated, founded as a conservative rival to *The* CRIMSON.

Harvard Lampoon   A humor magazine produced at HARVARD University.

Harvard Yard   The central quadrangle and oldest part of HARVARD, with dormitories reserved for freshmen.

Harveian Oration   (1657) An annual lecture given before the Royal College of Physicians in honor of William Harvey, on or about St Luke's Day. Oct. 18th. (St Luke is said to have been a physician.)

Harvey Berin A New York fashion house.

Harwell The UK ATOMIC ENERGY AUTHORITY's center for fundamental research into nuclear physics and nuclear energy; it has experimental reactors of various kinds such as Bepo, Bleep, Dido, Zephyr and Pluto. (Village in Berkshire, between Wantage and Didcot.)

Haryana An Indian state formed from the HINDI-speaking southern PUNJAB. See CHANDIGARH.

Hashemites Arab family claiming descent from Muhammad's uncle Hashim, as did Abdullah, the first King of Jordan, and his brother Feisal, first King of Iraq, sons of Hussein, Sharif of Mecca. The WAHABIS drove them out of Arabia.

Haslemere Festival (1925) (UK) An annual festival of early music and instruments, held in July at Haslemere, Surrey, where the Swiss Dolmetsch family of musicians and makers of harpsichords, clavichords, recorders etc. have long been established.

Hassan (1923) A melodramatic verse play by James Elroy Flecker about a fat confectioner of Baghdad and a pair of ill-starred lovers; spectacularly produced with ballets by Fokine and the music of Delius. It is remembered for its lyrics, notably the ode to Yasmin and 'The Golden Road to Samarkand'.

Hastings (1948) The HANDLEY PAGE long-range aircraft in service for many years with RAF Transport Command.

Hasty Pudding Club A HARVARD undergraduate dramatic club which since 1844 has staged annual burlesque shows. (From the cornmeal mush served at early meetings.)

Hatfield House The Jacobean home in Hertfordshire of the junior line of Cecils (Marquesses of Salisbury) since it was built by Robert Cecil, 1st Earl of Salisbury; in the grounds is the Tudor palace where Queen Elizabeth I lived.

Hatha Yoga The form of YOGA best known in the West.

Hathor Ancient Egyptian goddess of the sky, daughter of RA, whose symbol was a cow; she took many forms, and was associated with ISIS, OSIRIS and BAST.

Hatter's Castle (1931) A. J. Cronin's first best seller, about the career of an overambitious tradesman.

Hatton Garden The traditional center in the CITY of London of British trade in diamonds and, to a lesser extent, in other precious stones.

Hauksbee, Mrs A character who appears in many of Kipling's stories of life in India, Lucy Hauksbee is a clever little flirt, who loves to set the cat among the pigeons but is not bad at heart.

Haus der Kunst (Munich) The new art gallery and museum in which are housed the best of the famous collections from the Alte and Neue Pinakothek, which were destroyed in World War II. (German, 'arthouse'.)

Havana Declaration (1940) Made by the Pan-American Conference, in effect prohibited the transfer of colonies in the Western Hemisphere to Axis powers. See TRIPARTITE PACT.

Havering (1965) New London borough consisting of the former borough of Romford and the urban district of Hornchurch; headquarters at Romford, Essex.

Haviland china Wares made at LIMOGES, France, first (in 1842) by David Haviland to supply his retail china business in the US, and then by Charles Field Haviland who bought up the original French factory there (c. 1881), by Haviland & Co. (1892), by Theodore Haviland and finally, in 1936, by a Haviland factory in the US.

Hawaii standard time The same as ALASKA STANDARD TIME.

Hawarden A market town of Flintshire, west of Chester, where Gladstone's famous home (Hawarden Castle, 1572) is situated. The house contains St Deniol's Library of theological and historical works.

Hawk US ground-to-air defense missile for use against low-flying aircraft; range 25 miles.

Hawker Siddeley aircraft These include the COMET, TRIDENT, VULCAN, KESTREL, HUNTER, HARRIER, ANDOVER and NIMROD; the HS-748 (1966) short-range turboprop airliner for 40-60 passengers; and the HS-125, a 'business' jet. See next entry.

Hawker Siddeley Group A group of firms with factories in Britain, Canada, Australia, India and elsewhere, making aircraft (see last entry); missiles (SEASLUG, BLUE STEEL, BLUE STREAK); and a wide range of industrial equipment.

Hawkeye State Nickname of Iowa.

Hawks (1) Supporters of a militant foreign policy, in contrast to the DOVES. (2) The Atlanta Hawks, NATIONAL BASKETBALL ASSOCIATION.

Hawkshaw In American usage a synonym for 'detective', from the name of a character in an English melodrama, *The Ticket-of-Leave Man* (1863) by Tom Taylor. Hawkshaw also appeared in a comic strip by Gus Mager, but that was a burlesque of Sherlock HOLMES.

Hawley-Smoot tariffs (1930) Exceptionally high tariffs imposed by President Hoover despite protests at home and abroad; they led to tariff wars with the rest of the world.

Haworth The village near Keighley, Yorkshire, where the Brontës lived in the Parsonage, which is now preserved as a museum by the Brontë Society.

Hawthornden prize An annual award for the best imaginative work in prose or verse by a British author under 41.

Hay, Ian Pen name of Maj. J. H. Beith, author of *The First Hundred Thousand* (1915) about the British Expeditionary Force, and of many light novels.

Haydn's Dictionary of Dates A standard work on the subject, first published in 1841, last revised in 1910. (Joseph Haydn, editor until 1855.)

Hay Fever (1925) An early Noël Coward comedy about a large weekend party at the home of an ex-actress and her novelist husband.

Haymarket riot (1886) An incident during anarchist-fomented labor demonstrations in Chicago, when a bomb killed 7 police and wounded 66 others in the Haymarket Square.

Four people were hanged and a fifth committed suicide, but the bomb-thrower escaped. The labor movement, especially the Knights of Labor, was discredited and the founding of the rival American Federation of Labor was a result.

Hays Office (1934) A US censorship office set up by the motion-picture industry. (Established by Will Hays, president, Motion Picture Producers and Distributors of North America, and former Postmaster General.)

'Hay Wain' (1821) The most famous of Constable's paintings; now in the National Gallery, London.

H.C.E. The initials which recur throughout FINNEGANS WAKE, being the initials of the hero, H. C. Earwicker, and of key phrases such as Haveth Childer Everywhere, Here Comes Everybody etc.

H certificate A certificate formerly granted by the British Board of Film Censors to horror films unsuitable for children.

H.D. Initials used as pen name by the American poet Hilda Doolittle, perhaps the best of the IMAGISTS.

Headlong Hall (1816) Thomas Love Peacock's 'novel' on much the same lines as NIGHTMARE ABBEY.

Head of the River Race (1926) (UK) A timed race for eights over the University BOAT RACE course (but in the reverse direction), held at about the same date as that race; characterized by a very large entry. The name is also given to similar events elsewhere.

Hearst papers The 'yellow press' empire of sensational newspapers founded by the American Northcliffe, William Randolph Hearst (died 1951). He and his fantastic castle-home (the ENCHANTED HILL) at San Simeon, Calif., were portrayed in the movie CITIZEN KANE.

Heartbreak House (1919) Bernard Shaw's 'fantasia in the Russian manner', an indictment of the cultured leisured classes of Western civilization who obstruct the LIFE FORCE with their apathy and muddle. Capt. Shotover says in the play: Every drunken skipper trusts to Providence—and Providence runs them on the rocks.

Heartbreak Ridge The scene of bitter fighting in the KOREAN WAR, a strategic feature captured by US troops in Sept. 1951.

Heart is a Lonely Hunter, The (1940) The first work of a woman novelist, Carson McCullers, about the difficulty of knowing what is for the best or getting others to understand what it is. A socialist preaches to apathetic workers; a Negro doctor fails to arouse the Negroes of a small Southern town. In contrast, 2 deaf-mutes enjoy a serene friendship which comes to embrace the would-be proselytizers.

Heart of Midlothian (1818) Walter Scott's partly historical novel; see Jeanie DEANS. (Name of the prison or Tolbooth at Edinburgh, scene of a riot at the beginning of the book.)

Heart of the Matter (1948) Graham Greene's novel set in Freetown, Sierra Leone, of a girl whom Scobie succeeds in making utterly miserable by remorse for his deserted wife and the overwhelming sense of sin which so often obtrudes in this Catholic convert's novels.

Heathcliff The Liverpool gypsy boy adopted and brought up by the EARNSHAW FAMILY in WUTHERING HEIGHTS. Humiliated by young Hindley Earnshaw and, as he feels, by Hindley's sister Catherine whom he passionately adores, he disappears, but returns later to dominate the household and wreak his revenge.

Heath Robinson Name of a British cartoonist used adjectivally for anything resembling the whimsically intricate gadgetry to perform a simple operation which was the chief feature of his drawings for *Punch*. (W. Heath Robinson, died 1944.)

Heathrow (1946) The official name of London's main airport, commonly known as London Airport; used to distinguish it from London (Gatwick) Airport in Sussex. It lies east of Slough.

Heaven and Hell A book by Aldous Huxley; see DOORS OF PERCEPTION.

Heavenly Twins, The The stars CASTOR and POLLUX.

Heaviside layer The lower (E) layer of ionized gases in the ionosphere (see APPLETON LAYER) which reflects long-wave radio signals; sometimes used of the ionosphere as a whole. Also known as the Kennelly-Heaviside layer, since the US professor, A. E. Kennelly, first predicted it. (Oliver Heaviside, British Physicist.)

Hebdomadal Council The governing body of OXFORD UNIVERSITY, so named because it meets weekly. (Greek *hebdomas*, 'week'.)

Hebe In Greek legend, a daughter of ZEUS and HERA, and goddess of youth. She was cupbearer to the gods until GANYMEDE took over the post; she then married Heracles (HERCULES).

Hecate In early Greek legend the triple goddess of the sky, the earth and the Underworld; later chiefly regarded as the patroness of witches, associated with crossroads.

Hector In Greek legend, the chief Trojan hero, son of PRIAM and HECUBA, husband of ANDROMACHE. He killed PATROCLUS (see ILIAD), and was himself killed by ACHILLES.

Hecuba In Greek legend, wife of King PRIAM of Troy. At the fall of Troy she was carried off by the Greeks and saw 2 of her children killed. She appears in Euripides' *The Trojan Women* and *Hecuba*. In Shakespeare's play, seeing an actor moved to tears by her tragedy, HAMLET muses: What's Hecuba to him, or he to Hecuba,/That he should weep for her?

Hedda Gabler (1890) Ibsen's play in which Hedda tries, from selfish motives, to advance her husband's academic career by sacrificing that of a rival, Lövberg, who had once been in love with her. She steals the manuscript of Lövberg's new book, induces him to commit suicide, is found out, and kills herself.

Heep, Uriah The 'umble and greasy lawyer's clerk in DAVID COPPERFIELD, who blackmails his employer and is exposed by MICAWBER.

Hegelianism The philosophical view that everything in the universe (including thought and history) is a manifestation, striving towards perfection, of a cosmic spirit which operates through the dialectical process, i.e. every concept (thesis) implies and is in conflict with its opposite (antithesis), and their opposition is reconciled in a compromise (synthesis) between the two on a higher level; this synthesis in turn becomes the 'thesis' of the next stage of development. See DIALECTICAL MATERIALISM. (Hegel, German philosopher, 1770-1831.)

Hegira Anglicized name for the flight of MOHAMMED from Mecca to Medina in AD 622, the year from which the MUSLIM era starts. AH 1390 began in 1970. (Arabic *hijrah*, 'separation, departure from home'.)

Heidelberg Man Supposed early form of man, reconstructed from a massive jaw, about 400,000 years old, found near Heidelberg in 1907.

Heidi A children's story of life in the Swiss Alps, by Johanna Spyri (1827-1901); it was made into a movie.

'Heilige Nacht' A carol; see 'SILENT NIGHT'.

Heimwehr An illegal Austrian Fascist armed organization which fought against a similar Socialist body, the Schutzbund, in the 1920s and 1930s. (German, 'home guard'.)

Heinemann (W. H.) Bequest A fund, now administered by the Royal Society of Literature, from which awards are made primarily to authors of the less remunerative forms of literature: poetry, criticism, biography, history. There is also a prize for French authors, reciprocal to the French Stock prize.

Heinkel Name of manufacturer (abbreviated to He) given to a series of German aircraft, notably the He-178 which was the first jet plane (von Ohain turbojet) to fly, in Aug. 1939 (but see MESSERSCHMITT); and the He-176 powered by a liquid-fuel rocket motor, also tested in 1939 (June).

Heisenberg's Uncertainty principle (1927) That the more accurately the position of an atomic particle is determined, the less accurately can its momentum be determined, and vice versa. Also called the principle of indeterminacy. (Werner Heisenberg, German originator of quantum mechanics.)

Heisman Trophy (1935) An award presented to the outstanding college football player of the year.

Helen of Troy In Greek legend, the daughter of LEDA by ZEUS and wife of King Menelaus of Sparta; her face 'launched a thousand ships', i.e. started the TROJAN WAR, when PARIS carried her off to Troy. After the fall of Troy she returned to her husband.

Helicon, Mount See HIPPOCRENE.

Heligoland Bight (Aug. 1914) The first naval engagement of World War I, in which 3 German light cruisers were sunk and 3 crippled.

Heliopolis The center, near modern Cairo, of the worship of the sun-god RA during the OLD KINGDOM.

Helios The Greek sun-god, brother of SELENE and EOS; the Roman Sol.

Hellas The Ancient Greek name for Greece, still used today.

Hell Breughel Nickname of Pieter II (1564-1638), son of PEASANT BREUGHEL; so called because of his weird pictures of Hell.

Helleborus The genus that includes the Christmas Rose (*H. niger*) and the Lenten Rose (*H. orientalis*).

Hellenes The Ancient Greek name for Greeks.

Hellenistic Age (323-30 BC) The period during which a cosmopolitan Greek civilization, centered on Alexandria in Egypt, dominated the Near and Middle East and North Africa, from the death of Alexander the Great until the Roman defeat of CLEOPATRA, last of the PTOLEMIES.

Hellespont Ancient Greek name for the Dardanelles.

Hellfire Club (1745) Popular name for the Knights of St Francis, a club founded by Sir John Dashwood, Chancellor of the Exchequer. As its membership and activities were secret, sensational legends grew up about orgies at Medmenham Abbey on the Thames near Henley, and in the caves opposite Dashwood's home at West Wycombe Park, and their Rabelaisian motto *fay ce que voudras* ('do what you will'); but whether they have any basis in fact, is not known.

Hello, Dolly! (1964) A highly popular musical adapted by Michael Stewart from *The* MATCHMAKER; also a movie directed by Gene Kelly.

Hell's Angels The self-inflicted name of aggressive motorcycling fraternities that originated in California in the 1960s among young working- and middle-class dropouts. High speed is their drug and flamboyant rejection of society their motivation. The movement spread, in slightly less violent form, to Britain.

Hell's Corner (1940) Name given to the coast around Dover when it was being shelled by German guns from the coast opposite, as part of the BAT-TLE OF BRITAIN operation.

Helms World Trophy (1949) An award made annually to the foremost amateur athlete in each of the 6 continents; qualifying fields include baseball, football, track-and-field sports etc. The names of winners are inscribed on a 6-ft trophy of gold, silver and bronze. (Sponsored by the Helms Athletic Foundation, L.A.)

Heloïse and Abélard Peter Abélard was a popular theological teacher in Paris in the early 12th century who advocated a rational approach to religion, for which he was persecuted by the Cistercian, St Bernard. He fell in love with his pupil Héloïse, niece of Canon Fulbert, and married her secretly when she bore him a son. On learning this, Fulbert had him castrated. He became a monk, she a nun, exchanging letters of which 5 of his to her have been published. The story has been treated by many writers, including George Moore in his novel *Heloise and Abelard* (1921), Helen Waddel in *Peter Abelard* (1933) and Ronald Millar in his play *Abelard and Heloise* (1970).

Helsingfors Swedish name of Helsinki, capital of Finland.

Helsingör The site of Kronborg Castle, Denmark, the Elsinore of HAM-LET.

Helston Furry Dance (UK) A festival of pagan origin held on May 8th (Floral Day) at Helston, southwest Cornwall; the villagers dance through the streets to a traditional tune of great antiquity.

Helvetia The Latin name for Switzerland.

Hemiptera The parasitic bugs, an insect order which includes aphids

(e.g. greenfly), bedbugs, cochineal insects, leafhoppers and cicadas.

Hemlock and After (1952) Angus Wilson's satirical study of an aging writer who has failed to live up to his ideals.

Hendon (UK) A former MIDDLESEX borough, since 1965 part of the borough of BARNET.

Hendon Pageant (1920-37) An annual display by the RAF at Hendon aerodrome, London.

Hendon Police College (1934) The London Metropolitan Police college founded by Lord Trenchard when he was the Metropolitan Commissioner.

Hengist and Horsa The traditional, perhaps historical, leaders of the JUTES who settled in Kent in the 5th century AD.

Henley (1839) (UK) An annual regatta in July, the major rowing events at which are regarded as the unofficial world championships. (Henley on Thames, in Oxfordshire.)

Henlow The RAF Technical College, near Bedford; it provides training (including specialist training at postgraduate level) for officers of the RAF Technical Branch.

Henry, O. Pen name of W. S. Porter (1862-1910), an American master of the short story with an unexpected twist in the last paragraphs.

Henry Esmond (1852) Thackeray's novel set in the time of Queen Anne, in which the hero, banished from the home in which he was brought up and to which he is the rightful heir, serves in Marlborough's campaigns and returns to marry his foster father's widow, Lady Castlewood, and to claim his inheritance. Marlborough, Addison and Steele appear in the book. See ESMOND, BEATRIX; *The* VIRGINIANS.

Henry IV (1) Shakespeare's play (1598) in 2 parts, about the English King. (2) Pirandello's play (1922) about a man in modern times who takes on the personality of the 11th-century German Emperor Henry IV (see CANOSSA).

Henry VII's Chapel A Tudor chapel added to Westminister Abbey in the early 16th century, famed for its perfect fan vaulting. It contains a memorial to those who fought in the Battle of Britain, and the banners of the Order of the Bath.

Hephaestus The Greek god of fire, identified with the Roman Vulcan.

Hephzibah See BEULAH.

Hepplewhite Name given to furniture inspired by the book of designs which George Hepplewhite published in 1788. Adapted from ADAM STYLE designs, these were intended for middle-class furniture, mostly in mahogany. Heart-, shield- and oval-shaped chair backs are characteristic.

Heptameron, The (16th century) A collection of love stories written by Marguerite, Queen of Navarre. The title and setting of the tales were inspired by the DECAMERON. (Greek, 'seven days'.)

Heptarchy, The The 7 Anglo-Saxon kingdoms of England during the 5th-9th centuries: Northumbria, MERCIA, East Anglia, Essex, Kent, Sussex and WESSEX; they were not, however, permanent separate kingdoms throughout this period. (Greek, 'seven kingdoms'.)

Hera In Greek legend, sister and understandably jealous wife of ZEUS, mother of ARES; identified with the Roman Juno.

Heracles The Greek hero better known under his Latin name of HERCULES.

Herakleion An alternative spelling for IRÁKLION, capital of Crete.

Herald's College (or **Office**) Alternative names for the COLLEGE OF ARMS.

Herbert Commission (1957) A commission on the reorganization of the administration of GREATER LONDON. Its proposals for changing borough boundaries were not closely followed when the Greater London Council was established in 1965. (Sir E. Herbert, later Baron Tangley.)

Herblock Pen name of Herbert Lawrence Block, author and cartoonist, whose boldly drawn satirical cartoons became a feature of the Washington *Post* from 1946, providing a witty liberal commentary on current affairs.

Herculaneum An ancient Roman city overwhelmed by the eruption of Vesuvius which destroyed nearby POMPEII. Its existence was forgotten until the site was discovered by chance in the 18th century.

Hercules The Latin and better known name of the Greek Heracles, son of ZEUS and ALCMENE (the wife of AMPHITRYON), famous for his 'Twelve Labors'. He was killed by the shirt of NESSUS.

Hercules A Lockheed turboprop transport plane (the US C-130) now also in use by RAF Transport Command.

Here Comes Everybody (1965) The best attempt to explain James Joyce, by Anthony Burgess; see H.C.E.

Hereford cattle A hardy beef breed, used in crossing with dairy breeds; red with white face and markings.

Hereford round In archery, a match in which 6 dozen arrows are shot at distances ranging from 50 to 80 yards.

Hereros A tribe of cattle people in South West Africa who were almost exterminated (1903-07) in an early German exercise in genocide.

Hereward the Wake (1865) Charles Kingsley's semihistorical novel in which a Saxon outlaw, Hereward, defies the Normans from his hideout in the marshes of the Isle of Ely.

Heriot-Watt University (1965) Formerly a central institution (advanced college administered by an independent board of governors) in Edinburgh.

Hermes The Greek god of commerce, cunning and inventions, identified with the Roman Mercury. He was a son of ZEUS, and invented the lyre, among other things. As messenger of the gods he wore a winged hat and winged sandals, and carried a herald's beribboned staff.

Hermès A leading maker of luxury leather goods in Paris.

'Hermes of Praxiteles, The' (4th century BC) The only original statue by the Greek sculptor Praxiteles which has survived; HERMES is depicted with the infant DIONYSUS on his arm; it is in the museum at Olympia, where it was found.

Hermes Trismegistus The name given by 3rd-century AD neoplatonists to THOTH, identified with HERMES by the Greeks, as the author of the HER-METIC BOOKS. ('Hermes the thrice-greatest'.)

Hermetic books Books of unknown date and authorship attributed to HERMES TRISMEGISTUS but probably compiled in Greek at Alexandria in the first centuries of the Christian era. They dealt with alchemy, astrology and other occult subjects and have survived only through quotation (often extensive) in other authors. They show the influence of Jewish mysticism and NEOPLATONISM grafted onto Egyptian religious traditions.

Hermetic philosophy Alchemy. See HERMETIC BOOKS.

Hermitage A famous wine, both red and white, of the Rhone valley.

Hermitage, The (1) The chief art gallery in Leningrad. (2) The home and burial place of Andrew Jackson, near Nashville, Tenn., completed in 1835 only 10 years before his death.

Herne the Hunter A ghost in an English version of the widespread European legend of the Wild Hunter; he is a former keeper of Windsor Forest who walks at midnight in winter, destroying trees and cattle.

Hero and Leander In Greek legend Hero was a priestess of APHRODITE at Sestos, visited nightly by Leander, who had to swim across the HELLES-PONT from Abydos on the opposite shore. One stormy night he was drowned and Hero, in despair, threw herself into the sea. Marlowe retold the story in an unfinished poem (completed by Chapman), and Byron with a companion emulated the feat of swimming across the strait.

Herod, To out-Herod To surpass in wickedness even Herod the Great, who ordered the MASSACRE OF THE INNOCENTS. Originally, to rant louder than Herod in the old sacred plays (HAMLET, III, ii, 16).

Heroes and Hero-Worship, On (1841) A collection of Thomas Carlyle's lectures on history viewed as the life stories of great men.

Heron A small dinghy class, 11 feet 3 inches long, designed by Jack Holt

to be carried on the car top; usually home-built.

Herrenvolk A Nazi name for Germans; corrupted by Churchill to 'Herring-folk'. ('Master race'.)

Herries Chronicle, The (1930-33) A quartet of novels by Hugh Walpole, forming a family saga set in the Lake District.

Herstmonceux Alternative spelling of HURSTMONCEUX.

Hertzian waves An earlier name for electromagnetic waves. (First demonstrated in 1888 by the German physicist H. R. Hertz.)

Hesperides (1) In Greek legend, 3 nymphs variously said to live in a western island paradise or on Mount Atlas, where they guarded some golden apples belonging to HERA, which Heracles (HERCULES) wrested from them. (2) The collected poems (1648), mostly pastoral, of Robert Herrick. (So called because written in the West Country, i.e. Devonshire; see next entry.)

Hesperides, Islands of the Ancient Greek name for certain islands of the west, perhaps the Bissagos Archipelago south of Gambia, in West Africa; sometimes wrongly equated with the FORTUNATE ISLES. (Connected with the last entry by common derivation from the Greek for western'.)

Hesperus The Greek name for Venus when it is an evening star.

Hessen A Land of West Germany, capital Wiesbaden, formed from the old states of Hesse, capital Darmstadt, and Hesse-Nassau, a Prussian province of which Frankfurt was the chief town.

Hess landing (May 1941) The unheralded landing by parachute in Scotland during World War II of Hitler's deputy, Rudolf Hess, as a self-appointed ambassador to negotiate peace terms with Britain; he was interned.

Hestia See VESTA.

Heston and Isleworth (UK) A former MIDDLESEX borough, since 1965 part of the borough of HOUNSLOW.

Hetty Pegler's Tump A NEOLITHIC AGE chambered long barrow, at Uley, Gloucestershire, England.

HEW Initials used for the US Department of Health, Education and Welfare.

Heythrop College A leading Jesuit college near Chipping Norton, Oxfordshire, England.

Hiawatha (1855) Longfellow's poem of a legendary MOHAWK Indian chief and his DAKOTA wife, Minnehaha ('laughing water'). The simple meter and simple repetitive wording, though appropriate to the subject, cried aloud for parody—and got it, e.g. (on the subject of fur mittens): He, to get the warm side inside, / Put the inside skin side outside.

Hibbert Journal (1902) A British quarterly review of theology, philosophy, sociology and the arts, published at Oxford.

Hibernia Latin name of Ireland.

Hidcote Manor (UK) A NATIONAL TRUST property near Chipping Camden in the Cotswolds, particularly famous for its gardens, where rare exotic plants are grown.

Hidden Persuaders, The (1957) Vance Packard's entertaining attack on MADISON AVENUE's efforts to dragoon American consumers through 'motivational research' into buying what they neither need nor want.

Higgins, Professor A character in Shaw's PYGMALION, based on the phonetician Henry Sweet (died 1912).

High Church See ANGLO-CATHOLICISM.

High Court See LAW COURTS.

Highland Brigade Infantry brigade comprising: The BLACK WATCH (ROYAL HIGHLAND REGIMENT); The Queen's Own Highlanders (Seaforth and Camerons); The Gordon Highlanders; The Argyll and Sutherland Highlanders (Princess Louise's), the disbandment of which was announced in 1968. Since 1968, part of the Scottish Division.

Highland Clearances See The CLEARANCES.

Highland Division The 51st Division which surrendered when cut off at St Valéry-en-Caux in June 1940 and, reconstituted and merged with the 9th Scottish Division, covered itself with glory in the Western Desert (Egypt) and France.

Highland Jessie See 'CAMPBELLS ARE COMING'.

Highland Mary The girl invoked in several of Robert Burns's poems, perhaps a Campbell.

Highland (West Highland) cattle A shaggy hardy breed of high-quality beef cattle, with wide spreading horns and heavy dewlaps; bred in the Scottish Highlands.

High Renaissance (1500-27) The brief period when the Italian RENAISSANCE reached its peak in the time of Michelangelo, Raphael, da Vinci and Titian.

High Sheriff (UK) The chief executive officer of a county, appointed annually at a 'Pricking of the Sheriffs' ceremony, when the Queen pricks a list of nominations with a bodkin, being careful to prick the first name under each county. His duties, apart from receiving judges at ASSIZES, are mostly delegated to an undersheriff (a solicitor) or other officials.

High Wind in Jamaica, A (1929) A startling novel by Richard Hughes set in the early 19th century; a family of children who have survived a Jamaican hurricane are captured on their way to England by pirates, whose downfall they achieve by their utter absence of moral sense; one little girl commits murder.

Hijra A more correct spelling of HEGIRA.

Hikari A Japanese superexpress train on the New TOKAIDO LINE. There are 25 a day which, including 2 stops, do the 320 miles in 3 hr. 10 min., i.e. at an average speed of just over 101 m.p.h.

Hilary term (UK) The university or legal term beginning in January (called the Lent term at CAMBRIDGE UNIVERSITY). (St Hilary, commemorated on Jan. 17th.)

Hill, The (1) In USA, the Capitol Hill which dominates Washington, D.C., and where the Congress buildings and Supreme Court stand. (2) In Britain, a name for Harrow School at Harrow on the Hill, London.

Hillel Foundation lectures Given at various universities of Britain, USA and elsewhere to bring a knowledge of Judaism to students. (Founded in 1923 by the B'NAI B'RITH.)

Hillingdon London borough since 1965 consisting of the former borough of Uxbridge and the urban districts of Hayes, Ruislip-Northwood and Yiewsley-West Drayton; headquarters at Hayes.

Hill Samuel (1965) The biggest London merchant bank and acceptance house, formed by the merger of M. Samuel (1831) with Hill, Higginson, Erlanger (1907). The former was a family firm founded by Marcus Samuel who later founded Shell. The latter had concentrated on industry, with particular interests in Eagle Star Insurance, Nigeria and the Drayton group.

Hinayana The earlier of the 2 main forms of BUDDHISM, closer to BUDDHA's teaching; the 'Lesser Vehicle' (of Truth) or southern Buddhism of Ceylon, Burma, Siam, Indo-China and Indonesia. It is a pessimistic form of quietism, in contrast to MAHAYANA; more interested in morals than metaphysics, seeking the salvation not of all but of the individual. Buddha is venerated but not worshiped.

Hind and the Panther, The (1687) Dryden's poem written after he went over to Rome, in which the unspotted Hind is the Roman Catholic Church and the Panther the ANGLICAN CHURCH.

Hindenburg The last passenger airship on the transatlantic run; when it caught fire on landing in New Jersey, its sister ship GRAF ZEPPELIN was withdrawn from service.

Hindenburg Line (Siegfried Line) In World War I, the German defense line in FLANDERS to which they retreated in September 1918.

Hindi The form of HINDUSTANI which is the official language of India, spoken mainly by educated Hindus. Unlike URDU, it is written from left to right in the Devanagari script, and its vocabulary has been restocked with SANSKRIT words in recent centuries.

Hindle Wakes (1912) Stanley Houghton's play about a Lancashire mill girl who refuses marriage to a rich man whom she regards as unlikely to make a suitable husband, although she is quite happy to spend a weekend at Blackpool with him.

Hinduism The religion of most of India. BRAHMA was the chief god; BRAHMAN is the reality behind a world of illusion (maya), union with which is sought by release from karma and the chain of rebirth, through asceticism, meditation or YOGA. As in other religions, there is every level of practice, from mysticism and philosophical speculation through ascetic extremes down to idol worship.

Hindustani The lingua franca of northern India and West Pakistan, understood by Hindu and Muslim alike. It spread under the MOGULS, who adopted Persian as their court language, and is thus rich in Persian borrowings. URDU and HINDI are closely allied to it. (Hindustan, Persian name for India.)

Hippocleides A Greek betrothed to the daughter of the local ruler who, according to Herodotus, started to dance at his wedding feast and finally stood on his head. Gravely displeased, the ruler said 'You have danced your marriage away'; to which the young man made the famous retort: Hippocleides doesn't care!

Hippocratic oath The oath, still administered to doctors in some medical schools, to observe certain ethical standards, the chief point of interest to a layman being an undertaking not to divulge a patient's secrets. (Attributed to Hippocrates, Greek physician who died 357 BC.)

Hippocrene Greek legendary fountain on Mount Helicon, a part of the PARNASSUS range sacred to the Muses; hence used of poetic inspiration, as by Keats in his Ode to a Nightingale: O for a beaker full of the warm South,/Full of the true, the blushful Hippocrene. (Greek, 'horse-fountain', as created by a blow from the hoof of PEGASUS.)

Hippodrome (1905) A former New York playhouse for extravaganzas and spectaculars, at Sixth Avenue and 43rd Street; torn down about 1938.

Hippolytus In Greek legend, the virtuous son of THESEUS and an AMAZON queen. He was falsely accused by his stepmother, PHAEDRA, of trying to seduce her, for which his father cursed him and brought about his death, learning the truth too late. This legend is the theme of Euripides' *Hippolytus* (428 BC) and of Racine's *Phèdre.*

Hippopotamus song, The The best known of the Michael Flanders and Donald Swann animal songs, with the refrain: Mud, mud, glorious mud, / Nothing quite like it for cooling the blood!

Hiroshima bomb The first atomic bomb used in war, devastating the city on 6 Aug. 1945. (City of Honshu, Japan.)

Hiroshima, mon amour (1959) The first of the NEW WAVE movies directed by Alain Resnais (see LAST YEAR AT MARIENBAD), which deals with the impact of the heritage of World War II on a love affair between a Frenchwoman and a Japanese businessman.

Hispaniola Old name for the island where Columbus traditionally made his first landing in the New World; now divided between Haiti and the Dominican Republic.

Hissarlik Turkish name of the site of TROY, 20 miles southwest of Çanakkale, opposite Gallipoli.

Hiss case (1950) Whittaker Chambers, an American Communist, stated that Alger Hiss, one of Roosevelt's aides, had in 1938 given him a secret, though unimportant, document. Hiss was imprisoned for perjury when he denied this (released 1954). It was widely believed that he had been framed.

Hitachi (1920) The largest Japanese industrial group, with headquarters at Tokyo, which manufactures heavy electrical machinery, rolling stock, machine tools, computers, chemicals, atomic plant and electronic equipment.

Hitchcock chair American version of a late SHERATON-style chair, painted black and stenciled with fruit and flower designs. (Made in quantity by Lambert Hitchcock of Riverton, Conn., 1820-50.)

Hitlerite A Communist term of abuse for a Fascist.

Hitler-Stalin Pact (Aug. 1939) The nonaggression pact unexpectedly signed in Moscow a few days before World War II, sealing a secret agreement to partition Poland between them and to award the Baltic states to Russia. Stalin thus bought 22 months in which to prepare for the inevitable German invasion. Sometimes called the Ribbentrop-Molotov Pact, from the names of the 2 signatories.

Hitler Youth A German Nazi organization for the indoctrination of the young. (German, *Hitler Jugend.*)

Hitler Youth Quex and SA-man Brand Characters in Nazi propaganda books and movies representing idealized Nazi martyrs; Quex is murdered by Communists but on his deathbed converts his Communist father to the Cause.

Hittites An Indo-European people from the Caucasus who settled in ANATOLIA about 2000 BC, and founded an empire whose capital was Hattuses (now BOGHAZKÖY, Turkey); they were overthrown, possibly by Phrygians, c. 1200 BC.

HMV Name of a British phonograph and record company, from the initials of the words 'His Master's Voice', the caption to the early trademark, still used, of a dog listening to a phonograph. See EMI.

Hoare-Laval Pact (1935) An Anglo-French proposal, made soon after Mussolini's invasion of Abyssinia, to give most of the country to Italy and leave a little for the Emperor. Instantly denounced by British public opinion, it had to be abandoned, and Hoare resigned. (The Foreign Ministers, Samuel Hoare, later Lord Templewood: Pierre Laval, later VICHY GOVERNMENT leader.)

Hobbits The benevolent furry-footed people, living in burrows in the SHIRE, of the weird world of Tolkien's *The* LORD OF THE RINGS; their passion for food and tobacco, along with their other endearing traits, are becoming known to a large and international circle of readers.

Hobgoblin An alternative name for ROBIN GOODFELLOW.

Hobson-Jobson (1886) Title of a dictionary of Anglo-Indian words and phrases by Yule and Burnell. (Corruption of 'Ya Hasan! Ya Husain!', shouted at a MUSLIM festival, used by British soldiers in India as a name for the festival itself; chosen for the title as a typical example of what was in the book.)

Hobson's Choice (1) A phrase meaning 'no choice'. (Thomas Hobson, a 17th-century Cambridge man who hired out horses in strict rotation, giving his customers no choice of mount.) (2) Title of a play (1915) by Harold Brighouse (see MANCHESTER SCHOOL OF DRAMATISTS), a North Country dialect comedy about a Salford shoemaker.

Ho Chi Minh trail US name for the network of roads and paths through the jungle and mountains of southern Laos and eastern Cambodia, used as a supply route by the North Vietnamese. (Named after a North Vietnamese leader.)

Hock White wine from the valley of the Rhine where it meets the Main; the label sometimes gives the village of origin, vineyard, type of grape and quality, in that order. Hocks are richer and fuller-bodied than the MOSELLE type. (From the town of Hocheim.)

Hodgkin's disease A malignant disease of the lymph glands, which become enlarged; it is mainly confined to the young.

Hofburg (1275) The former Imperial Palace of the HAPSBURGS at Vienna; now a complex of buildings including the Presidential offices, state apartments open to the public, museums, a national library and the SPANISH RIDING SCHOOL.

Hofkirche (1563) The royal church of the Holy Roman Emperors at Innsbruck, containing the tomb of the Emperor Maximilian.

Hogarth chair An 18th-century English side chair, usually with hooped back and cabriole legs. (Named for the English artist William Hogarth.)

Hogmanay The Scottish name for New Year's Eve. (Derived through the French from Latin *hoc in anno*, 'in this year', part of the refrain of a song sung on that day.)

Hogsnorton A fictitious village where incredible events used to happen, recounted by the comedian Gillie Potter in a series of BBC radio sketches. (Name taken from a 17th-century proverb 'I think you were born at Hogs-Norton', i.e. 'your manners are atrocious'; from an Oxfordshire village now called Hook Norton.)

Hohenlinden (Dec. 1800) A battle in which the French and Bavarians under Moreau defeated the Austrians, who were forced to accept the peace of Lunéville which ended the SECOND COALITION and the French Revolutionary Wars. It was the theme of a poem by Thomas Campbell. (Village 20 miles east of Munich.)

Hohenstaufens A German dynasty which provided kings and emperors in the 12th-13th centuries.

Hohenzollern candidacy, The (1869) See EMS TELEGRAM.

Hohenzollerns (1415-1918) The dynasty which provided the ELECTORS of Brandenburg, Kings of Prussia (1701), and Emperors of Germany (1871); the main dynasty ended with Kaiser Wilhelm II's abdication, but the cadet branch of Hohenzollern-Sigmaringen ruled Rumania until 1947. (Descended from Count Zollern of Swabia, one of Charlemagne's paladins.)

Hohokam culture (c. 500 BC-c. AD 1500) The culture of the first people to irrigate the Arizona desert, in the Gila Valley area. Using tools of stone and wood, they dug remarkable irrigation channels and cultivated corn; equally remarkable are their clay figurines and other pottery, shells with designs apparently etched with acid, and a ball game for which they built courts. The PIMA may possibly be their direct descendants. See ANASAZI CULTURE. (Pima word for 'the ancient ones'.)

Hola prison camp A camp in Kenya where 11 MAU MAU prisoners died from violence, according to the findings of a coroner's inquest (1959).

Holborn A former London metropolitan borough, since 1965 part of the borough of CAMDEN.

Holcomb murders See IN COLD BLOOD.

Holinshed's Chronicles (1578) Histories and descriptions of England, Scotland and Ireland by several writers (Holinshed wrote the history of England), chiefly remembered as the source of many of Shakespeare's plots, and used also by other Elizabethan dramatists.

Holkham Hall The PALLADIAN home of COKE OF NORFOLK, at Wells, Norfolk; still the property of the Coke family (the Earls of Leicester).

Holland See NETHERLANDS.

Holland House (1605) The Kensington mansion which in the 18th and 19th centuries became famous as a salon of Whig politicians and writers. It is now public property, used for open-air concerts, and as a hostel. (Earl of Holland – the Lincolnshire Holland – former owner.)

Hollands Dutch gin; also called Hollands GENEVA.

Holloway The largest British prison for women, in North London.

Holloway's pills (1837) The first of the patent medicines, claimed to cure rheumatism, gout, 'paralysis', bronchitis, wounds, scrofula, etc., etc.; made of aloes, ginger and soap (as were BEECHAM'S PILLS). Thomas Holloway (died 1883) used some of the profits to found the Royal Holloway College, Egham, and the Holloway Sanatorium, Virginia Water.

Holly Abbreviation used locally for Hollywood, Calif.

Hollybush Summit (1967) Newspaper name for the meeting of President Johnson and Premier Kosygin, the first meeting for 6 years of the heads of state of USA and USSR. (Meeting held at Hollybush House, home of the president of Glassboro State College, N.J.)

Hollywood Used as a synonym for the American motion-picture industry, which made its headquarters there in California.

Hollywood Bowl (1919) A 50-acre natural amphitheater at Hollywood, Calif. where summer outdoor concerts are held, and an Easter sunrise church service.

Holmenkollen Hill A hill near Oslo, the Mecca of ski jumpers, where an international ski week is held in March.

Holmes, Sherlock The violin-playing, cocaine-addicted gentleman detective of Baker Street created by Conan Doyle and first appearing in *A Study in Scarlet* (1887). Tiring of him, the author had him killed off by MORIARTY in 1893, but popular demand forced his resurrection in 1903 in *The Empty House*. The author explained that Holmes had spent the intervening years in Tibet.

Holofernes See JUDITH AND HOLOFERNES and LOVE'S LABOUR'S LOST.

Holy Alliance (1815) An agreement by the rulers of Russia, Austria and Prussia reached after Napoleon's downfall, ostensibly to be guided in their policies by Christian principles, but actually to suppress liberal movements. The Pope and Britain refused to be parties to it. Also called the Metternich system. See CONCERT OF EUROPE; DREIKAISERBUND.

Holy Deadlock (1934) A. P. Herbert's satire on the English divorce laws which he was able to have amended 3 years later when, as an Independent MP, he introduced a Private Member's Bill leading to what became known as the Herbert Divorce Act.

Holy Ghost The Third Person of the TRINITY, the Divine Spirit. Jesus promised the Apostles that his Spirit would remain with them, and this was manifested on the day of PENTECOST. Thereafter the Holy Ghost guided the Church in its life and teaching. This doctrine was defined at the Council of Constantinople, 381. In art the Holy Ghost is represented as a dove.

Holy Ghost, The Sin against the A mysterious conception, based on *Matthew* xii, 31-32; its meaning is not there defined, but it is sometimes thought to refer to conscious thwarting of the good.

Holy Grail The chalice used by Christ at the Last Supper and traditionally brought by JOSEPH OF ARIMATHEA (*Matthew* xxvii, 57-60) to GLASTONBURY. In the versions of the legend by Chrestien de Troyes and Wolfram von Eschenbach, the Grail was located in the Hall of the Grail at Monsalvat, Spain.

Holy Innocents, Feast of December 28th, commemorating the MASSACRE OF THE INNOCENTS.

Holy Joe Armed forces chaplain.

Holy League (1) Name given to two 16th-century alliances directed against France and Spain respectively. (2) A Roman Catholic league against the HUGUENOTS formed by the GUISE family, backed by Philip II of Spain, and defeated by Henry IV of France, who himself then turned Catholic. See RELIGIOUS WARS, FRENCH.

Holy Living and Holy Dying (1650-51) A devotional work by Jeremy Taylor.

Holy Loch A Scottish loch in Argyll on the west of the Firth of Clyde, which from 1961 was used as a base for US POLARIS submarines. Compare FASLANE.

Holy Office (1) The INQUISITION. (2) The modern successor to (1), which keeps a watch on heretical literature. Its official name is the Congregation for the Doctrine of the Faith.

Holy Roman Empire In theory the unification of Europe with Papal blessing under a Christian Emperor, and a continuation of the Roman Empire. First founded by Charlemagne (800), it collapsed at his death; revived by Otto I (962), it fell (1273) into the hands of the HAPSBURGS, who extended its boundaries. As a result of the THIRTY YEARS WAR the Protestant German states broke away in 1648, although the title and pageantry of the Holy Roman Empire lingered on until 1806, when Napoleon ended it (see AUSTERLITZ, NAPOLEONIC WARS) and the last Holy Roman Emperor, Francis, became Emperor of Austria.

Holyroodhouse An ancient palace at the foot of Canongate, Edinburgh, reconstructed by Charles II; the British sovereign's official residence when in Scotland.

Holy See, The The Papacy; the Papal court; the authority and jurisdiction of the Pope.

Holy Spirit Synonymous with HOLY GHOST.

Holy Trinity of Steel See STEWART & LLOYDS.

Holy Week The week before Easter; also called PASSION WEEK.

Home Counties Those surrounding London, particularly those into which GREATER LONDON has encroached (Essex, Kent, Surrey and Hertfordshire); with the outward spread of the commuter belt, Buckinghamshire, Berkshire and Sussex have a claim to inclusion.

Home Guard (May 1940) The unpaid and at first voluntary force formed to repel German invasion of Britain; men up to the age of 65 were eligible, and were armed with what miscellaneous weapons were available. Later it was possible to develop it into a fully trained and armed force, units of which manned antiaircraft batteries. They stood down in November 1944.

Home Rule A term used from the 1870s for Irish internal self-government. An Act to establish it was passed in September 1914 but suspended for the duration of World War I. Another Act was passed in 1920 which, at the request of the 6 northern counties, provided separate parliaments for the Catholic South and the Protestant North.

Homestead Act (1862) Enacted that a head of family could claim up to 160 acres of public land, and having occupied and/or cultivated it for 5 years could claim exemption from its seizure for debt; he could also buy the land after 6 months for a nominal sum. The object was to attract surplus labor in the cities back to the land, but it had little effect.

'Home, Sweet Home' (1823) A song written by John Howard Payne to an old Sicilian tune for a now-forgotten opera. The theme is: Be it ever so humble, there's no place like home. In protest against WHITEHALL gobbledygook, Winston Churchill once rendered it 'Domestic habitation unit, sweet domestic habitation unit'.

Homo erectus The specific name first given to JAVA MAN, and now extended to cover all the PITHECANTHROPINES.

'Homo habilis' (Skillful Man) Professor Leakey's name for the creature of which he found remains, together with crude stone tools, at OLDUVAI GORGE in 1960-62. It is held by some to be a form of man though anatomically an AUSTRALOPITHECINE, and thus possibly a link in the evolution of man from ape. It has been dated to about 1,750,000 years ago.

Homo sapiens Modern man, thought to have appeared about 30,000 BC.

Honest John US truck-launched artillery rocket, with a range up to 15 miles, designed to take a nuclear warhead.

Hong Kong flu (1968-69) A pandemic of a mild form of influenza that spread from the Far East; the virus strain, named A2, differed from that in ASIAN FLU.

Hongroise Cooking term indicating the presence of paprika.

Hons, The A family society formed by the children of Lord Redesdale. According to one of them, Jessica Mitford in *Hons and Rebels* (1960), the popular derivation from 'Honorables' is incorrect; the name is a childhood corruption of 'hens' (which were apparently a major feature in the Redesdale domestic economy), and is pronounced as spelled.

Hood, HMS The largest British battleship, sunk in May 1941 by the BISMARCK.

Hoosier State Nickname of Indiana. (Derivation uncertain.)

Hoover Dam (1936) A huge dam, 726 ft high, on the Colorado River between Arizona and Nevada, creating Lake Mead; temporarily re-

named the Boulder Dam when President Hoover was out of favor; old name restored by President Truman in 1947.

Hoover moratorium (1931) The suspension of payment of intergovernmental debts and reparations proposed by President Hoover at the height of the DEPRESSION.

Hopalong Cassidy The romantic cowboy created by Clarence E. Mulford (1883-1956) in *Bar-20* (1907), a Western written 17 years before he ever set foot in the West. He reappeared in 28 other stories by Mulford and in countless scripts invented by others for movies and TV from 1934, creating a juvenile cult of Davy Crockett proportions.

'Hope' G. F. Watts's painting of Hope sitting blindfold on the globe, trying to extract music from the last remaining string of her broken lyre; now in the TATE Gallery, London.

Hope, Anthony Pen name of Anthony Hope Hawkins, author of novels about RURITANIA.

Hope, SS A famous US hospital ship which for over 10 years has been visiting countries in Africa, Asia and South America on teaching-treatment missions.

Hope diamond, The A 44-carat Indian diamond of a rare shade of blue, supposed to have been stolen from an idol and therefore to bring misfortune to its owners. It was sold to Louis XIV, bought by the Hope family, and after various changes of ownership came to rest in the Smithsonian Institution, Washington, D.C.

Hopetoun House An ADAM STYLE mansion, residence of the Marquesses of Linlithgow, at South Queensferry, near Edinburgh.

Hopewell culture The most advanced of the MOUND BUILDERS cultures, centered in southern Ohio but found over a wide surrounding region; authorities differ as to their date, the outside limits being 500 BC to AD 1300. Characteristics are banked earth enclosures, round burial mounds, and fine craftmanship, especially in copper but also in ceramics and stone. (Named for the first site, Hopewell Farm, Hamilton County, O., and thus unconnected with the next entry.)

Hopewell Village A national historic site (1938) in Pennsylvania, one of the finest examples of US 18th- and early 19th-century iron-making villages, with ruins of the old furnace.

Hopi A Shoshonean-speaking race (see SHOSHONI) of PUEBLO INDIANS; some 3500 survive in a reservation in Arizona and still perform a spectacular snake dance (with live rattlesnakes) every other year north of Winslow.

Horatio In Shakespeare's play, HAMLET, Hamlet's only true friend.

Horatio Alger (1) In American usage, an adjective meaning 'relating to, resembling the works of, Horatio Alger', an American clergyman (1832-99) who wrote 120 works of juvenile fiction on the theme newsboy (or bootblack) to riches, via hard work, self-reliance and all the virtues. Hence (2) the name of an award given by the American Schools and Colleges Association for achievement from humble beginnings.

Horatius, The brave The well-known hero who, 'facing fearful odds' held up LARS PORSENA at the gates of Rome.

Hornblower, Horatio The hero of a series of novels by C. S. Forester about the British Navy in Napoleonic times, the first of which was *The Happy Return* (1937). They cover Hornblower's career from midshipman to Admiral Lord Hornblower.

Horn Dance See ABBOTS BROMLEY HORN DANCE.

Hornet (1952) A national class of very fast 16-foot dinghy, designed by Jack Holt; exciting to race and frequently capsizes.

Horniman Museum (1897) A museum and library in Forest Hill, London, devoted to the history of the development of man, with a collection of early tools, dance masks, musical instruments etc.

Horniman theatre, The See MANCHESTER GAIETY.

Hornsey A former London borough, since 1965 part of the borough of HARINGEY.

'Horse Fair, The' (1853) One of the vigorous and accurate paintings of animals by the French artist Rosa Bonheur. (Presented by Cornelius Vanderbilt to the Metropolitan Museum of Art, NYC: a replica is in the National Gallery, London.)

Horse Guards (1) Used for the HOUSEHOLD CAVALRY or (2) specifically, The BLUES AND ROYALS; (3) in London, an 18th-century building in WHITEHALL, on the site of a former guard house to the Palace of WESTMINSTER, headquarters of the Army (London District), and long associated with the HOUSEHOLD CAVALRY. See next entry.

Horse Guards Parade The parade ground adjoining the HORSE GUARDS (3), where the ceremony of TROOPING THE COLOR is held on the Queen's Birthday.

Horse of the Year Show (1949) (UK) A show held at WEMBLEY each October, chiefly to determine the leading show jumpers of the year.

Horse's Mouth, The (1944) Joyce Cary's novel of the dedicated old artist, rogue and genius, Gulley Jimson.

Horse's Neck A long drink of ginger ale and brandy or other liquor.

'Horst Wessel Lied' (1933) The Nazi 'national anthem', written by Horst Wessel to an old music-hall tune; it began: Die Fahne hoch, die Reihen dicht geschlossen! ('Up with the flag and close the serried ranks').

Horus Ancient Egyptian hawk-headed god of the rising sun, opponent of the powers of darkness, son of ISIS and OSIRIS; equivalent to the Greek APOLLO.

Hoskinstown Site near Canberra, Australia, of the largest fixed telescope, set up in 1964.

Hosta The genus name of the Plantain Lily, also called *Funkia*.

HOTAC Abbreviated trading name of the London Hotel Accommodation Service in Baker Street, formed chiefly to assist visitors to London to find emergency accommodation even when most hotels are fully booked.

Hot Springs National Park (1921) A park in central Arkansas, surrounding the city of Hot Springs. There are

47 hot mineral springs, reputed from Spanish times to have therapeutic value, and bathhouses run under government supervision.

Hotspur Nickname of Sir Henry Percy (1364-1403), eldest son of the 1st Earl of Northumberland, a gallant and hot-tempered warrior who was killed fighting for Owen Glendower against Henry IV. He appears in Shakespeare's HENRY IV.

Hottentot bustle, The A nickname for steatopygy (immensely fat buttocks) characteristic of pure-blooded Hottentot women. See next entry.

Hottentots A South African community, now scattered, apparently akin to the BUSHMEN, whose distinctive KAFFIR CLICK they still retain. Unlike them they took to urban ways, and intermarried freely with BANTU, Dutch and other races. (Perhaps an AFRIKAANS word for 'stammerers'.)

Houdini A generic term for an 'escapologist', a person who, however carefully he is trussed up, can free himself. (From Harry Houdini, died 1926, an American conjuror and illusionist, who excelled at the art.)

Houghton and Gee spy case (1961) The arrest of Harry Houghton and Ethel Gee, both sentenced in the PORTLAND SECRETS CASE to 15 years imprisonment. Houghton was suborned by LONSDALE.

Houghton Meeting (UK) The last flat-race meeting of the season at Newmarket, in October, at which the Cambridgeshire is run.

Hound Dog US air-to-surface missile carried by the STRATOFORTRESS. It has a range of 575 miles.

'Hound of Heaven, The' (1893) Francis Thompson's devotional poem, in which he represents himself as in flight from God's love, pursued and overtaken. It begins: I fled Him, down the nights and down the days; / I fled Him, down the arches of the years.

Hound of the Baskervilles, The (1902) A Conan Doyle story presented as an early exploit of Sherlock HOLMES, whom the author had killed off in a previous story.

Hounslow London borough since 1965 consisting of the former boroughs of Heston-Isleworth-Hounslow and Brentford-Chiswick, and the urban district of Feltham.

House, The (1) (OXFORD UNIVERSITY) Christ Church (College). (2) (CITY of London) The Stock Exchange. (3) (Politics) The House of Commons. (4) The US House of Representatives.

House and Garden (1901) A Condé Nast monthly magazine.

House Beautiful A monthly magazine published in New York.

Houseboat manslaughter case (1956) (UK) The trial of Mrs Vikki Clark, alias Wright, sentenced to 3 years for the manslaughter of her two-year-old twin sons in a houseboat fire at South Benfleet, Canvey Island, Essex.

Household Cavalry The cavalry brigade of the HOUSEHOLD TROOPS, consisting of 2 regiments: The LIFE GUARDS and The BLUES AND ROYALS.

Household Troops The sovereign's personal guard, consisting of the HOUSEHOLD CAVALRY and the 3 senior Guards regiments, the GRENADIER, COLDSTREAM and Scots Guards.

House of Fraser A UK shop empire built up by Sir Hugh Fraser, a Glasgow draper, and including HARRODS, John Barkers and D. H. Evans; it also sells Eskimo foods.

House of the Dead (1861) Dostoevsky's novel based on his own experiences in a Siberian prison after his arrest as a revolutionary.

House of the Seven Gables, The (1851) Nathaniel Hawthorne's novel of a family under a curse; it is represented by an aging spinster who lives in the ramshackle old family mansion of the title, joined by her brother back from a long prison sentence for a murder committed by his cousin. The innocent suffer, the wicked prosper, until the cousin's sudden death; then, the sin of their ancestor expiated, the curse broken, brother and sister spend their last few years in peace.

House that Ruth Built, The The YANKEE STADIUM, as having been financed by the huge gates when BABE RUTH played.

Houston Astrodome (1965) The biggest indoor arena in the world, at Houston, Tex.; used for baseball and boxing matches etc. In the 'Astrodomain' are an Astrohall (for conventions) and the Astroworld (a Texan DISNEYLAND).

Houyhnhnms The race of horses which inhabited the last of the countries visited in GULLIVER'S TRAVELS, the embodiment of nobility, virtue and reason, who kept the YAHOOS in subjection.

Hovercraft A vehicle which floats a foot or two above ground or water on a cushion of air provided by a ring of air jets placed below it, all directed inwards. A British invention, by Christopher Cockerell, taken off the secret list in 1959. See SR-N.

Howard's End (1910) E. M. Forster's novel on the theme of his key aphorism, 'only connect', i.e. about bringing together people, classes and nations through sympathetic insight and understanding. The Wilcoxes (wealth and business), Schlegels (culture) and Bast (the poor bank clerk) are brought together in the country house which gives the book its title.

How Green Was My Valley (1940) Richard Llewellyn's popular novel about a Welsh mining village.

Howl (1956) Beatnik poems by the American, Allen Ginsberg. The title poem begins: I saw the best minds of my generation destroyed by madness, starving, hysterical, naked.

'How they brought the Good News from Ghent to Aix' (1845) Browning's dramatic poem, not based on historical fact, of 3 men galloping to save Aix: I galloped, Dirck galloped, we galloped all three.

How to Win Friends and Influence People (1955) A sensationally successful book by Dale Carnegie of Missouri, which was in effect a guide to salesmen on the techniques of persuasion, but apparently appealed to a much wider public.

Hoyle, According to According to the rules of the game. (Edmund Hoyle, who wrote an authoritative treatise on whist in 1742, later adding chapters on other card games; the name is perpetuated in *Hoyle's Games Modernised*, a standard work on all indoor games, including billiards, chess, roulette etc.)

H₂S Code name for airborne radar used for bombing through clouds in 1943.

Hub, The Nickname for Boston, Mass. Oliver Wendell Holmes went so far as to say that 'Boston Statehouse is the hub of the solar system'.

Hubble's Law (Astronomy) That the speed of recession of galaxies is proportional to their distance from an observer. See EXPANDING UNIVERSE THEORY.

Huckleberry Finn (1884) Mark Twain's masterpiece in which Huck, as he was called, a character from the earlier TOM SAWYER, escapes from his drunken father to float down the Mississippi on a raft with a runaway slave, Jim. The latter is captured, and Huck meets Tom Sawyer again.

HUD (1965) Initials used for the Federal Department of Housing and Urban Development, which deals with problems created by America's expanding and overcrowded cities.

Hudibras (1663-78) Samuel Butler's mock-heroic verse satire modeled on *Don Quixote*, in which Hudibras, a fat Presbyterian hunchback, sallies forth on an old nag with the INDEPENDENT, Ralpho, as his Sancho Panza, to put the world to rights, and especially to stop people enjoying themselves. They spend much of their time quarreling over trivial theological points. (Name taken from Spenser's FAERIE QUEENE.)

Hudson Institute (1961) An organization in New York State founded by Dr Herman Kahn when he left the similar RAND CORPORATION. Dr Kahn (who coined the term 'megadeath' for a unit of 1 million dead in nuclear war) carries out research on the likely direction of scientific progress in the far future, e.g. new methods of propulsion, sources of power and food, space travel and colonization, doubling man's allotted span—thus as a by-product providing SF writers with endless new material. The Hudson and Rand institutions are commonly called 'think factories' or 'think tanks'.

Hudson Memorial   See RIMA.

Hudson River School   (1825-1870s) The first distinctively American group of landscape painters, started by Thomas Cole (1801-52) who, on arrival from England, fell in love with the Catskills and settled by the Hudson. Other members were Thomas Doughty and A. B. Durand. They dedicated themselves to glorifying the magnificent scenery of the Hudson valley and adjacent areas.

Hudson's Bay blanket   A heavy woolen blanket with one or more broad stripes, usually black on red ground or varicolored on white, indicating its weight.

Hudson's Bay Company   (1670) Founded by Prince Rupert, chartered by Charles II and given the monopoly of the English fur trade with the Indians of North America in competition with the French. It is still the biggest fur trader in Canada, but derives most of its income from oil rights, department stores and other interests.

Hughenden Manor   Disraeli's home near High Wycombe, Buckinghamshire, now owned by the NATIONAL TRUST.

Hughes Medal   (1902) ROYAL SOCIETY medal awarded annually for original discovery in the physical sciences, especially electricity and magnetism.

Hughes missile   A US air-to-air missile of recent development.

Hugh the Drover   (1924) Vaughan Williams's ballad-opera set in the Cotswolds, full of English folk music. Hugh is accused of being a spy for Napoleon, but his reputation is cleared by the arrival of a sergeant whose life he had once saved.

Huguenots   French Protestants, mainly CALVINISTS; victims of the ST BARTHOLOMEW MASSACRE, tolerated

under the EDICT OF NANTES, and again persecuted on its revocation, they scattered to England and other Protestant countries. (Corruption of German *Eidgenossen*, 'confederates'.)

Huis-Clos   (1944) Sartre's long one-act play about a man and 2 women who have died and are shut up in one room to torture each other endlessly ('hell is other people'). Finally offered freedom, they find they have become indispensable to one another. (English title, *In Camera*; US title, *No Exit*.)

Huks, The   US abbreviation of Hukbalahap, the Filipino abbreviated name for the People's Army Against Japan, a Philippine underground guerrilla movement against Japanese occupation, which after World War II under Communist leadership maintained a most troublesome rebellion against the Philippine government until 1955.

Hull House   (1889) A pioneer social settlement modeled on TOYNBEE HALL, founded in Chicago by Jane Addams; leading social reformers took up residence there.

Hulot, Monsieur   The clumsy, gangling ever so apologetic character created and portrayed by the French cinema producer, Jacques Tati, in a series of near-silent comedies.

Humanae vitae   (1968) Pope Paul VI's encyclical which reaffirmed the Church's previous condemnation of birth control; it aroused sharp controversy within the Church. (Latin, 'of human life'.)

Humanism   See REVIVAL OF LEARNING.

Humanité, L'   (1904) A French Socialist newspaper founded by Jean Jaurès, which in 1920 became Communist.

Humble Petition and Advice   (1657) Presented by the second PROTECTORATE Parliament, offering the title of king to Oliver Cromwell, which he refused, and suggesting the restoration of a Second Chamber in Parliament, which he accepted.

Humboldt current   The cold current flowing from the Antarctic up the west coast of northern Chile and Peru, causing fogs and aridity in the coastal regions.

Hume-Setty case (1949) (UK) Donald Hume was sentenced to 12 years as an accessory to the murder of Stanley Setty, whose body was found in the Essex marshes. After his release, Hume confessed that he was the principal in the case, but in the meantime he had been given a life sentence in Switzerland for the murder of a taxi driver.

Humphrey Clinker (1771) Smollett's comic novel in the form of letters written by the Bramble family, whose servant Humphrey becomes; later it transpires that he is the illegitimate son of Mr Bramble. The book includes a picture of life at Bath ('Hot Wells').

Humpty Dumpty The egg of the rhyming riddle found, under various names, throughout Europe. In THROUGH THE LOOKING-GLASS he became the scornful character for whom words meant just whatever he chose them to mean.

Hunchback of Notre Dame Quasimodo; see NOTRE DAME DE PARIS.

Hundred Associates, The (1627-63) The Company of New France, a joint-stock company to which Cardinal Richelieu handed over the administration and trade monopoly of Canada in return for their promise to settle the St Lawrence Valley. This they failed to do, and their charter was revoked.

Hundred Days, The (1815) (1) The period between Napoleon's escape from ELBA in March and the Battle of WATERLOO in June. (2) The period of the special session of Congress (March-June 1933) which speedily passed the main NEW DEAL measures, including the AGRICULTURAL ADJUSTMENT Act, the NATIONAL INDUSTRIAL RECOVERY ACT and authorization for the TVA.

Hundred Flowers policy In China on 17 February 1957, CHAIRMAN MAO Tse-tung announced, 'Let 100 flowers blossom and 100 schools of thought contend', i.e. invited a flowering of public criticism of his regime. This turned out to be so virulent and widespread that the policy was abruptly reversed, and wholesale arrests followed.

Hundred Years War (1337-1453) An intermittent war waged by England, which claimed the French throne. Begun by Edward III, it ended in the reign of Henry VI, with England ejected from all its French possessions bar Calais. The main battles were CRÉCY, Poitiers, AGINCOURT, and the siege of Orléans raised by Joan of Arc.

Hungarian rising (Oct. 1956) A revolt against Russian domination, put down savagely by Russian troops. Kadar was installed as premier to replace Nagy, who was executed as ringleader.

Hungry Forties, The The 1840s, when bad harvests and the Irish potato famine, combined with the CORN LAWS, caused great distress in Britain.

Huns Mongolian horsemen who swept into Europe to form a short-lived empire from the Urals to the Rhine, which collapsed when Romans and GOTHS defeated Attila at Châlons-sur-Marne (451).

Hunter (1956) A HAWKER SIDDELEY sweptwing ground-attack and short-range Army-support aircraft, due for replacement by the HARRIER. It was designed by the same man as the HURRICANE.

Hunterston (1964) (UK) One of the earlier series of nuclear power stations, designed also to produce plutonium. A new AGR reactor is also projected. (Coastal site south of Largs, Ayrshire.)

Huntington Library (1919) A famous library at San Marino near Los Angeles; among its treasures are a GUTENBERG BIBLE, Caxton's first book in English and a MS of the *Canterbury Tales*. With it are administered an art gallery (containing many valuable paintings, e.g. the BLUE BOY), and botanical gardens with 1200 varieties of camellia and a collection of desert plants. (Collected and donated by Henry E. Huntington, a railroad magnate.)

Huntington's chorea A hereditary disease which appears in middle age, characterized by involuntary purposeless movements and mental deterioration.

Huntley-Brinkley Report A TV news and commentary program broadcast by NBC every weekday evening from 1956 to 1970; a merging of 'CHET HUNTLEY REPORTING' and 'DAVE BRINKLEY'S JOURNAL', with one reporting from New York, the other from Washington.

Hurlingham Club (1869) A London club at RANELAGH Gardens, originally but no longer a polo club, now providing facilities for tennis, swimming, squash, croquet etc. The Hurlingham Polo Association controls British polo.

Huron An Iroquoian race and confederacy of Indians who originally lived between Lakes Huron, Erie and Ontario; they cooperated in the French fur trade but their rivals, the FIVE NATIONS, who had Dutch support, dispersed them in the 17th century and they retreated as far as Wisconsin. Also known as Wyandot.

Hurricane The Hawker fighter which, with the Spitfire, won the BATTLE OF BRITAIN.

Hurricane Flora (1963) A hurricane which devastated Haiti and Cuba. (Hurricanes are given feminine names because of their unpredictability.)

Hurstmonceux The village in Sussex, near Eastbourne, to which the ROYAL GREENWICH OBSERVATORY was moved in 1958.

Husky An ESKIMO DOG; see also SIBERIAN HUSKY. (Possibly a corruption of 'ESKIMO'.)

Hussars The surviving regiments, all in the ROYAL ARMOURED CORPS, are: The Queen's Own Hussars; The Queen's Royal Irish Hussars; The Royal Hussars (Prince of Wales's Own); 13th/18th Royal Hussars (Queen Mary's Own); 14th/20th King's Hussars; 15th/19th The King's Royal Hussars.

Hussites Bohemian followers of John Huss, who developed from a party of religious reform to a nationalist party opposed to German and Papal domination. Successful in the Hussite War (1419-34), they won concessions from Sigismund, the Holy Roman Emperor. (John Huss, rector of Prague University, burned at the stake in 1415 as an agitator for religious reform.)

Hustler (1961) The US B-58 delta-winged medium bomber, built by CONVAIR. It was the first supersonic (Mach 2) bomber, a 3-seater with 4 turbojets.

Hutu A BANTU people of BURUNDI and RWANDA in Central Africa, constantly at feud with the TUTSI. Also called Bahutu.

Hwang Ho Chinese name of the Yellow River.

Hyades An open (or galactic) star cluster in TAURUS, which includes ALDEBARAN; when it rose with the sun it was thought to foretell rain. (Greek, 'the rainy ones', name of the daughers of ATLAS.)

Hyde Park (1) The well-known London park. (2) A village in New York State overlooking the Hudson River, where the Roosevelt family home is now classed as a national historic site, with a Franklin D. Roosevelt library and museum.

Hydra In Greek legend, a many-headed monster slain by Heracles (HERCULES) as one of his Labors.

Hyksos Kings Rulers of Semitic nomads who invaded Egypt in the late 18th century BC, introducing new weapons and horse chariots; they were expelled about 1570 BC by the founders of the NEW KINGDOM. (Egyptian, 'Shepherd Kings'.)

Hymen In Greek legend, the young god of marriage, son of APOLLO.

Hymenoptera An order of insects with 4 membranous wings, the bees, wasps and ants (not including termites).

Hymettus A mountain overlooking Athens, famous in olden times for honey and marble.

Hypatia A lecturer on Greek philosophy in 5th-century Alexandria, and the heroine of Charles Kingsley's historical novel of that name (1853). She was torn to pieces by a Christian mob who disapproved of pagan philosophy.

Hyperboreans In Greek legend, a people who lived in a fertile land far to the north, where the sun always shone.

Hypericum The genus name of the St-John's-Worts; *H. calycinum* is the Rose of Sharon.

Hyperion In later Greek legend, a TITAN, father of HELIOS (Sun), SELENE (Moon) and EOS (Dawn); originally (in Homer) the name of the sun-god.

Hyperion (1820) Keats's unfinished poem on the overthrow of the TITANS by the new Greek gods (representing his own revolutionary ideas); see last entry.

Hyperion Lord Derby's horse that in 1933 won the (Epsom) DERBY (in record time) and the St Leger.

I

Iachimo The villian of Shakespeare's CYMBELINE who persuades Imogen's husband that Imogen has been unfaithful.

IAEA See INTERNATIONAL ATOMIC ENERGY AGENCY.

Iago In Shakespeare's play, Othello's ensign who, from malevolence and jealousy, persuades OTHELLO that DESDEMONA has been unfaithful to him.

IATA (1945) The International Air Transport Association, the nongovernmental organization of scheduled airlines to promote safe and efficient transport; successor to the International Air Traffic Association (1919); headquarters, Montreal.

Ibadan University The first university to be established in Nigeria, in the southwest.

Iberia (1) The ancient name for the country of the River Ebro, hence the Spanish peninsula. (2) Name of the chief Spanish airline. (From *Iberus*, 'Ebro'.)

Iberians A dark-skinned race of small stature, not belonging to the Nordic or Alpine groups and speaking a language unrelated to any other known language, of whom the Basques are a remnant and traces survive in Wales, Ireland, Brittany etc.; thought to have occupied most of Western Europe in Neolithic times; also called Mediterranean or Eurafrican.

Iblis See EBLIS.

IBM Initials normally used for International Business Machines, with headquarters at Armonk, N.Y. and, in Europe, Paris. Its products include electric typewriters, dictating equipment, punched card accounting and electronic data-processing machines.

Ibn Arabic, 'son of'.

Ibo The dominant people, and semi-BANTU language, of eastern Nigeria. See BIAFRA REPUBLIC.

Ibrahim Arabic equivalent of ABRAHAM.

ICA See INTERNATIONAL COOPERATION ADMINISTRATION.

ICAO See INTERNATIONAL CIVIL AVIATION ORGANIZATION.

Icarus See DAEDALUS.

ICBM Initials commonly used for intercontinental ballistic missile, i.e. one with a range of over 5000 miles; compare IRBM. See MIRV.

ICC See INTERSTATE COMMERCE COMMISSION.

Ice Age The period of about a million years, ending 10,000 BC, when northern Europe and America had a permanent ice cover; also, a previous period of this kind.

Iceman Cometh, The Eugene O'Neill's play (1946), the Iceman being Death.

Iceni The ancient Britons of East Anglia who, under Boadicea, revolted against Roman rule in AD 62.

ICFTU Initials used for the (non-Communist) International Confederation of Free Trade Unions.

Ichabod A son of Phinehas, born just after the deaths of his father and grandfather (I *Samuel* iv, 21); the name means 'the glory is departed (from Israel)'.

I Chose Freedom (1946) The highly colored autobiography of a Russian, Victor Kravchenko, who defected to the West in Washington, D.C. (1944). It deals with the period of the STALINIST PURGES. The suggestion has been made that it is the work of a 'ghost'.

Ichthys The Greek word for 'fish'; the early Christians noticed that the letters formed the initials of the Greek for 'Jesus Christ, Son of God, Savior', and thus came to adopt the fish as a symbol of Christ.

ICI (1926) A UK firm which manufactures alkalis (Winnington, Cheshire), dyestuffs (Manchester), ammonia (Billingham), TERYLENE (Harrogate), paints (Slough) and has other factories at Wilton and Glasgow; among its other products are Perspex, Polythene and Paludrine. (Initials standing for Imperial Chemical Industries.)

Icknield Way A pre-Roman track running from near Marlborough through the Goring Gap on the Thames, to Letchworth and the Wash. (Possibly derived from IGENI, the tribe who lived in East Anglia.)

I, Claudius (1934) Robert Graves's novel in the form of Claudius's own story of the humiliations of his youth and, in the sequel *Claudius the God* (1943), his unwilling succession to Caligula as Roman Emperor.

ICM (Increased Capability Missile) A US ICBM due in service about 1973; it carries double the payload of MINUTEMAN over the same range and is designed to penetrate any defense as it is maneuverable during the reentry phase, when it will take an erratic but predetermined course. It will also have a multiple warhead of the MIRV type.

ICS The (former) Indian Civil Service.

IDA See INTERNATIONAL DEVELOPMENT ASSOCIATION.

Ida (1) A mountain near Troy. (2) A mountain in Crete in a cave of which ZEUS was brought up. (3) Mother Ida, apostrophized in Tennyson's *Oenone*, is (1), where the nymph Oenone fell in love with PARIS. (4) The Idaean Mother was CYBELE, associated with both (1) and (2).

Ida, Princess Heroine of Tennyson's fantasy, THE PRINCESS, and of the GILBERT AND SULLIVAN OPERA, *Princess Ida*, based on it.

Id al-Fitr, Id al-Kabir See BAIRAM.

IDB Initials used for illicit diamond buying or buyer.

IDC (1962) (UK) Initials used for the Industrial Development and Construction Co., with headquarters at Stratford on Avon, a group of industrial and commercial builders and building designers which operates at home and overseas.

ID card For Identification Card; any card, preferably official, that helps to identify its bearer by name, address etc. Used especially in checking a person's age before serving alcoholic beverages.

Ides of March March 15th in the Roman calendar; the fateful (or fatal) day, with reference to the day of Julius Caesar's assassination.

Idiot, The Prince Myshkin in Dostoevsky's novel of that name; a Christlike epileptic pauper prince, the type of the 'divine fool'.

Idiot's Delight (1936) Robert E. Sherwood's famous PULITZER-PRIZE play, produced 2 years before MUNICH. The outbreak of a world war finds a polyglot miscellany of tourists marooned in a Swiss Alpine hotel; they include American actors, a French arms manufacturer and his Russian mistress, English honeymooners and a German scientist. The Russian gives up her Frenchman and remains with the leading American actor, trapped in an air raid after the rest have left to join up.

Idler, The (1758-60) Dr Johnson's Addisonian essays, lighter in tone than those in the RAMBLER.

Idlewild Now Kennedy Airport, New York.

Idris Welsh legendary giant whose chair is the top of Cader Idris, a mountain in Merionethshire. He inspired poets and induced madness.

Idylls of the King (1859-85) Tennyson's version of ARTHURIAN LEGEND, based on Le MORTE D'ARTHUR; an allegory in which King ARTHUR represents the soul of man at war with the senses.

IFC See INTERNATIONAL FINANCE CORPORATION.

Ife heads (13th century) Bronze and terracotta heads of great artistic merit made at Ife, the center of YORUBA religion in Western Nigeria. The artistic tradition may have derived from the NOK CULTURE.

IFS See IRISH FREE STATE.

IFTU (1901-45) Initials used for the International Federation of Trade Unions, the first such body to be formed. It was succeeded by the WFTU.

If Winter Comes . . . (1920) A novel by A. S. M. Hutchinson which was immensely popular in its time. (A quotation from Shelley, which continues 'can Spring be far behind?')

IG Farben Abbreviated name of a major German chemical group, in 1945 split into BAYER, Hoechst and BASF. (German *Interessengemeinschaften*, a vertical trust in which profits are shared; *Farbenindustrie*, 'dyes industry'.)

Ightham A near-perfect ancient moated manor house at Ivy Hatch, near Sevenoaks, Kent; still occupied.

IGY See INTERNATIONAL GEOPHYSICAL YEAR.

IHS The first 3 letters of the name Jesus in Greek, in which long *e* resembles *H*; variously taken to represent the Latin phrases *Iesus Hominum Salvator* (Jesus, Savior of men), *In Hoc Signo* (*vinces*) (under this sign shalt thou conquer) or *In Hac* (*cruce*) *Salus* (in this Cross is salvation).

IJsselmeer The name given to the Dutch Zuider Zee when it was cut off from the sea by a barrage (1932).

Ikara An Australian-built antisubmarine weapons system carried by TYPE 82 DESTROYERS.

Ike Nickname of General (later President) Dwight D. Eisenhower.

Île de France The district round Paris bounded approximately by the Seine, Marne, Oise and Aisne, the French equivalent of the English HOME COUNTIES.

Ilford (UK) A former Essex borough, since 1965 part of the borough of REDBRIDGE.

Iliad, The Homer's epic poem about the events of a few days near the end of the TROJAN WAR. It begins with ACHILLES sulking in his tent and ends with a Trojan state funeral for HECTOR, whose corpse Achilles has been persuaded to return.

Ilium Another name for Troy. (Latin form of Greek name *Ilion*.)

'Ilkla Moor' A widely known song from Ilkley, Yorkshire, beginning:

Wheer wer' ta bahn w'en Aw saw thee / On Ilkla Moor baht'at?

Illustrated London News (1842) The pioneer in the sphere of illustrated weeklies.

Illyria Old name for the Adriatic coastal region of Yugoslavia, Albania and northern Greece, once a Roman province.

ILO (1919) A body set up at Geneva under the LEAGUE OF NATIONS as the International Labor Office and taken over by UNO (as the International Labor Organization). It promotes the improvement and standardization of labor conditions and living standards.

ILP (1893) Initials used for the Independent Labor Party, one of the elements which went to form the British Labour Party; it broke away in 1932 under James Maxton, who held it together until his death in 1946. It was consistently pacifist.

Ilyushin The name of a series of Russian civil and military aircraft, notably the Il-12, a twin-engined contemporary of the Viking, and the 4-engined Il-62, equivalent of the VC-10.

Imaginary Conversations (1824-53) A series of dialogues between historical characters down the ages, on various subjects, by Walter Savage Landor; one of them is a conversation between Dante and BEATRICE, for example.

Imagists (1910-18) An Anglo-American group of poets led by T. E. Hulme, Ezra Pound, H. D. (Hilda Doolittle) and her husband Richard Aldington; they used images supercharged with intellectual and emotional significance to construct brief crystalline poems.

Imam Arabic title applied to various religious leaders, from the earliest Caliphs and the leaders of the main MUSLIM sects down to the person who leads the prayers in a mosque. (Arabic, 'leader'.)

Imari pattern A Japanese style of decorating ceramics, with intricate patterns of underglaze blue, red and gold, made familiar to the West, where it was widely copied, by export wares in the late 17th and early

18th centuries. (Japanese port for the pottery district of Arita, where the KAKIEMON PATTERN also originated; these 2 together are sometimes called Arita ware.)

IMCO (1958) Initials standing for the Intergovernmental Maritime Consultative Organization, whose headquarters are in London. It fosters cooperation between governments in all matters concerning shipping, including safety at sea and the elimination of discriminatory practices.

IMF See INTERNATIONAL MONETARY FUND.

Imitation of Christ (1426) A mystical work on meditation thought to have been written by Thomas à Kempis or by a French preacher named Gerson. (Latin title, *De imitatione Christi*.)

Immaculate Conception The Roman Catholic dogma (1854) that the Virgin MARY was conceived and born without original sin.

Immelmann turn An effective aerobatic maneuver developed in World War I by the German air force, consisting of a half loop with a half roll at the top, the pilot thus gaining height and reversing direction. (Invented by Max Immelmann, shot down in 1916.)

Immortal Hour, The Rutland Boughton's CELTIC TWILIGHT OPERA (1914), which in Britain enjoyed an immense vogue as an escape from wartime realities.

Immortals, The Name given to the members of the ACADÉMIE FRANÇAISE.

Imogen See CYMBELINE.

Impatiens The genus name of the balsams, which include Busy Lizzie, the cottage houseplant.

Imperial Airways (1924-40) A merger of 4 British airlines with governmental participation, from which BOAC and BEA were eventually formed.

Imperial College of Science and Technology A unit of LONDON UNIVERSITY, comprising the Royal School of Mines, City and Guilds (engineering), and the Royal College of Science (physics); established in South Kensington.

Imperial Institute See COMMONWEALTH INSTITUTE.

Imperial Preference The policy of encouraging trade within the British Empire either, when Britain was still a FREE TRADE country, by imposing tariffs on foreign imports into Britain and the Empire or, after Britain had begun imposing tariffs (the McKenna duties (1915) and subsequent measures), by lowering them preferentially for Empire goods. Advocated by the TARIFF REFORM LEAGUE (1903) and introduced by the OTTAWA AGREEMENTS (1932).

Imperial War Museum (1917) A museum in Lambeth, London, devoted to all British military operations since 1914. In addition to exhibitions of military equipment, there are large libraries of books, films and photographs and a collection of paintings.

Importance of Being Earnest, The (1895) Oscar Wilde's last play, a brilliant, inconsequent fantasy about Jack Worthing who, since as a babe he was found in a handbag at Victoria Station, has difficulty in persuading Lady Bracknell that he is an eligible suitor for her daughter. He turns out to be an Ernest Moncrieff; hence the punning title.

Impressionism (1870s) An artistic movement, associated chiefly with Monet, Pissarro and Sisley, which aimed to capture fleeting impressions of color and the play of light, by painting outdoors with swift strokes of bright color what the painter's eye actually saw. The subjects were, necessarily, scenes of contemporary life, and did not tell a story. Whistler, Sickert and Wilson Steer, among many, were influenced by the movement. (Named after Manet's 'Impression, Sunrise' of 1872.)

Inca (1) Title of the Emperor of Peru, whose capital was Cuzco. (2) A member of the KECHUAN-speaking race dominant in Peru during the last 4 centuries before the Spanish Conquest (1532), by which time their rule extended to what are now Ecuador and northern Chile. See

MACHU PICCHU.

In Camera Sartre's play; see HUIS-CLOS.

In Cold Blood (1966) Truman Capote's account of the Holcomb murders; Dick Hickock and Perry Smith, former cell-mates in a Kansas prison, selected at random a Kansas farming family, and killed 4 of them for no reason at all. The book is based on the author's interviews with the accused, who were executed in 1965.

Independence Day The FOURTH OF JULY.

Independents A Protestant sect who, at first called BROWNISTS, gradually from Tudor times took the position of rejecting both rule by bishops and rule by presbyters; they believed in complete religious toleration and that each congregation should manage its own affairs (hence the later name CONGREGATIONALISTS). Under Cromwell, who supported them, they elected the BAREBONES PARLIAMENT.

Index, The (1557) Short title of the Index Librorum Prohibitorum, a list of books prohibited to Roman Catholics because they might endanger faith or morals, compiled by the HOLY OFFICE. The works of Gibbon, Chaucer and Milton appeared in it, and at one time Dante's. It was abolished in 1966.

Indianapolis '500', The (1911) The US Auto Club Championship 500-mile auto race, run in May at the Indianapolis motor speedway, Indiana.

Indian Bible, The The UP-BIBLUM GOD.

Indian giver Colloquialism for one who takes back a gift.

Indian hemp One of the many names for *Cannabis* (marijuana, 'pot').

Indian pudding A baked pudding of cornmeal, milk, sugar, butter, molasses and spices.

Indian rope trick A trick which apparently sober citizens claimed to have seen performed in India: a rope is thrown in the air and a man climbs up it. This traveler's tale has had a remarkably long life but is now perhaps finally dead.

Indians (1) The Cleveland Indians, AMERICAN (Baseball) LEAGUE, playing at the Municipal Stadium, the largest baseball park.

Indian Summer A period of mild sunny weather in October; see ST LUKE'S SUMMER.

Indian wrestling (1) An American Indian style in which contestants lie head to foot alongside, locking adjacent arms and legs, and each tries to turn the other on his face. (2) A parlor trial of strength; sitting face to face with elbows on the table and fingers interlocked, each contestant tries to force the other's arm down on the table.

Indienne (Cooking) Curried.

Individual Psychology Alfred Adler's system of psychoanalysis. Rejecting FREUDIAN PSYCHOLOGY, he stressed man's will to power and need to compensate for inferiorities, real or imagined, which he termed 'inferiority complex'.

Indo-China War (1946-54) A nationalist war to drive the French from Indo-China, started by a sudden raid on the TONKIN garrison and ended by DIEN BIEN PHU and the GENEVA AGREEMENTS.

Indo-European languages A group with 2 main divisions: (1) the eastern, including SANSKRIT and the modern north Indian and Pakistani languages derived from it, Persian, and the SLAVONIC LANGUAGES; (2) the western, including Ancient Greek and Latin and their modern derivatives (see ROMANCE LANGUAGES), CELTIC LANGUAGES, and Germanic languages (e.g. German, English, Scandinavian languages).

Industrial Christian Fellowship (1877) A society which works in industry in accordance with the principles of CHRISTIAN SOCIALISM.

Industrial Reorganization Corporation (1966) A body set up by Act of Parliament to help British industry to improve its competitive strength in overseas trade, e.g. by advising on mergers and rationalization. Government also took powers to form new companies and to infiltrate into or buy existing companies.

Industrial Workers of the World
(1905-18) A militant organization of workers founded by US syndicalists to carry on class warfare through industrial sabotage.

Indus Valley civilization (2500-1500 BC) A pre-ARYAN civilization of India possibly derived from MESOPOTAMIA. The 2 chief sites excavated are MOHENJODARO and Harappa. Naturalistic figures of animals and stylized human figures, including dancers, are characteristic and interesting as foreshadowing many features of later (Aryan) Indian art.

Indus waters agreement (1960) The settlement of a long-standing dispute between India and PAKISTAN over the sharing for irrigation purposes of the waters of the Indus and its 5 tributaries.

Indy Colloquial abbreviation for Indianapolis, Ind.

Indy, The Common abbreviation for the INDIANAPOLIS '500'.

'Inferno', Dante's See DIVINE COMEDY.

Ingoldsby Legends, The (1840) A collection of delightful and skillful light verse by the Rev. R. H. Barham, of which by far the best known is The JACKDAW OF RHEIMS.

Inherit the Wind A play by Jerome Lawrence and Robert E. Lee concerning the SCOPES TRIAL; also a movie (1960).

Inkerman (1854) A battle of the CRIMEAN WAR, 10 days after BALACLAVA, in which the Russians were thrown back by the British with heavy loss. (Ridge near Sebastopol.)

In Memoriam (1850) Tennyson's elegy on the death of his great friend Hallam and on the theme of personal immortality.

Inner City A new euphemism for 'slums', arising from the nationwide tendency in the US for the more prosperous elements of a city to move out to the suburbs, leaving the center to degenerate into slums and Negro ghettos, inhabited by the unemployable and the very poor.

Inner Mongolia The southern part of Mongolia, proclaimed an autonomous region of China by Chiang Kai-shek (1947); capital Huhehot (or Kweisui). See OUTER MONGOLIA.

Inner Temple (UK) The oldest and most richly endowed of the INNS OF COURT.

Inner Wheel clubs (1934) (UK) Clubs, formed by wives of ROTARY CLUB members, which are active in various kinds of social and charitable work. Compare ROTARY ANNS.

Innes, Michael Pen name assumed by J. I. M. Stewart when writing detective stories, e.g. The Journeying Boy (1949).

Innisfail A poetical name for Ireland.

Innisfree The 'Lake Isle' of W. B. Yeats's best-known poem (1895), a nostalgic recollection of his homeland written in London; it begins: I will arise and go now, and go to Innisfree, / And a small cabin build there, of clay and wattle made.

Innocents Abroad, The (1869) Mark TWAIN's novel exploiting the humors of provincial-minded American tourists traveling in Europe and the East.

'Innocent X' (1650) Velázquez' masterpiece of portraiture, in the Palazzo Doria, Rome.

Inns of Court Institutions founded in the reign of Edward I to train lawyers; 4 survive (INNER TEMPLE, Middle Temple, LINCOLN'S and GRAY'S INN), all in London, where law students keep 12 terms before being called to the bar (i.e. becoming barristers).

Inquisition, The (13th century) The HOLY OFFICE, a Papal tribunal set up to stamp out heresy, starting with the ALBIGENSIANS; it earned damaging notoriety, especially in Spain where it lingered on until 1834, by its use of torture to extract confessions and by public burnings at the stake (autos-da-fé).

INRI Initials standing for the Latin for 'Jesus of Nazareth, King of the Jews', the inscription on the Cross. (Matthew xxvii, 37; Iesus Nazarenus Rex Iudaeorum.)

INS (1909) Initials of William Randolph Hearst's International News

Service. See HEARST PAPERS, UPI.

Insectivora An order of small insect-eating, mostly nocturnal, mammals, including shrews, moles and hedge-hogs.

Institute for Strategic Studies, Ltd. (1958) A London organization, with international membership, that aims to promote discussion and research on problems of defense, disarmament and international security in the nuclear age. It publishes *Survival* (monthly), *Strategic Survey* (yearly) and other papers.

Intelsat The International Telecommunications Satellite Consortium, which in 1967 put up a family of synchronous satellites (see SYNCOM) providing TV, radio and telephone communications linking 32 nations. Its operations are managed by COMSAT.

Inter-American Development Bank (1960) One of 5 such regional organizations, operating independently of the WORLD BANK and covering the American continent; almost half its capital was found by the US.

Internal Revenue Service A division of the department of Treasury, formerly the Bureau of Internal Revenue, that collects income and excise taxes etc. and enforces revenue laws.

International Agencies The UN's specialized agencies, such as the ILO, FAO, UNESCO, WHO etc. A committee of the ECONOMIC AND SOCIAL COUNCIL acts as liaison between them and the GENERAL ASSEMBLY.

International Atomic Energy Agency A UN agency, with headquarters in Vienna, which promotes the peaceful use of nuclear energy. See ATOMS FOR PEACE.

International Bank for Reconstruction and Development Better known as the WORLD BANK.

International Bible Students' Association A name for JEHOVAH'S WITNESSES.

International Brigade The body of volunteers who fought against Franco in the SPANISH CIVIL WAR; they defeated an Italian force at Guadalajara (1937) and were engaged in heavy fighting on the Ebro in 1938.

Recruited from many countries, they included a contingent of British intellectuals who returned disillusioned by the ugly side of Spanish republicanism.

International Civil Aviation Organization A UN agency, with headquarters at Montreal, which promotes uniformity of standards in civil aviation.

International Cooperation Administration (1955-61) A US agency whose functions were taken over by the AGENCY FOR INTERNATIONAL DEVELOPMENT.

International Court of Justice (1946) The UN body which took over the functions of the Permanent Court of International Justice (1922); see HAGUE COURT. Its 15 judges of 15 different nationalities represent the major legal systems of the world and are elected for 9-year renewable terms by the GENERAL ASSEMBLY and the SECURITY COUNCIL.

International Date Line A line corresponding to longitude 180°, with deviations to keep all Siberia and Australia to the west of it. Time zones immediately to the west are 24 hours ahead of those to the east.

International Development Association (1960) An international organization, affiliated to the WORLD BANK, which makes interest-free loans to developing countries, repayable over terms of 50 years; the headquarters are in Washington, D.C.

International Dragon etc. For classes of boat see under DRAGON, etc. See also INTERNATIONAL FOURTEEN.

International Finance Corporation A UN agency, with headquarters in Washington, D.C., which in association with the WORLD BANK invests funds in productive private enterprises in developing countries.

International Fourteen Oldest of the modern dinghy classes, given international status in 1927; the design varies greatly between the many boatyards where it is built. They are meant to be tricky to handle and have no deck. The PRINCE OF WALES CUP (1927) is the leading championship.

International Geophysical Year (July 1957 to Dec. 1958) A concerted worldwide meteorological investigation of the forces acting on the Earth.

International Harvester The largest producer of agricultural machinery, with headquarters in Chicago; one of the 30 industrials that make up the DOW JONES Industrial Average.

International Horse Show, Royal (1907) A major show held at the White City or WEMBLEY, London, in July. Events include the KING GEORGE V, QUEEN ELIZABETH and PRINCE OF WALES CUPS, a coaching marathon, hound show, costers' turnout competition, and occasionally a display by the SPANISH RIDING SCHOOL.

International Hydrological Decade (1965) An international effort on the lines of the INTERNATIONAL GEOPHYSICAL YEAR, in which 60 UNESCO countries are cooperating in research on water supply, river control etc.

'Internationale, L" The Communist anthem written by Eugène Pottier and beginning: Debout, les damnés de la terre. It was the Soviet national anthem until 1946, and then became the Communist Party song.

International Labor Organization See ILO.

International Monetary Fund (1946) A fund set up after BRETTON WOODS to ease international payment difficulties, stabilize foreign exchange rates and liberalize trade; of the total subscriptions, in gold and national currencies, half came from USA and Britain.

International Nickel An important Canadian producer of nickel and copper, with its main mines around Sudbury, Ont., and operating the world's largest nickel refinery at Port Colburn, Ont. One of the 30 industrials that make up the DOW JONES Industrial Average.

International Paper The largest US paper group, based in New York; one of the 30 industrials that make up the DOW JONES Industrial Average.

International Publishing Corporation (1962) A group of newspaper and publishing companies formed by Cecil King, and including the Lon-

don *Daily Mirror, Reveille,* Odhams, Newnes, Iliffe, Temple Press, KELLY'S DIRECTORIES, *Stock Exchange Gazette,* Paul Hamlyn etc. Taken over by Reed Paper Group (1970).

International Quiet Sun Years (1964-65) The cooperative study by scientists of 71 countries of the sun and earth during a period of minimum sunspot activity.

International Refugee Organization (1947-51) An international body which repatriated or resettled some 5 million refugees and displaced persons before it was replaced by the UNITED NATIONS HIGH COMMISSIONER FOR REFUGEES.

International Student Conference (1950) A pro-Western body which broke away from the Communist-dominated International Union of Students.

International Telephone & Telegraph Co. See ITT.

International Workingmen's Association Earlier name for 2 bodies later known as the FIRST INTERNATIONAL and SECOND INTERNATIONAL.

Interpol The International Criminal Police Commission, an organization for cooperation between the Criminal Investigation Departments (or equivalent bodies) of member states; established in Vienna (1923) and reestablished in Paris (1946).

Interpreter's Bible, The (1952-57) A 12-volume edition of the Bible with copious commentaries and articles giving background information.

Interpublic An international holding company for a group of advertising and market research companies who operate in competition; the main units are the US companies McCann Erickson and Erwin Wasey, the British firm Pritchard Wood (1961), Marplan, a market research company, and Infoplan, a public relations firm.

Interstate Commerce Commission (1887) A powerful government body which exercises control over all forms of federal (as opposed to internal state) transport, by fixing rates, issuing licenses, prohibiting racial discrimination, and supervising finance and planning.

Intimations of Immortality (1807) Shortened title of Wordsworth's Ode: *Intimations of Immortality from Recollections of Early Childhood*, on the theme that we are born 'trailing clouds of glory' but 'shades of the prison house begin to close / Upon the growing boy'.

Intourist The Soviet state travel agency for foreigners.

Intrepid The name of the LEM used on the APOLLO 12 mission.

Invalides, Les (1676) Founded in Paris by Louis XIV as a home for disabled soldiers and still housing about 100 of them. In the same group of buildings are an important military museum and the Church of the Dome, where Napoleon, Foch and other military leaders are buried. (On the South Bank, south of the QUAI D'ORSAY.)

Inveraray Castle Headquarters of the Campbell clan on Loch Fyne, Argyll, and home of the Dukes of Argyll since the 15th century.

Invergordon Mutiny (Sept. 1931) A mutiny in the Royal Navy provoked by cuts in pay imposed by Ramsay MacDonald's National Government. (Naval base in Cromarty Firth.)

Invertebrates All animals that do not have backbones, e.g. snails, worms, flies, crabs, jellyfish, sponges and PROTOZOA.

Invincible, HMS (1908) The first battle cruiser, a type of capital ship in which armor was sacrificed to speed.

Invisible Man (1) An early SF novel (1897) by H. G. Wells. (2) The outstanding first novel (1952) of the American Negro writer, Ralph Ellison, about a young Negro's growing disillusion not only with white people but with his own race.

'Invitation to the Dance' A set of charming waltzes written by Weber for the piano, later orchestrated by Berlioz (among others) and in that form the inspiration of one of the most delightful of Diaghilev's early ballets, *Le Spectre de la rose*, with spectacular choreography by Nijinsky.

Io In Greek legend, a daughter of a king of Argos whom ZEUS turned into a heifer. The jealous HERA sent a gadfly to torment her, which made her run (or swim) all the way from Greece to Egypt, via the Bosporus ('cow ford') and the Ionian Sea (named after her). There she regained human form and bore Zeus a son.

Iolanthe (1882) A particularly tuneful GILBERT AND SULLIVAN OPERA in which the Queen of the Fairies, who has banished Iolanthe for marrying a mortal (now Lord Chancellor) and has been slighted by the Peers, takes her revenge by ordering Iolanthe's half-fairy son into Parliament, where he has a high old time leading both parties and passing any measures he pleases, e.g. one throwing the peerage open to competitive examination.

Ionic Order An order of Greek architecture intermediate between the DORIC and the CORINTHIAN in slenderness of columns and degree of embellishment and easily recognizable by the voluted capitals.

IOOF Initials used for the Independent Order of Odd Fellows; see ODD-FELLOWS.

Iphigeneia In Greek legend, daughter of AGAMEMNON and CLYTEMNESTRA. When the start of the expedition to Troy was delayed by contrary winds, her father sacrificed her to placate the gods. In a later version, ARTEMIS rescued her from the altar and spirited her away to the land of the Tauri (the Crimea) where she became a priestess and where her brother ORESTES found her. See next 2 entries.

Iphigeneia in Aulis (406 BC) Euripides' unfinished play about the sacrifice of IPHIGENEIA at Aulis. Racine wrote a play (1674) and Gluck an opera (1772) based on this. See also next entry.

Iphigeneia in Tauris (414 BC) Euripides' play in which IPHIGENEIA is found in the land of the Tauri by her brother ORESTES, and they escape together. Goethe wrote a play (1787) and Gluck an opera (1779) based on this. ('In Tauris' is the Latin form of the title, and means 'among the Tauri', the people of the Crimea.)

Ipomoea The genus that includes Morning Glory.

IQSY Initials used for the INTERNATIONAL QUIET SUN YEARS.

IRA Initials of the Irish Republican Army. (1) The force formed by the IRB under Michael Collins in January 1919 which, without the support of the SINN FEIN or authority of the DAIL, fought until 1921 for the independence of Ireland. (2) The hard-core remnant which rejected PARTITION and, under De Valera, waged civil war against the FREE STATERS under Collins, until they capitulated in 1923 (see FIANNA FÁIL). (3) The extremists still continued guerrilla warfare against successive Irish governments and organized bomb outrages on the ULSTER border and in England until (nominally) banned in 1962. Later the IRA turned to social agitation in the Republic and Ulster, infiltrating the civil rights movement in the latter (1969).

Iráklion (Heraklion) Capital of Crete, a Greek island formerly known by its Italian name, Candia.

Iraq Petroleum Co. An oil company, controlled by leading British, Dutch, French and US companies, which exploits the petroleum of Iraq and of many other Middle East countries.

IRB Initials of the Irish Republican Brotherhood, the revolutionary core of the 19th-century FENIAN movement; revived (1913) in USA and financed by Irish Americans, it formed the IRISH NATIONAL VOLUNTEERS, which in 1919 were reformed as the IRA. See EASTER RISING.

IRBM Intermediate range ballistic missile, i.e. one with a range of about 1500 miles; see ICBM.

IRC Initials used for the INDUSTRIAL REORGANIZATION CORPORATION.

Ireland, Republic of The official designation of Southern Ireland from 1949, when it seceded from the Commonwealth. See EIRE.

Irgun Zvai Leumi A Jewish terrorist organization in Palestine, contemporary with the STERN GANG; its survivors now support the Israeli 'liberal' party.

Iris In Greek legend originally the rainbow; later she appears as the messenger of the gods.

Irish coffee Coffee laced with Irish whiskey and topped with whipped cream.

Irish Free State The official designation of Southern Ireland while it had Dominion status (1922-37).

Irish Guinness Oaks The Irish equivalent to the OAKS, run at the CURRAGH in July.

Irish National Volunteers An irregular force raised by the IRB in November 1913 to counter the ULSTER VOLUNTEERS, to fight against PARTITION and (from 1914) against conscription. They were reconstituted as the IRA in 1919.

Irish Republican Army See IRA.

Irish Republican Brotherhood See IRB.

Irish setter A sporting dog, a dark mahogany or chestnut variety of setter developed in Ireland in the early 18th century.

Irish stew A stew consisting of layers of meat, onions and sliced potatoes, in thick gravy.

Irish Sweeps Derby The Irish equivalent of the DERBY, run at the CURRAGH in June. (Sponsored by the privately owned Hospitals Trust Ltd., which runs a world-famous sweepstake; one fifth of the profits go to Irish hospitals.)

Irlandaise (Cooking) With potatoes.

IRO See INTERNATIONAL REFUGEE ORGANIZATION.

Iron Age The period which succeeded the BRONZE AGE, when iron replaced bronze in making tools and weapons, a skill which spread from the Middle East about 1200 BC to reach Europe (HALLSTATT) about 700 BC.

Iron Chancellor Bismarck; see BLOOD AND IRON.

Iron Cross (1813) The best-known German military medal; the highest of its 4 classes, the Grand Cross, has been awarded only twice since 1813.

Iron Curtain A phrase symbolizing the barrier against Western cooperation raised by Stalin, and later the whole Communist bloc; first used by

Churchill in a telegram to Truman (May 1944) and, publicly, in his FULTON SPEECH.

Iron Duke (1) Nickname of the first Duke of Wellington. (2) Name of one of the earlier DREADNOUGHT-type battleships.

Iron Gates A narrow 2-mile gorge of the Danube on the Rumanian-Yugoslav border east of Belgrade; once a serious obstacle to navigation because of the rapids formed.

Iron Guard (1936) The Fascist party in Rumania.

Iron Maiden of Nuremberg A 17th century instrument of torture consisting of an iron box with spikes inside; when the door closed on a victim he was impaled on all sides. The original is now in Germany.

Ironsides A name given to Cromwell's army. (From a nickname given to Cromwell by the Royalists, alluding to that given to EDMUND IRONSIDE.)

Iroquois See FIVE NATIONS.

Irredentists (1) Originally, from 1878, an Italian movement calling for the recovery of all Italian-speaking districts, e.g. TIROL. (2) Applied to similar movements elsewhere, e.g. Hungarian claimants to Transylvania after World War I. (Italian *Italia irredenta*, 'unredeemed Italy'.)

IRS See INTERNAL REVENUE SERVICE.

Irvine (1966) (UK) A NEW TOWN in Ayrshire, 7 miles west of Kilmarnock, designed to take 80,000 inhabitants.

Irvingites (1835) A religious sect founded in London by a former minister of the Church of Scotland; it combines Roman Catholic ritualism, a belief in contemporary miracles and primitive elements from early Christianity. Properly styled the Holy Catholic and Apostolic Church, it still survives. (Edward Irving, founder.)

Irvin suit RAF flying suit used in World War II.

Isaac The second Hebrew patriarch, only son of ABRAHAM by Sarah, husband of REBECCA, and father of ESAU and JACOB. In youth he was saved from sacrifice by his father by the substitution of a ram caught in a thicket (*Genesis* xxii, 13).

Isaacs, Sir Rufus The 1st Marquess of Reading, Viceroy of India (as Viscount Reading) and Foreign Secretary (as Marquess).

Isabella color Off-white or dirty white. (Traditionally derived from Isabella of Austria, daughter of Philip II of Spain, who vowed not to change her linen until her husband had taken Ostend. The siege lasted 3 years, until 1603; but in fact the term was used before her time.)

Isaiah (8th century BC) One of the major prophets, and traditionally the author of the first 39 chapters of *Isaiah*.

Iseult (Ysolde, and many other spellings) In ARTHURIAN LEGEND daughter of a king of Ireland, who fell in love with TRISTRAM.

Ishmael (1) Son of ABRAHAM by HAGAR, whose 'hand will be against every man and every man's hand against him' (*Genesis* xvi, 12). The Arabs are traditionally descended from his 12 sons. (2) The narrator in Melville's MOBY DICK which begins with the arresting words: 'Call me Ishmael'; these were used as the title of Charles Olson's book about Melville.

Ishtar The Babylonian goddess of love (derived from the SUMERIAN goddess Inanna), object of the most widespread cult of the Mesopotamian world, worshiped with orgies and ritual prostitution. She brought back TAMMUZ from the Underworld each year. Identified with the planet Venus, she is represented in the Greek pantheon by APHRODITE.

Isis Ancient Egyptian cow-goddess, sometimes regarded as a Moon goddess, represented in art as having a human head with horns. Mother by OSIRIS of HORUS, she avenged the death of Osiris by killing SET. She became the great nature goddess of the Mediterranean world, identified with various local deities.

Isis, The (1) The Thames at Oxford, strictly only from its source to its junction with the Thame. (2) The OXFORD UNIVERSITY undergraduate magazine. (From ancient error which assumed that the Latin *Thamesis*, 'Thames', was a compound name formed from *Thame* and *Isis*.)

Islam The MUSLIM religion; the Muslim world. (Arabic, 'submission', i.e. to the will of Allah.)

Isles of the Blest Another name for the FORTUNATE ISLES.

Islington Inner London borough since 1965 consisting of the former metropolitan boroughs of Islington and Finsbury.

Ismaili sect A SHI'ITE sect which consider that in the 8th century the elder son (Ismael) of the 6th IMAM was wrongly disinherited by his father for drunkenness. The AGA KHAN is the spiritual leader of the sect, which has some 10 million adherents in India, PAKISTAN, the Middle East and East Africa.

Isolde See ISEULT.

Isonzo (June 1915-Sept. 1917) A river then in Italy, the scene in World War I of 11 battles between the Austrians and Italians. (Now the River Soca in Yugoslavia.)

Israel (1) The northern kingdom in Palestine, formed under Jeroboam, which seceded from the rule of King SOLOMON'S son (see JUDAH) in the 10th century BC; it was destroyed by the Assyrians in 722 BC. (2) The modern Jewish state.

Issus (333 BC) The battle in which Alexander the Great defeated the Persian Darius; see GAUGAMELA. (Town in southeast Cilicia, Asia Minor.)

Istanbul Turkish name of Constantinople. (Corruption of the Greek for 'into the city'.)

Istiqlal (1943) The Moroccan nationalist party. (Arabic, 'independence'.)

ISV The International Scientific Vocabulary, of words current in 2 or more languages and differing from New Latin in being adapted to the language in which they appear.

ITA Initials standing for Initial Teaching Alphabet, used with success in teaching infants to read; it consists of 43 phonetic characters. Once children have learned to read fluently in it, they are switched to the orthodox, far from phonetic, alphabet, which they quickly assimilate.

ITA (1954) (UK) Initials standing for Independent Television Authority, a body appointed by the Postmaster General to operate a public service for disseminating information, education and entertainment, to erect transmitters, license program contractors and to limit the proportion of advertising time in their programs. See ITV.

Italia express An evening train from Stockholm via Copenhagen, Hamburg, Frankfurt, Basle, Milan and Florence to Rome (reached in 44 hours).

Italia irredenta See IRREDENTISTS.

Italian East Africa (1936-41) The brief union of Ethiopia, ERITREA and Italian Somaliland under Italian rule.

Italian Renaissance (14th-16th centuries) The first stage of the RENAISSANCE in art and literature, which began in the age of Giotto, Dante and Petrarch and culminated in the HIGH RENAISSANCE.

Italia prize Awarded at an annual international competition for documentaries, musical works and plays written specifically for broadcasting.

Ithaca The island kingdom of ODYSSEUS (Ulysses) off the west coast of Greece. (In modern Greek spelled Ithaki.)

ITN (1967) (UK) Initials standing for Independent TV News, a, service which provides news bulletins for all the commercial TV services, given by a company owned jointly by the program contractors.

ITT (1928) Initials used for International Telephones & Telegraph, a company originally formed of various postal telegraph, cable and radio firms, now one of the world's largest electronics and communication combines. It absorbed numerous firms engaged in a wide range of other activities, including insurance, publishing and building. Standard Telephones and Cables is a wholly owned subsidiary with European headquarters in Brussels.

ITU (1934) Stands for International Telecommunication Union, a merger of the International Telegraph Union (1865) and International Radiotelegraph Union (1906), with headquarters in Geneva. Its chief function is to allocate radio frequencies; it also fosters international cooperation, development, increased public use, and low rates.

ITV (1955) (UK) Initials standing for Independent Television, the commercial service operated by the ITA through various regional program contractors, who pay rent to the Authority and part of their advertising revenue to government.

IUCD Initials used for intrauterine contraceptive device, i.e. a device inserted in the womb.

Ivanhoe (1819) Walter Scott's novel in which the hero Ivanhoe goes on crusade with Richard Coeur-de-lion. The main features of the book are the tournament at Ashby de la Zouche, at which Richard fights incognito, and the depiction of SAXON hatred for their NORMAN masters. ROBIN HOOD appears in this book.

Ivan the Terrible (1944) The title of an unfinished trilogy of movies, and of the first of them, by Eisenstein; he completed the second, *The Boyars' Plot*, in 1946. They describe, in a stylized technique with masklike makeup, the struggle of the young 16th-century Tsar to gain ascendancy over his boyars (feudal lords).

Iveagh Bequest A Robert Adam house at Kenwood, northwest London, bought with its art treasures for London by public subscription and a gift from the 1st Earl of Iveagh.

Ivrit The modernized form of Hebrew spoken in the Israeli Republic.

Ivy, Operation See ENIWETOK.

Ivy League (1) A College Athletic Conference comprising BROWN, COLUMBIA, CORNELL, DARTMOUTH, HARVARD, PENNSYLVANIA, PRINCETON, YALE. (2) The students and graduates of these universities. (3) Applied also to their style of dress—quiet and neat.

Iwo Jima landing (Feb. 1945) A particularly fierce engagement by US Marines against fanatical Japanese resistance, on an isolated volcanic island 700 miles southeast of Japan.

IWW See INDUSTRIAL WORKERS OF THE WORLD.

Ixion In Greek legend, a rascal who after being helped by ZEUS tries to seduce HERA, his wife. As a punishment he was chained to a burning wheel which rolled eternally through the skies or, in a later version, in Hades.

Izmir Turkish name for Smyrna, ancient Greek port on the Aegean, now Turkish.

Izvestia (1917) Soviet Russian daily newspaper, representing the government viewpoint (see PRAVDA) and reproducing government documents at length. (Russian, 'news'.)

J

'Jabberwocky' A nonsense ballad which Alice finds in a book in THROUGH THE LOOKING-GLASS. It begins: "Twas brillig and the slithy toves / Did gyre and gimble in the wabe'. There are many portmanteau words in it which have passed into common usage, e.g. 'burble', 'chortle', 'galumph' and 'uffish' (gruff + rough + huffy + -ish).

J'accuse (1898) The novelist Zola's trenchant attack on the handling of the DREYFUS CASE, in the form of an open letter to the French President published in a Paris newspaper.

Jack and Jill Characters in a nursery rhyme, and traditional names for any lad and lass. The rhyme has been unconvincingly linked with a Scandinavian myth about features visible on the Moon.

Jack and the Beanstalk A worldwide folk story, usually interpreted as follows. Jack (mankind) climbs the heaven-high beanstalk (YGGDRASIL), steals from a giant (God) a hen which lays golden eggs (the Sun), a harp (wind) and money (the fruit of rain, on which crops depend). He then shins down the stalk which he fells with an ax, bringing the pursuing giant crashing down to earth.

Jack Cade's rebellion (1450) A revolt of the men of Kent led by an Irish landowner who had settled there; it was put down by Henry VI.

'Jackdaw of Rheims, The' One of the INGOLDSBY LEGENDS. The Jackdaw steals the Cardinal's ring, and is cursed with bell, book and candle ('never was heard such a terrible curse!'). Reduced to a pitiable state, the unhappy bird returns the ring, reforms, and after his death is canonized as St Jim Crow.

Jackfield ware (1) Red earthenware covered with a jet-black glaze and decorated with gilt, made in the mid-18th century at Jackfield, Shropshire, England; also copied by WHIELDON and others. (2) A revival of this by various Staffordshire potteries about 1855, chiefly in the form of cow-creamers, tea wares and figures, sometimes with multicolored floral decorations etc.

Jack Horner A character in a nursery rhyme, said to be a historical Jack Horner sent by the Abbot of Glastonbury to appease Henry VIII at the DISSOLUTION OF THE MONASTERIES with a pie in which were concealed the title deeds of some manors; he stole one of them.

Jack-o-Lantern Will-o'-the-wisp or ignis fatuus, the flickering light seen in marshes and due to the spontaneous combustion of methane (marsh gas). Thought to be the work of mischievous spirits trying to lure travelers into the marsh, ignis fatuus ('foolish fire') and its synonyms came to be used of delusive hopes.

Jack Rose The standard applejack cocktail, with 8 parts apple brandy, 2 parts lemon juice, 1 part Grenadine.

Jacksonian democracy A further development of JEFFERSONIAN DEMOCRACY symbolized by the first self-made man to become US President—Andrew Jackson (1828-35); he believed that the good of the community as a whole would best be served by unrestricted majority rule, and went much further than Jefferson in appealing to the masses or 'common man'.

Jack Spot case (1955) (UK) The acquittal of Jack Comer, alias Jack Spot, accused of stabbing a man outside a SOHO nightclub. He successfully pleaded that he was the victim of a frame-up.

Jack Straw's Castle The name of several London pubs, alluding to one of the leaders of the PEASANTS' REVOLT.

Jack the Giant Killer A nursery story of a Cornishman who rid the country of giants, aided by a sword and other magic props.

Jack the Ripper (1888) The man, never conclusively identified, who in 4 months killed at least 4, and possibly 7, prostitutes in a small area of Whitechapel, London.

Jacob The third Patriarch, son of ISAAC, who cheated his twin, ESAU, of his birthright (*Genesis* xxv, 29-34) and of his father's blessing (*Genesis* xxvii, 19-29). His wives were Leah and Rachel. He became the father of 12 sons, founders of the 12 tribes of Israel. In *Genesis* xxxii, 24-32 he wrestled with an unknown 'man', possibly in the original legend the local river-god obstructing his entry into CANAAN, here transformed into an angel or Jehovah. See JACOB'S LADDER.

Jacobean period (1603-42) A convenient if inaccurate term for the reigns of James I and Charles I. Furniture was still made in TUDOR PERIOD style and in oak, but with lighter designs. Inigo Jones introduced PALLADIAN ARCHITECTURE to England.

Jacobins (1789-99) The extreme republicans of the FRENCH REVOLUTION, from whom the GIRONDINS broke away early. They were, under Robespierre and Marat, responsible for the Reign of TERROR. (Members of a club which met in an old Jacobin convent.)

Jacobites Tories, led by Henry St John, Viscount Bolingbroke, who after the GLORIOUS REVOLUTION still wanted a restoration of the exiled STUARTS. See OLD PRETENDER; YOUNG PRETENDER; FIFTEEN; FORTY-FIVE. (Jacobus, Latin form of James, i.e. James II and James the Old Pretender.)

Jacob's ladder The ladder reaching to heaven, with angels ascending and descending on it, seen in a dream by JACOB at BETHEL (*Genesis* xxviii, 12-15).

Jacob's Pillow (1933) The first dance center of its kind in America, founded by the young dancer and choreographer, Ted Shawn, after he separated from his wife Ruth St Denis with whom he had founded the earlier Denishawn School (1914). It developed from his Jacob's Pillow Dance Festival at Lee, Mass., and

became an internationally known center with its own school and theater.

Jacquard weave An intricate variegated weave made on a Jacquard loom and used for brocade, tapestry and damask. (Jacquard loom, named for the Frenchman who invented it, 1801-08; the mechanism is controlled by a chain of variously perforated cards.)

Jacquerie, The (1358) A desperate peasant rising in the north of France, marked by much bloodshed. (*Jacques Bonhomme*, French nickname for a peasant.)

Jaguar (1) (Aircraft) An Anglo-French high-performance tactical strike/advanced trainer aircraft developed by BAC and Bréguet (engines by Rolls Royce and Turboméca), due in service in 1971-72. Maximum speed Mach 1.7, radius of action 1000 miles, weapons load 10,000 lbs. (2) (Automobile) See E-TYPE.

Jainism An Indian religion founded by Mahavira in the same century as BUDDHISM (6th century BC), which it closely resembles, emphasizing compassion and nonviolence. (SANSKRIT *jaina*, 'one who has overcome', 'BUDDHA'.)

Jakarta The capital of Indonesia, formerly known by its Dutch name, Batavia.

JAL Signifies Japan Air Lines.

Jallianwala Bagh The scene of, and sometimes used for, the AMRITSAR MASSACRE. (Name of open space at Amritsar.)

James, Jesse (1847-82) The ROBIN HOOD of Missouri who, allegedly because Federal militia beat him and jailed his mother (1863), joined the Confederate guerrillas (see QUANTRELL); then, according to a ballad, 'And with his brother Frank he robbed the Chicago bank, / And stopped the Glendale train'. A youngster in his gang shot him in the back in Kansas City for the $10,000 price on his head. A popular symbol of resistance to injustice, he is said to have paid off a widow's mortgage and stolen the money back from the mortgagee.

James Dean legend The legend of the young HOLLYWOOD actor, James Dean (1931-55) who died young and became a symbol to the youth of America and elsewhere. His motion-picture career began only in 1950 and included appearances in *Sailor Beware*, *Rebel without a Cause*, *Giant* and *East of Eden* (1955).

Jameson Raid (1895) An unofficial British armed raid on the Transvaal Republic, led by Dr Jameson and supported by Cecil Rhodes. The cause was irritation at President Kruger's refusal to grant political rights to the UITLANDERS, whom he taxed heavily. It united the Boers against the British and led to the BOER WAR.

James Sixt and First Scots name for James I of England, see STUARTS.

Jammu and Kashmir The official name in India of Indian-held Kashmir (see AZAD KASHMIR), Jammu being the southwestern district of Kashmir where the Hindu minority live, forming one fifth of the total population of Jammu and Kashmir, which is predominantly MUSLIM. See KASHMIR DISPUTE.

Jamshid A legendary king of Persia who reigned for 700 years, and under whom all the arts of civilization were developed. Because of his overweening arrogance, the gods reduced him to utter destitution and misery. The RUBAIYAT refers to 'the Courts where Jamshid gloried and drank deep', which 'They say the Lion and the Lizard keep'.

Jane Eyre (1847) The name of Charlotte Brontë's study of selfless love surviving shocks, and of its shy heroine, governess to Mr ROCHESTER's ward.

Janissaries (14th century) Turkish bodyguard, at first recruited from Christian subjects; they waxed powerful and unruly, and were massacred at the instigation of the Sultan in 1826. (Turkish, 'new soldiers'.)

Jansenism (17th century) The view that man is so depraved that there is no salvation except through divine grace. Recognizing its affinity with the predestination doctrine of CALVINISM, the JESUITS fiercely attacked

this heresy, which was, however, supported by Pascal. The Jansenists had their headquarters at PORT-ROYAL. (Cornelius Jansen, Louvain professor, Bishop of Ypres.)

Jansky noise (1931) Radio signals from the MILKY WAY, first picked up by K. G. Jansky (USA) as a steady hiss on a shortwave band.

Janus Roman god who guarded doors, city gates and, in wartime, the city itself. He is represented with 2 heads, vigilantly facing past and future. January is named after him.

Jaques The 'melancholy' attendant on the Duke in AS YOU LIKE IT.

Jarley, Mrs The owner of a traveling waxworks show who befriended Little Nell in The OLD CURIOSITY SHOP.

Jarndyce v. Jarndyce The fictional Chancery case which 'dragged its dreary length' interminably through Dickens's BLEAK HOUSE.

Jarrow hunger march (1936) The best known of several marches to London organized by town councils to protest against unemployment resulting from the DEPRESSION. (A Tyneside town.)

Jarvie, Bailie Nicol The shrewd and cautious Glasgow magistrate who comes to Frank OSBALDISTONE's aid in Scott's ROB ROY.

Jasna Gora A place of pilgrimage of great national importance to Poles, an ancient monastery overlooking Czestochowa (between Warsaw and Krakow). Over the altar is an image of the Virgin (the Black Madonna) traditionally painted by St Luke. Pilgrimages to it have often been the occasion of demonstrations of unrest under Russian or Communist rule.

Jason The leader of the ARGONAUTS. The king of Colchis promised him the GOLDEN FLEECE if he plowed a field with fire-breathing bulls and sowed it with dragons' teeth. The king's daughter, MEDEA, helped him to do this by giving him a fire-resistant lotion, but the king broke his promise. Medea then put to sleep the dragon who guarded the Fleece and, together with Jason, fled with it from Colchis.

Jasper National Park (1907) The world's largest, situated in west-central Alberta on the British Columbia boundary, astride the main line from Edmonton to Prince Rupert. It is a mecca for mountaineers and skiers, and contains the COLUMBIA ICEFIELD.

Jasper ware (1775) Name given by Josiah Wedgwood to his fine stoneware stained blue (see WEDGWOOD BLUE) and decorated with white figures in relief in the style of Ancient Greek vases. Other colors were also used, and other potteries copied this ware, which is still made today by the Wedgwood firm.

JATO Initials used for jet-assisted takeoff.

Java Used as a synonym for coffee.

Java Man The first specimen of PITHECANTHROPINE to be found, in 1891 in Java.

Javelin (1955) The RAF Gloster fighter, replaced by the LIGHTNING.

Jax Colloquial abbreviation for Jacksonville, Fla.

Jaxartes Ancient name of the Syr Darya river, Kazakhstan, USSR.

Jayhawkers (1) Antislavery guerrillas of Kansas who raided Missouri before and during the Civil War. (2) Bandits who raided in the West after it. (3) People of Kansas. (As a state emblem Kansas invented the Jayhawk bird, said to fly backwards so it can see where it has been.)

Jayhawk State Kansas; see last entry.

Jazz Age A term for the 1920s in USA, popularized by Scott Fitzgerald; it was characterized by the complete emancipation of women, general absence of moral restraint and all the evils of the PROHIBITION period.

Jazz Singer, The The movie which ushered in the era of 'talkies' (1927), with Al Jolson in the title role.

JB (1958) A parable play in verse by Archibald MacLeish which put the Book of JOB into modern dress, in a circus setting; first produced at YALE and then by Elia Kazan on BROADWAY, where it was a major success. JB's questionings are given an unsatisfying answer by the Voice from the Whirlwind and he decides like Job that all he can do is endure and love.

JCC (1920) The Junior Chamber of Commerce; members ('Jaycees') are 21-36 years old and engage in projects for community betterment.

Jean-Christophe (1904-12) Romain Rolland's series of 10 novels in which France and Germany are seen through the eyes of the musician Jean-Christophe Kraft. The work explores the position of the artist in a corrupted modern society.

Jebru, Mythical Isle of (US army phrase, World War II) A far-off land to which GI JOES would claim that they were being sent, meaning, in effect, 'destination unknown'.

Jebusites (1) The pre-Israelite inhabitants of Jerusalem, later reduced to slavery. (2) Dryden's nickname for the JESUITS.

Jeeves The impeccable, imperturbable, sagacious gentleman's gentleman whose function in P. G. Wodehouse's books is to rescue Bertie WOOSTER from disaster and to restrain his sartorial extravagances.

Jeffersonian democracy The belief that people, who are born equal, free and with like potentialities, are well able to govern themselves through democratic institutions. The safeguarding of the rights of the individual, and of the individual state against a central federal government, was therefore of supreme importance. See JACKSONIAN DEMOCRACY. (Thomas Jefferson, 3rd US President, 1801-09.)

Jefferson Memorial (1943) On the Potomac shore, Washington, D.C., a large domed circular colonnade built in marble in the Classical style which Thomas Jefferson himself introduced to America; on the walls are inscriptions based on his writings.

Jehovah's Witnesses (1852) A US sect founded by Pastor Russell. It teaches that Christ returned, invisibly, in 1874; millions (i.e. Witnesses) now living will never die; all Churches and governments are of Satan; the Cross is a phallic symbol; vaccination and blood transfusion are evil. The chief goal of the Witnesses is the establishment of God's Kingdom which will be formed after ARMAGEDDON through the agency of Christ. Witnesses meet in Churches called Kingdom Halls and baptize by immersion. They are also indefatigable door-to-door evangelists and tract distributors.

Jehu (9th century BC) A King of ISRAEL who seized the throne from AHAB and slew all Ahab's descendants. He was a reckless chariot driver (2 Kings ix, 20); hence the name was applied to a cabby or coachman.

Jekyll and Hyde See DR JEKYLL AND MR HYDE.

Jellyby, Mrs A character in Dickens's BLEAK HOUSE, whose preoccupation with the sorry state of the heathen of Borrioboola-Gha (on the left bank of the Niger) led her to overlook her own family's needs.

Jelly Roll Morton Nickname of Ferdinand Morton (1885-1941), a New Orleans Creole pianist and composer who claimed to have originated jazz, the blues and the stomp.

Jemima Puddleduck (1908) A children's book written and illustrated by Beatrix Potter.

Jena, Battle of (Oct. 1806) After the Prussians had joined the THIRD COALITION, Napoleon defeated and destroyed them at Jena and Auerstädt; see TILSIT, TREATY OF. (Former capital of THURINGIA, now in East Germany.)

Jenkins, Nick The narrator in Anthony Powell's 'The MUSIC OF TIME' series.

Jenkins's Ear, War of (1739) A war between Britain and Spain precipitated by a Capt. Jenkins, who alleged that Spanish customs officials had torn off his ear while searching his ship for contraband, and produced the ear in evidence in the House of Commons. In fact it had been cut off by a pirate (punished by the Spaniards). Robert Walpole half-heartedly declared a war which achieved nothing.

Jephthah A judge of ISRAEL who swore that if he was victorious in battle he would sacrifice to Jehovah the first thing that met him on his

return. This proved to be his only daughter (*Judges* xi, 30-40). The story was the theme of an oratorio by Handel (1752) and various other works.

Jeremiad A long tale of woe, from LAMENTATIONS, a book of the Old Testament once attributed to JEREMIAH.

Jeremiah (6th century BC) A major prophet of ISRAEL, who opposed his country's policy of playing off Egypt against Babylon and rebuked it for irreligion; he was therefore very unpopular and often imprisoned. With the fall of Jerusalem he fled to Egypt. See last entry.

Jersey cattle The smallest breed of dairy cattle, producing rich milk; fawn or cream colored.

Jersey Lily, The Nickname of a minor but beautiful British actress, Lillie Langtry, Edward VII's friend. (Born in Jersey.)

Jersey Red A variety of apple.

Jerusalem Bible, The (1966) A new English translation of the Bible by 21 Roman Catholics, intended for use by all denominations; the notes and introduction are translated from the French *Jerusalem Bible* (1956). (The French translation was edited by a member of the Dominican Institute, Jerusalem.)

Jesse window A stained-glass window depicting a genealogical tree of Jesus' descent from Jesse, father of King DAVID.

Jesuitry Casuistry, equivocation, dissembling, speaking with mental reservations. (The JESUITS were thought to hold that the end justifies the means.)

Jesuits (1534) Members of the Society of Jesus founded in Paris by St Ignatius Loyola, St Francis Xavier and others. A religious order entered after long and rigorous training, ruled autocratically by a General, and chiefly engaged in missionary and educational work, and the Spiritual Exercises laid down by Loyola. They were prominent in the COUNTER-REFORMATION.

Jesus, Society of See JESUITS.

Jesus style A development of the FAIRBAIRN STYLE of rowing, with a powerful catch at the beginning of the stroke. (Jesus College, Cambridge.)

Jet Propulsion Laboratory The headquarters, near Pasadena, Calif., of the US unmanned space programs, e.g. LUNAR ORBITER and VOYAGER; a subsidiary of NASA, it is run under contract by the California Institute of Technology.

Jets The New York Jets, AMERICAN FOOTBALL LEAGUE. Became member of the AMERICAN CONFERENCE, NATIONAL FOOTBALL LEAGUE in 1970.

Jet Set An envious name conjuring up a picture of perfectly groomed creatures (the Beautiful People) taking jet flights from one luxury resort to another, only to discover that *coelum non animum mutant qui trans mare currunt* ('if it's a bore here it'll be a bore there').

Jetstream (1969) A HANDLEY PAGE twin turboprop 300-m.p.h. 'business' aircraft; there is also a military version.

Jeu de Paume Annex of the LOUVRE, Paris, devoted to IMPRESSIONISM. See TUILERIES.

Jeunes filles, Les (1936-39) A 4-volume work by the French novelist, Henri de Montherlant, giving scope to his view that the male is a noble virile creature beset by women bent upon his degradation.

'Jewel Song' An aria in Gounod's FAUST sung by MARGARET as she puts on her necklace and earrings before a mirror.

Jewish Agency (1919) A Zionist agency set up under the terms of the British mandate over Palestine, to advise on the establishment of a Jewish National Home there; now a world organization, with headquarters in Jerusalem and New York, acting as liaison between ISRAEL and Jewish communities elsewhere.

Jew Süss (1925) Lion Feuchtwanger's long historical novel about a German Jewish community in the 18th century.

Jezebel (9th century BC) The wife of AHAB, King of ISRAEL; she introduced BAAL worship (1 Kings xvi, 31) to Israel. An unscrupulous woman of loose morals (see NABOTH'S VINE-YARD), she was thrown, 'painted and tired', out of the window at JEHU's command and her carcass eaten by dogs (2 Kings ix, 30-37).

J.F.K. Initials used as nickname for John Fitzgerald Kennedy, 34th US President.

Jiggs A character in the comic strip *Bringing Up Father* (1913) by George McManus, widely syndicated, transferred to radio, movies and TV, and translated into 27 languages. An Irish laborer who suddenly strikes it rich, he is pushed frantically up the social ladder by his aggressive wife Maggie, and does his pathetic best to get back down where he belongs.

Jim Beams (1953) Whiskey bottles made in various shapes (such as animals, people, buildings etc.) by the James B. Beam Distilling Company. They are important collectors' items.

'Jim Crack Corn' An alternative title for 'BLUE TAIL FLY'.

Jim Crow A Negro or (adjectively) for Negroes. (A runaway slave who composed the song and dance — 'Wheel about, turn about, jump Jim Crow' — which gained wide popularity when adopted by a white American comedian named Rice in the 1830s.)

Jimmy O'Goblins Rhyming slang for gold sovereigns, and still used of pound notes.

Jimson, Gulley See *The* HORSE'S MOUTH.

Jimsonweed A very poisonous foul-smelling annual weed (Thorn Apple, *Datura stramonium*), native to tropical Africa and Asia, belonging to the nightshade family. (Corruption of Jamestown, Va.)

Jim Thorpe Trophy Awarded to the player adjudged to be the most valuable in the NATIONAL FOOTBALL LEAGUE, on the basis of a Newspaper Enterprise Association poll of all NFL players.

Jingle, Alfred An impostor in PICKWICK PAPERS, famous for his tall stories, which have to be pieced together from staccato fragments, e.g.: Tall lady, eating sandwiches —forgot the arch—crash—mother's head off — sandwich in her hand — no mouth to put it in, etc.

Job A rich patriarch in the Old Testament who is suddenly subjected to all the ills that flesh is heir to; he bears these with patience, staunch in his trust in God, and is rewarded (*Job* xlii, 10—17). See next entry and JB.

Job's comforter A friend to whom one turns in vain for consolation, getting a dusty answer. JOB'S 3 friends assure him that all his misfortunes are a punishment for sin (*Job* ii, 11).

Job's tears Pearly, white seeds, sold as beads, from a grass of the same name native to Asia but cultivated elsewhere.

Jocasta Mother and wife of OEDIPUS, by whom she became the mother of ANTIGONE. When she discovered that she had married her son, she hanged herself.

Jockey Club (1750) (UK) The self-constituted body of 50 members, with headquarters at Newmarket, which has autocratic control of British racing; it licenses and disciplines trainers, jockeys, handicappers etc., makes and amends rules, and works through an executive arm consisting of 3 Stewards.

Jodrell Bank (1957) A giant steerable radio telescope, 250 ft in diameter, in Cheshire, England; directed by Sir Bernard Lovell, it belongs to Manchester University. It tracked SPUTNIK I.

Joe Bananas Corruption of Joseph Bonanno, usually regarded as the head of COSA NOSTRA.

Joe Doakes The average citizen, man-in-the-street, so-and-so (in England called Snooks).

Joe Miller's Jestbook (1739) A book of jokes named after a DRURY LANE comedian who had died the previous year.

Joey Professional nickname for a circus clown. (From Joseph Grimaldi, the Anglo-Italian clown, who died in 1837.)

JOG (1950) (UK) Initials used for Junior Offshore Group, formed to provide less expensive ocean racing confined to boats with a waterline length between 16 and 20 ft. A second class for boats of 20-24 ft was later added.

'John Anderson, my Jo' A traditional song rewritten by Robert Burns, sung to her husband in old age by an affectionate wife. (*Jo* is dialect for 'sweetheart'.)

John Barleycorn A personification of beer and other drinks made from malted barley.

John Birch Society (1958) An extreme right-wing American group which advanced the view that the US government was threatened by a Communist take-over (in which Eisenhower and Foster Dulles were implicated) and urged the abandonment of the UN, NATO and foreign aid. It was founded by Robert Welch and named for a young American missionary turned intelligence officer, killed by Communists in China, 1954.

'John Brown's Body' (1) A song celebrating the martyr (in the eyes of abolitionists) of HARPER'S FERRY. The original words, attributed to Thomas B. Bishop, were set to an old Negro melody. New words were written to the tune in 1862 by Julia Ward Howe, beginning: 'Mine eyes have seen the glory of the coming of the Lord'. This version was called 'The Battle Hymn of the Republic'. (2) A very long narrative poem by Stephen Vincent Benét giving a realistic and impartially sympathetic account of the AMERICAN CIVIL WAR. Despite faults of composition and style, it won a PULITZER PRIZE and became widely popular.

John Bull Britain personified, a typical Britisher; from an anti-French satire by John Arbuthnot — a Scot — *The History of John Bull* (1721), in which he is represented as a bluff good-natured farmer.

John Bull's Other Island (1904) Bernard Shaw's play about Irish Home Rule, commissioned by Yeats, in which Tom Broadbent, representing England, establishes complete ascendancy over Larry Doyle, representing Ireland.

John Collins A COLLINS made with LONDON GIN.

John Doe and Richard Roe (UK) A legal phrase standing for any plaintiff and defendant in a case (originally with a specialized meaning).

John Dory Edible marine fish with large head, a large dark spot on either flank and an extensible mouth which can be shot forward to take food.

John Gilpin (1782) William Cowper's poem about a CHEAPSIDE linendraper whose horse bolted with him all the way to Ware and back again to Cheapside. Taught to every English child, perhaps because its thumping rhythm ('John Gilpin was a citizen / Of credit and renown') makes it easy to remember.

John Hancock Colloquialism for a signature; from the size and prominence of the signature appended to the DECLARATION OF INDEPENDENCE by the American statesman of that name.

John Henry A variant for JOHN HANCOCK.

'John Henry' A folk song about the 'Negro Paul BUNYAN', hero of the rock-tunnel gangs, who worked on the Chesapeake & Ohio Big Bend Tunnel in the early 1870s. In an epic competition with a steam drill he crushed more rock than the machine but died of the effort 'with his hammer in his hand'. Symbolizing man's last stand against machinery, he was not widely known until 1931 when ballads about him were published and Roark Bradford's novel *John Henry* appeared (turned into a musical by Jacques Wolfe).

John Inglesant See LITTLE GIDDING.

John Innes The name of formulae for standardized seed and potting composts consisting of loam, peat, sand and fertilizers. There is no copyright in them and the John Innes Horticultural Institution (now associated with the University of East Anglia) has no control over the many firms marketing composts under this name. John Innes Nos 1 and 2 are for seeds; JI No 3 is for plants needing rich compost. The Institution published the formulae in 1939.

John Law A policeman.

Johnny Appleseed Nickname of Jonathan (or John) Chapman (1775-

1847), born near Boston, eccentric SWEDENBORGIAN whose self-imposed task it was to plant apple seeds in the wilderness, especially in Ohio and Indiana, which he did for the last 46 years of his life.

Johnny-Come-Lately (1) New Zealand and Australian term for a recent and thus inexperienced immigrant. (2) Any newcomer, late or recent arrival.

Johnny Head-in-Air See STRUWWELPETER.

Johnny-on-the-spot Colloquialism signifying one who happens to be on hand and ready to perform a service or respond to an emergency.

John of Gaunt The Duke of Lancaster, fourth son of Edward III, ancestor of the LANCASTRIAN kings. (Born at Ghent, of which Gaunt is a corruption; died 1399.)

John o' Groats Traditionally (but not in fact) the northernmost point of mainland Britain. (Named after a Dutch immigrant, Jan Groot, whose house still stands.)

John Q. Public Colloquialism for a member of the public, or average citizen; also a personification of the public or community.

Johns Hopkins (1876) University at Baltimore, Md.

Johns-Manville A leading New York firm making building materials; one of the 30 industrials that make up the DOW JONES Industrial Average.

John Stiles Legal term for a party to proceedings whose true name is unknown; compare JOHN DOE AND RICHARD ROE.

Johnstown flood (1889) A disaster at Johnstown, southwest Pennsylvania, due to a reservoir bursting its banks; over 2300 people were drowned.

John Sullivans Slang for long pants or combinations. (John L. Sullivan, famous 19th-century prizefighter who, as was then the custom, wore them when boxing.)

Jolly Hotels A chain of over 50 good, and in some cases deluxe, hotels in Italy.

Jolyon See YOUNG JOLYON.

Jonah (8th century BC) A prophet of ISRAEL of whom the story is told in the 4th-century Old Testament book, *Jonah*, that when the ship in which he was traveling was struck by a mighty tempest the sailors cast lots to find out who was responsible for their plight. 'The lot fell on Jonah', who was thrown overboard and swallowed by a whale, which 'vomited out Jonah on the dry land'.

Jonathan See DAVID.

Jonathan An American variety of red apple.

Joneses, The The people next door, with whom it is necessary to keep up, according to ADMASS standards in the AFFLUENT SOCIETY. Thus, if the Joneses install central heating, the Smiths must, or lose caste. (Title of a US comic strip, 1913-31, by A. R. Momand.)

Jonkheer A Dutch title, equivalent to baronet.

Jordan See TRANSJORDAN.

Jordan, Mrs Stage name of the actress who was for many years the mistress of the Duke of Clarence (later William IV).

Jordans Meetinghouse (1688) One of the first legitimate Quaker meetinghouses, the burial place of William Penn, and now preserved as a place of historic interest, with relics and manuscripts about Quaker history. (Hamlet near Beaconsfield, Buckinghamshire.) See QUAKERS.

Jordan waters dispute The continuing dispute between Jordan and ISRAEL over sharing for irrigation purposes the waters of the River Jordan and its tributaries.

Jorrocks The indomitable sportsman and Cockney grocer who first appears in *Jorrocks' Jaunts and Jollities* (1838) by R. S. Surtees, and in subsequent novels becomes MFH of the Handley Cross pack.

Joseph JACOB's son, whom his jealous brothers sold into slavery in Egypt, sending his coat of many colors dipped in blood to Jacob as proof of his death (*Genesis* xxxvii). After the episode of POTIPHAR'S WIFE and his interpretation of Pharaoh's dreams, he rose to high office. In a time of famine Jacob, hearing that there was 'corn in Egypt', sent his sons to buy some; they were received kindly by Joseph, whom they failed to recognize, and who eventually persuaded the whole family to settle in Egypt (*Genesis* xlii-xlvii).

Joseph, Chief See NEZ PERCÉ WAR.

Joseph and his Brethren (1933-43) Thomas Mann's series of 4 novels, based on the Biblical story of JOSEPH.

Joseph Andrews (1742) Henry Fielding's novel, part parody of Samuel Richardson's PAMELA, part plea that a kind heart is more important than a strict morality.

Joseph of Arimathea The Jew who got Pilate's permission to take down Christ's body (*Matthew*, xxvii, 57-60) and, according to English late medieval tradition, brought Jesus as a boy to England and later took the HOLY GRAIL to GLASTONBURY, where he founded a church.

Joshua A book of the Old Testament which tells how Joshua, successor to Moses, led the Israelites into the PROMISED LAND.

Jourdain, M. See *Le* BOURGEOIS GENTILHOMME.

Journey's End (1928) R. C. Sherriff's play of World War I, set in the trenches; though realistic in detail it is romantic in spirit.

Journey to the End of the Night (1932) Louis-Ferdinand Céline's vituperative and rambling novel attacking the sickness of the world during and after World War I. (French title, *Voyage au bout de la nuit*.)

JPL Initials standing for JET PROPULSION LABORATORY, Pasadena.

Js, The A nickname used in Roman Catholic circles for the JESUITS.

Juan in America (1931) Eric Linklater's amusing modern picaresque satire.

Judah (1) The fourth son of JACOB and Leah, ancestor of one of the 12 tribes of ISRAEL. (2) The southern portion of Palestine, including Jerusalem, which remained loyal to SOLOMON's son, Rehoboam, when the northern part, as Israel, seceded in the 10th century BC. The kingdom was overrun by the Babylonians in 586 BC.

Judas Iscariot The disciple who betrayed Jesus with a kiss for 30 pieces of silver (*Matthew* xxvi, 14-15 and 48-49), and then hanged himself

(*Matthew* xxvii, 3-5). See ACELDAMA.

Judas Window, The (1938) A crime mystery by 'Carter Dickson' (see FELL, DR GIDEON). (Peephole in a door; also called a judas or judashole.)

Jude the Obscure (1896) Thomas Hardy's WESSEX novel of Jude Fawley and his cousin Sue Bridehead who, after unhappy marriages, live together and then return to their spouses, their children having been murdered by Jude's legitimate son.

Judges (mostly 7th century BC) An Old Testament book describing how the Israelites conquered CANAAN, their successive defeats by numerous enemies, their turning away from Jehovah to worship BAAL and ASHTORETH, and their intermarrying with Philistines and HITTITES. It includes the story of SAMSON. ('Judge', name given to various leaders of the Israelites, of whom JOSHUA was the first and SAMUEL the last, who rose to power in periods of crisis (c.1200-1020 BC); they were military commanders rather than judges.)

Judge's Story, The (1947) Charles Morgan's novel in which a retired judge is called on to resist various temptations put in his way by a taunting millionaire and to sacrifice all his wealth to screen his beloved ward from the results of her husband's folly.

Judgment of Paris In Greek legend, the decision whether the Apple of Discord inscribed 'to the fairest' should be given to HERA, ATHENE or APHRODITE, entrusted by ZEUS to PARIS. He awarded the apple to Aphrodite, she having promised him the loveliest of women (HELEN OF TROY). The best of Rubens's paintings of this scene is in the PRADO, Madrid.

Judith (2nd century AD) A book of the APOCRYPHA, which tells the story of JUDITH AND HOLOFERNES.

Judith and Holofernes A romance told in JUDITH. When Nebuchadnezzar (here represented as King of ASSYRIA) attacks ISRAEL, Judith captivates the enemy general, Holofernes, gets invited to a feast at which, when he is in a drunken stupor, she cuts off his head, and carries it back to the Israelites; inspired by this act, they put the Assyrians to flight. The story has no basis in fact.

Judy O'Grady A name familiar from Kipling's lines in 'The Ladies': For the Colonel's lady an' Judy O'Grady/ Are sisters under their skins!

Jugendstil See ART NOUVEAU.

Juggernaut A title of KRISHNA, whose idol was drawn round Jagannath (in Orissa) in a huge wagon under which, Europeans once believed, fanatics used to throw themselves to their death; hence anything which demands or is given blind sacrifice. (Corruption of Jagannath, 'lord of the world'.)

Juilliard School of Music (1924) A special school, at Lincoln Center Plaza, NYC, for students of exceptional talent, established by the Juilliard Musical Foundation; in 1926 the Institute of Musical Art, the oldest US music school, became affiliated to it as its undergraduate school. The Foundation was set up under the will of Augustus Juilliard (1840-1919).

Jukes, The A fictitious family name used in *The Jukes: A study in crime, pauperism, disease and heredity* (1877), on the life histories of the descendants of a family of sisters who lived in New York, written for a prison association; applied to those of low mentality. Compare KALLIKAKS.

Jules Rimet Trophy The official name of the soccer WORLD CUP, won in 1970 by Brazil. (Rimet, president of FIFA, who did much to encourage international soccer.)

Julian calendar The OLD STYLE calendar. (Introduced by Julius Caesar in 46 BC.)

Julienne (1) A clear vegetable soup; (2) garnished with slow-cooked matchstick strips of vegetable.

Juliet See ROMEO AND JULIET.

July Monarchy Alternative name for the ORLEANIST MONARCHY. (Began in July 1830.)

July Plot, The Alternative name for the OFFICERS' PLOT (1944).

Jumbo The name of an exceptionally large elephant sold by the London Zoo to the BARNUM & BAILY SHOW in 1882; now applied to anything large, from cigarettes to airliners.

Jumbo jet Nickname of the BOEING-747 airliner, in service from 1970 and designed to carry 350, and in one version up to 490, passengers at 600 m.p.h.

Jungian psychology A psychoanalytic theory which, like Adler's INDIVIDUAL PSYCHOLOGY, rejects FREUDIAN emphasis on 'sex'. It classifies man as introvert or extrovert, and suggests the existence of a collective unconscious to which all have access, containing racial memories and ancient basic ideas (archetypes) on death, immortality etc. Jung advocated the development of that part of the personality which is weakest, e.g. the intellectual should develop his emotional life. (Carl Jung, Austrian psychologist, 1875-1961.)

Jungle, The (1906) Upton Sinclair's best-known novel which showed up the lack of regard for hygiene among Chicago meat-packers and led to a government investigation of stockyard conditions. A Lithuanian immigrant with every natural advantage suffers a Joblike reversal of fortune—the loss of wife, child, job and health. He becomes a hobo, takes to crime and turns Socialist; but the dice seem loaded by Sinclair rather than by Fate.

Jungle Books (1894-95) Kipling's 2 books of children's stories of animal life, of which the central figure is MOWGLI.

Junior Achievement A scheme to give young people business experience through operating their own small businesses under the guidance of volunteers. Companies with an average capital of $100 provided by parents and teachers are set up each fall and dissolved in the spring. The organization, with headquarters in New York, operates in some 250 US and Canadian cities.

Junior League A league of young women organized for intelligent participation in civic affairs, especially through direct volunteer service. The first was founded in New York (1901) and 31 leagues were formed (1921) into the Association of the Junior Leagues of America.

Junius, Letters of (1769-72) A series of anonymous letters that appeared in a London journal, violently attacking the TORIES. The secret of their authorship was well kept, and speculation about it has tended to inflate interest in these unimportant writings. Sir Philip Francis is nowadays a favorite candidate for the authorship.

Junk Art A facet of POP ART in which Campbell soup cans, bicycle wheels and other assorted spare parts are superimposed on a painted canvas. A leading practitioner is Robert Rauschenberg.

Junkers (1) The autocratic large landowners of EAST PRUSSIA in the 19th century. (2) The typical jack-booted Prussian army officer caste sired by (1), which later became the ruthless elite of the German Imperial army.

Junkers aircraft German aircraft, including the Ju-52, one of the most successful civil and military transport planes; the Ju-88, a famous bomber of World War II; and the Ju-87, see STUKAS.

Juno Roman goddess equivalent to the Greek HERA.

Juno and the Paycock (1924) Sean O'Casey's comedy about the vain Paycock (Peacock) who solves all problems by having another drink, and his heroic wife Juno Boyle, battling not only with him but with the problems of slum poverty and the Irish TROUBLES, when 'the whole world is in a state of chassis' (chaos).

Jupiter Roman god equivalent to the Greek ZEUS.

Jupiter US Army's liquid-propelled IRBM, range 1500 miles, designed to carry a nuclear warhead. See JUPITER-C.

Jupiter Ammon A god combining the attributes of the Greek ZEUS (Jupiter) and the Egyptian AMON; he is particularly associated with the famous oracle visited by Alexander the Great, situated in a Libyan oasis.

Jupiter-C US 4-stage satellite launcher, used (1958) to put the first US satellite, EXPLORER I, into orbit.

Jupiter Symphony The name commonly used for Mozart's Symphony No. 41 in C major; there is nothing Olympian about it and the name, or rather misnomer, was probably given by J. B. Cramer.

Jurassic Period The middle period of the MESOZOIC ERA, lasting from about 200 to 150 million years ago. Fossils appear of flowering plants, the brontosaurus, Archaeopteryx and the pterodactyl (the first flying, reptilian creatures), crocodiles, lizards, frogs, snakes. Portland limestone was formed. (Named after the Jura mountains.)

Jurgen (1919) James Branch Cabell's novel of a pawnbroker magically restored to youth who embarks on an odyssey which takes him to heaven and hell; after fantastic adventures he is glad to return to his normal henpecked life.

Justice The British nonparty section of the International Commission of Jurists.

Justice (1910) Galsworthy's play criticizing prison administration, the processes of the law, and society, which join in victimizing a solicitor's clerk sentenced for forging a check to help a woman in trouble.

Justice of the Peace A lay magistrate, with powers to try minor civil and criminal cases and hold preliminary examinations in more serious cases; also to solemnize marriages etc. Usually elected in the US, but appointed by the LORD CHANCELLOR in England, where the term originated and was at first applied to local gentry appointed by the king to keep order in their districts.

Justinian code (AD 529-34) A codification and simplification of Roman law by the Byzantine Emperor Justinian I, the basis of the CODE NAPOLÉON and other continental systems, but described by Edward Gibbon as consisting of 'too often incoherent fragments'.

Just So Stories (1902) Kipling's illustrated book for children on such topics as 'How the Camel got his Hump'; it contains many phrases which passed into common use, e.g. 'the great grey-green greasy Limpopo River', 'the Cat that Walked by Himself', 'a man of infinite-resource-and-sagacity'.

Jutes The Teutonic invaders from the lower Rhine who, from the 5th century AD, settled in Kent and the Isle of Wight. They differed culturally from the ANGLES and SAXONS.

Jutland, Battle of (May 1916) A naval engagement in World War I in which the British Grand Fleet under Jellicoe, with a battle cruiser squadron under Beatty, lost 6 major ships to 2 of the German High Seas Fleet, causing Beatty to remark: There's something wrong with our bloody ships today, Chatfield. Despite its tactical success in the battle, the German fleet never again emerged, except to surrender in 1918.

Juvenile Courts Courts for the trial of persons up to the age of 18, which aim at rehabilitation rather than punishment, employing clinical and casework techniques.

K

K The narrator of Kafka's *The* CASTLE and, as Jozef K, of *The* TRIAL; a device supposedly indicating an autobiographical element in those novels.

K (1) Standard symbol for 'kilo' (a thousand), used colloquially in such phrases as 'annual salary of 15K'. (2) Abbreviation used for 'knighthood', as in 'he has at last got his K'.

Kaaba The Islamic holy of holies at Mecca, a windowless cubic building said to have been built by ABRAHAM; pilgrims circle it 7 times, kissing the Black Stone (a meteorite) in its walls which was traditionally given by Gabriel to Abraham. (Arabic, 'square house'.)

Kabaka Title of the former kings of Buganda, the province of Uganda inhabited by the Baganda. The last king became President of Uganda until he was exiled in 1966.

Kabuki A type of Japanese drama, deriving from the NŌ-PLAY, but less elaborate and stylized.

Kabyle A BERBER race of Algeria.

Kaffir click An indescribable suction sound used only in the languages of the HOTTENTOTS and BUSHMEN, and of 2 minor tribes in East Africa.

Kaffirs (1) Old South African name for the Bantu peoples, formerly spelled Caffres. (2) On the London Stock Exchange, colloquialism for South African mining shares. (Arabic *kafir*, 'infidel', i.e. non-MUSLIM.)

Kafkaesque Resembling the world created by Kafka in *The* CASTLE, *The* TRIAL and other novels.

Kai Lung The urbanely witty Chinese character created by Ernest Bramah (pen name of E. B. Smith) in his novels *The Wallet of Kai Lung* (1900) and *Kai Lung's Golden Hours* (1922).

Kailyard School A derogatory term for writers of sentimental dialect stories of Scottish peasant life, e.g.

J. M. Barrie, S. R. Crockett. (Scottish, 'cabbage patch'.)

Kajar dynasty The family which, after an interregnum, succeeded the SAFAVIDS and ruled Persia from 1794 until Riza Khan Pahlavi seized power in 1921.

Kakiemon pattern A Japanese style of decorating ceramics, with asymmetrical designs of flowers, birds (e.g. quails and pheasants), trees, children etc., enamel-painted with a wider palette of colors than IMARI PATTERN, including yellow, blue, green and orange. It was made familiar to the West through exports in the late 17th and early 18th centuries, and was copied by MEISSEN, CHANTILLY and CHELSEA PORCELAIN etc. (Name of a family of potters.)

Kalaupapa A small century-old leper colony on the island of Molokai, Hawaii.

Kalevala A Finnish epic poem probably embodying legends of very great antiquity but not committed to writing until the early 19th century. ('Land of Heroes'.)

Kali In HINDUISM, the bloodthirsty consort of SIVA, represented with matted hair, bloodstained ams and hideous fangs; also the object of a fertility cult, especially at Calcutta.

Kalinga prize A $2500 prize awarded by UNESCO for distinguished work in the popularization of science.

Kalinin A city of the USSR, formerly known as Tver.

Kaliningrad A city of the USSR, formerly known by its German name, Königsberg.

Kallikaks, The A fictitious name used in a sociological study of a New Jersey family of which one branch was predominantly intelligent and successful, another subnormal and prone to crime. Also used, rather inaccurately, for persons of low mentality; compare JUKES. (Concocted from the Greek, to mean 'good-bad'.)

Kamakura period (1185-1392) A militaristic period of early Japanese history which succeeded the peaceful FUJIWARA PERIOD.

Kamaraj plan (1963) The proposal that Indian CONGRESS PARTY leaders holding high office should resign office to devote themselves to Party work. Nehru used the suggestion both to rid himself of opponents and to give new life to the Party. Among those who resigned were Kamaraj himself and Nehru's successor, Shastri. (Kamaraj, then Chief Minister of Madras, later President of the Congress Party.)

Kama Sutra An ancient Indian treatise on sex, with no conceivable bearing on modern life but, judging by the placing of advertisements for it, bought by intellectuals. (Hindu *Kama*, the Indian Cupid; *sutra*, 'commentary'.)

Kanaka A South Sea Islander, applied particularly to forced labor formerly employed on the sugar plantations of Queensland, Australia. (Hawaiian, 'man'.)

Kanarese The DRAVIDIAN LANGUAGE spoken in Mysore and neighboring areas of Hyderabad and Madras, having some affinity with TELUGU. Also called Kannada.

Kangaroo (1923) A novel by D. H. Lawrence which vividly evokes the feeling that the infinitely ancient continent of Australia is under only temporary human occupation. There is also a plot of sex war and politics.

Kangaroos (London Stock Exchange) Colloquialism for Australian mining shares.

K'ang Hsi (1662-1722) An emperor of the CH'ING DYNASTY, whose reign is associated with the *famille verte* color scheme in decorating porcelain, and the beginnings of mass export of NANKING CHINA.

Kannada An Indian language; see KANARESE.

Kano School (16th-19th centuries) A school of Japanese artists who, under Chinese influence, evolved a vigorous new style, painting large bold designs, typically against a gold background. They worked mainly on decorating the houses of the SHOGUNS.

Kant's Critique of Pure Reason (1781) The most famous of Kant's philosophical works, which advances the view that the mind can record the appearance of a thing (phenomenon), which it fits into its own preconceptions; but it can never get at its cause, the thing-in-itself (*Ding-an-sich*), i.e. never know what the outside world is really like.

KANU (1946) Initials of the Kenya African National Union, Kenyatta's party, the successor to the banned Kikuyu Central Association; it won the struggle for power against KADU (Kenya African Democratic Party), later dissolved.

KAP Initials standing for the Chinese Ministry for Public Security, an internal secret police and external counterintelligence department; it has its own military force and runs concentration and labor camps. It is directly responsible not to CHAIRMAN MAO Tse-tung but to the State Council under the prime minister, Chou En-lai.

Kapital, Das (1867-94) The main work of Marx and Engels; it analyzes Capitalism which, they held, was doomed to inevitable self-destruction. See DIALECTICAL MATERIALISM.

K*a*p*l*a*n, H*y*m*a*n A character created by the Polish-born American humorist Leo Rosten (under the pen name Leonard Q. Ross) in a book (1937) based on his own struggle to teach immigrants English.

Kapp Putsch (1920) A German armed rising of FREIKORPS units under an American journalist, Wolfgang Kapp, which seized Berlin but was foiled by the declaration of a general strike. Some of the rebels wore swastikas, and their political views also foreshadowed the rise of the Nazi.

Karamazov, Mitya, Ivan and Alyosha See The BROTHERS KARAMAZOV.

Kariba dam (1960) A hydroelectric station run jointly by ZAMBIA and Rhodesia, situated on the Zambezi river, which divides the 2 countries.

Karlmarxhof (Vienna) A much-admired block of workers' flats built by a Socialist city council, and shelled by government forces in quelling a

Socialist revolt against the regime of Chancellor Dollfuss (1934).

Karl-Marx-Stadt A city of East Germany, formerly known as Chemnitz.

Karlovy Vary The Czech spa, formerly known by its German name of Carlsbad.

Karnak An Egyptian village on the site of ancient THEBES, with many temples of the MIDDLE KINGDOM and the NEW KINGDOM; once joined to LUXOR by an avenue of ram-headed Sphinxes.

Kärntnerstrasse The fashionable shopping street of Vienna, running from the city's center to the RINGSTRASSE, at the junction with which stands the Opera.

Kashmir dispute The struggle between India and PAKISTAN for possession of Kashmir, which broke into war in 1947-49 and 1965-66. At PARTITION, the Hindu Maharaja of Kashmir declared the accession of his state to India; Pakistan has never accepted this because Kashmir is predominantly MUSLIM and controls the main rivers of Pakistan (see INDUS WATERS AGREEMENT). See also AZAD KASHMIR; JAMMU AND KASHMIR.

Kaspar Old Kaspar, in Southey's poem, was unable to tell his grandchildren what good came of the Battle of BLENHEIM, 'but 'twas a famous victory'.

Kate Greenaway A fashion style characterized by long full skirt, short waist and sleeve, round neck and usually a sash. (From a famous illustrator of children's books, died 1901; see GREENAWAY (KATE) MEDAL.)

Katharina The shrew of Shakespeare's *Taming of the Shrew*, tamed and married by Petruchio after a long verbal fencing match.

'Kathleen Mavourneen' An 'Irish' song (composed by an Englishman in 1835) with the opening words: Kathleen Mavourneen! the grey dawn is breaking,/The horn of the hunter is heard on the hill.

Katowice A city of Upper Silesia, Poland, formerly Stalinograd.

Katyn massacre (April-May 1940) The massacre of 4253 Polish officers, generally attributed to the NKVD as a deliberate Russian attempt to weaken the Polish elite; the Commu-

nists accuse the German Nazis of the crime. (A wood near Smolensk in Russia, where their mass graves were found in 1943.)

Katzenjammer Kids, The (1897) The first real comic strip, with frames, balloons and a permanent cast, begun by Rudolph Dirks for Hearst and based on a German model of the 1860s, Wilhelm Busch's *Max und Moritz*. After a lawsuit (1912) there were 2 versions, *The Captain and the Kids* (Dirks) and another by Joe Musial. The chief characters are Mama, in ambiguous relationship with her lodger ('the Captain'), and her 2 little horrors, Hans and Fritz, all conversing in Anglo-German-Yiddish, e.g.: Mit dose kids, society is nix.

Kaunas A City in Lithuania, known also by its Russian name of Kovno.

Kay, Sir One of King ARTHUR'S knights, a braggart and a boor.

KC Initials used for Kansas City, Mo.

Kechuan The AMERICAN INDIAN LANGUAGE spoken by the ancient INCAS and still spoken in Peru. Also spelled Quechuan.

Kedar Son of ISHMAEL (*Genesis* xxv, 13) and traditional ancestor of the Bedouin. The black tents of Kedar (i.e. of the nomadic Arabs) are mentioned in the Psalms and in the *Song of Solomon*: I am black but comely . . . as the tents of Kedar.

Kedleston Hall (UK) The home near Derby of the Curzon family through 8 centuries, rebuilt by Robert Adam.

Keele University (1962) Formerly the University College of North Staffordshire (1951), at Keele, near Newcastle under Lyme.

'Keep Left' group (1949) (UK) A group of left-wing Labour MPs who opposed the Labour Foreign Secretary, Ernest Bevin, in his support for NATO, and advocated the formation of a European THIRD FORCE, led by Britain, standing neutral between capitalist USA and Communist USSR.

Keep the Aspidistra Flying (1936) George Orwell's comic novel about working-class life.

Keesing Short title of *Keesing's Contemporary Archives*, a weekly summary of world news, with a cumulative index; published in Bristol, England, since 1931.

Kefauver investigation (1950) A US Senate commission of inquiry into organized crime in interstate commerce. (Chairman, Estes Kefauver, Senator from Tennessee.)

Kellogg (W. K.) Foundation (1930) One of the largest US foundations; it makes grants for experimental programs in the fields of health, agriculture and education; the headquarters are at Battle Creek, Mich., the home of the Kellogg Corporation.

Kellogg Pact (1928) A pact for the renunciation of war as an instrument of policy, except in self-defense, signed by all the Great Powers (including USA and Russia which were not members of the LEAGUE OF NATIONS) and many others; also called the Kellogg-Briand Pact. (Suggested by the French Foreign Minister, Briand, to the US Secretary of State, Kellogg.)

Kells, Book of An illuminated Latin manuscript of part of the Gospels dating to about the 8th century, an outstanding example of Celtic Christian art, from the monastery of Kells, Co. Meath; now at Trinity College, Dublin.

Kelly gang (1878-80) Australian bandits led by Ned Kelly in Victoria Colony, who killed 3 police and for 2 years terrorized the countryside; Kelly was hanged in 1880, and the rest were killed.

Kelly pool A form of pool game in which each player draws a number and, while playing on the object balls in numerical order, aims to pocket the ball having his number on it. If his ball is pocketed by another player he loses his chance of winning.

Kelly's Directories (1799) A series of London, county and town directories published by Kelly's Directories Ltd., who also produce an annual *Handbook to the Titled, Landed and Official Classes* (1875).

Kelmscott Press (1890) The private press established by William Morris near his HAMMERSMITH home, Kelmscott House.

Kelvin scale A scale of absolute temperature in which 0°K is the lowest attainable temperature (−273°C). Conversion of °K to °C is made by adding 273 (or more precisely 273.16) to the latter.

Kelvinside The northwestern area of Glasgow around the University and Kelvingrove Park, where the upper middle-class residents were supposed to speak with a mincing ('Kelvinside') English accent, much despised by the true Scot.

Kemal Atatürk See ATATÜRK.

Kempe Short title for *Kempe's Engineers' Yearbook* (1895), a comprehensive annually revised reference book, indispensable to all types of engineer.

Kendo An ancient Japanese form of quarterstaff (fighting with a long pole), highly stylized and ceremonious.

Kenilworth (1821) Walter Scott's historical novel of the fate of Amy Robsart, married to Queen Elizabeth's favorite, the Earl of Leicester, and victimized by the evil Richard Varney, his protégé. The turning point of the plot takes place during the Queen's visit to Kenilworth Castle.

Kennecott Copper Corporation (1915) A large US concern with copper mines in several American states as well as in Chile and other countries.

Kennedy assassinations (1) Of President John Fitzgerald Kennedy at Dallas, 22 Nov. 1963, by a marksman presumed to be Lee Oswald, himself murdered by Jack Ruby 2 days later. (2) Of his brother, Senator Robert F. Kennedy, shot at Los Angeles, 5 June 1968 (died the next day), by a Jordanian immigrant, Sirhan Bishara Sirhan.

Kennedy Compound, The A name for the Kennedy family homes on Cape Cod, Mass.

Kennedy International Airport The new name of Idlewild, the New York City airport in Queens borough on Long Island.

Kennedy Memorial Award (1968) A prize of $10,000 awarded by the publishers, Harper & Row, to authors of books of general interest which throw light on the influence of individuals on their times and foster an understanding of USA or its world role. (Financed by profits from selling President J. F. Kennedy's *Profiles in Courage*.)

Kennedy Round, The (1964-67) A round of negotiations under the auspices of GATT, which ended in 1967 and aimed originally at the abolition of industrial tariffs on goods in which USA + COMMON MARKET + EFTA control 80% of world trade, and a 50% cut in all others. Further aims were limitation of subsidies to agriculture and a food aid scheme for needy countries. After hard bargaining, especially by France, and a failure to persuade USA that some of its tariffs were so high that even a 50% cut had little practical value, a package deal of untidy compromises was belatedly reached. (Suggested in 1961 by President Kennedy, who assumed an imminent merger of the Common Market and EFTA.)

Kennedy's Latin Primer A standard school textbook on the subject still, after nearly a century, a best seller. (Benjamin Hall Kennedy, CAMBRIDGE UNIVERSITY professor.)

Kennedy (John F.) Stadium The stadium in Philadelphia, where the Army-Navy football game is played.

Kennelly-Heaviside layer Alternative name for the HEAVISIDE LAYER.

Kenny polio treatment A system of treating poliomyelitis cases by sustained exercises rather than vaccine injections; it gradually won approval against professional opposition. (Introduced by Sister Kenny, an Australian nurse.)

Kensal Green A large Roman Catholic cemetery in Willesden, West London, referred to in G. K. Chesterton's 'The Rolling English Road': For there is good news yet to hear and fine things to be seen,/Before we go to Paradise by way of Kensal Green.

Kensington and Chelsea (Royal Borough) An inner London borough formed in 1965 from the royal borough of Kensington and the metropolitan borough of Chelsea.

Kensington Palace A palace on the west side of Kensington Gardens, bought by William III and altered by Wren; the birthplace of Queen Victoria and Queen Mary. Part is now used by the LONDON MUSEUM.

Kensington Stone, The A slab with a runic inscription dated 1362, found in Minnesota in 1898. Originally pronounced a forgery, it is now regarded as being possibly the genuine relic of a VIKING expedition.

Kent (sheep) A breed of long-wool sheep which produce a heavy fleece used in making blankets, knitting yarns etc. Also called Romney Marsh.

Kentish man (UK) A man born in Kent west of the Medway (which flows through Tonbridge, Maidstone and Chatham); those born east of it are called 'men of Kent'.

Kentucky Derby (1875) The most famous of the American classic horse races, run over a distance of 1¼ miles on the first Saturday in May at CHURCHILL DOWNS.

Kentucky rifle A long-barreled muzzle-loading flintlock of small caliber, made in the early 18th century near Lancaster, Penn., and a favorite with frontiersmen; also called Pennsylvania rifle.

Kent University (1965) (UK) A new foundation, at Canterbury.

Kenwood See IVEAGH BEQUEST.

Kenyapithecus africanus Name proposed (1967) by Dr Leakey for a species of very small hominid (manlike) creatures of which he found jaw and tooth fragments in Kenya. He considers them to be MIOCENE and 20 million years old, and in the ancestry of man but not of apes, thus pushing back the division in ancestry by some 15 million years. In 1960 he also found remains of what he called *Kenyapithecus wickeri*, 10 million years old.

Kepler's laws (1609) The 3 laws governing the orbit of planets round the Sun, announced by the German astronomer Kepler and later shown by Newton to arise from the law of gravitation.

Kepler's Star One of the 3 supernovae observed in the MILKY WAY, seen by Kepler and Galileo in the constellation Ophiucus in 1604.

Kerensky government See OCTOBER REVOLUTION.

Kermess In the LOW COUNTRIES, a

boisterous celebration of the anniversary of a church's foundation; a scene often painted by the Dutch and Flemish Masters. (Equivalent to ('kirk-mass'.)

Kermesse héroïque, La (1935) A film comedy directed by Jacques Feyder, about the Spanish occupation of FLANDERS in the 16th century. See last entry.

Kerry A breed of dual-purpose black cattle, found mainly in southwest Ireland.

Kerry blue (early 1800s) An Irish terrier with silky blue or blue-gray coat. (Co. Kerry).

Kerry Hill (sheep) A breed of short-wool sheep bred mainly in Wales and the English Midlands. It produces a soft wool, and has distinctive black and white markings on face and legs.

Kestrel (1965) The world's first VTOL aircraft, the P-1127, a ground-attack fighter with a jet lift, built by HAWKER SIDDELEY. It is a smaller version of the P-1154 which had double the thrust and was a long-range supersonic V/STOL fighter, canceled in 1964. See HARRIER.

Ketch, Jack (1) A public executioner who executed Monmouth (1685) and other famous people. (2) A generic nickname for a public hangman.

Kettle, Capt. The forceful mariner of many novels (1898-1938) by C. J. Cutcliffe Hyne.

Keynsian economics The doctrines of J. M. (1st Baron) Keynes, particularly his recommendation that governments should 'spend their way out of a slump', i.e. greatly increase public expenditure to provide employment and stimulate markets; an essential corollary was that governments should cut back expenditure in a boom period, but this has never been tried. See ECONOMIC CONSEQUENCES OF THE PEACE.

Keys, Ceremony of the A nightly ceremony at the TOWER OF LONDON, when the Chief Warder, with a Guards escort, locks the gates.

Keystone comedies (1916-26) Movies made at Hollywood by the Keystone Corporation under Mack

Sennett, in some of which Charlie Chaplin appeared.

Keystone State Nickname of Pennsylvania. (Center of the original 13 States.)

KGB The Soviet State Security Committee (i.e. secret police) which succeeded the MGB in 1953, with the same duties; it supervises the GRU and propagates Communism abroad.

Khadijah The rich widow who became the first wife of the Prophet MOHAMMED, and by him the mother of Fatima (see FATIMITES).

Khaki Campbell A popular breed of dual-purpose domestic duck.

Khaki election In the UK: (1) Liberals' name for the 1900 election forced by Lord Salisbury, in which the Conservatives increased their majority at a time when the BOER WAR appeared to be all but over. (2) The name is also sometimes given to the COUPON ELECTION (1918).

Khartoum, Fall of (1885) The capture of Khartoum, and the massacre of its defenders under Gen. Gordon, by the Mahdists after a 9-month siege; a relief force under Wolseley arrived 2 days too late. Gordon had been sent to withdraw the European and Egyptian population from the Anglo-Egyptian Sudan, after 10,000 men under Col. Hicks had been massacred in 1883. See MAHDI.

Khedive The title of the Turkish governor of Egypt (1867-1914). (Persian, 'ruler'.)

Khmer The language spoken at ANGKOR, related to the early Burmese languages called Mon. (Khmer, old name of Cambodia, which is a European corruption of the SANSKRIT *Kambuja*.)

Kid, The (1920) Charlie Chaplin's first feature length movie, in which he appeared with the boy actor, Jackie Coogan, in a comedy of slum life.

Kidnapped (1886) R. L. Stevenson's novel about David Balfour, defrauded of his inheritance by an uncle who has him kidnapped and sent to sea. With a Jacobite friend, Alan Breck, he is wrecked off the coast of Scotland, returns home and gets back his property. The sequel, CA-

TRIONA, relates their further adventures.

Kikuyu The BANTU race dominant in Kenya; their language.

Kilauea Crater The 'pit of eternal fire', lying at 4090 ft on the side of MAUNA LOA, Hawaii. It is one of the largest and most spectacular of all active craters, 2 miles across with walls 500 ft deep. The last eruption was in 1955.

Kilkenny cats The expression 'to fight like Kilkenny cats' is said to have originated from German mercenaries stationed at Kilkenny at the turn of the 18th century, who tied cats together so that they fought to the death.

Killiecrankie (1689) Battle between Highland JACOBITES led by John Graham of Claverhouse ('BLUIDIE CLAVERS') and Scottish troops under Mackay loyal to William III. Claverhouse won, but was fatally wounded. (Pass between Perth and Inverness.)

Kilroy Was Here Phrase scribbled everywhere by US troops in World War II; origin unknown. See MR CHAD.

Kim (1901) Kipling's story of Kimball O'Hara, an orphan who travels through India with an old Tibetan lama, absorbing an intimate knowledge of Indian life which, while still a boy, enables him to give valuable help to the British Secret Service.

Kimberley A town in Cape Province, South Africa, west of Bloemfontein, and famous for (1) its diamond mines, controlled by DE BEERS; (2) its relief by Gen. Sir John French in February 1900, after a long siege.

Kind Hearts and Coronets (1949) A Boulting Brothers movie based on a story by Roy Horniman (1907), in which the hero successfully murders all the 8 people who stand between him and the succession to a dukedom, only to give himself away at his moment of triumph. All the victims of this riotous farce were played by Alec Guinness. (Title taken from a Tennyson poem.)

King and I, The (1951) A Rodgers and Hammerstein musical based on Margaret Landon's novel *Anna and the King of Siam* about an English governess who went to Siam in the mid-19th century to teach the king's children, and the resultant clash between eastern and western standards. Attractive songs such as 'Getting to Know You', 'A Puzzlement' and 'Shall We Dance?' helped to make both stage and screen versions highly successful.

King Charles's head An obsessive idea which a person cannot keep out of his writings or conversation; see Mr DICK.

King Edwards Best known of the English main-crop potatoes, kidney-shaped with a white skin splashed red. (Named after Edward VII.)

Kingfish The nickname of a notorious governor of Louisiana, Huey Long, who was shot dead in 1935.

King George V Cup (show jumping; 1911) The chief competition at the Royal INTERNATIONAL HORSE SHOW, for individual men.

King George VI and Queen Elizabeth Stakes (1952) An international flat race run over 1½ miles in July at Ascot; its object is to bring the best 3- and 4-year-olds together at weight-for-age.

King George VI Steeplechase A race held on Boxing Day at Kempton Park.

Kingis quair (1453) An allegorical poem attributed to King James I of Scotland, telling of his first glimpse of his future wife from his prison window in the TOWER OF LONDON. (Quair = quire, 'a short literary work'.)

King James Bible Another name for the Authorized Version.

King Kong (1932) A giant ape who appeared in one of the earliest Science Fiction talkies, written by Merian C. Cooper, and in many sequels.

King Lear (1605) Shakespeare's tragedy in which the English king, misconstruing the character of his 3 daughters, leaves his kingdom to GONERIL and Regan, whose monstrous ingratitude sends him mad; too late he learns that CORDELIA was the one who loved him.

King Log and King Stork In AESOP'S FABLE, 'The Frogs Desiring a King',

Jupiter sent them a log; when they complained of its inertia he sent them a stork, which gobbled them up. Thus, a choice between lax and tyrannical rule etc.

King of Jazz   Nickname of Paul Whiteman, whose band (started 1919) became the most famous of the fashionable dance orchestras of its day. He did much to develop the commercialization of jazz, and also commissioned the RHAPSODY IN BLUE. The nickname is the title of a screen tribute to him (1930).

King of Rome   The title Napoleon gave to his infant son by Marie Louise; later he became the Duke of Reichstadt, and was called Napoleon II by Bonapartists.

King of Swing   Title awarded to Benny Goodman, Jewish clarinetist from Chicago, who gave new life to jazz in the 1930s.

King of the French   (1830) Title given to Louis Philippe to stress the fact that he had been elected king by the Chamber of Deputies; see ORLEANIST MONARCHY.

King Philip's War   (1675-76) The first war to break the 54-year peace between the earliest NEW ENGLAND colonists and the Indians, waged with mutual savagery against the son (known as King Philip) of the chief of the WAMPANOAGS who had made the original treaty (1621). Encroachment on their hunting grounds and suspicion of missionary activities were the chief causes. Some 500 colonists were killed or captured and the war ended only when Philip was taken and executed.

Kings   (6th cenutry BC) The name of 2 books of the Old Testament, completed at Babylon during the EXILE. 1 Kings tells of SOLOMON's reign and the stories of ELIJAH and AHAB; 2 Kings deals with events leading to the BABYLONIAN CAPTIVITY.

Kings   The Los Angeles Kings, NATIONAL HOCKEY LEAGUE.

Kings Canyon National Park   (1940) A Sierra Nevada wilderness in middle-eastern California, with numerous peaks (13-14,000 ft) and groves of giant sequoias.

King's College (London)   A unit, founded 1829, of LONDON UNIVERSITY and housed in a wing of SOMERSET HOUSE; it makes special provision for Anglican ordinands.

King's Cup   (1922) An annual air race held in July, originally intended to stimulate British aircraft design, and later thrown open to international competition. (Presented by King George V.)

King's Cup   (tennis) A cup presented by the King of Sweden as the trophy for a men's team championship of the world at lawn tennis. It is Europe's indoor equivalent of the DAVIS CUP.

King's Scholars   At Eton, the 70 foundation scholars, who live in college (and thus are known as 'Collegers'), in distinction from the rest of the school (OPPIDANS), who call them 'tugs'.

Kingston Lacy   (UK) A house near Wimborne Minster, Dorset, occupied by the Bankes family of Corfe Castle ever since it was built 300 years ago.

Kingston upon Hull   (UK) The official designation of the town commonly known as Hull.

Kingston upon Thames   London borough since 1965 consisting of the former boroughs of Kingston, Surbiton and Malden and Coombe.

Kingstown   English name of Dún Laoghaire, the port of Dublin.

King Street   The address of the headquarters of, and used for, the Communist Party of Great Britain (1920), in London WC2.

Kinsey reports   Two studies, of the sexual behavior of the human male (1948) and female (1951), compiled with a wealth of statistical detail by Alfred C. Kinsey and his colleagues at Indiana University.

Kinshasa   The new name given to the capital of the CONGO REPUBLIC, formerly known by its Belgian name, Léopoldville.

Kiowa   A nomadic tribe of PLAINS INDIANS of Kansas, who used to raid Mexico and were fierce fighters against the whites generally. They survive in Oklahoma, and hold an annual dance at Carnegie.

Kiplincotes Derby   (1519) (UK) Claimed to be the oldest horse race in the world, run in March over a 5-mile course through several parishes starting from South Dalton near Beverley, Yorkshire, and ending at Kiplincotes Farm. The stake money all goes to the runner-up, and usually exceeds the first prize in value.

Kiplinger Letter, The A newsletter published in Washington, D.C., and circulated privately to businessmen.

Kipps, Arty The hero of H. G. Wells's semiautobiographical novel *Kipps* (1905), the Folkestone draper's assistant who inherits a fortune, gets engaged to a superior girl who sets about grooming him, escapes to marry his boyhood love and, having lost his money to a fraudulent lawyer, is relieved to return to the quiet life of a shopkeeper.

Kirchner girls The favorite pinups of World War I.

Kirk, The Colloquial name for the Church of Scotland.

Kirk o' Field A house outside Edinburgh where Lord Darnley was found strangled in 1567, possibly at the instigation of his wife, Mary Queen of Scots, and her future husband, the Earl of Bothwell. See CASKET LETTERS.

Kirov murder (1934) The assassination of a leading Communist, the Party boss of LENINGRAD. He was supposed to be a close friend of Stalin, but the circumstances of his death were sufficiently mysterious to start rumors that Stalin or those close to him were responsible for it. It was the pretext for beginning the STALINIST PURGES.

Kirsch, Kirschwasser A liqueur brandy made from wild black cherries, chiefly in Germany.

Kisangani A town in the Congo, formerly Stanleyville.

Kiss Me, Kate (1948) Cole Porter's musical comedy based on *The Taming of the Shrew* (see KATHARINA).

Kitchener's Army The army of volunteers raised by Lord Kitchener as Minister of War at the outset of World War I. They totaled 3 million before conscription was introduced in 1916.

Kitemark The trademark of the BRITISH STANDARDS INSTITUTION, which manufacturers are permitted under license to use on goods conforming to a British Standard.

Kitimat See ALCAN.

Kitty Foyle (1939) A lively stream-of-consciousness novel by Christopher Morley in which a young Philadelphia MAIN LINER'S love for an Irish typist of not very gentle birth is sympathetically described.

Kitty Hawk The scene of the first flight of a heavier-than-air machine (1903), made by Orville Wright. (Village in northeast North Carolina.)

Kitty Hawk type Used colloquially of early types of missiles etc. (See previous entry.)

Kiuchuan Chinese missile site; see CHIUCHUAN.

Kiwanis (1915) An organization of American and Canadian clubs pledged to raise standards in industry, business and the professions. (Coined name.)

KKK The KU KLUX KLAN.

KLM (1919) The chief Dutch airline, almost wholly owned by government.

Klondike The district (and river) in Yukon Territory, Canada, on the Alaskan border, where the discovery of gold in 1896 led to the gold rush of 1897-98.

KMT Initials used for KUOMINTANG.

Knack, The (1961) Ann Jellicoe's comedy and movie about the impact of an innocent girl on 3 men, one of whom is an expert at seduction, another most inexpert.

Knesset The Israeli Parliament.

Knickebein German system of guiding night bombers over Britain by radio beams, introduced August 1940, and rendered ineffective by countermeasures.

Knickerbocker Club (1871) A New York social club. (Knickerbocker, a descendant of the early Dutch settlers in New York, and hence any New Yorker; also a pen name of Washington Irving, who mocked their pretensions.)

Knickerbockers The New York Knickerbockers, NATIONAL BASKETBALL ASSOCIATION.

Knicks Short for New York KNICKERBOCKERS.

Knightley, Mr   See EMMA.

Knight of the Burning Pestle, The
(about 1607) A Beaumont and
Fletcher comedy, with a grocer's
apprentice cast as a caricature of
DON QUIXOTE in a play within the
play.

Knight of the Rueful Countenance   A
name for DON QUIXOTE.

Knights, The   (424 BC) Aristophanes'
comedy in which he attacks the
powerful demagogue CLEON without
mercy — striking testimony to the
freedom of speech then prevailing in
Athens.

Knights Hospitallers   See KNIGHTS OF
ST JOHN.

Knights of Columbus   (1882) A US
Roman Catholic fraternal organization.

Knights of Malta   (1530) The name
given to the KNIGHTS OF RHODES after
they left Rhodes and were given
Malta by the Emperor Charles V.

Knights of Pythias   (1864) A US
fraternal organization founded at
Washington, D.C.

Knights of Rhodes   (1310-1525) The
name given to the KNIGHTS OF ST JOHN
during their stay in Rhodes after the
loss of the Holy Land.

Knights of St John   (11th century) A
religious nursing order, the Knights
Hospitallers of St John of Jerusalem,
which very soon became a military
crusading order and acquired extensive possessions in Palestine and
Europe; later they became the
KNIGHTS OF RHODES and KNIGHTS OF
MALTA. The original order survives
but was suppressed in England, to
be revived in the 19th century as a
benevolent association, which now
controls the ST JOHN AMBULANCE BRI-
GADE and Association.

Knight's Tale, The   In the CANTER-
BURY TALES, the story of PALAMON
AND ARCITE.

Knights Templars   (1) A religious
order founded (1118) by French
knights to protect pilgrims in the
Holy Land. They then became a military crusading order, wealthy and,
according to their enemies, corrupt
and insolent, and were suppressed
by the Pope in 1312, much of their
property passing to the KNIGHTS OF
ST JOHN. (Named after quarters given
them at Jerusalem on the site of SOL-
OMON'S TEMPLE.) (2) An order of
FREEMASONS.

Knole   One of the largest private
houses in England, at Sevenoaks,
Kent, mostly dating from the 15th
century; home of the Sackvilles, and
now the property of the NATIONAL
TRUST.

Knossos   Ancient city of Crete, excavated by Sir Arthur Evans; see MI-
NOAN CIVILIZATION.

Know-Nothing Party   A political society once prominent in American
politics (1852-60) which aimed at
continued WASP control of government by depriving naturalized
Americans and Roman Catholics of
political rights. It was formed in reaction to mass immigration of the
Irish, which was reaching its peak in
1830-60, and also of Germans, as
both these groups were resisting assimilation and criticizing US institutions. See Ned BUNTLINE. (So
called as originally a secret organization, all knowledge of which was
disclaimed by members.)

KO   Initials used in boxing for
'knockout'; compare TKO.

Köchel numbers   The numbers given
to Mozart's 626 compositions in the
standard catalogue of them compiled in chronological order by
Köchel.

Kodama   A Japanese limited express
train on the New TOKAIDO LINE.
There are 21 daily services which,
with 10 stops, do the 320-mile run
in 4 hours, i.e. at an average speed of
80 m.p.h.

Kodokan   (1882) Judo school founded by Dr Kano in Tokyo; now the
world headquarters of judo.

K of C   See KNIGHTS OF COLUMBUS.

K of K   Nickname for Earl Kitchener
of Khartoum, who gained his title by
recapturing Khartoum from the
MAHDI (1898); he was Minister of
War in World War I until his death
in 1916 (see HAMPSHIRE, HMS).

K of P   See KNIGHTS OF PYTHIAS.

Koh-i-noor diamond   One of the British Crown jewels, a huge diamond
dating back to at least the 14th century but of unknown origin, present-

ed to Queen Victoria after the annexation of the PUNJAB. (Persian, 'mountain of light'.)

Ko-Ko See MIKADO.

Koko Nor, Lake A Chinese army nuclear base (1966) in Tsinghai Province, some 200 miles northwest of LANCHOW, close to the Nan Shan (Ch'ilien Shan) mountains which have rich uranium deposits. Research on the hydrogen bomb is carried on there. See CHIUCHUAN. (Also called Lake Tsinghai.)

Kolapore Cup (1871) In full, the Rajah of Kolapore's Imperial Challenge Cup, a rifle-shooting competition for eights from the 'Mother Country' and the Dominions.

Kolyma The site in far eastern Siberia of a Soviet forced-labor camp where some 2 million people are said to have died in the Stalin era; it has been called 'the frozen AUSCHWITZ of Siberia'.

Komsomols (1918) Russian name for members of the All-Union Leninist Young Communist League.

Königgratz German name sometimes given to the Battle of SADOWA.

Königsberg German name of the city of Kaliningrad, USSR.

Kontiki Name of the balsa-log raft on which Thor Heyerdahl and 5 others sailed in 1947 from Lima to the Tuamotu group (east of Tahiti) to demonstrate that people from Peru could have colonized the Pacific islands in ancient times, and could account for the fair-skinned element in Polynesia. (Name of the pre-INCA sun god or king of Peru who, according to legend, sailed off into the Pacific with his white, bearded subjects.)

Köpenick hoax (1906) A Berlin ex-convict in search of a passport put on a Guards officer's uniform and, in the days when the officer class were all-powerful, was able to arrest the burgomaster and rifle his office but, not finding a passport, gave himself up. The incident was used in Zuckmayer's comedy, *Der Hauptmann von Köpenick* (1931). (Name of a Berlin suburb.)

Korean War (1950-53) A war due to the joint occupation of Japanese

Korea in 1945 by Russian and US troops, respectively north and south of the 38th parallel. When they went, the North Koreans, by then communized, invaded South Korea. The UN condemned the invaders, US troops returned and drove them back, but retreated when Chinese 'volunteers' joined in, despite reinforcement from other UN countries, including Britain. After great devastation and long negotiation a truce was signed, leaving the country divided as before.

Kossovo (1389) The decisive battle which began over 300 years of Balkan subjection to the OTTOMAN TURKS. A confederation of Christian SLAVS under Serbian leadership met with a crushing defeat; the Byzantines, unconscious of their own impending doom, gave no assistance to their fellow Christians. (Plain in southern Serbia.)

Kovno Russian name of Kaunas, former capital of Lithuania.

Kozhikode A seaport of Kerala, India, formerly known as Calicut.

KP Initials signifying Kitchen Police, i.e. enlisted men detailed to assist the cook in a military mess.

Krafft-Ebing The author's, name, sometimes used as a synonym for his main work, *Psychopathia Sexualis* (1886). (Baron von Krafft-Ebing, German neurologist.)

Krakatoa An island of Indonesia almost completely destroyed by a violent volcanic explosion in 1883, causing a tidal wave which killed 35,000 people in Java and Sumatra and reached as far as Cape Horn; dust affected the atmosphere all round the world. (Island between Java and Sumatra.)

Kraken Awakes, The (1957) A Science Fiction novel by John Wyndham, based on an old Norse legend (about which Tennyson wrote a poem) of a huge sea monster. In the novel a radio scriptwriter and his wife describe how the Kraken came to menace mankind.

Krapp's Last Tape (1958) Beckett's short play in which Krapp listens to a tape recording he made 30 years earlier and finds that it has lost all significance for him in old age.

K ration (US army) Emergency ration.

Krazy Kat (1911-44) George Herriman's innocent cartoon character who loves Ignatz, the worldly mouse, even (perhaps especially) when he succeeds in 'kreasing Kat's bean with a brick'. Offisa Pup, representing the law, loves Kat. This cartoon, set among the cactuses of Arizona, delighted the JAZZ AGE eggheads.

Kremlin Generic term for a Russian citadel; specifically the huge walled enclosure in Moscow containing buildings dating back to the 15th century; the seat of, and a synonym for, the Soviet government.

Kremlinology A 'science' generated by the secretiveness of the Soviet government, especially in Stalin's day. Its practitioners study Russian newspapers, broadcasts, press photographs etc. for indications of gain in, or loss of, favor by individual Soviet leaders, and for signs of shifts of emphasis in the Party line. (Jocular formation from 'Kremlin'.)

Kresge Foundation (1924) A foundation which supports religious, charitable and educational institutions; the headquarters are in Detroit.

Kretschmer's types (1925) A classification which tried to relate personality to types of physique, based on skeletal build (ignoring soft tissue). The 3 main types were (1) tall, slim men, tending to be introverted and serious (e.g. DON QUIXOTE and the 'lean and hungry Cassius'); (2) short, thickset (pycnic) men, tending to be extrovert and amiable (e.g. SANCHO PANZA), but liable to be manic-depressive in mental breakdowns; (3) the well-proportioned athletic type, rather negative in his reactions to life. (Ernst Kretschmer, German psychiatrist.)

Kreuger crash, The (1932) The downfall of the Swedish 'Match King', Ivar Kreuger, whose financial operations were on a huge scale, particularly in Sweden, USA and France. Detected in fraud and forgery, he committed suicide, leaving behind a trail of company failures.

Kreutzer Sonata (1) Beethoven's violin sonata, dedicated to a French musician of that name. (2) One of Tolstoy's later novels (1890), based on his own sex life.

Kriemhild In the NIBELUNGENLIED, GUNTHER's sister who unwittingly betrays her husband SIEGFRIED to HAGEN. Her death symbolizes the fall of the Burgundians.

Krim Tartars The TARTARS of the Crimea.

Krishna In HINDUISM, the eighth and most popular incarnation of VISHNU, god of fire, storms and the sun, the Indian APOLLO, particularly worshiped by women. Some sects worship him as the god of love in all its forms. He appears in the BHAGAVAD-GITA.

Kriss Kringle A German-American name for Santa Claus. (From German *Christkindl*, 'Christ-child', 'Christmas present'.)

Kristin Lavransdatter (1920-22) Sigrid Undset's trilogy of historical novels set in 13th/14th century Norway.

Kroger spy case (1961) The arrest of Morris and Lona Cohen (alias 'Peter and Helen Kroger'), both sentenced to 20 years imprisonment in the PORTLAND SECRETS CASE but released in 1969. They were also involved in the earlier ROSENBERG SPY CASE.

Krokodil Soviet Russian humorous periodical.

Kronstadt mutiny (1) A Russian mutiny against the Lvov government in July 1917. (2) A mutiny in 1921 put down by the Bolshevists with violence; one of the factors that led to the NEW ECONOMIC POLICY. (Russian island naval base in the Gulf of Finland, with a reputation for mutinies, e.g. also in 1825, 1905, 1906.)

Kruger telegram (1896) The Kaiser's telegram congratulating President Kruger on the failure of the JAMESON RAID.

Krupp Diamond A diamond formerly belonging to the KRUPPS which passed into the hands of the actress Elizabeth Taylor.

Krupps (1811) The huge German family firm with steel and engineering works at Essen; it armed Germany (1857-1945) and now makes locomotives, ships, transport aircraft, atomic plant, chemicals etc. The Allies failed to break up the group in 1945 as no buyers would come forward. In 1967 the last Krupp died and the firm, deeply in the red, 'went public'.

Kshatriyas The Hindu military caste, second only to the BRAHMINS in rank. (SANSKRIT, 'rulers'.)

K2 The Himalayan mountain peak now known as Mt Godwin-Austen, or Chobrum.

Kubla Khan (1797, published 1816) Coleridge's poem, which came to him in a dream after reading about Kubla in PURCHAS HIS PILGRIMES. He jotted down as much as he could before he was interrupted by 'a person from Porlock', and was unable to remember the rest of it. See XANADU.

Kuibyshev A city of the USSR, formerly Samara.

Ku Klux Klan An obscurantist secret society formed after the AMERICAN CIVIL WAR to maintain white supremacy in southern USA; suppressed in 1871, it was revived in 1915 to persecute not only Negroes, but Jews, Catholics, Darwinists, pacifists, etc. Bespectacled businessmen in city suits disguise themselves in white robes and hoods, and burn 'fiery crosses', one of the saddest sights in Christendom. (Illiterate misspelled derivation from Greek *kuklos*, 'circle'.)

Kulturkampf (1870s) German for 'cultural struggle', the name given to Bismarck's campaign to subordinate the Church to the State. He expelled the JESUITS, made civil marriage legal, and imposed restrictions on the Catholic Church, which he regarded as a threat to national unity.

Kümmel An old-established liqueur, now made in the Netherlands, Denmark and Latvia from grain or potato spirit flavored with caraway or cumin seeds.

Kunsthistoriches Museum A Vienna museum containing an exceptionally fine art collection.

Kuomintang (1912) The Chinese nationalist party founded by Sun Yat-sen which under his successor Chiang Kai-shek formed the Nanking government in 1927. It included people of every shade of political opinion (short of Communism), united only in determination to free the country from Japanese and Western dominance, but was weakened by internal corruption and inefficiency, and its continual struggle against the Communists, to whom it succumbed in 1949. Chiang Kai-shek then set up a government in Formosa. (Chinese, 'nation-people-party'.)

Kurdistan The land of the KURDS, in southeast Turkey, north Iraq and northwest Persia, with small adjoining areas of northeast Syria and southern Azerbaijan (USSR).

Kurds A nomadic Iranian mountain race of KURDISTAN, speaking an INDO-EUROPEAN LANGUAGE and preserving its racial integrity despite being divided between Turkey, Persia and Iraq. Russians in 1954 tried to set up a separatist Kurdish state in Persia, with a capital at Mahabad, and encouraged the Kurds of the rich Mosul oil-field area in Iraq, who had similar ambitions and still cause continual trouble to the Iraqi government.

Kurfürstendamm Berlin's fashionable shopping street. (German, 'Elector's causeway'.)

Kut, Siege of (Dec. 1915-Apr. 1916) The Turkish siege of Gen. Townshend's forces in a town on the Tigris in MESOPOTAMIA, which ended in British surrender. (Also called Kut el-Amara.)

Kuwait Oil Co. (1934) The company which was given the sole right to exploit the rich oil-fields of Kuwait on the Persian Gulf; it is controlled by BP and the Gulf Exploration Co. in equal partnership. Production did not begin until 1946.

KVD (1960) Soviet Committee for Internal Affairs, the successor to MVD.

Kwajalein Island A large atoll of the Marshall Islands, chosen as the site for tests starting in 1968 of the first complete experimental NIKE-X SYSTEM.

Kwangchow (Kuang-chou) Official Chinese name of Canton.

Kyrie eleison (1) The short supplication 'Lord have mercy' used in various Church services. (2) A musical setting of this. (Greek words.)

L

'L', The An alternative spelling of 'the EL.', i.e. the New York City elevated railway.

LA Initials used postally and colloquially for Los Angeles.

Labanotation A system of recording the positions and movements of a ballet. (Rudolf Laban, inventor.)

Labor Day In Canada and USA, a legal holiday on the first Monday in September.

Labrador Current A cold current which flows south along the Labrador coast from Baffin Bay and, fed by water from Greenland and Hudson Strait, often carries icebergs and even field ice to its confluence with the GULF STREAM off Newfoundland, causing local fogs there in spring and early summer. Also called the Arctic Current. See GRAND BANKS.

Laburnum Grove (1933) J. B. Priestley's comedy about a criminal who, when 'resting', lives the life of a highly respectable suburban householder.

Lacedaemonians See SPARTANS.

Lachesis One of the 3 FATES.

Ladakh crisis (1962) The Chinese incursion into the Ladakh enclave of Indian-held Kashmir which juts into Tibet following the MCMAHON LINE (which the Chinese have never accepted), in order to safeguard communications between Sinkiang and western Tibet. Having gained their objective the main Chinese forces withdrew.

'La donna è mobile' The famous aria from RIGOLETTO (Italian, 'Women are capricious') which plays a key part in the dénouement of the plot.

Ladrones Spanish name for the Marianas island group in the northwest Pacific. ('Thieves', the name given them by Magellan, whose crew suffered from their inhabitants' pilferings.)

Lady Baltimore cake A (usually white) butter cake with boiled frosting and a filling of frosting, chopped raisins, figs and nuts. (Probably named for the wife of the founder of Maryland.)

Lady Bird Family nickname of the wife of LBJ.

Lady Chapel A chapel in a cathedral or large church dedicated to the Virgin MARY, and normally situated behind the altar.

Lady Chatterly's Lover (1928) D. H. Lawrence's novel on the nature of sexual relationship, in which the aristocratic Connie runs away with her impotent husband's gamekeeper, Mellors. Its frankness was too much for the English courts until 1960 when Penguin, which had published it in cheap paperback form, forced the issue and was acquitted on the charge of publishing an obscene article.

Lady into Fox (1922) David Garnett's fantasy of a woman who turned into a fox and her subsequent relationship with her husband.

Lady Margaret Hall (1878) The oldest women's college at OXFORD UNIVERSITY. (Named after Lady Margaret Beaufort, mother of Henry VII.)

Lady of Shalott In ARTHURIAN LEGEND, the girl who died from unrequited love for LANCELOT; in Tennyson she is Elaine, the lily maid of Astolat (said to be Guildford).

Lady of the Camellias A ballet with music from Verdi's TRAVIATA, choreography by Antony Tudor and scenery and costumes by Cecil Beaton. See DAME AUX CAMÉLIAS.

Lady of the Lake (1) In ARTHURIAN LEGEND, the enchantress Vivien, mistress of MERLIN; she made EXCALIBUR, stole the infant LANCELOT from his parents, and imprisoned Merlin in a tower or thornbush, there to remain ready to conjure up King ARTHUR when Britain again has need of him. (2) Title of Walter Scott's poem about a very different lady, who lived by Loch Katrine.

Lady of the Lamp Florence Nightingale, who worked tirelessly and successfully at a hospital in Scutari

(Usküdar, opposite ISTANBUL) to raise the appallingly low standards of nursing of the sick and wounded in the CRIMEAN WAR. (Name referred to her night rounds of the hospital, lamp in hand.)

Lady or the Tiger?, The (1882) An ingenious novelette by Frank R. Stockton. A young man and a king's daughter fall in love. The king finds out and gives him the choice of opening one of two doors; behind one is a tiger, behind the second — another beautiful girl he is free to marry. The princess secretly promises to guide his choice; the book ends without disclosing which door she indicates.

Ladysmith, Relief of (28 Feb. 1900) An episode of the BOER WAR; Ladysmith, a township in Natal, was besieged for 4 months before it was relieved by Gen. Buller. It is now said that the hardships of the besieged were not great.

Lady's Not for Burning, The (1949) A verse comedy by Christopher Fry about a young witch in Elizabethan times.

Lady Windermere's Fan (1892) Oscar Wilde's comedy of manners in which a trivial plot about the runaway Lady Windermere's restoration to her husband by her (unknown) mother is a vehicle for the witty dialogue for which Wilde was later to become so famous.

Laertes (1) In Greek legend, the father of Odysseus. (2) In Shakespeare's HAMLET, the man who, to avenge the death of his father POLONIUS and his sister OPHELIA, fights a duel with Hamlet in which both die.

Laetare Medal (1883) A gold medal annually awarded to an American Roman Catholic for distinction in the arts, science, government or professional service etc., by a faculty committee of the University of Notre Dame, Ind., and announced on Laetare Sunday (the fourth in Lent). (Latin, 'rejoice'.)

'Lafayette, we are here' The closing sentence of Col. Charles E. Stanton's speech at Lafayette's tomb in Paris, on US entry into World War I in 1917. (A reference to the Marquis de Lafayette, the Frenchman who fought in the American and French Revolutions.)

Lafayette Squadron (Apr. 1916) A squadron of American volunteers which served with the French air force before USA joined in World War I.

La Guardia Airport An airport on Long Island, in the borough of QUEENS, New York City.

Lake Poets Wordsworth, Coleridge and Southey, who lived in the Lake District for varying periods; the name was originally meant to be derisive but has long ceased to carry any such implication. See ROMANTIC POETS.

Lakers The Los Angeles Lakers, NATIONAL BASKETBALL ASSOCIATION.

Lake Success A village in New York State, temporary headquarters of the UN before its move to MANHATTAN in 1952.

Lalique glass Glassware in ART NOUVEAU designs, produced in Paris on a factory scale from the early years of the 20th century. (Réné Lalique, 1860-1945.)

Lalla Rookh (1817) Thomas Moore's oriental tale in verse and prose of a daughter of the MOGUL Emperor and the legends told her by a Persian poet.

Lamaism The degenerate form of BUDDHISM which was the religion of Tibet until Communist China took over the country. See DALAI LAMA.

Lamarckism The view that habits (or, loosely, characteristics) acquired through adjustment to environment can be inherited. See BACK TO METHUSELAH. (Chevalier de Lamarck, French zoologist, 1744-1829.)

Lambaréné (1913) The site of the hospital village in Gabon, West Africa, founded by Dr Albert Schweitzer.

Lambeth Conference (1867) An assembly of bishops of the ANGLICAN CHURCH from all over the world, held at LAMBETH PALACE, London, normally every 10 years. The Archbishop of Canterbury presides over its deliberations as the spiritual head of the Church.

Lambeth Delft (1) Blue and white DELFT made at Lambeth from the early 17th century to 1790. (2) A revival of MAIOLICA by DOULTON POTTERY of Lambeth, also called Lambeth faience (1873-1914).

Lambeth Palace The London residence since the 12th century of the Archbishops of Canterbury, by Lambeth Bridge.

Lambeth Walk, The (1937) An English dance excellently characterizing the COCKNEY 'image' of nonchalant jaunty good humor, in the form of a strutting march cum square dance; a similarly characteristic song, 'Doin' the Lambeth Walk', went with it. (A London street south of the Thames.)

Lambs Club A distinguished social club in New York City.

LAMDA The London Academy of Music and Dramatic Art, in Kensington.

'Lame Duck' Amendment The 20TH AMENDMENT. Previously, after the November national elections there was a final session of the old legislature lasting normally from December to March 3rd, during which a President, Vice-President and all members who had failed to win reelection were necessarily ineffective 'lame ducks'.

Lamellibranchs See MOLLUSKS.

Lamentations (6th century BC) A book of the Old Testament formerly attributed to JEREMIAH. It laments the fall of Jerusalem in 586 BC (see BABYLONIAN CAPTIVITY).

Lamia (1820) Keats's narrative poem about a bridegroom who discovers on his wedding night that his bride is a lamia (a half-serpent monster who preys on human beings); a version of an old Greek legend, but taken by Keats from Burton's ANATOMY OF MELANCHOLY.

Lammas August 1st, the ANGLO-SAXON harvest festival; Scottish quarter day. (From Old English for 'loaf mass'.)

'Lamplight Portrait, The' Charles Willson Peale's portrait of his artist brother James (1749-1831). (Detroit Institute of Arts.)

Lancashire style (Wrestling) Another name for CATCH-AS-CATCH-CAN.

Lancaster British AVRO fast 4-engined long-range bomber, used in the first British-based raid on Italy (Milan) in October 1942.

Lancaster Herald An officer of the COLLEGE OF ARMS.

Lancaster House An early Victorian mansion in Stable Yard, St James's, London, now owned by the Ministry of Works; often used for conferences on Commonwealth affairs.

Lancastrians Descendants of JOHN OF GAUNT, Duke of Lancaster: Henry IV, V and VI (1399-1461), and Henry VII, who married a daughter of the YORKIST Edward IV; see WARS OF THE ROSES.

Lancelot One of King ARTHUR's knights, the lover of Queen GUINEVERE, loved by ELAINE.

Lancers The surviving regiments, all in the ROYAL ARMOURED CORPS, are: 9th/12th Royal Lancers (Prince of Wales's); 16th/5th The Queen's Royal Lancers; 17th/21st Lancers.

Lanchester (1896) The first British gasoline-driven car to have most of the essentials of a modern car. For many years a distinguishing feature was the use of a horizontal bar instead of a steering wheel.

Lanchow A center of Chinese nuclear development and research, with a uranium plant, large hydroelectric and thermal electric power resources, and a petrochemical industry. It is the capital of Kansu Province, on the Hwang Ho. See KOKO NOR; PAOTOW.

Land Commission (1967) A UK body armed with powers for the compulsory purchase of building land required in the public interest. It is financed by a levy (initially 40%) on development values.

Land League (1879-81) An organization of Irish farming tenants directed against their landlords and using the boycott in protest against evictions and high rents. One of the founders, Parnell, was arrested, but in the same year legislation was passed restricting rents and safeguarding security of tenure.

Ländler An Austrian country dance to slow waltz time, the forerunner of the true waltz. See SCHUHPLATTLER.

Land o' Cakes Scotland, a term used by Burns, referring to Scottish oatmeal cakes.

Land of Enchantment A nickname for New Mexico.

'Land of Hope and Glory' A song written by the novelist A. C. Benson to music by Elgar, part of the *Pomp and Circumstance* suite. At one time considered as a possible alternative UK national anthem, it was felt that the words 'Wider still and wider shall thy bounds be set; / God who made thee mighty, make thee mightier yet' had become inappropriate when successive governments were doing the exact opposite.

'Land of my Fathers' The Welshman's national anthem, written in Welsh.

Land of Opportunity A nickname officially given to Arkansas in 1953 in the face of declining population (which continued).

Land of 10,000 Lakes A nickname of Minnesota, actually an understatement.

Land of the Midnight Sun (1) Norway, as the phenomenon is most easily observed there. (2) A nickname for Alaska.

Land o' the Leal Heaven; title of a poem by Baroness Nairne, died 1845. (*Leal*, Scottish word for 'loyal', 'faithful', hence 'blessed'.)

Landrace The leading Scandinavian breed of bacon hog, in Britain usually crossed with the LARGE WHITE or other breeds.

Landseer's Lions (1868) The bronze lions at the base of Nelson's monument, TRAFALGAR SQUARE, London, the work of Sir Edwin Landseer.

Landsturm German name for the third-line reserve, consisting of untrained young men and ex-servicemen aged 39-45, i.e. all those not in the LANDWEHR or other forces. ('Land storm'.)

Landwehr German name for the second-line reserve, consisting of men under 39 years of age with 7 years' active service. ('Land defense'.)

Langley Medal Awarded by the SMITHSONIAN INSTITUTION for distinguished work in aerodynamics and its application to aviation.

Languish, Lydia In Sheridan's play *The Rivals*, a niece of Mrs MALAPROP who prefers romantic elopement with a penniless ensign rather than a humdrum marriage to the rich baronet's heir chosen for her. As these turn out to be one and the same person, no great harm is done.

Lansbury's Lido (1930) Open-air bathing place on the SERPENTINE in Hyde Park, London. See LIDO. (Established by George Lansbury, Labour Commissioner of Works.)

Lansdowne letter (1917) A letter published in the British press during World War I by the 5th Marquess of Lansdowne, a former Foreign Secretary (1900-06); it advocated a compromise peace with Germany lest Europe destroy itself.

Lanyon Quoit A NEOLITHIC tomb northwest of Madron, near Penzance, England.

Laocoön (1) In Greek legend the Trojan priest who offended APOLLO and was punished by being crushed to death by 2 huge snakes, together with his 2 sons. (2) The 2nd-century sculpture depicting this, discovered in 1506 in Rome, and now in the VATICAN. (3) Title of Lessing's essay 'on the limits of painting and poetry' (1776).

Laodicean Lukewarm in religion (or politics), like the Laodicean Church rebuked in *Revelation* iii, 15-16, for being 'neither cold nor hot'.

Lao Dong The Pan-Vietnam Communist Party. In 1962 a southern branch of it was established, called the People's Revolutionary Party to disguise the overall control exercised by North Vietnam over its supporters in South Vietnam. See VIETMINH. ('Workers' Party'.)

Laoighis A county of the Irish Republic, formerly Queen's County.

Laputa An imaginary flying island in GULLIVER'S TRAVELS inhabited by unpractical scientists and philosophers who have attendants to flap them in the face with bladders to bring them down to consideration of mundane matters.

Large White (1) A Yorkshire breed of bacon hog, from which the Middle White pork and bacon hog was evolved. (2) Another name for the Cabbage White butterfly.

Lari massacre (1953) The murder by MAU MAU in Kenya of nearly 100 fellow Kikuyu.

Lark Rise to Candleford (1939-43) Flora Thompson's trilogy (*Lark Rise, Over to Candleford, Candleford Green*), in which Laura (representing the author) gives a delightful description of 19th-century village life in the southeast Midlands of England.

Larousse A French encyclopedia-dictionary, first published over 100 years ago, and still a leading French reference book. (Pierre Larousse, 1817-75, lexicographer.)

Lars Porsena An Etruscan king who appears to have conquered Rome in the 6th century BC; the story in *Horatius*, one of Macaulay's *Lays of Ancient Rome*, follows the Roman legend which conceals this humiliation. Its opening lines (Lars Porsena of Clusium / By the nine gods he swore / That the great house of Tarquin / Should suffer wrong no more) are among the most familiar in English poetry.

Lascaux caves Caves near Montignac in the French Dordogne, discovered in 1940, with extremely impressive colored animal paintings on the walls, probably belonging to the MAGDALENIAN CULTURE. Opened to the public in 1948, they had to be closed in 1960 owing to deterioration of the paintings.

Lascelles Family name of the Earls of Harewood.

Lasker Medical Journalism Award An award of $2500, sponsored by the Lasker Foundation.

Lassen Peak The only recently active (1914-17) volcano in mainland US, 10,457 ft, south of Mt Shasta in the Sierra Nevada, northern California. At its last eruption it scattered ash as far as Reno. There are also hot springs and geysers in the Lassen Volcanic National Park (1916).

Lassie A collie which became a star of the screen, in movies and TV.

Last Days of Pompeii, The (1834) Bulwer-Lytton's famous historical novel set in the time when POMPEII was destroyed by an eruption of

Vesuvius in AD 79.

Last Enemy, The (1942) Richard Hillary's account of his wartime experiences in the RAF, published the year before his death.

Last Frontier, The A nickname for Alaska, the last mainland state to join the Union.

'Last Judgment' Michelangelo's fresco behind the altar of the SISTINE CHAPEL, Rome.

'Last of England, The' (1855) Madox Brown's Pre-Raphaelite painting of 2 emigrants taking their last look at England; now in the Birmingham Art Gallery.

Last of the Mohicans, The See LEATHERSTOCKING TALES.

Last of the Romans Title given to the 14th-century Roman patriot RIENZI, and later to Horace Walpole, Charles James Fox and others.

Last Puritan, The (1936) George Santayana's only novel, in which Oliver, an inhibited New Englander, is brought to grief by his austere perfectionism while the gay Mario has things all his own way. The author deplores excessive puritanism but prefers Oliver to Mario.

'Last Supper' (1497) Leonardo da Vinci's painting in oil on the refectory wall of the Dominican convent church of Sta Maria delle Grazie at Milan. It deteriorated even in his lifetime and had to be much restored. It depicted the moment when the Apostles were saying 'Lord, is it I?' (*Matthew* xxvi, 22).

Last Year at Marienbad (1961) A movie directed by Alain Resnais (see HIROSHIMA, MON AMOUR), for which the scenario was written by Alain Robbe-Grillet, French NEW WAVE novelist.

Las Vegas A town in Nevada, which since 1945 has become notorious for its mushrooming gambling casinos and nightclubs and for its battalions of one-arm bandits, now yielding in popularity to English bingo. Situated in the southeast corner of the state, it is only a few hours from Los Angeles.

Late George Apley, The (1937) John P. Marquand's study of the values prevailing in the NEW ENGLAND puritan and aristocratic society from which he himself came; it purports to be the memoir of a conventional Bostonian, whom he describes with ironic sympathy. With George Kaufman, Marquand turned the novel into a play (1946).

La Tène An improved IRON AGE culture developed from the HALLSTATT about 400 BC. (Named after a Celtic lakeside settlement in Switzerland.)

Lateran, The A former palace of the popes in eastern Rome, now a museum. (On the site of the house of the ancient Laterani family, confiscated by Nero and later given to the popes.)

Lateran Treaty (1929) A concordat and treaty between Mussolini and Pope Pius XI establishing the VATICAN CITY as a sovereign power, and ending the self-imposed imprisonment of the Popes in the Vatican begun in 1870.

Latin America Central and South America. (Countries speaking Latin languages, i.e. Spanish, Portuguese, French.)

Latin Quarter The LEFT BANK district of Paris where the SORBONNE University is situated; once the center of the city's artistic life. (For French *Quartier Latin*, as the medieval students used Latin as a lingua franca.)

Latter-Day Saints Members of the Church of Jesus Christ of the Latter-Day Saints, an American sect founded (1830) by Joseph Smith, with beliefs based on the Book of MORMON, and widely known as 'Mormons'. Their practice of 'plural marriage' caused public scandal and was abandoned in 1890 under governmental pressure. They are particularly numerous in and around Utah.

L'aubina A powder rich in protein developed in Lebanon as a diet supplement; it can be added to food such as rice to increase its protein value, as part of the campaign to solve the problem of adequately feeding the rapidly increasing world population.

Laughing Buddha The familiar Chinese porcelain figure of an excessively fat man displaying his navel; he is a BODHISATTVA and represents riches and contentment.

'Laughing Cavalier' (1624) The famous portrait by the Dutch painter, Frans Hals, of a swashbuckling officer; now in the WALLACE COLLECTION, London.

Laurasia Geologists' name for the northern supercontinent, once joined to GONDWANALAND, later separated from it by the Tethys Ocean, and divided into North America, Greenland and Eurasia (less India). Also called Laurentia, and named for the St Lawrence.

Laurel racetrack The venue of the Washington international flat race (1952) held in October, at Laurel, Md., near Washington, D.C.

Lausanne Treaty (1923) The postwar treaty with Turkey which replaced the SÈVRES TREATY. Turkey regained Smyrna and a little territory in Europe, but lost all the non-Turkish lands (Arabia, Palestine, Syria, Iraq and most of the Aegean Islands). The Dardanelles forts were demolished.

Lavengro (1851) George Borrow's partly autobiographical novel in which the gypsy, Jaspar Petulengro, appears; it also deals with the hero's life of struggling poverty in London. See ROMANY RYE. (Name given to the author by the original of Petulengro, meaning 'student of language'.)

Law Courts, The (London) Colloquial name for the Royal Courts of Justice, the building in the Strand which houses the Supreme Court (of Judicature); this comprises the Court of Appeal and the High Court (of Justice), the latter having 3 Divisions: QUEEN'S BENCH, CHANCERY and Probate, Divorce and Admiralty (PDA).

Law of December 1 (1934) The 'law', enacted on the day of the KIROV MURDER, which authorized the commencement of the STALINIST PURGES.

Law West of the Pecos, The The nickname for a camp saloonkeeper, Roy Bean, a comic scalawag who got himself appointed JP (1882-1903) at Langtry on the Texas-Mexico border. Holding court in the 'JERSEY LILY' saloon (named like the town for the actress), he specialized in finable cases and kept most of the fines for himself; a mass of stories, unbelievable but mostly true, gathered round his memory. (Refers to an earlier saying: There is no law west of the Pecos.)

Lay of the Last Minstrel, The (1805) Walter Scott's long narrative poem of how Baron Henry wooed Lady Margaret of Branksome Hall, despite the feud between their 2 families.

Lays of Ancient Rome (1842) Macaulay's ballads based on early Roman legends, e.g. that of LARS PORSENA.

Lazarus (1) The beggar full of sores, of the parable in *Luke* xvi, 19-31, who when he died went to ABRAHAM's bosom while DIVES lay in torment in hell. (2) The brother of MARTHA AND MARY whom Jesus raised from the dead (*John*, xi, 44).

LBJ Initials used as nickname for Lyndon B. Johnson, US President from 1963-69.

LDCs Abbreviation used in the financial press for Less Developed Countries, i.e. those which have been successively called undeveloped, underdeveloped and developing.

Leadenhall Market A 600-year-old London market in Gracechurch Street, now dealing mainly in poultry, but also in fruit, vegetables and groceries.

Leader of the House (UK) A Cabinet Minister who arranges the order of business in the House of Commons in consultation with the Speaker, Clerk, Whips and the Leader of the Opposition.

League Covenant (1919) The constitution of the LEAGUE OF NATIONS, which was incorporated in the VERSAILLES TREATY and all subsequent treaties made with ex-enemy powers.

League of Nations (1920-46) Established under the LEAGUE COVENANT as a world organization for peace, but weakened at the outset by US refusal to join, and later by the defection of Germany, Japan and Italy (1933-37); Russia was a member for only 5 years. Its only means of enforcing good behavior was by 'sanctions', and these failed completely against Japan (Manchurian crisis, 1931) and Italy (Abyssinian War, 1935). The League's main

achievements were the ILO and the MANDATES COMMISSION. The headquarters were at Geneva.

League of Nations Union A British society which tried to stimulate public interest in, and active support for, the LEAGUE OF NATIONS. Its main achievement was the PEACE BALLOT.

League of Women Voters A nationwide organization, with hundreds of local leagues, which encourages women to vote in elections and in general to play an ever-increasing role in public affairs.

Leander Greek legendary figure; see HERO AND LEANDER.

Lease-Lend (1)The US loan to Britain (1940) of 50 destroyers in exchange for bases in the West Indies; (2) US loans of arms and supplies (Mar. 1941 to 1945) to countries fighting Axis powers; repayment was partly by 'reverse lease-lend', mostly waived.

Leathernecks A nickname for US Marines.

Leatherstocking Tales, The (1823-41) James Fenimore Cooper's 5 famous novels (including *The Last of the Mohicans*), of 18th-century frontier life and the Redskins. The hero is Natty Bumppo, who prefers Indians to most whites and excels them as a hunter. One of his nicknames is Leatherstocking, meaning tough backwoodsman.

Leavenworth (1895) A federal and military prison in Leavenworth, northeast Kansas.

Leaves of Grass (1855) Walt Whitman's chief volume of verse, frequently revised and augmented. His poems sing ecstatic praises of America and advocate a breaking loose from cultural ties with Europe to form a distinctively American democratic way of life.

Lebensraum German for 'living-space', used in connection with Hitler's thesis that Germany was overpopulated and had a divine right as HERRENVOLK to conquer its neighbors so as to provide room for the surplus.

Le Bourget The international airport north of Paris, used by BEA among others. See ORLY.

Leclerc Nom-de-guerre of the French general, Vicomte de Haute-cloque, who led some 2500 FREE FRENCH 1500 miles across the Sahara from Lake Chad to join Gen. Montgomery's army in North Africa in February 1943.

Le Corbusier Pseudonym of the imaginative Swiss architect Charles Jeanneret (1887-1965); see UNITÉS D'HABITATION.

Leda In Greek legend, wife of a King of Sparta whom ZEUS, disguised as a swan, seduced while she was bathing. The result was CASTOR AND POLLUX, and HELEN OF TROY.

Leeds creamware The most famous of the cream-colored earthenwares, made at the Leeds Pottery (1760-1821) and characterized by pierced decoration, a deep buttery glaze, and very light weight. The products were usually left undecorated.

Left Bank The south bank of the Seine in Paris and the adjoining districts – the student world of the LATIN QUARTER and the Luxembourg, the Boulevard St Germain (libraries, publishers, printers), etc.

Left Book Club (1935) (UK) Founded by the publisher, Victor Gollancz, to produce cheap books on all aspects of Socialism. It was so successful that any politically minded person who did not wish to be labeled Fascist had to have a few on his shelves in the years before World War II.

Left Hand! Right Hand! (1945-50) The general title of Sir Osbert Sitwell's outstanding 5-volume autobiography, with its close-up of the author's eccentric father, Sir George, at Renishaw Hall, near Sheffield.

'Legend of Sleepy Hollow, The' One of the most famous stories in Washington Irving's SKETCH BOOK. The courtship of a gauche schoolmaster, Ichabod Crane, is rudely disturbed by a rival who, disguised as a headless horseman, scares him out of his wits. Sleepy Hollow is Tarrytown, N.Y.

Leghorn A hardy breed of domestic fowl, a prolific layer of white eggs. (Originally imported from Italy via Leghorn or Livorno.)

Legion of Honor (1802) A French order founded by Napoleon. It now has 5 classes: Grande Croix (restricted to 80 holders), Grand Officier (200), Commandeur (1000), Officier (4000), Chevalier (unlimited).

Legree, Simon A plantation overseer, the villain of UNCLE TOM'S CABIN.

Leguminosae A family of plants characterized by legume fruits, i.e. pods. All the British examples belong to the subfamily PAPILIONACEAE. Mimosas and acacias form another main group.

Lehigh University at Bethlehem, Penn.

Lehman Collection A collection, given in 1969 to the Metropolitan Museum of Art, NYC, of Western European paintings, bronzes, ceramics, jewelry, furniture and tapestries, covering the 12th-20th centuries. (Robert Lehman, investment banker.)

Leicester (sheep) A large heavy-fleeced breed of sheep from which most of the English lowland longwool breeds have been evolved (e.g. the BORDER LEICESTER).

Leicestershire plan (UK) An educational experiment designed to do away with the 11-PLUS without resorting to the COMPREHENSIVE SCHOOL. All children at 11+ go without examination to a 3-year 'high school', several of which are grouped to feed one major grammar school, to which children are sent, if their parents wish, at age 14, again without examination. (An experiment confined to parts of Leicestershire in the 1960s.)

Leighton Park School (1890) (UK) A school near Reading which specializes in bringing together boys from all parts of the world and educating them to become citizens of the world.

Leinster The eastern province of the Irish Republic, formerly the 2 Celtic kingdoms of North and South Leinster, now consisting of Carlow, Dublin, Kildare, Kilkenny, Laoighis, Longford, Louth, Meath, Offaly, Westmeath, Wexford and Wicklow.

Leipzig, Battle of (Oct. 1813) The

defeat of the French by the combined German, Austrian and Russian armies in the War of Liberation, which, while crushing and bloody, did not prevent Napoleon from gaining further victories against them in 1814. Also called the Battle of the Nations.

Leix A spelling of LAOIGHIS used by the Irish up to 1935.

Lélia (1952) André Maurois' biography of George Sand. (Title taken from a novel by George Sand.)

Lelystad The future chief town of the whole new IJSSELMEER Reclamation Area, in the Oost Flevoland Polder drained in 1957. (Lely, engineer in charge of the IJsselmeer scheme.)

LEM Lunar Excursion Module, used in the APOLLO SPACE PROGRAM to carry 2 astronauts from the mother craft down to the moon's surface; the bottom half serves as a launching pad for the return journey to the orbiting mother craft. (Also written LM.)

Le Mans Town southwest of Paris, the venue each summer of a 24-hour endurance race (1923) for GT (grand touring) and sports cars.

Lemberg Old German name of Lvov, now a city of the Ukraine; the Polish spelling is Lwow.

Lemuria Zoologists' name for a hypothetical continent now sunk beneath the Indian Ocean, once thought to have linked Madagascar to Malaysia, thus accounting for the strange distribution of the lemur, a primate found only in those 2 regions. See GONDWANALAND. Theosophists eagerly seized on such 'lost continents' (including ATLANTIS) and described their inhabitants who, they say, were far in advance of us, having not only jet planes but all the virtues too.

Lena goldfields dispute (1930) An arbitration court awarded Britain compensation for capital invested in the Lena goldfields of Siberia in Tsarist days; the Soviet government refused to pay.

Lend-Lease See LEASE-LEND.,

Lenin (1959) A Russian icebreaker, the world's first nuclear-powered surface vessel.

Lenin, Order of (1930) A high Soviet award made to individuals or associations for special services to the regime.

Lenin Canal (1952) A 63-mile ship canal linking the Volga and the Don south of Volgograd (Stalingrad), USSR.

Leningrad A city of the USSR, formerly St Petersburg and, briefly, Petrograd.

Leningrad, Siege of The German investment which lasted from September 1941 to January 1944.

Leningrad case (1949) The execution without trial of important followers of Zhdanov, the Party leader at LENINGRAD and possible successor to Stalin. Zhdanov himself died an apparently natural death in 1948. In 1954 Khrushchev said that Stalin, on false accusations supplied to him by Beria, had personally supervised the liquidation of these men.

Leninism See MARXIST-LENINISM.

Lenin Prize (1925) Russia's supreme award for achievements in science, technology, literature and the arts; called Stalin prize, 1940-54.

Lenin Stadium Moscow's arena for all sports.

Lenin's testament (1922) A letter written by Lenin to the Party Congress warning delegates against Stalin and suggesting his replacement as secretary-general of the Party.

Lents CAMBRIDGE UNIVERSITY spring college boat races. (Held Lent term.)

Leo The Lion, 5th of the constellations of the Zodiac, between CANCER and VIRGO; the sun enters it about July 21st. Astrologers claim that those born under this sign may be lazy, uncritical, romantic.

Leofric See GODIVA, LADY.

Leonora See 'FIDELIO.

Leonora Overtures Beethoven's 4 versions of the overture to his opera FIDELIO, all of them still performed.

Leopard, The (1956) The Prince of Lampedusa's novel of the attempts of an old Sicilian family to adapt itself to the social changes which followed the Garibaldi era.

Leopold and Loeb murder case (1924) Two wealthy American students kidnapped and murdered a small boy simply to show how easy it was; they received life sentences. Richard Loeb was killed in a prison brawl; Nathan Leopold was released in 1958.

Léopoldville Former name of the capital of (ex-Belgian) Congo, now renamed Kinshasa.

Lepanto (1571) A decisive naval victory over the Turks won by the combined forces of the Christian League (Spain, Venice, Genoa and the PAPAL STATES) under Don John of Austria. It was the last major engagement between fleets of oared galleys. (Italian name of the Greek port of Návpaktos, in the Gulf of Corinth.)

Lepidoptera The butterflies and moths, an order of insects with 2 pairs of large, scaly, colored wings; the caterpillars feed on plants, the adults on nectar.

Lesbian A female homosexual, so named from the Aegean island of Lesbos, where in the 7th century BC 'burning Sappho loved and sung' (Byron's DON JUAN).

Lesbia's sparrow The pet cage bird of his beloved Lesbia, on whose death Catullus (1st century BC) wrote a famous little elegy beginning: 'Mourn, ye Loves and Cupids'.

Lesotho The name taken on gaining independence (1966) by Basutoland, a former British protectorate in southern Africa.

Lestrade of Scotland Yard The Inspector whom Sherlock HOLMES continually forestalled and outwitted.

Lethe In Greek legend the river of forgetfulness, one of the rivers of the Underworld, where the dead drank and forgot the past.

Lettish The language spoken by the Letts of Latvia, closely related to LITHUANIAN.

Levant Company (1581) English chartered company formed to trade with Asia via the Mediterranean, with depots at Aleppo, Damascus and Alexandria, thus weakening the MUSCOVY COMPANY.

Levassor car engines See PANHARD-LEVASSOR.

Levelers A section of Cromwell's army, supported by many civilians, who (1648) advocated republican

government, manhood suffrage, religious toleration and social reform. They mutinied and were suppressed by Fairfax.

Leventritt Award An award for pianists and violinists who succeed in a competition organized by the Edgar M. Leventritt Foundation, NYC; the US counterpart of the Belgian CONCOURS DE LA REINE ELISABETH. The winner receives $1000 and makes guest appearances with major orchestras.

Leverhulme Medal (1960) ROYAL SOCIETY gold medal awarded every 3 years for research in pure or applied chemistry or engineering.

Leviathan (1651) Thomas Hobbes's work on the nature of government; he believed that as man is guided by pride and egoism it is essential for the individual to surrender his rights completely to a strong central government, to which he gives the name Leviathan, taken from *Job* xli, 34, where that unidentifiable monster is described as 'a king over all the children of pride'.

Levin See ANNA KARENINA.

Levis A form of blue jeans introduced in GOLD RUSH days in California, with copper rivets inserted to strengthen the pockets, in which miners were wont to put samples of ore. (Invented by Levi Strauss, who had a clothing shop in San Francisco.)

Levites The priestly caste in ISRAEL, traditionally descendants of the tribe of Levi.

Leviticus The third book of the PENTATEUCH, like *Deuteronomy* occupied with the law and priestly rules. ('The Levitical book', i.e. a manual for priests.)

Lewis and Clark Trail The first overland route to the Pacific, opened up by the Lewis and Clark expedition (1804-06) of 27 men; starting from St Louis they traveled down the Ohio, up the Missouri to its source, across the Rockies and down the Columbia. (Meriwether Lewis, 1774-1809; William Clark, 1770-1838.)

Lewis and Short (1879) Name of compilers used for their (still) standard Latin-English dictionary.

Lewisham Inner London borough since 1965 consisting of the former metropolitan boroughs of Lewisham and Deptford; headquarters at Catford.

Lexington (Apr. 1775) The first skirmish of the AMERICAN WAR OF INDEPENDENCE. British forces set out from Boston to seize a stock of ,arms at Concord, but MINUTEMEN, warned by PAUL REVERE, repulsed them. (Town near Boston.)

Leyte Gulf, Battle of the (Oct. 1944) The biggest naval battle of World War II, in which the US fleet inflicted heavy losses on the Japanese. On this occasion the Japanese first used *kamikaze* (suicide bombers). (A gulf in the east Philippines.)

Leyton (UK) A former municipal borough of Essex, since 1965 part of the borough of WALTHAM FOREST.

Liberal National Party See SIMONITES.

Liberator, The Simón Bolívar, who liberated Venezuela, Colombia, Ecuador, Peru and Bolivia from Spanish rule (1821-25).

Libermanism The views which Prof. E. Liberman of Kharkov University was allowed to put forward in 1962, advocating the reintroduction of the profit motive in USSR in order to raise quality and production, and decentralization to improve efficiency.

Liberty, Statue of A statue 300 feet high (with its pedestal) which stands on an island in the entrance to New York harbor.

Liberty Bell The bell in Independence Hall, Philadelphia, rung when the DECLARATION OF INDEPENDENCE was adopted in 1776.

Liberty Bonds War bonds issued by the US government during World War I.

Liberty Boys Another name for the SONS OF LIBERTY.

Liberty Hall A place where one is free to do what one likes. (From SHE STOOPS TO CONQUER, where Squire Hardcastle, puzzled by the extraordinary conduct of 2 young men, says: This is Liberty Hall, gentlemen.)

'Liberty or Death' speech (1775) Patrick Henry's speech to the Virginia Convention 2 months before LEXINGTON, urging resistance to the British and establishment of an army. It concluded: As for me, give me liberty or give me death!

Liberty ships Mass-produced cargo boats built at an immense rate in Kaiser's shipyards in USA during World War II to replace losses to German submarines.

Libra The Scales, 7th constellation of the Zodiac, between VIRGO and SCORPIO, which the sun enters at the autumnal equinox about September 21st. Astrologers claim that those born under this sign may be weak, pacific and changeable.

Library-Museum of the Performing Arts (1965) One of the institutions at the LINCOLN CENTER.

Library of Congress (1800) The US national library, in Washington, D.C., the nucleus of which was Thomas Jefferson's library; it is now one of the world's largest and includes collections of MSS, music and maps, besides being entitled to a copy of any book copyrighted in the US. Its Catalog Card Number system is internationally used.

Libya The former Turkish province of Tripoli, conquered by Italy in 1912 and divided (1919-29) into Tripolitania, west of Benghazi, and Cyrenaica to the east. After a period under AMGOT it became independent in 1951. (Greek name for Africa.)

Lick Observatory (1959) The University of California's observatory on Mt Hamilton, Calif., with a 120-inch reflector telescope.

Liddell and Scott (1843) Compilers' names used as the short title of the Greek lexicon which has been the standard Greek-English dictionary since it was first published.

Lidice (1942) A Czech mining village razed to the ground by the Germans. The men were all shot, the women taken to concentration camps, in reprisal for the assassination of the infamous Heydrich, German 'Protector' of Bohemia, in which the village was accused of being involved.

Lido An elongated sandy island covering the entrance to the Venice Lagoon; a popular and fashionable bathing place for at least 150 years. See also LANSBURY'S LIDO.

'Liebestraum' A beautiful Liszt piano piece, often murdered by sentimentality. (German, 'dream of love'.)

Liebfraumilch A name which can be given to any German Rhine wine of any quality. (Named after the Liebfrauenkirche, 'Church of Our Lady', at Worms.)

Life (1936) See TIME; LIFE INTERNATIONAL.

Life Force A translation of Bergson's *élan vital*, the spirit of energy and life by virtue of which all living things evolve and progress in a CREATIVE EVOLUTION. In Shaw's plays it becomes increasingly synonymous with the Will of God, or a sort of depersonalized Holy Ghost, which will not permit Man through apathy to obstruct its plans so that he may enjoy free will; rather would it be forced to replace Man by some more effective instrument — SUPERMAN.

Life Guards, The (1661) One of the 2 regiments of the HOUSEHOLD CAVALRY, originally formed from CAVALIERS who were with Charles II before the RESTORATION. They take precedence over all other regiments, wear scarlet tunics and white plumes.

Life International (1946-1970) A US fortnightly which consisted of selections from *Life* (see TIME) and *Fortune*, as well as original articles.

Lifemanship (1950) Stephen Potter's application of the principles of GAMESMANSHIP to the problems of gaining and keeping social ascendancy over one's fellows — problems further studied in ONE-UPMANSHIP.

Life with Father (1935) Clarence Day's amusing sketches about a New York family (in essentials, his own family), especially the father, an eccentric tyrant, and the mother, who has a feminine genius for getting her own way. A record-breaking Broadway hit was made out of it by Russel Crouse and Howard Lindsay (1939). *Life with Mother* (1936) was less popular.

Lightning (1957) The RAF's first supersonic fighter, a BAC sweptwing aircraft flying at twice the speed of sound, which replaced the Javelin and was succeeded by the PHANTOM.

Light of Asia, The (1879) Sir Edwin Arnold's life of BUDDHA in blank verse.

Light Sussex A light breed of domestic fowl much used for crossing.

Liguria The Italian coastal region around Genoa, briefly a Napoleonic republic. (*Ligures*, ancient tribe inhabiting this region and adjoining parts of France and Switzerland.)

Li'l Abner (1935) Al Capp's famous comic strip set in the hillbilly community of Dogpatch. The bashful hero, forever at odds with a corrupt world, Daisy Mae, who made him her husband, his pipe-smoking Mammy Yokum, Stupefyin' Jones, Joanie Phoanie and many others (often public figures thinly disguised) burlesque the American way of life. They proved so popular that they were promoted to a movie (1940) and a Broadway musical (1956). See SADIE HAWKINS DAY.

Liliaceae A very large family of mainly bulbous plants and a few shrubs; it includes lilies, tulips, bluebells, onions, aloe, yucca and asparagus.

Lilith (1) A Babylonian demoness of the night. (2) In *Isaiah* xxxiv, 14, a marginal note identifies her with the screech owl or night monster there mentioned. (3) In Jewish folklore, ADAM's first wife, who left him to become the 'devil's dam'. (Hebrew *lilatu*, 'night'.)

Lilliburlero Originally an Irish Catholic slogan ('Lilliburlero bullen-a-la'), later incorporated in an anti-Catholic, anti-Jacobite song to a tune resembling 'Hush-a-by Baby', and revived as a marching song by British Commandos in World War II.

'Lilli Marlene' (1938) A German song revived by Radio Belgrade in 1941, adopted by Rommel's AFRIKA KORPS and borrowed by the British 8th Army opposing them. The English version began: Underneath the lantern/By the barrack gate,/Darling I remember/The way you used to wait.

Lilliput The most famous of the 4

imaginary countries of GULLIVER'S TRAVELS. The inhabitants are as small-minded as they are small-bodied, divided into furious factions such as the BIG-ENDIANS AND LITTLE-ENDIANS (Catholics and Protestants), and the High Heels (TORIES) and Low Heels (WHIGS)—just like England.

Lilly Endowment (1937) One of the largest US foundations, which promotes higher education, religion and community services in Indiana, particularly in Indianapolis.

Lilongwe The projected new capital of MALAWI, at present headquarters of the central region.

Lily-Whites Name given to those who opposed Negro participation in politics; compare BLACK AND TANS (2).

Lima Declaration (1942) A declaration by the PAN-AMERICAN UNION that the Latin American republics would repel foreign attacks, i.e. adopting the MONROE DOCTRINE. See RIO TREATY.

Limburger A soft white cheese resembling CAMEMBERT but with a stronger smell and its own characteristic taste. (Originally made at Limburg, Belgium.)

Lime, Harry See THIRD MAN.

Lime Grove The site of, and used for, the original BBC TV studios. (Street just west of Shepherds Bush Common, West London.)

Limehouse A London dockland area once well known to tourists (see DIRTY DICK's) but now faded into oblivion. See next entry.

Limehouse oratory The kind used by Lloyd George in 1909 in the London dockland area of Limehouse, during a speech violently abusing landowners and big business.

Limoges Hard-paste porcelain made at the French town of Limoges (near a large source of kaolin), by numerous factories from 1783 onward. See HAVILAND CHINA.

Linacre (1962) A new college of OX-FORD UNIVERSITY.

Lincoln (sheep) A long-wool breed of sheep, the largest and heaviest in Britain.

Lincoln assassination (Apr. 1865) The shooting of President Lincoln by John Wilkes Booth at Ford's Theater, Washington, a few days after Robert E. Lee had surrendered at APPOMATTOX COURT HOUSE.

Lincoln Center (New York City) In full, the Lincoln Center for the Performing Arts, a complex of buildings on the upper west side of Manhattan; it was virtually completed in 1966 with the opening of the new METROPOLITAN OPERA HOUSE; it also contains the new Philharmonic Hall, the New York State Theater and the Vivian Beaumont Theater.

Lincoln County War (1877-81) A cattle war in the Pecos Valley, N.M., of which BILLY THE KID was the leading light until a sheriff shot him dead, aged 21.

Lincoln Memorial (1922) A Classical building in Potomac Park, Washington, D.C., with 36 columns representing the 36 states existing at Lincoln's death, and a 20-ft statue of him by the American sculptor Daniel Chester French.

Lincoln rocker A high-backed upholstered rocking chair with open arms, popular in the mid-19th century. (Named for Abraham Lincoln.)

Lincoln's Birthday February 12th, a legal holiday except in 9 of the former Confederate states and 8 others.

'Lincolnshire Poacher, The' An old English song with the refrain: Oh, 'tis my delight on a shining night, in the season of the year.

Lincoln's Inn (UK) One of the INNS OF COURT, attended particularly by CHANCERY lawyers.

Lindbergh baby case (1932) The trial of Bruno Hauptmann, who kidnapped and murdered the infant son of Charles Lindbergh, the transatlantic solo flyer; Hauptmann was executed in 1936.

Lindisfarne Gospels Illuminated manuscripts of the 7th century, the work of Irish monks on Lindisfarne (Holy Island) off Northumberland; now in the British Museum.

Lindy Hop An excessively athletic dance of Negro origin in which the man slings his partner round his neck, between his legs etc.; it is regarded as a forerunner of the (relatively) sober jitterbug. (For Charles Lindbergh; see SPIRIT OF ST LOUIS.)

Linear B script That used for inventories and trading accounts inscribed on tablets found at KNOSSOS and elsewhere; Michael Ventris deciphered them in 1953 and found them to be in archaic Greek.

Lingard, Capt. A character who appears in 3 of Joseph Conrad's novels: ALMAYER'S FOLLY, *An Outcast of the Islands,* and *The* RESCUE.

Ling-Temco-Vought A Dallas-based aircraft firm which came into greatly increased prominence postwar, and manufactures the CORSAIR and the CRUSADER.

Linlithgowshire The Scottish county now known as West Lothian.

Linnean Society (1788) A leading British natural history society, publishing journals and papers on botany and zoology. The headquarters are at BURLINGTON HOUSE. (Named after the Swedish naturalist, Linnaeus.)

Linotype A printing machine which composes type in solid lines (slugs), used in newspaper work.

Lion and the Unicorn, The The supporting figures in the royal arms of England and Scotland respectively; represented in the nursery rhyme as 'fighting for the crown'.

Lion in Winter, The (1966) James Goldman's unusual comedy about 24 hours in the life of Henry II. He summons to his court his long-imprisoned Queen, Eleanor of Aquitaine, and his 3 sons, Geoffrey, Richard Coeur de Lion and John, to discuss the future of the English crown, leading to threats by them of assassination and war. The play, though full of deliberate anachronisms, is based on historical fact; it was made into a successful movie.

Lion of the North, the A name for Gustavus Adolphus, King of Sweden; see THIRTY YEARS WAR.

Lions The Detroit Lions, NATIONAL FOOTBALL LEAGUE. Became member of the NATIONAL CONFERENCE, NATIONAL FOOTBALL LEAGUE in 1970.

Lions clubs Clubs primarily for businessmen under 50, who give practical help to less fortunate people — mainly the aged, the blind and the infirm — and also interest themselves in international relations and welfare. Lions International (1917), founded in Chicago, claims about 1 million members, and abroad is especially strong in Britain and Japan.

Lipizzaners (1580) A famous breed of horses, still used at the SPANISH RIDING SCHOOL, Vienna; shapely and nearly always white, with small heads, they make magnificent ceremonial carriage horses. (Named after the stud at Lipizza, near Trieste.)

Lithuanian A language closely related to LETTISH. These 2 languages are closer to SANSKRIT, and more archaic in structure, than any other living INDO-EUROPEAN LANGUAGE.

Lit. Hum. Abbreviation of Literae Humaniores, the final honor school in classical studies and philosophy at OXFORD UNIVERSITY; GREATS. (Latin, 'the more humane letters'.)

Little America (1) The base established (1928) by the Byrd Antarctic expedition on the Bay of Whales south of the Ross Sea, and used as winter quarters in Byrd's later expeditions and as an air base. (2) London Grosvenor Square and its environs, used as General Eisenhower's headquarters in World War II, and the site of the American Embassy (1962), President Roosevelt's statue, etc.

Little America's Cup (1961) An international catamaran challenge trophy, the chief world multi-hull match race, usually held off Thorpe Bay, Essex. The participants have been Britain, USA and Australia.

Little Bear Ursa Minor, a small northern constellation that contains the LITTLE DIPPER (including the NORTH STAR).

Little Big Horn, Battle of the See CUSTER'S LAST STAND. (A river in South Dakota.)

Little Boy Blue, of the nursery rhyme, has been doubtfully identified with Cardinal Wolsey who, as a butcher's son, may well have tended his father's livestock.

'Little Brown Church in the Vale, The' (1865) A nonsectarian hymn composed by William S. Pitts; its rhythmically chanted refrain 'Come, come, come, come' made it a favorite with revivalists. It was supposedly inspired by a church near Nashua, Ia., which now draws thousands of visitors each year.

Little Buttercup See PINAFORE, HMS.

Little Church Around the Corner, The An Episcopal church in MAN-HATTAN, which got its name in 1870 when the pastor of a fashionable Madison Avenue church who had refused to hold a burial service for an actor suggested trying 'the little church around the corner'; it then became a shrine for theater people. Officially it is the Episcopal Church of the Transfiguration.

Little Dipper The 7 bright stars in the LITTLE BEAR, forming a similar pattern to the BIG DIPPER, with the NORTH STAR at the tail.

Little Dorrit (1858) Dickens's novel much concerned with the MARSHAL-SEA PRISON, where little (Amy) Dorrit's father and her future husband spend some of their time, and she herself was born. See CIRCUMLOCU-TION OFFICE.

Little Entente (1920-39) An alliance between Czechoslovakia, Yugoslavia and Rumania, encouraged by France as helping to contain Germany on the east, and aimed primarily at preventing a HAPSBURG restoration (then being canvassed).

Little Eva In UNCLE TOM'S CABIN, the daughter of Tom's owner, to whom Tom is devoted.

Little Flower Nickname (translating his Christian name) of Fiorello La-Guardia, 3 times mayor of New York (1933-45).

Little Foxes, The (1939) Lillian Hellman's play about a Southern family watching industrialism creep in and, like 'the little foxes that spoil the vines' (*Song of Solomon* ii, 15), spoil their idyllic life. There was a sequel, *Another Part of the Forest* (1946).

Little Gidding A 17th-century Anglican lay religious community formed near Huntingdon by the family of Nicholas Ferrar and frequented by the poets George Herbert and Richard Crashaw. It is the setting for J. H. Shorthouse's novel *John Inglesant* (1881) and T. S. Eliot's poem 'Little Gidding' (1942) in *Four Quartets*.

Littlehampton, Lady (Maudie) The famous creation of the British cartoonist Osbert Lancaster, a frantic and featherbrained commentator on current affairs.

Little John (1) ROBIN HOOD's companion, a large man originally called John Little. (2) US tactical barrage rocket with a range of 10 miles.

Little King, The A cartoon character created (1934) by Otto Soglow in the NEW YORKER. As befits a constitutional monarch, the king never expresses an opinion — in fact he never speaks at all.

Little League (1939) A baseball league for boys aged 8-12, with numerous teams in most of the states of USA; it has its own World Series. (Sponsored by the US Rubber Co.)

Little Lord Fauntleroy (1886) A children's book written by a Manchester-born American, Frances Hodgson Burnett, about a horrible little mother's darling in black velvet and lace collar, who wins everybody's heart except the reader's.

Little Moreton Hall A 16th-century moated house near Congleton, Cheshire, owned by the NATIONAL TRUST.

Little Nell See The OLD CURIOSITY SHOP.

Little Orphan Annie A comic strip by Harold Gray (1924) in which the pathetic orphan gradually developed a certain bossiness and right-wing outlook.

Little Orphant Annie James Whitcomb Riley's poem, originally called 'The Elf Child' (1885), in the Hoosier dialect. It is a cautionary tale for children; if they don't behave 'the Gobble-uns'll git you / Ef you don't watch out!'

'Little Red Ridinghood' A fairy tale of a little girl eaten by a wolf disguised as her grandmother, to whom she was bringing a present. Common to the countries of Western Europe, it was printed in Perrault's MOTHER GOOSE'S TALES. The Grimms added a happy ending in which child and granny are restored to life.

Little Rhody Nickname of Rhode Island.

Little Rock The capital of Arkansas, with a public image of extreme opposition to racial integration. In 1957 Federal airborne troops had to be brought in to force Governor Faubus to allow Negroes to register at the high school.

Little Ruhr A nickname for the main industrial area of Czechoslovakia and Poland, corresponding to Upper Silesia and adjacent districts, and stretching from Ostrava through KATOWICE to Krakow and Czestochowa; economic coordination has been achieved there between the 2 countries. See RUHR.

Little Women (1868) A famous book by Louisa M. Alcott, based on her memories of childhood in NEW ENGLAND.

Little Wonder, The Nickname of Tom Sayers, an English boxer who fought the first international heavyweight championship (1860) against an American, the Benicia Boy, in a match stopped by police after 37 rounds.

Liu The slave girl in TURANDOT who sacrifices herself to save the Unknown Prince and his father.

Liver bird A mythical bird invented in the 17th century solely to explain the name Liverpool, and now adopted as the city's emblem.

Liverpool Delft (1710-85) DELFT made at Liverpool; it had a bluish tinge, and some of it was transfer printed.

Liverpool pottery and porcelain (1756-1841) The wares made by several factories at Liverpool, including the Herculaneum factory (1793-1840) which made pottery jugs, printed pottery, stoneware and, from 1800, bone china. Soft-paste porcelain was made by a firm founded in 1756. See LIVERPOOL DELFT.

Liverymen Members of the CITY of London's Livery Companies who are Freemen of London, and virtually elect the Lord Mayor. (From the distinctive ceremonial dress worn.)

Livingston (1962) (Scotland) A NEW TOWN in West Lothian, designed to take 100,000 inhabitants.

Liza of Lambeth (1897) Somerset Maugham's first novel, written from insights gained during his brief career as a doctor in the London slums.

Lizzie Borden murder case (1892) The acquittal of an American woman of gentle birth, accused of axing her father and stepmother to death at Fall River, Mass. Many continued to think her guilty, and several books, plays and ballads were written about her; also an anonymous summary of the case for the prosecution which ran: Lizzie Borden took an ax / And gave her mother 40 whacks. / When she saw what she had done, / She gave her father forty-one! See FALL RIVER LEGEND.

Llangollen, Ladies of (1778-1831) Two eccentric and autocratic Irish bluestockings who lived in a house they named Plas Newydd at Llangollen, Denbighshire, where they were visited by Wellington, Wordsworth and other notabilities.

Llareggub See UNDER MILK WOOD.

LLG Initials used for David Lloyd George (later Earl Lloyd George), Liberal leader and Prime Minister during World War I.

Lloyd-Baker estate Property in North London which has been kept intact in the Lloyd-Baker family for 400 years; almost all profits are plowed back, enabling rents to be steadily reduced. Tenants are personally selected by Miss Lloyd-Baker from a very long waiting list.

Lloyd George A favorite variety of raspberry, the New Zealand clone of which produces fruit of excellent flavor either in summer or in autumn—although it should not be allowed to fruit twice in the year.

Lloyd George Fund A political fund derived from the sale of honors and formed 'to promote any political purpose approved by Lloyd George'. The Conservative Party, while in coalition with Lloyd George's Liberals, was given its share; nevertheless the existence of the fund was used in propaganda to break up that coalition.

Lloyd's (1689) London's international market for 'non-life' insur-

ance (i.e. accident etc.) and center
for marine and airline intelligence,
now in Lime Street, off Leadenhall
Street. The underwriters are a self-
recruited body of rich men, each
with unlimited liability. (Named
after the coffeehouse where it began
life.)

Lloyd's Register of Shipping (1760)
A society formed to survey and clas-
sify ships, managed by a committee
of over 100 shipowners, shipbuild-
ers, underwriters etc. It publishes
Lloyd's Register Book, giving details
of all seagoing vessels, and also
Lloyd's Register of Yachts. (Named
after the coffeehouse; see last
entry.)

LM Lunar Module, an alternative
abbreviation for LEM.

LMS (UK) Initials of the London,
Midland and Scottish Railway,
which had London termini at Euston and St Pancras and ran the *Royal
Scot* service from London to Glasgow. It is now divided mainly between the London Midland and the
Scottish Regions of British Railways.

LNER (UK) Initials of the London
and North-Eastern Railway, which
had London termini at King's Cross,
Marylebone and Liverpool Street. It
ran the *Flying Scotsman* service
from King's Cross to Edinburgh, the
record for the journey being 5 minutes under 6 hours. it is now mainly
divided between the Eastern and
Scottish Regions of British Railways.

Lobster à l'Américaine Raw lobster
sautéd in oil with tomatoes. (Possibly a corruption of ARMORICAINE; not
connected with America.)

Lobster Newburg Lobster cooked in
sherry or Madeira, served with rice,
mushrooms and cream sauce, and
finished with Cognac.

Lobster Thermidor Lobster cooked
in butter and white wine, served in
the shell and covered with cheese
and mustard sauce, crusted.

Locarno Pacts (1925) A group of
treaties, suggested by Stresemann,
the German Foreign Minister, by
which France, Belgium and Germany, with Britain and Italy, jointly

guaranteed the existing Franco-
German frontier and also the demili-
tarization of the Rhineland. They
were denounced by Hitler in 1936.

Lochinvar The hero of a song in
Scott's MARMION who carries off the
fair Ellen at her wedding feast;
'They'll have fleet steeds that follow' quoth young Lochinvar.

Loch Ness monster A prehistoric
aquatic animal which has been reported on numerous occasions since
1934 as having been seen swimming
in Loch Ness, Inverness-shire.

Lockheed aircraft (1927) Civil and
military planes made by the Lockheed Co. of Burbank, Calif. Their
Constellations pioneered the regular
transatlantic service in 1946. Other
models include the STARFIGHTER,
Super-Constellation, U-2, GALAXY
and Tristar airbus.

Lockit, Lucy In the BEGGAR'S OPERA,
the daughter of the cruel governor of
Newgate prison, who falls in love
with Macheath, incarcerated there,
and helps him escape.

Locksley Hall (1832) Tennyson's
poem in which a man revisits his
childhood home and meditates on
the girl who rejected him for a richer
suitor, feeling 'That a sorrow's
crowning sorrow is remembering
happier things'. Turning to wider
issues, he is fortified by the thought:
'Yet I doubt not thro' the ages one
increasing purpose runs' and, later,
'Better fifty years of Europe than a
cycle of Cathay'.

Locofocos (1835) Nickname of the
radical faction of Democrats in New
York, earned because, when their
opponents cut off the gas during a
TAMMANY HALL meeting, they carried
on by candlelight, lighting the candles with locofocos, i.e. matches
(then a new invention).

Lodi A variety of apple.

Loeb editions (1912) An Anglo-
American standard series of the
Greek and Latin Classics, with an
English translation on the facing
page. (Founded by James Loeb, US
banker.)

Loftleidir The Icelandic international airline.

Logan, Mt The second highest peak

in North America (19,850 ft), in southwest Yukon Territory, Canada.

Logan Gardens (Scotland) Gardens at Port Logan, Stranraer, Wigtownshire, famous for the profusion and variety of their subtropical plants.

Log cabin to White House (1910) Title of W. M. Thayer's biography of James Garfield, 20th US President, who was born in an Ohio log cabin; he was assassinated shortly after assuming office in 1881.

Logical Positivism The view that philosophical statements are of value only if they can be tested by the experience of the senses. Thus, arguments on metaphysical problems (the existence of God, for example) are meaningless. This school owes its inspiration to Wittgenstein's TRACTATUS LOGICO-PHILOSOPHICUS; its chief British exponent is A. J. Ayer of Oxford.

Lohans Buddhist hermit saints, of whom many vigorous statues and statuettes were made in China from the 10th century onwards.

Lohengrin (1850) Wagner's opera in which Lohengrin, the son of Parsifal (PERCIVAL), comes to Antwerp in his swan-drawn boat to rescue a princess of Brabant. He marries her on condition that she does not ask him who he is because, as a Knight of the Grail, his name must not be divulged; when she does, he is forced to tell the truth and departs in his boat.

Loi-cadre (1956) French 'outline law' which empowered the government to grant political concessions to overseas territories (except Algeria), including universal suffrage and a single electoral college for elections both to local legislatures and to the French parliament.

Loki In Scandinavian mythology the god of mischief and evil who caused BALDER'S death. See GÖTTERDÄMMERUNG.

Lola Montez Stage name of an Irish dancer who captured the heart of Ludwig I, running Bavaria for him in 1847-48, until both of them were driven out.

Lolita (1958) A novel by the Russian-American writer Vladimir Nabokov, about Professor Humbert's love affair with a 12-year-old 'nymphet'; made into a movie (1962) by Stanley Kubrick.

Lollards The pre-Lutheran Reformers, followers of John Wyclif (1320-84). (From old Dutch word, meaning 'mutterers'.)

Loman, Willy The traveling salesman in Arthur Miller's *Death of a Salesman* (1949) who gradually comes to realize that his life has been a complete failure, and commits suicide.

Lombards (Longobardi) A Germanic race which ruled LOMBARDY from the 6th century until Charlemagne drove them out in 774.

Lombard Street A street in the CITY of London traditionally associated with banking; hence the London money market; financiers. (Street of the medieval LOMBARDY bankers.)

Lombard Street Curlicue 'The Crookedest Street in the World', a famous feature of San Francisco which climbs Russian Hill in 8 hairpin bends; formerly called Jacob's Ladder.

Lombardy The Italian Lake district between the Alps and the Po, bounded east and west by Piedmont and Venice; under French, Spanish and Austrian rule before incorporation in the Kingdom of Italy. The capital was Milan.

London, Secret Treaty of (1915) The Allies' bribe to Italy to enter World War I. They offered South Tirol, Adriatic ports, the Dodecanese and freedom to expand its African colonies. Published in 1918 by the Bolshevists, it caused considerable trouble at the Peace Conference.

London, The Abbreviation commonly used for the London Hospital, Whitechapel, E.1.

London blitz (7 Sept. 1940-May 1941) The series of night raids on London which developed from, and overlapped, the BATTLE OF BRITAIN and vividly presented to American listeners in Ed Murrow's on-the-spot broadcasts. (Blitz, short for BLITZKRIEG.)

London Bridge (1) Until 1750 the only Thames bridge in London, built in the 12th century and carrying houses, shops and a chapel.

(2) Its replacement (1831), now being reconstructed and widened. The facing stones, parapets etc. were bought by a Californian oil tycoon (1969) for transportation to the deserts of Arizona where he is building a new township, Lake Havasu City, for those who want to get away from it all. An artificial river had to be cut to provide something for it to bridge.

London Clinic A fashionable private hospital at the top of HARLEY STREET, run by a group of Harley Street consultants.

Londonderry, Siege of (1689) Three-month siege by Irish Catholic supporters of James II of Protestant-held Londonderry, lifted after much hardship and 10,000 deaths by the English navy. Commemorated each August by the Relief of Derry celebrations.

'Londonderry Air' An Irish traditional folksong from Co. Derry, first published in 1885 as 'Farewell to CUCHULAIN'. Since then the air has been arranged by various hands for all kinds of instrument.

London Gazette, The A twice-weekly government publication, listing official appointments and announcements, bankruptcies and, in wartime, casualties.

London gin Generic term for any dry gin.

London Group (1913) A school of British artists who broke away from the NEW ENGLISH ART CLUB and, under the influence of Cézanne, Gauguin and Van Gogh, endeavored to paint realistic interpretations of modern life. Sickert, Epstein, Wyndham Lewis and most of the CAMDEN TOWN GROUP belonged to it.

London Library (1841) A subscription library with half a million books, housed in St James's Square.

London Mercury (1919-34) An influential literary magazine founded and edited by Sir John Squire.

London Museum A museum with exhibits covering the history of London from the earliest times to the present, housed in KENSINGTON PALACE, where the State Apartments are also open to the public under the Museum's administration. It is planned to amalgamate it with the GUILD-HALL Museum in a new building at London Wall.

London Naval Conference (1) A meeting of the Powers (1930) which tried to apply the principles of the WASHINGTON NAVAL AGREEMENT to cruisers, destroyers and submarines, and to extend the naval holiday by 6 years. The resulting agreement was not ratified by France and Italy, and was denounced by Japan in 1934. (2) A further attempt (1936) to limit naval armament by fixing maxima for gun calibers in capital ships, tonnage of aircraft carriers etc. Italy and Japan rejected the agreement.

London Press Exchange (1893) The oldest London advertising agency, originally a news agency; its clients include Beechams and Cadburys. In 1969 Leo Burnett (USA) took over the overseas branches.

London School of Economics (1895) A branch of LONDON UNIVERSITY, near the Aldwych, founded by Sidney and Beatrice Webb and associated with Harold Laski and R. H. Tawney; many distinguished left-wing economists have been trained there.

London Stone A stone believed to have marked the point in the Roman forum of London from which distances along the Roman roads were measured. It is now set in the wall of the Bank of China, opposite Cannon Street Station.

London University A federation of nearly 30 colleges and institutes and a dozen medical schools scattered over London and the HOME COUNTIES, with headquarters at Malet Street, Bloomsbury.

London Weekend TV (1968) A program contracting company providing TV services for London from 7 p.m. on Friday until Sunday night; the headquarters are at Wembley Park. The company was formed with Aidan Crawley as chairman and a former BBC Controller of Programs as managing director; it is financed in part by the *Observer*, *Economist* and *Daily Telegraph*.

Loneliness of the Long-Distance Runner, The (1962) A movie made from the title story of a collection of short stories by Alan Sillitoe (1959); a Borstal governor (see BORSTAL SYS-

TEM) tries to use the athletic potentialities of one of his charges to turn him into a reformed character.

Lone Ranger, The Originally a comic-strip hero of the Old West, the Lone Ranger was created by Fran Striker and drawn by Flanders for King Features Syndicate beginning in 1939. His red shirt, black mask and Indian helper Tonto were his trademarks, as well as his rousing cry to his horse, 'Hi ho Silver! Away-y-y!'. The Lone Ranger later became a popular radio program and then appeared as a television series.

Lone Star State Nickname of Texas.

Longchamp Paris racetrack near the Seine in the Bois de Boulogne, where the PRIX DE L'ARC DE TRIOMPHE is run.

Long Day's Journey into Night (1956) Eugene O'Neill's autobiographical play, written in 1941 but not performed until after his death.

Long Drive, The The cattle drive from Texas to the railroads of Kansas and Nebraska along the CHISHOLM TRAIL. In the period 1865-79 4 million cattle made the journey and the Kansas cow towns such as Abilene, Dodge City and Wichita came into being.

Long Elizas Tall ladies painted on early Chinese export porcelain; copied on Dutch DELFT and later by most English factories, e.g. WORCESTER. (Corruption of Dutch for 'tall maidens'.)

Longest Bar in the World A once-famous 100-ft bar in what was the ultra-exclusive Shanghai Club, a meeting place for bankers, diplomats and other Westerners. It still survives, in what is now a social club for Chinese and foreign seamen; ping-pong is the chief entertainment there today.

Long Island duck A duck raised on Long Island, the source of 40% of US production.

Long John Scotch Whisky championship (1970) A match play golf championship instituted in succession to Britain's oldest golf event, the *News of the World* championship (1903). It is open to PGA members, with 8 places reserved for lead-ing European players. Prize money totals £10,000 and the 1970 venue was Moor Park, in August.

Long John Silver The smooth-tongued one-legged villain of Stevenson's TREASURE ISLAND who, having packed the crew with his own men, plans to stage a mutiny and take over command of the expedition.

Long Knives (1) Indian name for established settlers (especially Virginians), used to distinguish them from the English and referring to their swords; also Big Knives. (2) Nickname given to the US Cavalry in the Indian War of 1876.

Longleat House Tudor home near Warminster, Wiltshire, of the Marquess of Bath; to the attractions of pictures, furniture and books have now been added free-range lions.

Long March (Oct. 1934-Oct. 1935) The strategic retreat out of reach of Chiang Kai-shek of Mao Tse-tung's 1st Front Red Army of 100,000 men, from Juichin (their headquarters in Kiangsi) through Kweichow and Szechwan to Yenan (Wuch'ichen) in Shensi, which became their headquarters for the next 10 years; the distance covered was 6000 miles, and 70,000 men were lost on the way.

Long Parliament (1640-60) The Parliament which released the victims of Charles I's personal rule, had Strafford executed and Archbishop Laud imprisoned, abolished the STAR CHAMBER and ship money, and became the RUMP PARLIAMENT in 1649. Surviving members were recalled by General Monk in 1660, and voted for the RESTORATION.

Long-range Desert Patrol A British unit which in the North African campaign (1940-43) carried out sabotage behind the enemy's lines, on one occasion raiding Rommel's headquarters.

Longton Hall (1749-60) The earliest Staffordshire porcelain factory; most of its pieces were not particularly well made or decorated, but some now fetch high prices.

Long Trail A 260-mile trail following the crests of the Green Mountains across Vermont, popular with hikers and provided with camping sites.

Lonsdale Puissance championship (1947) A show jumping contest at the Royal INTERNATIONAL HORSE SHOW over high or difficult jumps.

Lonsdale spy case (1961) The trial of 'Gordon Lonsdale' (alias of a Russian GRU commander, Conon Molody), sentenced in the PORTLAND SECRETS CASE to 25 years imprisonment; he was exchanged for Greville WYNNE (1965).

Look (1937) A fortnightly magazine on the lines of *Life*, published in New York by Cowles Magazine Inc.

Look Back in Anger (1956) John Osborne's play which, set in a Midland bed-sitter, opened a new era of realism in the English theater, and featured Jimmy PORTER as the first ANGRY YOUNG MAN.

Look Homeward, Angel (1929) Thomas Wolfe's discursive but vigorous semiautobiographical novel (later made into a play) in which Eugene Gant tells of his upbringing in a town of North Carolina (where the author was born) and particularly of his parents, and how he eventually started on a journey which in the sequel, *Of Time and the River* (1935), took him to Harvard, New York and France.

Looking Backward: 2000-1887 (1888) A Utopian novel by Edward Bellamy which depicts Boston, Mass., under a future socialist regime.

Looking Glass World A world in which everything is back to front, as in THROUGH THE LOOKING GLASS; a mad, illusory world.

Loom of Youth, The (1917) A frank account of English 'public' school life by Alec, brother of Evelyn, Waugh, then 18; it was based on his own experiences at Sherborne.

Loop, The The main shopping center of Chicago, occupying 7 blocks on State Street; a notorious slum area lies behind it. (In a loop of elevated railroad tracks.)

Lop Nor, Lake China's proving ground for nuclear weapons, in eastern Sinkiang.

Loran towers Navigational aids for ships and aircraft in the form of towers up to 1400 ft high transmitting radio signals. By measuring the time displacement between signals from any 2 towers, a 'fix' is obtained. (Formed from initial letters of 'Long Range Navigation'.)

Lord Advocate The Scottish equivalent of the Attorney General.

Lord Chamberlain (UK) The chief officer of the Royal Household. He controls most of the staff of the royal household, is responsible for the appointment of royal tradesmen and until 1968 censored plays. Not to be confused with the Lord Great Chamberlain, a hereditary appointment, with ceremonial duties.

Lord Chancellor Short title of the Lord High Chancellor of England, Keeper of the Great Seal, who is the senior judge and head of the legal profession, Speaker of the House of Lords and the government's chief legal adviser in the Cabinet; he presides over the Judicial Committee of the PRIVY COUNCIL and the House of Lords sitting as the supreme court of appeal. He appoints judges, JPs and QCs. He vacates office on a change of government.

Lord Chief Justice The senior permanent member of the judiciary, ranking next to the LORD CHANCELLOR (a party appointment). He is president of the QUEEN'S BENCH DIVISION and may also sit on the Courts of Appeal and of Criminal Appeal.

Lord Haw-Haw Journalist's inapposite nickname for William Joyce, an Irish-American member of the BRITISH UNION OF FASCISTS who from Germany broadcast attacks on British morale during World War II and was hanged as a traitor in 1946. His accent was not Oxford (as implied by the name) but a curious invention of his own in which Germany, for example, was pronounced Jairmany. (The name was transferred from his predecessor, the 'Officer in the Tower'.)

Lord Jim (1900) Joseph Conrad's novel about a ship's officer who tried to live down an early act of cowardice (jumping off an apparently sinking pilgrim ship in the Red Sea), and atoned for it by the vicarious sacrifice of his life; as in other Conrad novels, the story is told indirectly through Capt. MARLOW.

Lord Lieutenant The sovereign's local representative in a county, largely an honorific appointment usually held by a peer or large landowner. As head of the county magistracy he submits nominations of Justices of the Peace to the LORD CHANCELLOR.

Lord Mayor's Show The annual procession on the second Saturday in November of the newly elected Lord Mayor of London to the LAW COURTS to be presented to the LORD CHIEF JUSTICE.

Lord of the Flies (1955) William Golding's novel about a group of boys stranded on a desert island after an airplane crash, and their reversion to primitive savagery.

Lord of the Rings, The (1954-56) A trilogy in which J. R. R. Tolkien, a Professor of English, has created a uniquely weird self-contained world of his own, inhabited by HOBBITS, Dwarves, Elves (who speak ELVISH) etc. The Dark Powers of evil from the Land of Mordor seek the gold Ruling Ring in the possession of Frodo Baggins (a HOBBIT), who travels through terrifying hazards to foil them (and thus save the world) by throwing the Ring into the Fiery Mountain. See also SHIRE, THE.

Lord Protector Title sometimes given to a Regent, specifically to: (1) PROTECTOR SOMERSET; (2) Oliver and, briefly, Richard Cromwell during the PROTECTORATE.

Lord Randal An ancient ballad which spread throughout Europe, perhaps from Scotland, about a hunter poisoned by his stepmother (or, in another version, 'true love') who comes home to his mother to die; Lord Randal has been variously identified.

Lord's (1814) The headquarters of the MCC and of the Middlesex County Cricket Club in St John's Wood, London. (Thomas Lord bought the ground for the MCC.)

Lord's Day, The Sunday, the Christian equivalent of the Jewish Sabbath (Saturday), and often itself called the Sabbath. Traditionally, it commemorates the RESURRECTION.

Lord's Day Observance Society (1831) (UK) A body devoted to ensuring, under 17th-century Puritan laws which politicians shirk repealing, that the traditional English Sunday gloom shall not be shattered by a game of cricket or suchlike revelry.

Lord Ullin's Daughter (1809) Thomas Campbell's ballad of a girl who elopes and is drowned before the eyes of her father who has come in pursuit.

Lord Warden See CINQUE PORTS.

Lorelei (1) A rock on the Rhine near Bingen, a danger to river traffic. (2) A legendary siren who lured boatmen to their doom there. (3) The gold-digging blonde of GENTLEMEN PREFER BLONDES.

Loreley express An early morning train from the Hook of Holland to Rome.

Lorenzo the Magnificent Lorenzo de' MEDICI (1449-92), ruler of Florence, poet and patron of the arts and learning.

Lorna Doone (1869) R. D. Blackmore's novel about the Doone family, outlaws of Exmoor in the West Country at the time of the MONMOUTH REBELLION. John Ridd marries Lorna, who had shielded him from the Doones, his father's murderers, and who turns out to be not a Doone but the kidnapped daughter of a Scottish nobleman.

Lorraine See ALSACE-LORRAINE.

Lorraine, Cross of A red cross with 2 horizontal crosspieces on a blue ground, the emblem used by Joan of Arc and adopted (1940) by de Gaulle for the FREE FRENCH.

Los In William Blake's private mythology, a Protean figure who appears to personify imagination, energy and creative genius, and has a regenerating influence on URIZEN.

Los Alamos Space research center in New Mexico, near Santa Fé; the MANHATTAN PROJECT was assembled there.

'Lost Colony, The' A pageant about the Roanoke settlement, given at

Manteo, N.C.; see ROANOKE ADVEN-
TURE.

Lost Generation, The The rootless
and disillusioned generation that
grew up during World War I, specifically the young writers who belonged to it, e.g. Hemingway, Scott
Fitzgerald and Dos Passos. (From
Gertrude Stein's remark to Hemingway: You are all a lost generation.)

Lost Horizon See SHANGRI LA.

'Lost Leader, The' Robert Browning's poem beginning 'Just for a
handful of silver he left us, / Just for
a riband to stick in his coat', attacking someone (perhaps Wordsworth)
he regarded as a turncoat.

Lost Tribes of Israel The tribes taken
as slaves to ASSYRIA from northern
Palestine in 721 BC (2 *Kings* xv, 29),
of whom nothing further is known,
although the fate of the victims of
the later BABYLONIAN CAPTIVITY is on
record. See BRITISH ISRAELITES.

Lot Nephew of ABRAHAM who was
allowed to escape from the destruction of SODOM AND GOMORRAH with
his family, but whose wife was
turned to a pillar of salt for disobey-
ing Jehovah's command 'look not
behind thee' (*Genesis* xix, 17 and
26).

Lothair (1870) Benjamin Disraeli's
political novel, in which many characters were thinly disguised contemporaries, about the competition
between the Roman and ANGLICAN
CHURCHES and Italian revolutionaries
for the financial support of the
wealthy young Lothair.

Lothario, The Gay The 'haughty,
gallant, gay' and heartless rake of
Nicholas Rowe's tragedy, *The Fair
Penitent* (1703).

Lotus-eaters, The In Greek legend,
the drowsy inhabitants of a land
where, in Tennyson's words, 'it
seemed always afternoon'; those
who ate the lotus fruit forgot their
homes and families and sank into
luxurious apathy. ODYSSEUS and his
men found this ancient COSTA BRAVA
a great temptation; those who succumbed had to be forcibly carried
aboard.

Louisbourg A national historic site
on Cape Breton Island, founded by

the French as Havre à l'Anglois, a
powerful fortress, once second only
to Quebec. The fortifications were
almost destroyed by British settlers
at the rival port of Halifax; their restoration was begun in 1961.

Louisiana Purchase (1803) The
treaty by which the USA doubled its
size through buying from Napoleon
for $15 million an undefined area of
the old French province of Louisiana lying between the Rockies and
the Mississippi, which later became
the states of Louisiana, Arkansas,
Missouri, Iowa, South Dakota, Nebraska, Colorado, Kansas etc.

Louisiana Story Virgil Thomson's
orchestral suite from music he composed for Robert Flaherty's semidocumentary film of that name (1948).
The suite is in 2 parts, the second
being 'ACADIAN Songs and Dances',
based on old Cajun tunes. See
FRENCH AND INDIAN WAR.

Louis Quatorze The age of BAROQUE,
in vogue in the reign of Louis XIV
(1643-1715), during which Versailles was finished. It was characterized by elaborate and costly furniture (some of it made in silver),
Boulle's tortoiseshell and brass
marquetry work (generally known as
buhl), and GOBELINS tapestries.

Louis Quinze The age of ROCOCO, in
vogue during the reign of Louis XV
(1715-74); rooms were smaller, furniture lighter and more colorful,
with wood marquetry, lacquer work
and ormolu mounts.

Louis Seize The Neoclassical (see
NEOCLASSICISM) reaction to the LOUIS
QUINZE style, in vogue during the
reign of Louis XVI (1774-93), inspired by the Latin styles discovered
during the excavations at POMPEII
and HERCULANEUM begun 20 years
before Louis XV died. Buhl (see
LOUIS QUATORZE) came back into favor, ormolu ornamentation was re-
fined and perfected, and furniture
was veneered with mahogany, some
of it decorated with porcelain.

Lourdes A town on the French side
of the Pyrenees, a major place of pilgrimage for the sick since a shepherd girl (St Bernadette) saw visions
of the Virgin MARY (1858) who told

her of the healing powers of the local waters.

Louvain A city of Brabant, Belgium, which at the beginning of World War I became a symbol of German 'frightfulness' when the fine old medieval buildings were deliberately razed in retaliation for civilian attacks on the occupation troops. The university library was rebuilt and restocked, only to be destroyed again by the Germans in 1940.

Louvre, The A huge museum and art gallery in Paris, on the site of a 12th-century castle and 16th-century royal palace, containing one of the finest collections of paintings, sculpture and antiquities in the world.

Love and Mr Lewisham (1900) H. G. Wells's partly autobiographical novel of a young science master in a Sussex school who sacrifices his high ambitions when he marries a very ordinary servant girl.

Loved One, The (1948) Evelyn Waugh's witty exposure of the extent to which the people of HOLLYWOOD were at that time in the clutches of the morticians, to whom vast sums were paid for elaborate funerals and paradisal burial grounds.

Love for Love (1695) A typically witty Restoration comedy by Congreve, in which a young man renounces his inheritance in favor of a younger brother in return for his father's settling his debts. He is rescued from the consequences of this act by the wiles of the girl who loves him.

Love's Labour's Lost (1594) Shakespeare's comedy in which a King of Navarre and his friends unsuccessfully endeavor to resist the charms of a visiting French princess and her entourage. A famous minor character is the tedious schoolmaster, Holofernes.

Love the Magician (1915) Falla's Andalusian gypsy ballet. (Spanish, *El amor brujo*.)

Low Church See EVANGELICALISM.

Low Countries The region around the deltas of the Rhine, Meuse (Maas) and Scheldt, i.e. Holland, Belgium and adjacent districts. (Translation of *Nederland*, 'Netherlands'.)

Lowestoft porcelain (1757-1803) English porcelain decorated in oriental or French styles, in underglaze blue (resembling BOW) or polychrome, and made for use rather than for show. Genuine pieces are rare. See CHINESE LOWESTOFT.

Low Sunday The Sunday after Easter.

Loyalties (1922) Galsworthy's play about an old solicitor, Jacob Twisden.

LP Initials used for long-playing phonograph records, usually of 12-inch diameter and played at 33 rpm; with the EP they replaced the old 78 rpm short-playing records in 1948.

LPE Initials used for LONDON PRESS EXCHANGE, an advertising agency.

LPN For Licensed Practical Nurse, licensed to assist an RN or doctor, as having practical nursing skill but lacking the statutory qualifications of an RN.

LSD Initials used for lysergic acid diethylamide, a drug producing hallucinations which appear to vary in content with the preoccupations of the individual concerned, from bliss to extremes of terror.

LST British-designed, American-built landing craft, first used, with the DUKW, in Sicily in July 1943. (Initials of 'landing ship, tank'.)

Lubin A character in Bernard Shaw's BACK TO METHUSELAH, said to be based on H. H. Asquith.

Lublin Committee Polish Communist Committee of National Liberation, first established in Moscow (July 1944), and at the end of the year proclaimed at Lublin, Poland, as the Polish provisional government, under Russian aegis.

Lubumbashi The Congolese name for Élisabethville, former capital of Katanga, now of Lower Katanga.

Lubyanka Prison A name of terror to Russians, being the Moscow prison used by the GPU, whose headquarters were also in Lubyanka Street.

Lucia di Lammermoor See BRIDE OF LAMMERMOOR.

Lucifer (1) Latin name for Venus as a morning star (Greek Phosphorus). (2) A fallen star in *Isaiah* xiv, 12, 'How art thou fallen from heaven, O Lucifer, star of the morning', which referred to the downfall of Nebuchadnezzar. (3) In Dante, the ruler of hell; in Milton, the name of the archangel expelled from heaven who became Satan.

Luck of Roaring Camp, The (1868) A collection of Bret Harte's short stories. The title story, published in his own periodical, *The Overland Monthly*, was the first to bring him national recognition. It is about gold miners, less rugged than they would wish to appear, who adopt a dying prostitute's child.

Lucky Jim Jim Dixon, the REDBRICK hero of Kingsley Amis's novel, who shambles hilariously through an understandably brief career as lecturer in history at a Welsh university.

Lucky Luciano The most powerful gangster in the history of COSA NOSTRA. In 1931, according to VALACHI, he led younger members in killing its founder and 40 other older leaders and then reorganized it. He allegedly helped the Allies in their invasion of Sicily and stopped US waterfront strikes during World War II; he also cashed in on wartime rationing and shortages, and was the first to join forces with non-Italian gangsters.

Lucrece In Roman legend, a married woman raped by the son of the Etruscan King of Rome. She committed suicide and the TARQUINS were driven out of Rome, which became a republic. The story is told in Shakespeare's *The Rape of Lucrece* (1594). (Anglicized form of Lucretia.)

Lucullus (Cooking) A name that may be added to any especially elaborate dish. (Roman epicure of 1st century BC.)

Lucy Cavendish College (1965) CAMBRIDGE UNIVERSITY's first graduate college for women, at present housed in temporary accommodation.

Lucy ring, The A successful spy ring set up before 1939 by dissident German officers under the Hitler regime; they infiltrated military headquarters and throughout the war passed vital information to the Allies through Switzerland, mainly to the Russians as the others doubted its authenticity. ('Lucy', code name of Rudolf Roessler, its leader.)

Luddites (1811-16) (UK) The machine wreckers of the Midlands and industrial north who protested against unemployment caused by new machinery brought in by the Industrial Revolution and against the enforcement of low wages and long hours; as there was no police force, the movement was suppressed by troops, and many rioters were hanged or transported. (Named after the leader called General Ludd, never identified, or a mad boy called Ned Lud.)

Lufthansa The chief German airline. (German *Luft*, 'air' + *Hansa*, see HANSEATIC LEAGUE.)

Luftwaffe The German Air Force.

Lüger A German automatic pistol used in both world wars, and also popular in the USA.

Lullingstone silk farm A famous silk farm housed in the cottage where Charles II's mistress, Nell Gwyn, lived, at Salisbury Hall, London Colney, Hertfordshire.

Lumpkin, Tony The mischievous character who causes all the trouble in Goldsmith's SHE STOOPS TO CONQUER.

Luna Roman moon-goddess, equivalent to the Greek SELENE.

Luna Name given to later Russian moon probes (see LUNIK). *Luna 9* made the first soft landing on the moon and relayed back high-definition pictures of the surface (Feb. 1966); *Luna 10* became the first moon satellite. *Luna 15* crashed on the moon while *Apollo 11* was there.

Lunar Orbiter The US program for putting TV cameras into orbit round the moon in order to pinpoint suitable landing sites for the APOLLO SPACE PROGRAM. In November 1966 *Lunar Orbiter 2* relayed the first landscape photograph of the moon's surface.

Lunik Name given to the Russian moon probes of 1959. *Lunik 1* passed near the moon and became the first solar satellite; *Lunik 2* was the first to hit the moon; *Lunik 3* relayed back the first photographs of the far side of the moon. See LUNA.

Lupercalia A Roman spring festival of expiation, later of fertility. (Latin *lupus*, 'wolf', identified with the wolf that suckled Romulus and Remus.)

Lupin, Arsène The master criminal created by the French journalist Maurice Leblanc in the early years of this century.

Lusitania Latin name for Portugal and western Spain.

Lusitania sinking (1915) The torpedoing without warning by a German submarine of a Cunard liner, with the loss of 1200 lives, including 124 Americans; this event influenced US opinion towards joining in the war against Germany.

Luther (1961) John Osborne's historical play, which shocked some by its literal rendering of that coarse monk's talk.

Lutheran Church The Protestant Church which, in contrast to the REFORMED CHURCH, accepts the AUGSBURG CONFESSION as the basis of its beliefs. In Germany it is now called the Evangelical United Brethren Church; it is the established episcopal Church of the Scandinavian countries, and is powerful in the American Middle West.

Lutine Bell A bell which hangs in 'The ROOM' at LLOYD'S in London; one stroke is sounded for bad, 2 for good news. (Salvaged from the frigate *Lutine*, sunk in 1799 at a cost to Lloyd's of some $1½ million.)

Luton Hoo (UK) An 18th-century country house at Luton which contains the WERNHER COLLECTION.

Lutz An ice-skating jump, of which there are various types.

Luxor The Egyptian tourist center on the site of ancient THEBES (south of KARNAK) where Amenhotep III built the Great Temple of AMON, to which Tutankhamen and Rameses II made additions. See also VALLEY OF THE KINGS.

Lvov A city now in the Ukraine; see LEMBERG.

LX Club CAMBRIDGE UNIVERSITY rugger club of the best 60 players in residence (elected for life). (LX, Roman numerals for 60.)

LXX Abbreviation for the SEPTUAGINT.

Lyceum melodrama Plays such as *The* BELLS, in which Henry Irving made his name at the Lyceum Theatre, London; he then took over the theater as manager, continuing to stage, and act in, both melodramas and Shakespeare.

Lycidas (1637) Milton's elegy on the death of his young friend Edward King. (Name of a shepherd in Virgil's ECLOGUES.)

Lydgate, Dr In George Eliot's MIDDLEMARCH, a young doctor with ideals who sinks to becoming a fashionable consultant.

Lydia Pinkham's Vegetable Compound Another competitor for PINK PILLS FOR PALE PEOPLE.

Lyonesse In ARTHURIAN LEGEND a country, now submerged near the Scilly Isles, particularly associated with TRISTRAM and Iseult.

Lyon King of Arms The Scottish equivalent of GARTER KING OF ARMS, with his own separate office.

Lyonnaise Cooking term indicating fried shredded onions.

Lyra The Harp, a northern constellation, which contains the Ring Nebula, the brightest of the planetary nebulae; alpha Lyrae is VEGA. (The lyre of ORPHEUS or of HERMES.)

Lyrical Ballads (1798) A book of poems written in collaboration by Wordsworth and Coleridge, in which they deliberately restricted themselves to the language and incidents of common life.

Lysenkoism The prostitution of science to political ends. In 1948 the Russian Academician T. D. Lysenko attacked colleagues who held the generally accepted view that acquired characteristics are not inherited, because this clashed with the current Stalinist version of MARXIST-LENINIST theory.

Lysistrata (415 BC) Aristophanes' comedy in which women on both sides of the PELOPONNESIAN WAR terminate it by the simple procedure of refusing their husbands their 'marital rights' until they stop fighting.

Lytton report   (1932) A report to the LEAGUE OF NATIONS which condemned the Japanese invasion of Manchuria (see MUKDEN INCIDENT) and recommended that they should be ordered to withdraw. The League Assembly approved the report but took no action on it — a failure sometimes regarded as the first sign of the disintegration of the League's morale.

M

'M' In Ian Fleming's novels, James BOND's service chief, modeled on the actual head of Britain's wartime secret service.

Mac In common use as an informal address to a man whose name is unknown.

Macaulay's New Zealander A reference to Lord Macaulay's glimpse of the distant future: When some traveler from New Zealand shall, in the midst of a vast solitude, take his stand on a broken arch of LONDON BRIDGE to sketch the ruins of St Paul's.

Macaulay's schoolboy The omniscient little boy implied in Lord Macaulay's phrase: Every schoolboy knows who imprisoned Montezuma and who strangled Atahualpa.

Macavity The Mystery Cat of whom T. S. Eliot wrote, in a mood of relaxation: 'There never was a Cat of such deceitfulness and suavity' and 'He's the bafflement of Scotland Yard, the FLYING SQUAD's despair: / For when they reach the scene of crime — Macavity's not there!' The poem appeared in *Old Possum's Book of Practical Cats* (1939).

Macbeth A historical 11th-century king who murdered King Duncan, seized the throne of Scotland, and was killed by Duncan's son Malcolm. In Shakespeare's play Macbeth also had BANQUO, Lady MACDUFF and her children murdered.

Macbeth, Lady The wife in Shakespeare's play who urges on MACBETH in his crimes but in the sleepwalking scene goes mad and commits suicide.

Maccabees A Jewish family who led a successful revolt in the 2nd century BC against the Syrian SELEUCID king, Antiochus IV Epiphanes, who tried to hellenize Palestine. The Maccabees formed a priest-monarchy which was overthrown by Rome in 63 BC.

Maccabees Two books of the APOCRYPHA, telling the story of the revolt of the MACCABEES.

McCarthyism Indiscriminate witch-hunting zeal against 'Communist' (i.e. left-wing) officials, as displayed by Senator Joseph McCarthy when chairman of a committee investigating subversive influences in government from 1951 until his policy was condemned by fellow Senators in 1954.

McCoy, The real Colloquialism for 'best of its kind'. (Probably originally McKay, referring to a Scotch whisky exported to North America in the 1880s, confused with the name of an American boxer, McCoy.)

McDonnell Douglas Corporation A merger of DOUGLAS AIRCRAFT and McDonnell Aircraft of St Louis, Mo., to form one of the largest US aircraft firms.

MacDowell Colony (1908) A workshop for musicians, writers and artists established in Peterboro, N.H., by the widow of the composer Edward Alexander MacDowell, in what had been their summer home. She survived her husband by 48 years (1908-56), and during this period large numbers found ideal conditions there for their work.

Macduff A former friend of MACBETH who joins Malcolm. When he hears this, Macbeth has Lady Macduff and their children murdered, and Macduff avenges them.

MACE A temporarily disabling liquid chemical used by police; squirted in the face, it causes tears, dizziness, confusion, immobilization, and sometimes nausea.

Macédoine (Cooking) A mixture of fruits or of vegetables. (Reference to the mixture of races in MACEDONIA.)

Macedonia A Balkan region which after the breakup of the Turkish Empire was partitioned between

Greece, Serbia (later Yugoslavia) and Bulgaria. The population is a mixture of at least 8 races, hence MACÉDOINE. See IMRO.

McGill Leading Canadian university, at Montreal.

McGuffey's Readers A series of school books written from 1836 by William Holmes McGuffey, into which he injected his own political conservatism; they were in use down to the 1920s.

Macheath, Capt. The highwayman hero of the BEGGAR'S OPERA.

Machiavellianism, Machiavellism (The practice of) the policy, deliberately and exclusively founded on self-interest, recommended in Machiavelli's The PRINCE.

Machu Picchu An INCA mountain city discovered in 1911 northwest of Cuzco, Peru, with well-preserved buildings and terraces skillfully constructed of huge stones.

McIntosh A medium-red dessert apple, grown especially in NEW ENGLAND and New York and accounting for about a tenth of the US crop.

McKay, The real See MCCOY.

McKinley assassination (1901) The shooting of President William McKinley at Buffalo, N.Y., by a Polish-born anarchist.

Mackinnon Cup (1891) A rifle-shooting competition for teams of 12 from Great Britain, Ireland and the Dominions.

'Mack the Knife' One of the big song hits of the THREEPENNY OPERA; Mack the Knife is a crook, the equivalent of MACHEATH.

Maclean Mission (Sept. 1943) The British mission led by Maj. Gen. Fitzroy Maclean, parachuted into German-occupied Yugoslavia to assist Tito and his PARTISANS.

Maclean's Magazine (1896) A leading Canadian weekly, published in Toronto, with general articles of Canadian and international interest.

Macleod, Fiona Pen name under which William Sharp wrote The IMMORTAL HOUR and other CELTIC TWILIGHT works. It was not until after his death in 1905 that it became known that these were written by Sharp, who had also published various biographies and poems under his real name.

Macleod of MacLeod The chief of the clan MacLeod, members of which come from all over the world to Skye to see the present chief, Dame Flora Macleod of MacLeod.

McLuhanism A vision of the world transformed by the electronic revolution (broadcasting, telephones, talkies) into a 'global village' where war and racialism will be unthinkable, and books no longer read. It is offered by Marshall McLuhan, the Canadian author of The Gutenberg Galaxy (1962) and Understanding Media (1964).

McMahon letters (1915-16) Letters (published in 1938) between the HASHEMITE Sherif Hussein of Mecca and the British High Commissioner in Egypt, McMahon. Hussein demanded independence after the war for the Arab lands which now comprise Iraq, Syria, Lebanon, ISRAEL, Jordan and SAUDI ARABIA. McMahon promised UK support except for an area corresponding to Lebanon and coastal Syria. The BALFOUR DECLARATION contradicted this, and moreover the LEAGUE OF NATIONS put the whole area under mandate except Saudi Arabia.

McMahon Line (1914) The boundary between Tibet and India which mainly follows the crest of the Himalayas. No Chinese government has ever accepted it, claiming that a Buddhist population having close ties with Tibet have been left on the wrong side of it in northern Kashmir. See LADAKH CRISIS.

M'Naghten Rules (1843) (UK) Rules laying down criteria for a successful plea of insanity in a criminal case; the chief rule was that the accused must either not have known what he was doing, or not have known that it was wrong. (Named after the accused in such a case; neither he nor anyone else knew for certain how his name should be spelled; sometimes given as M'Naughten or MacNaughten.)

MacRobertson Trophy An international croquet competition between Britain. Australia and New

Zealand.

MAC system Abbreviation for Multi-Access Computing system, by which one large computer can serve a wide variety of users, not only for calculations but for storing and retrieving information. It forms part of the British GPO's new National Data Processing Service.

Macy's (1858) A retail department store in Herald Square, NYC, said to be the 'world's largest' and a 'must' for tourists.

MAD Initials used for Magnetic Anomaly Detector, a US device enabling aircraft to pinpoint nuclear submarines at any depth; it is also mounted in the British NIMROD AIRCRAFT.

Madagascar The island. The state is now known as the Malagasy Republic.

Madame As a title in pre-Revolutionary France, see MONSIEUR.

Madame Bovary (1857) Flaubert's masterpiece, a realistic novel about the bored wife of a village doctor and her squalid love affair, written with the meticulous attention to details of style for which Flaubert was so renowned.

Madame Butterfly (1904) Puccini's opera about Lt F. B. Pinkerton, USN, who marries the Japanese GEISHA GIRL of the title, deserts her, and returns years later with his American wife to find her still waiting faithfully for him. Heartbroken, Butterfly takes her life.

Madame Tussaud's (1802) A London exhibition of waxworks, near Baker Street Station, famous for its CHAMBER OF HORRORS. (Name of French founder.)

Madeleine, The (1842) In Paris, the Church of St Mary Magdalen, near the Opéra, in external form a Greek temple.

Madeleine Smith case (1857) (UK) The trial in Glasgow of a Scots girl for the murder by arsenic of her lover, L'Angelier, a rather disreputable Channel Islander who was possibly blackmailing her; a verdict of not proven was returned, and the mystery was never solved.

Mad Hatter's Tea Party A perpetual tea party in ALICE IN WONDERLAND, at which the Hatter, March Hare and Dormouse sit at a long table so that they can 'move round when things get used up'.

Madhya Pradesh A state of India, formerly Central Provinces.

Madison Avenue The New York center since the 1940s for advertising and publicity firms, a street running between Fifth and Park Avenues, to both of which some of the leading firms have begun to move to escape the not entirely flattering Madison Avenue 'image'. (James Madison, 4th President.)

Madison Square Garden The New York indoor stadium famous primarily for boxing contests, but accommodating most sports; the 4th stadium of this name has been built over the Pennsylvania railway station, a long way away from Madison Square.

Madison Square Garden murder See THAW MURDER CASE.

Mad Mullah Nickname of the SOMALI rebel leader, Muhammad Abdullah Hasan, who kept up an intermittent campaign against the British administration in Somaliland from 1900 to 1920. A year later he died in his bed, having escaped to Abyssinia.

Madonna lily The white, *Lilium candidum*, associated in medieval art with the Madonna.

Madwoman of Chaillot, The (1945) Jean Giraudoux' tragicomedy and political parable in which an eccentric and innocent old spinster gets the better of materialistic forces represented by the capitalists of Paris. The play was made into a movie.

Maecenas Roman statesman and adviser of OCTAVIAN (Augustus), who was the patron of Virgil and Horace; hence any generous patron of literature.

Maenads See BACCHANTS.

Maeve (Medb) Legendary Queen of Connacht who attacked Ulster (see CUCHULAIN). Disgusted with CONCHOBAR's treachery to DEIRDRE, many of his RED BRANCH KNIGHTS deserted to Maeve.

Mae West Airmen's slang for an inflatable life jacket, named after a particularly buxom film star.

Mafeking, Relief of (May 1900) In the BOER WAR, the relief of a small British force under Baden-Powell after a siege of 7 months. London's riotous celebration of this event gave the word 'mafficking' to the language. (Town in northeast Cape Province.)

Mafia A secret society formed in Sicily in the 15th century, and still powerful; it specializes in vendetta, blackmail, 'protection' and murder. All attempts to suppress it have failed and, through emigrants, it has spread to USA as COSA NOSTRA.

Maga, The Abbreviated nickname of BLACKWOOD'S MAGAZINE. (Derived from the tradition that its founder used to refer to it, in his broad Scots, as 'ma maga-zine'.)

Magdalen See MARY MAGDALENE.

Magdalen College (1458) A college of OXFORD UNIVERSITY.

Magdalenean culture The last of the PALEOLITHIC cultures, perhaps lasting from 15,000 BC to about 8000 BC. Bone and antler carving was perfected, and cave painting brought to its highest level at LASCAUX by people who disappeared without trace at the end of the period. (La Madeleine, a rock shelter in the Dordogne, France.)

Magdalene College (1542) A college of CAMBRIDGE UNIVERSITY.

Magdalen Tower The tower of MAGDALEN COLLEGE, Oxford, on the roof of which the college choir sings at dawn on May 1st.

Magee University College See QUEEN'S UNIVERSITY.

Magellanic Clouds The 2 nearest galaxies (extragalactic nebulae), visible to the naked eye in the southern hemisphere. They are some 160,000 light-years away. (Named after Magellan, the first European to sail round South America.)

Magenta (1859) Napoleon III's costly defeat of the Austrians in Italy, where he had come to the aid of Cavour and the Piedmontese in the RISORGIMENTO. See SOLFERINO.

Maghreb, The Arabic name for Morocco. ('The land of the farthest west'.)

Magi, The The wise men from the east (i.e. CHALDEAN astrologers) who are described in *Matthew* ii as coming guided by a star to Bethlehem to worship the infant Jesus. Later legend confused them with the THREE KINGS. See EPIPHANY. (Latin, 'wise men'.)

Magic Circle, The The professional organization of British illusionists and conjurors, with its own club, theater, library and museum.

'Magic Fire Music' Music from the closing stages of the RING OF THE NIBELUNGS opera *Die Walküre*. Wotan punishes his daughter BRUNHILD for disobedience by ordaining that she shall lie asleep on a mountain until she is found by a man. She asks to be encircled by fire through which only a hero can pass (i.e. SIEGFRIED, in the sequel of that name).

Magic Flute, The (1791) Mozart's last opera, on a theme compounded of fairy-tale magic, broad comedy and hints of Masonic lore (at a time when Freemasonry was banned). (German title, *Die Zauberflöte*.)

Magic Mountain, The (1924) Thomas Mann's BILDUNGSROMAN in which dying Europe on the eve of World War I is symbolized by the polyglot TB patients isolated in a Swiss clinic. Some influence the young narrator towards an artistic, contemplative life (represented by the Mountain), others to a life of action. He is still undecided when he goes to join the German army on the outbreak of war.

Maginot Line The defenses on the German frontier built between the wars, behind which the French felt secure until the Germans easily outflanked them in 1940. (André Maginot, Minister of War.)

Magna Graecia The cities of southern Italy colonized by the Ancient Greeks, e.g. Tarentum (Taranto). SYBARIS, Locri, Rhegium (Reggio). (Latin, 'Great Greece'.)

Magnificat The Virgin MARY's song of praise after the ANNUNCIATION, given in *Luke* i, 46-55, and sung in church services. Of its many musical settings, the most famous is Bach's *Magnificat in D* (1723) for orchestra, chorus and soloists. (First word of the Latin for 'My soul doth magnify the Lord'.)

Magnificent Ambersons, The   (1918) Booth Tarkington's novel of snobbery in the Midwest, on which Orson Welles based a famous movie (1942).

Magnificent Mile, The   North Michigan Avenue, Chicago, where the fine Wrigley Building, Tribune Tower and Palmolive Building contribute to a dramatic skyline towering above Grant Park.

Magnitogorsk   A Russian city founded in 1931 near the Magnet Mountain at the southern end of the Urals. It is now the center of an important industrial area based on the large steel mills there.

Magnolia State   Nickname of the State of Mississippi.

Magnus, King   A character in G. B. Shaw's play The APPLE CART, a King of England of the last quarter of the 20th century. He upsets the Socialist government by his open criticisms of it and then threatens to abdicate in order to stand as candidate for the Royal Borough of Windsor. See PROTEUS.

Magoo   A character in a series of animated cartoons, a sort of latter-day DON QUIXOTE who because of his preternatural short sight, flounders hither and thither in a sea of perpetual misunderstanding.

Magyar   The language of Hungary, belonging to the FINNO-UGRIAN LANGUAGES.

Mahabharata   (500 BC) One of the 2 great Hindu epic poems (see also RAMAYANA), telling of the deeds of the gods, including the Trinity of BRAHMA, SIVA and VISHNU. It contains the BHAGAVAD-GITA.

Mahagonny   (1929) Abbreviated title of The Rise and Fall of the City of Mahagonny, Brecht's opera on the Marxian but not very operatic theme of the inevitable collapse of capitalism, represented here by the US town of Mahagonny.

Maharashtra   A Marathi-speaking state of India formed in 1960 from the southeastern portion of Bombay State; capital Bombay. See MAHRATTAS.

Mahatma   (1) In Buddhism, a sage or adept who by asceticism and medi-

tation has attained to exceptional wisdom and powers. (2) An honorific title bestowed on Gandhi. (Sanskrit, 'great-souled')

Mahayana   The later of the 2 main forms of Buddhism, which appeared about the beginning of the Christian era; the 'Greater Vehicle' (of Truth) or northern Buddhism of Tibet, China, Japan, Korea. It is optimistic and positive, in contrast to HINAYANA; believers must try to train themselves to become BODHISATTVAS and so save all mankind. Mahayana Buddhists tend to take an active part in politics.

Mahdi   A Muslim messiah, a title several times assumed, notably by the leader of the antiforeign movement which swept the Sudan in 1883. (Arabic, 'the guided one'.)

Mahrattas   A Hindu Marathi-speaking race; they formed a strong military confederacy in west and central India which weakened MOGUL power. They founded states such as Indore and Gwalior, and now predominate in the state of MAHARASHTRA.

Maid Marian   A character of the morris dance, who figures in the ROBIN HOOD legend as his sweetheart.

Maid of Orleans   A name for St Joan of Arc, who raised the British siege of Orleans in 1429.

'Maids of Honor, The'   A painting by Velázquez; see 'Las MEÑINAS'.

Maigret, Inspector   The strong-willed detective who first appeared in The Crime of Inspector Maigret (published in France 1930), by the Belgian-born writer Georges Simenon.

Maine, The   A US battleship sent to Havana to protect US lives there, and blown up in the harbor on 15 Feb. 1898, apparently by a submarine mine, with the loss of 260 officers and men. This tragedy triggered off the Spanish-American War, during which 'Remember the Maine!' became a war cry.

Main Liner   A Philadelphia suburbanite of aristocratic or rich family, as usually living in the stately homes built for 40 miles along the main line of the Pennsylvania Railroad, from Philadelphia to

Paoli.

Main Sequence stars The type to which most stars, including the sun, belong; in them hydrogen is being converted into helium, and the end product is the RED GIANT. See also OBAFGKMRNS.

Main Street (1920) Sinclair Lewis's novel recording the hopeless efforts of a doctor's wife to bring culture to the Midwest town of Gopher Prairie (based on the Minnesota birthplace of the author).

Maiolica (14th-17th centuries) Italian DELFT, decorated from the 16th century with elaborate historical, mythological and biblical scenes in brilliant colors; now rarely seen outside museums. See MAJOLICA. (Named after Spanish wares imported into Italy via Majorca.)

Maison Tellier, Le A famous short story of Maupassant's, a delightful account of an innocent Sunday outing in the country by the whole staff, including Madame, of a provincial brothel.

Maître d'hôtel (Cooking) Garnished with parsley, and perhaps with butter sauce and lemon juice.

'Maja desnuda' (?1798) Goya's painting of the Duchess of Alba in the nude; there is a companion picture of her fully clothed, but the popular story that this was done to allay her husband's suspicions of their relationship does not stand up to examination—he had died several years earlier. Many authorities think the Duchess is not the person represented in the pictures.

Majolica (1850) Confusing name (see MAIOLICA) given by Minton and other potteries to stoneware with opaque colored glazes, used in making display and utilitarian wares, tiles etc.

Major Barbara (1905) Bernard Shaw's play in which Major Barbara Undershaft of the SALVATION ARMY conducts a verbal battle with her father (see UNDERSHAFT, ANDREW). She resigns from the Army rather than accept his donation of 'tainted money', but finds much truth in some of his views. 'I stood on the rock I thought eternal; and . . . it crumbled under me.'

Major Generals, Rule of the (1654-55) Period during Cromwell's PROTECTORATE when the country was divided into 11 districts, each under a major general, who enforced the strictest Puritan standards of conduct; the origin of English mistrust of standing armies.

Majority card An identity card required by law in some states to show that the holder is over 21 and can be admitted to a bar serving alcohol.

Majuba, Battle of (1881) See SOUTH AFRICAN WARS.

Makerere (1950) A university of Kampala, Uganda.

Malade imaginaire, Le (1673) Molière's comedy in which 2 doctors batten on the hypochondriac Argon.

Malaga A strong sweet white wine from the Spanish province of that name, adjoining Gibraltar.

Malagasy Republic Official name of the island-state of Madagascar.

Malaprop, Mrs Aunt and guardian of Lydia LANGUISH in Sheridan's The RIVALS, famous for her enthusiastic misuse of the English language, as in 'Why, thou barbarous Vandyke!' Hence *malapropism*, a confusion of similar sounding words of very different meanings. (Name itself from French *mal à propos*, 'little to the point'.)

'Malaria' Jones See CAMPAGNA.

Malawi The name taken on gaining independence (1964) by Nyasaland, formerly a British colony of Central Africa.

Malay The language of Malaysia, one of the chief MALAY-POLYNESIAN LANGUAGES. It has borrowed heavily from SANSKRIT, Persian, Arabic and TAMIL, and is an exceptionally easy language for a foreigner to learn. See also BAHASA INDONESIA; TAGALOG.

Malayalam The DRAVIDIAN LANGUAGE, closely allied to TAMIL, spoken in Kerala.

Malay-Polynesian languages A widespread group of languages spoken from Madagascar to Hawaii and Easter Island. See MALAY; POLYNESIANS.

Malaysia, Federation of (1963) Formed from Malaya, Sarawak, Sabah and (until 1965 when it seceded) Singapore.

'Malbrouk s'en va-t-en guerre' An old French song about the wife of the warrior Malbrouk (not certainly Marlborough) awaiting his return from a war, in which he is killed. The tune resembles 'We won't go home till morning'. (French, 'Malbrouk goes off to war'.)

Malcolm See MACBETH.

Malcolm X An American Negro, born Malcolm Little, who was recruited in prison to the BLACK MUSLIMS, quarrelled with their leader, visited Africa and Mecca and became Malik el-Shabazz, a MUSLIM 'prophet', doubtfully converted to the view that all races form one great family. For this apostasy he was murdered in HARLEM (1965) by a Black Muslim. ('X' is used by Black Muslims instead of a (rejected) 'white' surname.)

Malden and Coombe (UK) A former municipal borough of Surrey, since 1965 part of the borough of KINGSTON UPON THAMES.

Maldon Scene of a 10th-century defeat of the men of Essex by Danish invaders, recounted in a contemporary poem, 'The Battle of Maldon'.

Male Animal, The (1940) James Thurber's best play, written in collaboration with Elliott Nugent.

Mali, Republic of The name taken on gaining independence (1960) by the former French colony of Sudan.

Malibu surfboard The finned fiberglass board that transformed surfing, rendering possible varied acrobatic feats in the standing position. (Named for Malibu Beach, the premier Californian surfing center, 25 miles west of Los Angeles.)

Malleus Maleficarum (1484) *The Hammer of the Witches*, a book published at Cologne by 2 professors of theology appointed by Pope Innocent VIII as Inquisitors into the practice of witchcraft (i.e. pre-Christian ritual). It constituted a guide for Inquisitors engaged in the wholesale persecution of 'witches' carried out by this Pope.

Mallory Cup The North American men's yachting championship.

Mallory Park (UK) An auto and motorcycle racing circuit near Hinckley, Leicestershire, at which international motorcycle races are held in June and September.

Malmaison The château west of Paris is where the Empress Josephine often stayed with Napoleon, and where she lived after their divorce. It now has a Napoleonic Museum.

Malplaquet, Battle of (1709) The final defeat of the French in the War of the SPANISH SUCCESSION, by Marlborough and Prince Eugène of Savoy, won at heavy cost and while Anglo-French peace talks were in progress. (Village near Mons, in France.)

Malta, GC The island was awarded the George Cross (1942) for the bravery of its people under continual air attacks, a unique award to a community.

Maltese Falcon, The (1930) The best of Dashiell Hammett's detective novels, in which a new type of tough private eye first appears—Sam Spade, who investigates the theft of a treasure which once belonged to the KNIGHTS TEMPLARS, the jewel-laden falcon of the title.

Malthusianism (1798) The theory that population increases in geometrical, food production only in arithmetical proportion, and that it is thus essential to keep down the rate of population increase by 'moral restraint', i.e. abstention from intercourse. (View put forward by the Rev. T. R. Malthus, economist.)

Malvern Festival (1929) A dramatic festival founded by Sir Barry Jackson in honor of Bernard Shaw, held annually until 1939 and revived occasionally since. Plays performed included not only the contemporary works of Shaw, Bridie, Priestley etc. but revivals of 16th and 17th-century classics.

Malvolio The pompous steward of OLIVIA in Shakespeare's TWELFTH NIGHT; BELCH and AGUECHEEK send him a forged letter which fools him into wearing cross-gartered yellow stockings ('a colour she abhors') to win his mistress' heart.

Mame (1966) A musical based on

the novel *Auntie Mame* by Patrick Dennis and the play by Jerome Lawrence and Robert E. Lee.

Mamelukes Originally the Sultan of Egypt's bodyguard, formed of CIRCASSIAN slaves. They rapidly seized power, and ruled Egypt from 1254 to 1517; thereafter they held subordinate high office under the Turkish viceroys. In 1811 the KHEDIVE Mehemet Ali lured them to Cairo and had them massacred. (Arabic, 'slaves'.)

Mammon (1) Aramaic word for 'riches' used in *Matthew* vi, 24 ('Ye cannot serve God and mammon') and *Luke* xvi, 9 ('mammon of unrighteousness'). (2) Mistakenly used by medieval Christians as the personification of greed and avarice, the god of the worldly.

Mammoth Cave Part of an extensive series of spectacular caverns and underground rivers, in Mammoth Cave National Park (1936), southwestern Kentucky. In the WAR OF 1812, niter was prepared here from guano to make gunpowder.

Managerial Revolution, The (1941) James Burnham's book putting the view that control of government and industry is passing from politicians and capitalists to trained administrators and technicians.

Man and Superman (1905) The play in which Bernard Shaw introduced to the British public the ideas of CREATIVE EVOLUTION and the LIFE FORCE, and of the SUPERMAN, put into the mouth of John TANNER, who in the dream of Act III becomes DON JUAN, representing the SUPERMAN he can never himself be.

Manassa Mauler, The Nickname of Jack Dempsey, world heavyweight boxing champion, 1919-26. (Born at Manassa, Col.)

Manchester Gaiety, The (1908-20) The theater where Miss Horniman set up the first modern repertory company in Britain, and where the MANCHESTER SCHOOL OF DRAMATISTS was launched.

Manchester Guardian (1821) A daily newspaper, renamed The *Guardian* in 1959.

Manchester School The advocates of FREE TRADE and laissez-faire, led

by John Bright and Richard Cobden, who in the 1840s were MPs respectively for Manchester and nearby Stockport.

Manchester school of dramatists Playwrights launched into fame by Miss Horniman at the MANCHESTER GAIETY; they included Stanley Houghton (HINDLE WAKES), Harold Brighouse (HOBSON'S CHOICE) and Alan Monkhouse.

Manchu Dynasty Another name for the CH'ING DYNASTY.

Manchukuo (1932-45) The puppet state set up in MANCHURIA by the Japanese, under the ex-Emperor Puyi, and turned by them into a major industrial area which supplied them with armaments.

Manchu language One of the ALTAIC LANGUAGES, under the CH'ING DYNASTY the official language of China, now spoken only in parts of northern Mongolia. See MANCHUS.

Manchuria The industrial area of China, in the northeast, now broken up into the provinces of Heilungkiang (capital Harbin), Liaoning (capital Mukden) and Kirin; other parts were incorporated into the Chinese province of Hopei and the autonomous republic of INNER MONGOLIA.

Manchus A Tartar people first mentioned in Chinese records of the 10th century. They conquered MANCHURIA and then all China; see CH'ING DYNASTY.

Mancini case (1941) The trial of Tony Mancini, who killed a man in self-defense at a London club. His counsel failed to plead that the death was the unpremeditated result of sudden affray, and Mancini was hanged. Another Tony Mancini was involved in the BRIGHTON TRUNK MURDERS.

Mandarin Foreigners' name for PUTUNG-HUA.

Mandarins, The (1954) Simone de Beauvoir's account, in fictional form, of her life among the Paris existentialists, including Sartre, Camus and Koestler.

Mandates Commission (1919-45) The organization set up by the LEAGUE OF NATIONS to supervise the administration of ex-German colonies (TANGANYIKA, South West Africa, Cameroons, Togoland, New Guinea) and ex-Turkish possessions (Iraq, Syria, Palestine, Transjordan). It was succeeded by the UN TRUSTEESHIP COUNCIL.

M. & B. 693 Sulfapyridine, one of the earliest sulfa drugs, discovered at May & Baker's pharmaceutical laboratories in 1938, and used as a cure for pneumonia, gonorrhea etc.

Mandelbaum Gate Until 1967 the control point for traffic between the Jordanian and Israeli sections of the divided city of Jerusalem.

Mandingo A group of languages which predominate throughout most of the region formerly known as FRENCH WEST AFRICA.

Man for All Seasons, A Robert Bolt's radio play (1954), stage play (1961) and movie in which an ironic Sir Thomas More tries warily to keep the overpowering Henry VIII at a distance but refuses to compromise his religious principles to save himself from the executioner's block.

Man Friday (1) The 'savage' whom ROBINSON CRUSOE rescues from death at the hands of cannibals and who becomes his general factotum. (2) Any faithful, versatile right-hand man. (So named because Crusoe found him on a Friday.)

Mangla dam A dam on the River Jhelum on the PAKISTAN-Kashmir border, a major work necessitated by the INDUS WATERS AGREEMENT to conserve floodwater from the Indus river system in Pakistan. It is planned to supplement it by building the Tarbela dam to the north-west, on the Indus itself.

Manhattan The island and borough which forms the central core of New York City; among its better-known features are CENTRAL PARK, GREENWICH VILLAGE, HARLEM, WALL STREET, BROADWAY, FIFTH and PARK AVENUES, WASHINGTON SQUARE and TIMES SQUARE.

Manhattan, The A 115,000-ton ice-breaking tanker, the first commercial vessel to pierce the NORTHWEST PASSAGE (1969) in an effort to open a route from the east to the Alaskan oil fields, via the Prince of Wales Strait. At one stage she was icebound off Melville Island, and further improvements in design were indicated before regular services would be practicable.

Manhattan clam chowder A chowder made with tomatoes and without milk, otherwise resembling NEW ENGLAND CLAM CHOWDER, but not accepted by staunch New Englanders as a true clam chowder.

Manhattan cocktail One made of rye whiskey and sweet vermouth, usually with bitters and a cherry.

Manhattan project US code name for the program to develop an atomic bomb, see TUBE ALLOYS.

Manichaeism A dualist religion founded by the Persian Mani, derived from ZOROASTRIANISM and with Buddhist elements. Mani claimed to be the latest of a succession of teachers (ABRAHAM, Zoroaster, Jesus); he was crucified by orthodox Zoroastrians (AD 275). The Perfect or Elect lived a secluded life of extreme asceticism, while those who lived in the world were called Hearers or Believers. The religion spread to India and China, and survived at Samarkand until the 14th century; it was the inspiration of the ALBIGENSIANS, CATHARI and BOGOMILS. (*Manichaeus*, Latinized form of Mani.)

Manifest Destiny A phrase probably first used in 1845 by John L. O'Sullivan in an editorial attacking foreign governments which opposed the annexation of Texas and 'our manifest destiny to overspread the continent allotted by Providence for . . . our yearly multiplying millions'. The phrase was then freely borrowed by journalists and politicians.

Manila Pact (1954) The treaty that led to the setting up of SEATO.

Man in the Iron Mask A man imprisoned by Louis XIV for 40 years at various places, including the Île Ste Marguerite off Cannes. When transferred to a new prison he wore a black velvet (not iron) mask. In Dumas' novel he is said to be the son of Cardinal Mazzini and the king's mother, but there are many other theories as to his identity.

Mankind 2000 (1967) An international organization founded by Dr Robert Jungk and backed by Lord Boyd Orr, Yehudi Menuhin, A. J. P. Taylor etc.; its object is to prepare people for the future by publicizing the latest scientific developments.

Mann Act (1910) The White Slave Traffic Act which prohibited interstate transportation of women for immoral purposes, at a time when white slaves were being imported from Europe and Asia and distributed through the states.

Manned Orbiting Laboratory See MOL.

Manned Spacecraft Center The NATIONAL AERONAUTICS AND SPACE ADMINISTRATION'S center, southeast of Houston, Tex., which includes the MISSION CONTROL CENTER, facilities for astronaut training etc.

Mannerheim Line (1939) The Finnish defense system on the Russian border. (Field Marshal Mannerheim, later President of Finland.)

Mannerism (1530–1600) The period in Italian art following the HIGH RENAISSANCE which, under the impact of the REFORMATION and COUNTER-REFORMATION, abandoned the serenity of Raphael for the distorted, elongated human figures of, e.g., El Greco, and deliberately broke the rules established by the Renaissance.

Manners, Lady Diana Maiden name of Lady Diana Duff Cooper, later Lady Norwich, a famous beauty of the 1920s who made her name as the Madonna in The Miracle, a religious mime directed by Max Reinhardt.

Mannlicher The famous Austrian big-game and sporting rifle.

Man of Aran (1934) Robert Flaherty's documentary film about the small fishing community on the Isles of Aran, off the Galway coast, Ireland.

Man of Destiny A name for Napoleon Bonaparte.

Man of La Mancha (1965) Dale Wasserman's long-run musical drama dealing with episodes in the lives of DON QUIXOTE and Cervantes; music by Mitch Leigh, lyrics by Joe Darion.

Manon Lescaut (1731) (1) The title of Abbé Prévost's novel, in which the faithless luxury-loving Manon ruins the career of the Chevalier des Grieux, a brilliant student who is infatuated by her. On her being transported to America, des Grieux follows her, fights a duel with the governor of Louisiana's son and then escapes to the desert, where Manon dies in his arms. (2) Puccini's opera (1893) based on (1); the story was also used in Massenet's opera Manon (1884).

'Man on the Flying Trapeze, The' A song, of which there are many modern versions, derived from 'The Flying Trapeze' (1868) by the English singer and comedian, George Leybourne, music by Alfred Lee. It became a favorite with circus clowns and also inspired William Saroyan's fantasy story, 'The Daring Young Man on the Flying Trapeze' (1934).

Man o' War A famous racehorse foaled at Belmont Stables, near Lexington, Ky.; in 2 years' racing (1919-20) he was only once beaten (as a 2-year-old) and went on to win about $1 million in prize money, stud fees and sale of foals.

Mansfield, Katherine Pen name of Kathleen Beauchamp (1888-1923), later Mrs Middleton Murry, a New Zealand writer of highly polished short stories of great sensitivity.

Mansfield judgment (1774) The court ruling in the case of the slave, Somerset, by which an English lawyer, Granville Sharp, succeeded in establishing his contention that slavery was illegal in England.

Mansfield Park (1814) Jane Austen's novel on the theme of the differing values prevailing in London and the country, as revealed to the heroine, Fanny Price, by the BERTRAM FAMILY, the Crawfords and Aunt NORRIS.

Mansion House (18th century) The official residence of the Lord Mayor of London, at the Bank; it contains a banqueting room called the Egyptian Hall.

Mansion House speech (1911) An important speech in which Lloyd George warned Germany that Britain stood by France in the AGADIR CRISIS.

Mantoux test A test for tuberculosis.

Man Who Came to Dinner, The (1939) A comedy by Moss Hart and George S. Kaufman in which the dinner guest is the entirely self-centered Sheridan Whiteside (a caricature of Alexander Woollcott), who breaks his leg and during his enforced stay manages to upset not only the family but the whole town. At last he is able to go—but breaks his leg again.

Man Who Was Thursday, The (1908) G. K. Chesterton's fantasy about anarchists and spies, with a Catholic moral.

'Man Without a Country, The' (1863) Edward Everett Hale's short story, in which a naval officer, Philip Nolan, after playing a part in the Aaron Burr conspiracy, angrily wishes he may never hear his country's name again. His wish is granted: for the rest of his life he is kept at sea and never allowed to land.

Man With the Golden Arm, The (1949) Nelson Algren's novel of the Chicago slums. The hero's golden arm is supreme with the pool cue and with dice but cannot rescue him from his environment; he escapes by heroin and then suicide.

'Man with the Hoe, The' (1) Millet's painting (1862) of a peasant resting from the labor of hoeing, in the middle of a bleak landscape. For this and similar works Millet was accused of Socialist leanings. (San Francisco Museum of Art.) (2) A successful poem (1899) by Edwin Markham, inspired by (1) and making its message abundantly clear: 'The emptiness of ages in his face. / And on his back the burden of the world'.

Manx The people, and the CELTIC LANGUAGE, of the Isle of Man.

Manzanilla A FINO sherry, paler, drier and lighter in body than AMONTILLADO.

MAOI A group of drugs used in treating depression, dangerous unless used under professional guidance. (Initials of monoamine-oxidase inhibitors.)

Maoism The Chinese version of Communist revolution preached by CHAIRMAN MAO. From the beginning it differed from Marxist orthodoxy in relying on the peasantry (not the urban proletariat) to undermine the existing regime by a protracted People's guerrilla war. Since attaining power, Mao has concentrated on maintaining a state of permanent revolution, i.e. constant vigilance against apathy, revisionism, deviation to left or right (unless by the leaders), and reaction. These policies were dictated by conditions in China, where the peasants, overwhelmingly in the majority, had always been conservative and apathetic.

Mapai Israeli Labor Party, based on the rural agricultural worker, and moderate in outlook. See next entry.

Mapam Israeli United Workers' Party, a left-wing Socialist party of urban workers. See last entry.

Maphilind Former Indonesian President Sukarno's name for his proposed union of Malaysia, the Philippines and Indonesia. (From the initial letters of those countries.)

Maple Leaf Flag, The Canada's national flag which replaced the Canadian red ensign in 1965; the design is a red maple leaf on a broad white ground between 2 vertical red borders.

'Maple Leaf Forever, The' (1867) The Canadian national anthem, beginning: In days of yore / From Britain's shore.

Maple Leafs The Toronto Maple Leafs, NATIONAL HOCKEY LEAGUE, one of the 3 Canadian teams in the League.

MAR (1964) A US radar system, the Multifunction Array Radar, moved electronically by computer to scan in all directions at once, and able to detect, identify and track 1000 objects simultaneously; for use in the KIKE-X SYSTEM.

Maracaña The world's largest sports stadium, at Rio de Janeiro, Brazil.

Maraschino A liqueur, originally Dalmatian, distilled from bitter black cherries. (Italian *amarasca*, 'bitter'.)

Marathas An alternative spelling of MAHRATTAS.

Marathi The INDO-EUROPEAN LAN-
GUAGE of the MAHRATTAS, and the
principal language of MAHARASHTRA.

Marathon (490 BC) (1) A decisive
battle in which the Greeks under
Miltiades defeated the much larger
Persian army sent by Darius the
Great. (2) A 26-mile race, so named
because the news of (1) was brought
to Athens from the field of battle by
a messenger who ran this distance
and dropped dead on arrival. (A
coastal plain north of Athens.)

Marat/Sade (1964) A convenient abbreviation for *The Persecution and
Assassination of Marat as Performed by the Inmates of the Asylum of
Charenton under the Direction of
the Marquis de Sade*, by Peter Weiss;
the title leaves little to add. Peter
Brook's production of it with the
Royal Shakespeare Co. at the Aldwych, London, was hailed with delight by the critics of the 'posh Sundays'. [Jimmy PORTER'S name for the
more intellectual London Sunday
papers]. 'The heart has its reasons
which reason knows nothing of.'

Marble Arch (A London arch, designed by John Nash for BUCKING-
HAM PALACE (1820), removed to the
northeast corner of HYDE PARK (1851)
and now marooned there on a traffic
island, inconspicuously housing a
police post with, nearby, SPEAKERS'
CORNER to keep them busy and the
site of TYBURN TREE to remind them
of times when Capital Punishment
was a popular entertainment.

Marble House, The (1892) A magnificent house (styled 'cottage') built
by Richard M. Hunt (see The
BREAKERS) for W. K. Vanderbilt at
Newport, R.I., lavishly decorated
with marble and gilding; it is open
to the public.

Marchand de vin (Cooking) Flavored with claret.

Marcher Lords The feudal lords
who held the troubled Scottish and
Welsh border areas; in the 13th
century called Earls of March (the
Mortimers on the Welsh, and the
Dunbars on the Scottish border).
(Germanic word *marko*, boundary;
whence margrave, marquess etc.)

March Hare A contentious

character prominent in the MAD HAT-
TER'S TEA PARTY, ably abetting the
Hatter in his mad logic. Alice was
surprised, since it was May, and the
old phrase 'as mad as a March hare'
implies that hares are only mad during their mating season in March;
but the CHESHIRE CAT had warned her
'We're all mad here' and 'You must
be, or you wouldn't have come here'.

'Marchioness, The' See SWIVELLER,
DICK.

March of Dimes The drive to raise
funds for the NATIONAL FOUNDATION,
held usually in the last week of January.

March on Rome (1922) The fanciful
name given in Italian Fascist mythology to Mussolini's journey to
Rome (by train) at the King's invitation, and the subsequent arrival of
thousands of Fascisti by bus, truck
and cart; the birth of Fascist Italy.

March through Georgia (1864) The
march of the Union troops under
Gen. William T. Sherman through
Georgia to capture the Confederate
arsenal at Atlanta, and on to the sea,
ruthlessly burning down towns on
their way. See AMERICAN CIVIL WAR.

Marconi affair, The (1912) The purchase by the Chancellor of the
Exchequer, David Lloyd George, on
the advice of the Attorney General, Rufus Isaacs (Lord Reading), of
$5000 worth of shares in the Mar-
coni Co. at a time when the Post Office was negotiating a contract with
it. The Liberal majority of a committee of inquiry acquitted both men
of indiscretion, the Conservative
members dissenting.

Marco Polo Bridge incident (July
1937) The Japanese-fabricated incident which provided the pretext
for the renewal of the Sino-Japanese
War which had begun with the MUK-
DEN INCIDENT. Also called the Peking
incident.

Mardi Gras (1) The French name for
Shrove Tuesday, the last day of the
Carnival which precedes Lent in
France and other Catholic countries.
(2) The carnival at New Orleans, La.,
the largest and most colorful Mardi
Gras in the US, lasting several days
with torchlight parades and balls;

also similar festivals at Mobile, Ala., etc. See FASCHING. (French, 'fat Tuesday'.)

Marengo (1800) The victory of Napoleon (as First Consul) over the Austrians. (Italian village in Piedmont near Alessandria.)

Mare Nostrum The Mediterranean; also used as the title of one of Blasco Ibáñez' novels (1918). (Latin, 'our sea'.)

Mareth Line Rommel's defense line on the southern frontier of Tunisia, originally built by the French to keep the Italians out; breached by Montgomery's 8th Army in March 1943.

Margaret In Goethe's poem, the ignorant young girl seduced by FAUST; she drowns their child and, in the Dungeon scene at the end of Part 1, though awaiting execution, refuses Faust's offer to rescue her, preferring to be saved through suffering. Also called Gretchen, the German diminutive of Margaret.

Maria Chapdelaine (1916) A popular novel about Quebec farmers written by a Frenchman, Louis Hémon, after a brief visit to Canada.

Maria Marten of the Red Barn The name of several Victorian melodramas based on a sensational murder at Polstead, near Ipswich, which caught the popular imagination in 1827.

Mariana of the Moated Grange (1) The girl who is rejected by Angelo in Shakespeare's MEASURE FOR MEASURE. (2) The subject of 2 poems by Tennyson's suggested by (1). (3) The title of a famous painting by Millais (1851).

Marianas Turkey Shoot A name for the Battle of the PHILIPPINE SEA.

Marianne The young woman, dressed in red, white and blue, who symbolizes the French Republic. (Named after a secret society formed during the SECOND EMPIRE to restore the Republic.)

Marian Persecution The wholesale burnings of Protestants (including Cranmer, Ridley and Latimer) as heretics, under Queen Mary I (1553-58).

Marianske Lázne See MARIENBAD.

Maria Theresa dollar A coin (the Austrain thaler), originally 90% sil-

ver and weighing an ounce, which became the chief unit of currency in ABYSSINIA until banned in 1946. Still minted today (dated 1780), it is widely used from SAUDI ARABIA to West Africa, as raw material for jewelry, as a unit of weight, or strung on necklaces.

Marienbad The German name of Marianske Lázne, now a Czech spa, with water containing Glauber salts.

Marina City Lofty apartments, in Chicago, Ill., a 61-story circular building with 588-ft towers.

Marineland The name of 2 open-air oceanaria, where whales and ocean fish are exhibited. The first to be established was the one 18 miles south of St Augustine, Fla. The other is in Los Angeles. Both are famous for their highly intelligent dolphins.

Mariner Name given to a series of US space probes. *Mariner 2* (1962) sent back data from near Venus indicating extreme heat and unsuitability for living things; *Mariner 4* (1965) relayed pictures of Mars taken at a range of 7800 miles, showing craters but no canals. *Mariner 5* (1967) passed near Venus (see VENUS space probe). *Mariner 6* and *7* in 1969 relayed close-range pictures of Mars over a distance of 58 million miles.

Mariolatry Undue preference to the worship of the Virgin MARY over that of Christ.

Maritimes, The The Maritime or Atlantic provinces of Canada, i.e. Newfoundland, Nova Scotia, New Brunswick and Prince Edward Island.

Marius the Epicurean (1885) Walter Pater's mannered novel about the development of a Roman of the 2nd century AD who, after sampling the various philosophies of his time, is finally attracted to Christianity.

Mark, King In ARTHURIAN LEGEND, a king of Cornwall who loses his wife ISEULT to TRISTRAM. In some versions he is a tragic and sympathetic figure, in others a poltroon.

Markham, Mrs Pen name of a Mrs Penrose who produced a celebrated period-flavored history of England for children in 1823.

Marks and Spencers The earliest British multiple chain store, founded in 1887 by Michael Marks, a Jewish refugee from Russia, and Tom Spencer, and still a family concern although a public company. Specializing in clothes and food, it won under the second-generation management of Lord Marks and Lord Sieff an outstanding reputation for giving value for money and has been described as having done more for social equality than the BUTLER ACT. Usually known as 'Marks and Sparks'.

Marlborough House (1710) A Wren house built for the 1st Duchess of Marlborough, later the home of Queen Mary, and since 1962 a Commonwealth Centre where conferences are held. It is open to the public.

Marlow, Capt. The narrator in several of Joseph Conrad's novels and stories, including LORD JIM and CHANCE, who assembles the evidence about the events recorded and tries to analyze the motives of the participants; this forms the basis of Conrad's oblique impressionistic approach, with the author aloof and skeptical in the background.

Marlowe, Philip The detective in Raymond Chandler's studies of American decadence, one of the earliest of the new style hard-boiled private eyes of the 1930s.

Marly A château, of which nothing survives, designed by Mansart for Louis XIV and built in a park near Versailles.

Marly horses A famous pair of Numidian horses made in bronze by W. Coustou (1677-1746) for MARLY; now at the Place de la Concorde entrance to the Champs Elysées, Paris.

Marmion (1808) Walter Scott's poem of FLODDEN Field and the manifold love intrigues of Marmion. But: 'Charge, Chester, charge! On, Stanley, on!'/Were the last words of Marmion.

Marne, Battles of the (1) *First Marne* (Sept. 1914), a decisive battle in which Anglo-French forces saved Paris by driving the Germans back to the Aisne. (2) *Second Marne* (July 1918), in which French and US troops again drove the Germans

back on the Aisne; together with Haig's attack at Amiens in August, it formed the final decisive counteroffensive of World War I.

Marplan A market research company; see INTERPUBLIC.

'Marriage à la Mode' (1745) Hogarth's masterpiece, a series of satirical oil paintings (From which engravings were made) in which the canvas is crowded with detailed figures whose gestures enact a drama in dumb show (as he explained).

'Marriage at Cana, The' A painting by Veronese ostensibly of the CANA MARRIAGE FEAST but, apart from the figure of Christ, a 16th-century Venetian banqueting scene; now in the Dresden gallery.

Marriage of Figaro, The (1786) Mozart's opera based on the second part of Beaumarchais' play (see BARBER OF SEVILLE). Count Almaviva, now tiring of his wife Rosina, foolishly tries to seduce her maid Susanna. Since the latter is engaged to FIGARO he is, of course, outwitted.

Mars Roman god equivalent to the Greek ARES.

Mars Name given to a series of Russian probes launched towards Mars but without success.

Marsala A Sicilian light-colored wine resembling sherry. (Port from which shipped.)

'Marseillaise, The' (1792) The French national anthem, sung by a Marseilles volunteer unit as they marched into Paris shortly before the Republic was proclaimed. It begins: Allons, enfants de la patrie,/Le jour de gloire est arrivé.

Marshall Aid US aid given under ERP (the European Recovery Program or Marshall Plan). (Proposed in 1947 by the Secretary of State, General George Marshall.)

Marshall Field (1865) A department store founded in Chicago by Marshall Field; see FIELD ENTERPRISES.

Marshall Space Flight Center At Huntsville, Ala., where, under the direction of von Braun (see V-2), the SATURN V rocket was developed.

Marshalsea A debtors' prison in Southwark, London, which was as notorious as the FLEET, and is described in Dickens's LITTLE DORRIT.

Marston Moor (1644) The biggest battle of the ENGLISH CIVIL WAR, in which Cromwell's newly raised cavalry decisively defeated Prince Rupert; it led to the loss of the north of England to Charles I's cause. (Moor near York.)

Marsupialia One of the 3 subclasses of mammals; the young are born in an undeveloped state and usually complete their development in a pouch (*marsupium*). The subclass includes the kangaroos, wallabies, wombats, koalas and Tasmanian devils of Australia, and the opossums of America.

Martel An Anglo-French air-to-ground precision tactical strike missile, carried by the BUCCANEER. One version is television-guided, another homes on enemy radar.

Martello towers Small round watchtowers built at various points on the coasts of southeast England when Napoleon threatened invasion. Many still survive, thanks to massive construction. (Inaccurately named after a similar tower captured at Cape Mortella, Corsica.)

Martha and Mary Two sisters of LAZARUS; when they were entertaining Jesus, Mary was intent on getting spiritual instruction from him, Martha was fussing about getting him a proper meal. This drew the comment: Martha, Martha, thou art careful and troubled about many things (Luke x, 41).

Martha Washington table A SHERATON-style sewing table with drawers and a hinged top, so named because Martha Washington was said to have had one at MOUNT VERNON.

Martian invasion panic (1938) (USA) The result of Orson Welles's little joke, when he broadcast the gist of H. G. Wells's WAR OF THE WORLDS as a news bulletin. People are said to have died of shock as he described the landing in America of men from Mars.

Martin Chuzzlewit (1844) Dickens's novel in which Martin is sent out into the world by his rich grandfather more or less penniless in the hope that hard experience may cure his selfishness. He goes to America

(of which Dickens paints a highly unflattering and unconvincing picture) with Mark Tapley, and comes back a sadder and wiser man. See also PECKSNIFF; Sairey GAMP.

Martini A cocktail of gin and dry vermouth ('gin and French') or (in Britain) sweet vermouth ('gin and Italian') — the former with an olive or lemon peel, the latter with a cherry.

Martini International Club A stroke play golf tournament, entries for which are by qualification and invitation, played in June. Prize money totals $17,000. (Sponsored by Martini and Rossi Ltd.)

Martin Luther King murder The assassination of 4 April 1968 at Memphis, Tenn., of the founder of the SOUTHERN CHRISTIAN LEADERSHIP movement, by James Earl Ray who, after extradition from England where he had fled, was given a 99-year sentence in 1969.

Martinmas November 11th, the feast of St Martin, in the Middle Ages the day when livestock were slaughtered and salted for the winter supply of meat. See ST MARTIN'S SUMMER.

Martinware (1873-1915) Individual pieces of salt-glaze stoneware grotesqueries in a wide range of subdued colors, made by the 4 Martin brothers of Southall, London; each piece is signed and dated. The most usual form is an owl-like bird with a detachable head; mask jugs and many kinds of vase decorated with strange fish, birds or dragons were also made.

Marxism The basis of Communism, the doctrine which sought to demonstrate by DIALECTICAL MATERIALISM that capitalism must inevitably destroy itself, to be succeeded by a classless socialist community in which the State would wither away. See COMMUNIST MANIFESTO. (Karl Marx, German theorist, 1818-83.)

Marxist-Leninism Theories arising from the adaptation of 19th-century MARXISM TO 20th-century facts, and in particular to the problems of governing Russia; it includes belief in 'SOCIALISM IN ONE COUNTRY' and peaceful coexistence with countries under different social systems, in contrast to TROTSKYISM. (Lenin, leader of the OCTOBER REVOLUTION.

Mary, The Virgin The mother of Jesus (*Matthew* i, 18), present at the Crucifixion, and last mentioned in *Acts* i, 14; venerated particularly in the Roman Catholic Church, as the Blessed Virgin Mary, the Madonna, the Mother of God, Our Lady, Mater Dolorosa and under many other names.

Mary Barton (1848) Mrs. Gaskell's novel depicting the hard lot of workers in the Manchester cotton mills.

Mary Celeste (1872) A deserted American ship found abandoned in the North Atlantic, 4 weeks after leaving New York for Genoa, with evidence of very recent occupation and no indication of a reason for her abandonment. The mystery was never solved.

Mary Gregory glass A style of glassware painted in white or colored enamels with scenes usually depicting children, on glasses, jugs, decanters etc. The best were made by a Czech firm, Hahn's, at Jablonec (1850-80), but the name of Mary Gregory, who did similar work at the Boston & Sandwich Glass Works, Sandwich, Cape Cod, came to be used of all products in this style.

Mary Jane (1) A low-heeled broadtoed patent-leather sandal with a single-buckle ankle strap, worn especially by young girls. (Originally a trademark.) (2) A colloquialism for marijuana.

Marylebone A former London metropolitan borough, since 1965 part of the borough of WESTMINSTER (City of). (Usual abbreviation of St Marylebone.)

Mary Magdalene The woman of Magdala from whom Jesus cast 7 devils (*Luke* viii, 2); identified in Christian tradition with the prostitute of *Luke* vii, 37, who anointed Jesus' feet; also mentioned as present at the Crucifixion and as the person to whom Christ first appeared after it (*John* xx, 1-18); the patron saint of penitents.

Mary Rose (1920) J. M. Barrie's play about Mary's 'Island that Likes to be Visited'.

Masai An African race of mixed Hamitic stock, living in southern Kenya and northern TANZANIA. Originally a nomadic cattle people, they are now settling to agriculture.

Masked Ball, The (1859) English title of *Un ballo in maschera*, Verdi's first fully mature opera. The plot was based on the assassination of the King of Sweden at a masked ball in 1792, but for political reasons the papal censor insisted on a non-European setting and colonial Boston was substituted for Stockholm (the opera was also played in Boston 2 years later).

Mason, Perry The lawyer-detective who first appeared (1933) in a novel by the American writer E. S. Gardner, and who became more widely known to the world through a TV series.

Mason-Dixon Line (1767) Originally the settlement of a boundary dispute between Pennsylvania and Maryland, which came to be regarded as the boundary between free and slave (or northern and southern) states. (Names of 2 British surveyors who demarcated it.)

Masonic Societies See FREEMASONS.

Mason jar A glass jar with airtight screw cap, for home canning. (After its 19th-century American inventor.)

Mason's Ironstone (1813) Tough highly decorated earthenware, of which octagonal jugs with snake handles are the commonest examples.

Masorah (6th-9th centuries AD) A Jewish commentary on the Old Testament text meticulously compiled by the Masoretes (biblical scholars) from oral traditions.

Masquerade (1950) A floribunda rose producing semidouble flowers which change from yellow to pink and then to red.

Massachusetts Institute of Technology See MIT.

Massacre of St Bartholomew See ST BARTHOLOMEW MASSACRE.

Massacre of the Innocents When Herod the Great, King of the Jews, heard that a child had been born in Bethlehem destined also to be King of the Jews, he ordered the massacre of all male children born there at that time; but Jesus escaped (*Matthew* ii, 16). See HOLY INNOCENTS.

'Massacre of the Innocents, The' A painting (see last entry) by PEASANT BRUEGHEL, thought by some to be a veiled reference to Spanish oppression of the NETHERLANDS, although the painter appears to have been on good terms with the regime.

Masséna (Cooking) With artichoke hearts and bone marrow.

Massey-Ferguson (1891) A Canadian firm, with headquarters at Toronto, which makes farming machinery, tools and implements.

Massey Report (1951) The report of a Royal Commission appointed to inquire into the state of Canadian culture; it recommended massive state aid to universities; see also CANADA COUNCIL. (Vincent Massey, Governor-General of Canada 1952-59.)

Mass Observation (1937) A London society founded by the sociologists Tom Harrisson and Charles Madge to gather through teams of observers objective facts about the British way of life and thought; these were then as far as possible reduced to statistical form. It was the first of a flood of surveys and opinion polls to be let loose on Britian.

Master Builder, The (1892) Ibsen's play about the architect Solness who kills himself in his attempt to achieve the impossible. The symbolism of the new house he has built tends to overburden the play.

Master-mind lectures Lectures given at the BRITISH ACADEMY and financed by the Henriette Hertz Trust, on the great writers and thinkers of the past.

Master of Ballantrae, The (1889) R. L. Stevenson's study of brotherly hate in the days of the FORTY-FIVE. The unscrupulous Master, James Durrie, fights for the YOUNG PRETENDER, flees abroad and is presumed dead. His younger brother, who fought on the other side, succeeds to the title and marries the unloving Alison who had been intended for James. James returns to plague both

of them for the rest of the novel.

Master of the Rolls (UK) One of the ex-officio judges of the Court of Appeal, and in practice its president; he ranks next below the LORD CHIEF JUSTICE.

Masters, The (1934) The leading US international golf tournament; entry is restricted to those invited by the Augusta National Golf Club, Ga., who ask the leading golfers of the year. The tournament is played on Bobby Jones's course at Augusta for prize money totalling $150,000. See also DUNLOP MASTERS.

Mastersingers, The (1868) Wagner's only comic opera, about a song contest in which the prize is a girl who, since this is comedy, is won by the right man after various machinations. (German title, *Die Meistersinger von Nürnberg*.)

Masterson, Bat A marshal of the Old West, famous as the hero in a TV series based on his supposed exploits.

Masurian Lakes, Battle of the (Feb. 1915) The 'winter battle' in World War I in which Hindenburg and Mackensen drove the Russians out of GALICIA, Lithuania and Courland, and went on to take Warsaw.

Mata Hari Alias of Margaret Zelle, a Dutch-born woman who posed as a Javanese and spied for Germany from 1905 until her execution in France in 1917.

Matapan, Battle of Cape (Mar. 1941) A British naval victory over an Italian force off southern Greece.

Match King, The See KREUGER CRASH.

Mater et Magistra (1961) Pope John XXIII's encyclical on social questions which, in contrast to RERUM NOVARUM, gave qualified approval to some forms of socialism. (Latin, 'Mother and Teacher'.)

Matchmaker, The (1955) A farce by Thornton Wilder, the basis of the musical, HELLO, DOLLY! (1964). It first appeared under the title *The Merchant of Yonkers* (1939), a version of a German farce by J. Nestroy (1801-62).

Mathias See BELLS, THE.

Mathis der Maler (1934) Hindemith's opera based on the life of the

16th-century German painter Mathias Grünewald, who was caught up in a peasants' revolt in the days of Luther. It deals with the creative artist's role in society. (German, 'Mathias the painter'.)

Matteotti murder (1924) The murder of a Socialist opponent by Fascists. Mussolini was forced by public reaction to have them arrested in 1926, but they were given only light sentences.

Matty, Miss The best-loved of the innocent but indomitable spinsters in CRANFORD.

Maud (1855) Tennyson's poem in which a man describes how he wooed the daughter of the squire who had ruined his family, killed her brother in a duel, and fled the country. It contains the familiar lyric 'Come into the garden, Maud'.

Maud Committee (1940-41) Code name of a UK committee under Sir George Thomson which finally recommended the development of a uranium bomb. This project was then handed over to TUBE ALLOYS.

Maud Muller (1854) Whittier's narrative poem about a rich judge who falls in love with a country girl; both make more suitable marriages but both sorrowfully wonder if this was for the best.

Mauler US antiaircraft missile, abandoned 1965.

Mau Mau A Kikuyu nationalist secret society, formed in Kenya possibly in 1944, not known to the authorities until 1950, or to the world till 1952, when it murdered its first European victim. Members were bound by oaths of degrading bestiality and freely murdered white settlers and Kikuyu opponents alike, in a terrorist campaign that lasted till 1960. (Kikuyu, 'get out! get out!'.)

Mauna Loa The world's largest active volcano (13,680 ft) which, with its extinct twin Mauna Kea (13,784 ft), lies in the Hawaii Volcanoes National Park. See KILAUEA CRATER. ('Long mountain'.)

Maundy money Specially minted coins, distributed in white leather purses by the Royal Almoner at Westminster Abbey, as a substitute

for the ceremony described under MAUNDY THURSDAY.

Maundy Thursday The day before Good Friday, on which popes and kings washed the feet of the poor in commemoration of Christ's washing the feet of the Apostles (John xiii, 14); see last entry. (Corruption of French and Latin words for 'command', i.e. Christ's command to love one another, John xiii, 34.)

Maurice debate (May 1918) (UK) A Commons debate on whether Lloyd George had misled the House as to the Army's strength in France. The official opposition under Asquith divided the House against the government, and lost the debate together with what prestige they had left. (Sir Frederick Maurice, director of military operations, who made the accusation.)

Mauritshuis (1644) The Dutch Royal Museum of Painting at the Hague.

Maurya dynasty (320-184 BC) An Indian military dynasty which, under the enlightened Asoka, united most of India and Afghanistan, adopting BUDDHISM as the national religion.

Mauser Name of the Prussian army rifle of 1871 and subsequent models which were sold to the armies of the world; also from 1898 of automatic pistols. (German firm at Oberndorf-am-Neckar.)

Mausoleum, The (352 BC) One of the SEVEN WONDERS OF THE WORLD, the tomb of Mausolus, King of Caria, built at the capital, Halicarnassus (now Budrum, in Turkey) by his widow.

Maverick A politician who does not toe his party line; an intellectual or other nonconforming individualist. (From Sam Maverick, a Texan pioneer who died in 1870. The basic idea is of unbranded calves on the open range that do not follow their mothers. Maverick is said to have left his calves unbranded, so that they were rounded up and branded by others; alternatively, it was he who branded other ranchers' strays.)

Max Gate The name of a house near Dorchester built in 1883 by the architect-writer Thomas Hardy, who lived there for most of the latter half of his long life.

Maxim's A Paris restaurant and nightclub which became a household name through a song in the MERRY WIDOW, 'Da geh'ich zu Maxim'. It is still going strong.

Mayan civilization That which flourished in Guatemala from the 3rd century AD and later in Yucatan, where the Mayans were joined by the TOLTECS. They invented a pictorial script in the 4th century, and had an accurate calendar reflecting a deep knowledge of astronomy. They were in an advanced state of decline by the time of the Spanish conquest. The AZTECS inherited their culture.

Mayan language The AMERICAN INDIAN LANGUAGE of the MAYAN CIVILIZATION and of the AZTECS.

Mayday English name of the international radiotelephone SOS signal used by ships and aircraft. (Anglicized form of pseudo-French m'-aidez, 'help me'.)

May Economy Committee (1931) (UK) A government committee which recommended drastic pay cuts for civil servants and the forces, and in the dole (unemployment pay), implemented by Philip Snowden. This led to the INVERGORDON MUTINY and the collapse of the second Labour ministry of Ramsay MacDonald.

Mayerling affair (1889) The Austrian Crown Prince Rudolf, only son of Emperor Franz Josef, together with his mistress were found dead at the prince's hunting lodge at Mayerling, near Vienna, after the Emperor had ordered him to break off the liaison. Finding the lodge surrounded by police, Rudolf shot her and committed suicide. (This is the most generally accepted version of what happened; but it has been questioned by some.)

Mayflower The ship in which the PILGRIM FATHERS sailed.

Mayflower Compact, The An agreement to set up a government, made by the PILGRIM FATHERS at a meeting on the MAYFLOWER 11 Nov. 1620.

Mayflower II (1957) A replica of the MAYFLOWER, which sailed from Plymouth (Devon) to Plymouth (Mass.) where it is permanently anchored.

May 4th Movement (1919) Chinese student revolt led by Westernized left-wing intellectuals; regarded as marking the final rejection of traditional Chinese ways and beliefs.

Mayo Clinic (1889) A large clinic at Rochester, Minn., attended by patients from all over the world; it is staffed by a voluntary association of doctors, surgeons and others engaged in medical research. The clinic comprises several hospitals, and hotels for outpatients. See also MAYO FOUNDATION. (Founded by W. W. Mayo and his 2 sons.)

Mayo composite aircraft (1938) A small float seaplane carried on top of a flying boat, from which it took off at a suitable height. The seaplane could thus carry a heavier load of fuel than it could take off with unaided. (Invented by R. H. Mayo in conjunction with Short Bros. at Rochester, Kent.)

Mayo Foundation In full, the Mayo Foundation for Medical Education and Research, a very large graduate medical school at Rochester, Minn., and part of the University of Minnesota. (See MAYO CLINIC.)

Mayor of Casterbridge, The (1886) A WESSEX novel by Thomas Hardy about Michael Henchard who, when drunk at a fair, sells his wife and baby to a sailor. He becomes Mayor of CASTERBRIDGE; his wife, and later the sailor, returns, the story of his wife's sale comes out, and he dies after experiencing every kind of misfortune and frustration.

May-week At CAMBRIDGE UNIVERSITY a period (now a fortnight in June) when the end of the academic year is celebrated with boat races, college balls etc.

MC Master of Ceremonies.

MCC (1) Initials used for the Marylebone Cricket Club, London, the controlling body of English cricket, which made its headquarters at LORD'S from 1814. (2) See MISSION

CONTROL CENTER.

MCPA A selective hormone weed killer for lawns.

Meadowbank A sports stadium at Edinburgh built to accommodate the Commonwealth Games of 1970.

Meals-on-Wheels A service which brings hot meals to the homes of aged and bedridden people who live by themselves.

Means Test (UK) An inquiry into a person's private income to determine eligibility for a state or local authority benefit — has been an issue ever since the MacDonald government proposed (1933) that unemployment benefit should be graded according to need. The issue has been revived whenever it is suggested that such benefits should not be granted irrespective of need.

Measure for Measure (1604) A late comedy of Shakespeare's, showing signs of disillusion; the happy ending, in which the 6 main characters are paired off in marriage after many frustrations, is contrived and artificial.

Meccano Trade name of an ingenious toy construction set introduced early in the century, consisting of perforated metal strips, nuts and bolts, wheels, pulleys etc. enabling young boys to build up an infinite variety of trucks, cranes etc. to their own design.

Mecklenburg An old German province on the Baltic, capital Schwerin, now divided up into districts of East Germany.

Medal of Freedom Founded in 1945 for meritorious acts by civilians in wartime and, renamed Presidential Medal of Freedom (1963), converted into the highest US civilian award, given for significant public or private endeavor.

Medal of Honor (1862) The highest US award for bravery in action, awarded by Congress. Usually called the Congressional Medal of Honor.

Medea Legendary sorceress, daughter of the king of Colchis who helped JASON win the Golden Fleece on his promising to marry her. To effect their escape she killed her brother, and on arrival at Jason's home she arranged the murder of PELIAS. When Jason deserted her she sent his new bride a robe which burned her to death, and also killed Jason's children. She then tried to poison Theseus.

Medes An ancient people of the Persian-Mesopotamian borders, whose capital was Ecbatana. In 550 BC their Persian subjects revolted and the Persian Cyrus the Great founded the kingdom of the Medes and Persians. The *law of the Medes and Persians* is one which 'altereth not' (*Daniel* vi, 8).

Medicaid A welfare health program for medical aid to the needy, administered by the Medical Services Administration.

Medicare (1966) The first cautious approach to an American national health service, restricted by strong professional lobbying to those over 65. Complemented by a Blue Cross-Blue Shield program of Senior care health insurance for persons over 65. The same name is used in Canada for a scheme introduced in 1968.

Medici, The An Italian family, originally bankers, which ruled Florence and Tuscany (1434-1737), provided 2 popes, and the wives of Henry II (Catherine) and Henry IV (Marie) of France. The first to rule Florence, Cosimo, and his grandson Lorenzo the Magnificent (1449-92) were great patrons of literature and the arts.

Medici 'Mercury', The (1580) A remarkable sculpture by the Fleming, Giovanni da Bologna, who settled in Florence; now in the Bargello Museum, Florence.

Medici prints Colored prints of OLD MASTERS and modern paintings, produced by the Medici Galleries, London.

Mediterranean A modernistic style of furniture blending French, Italian and Spanish styles.

Mediterranean climate A technical term in geography for a type of climate characterized by dry sunny summers and mild wet winters, usually found between latitudes 30°

and 40° north or south of the equator, especially on the western side of a continent. Examples are central coastal California, central Chile, southern Australia, Cape Town, and the Mediterranean itself.

Mediterranean race See IBERIANS.

Medmenham, Monks of See HELL-FIRE CLUB.

Médoc Claret (see BORDEAUX WINES) from the communes of Pauillac (notably from the Châteaux Latour, Lafite and Mouton-Rothschild), Margaux, St Julien and St Estéphe.

Medusa In Greek legend, one of the GORGONS, whose gaze turned the beholder to stone, even after PERSEUS had cut off her head, thus providing him with a secret weapon of which he made great use.

Meek, Private A character in G. B. Shaw's *Too True to be Good* said to be modeled on Lawrence of Arabia.

mehitabel See ARCHY AND MEHITABEL.

Meiji Restoration (1868) The restoration of the power of the Japanese Emperor, in abeyance during the TOKUGAWA SHOGUNATE. The Meiji period is the name given to the reign of Mutsuhito (1868-1912), during which Japan became a world power, absorbing the knowledge and techniques of the West.

Mein Kampf (1924) Hitler's political testament, written while he was in prison; in it he gave clear warning of his plans, but as he was then an obscure agitator few took notice of it at the time. (German, 'my struggle'.)

Meissen (1710) Porcelain of the first European firm to make true hardpaste porcelain. The early pieces are among the most highly prized (and priced) of all European porcelain, especially the COMMEDIA DELL'ARTE figures modelled by Kändler (1737-44); but in the 19th century quality declined as production rose. (Village near Dresden, Saxony; see DRESDEN PORCELAIN.

Meistersinger See MASTERSINGERS.

Melanesians The Negroid races of the Western Pacific, including the people of Papua-New Guinea, Fiji, the Solomons, New Hebrides and

New Caledonia. (Greek, 'black islanders'.)

Melba toast Narrow slices of very crisp thin toast. (Named after Dame Nellie Melba, Australian soprano.)

Melbourne Cup (1860) Australia's classic weight-for-age flat race, run at Flemington, Melbourne, in November, over a course of 2 miles.

Melchior One of the THREE KINGS, traditionally a King of Nubia.

Mellon Collection The nucleus of the art treasures of the NATIONAL GALLERY OF ART (Washington), donated in 1937 by the banker Andrew W. Mellon, who collected them specifically for this purpose. It includes examples of the major European and American schools from the 13th-19th centuries together with Italian Renaissance sculpture.

Mellon (Richard King) Foundation (1947) A foundation which supports religious, charitable, literary and educational programs; the headquarters are in Pittsburgh, Pa.

Mellors, Oliver See LADY CHATTERLY'S LOVER.

Melpomene The Greek muse of tragedy.

Melton Mowbray A town northeast of Leicester famous for (1) pork pies, (2) Stilton cheese, (3) its countryside hunted by 3 leading packs, the Quorn, Belvoir and Cottesmore.

Melungeons A small dark-skinned community living on a mountain ridge (Newman's Ridge) in Hancock County, north Tennessee, whose origin has long puzzled anthropologists. It has been suggested that they descend from the ROANOKE ADVENTURE settlers, or from marooned Portuguese sailors (*melungo* is said to be Afro-Portuguese for 'shipmate'). Also called Ridgemanites.

Memel Now Klaipeda, city of Lithuanian SSR.

Memoirs of a Fox-Hunting Man See SHERSTON'S PROGRESS.

Memoirs of a Midget (1921) Walter De La Mare's delicate and poetic fantasy of a world seen through the eyes of a midget heroine.

Memorial Day May 30th, also called Decoration Day, commemorating the dead of the armed forces, and from 1971 kept as a legal holiday on the last Monday in May.

Memphis Capital of ancient Egypt during the OLD KINGDOM, situated at the apex of the Nile delta on the opposite (right) bank of the river to GIZA and SAKKARA. To its north lay HELIOPOLIS.

Mendeleev's Periodic Law (1869) That the physical and chemical properties of the elements vary in a uniform way with their atomic weights. Mendeleev, on the basis of this law, compiled a Periodic Table classifying the elements, including those not then discovered; and this, with modifications and additions, is still valid. (Russian chemist.)

Mendelism (1860s) A theory of heredity which attracted no attention when published but was accidentally rediscovered in 1900 and is now the accepted basis of genetics. The idea of dominant and recessive characteristics played a part in it. (Gregor Mendel, Abbot of Brünn, who derived his theory from breeding experiments with sweet peas.)

Menelaus In Greek legend, a king of Sparta, brother of AGAMEMNON, husband of HELEN OF TROY.

'Meñinas, Las' (1656) One of the most famous of paintings by Velázquez, depicting the young Infanta of Spain with her maids of honor and her dwarfs, the painter at his easel, the King and Queen reflected in a mirror, and other figures; now in the PRADO, Madrid, (English title, "The Maids of Honor".)

Menin Gate (1927) A memorial at Ypres to the nearly 55,000 British soldiers gazetted as missing in the 3 battles of Ypres in World War I.

Mennonites Dutch and Swiss ANABAPTISTS, who founded communities in Russia and North America.

Men of Good Will (1932-47) Name given by Jules Romains to a continuous novel in 27 volumes, depicting many aspects of life in France in the period 1908-33. (French title, *Les Hommes de bonne volonté*.)

'Men of Harlech' A Welsh war song about fighting the SAXONS; there are several differing versions of the words in English.

Men of the Trees (1922) A society formed to encourage the protection, preservation and planting of trees throughout the world, and to educate the public regarding the advantages of afforestation. Its headquarters are in Hampshire, England.

Mensa A society of people who can show, through a standard test, that they have a high IQ.

Mensheviks The minority group of the Social Democrats which in 1903 split into the Mensheviks and BOLSHEVIKS. Led by Martov, they held that the RUSSIAN REVOLUTION should be directed not by the workers but by the bourgeois. The were themselves permanently split in 1914 between those who wanted to rally to the fatherland and those who opposed any participation in the war. (Russian, 'minority'.)

Mentor A wise old friend of ODYSSEUS; in the *Odyssey*, when TELEMACHUS is searching for his father, ATHENE goes with him in the guise of Mentor as counselor and guide.

Men, Women and Dogs (1943) A collection of James Thurber's drawings on his favorite themes of domineering wives driving their menfolk to the bottle and to the placid company of conspicuously nonpedigree dogs.

Mephistopheles The cynical, malicious Devil to whom FAUST sells his soul. (Traditionally a corruption of Greek words standing for 'hating the light'; sometimes abbreviated to Mephisto.)

Mer, La (1903-05) Debussy's symphonic sketch, with movements entitled 'From dawn to midday on the sea', 'Play of waves' and 'Dialogue of wind and sea'.

Mercantile System The 18th-century doctrine that government should regulate overseas trade, boosting exports and limiting imports, in order to amass gold and silver reserves, regarded as the only true wealth. Colonies, such as North America, should be used as sources of raw materials and as markets for

British products, local industry being discouraged. Adam Smith first demonstrated the fallacies in this then generally accepted theory, and the advantages of a laissez-faire policy.

Mercedes (1901) Name given to German DAIMLER cars to overcome French sales resistance to German products. Mercedes introduced the pressed-steel chassis and honeycomb radiator. A 1905 model reached 109 m.p.h. (Christian name of Daimler's daughter.)

Merchant Marine Academy, US A training college on the north shore of Long Island, at King's Point, N.Y. Applicants are nominated by Congressmen on a state quota basis and students graduate with a Merchant Marine license as deck or engineer officer, a BS degree, and a commission as Ensign in the Naval Reserve.

Merchant of Venice, The (1596) Shakespeare's comedy; see PORTIA; SHYLOCK.

Merchant Taylors' (UK) A boys' 'public' school which moved to Moor Park, near Northwood, Middlesex, in 1932. The northern branch of the school is at Great Crosby, near Liverpool.

Mercia A kingdom of central England, founded by the ANGLES in the 6th century.

Mercury Roman god equivalent to the Greek HERMES.

Mercury Project (1958) The first US project to put man into space; it achieved its first suborbital flight in 1961 (see FREEDOM 7), and the first orbital flight in 1962 (see FRIENDSHIP 7); followed by the GEMINI program.

Mercutio Romeo's mettlesome friend in Shakespeare's ROMEO AND JULIET, a man of sharp wit, killed by Tybalt in a duel.

Merion, Diana The heroine of DIANA OF THE CROSSWAYS.

Merlin (1) Historically, possibly a bard at ARTHUR'S court; (2) in ARTHURIAN LEGEND, a magician and seer sired by a fiend but baptized; see LADY OF THE LAKE.

Merlin-Rocket (1951) A national class of 14-foot dinghy, a merger of 2 designs by Jack Holt and Ian Proctor.

Mermaid Tavern A famous 17th-century tavern in CHEAPSIDE, London, frequented by Raleigh, Beaumont, Fletcher, Donne, Ben Jonson and possibly Shakespeare.

Mermaid Theatre (1959) The CITY of London's first theater for 300 years, built at Puddle Dock, BLACKFRIARS, on the site of a bombed-out warehouse by the actor-producer Bernard Miles to revive Elizabethan traditions.

Merovingians The dynasty founded by Clovis which ruled the Frankish kingdom (France) 481-752; succeeded by the CAROLINGIANS. (Named after Clovis's grandfather.)

Merrilies, Meg The queen of the gypsies in Scott's GUY MANNERING, who recognizes Harry Bertram on his return from India and helps him to defeat his enemies.

Merrill Lynch See The THUNDERING HERD.

Merrill's Marauders US equivalent of the CHINDITS, operating in Burma in 1944. (Brig. Gen. F. D. Merrill.)

Merrimac and Monitor Two ships which during the AMERICAN CIVIL WAR fought at Hampton Roads (1862) in the first action between ironclads. The Union *Monitor* was the first ship to have a revolving armored gun turret (with two 11-in guns). The action was indecisive.

Merriweather Post Contest A competition sponsored by the Washington National Symphony for violinists and cellists. The first prize is $1500 and a guest appearance with that orchestra.

Merriwell, Frank The athletic champion of YALE, embodiment of muscular Christianity and hero of over 200 dime novels written by Burt L. Standish between 1896 and 1931, when he sank to his true level in a comic strip, only to reappear as an adult in yet more stories from 1941. Sales are said to have topped 100 million.

Merry Andrew A clown. (Origin unknown.)

Merry Monarch A name for Charles II.

Merry Widow, The (1905) Franz Lehar's ever-popular operetta about the dashing young diplomat, Danilo.

Merry Wives of Windsor, The (1601) Shakespeare's comedy of the penurious FALSTAFF's efforts to court both Mrs Ford and Mrs Page, who put him in a dirty-linen basket and throw him in a ditch. Meanwhile Page's daughter Anne foils the advances of Dr Caius and Slender and runs off with Fenton.

Mers-el-Kebir (July 1940) French naval base at Oran, Algeria, where the British were forced to put the French fleet out of action to prevent its passing into German hands.

Mersey sound, The The type of pop music associated particularly with the Beatles who, with several other contemporary groups, hailed from Liverpool Merseyside. ('The sound' was jazz jargon for ultimate perfection in the rendering of rock music, as in MOTOWN SOUND.

Merton London borough since 1965 consisting of the former boroughs of WIMBLEDON and MITCHAM and the urban district of Merton-Morden; headquarters at Wimbledon.

Mesa Verde National Park (1906) A park in southwestern Colorado; in its canyons are the best-preserved relics of the CLIFF DWELLERS, including 'Cliff Palace' (173 rooms) and the 3-story Spruce Tree House (122 rooms).

Mesolithic Age (Middle Stone Age) The transitional period between PALEOLITHIC and NEOLITHIC Ages when with the end of the ICE AGE the steppe and tundra developed into forest and man turned from dependence on herds of reindeer etc. to fishing and collecting shellfish.

Mesopotamia The ancient name of the area now occupied by Iraq, and formerly by Akkad, SUMER, ASSYRIA and Babylonia; generally regarded as the cradle of Western civilization. (Greek, 'between rivers', i.e. the Tigris and Euphrates.)

Mesozoic Era The geological era lasting from about 240 to 70 million years ago, divided into the TRIASSIC, JURASSIC and CRETACEOUS PERIODS. The characteristic fossil is the ammonite (a marine cephalopod, ancestor of Nautilus). The climate was mild; it was the age of the great reptiles (dinosaurs etc.) which finally yielded place to mammals, and of ferns and evergreens which yielded to flowering plants. (Greek, 'middle life', i.e. middle era between PALEO-ZOIC and CENOZOIC.)

Messerschmitt Name of manufacturer (abbreviated to Me) given to a series of German aircraft, including the Me-262, the first jet fighter to go into action (1944) and the Me-109, the mainstay of the LUFTWAFFE in World War II. See HEINKEL.

Messiah (1) The savior and king who, according to Jewish belief from the 2nd century BC onwards, would appear when God had gathered his Chosen People into a new kingdom; the dead would rise again to share in its glories, and God would judge their oppressors. The MUSLIM equivalent is the MAHDI. (2) Jesus who, in Christian belief, was the promised Messiah of (1). (3) Hence, any liberator from oppression. (Hebrew, 'anointed', of which the Greek translation was *Christos*, 'the Christ'.)

Messiah, The (1742) Handel's oratorio on the life of Christ, using words from the Bible, mainly from Old Testament prophecy, and containing such famous airs as 'He shall feed his flock', 'I know that my Redeemer liveth', and the Hallelujah chorus.

Messina brothers Five Italian brothers who from the 1930s to the 1960s made a living out of procuring, housing and fleecing prostitutes in London, Belgium and Alexandria. All served prison sentences and were deported or fled from Britain. In 1967 it was revealed that some of the survivors still operated London brothels by remote control from Genoa.

Met, The Used as an abbreviation for the New York METROPOLITAN OPERA HOUSE.

Metamorphoses (1st century BC) Ovid's version in hexameter verse of Greek and Roman myths involving magical changes of form.

Metaphysical poets A group of 17th-century poets, led by John

Donne and including Vaughan, Marvell and George Herbert; criticized by Dr Johnson for using complex imagery, above the heads of the common reader, drawn from science, philosophy, the arts and theology, and for their innovations in meter. (The name was first used by Dryden.)

Meteor Name of a series of fighter aircraft built by the Gloster Aircraft Co. The E-28/39 was the first British jet plane, powered by a WHITTLE turbojet and tested in 1941. A development of this, the Meteor began active service with the RAF in 1944, and in 1946 set up a world speed record of 616 m.p.h. See JAVELIN.

Method acting A system taught at the New York Actors' Studio and developed from the STANISLAVSKY SYSTEM.

Methodism (1739) The revivalist movement within the Church of England started by John and Charles Wesley; it broke away from the Church in 1795 and subsequently split into various sects (Wesleyan, Primitive, United, Calvinist, Independent), some of which later reunited (see next entry). George Whitefield, an original cofounder, seceded to form the COUNTESS OF HUNTINGDON'S CONNECTION. (Originally 'Methodists' was the name given to the Wesleys' religious club at OXFORD UNIVERSITY, so named for its methodical rules of fasting and prayer.)

Methodist Church In the US, this represents a merger (1939) of the Methodist Episcopal Church, Methodist Episcopal Church South and Methodist Protestant Church. In Britain, the Wesleyan, Primitive and United Methodist Churches reunited in 1932 to form the Methodist Church. See last entry.

Methuselah Son of Enoch and grandfather of Noah; he died aged 969 according to Genesis v, 27.

Métis French for 'mongrel', used of people of mixed French-Canadian and Indian blood in western Canada who live as Indians. (Singular and plural, métis, feminine métisse.)

Métro (1) The Paris subway. (2) Montreal's new subway. (Short for 'Métropolitain'.)

Metro Centre In Toronto, the largest city center redevelopment in North America, scheduled for completion in the 1980s. The developers are the CPR and CNR, using ex-railroad land. There will be: (1) a residential area for 20,000; (2) a shop-office-hotel area; (3) a communications center; (4) a taxi-bus-automobile-train transportation complex.

Metroland The area served by the London Metropolitan District Railway, a nickname given added currency by Evelyn Waugh's fictional Lady Metroland, formerly Mrs BESTE-CHETWYND.

Metroliner Penn Central's heavily patronized (and subsidized) passenger train which averages 90 m.p.h. on the New York-Washington (D.C.) run.

Metropolitan Opera House (NYC) Premier US opera house, reopened (1966) in a new building in LINCOLN CENTER, replacing the 'Old Met' at Broadway and 39th Street.

Metropolitan-Vickers See AEI.

Metro-Vic Moscow trial (1933) The trial of 6 British engineers of the Metropolitan-Vickers Electrical Co., charged by Soviet Russia with espionage and sabotage.

Mets The New York Mets, NATIONAL (Baseball) LEAGUE, playing at Shea Stadium, QUEENS. In 1969, against all expectation, they emerged from comparative obscurity to beat the ORIOLES and become world champions.

Metternich System See HOLY ALLIANCE.

MEU Initials used for Fowler's Modern English Usage, a standard work of reference on the subject, first published in 1926 and revised by Sir Ernest Gowers in 1965.

Meudon, The Curate of A name for Rabelais.

Meursault See BURGUNDY.

Mexican War (1846-48) The year after the annexation of Texas, the US accused Mexico of shedding 'American blood on American soil', i.e. in a disputed area. General Zachary

Taylor captured Monterrey and General Winfield Scott captured Mexico City from Vera Cruz. Mexico recognized the RIO GRANDE frontier and ceded New Mexico and California (where gold had been found) for $15 million.

Mezzogiorno, Il Italian name for Italy south of Naples, until recently neglected and impoverished. ('Noon', 'south'.)

MGB (1945-53) The Soviet Ministry of State Security, the secret plain-clothes police employed in internal security, counterintelligence, and espionage throughout the world; renamed KGB.

MGM Initials used for Metro-Goldwyn-Mayer, a motion-picture company formed from Metro Pictures and Goldwyn Pictures by Marcus Loew, managed by L. B. Mayer. Sam Goldwyn resigned before it was formed. Its headquarters are at Culver City, a suburb of Los Angeles.

MHD Initials standing for magneto-hydrodynamic generator, a new means of generating electricity by sending a stream of hot ionized gas (plasma) through a magnetic field at several times the speed of sound; for use in conjunction with conventional generators.

Micawber, Mr Wilkins DAVID COPPERFIELD's penurious landlord, who lives in eternal hope that 'something will turn up', as indeed it does.

Michaelmas September 29th, the feast of the archangel Michael, and English quarter day, formerly celebrated by eating Michaelmas goose (see NOTTINGHAM GOOSE FAIR).

Michaelmas term (UK) The university and legal autumn term beginning after MICHAELMAS.

Michael X Pseudonym of Michael Abdul Malik né de Freitas, a West Indian BLACK POWER leader in Britain, sentenced to 12 months imprisonment in 1967 for stirring up racial hatred. The *Sunday Times* was fined £5000 for its version of his earlier career. See RACIAL ADJUSTMENT ACTION SOCIETY.

Michelson-Morley experiment (1887) A demonstration that the velocity of light was a universal constant for all observers irrespective of their motion; it was the starting point for EINSTEIN'S THEORIES.

Mickey Finn Any doctored drink intended to make the victim unconscious. (Originally used of 'knock-out drops' composed of liquid chloral and alcohol.)

Mickey Mouse (1) The hero of the first animated sound cartoon, made by Walt Disney (1928); his squeaky voice soon became known throughout the world. (2) RAF nickname for the electrical device which governs the release of a stick of bombs.

Micmac An Algonquian-speaking race of Indians who fished and hunted in the MARITIME PROVINCES of Canada, where they were probably seen by Cabot (1497). They acted as middlemen for the French, who converted them to Christianity, but they fought fiercely against the English. Some 4000, much intermarried, survive. ('Allies'.)

Microbiological Research Establishment A British institution concerned with chemical and biological warfare, with laboratories at Porton, northeast of Salisbury; it works in conjunction with the Chemical Defence Experimental Establishment, also at Porton, and a factory which makes the riot-control gas CS at Nancekuke, Cornwall.

Micronesians The mixed POLYNESIAN races inhabiting the groups of small islands north of Melanesia in the Pacific, including the Marianas, Marshalls, Carolines and Gilberts. (Greek, 'small-island people'.)

Midas In Greek legend, a king of Phrygia to whom DIONYSUS granted his request that everything he touched might turn to gold; but as 'everything' covered food and drink, he had cause speedily to regret his request.

Midas Name of a series of US early warning satellites, first launched in 1961, to detect exhaust gases from missiles at launching.

Middle Ages The period from the deposition of the last Western Roman Emperor, Romulus Augustulus, in AD 476, to the RENAISSANCE of the 14th century.

Middle Congo See CONGO, REPUBLIC OF.

Middle Earth The world of the HOBBITS, where the SHIRE is.

Middle English The form of English spoken from the 11th-14th centuries; by the end of this period the southeast Midlands and London dialect used by Chaucer had displaced the WESSEX dialect of OLD ENGLISH; it is the basis of the spoken and written form now called Received Standard (or the Queen's) English.

Middle Kingdom (Ancient Egypt) The period of some 400 years from about 2000 BC, the second period of Egyptian greatness, when the pharaohs of the 11th-14th Dynasties ruled at THEBES.

Middlemarch (1872) George Eliot's masterly, partly autobiographical, study of the Midlands society of her time, and the impact of new values brought by the Industrial Revolution on 2 young idealists, Dorothea BROOKE and Dr LYDGATE.

Middlesex A county west and north of London, abolished in 1965 and absorbed into GREATER LONDON.

Middle Temple See INNS OF COURT.

Middletown (1929) A study of a typical modern US city, by R. S. and H. M. Lynch.

Midgard In Scandinavian mythology the abode of man, joined to ASGARD by a rainbow bridge.

Midlothian campaigns (1879 and 1880) Gladstone's electoral campaigns which brought him back to Parliament and to his second term as Prime Minister. It was the first direct appeal to the electorate by a Prime Minister.

Midnight Steeplechase, The (UK) A legendary cross-country steeplechase allegedly ridden in nightshirts from the Cavalry barracks, Ipswich, to Nacton Church, in 1803. The only evidence for it is a famous painting by Henry Alken (1839). Also called the Moonlight Steeplechase. (Cross-country races with a church steeple as objective are recorded in Ireland as early as 1752.)

Midnight Sun, Land of the Scandinavia north of the Arctic Circle, where the sun is visible night and day from mid-May to late July.

Midsummer Night's Dream, A (1596) (1) Shakespeare's gentle comedy of 2 pairs of lovers in the woods near Athens, much bemused by PUCK's magic spells, as is TITANIA, who falls in love with BOTTOM, leading actor in the 'tedious-brief scene' of PYRAMUS AND THISBE. (2) Mendelssohn's famous overture (1826) on these themes.

Midway Island, Battle of (June 1942) A naval engagement fought mainly by carrier-borne aircraft, which ended in US victory over the Japanese, a decisive turning point in the war in the Pacific.

Midwich Cuckoos, The (1957) One of John Wyndham's Science Fiction novels, from which the movie The Village of the Damned was made. The matrons of Midwich find that they have mysteriously produced a generation of yellow-eyed children, human in looks but utterly alien and terrifying.

Mif Abbreviation for 'Milk In First'. According to the Mitford family, arbiters of U AND NON-U, putting milk in the cup before the tea is a terrible thing to do, and the sort of people who did it were dubbed Mif.

MI-5 (1909) The British Security Service, engaged in detecting, watching and foiling spies, saboteurs and subversive elements in Britain (see MI-6). When an arrest is necessary the case is transferred to the SPECIAL BRANCH of Scotland Yard, MI-5 is responsible to the Home Secretary but also has direct access to the Prime Minister.

MiG Name of a series of Russian fighter aircraft, including the outstanding MiG-15 (1948) jet plane used in the KOREAN WAR against US SABREJETS; the supersonic MiG-19 (1955), the highly specialized MiG-21 (1959) the MiG-23 (Mach 3), VTOL and swing-wing models. (Initials of Mikoyan-Gurevich.)

Mighty Atom, The (1896) A bestselling novel by Marie Corelli.

MIK For More In Kitchen, the opposite of FHB.

Mikado, The (1885) A GILBERT AND SULLIVAN OPERA. The Mikado orders his Lord High Executioner, Ko-Ko, to execute somebody—anybody—or forfeit office and life; POOH-BAH, Lord High Everything Else, is reluctant to volunteer, although assured that 'criminals who are cut in two can scarcely feel the fatal steel'; the Mikado's son, Nanki-Poo, offers himself, but Ko-Ko has to confess that he cannot bring himself to kill anyone, and bursts into tears. All, however, is eventually settled to the Mikado's satisfaction.

Mildenhall Treasure (1942) A hoard of 4th-century Roman silver tableware of great beauty and in excellent condition, found buried at West Row, near Mildenhall, Suffolk.

Milestones (1912) A comedy by Arnold Bennett and Edward Knoblock about resistance to new ideas through 3 generations. The pioneer of iron ships who is frustrated in Act 1 himself opposes steel ships in Act 2.

Milky Way, The The luminous band of stars and nebulae which encircles the sky; it is a cross section of the flattened plane in which are concentrated most of the stars of the spiral galaxy to which our solar system belongs. The diameter of this incomprehensibly vast galaxy is 100,000 light-years (600,000 million million miles); yet it is only one of perhaps 1000 million such galaxies ('extragalactic nebulae'), of which the MAGELLANIC CLOUDS and the galaxy in ANDROMEDA are visible examples. ('Galactic' comes from a Greek word meaning milky.)

Millamant The elegant witty flirt of Congreve's The WAY OF THE WORLD.

Mille Miglia (1927-57) A famous Italian road race for sports cars, run from Brescia to Cremona and back. (Italian, 'thousand miles'.)

Miller, The Affectionate name for the horse GOLDEN MILLER.

Miller's Tale, The In the CANTERBURY TALES, a typical medieval story of cuckoldry, in which a young lodger persuades his landlord to prepare for a second Flood, while he makes free with the wife.

Million, Le (1931) One of René Clair's early comedy movies.

Millionaires' Row Nickname for Kensington Palace Gardens, London, especially the part overlooking Palace Green, on the west boundary of Kensington Gardens. Formerly noted as the sanctuary of the very rich, it is now largely occupied by embassies, including those of the USSR and other Communist countries, and of France and Israel.

Mill on the Floss, The (1860) GEORGE ELIOT's novel about Maggie and her beloved brother Tom Tulliver who disapproves of the men she loves. The two are reconciled only at the moment of final disaster, when both are drowned in a flood at the mill. See TULLIVER AUNTS.

Milner report (1921) The report which recommended the grant of full independence to Egypt. (Alfred, 1st Viscount Milner.)

Milquetoast, Caspar The chief character in H. T. Webster's comic strip of the 1920s, The Timid Soul; his (and its) name sum him up, and Milquetoast has passed into American usage as a synonym for a man who dare not call his soul his own.

Milton Keynes (1967) (UK) The largest of all NEW TOWNS, in north Buckinghamshire, between Wolverton, Stony Stratford and Bletchley, designed to take 250,000 inhabitants.

Milton's Cottage The house at Chalfont St Giles, Buckinghamshire, where Milton finished Paradise Lost during the GREAT PLAGUE; now preserved as a museum.

Milton Work point count The method of valuing the hand used in most bridge systems: A,K,Q, J count 4,3,2,1, respectively.

Mimi See La BOHÈME.

Mincing Lane. A street in the CITY of London long associated with the tea trade, and later also with rubber and other commodities.

Minerva Roman goddess equivalent to the Greek ATHENE.

Ming dynasty (1368-1644) The Chinese dynasty which ended the Mongol rule of the YÜAN DYNASTY. In art the main features were blue and white porcelain, tall vases with brightly colored floral designs, and lacquer ware; in the 17th century porcelain specifically designed for the European market was first exported. The capital was moved from

Nanking back to Peking in 1421. The CH'ING DYNASTY followed.

Miniver, Mrs The fictional compiler of a diary showing the reactions of an upper-class English housewife to events of the period from Munich to the opening weeks of World War II; published as *Mrs Miniver* (1939) and written by Jan Struther, pen name of Joyce Anstruther.

Minnehaha See HIAWATHA.

Minoan civilization The BRONZE AGE civilization of Crete from 2500 BC till the destruction of the capital, Knossos, by fire, or possibly by MYCENAEANS, in 1400 BC. The Minoans may have originally come from the Anatolian mainland. (Named after MINOS.)

Minorca A medium-sized breed of domestic fowl, kept as an egg producer.

Minos In Greek legend, a King of Crete; see MINOTAUR; PASIPHAË. After his death he became the judge of the dead.

Minotaur In Greek legend the offspring of PASIPHAË, half man half bull, hidden by MINOS in the Labyrinth built by DAEDALUS at KNOSSOS; it was fed by the sacrifice of Athenian youths and maidens. THESEUS slew it. The legend was based on bull sports at Knossos, where paintings have been found of young men somersaulting over the horns of charging bulls. (Minos + Greek *tauros*, 'bull'.)

Mint, The The Royal Mint on Tower Hill, London, where coins of the realm and medals are made.

Mint, The (1955) T. E. Lawrence's diary of his life as Aircraftman Shaw of the RAF. It failed to live up to advance publicity about its revelations of character and motives.

Minton (1793) A still-existing English firm making earthenware and bone china, much influenced by SÈVRES in early years. It produced PARIAN WARE in the 1840s, Solon's extravagantly elaborate *pâte-sur-pâte* pieces from 1870 (they now fetch high prices), and a wide range of other products, e.g. MAJOLICA.

Minuteman (1958) The US cheap, solid-fuel, quick-firing ICBM in service as a retaliatory weapon to be launched from heavily protected, widely dispersed launching pits. Mark III has 'penetration devices' (MIRV) to defeat counter measures. It is due to be replaced by ICM. For the source of name, see next entry.

Minutemen Name given in the AMERICAN WAR OF INDEPENDENCE to the militia, as holding themselves ready at a minute's notice; especially applied to those who fought at LEXINGTON.

'Minute Waltz, The' A piece by Chopin (which cannot be played in a minute) that attained a wider popularity in the movie *A Song to Remember* (1945) about the composer's life, and was also the basis of 'Castle of Dreams', a foxtrot.

Miocene Epoch The third subdivision of the TERTIARY PERIOD, lasting from about 25 to 10 million years ago. PROCONSUL belongs to this epoch. The Alps were formed. See also KENYAPITHECUS AFRICANUS. (Greek, 'less of the modern', i.e. fewer of the modern forms of life are found.)

Mirabeau (Cooking) With anchovies and olives.

Mirabell See *The* WAY OF THE WORLD.

Miracle, The See MANNERS, LADY DIANA.

Mirage Name of a wide range of French military aircraft, including the Mirage IV strategic bomber, which carries atomic bombs. The 111G is a swing-wing fighter, speed Mach 2·1, approved in 1965 for construction by Dassault, the firm which backed out of the AFVG project.

Miranda In Shakespeare's *The Tempest*, PROSPERO's daughter.

MIRV Initials standing for Multiple Independently-targetable Reentry Vehicle, i.e. a ballistic missile with a warhead which, on reentry into the atmosphere, automatically breaks up into several smaller warheads aimed at different predetermined targets — a device to overcome antiballistic missile systems. See MINUTEMAN; SS9.

Misanthrope, Le (1666) Molière's comedy in which Alceste, disgusted with social convention and hypocrisy, resolves to act with complete honesty, with disastrous results.

Misérables, Les (1862) Victor Hugo's story of Valjean, who steals a loaf of bread and goes to the galleys for 19 years. He then begins a new life, succeeds in business, becomes mayor, but is recognized by the police and again arrested. There are famous chapters on the Battle of WATERLOO and Valjean's flight through the sewers of Paris.

Mishnah Oral instruction in the Jewish law, dating from the 2nd or 3rd centuries AD, later included in the TALMUD. (Hebrew, 'oral instruction'.)

MI-6 (1911) The British Secret Intelligence Service (SIS), engaged in spying abroad, often through disaffected nationals. The Foreign Secretary deals with Parliamentary questions about its work. Its US equivalent is the CIA. See MI-5.

Miss America Pageant (1921) An annual beauty contest held at Atlantic City, N. J.; competitors must have a high-school education, and a $10,000 scholarship is awarded to the winner.

Missa Solemnis (1823) Beethoven's *Mass in D*, written for choir and full orchestra, primarily for performance in church. (Latin, 'Solemn Mass', i.e. high mass in which the celebrant is assisted by a deacon and subdeacon.)

Miss Bianca A mouse who appears in a series of books for children by Margery Sharp, first in *The Rescuers* (1959), in which as a member of the Mouse Prisoners' Aid Society she won fame for heroic rescue work.

Mission Control Center The section of the Houston MANNED SPACECRAFT CENTER that monitors and controls all manned space missions.

Mississippi Bubble (1720) Rumors of gold and silver in the Mississippi valley led John Law, Scottish controller of finance in France, to found the Compagnie des Indes, which was allowed to issue its own unbacked currency to finance colonization there. In the year of the SOUTH SEA BUBBLE, public confidence broke and the French government was saddled with a debt of $340 million.

Miss Lonelyhearts (1933) A novel by Nathanael West about a man who writes a newspaper 'lonely hearts' column and in his private life tries to be as useful to his fellow creatures as he hopes his column is. He gets murdered for his trouble.

Miss Muffet The character in the nursery rhyme is said to be Patience Muffet, daughter of a 16th-century entomologist who studied spiders.

Missolonghi The site on the west coast of Greece of a monument to Lord Byron, who died there while working for Greek independence. (Traditional spelling of modern Mesolongion.)

'Missouri, I'm from' A phrase indicating considerable skepticism; from its use by a politician who said: 'I'm from Missouri, and you've got to show me'. See SHOW ME STATE.

Missouri Compromise (1820) An attempt to solve the controversy about whether slavery should be permitted in states newly admitted to the Union; it fixed latitude 36° 30' as the line between free and slave states, but Southern states resented this as an interference with states' rights. See DRED SCOTT DECISION.

Miss Universe Pageant An annual beauty contest held at Miami, Fla.; the winner gets $20,000 and a mink coat.

Mr and Mrs North A couple who, more by luck than good management, contrive to help the police in an amusing series of detective stories by Richard and Frances Lockridge which first appeared in the NEW YORKER (1936) and became the basis of a radio series.

Mr Bolfry (1943) James Bridie's witty play in which the Devil (in the guise of the Rev. Mr Bolfry) descends on a Scottish manse and gives everyone a lot to think about, especially after the umbrella he had left behind makes its own way after him.

Mr Bones The end man in a minstrel show who plays on the bones and, like MR TAMBO, carries on humorous dialogue with MR INTERLOCUTOR.

Mr Britling Sees it Through (1916) H. G. Wells's novel of how the coming of the war affected the life of a secluded Essex village, and especially of Mr Britling, whose son is killed in it.

Mr Deeds Goes to Town (1936) Frank Capra's film of the unsophisticated hero of the backwoods (played by Gary Cooper), who outmaneuvers the city slickers trying to cheat him of a large legacy.

Mr Dooley A national figure created by the journalist F. P. Dunne. Mr Dooley kept a saloon on Chicago's West Side and from 1898 to World War I kept up a caustic running commentary on politics and the American way of life, e.g. (when the Supreme Court denied the Philippines constitutional rights in 1900): No matther whether th' Constitution follows th' flag or not, th' Supreme Coort follows th' iliction returns. The sketches were collected as *Mr Dooley in the Hearts of His Countrymen* (1899), *Mr Dooley: On Making a Will and Other Necessary Evils* (1919) etc.

Mr Interlocutor The whiteface man in the middle of the line of performers at a minstrel show who puts questions to the end men, MR BONES and MR TAMBO.

Mr F.'s aunt In Dicken's LITTLE DORRIT, an elderly dotty widow supported by Mr F. (Finching), and given to remarking á propos of nothing: There's milestones on the Dover Road.

Mister Johnson (1939) Joyce Cary's novel about an African clerk whose imagination outruns his education. Believing his own lies, he finishes up on the scaffold. The story is set in Nigeria, where the author briefly served in the administrative service.

Mr Midshipman Easy (1836) One of the best known of Capt. Marryat's novels of British naval life.

Mr Moto The ingenious Japanese detective in stories by John P. Marquand, collected in *Thank You, Mr Moto* (1936), *Stopover Tokyo* (1957) etc.

Mr Norris Changes Trains (1935) Christopher Isherwood's novel of a corrupt, amoral Berlin between the wars. Mr Norris, pretending to be a Communist, is selling secrets to Nazis and foreigners.

Mr Perrin and Mr Traill (1911) Hugh Walpole's study of rivalry and hate in an English 'public' school Senior Common Room.

Mr Polly H. G. Wells's novel; see POLLY, ALFRED.

Mister Roberts (1946) A World War II novel by Thomas O. Heggen about tedium and tensions on board a US Navy cargo boat; Roberts is a popular lieutenant in an unhappy ship. It was made into a comedy by Joshua Logan (1948) and then into a movie.

'Mr Sludge the Medium' (1864) A poem in Robert Browning's *Dramatis Personae*, in which the fraudulent medium (representing an American, Daniel Dunglas Home, whose séances Browning had attended) makes his defense, putting some of the blame on the public's credulity.

Mr Tambo The end man in a minstrel show who plays the tambourine and, like MR BONES, is questioned by MR INTERLOCUTOR.

Mrs Beeton Abbreviated title for *Mrs Beeton's Cookery Book* (1861), a standard work on the subject, constantly revised and still published today, when the recipes no longer tend to start with 'Take a dozen eggs'.

Mrs Grundy A personification of the fear of what the neighbors will say, who developed into a symbol of English prudery. (A character in an 18th-century play, who never appears but is often invoked, in terms of 'What will Mrs Grundy say, or think?')

Mrs O'Leary's cow See CHICAGO FIRE.

Mrs Warren's Profession (1898) Bernard Shaw's play in which Mrs Warren confesses to her daughter Vivie that her education has been paid for by her mother's takings as a prostitute; the girl's sympathetic understanding lasts only until she realizes that her mother has not ceased to ply her profession.

Mistinguett Stage name of a star of the Paris music halls, whose legs were insured for a fabulous sum. Her real name was Jeanne Bourgeois (1873-1956).

MIT (1861) Initials commonly used for the Massachusetts Institute of Technology, which moved from Boston to Cambridge, Mass., in 1916. It gives higher education in all branches of engineering, architecture, the humanities and social science, but it is chiefly famed for its many research laboratories, uniquely well equipped with a nuclear reactor, supersonic wind tunnel, servomechanisms and electronic devices of all kinds. It has build up a world reputation as a research center.

Mit brennender Sorge Pope Pius XI's encyclical, written in German and addressed to the German nation, condemning anti-Semitism under Nazi rule. (German, 'with bitter sorrow'.)

Mitcham (UK) A former municipal borough of Surrey, since 1965 part of the borough of MERTON.

Mithraism The worship of the Persian bull god (later sun god) Mithras; this mystery religion became popular among the Roman legionaries who spread it over Europe, where it become a powerful rival to Christianity, to which it bore some resemblance. Remains of a temple of Mithras were unearthed in the CITY of London in 1954.

Mitre, The (1) A Fleet Street inn near Fetter Lane, London, frequented by Dr Johnson. (2) A Fleet Street inn west of (1), frequented by Ben Jonson and Pepys. (3) A leading Oxford hotel frequented by undergraduates.

Mitsubishi A group of Japanese firms ranking second to the MITSUI GROUP in its share of foreign trade. Its main interests are aircraft, motor vehicles, shipbuilding, machinery and metal mining.

Mitsui group (1947) A group of Japanese firms, re-formed after the war, which account for over 10% of the country's overseas trade; they build power stations and dams in various parts of the world, and are also engaged in mining, shipbuilding, chemicals, banking, insurance etc.

Mitteleuropa See PAN-GERMANISM.

Mitty, Walter A character in one of James Thurber's short stories who retreats from the realities of henpecked domesticity into daydreams of heroic deeds.

Mizpah The place where JACOB and Laban came to an agreement; the name meant 'watchtower' and Laban explains it in *Genesis* xxi, 49, as symbolizing 'The Lord watch between me and thee, when we are absent one from another', i.e. 'may he guard my daughters from your illtreatment'. But taken literally, and out of context, the name is engraved on rings by love-sick spouses.

MLF See MULTILATERAL FORCE.

M-number In astronomy, the Messier number given in a short list of star clusters, often used instead of the NGC NUMBER.

Moabite Stone (9th century BC) A monument put up by a King of Moab, bearing the earliest known PHOENICIAN inscription; now in the LOUVRE.

Moat Farm murder (1899) (UK) A famous case, depicted on Staffordshire pottery groups etc., in which an ex-soldier, S. H. Dougall, murdered a woman at Moat Farm, Clavering, near Chelmsford. He tried to cash a forged check of hers, and was arrested and executed in 1903.

Mobil Oil Corporation (1966) An oil company, originally Standard Oil of New York (1882), later Socony-Vacuum and Socony Mobil Co.

Möbius loop A model used in topology (the branch of mathematics which studies such subjects as the geometry of knots). A strip of paper is twisted and the ends glued together. If it is twisted through 180° there is only one edge; if through 360°, and cut down the middle, 2 interlocked loops result. It has other unexpected properties to delight mathematicians.

Moby Dick (1851) A novel by Herman Melville which combines a detailed description of every aspect of whaling with an allegorical story of Captain Ahab's obsessive hunt for the white whale, Moby Dick. See next entry.

Mocha Dick (1839) Subtitled *or, The White Whale*, a story by J. N. Reynolds which appeared in the *Knicker-bocker Magazine* 12 years before Melville's MOBY DICK, which it must have inspired.

Mocha ware (1784-1914) Pottery mugs and jugs for domestic and public-house use, with bright colored bands on a brown ground. All have feathery treelike designs, automatically traced out by the spreading of a drop of a preparation called mocha tea applied to the slip while still wet.

Mock Turtle, The A lachrymose character in ALICE IN WONDERLAND who teaches Alice the Lobster Quadrille to a song with the chorus: Will you, won't you, will you, won't you, will you join the dance?

Model T The first mass-produced car made by Henry Ford from 1908.

Moderations See MODS.

Moderator See PRESBYTERIANISM.

Modern Comedy, A (1929) The second trilogy of the FORSYTE SAGA, consisting of *The White Monkey, The Silver Spoon* and *Swan Song.* They tell the story of Fleur, daughter of Soames Forsyte and his second wife. There is also a third trilogy, *End of the Chapter* (1933).

Modern Greats Final BA examination at OXFORD UNIVERSITY in philosophy, politics and economics (PPE). See GREATS.

Modern Love (1862) George Meredith's irregular sonnet sequence on the tragic decline of a married couple's love, based on his own experiences during his first marriage.

Modern Pentathlon An annual world championship in which individuals and teams compete in all of 5 events: cross-country riding and running, épée fencing, pistol shooting and swimming. See MODERN TETRATHLON; PENTATHLON. (Greek, '5 contests'.)

Modern Tetrathlon The MODERN PENTATHLON without the riding contest. (Greek, '4 contests'.)

Modern Times (1936) A Charlie Chaplin comic film satire on the horrors of a mechanical age.

Modern Woodmen of America (1883) A large US fraternal organization.

Modred (Mordred) King ARTHUR'S treacherous nephew. According to Geoffrey of Monmouth, he seduced GUINEVERE; according to Malory and his French originals, she repulsed his advances. Subsequently, Modred mortally wounded Arthur and was himself killed in the last battle in LYONESSE.

Mods Abbreviation in common use for Moderations, the first examination for the degree of BA at OXFORD UNIVERSITY.

Modulor, Le An original system of architectural measurement, invented by Le Corbusier and used in his UNITÉS D'HABITATION; it is related to the proportions of the human body.

Moffat Bible A translation of the Bible into colloquial English by a Scotsman, the Rev. James Moffat. He completed the Old Testament in 1899 (revised edition 1924) and the New in 1925.

Moguls (1526-1857) The Indian MUSLIM dynasty founded at Delhi by Babur, who claimed descent from TAMBURLAINE (hence the name, a corruption of 'Mongol'). Under Akbar (died 1605) and the last great emperor, Aurungzebe (died 1707), the Mogul Empire extended over almost all India. Thereafter their power was broken by the MAHRATTAS, although they ruled at Delhi until the last nominal emperor was deposed by the British.

Mohacs Scene of 2 battles with the OTTOMAN TURKS: (1) In 1526 Suleiman the Magnificent defeated Hungary, which was under Turkish rule for the next 150 years. This led to the revival of the HOLY ROMAN EMPIRE under the HAPSBURGS as the champion of Europe in succession to Hungary. (2) In 1687 the Austrians defeated the Turks and drove them out of western Europe. (Hungarian town on the Danube, near the Yugoslav border south of Budapest.)

Mohammed (also **Mahomet**) Traditional English spellings of the Prophet's name, more correctly spelled Muhammad.

Mohawk One of the FIVE NATIONS; most of the survivors live in the Caughnawaga Indian Reserve near

Montreal, and others in New York State.

Mohenjodaro The chief center of the INDUS VALLEY CIVILIZATION, in PAKISTAN on the Indus north of Hyderabad; it is remarkable for its planned streets, water supply system and covered drains.

Mohicans A confederacy of ALGONQUIN Indians who formerly occupied the region of the upper Hudson.

Moho, The Abbreviation used for the Mohorovicić Discontinuity, the sharply defined boundary between the earth's crust and the mantle which envelops the inner core, at a depth varying from 30 miles below land to 5 miles under the ocean floor; see MOHOLE. (Named after a Czech scientist.)

Mohocks The well-born ruffians who infested London streets in the early 18th century. (Corruption of Mohawks.)

Mohole In the 1960s US scientists planned to drill a bore hole some 7 miles through the earths' crust on the ocean floor near the Pacific island of Guadalupe, down to the MOHO mantle; the project was abandoned for lack of funds.

Mohs scale A scale of hardness (H), in minerals, in which talc has H1, gypsum H2, calcite H3, fluorspar H4, apatite H5, feldspar H6, quartz H7, topaz H8, sapphire H9, and diamond H10. Each can be scratched by all those above it in the scale. A penknife has H6.5.

MOL Manned Orbiting Laboratory, originally a US Air Force project, now under NASA; it is designed to give better earth reconnaissance and space surveillance, and will be manned by astronauts rendezvousing with it in GEMINI spacecraft.

Moldau, The Smetana's symphonic poem, one of the most popular of a cycle of 6 entitled *My Country* (1874-79). (German name of the Vltava, which flows through Prague.)

Moll Flanders (1722) Daniel Defoe's picaresque novel of a lady of easy virtue who becomes an accomplished thief and, after transportation to Virginia, 'at last grew rich, liv'd Honest, and died a Penitent'.

Mollie Parnis A New York fashion house.

Mollusks A phylum of mostly aquatic creatures with nonsegmented bodies, including gastropods (snails, slugs, limpets), lamellibranchs or bivalves (mussels, oysters) and cephalopods (octopuses, squids, cuttlefish).

Molly Maguires (c. 1854-77) A secret society of Irish anthracite miners in east Pennsylvania which terrorized management and workers until, with the help of PINKERTON'S, the leaders were arrested and 10 hanged for murder. The society derived from the Ancient Order of Hibernians which fought the landlords in Ireland (1835-55).

Molly Pitcher Nickname of Mary Hays McCauley who during the Revolutionary War carried water to the troops during the hot weather in which the battle of Monmouth was fought (1778). When her then husband, John Hays, was prostrated by heat she is said to have taken his place and manned his cannon.

Molniya Name of a series of Russian telecommunication satellites; one was used to transmit color TV between Moscow and Paris.

Moloch (1) A Canaanite god mentioned in *Leviticus* xviii, 21, and 2 *Kings* xxiii, 10, to whom the Israelites sacrificed children as burnt offerings at TOPHET. (2) Anything calling for terrible sacrifice, e.g. war. (From *melek*, 'king'; also spelled Molech.)

Molony report (1962) (UK) A report on consumer protection which led to the setting up of the CONSUMER COUNCIL.

Molotov Former name of Perm, a city of the USSR.

Molotov cocktail A homemade anti-tank bomb, first used by the Finns against the Russians in 1940. (Named ironically after Soviet Foreign Minister Vyacheslav Molotov.)

Momus The Greek god of savage mockery.

Mona An island mentioned by Tacitus as being associated with the DRUIDS; it may have been the Isle of Man or Anglesey.

Monaco Grand Prix An auto race
run in May over the Monaco circuit
of about 2 miles round the streets of
Monte Carlo.

'Mona Lisa' (about 1500) Leonardo
da Vinci's portrait of the wife of a
Florentine official, Francesco del
Giocondo (hence the alternative
name, 'La Gioconda'), famous for her
enigmatic smile. It is in the LOUVRE
at Paris, whence it was stolen in
1911 (recovered 1913).

'Monarch of the Glen, The' One of
numerous stag paintings by Sir Edwin Landseer, Queen Victoria's favorite painter. His animal studies
are well observed and well painted,
and possibly this picture should not
have been singled out, as it has been,
for scorn as typical of the philistine,
sentimental taste of the Victorian
age.

Mona's scale (Angling) A scale for
assessing the weight of landed fish
from their length, assuming average
condition.

Monckton Report (1960) A report on
the Federation of Rhodesia and Nyasaland, which recorded African
opposition to the federation formed
in 1953, and recommended the grant
to member countries of the right to
secede from it.

Mondrian A type of design taken
from the paintings of Piet Mondrian
and used in fabrics, decor etc. See
'BROADWAY BOOGIE-WOOGIE'.

Monégasque Of Monaco, the principality at Monte Carlo.

Mongolia See INNER MONGOLIA; OUT-
ER MONGOLIA.

Mongolism A type of mental defi-
ciency associated with translocation
involving the twenty-first chromo-
some marked by MONGOLOID facial
characteristics.

Mongoloid Term applied to races
with MONGOL characteristics—yellow skin, straight hair, slant eyes,
high cheekbones and flat noses
—found in Asia and Europe east of
a line from Lapland to SIAM.

Mongols An Asian nomadic race of
obscure origin, first mentioned by
the Chinese in the 6th century AD.
They emerged suddenly into history

in the 12th century, and under
Genghiz Khan (1206-27) conquered
MANCHURIA, northern India and
south Russia. In the same century
they overran eastern Europe, established the GOLDEN HORDE and founded the YÜAN DYNASTY in China. In
the 14th century TAMBURLAINE created a second empire which collapsed at his death (1405); the Mongols then reverted to nomadic life.
See MOGULS; MONGOLOID; TARTARS.

Monitor (Union ship) See MERRIMAC
AND MONITOR.

Monkey Trial Another name for the
SCOPES TRIAL. (It was wrongly
thought that Darwin held that man
was descended from the monkey.)

Monk Lewis Name given to M. G.
Lewis, author of *Ambrosio or the
Monk* (1795), a psychological development of the GOTHIC NOVEL. A
demon in the form of a monk turns
into a woman and tempts the Abbot
Ambrosio, who is condemned by the
INQUISITION; the Devil rescues Ambrosio but later destroys him.

Monmouth's rebellion (1685) A rising against James II by the Protestant
Duke of Monmouth, illegitimate son
of Charles II, who landed at Lyme
Regis from Holland and was defeated at SEDGEMOOR. See BLOODY ASSIZE.

Monomark An anonymous registered address, in the form BM/XYZ,
London, WC1, obtainable by annual
subscription to British Monomarks,
who redirect letters from it.

Monophysite heresy (5th century
onwards) The view that Christ's
human and divine nature were one
and the same; condemned by the
Council of CHALCEDON, and still held
by the Coptic Church of Egypt and
Abyssinia.

Monopoly A table game belonging to
the snakes and ladders family, in
which rewards and hazards are such
as might occur in the course of large-
scale financial operations.

Monotremata A subclass of primitive egg-laying mammals, represented now only by the duckbill platy-
pus and spiny anteaters of Australia.

Monroe Doctrine (1823) A declaration by President Monroe that, as

USA would not intervene in European affairs, so it expected European countries not to intervene in any country of the Western Hemisphere, other than existing colonies.

Monrovia group (1961) An association of African states formed when Nigeria and Liberia joined with the BRAZZAVILLE GROUP to create a moderate bloc.

Mons (23 Aug.-5 Sept. 1914) The first major engagement of the British Expeditionary Force in World War I, in which the British delayed the German advance to good effect, but were then forced to retreat.

Monsanto (1901) A large plastics and chemicals firm, with headquarters at St Louis, Mo.

Monsieur In pre-Revolutionary France, a title specifically given to the King's second son (the eldest was called the Dauphin) or to the eldest of the King's brothers. His wife was referred to as 'Madame'.

Monsieur Beaucaire (1900) A novel by Booth Tarkington about the adventures in 18th-century Bath of a cousin of Louis XV's, disguised as a barber. A play (1901) and an operetta (1919) were based on it.

Mons Meg A 15th-century big gun at EDINBURGH CASTLE. (Perhaps made at Mons.)

Mons Officer Cadet School (1949) (UK) Originally a school to train national servicemen for commissions in all branches of the army except infantry; since EATON HALL closed (1958) it has also taken over infantry training, and trains candidates for short-service regular commissions, as well as African and Asian officer cadets.

Mons Star See 1914 STAR.

Monstrous Regiment of Women, First Blast of the Trumpet against (1558) The CALVINIST John Knox's attack on the rule of Catholic Queen Mary in England and of the Scottish Regent, Mary of Lorraine; of no importance save for the magnificent title, which has passed into everyday use in the incorrect sense of 'monstrous tribe of women'. ('Regiment' meant 'rule'.)

Montacute House An E-shaped Elizabethan house near Yeovil, Somerset, now owned by the NATIONAL TRUST.

Montagues (Romeo's family) See CAPULETS.

Montagu Motor Museum A collection of VETERAN and VINTAGE CARS and motorcycles at BEAULIEU.

Montaigne's Essays (1580, 1588) The great work of the French inventor of the modern essay, published in 3 volumes 17 years before Bacon's Essays. Theological dogma and academic preconceptions were discarded in an unprejudiced survey of the main topics affecting man in his daily life. An English translation by John Florio was published in 1603.

Monte Bello Islands The scene of the detonation (1952) of the first British atomic bomb, in a ship in the Indian Ocean about 100 miles from North-West Cape, Western Australia.

Monte Carlo Rally A testing car event held in January; individual competitors and teams entered by car manufacturers, from a choice of starting points in Europe and Britain race through mud, snow and mountains to Monte Carlo, where they are assessed for condition on arrival, punctuality at checkpoints etc.

Monte Cassino A hill between Naples and Rome, crowned by a 6th-century Benedictine monastery, destroyed (Feb. 1944) by Allied bombing and rebuilt in 1956. The hill and town of Cassino were the scene of fierce fighting lasting until May, in which Polish forces greatly distinguished themselves.

Montesi case (1957) A manslaughter trial at Venice in which a girl's death was alleged to involve various personalities in Italian high social and political circles; it ended in the acquittal of all the principal accused.

Montessori system A further development of the PESTALOZZI and FROEBEL SYSTEMS, emphasizing self-education by the children themselves through play, minimum teacher control, and the training of hand and eye. (Maria Montessori, Italian educationist, 1870-1952.)

Montezuma Castle One of the best-preserved relics of the CLIFF DWELL-ERS, by the Verde River, Ariz. Built in 5 stories (C. AD 1300), it is now a national monument.

Montgomery bus boycott (1955-56) A Negro boycott of bus services, in protest against racial segregation at bus terminals, organized by Martin Luther King at Montgomery, Ala. where he was a Baptist pastor. See SOUTHERN CHRISTIAN LEADERSHIP.

Montgomery Ward (1872) A large Chicago mail-order firm, with a chain of retail stores.

Monticello (1769-1809) The house designed for himself by Thomas Jefferson, near Charlottesville, central Virginia. It is in a beautiful New World version of PALLADIAN ARCHI-TECTURE modified by the brick-building tradition of the Dutch and English RENAISSANCE.

Montlhéry A banked auto-racing track south of Paris.

Montmartre A hill and a quarter of Paris dominated by the SACRÉ CŒUR. Throughout the 19th century it was the artists' and writers' quarter, and a few still live there, though most have moved to MONTPARNASSE. It is now chiefly associated with night life.

Montmorency Falls A tourist attraction and the source of Quebec's electricity, at the mouth of the Montmorency River where it enters the St Lawrence near Quebec.

Montparnasse The area of Paris (southwest of the LATIN QUARTER) to which most artists and writers moved from MONTMARTRE during the present century, others going to Montsouris further south. Like MONTMARTRE, Montparnasse is also famous for its night life, and the great outdoor cafés such as the Dôme, Rotonde and Coupole.

Montrachet See BURGUNDY.

Montreux Convention (1936) An international agreement to permit Turkish refortification of the Dardanelles, and to prohibit the passage of specified types of warship in peacetime; it modified the STRAITS CON-VENTION (1841).

Montreux Festival See GOLDEN ROSE.

Monty Field Marshal Viscount Montgomery of Alamein.

Monument, The (1677) A 202-ft column designed by Wren and erected at Fish Street Hill, BILLINGSGATE, London, to commemorate the GREAT FIRE of 1666. The energetic can climb the 311 steps to the top for a view of London.

Monza (Park) A banked auto-racing track near Milan, built in 1921; the home of the Italian Grand Prix.

Moo-Cow Contemporary nickname for the 1925 MORRIS-COWLEY car.

Moodies cards (Stock Exchange) Summaries of significant data about firms whose shares are quoted on the exchange, provided by Moody's Investors Service, NYC, and Moodies Services Ltd of London.

Moody Foundation (1942) One of the largest US foundations, which supports educational, religious, scientific and charitable activities in Texas; the headquarters are in Galveston.

Moog An electronic computerized portable sound-effects machine which, it is claimed, can make 11 million different sounds, but only one at a time, and hence chiefly of use for sound tracks and records, although it has been demonstrated in such recordings as 'Switched-on Bach', and 'And the Plastic Cow Goes Moo-oo-oo-G'. Invented by Robert Moog (rhymes with 'rogue') of Trumansburg, NY.

Moon and Sixpence, The (1919) Somerset Maugham's novel, suggested by the life of Gauguin, here represented by Charles Strickland, who abandons his career as a London stockbroker to take up painting, and dies in Tahiti of leprosy.

Moon Hoax, The (1859) The account by Richard Adams Locke of a hoax perpetrated in 1835 when the New York Sun carried a series of articles entitled 'Great Astronomical Discoveries, lately made by Sir John Herschel' which announced that a vast human population had been discovered on the moon. Thousands were taken in.

Moonlight Sonata, The (1801) A misleading name given by a critic to the most popular of the piano sonatas by Beethoven, who intended it to reflect melancholy rather than romantic sentiment.

Moonlight Steeplechase See MID-NIGHT STEEPLECHASE.

Moon Mullins (1919) A comic strip well drawn by Frank Willard; each installment is a self-contained episode in the tenement life of a group of people who have come down in the world.

Moonstone, The (1868) The first English detective novel, by Wilkie Collins, in which the first fictional detective, Sergeant Cuff, solves the mystery of the loss of a huge diamond taken from an Indian idol.

Moor, The (UK) Colloquialism for Dartmoor prison at Princetown.

Moors (1) The BERBERS of northwest Africa (Morocco, Algeria and Tunis) who were conquered by the Arabs in the 7th century and converted to Islam. (2) The Arabs and Moors who dominated Spain from AD 711 to 1238, and Granada until 1492. See MORISCOS. (From Spanish *Moros* from Latin *Mauri*, 'BERBERS'.)

Moors Murder case (1966) (UK) The murder of at least 3 young people by Ian Brady and Myra Hindley as pointless exercises in sadism directly inspired by Sade. The bodies were buried on the moors near Manchester; Brady and Hindley were given life sentences.

Moose, Loyal Order of (1888) A US fraternal organization with Masonic-type rites.

Moral Rearmament (MRA; 1921) A US revivalist movement founded by Dr Frank Buchman which spread to many countries, as BUCHMANISM or the OXFORD GROUP. Its members, committed to absolute purity and honesty, practice group confession and meditation ('quiet times').

Moravians (18th century) A HUSSITE sect founded by Moravians settled in Saxony. It made converts in Britain and America, and is still active in mission work.

Mordred See MODRED.

Morey's Pub A club and bar at YALE

University for Junior and Senior undergraduates; graduates are not admitted.

Morgan A breed of stylish light carriage and saddle horse, about 15 hands, probably a blend of THOROUGHBRED, ARAB and other elements. (Named for the original sire, foaled *c.* 1789, which was given the name of its owner, Justin Morgan, a NEW ENGLAND teacher.)

Morgan le Fay King ARTHUR'S fairy sister, who revealed to him LANCELOT'S amour with GUINEVERE, and carried the dead king to AVALON.

Morgenthau Plan A proposal to 'pastoralize' Germany after World War II (i.e. to destroy its industrial potential), accepted at the OCTAGON (second Quebec) Conference (Sept. 1944) but later rejected. (Put forward by Henry Morgenthau, US Secretary of the Treasury.)

Moriarty, Professor The Napoleon of crime, locked in whose arms Sherlock HOLMES fell to his (apparent) death in 1893.

Moriscos The MOORS who stayed on in Spain after the Spaniards had regained control of the country. The Moriscos were expelled in 1609.

Morland, Catherine The chief figure in Jane Austen's NORTHANGER ABBEY, her mind empty except for romantic fancies derived from too much reading of novels, especially GOTHIC NOVELS.

Mormon, Book of The supplementary bible of the LATTER-DAY SAINTS, a history of America from the time of Babel, predicting the Millennium and the foundation of a New Zion in America; it was written on gold plates in 'reformed Egyptian' and revealed to Joseph Smith. Smith returned the plates to an angel after he had translated them. (Coined name.)

Mormon cricket A katydid of the western states, destructive to crops and range grasses; so named as found where the MORMONS settled.

Mormons Name given by nonmembers to members of the Church of Jesus Christ of LATTER-DAY SAINTS. See MORMON, BOOK OF.

Mormon Trail The old trail from Nauvoo on the Mississippi in west

Illinois through Iowa, joining the OREGON TRAIL through Nebraska and Wyoming, and branching south to Salt Lake City.

Mornay sauce A Béchamel-type sauce prepared with cheese.

Morning Post, The (1772) A High Tory London daily, absorbed by the *Daily Telegraph* in 1937.

Moroccan Crisis (*First*) created when in 1905 Kaiser Wilhelm landed at Tangier and made a speech supporting Moroccan independence and, by implication, against France. (*Second*) an alternative name for the AGADIR CRISIS.

Morpheus In classical mythology, the god of dreams, son of Hypnus, the god of sleep.

Morris chair A large armchair with movable back and loose cushions, the forerunner of modern reclining chairs, designed by William Morris, the English artist-designer and poet (1834-96).

Morris-Cowley (1925) The first cheap British car, selling at £200, complete with what were called balloon tires. It was known by its 'bull-nose' radiator, which had however also been a feature of the 1913 Morris-Oxford. (Named after the firm of W. R. Morris, later Lord Nuffield, at Cowley, Oxford.)

Morte d'Arthur The 15th-century version of ARTHURIAN LEGEND written by Sir Thomas Malory, using English and French sources. The original MS, discovered in the Winchester College library within the last 30 years, and first published in 1947, differs substantially from the version prepared by Caxton, and is now accepted as the authentic text.

Morton's Fork The view that the rich can well afford to pay taxes, and those who appear poor must have saved enough to do so, used by Bishop Morton to extort more revenue for Henry VII.

Moscovite (Cooking) Served with caviar.

Moscow, Retreat from (1812) Napoleon's winter retreat from a burned-out Moscow, begun on October 18th, during which the GRANDE ARMÉE was virtually annihilated,

more by indiscipline than by winter conditions.

Moscow Conference (Oct. 1944) Known by the code name Tolstoy, a meeting at which Churchill and Stalin decided to impose the CURZON LINE on Poland.

Moselle German light wines from the Moselle valley, including Berncasteler; they are less potent than HOCK.

Moslem See MUSLIM.

Mosleyites Name given to the BRITISH UNION OF FASCISTS.

Mosquito (1940) The DE HAVILLAND twin-engined fast fighter-reconnaissance-bomber, built of plywood for speedy mass production and used with success by the RAF in World War II.

Moss Bros. A London firm which built up a reputation by hiring out men's attire for formal occasions.

Moss Bros. championship An international show-jumping puissance competition, i.e. one in which the fences are high or difficult, held at the Royal INTERNATIONAL HORSE SHOW.

Moth (1925) A famous light aircraft made by DE HAVILLAND, from which were developed the Gipsy Moth (1928) and the Tiger Moth.

Mother Bell Affectionate name (sometimes shortened to Ma Bell) for the Bell Telephone Company; see BELL SYSTEM.

Mother Carey's chickens Sailors' name for storm petrels and, formerly, for snow. (Perhaps from Italian *madre cara*, dear mother, i.e. the Virgin MARY.)

Mother Courage (1938) Brecht's play about a camp-following mother whose children one by one meet violent death, in the THIRTY YEARS WAR.

Mother Goose rhymes A name used in the US for 'nursery rhymes' and derived from a legend invented, with much circumstantial detail, in 1860 by a man who claimed to be descended from a Boston printer named Fleet who married the daughter of a real Mrs Goose. Fleet was said to have printed *Songs for the Nursery* or *Tales from Mother Goose* in 1719, but no 18th-century copy was ever traced. See next entry.

Mother Goose's Tales The subtitle of a collection of fairy tales made by the Frenchman Charles Perrault in 1697 including such famous tales as CINDERELLA, BLUEBEARD etc. (French title, *Contes de ma mère l'oye*.)

Mother Hubbard (1) A folklore character, accompanied by a dog, known long before the nursery rhyme was composed in 1804. (2) A long shapeless dress, as depicted in illustrations of the rhyme; much favored by missionaries in clothing Pacific islanders in the 19th century.

Mothering Sunday The fourth Sunday in Lent, the day when apprentices were allowed to go home for the day in medieval times. See MOTHER'S DAY.

Mother of Presidents The nickname of Virginia, the native state of 8 Presidents, including 4 of the first 5 (Washington, Jefferson, Madison, Monroe) and Woodrow Wilson.

Mother of the Gracchi (2nd century BC) Cornelia, mother of 2 famous Roman tribunes, Tiberius and Gaius Gracchus; hence a mother of brilliant children.

Mother of the Red Cross Clara Barton, who organized supplies for the wounded in the Civil War, helped to run hospitals during the FRANCO-PRUSSIAN WAR and returned to the US to press for the establishment of the American RED CROSS, of which she became the first president in 1881. Also called The Angel of the Battlefields.

Mother's Day (1913) A US custom of recent invention enshrined in an Act of Congress setting aside the second Sunday in May for remembering mothers. Brought to Britain by US troops in World War II, and inextricably confused with MOTHER-ING SUNDAY, it has been propagated by all the weapons of modern commercialism.

Mother Shipton (1488-1561) A Yorkshire prophetess, whose prophecies were not published until long after her death. Successive editions were 100% accurate on the past but not on the future; the famous line 'Carriages without horses will go'

was inserted by the 1862 editor, being by that time a safe bet.

Motif No. 1 Designation facetiously applied to the natural composition at the wharf in Rockport, Mass., made by a little sail loft with a siding of vertical brown planks, which juts out into the harbor, and a small vessel usually tied alongside, because the scene has been so often painted by artists.

Motown sound Rock music from Detroit, the 'motor town'.

Moulin Rouge A Paris dance hall, with a show which traditionally begins and ends with a spirited *can-can*; it became famous when Toulouse-Lautrec designed posters for it.

Mound Builders A 19th-century name given to prehistoric American Indian peoples who built large earthworks and burial mounds in many regions between the Great Lakes and the Gulf of Mexico. Later it was found that these comprised several quite separate cultures (e.g. the HOPEWELL CULTURE). The burial mounds possibly date from 1000 BC; the 'temple' or pyramid-shaped mounds of the Mississippi valley from AD 700 to early historic times; the huge Great Serpent Mound in Ohio from AD 500 or earlier.

Mountain, The In the FRENCH REVO-LUTION, the extreme republican minority which, led by Danton and Robespierre, dominated the PLAIN and won complete control of the CONVENTION. (So called because they occupied the highest seats in the assembly hall; in French, *La Montagne, Les Montagnards*.)

Mountain Men, The Fur trappers and traders who in the 1820s and 1830s explored the regions west of the Rockies. They lived in the wilds in primitive conditions, often with Indian spouses, their only contact with the outside world being the annual rendezvous arranged by the ROCKY MOUNTAIN FUR COMPANY.

Mountains of the Moon The legendary source of the Nile, so named from at least the 2nd century AD. Eventually they were identified by H. M. Stanley as the Ruwenzori Mountains just north of the equator on the Uganda-Congo border.

Mountain standard time   The civil time of the 105th meridian, 2 hours slower than EASTERN STANDARD TIME; observed in west-central USA, Alberta and Saskatchewan.

Mountain State   A nickname of West Virginia, the most mountainous state east of the Rockies.

Mount Athos   A peninsula in MACEDONIA, Greece, occupied by numerous long-established monasteries of the EASTERN ORTHODOX CHURCH. It is said that no woman or female domestic animal is allowed entry.

Mount Badon   The site of King ARTHUR's last battle against the West SAXONS at the turn of the 6th century. (Possibly Liddington Camp, Badbury, near Swindon.)

Mountbatten   Family name of the Duke of Edinburgh, the Marquesses of Milford Haven and Earl Mountbatten of Burma. See BATTENBERG.

Mount Holyoke   (1837) The first women's college in the US, at South Hadley, Mass., one of the SEVEN SISTERS.

Mounties   Abbreviated name of the Royal Canadian Mounted Police, before 1920 the Royal North-West Mounted Police.

Mount McKinley National Park   (1917) A nature reserve in south-central Alaska which includes the highest peak in North America (Mt McKinley, 20,320 ft) and where DALL SHEEP, caribou, grizzlies and other unusual wildlife are found.

Mount Palomar Observatory   (1948) The California Institute of Technology's observatory on Mount Palomar, California, with a 200-inch Hale reflector telescope, for long the largest in the world. It is about 100 miles from MOUNT WILSON OBSERVATORY, with which it is administered.

Mount Rainier National Park   (1899) A park in the Cascades, west-central Washington, containing Mt Rainier (14,410 ft), the greatest single-peak glacial system in the US.

Mount Rushmore National Memorial   (1929) The colossal (465-ft high) profiles of 4 Presidents (Washington, Jefferson, Lincoln, Theodore Roosevelt) at 6000 ft in the Black Hills, S. Dak. They were formed (1927-41) by a team of ex-miners under the direction of Gutzon Borglum, using rock drills and gelignite.

Mount Vernon   George Washington's PALLADIAN home, on the Potomac near Alexandria, Va. He was buried there and it is a national monument. (Named for British Admiral Vernon.)

Mount Wilson Observatory   (1917) The Carnegie Institution's observatory on Mount Wilson, near Pasadena, Calif., with a 100-inch reflector telescope; administered with the MOUNT PALOMAR OBSERVATORY.

Mourning Becomes Electra   (1931) Eugene O'Neill's trilogy of plays in which he refashions the story of the ORESTEIA in the 19th-century setting of Puritan NEW ENGLAND.

Mouse That Roared, The   (1955) A satirical novel in which the minute duchy of GRAND FENWICK acquires the secret of a nuclear device and wages war on the US in order to lose, and to insure itself of a permanent income and world peace. In its sequel, *The Mouse on Wall Street*, the duchy makes huge profits by selling gum flavored with its local wine. The Grand Duchess, trying to lose this wealth on Wall Street, multiplies it. A world crisis follows, solved when Grand Fenwick gives its money away.

Mousetrap, The   (1952) Agatha Christie's thriller which has enjoyed by far the longest run in English theater history.

Mousterian culture   The main culture of the middle PALEOLITHIC period, perhaps lasting from 150,000 to 70,000 BC, when NEANDERTHAL MAN appeared, living in caves, making implements of mammoth and reindeer bones, and burying the dead. (Le Moustier, a rock shelter in the Dordogne, France.)

Mowgli   An Indian boy in Kipling's JUNGLE BOOKS who is brought up in the jungle by a wolf, but is later rescued.

Mozambique   The official name of Portuguese East Africa.

MRA   Initials commonly used for the MORAL REARMAMENT movement.

MRP In France, initials standing for Mouvement Républicain Populaire, a progressive Catholic or Christian Democratic party, now replaced by the CD.

MSA See MUTUAL SECURITY AGENCY.

MSG Monosodium (or sodium) glutamate, a white crystalline powder used especially to intensify what remains of the flavor of foods processed for canning, freezing etc. It is derived from the protein gluten, found in wheat. See CHINESE RESTAURANT SYNDROME.

MST See MOUNTAIN STANDARD TIME.

MT Mountain Time, i.e. MOUNTAIN STANDARD TIME.

Much Ado about Nothing (1598) One of the 3 comedies of Shakespeare's later years, mainly in blank verse; see BEATRICE; BENEDICK.

Mufti of Jerusalem Haj Amin el-Huseini, a pro-German Arab rebel in Palestine who was a thorn in the flesh of the British administration throughout and after World War II.

Mug Books The (presumably ambiguous) name given to hundreds of county histories compiled in 1870-1900, with photographs of businessmen and farmers who wanted to see their pictures in a book.

Muggletonians (1651) A sect founded by Muggleton and Reeve, who claimed to be the 2 witnesses of *Revelation* xi, 3. It survived for 200 years, although their subsequent careers must have been difficult to reconcile with the succeeding verses.

Mughal Persian spelling of MOGUL.

Mugwump (1884) A voter who does not support his party's candidate; one who is too detached to satisfy US standards of party fanaticism. (Algonquin Indian word, 'great man'.)

Muhammad Ali See CLAY, CASSIUS.

Mukden Old name of the former capital of MANCHURIA, now called SHENYANG.

Mukden incident, The (Sept. 1931) An explosion used by the Japanese as an excuse for the seizure of MUKDEN, which began their conquest of MANCHURIA and the undeclared Sino-Japanese War destined to last until 1945. See MARCO POLO BRIDGE INCIDENT.

Mulberry Code name for the artificial harbors used in the Normandy landings, 1944.

Müllerliede See SCHÖNE MÜLLERIN.

Mulliner, Mr A P. G. Wodehouse character, always ready to cap anyone's story with a quite incredible 'true' story of his own.

Multilateral Force (MLF; 1964) A projected force of surface vessels armed with POLARIS missiles and manned by mixed crews from NATO navies. It was opposed by France which wanted to develop its own nuclear force, and an ATLANTIC NUCLEAR FORCE was then suggested.

Mummers' Parade An annual parade held on January 1st in Philadelphia, Penn., in which, following German medieval custom on TWELFTH NIGHT, bands, groups and organizations parade for hours in colorful costumes.

Münchausen, Baron A historical person who served in the Russian army and had a weakness for telling the tallest of tall stories, e.g. of snow so deep that he tethered his horse to what he took for a fence and found him next morning dangling from the top of a church steeple. R. E. Raspe compiled an English version of these tales in 1785.

Munich (30 Sept. 1938) A name symbolizing the agreement signed by Neville Chamberlain, Daladier, Mussolini and Hitler, under which Hitler occupied Czech SUDETENLAND, and described by Chamberlain as bringing 'peace in our time'; hence any shameful act of appeasement and betrayal.

Munich Putsch (Nov. 1923) A premature and ill-prepared rising staged by Hitler to overthrow the Bavarian government with the help of Gen. Ludendorff. Hitler was arrested and given a 5-year sentence, during which he wrote MEIN KAMPF. (Plotted in a Munich beer hall; hence its alternative name, the Beerhall Putsch.)

Munsinger case (1966) A Canadian political scandal arising from the association of Conservative Ministers with an alleged German spy, a woman named Munsinger. As in the PROFUMO CASE, the security risk was shown by a judicial inquiry to be minimal, and after bitter party recriminations the whole affair was seen to be best forgotten.

Munster The southwestern province of Ireland, formerly a Celtic kingdom, now consisting of Clare, Cork, Kerry, Limerick, Tipperary and Waterford.

Murano glass Venetian glass; the 11th-century factories were transferred in 1291, for fear of fire, from Venice to the nearby island of Murano, and have remained there ever since. The best was the clear crystal glass made in the period from the 16th to 18th centuries, which was followed by a decline and a revival in the 1850s. Characteristics are light weight, attractive colors, lacelike designs of opaque white threads (*latticinio*) and other ingenious innovations.

Murder Inc. The assassination squad of the Crime Syndicate, a loose nationwide association of Unione Siciliano mobs, reputed to have displaced COSA NOSTRA as the chief thugs of USA. Its main interests are prostitution, gambling, labor-union rackets and politicking. Joe Valachi (see VALACHI PAPERS) revealed its existence to a Senate committee.

Murder in the Cathedral, The (1935) T. S. Eliot's first verse play, on the Thomas à Becket story. There is a chorus of Canterbury Women, and 4 knights offer him temptations in modern guise and language, which Becket rejects. They then become his executioners, addressing their comments on the event directly to the audience.

'Murders in the Rue Morgue, The' (1841) A story by E. A. Poe, published in a Philadelphia magazine, in which the murder of a mother and daughter is solved by AUGUSTE CHEVALIER DUPIN in what is generally regarded as the first detective story.

Murder Squad A small branch of the CRIMINAL INVESTIGATION DEPARTMENT at Scotland Yard to whom murder cases of particular difficulty are referred; officially known as C1 Branch.

Murphy bed A bed which can be folded back into a closet when not wanted. (Invented by William L. Murphy.)

Murrayfield The Edinburgh headquarters of Scottish rugger; the ground is also used for the Highland Games.

Muscat of Alexandria The sweetest variety of grape, provided it is grown in a well-heated greenhouse.

Muscle Shoals A stretch of 37 miles of rapids on the Tennessee River, northwest Alabama, once a barrier to navigation between Knoxville and the Ohio; now submerged by Wilson Lake created by the Wilson Dam (1925) which later came under TVA administration.

Muscovy Company (1555) English chartered company formed to trade with Russia; it opened up trade with Asia via Russia and Persia.

Music of Time, (A Dance to) The A still unfinished series of novels by Anthony Powell (started in 1951), forming a witty study of upper-class attitudes as they have developed since World War I, exemplified by a host of characters who drift in and out of each novel: NICK JENKINS, the narrator, Lady Molly, Stringham, the composer Moreland and the revolting, unaccountably successful, Widmerpool.

Muskogean Indians A language group of the southeast, of whom the CHOCTAW, CHICKASAW, CREEK and SEMINOLE formed (with the non-Muskogean CHEROKEE) the FIVE CIVILIZED NATIONS.

Muslim A follower of the religion of ISLAM; also, as an adjective, 'of Islam'. The more usual Western name, 'Muhammadan' is not liked by Muslims as it implies that they worship Mahomet rather than the one God, Allah. Also spelled Moslem.

Muslim Brotherhood (1929) In Egypt, a politico-religious party even more fanatically anti-West than the WAFD; it was banned in 1954, the year Nasser came to power, and moved its headquarters to Damascus.

Muslim League (1906) Originally an all-Indian religious movement to protect MUSLIM interests in British India; under Jinnah it broke with the Hindu CONGRESS PARTY, (1935) and became a political party in opposition to it, demanding PARTITION (1941). The League continues to function both in PAKISTAN (where its influence has waned) and in India.

Mustapha Kemal See ATATÜRK.

Mut The Egyptian mother-goddess, wife of AMON, usually depicted with the head of a vulture.

Mutt and Jeff (1) Characters in the first daily strip cartoon, Bud Fisher's 'Mr Mutt', published in San Francisco in 1907. (2) Nickname for the British War and Victory medals given to most of those who served in World War I.

Mutual Fund An open-end investment company which makes a continuous offering of new shares and redeems shares on demand at or near net asset value; in contrast to closed-end companies (British 'investment trusts') with fixed capitalization, whose shares are bought and sold by the investor on the market. The British name is Unit Trust.

Mutual Security Agency (1951-53) A US body which replaced the ECONOMIC COOPERATION ADMINISTRATION after MARSHALL AID stopped. After many changes of name its functions were taken over by the AGENCY FOR INTERNATIONAL DEVELOPMENT.

MVD (1946-60) The Soviet Ministry for Internal Affairs which succeeded the NKVD. Its uniformed personnel carried out police, licensing and registration duties and also supervised frontier troops; it issued passports to Russians and visas to foreigners. It was succeeded by the KVD but the title came into use again in 1968.

Mycenaean civilization That which arose in southern Greece *c*. 1600 BC, centered on Mycenae and neighboring Tiryns; it was partly influenced by the MINOAN CIVILIZATION. After a disastrous raid by unknown people *c*. 1200 BC, it declined into the dark age from which the DORIAN states, including Sparta, emerged into the light of history in the 8th century BC. The legendary founder was PERSEUS.

My Fair Lady See PYGMALION.

'My Old Dutch' An old COCKNEY music-hall song sung by Albert Chevalier. ('Dutch' for Duchess = wife.)

'My Old Kentucky Home' (1853) Stephen Foster's nostalgic and sympathetic Negro song; as he thought it was not in his style he let Christy of the CHRISTY MINSTRELS put his name to it in return for $15.

Myrmidons In Greek legend, ants (Greek *murmekes*) turned into human beings by ZEUS; later, the warlike, brutal race of Thessaly led by ACHILLES at Troy. Hence used of a swarm of people, especially underlings or hired ruffians.

Myshkin, Prince See *The* IDIOT.

Mysteries of Udolpho, The (1794) A GOTHIC NOVEL by Mrs Ann Radcliffe, of a heroine kept in durance vile in an Apennine castle by a villainous stepuncle.

Mysterious Universe, The (1930) A masterly popular exposition of cosmogony by Sir James Jeans, now rendered rather out of date by subsequent discoveries.

Mystic Seaport The replica of a 19th-century coastal village, recreated by the Marine Historical Association at Mystic, Conn. Among the exhibits are the whaleship *Charles W. Morgan*, the square-rigged *Joseph Conrad* and an outstanding collection of nautical relics.

N

NAACP (1909) Initials of the National Association for the Advancement of Colored People, a Negro middleclass movement that seeks equal citizenship rights and opportunity for Negroes through direct and legal action, legislation and education.

Nabataeans A people who came from south Arabia to Palestine and, before the Christian era, were able to make the Negev desert flower by an ingenious system of irrigation, and to found an advanced civilization centered on PETRA. They traded widely, learning to speak Greek and ARAMAIC.

Naboth's vineyard An object so coveted that one will commit any crime to get it. (In 1 Kings xxi Naboth is stoned to death at JEZEBEL's instigation so that her husband, King AHAB, can confiscate his vineyard.)

Nadge Abbreviation for Nato Air Defense Ground Environment, an early warning system to detect and track aircraft and feed data to anti-aircraft missile sites and to interceptor aircraft. It is scheduled for construction during the early 1970s in various countries of Western Europe and Turkey, built by an international consortium of firms.

NAFTA Initials used for North Atlantic Free Trade Area, a suggested alternative to Britain's entry into the COMMON MARKET, involving a link with USA and Canada.

Nagas A MONGOLOID people of eastern Assam; although numbering only a million, they began in 1956 an armed revolt for independence of India. Nagaland was formed as a separate Indian State in 1963.

Nagasaki bomb The second and final atomic bomb of World War II, dropped on 9 Aug. 1945. (City of Kyushu, Japan.)

Nailsea glass (1788-1873) English glassware with brightly colored stripes, made into walking sticks, rolling pins, flasks etc., originally at the village of Nailsea near Bristol, but much copied elsewhere.

Naked and the Dead, The (1948) Norman Mailer's novel of World War II, about a US attack on a Japanese-held Pacific island.

Naked Lunch (1959) William Burroughs's beatnik novel which, like the drug addiction it deals with, is an acquired taste, probably *pari passu*.

Naming (House of Commons) The SPEAKER's last resource in dealing with a recalcitrant member; he calls him by his surname (instead of his constituency) and the LEADER OF THE HOUSE then moves the suspension of the offender.

NANA Initials standing for North American Newspaper Alliance, a syndicated news and features agency which includes the Kemsley Foreign News Service.

Nanking china European name for the Chinese underglaze blue and white ware made in great quantity in the 18th and 19th centuries for European markets. (In USA called CANTON CHINA.)

Nanki-Poo See MIKADO.

Nanook of the North (1922) Robert Flaherty's documentary film about the ESKIMOS.

Nantes, Edict of See EDICT OF NANTES.

Nantgarw (1813-23) A porcelain factory founded at Nantgarw in the Taff Vale, South Wales, by Billingsley (see BILLINGSLEY FLOWERS); it produced much work resembling SÈVRES. See SWANSEA PORCELAIN.

Nantucket sleighride A colloquialism for a run in a whaleboat fast to a harpooned whale.

Napier An early British car which won the GORDON BENNETT CUP in 1902 and put up a 24-hour record at BROOKLANDS in 1907 which remained unbeaten until after World War I.

Napoleon A rich pastry consisting of several oblong layers of puff paste filled with cream, custard or jelly.

Napoleon The boar who is the Stalin of Orwell's ANIMAL FARM.

Napoleon brandy A term used by some firms to indicate age and high quality; having no defined meaning it can be used indiscriminately.

Napoleonic Wars (1805-15) The wars waged from the time Bonaparte became Emperor Napoleon, comprising campaigns against Austria (1805, AUSTERLITZ); Prussia (1806, JENA); the PENINSULAR WAR (1808-14); Austria (1809, WAGRAM); the invasion of Russia (1812); the German War of Liberation (1813, LEIPZIG); and WATERLOO (1815). More loosely, the term is extended to cover the wars waged from the time Bonaparte became First Consul in 1799.

Napoleon of Notting Hill, The (1904) G. K. Chesterton's fantasy novel about a future kingdom of London which, from boredom, had reverted to medieval customs. The borough of Notting Hill under 'Napoleon' fights the rest of London over the building of a road.

'Napoleon II' See KING OF ROME.

Narcissus In Greek legend, a beautiful youth who pines away from hopeless love for his own reflection seen in pools, and is turned into the narcissus flower.

Narraganset An Algonquian Indian race, now extinct, which lived in Rhode Island and were almost exterminated in KING PHILIP'S WAR.

NASA See NATIONAL AERONAUTICS AND SPACE ADMINISTRATION.

NASCAR racing Auto racing under the auspices of the National Association for Stock Car Auto Racing, using standard street models adapted within specified limits for racing purposes. The season runs from January to September. See SOUTHERN 500.

Naseby (1645) The first battle fought by the NEW MODEL ARMY, which decisively defeated the CAVALIERS. (Village near Northampton.)

Nash terraces The terraced stucco houses round Regent's Park, London, designed by John Nash and Decimus Burton in the 1830s. Internally, the lofty rooms and long climbs to upper floors make them inconvenient and uneconomic in modern conditions, but a move to replace them was strongly opposed on aesthetic grounds.

Nasmyth's steam hammer (1838) A power-driven hammer, similar in operation to the modern pile driver, used in making heavy forgings, the manufacture of which it revolutionized.

Nassau A former German duchy incorporated in Prussia, see HESSEN; ORANGE; ORANGE-NASSAU.

Nassau Conference (1962) A meeting between President Kennedy and Harold Macmillan at which Britain accepted the offer of POLARIS instead of the canceled SKYBOLT missiles, having just rejected de Gaulle's offer of cooperation in developing an Anglo-French substitute. This convinced de Gaulle that Britain was submitting to a US dominance which he himself was almost obsessively resisting.

Nasser, Lake The name given to the lake impounded by the ASWAN HIGH DAM.

Natasha (Rostova) See WAR AND PEACE.

Natchez Trace Historical road from Nashville, Tenn., to Natchez, Miss., important in early travel. The Natchez Trace National Parkway closely follows this route.

Nation, Carry See CARRY NATION'S HATCHETATIONS.

National, The Common abbreviation for the GRAND NATIONAL.

National Academy of Sciences (1863) An organization set up in Washington, D.C., by Congress to advise the government on scientific matters, with members chosen for distinction in research. It awards gold medals and makes grants for research. In 1916 a National Research Council was established under it to coordinate research resources, and this played an important part in America's military development, in addition to its nonmilitary functions.

National Aeronautics and Space Administration (1958) US government body which controls research and development in the nonmilitary aspects of these fields. (NASA.)

National Arboretum A 400-acre botanical garden just outside Washington, D. C., set aside by Congress for the study of trees and plants; administered by the Secretary of Agriculture, and open to the public.

National Archives A part of the General Services Administration in Washington, D.C., which supervises the preservation of government records, and also the Roosevelt Library at HYDE PARK and the Truman Library at Independence. On display at the headquarters building are the DECLARATION OF INDEPENDENCE, the CONSTITUTION OF THE US and the BILL OF RIGHTS, sealed in glass and bronze cases filled with helium.

National Assembly (French history) Name adopted by the THIRD ESTATE of the STATES-GENERAL (10 June 1789) when it broke away from it. Banned by Louis XVI, it took the TENNIS COURT OATH but dissolved itself when Louis accepted a constitution in 1791. The name was revived in 1946 for the reconstituted Chamber of Deputies.

National Basketball Association (1949) One of the 2 major professional basketball associations (BRAVES, BUCKS, BULLETS, BULLS, CAVALIERS, CELTICS, HAWKS, KNICKERBOCKERS, LAKERS, PISTONS, ROCKETS, ROYALS, 76ERS, SUNS, SUPERSONICS, TRAIL BLAZERS, WARRIORS).

National Collegiate Athletic Association (1905) Founded as an advisory body for collegiate sports at a time it was being suggested that college football should be abolished as players were being killed. At first it fixed rules for eligibility and competitions, but from 1921 it conducted championships in various sports. In 1948 it tackled excesses in college recruiting policies, punishing schools which violated its code. See AMATEUR ATHLETIC UNION.

National Conference (1970) One of the 2 conferences of the NATIONAL FOOTBALL LEAGUE (BEARS, CARDINALS, COWBOYS, EAGLES, FALCONS, 49ERS, GIANTS, LIONS, PACKERS, RAMS, REDSKINS, SAINTS, VIKINGS).

National Convention (US politics) A convention of a political party, usually composed of delegates chosen by state primaries or conventions and meeting primarily to nominate candidates for President and Vice-President and to adopt a platform.

National Debt The total debt of a nation's central government. In the US (where it does not include the debts of the individual states), the National Debt increased a hundredfold between 1865 and 1955 and in 1970 topped $370 billion. In Britain (where it is managed by the BANK OF ENGLAND) it has risen fiftyfold since the eve of World War I and stands at about £30 billion, comprising all government stocks, National Savings securities and the floating debt of short-term loans (e.g. Treasury Bills).

National Defense Student Loan Program A scheme whereby repayment of half a loan to a student is waived if he takes up public-school teaching.

National Democratic Party (West Germany) See NPD.

National Education Association (1857) The most influential teachers' association in the US; it promotes the interests of teachers and improvements in education generally. The headquarters are in Washington.

National Enterprise etc. For classes of boat see under ENTERPRISE etc. See also NATIONAL TWELVE.

National Film Theater The British Film Institute's experimental and research cinema which was developed from the Telekinema built for the FESTIVAL OF BRITAIN, and occupies the same site under Waterloo Bridge on the South Bank of the Thames.

National Football League (1920) (1) One of the 2 major professional football leagues through 1969 (BEARS, BROWNS, CARDINALS, COLTS, COWBOYS, EAGLES, FALCONS, 49ERS, GIANTS, LIONS, PACKERS, RAMS, REDSKINS, SAINTS, STEELERS, VIKINGS). (2) Major professional football league formed in 1970 by a merger of the AFL and the NFL consisting of the NATIONAL

CONFERENCE and the AMERICAN CON-
FERENCE.

National Foundation (1938) Founded by Franklin Roosevelt as the National Foundation for Infantile Paralysis, Inc.; the name was changed in
1958. (Roosevelt contracted poliomyelitis in 1921.)

National Front (UK) A newly formed and ambitiously named grouping
of the League of EMPIRE LOYALISTS
and the British National Party,
pledged to extreme rightwing, ra-
cialist and anti-Semitic views.

National Gallery of Art (1941) The
Washington (D.C.) gallery authorized by Congress in 1937 and built
with funds provided by Andrew W.
Mellon, who also supplied the nucleus of its contents (see MELLON
COLLECTION). Other collections are
the WIDENER, Chester Dale (mainly
French Impressionists) and Kress,
together forming a comprehensive
representation of the major European and American schools.

National Geographic Society (1888)
The world's largest nonprofit scientific and educational institution,
with over 5 million members; headquarters Washington, D.C. It publishes the internationally famous
National Geographic Magazine
(monthly) as well as monographs,
maps, TV and other educational
material. In Explorers Hall are exhibits from its scientific expeditions, e.g. that which discovered
MACHU PICCHU. It also compiled a
sky atlas (1949-56) from observations at MOUNT PALOMAR OBSERVA-
TORY.

National Guard A civilian armed
force recruited and controlled by
each individual state (and the District of Columbia), but equipped and
paid by the Federal government;
they are also liable for service in the
Federal army.

National Health Service (1948) (UK)
The welfare service set up by the
Labour government and established
under Aneurin Bevan as Minister of
Health, financed partly by compulsory contributions but mainly from
general taxation, providing virtually
free medical, dental and allied services for all.

National Hockey League (1917)
Major professional ice-hockey
league. Originally a league of Cana-
dian ice-hockey teams; it now com-
prises 3 Canadian teams and 11 US
teams (BLACK HAWKS, BLUES, BRUINS,
CANADIENS, CANUCKS, FLYERS, KINGS,
MAPLE LEAFS, NORTH STARS, PEN-
GUINS, RANGERS, RED WINGS, SABRES,
SEALS).

National Horse Show (1883) An
annual 8-day show held at MADISON
SQUARE GARDEN, NYC. It includes the
New York Grand Prix international
jumping competition (1909).

National Industrial Recovery Act
(1933) A NEW DEAL measure to reduce unemployment and stimulate
the economy by establishing the
NATIONAL RECOVERY ADMINISTRATION
and the PUBLIC WORKS ADMINISTRA-
TION. The Supreme Court ruled
(1935) that important parts of it were
unconstitutional.

National Labor Relations Board
(1935) The key government agency
of the several dealing with labor
matters, set up during the NEW DEAL
period and continued under the
TAFT-HARTLEY ACT. It determines
'bargaining units' (one union only
represents the employees in the
unit), deals with complaints of unfair labor practices by unions or employers etc.

National League One of the 2 major
professional baseball leagues. Originally the National League of Professional Base Ball Players, founded in
New York in 1876, and thus the older major league (ASTROS, BRAVES,
CARDINALS, CUBS, DODGERS, EXPOS,
GIANTS, METS, PADRES, PHILLIES, PI-
RATES, REDS).

National Library of Medicine Located in the Washington suburb of Be-
thesda, Md., where are also the National Institutes of Health and the
Naval Medical Research Institute.
Since 1963 it has operated a computerized record of world medical literature.

National Maritime Museum See
QUEEN'S HOUSE.

National Medal of Science An
award established by Congress for

distinguished contributions to physics, biology, mathematics or engineering.

National Mediation Board (1934) An independent US Federal agency which mediates in disputes likely to interrupt interstate commerce by rail or air.

National Merit Scholarship (1955) A scholarship given to those who have shown exceptional ability to benefit from a college education; its value varies according to need. The scheme is financed by the Ford FOUNDATION and the Carnegie Corporation.

National Park Service (1916) The US government agency that since 1933 has administered all national parks, monuments, memorials etc.

National Physical Laboratory (1900) A British government institution at Teddington, London, under the Ministry of Technology, engaged in research on industrial applications of the physical sciences, with divisions specializing in molecular science, autonomics, aerodynamics, metallurgy etc. It works in close association with the ROYAL SOCIETY.

National Prohibition Act The official designation of the VOLSTEAD ACT.

National Recovery Administration (1933) One of the NEW DEAL organizations, set up under the NATIONAL INDUSTRIAL RECOVERY ACT, intended to stimulate industry, reduce unemployment and control industrial competition.

National Recreation Centre (UK) See CRYSTAL PALACE.

National Register of Historic Places (1969) A list of over 1100 properties significant in history, architecture or culture, managed by city, county, state, Federal government, private agencies or individuals.

National Research Development Corporation (NRDC) A British government body set up after World War II to finance the development of promising inventions, chief of which has been the HOVERCRAFT.

National Science Foundation A US government body formed after World War II to stimulate, coordinate and assess fundamental scientific research and, with the NATIONAL ACADEMY OF SCIENCES and the President's Science Advisory Committee, to advise the government on such matters.

National Security Agency (1952) The US government agency, under the Defense Department, responsible for code making and breaking, radio monitoring, reconnaissance by satellite and U-2 AIRCRAFT, and other forms of 'electronic intelligence' (see ECM). Its heavily guarded headquarters are at Fort Meade, Md.

National Theatre (1963) (UK) Formed by the National Theatre Company under Sir Laurence Olivier, and temporarily housed in the Waterloo Road premises of the OLD VIC, which it replaced, pending the completion of a new theater on the South Bank of the Thames, begun in 1969.

National Trust (1895) A British organization incorporated by Act of Parliament but financed by membership subscription and voluntary gifts, which promotes the preservation of land and buildings of historic interest or natural beauty for the benefit and access of the people. It owns many famous country houses, gardens, homes of great men, ancient monuments, and whole stretches of countryside and parks.

National Twelve The most popular restricted class of dinghy, for use in inland and coastal waters. 'Twelve' refers to the overall length of 12 feet. It costs about $500.

NATO (1949) The North Atlantic Treaty Organization set up by the ATLANTIC PACT as a defensive measure against the Communist bloc. After the virtual withdrawal of France in 1966, the headquarters were moved from Paris to Evere, near Brussels airport, pending the completion of permanent quarters at Heysel. The organization is directed by a Council of Foreign Ministers; the military headquarters is known as SHAPE.

Nat Turner's insurrection (1831) A slave revolt in Southampton County, Va., led by a Negro Baptist

Sea, father of the NEREIDS.

Neroni, Signora Madeline An exotic creature in Trollope's BARCHESTER NOVELS. The daughter of Prebendary Stanhope, she claims to be the mother of the last of the Neros by a husband she mysteriously left behind in Italy after 6 months of marriage.

Nesselrode An ice pudding with marrons glacés (candied chestnuts).

Nessus In Greek legend, a CENTAUR shot by HERACLES with a poisoned arrow for trying to abduct his wife Deianira. Later she gave Heracles a shirt stained with the blood of Nessus, who had told her that it would act as a love charm; instead it killed Heracles.

Nestlé The largest Swiss firm, with headquarters at Cham and Vevey, which carries on an international trade in tinned milk, chocolates, frozen foods, ice cream and instant drinks.

Nestor In Greek mythology, a King of Pylos who lived to a great age and whose advice, whether because it was wordy or because it was usually wrong, was esteemed equal to that of the gods.

Nestorian heresy That Christ had 2 distinct natures, and that MARY was not the mother of God but only of the human Jesus; condemned by the Council of EPHESUS. The Nestorian Church still exists in Syria, Iran, Iraq and India. (Nestorius, patriarch of CONSTANTINOPLE, 428-31.)

NET National Educational TV, which by 1967 was broadcasting from 126 educational stations. The high cost of linking these to give a coordinated service led to alternative suggestions of joining forces with PBL and the use of a satellite link.

Netherlands (1) Historically, the region of the Rhine, Meuse and Scheldt deltas (equivalent to modern Holland, Belgium, Luxembourg and adjacent areas of France and Germany); see AUSTRIAN NETHERLANDS; SPANISH NETHERLANDS. (2) The kingdom more usually called in English (and often by Dutchmen) by the name of its 2 richest provinces — Holland.

Netherlands Borneo Now Kalimantan, Indonesia.

Netherlands East Indies Now Indonesia.

Netherlands Guiana Now Surinam, South America.

Netherlands New Guinea Now Irian Barat, or West Irian, Indonesia.

Nets The New York Nets, AMERICAN BASKETBALL ASSOCIATION.

Neuilly, Treaty of (1919) The postwar treaty with Bulgaria, which came off lightly, but lost access to the Aegean by having to cede Western Thrace to Greece.

Neuve Chapelle (1915) In World War I the scene of heavy indecisive fighting in which British and Indian troops suffered severe casualties. (Village southwest of Armentières, France.)

Nevsky Prospekt One of the main avenues of LENINGRAD, USSR, which radiate from the 18th-century Admiralty; 2½ miles long.

Newbery Medal The US equivalent to the Library Association's CARNEGIE MEDAL.

New Bridge, The (UK) A voluntary organization which helps discharged prisoners to find jobs and in general to reintegrate themselves into society; there are branches in many parts of England.

Newcastle disease A virus disease of chickens which reduces egg production and paralyzes chicks; preventable by vaccination.

New Catholic Edition (1949) An American edition of the DOUAI BIBLE.

Newcomen engine (1705) An early form of steam engine, used for pumping water in mines; it was while repairing one of them 60 years later that James Watt hit on the idea for his improved model.

Newcomes, The (1855) Thackeray's family saga. The patient, honest, Col. Newcome loses his fortune and retires to the CHARTERHOUSE; his artist son, Clive, first marries the vulgarian Widow Mackenzie and, when she dies, at last wins his cousin Ethel, destined by her family for a richer marriage.

New Deal (1933-39) A series of measures to deal with the DEPRESSION. introduced by F. D. Roosevelt on first taking office, and much hampered by an obscurantist Supreme Court which ruled that the AGRICULTURAL ADJUSTMENT ADMINISTRATION and the NATIONAL RECOVERY ADMINISTRATION were unconstitutional. Other measures included the WAGNER ACT, TVA and a SOCIAL SECURITY ACT. ('A new deal for the American people', a phrase from a pledge made by Roosevelt in 1932 before his election as President.)

Newdigate prize (1806) An annual prize for English verse, open to OXFORD UNIVERSITY undergraduates.

New Economic Policy (1921-29) A temporary compromise policy instituted by Lenin in the face of urban and rural rioting in Russia. It halted the forced levy of food for the cities, and permitted trading for private profit, sale of some farm produce on the free market, and small-scale private industry.

New England Name given to the area now comprising the states of Massachusetts, Connecticut, Vermont, New Hampshire, Maine and Rhode Island, where the first settlers were of English PURITAN stock; for long a center of stability and culture in American life.

New England Almanac (1773-1968) An annual published by the Daboll family of New London, Conn., and then absorbed in the OLD FARMER'S ALMANAC.

New England boiled dinner Boiled meat (e.g. corned beef or ham) cooked with variety of vegetables as turnips, onions, potatoes, cabbage, parsnips, carrots.

New England clam chowder A chowder comprising chopped clams, potatoes, onions etc., and made with milk. Compare MANHATTAN CLAM CHOWDER.

New England Colonial The American architectural style derived from 17th-century southeast England, predominantly using wooden construction, hand-hewn oak frames and clapboard sidings.

New English Art Club (1886) A movement founded by British artists who under French influences became dissatisfied with the standards of the ROYAL ACADEMY. Steer and Sickert were among the leading founder-members of the group, which became closely associated with the SLADE SCHOOL. In 1911 some members founded the CAMDEN TOWN GROUP and later the LONDON GROUP.

New English Bible A translation of the Bible by a British interdenominational committee; the New Testament was published in 1961 and the Old in 1970.

New English Dictionary Earlier name of the OED.

Newfoundland standard time The civil time observed in Newfoundland, ½ hour faster than ATLANTIC STANDARD TIME.

New Frontier (1961) A form of liberal NEW DEAL program first put forward by President Kennedy in a TV program ('The Great Debate').

Newgate An old London prison, outside which public hangings took place until 100 years ago; the site is now occupied by the OLD BAILEY.

New Granada Preliberation name of Colombia.

New Grange A megalithic chambered round barrow of unusual size, in a circle of tall monoliths, near Drogheda, Ireland.

New Hall (1954) A women's college of Cambridge University.

New Hall (1781-1825) One of the 3 English hard-paste porcelain factories, at Shelton, Staffordshire, the patent having been bought from Bristol (see BRISTOL PORCELAIN). Most of it imitated Chinese decoration, pink and orange mandarins being typical. The firm also made inferior bone china from 1810.

Newham (1965) New London borough consisting of the former county boroughs of East Ham and West Ham, with the part of the former metropolitan borough of Greenwich that lies north of the Thames; headquarters at East Ham.

New Kingdom (Ancient Egypt) The period of 500 years from about 1570 BC when the pharaohs of the 18th-20th Dynasties ruled at Thebes; Egyptian power was extended

southwards and as far as the Euphrates to the east; it was the age of
the great conqueror Thothmes III
and of Rameses I and II.

Newlands Corner (England) A famous beauty spot near Guildford,
overlooking the Dorking-Guildford
valley.

New Learning The English form of
the REVIVAL OF LEARNING, inspired by
Erasmus, Colet and More and influencing the English REFORMATION
movement.

New Left A phenomenon of the
1960s, also called the Movement or
the New Radicals, composed of the
children of permissive middle-class
families and given to self-righteous-
ness and the denigration of all ideo-
logies. Its origins lie in the BEAT
GENERATION, the student sit-ins,
VIETNAMESE WAR protest marches
and attempted (but rejected) solidarity with BLACK POWER and the
workers. Variously inspired by Mar-
cuse, MCLUHANISM, Bob Dylan, MAL-
COLM X, Che Guevara, Noam Chom-
sky and Lukács, it regards Russia
and the US (and sometimes even
Mao) as equally imperialistic. Originating in the US, it spread to Britain,
France and elsewhere. Its spearhead
is the SDS (or equivalents).

New Look (1947) A reaction in fashion introduced by DIOR, with long
billowing skirts as a welcome
change from the austerities of wartime and postwar clothes rationing;
the term was later applied *ad nau-
seam* to any change or new development.

New Model Army (1645) The
ROUNDHEAD army as reorganized
under Sir Thomas Fairfax after the
SELF-DENYING ORDINANCE, with Oliver Cromwell in command of the
cavalry; it won its first victory at
NASEBY.

Newnham (1871) The second oldest
college for women at CAMBRIDGE UNI-
VERSITY.

New Order in Europe Hitler's plan
to consolidate the whole of Europe
under German leadership; see TRI-
PARTITE PACT.

New Party (1931) (UK) A short-lived
political party formed by Oswald

Mosley when he left the Labour
Party, which had rejected his plan
to remedy unemployment and economic depression; it was joined
briefly by John Strachey.

Newport, Ind. The site of a factory
which makes SARIN nerve gas and
loads it in shells, rockets and mines.

Newport Tower A round stone
structure at Newport, R.I., thought
by some to have been built by early
VIKINGS.

News of the World Championship
See LONG JOHN SCOTCH WHISKY CHAM-
PIONSHIP.

News of the World Cup The British
short-range championship held under the auspices of the National
Small-bore Rifle Association.

Newstead Abbey Byron's home at
Linby, Nottinghamshire, now owned
by the Nottingham Corporation.

New Stone Age See NEOLITHIC AGE.

New Style The present or Gregorian
calendar; see OLD STYLE.

Newsweek (1933) The sole survivor
of the many weeklies modeled on
TIME magazine; published in New
York.

New Thought A mental and healing
movement started by Phineas P.
Quimby (1802-66) who after experi-
menting with hypnosis advanced
the theory that physical and mental
illness results from mistaken beliefs
and is cured by recognizing that fact
and adopting a positive outlook resembling that advocated in COUÉISM.

Newton Aycliffe (1947) (UK) A NEW
TOWN in Co. Durham, 6 miles northwest of Darlington, designed to take
45,000 inhabitants.

Newton's laws of motion (1) A body
remains in a state of rest or of
uniform motion in a straight line
unless acted on by an external force.
(2) The rate of change of momentum
is proportional to the force causing
it and is in the same direction. (3) To
every action there is always an equal
and opposite reaction.

New Towns (UK) Overspill towns to
take surplus population from conur-
bations, built in most cases by development corporations under various New Towns Acts (1946 onwards); they are taken over by the

New Towns Commission (1961) when development is complete, as with Crawley (Sussex), Hemel Hempstead, Hatfield and Welwyn Garden City (Hertfordshire).

New Wave, The A movement in French novels (the New Novel), drama (the New Theater) and films which began in the late 1950s and appears to be the reverse of the interior-monologue approach, concentrating on objective description, or cryptic, laconic dialogue, from which character and motive have to be deduced. LAST YEAR AT MARIENBAD and GODOT are examples. (Translation of French *La Nouvelle Vague*).

New World Symphony (1893) Dvořák's fifth and last symphony, written after a sojourn in New York, and in part inspired by Negro tunes; there are for example echoes of 'Swing Low, Sweet Chariot' in the 2nd movement.

New York cut Beef sirloin cut with the hipbone included.

New Yorker (1925) An internationally famous weekly which combines political satire, cartoons, humorous verse and outstanding short stories; many famous writers have graduated in its pages.

Nez Percé War (1877) Waged by Chief Joseph of the Nez Percé race of the Snake River area in Oregon and Idaho, who tried to lead his people into Canada but was defeated after a long and wide-ranging campaign against superior US forces. The survivors were settled first in Oklahoma and then in Idaho. (French name, as wearing nose-rings.)

NFL See NATIONAL FOOTBALL LEAGUE.

NGC number In astronomy, the number given to star clusters, galaxies and clouds of gas, in the New General Catalogue, a 19th-century revision of Herschel's list. See M-NUMBER.

NHL See NATIONAL HOCKEY LEAGUE.

Niagara Falls (1) Twin cataracts divided by Goat Island into the Horseshoe Fall (Ontario) and the American Fall (New York State), together carrying the world's greatest volume of water. The height of the falls var-

ies by as much as 30 ft according to the amount of water taken to supply the world's largest concentration of hydroelectric power. (2) Name of twin US and Canadian towns on either side.

Nibelungenlied (Lay of the NIBELUNGS) A 13th-century German epic poem based on stories in the Scandinavian VOLSUNGA SAGA and the EDDA, combined with legends of Germanic westward migrations under pressure from the HUNS. It tells the story of SIEGFRIED, HAGEN and KRIEMHILD. See next entry.

Nibelungs (1) In Scandinavian mythology a race of dwarfs who possess a hoard of gold. (2) In the NIBELUNGENLIED the name passed to successive owners of the gold, i.e. SIEGFRIED's men and the Burgundians. See RING OF THE NIBELUNGS.

Nicaea, Council of (325) The first Ecumenical Council, summoned by the Emperor Constantine the Great to crush the ARIAN HERESY; it issued the NICENE CREED defining the mystery of the TRINITY and affirming the consubstantiality of the Son of God; it also fixed the date of EASTER. (Nicaea in Bithynia, Asia Minor; now Iznik, Turkey.)

Nicene Creed The one creed that unites the Roman Catholic, ANGLICAN and EASTERN ORTHODOX CHURCHES (the last introducing modifications), drawn up by the Council of NICAEA to combat the ARIAN HERESY, and enlarged by the Council of Constantinople. Used at Mass and Holy Communion.

Nicholas Nickleby (1839) Dickens's novel in which the hero goes around rescuing the victims of improbable cruelty; redeemed in part by the picture of Wackford SQUEERS at DOTHEBOYS HALL and other minor characters.

Nicol prism An optical device for producing plane-polarized light.

Niehan clinic A Swiss clinic where Dr Niehan gave transfusions to keep old age at bay, attended by many very prominent personalities in the 1950s.

Nietzschean Connected with Nietzsche's view, deduced from nature, that the force behind life is not desire for happiness and well-being but a drive towards transformation, strength and growth, which he called 'the will to power'. See SUPERMAN. (Friedrich Nietzsche, German philosopher, 1844-1900.)

Nigger of the 'Narcissus', The (1897) Joseph Conrad's sea story of James Wait, a Negro dying of tuberculosis, and of Donkin, the mean-spirited offspring of the slums who nearly starts a mutiny.

'Night' and 'Day' (1929) Epstein's stone carvings on the outside walls of the headquarters of London Transport, in Broadway, Westminster.

'Night before Christmas, The' (1823) Clement Clarke Moore's poem, also known as 'A Visit from St Nicholas', which became the standard version of the Santa Claus legend.

Nightmare Abbey (1818) Thomas Love Peacock's plotless novel, characteristically replete with delightful satire on the current absurdities of his day, and especially on Coleridge, Byron and Shelley.

Night of the Long Knives (30 June 1934) A name given to the massacre on Hitler's orders of Röhm and other Storm Troopers (see SA).

Night Thoughts, Young's (1742-45) In full, Edward Young's *The Complaint: Night-Thoughts on Life, Death, and Immortality*, verse of portentous solemnity and deep melancholy, tailored to suit the contemporary taste.

'Night Watch, The' (1642) Rembrandt's painting of a militia company of musketeers about to set out; it was commissioned by the officers, who were not at all pleased with it. Now in the Rijksmuseum, Amsterdam.

Nike (1953) US surface-to-air interceptor missile, which became the chief antiaircraft weapon guarding American cities and strategic points. See next entry.

Nike-Ajax US missile, the first to intercept an aircraft (1951); range 30 miles. See NIKE-HERCULES.

Nike Apteros Wingless Victory, or Athene-Nike, to whom the small but lovely temple at the entrance to the Acropolis is dedicated. ATHENE is called 'wingless' in distinction from the goddess Nike (Victory) herself, who was represented as winged. (Greek name.)

Nike-Hercules (1958) US Army's solid-fuel surface-to-air guided missile which superseded NIKE-AJAX; it travels at 3 times the speed of sound over a range of 75 miles and is designed to carry a nuclear warhead. It was reported to have destroyed a target at 70,000 feet.

Nike-X system A development of the NIKE-ZEUS SYSTEM using MAR radar and SPARTAN and SPRINT missiles.

Nike-Zeus system (1963) An antiballistic missile (ABM) system developed experimentally from SAGE, using ZEUS ABMs to intercept missiles several hundred miles away at heights of 60 miles. Its construction was delayed by cost and other considerations, and it then became obsolete, since it would not have given protection against the latest penaids (penetration aid devices); see NIKE-X.

Nile, Battle of the (1798) Nelson's victory off Abukir, which cut off Napoleon's forces in Egypt.

Nimbus (1964) A series of weather satellites which supplements the TIROS series by sending back infrared pictures of the night side of the earth. *Nimbus 3* (1969) was the first NASA spacecraft to use a nuclear power system, a SNAP generator, as part of its equipment.

Nimrod (1) Described in Genesis x, 9-11, as ruler of Shinar (Sumeria) and a mighty hunter (i.e. of men) before the Lord; he has not been identified from local records. (2) Pen name of C. J. Apperley (1779-1843), the sporting writer who wrote, in particular, about the prodigious John Mytton. His books were illustrated with ALKEN PRINTS.

Nimrod accelerator See RUTHERFORD LABORATORY.

Nimrod aircraft The world's first all-jet sea-reconnaissance aircraft, a HAWKER SIDDELEY version of the COMET 4C which replaced the SHACKLETON (1969). They carry MAD and other detector devices.

Nimrud The earliest capital of the ASSYRIAN empire, near NINEVEH, during a period of expansion in the 9th century BC under Ashurbanipal II and his successors.

Nine Tailors A bellringing term which became known outside the world of bellringers through Dorothy L. Sayers's murder story of that name, the plot of which (elucidated, as usual, by Lord Peter WIMSEY) is interwoven with a study of the subject. (Tailor for 'teller', a stroke on the bell at a funeral; 6 for a woman, 9 for a man.)

1984 (1949) George Orwell's terrifying novel of a future totalitarian state where citizens are watched through a TV system installed in every home ('Big Brother is watching you'); words are twisted to mean their opposite ('newspeak'); the Party line is continually changed, creating mutually contradictory dogmas which nevertheless have to be accepted (by a process he calls 'doublethink'); and those who fall from grace become 'unpersons', all mention of whom is systematically expunged from the records.

1914 Star (Mons Medal) The medal given to members of the British Expeditionary Force who served in France or Belgium before 23 November 1914.

Nineteen Propositions (1642) The LONG PARLIAMENT's demand for control of government, the immediate cause of the ENGLISH CIVIL WAR.

19th Amendment (1920) The amendment to the American Constitution which introduced women's suffrage.

Nineveh The ASSYRIAN capital in succession to NIMRUD, from the 8th century until it was destroyed by the MEDES in 612 BC. Its site is on the Tigris near Mosul, at a place now called Kuyunjik.

Ninth Commandment 'Thou shalt not bear false witness' (Exodus xx, 16). To Roman Catholics this is the Eighth Commandment.

Niobe In Greek legend, wife of AMPHION; because she boasted that she had more children than their mother, APOLLO and ARTEMIS killed all 12

of them. Niobe returned to her country Lydia and asked ZEUS to turn her to stone; this he did, and her tears ran eternally down the rock face.

Nipmuck An Indian hunting tribe of the Rhode Island region who were almost exterminated in KING PHILIP'S WAR.

Nipponese The Japanese; Nipponism, the spirit of self-sacrificial patriotism. (Japanese nippon, 'Japan'.)

NIRA See NATIONAL INDUSTRIAL RECOVERY ACT.

Nirvana A Buddhist concept, not clearly defined by BUDDHA, which to some means complete annihilation of the individual self, and to others the absorption of self in 'the All', a state of perfect serenity attained by the eradication of all desire for the things of the senses through following Buddhist precepts.

Nisei A person of Japanese descent born in USA.

Nissen hut (1916) A tunnel-shaped hut, similar to a QUONSET HUT, of corrugated iron on a cement foundation, invented by Col. Nissen (RE), and first used on the Western Front in World War I.

Nivelle offensive (Apr.-May 1917) An ambitiously planned all-out attack on the line of the River Aisne (including the CHEMIN DES DAMES) in World War I by the overconfident French General Nivelle. French losses were enormous, and 54 Divisions mutinied; Pétain replaced Nivelle and succeeded in restoring discipline. Sometimes called Second Aisne.

Nivernaise (Cooking) With carrots.

Nizhni Novgorod Old name of Gorki, a city of the USSR.

NKVD (1935-46) The Soviet People's Commissariat for Internal Affairs, which absorbed the OGPU and included the Administration for State Security. It was responsible under the 3 successive leaders, Yagoda, Yezhov and Beria, for waves of mass purges and the running of the slave-labor camps. It was renamed the MVD.

NLF Initials used for National Liberation Front. (1) In VIETNAM, an organization (1960) that includes non-Communist nationalists but is controlled by Communists. In 1969 it was given the status of 'provisional government of (all) Vietnam'. (2) In Yemen, the political party which came out on top when South Yemen became independent (1967).

NLRB See NATIONAL LABOR RELATIONS BOARD.

NN A voluntary organization in London to help mental patients discharged from hospital to refind their place in society. (Initials of Neurotics Nomine.)

Nobel prizes Founded by the Swedish inventor of dynamite, Alfred Nobel (died 1896), and awarded for the year's most outstanding work in literature, physics, chemistry, medicine or physiology, and the promotion of peace; they are worth some $70,000 each.

Nob Hill One of the hills of San Francisco, rising almost from the water's edge, famous for its large Victorian houses of bizarre extravagance built there by 19th-century tycoons.

Nod, Land of A name from *Genesis* iv, 16: 'Cain . . . dwelt in the land of Nod, on the east of Eden'. Swift first used it in the sense 'sleep', since when it has become standard usage in the nursery.

Nok culture (5th century BC-2nd century AD) The culture of a region of Northern Nigeria, southwest of Jos, where numerous remarkable terra-cotta heads were found in the 1940s.

Noli me tangere Name given to paintings of Christ appearing to MARY MAGDALENE at the Sepulcher. (Latin for 'touch me not', the phrase used by Jesus in *John* xx, 17.)

Noll A nickname for Oliver Cromwell, also called Old Noll; see next entry.

Nolly A now obsolete abbreviation for Oliver; applied particularly to Goldsmith; of whom David Garrick wrote unkindly: Here lies Nolly Goldsmith, for shortness called Noll, / Who wrote like an angel but talk'd like poor Poll.

Nomanhan incident (May 1939) The first of a series of little publicized Japanese attempts to invade Siberia from the Mongolia-MANCHUKUO bor-

der, decisively repulsed by Zhukov.

Nonconformist conscience, The The moral rectitude of NONCONFORMISTS, especially as manifested in British politics during the period (up to the time of Lloyd George) when they were a main source of Liberal Party strength.

Nonconformists Protestants who would not conform with the principles of the Established Anglican Church, in particular rejecting the rule of bishops. They include the BAPTISTS, INDEPENDENTS, (English) PRESBYTERIANS (see EPISCOPALIANS), and METHODISTS. Up to the RESTORATION, they were called PURITANS or Dissenters.

Nonintervention Committee (1936-39) A farcical committee, mainly Anglo-French, set up to stop foreign intervention in the SPANISH CIVIL WAR. Supplies, arms, troops, planes and volunteers continued to pour into Spain from many quarters, and Italian submarines sank shipping in the Mediterranean, while the committee pursued its endless deliberations.

Non-Proliferation Treaty (1968) An international treaty signed after 10 years of negotiation, by which the nuclear powers undertake not to help others to manufacture or acquire nuclear weapons, and nonnuclear-weapon states undertake not to try to acquire them. (Sometimes abbreviated to NPT.)

Nonsuch (1539) A huge palace built for Henry VIII in Nonsuch Park, on the Epsom road near Ewell, Surrey; only the foundations remain.

No Orchids for Miss Blandish (1939) A novel by J. Hadley Chase for the tough sex market; it is an admitted English plagiarism of William Faulkner's potboiler, *Sanctuary* (1931).

Nô play A highly stylized 17th-century Japanese form of historical drama; the 2 main actors wear masks and elaborate costume, and are assisted by dancers, singers and a narrator; the performance lasts some 7 hours.

'No Popery' riots Another name for the GORDON RIOTS.

Norad Initials standing for the North

American Air Defense Command, which has a control center and command post near COLORADO SPRINGS, Col., coordinating the air defense of Canada and the USA. See CHEYENNE MOUNTAIN.

Nordic A term sometimes applied to the tall fair-haired racial type of Scandinavia. There is a small Nordic element in Germany (as there is in Britain), and Nazi theorists were able to persuade themselves that the Germans were, under the leadership of the dark and undersized Hitler and Goebbels, essentially Nordic. See ARYAN MYTH.

Nordic Council A body formed by the governments of Scandinavia, Finland and Iceland which has achieved a certain degree of economic coordination between these countries.

Nordic events (Skiing) Cross-country skiing races, and ski jumping; see ALPINE EVENTS.

Nore Mutiny (1797) A mutiny in the British North Sea Fleet following a mutiny a month earlier in the Channel Fleet at Spithead, which had won pay increases. At the Nore, however, some of the mutineers, inspired by the FRENCH REVOLUTION, demanded not only improved conditions but political reforms. Their leaders were hanged, and the fleet put to sea the same year to win CAMPERDOWN. (Anchorage near Sheerness in the Thames Estuary.)

Norfolk A naval base in southeast Virginia, headquarters of the Supreme Allied Commander, Atlantic, a NATO command.

N or M The answer to the first question (What is your name?) in the Anglican catechism. (Stands for 'state your name or names'; M is a corruption of NN; N stands for Latin *nomen*, 'name', and its duplication is the medieval copyists' shorthand method of indicating the plural.)

Norma (1831) Bellini's opera set in Roman Gaul. The DRUID high priestess, Norma, falls in love with a Roman proconsul and sacrifices her life for him.

Norman architecture (11th-12th centuries) The English form of RO-

MANESQUE ARCHITECTURE, exemplified in Winchester, Durham and St Albans cathedrals, and the Abbey Church of Tewkesbury.

Normande (Cooking) With shellfish or fish sauce; or with apples.

Normans See VIKINGS.

Norns The 3 Fates of Scandinavian mythology who water YGGDRASIL.

Norris, Aunt In Jane Austen's MANSFIELD PARK, the selfish, poisonous aunt of the BERTRAM FAMILY, who bullies the heroine, Fanny Price.

Norsemen See VIKINGS.

North and Hillard Names of coauthors used as short title of a standard school textbook on Latin prose.

Northanger Abbey (1818) Jane Austen's novel; see MORLAND, CATHERINE.

North Atlantic Treaty (1949) See ATLANTIC PACT.

Northcliffe Lectures in Literature Annual lectures on English and foreign literature, given under the auspices of the UNIVERSITY COLLEGE, LONDON UNIVERSITY. (Named after Lord Northcliffe, newspaper proprietor.)

Northcliffe Press The London *Daily Mail* (1896), *Daily Mirror* (1903) and other papers started or owned by Alfred Harmsworth (Lord Northcliffe), who died in 1922. For a few years he also controlled *The Times*, but this would hardly be included by the term, which stood for cheap sensational journalism. Later the group was named the Amalgamated Press.

Northeastern University (1898) At Boston, Mass.

Northeast Passage Sea route north of Russia, the search for which began with Chancellor's voyage to the White Sea (1553) but was not successful until 1879.

Northern Earls, Rising of the (1569) One of several Roman Catholic plots to dethrone Elizabeth I.

Northern Lights Another name for the AURORA BOREALIS.

Northern Rhodesia Renamed Zambia in 1964 on gaining independence.

Northern Spy A red-striped late-keeping American apple used for cooking, dessert and canning.

North German Confederation (1866-71) A grouping of the German states north of the Main (i.e. excluding Baden, Württemberg and Bavaria) under the King of Prussia as President, with Bismarck as Chancellor; incorporated in the German Empire in 1871.

North of Boston (1914) A collection of Robert Frost's poems published in England, containing some of his best-known works, e.g. 'Mending Wall' ('Good fences make good neighbors'), 'The Death of the Hired Man', 'Home Burial'.

North Rhine-Westphalia A *Land* of Western Germany, capital Düsseldorf, formed from WESTPHALIA and part of the old RHINE PROVINCE.

North Star Polaris, the Pole Star, a bright star in the LITTLE DIPPER to which the Pointers of the GREAT BEAR point.

North Stars The Minnesota North Stars, NATIONAL HOCKEY LEAGUE.

North Star State Nickname of Minnesota.

Northstead, Manor of (UK) The stewardship of this manor (in Yorkshire) is a fictitious office serving the same purpose as the CHILTERN HUNDREDS.

Northwestern University (1851) At Evanston, Ill.

North-West Frontier Province An Indian province created (1901) for the better administration of the troublesome PATHANS on the Afghan border; now part of West PAKISTAN.

Northwest Passage Sea route north of Canada, sought from Tudor times as a possibly shorter route to the East; discovered by Franklin (1847) but not traversed till 1905.

Northwest Passage (1937) A carefully researched historical novel by Kenneth Roberts based on the account by Major Robert Rogers (a Loyalist American soldier) of his search for an overland route to the northwest in the 1760s.

Northwest Territories The largest administrative unit of Canada, almost uninhabited (population 33,000), extending right across the north and including the Arctic islands (e.g. Baffin, Ellesmere) and areas of tundra and permafrost. Hardy tourists go there for the fishing (including ice fishing), hunting and sailing.

Norwich School (1803) A school of English landscape painters founded by J. S. Cotman and John Crome, who both lived at Norwich. They had many followers, including their sons.

Nosey Parker A colloquialism for 'inquisitive busybody'.

Nostradamus Occasionally used as a synonym for 'prophet'. (From the Latinized name of a French doctor, de Nostredame, who in 1555 published some remarkable verse apparently referring to such future events as the FRENCH REVOLUTION, Hitler's regime and air bombardment.)

Nostromo (1904) Joseph Conrad's best novel, about the demoralizing effect of the greed for riches (represented by the local silver mines) on a closed community in a small South American republic. (For Italian *nostr' uomo*, 'our man', i.e. the mining firm's chief stevedore, a central character.)

Notes and Queries (1846) A British monthly, formerly weekly, paper devoted to oddments of information likely to be of interest to antiquaries and literary men; it also provides a forum in which they can answer one another's questions.

Notes of a Native Son (1955) James Baldwin's angry indictment of the treatment of Negroes in America; it was followed by *More Notes of a Native Son* (1961).

Notre-Dame The name in French-speaking countries of many churches dedicated to Our Lady, but used specifically of the cathedral in Paris.

Notre Dame de Paris (1831) Victor Hugo's novel, set in the 15th century, about Quasimodo, the hunchback bell ringer of NOTRE-DAME, who saves the gypsy dancer Esmeralda from the lustful Archdeacon Frollo, whom he hurls to his death from the top of the cathedral.

Nottingham Club A calling system at bridge in which an opening bid of 1 club indicates great strength.

Nottingham Goose Fair (1284) A fair

held on the first Thursday of October, in olden times lasting 3 weeks and selling huge quantities of geese; the only survivor of several goose fairs held at MICHAELMAS, now chiefly of historical interest and not selling geese.

Nottingham ware (1690-1800) (UK) A fine lustrous salt-glaze stoneware, also called brownware, variously decorated. Jugs and mugs were the commonest form. The name is also given to the inferior products of numerous factories in the Nottingham district.

Nouvelle Vague, La See NEW WAVE.

Novum Organum Francis Bacon's revolutionary work (1620) stressing the superiority of inductive reasoning, from particular instances to general laws, over the prevailing ARISTOTELIAN METHOD. (Latin, 'new instrument', i.e. for scientific and philosophical investigations.)

Now Generation A name for the youth of the 1960s.

NPD (1965) The West German right-wing National Democratic Party. (Initials of Nationaldemokratische Partei Deutschlands.)

NQU Initials used in some families for 'not quite us', i.e. deemed slightly lower in the social pecking order. There are numerous variants.

NRA (1) National Rifle Association. (2) NATIONAL RECOVERY ADMINISTRATION.

NSA (1) See NATIONAL SECURITY AGENCY. (2) The National Student Association, a body of American college students regarded as revolutionary at home but accused in 1967 of having long been subsidized by the CIA to oppose Communists at international youth congresses.

NSDAP Nationalsozialistische Deutsche Arbeiterpartei, The National Socialist German Workers' Party, i.e. Hitler's Nazi party.

NSF See NATIONAL SCIENCE FOUNDATION.

NSMAPMAWOL Initials of 'Not so much a programme, more a way of life', the BBC's successor to TW3.

NTSC Initials standing for the American system of color TV, which resembles PAL. (National Television System Committee.)

Nuffield College, OXFORD (1937) A postgraduate college to encourage research, especially in social studies, founded by Lord Nuffield.

Nuffield Foundation (1943) Endowed by Viscount Nuffield (William Morris, the car manufacturer) with $25 million of stocks in his companies, it promotes, primarily, medical and sociological research; it represents only part of the money he gave away during his lifetime, estimated to total about $70 million.

Nuits-St Georges See CÔTE DE NUITS.

Number One, London The proud old postal address of APSLEY HOUSE in Piccadilly, the First Duke of Wellington's home.

Numbers The fourth book of the PENTATEUCH, recounting the wanderings of the Israelites in the desert and their invasion of CANAAN. (The title refers to the census of the people, *Numbers* i, 2.)

'Number 2, The Pines' (1920) Max Beerbohm's miniature masterpiece, a biographical sketch of Swinburne and Watts-Dunton, named after the Putney house where they lived together (1879-1909). It appears in a volume of essays, *And Even Now*.

Numidians See BERBERS.

Nunc Dimittis The first words, used as the title, of the canticle taken from *Luke* ii, 29: 'Lord, now lettest thou thy servant depart in peace'; used as a noun phrase meaning 'readiness to die'. (Latin, 'now dismiss thou'.)

Nunn May spy case (1946) (UK) The trial of Alan Nunn May, sentenced to 10 years imprisonment for passing information to Russia regarding the atomic bomb, 'as a contribution to the safety of mankind'; released 1952. See OTTAWA SPY RING.

Nun's Priest's Tale, The In the CANTERBURY TALES, the story of how CHANTICLEER AND PERTELOTE outwit a fox.

Nürburgring A GRAND PRIX motor racing circuit in the Eifel mountains, south of Bonn, West Germany.

Nuremberg Laws (1935) Nazi legislation which deprived the Jews of all civic rights, and prohibited their intermarriage with 'Aryan' Germans. See ARYAN MYTH.

Nuremberg rallies (1933) Annual mass rallies of the Nazis, which Hitler made the occasion of some of his major speeches. (Ancient Bavarian city, north of Munich.)

Nuremberg trials (1945-46) The trials of German war criminals; Ribbentrop and Streicher, among others, were executed; Goering committed suicide before execution; Hess was sentenced to life imprisonment.

Nutcracker Man See ZINJANTHROPUS.

Nutcracker Suite, The See CASSE-NOISETTE.

Nutmeg State Nickname of Connecticut. (The early inhabitants were traditionally the sort of people who would sell wooden nutmegs as real.)

Nyasaland Now renamed MALAWI.

NYC New York City.

Nye Familiar name for Aneurin Bevan, the British Labour Minister of Health who introduced the NATIONAL HEALTH SERVICE.

Nymphenburg porcelain (1753) The products of a factory near Munich, perhaps second in prestige to MEISSEN, and especially famous for figures modeled by Anton Bustelli in 1754-63. The factory still operates today.

NYSE Signifies New York Stock Exchange; compare ASE.

O

Oak-apple Day May 29th, Charles II's birthday, named after the oak apples (or oak leaves) worn by Royalists in memory of his escapade at BOSCOBEL. (Oak apples, the small round galls found on oak leaves attacked by the gallfly.)

Oak Ridge A Tennessee town where wartime atomic research took place; now the site of ORINS (Oak Ridge Institute of Nuclear Studies), which has a fuel enrichment plant, and the Oak Ridge National Laboratory of the ATOMIC ENERGY COMMISSION, a center for research on the effects of radiation on plants and animals.

Oaks, Boysie The antihero of John Gardner's tongue-in-cheek thrillers, a James BOND with all the aggressiveness of FERDINAND THE BULL.

Oaks, The The English classic flat race for 3-year-old fillies, run over $1\frac{1}{2}$ miles at Epsom.

O and M Initials used for Organization and Methods, a name given to the systematic streamlining of procedure in office or factory by consultant 'O and M men'. An earlier name was 'common sense and efficiency'.

OAS (1) Initials of the French title of the terrorist Organization of the Secret Army, founded (1961) by Gen. Salan after the failure of the REVOLT OF THE FOUR GENERALS, in a last desperate attempt to establish an *Algérie française*. It perpetrated numerous bomb outrages in Algeria and Paris but died out when Algeria became independent (July 1962). (*Organisation de l'Armée Secrète*.) (2) See ORGANIZATION OF AMERICAN STATES.

OBAFGKMRNS The Draper classification of stars in descending order of surface temperature and absolute magnitude (intrinsic brightness), and ranging in color from blue to red. Most stars (the MAIN SEQUENCE STARS) fit into this classification. Examples are: ALGOL (B), SIRIUS (A), Pole Star (F), Sun (G), ALDEBARAN (K). BETELGEUSE (M). In an older (Ptolemaic) classification the brightest are called 1st magnitude, the faintest 6th magnitude stars. (A useful mnemonic is: Oh! be a fine girl, kiss me right now, Sweet!)

Oberammergau A Bavarian village in the Alps south of Munich, famous for its PASSION PLAY performed by a huge cast (1250) of the villagers every tenth year (normally) since 1633 (e.g. in 1970) as an act of gratitude for escape from a plague epidemic.

Oberon (1) King of the Fairies, husband of TITANIA or Queen Mab. The name is derived from the German ALBERICH through the French form, Auberon. (2) Title of Weber's opera (1826).

Obie Award An award of $500 made by a GREENWICH VILLAGE newspaper, the *Village Voice*, for the best OFF-BROADWAY show of American origin. (From the initials of Off-Broadway.)

Oblómov (1858) Goncharov's best novel. Oblómov is a typical Russian whose gifts and virtues are shrouded by innate lethargy. His name has passed into the Russian language as a symbol of Russian passivity and inertia.

O'Brien, Flann Pen name of the Irish writer Brian O'Nolan (1911-66); see AT SWIM-TWO-BIRDS.

Occam's razor The principle that the guiding rule in philosophical speculation should be simplicity; the number of assumptions made should be kept to the minimum, all inessential concepts being cut out as with a razor. (Advanced by William of Ockham, or Occam, 14th-century English theologian.)

OCD Signifies Office of Civil Defense.

Ochrana See OKHRANA.

O'Connell Street A principal street of Dublin, better known under its old name, Sackville Street. (Named after 'The Liberator', Daniel O'-Connell (died 1847), who founded a movement for Irish independence.)

Octagon Code name of the second Quebec Conference (Sept. 1944), a meeting at which Churchill and Roosevelt discussed strategic policies and the MORGENTHAU PLAN.

Octavian Gaius Octavius, who was renamed Gaius Julius Caesar Octavianus when adopted by Julius Caesar, and in 27 BC given the title of Augustus when he became the first Roman Emperor (in all but name).

October Manifesto (1905) Tsar Nicholas II's promise to permit an elected DUMA, extracted from him after Trotsky had set up a workers' soviet at ST PETERSBURG and called a general strike.

October Revolution (1917) The Bolshevik revolution of 7 Nov. 1917 (25 Oct. Old Style), led by Lenin and Trotsky; to be distinguished from the February Revolution (March New Style) which established a republic under a provisional government led by Prince Lvov and later by Kerensky.

Odd Couple, The (1965) Neil Simon's eccentric and most amusing comedy in which 2 deserted husbands are forced by circumstances to keep house together; turned into a movie by Gene Saks.

Oddfellows, Independent Order of (Manchester Unity) (1810) A large friendly society, a revival of earlier Oddfellow societies, with central headquarters at Manchester and lodges in the UK, USA, the Dominions, and various European countries. It has a Masonic-type ritual. (Explained as derived from the fact that the earliest founders were regarded as odd fellows.)

Oddjob The impassive Korean who guards GOLDFINGER, his main weapon of offense a steel bowler hat.

Oder-Neisse line The current boundary between them formally recognized by East Germany and Poland under the Görlitz agreement (1950), but not recognized by West Germany and the Western Powers. It is formed by the River Oder (Odra) and its tributary the western Neisse

(Nisa), and gives a fifth of prewar Germany to Poland, including EAST PRUSSIA and German SILESIA, and notably the cities of Stettin and Breslau.

ODESSA Nazi organization for helping senior members of their party to escape from Germany at the end of World War II and to evade arrest thereafter. (Initials of German for Organization of SS Members.)

'Ode to a Nightingale' (1819) Keats's poem pensively contrasting his own mortality with the immortality of the bird's song — the same, he surmises, as may have been heard by Ruth 'amid the alien corn' and have often 'charm'd magic casements, opening on the foam / Of perilous seas, in faery lands forlorn'.

Odette de Crécy In Proust's REMEMBRANCE OF THINGS PAST, a cocotte who becomes SWANN's mistress and later his wife, and the mother of GILBERTE. Widowed twice, she eventually becomes the mistress of the Duc de GUERMANTES.

Odin, Woden, Wotan Chief god of Scandinavian mythology, god of wisdom and of war. Wednesday is named after him.

Odtaa (1926) A novel by John Masefield; the title is made up of the initials of 'One damn thing after another'.

Odysseus (Ulysses) In Greek legend, King of ITHACA and one of the Greek leaders in the TROJAN WAR. After the adventures described in the ODYSSEY, he returned in disguise to Ithaca, slew PENELOPE's suitors and was reunited to his wife. In Homer he is wise and resourceful, in later authors crafty and treacherous. Tennyson's splendid poem 'Ulysses' represents him as still restless for adventure in his old age: How dull . . . to rest unburnish'd, not to shine in use'.

Odyssey, The Homer's epic poem recounting the adventures of ODYSSEUS on his return voyage from Troy, e.g. those involving CALYPSO, NAUSICAA, the LOTUS-EATERS, POLYPHEMUS, CIRCE, and SCYLLA AND CHARYBDIS.

OECD (1961) The Organization for Economic Cooperation and De-

velopment, an improved organization replacing OEEC, with USA and
Canada as full members.

OED   Initials used for the *Oxford
English Dictionary*, completed in 10
volumes (1928) and now under revision.

Oedipus   Greek legendary hero who,
after solving the riddle of the Sphinx
which plagued THEBES, was made
King of Thebes. Unknowingly, he
killed his father and married his
own mother, JOCASTA. When TIRE-
SIAS revealed his true identity, Oedipus blinded himself, cursed his sons
(see SEVEN AGAINST THEBES), and was
led by his only faithful child, ANTI-
GONE, to Colonus. He appears in
Sophocles' plays *Oedipus Rex* and
Oedipus at Colonus.

Oedipus complex   Freud's term for
the psychological results of a boy's
excessive attachment to his mother
and consequent (often unconscious)
jealousy of and hostility to his father. See ELECTRA COMPLEX. (See
OEDIPUS.)

OEEC   (1948-61) The Organization
for European Economic Cooperation, established to allocate funds
under ERP, coordinate economic and
reconstruction programs and reduce
tariffs and quotas; replaced by OECD.

Oerlikon   Swiss light quick-firing 20-
mm antiaircraft gun, used by both
sides in World War II. (Name of
town where made.)

Offaly, Ireland   Formerly King's
County.

Offa's Dyke   An earth and stone
rampart from the mouth of the Wye
at Beachley to the mouth of the Dee
in Flint, traditionally built by Offa,
8th-century king of MERCIA, to keep
out the Welsh, but probably earlier.

Off-Broadway theater   The small
New York theaters where, from the
1950s, experimental plays and revivals of classics have been staged
which were of too limited an appeal
to pay their way on Broadway.

Officers' Plot   (July 1944) An attempt
on Hitler's life by Gen. von Stauffen-
berg and other officers. He left a
bomb in a briefcase near Hitler at the
WOLF'S LAIR; it caused extensive
damage, but Hitler was only slightly

injured.

Of Human Bondage   (1915) Somerset
Maugham's most ambitious novel, a
forthright semiautobiographical story about Whitstable, where he was
brought up, Canterbury, where he
went to school, and London, where
he qualified in medicine.

Oflag   German prisoner-of-war camp
for officers. (Abbreviation of *Offizier*
and *Lager*, 'camp'.)

OFM   Initials placed after their
names by FRANCISCANS. (For Order of
Friars Minor.)

Of Thee I Sing   (1931) A musical
comedy with music by George
Gershwin and book by George Kaufman, Morrie Ryskind and Gershwin's brother Ira; the title is taken
from a national hymn, 'AMERICA'.
The first musical to win a PULITZER
PRIZE, it staged a brilliant burlesque
of a NATIONAL CONVENTION. The presidential candidate Wintergreen,
whose platform (anticipating a generation then unborn) is Love, is supposed to marry the winner of an Atlantic City beauty contest.

Ogam (Ogham)   A Celtic alphabet
consisting of groups of lines, used in
inscriptions on memorial stones dating from about the 5th century AD,
found mainly in southwest Ireland
but also elsewhere in the British
Isles.

OGO   (Orbiting Geophysical Observatory) A series of US satellites to
analyze the earth's belts of radiation,
including one (EOGO) in eccentric
orbit over the Poles. First launched
in 1964.

Ogpu   (1924-34) The name given to
the GPU when it was given all-Union
status; replaced by the NKVD. (Initials of the Russian for 'All-Union
State Political Organization'.)

O'Hara, Scarlett   The hot-tempered
heroine of GONE WITH THE WIND.

O'Hare   The Chicago international
airport, the busiest in the world.

Oh Dad!   (1961) Short title of *Oh
Dad, Poor Dad, Mama's Hung You
in the Closet and I'm Feeling So
Sad*, Arthur Kopit's undergraduate
fantasy play about a phenomenally
possessive mother, who carries her
dead husband about with her in a

coffin, and her son who has not the courage to escape her thrall.

Ohm's law At a given temperature, the ratio of the potential difference between 2 points of a conductor and the current flowing between them is a constant. For a potential difference of E volts and a current of I amps, the resistance (R) in ohms is E/I.

Oh, What a Lovely War! (1963) A musical revue produced by the THE-ATRE WORKSHOP, satirizing attitudes towards World War I; made into a movie (1969).

Oilers The Houston Oilers, AMERICAN FOOTBALL LEAGUE. Became member of the AMERICAN CONFERENCE, NATIONAL FOOTBALL LEAGUE in 1970.

Oiseau Bleu, L' A nonstop evening express train from Paris to Brussels, reached in under 3 hours.

Ojibwa An ALGONQUIAN-speaking race of Indians, originally of the Great Lakes region. They are now the most numerous of surviving Indian groups, with some 30,000 in USA (Minnesota, Wisconsin, North Dakota, Montana, Michigan) and 20,000 in west-central Canada. Their customs were borrowed as background material for Longfellow's HIAWATHA (who was, however, a MOHAWK). The name is also spelled Ojibway, and corrupted to Chippewa.

Okhrana (1881-1917) The Russian Imperial secret police, originally formed to check terrorism.

Okie A migrant agricultural worker, especially one from Oklahoma (compare ARKIE) forced out by DUST BOWL conditions or loss of land. The Joads of GRAPES OF WRATH were Okies.

Okinawa The largest of the Ryukyu Islands, it was the site of a successful US assault (Apr.-June 1945) against fanatical Japanese opposition in World War II. Several major US military bases were constructed on the island.

Oklahoma! (1943) A record-breaking musical, the first Rodgers and Hammerstein smash hit, and the first in which a ballet was successfully integrated into the plot by Agnes de Mille. Among its hit songs

were 'The Surrey with the Fringe on Top' and 'Oh, What a Beautiful Mornin'!' It was based on a folk drama, *Green Grow the Lilacs* (1931) by Lynn Riggs.

Old Adam, The The original sin inherent in man.

Old Bailey The Central Criminal Court, London. See ASSIZES. (Name of the street it is in.)

Old Believers See RASKOLNIKI.

Old Bill A walrus-moustached veteran of the FLANDERS mud, the creation of the British cartoonist Capt. Bruce Bairnsfather in World War I; his most famous cartoon showed Bill and another Tommy under fire in a waterlogged shell hole in no-man's-land, with the caption: Well, if you knows of a better 'ole, go to it!

Old Boy net (UK) The means of getting what one wants through the freemasonry of 'public' school Old Boys (i.e. alumni); or (by extension) through knowing the right people in the right places.

Oldbury on Severn (UK) One of the earlier series of nuclear power stations. (Coastal village, opposite Chepstow, in Gloucestershire.)

Old Carthusian See CARTHUSIANS (2).

'Old Chisholm Trail, The' A cowboy folk song beginning 'Come along boys and listen to my tale, / I'll tell you of my troubles on the old Chisholm trail', and a ki-yi-yippy refrain. Succeeding couplets were improvized by the cowboy as he rode along. See CHISHOLM TRAIL; LONG DRIVE.

Old Colony State See BAY STATE.

Old Contemptibles The British Expeditionary Force which fought at Mons (1914). (From the phrase, doubtfully attributed to the Kaiser, 'the contemptible little British army'.)

Old Crome Name given to the painter John Crome to distinguish him from his son J. B. Crome, also a member of the NORWICH SCHOOL.

Old Curiosity Shop, The (1841) Dickens's sentimental novel about Little Nell and her grandfather whose London curiosity shop is seized by QUILP for debt, and who flee together to wander through the countryside until after many adventures they settle in a quiet village. The antique and gift shop off Kingsway is connected with the novel only by name.

'Old Dan Tucker' (1843) Dan Emmett's minstrel song, still very popular for folk dancing, with the belligerent refrain 'Get out de way'. The hardened sinner Dan is believed to be a historical character, possibly a white man.

Old Dominion, The Nickname of Virginia.

Old Dominion Foundation (1941) A foundation established by Paul Mellon with special interests in Virginia (the Old Dominion) which also supports programs elsewhere, especially in the fields of liberal education, the arts, conservation and mental health.

Old English Also called Anglo-Saxon, the language of the ANGLES and SAXONS from their arrival in England in the 5th century AD until it was modified into MIDDLE ENGLISH in the 11th century. The Saxon dialect of WESSEX predominated in this period.

Old Faithful The most famous, though not the largest, geyser in the YELLOWSTONE NATIONAL PARK. It spouts a graceful 150-ft column of hot water and steam for a few minutes at near-regular intervals of about an hour, year in and year out.

Old Farmer's Almanac (1793) An annual first published in Massachusetts by R. B. Thomas and still going strong, having absorbed the NEW ENGLAND ALMANAC (1968). Its chief contents are a farmer's calendar, a weather forecast for the year, planting and gestation tables, game laws, recipes, anecdotes, horoscopes etc.

'Old Folks at Home' (1851) Stephen Foster's Negro song about the 'SWANEE Ribber'.

Old Ghana (8th-11th centuries AD) A kingdom of the Sudan, west of Timbuktu, conquered by the ALMORAVIDS. Modern Ghana has no connection with it, racially or geographically.

Old Glory The STARS AND STRIPES.

Old Grog Admiral Vernon, who ordered (1740) that the rum ration should be diluted, in which form it became known as grog, in his memory. (From his coat of grogram, a coarse cloth of wool and mohair.)

Old Hickory Nickname of Andrew Jackson; see JACKSONIAN DEMOCRACY.

Old Hundred The tune, of uncertain origin, now attached to the metrical version of the hundredth psalm, 'All people that on earth do dwell'.

Old Ironsides Nickname of USS *Constitution*, earned when in 1812 she sank the British frigate *Java* off Brazil. When there was talk of breaking her up, Oliver Wendell Holmes wrote a poem of protest with this title (1830) and the proposal was dropped.

Old King Cole The merry old soul of the nursery rhyme, variously identified with a 3rd-century prince who built Colchester, a rich Reading clothier named Colebrook, and others.

Old Kingdom (Ancient Egypt) The period of some 500 years from about 2800 BC, when the 3rd-6th Dynasties ruled at MEMPHIS; the Age of the Pyramids.

Old Lady of Threadneedle Street The BANK OF ENGLAND, which is in that street.

Old Line State A nickname for Maryland on account of the prowess of its regular 'troops of the line' at the Revolution.

Old Man and the Sea, The (1952) A novel in which Ernest Hemingway, in the guise of a Cuban fisherman battling alone with the elements, turned his back on the world which had spurned his previous work, *Across the River and into the Trees* (1950).

Old Man of the Mountain (1) The name given to the founder of the ASSASSINS sect in Persia (around AD 1100) after he had moved his secret headquarters to Mount Lebanon. (2) A rock formation on the upper cliffs of Profile Mountain, in the White Mountains, N.H. Also known as the Great Stone Face, the title of one of Nathaniel Hawthorne's stories in which it figures.

Old Man of the Sea The troublesome character in the ARABIAN NIGHTS who climbed on the back of SINBAD THE SAILOR; a person one cannot shake off; an incubus.

Old Marshal, The Chang Tso-lin, governor of MANCHURIA, which he declared independent of China in 1921 and ruled ruthlessly but efficiently until he died of wounds received in a Japanese air raid in 1928.

Old Masters The great European painters from Giotto to the 18th century; extended to include the acknowledged great of the 19th century; the works of these.

'Old Models' A painting by William M. Harnett (1848-92), in the Boston Museum of Fine Arts and used for the design of a US postage stamp (1969). Like many of his works, it is a realistic still life of musical instruments etc.

Old Moore's Almanac Name given to at least 4 modern imitations of a 17th-century publication by Francis Moore, quack and astrologer.

Old Mortality (1816) Walter Scott's novel, and the nickname of the old man in it who tries to keep green the memory of the COVENANTERS who fell victims to BLUIDIE CLAVERS by tending their graves all over Scotland.

Old Mother West Wind (1910) The first of a series of animal stories written for children by Thornton Burgess, originally for *Good Housekeeping.*

Old National Road See CUMBERLAND ROAD.

Old Ones A name for the CLIFF DWELLERS (see ANASAZI CULTURE).

Old Parr Thomas Parr, a Shropshire man said to have died aged 152 in 1635, lived under 10 reigns, married a second wife at 120 and had a child by her.

Old Possum The name taken by T. S. Eliot in writing his whimsical *Old Possum's Book of Practical Cats* (1939). See MACAVITY.

Old Pretender James Stuart, 'James III', son of James II by his second wife. He died in Rome, 1766. See FIFTEEN.

Old Red Sandstone The freshwater deposits of the DEVONIAN PERIOD, in which red sandstone predominates; rich in fossil fishes and marsh plants.

Old Rowley Nickname of Charles II, from one of his racehorses; hence the Rowley Mile at Newmarket. (Not connected with Anthony Rowley, of the nursery rhyme 'A frog he would a -wooing go'.)

Old Sarum The original site of Salisbury, 2 miles north of the present town; famous as a 'rotten borough'. (Corruption of the Latin name *Sarisburia.*)

Oldsmobile (1902) The first US mass-produced car, made by R. E. Olds.

Old Stone Age See PALEOLITHIC AGE.

Old Style The JULIAN CALENDAR, abandoned in Britain in 1752, when September 3rd became by law September 14th (NEW STYLE); and in Russia in 1918.

Old Tippecanoe Nickname of General Harrison; see TIPPECANOE, BATTLE OF.

Old Tom gin Generic term for a gin sweetened with sugar or glycerine.

Olduvai Gorge A site in the Serengeti plains, north TANZANIA, where remains were found of ZINJANTHROPUS and 'HOMO HABILIS'.

Old Vic A London theater in the Waterloo Road which from 1914 under Lilian Baylis staged Shakespeare's plays and later, until SADLER'S WELLS was opened, opera. After World War II, it became an unofficial national theater with an all-around classical repertoire, and finally in 1963 was replaced by the NATIONAL THEATRE.

Old Wives' Tale, The (1908) The best of Arnold Bennett's FIVE TOWNS novels, telling the life story of Constance Baines, draper's daughter, who stays in, and marries into, the business; and of her sister Sophia, who elopes with a rascally traveling salesman, runs a *pension* in Paris during the FRANCO-PRUSSIAN WAR, and returns to spend her last years with the now widowed Constance.

Old World The Eastern Hemisphere, specifically Europe.

Oleaceae The olive family of trees and shrubs, which includes the olive, ash, jasmine, privet and lilac.

O level The GCE examination taken at age 16 or earlier, requiring a higher standard than the old School Certificate. (O for Ordinary.)

Oligocene Epoch The second subdivision of the TERTIARY PERIOD, lasting from about 50 to 25 million years ago. Present-day mammals began to appear, e.g. cats and dogs, and primitive apes, as well as the saber-toothed tiger. (Greek, 'few of the modern', i.e. a few modern forms of life found.)

Oliver See ROLAND.

Oliver Twist (1838) Dickens's novel about the foundling Oliver's persecution by BUMBLE in a workhouse, his subsequent adventures with FAGIN and Bill SIKES, further persecution by his half-brother out to deprive him of his inheritance, and his final adoption by the kindly Dr Brownlow.

Olivia A character in Shakespeare's TWELFTH NIGHT who falls in love with VIOLA, disguised as a page.

Olney hymns (1779) Those written, in collaboration with John Newton, by William Cowper when he was living at Olney, Buckinghamshire.

Olney Pancake Race (1445) Run on Shrove Tuesday at Olney, Buckinghamshire, by housewives carrying a pancake in a frying pan.

Oloroso One of the 2 main types of sherry (see FINO), full-bodied, deep gold or brown; in its natural state, dry; but for export blended with sweet wine to form, in order of increasing sweetness, Amoroso, Cream, Golden and Brown dessert sherries.

Olympia (1) See OLYMPIC GAMES; (2) exhibition buildings in HAMMERSMITH, London, opened in 1886. The Ideal Home Exhibition and Dairy Show are staged there.

Olympia Name of the West German communications satellite program.

Olympiad The 4-year period between OLYMPIC GAMES.

Olympic Games (1) The Ancient Greek celebration in honor of Olympian ZEUS at Olympia in the Peloponnesus, at which there were contests in drama, music and athletics; (2) the modern revival of the athletics section of these, begun in Athens in 1896.

Olympic National Park (1938) A park in northwestern Washington containing the finest surviving forests, including rain forest, of the Pacific Northwest, and several glaciers. It is the summer feeding ground of the ROOSEVELT ELK.

Olympus The home of the Greek gods, identified with the 10,000-ft mountain at the eastern end of the range that separates Greece and MACEDONIA.

OM Initials placed after the name of a recipient of the Order of Merit, a British Order limited to 24 members, for people of special distinction; instituted in 1902.

Omaha Beach Code name of a beach northwest of Bayeux, one of the US landing sites on D-Day.

Omar, Mosque of A mosque on the site of SOLOMON'S TEMPLE at Jerusalem; originally a Byzantine church.

Omayyads The dynasty of Caliphs who ruled at Damascus (661-750) and in Spain (756-1031).

Ombudsman An official appointed by government to investigate complaints by individuals against oppressive bureaucratic action; appointed in Sweden in 1809, New Zealand 1962 and Britain 1966, where he is called the Parliamentary Commissioner for Administration.

Omnium, Dukes of The first Duke appears in Trollope's FRAMLEY PARSONAGE as a very rich, self-assured and scandalously unscrupulous character. His nephew, Plantagenet Palliser ('Planty Pall'), married to the admirable Lady Glencora, inherits the title and becomes Prime Minister in the PHINEAS FINN series of novels. In contrast to the first Duke, he is a sensitive, honorable man.

One-Eleven (1965) A BAC short-haul airliner which, like its US rival the DOUGLAS DC-9, has twin tail-mounted jets.

'One-Hoss Shay' (1858) The more familiar title of Oliver Wendell

Holmes's poem 'The Deacon's Masterpiece, or the Wonderful One-Hoss Shay'. The Deacon builds a shay (symbolizing Calvinism, inflexible dogma, or any overlogical thesis) 'in such a logical way / It ran a hundred years to a day'—and then suddenly fell to pieces.

Oneida A fierce Iroquoian race, one of the FIVE NATIONS, who lived around Oneida Lake (N.Y. State); they were almost the only Iroquois to fight the English in the Revolution. Most of the 3000 survivors now live in Wisconsin. ('People of the rock'.)

Oneida Community (1847-79) A small communistic society which formed and successfully managed a farm settlement at Oneida Creek, N.Y.; at first polygamy and polyandry were permitted. They were also called the Perfectionists.

One Thousand Guineas A classic English flat race for 3-year-old fillies run over the ROWLEY MILE at the first Spring meeting, Newmarket.

One Ton Cup (1898) An international ocean-sailing team race, originally for yachts in the one ton class, but now for those not exceeding 22 ft. (RORC RATING); held in July.

One-Upmanship (1952) Stephen Potter's sequel to LIFEMANSHIP, a study of the art of disconcerting one's fellows. For example, if a man has just bought a large country house, the Lifeman will ask him patronizingly: 'Well, how's the cottage?' If the proud householder is also a Lifeman, he will reply: 'What with those NATIONAL TRUST fellows and the Society for the Preservation of Ancient Buildings nosing around, I'm beginning to regret I ever bought it'.

One-Way Pendulum (1959) N. F. Simpson's contrived fantasy play satirizing suburban distortions of values and proneness to obsessions. Upstairs, Kirby has taught all but one of a battery of 'speak-your-weight' machines to sing the Hallelujah Chorus (the one sticks grimly to '15 stone 10 lb.'); below, his father has constructed a model of the OLD BAILEY, where he puts his son on trial for multiple murder.

One World (1943) A plea for international cooperation when war ended, written by the REPUBLICAN leader Wendell Wilkie after he had visited Russia and China in 1942.

Only in America (1958) One of 3 collections of mildly satirical sketches written by Harry Golden for his famous newspaper, the *Carolina Israelite*, and later adapted for Broadway.

Only Way, The (1899) A dramatized version by Freeman Wills of Dickens's TALE OF TWO CITIES, in which Sir John Martin Harvey acted the part of Sydney CARTON.

Onondaga An Iroquoian race, a leading member of the FIVE NATIONS, who lived fairly peaceably in central New York State. Very few survive. ('Mountain-dwellers'.)

On the Beach (1957) Nevil Shute's novel about the last survivors of the complete destruction of the inhabited globe after an atomic war.

'On the Mall' (1923) A march written by the American band conductor and composer, Edwin Franko Goldman.

On the Road (1957) The best known of the BEATNIK novels, by Jack Kerouac, in what he called 'spontaneous prose'.

On the Spot (1931) An Edgar Wallace thriller inspired by the career of SCARFACE AL CAPONE.

Oom Paul Nickname of Paul Kruger, President of the Transvaal and Boer leader in the BOER WAR (AFRIKAANS *oom*, 'uncle'.)

007 The Secret Service designation of James BOND; the 00 signifies a license to kill when necessary.

OP (1) Initials placed after their name by DOMINICANS. (For Latin. *Ordinis Praedicatorum*, 'of the order of preachers', the Dominicans being also known as Friars Preachers.) (2) (Theater) Opposite Prompt side, i.e. on the left of the theater stage as viewed by the audience.

Op art (1965) Designs on fabrics, tableware etc., and to a less important extent paintings, often in black and white or fluorescent color, which exploit effects of afterimages and optical illusion, so that the whole or part of the design appears to move. ('Op' for 'optical'; no connection with Pop art.)

OPEC (1961) Initials used for the Organization of Petroleum Exporting Countries, formed by Venezuela and the oil-producing states of the Middle East to protect themselves from unfair exploitation by the large Western oil companies. LIBYA and Indonesia joined it later.

Open-door policy Trade access on equal terms to all nations without discrimination. When foreign powers were carving out spheres of influence in a weakened China, the British suggested that this policy should guide them; it was adopted and enunciated by the US Secretary of State John Hay (1899). Later it was applied elsewhere in the Far East.

Ophelia In Shakespeare's HAMLET, the daughter of POLONIUS; driven mad by Hamlet's treatment and her father's death, she drowns herself.

Ophir, Land of According to 1 Kings x, 11, the source of the gold and precious stones brought to King SOLOMON; probably somewhere in Arabia. The early Portuguese explorers sought it in central Africa, the Spanish in the Pacific (hence the name Solomon Islands).

Opium War (1839-42) An extraordinary war in which the British fought for the right to import opium from India into China, bombarding CANTON and occupying Hong Kong. It was considered that Chinese confiscation of opium belonging to British merchants justified this.

Oppenheimer case (1954) The suspension of Dr Robert Oppenheimer, chairman of the advisory committee to the ATOMIC ENERGY COMMISSION, because he had failed to disclose alleged Communist interests in earlier years. Although he had supervised the making of the first atomic bomb, he opposed the development of the hydrogen bomb, and so fell a victim to MCCARTHYISM, and was not rehabilitated until 1963.

Oppidans All boys at Eton College other than KING'S SCHOLARS. (Latin *oppidum*, 'town'; they live in boarding houses in the town, the scholars live in college.)

Opus Dei (1928) An international Roman Catholic organization, mostly of laymen, dedicated to the inconspicuous dissemination of the ideals of Christian living by the example of their own lives. It was founded in Spain. (Latin, 'work of God'.)

OR Initials used for Operational Research, the mathematical analysis of complex problems, whether managerial or military, that can be set out in quantitative terms, usually performed by computers. The term covers war games or 'scenario analysis' (working out the possible results of various combinations of moves and countermoves) and cost-effectiveness analysis (deciding the best way to achieve an objective with given resources). This shuffles off the burden of 'decision-taking' (the current term for deciding what to do) onto a machine which may well give the wrong answer, since it will often not have been fed with all the requisite data, and it cannot take account of human factors.

Oracle, Sir A reference to Gratiano's lines in Shakespeare's *Merchant of Venice*, in which he rebukes his friend ANTONIO: As who should say, 'I am Sir Oracle, / And when I ope my lips let no dog bark'.

Oradour massacre (1944) The massacre by German soldiers of nearly all the inhabitants of Oradour-sur-Glane, near Limoges, France, on the grounds that arms had been found hidden there. The Germans had apparently confused it with another Oradour, where RESISTANCE MOVEMENT forces had been active.

Oran See MERS-EL-KEBIR.

Orange A town north of Avignon in France; formerly an independent principality governed (1530-1673) by the Dutch House of ORANGE-NASSAU.

Orange Bowl (1) Sports stadium at Miami, Fla. (2) The invitational BOWL GAME played in the Orange

Bowl usually with one team from the BIG EIGHT Conference.

Orangemen Members of the Orange Society, formed by Irish Protestants (1795) to protect the ASCENDANCY and the Protestant religion against Wolfe Tone's Society of United Irishmen, by then turned republican and seeking aid from the French DIRECTORY; now used generally for Ulster Protestants. (Named after William III of England, Prince of Orange.)

Orange-Nassau, House of The dynasty founded by William the Silent, to which William III of England belonged; it is still the Royal House of the Netherlands. See ORANGE; NASSAU.

Orange Pekoe (1) Originally, a high-quality China tea manufactured from the youngest leaves and scented with orange blossom, (2) Now a trade term merely indicating a grade of tea rather better than Pekoe. (Chinese, 'white hair', referring to the down on the young leaf.)

Orangerie Paris art gallery, see TUILERIES.

Orc (1) In William Blake's private mythology, the spirit of rebellion, violence and passion, which continually strives to loosen the shackles of URIZEN. (2) One of a host of evil beings in The LORD OF THE RINGS.

Ordeal of Gilbert Pinfold, The (1957) Evelyn Waugh's diary of a man plagued by hallucinations; it is based on a personal experience.

Ordeal of Richard Feverel, The (1859) George Meredith's partly autobiographical novel of a father who tries to give his son the perfect upbringing; the latter, however, marries a girl his father refuses to receive, and the consequences are disastrous to all.

Ordovician Period The second earliest period of the PALEOZOIC ERA, lasting from about 500 to 450 million years ago. Fossils are found of the earliest vertebrates (primitive fishes) and land plants (algae). (Latin *Ordovices*, tribe of North Wales.)

Oregon Trail The old trail from Independence on the Missouri, via Nebraska (where it joined the MORMON TRAIL and followed it via Fort Laramie to Fort Bridger in southwest Wyoming) and on through Idaho to Fort William (Portland), Oregon.

Oresteia, The (458 BC) The only complete trilogy of Greek drama to survive, comprising *Agamemnon*, *Choephoroi* ('Libation-pourers') and *Eumenides* ('The Furies'), by Aeschylus. It records the murder of AGAMEMNON, his son ORESTES' revenge on CLYTEMNESTRA, and his acquittal.

Orestes In Greek legend, the son of AGAMEMNON and brother of ELECTRA; they avenge their father's murder by killing Aegisthus and CLYTEMNESTRA and are acquitted by matricide by the intervention of APOLLO and ATHENE. Orestes appears in the ORESTEIA, Sophocles' *Electra* and in 4 plays of Euripides.

Orford Club A major English polo club in Suffolk near the coast.

Organisation Européen pour la Recherche Nucléaire See CERN.

Organization for Economic Cooperation and Development Better known as the OECD.

Organization for European Economic Cooperation Better known as the OEEC.

Organization of American States (1948) An organization of the USA and all the independent states of Central and South America (excluding Cuba, expelled in 1962, and Bolivia which seceded in 1963). It tries to ensure the peaceful settlement of internal disputes and to coordinate external policies. Canada is not a member.

Oriana See AMADIS DE GAUL.

Orient Express A train from Calais via Paris, Lausanne, Milan, Venice and Trieste, to Yugoslavia, Greece and Turkey.

Origin of Species, The (1859) Short title of Darwin's On the Origin of Species by means of NATURAL SELECTION, or the Preservation of Favoured Races in the Struggle for Life. In contrast to the then prevailing view that each species was separately created, this was the first clear formulation of the theory that the entire animal kingdom has in the course of time evolved from one primitive form of life. See DARWIN'S FINCHES.

ORINS Initials used for the OAK RIDGE Institute of Nuclear Studies.

Orioles Baltimore Orioles, AMERICAN (Baseball) LEAGUE, playing at the Memorial Stadium. Until 1954 they were the St. Louis Browns; the original Baltimore Orioles moved to New York in 1903 and were later renamed the New York GIANTS.

Orion In Greek legend, a mighty hunter, son of POSEIDON, who is blinded but has his sight restored. His death is engineered by APOLLO, who fears that ARTEMIS may fall in love with him; with his belt and sword, he then takes his place among the constellations (see next entry).

Orion The Hunter, the most conspicuous northern constellation; the Belt consists of 3 second magnitude stars across the center; below the Belt is the Great Galactic Nebula, visible to the naked eye. BETELGEUSE and RIGEL are the brightest stars in Orion.

Orlando Italian form of ROLAND, the medieval hero.

Orlando (1928) Virginia Woolf's unclassifiable fantasy in which Orlando starts as a young Elizabethan male poet and grows into a modern woman poet. This race through the centuries affords opportunities for satirical digressions on literary and social themes.

Orlando Furioso (1532) Ariosto's epic poem, with stories of monsters, a trip to the moon in Elijah's chariot, and other such fantasies, having in fact little to do with Orlando (ROLAND). (Italian, 'Orlando mad'.)

Orleanist Monarchy (1830-48) In French history the reign of Louis Philippe, KING OF THE FRENCH; also called the July Monarchy. (Louis was the son of PHILIPPE ÉGALITÉ, Duke of Orleans.)

Orleans, Duke of A 14th-century title which became extinct but was revived in 1661 by Louis XIV, who bestowed it on his brother. PHILIPPE ÉGALITÉ was one of the line; see last entry.

Orlon A man-made fiber manufactured by DU PONT and used as a wool substitute in knitwear.

Orly The international airport south of Paris, comprising Orly-Sud and Orly-Ouest, used by Air France among others. See LE BOURGET.

Ormuzd, Ormazd See AHURA MAZDA.

Orphée (1946) Jean Cocteau's movie about a poet who had lost his inspiration, and a princess who represents his own personal death. He also wrote a play with this title in 1926. (French spelling of ORPHEUS.)

Orpheus A legendary Greek musician, the son of a king of Thrace and one of the Muses, who was given a lyre by APOLLO with which he charmed even the trees and stones (and see EURYDICE). His grief over his loss of Eurydice was so prolonged that the women of Thrace took it as an insult, and the Maenads (BACCHANTS) tore him to pieces as having offended DIONYSUS.

Orpheus and Eurydice (1762) Gluck's first opera, which broke completely with the traditions of Italian opera.

Orpheus in the Underworld (1858) Offenbach's comic operetta in which Orpheus, a popular violinist, reluctantly rescues his wife from the Underworld at the insistent demand of his public.

Orphic Mysteries A Greek cult of the 6th century BC associated with the name of ORPHEUS. Devotees preached purity, asceticism and atonement for sin, believed in an afterlife, and worshiped the man-god ORPHEUS who had suffered torment on earth. The cult influenced Pythagoras and Plato, and foreshadowed Christian beliefs.

Orpington A large and hardy dual-purpose breed of domestic fowl, typically buff colored ('Buff Orpington'). (Orpington, Kent.)

Orrefors glass Modern Swedish art glass made near Kosta in Småland, a famous glass district since 1742.

Orthodox Church Another name for the EASTERN ORTHODOX CHURCH.

Orthoptera An order of insects with mouths equipped to bite, and which run and jump but do not always fly; the cockroaches, locusts, crickets, grasshoppers etc.

Orwellian Resembling the world created by George Orwell in the novels 1984 and ANIMAL FARM.

OSA Initials placed after their names by AUGUSTINIANS. (Initials of Latin for Order of St Augustine.)

Osagyefo The title assumed by Nkrumah when President of GHANA. ('Redeemer'.)

OSAL Initials used for the Communist Organization of Latin American Solidarity, sponsored by Castro's Cuba, and formed to carry out subversion in Latin America. It is closely allied with OSPAAL.

OSB Initials placed after their names by BENEDICTINES. (Initials of Latin for Order of St Benedict.)

Osbaldistone, Frank The hero of Scott's ROB ROY who marries Diana Vernon. His cousin Rashleigh Osbaldistone is his bitterest enemy and, after betraying his fellow JACOBITES, is killed by Rob Roy.

Osborne House Originally a royal residence, near Cowes in the Isle of Wight, where Queen Victoria died; it then became a Royal Naval College (1903-21) and later a hospital for officers.

Oscar A gold-plated figurine annually awarded by the Academy of Motion Picture Arts and Sciences, HOLLYWOOD, for the highest achievements in motion-picture production; (loosely) a similar award for acting or scenario writing. (Name chosen arbitrarily.)

Oscar de la Renta A New York fashion house.

Osiris Ancient Egyptian ox-god, sometimes regarded as a Sun-god but also as a god of the dead, represented in art as a crowned mummy. ISIS was his sister and wife, and he was killed by his brother SET, but was resurrected. His worship developed into a fertility cult resembling that of TAMMUZ and DIONYSUS.

OSO (Orbiting Solar Observatory) A series of US research satellites, first launched in 1962, to collect data on gamma rays and X rays from the sun.

OSPAAL (1966) Initials used for the Communist Organization of the Solidarity of the Peoples of Africa, Asia and Latin America, founded at a conference in Havana, Cuba, which called for world revolution against (US) imperialism. It is closely allied with OSAL.

Osprey (1952) A national class dinghy designed by Ian Proctor and raced, mainly in southwest England, by a crew of 2 or 3; overall length 17 feet 6 inches.

OSS (1941) The US Office of Strategic Services, forerunner of the CIA, formed by General 'Wild Bill' Donovan; the equivalent of the British SOE, it parachuted many trained agents and saboteurs into France during World War II.

Ossian In Irish legend, the son of FINN, also spelled Oisin; he lived to tell, aged about 150, the old Irish legends to St Patrick.

Ossianic poems (1760-63) Spurious poems by a Scottish MP, James Macpherson, partly translated from GAELIC and ERSE originals, but mostly cleverly invented by him and passed off as authentic. See also OSSIAN.

Osterley Park House A Robert Adam house near the Great West Road, Osterley, near London, administered by the Victoria and Albert Museum.

Ostrogoths Eastern GOTHS, who ruled Italy from 493 until the Emperor Justinian drove them out in 534.

OTC (1908) (UK) Initials used for Officers' Training Corps, the cadet force at 'public' schools and universities. At the outset of World War II it was divided into a junior (schools) branch which was later merged with the Combined Cadet Force, and a senior branch which remains the University OTC.

Otello (1887) Verdi's opera, based on Shakespeare's OTHELLO.

Otéro, La Belle (1868-1965) A Spanish grande cocotte of the BELLE ÉPOQUE, loved by kings and grand dukes.

OTH   Initials used for Over The Horizon radar, a US system which gives 15 minutes' warning of attack by FOBS.

Othello   The Moor who in Shakespeare's play (1604) of that name is led by IAGO to suspect DESDEMONA's fidelity.

Ottawa agreements   (1932) These established IMPERIAL PREFERENCE between Britain and the Dominions and (1933) the Colonies, marking Britain's final abandonment of FREE TRADE in the face of the World DEPRESSION. In practice Britain had to tax vital foreign foodstuffs (e.g. US wheat and Argentine meat) to assist the Dominions, who gave little compensation by granting preference, but by no means free entry, for British manufactures.

Ottawa spy ring   (1945) The network uncovered by the defection of a Soviet diplomat, Igor Gouzenko, at Ottawa; it led to the arrest of FUCHS, NUNN MAY and the ROSENBERGS.

Otterburn   (1388) A border battle between the Douglases and the Percys, the subject of an old ballad.

Ottoman Turks   (1300-1920) The second wave of Turks, who displaced the SELJUK TURKS and ruled until Turkey became a republic; also called Osmanlis. In the 15th century they destroyed what was left of the BYZANTINE EMPIRE, and reunified the Islamic world from the Balkans to Tunis. (Named after the founder, Othman, also spelled Osman or Usman.)

Oudenarde, Battle of   (1708) Third victory over the French in the War of the SPANISH SUCCESSION, won by Marlborough and Prince Eugène of Savoy. (Town near Ghent in east FLANDERS, Belgium.)

OUDS   (1885) Initials commonly used for the OXFORD UNIVERSITY Dramatic Society, which usually restricts itself to performances of Shakespeare and the classics.

Ouida   Pen name of Louise de la Ramée, English-born half-French author of UNDER TWO FLAGS (1867) and many other melodramatic novels; she is remembered with delight for her gorgeous young Guards officers, with their moustaches drenched in scent, and the remark (to be fair, wrongly attributed to her and coming from Desmond Coke's parody, *Sandford of Merton*): All rowed fast, but none so fast as stroke. (Nursery pronunciation of Louise.)

Our Dumb Friends   See BLUE CROSS.

Our Mutual Friend   (1864) Charles Dickens's last complete novel. John Harmon is left a fortune on condition that he marry Bella Wilfer, whom he has never met. He therefore arrives under an assumed name to see how the land lies, and eventually marries her. The story is heavy with symbolism and brooding melancholy.

Our Town   (1938) Thornton Wilder's play sympathetically depicting everyday life in a small New Hampshire town at the turn of the century, remarkable for the device of a voluble Stage Manager commenting to the audience on the progress of the play. In the last act, set in a cemetery, the dead proclaim their faith in the age-old values and in the essential harmony of the universe. The play was made into a movie (1940) with music by Aaron Copland.

Outer Mongolia   The northern part of Mongolia, formerly Chinese, which proclaimed itself the Mongolian People's Republic (1924) and was recognized by Chiang Kai-shek in 1946; capital, Ulan Bator.

Outer Seven, The   Another name for EFTA.

Outline of History, The   (1920) H. G. Wells's remarkable and original history of mankind from prehistoric times down to his own day.

Outsider, The   (1956) A book of essays by Colin Wilson analyzing the pessimism of contemporary culture and discussing 'social misfits' such as Van Gogh, Nijinsky and Col. Lawrence. It became, without due cause, associated with the ANGRY YOUNG MEN image and, after acclaiming it with rapture, the critics turned their backs on it.

Outward Bound   (1923) Sutton Vane's play in which a small group of passengers find themselves in a liner bound for heaven or hell, and gradually come to realize that they are dead.

Outward Bound Schools (1941) Run by a Trust, in Wales, the Lake District and overseas, where boys and girls are taught to face hazards and hardships on mountain and sea, and trained in rescue work. Inspired by Kurt Hahn, of GORDONSTOUN and the ATLANTIC COLLEGE Council.

Overloaded Ark, The (1953) The first of several delightful accounts by the zoologist, Gerald Durrell, of his travels in various parts of the world in search of animals for the Jersey zoo.

Overlord Code name of the final plan for the landings in Normandy in 1944.

'Over There' (1917) A song which, with its last line 'We won't come back till it's over over there', was expressly written to boost morale in World War I. Composed by George M. Cohan its popularity won him a special Congressional medal, and it was even recorded by Caruso.

Ovra The Italian Fascist secret police. (Initials of Italian for 'Security organization for the repression of anti-Fascism'.)

Owens Illinois (1909) The world's largest bottle manufacturers and from 1931 pioneers in the US in making glass fibers; founded by Michael J. Owens and Edward D. Libbey. One of the 30 industrials that make up the DOW JONES Industrial Average.

'Owl and the Pussy-Cat, The' One of Edward Lear's Nonsense Songs.

Ox-Bow Incident, The (1943) A somber movie, based on an American novel, on the subject of lynching. It was released in Britain as *Strange Incident*.

Oxbridge A portmanteau word for OXFORD and CAMBRIDGE UNIVERSITIES.

OXFAM (1942) (UK) A voluntary organization with headquarters at Oxford which helps to relieve poverty and suffering in all parts of the world by providing food, clothing, medical attention, shelter, training and education. (For Oxford Famine Relief.)

Oxford Group, The An early nickname for BUCHMANISM. (Dr Buchman formed a group, one of many, when he visited Oxford in 1921; there was no special association of the movement with Oxford.)

Oxford Movement (1833) The movement towards ANGLO-CATHOLICISM started by J. H. (later Cardinal) Newman and John Keble. They tried to revive pre-REFORMATION religion in the Church of England, with emphasis on ritual, sacraments, the confessional etc.

Oxford shoe An ordinary laced shoe.

Oxford University One of the 2 leading English universities, a center of learning since c. 1167, now consisting of 34 separately administered residential colleges (including 5 for women), the oldest being University College (1249), Balliol (1263) and Merton (1264). A HEBDOMADAL COUNCIL administers the university's affairs. There are some 10,000 in residence. See also ALL SOULS, OXFORD.

Oxon. Abbreviation for (1) (Bishop) of Oxford, (2) of OXFORD UNIVERSITY. (For Latinized name *Oxoniensis*, from older name Oxenford.)

Oxonian Of Oxford; see OXON.

Oxus Ancient name of the Amu Darya river, USSR.

Oxyrhynchus papyri See SAYINGS OF CHRIST. (Oxyrhynchus, a city of Middle Egypt, where early Christians settled, about 120 miles south of Cairo.)

Oysters Rockefeller Oysters baked with a spinach and herb mixture, a specialty of ANTOINE'S.

Oz, The Wizard of See WIZARD OF OZ.

'Ozymandias' (1818) Shelley's sonnet on the ruins of a mighty statue set up in the desert by some ancient tyrant, with the inscription; 'My name is Ozymandias, King of Kings: / Look on my works, ye Mighty, and despair'. On which Shelley commented: Nothing beside remains . . . / The lone and level sands stretch far away. (Ozymandias is probably Rameses II.)

P

Pace Egging An English Easter Monday celebration in Lancashire, Yorkshire and Cheshire, marked by a children's performance of a 16th-century play with traditional characters (St George, Bold Hector, Bold Slasher etc.); the Toss Pot, wearing a top hat, goes round with a basket collecting eggs (money is now an acceptable substitute) from the spectators. (Presumably from Paschal or Pâques.)

Pacem in terris (1963) Pope John XXIII's encyclical on the role of the Church in the nuclear age and on the supreme need for world peace. (Latin, 'peace on earth'.)

Pacers The Indiana Pacers, AMERICAN BASKETBALL ASSOCIATION.

Pacific Charter (1954) A declaration of aims by the SEATO powers.

Pacific Crest Trail A 2300-mile foot and horseback trail in the West.

Pacific Eight A College Athletic Conference, comprising California, Oregon, Oregon State, Southern California, Stanford, UCLA, Washington, Washington State. One team plays each year in the ROSE BOWL against a team of the BIG TEN Conference. See BOWL GAMES.

Pacific Security Pact See ANZUS.

Pacific standard time The civil time of the 120th meridian, 3 hours slower than EASTERN STANDARD TIME; observed in western USA and British Columbia.

Pacific Union Club An exclusive men's club in San Francisco.

Packers The Green Bay (Wis.) Packers, NATIONAL FOOTBALL LEAGUE. Became member of the NATIONAL CONFERENCE, NATIONAL FOOTBALL LEAGUE in 1970.

Pact of Steel (May 1939) The full military and political alliance between Italy and Germany which developed from the ROME-BERLIN AXIS.

Paddington A former London metropolitan borough, since 1965 part of the borough of WESTMINSTER (City of).

Padres The San Diego Padres, NATIONAL (Baseball) LEAGUE, playing at the San Diego Stadium.

Pagliacci, I (1892) Leoncavallo's opera in which Canio, the clown, stabs his faithless wife to death in the course of a 'play within a play', a production of COLUMBINE and HARLEQUIN. See CAV. AND PAG. (Italian, 'the strolling players'.)

Painted Desert A region in Arizona which extends 300 miles along the Little Colorado River, with red, brown, blue, yellow and white sandstone and other rocks; part of it is in the PETRIFIED FOREST NATIONAL PARK.

Painterly Abstraction Alternative name for ABSTRACT EXPRESSIONISM. (Painterly, translation of German *malerisch*, in the sense that the emphasis is not on line but on form and color.)

Paisleyism (1966) An extremist Ulster Protestant movement led by the Rev. I. R. K. Paisley, who describes himself as a fundamentalist CALVINIST.

Paisley pattern The characteristic peacock-feather design, originally used in the imitation cashmere shawls first made at Paisley. (County town of Renfrewshire, near Glasgow.)

Pakeha Maori name for Europeans.

Pakistan A name coined in 1933 from the initials of PUNJAB, Afghan (i.e. the PATHANS of the North-West Frontier Province) and Kashmir, and the termination of Baluchistan; the case for its adoption was strengthened by the fact that it could well come from Persian *pak*, 'pure', 'holy' + *stan*, 'land'.

Pal The West German Telefunken system of 625-line color TV adopted by Britain for use in 1967. (Stands for Phase Alternation line.)

Palaeologus The name borne by the last dynasty of Byzantine emperors, who ruled from 1261 until the fall of CONSTANTINOPLE (1453).

Palais-Bourbon (1728) In Paris, the seat of the NATIONAL ASSEMBLY, on the LEFT BANK.

Palamon and Arcite Two Theban knights captured by Duke Theseus of Athens, who fall in love with their captor's daughter; a tale told by Boccaccio and by Chaucer in *The* KNIGHT'S TALE.

Palatinate Specifically, the Rhine Palatinate, formerly ruled by the Count Palatine of the Rhine (an ELEC-TOR); divided into the Rhenish (Lower) Palatinate, capital Heidelberg, since 1946 merged in the *Land* RHINELAND-PALATINATE, and the Upper Palatinate, capital Amberg, now in Bavaria. (See next entry.)

Palatine A German count (Count Palatine) or English earl (Earl Palatine; see COUNTY PALATINE) having supreme, almost royal, jurisdiction within his fief in medieval times. See last entry. (Derived ultimately from Latin *Palatium*, 'PALA-TINE HILL'.)

Palatine Hill One of the 7 hills of Rome, where the first Roman settlements were made, and the site of the palaces (so named after it) of the early Roman Emperors.

Pale, The An area around Dublin where from the 12th century to Tudor times England imposed direct rule and banned Irish law and custom. Hence 'beyond the pale', of outrageous conduct etc.

Paleolithic Age (Old Stone Age) The period of perhaps a million years, covering the ICE AGE and ending about 8000 BC, during which early forms of man learned to walk upright, speak, make fire and make tools, and the first types of *Homo sapiens* produced remarkable cave paintings, such as those of ALTA-MIRA.

Paleozoic Era The geological era lasting from about 600 to 240 million years ago, divided into the CAMBRIAN, ORDOVICIAN, SILURIAN, DEVONIAN, CARBONIFEROUS and PERMI-AN PERIODS. During this era fossils become abundant and include fishes, amphibians, reptiles, insects and

primitive plants. The climate was at first mild, but there was a long spell of cold at the end. (Greek, 'ancient life'.)

Paley's Evidences Short title of *View of the Evidences of Christianity* (1794) by William Paley, the study of which was prescribed for entrants to CAMBRIDGE UNIVERSITY until well into the 20th century.

Palgrave See GOLDEN TREASURY.

Pali The Aryan dead language of northern India in which the Buddhist scriptures are preserved in Ceylon and Burma.

Palinurus A pilot in Virgil's AENEID who fell asleep at the helm and was swept overboard; he reached the shore, but was there murdered.

'Palinurus' The pen name under which the English critic Cyril Connolly wrote *The Unquiet Grave* (1945), a handbook for pessimists.

Pal Joey (1941) A modern BEGGAR'S OPERA by Rodgers and Hart based on stories serialized in the NEW YORKER by John O'Hara and published in book form in 1940. There was a strong plot, unusual in musicals, woven round the escapades of the egregious heel of the title. Song hits included 'Bewitched, Bothered and Bewildered' and 'I Could Write a Book'.

Palladian architecture A style developed for town and country houses in northern Italy by Antonio Palladio (1508-80), who had made a close study of classical Roman architecture. It was introduced to England by Inigo Jones in the 17th century, and revived there by William Kent in the 18th. Symmetrical facades with classical columns were the main characteristics.

Pallas An epithet frequently applied to ATHENE; its meaning is disputed, the most usual translations being 'virgin' or 'brandisher of the spear'.

Pall Mall A London street linking TRAFALGAR SQUARE to ST JAMES'S PAL-ACE, and with St James's Street the home of the more prestigious social clubs ('clubland'). (Named for Charles II's favorite *pallamaglio* ('ball and mallet'), probably the earliest form of croquet, played in St James's Park nearby.)

Palmetto State Nickname of South Carolina.

Palm Sunday The Sunday before EASTER, commemorating Jesus' entrance into Jerusalem, when the people welcomed him with branches of palm trees strewn in his way (*John*, xii, 13); palm fronds figure in processions and ceremonies on that day.

Palm-wine Drinkard, The (1952) The first novel of the Nigerian Amos Tutuola, and the first novel from Black Africa to receive general acclaim from British critics. As the title indicates, it molds English to African uses in telling a traditional spook-ridden story of West Africa.

Palmyra The former capital of the state of Palmyra, where Queen Zenobia reigned in the 3rd century AD; its ruins are in the desert northeast of Damascus.

Palomares bombs (1966) Hydrogen bombs from a US bomber which crashed near a Spanish Mediterranean village. A large task force was sent to find them, 3 on land, the fourth—most difficult to trace—eventually recovered from the sea. Some plutonium was released and, despite extensive decontamination, the possibility of long-term harmful effects cannot be dismissed.

Palomino horse A rare color breed of (mainly) parade horse, bred in southwestern USA and elsewhere. They vary from shades of yellow or gold to pale cream, and have long white or silver manes and tails. (Spanish, 'dove-like'.)

Pamela (1740-41) Sometimes regarded as the first novel, written by Samuel Richardson in the form of letters from a sanctimonious maidservant who persuades her amorous 'young master' to marry her.

Pan The Greek god of shepherds and flocks, with goat's feet, horns and prick ears. He invented the 7-reed syrinx or Pan's pipe, and liked to startle travelers in lonely places (hence 'panic fear').

Pan-Africanist Congress (1959) Formed by the more militant members of the AFRICAN NATIONAL CONGRESS, led by Robert Subukwe.

Pan Am Pan American (World) Airways, the pioneer US airline that in 1927 started a service between Key West and Havana, and then inaugurated services to Chile (1929), and across the Pacific (1935) and Atlantic (1939).

Panama scandal (1888-92) A French political scandal arising from a project to build a canal in Panama. Ferdinand de Lesseps, who had built the Suez Canal, was put in charge, though already in his 70s. He misjudged the difficulties of the terrain and the company formed to build the canal went bankrupt. It then transpired that several leading politicians who supported a last-minute scheme to save it had sold their votes. Lesseps was, unjustly, one of those accused of bribery and corruption. Many Jews were involved, and French anti-Semitism increased.

Pan-American Highway An all-season road network from Texas via Mexico City, Panama and Valparaiso to Buenos Aires, projected in 1923 and now linking all the Latin-American capitals. The system includes various alternative routes.

Pan-American Union (1910) A successor to the International Union of the American Republics (1890) and the predecessor of the ORGANIZATION OF AMERICAN STATES.

Panay incident (1937) An international crisis which arose when Japanese aircraft sank the US gunboat *Panay* in the Yangtze.

Pancake race A Shrove Tuesday race run at Liberal, Kan., similar to the OLNEY PANCAKE RACE.

Panchen Lama The Tibetan priest who ranks second only to the DALAI LAMA, and was formerly the abbot of a monastery in western Tibet; also called the Tashi Lama.

Pandarus (1) A Trojan leader in the TROJAN WAR. (2) In Chaucer and Shakespeare, the uncle of Cressida, from whose name the word 'pander' is derived. See TROILUS AND CRESSIDA.

Pandit A title of esteem in India, bestowed e.g. on Jawaharlal Nehru.

(Hindu spelling of 'pundit'.)

Pandora's box In Greek legend, a box containing all the evils, which ZEUS gives to Epimetheus ('afterthought') on his marriage to the Greek Eve, Pandora ('all-gifted'). She opens the box and the evils escape to plague the world, leaving only Hope (which also escapes, in some versions). This was Zeus's revenge on man for having obtained the gift of fire from PROMETHEUS.

Pan-Germanism Advocacy of the integration of all German-speaking people into one State, i.e. German claims to absorb Austria, ALSACE-LORRAINE, Luxembourg, and parts of Czechoslovakia, Switzerland, Poland and FLANDERS. The names Mitteleuropa and Grossdeutschland were used of such a projected state. See NEW ORDER IN EUROPE.

Pangloss, Dr The tutor in Voltaire's CANDIDE who, in the teeth of all evidence, persists in his assertion that 'all is for the best in the best of possible worlds'—a caricature of Leibniz's views.

Panhandle State Nickname of West Virginia. (Has panhandle-shaped projections into neighboring states.)

Panhard-Levassor (1892) A French firm of car manufacturers who at first used DAIMLER engines mounted in front of the chassis, and introduced the front radiator, a transmission shaft to the rear wheels, and a clutch. The Panhard 70 (1902) was their most famous car, and an earlier type in 1899 won a 354-mile race at 34 m.p.h.

Panjandrum, The Grand Mock title for a pompous busybody. (Coined by the 18th-century actor Samuel Foote when composing a nonsense speech to test the memory of a fellow actor. This piece, beginning 'So she went into the garden to cut a cabbage leaf to make an apple pie' became surprisingly well known.)

Panmunjom The scene in Korea from 1951 of protracted negotiations for a settlement of the KOREAN WAR. Although an armistice was signed in 1953, emissaries from the states concerned still meet for ritual exchanges

of abuse matches, 'the world forgetting, by the world forgot'.

Pantagruel The son of Gargantua. See GARGANTUA AND PANTAGRUEL.

Pantaloon A stock character of the COMMEDIA DELL' ARTE, a foolish old merchant of Venice, wearing spectacles, slippers and pantaloons, the butt of the Clown. (Venetian patron saint, Pantaleone.)

Panthéon (1789) A building in the LATIN QUARTER of Paris; originally conceived as a church, it became on completion at the Revolution a Hall of Fame, where the remains of Mirabeau, Voltaire and Rousseau were buried. Thereafter, now church, now Hall of Fame, according to the regime in power, it assumed the latter (and present) function in 1885, on the burial there of Victor Hugo. (Greek, 'temple of all the gods'.)

Panther (1942) A German cruiser tank of World War II: 44 tons, 700 h.p., 30 m.p.h. It had a short mechanical life.

Panthers See BLACK PANTHER.

Panurge A character in Rabelais' GARGANTUA AND PANTAGRUEL; unable to decide whether to marry, he accompanies Pantagruel to Cathay to consult the oracle of the Holy Bottle, which answers his question with the one word: Drink. (Greek, 'all-doer'.)

Paolo and Francesca Two lovers put to death for adultery in 1289 in Ravenna, he being the handsome young brother of the unattractive man she had been forced by her parents to marry. Their story is told by Dante and many other writers, in poems, plays and opera.

Paotow One of the centers of Chinese nuclear development, with 2 plutonium-producing reactors; it is in Suiyuan, Inner Mongolia, on the Hwang Ho in northwest China, at the terminus of the Gobi Desert caravan routes. See LANCHOW.

Papa Doc Self-imposed nickname of François Duvalier, dictator of Haiti from 1957 to 1971, who managed to retain power through his TONTONS MACOUTES. 'Doc' refers to his claim to have been a doctor in country practice; he was never that, but a US sanitary mission once employed him as public-health officer.

Papal Infallibility (1870) The dogma announced by Pope Pius IX that the Pope cannot err when he speaks *ex cathedra*, i.e. when solemnly enunciating, as binding on all Catholics, a decision on a question of faith or morals.

Papal States The territory of central Italy, stretching across the peninsula and from Tuscany to the Kingdom of Naples, over which the Pope was nominally temporal sovereign from the 8th century until 1870, when it was incorporated into Italy. See VATICAN CITY.

Papaveraceae The poppy family, characterized by the narcotic milky juice; it includes meconopsis and eschscholtzia.

Paphos An ancient city of Cyprus associated with APHRODITE; hence Paphian, of illicit love.

Papilionaceae The pea-flower sub-family which includes all the British specimens of LEGUMINOSAE. It is characterized by a butterfly-shaped flower; typical examples are the sweet pea, bean, clover, vetch, groundnut, lupin, gorse, laburnum, wisteria. (Latin *papilio*, 'butterfly')

Papua Southeast New Guinea, formerly called British New Guinea; renamed Territory of Papua (1906) and put under joint Australian administration with ex-German New Guinea as Papua-New Guinea (1949).

Pará A Brazilian seaport, also known as Belém.

Paracelsus Name adopted by a Swiss physician, alchemist and astrologer, Theophrastus von Hohenheim (1493-1541).

Paraclete The HOLY GHOST; literally, the Advocate; the Comforter of *John* xiv, 26.

Paradise A term used in the Greek SEPTUAGINT to translate 'Garden of Eden'; since life there was perfect it came to be used of the perfect life after death. (Persian word.)

Paradise Lost (1667) Milton's great epic on the Old Testament theme of 'Man's first disobedience' in the Garden of Eden, of which Satan is the dominant character throughout.

Paradise of the Pacific A nickname for Hawaii.

Paradise Regained (1671) Milton's lesser epic on the New Testament theme of Christ's triumph over temptation.

Paraguay tea Maté.

Paranthropus See ZINJANTHROPUS.

Parcae Latin name for the FATES.

Parent-Teacher Association An association to promote cooperation between parents and teachers in the interests of the children at a particular school.

Parian marble Fine-textured marble from the Aegean island of Paros.

Parian ware A form of porcelain which can be molded in liquid state but looks like marble when set; used in the mass production of classical busts for the cottager, first by COPELAND & GARRETT (1840). Early examples were good but later work deteriorated into sentimentality. This ware was used by MINTON and others, and for some kinds of domestic china.

Paris In Greek legend, son of PRIAM, who carried off HELEN OF TROY, thus starting the TROJAN WAR, in which, though a coward, he killed ACHILLES but was himself killed by PHILOCTETES. See JUDGMENT OF PARIS.

Paris, School of A vague term applied to 20th-century artists who worked in Paris; in fact they belonged to various schools — or none.

Paris, Treaty of The name of several peace treaties, including those which ended (1) the SEVEN YEARS WAR (1763) and (2) the SPANISH-AMERICAN WAR.

Paris Commune (1) (1792-94) The revolutionary municipal government of Paris, which played a large part in the Reign of TERROR. (2) (March-May 1871) The Socialist government of Paris set up when the Germans withdrew after the FRANCO-PRUSSIAN WAR; besieged by French government troops ('Versaillists'), its overthrow was followed by a 'Week of Blood'.

Paris green An insecticide derived from arsenic.

Paris-Match (1949) A leading French illustrated weekly with an international reputation for its brilliant articles and illustrations.

Paris Peace Conference (1) The conference (1919-20) of Allied Powers after World War I which, with great difficulty, framed the treaties of VERSAILLES, ST GERMAIN, TRIANON, NEUILLY and SÈVRES. (2) The conference (1946) after World War II which framed treaties with Italy, Rumania, Hungary, Bulgaria and Finland.

Paris Summit Conference (1960) A projected meeting of Eisenhower, Khrushchev, Macmillan and de Gaulle, canceled at the eleventh hour by Khrushchev because of the U2 INCIDENT.

Paris Treaty (1952) The treaty under which the EUROPEAN DEFENSE COMMUNITY was to have been established.

Park Avenue The New York street running north from Park Avenue South (Fourth Avenue), once the site of the luxury apartments of the FOUR HUNDRED set, now largely taken over by new office blocks.

Parke-Bernet An art gallery and antiques auction room on MADISON AVENUE, NYC, owned by SOTHEBY'S.

Parker House roll A roll made by folding half of a flat circular piece of dough over the other half. (Name of a hotel in Boston.)

Parkhurst prison (UK) A prison in a suburb of Newport, Isle of Wight, used for long-sentence prisoners and noted for strict discipline; a special security block for men serving very long sentences was added in 1966.

Parkinsonism A condition very like PARKINSON'S DISEASE, found as a sequel to sleeping sickness.

Parkinson's disease Paralysis agitans or shaking palsy; a condition characterized by trembling hands, expressionless face and a shuffling gait. (James Parkinson, 1755-1824, British neurologist.)

Parkinson's law (1958) 'Work expands so as to fill the time available for its completion' and 'subordinates multiply at a fixed rate regardless of the amount of work pro-

duced'. (Discovered by C. Northcote Parkinson, historian and wit.)

Parkman (Francis) prize A US literary prize for a work of history; it carries great prestige. (US historian, died 1893.)

Parliamentary Private Secretary (UK) An MP appointed by a Minister to assist him in maintaining contact with backbenchers and in assessing the feeling of the House generally. The post is unpaid. See PARLIAMENTARY SECRETARY.

Parliamentary Secretary (UK) A Junior Minister appointed as a Minister's deputy; he also acts as his chief liaison official with MPs of his party. The post is paid; the head of a large department may have more than one Parliamentary Secretary. Parliamentary Undersecretary of State is the corresponding title when the Minister is a Secretary of State. See PARLIAMENTARY PRIVATE SECRETARY.

Parliament of Saints Another name for the BAREBONES PARLIAMENT.

Parmentier (Cooking) With potatoes. (Name of man said to have introduced the potato to France.)

Parmesan A very hard dry granular cheese, used in grated form in soups and with macaroni. There are 2 distinct kinds, made in the North Italian provinces of Emilia (where Parma is) and LOMBARDY. (Originally made in the Duchy of Parma.)

Parnassians A group of 19th-century French poets led by Leconte de Lisle who, reacting against the excessive emotionalism of their predecessors, turned to cold and pessimistic objectivity and an obsession with form. Some of them later transferred their loyalties to the SYMBOLISTS. (From Le Parnasse contemporain, 1866-76, an anthology of their work.)

Parnassus A mountain in Greece north of DELPHI, one of the traditional homes of the Muses; also sacred to APOLLO and DIONYSUS.

Parnell divorce, The (1889) C. S. Parnell, leader of the Irish Nationalist Party holding the balance of power at Westminster, persuaded Gladstone to offer HOME RULE but, on being involved in a divorce, lost the support both of Gladstone's NONCONFORMIST followers and of the Irish Catholics.

Parsifal (1) German spelling of PER-CIVAL; (2) the title of Wagner's opera on the story of the HOLY GRAIL.

Parsis A small Indian community settled around Bombay, descendants of Persians who fled from MUSLIM persecution in the 8th century. They retain some beliefs of ZOROASTRIANISM but have been influenced by HINDUISM. (Also spelled Parsees.)

Parthenon, The (438 BC) The temple of ATHENE on the ACROPOLIS at Athens, built by Pericles to house a famous chryselephantine (i.e. gold and ivory) statue of her. It became in turn a church, a mosque, and an ammunition store which blew up, but much of it still stands, a noble monument to the Golden Age of Greece. Some of the ELGIN MARBLES came from this source. (Greek, 'temple of the maiden goddess'.)

Parthians A Scythian people of the Caspian region, famous as mounted archers who closed on their enemies (notably the Romans) shooting off their arrows, and continued to shoot, backwards, as they fled again; hence a 'Parthian shot' for a parting shot, repartee or invective uttered on departure and affording no opportunity for reply.

Partington, Dame According to the Rev. Sydney Smith, king of wits, in a political speech at Taunton, a lady with a house on the beach at Sidmouth, Devon, who during a great storm in 1824 was seen with her mop vigorously sweeping back what Smith calls the 'Atlantic Ocean'. He compared her action to the efforts of the House of Lords to obstruct the REFORM BILL of 1832.

Partington, Mrs An American counterpart to Mrs MALAPROP—the name being borrowed from Sydney Smith (see last entry)—created (1847) by Benjamin Penhallow Shillaber in the Boston Post in a series of sketches about her misadventures and her views on most topics under the sun; they were collected as The Life and Sayings of Mrs Partington (1854).

Partisans In World War II a name given to the Communist-led guerrilla forces built up by Tito in Axis-occupied Yugoslavia; among others.

Partition (1) Of Poland by Russia, Austria and PRUSSIA in 1772, 1793 and 1795, and in 1939 by Germany and Russia; (2) of Ireland (1921) into the IRISH FREE STATE and Northern Ireland; (3) of India (1947), into India and PAKISTAN; (4) of Palestine (1948), into Israel and Jordan.

Partridge Shorthand title for Eric Partridge's A Dictionary of Slang and Unconventional English, first published in 1937 and several times revised and enlarged; also, to a lesser extent, for any of his other lexicographical works.

Pascal's Pensées A collection of random notes by Blaise Pascal, the French mathematician and JANSEN-IST, on religion, philosophy and morals. Since his death in 1662, numerous editions of the Pensées, the first in 1670, have appeared.

Pascendi (1907) Pope Pius X's encyclical, which took a conservative stand against the growing modernist movement in the Church.

Pasht Egyptian goddess; see BUBAS-TIS.

Pasionaria, La Nom de guerre of the Joan of Arc of the SPANISH CIVIL WAR; a miner's daughter and a dedicated Communist, whose real name was Dolores Ibarruri. After Franco's victory she went into exile in Moscow. (Spanish, 'passion flower'.)

Pasiphaë In Greek legend, the wife of Minos who got DAEDALUS to make a wooden cow into which she climbed to mate with POSEIDON'S sacred bull. The result was the MINOTAUR.

Passage to India, A (1924) E. M. Forster's novel on the barriers to mutual understanding between individuals and races, demonstrated in the reactions of the Indian and British communities in a small township to an Englishwoman's hysterical accusation against an Indian, Dr Aziz. See FIELDING, CYRIL.

Passchendaele A Belgian village near YPRES, scene of one of the bitterest and costliest struggles of World War I from July to Nov. 1917, in which the Canadians captured the ridge overlooking it but suffered very severe casualties. The Battle of Passchendaele is properly a part of the 3rd Battle of Ypres, but is sometimes used as a synonym for it.

Passfield, Baron The title given to the distinguished Socialist economist Sidney Webb so that he could serve in the Cabinet without standing for election; Beatrice Webb, his wife and collaborator in many books, refused to use the title.

Passion, The The sufferings of Jesus Christ on the Cross. (Latin, 'suffering'.)

Passion Play A miracle play on the PASSION; see OBERAMMERGAU.

Passion Sunday The second Sunday before Easter; see PASSION, The.

Passion Week (1) The week following PASSION SUNDAY. (2) In the ANGLICAN CHURCH, the week after (1), i.e. HOLY WEEK.

Pass Laws The South African laws which require all Africans to carry passes (identification cards); organized opposition to them was first demonstrated by a resolution of the AFRICAN NATIONAL CONGRESS in 1919.

Passover Jewish feast, celebrated in the spring, commemorating the sparing ('passing over') of the Jewish firstborn described in *Exodus* xii.

Paston Letters (1434-1509) Family letters of the Pastons of Norfolk, not meant for publication, written in the time of the WARS OF THE ROSES, and published in the 18th century.

Pastoral Symphony, The (1808) Beethoven's Sixth Symphony, on themes of the kind indicated by its title, e.g. birdsong, a storm, a shepherd's hymn.

PA system Abbreviation for Public-Address system.

Pathans The Muslim PUSHTU-speaking people of Afghanistan, fierce warriors who used to give much trouble on the northwest frontier of British India.

Pathétique, The (1) Beethoven's piano sonata (1798), so named by its publisher on account of its depiction of passionate feeling and suffer-

ing. (2) Tchaikovsky's last symphony, No. 6, first performed a few days before his death (1893), instinct with prophetic foreboding.

Pathet Lao Nationalist party in Laos which, supported by the VIETMINH, was prominent in the fight for independence from 1953 onwards.

Pathfinder, The Nickname of John C. Frémont, referring to his expeditions to Oregon and California (1842-48). He was the first (and unsuccessful Presidential candidate put up by the new REPUBLICAN PARTY (1856) with the slogan 'Free soil, free men, free speech, Fré-mont!'

Pathfinder force Specially selected and trained RAF pilots and navigators of bombers which dropped flares over a target area to guide the main attacking force, first used in raids on Germany in the autumn of 1942.

Path to Rome, The (1902) Hilaire Belloc's discursive description of his walk from France across the Alps to Rome.

Patience (1881) A GILBERT and SULLIVAN OPERA satirizing the aesthetic movement of the day in the person of BUNTHORNE, the fleshly poet. Patience, a milkmaid, dithers between him and a rival poet, Grosvenor, who describes himself as the apostle of simplicity. There is a chorus of Rapturous Maidens and Officers of the Dragoon Guards.

Patmos The Aegean island where, according to *Revelation* i, 9, St John had his vision of the APOCALYPSE.

Patna rice A trade term for high-quality long-grain rice of the kind served with curries. (A district of Bihar, India.)

Patriarchs, The In New York City, a club of the extremely rich founded by one of the Astor family and Ward McAllister (see FOUR HUNDRED); it holds an annual Patriarchs Ball.

Patriots The Bay State Patriots, AMERICAN FOOTBALL LEAGUE. Became member of the AMERICAN CONFERENCE, NATIONAL FOOTBALL LEAGUE in 1970.

Patriots' Day April 19th, a legal holiday in Maine and Massachusetts commemorating the Battle of LEXINGTON.

Patroclus   The cousin and bosom companion of ACHILLES.

Patterne, Sir Willoughby   The conceited and humorless man whose character gives its name to George Meredith's The Egoist (1879); his egoism loses him 2 fiancées.

Paul et Virginie   (1787) A pastoral romance of Bernardin de Saint-Pierre about 2 orphans brought up in idyllic surroundings in Mauritius.

Paul Jones   A dance which, under the direction of a 'caller', affords opportunity to change partners at intervals. (Named for the Scot who fought in the Continental navy in the Revolution and later joined the Russian navy.)

Paul Revere   (The Midnight Ride of) Longfellow's ballad on the American hero who rode from Boston to LEXINGTON in 1775 to give a warning of British troop movements that ensured victory in the first engagement of the War of Independence.

Pavlovian reflex   A phrase in popular use for a reflex action such as a dog's salivation at the sight of food or, more accurately, for salivation at a signal which he has learned to associate with food (i.e. a conditioned reflex). (I. B. Pavlov, Russian physiologist, died 1936.)

Pawnee   A 'blanket' Indian nomadic tribe and confederacy, one of the oldest groups of PLAINS INDIANS, who lived in Nebraska. They provided scouts for the whites and fought against the SIOUX. A few survive in Oklahoma, where they hold an annual powwow at Pawnee.

PBL   Public Broadcasting Laboratory (1967), established by the FORD FOUNDATION as an experiment in broadcasting noncommercial programs from over 80 educational stations; see PTV; NET.

PCM   Initials standing for Pulse Code Modulation, a telephone device to permit 24 conversations to be transmitted simultaneously over 2 circuits by sampling each in turn at 8000 times a second. This increases the capacity of existing services without additional cable laying and its concomitant street excavations.

PDQ   Initials for pretty damned quick, meaning 'at once if not sooner'.

Peabody (George Foster) Awards   Given for enlightened achievement in TV and radio, e.g. in the fields of international understanding, programs for the young, education, documentaries and news, as well as in entertainment.

Peabody's Buildings   Blocks of apartments built for the London poor by an American expatriate philanthropist, George Peabody (died 1869).

Peace   (1942) A hybrid tea rose which produces very large pale yellow flowers with pink edges.

'Peaceable Kingdom, The'   (c. 1835) A painting, of which he made many versions, executed for his fellow QUAKERS in Pennsylvania by the visionary 'primitive' artist Edward Hicks, a sign painter by trade. It shows a large group of wild and domestic animals, with children. (Brooklyn Museum.)

Peace Ballot   (1935) A British national ballot organized by the LEAGUE OF NATIONS UNION; 10 million people voted in favor of reducing armaments; the result was said to have encouraged Hitler.

Peace Corps   A body of American volunteers recruited (1961) by President Kennedy to provide teachers, doctors, agriculturalists and other trained staff to work in underdeveloped countries at subsistence rates of pay; similar corps were formed in other Western countries.

Peach Melba   Peach slices with ice cream and cream; in hotel French, Pêche Melba. (Named after Dame Nellie Melba, Australian soprano.)

Peach State   A nickname for Georgia, where peaches are now a valuable crop in the center and south.

Peachum, Polly   In the BEGGAR'S OPERA, the daughter of a receiver of stolen goods who marries Capt. MACHEATH.

Peake's Commentary   (1919) Short title of a commentary on the Bible by A. S. Peake. A revised edition was published in the 1950s.

Peanuts (1950) Charles Schulz's comic strip in which tiny children with yapping mouths act out adult foibles at a new pitch of intensity. CHARLIE BROWN is the leader, plagued by the bullying Lucy, and accompanied by his dog SNOOPY.

Pearl Harbor The US naval base on the island of Oahu, Hawaii. The surprise attack (7 Dec. 1941) by Japanese naval aircraft on the US fleet based there brought the USA into World War II.

Pearly King and Queen (London) The winners of competitions held from time to time (e.g. at the INTERNATIONAL HORSE SHOW) for the best examples of the COCKNEY costermongers' traditional ceremonial dress ('Pearlies'), covered with mother-of-pearl buttons from top to toe.

Peasant Brueghel Nickname of Pieter Brueghel I (1525-69), the greatest of a family of Flemish painters, father of VELVET BRUEGHEL and HELL BRUEGHEL. He was so called because his favorite subject was peasant life; he himself was far from being a peasant. See 'MASSACRE OF THE INNOCENTS'. (Also spelled Breughel or Breugel.)

Peasants' Revolt, The (1381) A rising in Kent and Essex led by John Ball, Wat Tyler and Jack Straw, who captured London and compelled Richard II to abolish serfdom. After Tyler's murder the rising was put down and all concessions canceled.

Peat, Marwick, Mitchell A leading firm of London accountants, with branches in many US cities.

Peck's Bad Boy A humorous chronicle written by George Wilbur Peck for the Milwaukee Sun, which he owned and edited (1878-90); the sketches were later published in book form and the title passed into common use.

Pecksniff The arch-hypocrite of Dickens's MARTIN CHUZZLEWIT, a relative of Martin's, with 2 famous daughters, Charity and Mercy.

Pecos Bill The Paul BUNYAN of southwestern cowboys, whose mother killed 45 Indians with a broom one day and weaned him on moonshine. With such a background it is not surprising that he dug the RIO GRANDE, hugged two grizzlies to death, taught broncos to buck and invented tarantulas as a joke. His horse, Widow-maker, nurtured on nitroglycerine and barbed wire, once threw a man so high he landed on Pike's Peak. Bill's end was sad; he met a Bostonian in a mail-order cowboy outfit — and died laffing.

Peculiar People, The (1838) A sect founded in London, without creed or clergy, who in illness rely on prayer, rejecting medical aid. (From Titus ii, 14, 'to purify unto himself a peculiar people'.)

Peeler Old name for a policeman. (After Sir Robert Peel, who founded the London Metropolitan Police in 1829; the alternative nickname, 'bobby', comes from his Christian name.)

Peelites Those who supported Sir Robert Peel when he repealed the CORN LAWS (1846) in the teeth of opposition, led by Disraeli, from his own Conservative Party. They then formed a third party which in 1859 was mainly absorbed into the Liberal Party. Gladstone was a leading Peelite.

Peel Report (1937) The report of a Royal Commission which recommended the partition of Palestine.

Peenemünde The research station on the northeast coast of Germany where the Germans developed (1937-45) liquid-fuel rockets (including the V-2) and guided missiles; bombed by the RAF in August 1943.

Peeping Tom In a late addition to the Lady GODIVA legend, the tailor who peeped at her as she rode naked through Coventry, and was struck blind.

Peer Gynt (1867) Ibsen's verse fantasy in many episodes of a warm-hearted but irresponsible peasant lad who, feeling unworthy of the virtuous SOLVEIG, sets out to taste all experience. His character deteriorates during his adventures in many lands, which include successful slave trading. He comes back to find a mysterious Button Molder waiting to melt him down as useless dross, but is redeemed by Solveig's continuing love for him.

Peer Gynt Suite (1876) Grieg's incidental music for Ibsen's drama (see last entry), commissioned by Ibsen. It includes the well-known 'Death of Åse', 'ANITRA'S Dance' and 'SOLVEIG'S Song'.

Pegasus In Greek legend a winged horse caught by BELLEROPHON.

Peggotty, Clara In Dickens's DAVID COPPERFIELD, David's nurse, member of a Yarmouth fisherman's family which plays a prominent part in the story.

Peiping Name (meaning 'northern peace') given to Peking (meaning 'northern capital') by Chiang Kaishek when he set up his capital at Nanking (1928); the Communists restored the ancient name in 1949.

Peking incident, The See MARCO POLO BRIDGE INCIDENT.

Peking Legations, Siege of (1900) The culmination of the BOXER MOVEMENT, when the Boxers besieged the foreign communities in Peking for 2 months, with the secret support of the Dowager Empress. They were relieved by an international force, including British, US, Japanese and Russian troops.

Peking Man A specimen of PITHECANTHROPINES found 1927–29 near Peking, China.

Pekoe See ORANGE PEKOE.

Pelagianism The Christian doctrine of those who denied original sin and the eternal damnation of unbaptized infants; they believed in free will and that the first steps toward salvation could be taken by the human will ('justification by works') unaided by God's mercy ('grace'), a view contrary to that of St Augustine but to which the JESUITS tended. (Pelagius, Latin name of a 5th-century British monk called Morgan, who taught in Rome and was condemned by the Pope.)

Pelargonium See GERANIUM.

Pele The POLYNESIAN goddess of volcanoes; threads of spun glass formed from cooling lava and seen in some eruptions are called Pele's Hair. Confusingly, a type of explosive eruption is named Peléan, after the Mt Pelée eruption in 1902; this mountain is in the West Indies, and the similarity of name must be assumed to be coincidental.

Pelegrina, La A fabulous pearl, twin of La PEREGRINA, which was retained by the Queen of Spain when the Spanish monarchy ended in 1931.

Pelican books See PENGUINS.

Pelican State Nickname of Louisiana.

Pelion and Ossa Two mountains of Greece; according to legend giants, variously named, piled Pelion on Ossa in order to reach the abode of the immortals and rape HERA and ARTEMIS. They were defeated and imprisoned under the earth, where they cause earthquakes and volcanic eruptions.

Pelléas et Mélisande Title of Maeterlinck's play (1892) and Debussy's opera (1902) based on it. Mélisande falls in love with Pelléas, the brother of her husband, who kills him; she dies after giving birth to Pelléas's child.

Pelmanism (1) A system of memory training introduced about the time of World War I. (2) A memory-testing card game. (Proprietary name.)

Peloponnesian War (431–404 BC) The war between Athens and Sparta caused by dislike of Athenian imperialism. It destroyed forever Athenian political dominance of Greece. The great *locus classicus* of the War is the incomparable History by Thucydides.

Pelops In Greek legend, the son of TANTALUS and founder of the dynasty which ruled the Peloponnesus. He won his wife by bribing a charioteer to lose a race to him, but murdered him when he claimed his reward. This was the origin of the curse of Pelops inherited by the House of ATREUS, who was his son.

Pelton wheel One of the 3 main types of wheel used in hydroelectric plant; the rim is fitted with cupshaped paddles which are struck by high-pressure jets of water.

Pembroke table Elegant occasional table with short drop leaves supported by brackets, designed by CHIPPENDALE, HEPPLEWHITE and SHERATON, notable for fine cabinetwork and veneering, and today fetching very high prices.

PEN Club (1921) An international association of writers. (Initials stand for: Poets, Playwrights, Editors, Essayists, Novelists.)

Pendennis (1850) Thackeray's novel about Arthur Pendennis, an idle and conceited writer who gets himself involved with various women, including the daughter of a blackmailing escaped convict about whom his uncle, Major Pendennis, misadvises him. In the end he marries the girl with whom he was brought up, Laura Bell.

Pendleton Roundup A rodeo classic held in September at Pendleton, Ore.

Penelope In Greek legend, the faithful wife of ODYSSEUS. She spent his 20-year absence bringing up their son TELEMACHUS and fending off her suitors (Odysseus was presumed dead) by promising to marry one of them when she had finished weaving a shroud for her father-in-law; this she wove all day and unravelled each night.

Penfold, The (UK) A stroke-play golf tournament for PGA members, and amateurs with a handicap of scratch or better, played in May. Prize money totals $10,000 (Sponsored by Golf Balls Developments Ltd.)

Penguin Island (1908) Anatole France's amusing novel of a blind monk who blesses a colony of penguins thinking they are human, which they miraculously become. The account of their subsequent development affords the author opportunity to satirize French history, with special reference to the DREYFUS CASE. (French title, *L'île des pingouins*.)

Penguins Early paperback editions, originally of reprints; to these other series were later added, such as Pelicans (cultural and scientific, including commissioned books), Puffins (for children) etc. (Firm founded by Allen Lane.)

Penguins The Pittsburgh Penguins, NATIONAL HOCKEY LEAGUE.

Peninsular War (1808-14) Begun by a Portuguese appeal for help after invasion by France, and the placing of Napoleon's brother Joseph on the Spanish throne. Wellesley (the future Duke of Wellington) defeated the French in Portugal; Sir John Moore went to Spain (see CORUNNA); Wellington returned and drove the French out of Spain, after victories at Salamanca and Vittoria.

Peninsula State Nickname of Florida.

Penkovsky spy case (1962) The case of the Soviet Colonel, Oleg Penkovsky, who for a year leaked important information to the West through Greville WYNNE. He may have disclosed Russian intentions in the CUBAN CRISIS.

'Penn's Treaty' (1772) Benjamin West's painting of a scene from Pennsylvanian history, 'William Penn's Treaty with the Indians'. (Independence Hall, Philadelphia.)

Pennsylvania, University of (1740) One of the IVY LEAGUE, at Philadelphia.

Pennsylvania Academy of the Fine Arts (1805) The oldest US art institution, in Philadelphia, with unofficial beginnings dating back to 1791. Its collection displays the evolution of American art down to modern times, and its schools have trained many leading artists.

Pennsylvania Avenue The wide tree-lined avenue in Washington, D.C., that runs from the Capitol past the WHITE HOUSE and on toward GEORGETOWN. The original plan was somewhat spoiled when the road was blocked by the Treasury and LIBRARY OF CONGRESS buildings.

Pennsylvania Dutch Name given to ANABAPTIST refugees from the Rhineland; their descendants; their dialect. The earliest settled (1683) in and around what is now Lancaster County, southeast Pennsylvania. Famous for their industrious, religious, Spartan way of life, they still speak a German dialect and wear old-fashioned clothes. Also applied to their distinctive painted softwood furniture, often with floral patterns, which combined English and German peasant styles.

Penny Black (1840) The first adhesive postage stamp, but by no means the rarest; it bears the head of Queen Victoria.

Penrod (1914) The Indiana novelist Booth Tarkington's humorous novel about the escapades of young Penrod Schofield in a typical Midwestern setting; there were 2 sequels, and the trilogy was republished as *Penrod: His Complete Story* (1931).

Penseroso, Il See ALLEGRO, L'.

'Penseur, Le' Rodin's sculpture of a seated figure, originally intended to represent Dante in a larger work. (French, 'the thinker'.)

Penshurst Place A large country house near Tunbridge Wells, Kent, dating back to the 14th century; the birthplace of Sir Philip Sidney and still the home of the Sidney family (Viscount De L'Isle).

Pentagon, The The Defense Department, a huge complex of 5 concentric pentagons of buildings, completed in 1942 at Arlington, Virginia, across the Potomac from Washington, D.C.

Pentateuch The first 5 books of the Old Testament, traditionally written by Moses, compiled in the 4th century BC. (Greek, 'five books'.)

Pentathlon An Olympic contest for women in which individuals compete in all of 5 events: high and long jump, putting the weight, hurdle race, 200 meters. Also a similar men's contest (dropped from the OLYMPIC GAMES) in long jump, discus, javelin, 200 and 1500 meter events. (Greek, '5 contests'; see MODERN PENTATHLON.

Pentecost (1) Jewish harvest festival, held on the 50th day after the 2nd day of the PASSOVER (*Leviticus* xxiii); this came to be associated also with the celebration of the giving of the Law to Moses on Mount Sinai. (2) Earlier name of the Christian celebration on WHITSUNDAY. (Greek, '50th'.)

Pentecostalism (1909) A revivalist religion based on belief in 'speaking with tongues' (*Acts* i, 4-13), i.e. miraculous speech in languages unknown to the speaker. At first virtually confined to the INNER CITY areas of the US, it has been spreading in Latin America, Africa and Western Europe; in the 1960s it was even being adopted by students in American colleges. There are hundreds of denominations with different names, including the Assemblies of God (the largest in the US), and the world total of Pentecostals has been put as high as 35 million. (See WHITSUNDAY.)

Pentothal A general anesthetic, given by injection.

People's A Communist catchword, applied to republics, 'democracy' and every kind of organization; in so far as it has any meaning, it means that the People have considerably less say than in the corresponding organizations not so named, but that the autocrats who run them do try, or pretend, to put the interests of the masses first.

People's Commissars Early designation, abolished by Stalin in 1946, of Ministers of the USSR.

Pepys's Diary The uninhibited diary of Samuel Pepys (1633-1703), a highly efficient Secretary to the Admiralty for many years and a President of the ROYAL SOCIETY. Written in his own private shorthand, which was not deciphered until 1825, it covers the 9 years of his life from 1660 until his sight failed. Almost the whole of it was published in 1896.

P/E ratio (Stock Exchange) The price/earnings ratio of a stock, i.e. its price divided by the net earnings per unit.

Percheron A continental breed of farm horse of mixed ancestry, very large but handy. (La Perche, Normandy.)

Percival (Perceval, PARSIFAL) The pure knight of ARTHURIAN LEGEND to whom the HOLY GRAIL was revealed.

Percy's Reliques A collection of traditional ballads rescued from oblivion by Bishop Percy in his *Reliques of Ancient English Poetry* (1765).

Perdita and Florizel (1) Characters

in Shakespeare's The WINTER'S TALE; Perdita is marooned on what Shakespeare calls 'the seacoast of Bohemia', and at the end of the play marries the King of Bohemia's son, Florizel. (2) Nicknames of Mrs. Robinson, mistress of the PRINCE REGENT (George IV), an actress who made her name playing the part of Perdita, and of the Prince. (Latin, 'lost (i.e. marooned) woman'.)

Père Goriot (1834) One of the novels of Balzac's COMÉDIE HUMAINE, in which a foolishly fond father squanders his last sou on a pair of preternaturally cold, ungrateful daughters, both of whom have made rich marriages.

Peregrina, La A fabulous pearl, twin of La PELEGRINA, which once belonged to the King of Spain and was later bought by Richard Burton.

Perfidious Albion A phrase attributed to Napoleon (but he was not the first to call England 'perfidious').

Pergamum An important city of Asia Minor (north of modern IZMIR) in the 3rd-2nd centuries BC, where parchment, named after it, was made; famous for its library and sculptures.

Pericles, Prince of Tyre (1608) Shakespeare's play in which Pericles is parted from his wife and then daughter in circumstances which lead him to presume them dead, but at last is reunited to both.

Périgord (Périgueuse) Cooking term for dishes served with truffles.

Perissodactyla An order of hoofed mammals with an uneven number of toes (see ARTIODACTYLA), including the horse, rhinoceros, ass, tapir and zebra.

Perm A city of the USSR, for a time known as Molotov.

Permian Period The most recent of the periods of the PALEOZOIC ERA, lasting from about 275 to 240 million years ago. (Permia, an ancient kingdom east of the Volga.)

Peronista Party The party which supported Peron, Argentine President (1946-55) until his exile to Spain. In 1965 a neo-Peronista Party gained a quarter of the seats in the House of Deputies.

Perpendicular (1375-1575) The final stage of English GOTHIC ARCHITECTURE, most easily recognized by the vertical lines running right through the windows from bottom to top. The effect of loftiness was often enhanced by elaborate fan vaulting, of which one of the finest examples is King's College Chapel, Cambridge.

Perry Oaks A new terminal at London Airport (HEATHROW), west of the central area.

Perseid meteors A shoal of meteors which orbit the sun and through which the earth passes each August, producing a display of shooting stars emanating from the direction of PERSEUS.

Persephone Greek goddess of the seed corn or sown corn (Roman Proserpina), daughter of ZEUS and DEMETER. She spends 8 months of each year on earth, personifying the sown corn (see ELEUSINIAN MYSTERIES), and in this capacity was called the Maiden (Koré). After the 'Death of the Maiden' (i.e. harvest) in May (in Ancient Greece) she was abducted to the Underworld by HADES, during the 4 hot months when Demeter withers vegetation, to reign as Queen of the Underworld (i.e. she represents the seed corn buried underground in sealed jars to await September sowing). Compare ADONIS; TAMMUZ.

Persepolis The ACHAEMENID capital of Persia begun by Darius I, and today an impressive ruin northeast of Shiraz.

Perseus A major hero of Greek legend, son of ZEUS by DANAË, and legendary founder of the MYCENAEAN CIVILIZATION. He cut off MEDUSA'S head, with which he turned ATLAS into a mountain, and other enemies into stone. He rescued ANDROMEDA, and their son was the traditional ancestor of the Persians.

Perseus A northern constellation between CASSIOPEIA and TAURUS, representing PERSEUS holding MEDUSA'S head in his left hand. In the head of Medusa are ALGOL (beta Persei) and the nova observed in 1901. See last entry.

'Perseus' (1554) Cellini's bronze sculpture of PERSEUS holding up the severed head of the GORGON; now standing in the Loggia dei Lanzi, Florence.

Pershing A US tactical ground-to-ground ballistic missile, with a range of 400 miles.

'Persistence of Memory, The' (1931) A weird SURREALIST painting by Salvador Dali, depicting a limp watch hanging on a tree. (Museum of Modern Art, N.Y.C.)

Persuasion (1818) Jane Austen's last novel, based in part on her own experiences. Anne Elliot is overpersuaded by a friend into rejection of her suitor Frederick Wentworth, a naval officer, but after many vicissitudes and misunderstandings accepts him.

Pestalozzi Children's Village Trust Formed to provide care and education for deprived children from the less-developed countries; runs a children's village at Sedlescombe, Sussex. See next entry.

Pestalozzi system The earliest of a series of schemes (see MONTESSORI SYSTEM) for reforming infant education, based on learning by doing, nature study and other forms of accurate observation to promote accurate thinking; aimed at the full development of the potentialities of each individual. (Johann Pestalozzi, Swiss educationist, 1746-1827.)

Peter and the Wolf (1940) Prokofiev's orchestral piece in which a narrator tells a fairy tale against the musical background. The characters are each represented by a particular instrument, e.g. Peter by the violins.

Peter Bell (1819) A poem by William Wordsworth of how a thief about to steal a donkey is converted to a new life by observing the donkey's devotion to its master; its critics, including Shelley, felt that the poet had strayed too far along his chosen path of sublime simplicity.

Peter Grimes (1945) Benjamin Britten's opera based on a poem by Crabbe (1810), who was born in Aldeburgh where Britten settled. Grimes is a fisherman suspected of having brought about the death at sea of his apprentice. He is too proud and stubborn to accept the help offered him in establishing his innocence.

Peterlee (1948) (UK) A NEW TOWN 11 miles east of Durham, designed to take 30,000 inhabitants.

Peterloo (1819) (English history) An incident at St Peter's Fields (now the site of the Free Trade Hall), Manchester, when a large but orderly working-class crowd listening to a speech on political reform was broken up by cavalry; in the confusion, some were killed and many were injured (the figures were never established), but the Manchester magistrates were congratulated by the Home Secretary for ordering out the troops. (Coined derisively on the analogy of WATERLOO.)

Peter Pan (1904) J. M. Barrie's evergreen play for children, in which Peter Pan, the boy who wouldn't grow up, and the fairy Tinker Bell, whisk off Wendy and her brothers to Never-Never Land, full of pirates and Indians, not to mention a crocodile which has swallowed an alarm clock. There is a statue to him in Kensington Gardens.

Peter Principle, The (1969) A book subtitled 'Why Things Always Go Wrong' which states that 'in a Hierarchy, every employee tends to rise to his level of incompetence', i.e. a man who does his job well is promoted until he reaches one he cannot cope with, and there he sticks. He can be removed by pseudopromotion, e.g. Percussive Sublimation (i.e. kicked upstairs) or Lateral Arabesque (i.e. given a larger desk and thicker carpet in some remote part of the building out of harm's way). (By Canadian-born US professor, L. J. Peter.)

Peter Rabbit (1901) A children's book written and illustrated by Beatrix Potter.

Peter Simple (1834) The best of Capt. Marryat's vigorous naval stories, notable for its lively characterizations.

Peter's Pence (1) A tax of a penny per householder collected in England from ANGLO-SAXON times un-

til the REFORMATION as a gift to
the Pope. (2) Now used of voluntary contributions to the Papal
treasury.

Petit Caporal, Le Napoleon I's nickname among his soldiers.

Petition of Right (1628) A request by
Parliament for the abolition of illegal taxation, imprisonment and bil-
leting, accepted by Charles I.

Petit Trianon A château in the park
at Versailles, a few hundred yards
from the GRAND TRIANON; built by
Louis XV for Mme de Pompadour,
given by Louis XVI to Marie Antoi-
nette and by Napoleon to Marie
Louise.

Pet Marjorie Margaret Fleming, who
died in 1811 aged 8, but not before
she had penned the immortal lines
(of a pug dog): His noses cast is of
the roman/He is a very pretty
weoman/I could not get a rhyme
for roman / And was oblidged to call
it weoman.

Petra John Burgon's 'rose-red city
half as old as Time'; its ruins can
still be seen south of the Dead Sea in
the Jordanian desert. It was first the
Edomite, then the NABATAEAN capital.

Petrified Forest, The (1935) Robert
Sherwood's melodrama on his favorite theme of sacrifice. A NEW
ENGLAND writer, disillusioned by
failure, arrives at a sleazy lunch
bar in the Arizona desert and hires
a gangster to kill him, after amend-
ing his insurance policy in favor
of the proprietor's daughter so that
she can escape from her surroundings.

Petrified Forest National Park
(1962) A park in Arizona, northeast
of Phoenix, containing spectacular
petrified trees of the MESOZOIC age in
a desert setting, part of the PAINTED
DESERT, the Blue Forest and American Indian ruins.

Petrov spy case (1954) Vladimir Petrov, a Soviet spy in the Soviet embassy in Australia, defected and disclosed the existence of a Russian spy
ring in that country.

Petruchio See KATHARINA.

Petrushka (1911) The most popular
of Stravinsky's ballets, about pup-

pets which come to life; the setting
is a fair at ST PETERSBURG.

Petticoat Lane The most famous of
London street markets, in Middlesex
Street, E.1, between Liverpool Street
and Aldgate Stations, where on Sundays a wide range of secondhand
goods is sold.

Petty Cury (UK) A short narrow
street in the center of Cambridge,
leading to the marketplace. ('Little
street of the cooks', from Latin *cur-
are*, 'to preserve meat'.)

Petty Sessions (UK) Magistrates'
(popularly called Police) Courts, the
lowest courts, with summary jurisdiction (i.e. without jury) in minor
offenses and powers up to 6 months'
imprisonment for any one offense.
In small towns they comprise not
less than 2 JUSTICES OF THE PEACE assisted by a magistrate's clerk, usually a solicitor; in bigger towns, a
stipendiary magistrate, who is a barrister and sits alone; in London, a
metropolitan police magistrate. All
these also hold preliminary inqui-
ries into more serious cases which
may have to go to QUARTER SESSIONS
or ASSIZES; and they deal with various civil matters (e.g. maintenance
orders, licenses).

Petulengro A gypsy in George Borrow's LAVENGRO and The ROMANY
RYE. (Gypsy, 'shoesmith'.)

Petworth House A country house at
Petworth, Sussex, dating mainly
from the 17th century, which has
one of the finest art collections in
Britain, and notable Grinling Gibbons carving.

Peulhs See FULANI.

Peyton Place (1956) The seamy story
of a decayed textile town in New
Hampshire, written by Grace Meta-
lious, who was born in Manchester,
N.H.

PGA Initials commonly used for
Professional Golfers' Association (of
Britain, Ireland, USA etc.).

PGA Order of Merit A list of leading
professional golfers drawn up on the
basis of points gained in various
specified tournaments, by a PGA.

PGR Initials used for psychogalvan-
ic reflex, a change in electrical potential on the skin caused by emo-

tion. It is recorded through electrodes placed on the hands, and is one of the changes measured by a lie detector.

Phaedra In Greek legend, a daughter of MINOS and the wife of THESEUS. APHRODITE made her fall in love with her stepson, HIPPOLYTUS, who rejected her. She then accused him of trying to seduce her. The story is told in Racine's *Phèdre* (1677).

Phaedra complex A psychoanalytic term for the emotional reactions between stepparents and stepchildren, especially (since the mother usually has the custody of her children) between a teen-age girl and her stepfather. By appealing to him, she tends to win any dispute with her mother; *per contra*, he is jealous of her boyfriends. See also PHAEDRA.

Phaethon In Greek legend, son of HELIOS who, allowed to drive his father's chariot of the sun, was unable to control the horses. ZEUS struck him dead with a thunderbolt lest he should burn up the earth.

Phantom (1961) US high-performance tactical strike aircraft; speed Mach 2, range 1000 miles, built by McDonnell. A British version partly produced in the UK, with Rolls Royce turbofan engines, began service with the Royal Navy and the RAF in 1968.

Pharisees A Jewish sect which arose in the 2nd century BC, strict observers of the Law, in conflict with the SADDUCEES; certain Pharisees were sharply attacked in the Gospels. The Jews of modern times regard themselves as descendants of this sect. (Hebrew, 'the separated ones'.)

Pharos A lighthouse at Alexandria built during the reign of the PTOLEMIES and numbered among the SEVEN WONDERS OF THE WORLD. The light was provided by torches or fires.

Phèdre (1677) Racine's play about the PHAEDRA legend.

Phi Beta Kappa (1776) A US fraternity or 'honor society' for those distinguished in the field of general scholarship, founded at WILLIAM AND MARY COLLEGE; the first fraternity to use Greek letters.

Phi Kappa Phi (1897) A US fraternity or 'honor society' for those distinguished in general scholarship.

Philadelphia lawyer Colloquialism for a very competent and learned lawyer, or a very shrewd person; used in such phrases as 'It would puzzle a Philadelphia lawyer'.

Philadelphia Mint (1792) The first US Mint, Philadelphia then being the US capital; see BUREAU OF THE MINT.

Philadelphia Story, The (1931) A sophisticated comedy by Philip Barry; the rebellious heiress of a conventional Philadelphia family, on the brink of a second and unpromising marriage, is rescued by her first husband who remarries her.

Philby spy case (1963) The defection of H.A.R. ('Kim') Philby to Russia in 1963. He was recruited by the Russians as a Communist sympathizer on coming down from CAMBRIDGE UNIVERSITY in 1933, rose high in MI-6 during World War II, acted as liaison with the CIA, tipped off BURGESS AND MACLEAN in 1951, and was still in British government pay when he fled from Beirut, where he was an *Observer* correspondent.

Philemon and Baucis In Greek legend a poor DARBY AND JOAN couple whose wish that they should remain together even in death is granted when ZEUS turns them into 2 trees with intertwining branches, as a reward for the hospitality they had offered him.

Philip drunk and Philip sober According to tradition, a woman condemned by Philip of Macedon (father of Alexander the Great) when he was drunk told him she would appeal when he was sober; hence 'an appeal from Philip drunk to Philip sober'.

Philippe Égalité The Duke of Orleans who at the FRENCH REVOLUTION adopted the name Égalité and voted for the execution of his own cousin, Louis XVI; but was himself guillotined later. His son was Louis Philippe, KING OF THE FRENCH.

Philippi (42 BC) The battle in which Mark Antony and OCTAVIAN (the future Augustus) defeated Brutus and Cassius who, 2 years earlier, had assassinated Julius Caesar. (City of

Macedonia.)

Philippine Sea, Battle of the (June 1944) A decisive US naval victory over the Japanese in the Marianas.

Phillies The Philadelphia Phillies, NATIONAL (Baseball) LEAGUE, playing at the Connie Mack Stadium.

Phillips curve A mathematical method applied by the London economist, A. W. Phillips, in an attempt to establish the relationship between the level of unemployment and the rate of change of money wages. As it appeared to show that wage stability entails a high rate of unemployment (17% in the US), economists have been busy since trying to prove that 'it ain't necessarily so'.

Phillips (Sarah Tryphen) lectures (1961) Lectures given on American history and literature, under the auspices of the BRITISH ACADEMY.

Philly Short for Philadelphia, Penn.

Philoctetes A hero of Greek legend abandoned on the island of Lemnos suffering from a terrible wound. He has HERACLES' bow and arrows, without which Troy cannot be taken; in Sophocles' play *Philoctetes* he is persuaded to come to Troy, where he kills PARIS.

Philomela In Greek legend, a princess of Athens raped by her brother-in-law Tereus, and changed into a nightingale. Her sister Procne becomes a swallow.

Phineas Finn (1869-80) Collective title of Trollope's 'parliamentary' novels, consisting of *Phineas Finn, Phineas Redux, The Prime Minister* and *The Duke's Children*. Phineas is a penurious Irishman of great charm who comes to London and eventually becomes Undersecretary of State for the Colonies. See OMNIUM, DUKES OF.

Phiz The pseudonym of Hablot Browne (1815-82), who illustrated Dickens's novels and the first JORROCKS novel of Surtees.

Phlegethon In Greek legend the river of flames, one of the rivers of the Underworld.

Phoebe lamp American pioneers' name for a primitive tallow-and-wick lamp of the type used down the ages, e.g. by the Ancient Greeks.

(Phoebe, Greek moon goddess.)

Phoebe Snow The name taken in the early 20th century by the Lackawanna Railroad, officially the Delaware, Lackawanna & Western, since 1960 renamed the Erie-Lackawanna Railroad. Also the name of its crack daily express on the 397-mile New York-Buffalo run. (From a white-clad cartoon character, adopted as a symbol of cleanliness; it was once also known as the Delay, Linger & Wait.)

Phoebus See APOLLO.

Phoenicians Greek name for the Semitic people of the coastal cities (Tyre, Sidon, Byblos, Megiddo) of what is now Lebanon; the Canaanites of the Bible. Confined by mountains to their coastal strip, they turned to seafaring, and founded Carthage. They were excellent goldsmiths and jewelers, and famous for their Tyrian-purple dye.

Phoenix Park A large Dublin park containing a zoo, racetrack, polo ground and the official residence of the President of Ireland.

Phoenix Park murders (1882) The assassination by FENIANS of the British Chief and Undersecretaries for Ireland, in Dublin. See also PHOENIX PARK.

Physicists, The (1962) Friedrich Dürrenmatt's play in which 3 of the world's leading scientists take refuge in an asylum in order to keep their latest discoveries from mankind.

Physiocrats A group of 18th-century French economists led by Quesnay, who held that agriculture was the sole source of wealth, deprecated commerce, and advocated a single land tax paid by all.

Piat The British equivalent of the US bazooka, a very effective antitank rocket gun developed by Imperial Chemical Industries. (Initials of projector, infantry, antitank.)

PIB Initials used for the PRICES AND INCOMES BOARD.

Picardy A former province of France, capital Amiens. It corresponds to the modern *département* of Somme and neighboring parts of Artois, Oise and Aisne.

Piccadilly Circus The center of

London's West End, once regarded as 'the hub of the Empire' but now slipping socially; the junction of Piccadilly, REGENT STREET and Shaftesbury Avenue (the theater district behind which lies SOHO) and adjacent to Leicester Square. In the center is 'EROS', beneath which the world's hippies gather to plan their next demo or trip to Katmandu. (The derivation of the name is uncertain; various suggestions are amusing rather than well founded.)

Piccadilly stroke-play tournament A tournament played at the Wentworth Club, Surrey, in October by the leading 40 players in the PGA ORDER OF MERIT, for prize money totalling $10,000. (Sponsored by Carreras.)

Piccadilly World match-play tournament A 36-hole golf tournament played at the Wentworth Club, Surrey, in October, by the 8 leading golfers of the world for a trophy and prize money totalling $38,000. (Sponsored by Carreras.)

Pickwick Papers, The (1837) Dickens's best-known novel, a series of episodes in the lives of members of the Pickwick Club. See BARDELL V. PICKWICK; DINGLEY DELL; EATANSWILL; JINGLE; WARDLE; the WELLERS.

Picts A probably pre-Celtic race in central Scotland, absorbed by the Scots.

Picture Post (1938-57) A London weekly illustrated magazine on the lines of *Life*.

Pictures at an Exhibition (1874) Musorgski's piano suite describing 10 pictures in an exhibition held after the death of his artist friend Hartmann. It is heard at its best in the orchestral version by Ravel.

Piedmont A region of northern Italy between the Alps and the Apennines, capital Turin; it was under the House of SAVOY from the 11th century.

Pied Piper of Hamelin In German legend a stranger who rid Hamelin Town in Brunswick of rats by playing his pipe; when the townsfolk refused to reward him, he piped their children away. The best-known version is Robert Browning's poem (1842); the legend was also

used in an early Walt Disney film.

Pierre (Bezukhov) See WAR AND PEACE.

Pierrot A late addition to the stock characters of pantomime, created in Paris in the early 19th century; a whiteface melancholy figure in loose white fancy clothes.

Piers Plowman, Vision Concerning (14th century) William Langland's alliterative poem, a religious allegory castigating the evils of Church and society, and painting a vivid picture of his times.

Pietà In art, a representation of the Madonna mourning the dead Christ. Among the most famous are Michelangelo's versions in Florence Cathedral, Milan and St Peter's Rome; and a Tintoretto (1571) at Milan. (Italian, 'pity'.)

Pig and Whistle An inn sign, corruption of Piggin and Wassail. (*Piggin*, a small wooden drinking vessel.)

Pike's Peak or bust! The motto of those who took part in the GOLD RUSH (1859) around what is now Denver. (A ROCKY MOUNTAIN peak in Colorado.)

Piledriver A mixed drink of vodka, bitters and an orange liqueur.

Pilgrimage of Grace (1536-37) A revolt in the north of England, after the DISSOLUTION OF THE MONASTERIES, of nobles, clergy and peasants. Under Robert Aske they took York and Doncaster, but withdrew on a promise of pardon which was not honored.

Pilgrim Fathers (1620) PURITANS who fled from England to Leyden in Holland in the early years of James I's reign and, led by John Bradford, sailed thence, called at Plymouth where they were joined by others, and crossed the Atlantic in the MAYFLOWER to found the first of the NEW ENGLAND (and second of the American) settlements, at (New) Plymouth, now in Massachusetts.

Pilgrims, The (1902) A club founded in memory of the PILGRIM FATHERS, with premises in London (Pilgrims of Great Britain) and New York (Pilgrims of the US; 1903).

Pilgrim's Progress (1678) John Bunyan's description of Christian's allegorical journey from the City of Destruction to the CELESTIAL CITY. See DOUBTING CASTLE; SLOUGH OF DESPOND; VANITY FAIR.

Pilgrim Trust (1930) Founded by the US railway magnate, banker and philanthropist, Edward S. Harkness, who left $5 million to be spent for the benefit of Britain. It is used for the preservation of ancient buildings, grants to learned societies, the NATIONAL TRUST and social welfare schemes, and for the purchase of works of art.

Pilkington Report (1962) (UK) A report on broadcasting which severely criticized the low moral and intellectual standards of commercial TV and recommended that the planning of its programs should be handed over to the ITA, who would sell advertising time to the TV companies. No significant action was taken on this, but a recommendation that the next new TV service should be allotted to the BBC, not to ITV, was implemented by the establishment of BBC-2.

Pill, The An oral contraceptive. After 10 years' public use the medical profession was still uncertain of the incidence of its side effects, alleged by some to include blood clotting, high blood pressure, jaundice, diabetes and neurotic symptoms, while others reported increased well-being.

Pillars of Hercules The Greek name for the Straits of Gibraltar.

Pillars of Society (1877) Ibsen's play about a corrupt and hypocritical industrialist.

Pillnitz, Declaration of (Aug. 1791) The announcement by the Emperor of Austria and the King of PRUSSIA that the cause of Louis XVI was the cause of monarchies everywhere; the chief reason for the French Revolutionary Wars, see VALMY.

Pilsen German name of the Czech city, Plzen. See next entry.

Pilsener Originally beer brewed at PILSEN; now a generic term for pale beer strongly flavored with hops.

Piltdown Man The type of early man deduced from the faked fossil of a skull constructed of ape jaw and human cranium by Charles Dawson. He announced its discovery in 1912, and fooled most of the anthropological world until 1953, when it was proved to be a hoax. (Piltdown, a Sussex village where he claimed to have found it.)

Pima A Shoshonean-speaking race (see SHOSHONI) of Indians who in the 13th century lived in north Mexico and south Arizona. They fought fiercely against the Spanish in the 18th century; they are now noted farmers and makers of basketwork and pottery, numbering about 7000. See HOHOKAM CULTURE.

Pimms Proprietary name of a series of alcoholic long drinks, more potent than they taste, of which the formula is secret. The most popular is Pimms No. 1, with a gin base, but there are varieties numbered 2 and 3. They should be served with cucumber-tasting borage and other embellishments.

Pimpernel See SCARLET PIMPERNEL.

Pinafore, HMS (1878) A GILBERT AND SULLIVAN OPERA. Able Seaman Ralph Rackstraw falls in love with his Captain's daughter, to whom the First Lord of the Admiralty is paying court. His case seems hopeless until Little Buttercup, a Portsmouth bumboat woman, reveals that she switched Ralph and the Captain when they were babies. Not only does Ralph get his girl, but the Captain is happy to marry Little Buttercup.

Pinakothek (Munich) See HAUS DER KUNST. (German from Greek for 'picture depository'.)

Pindaric odes (5th century BC) Odes written by the Greek poet Pindar, commissioned by the victors in the Olympic, Pythian and other similar Games, whose praises he sang.

Pine Bluff Arsenal A 15,000-acre installation in Arkansas, where riot-control and poison gases are made.

Pine Tree State Nickname of Maine.

Pinewood Studios Rank's film studios at Iver, near Slough, Buckinghamshire, England.

Pinfold, Gilbert See ORDEAL OF GILBERT PINFOLD.

Pinkerton, Lt See MADAME BUTTERFLY.

Pinkerton, The Misses In Thackeray's VANITY FAIR, the dignified sisters who ran an academy for young ladies in Chiswick Mall, where Becky SHARP was educated and taught French.

Pinkerton's   A private detective agency in Chicago which first achieved world fame through its activities in the Civil War.

Pink Lady   A mixed drink of gin, cider, grenadine and egg white.

Pink Pills for Pale People, Dr Williams's   A US competitor for BEECHAM'S PILLS, on much the same level of efficacy.

Pink 'Un, The   The London *Sporting Times*, now defunct, printed on pink paper and regarded by its Edwardian addicts as very 'naughty'.

Pinkville massacre   (1968) The alleged slaughter in cold blood by US troops of Vietnamese civilians in the hamlet of My Lai (of which the military code name was Pinkville). The allegation was made in 1969 by one of the soldiers present.

Pinocchio   (1943) Walt Disney's feature-length cartoon, based on a 19th-century Italian tale of a puppet who comes to life, and whose nose grows bigger whenever he lies.

Pinto Collection of Wooden Bygones   A unique collection of every kind of wooden implement and gadget, illustrating the social history of wood down the ages. Until recently it was on display at the home of the collector near Watford; it is now in the Birmingham Museum.

Pioneer   Name of a series of US lunar probes. *Pioneer 4* (1959) passed near the moon and went into orbit round the sun. *Pioneer 5* (1960) relayed signals from 22 million miles away and gave important information about interplanetary magnetic fields and their effect on cosmic rays.

Piozzi, Hester   The name, after her second marriage, of Mrs Thrale, friend of Dr Johnson, about whom she published her *Anecdotes* 2 years after his death.

Pippa Passes   (1841) Robert Browning's dramatic poem of a girl who goes singing through the streets songs by which, unknowingly, she changes the lives of 4 people who overhear her, and, incidentally, her own. The most famous of her songs

ends: 'God's in His heaven—/ All's right with the world!', expressing Pippa's (not Browning's) innocent optimism.

Pirates   The Pittsburgh Pirates, NATIONAL (Baseball) LEAGUE, playing at Three Rivers Stadium.

Pirates of Penzance, The   (1879) A GILBERT AND SULLIVAN OPERA. Frederic, indentured by mistake to a very gentle and unsuccessful band of pirates, has completed his apprenticeship and feels bound to denounce them. They quite understand, and when the police order them to yield in the Queen's name they kneel in homage to their Sovereign. It is then revealed that they are in fact delinquent noblemen, and are at once released to take their rightful places in the House of Lords.

Pisces   The Fishes, 12th of the constellations of the Zodiac, between ARIES and AQUARIUS; the sun enters it about February 21st. Astrologers claim that those born under this sign may be weak, unpractical, restless, affectionate.

Pisgah   Mount Pisgah, northeast of the Dead Sea, from which at Jehovah's command Moses gazed upon the PROMISED LAND that he himself would never enter (*Deuteronomy* iii, 27).

Pistol   A cowardly braggart who, with BARDOLPH, follows FALSTAFF in the MERRY WIVES and HENRY IV, and reappears in *Henvy V*; he marries Mistress QUICKLY.

Pistons   The Detroit Pistons, NATIONAL BASKETBALL ASSOCIATION.

Pithecanthropines   ('ape-men') Middle PLEISTOCENE creatures living some 400,000 years ago, with brains twice as large as AUSTRALOPITHECINES; they made stone tools, used fire and hunted. Some regard them as probably true men but of a different species from ours, and group them under the specific name *Homo erectus*. They include JAVA MAN and the later PEKING MAN.

Pitt, The Elder   William Pitt, the Great Commoner (1708-78), Prime Minister under George II and under George III until 1767, and Earl of Chatham from 1766. He was the father of the Younger Pitt (1759-1806), twice Prime Minister under George III.

Pitti One of the 2 great art galleries in Florence (the other is the UFFIZI).

Pitt Professor The holder of the chair of American History and Institutions at CAMBRIDGE UNIVERSITY.

Pitt-Rivers Museum (1883) An ethnological museum at OXFORD UNIVERSITY.

PK effect Initials used for psychokinetic effect, a term invented by Dr Rhine (see ESP) for the supposed ability of some people to influence (e.g. to move) inanimate objects by mental effort alone. See PSI FORCE.

PKI Initials used for the Indonesian Communist Party.

PLA (1909) Initials used for the Port of London Authority, with headquarters near Tower Hill. It administers the main docks and controls all shipping, stevedores, dockers and lightermen in the PORT OF LONDON. It comprises representatives of the Ministries of Defense and Transport and Trinity House, together with members elected by wharfingers, ratepayers etc.

PLA Initials used for the Chinese People's Liberation Army, formerly known as the Red Army, formed in May 1928 by Mao Tse-tung.

Plague, The (1947) Albert Camus's novel about an outbreak of plague at Oran. The hero is a doctor who does what he can, knowing (like the author) that most of what he does will be unavailing but hoping that a little of it may prove of value. (French title, *La Peste*.)

Plaid Cymru (1925) The Welsh nationalist party, first represented in the House of Commons in 1966. (Welsh, 'Welsh party'.)

Plain, The In the French Revolution, the moderate, but ineffective, middle-class Girondist majority of the CONVENTION. (So called in contrast to the MOUNTAIN; in French, *Le Marais*.)

Plain Bob One of the principal methods of change ringing of church bells.

Plains Indians Indians of very varied origin who subsisted by hunting bison on the plains of the Middle West and the Alberta-Saskatchewan region. The introduction of the horse by the SHOSHONI made the killing of bison so easy that by 1885 there were hardly any left. The settlement of the West led to frequent clashes with the whites, especially in the 1870s (see SIOUX WARS).

Plains of Abraham The site outside the walls of the upper town of Quebec, on a plateau overlooking the St Lawrence, to which General Wolfe made a surprise ascent in 1759 to defeat Montcalm during the SEVEN YEARS WAR. Both generals were killed; Quebec surrendered a few days later. The site is now a National Battlefield Park.

Plain Tales from the Hills (1887) Kipling's collection of early stories of life in India, including the first appearance of the heroes of SOLDIERS THREE.

Planck's constant (1900) In quantum theory a constant which, multiplied by the frequency of a radiation, gives its quantum of energy; its symbol is h. (Max Planck, German physicist.)

Planetarium, London (1958) A hall adjoining MADAME TUSSAUD's, Baker Street, which houses the only English planetarium. The movements of the stars and planets are demonstrated by a lecturer with the aid of moving images projected onto the domed ceiling.

Plantagenets (1154-1399) The kings of England from Henry II to Richard II; also called the Angevins ('of ANJOU'). (Nickname of Geoffrey, Count of Anjou and father of Henry II, from the Latin *planta genista*, 'broom', which he wore in his hat.)

Plantation Colonies Virginia (1607); Maryland (1632), a Catholic settlement founded by Lord Baltimore; North and South Carolina (1663), founded by Lord Clarendon; Georgia (1732), by General Oglethorpe.

Plantations, The The settlement in the 1550s of Englishmen and 'loyal' Irish in King's County (OFFALY) and Queen's County (LAOIGHIS) in Mary's reign after the suppression of the revolt of the O'Mores and O'-Connors, a policy continued in later reigns in other parts of Ireland, e.g. Ulster in 1608 (see ULSTER, PLANTA-

TION OF). See also CROMWELLIAN SET-
TLEMENT.

Plassey (1757) Clive's defeat of Suraj
ud Dowlah after the BLACK HOLE OF
CALCUTTA.

Plataea (479 BC) The final defeat of
the Persians by the Greeks after SAL-
AMIS. (City of Boeotia.)

Platyhelminths Flatworms, a phylum (Platyhelminthes) which includes the Trematodes (liver flukes
parasitic on sheep) and Cestodes
(tapeworms, parasitic on man and
other animals).

Play (1963) Beckett's play in which
the 3 characters speak their lines
buried to the neck in urns. The
whole play lasts 10 minutes, and is
then repeated *in toto, verbatim,*
which must, critics feel, be the *re-
ductio ad* something or other.

Playboy (1960) A monthly magazine
published in Chicago by Hugh Hef-
ner, founder of the Bunny-Girl
Playboy-Club look-but-don't-touch
school of eroticism. It has a center-
page foldout pinup for voyeurs,
a correspondence column which
touches on many subjects, and it is
said to publish some quite good
short stories.

Playboy of the Western World, The
(1907) J. M. Synge's play of the timid
boy, Christie Mahon, who thinks he
has 'destroyed his da' and finds
himself regarded as a hero on that
account; this goes to his head — until
the old man turns up in pursuit of
him.

Players Club (1888) A distinguished
social club in GRAMERCY PARK,
NYC, founded by the actor Edwin Booth, brother of Lincoln's assassin.

Plays: Pleasant and Unpleasant
(1898) Two volumes of Bernard
Shaw's plays. The Pleasant comprise ARMS AND THE MAN, CANDIDA,
The Man of Destiny and YOU NEVER
CAN TELL; the Unpleasant, *The Phi-
landerer*, MRS WARREN'S PROFESSION
and WIDOWERS' HOUSES.

Plaza-Toro, Duke of A Spanish
grandee in Gilbert and Sullivan's
GONDOLIERS; when there was any
fighting 'he led his regiment from
behind — he found it less exciting'.

Pléiade (16th century) A group of 7
French poets, including Ronsard
and du Bellay, who set out to reform
the vocabulary of French poetry,
drawing extensively on Classical
models. See PLEIADES.

Pleiades In Greek legend, the 7
daughters of ATLAS, who give their
name to a constellation (see next
entry).

Pleiades The best-known open (or
galactic) star cluster, containing several nebulae; eta-Tauri (Alcyone) is
the brightest. It is mentioned in *Job*
xxxviii, 31. See previous entry.

Pleistocene Epoch The earlier subdivision of the QUATERNARY PERIOD,
lasting from about one million to
25,000 years ago. It coincided with
most of the Great ICE AGE and of the
PALEOLITHIC AGE; PITHECANTHROPINES
and early man (NEANDERTHAL MAN,
HOMO SAPIENS) developed. (Greek,
'most of the modern', i.e. most modern forms of life developed.)

Plessey British telecommunications
and electronics firm whose interests
include radio, radar, air defense systems, automation and a stake in International Computers Ltd.

Plimoth Plantation A replica of the
original Pilgrim colony village, 2½
miles south of PLYMOUTH, Mass.,
open to the public except in winter.
See MAYFLOWER II.

Plimsoll mark A ship's maximum
summer load line, a circle intersect-
ed by a horizontal line, painted
amidships; also used of similar
markings for winter, tropical seas,
fresh-water etc. load lines. (Named
for 19th-century English campaigner
for shipping safety.)

Pliocene Epoch The most recent
subdivision of the TERTIARY PERIOD,
lasting from about 10 to one million
years ago. The earliest fossil remains
of AUSTRALOPITHECINES and of HOMO
HABILIS date from this epoch. (Greek,
'more of modern', i.e. more of the
modern forms of life are found.)

Plon-Plon Nickname of Prince Napoleon Joseph Charles Bonaparte,
son of Napoleon's youngest brother,
gained in the CRIMEAN WAR. (Corruption of *Craint-plon*, 'fear-bullet'.)

Plow, The In Britain, the commonest

name for the BIG DIPPER; sometimes incorrectly used for the whole constellation of the GREAT BEAR.

Plowden report (1965) A report on the reorganization of the British aircraft industry which recommended State control of the 2 main aircraft companies (BAC and HAWKER SIDDELEY), and European cooperation in future development. (Baron Plowden, former chairman of the ATOMIC ENERGY AUTHORITY.)

Plumed Serpent, The (1926) D. H. Lawrence's novel of Mexico, full of highly evocative nature descriptions combined with all but incoherent philosophizing based on a revival of the bloodstained religion of the AZTECS by a Nietzschean SUPERMAN type. (The title is a translation of Quetzalcoatl, the Aztec god.)

Pluto A Greek god. See HADES.

Pluto Code name for the submarine pipelines conveying gasoline across the English Channel for the Normandy landings, 1944. (Initials of 'pipeline under the ocean'.)

Plymouth Brethren (1828) A CALVINISTIC sect founded by an Irish curate, J. N. Darby, and established in 1831 at Plymouth, England. They have no clergy and meet in a 'room' each Sunday for the 'Breaking of the Bread'. Many splinter groups have seceded from the main body, e.g. the EXCLUSIVE BRETHREN.

Plymouth gin Generic term for a gin with a distinctive flavor said to be due to the addition of sulfuric acid before distillation; originally made in the English West Country.

Plymouth mail robbery (1962) The largest cash robbery in the history of American crime. A gang held up a US mail truck near Plymouth, Mass., and stole $1,551,277.

Plymouth porcelain (1768-70) The earliest hard-paste wares made in England. The secret of their manufacture was discovered by William Cookworthy, who moved to Bristol after only 2 years. See BRISTOL PORCELAIN.

Plymouth Rock (1) Rock at Plymouth, Mass., on which the PILGRIM FATHERS are said to have first stepped ashore. See PLIMOTH PLANTATION.

(2) US breed of poultry. (3) Derogatory term for a Plymouth Brother.

Plzen A Czech city, formerly known by its German name, PILSEN.

PMA A drug similar to STP.

PNEU (1888) (UK) Initials used for the Parents' National Educational Union, a society formed to propagate the views of Charlotte Mason on education, including character forming, through various schools in the UK and overseas, and to provide guidance in home tuition for individual parents and small communities serving abroad where no suitable schools are available.

Pobble Who Has No Toes, The A nonsense poem by Edward Lear; see RUNCIBLE CAT.

POD Initials used for Post Office Department.

Podoloff (Maurice) Trophy Awarded to the most valuable player in the NATIONAL BASKETBALL ASSOCIATION.

Podsnap A character in Dickens's OUR MUTUAL FRIEND who had the courage of all his convictions; anyone or anything that interfered with them was swept on one side.

Podunk (1) A small tribe of Indians who used to live in northern Connecticut. (2) A derisive term for a small, unimportant, isolated town. In 1934 some humorist officially christened a one-horse Iowa settlement 'Podunk Center'.

Poet and Peasant A popular overture to an otherwise unremembered operetta by the 19th-century Austrian composer Suppé.

Poetry Bookshop, The (1912) Founded in Bloomsbury, London, by the poet Harold Monro, as a place where poets could meet, hold poetry readings and, if they wished, lodge for a minute rent. See GEORGIAN POETRY.

Poets' Corner An area of the south transept of Westminster Abbey filled with tombs or other memorials to the great British poets and writers, from Chaucer onwards.

Poets' Poet, The A name given to Edmund Spenser, as a poet to be fully appreciated only by fellow poets.

Pogo (1948) Rich political satire in the form of a comic strip by Walt

Kelly. Pogo is the sophisticated possum of Okefenokee Swamp, Ga., who ran for president on an independent ticket in 1952. Kelly won liberal hearts by introducing the character Joe Malarkey when MC-CARTHYISM was still rampant; such as Barry Goldwater and George Wallace have also appeared, all in animal guise, together with Dr Howland Owl, Albert the Alligator and the Jack Acid (John Birch) Society. Verbal dexterity and intelligent comment on matters of real moment have made *Pogo* the eggheads' delight.

Poil de Carotte A story by Jules Renard, turned into an outstanding French movie by Julien Duvivier, using a nonprofessional cast in a village setting. (French, 'carroty-head'.)

Point Counter Point (1928) Aldous Huxley's novel of hate in which few features of contemporary society go unscathed. Many characters are based on leading figures of the day and of the past, while the author himself appears as Philip Quarles.

Point-Four Program (1947) The US program for technical and financial aid to underdeveloped countries, especially for health, educational and agricultural projects; later integrated into the general foreign aid program. (4th point of President Truman's inauguration address.)

Poirot, Hercule The Belgian detective who first appeared in Agatha Christie's *Mysterious Affair at Styles* (1920), when he had already drawn a police pension for 16 years, making him about 130 today. Splendidly conceited and glorying in his preposterous moustache, age has not withered him nor custom staled his infinite variety.

Polaris (Astronomy) Latin name for the Pole star or NORTH STAR.

Polaris An ICBM designed for firing from a submerged POLARIS SUBMARINE; it was so fired in 1960, and is the only ICBM to be tested with a nuclear warhead. A1 has a range of 1200 miles, A2 1400 miles (with an 800 kiloton warhead), and A3 a range of some 2500 miles. See POSEIDON.

Polaris submarines Nuclear submarines each armed with 16 POLARIS A3 missiles. The US completed their 41st and last Polaris submarine in 1966. The Royal Navy has 4 (see RESOLUTION), built in the UK but with the complete weapon system supplied by USA; the missiles are kept in USA. Their role is to take over the British deterrent from the RAF's V-bombers.

Polaroid Proprietary name for a thin transparent plastic sheet which plane-polarizes light; used in spectacles and car windshields to prevent glare.

Poldhu The site in southwest Cornwall from which the first transatlantic radio signal was transmitted, in 1901. (North of Mullion Cove.)

Polesden Lacey A Regency villa near Dorking, Surrey, owned by the NATIONAL TRUST and housing the Greville art collection.

Pole Star See NORTH STAR.

Polish Corridor (1919-39) A strip of territory dividing EAST PRUSSIA from the rest of Germany, given under the VERSAILLES TREATY to an otherwise landlocked Poland to permit access to the free port of Danzig and to Gdynia on the Baltic. Hitler took the first opportunity to recapture it for Germany. It is now part of Poland again.

Polish October (1956) An uprising against Russian dominance in Poland, which led to the return of Gomulka (who had been in disgrace for supporting Tito) and the dismissal of the Russian-born Polish Minister of Defense, Marshal Rokossovsky.

Politburo The supreme policy-making body of the Soviet Communist Party, renamed in 1952 the Presidium of the CENTRAL COMMITTEE, but reverting to the old title in 1966. (Abbreviation of Russian for Political Bureau.)

Pollux The second brightest of the 2 stars in the heads of the GEMINI 'twins' (the first being CASTOR).

Polly, Alfred The small tradesman of H. G. Wells's *The History of Mr Polly* (1910), who escapes from his dreary home (which he burns down) and from his horrible wife, to taste the joys of freedom; together with his Uncles Pentstemon and Jim forming a trio of Wells's most memorable creations.

Pollyanna An absurdly optimistic person, from the heroine of Eleanor Porter's novel *Pollyanna* (1913), who was given to playing 'the glad game', i.e. looking on the bright side no matter what.

Polonaise (Cooking) With beetroot and sour cream.

Polonius In Shakespeare's HAMLET the aged Lord Chamberlain, father of OPHELIA and LAERTES, killed accidentally by Hamlet when lurking behind the arras; in playing his part his worldly wisdom used to be stressed, but now his sententious wordiness gets more attention.

Polycentrism Freedom for national Communist parties to adapt their methods to local conditions, provided the ideological unity of the movement is not thereby weakened. (Idea and name proposed by the Italian Communist leader Togliatti, 1956.)

Polycrates, Ring of According to a story in Herodotus, Polycrates, a tyrant of Samos in the 6th century BC, waxed rich on piracy and was advised to throw away his most treasured possession to avert NEMESIS. He threw a ring into the sea, but it reappeared in a fish served up to him. So Nemesis overtook Polycrates, who died a violent death.

Polydeuces See CASTOR AND POLLUX.

Polyeucte Hero of Corneille's play of that name, a Christian convert executed by Félix, his father-in-law and Roman governor of ARMENIA; his martyrdom results in the repentant conversion of both Félix and his own widow.

Polynesians A group of Pacific races, including the Maori and the peoples of Hawaii, TONGA, Samoa, Tahiti and the Marquesas. See MALAY-POLYNESIAN LANGUAGES. (Greek, 'many-island people'.)

Polyphemus In Greek legend a CYCLOPS, a one-eyed giant, who shut up ODYSSEUS and his men in a cave. Odysseus blinded him and they escaped by clinging underneath the giant's flock of sheep, but only after Polyphemus had eaten 6 of their companions.

Polytechnic, The (1882) The first of many polytechnics, in Upper Regent Street, London, founded by Quintin Hogg and now officially called the Royal Polytechnic Institute. It was a pioneer experiment in providing part-time education for the young and for adults, and holds day and evening classes in a very wide range of subjects.

Pomerania A former German Baltic province, now divided between East Germany and Poland. (German, Pommern; Polish Pomorze.)

Pomerol Claret similar to, but not generally so good as, that from nearby ST ÉMILION.

Pommard See CÔTE DE BEAUNE.

Pomona The Roman goddess of fruit trees; she has no Greek equivalent.

Pompadour A name usually linked with the ROCOCO style, although Mme de Pompadour, Louis XV's mistress, was a leading advocate of a return to classical models (NEOCLASSICISM); also used of a rolled-back hairstyle she affected, and of a claret-purple color she liked.

Pompeii An ancient Roman port and pleasure resort, buried beneath lava from Vesuvius (see LAST DAYS OF POMPEII). Excavations begun in 1763 and now near completion have revealed much of the city as it was on the day of the disaster.

Ponderevo, Uncle See TONO-BUNGAY.

Pondicherry State (1955) A territory of the Union of India administered since 1962 directly from Delhi, and consisting of the former French settlements transferred to India in 1954.

Pons Asinorum Old nickname for the fifth theorem in Euclid's geometry, a stumblingblock for beginners. It states that 2 equal sides of any triangle make equal angles with the third side. (Latin, 'asses' bridge'.)

Pontecorvo spy case (1950) Dr Bruno Pontecorvo, employed in Canada on atomic research, defected to Russia.

Ponte Vecchio The old bridge at Florence, forming a street across the

River Arno for pedestrians only, lined on both sides with quaint old shops clinging onto it precariously. It survived World War II but was damaged in the floods of 1966.

Pontine Marshes The marshes of the CAMPAGNA around Rome. Mussolini was aptly nicknamed the Bullfrog of the Pontine Marshes, although it has to be said for him that he did drain them.

Pont l'Évêque A semihard cheese of Normandy.

Pont Street Dutch One of Osbert Lancaster's wittily named categories of modern 'architecture'. (Pont Street, Knightsbridge, London.)

Pony Express (1860-61) A fast mail service from St Joseph, Mo., to Sacramento, Calif. Mail was carried at the gallop, horses being changed at 190 relay stations spaced at 12-mile intervals. With the establishment of a telegraph line, the service closed down after only 18 months' operation. Among the riders were BUFFALO BILL and WILD BILL HICKOK.

Pooh-Bah In Gilbert and Sullivan's MIKADO, the Lord High Everything Else; hence applied to a jack-of-many-offices.

Pool of London The Thames immediately below LONDON BRIDGE, the highest point for vessels of medium size.

Poor Bitos (1956) Anouilh's play in which aristocrats torment poor Bitos, a self-made man who, however, deserves little sympathy.

Poor Richard's Almanack (1732-57) An annual almanac compiled by Benjamin Franklin under the name Richard Saunders and famous for its pawky aphorisms, many of them borrowed from the OLD WORLD and Americanized. Among them were: 'God helps those who help themselves'; 'Three may keep a secret, if two of them are dead'; and 'Some are weather-wise, some are otherwise'. They were collected under the title *Way to Wealth*.

Pooter, Mr The kind, dim, highly respectable London clerk invented by the brothers George and Weedon Grossmith in *The Diary of a Nobody* (1894), which sympathetically describes the very minor crises of life at The Laurels, Brickfield Terrace, Holloway, in the 1880s.

Pop Art A term which can have no settled meaning, as the essence of POP CULTURE is its ephemerality. It is however used of semiabstract paintings and collages full of allusions to modern urban life, e.g. its advertisements, fashions in dress, industrial design etc.

Pop culture The product among the younger generation of urban life, mass production, ample spending money and a general revolt against the standards of older people. It is characterized by ephemerality (e.g. last week's eagerly sought top of the pops record will be forgotten next week), living for the moment, overriding horror of being thought out-of-date, a superficial approach to problems of the day and, a redeeming feature, absence of class or race consciousness.

Pope Joan (1) A legendary female pope of the 9th century, an Englishwoman who died in childbirth during a papal procession. The story was widely believed in the Middle Ages. (2) A card game; the name is said to have no connection with (1).

Popeye The internationally famous one-eyed sailorman with a corncob pipe, created by Elzie Segar in 1929 and continued by others in strip, movie and radio form. A tin of spinach would suffice to give him superman strength and Crystal City, Tex., the spinach center, gratefully put up a monument to him. His stringy girl friend Olive Oyl and his friend WIMPY are no less well known.

Popish plot (1678) A plot invented by Titus Oates, a renegade Anglican clergyman; he alleged that the JESUITS planned with French assistance to kill Charles II and put James II on the throne; many innocent Catholics were hanged on his evidence.

Poplar A former London metropolitan borough, since 1965 part of the borough of TOWER HAMLETS.

Poplarism (UK) Defiance of central government or authority by local authorities. Named for the refusal (1921) of the POPLAR borough council, east London, to pay its share of London County Council expenses, protesting inequality of rates between rich and poor boroughs; they also paid wages and unemployment relief at higher than authorized scales. Led by George Lansbury (a future leader of the Labour Party), 30 councillors went to prison rather than give way.

Popolo d'Italia (1914) An Italian newspaper founded by Mussolini and edited by him until 1922; it became the chief Fascist daily.

Poppy Day (1921) The traditional collection for Earl Haig's Fund on REMEMBRANCE SUNDAY. The poppies, made by disabled veterans, represent the characteristic flower of the fields of Flanders where so many British soldiers of World War I lie buried. The idea also caught on in the US.

Popski's Private Army Nickname of a unit of the LONG-RANGE DESERT PATROL formed (Oct. 1942) by Vladimir Peniakov, a Russian-born Belgian subject serving with the British army.

Popular Front (1935) A Communist device recommended to non-Communist countries by the Comintern for strengthening opposition to Fascism by sinking differences between Socialist parties and the Communists to form a (temporary) common front. (For 'popular', see PEOPLE'S.)

Populist Party (1891) Formed in Kansas during an agricultural slump in western states, it brought together discontented workers, westerners who mistrusted the financial and commercial dictatorship of the northeast, and the GRANGE, among other groups, and demanded state control of communications and land tenure, improved work conditions, immigration restrictions, monetary reform etc. After its presidential candidate had failed to get more than 22 electoral votes (1892), it supported the unsuccessful candidacy of the Democrat, William Jennings Bryan, in 1896.

Poqo A terrorist offshoot in South Africa of the banned PAN-AFRICAN CONGRESS, operating mainly in the TRANSKEI, where it attacked both whites and African members of the Transkei Authority. (XHOSA *Ukupoqa*, 'independence'.)

Porgy and Bess (1935) George Gershwin's Negro opera set in Charleston, S.C.

Pork and Beans War (1838-39) Nickname for the undeclared Aroostook 'war' over territory on the New Brunswick-Maine border disputed between Canadian and US lumberjacks. Militia were called out by both sides but did not fight. The boundary was settled provisionally in 1842 but finally not until 1910. (Refers to Canadians' staple diet in those days.)

Port Arthur Chinese naval base (renamed Lüshun), now grouped with DAIREN as the conurbation of Lüta.

Porter, Jimmy The original ANGRY YOUNG MAN, the chief character of LOOK BACK IN ANGER.

Porterhouse steak A large steak cut from the thick end of the short loin, containing a T-shaped bone and a large piece of tenderloin. (A porter house served steaks, chops and the dark beer called porter.)

Portia (1) The ingenious heiress of Shakespeare's *Merchant of Venice* who, disguised as a lawyer, resists SHYLOCK's claim, and marries BASSANIO. (2) In Shakespeare's *Julius Caesar* the wife of BRUTUS.

Portland Club (1816) A London club in Charles Street, the recognized authority on bridge which drew up the first authoritative rules of the game.

Portland Club Cup A British Bridge competition for mixed pairs.

Portland secrets case (1961) (UK) The trial of LONSDALE, HOUGHTON AND GEE, and the KROGERS for espionage on behalf of Russia in connection with work at the Underwater Weapons Establishment, Portland, where equipment for the nuclear submarine DREADNOUGHT was being developed.

Portland Vase A Greek urn of dark-blue glass ornamented with figures in white, found in the 17th century near Rome in a grave of the 3rd century AD. The Duke of Portland lent it to the British Museum, where it was smashed to pieces in 1845 by a madman, but skillfully put together again.

Portobello Road   A London street in Notting Hill with many antique shops, supplemented on Saturdays by street stalls, frequented by tourists as well as dealers.

Port of London   The Thames from Teddington Lock to the Nore, administered by the PLA.

Port of New York Authority   (1921) The joint New York-New Jersey state agency that operates many of the transportation facilities (including marine and bus terminals, bridges, and airports) in the bistate Port of New York area; it also sponsored the WORLD TRADE CENTER.

Porton   See MICROBIOLOGICAL RESEARCH ESTABLISHMENT.

Porto Rico   The name until 1932 of Puerto Rico, a group of West Indian islands ceded to USA in 1898.

Portrait of the Artist as a Young Man   (1916) James Joyce's autobiography of his childhood and early manhood, in which he appears as Stephen DEDALUS. Using the 'interior monologue' technique of ULYSSES, he describes how he came to reject family, religious and patriotic ties to achieve freedom as an artist.

Port-Royal   An abbey near Versailles, headquarters of JANSENISM; it was razed by Louis XIV.

Port Salut   A soft pale yellow cheese of France with a very mild but distinctive and attractive flavor.

Portsmouth, Treaty of   (1905) The treaty that ended the Russo-Japanese War. (Portsmouth, N.H.)

Portugaise   (Cooking) With tomatoes and onion or garlic.

Poseidon   Greek god of the sea, all other terrestrial waters, earthquakes and horses; the Roman Neptune. See also PASIPHAË.

Poseidon   A bigger version of POLARIS, to carry twice the payload, due in service in the 1970s. It is a 'doomsday weapon', i.e. for use in a 'second strike' retaliation, and has penetration devices, such as multiple warheads (see MIRV), to defeat enemy defense measures, thus giving it what is called 'assured destruction capability'.

Posen   German spelling of the Polish city, Poznań.

Positivism   The 'religion' of Auguste Comte (1798-1857). Mankind had tried unsuccessfully to explain the universe in terms first of theology and then of philosophy. Comte advocated a scientific approach, seeking objective 'positive' truth. He tried, and failed, to found a church, the god of which was Humanity, with his own liturgy and a calendar of saints (i.e. those who had most benefited mankind).

Possessed, The   Dostoevsky's novel; see STAVROGIN.

Postimpressionism   (1910) A movement of reaction against IMPRESSIONISM, associated with Van Gogh, Gauguin and Cézanne. Dissatisfied with impressionistic sketches, they tried to stress the permanent element in their subjects. (Name given by Roger Fry.)

Post Office Tower   (1965) A high tower in London built to house the main link in a countrywide network of microwave towers to provide telephone circuits and TV channels supplementing those already in existence. At the top is a revolving restaurant affording panoramic views.

Postumus   A friend of Horace to whom he addressed one of his most famous odes: *Eheu fugaces, Postume, Postume, / Anni labuntur.* This was freely translated in one of the INGOLDSBY LEGENDS: Years glide away, and are lost to me, lost to me!

Potato Famine   (Irish) In 1845-47 blight caused a total failure of Ireland's staple crop, the death from hunger and typhus of perhaps a third of the population, and mass emigration to America.

Potemkin, Battleship   (1925) A historic Russian film directed by Sergei Eisenstein; a realistic story of the naval mutiny of 1905.

Potiphar's wife   The wife of Pharaoh's captain of the guard who, having failed to seduce JOSEPH, accused him of having tried to seduce her; he was put in prison (*Genesis* xxxix, 17-20).

Potomac Heritage Trail An 825-mile trail following the course of the Potomac.

Potsdam Conference (July-Aug. 1945) A conference attended by Truman, Stalin, Churchill and Attlee (who had just become Prime Minister), which discussed postwar settlements and issued a demand for unconditional surrender by Japan. As the conference began, Truman heard of the test explosion of the first atomic bomb.

Potteries, The The FIVE TOWNS of Stoke on Trent, north Staffordshire, where the potteries of WEDGWOOD, MINTON, DOULTON, LONGTON and many others were established.

Potterism (1920) Dame Rose Macaulay's novel about Mr Potter, a successful newspaper proprietor, and his best-selling novelist wife. They represent the prostitution of talents in a philistine pursuit of commercial success, a policy opposed by their children who form an Anti-Potter League. The author attacks both sides alike.

Pott's fracture A combined dislocation and fracture of the ankle, caused by twisting the foot.

Poughkeepsie regatta Premier US rowing event. (On the Hudson, in southeast New York.)

Pouilly-Fuissé See BURGUNDY.

Poujadists (1955-58) Members of a French petit-bourgeois political party whose program, against parliamentary government, taxes and any concessions to nationalism in North Africa, won them 2½ million votes in 1956; by 1958 they had disappeared. (Founded by Pierre Poujade.)

Pour le Mérite (1740) A Prussian, later German, order of merit. The military division (the badge of which was known as the Blue Max) ceased to exist after 1918. The civil division, awarded for distinction in science or art, survives.

POW Initials standing for prisoner of war.

Powderham Castle The home near Exeter of the Earls of Devon, dating back to the 14th century.

Powder River A famous cowboy yell, especially in 'Powder River — let' er buck'. (The river referred to is probably the one in Montana.)

Powellism (UK) Policies put forward in the late 1960s by the Conservative MP, Enoch Powell; they include the stricter control of immigration, sharp reductions in taxation offset by reductions in public investment and government subsidies, withdrawal of the British 'presence' east of Suez, and increased attention to winning the workers' votes.

Power of Positive Thinking, The (1952) A best seller by Norman Vincent Peale, a REFORMED CHURCH clergyman, in which the findings of psychiatry are given practical application in advice on everyday personal problems.

Poynings' Law (1495) An Act applying all English laws to Ireland and severely restricting the Irish Parliament's powers; repealed 1782.

Poyser, Mrs A character in ADAM BEDE who looks after her husband's niece, Hetty Sorrel. Garrulous, kind-hearted but sharp-tongued, she is said to be a portrait of George Eliot's mother.

Poznań A city of Poland, half way between Berlin and Warsaw, formerly known by its German name POSEN.

Poznan riots (June 1956) The agitation against Soviet domination which preceded POLISH OCTOBER. See last entry.

PPE (OXFORD UNIVERSITY) Initials standing for philosophy, politics and economics; see MODERN GREATS.

PPP (OXFORD UNIVERSITY) Initials standing for Psychology, Philosophy and Physiology, a course for the final BA examination of exceptional difficulty.

PPS (Parliament) Initials used for PARLIAMENTARY PRIVATE SECRETARY.

PQ Parliamentary Question (see QUESTION TIME), initials commonly used in WHITEHALL, where the production of an answer is given high priority, whether or not the matter raised is important.

PR Initials used for public relations; a PR man is a publicity man who is paid to project, with some degree of verisimilitude, a favorable image of his client (a person, firm, political party, foreign government etc.) through the appropriate media (press, TV etc.) and to the extent necessary (and often far beyond it).

Prado (1819) The Spanish national art gallery at Madrid, containing the treasures collected by the Spanish HAPSBURGS.

Pragmatic Sanction (1) An imperial decree; (2) specifically, the Emperor Charles VI's decree (1713) setting aside the SALIC LAW so that his daughter Maria Theresa could inherit the HAPSBURG dominions of Austria. (Translation of an old Latin legal term.)

Pragmatism (1896) A school of philosophy founded by the American, William James. If an idea (e.g. the idea of God) 'works', it is expedient to believe it; whether it is objectively true is a minor consideration.

Prairie Provinces The Canadian provinces of Alberta, Saskatchewan and Manitoba.

Prairie Schooner See CONESTOGA WAGON.

Prairie State A nickname for Illinois given by pioneers, who first encountered prairie there; there is in fact less of it in Illinois than in many states to the west.

Praise-God Barebones Nickname of a fanatical PURITAN member, Barbon, who gave its name to the BAREBONES PARLIAMENT.

Prater A large park in Vienna by the Danube.

Prattware (1) Generic term for primitive Staffordshire earthenware figures, jugs, teapots etc. (1790-1830) decorated with a distinctive range of underglaze colors which could withstand the heat of the glazing kiln —ochre, blue, green, brown, purple —made by Felix Pratt of Fenton and many others. (2) Plates etc. decorated with transfer prints of the potlid type made (1840-80) by Felix Pratt's son at the Fenton factory.

Pravda (1912) Soviet Russia's chief daily newspaper, representing the party viewpoint (see IZVESTIA). (Russian, 'truth'.)

PRB Initials originally and still sometimes used for PRE-RAPHAELITE BROTHERHOOD.

Preakness, The (1873) One of the 3 US classic flat races for 3-year-olds, run in May over a distance of 1 mile 1½ furlongs at the Pimlico racetrack, Baltimore, Md.

Precambrian Era The geological era earlier than the CAMBRIAN PERIOD, i.e. earlier than about 600 million years ago. Fossils are rare, but traces of sponges, seaweeds, mollusks and other marine life have been found. Rocks rich in metallic ores were formed.

Précieuses ridicules, Les (1659) Molière's one-act comedy of the 2 snobbish daughters whose rejected suitors avenge themselves by introducing their 2 valets as noblemen; the girls mistake their extravagant manners for the height of fashion. (French, 'the ridiculous BLUESTOCKINGS'.)

Precious Bane (1924) Mary Webb's novel about the gloomy rustics of the Worcester-Shropshire border. It leapt into fame when praised by the Prime Minister, Stanley Baldwin (a Worcestershire man). It may well have been the chief inspiration of COLD COMFORT FARM.

Preedy, George R. One of the many pen names used by Marjorie BOWEN.

Prelude, The (1799-1805, published 1850) Wordsworth's autobiographical poem about the 'growth of the poet's mind', his passionate attachment to Lakeland, and 'the self-sufficing power of Solitude'. The original (1805) version was published in 1926.

Premium Bonds (1956) (UK) Premium Savings Bonds, a semilottery device for raising capital introduced by Harold Macmillan; numbered bonds in units of £1, redeemable at par and bearing no interest, but eligible for prizes for the numbers selected each month by an electronic device called Ernie. Later, one large weekly prize was added.

Prensa, La (1869) An Argentine daily newspaper with an international reputation; suppressed during the

PERONISTA PARTY'S regime.

Prentice Cup Lawn tennis match between teams of 6 from OXFORD and CAMBRIDGE and from YALE and HARVARD, played in alternate years and in Britain and the USA alternately.

Pre-Raphaelite Brotherhood (1848-53) The misleading nickname of a group of English painters, notably Rossetti, Holman Hunt, Millais and Burne-Jones, who, inspired by what little they knew of the Italian painters before Raphael (i.e. before the 16th century), depicted serious biblical and literary themes in bright colors and meticulous detail. The name clung to them after they had broken up and gone their separate ways, and especially to those who like Burne-Jones turned to romantic medieval subjects.

Presbyterianism A form of Church governance adopted by the Church of Scotland and various Churches in England, Ireland and USA. It comprises the kirk sessions of the individual churches; presbyteries; synods; and a general assembly presided over by an annually elected moderator. Ministers (presbyters) are all of equal rank and are elected by their congregations, as are the lay elders who watch over the spiritual and moral welfare of church members. See COVENANTERS; WESTMINSTER CONFESSION.

President's Cup (Show jumping) A world championship based on points awarded to national teams for wins in various international events.

Presidium (of the Supreme Soviet) (USSR) The elected body to which the SUPREME SOVIET delegates its powers; its chairman is the President of the USSR. The POLITBURO directs its actions through Party members on the Presidium.

Press Barons (UK) Name for the newspaper proprietors raised to the peerage during this century: e.g. Lords Northcliffe, Rothermere, Beaverbrook, Kemsley, Thomson.

Pressburg German name of the Czech city of Bratislava.

Press Council (1963) (UK) A council with chairman and some members unconnected with the press, the rest representing proprietors, editors and journalists. It aims to discourage encroachments on the freedom of the press, monopolistic mergers, and unwarranted intrusions into the private lives of individuals.

Prester John A legendary 12th-century Christian king in the East or, in later versions, in Abyssinia. (John the Priest or Presbyter.)

Preston, Battle of (1648) An engagement in which Cromwell defeated the northern Royalists and their Scottish allies, ending the second phase of the ENGLISH CIVIL WAR.

Prestonpans See FORTY-FIVE.

Prestwick International airport 3 miles north of Ayr on the Scottish coast; also the site of a famous golf course.

Previous (examination) (UK) Another name for RESPONSIONS; also the official name at CAMBRIDGE UNIVERSITY of the LITTLE-GO.

Previous Question, The (UK) A Parliamentary device, the question being whether a vote should be taken on the subject under debate; used when the House cannot come to a decision, it takes the form of a motion such as: That the Question be not now put.

Priam In Greek legend, King of Troy, husband of HECUBA, father of 50 sons, including PARIS and HECTOR, and several daughters, including CASSANDRA. He was killed when Troy fell.

Priapus The Greek god of fertility and eroticism, the son of APHRODITE and DIONYSUS.

Price, Fanny See MANSFIELD PARK.

Prices and Incomes Board (1965) A British board set up to replace the National Incomes Commission; its duties are to make recommendations to government regarding any proposed rise in prices, wages, income from any other source, interest rates etc., and regarding productivity agreements. (Officially styled the National Board for Prices and Incomes.)

Price, Waterhouse The biggest firm

of London accountants, with offices in many US cities.

Pride and Prejudice (1813) The most famous of Jane Austen's novels of '3 or 4 families in a country village'; see the BENNET FAMILY.

Pride's Purge (1648) The occasion when the military rulers sent Col. Pride with a regiment to purge the LONG PARLIAMENT of those who opposed the trial of Charles I; the remainder became known as the RUMP PARLIAMENT.

Priestley Medal The highest honor in chemistry in the US. Named for the English discoverer of oxygen, Joseph Priestley, who spent his last 10 years (1794-1804) at Northumberland, Pa.

Primate, The The Archbishop of Canterbury, strictly the Primate of All England, to be distinguished (if logically possible) from the Primate of England, who is the Archbishop of York.

Primates The highest order of mammals, ranging from lemurs and monkeys to man.

'Primavera' (1477) Botticelli's painting in which MERCURY heralds the approach of Spring, who is ushered by Flora (goddess of flowers) and Zephyrus (the west wind) into the presence of VENUS, while CUPID aims his arrow at the Three Graces. Now in the UFFIZI, Florence. (Italian, 'spring'.)

Prime of Miss Jean Brodie, The (1961) A novel by the Scottish Catholic convert Muriel Spark about an unorthodox Edinburgh schoolmistress with Fascist leanings who has advanced views on introducing her girls to the problems of adult life. It is the basis of a play by Jay Allen and a popular movie was made of it.

Primrose, Dr See VICAR OF WAKEFIELD.

Primrose League (1883) A political association founded in memory of Disraeli by Lord Randolph Churchill to propagate the principles of TORY DEMOCRACY. The headquarters are at Storey's Gate, Westminster.

Prince, The (1513) The Florentine philosopher Machiavelli's handbook for princes on how to retain power by exploiting the greed and other weaknesses of mankind, by hypocrisy, bad faith, terror and any other methods that may seem expedient. See MACHIAVELLIANISM.

Prince Albert US name for a frock coat, as worn by Queen Victoria's consort.

Prince and the Pauper, The (1880) Mark TWAIN'S historical novel which became a children's favorite. The little pauper briefly changes places with the 10-year-old Prince Edward just before he succeeds his father, Henry VIII, as Edward VI.

Prince Charming The prince in the CINDERELLA story; hence it has come to mean a suitor who fulfills the dreams of his beloved or a man of often specious affability and charm toward women.

Prince Igor (1889) (1) Borodin's unfinished opera based on a contemporary poem about a historical event. In 1185 the Prince of Novgorod, Igor, raided the nomadic Polovtsky and was taken prisoner but escaped. The opera was completed by Rimsky-Korsakov and Glazunov. (2) A Diaghilev ballet, choreographed by Fokine and using the Polovtsian Dances from Act III of the opera, where they form part of a gypsy entertainment celebrating Prince Igor's capture.

Prince Monolulu A racing tipster seen until his death in the 1960s on most British racetracks, dressed in Red Indian garb. Punters, but not horses, responded to his slogan 'White man for pluck; black man for luck'.

Prince of Peace Christ. (From *Isaiah* ix, 6: For unto us a child is born . . . The Prince of Peace.)

Prince of Wales Cup (1927) Sailing championship for INTERNATIONAL FOURTEENS, raced at Cowes in July.

Prince of Wales Cup (show jumping; 1909) A competition at the Royal INTERNATIONAL HORSE SHOW for teams of 4 amateurs of the same nationality. (Formerly, the King Edward VII Cup.)

Prince Regent A prince who acts as regent; applied specifically to the Prince of Wales who acted (1811-20) for his father George III during his mental illness, until he succeeded to the throne as George IV.

Princes in the Tower Edward V (who reigned for 3 months) and his brother Richard, murdered in the Tower of London (1483), according to Tudor tradition by their uncle the Duke of Gloucester, who seized the throne as Richard III.

Princess, The (1847) A 'medley' by Lord Tennyson, chiefly remembered for the exquisite lyrics inserted in a later edition. See IDA, PRINCESS.

Princesse (Cooking) With asparagus.

Princess Ida See IDA, PRINCESS.

Princess Victoria A British Railways ferryboat which sank off Ireland in 1953 with passengers and crew.

Princeton (1746) One of the IVY LEAGUE universities, at Princeton, N.J.

Principalities An order of angels according to a 4th-century work, grouped with archangels and angels. See DOMINIONS AND POWERS.

Principles of Human Knowledge (1710) Bishop Berkeley's main work. He held that all we know, all our ideas, come through the senses; apart from what goes on in our own minds there is nothing of which we have knowledge. Thus there is no reason to suppose that matter exists at all. A critic has commented: . . . God / Must think it exceedingly odd / If he finds that this tree / Just ceases to be / When there's no one about in the Quad. To which an anonymous wit replied: Dear Sir, Your astonishment's odd:/I am always about in the Quad. / And that's why the tree / Will continue to be, / Since observed by Yours faithfully, God.

Pringle of Scotland, The A stroke-play golf tournament open to PGA members, and amateurs with a handicap of 1 or better, played in June at Royal Lytham and St Annes, Lancashire. Prize money totals $10,000. (Sponsored by Pringle of Scotland.)

Prinny Nickname of the PRINCE REGENT (later George IV).

Printanière (Cooking) With early spring vegetables.

Printemps, Au A large Paris department store near the Opéra.

Printing House Square The site of the offices of, and used in allusion to, the London *Times*.

Prisoner of Zenda, The (1894) Anthony Hope's novel of RURITANIA.

Private Angelo (1946) Eric Linklater's amusing novel of the reluctant Italian warrior who finds little difficulty in dodging war service in a land where unthinking patriotic self-sacrifice is not very highly esteemed.

Private Life of Henry VIII, The (1933) A famous film directed by Alexander Korda, which launched Charles Laughton into world fame in the title role.

Private Lives (1930) One of the most typical of the early Noël Coward comedies; a divorced couple find themselves on honeymoon in adjacent rooms of a hotel in the South of France, each having in desperation married an extremely dull partner.

Privy Council Developed from the Norman King's Council and powerful in Tudor and Stuart times; apart from its Judicial Committee, it now has only formal powers, and consists of holders of certain offices, Cabinet ministers, and distinguished persons nominated to it.

Prix de L'Arc de Triomphe An international flat race over 1½ miles, run at LONGCHAMP in October.

Prix des Nations An international jumping event held at recognized International Horse Shows. Teams of 4 from each competing country jump over the same course twice in a day; each competitor rides one horse only.

Prix Goncourt (1903) An annual prize of 5000 francs awarded to a novelist, preferably young, by the Académie Goncourt founded by Edmond Goncourt in 1896.

PRO (1) Public relations officer, a PR official acting for a government department, public utility, local government etc. (2) PUBLIC RECORD OFFICE.

Proconsul A MIOCENE fossil ape living some 20 million years ago, the first fragments of which were found in Kenya in 1926; thought to belong to the common ancestry of man and modern anthropoid apes.

Procrustes   In Greek legend, a bandit who tied his victims to a bed. If they were too long for it, he lopped off their feet; if too short, he stretched them until they fitted it.

Procter & Gamble   A merger of 19th-century soap and candle firms which now leads in the detergent and allied fields, with headquarters in Cincinnati; one of the 30 industrials that make up the DOW JONES Industrial Average.

Profile, The   Another name for the OLD MAN OF THE MOUNTAIN (2).

Profiles in Courage   (1956) Essays by Senator J. F. Kennedy (as he then was) on leaders of Congress who, in times of crisis, had put conscience before political expediency. It won a Pulitzer prize.

Profumo case   (1963) The resignation of the British Secretary of State for War, John Profumo, when it was found that he had been associating with the mistress of a Russian naval attaché.

Progress, Reporting   (UK) A Parliamentary device used when a committee of the whole House, which cannot adjourn itself, moves 'That the Chairman report Progress'; this brings the Speaker back, and he can then adjourn the sitting.

Prohibition   The period 1920-33 during which the sale of intoxicating liquor was made illegal, leading to bootlegging and gangster warfare; ended by the 21st Amendment. See 18TH AMENDMENT.

Promenade des Anglais   The seafront at Nice, built at the expense of English visitors as a token of gratitude for hospitality received.

Prometheus   In Greek legend, a Titan who at Zeus's command fashioned men out of mud. He became their benefactor, stealing fire from heaven to improve their miserable lot. Zeus punished him by chaining him to a Caucasus mountain, where an eagle pecked his liver all day, the liver being renewed each night; he punished man by PANDORA'S BOX. The idea that the gods begrudge man-

kind any knowledge that will increase their independence is found in *Genesis* iii, 22, where Jehovah complains that 'man is become as one of us' and casts Adam and Eve out of Eden. See TREE OF KNOWLEDGE. See next 2 entries. (Greek 'forethought'.)

Prometheus Bound   Aeschylus' tragedy which portrays the sufferings of PROMETHEUS chained to the mountain. He prophesies that Zeus will be overthrown by his own son, the identity of whose mother (Thetis) is known to Prometheus alone; when he refuses to reveal this secret, Zeus hurls him into Tartarus. In the sequel, *Prometheus Unbound* (now lost), he reveals it and is released. See next entry.

Prometheus Unbound   (1820) Shelley's dramatic allegorical poem in which PROMETHEUS symbolizes those who fight for freedom against tyranny.

Promised Land, The   (1) CANAAN, as promised to Abraham and his descendants (*Genesis* xii, 7; xiii, 15 etc.). (2) Heaven.

Proms, The   (1895) Colloquial abbreviation for the London Promenade Concerts at Queen's Hall, and later Albert Hall; no seats were provided on the ground floor so as to accommodate as many musical enthusiasts as possible at a minimum entrance charge. Sir Henry Wood was the prime instigator. ('Promenade' because it was possible to walk about during the performance.)

Prophet, The   Nickname for TECUMSEH's brother, Tenskwatawa, who was defeated at the Battle of TIPPECANOE.

Propylaea   The entrance to the ACROPOLIS at Athens. (Greek, 'before the gates'.)

Proserpina   See PERSEPHONE.

Prospero   In Shakespeare's *The Tempest*, the rightful Duke of Milan and the father of Miranda, blessed with magic powers which enable him to call on the services of ARIEL, control CALIBAN, engineer his usurping brother's repentance and his own rescue from the island on which he is marooned with Miranda.

Protection The economic doctrine, opposed to FREE TRADE, that home industry should be protected from foreign competition by the imposition of import duties or quotas. It was not adopted by the British government until 1932, when Neville Chamberlain introduced the Protective Tariff Act. See IMPERIAL PREFERENCE.

Protectorate, Cromwell's (1653-59) The name given to the later period of Oliver Cromwell's rule under a written constitution which he had to abandon for lack of a competent or cooperative Parliament; and to a brief period under his son Richard.

Protector Somerset Edward Seymour, Duke of Somerset, Protestant leader, who ruled England as LORD PROTECTOR (1547-49) during the first years of the minority of his nephew, Edward VI, until displaced by John Dudley, Earl of Warwick (later Duke of Northumberland).

Proterozoic Period Term sometimes used for the later stages of the PRE-CAMBRIAN ERA. (Greek *proteros*, 'earlier', *zoé*, 'life'.)

Protestantism A generic term for the religion of the Lutheran, Reformed, the Anglican and Nonconformist Churches.

Proteus (1) In Greek legend, a prophet who tended POSEIDON'S seals. He could assume any shape he chose, and the only way to force him to prophesy the truth was to catch him and hold him fast. (2) A character in Bernard Shaw's The APPLE CART, said to represent Ramsay MacDonald.

Protocols of Zion (of the learned elders of Zion) A forgery purporting to be a report of Zionist meetings at Basle in 1897, at which plans were laid for Jews and FREEMASONS to overwhelm Christendom. They were concocted by the Russian Secret Police from a French satire covertly attacking Napoleon III, and were published in 1903.

Proton Name given to a series of Russian research satellites. *Proton* 3 was launched in 1965 to hunt for quarks (believed to be most elementary of subnuclear particles).

Protozoa A phylum of one-celled microscopic animals, including amoebas and the Sporozoa (e.g. malaria, sleeping sickness and other parasites).

Proudie, Mrs The forceful wife of the Bishop of Barchester (who first appears in Barchester Towers, See BARCHESTER NOVELS), who dominates not only her husband but the whole diocese, vanquishing her only rival, Mr SLOPE.

Proustian Resembling the world created by Proust in REMEMBRANCE OF THINGS PAST, or his literary style.

Provençale (Cooking) Rich in garlic and olive oil.

Provence An old province of southeast France now divided between the *départements* of Var, Bouches-du-Rhône, Basses-Alpes and part of Vaucluse. The old capital was Aix. (Latin, *Provincia*).

Provos (1966) Nickname of youngsters of Amsterdam ('the Provotariat') who, dissatisfied with life as they found it, indulged publicly in practical jokes and whimsies such as leaving white-painted bicycles about the city for use by any who wanted them. After a surfeit of publicity they sank progressively to demonstrations, riots and molesting the public. They had no leader or program. (Abbreviation of Dutch for 'provokers'.)

Prufrock, J. Alfred A character who appears in T. S. Eliot's The Love Song of J. Alfred Prufrock (1915). He is a very ordinary man but, vaguely aware that his life is meaningless and empty, he struggles to rise above it, but too halfheartedly to succeed.

Prunier A Paris restaurant near the Opéra specializing in seafood; there is also a Prunier Traktir in the Avenue Victor-Hugo, and a London Pruniers, both fish restaurants par excellence.

Prussia A former German kingdom, capital Berlin, consisting of the land of the TEUTONIC KNIGHTS (Prussia proper) and BRANDENBURG, which later established domination over a unified Germany. It ceased to be a political entity under the Nazis, and its territories are now divided between West and East Germany and (EAST PRUSSIA, former capital, Königsberg) between Poland and USSR.

Psi force A term invented by Dr Rhine for the faculty used in the phenomena of ESP and the PK EFFECT. (Greek *psi*, name of the first letter of the Greek word from which 'psychic is derived.)

Psmith The hero of the pre-WOOSTER novels of P. G. Wodehouse, such as *Psmith in New York* and *Leave it to Psmith* (1923).

PST See PACIFIC STANDARD TIME.

Psyche In later Greek legend, a beautiful girl who personifies the soul purified by suffering to become worthy of true love, see CUPID AND PSYCHE. (Greek, 'breath', 'soul'.)

PT Pacific Time, i.e. PACIFIC STANDARD TIME.

PTA See PARENT-TEACHER ASSOCIATION.

PT boat US Navy Patrol Torpedo boat, usually unarmored, lightly weaponed but very fast, and designed to torpedo shipping in coastal waters; the equivalent of the British MTBs and the German E BOAT.

Pteridophyta An obsolescent term for the seedless plants, most of them extinct, but including ferns, horsetails and club mosses.

Ptolemaic system The system of astronomy in which the earth was regarded as the center of the universe, around which the sun revolves. It is named after Ptolemy, an astronomer of Alexandria in the 2nd century AD. See COPERNICAN THEORY.

Ptolemies (332-30 BC) A dynasty of Macedonian rulers of Egypt founded by one of Alexander the Great's generals; the last to rule was Cleopatra (see ACTIUM).

PTV Public Television. The Public Television Act (1967) provided government support for noncommercial TV and radio programs free from Federal interference and fostering regional diversity. The Corporation for Public Broadcasting was constituted in 1968 to implement the Act. See also NET; PBL.

Public Debt (US) The NATIONAL DEBT.

Public Enemy No. 1 A phrase used when the FBI first started a genuine campaign to stamp out thuggery in Chicago, giving this title to the chief surviving thug, against whom they concentrated their attention; applied specifically to J. H. Dillinger, shot dead by the FBI in 1934, after he had terrorized Chicago for 14 months.

Public Health Service (1912) A US government agency that had its origins in the Marine Hospital Service and the Quarantine Act.

Public Record Office (UK) The official repository of the national records, which date back to the Conquest and include the Domesday Book; the office is in Chancery Lane, London.

Public Trustee Office (1908) A British government office which acts as executor and trustee if so appointed by a court order or under the terms of a will. In 1966 it was administering or had accepted trusts totaling $1.7 billion.

Public Works Administration (1933) An organization set up under the NATIONAL INDUSTRIAL RECOVERY ACT to prime the economic pump by a comprehensive building program which included roads and vast dam projects in the West. It spent $5000 million during the NEW DEAL period, but too hesitantly to have all the effect anticipated.

Pucelle, La A name for Joan of Arc, used by Shakespeare and Voltaire among others. (French, 'the maid'.)

Puck (1) A generic name for all kinds of elf. (2) By Shakespeare in MIDSUMMER NIGHT'S DREAM converted into a proper name for ROBIN GOODFELLOW; his Puck is a mischievous spirit who can 'put a girdle round about the earth / In forty minutes'. (Connected with the West Country word *pixie*, with similar forms in other languages.)

Puck of Pook's Hill (1906) Rudyard Kipling's book of short stories in which the fairy PUCK appears and takes 2 children on a conducted tour down through English history.

Pueblo incident (Jan. 1968) The seizure of a US spy ship by North Korean gunboats; the 82 men aboard were brutally beaten and tortured by their captors but released after long negotiations. The ship's captain was at first criticized for not resisting capture or destroying secret equipment, but was not court-martialed as it became clear that he had no reasonable alternative.

Pueblo Indians American Indians of various tribes who from 500 BC settled in the semidesert regions of New Mexico and Arizona, and adjacent areas of Texas and Mexico, building communal homes of adobe and stone on cliff tops. Some 30,000 survive, speaking Spanish. (Spanish *pueblo*, 'town'.)

Puff A 'practitioner in panegyric' in Sheridan's comedy The Critic (1779).

Pugwash movement (1957) A movement inspired by Einstein and Bertrand Russell, which brings together scientists of all nations to discuss the diversion of scientific effort from destructive to constructive purposes; it promotes international cooperation in space and other forms of research, help to developing countries, exchange of scientists and information etc. See also VIENNA DECLARATION. (Pugwash, Nova Scotian town where the first conference was held.)

Pulcinella A stock character of the COMMEDIA DELL' ARTE, with a hooked nose, from which the hump-backed hero of the Punch and Judy show is derived. (Neapolitan, 'little turkeycock'; French spelling, Polichinelle; older English form, Punchinello.)

Pulitzer prizes Awarded annually by the trustees of COLUMBIA UNIVERSITY, NYC, for American works of fiction, history, biography, poetry, journalism etc. (Endowed by Joseph Pulitzer, newspaper proprietor.)

Pullman Railroad passenger car with specially comfortable furnishings for day or (particularly) for night travel. (George M. Pullman, their inventor; died 1897.)

Pulsars Dozens of usually invisible stellar objects which are characterized by the emission of very intense radio energy at highly regular intervals (as from about .033 to about 3.5 seconds) but whose exact nature is not known. Some astronomers believe that they are neutron stars resulting from the explosion of supernovae.

Pulteney Bridge (1771) A Florentine bridge at Bath, Somerset, designed by Robert Adam, with shops on either side.

Pumpernickel Malted whole meal rye bread, originally from WESTPHALIA.

Punch See PULCINELLA.

Punchestown Races A famous point-to-point meeting at Kildare, Ireland, held in April.

Punic faith Treachery, the Carthaginians (see next entry) having a reputation for this among the Romans.

Punic Wars Three wars between Rome and the PHOENICIAN colony of Carthage. First (265-242 BC): the Romans defeated Hamilcar at sea, became the strongest naval power in the Mediterranean, and won Sicily. Second, or Hannibalic War (218-201): Hannibal crossed the Alps and crushed the Romans at Lake Trasimenus (217) and Cannae (216), but was defeated in Africa near Zama. Third (149-146): the Romans utterly destroyed Carthage itself. (Punic, from Latin Punicus from Greek Phoenix, 'Phoenician'; Carthage was about 10 miles north of modern Tunis.)

Punjab (1) A former Indian province, now divided between West Punjab (in PAKISTAN), HARYANA and PUNJABI SUBA. (Persian, '5 rivers', i.e. the Indus and its 4 main tributaries.) (2) A character in LITTLE ORPHAN ANNIE.

PUO Doctors' shorthand for pyrexia (i.e. fever) of unknown origin—a common 'diagnosis'.

Purbeck marble A hard limestone quarried in England on the Isle of Purbeck, the Dorset peninsula near Swanage; it was used particularly in medieval churches.

Purchas his Pilgrimes With his earlier works under similar titles, a continuation (1625) by another clergyman, Samuel Purchas, of HAKLUYT'S VOYAGES.

Purdy A name associated with excellence in shotguns. (US 19th-century gunsmith.)

Purgatory The place where the souls of the departed undergo purification and preparation for life in Heaven; a medieval addition to Christian beliefs still accepted by Roman Catholics, who hold that the duration of stay can be shortened by the prayers of the living.

Purim Jewish festival held a month before the PASSOVER, in celebration of the deliverance of the Jews in Persia; see ESTHER.

'Puritan, The' (1887) A statue of Deacon Chapin by Saint-Gaudens, represented with a Bible in one hand and a stout cudgel in the other, the embodiment of the uncompromising vigor of early NEW ENGLAND Puritanism. (In Springfield, Mass.)

Puritans Dissenters; earlier name for NONCONFORMISTS; also used generally of the strictly religious and/or moral.

'Purple Cow, The' A nonsense quatrain by Gelett Burgess (1866-1951): I never saw a Purple Cow./I never hope to see one,/But I can tell you, anyhow, / I'd rather see than be one. It became so famous that he was moved to add later: Ah, yes! I wrote the 'Purple Cow'— / I'm sorry now I wrote it./But I can tell you, anyhow,/ I'll kill you if you quote it! Burgess also invented the words GOOP, bromide (for a bore or his platitudes) and blurb.

Purple Heart (1) US army medal awarded to those wounded on active service. (Silver heart with a purple ribbon.) (2) A stimulant tablet, a mixture of amphetamine ('pep pill') and barbiturate (sleeping pill). (Heart-shaped.)

Pursuivants Four officials of the COLLEGE OF ARMS bearing the titles: Bluemantle, Portcullis, Rouge Croix, Rouge Dragon. (Norman-French, 'followers'.)

PUS (UK) Abbreviation used for Parliamentary Undersecretary of State; see PARLIAMENTARY SECRETARY.

Puseyites A name for members of the OXFORD MOVEMENT. (E. B. Pusey, one of its leaders.)

Pushtu The official language of Afghanistan, spoken by the PATHANS. It is related to Persian. Also spelled Pashtu.

'Puss in Boots' A fairy tale of some antiquity about a youngest son who inherits only a cat from his father. This cat, however, turns out to be an ingenious and unscrupulous ally who by various ruses secures for his master a princess and a fortune.

Pussyfoot Johnson William E. Johnson, a temperance reformer and chief architect of PROHIBITION, who won his nickname as Federal agent appointed by Theodore Roosevelt to enforce the liquor laws in Oklahoma, where his stealthy ('pussyfoot') methods secured the arrest of thousands of bootleggers (1905-11).

Putain respectueuse, La (1946) Sartre's play set in the southern states of USA on a racial theme about a trumped-up charge against a Negro. (French, 'the respectful prostitute'.)

Putung-hua The form of Chinese spoken by the educated classes, based on the Peking dialect; called by foreigners 'Mandarin'.

PVO (USSR) Initials standing for Antiaircraft Defense Command.

PWA See PUBLIC WORKS ADMINISTRATION.

PX Initials used for Post Exchange, a retail store on an army post selling merchandise and services to military personnel and authorized civilians.

Pye Group A UK group of radio engineering firms, including Pye of Cambridge, E. K. Cole (Ekco) and FERRANTI Radio and TV. It was taken over by Philips.

Pygmalion (1913) Bernard Shaw's play in which the phonetician, Professor HIGGINS, as a Pygmalion (see next entry) creates an elegant lady out of the Covent Garden flower seller, Eliza Doolittle; she, to his dismay, falls in love with him. The basis of the record-breaking musical, *My Fair Lady* (1956).

Pygmalion and Galatea In Greek legend Pygmalion is a sculptor of Cyprus who makes an ivory statue of a woman; he finds it so beautiful that he gets APHRODITE to bring it to life. He then marries his own creation, calling her Galatea. See last entry.

Pyle (Ernie) Memorial Award An

award of $1000 made by SCRIPPS-HOWARD Newspapers to the journalist who most nearly exemplifies the style and craftsmanship of Ernie Pyle, a war correspondent killed in 1945 near Okinawa.

Pyramids, Battle of the (1798) Napoleon's defeat of the MAMELUKES outside Cairo.

Pyramus and Thisbe Two lovers of Babylon who arrange a secret tryst, from which Thisbe flees, frightened by a lion which bespatters with blood a garment she had dropped. Seeing it, Pyramus assumes she has been killed and commits suicide; Thisbe, returning to find her lover dead, does likewise. The story is told by Ovid and Chaucer, and a parody of it is played by BOTTOM and company in Shakespeare's MIDSUMMER NIGHT'S DREAM.

Pyrex Proprietary name of a heat-resistant glass.

Pythagoras's theorem That in a right-angled triangle the square on the hypotenuse is equal to the sum of the squares on the other 2 sides. (Greek philosopher of the 6th century BC.)

Pyx, Trial of the (UK) The test of samples of all coins from the MINT, held each March at the Goldsmiths Hall by the Goldsmiths' Company. (*Pyx*, the box in which the coins are put.)

Q

Q Pen name of Sir Arthur Quiller-Couch, Professor of English Literature, CAMBRIDGE UNIVERSITY (1912).

Qajar See KAJAR.

Qantas Initials of the Queensland and Northern Territory Air Service which served the outback regions of Australia, and later developed into the Australian international airline.

Q-boats (1915) Armed ships disguised as trading vessels, used by the British in World War I as decoys for German submarines.

Q-cars Patrol cars used by the CRIMINAL INVESTIGATION DEPARTMENT of the London Metropolitan Police.

Qiana (1968) Proprietary name of DU PONT's high-quality nylon fiber, 5 times the price of ordinary nylon and intended for the luxury fashion trade. It is washable and takes a wide range of dyes.

QSGs (1965) Initials used for Quasi-Stellar Galaxies, objects in far distant parts of space discovered by MOUNT PALOMAR OBSERVATORY; they are powerful emitters of ultraviolet and blue light, but their nature has yet to be explained.

QT Abbreviation for 'quiet', used in the phrase 'on the QT'.

Quadragesimo anno (1931) Pope Pius XI's encyclical on politics and the working classes and, issued after the LATERAN TREATY, supporting a Christian CORPORATIVE STATE. (Latin, 'in the 40th year'.)

Quadrant (Aug. 1943) Code name of the wartime conference at Quebec at which Churchill and Roosevelt discussed the relative priority of OVERLORD and the Italian campaign, and agreed on ANVIL.

Quadruple Alliance (1815) See CONCERT OF EUROPE.

Quai d'Orsay Site of, and used for, the French Foreign Office in Paris. (Name of a Seine-side street; *quai* = quay.)

Quaker Cousinhood, The A name given to the group of English Quaker families who since the 17th century have exercised much influence in the UK in many fields: the Lloyds of Lloyds Bank and Stewart & Lloyds, the Barclays of Barclays Bank and the brewery, the Frys and Cadburys of the chocolate firms, together with the Hoares, Buxtons, Butlers etc.

Quakers Common name for the Society of Friends, a Protestant sect which follows the teaching of George Fox (1624-91), rejects priesthood, sacraments and all dogma, eschews oaths and violence, and believes that each individual is guided by the inner light of the Holy Ghost. Quakers hold 'meetings' addressed by any member moved to do so. Although pacifist, they have a find record of service in ambulance corps in time of war. (Name derives from Fox's bidding a magistrate to 'quake at the word of the Lord'.)

Quality Street (1901) J. M. Barrie's play set in Napoleonic times when spinsters were 'put on the shelf' at an absurdly early age. The heroine, Phoebe Throssel, jumps off the shelf, with satisfactory results.

'Quantrell' A folk ballad about a Confederate guerrilla raid (1863) on the hamlet of Lawrence in nonslavery Kansas, led by William Quantrill (properly so spelled). They burned the place and massacred 150 unarmed men and boys. This was an episode in the long and bloody war between Missouri and Kansas, Lawrence being a stage on the escape route for slaves from Missouri.

Quare Fellow (1956) A play set in a prison just before an execution, produced by THEATRE WORKSHOP from a script by Brendan Behan.

Quarterly Review (1809) A London publication which began life as the Tory rival to the Whig EDINBURGH REVIEW; it was founded by John Murray with the support of Sir Walter Scott.

Quarter Sessions (UK) Criminal

courts held quarterly (or oftener), intermediate in jurisdiction between PETTY SESSIONS and ASSIZES. In counties they consist of 2 or more JPs presided over by a paid lawyer-chairman; in boroughs, of a Recorder, usually a barrister. Trial is by jury. These courts also hear appeals from PETTY SESSIONS.

Quartier Latin See LATIN QUARTER.

Quasars Astronomers' abbreviation for 'quasi-stellar radio source', first observed in 1963. Although in an optical telescope they look like individual stars, they emit far more energy than most galaxies. The initial theory was that they must be the most distant objects in the universe, but this was soon challenged, and their contradictory properties have generated many contradictory theories. Over 100 have been identified, but their nature is still an unsolved problem.

Quasimodo The hunchback of Notre-Dame; see NOTRE DAME DE PARIS.

Quatermain, Allan A principal figure in several of Rider Haggard's adventure stories, including one named after him.

Quaternary Period The later period of the CENOZOIC ERA, lasting from about one million years ago down to the present; subdivided into the PLEISTOCENE and Recent Epoch.

Quattrocento Italian for '15th century', the period of RENAISSANCE art (excluding the HIGH RENAISSANCE) and of the REVIVAL OF LEARNING. See CINQUECENTO. (Italian, '400' for '1400', i.e. the 1400s.)

Quebec Act (1774) A British Act which gave French Canadians freedom of religion and the retention of the French civil code; it kept them from joining the American Revolution, and is still regarded as their charter of liberty. It also extended Quebec's boundaries to include much of the land between the Ohio and Mississippi claimed by colonists of NEW ENGLAND, New York and Virginia.

Quebec Conferences (1943-44) See QUADRANT; OCTAGON.

Quechuan An AMERICAN INDIAN LANGUAGE; see KECHUAN.

Queen, Ellery The pseudonym of Frederic Dannay and Manfred Bennington Lee, the joint authors of, and also the name of the detective in *The Roman Hat Mystery* (1929) and many subsequent stories; the authors also published *Ellery Queen's Mystery Magazine* from 1941. See ROSS, BARNABY.

Queen Anne period (1702-14) The period when a distinctively English style of furniture was developed, characterized by elegance, comfort and simplicity. Walnut veneer and the cabriole leg were the hallmarks, and the bureau the typical product. Marquetry and lacquer were used.

Queen Charlotte's Ball The occasion in May when debutantes officially 'come out' at the beginning of the London SEASON, now that they are no longer (since 1958) presented at Court; dressed in white, they curtsy to a huge ceremonial birthday cake.

Queen Elizabeth Cup (show jumping) A competition at the Royal INTERNATIONAL HORSE SHOW for individual ladies, virtually constituting a world championship.

Queen Elizabeth II (1969) Cunard liner, third of the QUEENS. Because of airline competition on the Atlantic run, she was designed for cruises as well as the transatlantic service (Popularly called the QE2.)

Queen Mab The wife of Oberon, called by Shakespeare TITANIA.

Queen Mary's College A unit of LONDON UNIVERSITY, in the Mile End Road.

Queen of Hearts, The A formidable lady in ALICE IN WONDERLAND whose cry 'Off with his/her head' rings through the latter half of the book; the rest of her conversation is equally trenchant.

Queens A borough of New York City at the west end of Long Island.

Queens, The The Cunard liners *Queen Mary, Queen Elizabeth* and QUEEN ELIZABETH II

Queen's Beasts, The The supporters of the Royal Arms, of which replicas were made for Queen Elizabeth II's coronation. They comprise the Lion of England, Unicorn of Scotland, White Horse of Hanover, Greyhound and Red Dragon of the Tudors, Black Bull of Clarence (son of Edward III), White Lion of the Mortimers, Yale of the Beauforts, Falcon of the Plantagenets, and the Griffin of Edward III.

Queen's Bench Division (UK) A division of the High Court of Justice. It deals with common-law cases such as debt, breach of contract, damages for injury, defamation. The Court of Criminal Appeal has the same panel of judges, 3 forming a quorum.

Queensberry Rules (1867) Boxing rules compiled by J. G. Chambers, laying down the 3-minute round with 1-minute rest etc., still used, with modifications. (Named after their sponsor, the 8th Marquess.)

Queen's College An OXFORD UNIVERSITY College. (Apostrophe before the s; named after Edward III's Queen.)

Queens' College A CAMBRIDGE UNIVERSITY college. (Apostrophe after the s; founded by Henry VI's Queen and refounded by Edward IV's.)

Queen's Counsel (UK) A senior barrister (a 'silk') appointed by the LORD CHANCELLOR, nominally as Counsel to the Crown; any barrister of 10 years' standing may apply 'to take silk', as it is called. A QC wears a silk gown and in court must be accompanied by a junior barrister, to whom he will often leave the conduct of the case, and who gets two-thirds of the brief fee up to a certain limit, thus adding to a litigant's expenses and contravening the principles of restrictive practices legislation.

Queen's . County Former English name for LAOIGHIS, Irish Republic.

Queen's Guide The equivalent in the Girl Guides to the QUEEN'S SCOUT.

Queen's House, The Inigo Jones's PALLADIAN masterpiece at Greenwich Park, London, built for Charles I's Queen; now the central part of the National Maritime Museum.

Queen's Lawn The most exclusive part of the ROYAL ASCOT ENCLOSURE, where the old rule banning divorcées still obtains.

Queen's lecture (1965) An annual lecture, delivered in West Germany by a distinguished British figure, instituted after the Queen's German State Visit in 1965.

Queen's Park The only amateur soccer team in the Scottish League; it plays at HAMPDEN PARK, Glasgow.

Queen's Plate (1860) Canada's oldest and chief flat race, for Canadian-bred-3-year-olds over a course of 1¼ miles. (Prize augmented by a purse given by the Queen.)

Queen's Prize (1860) The premier award for rifle shooting at Bisley, open to all subjects of the Queen; consists of a gold medal and badge, $600 and a signed portrait of the Queen. (Known as the King's Prize when a king reigns.)

Queen's Remembrancer An officer of the British Supreme Court who represents the Exchequer in the collection of debts due to the Crown. See QUIT RENTS CEREMONY.

Queen's Scout A Scout rank attained only by the highest efficiency.

Queen's Speech The UK government's program of Parliamentary business for the forthcoming session read, normally by the Queen, at the State Opening in the House of Lords, where both Houses are assembled for the occasion; it is drafted in Cabinet.

Queen's University (1908) The university at Belfast, founded (1849) as a college of the Queen's University of Ireland. Magee University College, Londonderry, until 1950 a college of the University of Dublin, is now a college of Queen's.

Queen Victoria (1921) Lytton Strachey's second essay in debunking biography; but he fell under the spell of his subject, who emerges as almost a heroine.

Quemoy crisis (1958) The intermittent shelling by Chinese Communists of an offshore island almost enveloped by mainland China; Quemoy is held by the Formosan forces of Chiang Kai-shek. Wrongly assumed to be a prelude to the invasion of Formosa, where the regime rests solely on US support, it led to international tension.

Quentin Durward (1823) Scott's novel in which Quentin is an archer in the Scottish Guard of King Louis XI of France, of whom the novel gives a vivid presentation.

Quest for Corvo (1933) A. J. A. Symons's biography of the self-styled Baron CORVO, which started a vogue for the eccentric man's works, notably *Hadrian the Seventh*.

Question Time (UK Parliament) The daily period (2.45-3.30 p.m.), while the Commons is in session, at which members may put questions, of which they have given previous notice, to the member of government concerned; questions may also be put down for written reply. See PQ.

Quetzalcoatl The TOLTEC god who was adopted by the AZTECS as their chief god. ('Plumed serpent'.)

Quiche Lorraine Bacon and egg flan.

Quickly, Mistress The gullible hostess of FALSTAFF's favorite Boar's Head Tavern, who marries PISTOL.

Quicunque vult Alternative name for the ATHANASIAN CREED. (First words in Latin, 'Whoever wishes (to be saved)'.)

Quiet Flows the Don, And (1934) A two-volume work by Mikhail Sholokhov about the mixed reception given to the Communist Revolution by the Don Cossack villages in the Kuban, his birthplace. A sequel, *The Don Flows Home to the Sea*, was completed in 1940. The work comprises 4 volumes in Russian.

Quilp The replusive dwarf who relentlessly pursues LITTLE NELL and her grandfather in *The* OLD CURIOSITY SHOP.

Quirinal One of the hills of Rome, site of the royal palace (1870-1947), now the President's official residence. (From Latin *Quirinus*, name given to Romulus after he was deified.)

Quisling A traitor who collaborates with the enemy. (From Major Quisling, who ruled German-occupied Norway from 1940 until he was executed in 1945.)

Quito Pre-Liberation name of Ecuador, and still the name of its capital.

Quit Rents ceremony (Oct.) (UK) A quaint ceremony at the Law Courts, of medieval origin, at which the Corporation of London presents the QUEEN'S REMEMBRANCER with horseshoes, billhooks etc. as rent for 2 pieces of land which can no longer be identified.

Quonset hut A hut with a semicircular arching roof of corrugated metal and insulation on a foundation of bolted steel trusses.

Quota clubs Women's service clubs of executives in a business, profession, organization or government unit, linked through Quota Club International (1919) with similar clubs in Canada, Mexico and Australia. Their primary purpose is to give aid to the hard of hearing.

Quo Vadis? (1895) A historical novel by Henry Sienkiewicz, a Polish writer, set in Nero's Rome. One of the major characters is the pagan Petronius Arbiter. The Christian heroine is thrown to the lions in the arena but escapes to marry a man converted by Peter and Paul. (Latin, 'whither goest thou?')

R

R The film rating signifying 'restricted — persons under 17 not admitted unless accompanied by parent or adult guardian', under the
Motion Picture Code of Self-Regulation.

Ra The sun-god of the ancient Egyptians, depicted with the head of a
hawk. The early pharaohs were his
sons and representatives on earth,
and received the law from him. See
AMON.

Race for the Sea, The (Sept-Nov.
1914) In World War I, the name giv-
en to the northward extension of the
battle line by both sides on the Western Front until it reached the Channel ports.

Race Relations Board (1966) (UK) A
body set up by Parliament with
power to intervene in any instance
of racial discrimination which a local conciliation committee has been
unable to settle; if necessary it reports the matter to the Law Officers
of the Crown.

Rachmanism (1963) (UK) A term
comprehending extortionate rents
extracted by terroristic methods, and
in particular the brutal exploitation
of the housing needs of prostitutes
and colored immigrants, symbolized
by the operations in PADDINGTON,
London, of a Polish property owner
named Peter Rachman, whose mis-
deeds came to light through the
PROFUMO CASE, some of the women
in which had been his mistresses.
The revelations, a year after his
death, were put to political use by
opponents of the Conservative government's rent policies.

Racial Adjustment Action Society
Britain's counterpart to the BLACK
MUSLIMS, led by a Trinidadian, MI-
CHAEL X (Michael de Freitas).

RADA (1904) Initials normally used
for the Royal Academy of Dramatic
Art, Gower Street, London, a leading
school of acting.

Radames See AÏDA.

Radcliffe (1879) One of the SEVEN
SISTERS colleges, at Cambridge, Mass.

Radcliffe Camera A general library
at OXFORD UNIVERSITY. (Founded by
Dr Radcliffe, 1650-1714.)

Radcliffe Reports In the UK: (1) In
1956 on Cyprus; (2) in 1959 on the
working of the monetary and credit
system, recommending changes in
the relationship between the BANK
OF ENGLAND and the Treasury; (3) in
1962 on the extent of Communist
infiltration into the British civil
service and trade unions. (Lord Radcliffe.)

Radcliffe Tribunal (1963) (UK) An
investigation into the circumstances
which led to the VASSAL CASE; in the
course of it 3 journalists were committed to prison for refusing to reveal sources of information. (Lord
Radcliffe.)

Radical Students' Alliance (RSA) A
militant movement of British university students which advocates
student control of their own education; it also aims to make a mutual assistance pact with militant
groups of workers. Its heroes are
CHAIRMAN MAO, Fidel Castro and
Che Guevara.

Radio and Space Research Station
A British organization under the SCI-
ENCE RESEARCH COUNCIL, with head-
quarters at Ditton Park, Slough,
Buckinghamshire.

Radio Caroline First (1964) of the
programs broadcast from ships anchored outside British territorial waters to evade the ban on commercial
radio, and consisting almost exclusively of pop music and advertising.
Closed down in 1967.

Radio City A complex of buildings
in the ROCKEFELLER CENTER, used by
RCA and NBC.

Radio Free Europe A private network of 5 radio stations financed
by voluntary contributions which
broadcasts to the Communist countries of Europe where it claims a
regular audience over twice the size
of VOICE OF AMERICA's. Munich is the

headquarters.

Raf Colloquialism for Royal Air Force.

RAF Commemoration Day (Sept. 15th) The day in the 1940 BATTLE OF BRITAIN when an exceptional number of German planes were shot down.

Raffles The gentleman burglar and cricketer of E. W. Hornung's *The Amateur Cracksman* (1899).

Raffles Hotel A famous hotel in Singapore, named after Sir Thomas Stamford Raffles (1781-1826) who governed Java and Sumatra, and advised the annexation of Singapore.

Ragley Hall A 17th-century house near Alcester, Warwickshire, belonging to the Marquesses of Hertford. It has many art treasures, and a variety of sporting events are staged there.

Ragnarok The GÖTTERDÄMMERUNG of Scandinavian mythology.

Ragusa Italian name of the Yugoslav port of Dubrovnik.

Raiders The Oakland Raiders, AMERICAN FOOTBALL LEAGUE. Became member of the AMERICAN CONFERENCE, NATIONAL FOOTBALL LEAGUE in 1970.

Rail Splitter A nickname for Abraham Lincoln who, when the family moved to Illinois (1830), helped his father clear and fence his new farm. (One who splits logs into fence rails.)

Rain (1922) Somerset Maugham's play, based on his short story *Miss Thompson*, about a missionary in the South Seas who first converts and then seduces a prostitute, Sadie Thompson. Filled with remorse, he kills himself.

Rainbow, The (1915) D. H. Lawrence's novel introducing the BRANGWEN family, some of whom reappear in WOMEN IN LOVE. It displays the usual Laurentian characteristics: powerful, moving descriptions of nature, and tortuous nonsense about dark fecund forces.

'Rainbow' bomb (1962) A US hydrogen bomb exploded at a height of 250 miles over Johnston Island (southwest of Hawaii), so called because of the spectacular artificial aurora it created. It stopped transmissions from 3 satellites.

Rainbow Bridge The world's largest natural bridge, in south Utah; 309 ft high, 278 ft span, now a national monument.

Rainbow Corner, London A famous resort of US forces during World War II, previously Lyon's Corner House, Shaftesbury Avenue. (Named in memory of the RAINBOW DIVISION.)

Rainbow Division The US 42nd Division, prominent in World War I and so named because they were recruited from all sections of the community.

Rainbow Girls Members of an organization for girls corresponding to the DEMOLAY Order for boys.

Rainbow Room A restaurant in ROCKEFELLER CENTER, New York.

Rains Came, The (1937) A novel by Louis Bromfield set in Malabar, India; and an equally famous movie version (1939).

Rajputs A Hindu landowner-warrior caste of northwest India which founded the states of Jodhpur, Jaipur, Bikaner and Udaipur, now grouped in the state of Rajasthan.

'Rake's Progress, The' (1735) (1) Hogarth's series of satirical oil paintings, in the style of MARRIAGE À LA MODE. (2) Stravinsky's opera (1951) inspired by (1). (3) Ballet on theme of (1) to music by Gavin Gordon.

Ralph Roister Doister (1533) The earliest English comedy, written by a headmaster of Eton, Nicholas Udall; a naïve, robust play in doggerel verse about Ralph's unsuccessful wooing of the Widow Custance.

Rama An incarnation of VISHNU; see RAMAYANA.

Ramadan The MUSLIM month during which the faithful fast from sunrise to sunset, and ending with the Lesser BAIRAM feast when the new moon is seen; it begins in October (1970). It is traditionally the month when Allah sent down the Koran to earth.

Ramayana (500 BC) One of the 2 great Hindu epic poems (see also MAHABHARATA), recounting the wars of Rama, an incarnation of VISHNU;

representing perhaps ARYAN incursions into south India. (SANSKRIT, 'deeds of Rama'.)

Rambler, The (1750-52) A periodical amost entirely written by Dr Johnson, consisting of overdidactic essays on books and ethics.

Rambouillet A 14th-century royal château, in the forests halfway between Versailles and Chartres, used by Catherine de MEDICI and the place where Napoleon spent his last night of freedom; now the official summer residence of the French president, but usually open to the public.

Ramillies, Battle of (1706) Marlborough's second victory over the French in the War of the SPANISH SUCCESSION, which resulted in the expulsion of the French from the NETHERLANDS. (Village in Brabant, north of Namur, Belgium.)

Rams The Los Angeles Rams, NATIONAL FOOTBALL LEAGUE. Became member of the NATIONAL CONFERENCE, NATIONAL FOOTBALL LEAGUE in 1970.

R & A See ROYAL AND ANCIENT.

Rand Corporation (1946) A US nonprofit research organization or 'think factory' largely financed by the Air Force, with headquarters at Santa Monica, Calif. It does research on military planning through 'war games' (i.e. working out the relative advantages of all possible combinations of strategic moves and countermoves, e.g. in controlled escalation), a mechanistic approach later extended to politico-military problems, e.g. the biological and environmental effects of nuclear war on populations. See HUDSON INSTITUTE.

R and D costs Abbreviation used for 'research and development costs', a particular problem in designing aircraft for example, when they may be extremely heavy and incurred years before any profit can accrue.

Ranelagh Once a famous English polo ground, adjoining HURLINGHAM, but now a derelict waste.

Ranger The US program for photographing the moon at close quarters as a preliminary to SURVEYOR. Ranger 6 crashed into the far side of the

moon in 1962; Ranger 7-9 all sent back close-up pictures of the moon in 1964-65.

Rangers The New York Rangers, NATIONAL HOCKEY LEAGUE.

Rangers, The A Glasgow professional soccer team that plays at Ibrox Park; see CELTIC.

Rangers, US In World War II, commandos, who first saw action in the 1942 DIEPPE RAID. (Name borrowed from units of various kinds in earlier US history.)

Rank Organization A group built up by J. Arthur (later Lord) Rank, concerned with motion-picutre production and distribution. Gaumont-British, PINEWOOD STUDIOS, Odeon cinecameras (Rank Precision Industries), XEROX, bingo halls, automation and data processing.

Ranunculaceae The buttercup family, characterized by indented leaf patterns and conspicuous flowers; it includes meadow rue, monkshood, larkspur, columbine, clematis.

Rapacki plan (1958) A proposal to create a neutral zone in Central Europe (Germany, Czechoslovakia and Poland) where nuclear arms would be prohibited. It was supported by USSR and rejected by the West. (Named after its sponsor, the Polish Foreign Minister.)

Rapallo Treaty (1) Treaty between Italy and Yugoslavia (1920) allotting Dalmatia to Yugoslavia and Trieste to Italy, declaring Fiume independent, and pledging joint opposition to a HAPSBURG restoration (then much mooted). (2) The 1922 treaty by which Germany became the first state to recognize Soviet Russia, a huddling together of 2 nations who felt slighted by the Great Powers. (Italian coastal resort near Genoa.)

Rape of Lucrece See LUCRECE.

Rape of the Lock, The (1714) Pope's burlesque poem on a contemporary family feud caused by Lord Petre's cutting off a lock of a girl's hair.

Rape of the Sabines, The ROMULUS'S method of providing wives for the settlers in the new Rome. At his invitation the neighboring Sabines attended a feast, leaving their womenfolk behind; the Roman youths took advantage of this to kidnap the younger women.

Raphael One of the chief angels in Jewish tradition, who appears in TOBIT and PARADISE LOST. In paintings he is often shown carrying a pilgrim's staff or the fish that restored Tobit's sight.

Rapier (1967) BAC mobile air-portable surface-to-air guided weapons system for use by ground forces against low-level attacks.

Ras Ethiopian title of a royal prince; e.g. the Emperor Haile Selassie was Ras Tafari before he succeeded to the throne.

Rashomon (1951) The first and most famous Japanese movie to reach the Western world, at the Venice festival; in it, grunting warriors duel ritualistically in an atmosphere so bizarre as to be, temporarily, fascinating.

Raskolniki The Old Believers or Russian dissenters who in the 17th century refused to accept the patriarch Nikon's reform of the services of the Russian EASTERN ORTHODOX CHURCH.

Raskolnikov Atheist hero of Dostoevsky's *Crime and Punishment* (1866) who committed murder to prove to himself that he was 'beyond good and evil', yet was driven by his 'irrational' subconscious to a voluntary confession of the deed.

Rasselas The Prince of ABYSSINIA who, in Dr Johnson's philosophical romance, escapes from his father and the paradise of Happy Valley and goes to Cairo, where he finds that the usual recipes for happiness prove worthless; chastened, he returns to father.

Rastafarians A Negro sect which flourishes in the Jamaican slums, founded when Ras Tafari (see RAS) became Emperor of Ethiopia in 1930. They adopted the idea of a return to Africa, first propagated by Marcus Garvey, and grew beards in imitation of Ras Tafari, whom they chose as their future African patron.

Rastignac, Eugène de A character whose career is traced in several novels of Balzac's COMÉDIE HUMAINE, from penurious law student to rich statesman. Like the equally destestable Sorel in LE ROUGE ET LE NOIR, he makes ruthless use of women to advance the only cause dear to him — his own success.

Ratisbon The French name of REGENSBURG, derived from the original Celtic name.

'Raven, The' (1845) E. A. Poe's poem with the refrain: Quoth the Raven, 'Nevermore'. The poet is lamenting the death of 'the rare and radiant maiden whom the angels name Lenore', and hears the raven give this one dread answer to all his desperate hopes of reunion with her in some future life.

RBI (Baseball) Runs batted in.

RCA The Radio Corporation of America, one of companies which joined to form NBC. Other interests include the manufacture of electrical and electronic equipment, and publishing.

REA Signifies the US Rural Electrification Administration.

Reader's Digest (1922) A US and international monthly pocket-size magazine, containing condensed versions of material from world periodicals; it carried no advertisements until 1955. It is now published in 13 languages, with a world circulation of some 21 million. The company also publishes condensed and unabridged books.

Real Presence The presence of the body and blood of Christ at the Eucharist either by TRANSUBSTANTIATION, Consubstantiation (a slightly different, Lutheran, doctrine) or 'after an heavenly and spiritual manner' (Anglican definition).

Reaumur scale A temperature scale in which 0° is the freezing point of water, 80° its boiling point.

Rebecca ISAAC's wife, selected by ABRAHAM's servant at a well in MESOPOTAMIA (*Genesis* xxiv, 12-15). Of their children, she preferred JACOB above ESAU.

'Récamier, Mme' (1800) J. L. David's portrait of a lady reclining on a Neoclassical couch; the sitter went off in a pet before he had finished it. She was a famous beauty whose salon was much frequented under the DIRECTORY and First Empire. Now in the LOUVRE. See DIRECTOIRE.

Recessional   The music, or words to which it is set, played when the clergy and choir leave at the end of a service. See next entry.

'Recessional'   (1897) Kipling's poem published in The London Times on the occasion of Queen Victoria's Diamond Jubilee; it begins: God of our fathers, known of old,/Lord of our far-flung battle line.

Rechabites, Independent Order of (1835) A large friendly society for total abstainers founded at Salford, Lancashire; its lodges are called 'tents'. (From the Biblical Rechabites, a nomadic tribe who abstained from wine, Jeremiah xxxv, 6-8.)

Recherche du temps perdu, À la See REMEMBRANCE OF THINGS PAST.

Recife   The 'Brazilian Venice', capital and chief seaport of the province of Pernambuco; the city itself was formerly known as Pernambuco.

Reconstruction   The period (1865-77) after the AMERICAN CIVIL WAR when the Confederate states were rehabilitated under military rule and northern 'carpetbaggers' exploited the defenseless inhabitants for personal gain; called the Black Reconstruction in the South.

Rector of Justin, The   (1965) A novel by Louis Auchincloss about how a young teacher learns to adjust himself to life in a NEW ENGLAND boarding school dominated by the giant octogenarian rector.

Recusants   Roman Catholics and others who refused to attend Church of England services in the 16th-17th centuries.

Red Arrows, The   The leading aerobatic squadron of the RAF.

Red Badge of Courage, The   (1895) A psychological novel which brought Stephen Crane lasting literary fame and was remarkable for graphic descriptions of battle in the Civil War, of which the author had no firsthand knowledge. The hero enters the war with romantic illusions about his courage, quickly learns fear, runs away and, after an unmerited decoration, progresses through humility to real courage.

Red Baron   Nickname of Baron von Richthofen, see RICHTHOFEN CIRCUS; SNOOPY. (His plane was painted red.)

Red Biddy   A Glasgow Irish name for cheap red wine laced with methylated spirits, a favorite in the city's slums at one time; the name and the drink spread elsewhere, and is now applied to other nauseous concoctions of the kind.

Red Branch Knights   The army of CONCHOBAR, King of ULSTER, so named from their emblem, a rowan branch with red berries.

Redbrick   Name applied to any modern British university, in contrast to OXFORD and CAMBRIDGE universities and other ancient foundations.

Redbridge   (1965) Newly formed London borough consisting of the former boroughs of Wanstead-Woodford, Ilford and part of Dagenham, together with the urban district of Chigwell; headquarters at Ilford, Essex.

Redcoat   A British soldier in the days when red uniforms were worn.

Red Cross, American National (1881) A nationwide organization, part of the International Red Cross, with over 33 million members and 2.3 million active volunteers in over 3700 local chapters; it is the principal blood-collecting agency for hospitals, provides services to armed forces and veterans, engages in disaster relief and promotes large-scale training programs in safety and first aid.

Red Dean, The   Dr Hewlett Johnson, Dean of Canterbury (1931-63), who wrote the best-selling The Socialist Sixth of the World (1939), and persuaded himself that there was much good even in Stalinist Russia, which he often visited.

Red Devils   Nickname of the SPECIAL AIR SERVICE Regiment of the British Army.

Redditch   (1964) (UK) A NEW TOWN situated around the existing town, designed to take 70,000 new inhabitants.

Red Douglas   Nickname given to the Earls of Angus, in distinction from the Earls of Douglas, called BLACK DOUGLAS. The 2 branches of the family were united in the Dukedom of Hamilton.

Redeye US man-portable short-range antiaircraft weapon.

Red Flag, Order of the A Soviet order awarded for services to international revolution, i.e. for successful interference in other countries' affairs.

'Red Flag, The' The British Labour Party's 'school song', composed by an Irishman, sung at the annual conference – with less than universal enthusiasm since it contains such antiquated gems as: 'Come dungeon dark or gallows grim, / This song shall be our parting hymn.' and 'Though cowards flinch, and traitors jeer, / We'll keep the Red Flag flying here'.

Red Giant The type of star formed when most of the hydrogen in a MAIN SEQUENCE STAR has been used up. The interior contracts and heats up, the exterior expands, cools and glows red. BETELGEUSE is a typical example, with very low density and a huge diameter of some 200 million miles. The next stage of development is the WHITE DWARF.

Red Guards Mobs of undisciplined young Chinese who were set to enforce MAO'S CULTURAL REVOLUTION from 1966 onwards, each carrying a little red book of Mao aphorisms as badge of office.

Red Mill, The (1906) An operetta by the Irish-American Victor Herbert; its songs were so popular that it was revived in 1945.

Redouté roses Perhaps the most famous rose paintings ever made, published in Les Roses (1817–24) by Pierre Redouté, who also produced numerous volumes of equally skillful paintings of other flowers. There are cheap modern reproductions to trap the unwary.

Red Poll A breed of red dual-purpose cattle developed in East Anglia.

Red Power The American Indian counterpart to BLACK POWER, with the slogan 'Integrity not Integration'. After Roosevelt's Indian Reorganization Act (1934) and after

serving in both World Wars and the Korean War, Indians hoped that the tide would turn in their favor, but the 1950s policy of winding up the reservations proved disastrous and in the 1960s they began to engage in well-planned little demonstrations, such as occupying ALCATRAZ and offering to buy it for $24 in beads and cloth.

Red Queen, The A character in THROUGH THE LOOKING GLASS intended by Lewis Carroll to be 'the concentrated essence of all governesses'.

Red River uprising (1869–70) A rebellion by Canadian MÉTIS, led by Louis Riel (of French, Irish and Indian blood), who captured Fort Garry (i.e. Winnipeg) and set up a provisional government; the rebels dispersed without bloodshed when troops under Col. Garnet Wolseley arrived. The revolt was triggered off by fears arising from the purchase of the NORTHWEST TERRITORIES from the HUDSON'S BAY COMPANY.

Reds The Cincinnati Reds, NATIONAL (Baseball) LEAGUE, playing at Riverfront Stadium. The Cincinnati Red Stockings were the first all-professional baseball team, in the 1860s.

Redshirts, Garibaldi's See GARIBALDI'S THOUSAND REDSHIRTS.

Redskins The Washington (D.C.) Redskins, NATIONAL FOOTBALL LEAGUE. Became member of the NATIONAL CONFERENCE, NATIONAL FOOTBALL LEAGUE in 1970.

Red Sox The Boston Red Sox, AMERICAN (Baseball) LEAGUE, playing at FENWAY PARK.

Red Star The Soviet Defense Ministry's newspaper.

Redstone US Army's liquid fuel, surface-to-surface missile, range 200 miles, designed to carry a nuclear warhead; also used in launching the first American into suborbital flight (see MERCURY PROJECT).

Red Top An air-to-air homing missile made by HAWKER SIDDELEY for the LIGHTNING. See FIRESTREAK.

Redwing A national class of one-design clinker-built 14-foot dinghy, designed by Uffa Fox especially for use in the English West Country;

the sails are always red.

Red Wings   The Detroit Red Wings, NATIONAL HOCKEY LEAGUE.

Reeder, J. G.   The elderly detective who appears in many of Edgar Wallace's crime stories.

Reeve's Tale, The   In the CANTERBURY TALES, a ribald story of how 2 students seduce a miller's wife and daughter.

Reformation, The   The Protestant revolt, part religious, part nationalist, against the supremacy of the pope, brought to a head in 1517 by Luther in Germany, followed by Zwingli and Calvin in Switzerland and John Knox in Scotland. They wanted reform of the priesthood, an end to the sale of indulgences (i.e. buying salvation from priests), the translation of the Bible and prayer book into languages that could be understood; they repudiated transubstantiation and the worship of the Virgin MARY; but believed in salvation through faith alone as opposed to 'justification by works' (salvation through doing good deeds or buying indulgences). In England Henry VIII took the middle way, retaining Catholic doctrine but severing all ties with the Pope.

Reformation Parliament   (1529-36) Summoned by Henry VIII when the Pope refused to sanction his divorce from Catherine of Aragon, it passed legislation which carried through the English REFORMATION.

Reform Bills   Bills extending the franchise, particularly (1) the Whig measure (1832) which gave the vote to the middle classes and abolished rotten boroughs; (2) Disraeli's Bill (1867) which extended the vote to the urban working class.

Reform Club   (1832) A London club in PALL MALL founded in the year of the great REFORM BILL, to which members must still make a token obeisance, although the membership is no longer radical; it is frequented by Treasury officials, economists and judges with a propensity for writing letters to the London Times, and wields considerable political influence.

Reformed Church   The CALVINIST Church, which separated from the main LUTHERAN movement after Calvin and Luther had disagreed on the significance of the Last Supper. It became particularly strong in Switzerland, Holland (the DUTCH REFORMED CHURCH) and France (the HUGUENOTS).

Regan   One of the 2 evil daughters of KING LEAR; see GONERIL.

Regency period   In the English decorative arts, a term applied to the period (about 1790-1830) overlapping the regency (1811-20) of the future George IV. It corresponded with and was influenced by the French EMPIRE STYLE and was characterized in furniture by rosewood, brass inlay, and copies of ancient Roman and Egyptian models.

Regensburg   The German name of a city, formerly capital, of Bavaria, known in history as RATISBON.

Regent Street   One of London's principal shopping streets, which began life in 1812 as part of Nash's Via Triumphalis to link his Regent's Park to the PRINCE REGENT's palace, Carlton House (later rebuilt as CARLTON HOUSE TERRACE). The chief feature was the curving colonnaded Quadrant, rebuilt in the 1920s.

Regicides, The   (1649) The men who condemned Charles I to death, including Cromwell and Ireton.

Regulation 18b   A clause of a British Emergency Powers Act under which, at the beginning of World War II, persons such as Sir Oswald Mosley who were considered to be security risks were interned in a concentration camp in the Isle of Man.

Reichenbach Falls   Waterfall near Interlaken, Switzerland, perhaps most famous in Britain as the scene of Sherlock HOLMES's first death in 1891.

Reichsführer   The title taken by Hitler in his dual capacity of head of state and supreme commander of the armed forces. (German, 'state leader'.)

Reichstag fire   (Feb. 1933) The burning down of the German Parliament house, which gave Hitler the excuse to establish a one-party regime, declaring that the state was threatened by a Communist conspiracy. The fire was started on Hitler's orders but blamed on a Dutch half-wit, Van der Lubbe, who was executed.

Reichswehr The old name for the German Army, now called BUNDES-WEHR. (German, 'state defense'.)

Reid Professor Holder of the chair of Music at Edinburgh University.

Reign of Terror See under TERROR.

Reivers, The (1962) William Faulkner's humorous PULITZER-PRIZE novel, in which a man recalls a childhood escapade. With an Indian half-caste and a Negro servant, he ran away in his grandfather's car, and exchanged it for a sorry-looking nag which proved to be a race winner. ('Reiver' is Scotch for 'raider'.)

Religio Medici (1643) Sir Thomas Browne's learned meditations on a wide range of subjects, such as religious belief, nature, superstition, life and death. Although a devout Anglican, he had had, as a physician, scientific training, and therefore tempered reverence with skepticism.

Religious Wars, French (1562-98) A series of civil wars fought on religious issues, ended by the EDICT OF NANTES. See HOLY LEAGUE; HUGUE-NOTS; ST BARTHOLOMEW MASSACRE.

Remagen The bridge over the Rhine between Cologne and Koblenz, where an armored division of the US 1st Army made the first Allied crossing of that river, March 1945.

Remembrance Day November 11th, originally ARMISTICE DAY, renamed in Canada after World War II; see REMEMBRANCE SUNDAY.

Remembrance of Things Past (1913-27) Marcel Proust's immensely long masterpiece, a study of Parisian society as seen by the narrator, Marcel, like the author a hypersensitive, introspective young man. He traces the lowering of barriers by the aristocratic GUERMANTES family, who eventually accept, even in marriage, the VERDURINS, SWANN'S daughter GILBERTE and his widow, ODETTE DE CRÉCY. (The French title is À la Recherche du temps perdu, published

in 7 parts.)

Remembrance Rock (1948) Carl Sandburg's giant historical novel which traces the history of a family from the England of 1608 via Plymouth Rock to World War II; it is a masterly recapitulation of American aspirations and achievements, annotated by the poet-author's sage philosophizing.

Remembrance Sunday The Sunday before, on, or on the morrow of, November 11th (ARMISTICE DAY), when the dead of 2 world wars are remembered.

Renaissance (Renascence) Primarily the rebirth of classical learning and art, which began in north Italian city-states in the 14th century and spread to England, France and Spain; extended to cover the transition from the feudal, monastic Middle Ages to the secular urban civilization of the modern West, which coincided with the discovery of America, printing and the COPERNI-CAN THEORY.

Renaissance architecture (15th-17th centuries) The European revival of the classical orders and the rounded Roman arch which, pioneered by the buildings of Brunelleschi in Italy, gradually replaced Gothic. It did not reach England until a century later, coming to full development in the work of Inigo Jones, Wren and the Adam brothers.

Renishaw A country house near Sheffield on the Yorkshire-Derbyshire border, the home of the Sitwell family, well known through Osbert Sitwell's autobiographies, see LEFT HAND! RIGHT HAND!

Reno divorce The easy divorce obtainable under the state laws of Nevada, which accept many trivial grounds and only 6 weeks' residence; associated particularly with Reno as being the state's largest city, situated on the Californian border and thus convenient for HOLLYWOOD film stars etc.

Renown, HMS British POLARIS SUB-MARINE. Commissioned 1968.

Rentenmark (1923) Temporary German currency introduced to stabilize money during the inflationary period that followed World War I.

Repington Diaries Published in 1920-22 by a British war correspondent, Col. Charles Repington, and containing reminiscences of World War I regarded, by the standards of the day, as highly indiscreet.

Representative, The (1963) Hochhuth's Theater of FACT play attacking Pope Pius XII for, according to the German playwright, not having condemned Hitler's anti-Semitism.

Republican Party (1828) The party (at first called Whigs) which seceded from the old Republican Democratic Party to campaign for high tariffs. Strengthened by a further secession of Northern Democrats who stood for the abolition of slavery, they became the party of big business and economic imperialism, and after Woodrow Wilson's presidency (see DEMOCRATIC PARTY), brought the country back to isolationism. Their influence was crippled by failure to deal with the Great DEPRESSION in the 1930s and they remained out of power until 1969, except under Eisenhower whose election was on personal rather than party grounds. They were further weakened by the GOLDWATER CAPER.

Repulse, HMS British POLARIS SUBMARINE commissioned 1969.

Requiem (1) First word of a prayer used in the Roman Catholic requiem mass, a service for the souls of the dead. (2) A musical setting for this, e.g. Mozart's, Verdi's. (3) A similar setting for a special occasion, e.g. Brahms's *German Requiem*, written after his mother's death. (*Requiem aeternam dona*, 'grant them eternal rest'.)

Rerum novarum (1891) Pope Leo XIII's encyclical on social questions, specifically approving legislation which improved the lot of the working class, but attacking socialism.

Rescue, The (1920) Joseph Conrad's novel in which Capt. LINGARD reappears, faced with a choice between duty and love.

Resistance movement Name given, especially in France, to the underground movement of resistance and sabotage in German-occupied territory during World War II.

Resolution, HMS The first of the Royal Navy's 4 POLARIS SUBMARINES, commissioned in 1967. Displacement 7000 tons; built at Barrow-in-Furness by Vickers-Armstrong.

Responsions The first of the 3 examinations for the degree of BA at OXFORD UNIVERSITY; candidates with good academic qualifications are exempted from taking it.

Restoration, The (1660) The restoration of the monarchy, in the person of Charles II, after the ENGLISH CIVIL WAR.

Restoration period (1660-89) In English decorative arts, a period of reaction from Cromwellian austerities typified by walnut furniture with elaborate carving and barley-sugar turning. Veneering, marquetry, lacquer, gilding, glued joints, cane-seated chairs, glass-fronted bookcases, and daybeds all came into vogue. Grinling Gibbons's carvings were much in demand.

Restoration plays Comedies produced during the Stuart RESTORATION period (1660-1714), notably those by Dryden, Wycherly, Vanbrugh, Congreve and Farquhar, characterized in general by polished wit, licentiousness, artificiality and heartlessness — in natural reaction from a surfeit of Puritan austerity.

Resurrection (1) The rising of Christ from the tomb on the third day, commemorated on Easter Sunday; (2) the general resurrection of the dead.

Resurrection City (1968) A tent city erected in a park in Washington, D.C., for a protest gathering of the poor in May and June. Most were Southern Negroes, others were Indians, Mexican-Americans and poor whites from APPALACHIA. The demonstration was suggested by Martin Luther King just before his assassination and sponsored by his SOUTHERN CHRISTIAN LEADERSHIP CONFERENCE.

Resurrection Men A term first applied to BURKE AND HARE, and then used generally of grave robbers.

Retreat, The One of the world's leading hospitals for mental disorders, at York, England.

Return of the Native, The (1878) Thomas Hardy's WESSEX novel of Clym Yeobright who, to escape city life, opens a school on EGDON HEATH; he loses his sight, becomes first a furze cutter and then an itinerant preacher, his fickle wife having drowned herself.

Reuben Award The National Cartoonists' Society's award to the outstanding cartoonist of the year, named for RUBE GOLDBERG, to whom they gave it in 1968.

Reuter (1849) An international news agency, since 1941 a trust owned by British and Australian newspapers and handling nondomestic news. (Founded by Baron de Reuter.)

Revenge, HMS Last of the 4 British POLARIS SUBMARINES, commissioned 1969.

Revenge, The (1880) Tennyson's poem of Sir Richard Grenville's fight (1591) with the Spanish fleet at Flores in the Azores. It contains the oft-quoted: 'Sink me the ship, Master Gunner— / Sink her, split her in twain!'

Revere, Paul See PAUL REVERE.

Revised Standard Version An American version of the Bible (New Testament 1946; Old 1952) prepared by Protestant scholars but approved for both Protestant and Catholic use. It preserves the sentence structure of the KING JAMES BIBLE but substitutes modern American idiom for archaisms where necessary.

Revised Version A revision of the AUTHORIZED VERSION made by English and American scholars, completed in 1885 (APOCRYPHA, 1895).

Revival of Learning (or **Letters**) The literary aspect of the RENAISSANCE, the study of the literature, language and antiquities of Greece and Rome; Humanism. See NEW LEARNING.

Revolt of the Four Generals (Apr. 1961) The seizure of power in Algiers by Generals Jouhaud, Salan, Challe and another, quickly suppressed by de Gaulle.

Revolutionary War See AMERICAN WAR OF INDEPENDENCE.

Revolutions of 1848 An uncoordinated series of European revolutions, in Paris, Vienna, Prague, Budapest, the Italian and German states and elsewhere, mainly led by middle-class intellectuals inspired by the FRENCH REVOLUTION; their occurrence in one year was chiefly due to an economic slump and bad harvests. The English manifestation of this unrest was Chartism (see CHARTISTS).

Revue des deux mondes (1829) A leading French literary and political review, published fortnightly in Paris.

Rexists (1936) Belgian party formed by Léon Degrelle, inspired by the example of Nazism, and collaborationist during the war. (From *Christus Rex*, 'Christ is King', slogan of a Roman Catholic Young People's Society.)

Reynard the Fox A cycle of medieval tales of Reynard's stratagems to ensure survival in the animal world, a vehicle for satire on human affairs used in many languages and styles.

Reynard the Fox (1919) John Masefield's poem of a fox hunt, as seen by the hunters and the hunted.

RFD Initials used for rural free delivery, i.e. free mail delivery in outlying country areas.

Rhadamanthus In Greek legend, a brother of MINOS; wise and just on earth, he was appointed one of the judges of the Underworld.

Rhaetia An ancient Roman province extending over the modern Grisons canton of east Switzerland and part of Tirol. It gave its name to the Rhaetic Alps (which run parallel with the ENGADINE) and the Rhaeto-Romanic dialects of that region (Swiss Romansh and Tirolese Ladin); see ROMANCE LANGUAGES.

Rhapsody in Blue (1924) The first important orchestral composition in the jazz style, the title referring to the prominent use of the blue notes and chords characteristic of jazz. It was written for Paul Whiteman by George Gershwin, and orchestrated by Ferde Grofé.

Rhea   The Greek equivalent to CY-BELE.

Rhea Silvia   In Roman legend, a VES-TAL VIRGIN, the mother of ROMULUS AND REMUS by MARS.

Rheingold, Das   (1869) The prologue to Wagner's RING OF THE NIBELUNGS cycle. The Rhine Gold is the hoard of the NIBELUNGS, guarded by the RHINE MAIDENS.

Rheingold express   An early morning train from the Hook of Holland to Milan.

Rh factor   An agglutinating agent in the blood; its presence or absence is an inherited characteristic, of importance in certain rare conditions and in blood transfusions. See ABO BLOOD GROUPS. (Rh for *Rhesus* monkey, in which it was first observed.)

Rhineland-Palatinate   A *Land* of Western Germany, capital Mainz, formed from the Rhine PALATINATE, the southern part of the RHINE PROVINCE, and parts of Hesse and Hesse-Nassau.

Rhine Maidens   In Wagner's RING OF THE NIBELUNGS cycle, the guardians of the NIBELUNGS' hoard of gold buried in the bed of the Rhine. ALBERICH steals this and makes a magic ring from it, which at the end of the cycle returns to the eternal possession of the Rhine Maidens.

Rhine Province   A former Prussian province, capital Cologne, including Saarland and part of the RUHR. The northern districts are now in North Rhine-Westphalia, the southern in the RHINELAND-PALATINATE.

Rhinoceros   (1958) Ionesco's Theater of the ABSURD play on the theme of the urge to conform with mass fanaticism. One by one a town's inhabitants opt to become rhinoceroses, until only one (Bérenger) is left with the courage of his convictions, listening to the herd stampeding up and down the main street.

Rhode Island Greening   A greenish-yellow apple used in cooking and processing, grown especially in NEW ENGLAND and New York.

Rhode Island Red   See RIR.

Rhodesia and Nyasaland, Federation of   (1954-63) A short-lived federation of what were then the colonies of Northern and Southern Rhodesia and Nyasaland. After it broke up it resolved itself into its component parts, which were renamed ZAMBIA, Rhodesia and MALAWI respectively.

Rhodes scholarships   Endowed by Cecil Rhodes (died 1902) for students at OXFORD UNIVERSITY from USA, the Commonwealth, South Africa and (originally) Germany.

Rhys (John Llewellyn) Memorial Prize   An annual prize of $120 for a memorable work by a citizen of the Commonwealth under 30. (In memory of an RAF pilot killed in 1940 and awarded a HAWTHORNDEN PRIZE posthumously.)

Rialto   (1591) A famous bridge over the Grand Canal at Venice; the neighboring district, which has many markets.

Ribbentrop-Molotov Pact   (1939) See HITLER-STALIN PACT.

Ribston Pippin   One of the best dessert apples, with yellow and red fruit ripening in November. (Ribston, Yorkshire, where first introduced from Normandy in the 18th century.)

RIC   (1867-1922) Initials used for the Royal Irish Constabulary, an elite force which policed Ireland until PARTITION; their successors are the Royal Ulster Constabulary.

Ricardo's theory of rent   Population increases with the increase of capital; demand for land from which to feed the increased population becomes more insistent, forcing up rents to the benefit of landowners, who become the blameless and passive recipients of ever-increasing wealth in accordance with an economic law over which they have no control and for which there is no remedy. (David Ricardo, British economist, 1772-1823.)

Rice, Archie   The third-rate music-hall comic of John Osborne's disenchanted play *The Entertainer* (1957).

Riceyman Steps   (1923) Arnold Bennett's drab novel of a miserly secondhand bookseller in Clerkenwell, north London, who starves himself to death.

Richard of Bordeaux See DAVIOT, GORDON.

Richardson, Henry Handel The pen name of Henrietta Richardson; see FORTUNES OF RICHARD MAHONEY.

Richmond, NYC A borough comprising Staten Island and other islands in New York Harbor, linked by bridges to the New Jersey mainland and by the VERRAZANO-NARROWS BRIDGE to BROOKLYN.

Richmond Herald An officer of the COLLEGE OF ARMS.

Richmond Palace (14th century) The royal palace by the Thames at Richmond, Surrey, of which only a gateway now remains. Originally called Sheen, it was renamed Richmond by Henry VII. Queen Elizabeth died there.

Richmond upon Thames London borough since 1965 consisting of the former boroughs of Richmond, BARNES and TWICKENHAM, with headquarters at Twickenham.

Richter scale A scale used in measuring the severity of earthquakes.

Richthofen Circus A famous German fighter squadron in World War I, which introduced new team tactics to replace the individual 'dogfights' hitherto prevailing. (Led by Baron von Richthofen, shot down in 1918; 'circus' because their planes were painted in vivid colors.)

Rickettsiae Minute organisms intermediate in size between bacteria and viruses. Injected into the blood by lice, they cause typhus.

Riddle of the Sands, The (1903) A spy story in which the future Irish rebel, Erskine Childers, did much to alert Britain to the possibilities of a German invasion.

Rideau Hall The residence of the Governor-General of Canada, in the Ottawa suburb of New Edinburgh.

Riders of the Purple Sage (1912) The most famous and successful of Zane Grey's westerns; movie versions were made in 1931 and 1941.

'Riders on the Beach' A painting by Gauguin of Tahitians on horseback riding towards the sea. (Niarchos Collection.)

Riders to the Sea (1904) J. M. Synge's grim one-act tragedy of old Maurya, who one by one loses all her menfolk.

Ridgemanites See MELUNGEONS.

Ridolfi plot (1571) A Roman Catholic plot to dethrone Elizabeth I and, with Spanish help, to replace her by Mary Queen of Scots, who was to marry the Duke of Norfolk. (Italian banker, one of the conspirators.)

Riemannian geometry A non-Euclidean elliptic geometry which, not being confined to a 3-dimensional space, was invaluable to Einstein in formulating his relativity theories. It is based on the assumption that the sum of the angles of a triangle is less then 2 right angles. (G. F. B. Riemann, German mathematician, 1826-66.)

Rienzi (1835) Lord Bulwer-Lytton's historical novel about the LAST OF THE ROMANS; SEE ROMAN REPUBLIC (2).

Riesling The best of the types of grape used in making hock and similar wines.

Rievaulx Abbey (1131) An abbey near Helmsley, Yorkshire, formerly the best example of CISTERCIAN architecture in England, now largely in ruins.

Riffs The BERBER tribe of the Rif Mountains in Morocco who in 1909 first rebelled against the Spanish, whom they defeated at ANUAL, and later against the French, who under Pétain ended the rebellion in 1926, capturing its leader Abd-el-Krim.

RI Galleries (1881) Art gallery in Piccadilly, London, built for the Royal Institute of Painters in Water Colour; now also the home of the Pastel Society, the National Society of Painters, Sculptors and Engravers, and similar societies, which all exhibit there.

Rigel Beta-Orionis, 7th brightest star, in the foot of ORION; an 'energetic' star for which a relatively short life is predicted.

Rights of Man, The (1) Thomas Paine's defense (1791-92) of the French and American revolutions and his suggestions for social reform, which included many of the features now found in a welfare state; he also suggested the limitation of armaments, and graduated income tax. (2) See DECLARATION OF THE RIGHTS OF MAN.

Rigoletto The Duke of Mantua's hunchbacked jester whose daughter Gilda the Duke seduces, in Verdi's opera of that name (1851). Rigoletto plots to murder him, but Gilda sacrifices her own life to spare his; it is not until Rigoletto hears the Duke he thought dead singing the famous aria 'La donna è mobile' that he begins to realize that he has brought about his own daughter's death. The plot is derived from Victor Hugo's Le Roi s'amuse.

Rig-Veda Chief of the VEDAS, containing 1000 hymns of varying antiquity. (SANSKRIT rik, 'praise'.)

Rijeka A Yugoslav city and port, formerly known by its Italian name of Fiume.

Rikki-Tikki-Tavi A mongoose adopted as a pet, in one of the stories of Kipling's JUNGLE BOOKS.

Riksdag The Swedish Diet, or Parliament.

Rillington Place murders (1953) The murder in Notting Hill, London, of at least 6 women by J. R. H. Christie, who was hanged. In 1966 a judicial inquiry found that he had probably murdered the baby daughter of Timothy Evans, living at the same address. Evans, who had been hanged for this, was given a posthumous free pardon, but the same inquiry found that he probably strangled his wife, a crime of which he had not been convicted.

Rima (1) An Indian 'bird-girl' in W. H. Hudson's Green Mansions, a romantic tale of the South American jungle. (2) The W. H. Hudson Memorial by Epstein (1925) in the bird sanctuary of Kensington Gardens, London.

Rimmon A Babylonian god of storms; in II Kings v, 18, the Syrian general Naaman, who had been cured of leprosy through the agency of Elisha and thus converted to the religion of Israel, asks Elisha's permission to 'bow down in the house of Rimmon' when he goes there with

his king. Hence this phrase is used of doing what is wrong but expedient.

Rinaldo A hero of medieval romance, paladin of Charlemagne, cousin of ROLAND, owner of the horse BAYARD (Baiardo), bold, unscrupulous, rapacious. (Also spelled Renault, Reynold.)

Ring and the Book, The (1869) Robert Browning's poem giving differing versions of a famous 17th-century crime, as told by 12 people involved (the criminal, the victims, the Pope etc.). A bankrupt Florentine count, Guido, marries for money and then murders his wife and her putative parents.

Ring of the Löwenskölds, The (1925) The first volume of a trilogy by the Swedish novelist Selma Lagerlöf, a family chronicle.

Ring of the Nibelungs (1869-76) Wagner's Ring Cycle of 4 operas — Das RHEINGOLD, Die Walküre, Siegfried and GÖTTERDÄMMERUNG, first performed at Bayreuth in 1876. The story is based on the NIBELUNGENLIED and earlier Scandinavian sagas.

Ring Round the Moon (1947) Christopher Fry's translation of Anouilh's frivolity about twin brothers, one good, one wicked. (French title, L'Invitation au château.)

Ringstrasse (1860) The 2-mile tree-lined boulevard which encircles inner Vienna.

Rintelen spy ring An organization for espionage and sabotage formed (1915) in USA by the German naval captain, Franz von Rintelen, during World War I; he was arrested in 1917.

Rin-Tin-Tin The first animal to become a film star, making a fortune for Warner Brothers just after World War I. The dog was found in a German dugout near Metz, France, by Capt. Duncan who brought him home to Los Angeles. Rin-Tin-Tin died in 1932. A later dog of the same name was the heroic canine of "The Adventures of Rin-Tin-Tin" TV series.

Rio Grande The river which forms the Texas-Mexican boundary, properly the Rio Grande del Norte, to distinguish it from other rivers of the name.

Riom trials (1942) The VICHY GOVERNMENT's attempt to pin the blame for the fall of France on to their leading opponents, e.g. Blum, Paul Reynaud and Daladier. The trial was suspended by Laval, but the defendants remained in prison. (Town of central France; also spelled Riyom.)

Rio Tinto-Zinc Corporation (1962) A London-based mining, chemical, steel, aluminum and industrial group, whose main interests are in North America, Australia, Spain and Africa (especially the COPPERBELT).

Rio Treaty (1947) A reaffirmation of the LIMA DECLARATION, whereby the American republics (except Ecuador and Nicaragua) agreed that an attack on one of them was to be considered as an attack on all.

Ripley Name associated with the US 'Believe it or Not' syndicated newspaper column, consisting of improbable but true facts of all kinds; the work of R. L. Ripley (1893-1949).

Rip Van Winkle A character in a story in Washington Irving's SKETCH BOOK who sleeps for 20 years and wakes as an old man to find that America has become independent and his nagging wife is dead; applied to a person who is impossibly old-fashioned.

Rip Van Winkle gas A gas, for use in warfare, that deprives the enemy of aggressive instincts but inflicts no permanent injury. See last entry.

RIR Abbreviation for Rhode Island Red, a popular breed of reddish-brown dual-purpose poultry.

Rising Tide of Color (*against White World-Supremacy*) (1920) A once widely read book by an American, Lothrop Stoddard. It gave added encouragement to NORDIC racial theories.

Risley Headquarters of the UK ATOMIC ENERGY AUTHORITY's Reactor Group, responsible for the design and construction of nuclear power station reactors; also headquarters of the Authority's Engineering Group,

responsible for the erection of buildings for them. (Town near Warrington, Lancashire.)

Risorgimento The 19th-century Italian nationalist movement which, under Mazzini, Cavour and Garibaldi, drove the Austrians from the north and the Bourbon BOMBA from the south (the Kingdom of the TWO SICILIES), created the Kingdom of Italy (1861) under Victor Emmanuel II of Sardinia, and completed the unification of Italy by occupying Rome (1870) and ending the temporal power of the Pope, who was confined to the VATICAN. (Italian, 'resurgence'.)

Rite of Spring, The (1913) Stravinsky's ballet, considered revolutionary and discordant when first produced in Paris, with Nijinsky. It depicts a solemn pagan rite, a circle of seated elders watching a girl dance herself to death in propitiation of the god of spring. (French title, *Le Sacre du printemps*.)

'Ritual Fire Dance' A gypsy dance in Falla's LOVE THE MAGICIAN and included in the orchestral suite made from it.

Rivals, The (1775) Sheridan's comedy; see Lydia LANGUISH; Sir Anthony ABSOLUTE; Mrs MALAPROP.

River Plate, Battle of the (Dec. 1939) The naval engagement in which British cruisers attacked the German battleship GRAF SPEE, and forced her to take refuge in Montevideo harbor.

Riverside Drive A New York street with fine views over Riverside Park and the Hudson River, once an expensive and exclusive residential area.

RLS Initials standing for Robert Louis Stevenson.

RMA Initials used for the ROYAL MILITARY ACADEMY.

R month The months September-April when oysters are traditionally in season in the northern hemisphere, i.e. are safe to eat. (All these months, and none of the others, are spelled with an r.)

RN (1) Royal Navy. (2) Registered Nurse, a graduate nurse who has passed a state board examination and is licensed to practice as a nurse; compare LPN.

RNA Initials standing for ribonucleic acid, a complex molecule which, with DNA, passes on hereditary factors from one generation to another.

Road to Wigan Pier, The (1937) George Orwell's documentary novel about working-class conditions in the Great DEPRESSION.

Roanoke adventure (1585-87) The first and unsuccessful American colony, of mostly unsuitable men, sent out by Sir Walter Raleigh; they settled on Roanoke Island off the northeast coast of North Carolina, but soon disappeared without trace, leaving a vague Indian tradition of dispersal among them. See MELUNGEONS.

Roaring Forties, The The belt of southern ocean around and south of the 40th parallel where, unobstructed by landmasses, west winds blow strongly all the year round, making eastward circumnavigation preferable for sailing ships, although the early explorers, e.g. Magellan and Drake, went the hard way — westward round Cape Horn.

Roaring Twenties, The The 1920s, referring to the JAZZ AGE and the boom years on the stock market before the WALL STREET CRASH.

Robbins report (1963) (UK) A report on higher education which recommended that CATS should be given university status and enlarged to take 3-4000 students each; and that teacher training colleges should also be enlarged and renamed Colleges of Education.

Robert the Devil (1831) Meyerbeer's opera on Robert le Diable, father of William the Conqueror, a bold and cruel Duke of Normandy. (Italian title, *Roberto il diavolo*.)

Robin Goodfellow A mischievous spirit who can also be friendly and do odd chores about the house during the night; the equivalent of the German Knecht Ruprecht ('Servant Robin'); also called Hobgoblin, and by Shakespeare PUCK.

Robin Hood A legendary outlaw and crack shot with the bow and arrow, who lived in SHERWOOD FOREST, Nottinghamshire, where he robbed the rich to help the poor; he was supposed to have lived in the 12th-13th centuries, and many attempts were made to identify him with historical characters, e.g. an Earl of Huntingdon.

Robinson Crusoe (1719) Daniel Defoe's classic desert island story, based on Alexander Selkirk's experiences when Dampier landed him on the island group of Juan Fernández, off Chile, from which he was rescued by Woodes Rogers $4\frac{1}{2}$ years later in 1709. Defoe later claimed that the novel was an allegory of his own struggles with his conscience and with the external world.

Robophone A device which records telephone messages in the absence of the subscriber.

Rob Roy A cocktail of Scotch, sweet vermouth and bitters, served with a cherry. (Presumably so named because it would take a hero such as Rob Roy to swallow such an extraordinary mixture.) See next entry.

Rob Roy (1817) Walter Scott's novel based on the history of Rob Roy Macgregor, the Scottish Robin Hood who died in 1734. He is responsible for the final triumph of Frank OSBALDISTONE, whose cousin Rashleigh he kills. ('Robert the Red'.)

Robsart, Amy See KENILWORTH.

Roch Cup A skiing championship at Aspen, Col., for men and women, downhill and slalom.

Rochdale Pioneers (1844) The first cooperative society, founded by weavers at Rochdale, near Manchester, Lancashire.

Rochester, Mr (Edward) The moody hero of JANE EYRE, with a wife in the attic of whom Jane learns only on the day they are to marry.

Rockefeller Center (1947) New York City's 13-acre privately owned business and amusement center (including RADIO CITY), housed in 15 buildings between FIFTH AVENUE and Sixth Avenue.

Rockefeller Foundation (1913) Established by John D. Rockefeller Sr 'to promote the welfare of mankind throughout the world'.

Rockets (1) The San Diego Rockets, NATIONAL BASKETBALL ASSOCIATION. (2) The Denver Rockets, AMERICAN BASKETBALL ASSOCIATION.

Rockettes, The A famous precision dance group at RADIO CITY Music Hall.

Rockingham A term more indiscriminately used than most in the antique trade. True Rockingham consists of (1) earthenware (1778-1820), a typical product being brown-glazed CADOGAN TEAPOTS; and (2) bone china (1820-43) tea services etc. with buff, grey or pale-blue grounds and gilding. Contrary to popular beliefs, decoration was not usually over-elaborate, there is probably no such thing as a Rockingham cottage, and genuine Rockingham is usually marked. (Made on the estate of the Marquis of Rockingham at Swinton, near Rotherham.)

Rocky Mountain Arsenal Site near Denver, Col., of a factory which makes nerve, mustard and incapacitating gases, together with defoliants and herbicides for use in warfare, and the weapons to disseminate them. They include BZ, DM (which causes vomiting and sneezing), and the less potent CS and CN gases. See also SARIN.

Rocky Mountain Fur Company (1822-34) The fur-trading company that originated the rendezvous system (in contrast to trading posts); the MOUNTAIN MEN assembled each spring at a prearranged place in Wyoming, Utah or Idaho to meet the firm's caravans which brought supplies and trade goods and collected the skins. It dominated the trade in the central Rockies until the AMERICAN FUR COMPANY took the lead.

Rocky Mountains The Rockies extend 3200 miles from Alaska to New Mexico, with the highest peaks in Canada (Mt Logan) and Alaska (Mt McKinley). They form North America's main watershed, the GREAT DIVIDE. At the heart of the range is the Rocky Mountain National Park (1915) in north-central Colorado, containing 65 peaks over 10,000 ft. See also GRAND TETONS.

Rococo (1700-60) The frivolous final stage of BAROQUE, which flourished particularly in Vienna, Prague, Munich, Dresden and Paris; the characteristics were shell motifs, scrolls, arabesques and curves in general, used in architecture (notably in Bavarian churches), art (Watteau, Boucher, Fragonard), silver, porcelain, furniture etc. It was succeeded by a NEOCLASSICAL reaction. (French *rocaille*, 'shell-work'.)

Rodeo (1942) One of the most successful American (one-act) ballets, with music by Aaron Copland, choreography and book by Agnes de Mille. A young cowgirl, suddenly aware of men, tries to win their attention by competing with the cowboys on their own ground; unfortunately, she outshines them at bronco busting and is consequently most unpopular—until she meets her match.

Roderick Hudson (1876) Henry James's first novel, on what was to become his favorite theme, the impact of Europe on the sensitive American. Roderick is a sculptor who comes from NEW ENGLAND to Rome and fails to adapt himself to his new life.

Roderick Random (1748) Tobias Smollett's picaresque novel in which the hero seeks adventure at sea, in France and finally in South America, where he finds his long-lost father and returns enriched to marry the girl of his choice. See BOWLING, TOM.

Rodrigo See El CID.

Roentgen rays Another name for what Professor Roentgen himself, who discovered them, called X rays.

Rogation Days The 3 days before ASCENSION DAY when, in the Roman Catholic Church, the litany is chanted in public procession. (From Latin for 'supplication', 'litany'.)

Roger Code word used in radiotelephony for 'understood', from the morse letter 'R' used similarly in telegraphy, called Roger in a now obsolete phonetic alphabet.

Roget's Thesaurus (1852) Short title of a *Thesaurus of English Words and Phrases*, a dictionary of synonyms and antonyms, often revised and published in various modern forms. (British physician and a founder of LONDON UNIVERSITY.)

Rois faineants The later MEROVINGIAN Kings of the Franks, who allowed their powers to be usurped by the Mayors of the Palace, the greatest of whom was Pepin, father of Charlemagne and founder of the CAROLINGIAN dynasty which ousted them. (French, 'do-nothing kings'.)

Roi Soleil A name given to Louis XIV, during whose reign (1643-1715) the arts and literature flourished but France was bankrupted by extravagance and wars. (French, 'the Sun King'.)

Rokeby Venus Common name of Velázquez' only painting of a female nude, properly called 'The Toilet of Venus'. It is in the National Gallery, London, where, in 1914, it was slashed by a suffragette. (Named after Rokeby, Yorkshire, where its former owners, the Morritt family, lived.)

Roland (Italian, Orlando) In troubadour songs, the nephew and chief paladin of Charlemagne who through treachery is ambushed and slain with his friend Oliver at RONCESVALLES. See next entry.

Roland for an Oliver Tit for tat; an effective retort. ROLAND and Oliver were close friends, who emulated each other's exploits; once they fought each other for 5 days.

ROLF Stands for Remotely Operated Longwall Face machine, a British electronically and remote-controlled 'miner' which seeks out coal by gamma rays, plows along the seam, throws the coal on to a conveyor belt, and inserts pit props as it moves forward. In use at BEVERCOTES.

Rollright Stones A stone circle, perhaps Druidic, between Great and Little Rollright, Oxfordshire.

Romance languages Modern languages derived from Latin, e.g. French, Spanish, Italian and Rumanian, together with older languages such as Provençal. They stem from the 'vulgar Latin' used by the Roman legionaries and the common folk under Roman rule.

Roman Club A complicated Italian calling system at bridge, with numerous artificial bids. The opening bid indicates distribution rather than strength, in contrast to the NEAPOLITAN CLUB system.

Roman de la Rose A 13th-century romantic poem by 2 authors; part 1 is an allegory distantly based on Ovid's *Ars Amatoria*, part 2 consists of vigorous satire and, for its time, daring philosophical speculation. It was imitated by Chaucer (*Romaunt of the Rose*) and others, and greatly influenced European literature.

Romanée-Conti See CÔTE DE NUITS.

Roman Empire (31 BC-AD 395) The empire ruled from Rome from the time of Augustus until it was divided in two (see BYZANTINE EMPIRE); at its height it extended from Britain to the Persian Gulf and the Caspian, bounded on the north by the Rhine and Danube, and on the south by the North African littoral. The Western Empire (AD 395-476) continued in nominal existence until the deposition of its last Emperor, Romulus Augustulus, and then came under Byzantine rule.

Romanesque architecture (10th-13th centuries) The West European style which preceded GOTHIC ARCHITECTURE and is characterized by the round arch and massive construction. In England it is called NORMAN ARCHITECTURE.

Roman holiday The phrase 'Butchered to make a Roman holiday' comes from Byron's CHILDE HAROLD, and refers to gladiators made to fight to the death in Roman arenas to entertain the mob.

Romanovs (1613-1917) Name given to the dynasty that ruled Russia until the Revolution, though from the 18th century the Tsars were mainly of German blood, connected with the Romanovs only in the female line. See EKATERINBURG.

Roman Question, The The problems raised by the opposition of the Italian people to the pope's position as temporal ruler of the city of Rome. It came to a head in 1848 when Pope Pius IX was temporarily ejected, and Mazzini and Garibaldi proclaimed a

ROMAN REPUBLIC; it was not finally settled until 1929, by the LATERAN TREATY.

Roman Republic (1) The period in ancient Roman history (509-31 BC) from the final ejection of the TARQUINS to the beginning of the ROMAN EMPIRE. (2) The republic of the city of Rome proclaimed by RIENZI (1347) during the AVIGNONESE CAPTIVITY; it lasted only a few months. (3) The republic declared by Mazzini in 1849 (see ROMAN QUESTION) which also lasted only a few months.

Romantic composers Weber, Schumann, Chopin, Wagner, Berlioz, among many others. See ROMANTICISM.

Romanticism The reaction from Classicism, emphasizing individualism and revolt, emotion, imagination; humor and pathos rather than wit; creativeness rather than criticism; content rather than form. The 2 attitudes to art existed side by side, and sometimes in the same person at different periods. In Europe Romanticism was inspired by Rousseau and the FRENCH REVOLUTION, and its founders are generally regarded as Weber in music, Delacroix in art and Goethe in literature. See next and last entries.

Romantic poets Leading figures include (1) *English*: Wordsworth, Coleridge, Scott, Byron, Shelley, Keats; (2) *French*: Lamartine, Hugo, Musset, Vigny; (3) *German*: Goethe, Schiller, Heine. See ROMANTICISM.

Romantic Revival The name sometimes given to the period of the full flowering of ROMANTICISM in literature. Apart from the work of the ROMANTIC POETS, typical examples include the novels of Goethe, Scott and Hugo, as well as the GOTHIC NOVELS.

Romany The Gypsies' own name for Gypsy and for their language. (Gypsy *rom*, 'a Gypsy', *romany* being the adjective.)

Romany rye (1) One who identifies himself with the Gypsies. (2) Title of George Borrow's sequel (1857) to LAVENGRO. (*Rye*, 'gentleman'.)

Rome, Sack of (1527) An episode in the conflict between the HOLY RO-MAN EMPIRE and France, when Charles V's troops took Rome and imprisoned the Pope, who had allied himself with Francis I of France.

Rome, Treaty of (1957) The agreement to set up the COMMON MARKET.

Rome Beauty A medium-red cooking apple, forming one of the main US crops.

Rome-Berlin Axis (1936) The name coined by Mussolini for the alliance formed by Italy and Germany when the LEAGUE OF NATIONS imposed sanctions on Italy, which had invaded ABYSSINIA; extended to Japan in 1940 (the Rome-Berlin-Tokyo Axis) by the TRIPARTITE PACT. See also PACT OF STEEL.

Romeo and Juliet (1595) (1) Shakespeare's play of the feud between Montagues and CAPULETS at Verona. The Montague Romeo is secretly married to the Capulet Juliet by Friar Laurence, kills her cousin to avenge his friend MERCUTIO's death, and is banished. Their joint suicide leads to a reconciliation between the families. Gounod wrote an opera (1867) based on this play. (2) Tchaikovsky's overture fantasy for a projected opera, and his finest symphonic poem, portraying the characters and emotions of Shakespeare's play. Ten years separated the original and final versions of Tchaikovsky's work. The final version was first performed in 1880.

Rome Protocols (1934) Agreements that embodied plans for a Danubian bloc of Italy, Austria and Hungary, directed against France and the LITTLE ENTENTE, and also against Hitler's ambition to unite Austria with Germany.

Romer report (1961) (UK) A report on the breaches of security disclosed by the PORTLAND SECRETS CASE, which severely criticized the Admiralty.

Romford ((UK) A former municipal borough of Essex, since 1965 part of the borough of HAVERING.

Romford, Facey The hero of Surtees' *Mr Facey Romford's Hounds* (1865).

Romney Marsh (sheep) See KENT (sheep).

Romola (1863) GEORGE ELIOT's novel
set in medieval Florence in the time
of the reformer Savonarola, under
whose influence Romola comes after
the failure of her marriage to the de-
ceitful and selfish Tito Melema.

Romulus and Remus The legendary
founders of Rome, who were exposed in accordance with custom
because they were borne by a VESTAL
VIRGIN, but were rescued and suckled by a wolf. They lived to restore
their grandfather, Numitor, as ruler
of Alba. Romulus killed Remus, and
was responsible for the RAPE OF THE
SABINES.

Roncesvalles (778) The scene of the
defeat by BASQUES of the rearguard of
Charlemagne's army returning from
Spain. The troubadours turned this
into a story of treachery and ambush
by a huge SARACEN army; see ROLAND.
(A pass in the Pyrenees.)

Ronchamp chapel (1955) Notre-
Dame du Haut on a hill in the Haute-
Sâone, a remarkable building designed by LE CORBUSIER; the hill is
an ancient place of pilgrimage.

Ronde, La (1950) Max Ophüls's film
version of a play (1902) by the
Austrian Arthur Schnitzler, in
which in successive scenes 10 couples make love, one of each pair
appearing in the next scene; the last
scene is linked to the first by the
prostitute who appears in both. A
cynical observer with a merry-go-
round comments on the proceedings. Other stage and film versions
have been produced.

R-101 A British airship which
crashed in flames at Beauvais on a
flight to India (1930); the disaster
ended the development of airships
in Britain.

Roof of the World Translation of the
local name of the Pamirs, a mountainous region, in Tadzhikistan SSR,
Afghanistan and China.

Rooinek (Roinek) AFRIKAANS name
for the British in the BOER WAR; now
extended generally to include new
immigrants from Europe. (Afrikaans, 'red-neck'.)

Room, The The underwriting room
at LLOYD's, where the LUTINE BELL

hangs.

Room at the Top (1957) John
Braine's success story of a ruthless
young man with business and social
ambitions, set in a Yorkshire town.

Room of One's Own, A (1929) Virginia Woolf's plea for women's economic independence.

Room with a View, A (1908) E. M.
Forster's novel of central Italy, on
the themes of the clash of Latin passion and Anglo-Saxon puritanism,
and of upper-class prejudice with
less shallow emotions.

Roosevelt elk A rare species of elk,
surviving in parts of the Rockies and
Cascades; see OLYMPIC NATIONAL
PARK. (Named for Theodore Roosevelt, a great naturalist and hunter.)

Root and Branch Bill (1641) A bill
for the abolition of bishops, which
led to sharp and continuing dissen-
sion in the LONG PARLIAMENT.

Roquefort A semihard blue cheese
made of ewe's milk and ripened in
limestone caves at Roquefort; the
name is officially restricted to
cheeses so made, but there are imitations. Genuine Roquefort at the
right stage of maturity has a pungent
flavor much admired by the con-
noisseur. (Roquefort-sur-Soulzon, a
village in the Aveyron *département*
of south-central France; there is
another village of Roquefort in
southwest France.)

Roquefort dressing A dressing made
of Roquefort cheese mixed with
mayonnaise and a dash of WORCES-
TERSHIRE SAUCE.

RORC (1925) Initials used for the
Royal Ocean Racing Club, founded
after the success of the first FASTNET
race had indicated public interest in
offshore racing. See RORC RATING.

RORC rating A yacht handicapping
formula which superseded the TM; it
is based on waterline length and sail
area (which increase speed) as well
as beam and draft (which de-
crease it). The Cruising Club of
America has a different formula. (Introduced by the RORC.)

Rorke's Drift (1879) A battle in the
Zulu War in which a horde of ZULUS
under Cetewayo fanatically charged

a handful of British troops and were mowed down by machine guns. This avenged an earlier disaster, and a record number of VCs were awarded. (Site in Natal, South Africa.)

Rorschach inkblot test A psychoanalytical test in which patients are asked to describe what a series of complex inkblots suggest to them; their answers are said to reveal character, intelligence and emotional state. (H. Rorschach, Swiss psychoanalyst, 1884-1922.)

Rosaceae The rose family, which includes the genus *Prunus*, various berry-bearing plants (strawberry, raspberry, blackberry), fruit trees such as the apple and pear, as well as hawthorn, rowan, spirea, japonica etc.

Rosalind The daughter of the Duke in Shakespeare's AS YOU LIKE IT who falls in love with Orlando.

Rosamunde overture A well-known overture composed by Schubert, originally for a play called *The Magic Harp*, but then substituted for one he had written, together with a ballet and incidental music, for an otherwise unimportant play about a Princess Rosamunde.

Roscius A name applied to various great actors, including Garrick. (Quintus Roscius, a Roman actor of the 1st century BC.)

Rose Bowl Sports stadium at Pasadena, Calif., where the first BOWL GAME was played. See BIG TEN. (Named after the Tournament of Roses celebrated there annually on New Year's Day from 1890, inspired by the BATTLE OF FLOWERS at Nice.)

Roseires dam (1967) A dam in the Sudan on the Blue Nile, 130 miles south of the GEZIRA SCHEME, to which it adds a further million acres of irrigated land.

Rose Medallion A chiefly 19th-century enamel-decorated Chinese porcelain with medallions of oriental figures surrounded and separated by panels of flowers and butterflies.

Rosenberg spy case (1950) The FBI's arrest, arising from the FUCHS CASE, of Julius and Ethel Rosenberg, executed (1953) for passing atomic

secrets to Russia. The KROGERS were involved but escaped.

Rosencrantz and Guildenstern Two obsequious, hypocritical courtiers in Shakespeare's HAMLET.

Rosencrantz and Guildenstern Are Dead (1967) A play by a young Englishman, Tom Stoppard, in which these 2 characters from HAMLET (see last entry) meditate on their role in the ELSINORE dynastic struggle and on human affairs in general.

Rosenkavalier, Der (1911) Richard Strauss's half sentimental, half ironic opera of the bluff and hearty Baron Ochs who loses his girl to a younger rival, in an 18th-century Vienna setting.

Rosetta Stone (2nd century BC) A slab of black basalt, now in the British Museum, discovered by a Frenchman in 1799, which first supplied the key to the deciphering of Egyptian hieroglyphics, being inscribed in 3 languages including Greek. (Found near Alexandria at the Rosetta mouth of the Nile.)

Rosh Hashanah The Jewish New Year, falling in September or October in the Gregorian calendar.

Rosicrucians Originally a medieval society of alchemists and magicians, about which almost nothing is known. The name was subsequently borrowed by FREEMASONS and others, including a correspondence course in mysticism which confers supernatural powers (and riches) for a few dollars. (Variously derived from Latin *rosa crucis*, 'rose of the Cross', the old society's emblem, or the Latinized name of the alleged German founder, Christian Rosencreuz.)

Rosinante DON QUIXOTE's scraggy old horse.

Ross, Barnaby The pen name used by the 2 writers better known as Ellery QUEEN, in stories about the detective Drury Lane, e.g. *Drury Lane's Last Case* (1933).

Ross, J. H. The name T. E. Lawrence assumed when he first joined the RAF as an aircraftsman (1922) to escape publicity; later he changed his name to T. E. SHAW.

Ross, Martin Pen name of Violet

Florence Martin (1862-1915), one of the coauthors of EXPERIENCES OF AN IRISH RM.

Rossini (Cooking) With foie gras and truffles. (Named after the composer.)

Rotary Anns Unofficial name for wives of ROTARY CLUB members. See also INNER WHEEL CLUBS. (A pun on 'Rotarians'.)

Rotary Club (1905) A club started in Chicago, consisting of one representative of each profession and trade of the city, to encourage a spirit of service to others and promote the city's trade and other interests. The movement spread all over the world. Members are called Rotarians. (So named because the original club met at each member's place of business in rotation.)

ROTC The Reserve Officers' Training Corps (1917), a government-subsidized corps in colleges (senior division) and high schools (junior) for military training. The Air Force and the Navy also have ROTC units.

Rothermere Press See ASSOCIATED NEWSPAPERS. (Founded by Lord Rothermere, brother of Lord Northcliffe.)

Rothschild, N. M. (1804) A London merchant bank and acceptance house, founded by Nathan Rothschild, a Manchester cotton merchant; it once financed Wellington's army in Spain, and is now interested in hire purchase, unit trusts (i.e. MUTUAL FUNDS), and the Sun Alliance group of insurance firms. See next entry.

Rothschild dynasty A financial family dynasty founded by M. A. Rothschild of Frankfort on Main (died 1812). Of his 10 sons, 4 scattered in Napoleonic times to Paris, Vienna, Naples and London (see last entry), and a fifth remained in Frankfort. These subdynasties are symbolized in the family sign of 5 arrows.

Rôtisserie de la Reine Pédauque (1893) Anatole France's novel which introduces his mouthpiece, the Abbé Coignard, a modern Rabelais. (The title is the name of a restaurant.)

Rotten Row (London) A riding track running along the south side of HYDE PARK from Hyde Park Corner to Kensington Gardens; also called The Row. (Traditionally a corruption of *route de roi*, 'king's way'.)

Rotterdam blitz (May 1940) The purposeless German destruction of the center of Rotterdam by systematic air attack.

Rouge et le noir, Le (1830) Stendhal's novel of a repellent young man, Julien Sorel, who uses women to win advancement in the Church, the only career which he thinks likely to provide him with the power he seeks. (*Rouge* represents the military career, *noir* the clerical.)

Rougemont, Louis de Assumed name of a Swiss-born rogue who achieved fame by addressing the British Association in 1898 on his experiences among the Australian aborigines, later shown to be entirely imaginary. He also wrote an equally bogus account of Eskimo life.

Rouges (1848) Nickname of the French-Canadian Parti Démocratique which was formed under the influence of Papineau and included universal suffrage in its platform. It was absorbed into the Liberal Party. Compare BLEUS.

Rough Riders The 1st US Volunteer Cavalry Regiment. Theodore Roosevelt helped to raise it and as its Lt. Col. led the charge it made in a decisive battle in Cuba during the SPANISH-AMERICAN WAR (1898).

Roundheads In the ENGLISH CIVIL WAR the name given to the Parliamentary Party, mostly PURITANS, who fought against Charles I, or for Parliamentary rights, for the abolition of bishops or against Charles's Catholic supporters; strong in the south and east, controlling London and the ports. (From their close-cropped hair, a reaction against Royalist curls.)

Round Table (1) In 12th-century additions to ARTHURIAN LEGEND, the table made for UTHER PENDRAGON by MERLIN; also a feature of other medieval romances. (2) An informal literary and artistic club formed by habitués of the Algonquin Hotel, N.Y.C. Leading members included Alexander Woollcott, Robert Benchley, Franklin P. Adams and prominent artists and musicians.

Round-table Conference A conference seated at a round table, so that no problems of precedence arise (an idea borrowed from King ARTHUR'S ROUND TABLE); specifically applied to a series of conferences (1930-32) on constitutional reform for India.

Round the World in Eighty Days (1873) Jules Verne's novel about the feat of Phileas FOGG and his valet, Passepartout.

Round-up Code name for a proposed Allied landing in France in 1943 (subsequently converted to OVERLORD.)

Route 66 Highway running 2200 miles from Chicago to Los Angeles, through 6 states.

Rover Boys, The The heroes of a series of over 30 boys' books begun in 1899 by Arthur M. Winfield (pen name of Edward Stratemeyer) about preparatory school and college life. See TOM SWIFT.

Rowell-Sirois Report (1940) The report of a Royal Commission which analyzed inequalities in development between the various regions of Canada and made sweeping proposals for reform, partly frustrated by political disputes and then by World War II, but productive of many postwar improvements. (Names of successive chairmen.)

Rowlandson cartoons Ferocious political caricatures (many aimed at Napoleonic France) and scenes of low life by Thomas Rowlandson (1756-1827), who also illustrated the books of various novelists and produced a celebrated series on DR SYNTAX.

Rowland Ward (1892) Abbreviated title used for *Records of Big Game* published by Rowland Wards, the London taxidermists; it gives detailed measurements of outstanding specimens of big game shot by sportsmen.

Rowley Mile The mile course at Newmarket, named after OLD ROWLEY. The ONE THOUSAND GUINEAS and TWO THOUSAND GUINEAS are run over this.

Rowley poems, The See BRISTOL BOY.

Rowton Houses 'Poor man's hotels', the first of which was opened in London (1892) and was so successful that a company was formed to build others, to provide decent accommodation for the poor at no higher price than was charged for the dormitory accommodation then available in the common lodging house. (Lord Rowton, 1838-1903, who financed the scheme.)

Roxana, Roxane (1) The Bactrian wife of Alexander the Great. (2) Sultana of Turkey. See BAJAZET. (3) The heroine of Rostand's CYRANO DE BERGERAC. (4) The 'heroine' of Defoe's *Roxana* (1724).

Royal, The (1839) Common abbreviation for the Royal Agricultural Society's show, until 1967 held in a different part of the country each year, and now having a permanent home at the National Agricultural Centre, Kenilworth, Warwickshire. It provides a shopwindow for British agriculture and agricultural machinery.

Royal Academy (1768) Shortened title of the Royal Academy of Arts, London, which holds an annual summer exhibition of contemporary painting and scultpure, and occasional exhibitions of the art of a particular country or period. There are 40 Royal Academicians (RAs), who become Senior Academicians at 75 to create vacancies for younger men. See BURLINGTON HOUSE.

Royal Academy of Music (1822) The senior college of music, in MARYLEBONE, London; admission is by examination. See ROYAL COLLEGE OF MUSIC.

Royal and Ancient, The (1754) The ST ANDREWS Golf Club, recognized outside the USA as the world headquarters of golf.

Royal Armoured Corps (1939) Now comprises all the former cavalry regiments (except the HOUSEHOLD CAVALRY), and the Royal Tank Regiment. See DRAGOONS; DRAGOON GUARDS; HUSSARS, LANCERS.

Royal Ascot The 4-day race meeting at Ascot in June, a fortnight after the DERBY, a social event marked by considerable ceremonial, e.g. the Royal party's ride in state from nearby Windsor and down the course.

Royal Ascot Enclosure Formerly the Royal Enclosure, a part of the stands at ROYAL ASCOT closed to all who have not obtained entry badges through the EARL MARSHAL's office.

Royal Assent After a bill has passed all stages in both Houses of Parliament it is remitted to the Queen for the Royal Assent, which has not been withheld since the reign of Queen Anne. The bill then becomes an Act of Parliament.

Royal Automobile Club (1897) A very large London Club in PALL MALL, founded in the early days of motoring; it has a swimming pool and squash courts, and a country club outside London. It also acts as the national motoring authority which controls motor racing. Irreverently known as 'The Chauffeurs' Arms'.

Royal Ballet, The (1957) The title under which the SADLER'S WELLS Ballet (COVENT GARDEN), the Sadler's Wells Theatre Ballet (the junior company at Sadler's Wells Theatre), and the Sadler's Wells ballet school (see next entry) were merged.

Royal Ballet School (1957) Originally the SADLER'S WELLS ballet training school (1931) which teaches ballet to children from the age of 9 at the WHITE LODGE and elsewhere.

Royal Botanic Gardens Official name of Kew Gardens (London) and another garden at Edinburgh.

Royal College of Art A London college at Kensington Gore, given university status in 1967. It has a faculty of fashion designing.

Royal College of Music (1883) A college in Kensington, London, which combines with the ROYAL ACADEMY OF MUSIC and colleges in Manchester and Glasgow in holding local examinations.

Royal Commonwealth Society (1868) A London club, originally the Royal Colonial Institute, later the Royal Empire Society, with a specialist library for those interested in Commonwealth affairs.

Royal Courts of Justice See LAW COURTS.

Royal Court Theatre See ENGLISH STAGE COMPANY.

Royal Dragoon Guards, 4th / 7th (1922) A regiment of the ROYAL ARMOURED CORPS, an amalgamation of The 4th Dragoon Guards and The Princess Royal's 7th Dragoon Guards.

Royal Dragoons (1st Dragoons), The (1661) The oldest cavalry regiment in the British Army, now a regiment of the ROYAL ARMOURED CORPS; the Royals.

Royal Dutch / Shell (1906) The full title of the company generally known as Shell; a merger by Henri Deterding of Holland and Marcus Samuel, now the second largest petroleum group, with headquarters in London and the Hague. There are several hundred subsidiaries established in most countries of the world and given very considerable independence. British stockholders are in the majority, followed by American and Dutch. See SHELL TRANSPORT AND TRADING.

Royal Enclosure (Ascot) See ROYAL ASCOT ENCLOSURE.

Royal Festival Hall (1951) A London concert hall built on the South Bank of the Thames for the FESTIVAL OF BRITAIN, and later extended according to plan. Particular attention was paid to the acoustics.

Royal Fine Art Commission (1924) A government-appointed body which has powers (not apparently used to any great effect) to draw attention to any planning which appears likely to affect public amenities adversely, and to call for information regarding such planning. There is a separate commission for Scotland.

Royal George, The Admiral Kempenfelt's ship, which capsized at Spithead and sank with all hands (1782); celebrated in William Cowper's poem of that name; see SCIPIO MARCH.

Royal Greenwich Observatory (1675) An observatory founded at GREENWICH but moved to HURSTMONCEUX. The buildings at Greenwich are now occupied by the National Maritime Museum.

Royal Horse Guards Now called The BLUES AND ROYALS.

Royal Hospital, Chelsea See CHELSEA HOSPITAL.

Royal Humane Society (1774) A society which makes awards (of which the Stanhope Gold Medal is the highest) for exceptional bravery in saving people from drowning, mining disasters etc. It also promotes training in lifesaving.

Royal Hunt Cup A flat race run at Ascot in June over a distance of 7 furlongs, 155 yd.

Royal Institute of British Architects (1834) The professional body which supervises the training of architects, lays down scales of fees etc. Its headquarters building in Portland Place, London, is a surprising example of nonfunctional architecture.

Royal Institute of International Affairs, The Chatham House, a London association for the study and discussion of international affairs, with a library of books and world press cuttings on the subject. Its US counterpart is the Council of Foreign Relations.

Royal Institution (1790) A London association for the Diffusion of Science and Useful Knowledge, which has endowed 4 professorships (of natural philosophy, astronomy, chemistry and physiology) and sponsors public lectures, including Christmas lectures for schoolchildren.

Royal Mile, The A comprehensive name for the principal street in the Old Town, Edinburgh, leading from the Castle to HOLYROOD HOUSE, each section having its specific name, e.g. Canongate.

Royal Military Academy (1) Until 1946 the WOOLWICH ROYAL MILITARY ACADEMY. (2) From 1946, SANDHURST.

Royal Military College of Canada (1867) A college at Kingston, Ont., which trains officers for all 3 services and also confers graduate degrees.

Royal Oak Name of warships and inns, derived from Charles II's oak at BOSCOBEL.

Royal Opera House See COVENT GARDEN.

Royal Overseas League (1910) A club founded by Sir Evelyn Wrench, with headquarters off St James's Street, London, and branches elsewhere. It provides hospitality for overseas visitors and has a large membership, chiefly of those who have served overseas.

Royal Parks (London) This term includes HYDE, St. James's, Regent's, Greenwich, Richmond, HAMPTON COURT and Bushy parks, and Kensington Gardens.

Royal Pavilion, Brighton The PRINCE REGENT's fantasy palace in MOGUL style with Chinese decor, built by Holland and Nash. The original furniture has been put back in the State Apartments, which are open to the public.

Royal Road (500 BC) A strategic road built by Darius I to link Susa (then the Persian capital) and Sardis, capital of Lydia in western ANATOLIA and the entrepôt for trade between Persia and Europe.

Royals (1) The Kansas City (Mo.) Royals, AMERICAN (Baseball) LEAGUE, playing at the Municipal Stadium. (2) The Cincinnati Royals, NATIONAL BASKETBALL ASSOCIATION.

Royal St George's The championship golf course at Sandwich, Kent.

Royal Scot See LMS.

Royal Scots (The Royal Regiment), The (1633) The oldest regiment in the British Army, and therefore the 1st Foot. Now a regiment of the Lowland Brigade.

Royal Shakespeare Theatre Co. (1960) A company which derived from the SHAKESPEARE MEMORIAL THEATRE at Stratford and also took over the Aldwych Theatre (1961) in London pending the construction of a new theater in the Barbican. Under Peter Hall, director since 1960, all sorts of weird modern plays have been staged, and the link with Shakespeare seems tenuous.

Royal Society, The (1645) The oldest and leading scientific society in Britain; its full title is The Royal Society for Improving Natural Knowledge. The Fellowship (FRS) is a high distinction, and the COPLEY and other medals it awards also carry great prestige. The papers read at BURLINGTON HOUSE are published in the *Proceedings* or *Philosophical Transactions* of the Society.

Royal Society Medal Award instituted by George IV; 2 medals annually for the most important contributions to science published in the British Commonwealth.

Royal Society of Arts (1754) A London learned society formed to foster the application of scientific knowledge to the arts, manufacture and commerce, which now deals mainly with industrial design, exercising influence through lectures, exhibitions and awards. It is housed in an Adam building in the ADELPHI, near CHARING CROSS.

Royal Society of Literature Award See HEINEMANN (W.H.) BEQUEST.

Royal Society Research Professorships Eight professorships in the grant of the ROYAL SOCIETY for research scientists for whom no university chair is available.

Royal Sovereign The general favorite among strawberries, producing fruit of excellent flavor and flourishing everywhere except in very light soils.

Royal Variety Show (UK) An annual command performance by the pick of the music-hall artists, given in aid of the Variety Artists' Benevolent Fund and attended by Royalty.

Royal Worcester Porcelain Co. The name of the chief WORCESTER PORCELAIN factory from 1788 to 1793, and again from 1862 until today.

RPM Initials commonly used for resale price maintenance, the fixing of retail prices by manufacturers; restricted in the UK by legislation passed in 1965.

RSC Initials used for the ROYAL SHAKESPEARE THEATRE CO.

RST Initials used for Roan Selection Trust, a largely American-controlled mining group which operates the Mufulira and other mines in the Zambian COPPERBELT.

RSV See REVISED STANDARD VERSION.

Ruanda-Urundi A former Belgian Trust Territory in Central Africa, now divided between the 2 states of Burundi and Rwanda.

Rubaiyat of Omar Khayyam, The A 12th-century Persian poem on the general theme of *'carpe diem'* (make merry while you may) rendered familiar through Edward Fitzgerald's memorable translation (1859). Some stanzas have been set to music (e.g. Myself when young did eagerly frequent / Doctor and Saint and heard great argument). See JAMSHID.

Rube Goldberg A cartoonist whose name, like the English HEATH ROBINSON, is applied to the crazy contraptions such as both these cartoonists delighted to draw. Goldberg, who first attracted attention in 1906, added verbal to visual slapstick, and introduced 'baloney' to the English language. He was awarded a PULITZER PRIZE for his cartoons and was also a sculptor and writer. See REUBEN AWARD.

Rubicon, The A small river forming the boundary between Julius Caesar's province, CISALPINE GAUL, and Italy. In 49 BC Caesar crossed it, declaring 'the die is cast', and this decisive step started the civil war in which he triumphed over his rival, Pompey.

Ruddigore (1887) A GILBERT AND SULLIVAN OPERA about the Baronets Murgatroyd who under an old curse must commit a crime a day or die in agony; they find the obligation increasingly tiresome, and the latest of the line is rebuked by his ancestors, who step out of their frames in the Picture Gallery to point out that his crimes do not come up to the required standard. Thus pressed, he finds an ingenious solution to his dilemma.

Rüdesheimer A hock from Rhineland vineyards at Rüdesheim, darker and with a fruitier flavor than other hocks.

Rudi Gernreich A New York fashion

designer.

Rudolph Valentino Association A still active society dedicated to the remembrance of the handsome young film star of THE FOUR HORSE-MEN OF THE APOCALYPSE, who died in 1926.

Ruff's Guide (1842) Short title for *Ruff's Guide to the Turf*, a British race-goers' annual combined since 1959 with the *Sporting Life Annual*.

Ruhr, The The center of German heavy industry, the Dortmund-Essen-Duisburg area along the River Ruhr, a tributary of the Rhine.

Rumford Medal (1796) ROYAL SOCI-ETY biennial award for the most important discoveries in heat or light.

Rum Jungle The site south of Darwin, Northern Territory, Australia, where an important source of uranium was discovered in 1949.

Rumpelmeyers A Paris tea shop in the Rue de Rivoli long famous for its magnificent confectionery; it now carries on under a new name. There used also to be a Rumpelmeyers in London.

Rumpelstiltskin In German folklore a dwarf who taught a girl to spin gold from straw in return for her firstborn, but then promised to release her from the bargain if she could find out his name. He inadvertently gave it away himself, and killed himself in a rage.

Rump Parliament (1649-59) What was left of the LONG PARLIAMENT after PRIDE'S PURGE; it voted for a republic and abolished the House of Lords, was dissolved by Oliver Cromwell (1653) but recalled by Richard Cromwell to abolish the PROTECTORATE.

Runcible Cat, The Mentioned in Edward Lear's *The Pobble Who Has No Toes*: He has gone to fish for his Aunt Jobiska's / Runcible Cat with crimson whiskers.

Runcorn (1964) (UK) A NEW TOWN in Cheshire situated near the existing town, designed to take 70,000 new inhabitants.

Runnymede A meadow on the Surrey side of the Thames near Egham, the site (1) where King John signed Magna Carta (1215); and (2) of Sir Edward Maufe's memorial, on a hill above it, to those members of the Air Forces of the Commonwealth who have no known grave.

Rupert of Hentzau (1898) Anthony Hope's novel of RURITANIA.

RUR (1921) Karel Capek's play about Rossum's Universal Robots, half-human automatons which threaten world destruction while the Managing Director of the firm who manufactured them gloats over his profits from their sale. (*Robot*, an old Slav word for serf labor.)

Rural Rides (1830) A vigorous commentary on English rural life by William Cobbett, journalist and radical politician.

Ruritania The central European country invented by Anthony Hope as a setting for his romances of adventure and court intrigue, *The Prisoner of Zenda* and *Rupert of Hentzau*; hence any state where the intrigues of a reactionary court dominate politics, as in the old Balkan kingdoms.

Ruskin College (1899) The first residential college for working men (and later, women), founded at OX-FORD UNIVERSITY by an American and supported by trade unions etc. (Named in honor of John Ruskin, British radical writer and art critic.)

Russellites A name for JEHOVAH'S WITNESSES.

Russian dressing Mayonnaise with pungent additions, e.g. chili sauce, chopped pickles, pimientos.

Russian Hill A hill in San Francisco; see LOMBARD STREET CURLICUE.

Russian Revolutions (1) Workers' revolt in 1905 resulting from the RUSSO-JAPANESE WAR, quickly suppressed; see BLOODY SUNDAY. (2) The MENSHEVIK revolution of February 1917. (3) The BOLSHEVIK revolution of November 1917; see OCTOBER REVOLUTION.

Russian roulette A suicidal gamble in which a six-shooter is loaded with one bullet, the cylinder spun round, the revolver placed to the temple and fired, thus giving a 5-1 chance of survival.

Russo-Japanese War (1904-5) A war which arose from rival claims to

Korea and MANCHURIA, and ended in Russia's crushing defeat at TSU-SHIMA.

Rutgers (1766) University at New Brunswick, N.J.

Ruth A brief book of the Old Testament telling how Naomi lost her husband and sons in Moab, whither they had migrated from Bethlehem. One of her daughters-in-law, Ruth, a Moabitess, refused to desert her and went back with her to Bethlehem, where she became a gleaner 'amid the alien corn' (in the words of Keats) in the fields of Boaz, whom she later married. Their son was the grandfather of DAVID.

Ruth, Babe See BABE RUTH.

Ruth Draper garden One which was a mass of color last month and will be so next month, but right now appears to be a dying wilderness; the product of the fertile imagination of the American *diseuse* Ruth Draper (1884-1956) in one of her best-known sketches.

Ruth Ellis case (1955) The trial of the last woman to be hanged in Britain, found guilty of murdering her lover, David Blakely.

Ruthenia A former region of Austria-Hungary dominated by the Carpathians; it was divided in 1918 between Czechoslovakia, Poland and Rumania. After World War II Soviet Russia seized all 3 parts and incorporated them in the Ukraine.

Rutherford, Mark Pen name of William Hale White (1831-1913), a British novelist and lapsed CONGREGATIONALIST who in *The Autobiography of Mark Rutherford* (1881) and other works gives a sincere portrait of a DISSENTER in revolt against provincial narrowmindedness.

Rutherford Laboratory A British government laboratory for research in high-energy nuclear physics, with a powerful proton accelerator, Nimrod, at Chilton, a village near Didcot, Berkshire. See DARESBURY LABORATORY.

Ruthless Rhymes for Heartless Homes An illustrated book by Harry Graham (1874-1936) of light-heartedly cold-blooded little verses, typified by: Philip, foozling with his cleek, / Drove the ball through Helen's cheek; / Sad they bore her corpse away, / Seven up and six to play.

Ruy Blas (1) A poor play by Victor Hugo (1838), chiefly remembered through (2) Mendelssohn's overture (1839) written for it.

Ruy Lopez A conventional opening in chess.

Rwanda One of the 2 territories formed from the former Belgian Trust Territory of Ruanda-Urundi.

RWS (1804) Initials used for the Royal Society of Painters in Water Colour, which has galleries in Conduit Street, London, where spring and autumn exhibitions are held.

Rya A handwoven deep-pile rug of Scandinavian design, using 100% Persian lamb's wool yarns.

Ryder Cup (1927) Professional golf contest between Britain and USA, held in alternate years, with 4 foursomes and 8 singles.

Ryecroft, Henry The hero of *The Private Papers of Henry Ryecroft* (1903) by George Gissing, a semi-autobiographical account in diary form of escape from poverty and city life.

Rye House Plot (1683) An alleged WHIG plot, for which there is little evidence, to kill Charles II and the future James II. (Rye House Farm, Hertfordshire, where the conspirators are said to have met.)

Ryswick, Treaty of (1697) See AUGSBURG, WAR OF THE LEAGUE OF.

S

SA (1) Initials of the German name of the mass organization of Hitler's followers, founded 1922. Its leaders were massacred in 1934 (see NIGHT OF THE LONG KNIVES) at Hitler's command, and the SS then became supreme. Also called Brownshirts. (German *Sturmabteilung*, 'Storm troops'.) (2) SALVATION ARMY.

SAAB A Swedish aircraft firm which also makes motor vehicles, missiles and electrical equipment.

Saar plebiscites (1935 and 1957) Those held after the 2 world wars, in which the inhabitants of the Saar voted for return to Germany after French occupation and exploitation of its coal mines as a form of reparations. (Small area on the Franco-German border, capital Saarbrücken.)

Sabbath chain A chain across a road in Israel to prevent its use for vehicles on the Sabbath.

Sabbath Day's journey The distance, equivalent to less than ¾ mile, prescribed by Jewish tradition based on *Exodus* xvi, 29, as the maximum to be traveled on the Sabbath.

Sabbatical Year (1) The 7th year, when under Mosaic law land must be left fallow (*Exodus* xxiii, 11) and a moratorium on debts declared (*Deuteronomy* xv, 1-2). (2) At certain universities, a year's vacation from teaching, to be devoted to travel or research, granted to professors and other teaching members of the university, originally every 7th year.

Sabena (1923) The chief Belgian airline. (Initials of Société anonyme Belge d'exploitation de la navigation aérienne.)

'Sabine Women, The' (1799) J. L. David's painting of the RAPE OF THE SABINES in which he emphasizes the courage of the women, in gratitude to his estranged wife who had pleaded for his release from prison, where he had been sent for revolutionary activities; now in the Louvre.

Sabin vaccine A poliomyelitis vaccine made of living viruses, which can be taken orally and is effective over a long period. (Dr Albert Sabin, US scientist.)

'Sabre Dance' (1943) A melody from a Caucasian patriotic folk ballet by Khachaturian, *Gayane* (or *Gayne*), the name of a lovely Armenian with a brutal anti-Soviet husband. The tune became extremely popular, even reaching the jukeboxes.

Sabrejets (1952) US fighter planes, used in particular against MIG-15s in the KOREAN WAR.

Sabres The Buffalo Sabres, NATIONAL HOCKEY LEAGUE.

Sabrina The nymph of the River Severn, mentioned in Milton's COMUS, about whom an English legend was told to account for the Latin name of the river.

Sac Another spelling of SAUK.

SAC Initials used for Strategic Air Command, which provides a permanently airborne force ready for countermeasures against nuclear attack. The B-52 STRATOFORTRESSES are used, with about 24 aircraft in the air at any one time, flying from bases in USA (including Alaska), Pacific islands, Turkey and Siam. SAC was said in 1967 to have about 2000 hydrogen bombs as well as other nuclear weapons and warheads. The headquarters are at Offutt AFB, near Omaha, Neb.

Sacco and Vanzetti Two Italian anarchist immigrants found guilty of murder by a Massachusetts court (1921) but not executed till 1927, after many appeals and accusations of judicial prejudice.

SACEUR Supreme Allied Commander, Europe, the general in command of NATO land forces.

Sacher's A Vienna hotel once frequented by the aristocracy of Imperial Austria.

Sachertorte A rich chocolate sponge cake with jam filling, named after

SACHER'S.

Sachsenhausen A Nazi concentration camp.

Sackville Street A principal street of Dublin, now renamed O'CONNELL STREET.

SACLANT Supreme Allied Commander, Atlantic, the admiral in command of NATO naval forces.

Sacré Coeur (1914) The white church on top of MONTMARTRE in Paris, work on which began in 1876 as an expression of contrition and hope after the disastrous FRANCO-PRUSSIAN WAR of 1870.

'Sacred and Profane Love' (1510) Titian's painting now in the Borghese Gallery, Rome, with one clothed and one nude female figure, variously interpreted as representing Earthly and Heavenly Love or Grace and Truth (or Beauty).

Sacred College The college of Cardinals, whose duty it is to elect one of their number as Pope when the throne falls vacant.

Sacre du printemps, Le See RITE OF SPRING.

Saddleback A hardy breed of black baconer hog (Essex and Wessex) with a white 'saddle' over the shoulders and forelegs; mainly used for crossing purposes.

Sadducees An ancient Jewish sect, the priestly caste, opposed to the PHARISEES, not accepting the oral traditional law, denying the existence of angels and the immortality of the dead. (Said to be named after ZADOK THE PRIEST.)

Sadhu Indian title for an ascetic or holy man. (SANSKRIT, 'good'.)

Sadie Hawkins Day The first Saturday after November 11th, a day appointed by the mayor of Dogpatch (see LI'L ABNER) for a race in which girls chase the boys to catch a husband. Originally invented for the benefit of Sadie, 'the homeliest gal in all them hills', it is now a national institution.

Sadler's Wells (1931) A theater in Rosebery Avenue, FINSBURY, opened by Lilian Baylis to do for North London what the OLD VIC had done for South London, i.e. provide good plays at cheap prices. It then concentrated on opera in English (absorbing the CARL ROSA OPERA COMPANY) and (Dame) Ninette de Valois' ballet companies (see ROYAL BALLET). In 1968 the Sadler's Wells Opera was rehoused at the London Coliseum, St Martin's Lane, WC2. The Sadler's Wells Theatre is now used for visiting opera and ballet companies. (Site of a well, named after its owner, which was developed into a spa, where a theater was built in 1756.)

Sadowa (1866) The battle that ended the SEVEN WEEKS WAR, in which the Prussians under Moltke, using a new breech-loading rifle, defeated the Austrians; it marked the decline of Austria and the rise of Prussia as dominant in Central Europe. (Village near Königgratz, by which name the battle is also known; the latter town is now called Hradec Kralove and is 65 miles east of Prague.)

Sad Sack George Baker's strip cartoon depicting the trials of a peaceable citizen pitched into the alien atmosphere of the barrack room by World War II, and his subsequent return to civil life.

Safavids (1502-1736) A dynasty which presided over a renaissance of Persian art, building a magnificent new capital at Isfahan in the reign of Shah Abbas the Great.

Sagamore Hill The home (1887-1919) of Theodore Roosevelt, at Oyster Bay, L.I., N.Y., now a national historic site.

SAGE US precursor of BMEWS devised in the 1950s but outdated before completion; an automated, computerized defense system against bomber attack.

Sagebrush State Nickname of Nevada.

Sagittarius The Archer, 9th of the constellations of the Zodiac, between SCORPIO and CAPRICORNUS, representing a centaur drawing a bow; the sun enters it about November 21st. It contains many novae and planetary nebulae and may be the center of our galaxy. Astrologers claim that those born under this sign may be adventurous, extravagant and unreliable.

Saguenay A legendary kingdom up the Ottawa River sought by the French 16th-century navigator Jacques Cartier; name subsequently given to a river in Quebec.

Saigon Capital of, and used as a synonym for the government of, South VIETNAM.

SAINT Contraction for Satellite Inspection Technique, a US device designed to approach satellites in orbit and inspect them by TV camera and radiation sensors to determine whether they carry nuclear weapons. Development abandoned in 1962.

Saint, The The gentleman-burglar, Simon Templar, created by Leslie Charteris in 1928. His symbol, on the dust covers of some 40 novels, is a haloed stick figure.

St Agnes's Eve See EVE OF ST AGNES.

St Andrews Royal burgh on the east coast of Scotland, famous for its ancient university and as the home of the ROYAL AND ANCIENT.

St Anne's (1952) A women's college at OXFORD UNIVERSITY.

St Bartholomew Massacre (1572) The massacre of French HUGUENOTS begun in Paris on St Bartholomew's Day, ordered by Catherine de MEDICI, mother of the young King Charles IX. See GUISE, HOUSE OF.

St Brendan's Isle In medieval Irish legend, an island paradise discovered in mid-Atlantic by the 6th-century Irish saint of that name (also spelled Brandan).

St Clement Danes (17th century) One of the island churches in the Strand, London, restored after World War II as the church of the RAF; it is the church of the nursery rhyme 'Oranges and Lemons'. (Thought to have been built on the site of a Danish settlement.)

St Cross (1) A new college (1965) of OXFORD UNIVERSITY. (2) A religious and charitable foundation near Winchester, founded by Henry de Blois (1133).

Saint-Cyr (1806) The French WEST POINT, founded on the site of Mme de Maintenon's convent near Versailles, destroyed in World War II, and now at Coëtquidan near Rennes,

the capital of Brittany.

Ste Anne de Beaupré A shrine and basilica in a village of that name 20 miles from Quebec. A chapel was built on the site in 1658 by rescued sailors, and miraculous cures were reported. The basilica, begun in 1923, is visited by Canadian and US Catholics.

St Émilion A dark claret; Château Cheval Blanc and Château Ausone are among the best.

St George and the Dragon A legend of obscure origin. Nothing is known for certain about St George, the patron saint of England; the Dragon is simply the embodiment of evil. Gibbon's identification of him with St George of Cappadocia, fraudulent supplier to the Roman forces, is highly dubious.

St George's Chapel (15th century) The PERPENDICULAR chapel at Windsor Castle, famous for its fan vaulting. The GARTER CEREMONY is held here.

St George's, Hanover Square An 18th-century London church, famous throughout its history for fashionable weddings.

Saint-Germain (Cooking) With peas.

St Germain, Treaty of (1919) The postwar treaty with Austria (a separate, TRIANON, treaty was made with Hungary) which broke up the Austro-Hungarian Empire. Austria ceded huge areas to the new states of Czechoslovakia, Yugoslavia and Poland; lost South Tirol to Italy; and was left a scarcely viable state cut off from access to the sea, with only a quarter of its prewar population.

St Giles's Fair An ancient English Midlands market, held at Oxford after St Giles's Day (Sept. 1st), which survives as a pleasure fair.

St Helena The island in the South Atlantic associated with Napoleon as the place where he lived in exile from 1815 until his death.

St Hilda's (1893) A women's college at OXFORD UNIVERSITY.

Saint-Hubert (Cooking) With game.

St Hugh's (1886) A women's college at OXFORD UNIVERSITY.

St James's Palace The building, facing St James's Street, which succeeded WHITEHALL in the Hanoverian period as the principal royal palace in London until Queen Victoria moved to BUCKINGHAM PALACE. It was then used as a residence for royal princes and for levees. Ambassadors are still officially accredited to 'the Court of St. James's'.

Saint Joan (1923) Bernard Shaw's play which characteristically portrays the newly canonized Joan of Arc as an early nationalist and Protestant whose views are a menace to contemporary Church and society, and therefore meet to be burned.

St Joe Short for St Joseph, Mo.

St John Ambulance Brigade (UK) A voluntary organization which provides first aid, nursing and welfare services in hospitals, homes, at public and sporting events where first aid may be required, and in times of emergency. See KNIGHTS OF ST JOHN.

St John of Jerusalem, Order of See KNIGHTS OF ST JOHN.

St Lawrence Seaway The improved system of canals and locks, completed 1959, which opened up the Greak Lakes to seagoing vessels.

St Leger (1776) The last classic of the British flat-racing season, for 3-year-olds over a course of more than 1¾ miles at Doncaster.

Saint-Loup, Marquis de In Proust's REMEMBRANCE OF THINGS PAST, a member of the GUERMANTES family; at first infatuated with a prostitute, Rachel, he turns homosexual and wins Morel from CHARLUS. He then marries GILBERTE.

St Luke's Summer The English equivalent of the US INDIAN SUMMER. (St Luke's Day, Oct. 18th.)

St Margaret's, Westminster (1523) A London church in Parliament Square, since 1614 the official church of the House of Commons.

St Mark's The part-Byzantine cathedral which is the focal point of Venice.

St Martin-in-the-Fields (1726) A London church in TRAFALGAR SQUARE, famous as the church whose vaults were thrown open to the poor and homeless, and for the Rev. Dick Sheppard's sermons broadcast from

it when he was vicar (1914-27).

St Martin's Summer A period of mild sunny weather in November; compare ST LUKE'S SUMMER. (MARTINMAS, Nov. 11th.)

St Marylebone See MARYLEBONE.

St Nazaire raid (Mar. 1942) A small British commando raid on the repair docks at St Nazaire, at the mouth of the Loire, carried out successfully but with heavy loss.

Saint of Bleecker Street, The (1954) Gian-Carlo Menotti's most ambitious work (awarded a PULITZER PRIZE), a modern folk opera set in New York's Italian quarter, with a tragic story of a young man's love for his sister, who sees visions and receives the stigmata.

St Pancras A former London metropolitan borough, since 1965 part of the borough of CAMDEN.

St Pete Short for St Petersburg, Fla.

St Peter's, Rome The chief cathedral of the Roman Catholic Church, situated in VATICAN CITY.

St Petersburg The capital of Imperial Russia; renamed after the Revolution Petrograd, and later Leningrad.

Saints The New Orleans Saints, NATIONAL FOOTBALL LEAGUE. Became member of the NATIONAL CONFERENCE, NATIONAL FOOTBALL LEAGUE in 1970.

Saints, The A nickname for the CLAPHAM SECT.

St Stephen's The entrance to the House of Commons, originally a chapel and later the place where the House sat. Used as a synonym for the House of Commons.

St Valentine Day massacre (1929) The murder of leaders of Bugs Moran's gang, which left SCARFACE AL CAPONE supreme in the Chicago underworld.

Saki Pen name of H. H. Monro (1870-1916), writer of numerous satirical sketches.

Sakkara (Saqqara) The necropolis of MEMPHIS, south of Cairo; it is the site of the Step Pyramid of Zoser (3rd Dynasty), earliest known pyramid of the Pharaohs.

Saks Fifth Avenue A New York specialty store, featuring clothes for men and women. It was formed by a merger of the GIMBEL and Saks families' New York stores and was opened in 1924.

Salamis (480 BC) The Greek naval victory over the Persians (following THERMOPYLAE). (An island in the Gulf of Aegina, near Athens.)

Salchow An ice-skating jump, of which there are various types.

Salcombe Week The chief English West Country regatta, held in South Devon.

Salem rocker An early 19th-century Salem (Mass.) variant of the Windsor rocker, with a lower back than the BOSTON ROCKER.

Salem witch-hunt (1692) A hysterical outburst at Salem, Mass., started by a maid, dismissed by her master and ex-lover, denouncing her mistress as a witch. As a result 19 people were hanged for witchcraft.

Salerno (Sept 1943) Allied landing in Italy south of Naples, at a point north of the British 8th Army which had crossed from Sicily a few days earlier; made just after the Italian surrender, it met with stiff German opposition.

Salic Law An ancient law of the FRANKS, later interpreted to include a prohibition against a woman's accession to the French throne; this prohibition was adopted by other states of Europe. See PRAGMATIC SANCTION. (From name of a tribe of Franks from which the MEROVINGIANS descended.)

Salk vaccine (1954) The first effective vaccine against poliomyelitis; prepared from dead viruses, it is given in repeated injections; see SABIN VACCINE. (Dr Jonas Salk, USA.)

Sally Army A colloquial abbreviation for the SALVATION ARMY.

'Sally in Our Alley' An 18th-century ballad of which the words were written by Henry Carey but set to an older traditional air.

Sally Lunn A kind of tea cake, named after the woman who made them at Bath in the 18th century.

Salome In the New Testament story, Salome asked her stepfather Herod Antipas for the head of John the Baptist, who had denounced her mother for her incestuous second marriage (*Matthew* xiv, 8). See next entry.

Salome The title of a play by Oscar Wilde and an opera based on it by Richard Strauss, which add to the Biblical story (see last entry) the suggestion that Salome was in love with John, and Herod with Salome.

Salon des refusés (1863) An exhibition of works refused by the Salon, the French equivalent of the ROYAL ACADEMY; organized by Manet and his friends, with the approval of Napoleon III, it was a protest against the conservativism of the Salon jury.

Salonika The usual English name for the Greek port of Thessalonica.

Salop Alternative name for Shropshire. See also SALOPIAN.

Salopian (1) Of Shropshire. (2) Of Shrewsbury School. (From Anglo-Norman name of Shrewsbury.)

Salopian porcelain See CAUGHLEY.

Salt Abbreviation for Strategic Arms Limitation Talks, begun by the US and Russia at Helsinki in November 1969.

Salteena, Mr The butcher's son with social ambitions in *The* YOUNG VISITERS, who said of himself: I am not quite a gentleman but you would hardly notice it.

Salvation Army (1877) An organization for the relief of the destitute, originally called the East End Revival Society; it was founded by William Booth, a Methodist, who reorganized it as an 'army', with uniforms, brass bands and military ranks. The movement spread from London to most countries of the world.

Salzburg Festival An annual festival of Mozart's music held in July and August at the composer's birthplace.

Salzkammergut The Austrian mountain lake district east of Salzburg. (German, 'salt domain'.)

Sam The underdisciplined private of Stanley Holloway's monologue who refused to pick up the musket knocked out of his hand by Sergeant, until the Duke of Wellington rode up (on a lovely white 'orse) to plead with him to do so 'just to

484   Samaritaine ✳ 'Sanctus'

please me'.

Samaritaine A large Paris department store near the LOUVRE.

Samaritans, The (1953) A voluntary organization which gives help and advice to people in distress, particularly to those who appear to be contemplating suicide; it has over 70 branches in the UK. (See GOOD SAMARITAN.)

Sam Browne The military belt originally designed to carry an officer's sword, the wearing of which was made optional in the British Army at the beginning of World War II. (Named after Gen. Sir Sam Browne, VC, died 1901.)

Samian ware The red-clay domestic crockery of Ancient Rome; examples of it have been found all over the Empire, normally in fragments as it broke very readily.

Samian wine One of the favorite wines of Ancient Rome. (Made in Samos.)

Sam McGredy (1937) A hybrid tea rose with very large perfectly formed cream or buff flowers.

Samos US satellite with infrared cameras and special equipment for relaying extremely high definition pictures of the earth; used for military reconnaissance; launched in 1961.

Sam Slick the Clockmaker The hero of a classic humorous chronicle by Thomas Haliburton, a Nova Scotian judge. Sam is a shrewd and unscrupulous peddler who finds easy pickings among the slow and lazy Nova Scotians. In racy dialect he lambastes Nova Scotian backwardness, American democracy and British institutions impartially. The sketches were collected in numerous volumes, beginning with *The Clockmaker* (1837) and ending with *The Attaché; or Sam Slick in England* (1844).

Samson The HERCULES of the Israelites; rendered powerless when DELILAH cut off his hair, he was captured by the Philistines who blinded him and took him to Gaza (EYELESS IN GAZA). There he pulled down the pillars of a temple, which collapsed on him and all the lords of the Philistines (*Judges* xvi, 21-31). See next entry.

Samson Agonistes (1671) Milton's dramatic poem on the blind SAMSON's defiant act of self-destruction. (Greek *agonistes*, 'struggler'.)

Samson reproductions (1845) Brilliantly accurate copies of MEISSEN, CHELSEA, DERBY etc. porcelain, made in Paris by the firm of Samson (still in production). Many of the early (and all the modern) bear an honest 'S' (sometimes erased by the unscrupulous) in addition to the copied factory mark, and fetch high prices on their own merits.

Samuel The prophet whose life story is told in I *Samuel*. As a child he heard Jehovah's voice one night, and was sent to become a priest under Eli at SHILOH. He rallied the Israelites after their defeat by the Philistines, and became their 'judge' or ruler; but they demanded a king, and he reluctantly anointed SAUL as the first King of ISRAEL (I *Samuel* x, 1). See next entry.

Samuel (mostly 7th century BC) The name of 2 books of the Old Testament. I *Samuel* opens with the defeat of the Israelites by the Philistines, who captured the ARK OF THE COVENANT, and tells the stories of SAMUEL, SAUL and the early years of DAVID. II *Samuel* deals with the later years of David's reign.

Samuel, M. A London merchant bank; see HILL SAMUEL.

Samurai The military caste which dominated Japan during the TOKUGAWA SHOGUNATE; replaced after the MEIJI RESTORATION by a conscript army. See BUSHIDO.

Sancho Panza DON QUIXOTE's rustic squire who accompanies him on the donkey, Dapple; he is chiefly interested in food, drink and sleep, but indulgent to his master's whims. (Spanish *panza*, 'paunch'.)

'Sanctus' The hymn beginning 'Holy, Holy, Holy' which marks the end of the Preface to the Eucharist service, and during which the Sanctus bell is tolled. (Latin, 'holy'.)

Sand, George Pen name of the French novelist Baronne Dudevant (died 1876), mistress of Alfred de Musset and Chopin.

Sanders of the River (1911) Edgar Wallace's story of an intrepid empire builder in West Africa.

Sandhurst (1759) The ROYAL MILITARY ACADEMY (formerly College) at Camberley, Surrey, where army officer cadets are trained for commissions, originally in the cavalry and infantry only but, after amalgamation with the RMA Woolwich (1946), in all army units.

Sandwich glass (1825-80) Colored pressed glassware, particularly pieces with lacy patterns, made at Deming Jarves's Boston & Sandwich Glass Co. factory at Sandwich, Mass. Some were decorated with the American Eagle or the heads of Presidents; others with flowers etc.

SANE The Committee for a Sane Nuclear Policy, the US equivalent of the CND, under the chairmanship of Dr Spock (see SPOCK BOOK).

San Francisco Assay Office Since 1965 authorized to mint coins; see BUREAU OF THE MINT.

San Francisco Conference (1945) The international conference that adopted the UNITED NATIONS CHARTER.

San Francisco earthquake (1906) An earthquake which almost completely destroyed the city, though with comparatively small loss of life.

Sanger (Margaret) Award An award for contributions to the medical aspects of contraception. (Named for the woman who coined the term 'birth control' in her monthly magazine, *The Woman Rebel*, in 1914.)

Sanger's Circus An English circus developed from Astley's Circus (1768) by 'Lord' George Sanger, who took it over in 1871.

Sanhedrin The priests and elders of the Israelites sitting together as the highest court of law from about the 3rd century BC until AD 70; after that their jurisdiction was restricted to religious matters only. (Hebrew from Greek, 'sitting together'.)

Sankey and Moody hymns Those written or collected by Sankey and used by Moody in his evangelical campaigns in USA and later in Britain.

San Michele, The Story of (1929) Dr Axel Munthe's anecdotal autobiography, which includes his account of how he built himself the villa of San Michele on Capri.

San Siro Stadium The municipal sports arena at Milan, Italy.

Sanskrit The oldest known INDO-EUROPEAN LANGUAGE, still the scriptural language of HINDUISM. It is the parent of HINDUSTANI.

Sans Souci (1747) Name given by Frederick the Great to the palace he built at Potsdam. (French, 'without a care'.)

Santa Anita A racetrack at Arcadia, (Calif.) on the outskirts of Los Angeles.

Santa Fe Trail An 800-mile wagon route which linked Santa Fe, N.M., via Fort Dodge (near Dodge City) and Kansas City, almost in a straight line to Independence on the Missouri; of great importance from 1821 until the Santa Fe railroad was completed in 1880.

Santa Maria incident (1961) The seizure at sea of the Portuguese liner, *Santa Maria*, by a body of Portuguese passengers led by Capt. Galvão, as a propagandist gesture against the Portuguese dictatorship.

Santa Sophia (AD 537) One of the most famous and characteristic of Byzantine churches, at ISTANBUL; long since converted into the Great Mosque.

Santo Domingo (1) Old name of the Dominican Republic, in eastern Hispaniola. (2) Name of its capital, except for the period 1936-61 when it was called Ciudad Trujillo.

Santone Short for San Antonio, Tex.

Sapper Pen name of Cyril McNeile, a colonel in the Royal Engineers, author of BULLDOG DRUMMOND.

Sapphira Wife of ANANIAS.

Saracens Name, of obscure origin, for (1) Bedouins; (2) MUSLIMS; (3) the SELJUK TURKS against whom the Crusaders fought; (4) the Muslim pirates who in the 9th and 10th centuries terrorized Mediterranean shipping.

Saragossa English spelling of Zaragoza, a city of northern Spain.

Sarah ABRAHAM'S wife, mother of ISAAC.

Sarajevo assassination (28 June 1914) The assassination of the Archduke Franz Ferdinand, heir to the Austro-Hungarian throne, by a Bosnian Serb, Gavrilo Princip; the proximate cause of World War I. (Town in Bosnia, Yugoslavia.)

Saratoga, Battle of (1777) A battle in the AMERICAN WAR OF INDEPENDENCE which frustrated British attempts to isolate the NEW ENGLAND colonies; Gen. Burgoyne's force moved down from Canada to join up with Gen. Howe, but was cut off and forced to surrender. (A town in New York state, now called Schuylerville, near Saratoga Springs.)

Saratoga Trunk (1941) Edna Ferber's novel, made into a play (1960), with an 1880s setting at Saratoga, where a cowboy gambler meets a Creole adventuress. (A large trunk, usually with rounded top, a late 19th-century phenomenon in which ladies could pack masses of clothes for display at such places as Saratoga Springs, N.Y.)

Sardanapalus (1) Greek name of the last King of ASSYRIA. According to Greek stories he was effete and pleasure-loving, but capable of vigorous action when required. Defeated by rebels, he set fire to his palace and was burned to death together with his women and servants. This scene inspired Delacroix's great canvas in the LOUVRE. Sardanapalus is usually identified with the historical Ashurbanipal (7th century BC). (2) Byron's tragedy (1821) on this theme.

Sardi's A famous New York restaurant in the BROADWAY theater area, with a primarily theatrical *cachet*.

Sarin US lethal nerve gas (also called GB), causing death in from 2 minutes to 2 hours. Made at NEWPORT, IND.

Saros Name of the French communications satellite program.

Sarsen stones The sandstone boulders, quarried locally, which were used for the largest features (trilithons) of STONEHENGE. (Corruption of SARACEN, applied in about the 17th century to the sandstone boulders which, scattered on the Wiltshire chalk downs, looked 'outlandish'.)

Sartor Resartus (1836) Thomas Carlyle's work of which the first part consists of the views of the imaginary German Professor Teufelsdröckh on the philosophy of clothes; the second purports to be the professor's autobiography, actually an account of Carlyle's own spiritual crisis. (Latin, 'the tailor repatched'.)

Sarum Ecclesiastical name of Salisbury, used in the Bishop of Salisbury's signature.

SAS (1) Initials used for Scandinavian Airlines System (1946), jointly owned by Sweden, Norway and Denmark in the proportion 3 : 2 : 2. In 1954 it inaugurated a route to Los Angeles over the North Pole. (2) See SPECIAL AIR SERVICE.

Sasquatch The Pacific Northwest's version of the Himalayan ABOMINABLE SNOWMAN, a very tall hairy manlike creature said to have been sighted in the foothills of the Rockies near Nordegg, Alberta.

Sassanids (AD 226-641) A Persian dynasty, capital Ctesiphon, who conquered the PARTHIANS and MEDES and continually warred with Rome until they succumbed to MUSLIM invasions. The founder was Ardashir (Artaxerxes), son of Sassan.

Sassenach Scottish name for an Englishman; from the Gaelic *Sasunnach*, 'SAXON'.

Satchmo Nickname of Louis Armstrong, the American Negro jazz trumpet virtuoso, born in New Orleans in 1900. (Possibly for 'satchelmouth'.)

Satsuma ware (1) 18th-century Japanese cream-colored crackleware tastefully decorated in enamel colors and gilt; not exported. (2) Japanese ware made specially for Western markets in the 1870s and 1880s, smothered with gaudy decoration and worthless.

Saturday Evening Post (1728) A popular US illustrated magazine, carrying general articles and short stories dealing with American life; published in Philadelphia; ceased publication 1969; revived as a quarterly in 1971.

Saturn Roman god equivalent to the Greek CRONUS.

Saturn Name given to a series of US rockets, of which Saturn 5 was used to launch moon rockets in the APOLLO SPACE PROGRAM. It is claimed that it could put 36 men into orbit, and was first tested in 1967.

Saturnalia A major festival held in late December in Ancient Rome, possibly to celebrate the end of the vintage. Slaves were treated as equals during this period, which was marked by considerable license. It was adopted by the early Christians and transformed into the Christmas festivities; the custom of exchanging presents was common to both celebrations.

Satyricon A satirical novel written by Petronius, Nero's director of entertainments, in prose and verse. Parts of it have survived, including a description of the banquet given by the upstart Syrian, Trimalchio.

Sauchiehall Street One of the main shopping streets of Glasgow.

Saudia An alternative name for SAUDI ARABIA.

Saudi Arabia The name given by ibn-Saud in 1932 to the kingdoms of Hejaz and Nejd which he had united in 1927.

Sauk An Algonquian-speaking Indian tribe of the Wisconsin-Illinois region. They allied with the Fox tribe to regain their lands but were defeated in the BLACK HAWK war (1832). A few survive in Oklahoma. (Also spelled Sac.)

Saul The first King of ISRAEL, anointed by SAMUEL. He was jealous of his son Jonathan's love for his harpist DAVID. The phrase 'Is Saul also among the prophets?' (I Samuel x, 11-12) is used of one who unexpectedly supports what he had previously attacked.

Saul of Tarsus St Paul's name before he was converted (Acts ix, 18).

Sault Ste Marie Canals Better known as the Soo; 2 ship canals, one in Canada, one in the US, north and south of rapids between Lakes Huron and Superior; they are claimed to be the world's largest and busiest. (Name of twin towns, one in Michigan, the other in Ontario.)

Sauternes A sweet white Bordeaux wine from grapes left to shrivel on the vine; includes the highly regarded Château d'Yquem, and Château Guiraud.

Savage Club (1857) A London club in CARLTON HOUSE TERRACE, markedly bohemian in tone; the members, who call themselves Brother Savages, are mostly artists, actors, comedians or broadcasting personalities.

Savannah (1) The first steamer to cross the Atlantic (1819), a voyage which, aided by sail, took 25 days. (Built at Savannah, Ga.). (2) The first nuclear-powered merchant vessel, launched in 1959.

Save the Children Fund (1919) A voluntary organization to help sick, deprived and hungry children, with 500 branches in the UK.

Savidge Inquiry (1928) (UK) An investigation which followed the acquittal of Sir Leo Chiozza Money on a charge of indecent behavior with Irene Savidge in HYDE PARK. It was alleged that 2 police had perjured themselves and that in a subsequent police inquiry third degree methods had been used against Miss Savidge. The police were criticized but not prosecuted. Shortly afterwards Money was convicted of assaulting a woman on a train.

Savile Club (1868) A London club in Brook Street, with a membership including authors, publishers, actors and broadcasters, less staid than the GARRICK, more so than the SAVAGE.

Savile Row, London The world center for men's tailoring.

Savoy An ancient duchy south of Lake Geneva, the major part of which was ceded to France by the

King of Sardinia (1860); the Italian Royal family belonged to the House of Savoy.

Savoyard A member of the cast of a SAVOY OPERA.

Savoy Chapel The Queen's Chapel of the Savoy, Savoy Street, Strand, the private property of the British monarchy, inherited from JOHN OF GAUNT; headquarters of the Royal Victorian Order.

Savoy Hill The British Broadcasting Company's London station (1923-32) in the Strand. Its call sign was 2LO.

Savoy operas Another name for GILBERT AND SULLIVAN OPERAS, as produced at the Savoy theater; see D'OYLY CARTE OPERA CO.

Sawyer, Bob A happy-go-lucky medical student who with his fellow medico Ben Allen figures in the final episodes of Dickens's PICKWICK PAPERS.

Saxons The Teutonic invaders from northwest Germany who, from the 5th century AD, settled in Essex, MIDDLESEX, Sussex and WESSEX.

Saxony A former kingdom and province of Germany, capital Dresden. Half the kingdom was given to Prussia in 1815 and, with the Duchy of Anhalt, became the *Land* of Saxony-Anhalt, now in Eastern Germany. Lower Saxony, capital Hanover, is a *Land* of West Germany, and was formed from Hanover, Brunswick and Oldenburg.

Sayings of Christ A few brief statements attributed to Christ in some fragments of papyrus found at OXYRHYNCHUS in Egypt in 1897 and 1903. The manuscripts date to the 3rd century, but the sayings themselves may have been first written down in the 1st or 2nd centuries.

SBA See SMALL BUSINESS ADMINISTRATION.

Scala, La (1778) The Milan opera house, one of the largest in the world.

'Scandal in Bohemia, A' (1891) The first of many Sherlock HOLMES short stories to be published in the *Strand Magazine*.

Scanderbeg Turkish name of a 15th-century Albanian patriot who suc-cessfully rebelled against the OTTOMAN TURKS and held out against them until his death. (Corruption of Iskender Bey, i.e. Lord Alexander.)

Scapa Flow A strait in the Orkney Islands, Britain's chief naval base until it was closed in 1957, and the scene of the scuttling of the German fleet in 1919.

Scapin The ingenious and unscrupulous valet in Molière's comedy, *Les Fourberies* ('trickeries') *de Scapin* (1671).

Scaramouche A Spanish 'don' dressed in black, the cowardly braggart of the COMMEDIA DELL' ARTE, constantly belabored by HARLEQUIN. (Italian *scaramuccia*, 'skirmish'.)

Scarface Al Capone The most notorious of the Chicago gang leaders in the PROHIBITION days; he was not brought to justice until 1931 when BIG BILL THOMPSON's reign ended, and then only on an income-tax charge, for which he got 10 years.

Scarlet Letter, The (1850) A novel by Nathaniel Hawthorne about 17th-century Boston. The title refers to the red letter A which the heroine is condemned to wear because of her adultery. Her husband devotes himself to mercilessly tracking down the clergyman who had seduced her, and is shown in the process to be the greater sinner of the two.

Scarlet Pimpernel, The (1905) A novel by the Hungarian-born English writer, Baroness Orczy, in which Sir Percy Blakeney, to outward appearance a brainless fop, is the intrepid and 'demned elusive' Scarlet Pimpernel, who rescues victims of the FRENCH REVOLUTION and smuggles them to England. There were many sequels.

Scarpia, Baron The villain of TOSCA.

Scarteen Black and Tans, The An Irish fox-hunting pack with kennels at Scarteen near Knocklong, Tipperary, which hunts country on the Limerick-Tipperary border. It has been in the hands of the Ryan family for over 200 years, with the same strain of hounds, which have a characteristic bay.

Scheduled Castes See UNTOUCH-ABLES.

Scheherazade The daughter of the Vizier of the Indies who marries the Shah of an unspecified country. He, after discovering his first wife's infidelity, has sworn to marry a new wife each day and strangle her next morning. Scheherazade, by telling her stories (the ARABIAN NIGHTS) by installments, always breaking off each night before the denouement, retains the Shah's interest for 1001 nights, after which he cancels his threat.

Scheherazade (1) An orchestral suite by Rimsky-Korsakov. (2) A ballet set to this by Fokine. See last entry.

Schicklgruber The name borne by Adolf Hitler's illegitimate father, until he proved that his real name was Hitler; used in derision of Adolf by early political opponents.

Schick test A skin test to determine whether a patient is immune to diphtheria.

Schipperke A small tailless dog with smooth black coat, originally developed in FLANDERS as a barge watchdog. (From Dutch *schipper*, 'boatman'.)

Schlegel-Tieck prize (1964) An award of $700 for the best translation into English of a 20th-century West German work; administered by the (British) Society of Authors and the Translators' Association.

Schlieffen plan (1905) The German plan of campaign for a war on 2 fronts, put into partial operation in World War I; swift victory was to be achieved over France by a sweep through Belgium and force then concentrated on the eastern front. (Count von Schlieffen, German chief of staff.)

Schnauzer A German wire-haired terrier, bred in 3 sizes (including a miniature) and various colors, mainly black or gray.

Schneider Trophy (1913) An international race for seaplanes. In 1931 Britain, after setting up several world speed records in it, won the trophy outright by 3 successive victories with Supermarines. (Founded by a Frenchman, Jacques Schneider.)

Scholar-Gypsy, The (1853) Matthew Arnold's poem of a legendary Oxford student who joined the gypsies.

Scholasticism (1) The doctrines of the SCHOOLMEN. (2) Unimaginative emphasis on the trivial in teaching theological dogma and tradition.

Schönbrunn (1696) A ROCOCO royal palace in a park on the outskirts of Vienna.

Schöne Müllerin, Die (1823) Schubert's cycle of songs about a miller's love for a girl who has been spirited away by a mysterious huntsman; the 20 songs are held together by the sound of the millstream heard in the accompaniment. Also known as the *Müllerliede* (miller songs), especially as they were written by a Wilhelm Müller. (German, 'the fair maid of the mill'.)

School for Scandal, The (1777) R. B. Sheridan's comedy in which, amid various love intrigues and backbiting gossip, the rich Sir Oliver Surface discovers that, of his 2 nephews, Joseph is only after his money and the reckless Charles has at least some good points.

Schoolmen (1100-1500) The philosophers and theologians of Western Europe who tried to reconcile Aristotle with the Bible, reason with faith. Of these the greatest were Abélard (see HÉLOÏSE), Albertus Magnus, Aquinas (see THOMISM), Duns Scotus and Ockham (see OCCAM'S RAZOR). In the 14th century the Schoolmen descended to trivial disputation (see SCHOLASTICISM), and disappeared with the coming of the RENAISSANCE.

Schreiber Collection An important exhibition of porcelain on permanent display at the Victoria and Albert Museum, London.

Schuhplattler The Tirolean and Bavarian traditional courtship dance, in which the dancer slaps thigh, buttock and knee to LÄNDLER-style music.

Schuman plan (1950) The plan which led to the formation of the EUROPEAN COAL AND STEEL COMMUNITY in 1952, and so to the COMMON MARKET. (Robert Schuman, French

Foreign Minister.)

Schweik in the Second World War (1943) Brecht's play using the hero of Hasek's novel, the GOOD SOLDIER SCHWEIK.

Schweitzer (Albert) Professor Holder of the chair of the Humanities, University of the City of New York. See also LAMBARÉNÉ.

Schweppes A British firm best known for its effervescent drinks, but also making Rose's soft drinks and, through its food division, Chiver's jams and (from 1968) Typhoo tea, among other products. In 1969 it took over the Cadbury chocolate firm.

Schweppes championship A stroke-play golf championship for PGA members, and amateurs with handicaps of 1 or better, played in April at Hunstanton, Norfolk. Prize money totals $12,000. Sponsored by SCHWEPPES (Home) Ltd.

Science and Health with Key to the Scriptures (1875) The scripture of the Christian Scientists, frequently revised by its author, Mrs Eddy, the founder of the sect.

Science Research Council (1965) A UK body which took over from the Department of Scientific and Industrial Research the ROYAL GREENWICH OBSERVATORY, space research and the National Institute for Research in Nuclear Science.

Scilla The genus of squills or wild hyacinths, including the common English bluebell; see CAMPANULA.

Scipio march, The The march from Handel's opera *Scipione*, to which the words of William Cowper's 'The loss of the ROYAL GEORGE' were later set.

SCOD (1955) Initials used for South Coast One Design, an English auxiliary BERMUDIAN RIG cruising boat to sleep four; waterline length 21 feet; cost around $7000.

Scone Stone The ancient Scottish coronation stone taken by Edward I from Scone Castle (near Perth) and placed beneath Edward the Confessor's Chair in Westminster Abbey; removed by a Scottish nationalist in 1950 but returned a few months later. It was supposed to be JACOB's pil-

low (Genesis xxviii, 11).

Scopes Trial (1925) A deliberately sought test case in which a schoolmaster, J. T. Scopes, was accused of teaching Darwinism contrary to Tennessee law, and fined $100 (later remitted).

Scorpio The Scorpion, 8th of the constellations of the Zodiac, between LIBRA and SAGITTARIUS; the sun enters it about October 21st. Astrologers claim that those born under this sign may be masterful, possessive and intuitive.

Scorton Arrow (1673) A silver arrow, the trophy in an archery contest held in Yorkshire, presented to the first to hit a 3-inch bull's-eye at 100 yd. He becomes Captain and chooses next year's venue. (Traditionally first presented by Queen Elizabeth I, lost, and found later at Scorton, near Richmond, Yorkshire.)

Scotch Cup (1959) An international curling championship.

Scotch woodcock Scrambled eggs on toast, with anchovy paste.

Scotland Yard The WHITEHALL headquarters from 1890 of the London Metropolitan Police, and later also of the CRIMINAL INVESTIGATION DEPARTMENT; name retained to cover New Scotland Yard (opposite the House of Commons) and new buildings (1966) in Broadway nearby.

'Scots, wha hae' (1793) The Scotsman's national anthem, composed by Robert Burns, beginning: Scots, wha hae wi' Wallace bled, / Scots wham Bruce has aften led,/Welcome to your gory bed,/Or to victorie.

Scott expedition (1910-12) The Antarctic expedition which reached the South Pole (shortly after Amundsen) and in which Captain Scott and his 4 companions lost their lives.

Scottish Blackface A widely distributed longwool breed of hill sheep.

Scottish Nationalist Party (1928) A movement for Scottish Home Rule, which has had the support of Scottish writers such as Hugh MacDiarmid, Compton Mackenzie etc.

Scott-Moncrieff prize (1964) An award of $700 for the best translation into English of a 20th-century French work; administered by the

(British) Society of Authors and the Translators' Association.

Scottsboro trials (1931-32) The trials of a group of young Negroes found in a railroad freight car with some poor-white prostitutes. To save what there was of their reputation the women accused them of rape; the men were given death sentences commuted on appeal to long terms of imprisonment, but in the face of public outcry were eventually released. (Town in Alabama.)

Scourge of God, The A name for Attila, King of the HUNS who swept through the ROMAN EMPIRE in the 5th century.

Scouse Liverpudlian (i.e. a citizen of Liverpool), originally a nautical nickname of long standing. (From *lobscouse*, some kind of Lancashire hot pot.)

Scrabble A spelling game in which words are built up on a squared board with lettered counters having scoring values graded according to frequency of occurrence.

Scrap of Paper, The Bethmann-Hollweg's description (1914) of the Treaty of London (1839) by which Prussia, Austria, Britain and France guaranteed the neutrality of Belgium; he was protesting against Britain's declaration of war when Germany invaded Belgium.

Screwtape Letters, The (1941) A seriocomic book by C. S. Lewis in which Screwtape, a devil, teaches a subordinate how to lead human beings to damnation.

Scriblerus Club (1713) A group of writers, led by Pope, John Arbuthnot, Swift, Gay and Congreve, who met to discuss the pedantry and poor literary taste of their day. One by-product was the memoirs of the fictitious Martinus Scriblerus, who had read not wisely but too much, and who embodied all they deplored.

Scribner's Magazine (1887-1939) An illustrated magazine of high quality.

Scripps-Howard press The first chain of US newspapers, started by the Scripps family with the Cleveland *Press* (1878) and joined by R. W. Howard of UP (also founded by Scripps) in 1920. One of its chief acquisitions was the New York *World Telegram*.

Scrooge, Ebenezer The supreme miser and misanthrope who in Dickens's *A Christmas Carol* (1843) becomes a reformed character after the ghost of his deceased partner visits him on Christmas Eve and he has visions of his past and of his probable future if he does not change his ways.

Scrophulariaceae The snapdragon (antirrhinum) family, which includes many common wildflowers and garden plants, e.g. foxglove, speedwell (veronica), mullein (verbascum), toadflax. (Named after a plant once used as a remedy for scrofula.)

Scrutiny (1932-53) An English literary review, the sounding board of the F. R. Leavis or Cambridge school of critics which handed down ukases on what one should read and how. Their oddly asorted twin idols were George Eliot and D. H. Lawrence. Since the review's demise Cambridge has been able to resume the freedom of thought normally found in a great university while Leavis has been able to concentrate on flaying C. P. Snow for his TWO CULTURES concept.

Scuba Initials of Self-Contained Underwater Breathing Apparatus.

Scutari Former Italian name of (1) the Turkish city of Uskudar; (2) the Albanian town of Shkoder.

Scylla and Charybdis In Greek legend, the 2 monsters who sat on either side of the Straits of Messina between Italy and Sicily, and destroyed any ships that came too close. Hence 'between Scylla and Charybdis' means 'between the Devil and the deep blue sea'.

SDS (1960) Students for a Democratic Society, a radical organization of student protest, particularly against 'the System' (the military-industrial-financial complex), the draft and the VIETNAMESE WAR; it became increasingly militant in 1969 and split into various groups, e.g. the extremist Weathermen and a Marxist

Student-Worker Alliance. It is a main constituent of the NEW LEFT.

Seabees Nickname given to the US naval construction battalions (first formed in World War I, revived in 1941), units of highly skilled workmen under engineer officers who not only performed invaluable service in building airfields, naval bases, floating docks etc., but were given combat training to defend them when necessary. (From initials of 'Construction Battalion', plus puns on 'sea' and 'busy bees'.)

Sea Beggars, The The 16th-century Protestant Dutch sailors who raided Spanish shipping and plundered Roman Catholic churches, putting new heart into the struggle to throw off Spanish domination of the NETHERLANDS. (French *Les Gueux*, 'beggars', a name given to the Dutch CALVINISTS who in 1566 signed a 'Compromise', a pledge to drive out the Spaniards.)

Sea Cadet Corps (1942) The Royal Navy's voluntary youth organization for boys aged 14-18 likely to be interested in a career at sea.

Seacat A British short-range missile launcher, mounted in fours in *County* class ships.

Seadart A surface-to-air guided weapon, designed for use in TYPE 82 DESTROYERS, with a range of about 20-30 miles.

Seagram Building The House of Seagram on Park Avenue, NYC, the elegant 525-ft 38-story building designed by Mies van der Rohe and Philip Johnson.

Sea-green Incorruptible, The Carlyle's name for Robespierre, who in the FRENCH REVOLUTION kept to his own democratic principles, refusing to compromise with the more moderate GIRONDINS or the terrorists, and thus making so many enemies that he ended on the scaffold. (Carlyle mistakenly thought that he had an unhealthy complexion; hence 'sea-green'.)

Seagull, The (1896) Chekhov's play of the young writer Trepliov's jealousy of the successful Trigorin who walks off with, but then abandons, Nina, the girl he loves. She returns and compares herself with the sea gull Trepliov had shot earlier in the play and given to her as a token of his ruined ambitions after the humiliating failure of his first play.

Sea island cotton A fine quality long-staple cotton, originally cultivated on islands off the coast of South Carolina and Georgia.

Sea King A Royal Navy Westland helicopter equipped with antisubmarine weapons and sonar.

Sealab The underwater vessel used in experiments under the US Navy's Man-in-the-Sea program. In 1964 4 men remained submerged in it for 10 days at a depth of 193 ft; longer periods at greater depths were later achieved.

Sea Lion German code name for the proposed invasion of southern England in 1940.

Seals The California Golden Seals, NATIONAL HOCKEY LEAGUE.

Séamas Irish name equivalent to James.

Sean Irish form of the name John.

Sea of Tranquillity The area where the first two men landed on the moon, from APOLLO 11.

Searchlight Tattoo A spectacular pageant by the British armed forces, with massed military bands, now held each August at the White City, London, in aid of Service charities. It developed from the ALDERSHOT Tattoo of the 1920s at Rushmore Arena, at which searchlights played a prominent part.

Sears Cup The North American junior yachting championship.

Sears Roebuck The largest mail-order firm in the world, with headquarters at Chicago; since the 1920s it has also owned a chain of retail stores. One of the 30 industrials that make up the DOW JONES Industrial Average.

Seaslug British naval antiaircraft missile mounted in *County* class ships, the equivalent of the Army's THUNDERER; Mark I (1953) was replaced from 1966 by Mark II.

Season, The The London Season which begins in May with the ROYAL ACADEMY's Private View Day and

QUEEN CHARLOTTE'S BALL, and ends with COWES WEEK in August.

Seasons, The (1726-30) James Thomson's long poem in blank verse, chiefly notable as the first example of nature description 'on location' instead of through the study window, based on intimate knowledge of his native Teviotdale in Roxburghshire, Scotland.

SEATO (1954) Initials used for the Southeast Asia Treaty Organization, a mutual defense pact to counteract Communist aggression in that area (FORMOSA and Hong Kong being implicitly excluded), signed by USA, Britain, France, Australia, New Zealand, the Philippines, Siam and PAKISTAN. Indonesia held aloof. The headquarters are at Bangkok. See GENEVA AGREEMENTS.

Seaton Carew (UK) Site of a 1250-MW nuclear power station authorized in 1968 to be built south of West Hartlepool on the Durham coalfield.

Seaton Delaval Hall The last country house to be designed by Sir John Vanbrugh, near Whitley Bay on the Northumberland coast.

Seawanhaka Cup (1895) An international race for 6-meter yachts. (Cup presented by the Seawanhaka-Corinthian Yacht Club of Oyster Bay, Long Island, N. Y.)

Sea Wolf, The (1904) Jack London's novel about a NIETZSCHEAN SUPERMAN of a schooner skipper, Wolf Larsen, brought into enforced contact with 2 literary men with whom he is wrecked on a desert island. Larsen goes blind and dies, still captain of his soul; the others are rescued.

Sebring (1952) A 5-mile auto-racing circuit, 160 miles from Miami, Fla., where a 12-hour international endurance race is held each year, one of the events comprising the Sports-GT championship.

SEC Initials used for the US Securities and Exchange Commission, the governing body for all the American stock exchanges.

Second Coalition (1799) An alliance of Britain, Austria and Russia which drove the French out of Italy, Switz-

erland and the German states but disintegrated when Russia and Austria quarreled and was ended by Moreau's victory over Austria in 1800 at HOHENLINDEN.

Second Coming The return of Christ to earth; see ADVENTISTS.

Second Commandment 'Thou shalt not make . . . any graven image' (*Exodus* xx, 4-6). Regarded as part of the First Commandment by Roman Catholics.

Second Empire (1852-70) In French history the reign of Emperor Napoleon III which intervened between the SECOND and THIRD REPUBLICS, and ended with the French defeat in the FRANCO-PRUSSIAN WAR.

Second Front The name given to the concept of an attack on Europe by the Western Allies after the fall of France in 1940; Stalin never ceased to press for this, regarding the North African campaign as a minor operation, and suspecting that the West was content to watch the Germans and Russians destroy each other.

Second International (1) A Workingmen's Association formed in Paris (1889); it lost influence when it failed to unite Socialist parties to prevent World War I. (2) A federation of nonrevolutionary Socialist political parties formed after that war (Socialist International). See SOCIAL DEMOCRATS.

Second Mrs Tanqueray, The (1893) Pinero's immensely popular play about a woman with a past whose former lover gets engaged to her stepdaughter, leading to revelation, recrimination and Mrs Tanqueray's suicide.

Second Reading (Parliament) The main stage in the passing of an Act. The House debates the principles of the Bill which, if the majority so decides, is referred to a committee, usually of the whole House, for detailed consideration, clause by clause, and amendment (the Committee stage). See THIRD READING.

Second Republic (1848-52) In French history, the republic set up after the revolution which deposed Louis Philippe, KING OF THE FRENCH; it ended when President Louis Napoleon became the Emperor Napoleon III (see SECOND EMPIRE).

Second Sea Lord   (UK) A post combined with that of Chief of Naval Personnel, under the Minister of Defense for the Royal Navy.

Secret Agent, The   (1907) Joseph Conrad's story of London East End anarchists; Stevie is persuaded by Verloc, an agent provocateur, to blow up Greenwich Observatory, and succeeds in blowing himself up. His wife kills Verloc and then commits suicide.

Secret Doctrine, The   (1888) The bible of the theosophists, written by Mme Blavatsky; see THEOSOPHICAL SOCIETY.

Security Council   The supreme body of UN, comprising 5 permanent members (USA, USSR, UK, France and the island of Formosa, any of which can veto a decision of the rest of the council) and 10 members elected for 2-year terms.

Sedan   (1870) The defeat of the French in the FRANCO-PRUSSIAN WAR; Napoleon III was taken prisoner. (French frontier fortress in the Ardennes; the Germans again broke through there in 1940.)

Seddon murder case   (1912) (UK) The trial of Frederick Seddon and his wife, charged with murdering their aged lodger, Miss Barrow, by poison. Seddon was executed but his wife, defended by Marshall Hall, was acquitted.

Sedgemoor, Battle of   (1685) The engagement which ended MONMOUTH'S REBELLION. (Marsh near Bridgwater, Somerset.)

Sedley, Jos   In Thackeray's VANITY FAIR a spineless retired Collector from India, whom Becky SHARP cheats out of his money.

Sedum   The genus name of the stonecrops.

Seebohm report   (1968) (UK) A report which recommended that major local authorities should establish unified departments combining children's and welfare services with some of the social services of the health, education and housing departments; also a new central government department to oversee them. It commented on the relative neglect of the very old, the underfives, the physically and mentally handicapped, disturbed adolescents, and 'the flotsam and jetsam of society'.

Seeing Eye, The   (1929) A nonprofit organization at Morristown, N.J., which pioneered the training and supply of guide dogs for the blind (Seeing-Eye dogs).

Segrave Trophy   An award made annually by the ROYAL AUTOMOBILE CLUB to the British subject who has done most to demonstrate the possibilities of transport by air, land or water. (In memory of Sir Henry Segrave, who put up car and motorboat speed records; died 1930.)

Sejm   The Polish legislative assembly. (Polish, 'assembly'.)

Selborne   See NATURAL HISTORY AND ANTIQUITIES OF SELBORNE.

Selective Service Act   (1948) A measure which provides for conscription into the armed forces of men aged 18½-25, by lottery number. Some categories (e.g. students, workers in key industries) have, in normal times, been granted exemption or deferment. Conscripts serve 2 years plus 4 on the Reserve; most go to the Army, the requirements of the other services being usually met by volunteers.

Selective Service System   The Federal agency that administers all activities concerning compulsory military service; see last entry.

Selene   The Greek moon-goddess, sister of HELIOS and EOS; the Roman Luna. Later she became identified with ARTEMIS.

Seleucids   (312-64 BC) A dynasty of kings of Syria founded by Seleucus I, one of Alexander the Great's generals; at times they ruled over MESOPOTAMIA, but lost it after transferring their capital to ANTIOCH.

Self-Denying Ordinance   (1645) The measure under which the ROUNDHEAD members of both Houses of Parliament resigned their military commissions to permit the formation of the NEW MODEL ARMY under competent leadership.

Self-Help (1864) A work by Samuel Smiles, given as a prize to many an unfortunate Victorian schoolboy; it inculcates the complacent doctrine that God helps those that help themselves.

Seljuk Turks The first wave of Turks to move west from Turkestan, in the 11th century conquering Persia and ANATOLIA, and taking over the temporal powers of the ABBASID Caliphs of Baghdad; they are the 'infidel' SARACENS in Palestine against whom the CRUSADES were sent. At the end of the 13th century they were displaced by the OTTOMAN TURKS. (Named after the first ruler.)

Semele (1) In Greek mythology, the mother of DIONYSUS by ZEUS, who was resurrected from the Underworld each spring. (2) Dramatic cantata by Handel, containing the beautiful aria 'Where'er you walk'.

Seminole A MUSKOGEAN INDIAN race, one of the FIVE CIVILIZED NATIONS, who split off from the CREEK in the 18th century, settled in Florida and now survive in Oklahoma. They are mostly Roman Catholics. See next entry.

Seminole Wars (1) The war of 1817-18 in which the SEMINOLE were defeated by Andrew Jackson. (2) The war of 1835-42 in which 3000 Seminole, exploiting the natural advantages of the EVERGLADES, were able to avoid defeat for many years. They were then transported to Oklahoma.

Semiramis (1) A historical Queen of ASSYRIA of whom little is known except that she wielded great influence. (2) A legendary version of (1), later identified with ISHTAR, to whom was attributed the building of Babylon and other cities. She is the heroine of several plays and of Rossini's opera *Semiramide*.

Semites (1) The peoples, traditionally descended from SHEM, who speak SEMITIC LANGUAGES. (2) Used (incorrectly) as a synonym for the Jews, as in 'anti-Semitism'.

Semitic languages A group of languages spoken in the Middle East and adjacent countries; they include Akkadian (Assyrian, Babylonian), Hebrew, ARAMAIC, Phoenician, Arabic and AMHARIC (in Abyssinia). They share a neat system whereby basic ideas are expressed by 3-consonant roots which, modified by vowel changes and prefixes, express all shades of derivative meanings — e.g. k-t-b ('writing') forms, in Arabic, *kitab*, 'book'; *kataba*, 'he wrote'; *maktub*, 'letter'; *maktab*, 'office', etc.

SEN See STATE ENROLLED NURSE.

Senators The Washington (D.C.) Senators, AMERICAN (Baseball) LEAGUE, playing at the Robert F. Kennedy Memorial Stadium.

Seneca An Iroquoian Indian tribe of western New York which became the most powerful and numerous of the FIVE NATIONS. About 4000 survive in New York, and a few in Canada.

Senior Service tournament (1962) A stroke-play open golf tournament with a prize fund totalling around $30,000. (Sponsored by Gallahers, makers of Senior Service cigarettes.)

Sense and Sensibility Jane Austen's novel; see DASHWOOD FAMILY.

Sentimental Journey through France and Italy, A (1768) Laurence Sterne's unfinished account of his travels (he died before he reached the description of his experiences in Italy). He wrote it under the name of YORICK. See also SMELFUNGUS.

Senussi A MUSLIM puritan sect in LIBYA, founded in the 19th century by Muhammad al-Senussi; they led several revolts against Italian rule before and after World War I. Their leader became the first king of Libya in 1952.

Sephardim The Jews of southern Europe, especially Spain and Portugal, speaking the Sephardic dialect of Hebrew which now predominates in Israel. They are descended from the Spanish Jews who preferred expulsion to conversion when offered the option in 1490. See ASHKENAZIM. (Sepharad in *Obadiah* 20.)

Sepoy Mutiny Name (chiefly US) for the INDIAN MUTINY.

September Massacres (2-5 Sept. 1792) In the FRENCH REVOLUTION, the wholesale butchering of a large number of political prisoners, in Paris and some provincial towns, suspected of disloyalty to the republic; the result of panic after the Prussians had reached Verdun.

'September Morn' (1912) A painting by Paul Chabas. (Metropolitan Museum of Art, NYC.)

Septuagint Greek translation of the Old Testament and APOCRYPHA, traditionally begun by Palestinian Jews working at Alexandria in the 3rd century BC, but not completed until early Christian times. (Latin *septuaginta*, 70; according to legend, the PENTATEUCH was translated by 72 men in 72 days.)

Sequoia National Park (1890) A park in the Sierra Nevada, east-central California, famous for its giant sequoias and magnificent mountain scenery; it includes Mt Whitney (14,494 ft).

Sequoya Indian name of George Guess (or Gist), a half-caste who created the CHEROKEE alphabet (1821). The Sequoia tree is named for him.

Seraphim First mentioned in *Isaiah* vi, 2, as having 6 wings; later regarded as the highest order of angels, grouped with CHERUBIM and Thrones. (Plural of *seraph*, perhaps 'fiery serpent'.)

Serapis An Egyptian god; see APIS.

Serbo-Croat The South Slavonic languages spoken in Yugoslavia (in Serbia, Bosnia, Dalmatia, Croatia), closely akin to SLOVENIAN.

Serbonian bog A place mentioned in Milton's PARADISE LOST: 'A gulf profound as that Serbonian bog /... Where armies whole have sunk'. It was, historically, a bituminous lake on the Egyptian coast in which part of a Persian army was swallowed up in 350 BC.

Serendip An old name for Ceylon. *The Three Princes of Serendip* is a fairy story in which the princes were always finding delightful things by sheer chance; from it Horace Walpole coined the useful word 'serendipity', the faculty of doing this.

Seretse Khama case (1948) Seretse Khama, then a Bamangwato chief in Bechuanaland, having married an English wife against the wishes of his uncle and Regent, Tshekedi Khama, was exiled but allowed to return in 1956. (Subsequently he became the first President of the Republic of BOTSWANA.)

Sergeant US Army's ground-to-ground guided missile, range 75 miles, designed to carry a 100-kiloton warhead.

Sgt Mike A VIETNAMESE WAR cartoon series by Hodgson.

'Sgt Pepper's Lonely Hearts Club Band' The most influential of the rock-'n'-roll albums issued by the Beatles, marking pop's coming-of-age and general acceptance.

Serialism A theory of time advanced by J. W. Dunne, British aircraft designer, mathematician and philosopher, in his *An Experiment with Time* (1927) and later books. By inducing friends to keep bedside notebooks for instant record of dreams, he showed that many people dream of future events. This he attributed to the contents of time being as real as those of space, and built round this hypothesis a mathematical theory of a 4-dimensional space-time which individuals observe in sleep and could, but for habit, observe when awake.

Seringapatam (1799) The capital of the Sultan of Mysore, Tippoo Sahib, who was killed when the town was taken by the British after a siege in which the Indians made effective use of an early form of military rocket.

Serjeant Musgrave's Dance (1959) A play by John Arden in which 19th-century army deserters react to the horrors of war.

Serpentine, The The lake in HYDE PARK, London, which provides boating, skating, fishing and, for the hardy few, year-round bathing.

Serpukhov Site south of Moscow of a high-energy physics laboratory where a very large proton accelerator is being built.

Servicemen's Readjustment Act (1944) The official designation of the first GI BILL OF RIGHTS.

Sesame and Lilies (1865) A popular

work by John Ruskin consisting of lectures on reading, education and the role of educated women in society.

Sesostris Greek name for the Pharaoh Rameses II, and for 3 kings of a much earlier Egyptian dynasty.

Sestos and Abydos Towns on opposite shore of the HELLESPONT; see HERO AND LEANDER.

Set Ancient Egyptian god of night and of evil, who killed OSIRIS; portrayed in art with a snout and donkey's ears. Equivalent to the Greek Typhon.

Settebello, The Italian luxury train running daily between Milan-Bologna - Florence - Rome - Naples; first-class only, all seats reserved, 50% surcharge.

Seuss, Dr Pen name of Theodor Seuss Geisel (born 1904), author and illustrator of amusing and popular children's books.

Seven, The (or **The Outer Seven**) Names for EFTA.

Seven against Thebes, The (467 BC) Aeschylus' play about a legendary war in which 7 ARGIVE heroes fight to restore the rightful· King of THEBES. The rival claimants to the throne are the sons of OEDIPUS and, under the influence of his curse on them, fight in single combat in which both are killed.

Seven Bishops, Trial of the (1688) The acquittal of the Archbishop of Canterbury and 6 others, charged with seditious libel for opposing James II's DECLARATION OF INDULGENCE to Roman Catholics; the attempt to secure their conviction was a prime cause of the GLORIOUS REVOLUTION.

Seven Cities of Cibola The ZŪNI pueblos west of Albuquerque, N.M. Believing false reports of their great wealth, a minor Conquistador, Coronado, subjugated them in 1540 and, disillusioned, pressed on across the Arkansas River into Kansas, still seeking nonexistent riches.

Seven Deadly Sins Classified by early Christians as pride, covetousness, lust, anger, gluttony, envy and sloth.

Seven Lamps of Architecture, The (1849) John Ruskin's discussion of the 7 principles of architecture and his defense of the Gothic style.

Seven Pillars of Wisdom, The (1926) T. E. Lawrence's description of his desert campaign against the Turks in World War I; he also wrote an abridged version, *Revolt in the Desert* (1927).

Seven Sages, The Name given in ancient times to Thales of Miletus (the founder of Greek philosophy), Solon (the lawgiver of Athens) and other wise men of Greece, to whom some of the traditional Greek mottoes (such as 'know thyself', 'nothing in excess') were attributed, in most cases erroneously.

Seven Seas, The The North and South Atlantic, North and South Pacific, Indian, Arctic and Antarctic Oceans.

Seven Sisters (1) Translation of an ancient Greek name for the PLEIADES. (2) The 7 women's IVY LEAGUE colleges: BARNARD, BRYN MAWR, MOUNT HOLYOKE, RADCLIFFE, SMITH, VASSAR, WELLESLEY. (3) A name for the 7 biggest oil firms, originally STANDARD OIL OF NEW JERSEY, STANDARD OIL OF CALIFORNIA, MOBIL OIL, Shell, BP, TEXACO and Gulf. At one time they controlled three-quarters of world production.

Seven Sleepers, The Seven legendary Christians of Ephesus who, mewed up in a cave at a Roman Emperor's command in the 3rd century, fell into a miraculous sleep which lasted until the 5th century. Discovered by chance, they awoke, told their tale, and fell dead. The story, apparently of Syrian origin, is also found in the Koran.

Seven Storey Mountain, The (1948) The best-selling autobiography of the Anglo-American, Thomas Merton, brought up in France who in 1941 became a TRAPPIST monk in Kentucky.

1776 A historical and satirical musical, lyrics and music by Sherman Edwards, book by Peter Stone, about the signatories to the DECLARATION OF INDEPENDENCE.

17th Amendment (1913) An amendment to the US Constitution which enacted that Senators should be elected by popular vote.

17th Congress   (USSR) The Congress held in 1934, at which Stalin admitted that the peasantry had slaughtered half the country's livestock in protest against collectivization.

17th Parallel   (of latitude) The boundary fixed between North and South VIETNAM (1954).

Seventh Avenue   The heart of the fashion and garment district in mid-Manhattan.

Seventh Commandment   'Thou shalt not commit adultery' (*Exodus* xx, 14). To Roman Catholics this is the Sixth Commandment.

Seventh-Day Adventists   (1863) The largest of the American ADVENTIST sects, founded by William Miller after Christ had failed to appear in 1843 as he had prophesied. They still believe that the SECOND COMING is imminent, and keep Saturday very strictly as their Sabbath.

Seven Types of Ambiguity   (1930) A book written by William Empson, aged 21, giving a detailed analysis of the rich store of verbal nuances, allusions, double meanings etc. to be found in English poetry.

76ers   The Philadelphia 76ers, NATIONAL BASKETBALL ASSOCIATION.

'Seventy-six Trombones'   (1957) A melody taken from Meredith Willson's musical comedy (and movie, 1962), *The Music Man*.

Seven Weeks War   (1866) A Prussian attack on Austria to secure leadership of the NORTH GERMAN CONFEDERATION. The Austrians were defeated at SADOWA but were more successful against PRUSSIA's Italian allies.

Seven Wonders of the World   Various lists were given in ancient times, which usually included the HANGING GARDENS OF BABYLON, the COLOSSUS OF RHODES, the MAUSOLEUM, the PHAROS (lighthouse) at Alexandria, the Pyramids and the Temple of DIANA at Ephesus.

Seven Years War   (1756-63) A war precipitated by the King of PRUSSIA, Frederick the Great, in which he triumphed, against all expectation, over France, Austria and Russia. England, which had subsidized him, took the opportunity while France

was thus engaged to strengthen the foundations of its dominion in Canada and India through Wolfe and Clive.

Severn bore   (UK) A tidal bore producing a wave of up to 5 ft in height in the lower reaches of the River Severn at the spring tides.

Sèvres   Products of a French porcelain factory founded at VINCENNES and moved (1756) under royal patronage to Sèvres, southwest Paris, where it still operates today. The characteristic wares were decorated with panels of landscapes, flowers, exotic birds etc. on the famous colored grounds of green, *bleu de roi*, *rose Pompadour* etc. At first soft, and from 1769 hard, paste porcelain was made. Their styles were imitated by many English factories, and extensively faked.

Sèvres Treaty   (1920) The postwar treaty with Turkey which Mustapha Kemal (ATATÜRK) refused to ratify and was replaced by the LAUSANNE TREATY.

Seward's Folly   Alaska, the seemingly valueless territory which Secretary of State William Henry Seward succeeded in buying from Russia (1867) for 2 cents an acre only 30 years before the KLONDIKE gold rush.

Sex and Morality   (1966) A report commissioned by the British Council of Churches, which took a very liberal view on problems of sexual morality.

SF   Common abbreviation for Science Fiction.

SGHWR   Initials standing for steam-generating heavy-water reactor; see WINFRITH.

Sgraffito ware   A type of pottery, probably of Italian origin, in which colored clay is coated with clay of another color, and a design produced by cutting away the outer layer. (Italian, 'scratched'.)

's Gravenhage   Dutch name of The Hague.

Shackleton   British long-range maritime-reconnaisance aircraft developed from the LANCASTER, later fitted with an auxiliary jet engine to increase range; succeeded by NIMROD

AIRCRAFT.

Shadrach, Meshach and Abednego
Three Jews who refused to worship
the golden image set up by Nebuchadnezzar, and emerged unscathed
from the fiery furnace to which he
consigned them (*Daniel* iii, 12-30).

SHAEF Initials used for Supreme
Headquarters, Allied Expeditionary
Force, established in London early
in 1944 under General Eisenhower
to prepare for D-DAY.

Shakers, The (1747) A sect which
seceded from the QUAKERS and
formed a communistic settlement
near Albany, N.Y. They believed in
a male and a female Christ, the latter
being 'Mother Anne' who joined
them from Manchester in 1758. By
the 1860s the movement had died
out. The fashionable suburb of Sha-
ker Heights, Cleveland, O., was
named for a community founded
there in the early 19th century. (So
called because they trembled in religious ecstasy.)

Shakespeare Memorial Theatre The
old name of what is now the ROYAL
SHAKESPEARE THEATRE, Stratford on
Avon, England. See also STRATFORD
SHAKESPEAREAN FESTIVAL.

Shallow, Justice A fool of a JP, always boasting of his imaginary exploits, who appears in Shakespeare's
MERRY WIVES with his cousin Slender, a country bumpkin. He also
figures in HENRY IV *Part II* with his
fellow justice Silence.

Shamanism The belief that the
world is governed by good and evil
spirits which can be propitiated
through a *Shaman* (witch doctor).
The name was first applied to the
beliefs prevailing among the Ural-
Altaic peoples of Siberia, and then
to the Indians of Northwest America
and to others. (Word of Slavonic origin.)

Shambles, The A medieval street in
the center of York, England, which
has been associated with butchers
for a thousand years.

Shamrock The name of the 5 yachts
with which Sir Thomas Lipton
made successive attempts to win the
AMERICA'S CUP (1899-1930).

Shang dynasty (16th-11th centuries

BC) The earliest Chinese dynasty of
which we have any record; ritual
bronze vessels and jade work had
already reached a high standard of
artistry. See ANYANG.

Shangri La The name given by
James Hilton in his novel *Lost Hori-
zon* (1933) to a mythical Himalayan
UTOPIA.

Shannon Airport A transatlantic
airport, west of Limerick, on the
Shannon estuary, Co. Clare, Ireland.

Shans A MONGOLOID people of Burma, akin to the Siamese, who live in
the Shan States bordering on China,
Laos and Siam.

SHAPE Supreme Headquarters, Allied Powers, Europe, the military
headquarters of NATO, moved
(1967) to Casteaux, near Mons, Belgium.

Shape of Things to Come, The
(1933) H. G. Wells's novel giving a
glimpse of a science-dominated,
aseptic space age of the future.

Sharon Tate murders (1969) The
murder in California of the actress
Sharon Tate and 4 others, allegedly
by 5 persons (including 3 young
women). Arrests made in DEATH
VALLEY revealed that those charged
regarded themselves as hypnotized
slaves of Charles Manson, self-styled
Satan-God-Jesus, alleged leader of a
'family' of about 35 hippie drug addicts who claimed they stabbed their
rich victims to 'liberate' them. Five
other grotesque butcheries, apparently dictated by envy of riches or
personal spite, were also attributed
to this group.

Sharp, Becky The adventuress of
Thackeray's VANITY FAIR. A governess, she secretly marries her employer's son, Rawdon CRAWLEY, who is
disinherited; she, however, is kept
by Lord Steyne until forced abroad
to live by her wits. There she meets
again the man she first set her cap at,
Joseph SEDLEY, her school friend's
rich brother, and ruins him. See also
BECKY SHARP.

Sharpville shootings (Mar. 1960)
The shooting by Transvaal police
of 72 Pan-Africanist demonstrators
against the PASS LAWS. The banning
of the AFRICAN NATIONAL CONGRESS

followed this incident.

Shaston A town in Thomas Hardy's WESSEX novels, meant to represent Shaftesbury.

Shavian Adjective used in reference to George Bernard Shaw.

Shaw, T. E. The name T. E. Lawrence assumed when he joined the Tank Corps (1923), and subsequently adopted by deed poll. See J. H. ROSS.

Shawnee A nomadic race of Algonquian-speaking Indians, originally of eastern America; a few survive in Oklahoma. See TECUMSEH; The PROPHET.

Shaw's Corner G. B. Shaw's home at Ayot St Lawrence, Hertfordshire, from 1906 till his death, preserved by the NATIONAL TRUST.

Shays' Rebellion (1786-87) A revolt of debt-ridden farmers centered on Springfield, Mass., led by Daniel Shays, and quelled by State troops called in to protect the Springfield arsenal. Shays was later pardoned and some of his demands regarding tax, court fees and debt collection were met, but the main result was to emphasize the need for a strong Federal government.

She Rider Haggard's novel; see AYESHA.

Shearwater The only national class (1961) catamaran, a very popular type with one-design hulls; overall length 16 feet 6 inches. There are world and national championships.

Sheba, Queen of The Queen of ancient Sheba (the Yemen), who visited SOLOMON to see for herself whether the stories of his wisdom and riches were true (I Kings x, 1-13); according to Ethiopian tradition she bore him a son, David or Menelek, ancestor of the Abyssinians.

Sheffield plate (1743) Wares made in silver-plated copper (i.e. with sheets of sterling silver fused to a copper base), an English invention intended to provide a 'poor man's silver' but now highly prized. Many marks (e.g. 'Sheffield plated') on imitations were designed to mislead.

Sheldonian The Sheldonian Theatre, the OXFORD UNIVERSITY Senate House, designed by Wren. (Named after a 17th-century Archbishop.)

Shell See ROYAL DUTCH / SHELL.

Shell Chemicals (1959) A company now entirely independent from ROYAL DUTCH / SHELL.

Shell Transport and Trading The British parent company of ROYAL DUTCH / SHELL; there is a second, Dutch, parent.

Shem Eldest of Noah's sons, and traditional ancestor of the SEMITES.

'Shenandoah' An old capstan and windlass chantey with the words: 'Oh Shenandoah, I love your daughter; / Away, you rolling river'. The name is that of a famous Red Indian chief and of several rivers and a town called after him; but 'Shenandoah' and, later in the song, 'Missouri' were names arbitrarily chosen merely because they sounded good.

Shenandoah National Park (1935) A scenic park at the heart of the tree-covered Blue Ridge Mountains in northern Virginia, traversed by the SKYLINE DRIVE following the crests and affording magnificent views. See also BLUE RIDGE PARKWAY.

Shenyang The modern name of Mukden, former capital of MANCHURIA, now of the Liaoning Province of China.

Sheol A Babylonian and Hebrew name signifying both Death personified and the abode of the dead, regarded as a dark hollow ('pit') under the earth. The word was often mistranslated as 'Hell' in the AUTHORIZED VERSION of the Old Testament.

Shepheard's Hotel A famous hotel in Cairo which, as an exclusive rendezvous frequented by British 'imperialists', was burned down in the Black Saturday riots of 1952.

Shepherd Kings See HYKSOS KINGS.

Shepperton Studios The BRITISH LION film studios near Staines, one of which is the largest in Europe; there is also a giant tank for shooting sea scenes.

Sheraton Name given to furniture resembling designs published by Thomas Sheraton (1751-1806), who did not himself make furniture. Characteristic are satinwood, designs inspired by NEOCLASSICISM, slender elegance, tapering legs, and a preference for straight lines.

Sheriffmuir See FIFTEEN, THE.

Sherman (1942) A US cruiser tank of World War II: 30 tons, 400 h.p., 24 m.p.h.

Sherman Antitrust Act (1890) The first trust-busting Act, which forbade every monopolist combination in restraint of trade. Courts, presidents and state legislation saw to it that it became and remained inoperative. (John Sherman, Republican politician.)

Sherpas A MONGOLOID mountain race of Nepal, who have provided guides and carriers for many Himalayan expeditions. Tensing Norkey, a Sherpa, was the first man to reach the summit of Everest (with Hillary), in 1953.

Sherry Familiar name of Richard Brinsley Sheridan (1751-1816), Irish playwright and politician.

Sherry Cobbler Name given to a variety of drinks based on sweet sherry, with added port, spirit or liqueur, and decorated with fruit.

Sherston's Progress (1928-36) A trilogy of fictionalized autobiography by Siegfried Sassoon: *Memoirs of a Fox-hunting Man, Memoirs of an Infantry Officer* and *Sherston's Progress*; they depict the life of an English country gentleman in war and peace.

Sherwood Forest An ancient royal forest, mainly in Nottinghamshire and associated with ROBIN HOOD, of which patches still survive between Worksop and Nottingham.

She Stoops to Conquer (1773) Goldsmith's comedy in which the plot turns on 2 young men, Marlow and Hastings, misdirected by Tony LUMPKIN, mistaking Squire Hardcastle's house for an inn. See LIBERTY HALL.

Shetland pony A breed of small stocky hardy ponies, with long mane, tail and rough coat; also called Sheltie. (Originated in the Shetland Isles.)

Shiites (Shias) Members of one of the 2 major MUSLIM sects. They seceded from the orthodox SUNNITES because they do not recognize the authority of the Sunna or the first 3 Caliphs, regarding Muhammad's son-in-law Ali (fourth Caliph) as the first. They are found mainly in Persia. (Arabic *shi'ah*, 'sect'.)

Shiloh (1) A town in Palestine, near Jerusalem, where the ARK OF THE COVENANT was kept; Shiloh was destroyed by the Philistines. (2) A name for the Messiah.

Shiloh, Battle of (6-7 April 1862) The second major engagement of the Civil War, a bitter but indecisive battle between inexperienced troops with heavy losses on both sides; the Confederate general, A. S. Johnston, was killed. (Shiloh Church, near Pittsburg Landing, Tenn., on the Tennessee River opposite Corinth, Miss.)

Shinar, Plain of A Biblical name for Babylonia or MESOPOTAMIA.

Shinto Chinese name for the Japanese religion of ancestor and nature worship, to which were later added BUDDHISM and reverence for the Mikado as the descendant of the sun-goddess. After the MEIJI RESTORATION Shinto became state-sponsored, nationalistic and militaristic, but it was deflated after World War II by the Emperor Hirohito's public renunciation of his divinity. ('Way of the gods'.)

Ship of Fools (1962) A best-selling novel by Katherine Anne Porter, a Roman Catholic from Texas, published when she was nearly 70 and had been working on it for nearly 30 years. A microcosmic German ship sails from Mexico to Germany in 1931, with a JUNKER skipper, a priest, a mob orator, an anti-Semite, and proles in the steerage; by the end of the voyage they present a sorry spectacle. (Title from Sebastian Brant's poem in Alsatian dialect, published 1494.)

Shiraz rugs Rugs, similar to CAUCASIAN RUGS, made by the Kashkai nomads northwest of Shiraz, Persia. Diamond medallions are characteristic, and the red or blue grounds are rather garish.

Shire An English Midland breed of farm and cart horse, similar in color to the CLYDESDALE but coarser in build.

Shire, The The peaceful, pleasant HOBBIT country, based on the author's recollections of an unspoiled country district in the English West Midlands where he was brought up.

Shirley (1849) Charlotte Brontë's novel set in Yorkshire at the time of the LUDDITE RIOTS, in which the heroine, Shirley Keeldar, is based on the author's sister Emily.

Shock-Headed Peter See STRUWWEL-PETER.

Shogun Former title of the hereditary commander-in-chief of the Japanese army; see TOKUGAWA SHOGUNATE.

Sholem Aleichem The pen name of Solomon J. Rabinowitz (1859-1916), Russian-born author of highly praised humorous Jewish stories. See FIDDLER ON THE ROOF. (Yiddish for 'Peace be with you'.)

Shop, The (1) The former ROYAL MILITARY ACADEMY, Woolwich. (2) The London Stock Exchange.

Shoran A navigational aid system in which ships and aircraft use radar equipment to measure distances to 2 responder beacon stations. (For 'Short Range Navigation'; compare LORAN TOWERS.)

Shoreditch A former London metropolitan borough, since 1965 part of the borough of HACKNEY.

Shorthorn The most popular breed of English beef cattle, from which Polled Shorthorns and Dairy Shorthorns have also been developed; red and white in varying proportions, or roan.

Short Parliament (1640) A 4-week Parliament, the first convened by Charles I for 11 years, dismissed for being as stubborn as the ADDLED PARLIAMENT.

Shoshoni A group of PLAINS INDIANS speaking languages distantly related to that of the AZTECS, and once found in an area extending from Wyoming and Idaho to Mexico. Many of them were fighting tribes and several raided the Spanish for horses, which they introduced to the other PLAINS INDIANS from c. 1700. They included the UTE, COMANCHE, PIMA and HOPI.

Shotover, Capt. See HEARTBREAK HOUSE.

Shoulder Arms (1918) An early Charlie Chaplin comedy about life in the trenches in World War I.

Show Boat (1) Edna Ferber's novel (1926) about a theatrical family founded by the owner of a Mississippi showboat. (2) A highly successful musical (1927) based on it by Oscar Hammerstein and Jerome Kern. (A river steamboat equipped as a traveling theater to stage shows at stopping places.)

Show Me State Nickname of Missouri. See 'MISSOURI, I'M FROM'.

Show-off, The (1924) George Kelly's comedy satirizing American success stories.

Shrewsbury cake A rich sweet cracker, a speciality of Shrewsbury, Shropshire.

Shrine, The (1870) Short title of The Ancient Arabic Order of Nobles of the Mystic Shrine of North America, a secret fraternal society of KNIGHT'S TEMPLARS and 32nd-degree Masons who in various parts of the States parade in red fezzes and jewelled fancy dress to collect funds for its hospitals for crippled children of all races and creeds. (Originally it claimed descent from an ancient Arab secret society, as a gimmick in a worthy cause.)

Shrivenham The Royal Military College of Science, transferred from Woolwich in 1946, where officers of the Home and Overseas Services take courses in engineering and science. (Village near Swindon, Wiltshire.)

Shropshire Lad, A (1896) A. E. Housman's book of pastoral verse, noted for its brooding pessimism.

Shrovetide The 3 days before Lent, when Christians were shriven (i.e. made their confessions); it was marked by a final bout of festivities on Shrove Tuesday (the day before ASH WEDNESDAY), now represented only by the eating of pancakes in England; but see BATTLE OF FLOWERS; FASCHING; MARDI GRAS.

Shylock The Jewish moneylender of Shakespeare's *Merchant of Venice* who demands a pound of ANTONIO's flesh in default of repayment of a debt, and is foiled by PORTIA.

Sial (Geology) The relatively light rocks (e.g. granite) forming the continents; see SIMA. (Coined from their

characteristic elements, silicon and
aluminum.)

Siam An alternative name for Thailand.

Sian incident (1936) Chiang Kaishek was kidnapped by his own
deputy in a (successful) attempt to
persuade him to form a common
front with the Chinese Communists
against Japan; this coup is said to
have been suggested by Stalin.

SIB Initials used for the Special Investigations Branch of the Royal
Military Police, who investigate
cases of serious crime in the army,
and also operate during peacetime
crises such as those in recent years
in Cyprus and Aden.

Siberian Husky A sledge dog, usually gray with white and black markings, weighing 40-65 lbs, rather
smaller than the ESKIMO DOG. It is in
common use in Alaska, and is also
trained for military purposes.

Sibylline Books (1) Books of prophecies bought from the Cumaean Sibyl
(priestess of APOLLO's temple near
Naples) by King Tarquin of Rome.
Accidentally burned, they were replaced by a new version compiled
from other sources, itself burned in
Nero's reign. The Romans consulted
them in times of crisis. (2) A collection of Jewish and Christian prophecies compiled in the 2nd century AD
and much consulted in the Middle
Ages.

Sicilian Vespers, The (1282) A revolt against the harsh rule of Charles
I of ANJOU, King of the TWO SICILIES,
in which the Sicilians massacred the
French troops as the bells tolled for
vespers on Easter Monday. They
then summoned the help of the Aragonese of Spain, who took the place
of the Angevin rulers.

Sick Man of Europe A name for
Turkey in its 19th-20th century decline. See EASTERN QUESTION.

SID Initials standing for Space Intruder Detector, a burglar alarm
which, using a VHF transmitter and
receiver, reports movement anywhere in a building.

Sidcott A fireproof and waterproof
overall flying suit. (From name of
designer, Sid Cotton.)

'Sidewalks of New York, The'
(1894) A song with words by James
W. Blake and music by Charles Lawlor, which became widely popular
and is now the unofficial anthem of
New York City. 'East Side, West
Side', the opening line of the refrain,
is an alternative title.

Sidewinder US Navy's solid-fuel
air-to-air missile, mounted in Starfighters; it was used by the Chinese
Nationalists of FORMOSA against
China in 1958.

Sidhe Irish name for fairies. ('People
of the hills'.)

Sidney Street siege (1911) The
'siege' by a handful of troops of a
house in Sidney Street, Whitechapel, London, where some foreign
anarchists were resisting arrest.
Winston Churchill, then Home Secretary, watched the proceedings,
and was accused by political opponents of courting publicity by doing so.

Sidon, HMS A submarine which
sank at Portland, England (1955)
after an explosion.

Sidonia The enormously rich Spanish Jew who appears in Disraeli's
CONINGSBY and TANCRED. A banker
and philosopher, cold and aloof, he
is said to be based partly on one of
the Rothschild family and partly on
the author himself.

Siegfried (Sigurd) A hero of Scandinavian myth who seized the NIBELUNGS' gold from Fafnir. In the NIBELUNGENLIED he is a prince of the
lower Rhine who, aided by a cloak
of invisibility, wins BRUNHILD for
GUNTHER, who gives him his sister
KRIEMHILD in marriage. He is killed
by HAGEN.

Siegfried Idyll (1870) Wagner's
exquisite serenade for small orchestra, on themes from the finale of his
RING OF THE NIBELUNGS opera Siegfried; written as a surprise birthday
present for Cosima (whom he had
married that year) and also to celebrate the birth of their son Siegfried,
it was not intended for publication.

Siegfried Line (1) In World War I,
another name for the HINDENBURG
LINE. (2) In World War II, the British
name for the WEST WALL.

Siegfried's Journey (1938-45) A 3-volume autobiography by Siegfried Sassoon, covering the same period as SHERSTON'S PROGRESS.

Siemens, House of (1847) A German firm engaged in all branches of electronics and electrical engineering, from microminiature devices to power stations. It has close links with Bosch (household appliances) and AEG-Telefunken (high-voltage current production).

Sigma Delta Chi A US honorary press fraternity.

Sigma Xi (1886) A US fraternity or 'honor society' for those distinguished in the field of scientific research.

Sikes, Bill A generic term for a burglar, from the associate of FAGIN in OLIVER TWIST, who murders his mistress, Nancy.

Sikhs An Indian religious sect of the PUNJAB founded by Guru Nanak at the end of the 15th century. He tried, unsuccessfully, to bring Hindu and MUSLIM together under one monotheistic religion which rejected the Hindu caste system. In the 17th century the Sikhs developed into a military race fighting against MOGUL rule. They have since provided the British Army with soldiers as renowned as the GURKHAS, identifiable by their distinctive turban, beard and comb. See GRANTH. (Hindu, 'disciple'.)

Silas Lapham, The Rise of (1885) Dean Howells's best novel, in which Silas, who has made his pile in the sawmills, tries to move into Boston society; he finds the going very hard, and learns more about ethics than etiquette; meanwhile his daughter finds her own way to happiness.

Silas Marner (1861) GEORGE ELIOT'S novel in which Silas, a village weaver embittered by a false accusation of theft, turns recluse and miser. His faith in God is restored through chancing upon and bringing up a foundling girl, Eppie, who remains true to him even when her father comes to claim her many years later.

Silent Majority, The A term used in 1969 by Vice-President Spiro Agnew for students, trade unionists etc. who oppose left-wing agitation, but only silently, thus leaving the field clear for small but vociferous minorities of troublemakers to claim majority backing.

'Silent Night' (1818) A carol composed by an Austrian village schoolmaster, which became world famous. (Original title, 'Heilige Nacht', 'holy night'.)

Silent Spring, The (1963) Rachel Carson's book which first awakened the lay world to the destruction of wildlife and the danger to human life resulting from man's vastly increased use of chemical pesticides and weed killers.

Silenus In Greek mythology, a drunken old coward who accompanies DIONYSUS.

Silesia A former region of PRUSSIA (and to a less extent of Austria), fertile and rich in minerals, divided into Upper (eastern) Silesia, capital Katowice, and Lower (western) Silesia, capital Breslau (Wroclaw). In 1919 part was ceded to Poland and Czechoslovakia; in 1945 the rest of it east of the ODER-NEISSE LINE was ceded to Poland. Both countries expelled the German inhabitants. (Polish, Slask; Czech, Slezsko.)

Silk Road The ancient trade route linking China and Europe via Bokhara, Samarkand and a series of oases across the deserts north of Tibet to Peking. Chinese merchants carried silk to the West and brought back amber.

Silly Season Traditionally August, when daily papers, short of news in the holiday season, would blow up any trivial incident to make a headline. The years 1914 and 1939 have rather dented the tradition.

Silurian Period The third period of the PALEOZOIC ERA, lasting from about 450 to 410 million years ago. Fossils for the first time become abundant. (Latin *Silures*, Welsh tribe of the Ludlow border area, where the rocks of this period were first studied.)

Silver Box, The (1907) Galsworthy's first play, about a charwoman, Mrs Jones, at the house of a Liberal MP whose son, when drunk, unknowingly brings the char's husband into the house one night. Jones steals the silver cigarette box of the title.

Silver Ghost (1907-27) A famous early Rolls-Royce car, an exceptionally silent 6-cylinder 40/50 model made for 20 years almost without change.

Silver Ring (UK) The cheaper enclosure at a racetrack; so named because its patrons would normally bet in silver coins rather than in the golden guineas of TATTERSALL's.

Silver Star US armed forces award for gallantry in action not warranting the award of the MEDAL OF HONOR or the DISTINGUISHED SERVICE CROSS.

Silver State A nickname for Nevada, on account of the COMSTOCK LODE.

Silverstone (1948) The auto-racing circuit near Towcester, Northamptonshire, which became the chief British circuit after BROOKLANDS and Donington were closed; often the venue for the British GRAND PRIX.

Silver Vaults, The An underground arcade of small shops beneath Chancery Lane, London, where antique silver is sold.

Sima (Geology) The dense, heavy rocks (e.g. basalt) under the oceans and under SIAL. (Coined from their characteristic elements, *s*ilicon and *m*agnesium.)

Simbas Name given to the Congolese rebels who under Gizenga waged guerrilla war on the government in 1964 in the Stanleyville area.

Simca-Ford The French automobile firm, with a large factory at Poissy, northwest of Paris.

Simnel Rebellion (1487) A Yorkist attempt to place a rogue named Lambert Simnel on the English throne as Edward VI. A force of Irishmen and Flemish mercenaries was defeated at Stoke on Trent by Henry VII.

Simon Boccanegra (1857) Verdi's somber opera, full of sinister plotting but not without lighter touches.

Simon Fraser University (SFU) A new Canadian university built on top of Burnaby Mountain near Vancouver, British Columbia; sometimes called the 'instant university' as it is open all the year round, with

3 long terms, to expedite the production of graduates.

Simon Magus A sorcerer of Samaria mentioned in *Acts* viii, 18-21, as having offered Peter and John money for the power of laying on hands (hence 'simony', trafficking in ecclesiastical offices). Many legends were later added to this story.

Simon Population Trust (1961) (UK) Founded to promote research and action on the problems of world population in relation to world resources. (1st Baron Simon of Wythenshawe.)

Simon report (1930) A report on India which recommended the replacement of Dyarchy by responsible provincial government and the retention of separate ('communal') electorates for the various religious and racial communities. (Sir John Simon.)

Simplicissimus (1896) A satirical German periodical famous for its savage cartoons of Queen Victoria during the BOER WAR period, and of the German military caste.

Simplon express An evening train from Paris via the Simplon Tunnel, Milan and Rome (reached at lunchtime) to Naples (afternoon).

Sinbad the Sailor A merchant mariner in the ARABIAN NIGHTS who recounts a series of tall stories of magical adventures on his voyages. In one, he kills the OLD MAN OF THE SEA, in others he encounters the ROC, a bird with a wingspan which enables him to carry off elephants to his nest.

Singhalese The INDO-EUROPEAN LANGUAGE of southern Ceylon, closely related to PALI but with many borrowings from DRAVIDIAN LANGUAGES. Attempts to impose it on the TAMIL population as the only official language have led to much unrest. Also spelled Sinhalese.

Sing Sing (1825) A state prison at Ossining, New York.

Sinister Street (1913-14) Compton Mackenzie's 2-volume autobiographical novel of childhood, school and OXFORD UNIVERSITY, giving an insight into the minds of the young people who were shortly to be plunged into World War I.

Sinn Fein (1902) An Irish nationalist organization founded by Arthur Griffith; in the 1918 election most Irish seats were won by its candidates, who declined to go to Westminster and formed an unofficial DÁIL; in 1921 they accepted PARTITION and DOMINION STATUS. (Erse, 'ourselves alone'.)

Sino- The combining form for the word 'Chinese', as in 'Sino-Soviet dispute'. (From the Greek name for the Chinese.)

Sino-Tibetan languages A family of languages with 2 main divisions: (1) Siamese and Chinese; (2) Burmese, Tibetan and Nepalese.

Sioux A DAKOTA tribe of American Indians, once found from Saskatchewan to southern USA.

Sioux State Nickname of North Dakota.

Sioux Wars (1) The war of 1862-68, when SITTING BULL led attacks on whites in Iowa and Minnesota during the Civil War and was finally forced to accept Sioux reservation in Dakota Territory. (2) The war of 1875-76, caused by threatened encroachments on their new reserves. Allied with the CHEYENNE, Sitting Bull and Crazy Horse won the Battle of Little Big Horn (CUSTER'S LAST STAND) in 1876, but were eventually defeated.

Sirdar Title of the British governor and commander-in-chief of Egypt (1882-1936). (Urdu-Persian, 'chief commander'.)

Sirens In Greek legend, 2 sea nymphs who lure sailors to destruction by the beauty of their singing. ODYSSEUS got by through tying himself to the mast and filling the ears of his crew with wax. This so upset the Sirens that they drowned themselves. In URN BURIAL Sir Thomas Browne rashly says: What song the Syrens sang . . . is not beyond all conjecture.

Sirius The Dog Star, the brightest star in the heavens, in CANIS MAJOR; it has a companion star, a WHITE DWARF. (Greek, 'scorching'.)

'Sir Patrick Spens' A 15th-century historical ballad beginning: 'The king sits in Dunfermline town /

Drinking the blude-red wine'. The king sends Sir Patrick ('the best sailor that ever sail'd the seas') to fetch the King of Noroway's daughter, but the ship sinks with all hands.

Sir Winston Churchill, HMS The Royal Navy's fourth Fleet submarine, see VALIANT SUBMARINES.

SIS Initials standing for (British) Secret Intelligence Service, an older name for MI-6.

Sisera The captain of the Canaanite army who was defeated by Barak. Jael offered him asylum in her tent and then killed him by nailing his head to the ground while he slept (Judges iv, 21). See DEBORAH.

Sister Aimee Aimee Semple Macpherson, who founded the PENTECOSTAL Fundamentalist International Church of the Four-Square Gospel in Los Angeles. At her temple, thousands received total immersion. In 1926 she began to hint at her imminent demise and then disappeared, only to return with a story of having been kidnapped, but was later alleged to have stayed at various places under assumed names with a boyfriend. In 1944 she died of an overdose of drugs.

Sister Anne The phrase 'Sister Anne, Sister Anne, do you see no one coming?' was uttered by BLUEBEARD's last wife when anxiously awaiting rescue by her brothers.

Sistine Chapel The Pope's private chapel adjoining St Peter's, Rome, decorated with Michelangelo's ceiling fresco of the Creation, and his 'LAST JUDGMENT'. (Named after Pope Sixtus IV.)

Sistine Madonna Raphael's 'Madonna' (1513), formerly at Dresden, now in Russian possession. (Named after the Church of St Sixtus, Piacenza, where it once was.)

Sisyphus In Greek legend, a man who for his crimes on earth is condemned to roll up a hill a huge stone which always rolls back before he gets to the top. Hence a Sisyphean task, an unending task on which immense energy is expended with little to show for it.

Sittang River disaster (Feb. 1942) An incident during the Japanese invasion of Burma. Orders were prematurely given to blow up the only bridge across the river before the main body of British and Indian troops had reached it in their retreat.

Sitting Bull The SIOUX (DAKOTA) chief who after CUSTER'S LAST STAND (see SIOUX WARS) fled to Canada, returned in 1881, and was killed 9 years later by police who were trying to arrest him. (More accurately, his name was 'The Bull in possession'.)

Siva, Shiva One of the 2 main gods of modern HINDUISM, and one of the Trinity formed with VISHNU and BRAHMA. He is the ruthless destructive principle in life, and also the regenerative force that follows destruction; often represented with 4 arms, 3 eyes or several faces. He also appears as the consort of KALI, worshiped as a phallic god, especially at BENARES.

Siwash (1) Cowboys' disparaging term, derived from the CHINOOK language, for American Indians, especially in northwestern USA. (2) US generic nickname (often 'Old Siwash') for small provincial colleges or universities.

Six, The A name for the member countries of the COMMON MARKET.

Six Characters in Search of an Author (1921) Pirandello's play in which actors rehearsing an earlier play of his are interrupted by 6 people claiming to be the characters in it; they want to add to the play parts left out by the author. Unfortunately, their versions of the same events differ widely, and all ends in a tangle of illusions and illusions of illusions, which takes some sorting out.

Six Counties, The Northern Ireland, which consists of 6 of the counties of ULSTER.

Six-day War (1967) Between Israel and Egypt (supported by Jordan, Syria, Lebanon and Iraq). In May Egypt had secured the withdrawal of the UN force on the Israeli border and closed the Gulf of Aqaba to Israel. On June 5th Israel opened a preemptive blitzkrieg by destroying first the air forces (in a matter of hours) and then the armies of Egypt, Jordan and Syria. Nasser accepted a cease-fire on the 8th but Israel, alleg-

ing breaches of it, continued to attack Syria until the 10th. Israel conquered the West Bank of Jordan (with 650,000 inhabitants), the GAZA STRIP and Sinai peninsula (to the Suez Canal), the old city of Jerusalem and the Golan Heights in Syria. Some 2-300,000 Arabs became refugees; Israel lost 803 dead. The Arabs, because of an apparently genuine misunderstanding, falsely accused the US and UK of providing air cover for the Israeli attack. The Soviet Union supported the Arabs.

16th Amendment (1913) The amendment to the US Constitution which introduced Federal Income Tax.

Sixth Commandment 'Thou shalt not kill' (*Exodus* xx, 13). To Roman Catholics this is the Fifth Commandment.

Sixty-four-dollar question The crucial question. (The highest award in the CBS radio quiz show "Take It or Leave It', 1941-48.)

Sizewell (UK) The site of a very large nuclear power station; one unit began to operate in 1968. (Coastal village north of Aldeburgh, Suffolk.)

SJ Initials placed after their names by members of the Society of Jesus (i.e. JESUITS).

Skate, USS A nuclear-powered submarine, in 1959 the first to surface at the North Pole, and later the first to cross the Atlantic both ways submerged.

Skaters, The English name for *Les Patineurs*, a ballet arranged by Constant Lambert with music from several of Meyerbeer's operas, especially from the skating scene which appears incongruously in *Le Prophète*, an opera about an ANABAPTIST'S martyrdom. Frederick Ashton did the choreography.

Skelmersdale (1962) (UK) A NEW TOWN in Lancashire, west of Wigan, designed to take 80,000 inhabitants.

Skerryvore (1844) A lighthouse and rock southwest of Tiree Island in the Inner Hebrides off the coast of Mull. The light is 158 ft above sea level.

Sketch Book, The (1819) A collection of tales and sketches by Washington Irving (writing as 'Geoffrey Crayon, Gent.'). It includes the earliest American short stories, e.g. RIP VAN WINKLE, LEGEND OF SLEEPY HOLLOW, together with sketches of English landscape and customs.

SKF Initials used for the Swedish Ball-Bearing Co., which also makes roller bearings, steel and castings, and has mines and ironworks of its own. (Svenska Kullagerfabriken.)

Skid Row A district or community of people 'on the skids', i.e. at or near the bottom of the downward path. (From the 'Skid Road' in Seattle, made of greased logs over which lumbermen skidded timber; 'road' corrupted to 'row'.)

Skimpole, Harold A character in Dickens's BLEAK HOUSE, supposed to represent Leigh Hunt. An artist of charm but completely self-centered, he assumes that his friends will always be happy to help him out of his perennial financial difficulties and will not expect to be thanked for it.

Skin Game, The (1920) Galsworthy's play about the efforts of the nouveau riche industrialist, Hornblower, to gain social recognition by the aristocratic Hillcrists. Failing, he threatens to build a factory to ruin the view from the Hillcrists' mansion; a by-product of the struggle is the attempted suicide of a girl used as a pawn in it.

'Skipper Ireson's Ride' (1857) A dialect poem of Whittier's describing the tarring and feathering of a skipper who had left his crew to drown, carried out by the angry widows of Marblehead, Mass.

Skopje (Skoplje) Capital of MACEDONIA, Yugoslavia. Almost completely destroyed by an earthquake in 1963, it is being rebuilt on an adjacent site. Formerly known by its Turkish name, Üsküb.

Skua (UK) A rocket designed by Bristol Aero Jets Ltd for the Meteorological Office's space probes launched from the South Uist rocket range.

Skull and Bones (1832) The oldest of the senior secret societies at YALE.

Skybolt US air-to-ground nuclear ballistic missile, the development of which was abandoned (1962), creating a crisis in Britain to whom it had

been promised. The seaborne POLARIS was offered as a substitute at the NASSAU CONFERENCE.

'Skye Boat Song' A song about Bonnie Prince Charlie; the air is based on an old sea chantey, the words by Sir Harold Boulter (1859-1935): 'Speed, bonny boat, like a bird on the wing . . . / Over the sea to Skye'. R. L. Stevenson wrote another version.

Skylark A British solid-fuel research rocket used during the IGY, and made by BAC for ESRO; altitude 95 miles.

Skyline Drive A 105-mile road with exceptionally extensive views, running the length of the SHENANDOAH NATIONAL PARK, Va., along the watershed from Front Royal in the north to Jarman Gap in the south.

Skynet A series of British but US-built communications satellites launched by the US Air Force, to provide reliable long-distance defense communications between London and overseas units. The first, in stationary orbit over the western Indian Ocean, was launched in 1969.

Slade School (1871) A school of art, now attached to UNIVERSITY COLLEGE, LONDON University. (Named after Felix Slade, art collector, died 1868.

Slant Group A Roman Catholic group, mainly of Cambridge graduates, who advocate a Marxist or Socialist approach to Christianity.

Slaughter on Tenth Avenue (1936) A satirical modernistic ballet in the musical On Your Toes, choreographed by Balanchine, music by Richard Rodgers.

Slavonic languages A group of INDO-EUROPEAN LANGUAGES including Russian, Polish, Ukrainian, Bulgarian, and the languages of Czechoslovakia and Yugoslavia.

Slavs A people of Asian origin who, by settling round the inaccessible Pripet marshes in Russia managed to keep out of the way of successive invasions of Europe for hundreds of years. About the 5th century AD they began to migrate to south Russia, to the Balkans, and via Hungary to the Baltic coast. They were the ancestors of the numerous peoples who speak

SLAVONIC LANGUAGES.

Slazenger Championship (1946) A professional lawn tennis championship played at Devonshire Park, Eastbourne, England.

Slazenger Trophy A golf contest between Britain and a team representing the Commonwealth and Empire; it comprises foursomes and singles.

'Sleeping Beauty, The' A fairy tale of a princess put into an enchanted sleep in her father's castle, round which a dense forest springs up to protect her. A good fairy arranges that after 100 years she shall be waked by a kiss from a handsome prince brave enough to penetrate the forest. The earliest version is in Perrault's collection and is entitled 'La Belle au bois dormant'.

Sleeping Beauty, The (1889) Tchaikovsky's ballet, which introduces various figures from nursery tales, e.g. LITTLE RED RIDINGHOOD, CINDERELLA, PUSS IN BOOTS.

'Sleeping Gypsy' (1897) A large and imaginative painting by the Douanier Rousseau. (Museum of Modern Art, NYC.)

Sleep of Prisoners, A (1951) A religious verse drama by Christopher Fry, designed to be produced in a church.

Slivovitz A plum brandy made in Yugoslavia and Hungary.

Sloan (Alfred P.) Foundation (1934) A large foundation which makes grants to promote education and research in economics, business management, physics and medicine, and also for general purposes in such institutions as MIT, COLUMBIA and New York Universities etc.

Slope, Mr In the BARCHESTER NOVELS, Bishop Proudie's scheming hypocrite of a chaplain who dares to dispute the hegemony established by Mrs PROUDIE over her husband and the diocese—a forlorn enterprise.

Slough of Despond The quagmire into PILGRIM'S PROGRESS into which CHRISTIAN flounders, unable to escape unaided because of the burden of sin on his back.

Slovak The SLAVONIC LANGUAGE spoken in eastern Czechoslovakia

(in Slovakia and south Moravia, a region formerly under Hungary), closely allied to Czech.

Slovenian The SLAVONIC LANGUAGE spoken in northwest Yugoslavia (a region formerly under Austria), akin to SERBO-CROAT but more archaic.

Slump, The (1930s) Colloquial term for the worldwide effects of the WALL STREET CRASH. Also called the (Great) DEPRESSION.

Small Back Room, The (1943) Nigel Balchin's novel about the back-room boys or boffins, i.e. men engaged on secret scientific research in wartime.

Small Business Administration (1935) A US government agency that grants or guarantees long-term loans for small businesses.

Smelfungus Sterne's name in his SENTIMENTAL JOURNEY for Smollett, whom he represents as an ill-tempered traveler.

Smerdyakov See The BROTHERS KARAMOZOV.

Smersh According to Ian Fleming's *From Russia with Love* (a James BOND novel), the nickname among its personnel for the 'Soviet murder organization, operating at home and abroad'. (Said to be from Russian *Smeart Spionam*, 'death to spies'.)

Smitane (Cooking) With sour cream and onions.

Smith (1871) One of the SEVEN SISTERS colleges, at Northampton, Mass.

Smith Act (1940) An Act to suppress Fascist organizations in the US.

Smith (W.H.) & Son Award An annual literary prize of $2400 for the most outstanding contribution to literature by a British or Commonwealth author.

Smith & Wesson (1852) The first successful automatic-ejecting revolver, made at Springfield, Mass. The same firm later developed high-velocity Magnum models of .38 and (1956) .44 caliber.

Smith-Connally Act (1943) A wartime antistrike Act making the instigation of strikes in US government factories or in mines a criminal offense.

Smithfield ham Uncooked ham cut with the long shank attached, dry-cured, cold-smoked, and aged by hanging. (Smithfield, southeast Virginia.)

Smithfield Market A historic London market, now specializing in meat and poultry.

Smithsonian Institution (1846) An institution at Washington, D.C., which comprises a national museum (mainly of ethnology and zoology), zoo, art gallery and an astrophysical observatory. (Endowed by James Smithson, mineralogist, illegitimate son of a Duke of Northumberland.)

Smith Square The London square where the headquarters of all the three main British political parties are situated.

Smoke, The A name for London, also called the Great (or Big) Smoke.

Smokey the Bear The admonitory figure on National Park notices who warns against the dangers of forest fires; e.g. 'Smokey the Bear says "Put out your cigarette"'.

Smyrna Ancient Greek port in Asia Minor, now Turkish and known as Izmir. `

SNAP Initials used for Systems for Nuclear Auxiliary Power, the US ATOMIC ENERGY COMMISSION'S program to develop nuclear generators and reactors for use in space, on land or at sea. On the second moon landing *Apollo 12* left behind a collection of instruments (ALSEP, Apollo Lunar Surface Experiments Package) powered by SNAP-27 (using plutonium-238) for continuous 1-year operation. See also NIMBUS.

Snark A US robot-controlled pilotless bomber.

Snark, The The creature sought by the BELLMAN's crew in Lewis Carroll's poem *The Hunting of the Snark*. Some Snarks have feathers and bite, other have whiskers and scratch, but the only kind to dread is the BOOJUM.

SNCC Initials of the STUDENT NONVIOLENT COORDINATING COMMITTEE.

Snick Abbreviation used for the STUDENT NONVIOLENT COORDINATING COMMITTEE.

Snipe An international class of dinghy, the largest one-design class in the world, 15 feet 6 inches overall

and rather sluggish; designed in Florida in 1931.

Sno-cat A treaded vehicle used to draw sled trains in the Antarctic.

Snodgrass, Augustus The poetical young companion of Pickwick, in Dickens's novel.

Snoopy (1) The widely read (but unfortunately voiceless) canine philosopher of PEANUTS, subject to wild fantasies in which he is a World War I air ace scouring the skies for the RED BARON, the subject of songs and a musical. (2) Astronauts' nickname for the APOLLO 10 LEM.

Snow Baby, The Eskimos' nickname for the daughter born in inhospitable northeast Greenland in 1893 to Commander Peary's wife, who accompanied him on several of his exploring expeditions.

Snowball A character in Orwell's ANIMAL FARM who represents Trotsky.

Snowball A mixture of Advocaat and a lemon drink.

Snow-Bound (1866) Whittier's long poem giving a classic picture of winter life in rural Massachusetts, based on his own boyhood memories.

Snowdonia (1951) The National Park surrounding Snowdon in North Wales.

'Snows of Kilimanjaro, The' (1938) Hemingway's outstanding short story about a writer on safari in Africa with his rich mistress; he contracts gangrene and as he lies dying he dreams of a huge frozen leopard on Mt Kilimanjaro, a symbol of his own destruction through failure to match his achievements to his ideals and talents.

Snow White and the Seven Dwarfs (1938) The first feature-length animated cartoon in color, made by Walt Disney.

Soanes Museum A collection of antiquities, pictures and architectural drawings exhibited in the founder's home at Lincoln's Inn Fields. (Sir John Soanes, British architect, died 1837.)

Soap Box Derby A race for boys 11–15 in which they drive homemade motorless vehicles down a sloping course. Local winners compete in August at Akron, Ohio, for scholarships and savings bonds.

Soap opera A radio or TV serial with stock domestic situations, often melodramatic or sentimental. (Probably as often formerly sponsored by soap manufacturers.)

Sobranje The Bulgarian elective national assembly. (Bulgarian, 'assembly'.)

Social Contract, The (1762) Jean-Jacques Rousseau's plea for government by the whole sovereign people, in whose natural goodness he believed. It contains the phrase: 'Man is born free and is everywhere in chains'. Rousseau was the Karl Marx of the FRENCH REVOLUTION.

Social Credit An economic theory advanced by a Canadian, Major C. H. Douglas, suggesting that universal prosperity could be based on the payment to all of an annual 'national dividend' varying with a country's wealth. See next entry.

Social Credit Party (1920) A Canadian political party at first advocating SOCIAL CREDIT, now abandoned; in power in Alberta since 1935, and later in British Columbia.

Social Democrats The name adopted in 1869 by a German party which accepted Marxist theory but rejected Marxist revolutionary strategy. It has been used since by parties in many countries which are prepared to work for Marxist ends by democratic means through parliament, i.e. by patiently undermining, rather than violently overthrowing, Capitalism. Their international organization is the Socialist or SECOND INTERNATIONAL.

'Socialism in one country' The doctrine of Lenin and Stalin, vigorously opposed by Trotsky; see TROTSKYISM.

'Socialism in our time' (UK) The slogan with which Ramsay MacDonald won the 1929 general election, only 2 years before almost the whole Labour Party accused him of abandoning Socialism altogether.

Socialist International See SECOND INTERNATIONAL.

Socialist Realism The form of art and literature officially approved by the Soviet government, typified by pictures of muscle-bound workmen wielding axes, and stories of muscle-bound workmen sacrificing all to reach a productivity norm.

Socialist Sixth of the World, The See RED DEAN.

Social Realism A movement in the art and literature of Western countries, unconnected with SOCIALIST REALISM. The American name 'ASH-CAN SCHOOL' and the English, 'Kitchen Sink school', indicate its content; its aim is emphatic criticism of modern Western urban society.

Social Register Trademark title for publications listing the socialites of a city or region, giving their addresses, clubs etc.

Social Security, Ministry of (1966) (UK) A merger of the Ministry of Pensions and National Insurance and the National Assistance Board; its Supplementary Benefits section handles both contributory and noncontributory benefits, thus removing any invidious distinction between payments by right and charity to the poor. In 1968 it was further merged with the Ministry of Health.

Social Security Act (1935) One of the NEW DEAL measures; it introduced old-age pensions and unemployment benefits, financed by taxes on employers and employees.

Social Surveys (Gallup Polls) Ltd. See BRITISH INSTITUTE OF PUBLIC OPINION.

Society for Psychical Research (SPR) A body set up in London in 1882 to investigate all paranormal phenomena, including hypnotism, in a scientific spirit.

Socony Mobil Co. See MOBIL OIL CORPORATION.

Socratic irony The pretense of ignorance by a teacher, designed to encourage pupils to air their own views and thus display their own real ignorance; a major feature of the SOCRATIC METHOD.

Socratic method A method of instruction peculiar to Socrates; he would put a series of questions so chosen as to force his pupils step by step to the one logical solution of the problem posed, a process Plato called 'midwifery'. See last entry.

Sodom, Apple of See DEAD SEA FRUIT.

Sodom and Gomorrah (1) The Cities of the Plain destroyed by fire and brimstone for their wickedness, and now lying beneath the Dead Sea. (*Genesis* xviii, 20-xix, 25.) (2) The title of Part iv of Proust's REMEMBRANCE OF THINGS PAST.

SOE See SPECIAL OPERATIONS EXECUTIVE.

Soho A section of London between Oxford Street, Shaftesbury Avenue and REGENT STREET, famous for foreign-cuisine (especially Italian) restaurants, delicatessens, street markets, traffic jams, call girls and crime. The first foreigners were 17th-century French HUGUENOT refugees. Soho Square was laid out in 1681. (Anglo-French hunting cry, *ça ho!*, uttered on sighting the quarry.)

Sohrab and Rustum (1853) Matthew Arnold's epic fragment based on the legend of how Rustum, the Persian HERCULES, unwittingly killed his son Sohrab.

Soissonaise (Cooking) With French white beans (haricots blancs).

Sol Roman sun-god, equivalent to the Greek HELIOS.

Solanaceae The nightshade family, many members of which contain alkaloids, e.g. belladonna or atropine in deadly nightshade, hyoscine in henbane. Other members are the potato, tomato, capsicum, Cape gooseberry, tobacco plant, petunia, salpiglossis.

'Soldier, The' Rupert Brooke's poem beginning: If I should die, think only this of me: / That there's some corner of a foreign field / That is for ever England.

Soldier Field (1926) Large sports stadium at Chicago.

Soldiers, The Hochhuth's Theater of FACT (or rather in this case 'fact') play about the guilt of those who ordered the mass bombing of Germany; in it Churchill is accused of planning the air crash in which the Polish statesman Gen. Sikorsky was killed in 1943. The (British) NATIONAL THEATRE thought this a suitable play to stage; the LORD CHAMBERLAIN

disagreed.

Soldier's Medal A US Army award for services in peacetime or for heroism not involving actual conflict with the enemy; equivalent to the Navy and Marine Corps Medal and the Air Medal.

Soldiers Three (1888-89) Kipling's collection of early short stories about Ortheris, Learoyd and Mulvaney, serving in the Indian Army; they had already appeared in PLAIN TALES FROM THE HILLS.

Solemn League and Covenant See COVENANTERS.

Solera A system of blending sherry from wines of many vintage years; as a term on a bottle label it has no significance.

Solferino (1859) The second French victory over the Austrians in Italy (after MAGENTA); the casualties in both battles were so high on both sides that Napoleon III offered an armistice, which was accepted. The Red Cross owes its origin to the battle.

Solid South, The The Southern States, which until recent years could be relied on to vote solidly for the DEMOCRATIC PARTY.

Soling A Norwegian-designed 3-man glass-fiber keelboat which suddenly leaped into international and Olympic status in the late 1960s. It has a rigorous one-design specification, is far cheaper than the comparable DRAGON, and is essentially a yacht for young acrobats.

Solo (1955) A national class dinghy designed by Jack Holt, primarily for racing single-handed; overall length 12 feet 4½ inches.

Solomon Son of DAVID and BATHSHEBA, a King of ISRAEL of the 10th century BC who gained a legendary reputation for wisdom and wealth, not apparently justified by historical fact. See next 2 entries and SHEBA, QUEEN OF.

Solomon, Judgment of In a dispute between 2 harlots about the ownership of a child, King SOLOMON proposed to divide the child and give half to each. One woman agreed; the other begged the king to give it to her adversary rather than slay it, and was adjudged the true mother. (I Kings iii, 16-28.)

Solomon's Temple (1006 BC) The Israelites' chief temple, built by King SOLOMON (2 Chronicles iii) on Mount Zion, Jerusalem. Destroyed by Nebuchadnezzar (6th century BC), it was restored by Herod the Great (20 BC) and finally destroyed by Titus (AD 70). The site is now occupied by a mosque and the only remaining portion is the WAILING WALL.

Solutrean culture A period of the PALEOLITHIC AGE, perhaps lasting from 18,000 to 15,000 BC, during which the making of flint tools and spearheads was perfected. (La Solutré, near Mâcon, France.)

Solveig The peasant girl who loves PEER GYNT; her song was set to music by Grieg.

Somali A CUSHITE race (see HAMITES), originally and still mainly a nomadic cattle people of SOMALIA and French Somaliland; the Somali of northern Kenya and of Abyssinia occasionally agitate for union with Somalia.

Somalia (Somali Republic) Formed (1960) from the union of former British and Italian Somaliland.

Somerset Club An exclusive men's club in Boston.

Somerset Herald An officer of the COLLEGE OF ARMS.

Somerset House The Thames-side building which now houses the Board of Inland Revenue, Probate Registry, Registrar General's Office, and KING'S COLLEGE, LONDON UNIVERSITY. (Duke of Somerset, the PROTECTOR.)

Somerset Maugham Award A literary prize of $1200 awarded annually to a young British author who has published a literary work of outstanding promise; the money is intended to be used for travel.

Somerville (1879) A women's college at OXFORD UNIVERSITY.

'Something Has Gone Wrong with my Sister's Ideology' The hit song of a 1960s Chinese opera, Two Sisters on a Mountain.

Somme Battle (July-Nov. 1916) One of the costliest engagements of World War I, in which 60,000 were killed on the first day alone. The British used tanks for the first time, but in too few numbers and with too little faith in them. Cooperation between the RFC (the future RAF) and the army was another new feature. The battle achieved nothing.

Son et Lumière (1950s) A tourist attraction consisting of selective floodlighting of a famous building (such as the PARTHENON at Athens) synchronized with features of its history broadcast over loudspeakers to an outdoor audience. (French, 'sound and light'; first used by the French at the Loire châteaus.)

Song of Songs, The (3rd century BC) A collection of love songs which strayed into the Bible inadvertently. Early Christians expended much ingenuity on trying to assign allegorical meanings to them. Also called The Song of Solomon, but not the work of SOLOMON.

Song of the Earth, The (1908) Mahler's song cycle for solo voices and orchestra, with words translated from the Chinese. (German title, Das Lied von der Erde.)

'Song of the Shirt, The' (1843) Thomas Hood's poem about a poor drudge of a seamstress, 'Sewing at once with a double thread, / A shroud as well as a shirt'. The poem called attention to sweated labor in early 19th-century English cottage industries, and helped to improve conditions.

Sonnambula, La (1831) Bellini's opera about the adventures of the sleepwalking Amina when staying at an inn.

Sons and Lovers (1913) D. H. Lawrence's largely autobiographical novel of the Nottinghamshire coalfields where he was born, and of Paul Morel's (i.e. his own) emotional attachment to his mother.

Sons of Liberty (1765) A group of loosely knit, at first secret, organizations, particularly strong in Massachusetts and New York, which led the campaign against the STAMP ACT, playing a principal part in the BOSTON TEA PARTY and its sequel.

Sooner State Nickname of Oklahoma. (Sooners, those who evaded regulations and occupied the best land before the law-abiding arrived.)

Sopwith Camel (1917) A later development of the SOPWITH PUP, faster and with longer range.

Sopwith Pup (1916) The best-known of the British fighter aircraft of World War I. (Made by the firm founded by T. O. M. Sopwith, later chairman of the HAWKER SIDDELEY GROUP.)

Sorbonne, The (1253) The leading French university, in Paris. (Founded as a theological college by Richard de Sorbon.)

Sorcerer's Apprentice, The (1897) Dukas's symphonic scherzo, based on a ballad by Goethe. To save himself trouble, the Apprentice misuses his master's magic and finds himself overwhelmed by a flood of water which he is powerless to stop. (Translation of *L'Apprenti sorcier*.)

Sorel, Julien See Le ROUGE ET LE NOIR.

Sorge spy case The arrest by the Japanese and execution (1944) of Richard Sorge, German press correspondent in Japan, a member of the Nazi Party but also a Communist and Russian spy. He had supplied Russia with information on German plans before and after Hitler's attack on Russia.

Soroptimist clubs Women's clubs consisting of one member only from each profession or business. Members must be over 25 years old and of high standing in their calling. They engage in work for handicapped children, the aged and others in need of help. There is a Soroptimist International Association.

Sorrel, Hetty See ADAM BEDE.

Sorrows of Satan, The (1895) One of Marie Corelli's best-selling novels.

Sorrows of Young Werther, The (1774) Goethe's short sentimental novel in the form of letters, about a maundering German student who shoots himself because he cannot win his neighbor's wife.

Sotheby's London's chief auction rooms for antiques, paintings, first editions etc., situated in New Bond Street.

Soubise (Cooking) With onions.

Souchong Once a name associated with high-quality China tea; now a trade term for a grade of tea poorer than ORANGE PEKOE or Pekoe.

Sound of Music, The (1960) The last of the Rodgers and Hammerstein musicals (and movies), in which Maria, during a not very promising novitiate at the local nunnery, becomes governess to Captain Trapp's 7 children and with them escapes from the Austrian Nazis. Among many charming songs were 'My Favorite Things', 'Do-Re-Mi' and 'Edelweiss'.

Sourdough (Originally, in western USA) a prospector, pioneer; (Canada and Alaska) one who has spent more than one winter in the Arctic; an old-timer. (From their use of sourdough kept from one batch of baking to the next.)

Sousa marches Famous military marches composed by the bandmaster of the US Marines, J. P. Sousa (died 1932); among the best-known are 'Liberty Bell', 'STARS AND STRIPES FOREVER' and 'The Washington Post'.

Sous les Toits de Paris (1930) One of the earliest talkies of merit, made by René Clair, with a well-known accordion theme tune.

South African Wars (1) *First* (1881); caused by British vacillation over withdrawing from the Transvaal after helping to quell ZULU risings. The Boers inflicted a sharp defeat on a small British force at Majuba Hill and regained independence for the 2 Boer republics. (2) *Second*, see BOER WAR.

Southall (UK) A former municipal borough of MIDDLESEX, since 1965 part of the borough of EALING.

Southcottians Those who believed the claims of a Devonshire farm servant, Joanna Southcott (died 1814), to prophetic powers. She left a box, to be opened only in time of national crisis and in the presence of all the bishops. There was some public demand for this during World War I, but it was not till 1927 that a bishop could be found to assist in the ceremony. Inside were some odds and ends, including a pistol; but even this did not kill the legend.

South Devon (South Ham) cattle A large red dual-purpose breed, producing excellent beef, and milk from which Devonshire cream is made.

Southdown A breed of short-wool sheep noted for its meat and for its close fine wool which covers face and ears. It has been much used in producing the DOWN BREEDS. (Originally local to the Sussex Downs.)

Southeastern Conference A College Athletic Conference, comprising Alabama, Auburn, Florida, Georgia, Kentucky, LSU, Mississippi, Mississippi State, Tennessee, Vanderbilt.

Southern Christian Leadership Conference (1954) A Negro civil rights movement begun by Martin Luther King; it supported the NAACP and organized such demonstrations as the MONTGOMERY BUS BOYCOTT. See RESURRECTION CITY.

Southern Cross (Crux Australis) The most conspicuous constellation of the southern hemisphere, within the Antarctic Circle, with 4 bright stars forming a cross. It contains the Coalsack, a dark nebula.

Southern Cross (1928) The name of the FOKKER monoplane used in the first transpacific flight, made by the pioneer Australian airman Sir Charles Kingsford-Smith.

Southern 500 The last major stock-car race of the season, run in September at Darlington raceway, Darlington, SC, the birthplace of stock-car racing. See NASCAR RACING.

Southern Rhodesia The colony which became Rhodesia when Northern Rhodesia was renamed ZAMBIA. See UDI.

Southern TV The commercial company serving southern England, and owned by the RANK ORGANIZATION, ASSOCIATED NEWSPAPERS and D. C. Thomson.

Southgate (UK) A former municipal borough of MIDDLESEX, since 1965 part of the borough of ENFIELD.

South Pacific (1949) A Rodgers and Hammerstein musical (made into a movie in 1958), with a love story in a Pacific island setting peopled by US sailors during World War II, and adapted from James A. Michener's PULITZER-PRIZE winning *Tales of the South Pacific.* Among the many endearing songs were 'Bali Ha'i', 'Some Enchanted Evening', 'I'm Gonna Wash That Man Right Outa My Hair' and 'A Wonderful Guy'.

South Riding (1936) Winifred Holtby's best-selling novel about her native Yorkshire; also a movie made from it.

South Sea Bubble (1720) The collapse of the South Sea Co. formed in 1711 to trade with Spanish America on the favorable terms expected to result from the ASIENTO and the Treaty of UTRECHT. Speculation in its stocks reached frenzied heights and created the atmosphere for the floating of numerous harebrained schemes in other spheres (see MISSISSIPPI BUBBLE). The inevitable crash involved the government, the royal family and thousands of small investors, and brought Sir Robert Walpole to power.

South Tirol See ALTO ADIGE.

Southwark Inner London borough since 1965 consisting of the former metropolitan boroughs of Southwark, Bermondsey and Camberwell.

Southwest Conference A College Athletic Conference, comprising Arkansas, Baylor, Texas, Texas A & M, Texas Tech, TCU, Rice, SMU.

South Wind (1917) Norman Douglas's witty novel depicting the losing battle fought by a prewar English colony against the assimilation of their standards to those of the natives of a Capri-type island.

South Yemen The name adopted at Independence (1967) by the People's Republic formed from the Federation of South Arabia (i.e. Aden and the neighboring British protectorates).

Sovereign's Parade The graduation ceremony for SANDHURST cadets, at which the Sword of Honor is presented to the cadet adjudged the most meritorious of his year.

Sovetsk Modern Russian name for TILSIT.

Soviet Academy of Sciences A body

which until 1961 had executive power over all activities in the fields of pure and applied science in USSR, and managed all research institutions; it is now restricted to theoretical research.

Soviet-German Nonaggression Pact See HITLER-STALIN PACT.

Soviet Russia A term for the USSR (the Union of Soviet Socialist Republics), a country administered at all levels, from the village to the constituent republics and the Union itself, by soviets ('councils'), since 1936 elected directly by the whole electorate concerned. (Originally 'soviet' was used of the councils of workers, peasants and soldiers formed during the 1905 RUSSIAN REVOLUTION.)

'Sower, The' Millet's painting of a peasant scattering seed, personifying the dignity of labor and also the Present sowing the Future.

Soyuz A series of Russian spacecraft. Soyuz 1 crash-landed on return to earth (1967) as the parachute failed; it killed the cosmonaut, the first to die on a space mission. Soyuz 4 and 5 effected the first docking and transfer in space, January 1969. Soyuz 6, 7 and 8 were in simultaneous orbit, during which welding operations were carried out, October 1969.

Space Center (1) The MANNED SPACE-CRAFT CENTER, near Houston. (2) The MARSHALL SPACE FLIGHT CENTER at Huntsville, Ala., where SATURN and other space rockets are built.

Space City, USA A name for Houston, Tex.; see SPACE CENTER.

Space Needle (1962) A slender tower in Seattle, Wash., built for the Century 21 Exposition; it has a revolving restaurant at its summit.

SPADATS Space Detection and Tracking System, US defensive system to keep watch on orbiting satellites.

Spalding Tulip Time A tourist attraction in April and May in Kesteven and Holland, the bulb-farming Fenland districts of Lincolnshire, England, of which Spalding is the center.

Spandau The quarter of West Berlin which gives its name to the jail where German war criminals were imprisoned.

Spanish-American War (1898) A war which arose from the complaints of US business interests in Cuba about conditions there under Spanish rule, and was triggered off by the tragedy of the MAINE. An expeditionary force to Cuba (see ROUGH RIDERS) and naval operations, particularly in Manila Bay, quickly resulted in Spanish defeat, and the US gained the Philippines, Guam, Puerto Rico and (pending the declaration of an independent republic) Cuba. The Hearst press played a role in exacerbating American opinion before the war, and liberals today tend to date the beginning of American imperialism from this possibly unnecessary and unjustified war.

Spanish Bourbons See BOURBONS.

Spanish Civil War (1936-39) A war to overthrow the latest of a series of ineffective left-wing governments. Gen. Franco invaded Spain with Moroccan troops but failed to take Madrid, despite support from the Church, the upper classes, German planes and Italian troops. In 1938 he gradually drove a wedge between the Republican forces (sparingly aided by Russia) around Madrid and those around Barcelona, and moved in for the kill in March 1939. See BURGOS; GUERNICA; INTERNATIONAL BRIGADE; NONINTERVENTION COMMITTEE.

Spanish Farm (1924-27) A trilogy of novels by R. H. Mottram about World War I.

Spanish flu (Apr.-Nov. 1918) The influenza world epidemic which killed perhaps 20 million people all over the world, and seriously weakened the fighting forces on both sides in the last phases of World War I.

Spanish fly The metallic-green CANTHARIDES beetle (*Lytta* — formerly *Cantharis* — *vesicatoria*) which forms blisters on the skin that break, forming several more blisters. The blistering agent, called cantharidin, is used as a diuretic, and once had a (spurious) reputation as an aphrodisiac.

Spanish Guinea In 1935 split into 2 territories: (1) Rio Muni on the West African mainland; (2) Fernando Po. Now the republic of Equatorial Guinea.

Spanish Main (1) The South American mainland between Panama and the Orinoco; (2) the adjoining Caribbean Sea, where 16th-17th century English pirates harried Spanish shipping. (*Main* in the old sense 'wide expanse of land or sea'.)

Spanish Netherlands The NETHERLANDS countries (modern Belgium, Holland and Luxembourg) under the Spanish HAPSBURGS from the time of Emperor Charles V (1516) until the revolt of the northern Protestant Dutch as the UNITED PROVINCES (1581); thereafter the Belgian Catholic region in the south until the Treaty of UTRECHT (1713), when it became the Austrian Netherlands.

Spanish Riding School The 16th-century Viennese school, for which the Riding Hall was built in 1735, and which used and still uses only LIPIZZANER horses; it continues to be the chief school for classical or *haute école* riding. (So named after the horses, of Spanish origin.)

Spanish Steps (18th century) A mecca for British and American tourists in the artists' quarter of Rome, a wide flight of 137 steps ascending to a church. At the foot are the house where Keats died (with the Keats-Shelley Memorial Museum), a fountain by Bernini and an English tea shop.

Spanish Succession, War of the (1701-13) A war fought by the GRAND ALLIANCE to prevent the union of France and the Spanish Empire (Spain, Netherlands, Spanish America, Naples and Milan) under one crown after the succession of Louis XIV's grandson as Philip V of Spain. The main battles were fought by Marlborough, who won BLENHEIM, RAMILLIES, OUDENARDE and MALPLAQUET before he lost favor with Queen Anne and was dismissed (1711).

The war ended with the Treaty of UTRECHT. Philip remained King of Spain on condition that he did not inherit the French throne.

Spanish Tragedy, The (1594) Thomas Kyd's tragedy in blank verse, an early example of the 'revenge' plays popular at the time. The hero exacts an elaborate and spectacular revenge on the murderers of his son and then takes his own life.

Spar A member of the women's reserve of the US COAST GUARD. (From the Coast Guard motto Semper Paratus, 'always ready'.)

Sparkenbroke (1936) Charles Morgan's allegorical novel in which the passionate search of the hero, the poet Lord Sparkenbroke, for mystical illumination is represented by his lifelong love affair, never consummated, with his best friend's wife.

Spartacists (1919) The German Communist Party founded by Karl Liebknecht and Rosa Luxemburg which tried to seize Berlin. The rising was suppressed by the FREIKORPS, who murdered the 2 leaders. See SPARTACUS RISING.

Spartacus rising (73-71 BC) A revolt of Roman gladiators and slaves led by Spartacus. They held several Roman armies at bay while they ravaged most regions of Italy, but finally Spartacus was killed and his followers crucified.

Spartan (1965) A US long-range antimissile missile developed from ZEUS, designed to intercept incoming ICBMs in space and destroy them; for use, with SPRINT, in the NIKE-X SYSTEM.

Spartans The DORIC people of the ancient Greek state of Laconia (capital, Sparta) in the southern Peloponnesus, noted for bravery, frugality, stern self-discipline, 'laconic' terseness, and the dependence of their economy on conquered alien serfs (helots). Also called Lacedaemonians.

Spasur Abbreviation for Space Surveillance, a defensive line of stations in southern USA which can detect any satellite passing over it.

SPCA Signifies the Society for the Prevention of Cruelty to Animals; the British equivalent is the R ('Royal') SPCA.

SPCC Signifies the Society for the Prevention of Cruelty to Children; the British equivalent is the R ('Royal') SPCC.

SPD Initials of the German name of the SOCIAL DEMOCRATIC or Labor party of West Germany.

Speaker, The The presiding officer of the House of Representatives, House of Commons etc., responsible for order and discipline, elected by agreement between the parties at the beginning of each Congress or Parliament. In the US (but not in Britain) he may vote and take part in debate.

Speakers' Corner A site in HYDE PARK, near MARBLE ARCH, London, where street orators of all hues and persuasions unburden themselves of their pet obsessions to crowds of amiable hecklers. The name is also given to similar rendezvous on Tower Hill and at Whitestone Pond, Hampstead Heath.

Special Air Service (1940) British uniformed paratroops used on sabotage missions in enemy territory in World War II, and later e.g. in Malaya against Communist rebels. In 1950 they became a permanent regiment of the regular army.

Special Branch (Scotland Yard) The nearest equivalent in Britain to secret police, which deals, in cooperation with MI-5, with offenses against the state (e.g. treason, sabotage, subversive activities), investigates aliens, and guards foreign VIPs visiting Britain; first founded in 1886 to deal with the IRA; its strength is an official secret.

Specialized Agencies (UN) Now called the INTERNATIONAL AGENCIES.

Special Operations Executive (1940) A British secret organization set up on the fall of France, originally to train men to act as a fifth column in enemy-occupied territory, and later to coordinate or initiate subversion and sabotage against the enemy.

Spectator, The (1711-14) The successor to *The* TATLER, edited by Steele and Addison, reporting their views through the mouths of members of the fictional Spectator Club, one of whom was Sir Roger de COVERLEY. The modern *Spectator* was started in 1828.

Speke Hall An Elizabethan black-and-white manor house, near Liverpool Airport, leased from the NATIONAL TRUST by Liverpool Corporation.

Spencerianism (1) The view that everything must, or should, be left to natural laws of evolution; see SURVIVAL OF THE FITTEST. (2) The optimistic view that progress is not an accident but a natural law, at work everywhere through an evolution from the simple to the complex. (Herbert Spencer, English philosopher, 1820-1903.)

Spengler's Decline of the West (1918) A book in which the German philosopher Oswald Spengler developed a theory of the inevitable eclipse, already begun, of the Western world, after a period of 'Caesarism'.

Spenlow and Jorkins The partners in a legal firm in DAVID COPPERFIELD. Spenlow was, he said, the most generous of men but was unfortunately always restrained by the stern, unbending (and invisible) Jorkins.

Sphinx, The (1) In Greek legend, a winged lion with the head and breast of a woman, which plagued THEBES and ate those who could not solve her riddles. OEDIPUS was the first to solve one, whereupon she destroyed herself. (2) In Egyptian legend, a lion with a man's head, origin of the Greek legend. Of the many Sphinx statues in Egypt, the most famous is that at GIZA.

Spice Rack project A US Air Force chemical warfare research project; see SUMMIT PROJECT.

Spiegel, Der (1947) A popular West German weekly magazine, published in Hamburg; it has a reputation for fearless exposure of matters embarrassing to left-wing governments. See DER SPIEGEL CASE.

Spinoza's God A pantheistic conception, a God who reveals himself in the harmony of all being but is without personality or consciousness and does not concern himself with the actions of men. (Spinoza, 17th-century Dutch Jewish philosopher.)

Spion Kop (1) A hill for which a battle was fought (1900) during the siege of Ladysmith in the BOER WAR. (Near Ladysmith, in Natal.) (2) Name of the DERBY winner in 1920.

Spiraea The genus name of the meadowsweet and of the bridal wreath.

Spirit of St Louis The name of the aircraft in which Lindbergh made his solo flight across the Atlantic (1927).

Spitfire The Supermarine fighter which made its name in the BATTLE OF BRITAIN, and by the end of the war had attained altitudes of 45,000 ft.

Spithead Mutiny (1797) See NORE MUTINY.

Spithead Review An annual assembly of the Grand Fleet in the Solent off Portsmouth. The last, held just before World War I, is famous because Churchill, as First Lord of the Admiralty, on his own initiative ordered the ships not to disperse. The Fleet was thus in a state of covert mobilization long before the Cabinet decided to declare war on Germany.

Split A Yugoslav port, formerly known by its Italian name, Spalato.

Spock book, The The *Commonsense Book of Baby and Child Care* by Dr Benjamin Spock, which sold 9 million copies in its first 9 years.

Spode (1770-1847) A Staffordshire firm founded by Josiah Spode I, at first making domestic earthenware, later decorated with underglaze transfer printing. In 1794 he introduced bone china, which soon became and still is the standard form of porcelain. Under Josiah II (1797-1827) the firm excelled in accurate reproductions of MEISSEN, French, Chinese and leading English styles in the new material. See COPELAND & GARRETT.

Sponge, Mr The hero of *Mr Sponge's Sporting Tour* (1853) by R. S. Surtees. He is a horse coper who clings like a leech to any hospitality he can grab, impervious to all hints and snubs, driving his unwilling hosts to distraction.

Spoonerism The inadvertent transposition of sounds from one word to another, as in 'lean of leist resistance'. (Named after the Rev. W. A. Spooner, Warden of New College, OXFORD UNIVERSITY; in 1879 he announced the hymn 'Kinquering congs their titles take'.)

Spoon River Anthology, The (1915) Edgar Lee Masters's series of free-verse commentaries in which deceased inhabitants of the Midwest village of Spoon River correct and add to the epitaphs on their tombstones.

Sporozoa See PROTOZOA.

Sport of Kings, The Horse racing, as owing much to the early support of the Stuarts from James I onwards.

Spring Awakening (1891) The German Wedekind's play on problems of adolescent sex, amazingly outspoken for 1891 and banned in England until recently.

Spring Double (UK) A bet on the Lincolnshire and the GRAND NATIONAL, both run in March.

Springer empire The West German newspaper and periodical group built up since the war by Axel Springer. The chief units are the mass-circulation *Bild Zeitung* (1952) and the influential quality daily *Die Welt* (bought 1953), together with their Sunday counterparts. It came under violent attack from left-wing students in 1968.

Springfield rifle (1855) A repeating rifle made at the US Armory, Springfield, Mass. See GARAND RIFLE; SMITH & WESSON.

Springfields Site of one of the UK ATOMIC ENERGY AUTHORITY Production Group's factories for producing uranium and plutonium. (Village in Lancashire.)

Sprint A US short-range antimissile missile with very high initial speed, designed for use in the NIKE-X SYS-

TEM to intercept at altitudes of about 20 miles any missiles which evade SPARTAN.

Sputnik Russian name for their first series of earth satellites. *Sputnik 1*, launched 4 Oct. 1957, was the first man-made satellite to orbit the earth, and *Sputnik 2*, a month later, the first to carry a living creature (a dog). (Russian, 'traveling companion'.)

Spy Pseudonym of the caricaturist Sir Leslie Ward (1851-1922), whose work was published in *Vanity Fair*.

Spy who Came in from the Cold, The John Le Carré's disillusioned novel about the seamy side of spying, set in Berlin; it was made into a successful movie.

Square Mile, The A name for the CITY of London.

Squeers, Wackford The illiterate rogue in Dickens's NICHOLAS NICKLEBY who runs DOTHEBOYS HALL.

Squires The Virginia Squires, AMERICAN BASKETBALL ASSOCIATION.

Squire Toby A rarer form of Toby jug in which a handsome squire, sitting in a corner chair and holding a churchwarden pipe, replaces the TOBY FILLPOT of the standard jug.

Squirrel Nutkin (1903) A children's book written and illustrated by Beatrix Potter.

Squirt's Guide (London Stock Exchange) The *Jobbers' Industrial Index*, published by a firm of brokers, which gives the names of the jobbers who specialize in the various stocks quoted on the Stock Exchange.

SR-N Designation of a series of HOVERCRAFT. SR-N1 was the first to cross the English Channel; -N3 a large version designed for antisubmarine use; -N4 (Mountbatten class), over 100 tons, built for cross-Channel service (1968); -N6 a smaller version built for the same purpose, and in operation from 1966. (SR for Saunders-Roe, the original manufacturers.)

SRO Initials used for standing room only.

SS Hitler's personal army, originally a small and highly disciplined section of the SA. In 1936 they were merged with the GESTAPO. They kept close watch on Army officers and officials of the Nazi Party and government; organized the FINAL SOLUTION; staffed the concentration camps; and terrorized occupied countries. See also WAFFEN-SS. (Schutzstaffeln, 'security units'; also called Blackshirts, although they wore brown shirts, with black uniform.)

SS11 A Russian liquid-fuel missile smaller than SS9, thought to be targeted against US cities but not sufficiently accurate to destroy missile sites. An estimated 800-1000 were deployed by 1969.

SS9 A Russian ICBM test-fired in April 1969; payload 25 megatons or 3 MIRVs of 5 megatons each; range 5000 miles. An estimated 200 were deployed in 1969. Since it has a far greater capability than MINUTEMAN, its appearance led to an agonizing reappraisal of countermeasures. See SS11.

SST Initials used for Supersonic Transport, and the provisional name of the American rival to the Anglo-French CONCORDE. In 1966 it was announced that this would be made by BOEING (airframe) and GE (engines), and was designed to be faster (1800 m.p.h.) and to carry far more passengers (300), but would not be operational until 1978, several years after Concorde. Production was halted in 1971 by Congress.

SS13 A solid-fuel version of the SS11.

Stabat Mater (dolorosa) A 13th-century hymn on the 7 sorrows of MARY at the Cross, of which there are musical settings by Palestrina and many other composers. (Latin, 'The Mother stands mourning', the first words.)

Stade Roland Garros The French and international hard-court tennis open tournament at Auteuil, southwest Paris. The stadium is also used for other sports.

'Stag at Bay, The' One of the most popular of Landseer's paintings; see 'MONARCH OF THE GLEN'.

Stagecoach (1939) The classic Western movie, directed by John Ford and based on E. Haycox's *Stage to*

Lordsburgh.

Stakhanovite A title of honor in Soviet Russia for a worker whose output greatly exceeds the norm. (Alexei Stakhanov, a coal miner who in 1935, by a combination of hard work and intelligent time and motion study, produced phenomenal outputs.)

Stalag German prisoner-of-war camp for NCOs and men. (Abbreviation of *Stamm*, 'main body', and *Lager*, 'camp'.)

Stalingrad A city in the USSR, now renamed Volgograd. See next entry.

Stalingrad, Battle of (Aug. 1942-Feb. 1943) The successful Russian defense of the city now known as Volgograd against German assault, the turning point in Hitler's Russian campaign.

Stalinist purges (1934-40) A series of mass purges of leading Russian Communists during Stalin's regime, under successive heads of the secret police: under Yagoda (1934-36), started by the LAW OF DECEMBER 1; under Yezhov (1936-38; see YE-ZHOVSHCHINA); and under Beria (1939-40). A peculiar feature was the extraction of public 'confessions' of treason from some of the victims, who were shot whether or not they confessed.

Stalino A Ukrainian city, now renamed Donetsk.

Stalinograd A city of Upper Silesia, Poland, now renamed Katowice.

Stalin Prize Name given to the LENIN PRIZE, 1940-54.

Stalky and Co. (1899) Kipling's fictionalized account of his school days at the United Services College, Westward Ho!, Devon. Of the main characters, Stalky is the future commander of DUNSTER FORCE, Beetle is the author and McTurk is George Charles Beresford.

Stalwart A British amphibious military vehicle with giant tires, built by the Alvis branch of the BRITISH LEYLAND MOTOR CORPORATION.

Stamboul An earlier form, used by Europeans, of the name ISTANBUL (Constantinople).

Stamp Act (1765) The British government's measure imposing stamp duty on newspapers, legal documents etc., the most resented of the Acts of 1764-67 (Sugar, Customs Collecting, Revenue, Tea) and the least wise, since it upset those ever-vocal elements, the lawyers, editors and land speculators. Opposition centered on James Otis's slogan 'No taxation without representation'; the Act was repealed the next year, but the damage was done and events moved inexorably on to the BOSTON TEA PARTY.

Standardbred The breed of trotting and pacing horses used chiefly for harness racing but also as hunters; developed in eastern USA after the Revolution and descended from the English THOROUGHBRED Messenger (1780), whose famous great-grandson was HAMBLETONIAN (1849). Bred for speed at trot or pace, they are longer in the body, lower to the ground and heavier of bone than the Thoroughbred. (So called because they were required to trot or pace a mile in a standard of time.)

Standard Oil of California (1926) An oil company, with headquarters at San Francisco, which operates throughout the Americas and in Saudi Arabia, LIBYA etc.; one of the 30 industrials that make up the DOW JONES Industrial Average; see BAHREIN PETROLEUM CO.

Standard Oil of New Jersey (1882) J. D. Rockefeller's oil giant which controls ESSO, Cleveland Petroleum, Imperial Oil etc., and operates in most parts of the world; one of the 30 industrials that make up the DOW JONES Industrial Average.

Standfast, Mr A character in Part II of PILGRIM'S PROGRESS who formerly lived by hearsay and faith 'but now I go where I shall live by sight'.

Stanford (1885) University near Palo Alto, California.

Stanford Research Institute (1946) A nonprofit think tank (see HUDSON INSTITUTE) at Menlo Park and South Pasadena, Calif., with branches in Washington, New York, Chicago, Huntsville (see MARSHALL SPACE FLIGHT CENTER), Zurich, Tokyo and Stockholm. It carries out research in economics, industrial and agricultural problems, pure and applied science etc. and is much used by government.

Stanhope Gold Medal   See ROYAL HUMANE SOCIETY.

Stanislavsky system   A rigorous system of training, introduced at the Moscow Art Theater, by which an actor is taught to sink his personality completely in his role; the source of the American METHOD ACTING.

Stanley Cup Playoffs   (1894) The annual ice-hockey championship playoff series in the NATIONAL HOCKEY LEAGUE. (Donated·by Lord Stanley, Governor-General of Canada; originally a purely Canadian event.)

Stanley Gibbons   (1856) A London firm of stamp dealers, one of the largest in the world, and a household name in international philately.

Stansted   An airfield near Bishop's Stortford, Essex. Its selection in 1967 for expansion as the second subsidiary of London Airport (the first being Gatwick) aroused vociferous opposition, and protracted consideration was given to alternatives.

Star   (1923) A 15½-ft Bermudian-rigged keelboat for 2-man crews which has recently attained Olympic status.

Star Chamber   A court manned by royal councillors, first effectively used by the Tudors to try cases affecting Crown interests; abused by Charles I to persecute opponents, and abolished in 1641. (Met in room with ceiling decorated with stars.)

Starfighter   The US LOCKHEED F-104, a single-seat multi-purpose supersonic fighter; very many of those in service with the LUFTWAFFE crashed.

Star of David   A 6-pointed star, emblem of Judaism; also the yellow cloth badge (German, *Schandenband*, 'shame-band') in this shape which Nazis forced Jews to wear.

Star of India   The largest star sapphire in the world (563 carats), stolen (1964) from the American Museum of Natural History and later recovered.

Starr   A variety of apple.

Stars   The Utah Stars, AMERICAN BASKETBALL ASSOCIATION.

Stars and Bars, The   The flag adopted by the CONFEDERATE STATES OF AMERICA, with 3 red-white-red horizontal stripes and, on a blue union, one white star for each state.

Stars and Stripes, The   (1) The flag of the United States, with 13 red and white horizontal stripes representing the original seceding colonies (Mass., R.I., Conn., N.H., N.Y., N. J., Penn., Del., Md., Va., N.C., S.C., Ga.) and, on a blue union, one white star for each state. (2) The chief US Armed Forces daily, which first appeared in France in 1918 and was reborn in London (1942), eventually with special editions for the various war fronts.

'Stars and Stripes Forever, The'   (1897) One of the SOUSA MARCHES.

'Star-Spangled Banner, The'   Officially proclaimed the US national anthem in 1931, with words written in 1814 by Francis Scott Key to the 18th-century English melody (attributed to John Stafford Smith) of an academic *jeu d'esprit* entitled 'To Anacreon in Heaven'. Towards the end of the WAR OF 1812, Key bearded an English admiral aboard his flagship to plead for a friend's release, and thus became an involuntary spectator of the Royal Navy's unsuccessful night bombardment of Fort McHenry (Baltimore). As dawn broke he was overjoyed to see the Stars and Stripes still flying from the fort and, inspired by its defenders' refusal to capitulate, began then and there to scribble down the words of his poem on the back of an old letter. Under the title 'The Defense of Fort McHenry' it was published in a Baltimore paper a few days later; the modest author 'believed it to have been favorably received'.

State Department   The US department under the Secretary of State concerned with maintaining friendly relations between the US and foreign countries; this corresponds to the British Foreign Office.

State Enrolled Nurse   (UK) A qualification obtainable after a simpler course of training than for SRN

(State Registered Nurse).

Stately Homes The great English country houses. (From the opening line of a poem by Mrs Hemans resuscitated in a Noël Coward parody.)

State of the Union message The speech at the beginning of each session of Congress in which the President outlines the program of legislation that has been prepared for its consideration; equivalent to the QUEEN'S SPEECH in Britain.

State Opening The ceremonial opening of Parliament by the Queen at the beginning of the new session in late October or early November, and when a new Parliament assembles after a general election. It is the occasion of the QUEEN'S SPEECH.

States General The French assembly of the 3 Estates: Nobility, Clergy and Commons (THIRD ESTATE); Louis XVI was forced to summon it in 1789, for the first time since 1614, to pass measures necessitated by the country's bankruptcy.

Statesman's Year Book A standard book of reference giving statistical and other information about the countries of the world, published annually since 1863.

States' Rights Party See DIXIECRATS.

Stations of the Cross A series of 14 images or pictures on the walls of Roman Catholic churches, representing scenes from the last hours of Christ, from the condemnation to death to the placing of the body in the tomb; prayers are offered at each station. Also called the Via Crucis (Way of the Cross).

Stavisky scandal (1933-34) The revelation of large-scale frauds by a French financier, Alexandre Stavisky, which led to his suicide, the fall of the government (a minister being involved) and right-wing riots in Paris.

Stavrogin The chief character of Dostoievsky's *The Possessed* (1872), a member of the upper class who gets involved with Nihilists and who, after confessing to being the cause of a young girl's suicide, hangs himself.

STD (UK) Abbreviation for Subscriber Trunk Dialing, the telephone system which enables long-distance ('trunk') calls to be made without the intervention of an operator.

Steady State theory (1948) A cosmological hypothesis that continuous creation of matter produces new galaxies which force older galaxies ever outwards; put forward by Bondi and Gold and supported for a time by Fred Hoyle. It postulates a universe that has always existed and will always exist, in contrast to the BIG BANG THEORY, and was suggested by the EXPANDING UNIVERSE THEORY.

Stedman One of the principal methods of the change ringing of church bells. (Fabian Stedman of Cambridge, its 17th-century inventor.)

Steelers The Pittsburgh Steelers, NATIONAL FOOTBALL LEAGUE. Became member of the AMERICAN CONFERENCE, NATIONAL FOOTBALL LEAGUE in 1970.

Steerforth In Dickens's DAVID COPPERFIELD, a rich young cad who leads Little Em'ly Peggotty astray and is drowned at sea. His rival, Ham Peggotty, is drowned trying to save him.

Stella Jonathan Swift's name for his friend Esther Johnson (whom he may later have married). His letters to her, written 1710-13 and not meant for publication, were posthumously published in 1766-68 as the *Journal to Stella*.

Stentor A Greek herald in the TROJAN WAR whom Homer credited with the voice of 50 men; hence stentorian, 'loud-voiced'.

Stepney A former London metropolitan borough, since 1965 part of the borough of TOWER HAMLETS.

Sterling Area (1931) The 'scheduled territories', including the British Commonwealth (except Canada) and colonies, Eire, Iraq, Jordan, Libya, Burma and Iceland, which agree to keep their exchange assets at the BANK OF ENGLAND and to align their currencies with sterling.

Stern gang An anti-British terrorist organization active in Palestine in the 1940s; they blew up the British headquarters at the King David Hotel in Jerusalem (1946) and assassinated the UN mediator, Count Bernadotte (1948). At the time they were denounced by Zionist leaders as murderers and bandits, but are now not without honor in Israel. (Led by Abraham Stern, fighting under the nom-de-guerre Yair; killed by the British CRIMINAL INVESTIGATION DEPARTMENT in 1942.)

Stetson The 10-gallon cowboy hat. (John B. Stetson hat company.)

Stettin The German name of the city of Szczecin, now in Polish POMERANIA.

Steuben glass Tableware and ornamental pieces of brilliant white crystal, designed for the CORNING GLASS Company by leading American artists, handmade and individually signed. It is sold at the firm's own store on FIFTH AVENUE.

Stevenage (1946) (UK) One of the earliest NEW TOWNS, adjoining the existing town in Hertfordshire, with a population of about 60,000.

Stewart & Lloyds (1903) A British steel firm with headquarters at Corby, Lincolnshire. It has interlocking directorships with UNITED STEEL and John Summers, forming the 'Holy Trinity of Steel'.

Steyne, Lord See Becky SHARP.

Stiegel glass A comprehensive term for American glass of various types blown in pattern molds, specifically the blue, green or amethyst flint glass made by the German-born H. W. Stiegel at one of his 3 factories, at Mannheim, Penn. (1769-74). Also loosely applied to enameled glass bottles and jugs coarsely painted with flowers and birds.

Stiffkey, Rector of (1932) The Rev. Harold Davidson, who was unfrocked for immoral conduct and then went round the fairs exhibiting himself in a barrel etc., until killed by a circus lion.

Stilton The queen of British cheeses, a semihard blue cheese made in Leicestershire which gets its name from the original main-road selling point, Stilton, in Huntingdonshire. The belief that it is improved by adding port or beer is baseless.

Stirling (1941) A heavy 4-engined Short bomber used by the RAF in World War II.

Stockbroker Belt The outer ring of suburbs round London (or other cities) with prosperous-looking houses standing well back from the road, of the kind that imagination peoples with stockbrokers and their 'income-bracket' like.

Stock-car racing See NASCAR RACING.

Stockholm Appeal (1950) An appeal to ban the atomic bomb, allegedly signed by 500 million people, not all of them Communists.

Stockholm Treaty (1959) The treaty under which EFTA was established.

Stockwell Ghost (1772) A hoax perpetrated in Stockwell, London, by a servant girl, similar to the COCK LANE GHOST.

Stoke Newington A former London metropolitan borough, since 1965 part of the borough of HACKNEY.

Stokes-Adams syndrome A condition resembling epilepsy in which the ventricles of the heart stop beating long enough to produce loss of consciousness. It is a possible sequel to myocarditis (disease of the heart muscle).

Stokes (Thomas L.) Award An award of $500 for the best article in a daily newspaper on the development and conservation of natural resources.

Stokes mortar (1915) A British trench mortar, used in both world wars to lob small HE (high-explosive), gas, smoke or incendiary bombs into enemy positions. (Sir Frederick Stokes.)

Stonehenge A circular setting of large upright stones near Salisbury, Wilshire, England, believed to have been constructed around 1800-1400 BC, possible as a place of worship. It originally consisted of two concentric circles of stones enclosing two horseshoe-shaped rows with a central 'altar' stone. Some of the stones are up to 30 feet long and weigh up to 50 tons, and many were brought from over 100 miles away.

Stone Mountain The world's largest granite monolith, near Atlanta, Ga.;

it covers 583 acres and rises to 1680 ft above sea level.

'Stonewall' Jackson A Southern general in the Civil War, Thomas Jonathan Jackson, nicknamed for his stubborn resistance in the first Battle of BULL RUN (1861).

Stormont The seat of the Parliament of Northern Ireland, near Belfast.

Storm over Shanghai See CONDITION HUMAINE.

Storm Troops A name for the Nazi SA.

Storting The Norwegian Parliament.

Story of Civilization, The A multi-volume popular world history begun in 1935 by Will Durant with the last four volumes produced in collaboration with his wife, Ariel; the 9th volume (*The Age of Voltaire*) was published in 1965, when he was 80, and volume 10 (*Rousseau and Revolution*) was published in 1967.

Story of Mankind, The (1921) Hendrik Van Loon's best-selling world history, amusingly illustrated by the author.

Stouffer Prize An award of $50,000 by the Vernon Stouffer Foundation for an important contribution to the prevention or treatment of high blood pressure or hardening of the arteries.

Stowe An 18th-century PALLADIAN country house near Buckingham, since 1923 housing the 'public' school of that name.

STP A drug derived from the amphetamine of 'pep' pills and producing short-lived hallucinations.

Stradivarius Name given to violins made at Cremona, Italy, by Antonio Stradivari (1644-1737), reputed to be the best ever made.

Straffen murder case (1951) (UK) The trial of John Thomas Straffen, market gardener, found unfit to plead to the charge of strangling 2 small girls at Bath and sent to Broadmoor, from which he escaped. Charged with strangling another small girl, he was found fit to plead, sentenced to death but reprieved, and imprisoned.

Straits Settlements (1826-1946) The British Crown Colony consisting of Singapore, Penang, Malacca, Labuan and various small islands; capital Singapore.

Straker, Henry A chauffeur in Shaw's MAN AND SUPERMAN. Writing in 1903, Shaw chose him as the representative of a new class whose imminent rise to importance he foresaw—the skilled mechanic, well but self-educated, politically minded and able to keep his employers in their place.

Strange Interlude (1928) A 9-act play in 2 parts in which Eugene O'Neill introduced stream-of-consciousness techniques to the stage, using soliloquies and asides, and psychoanalyzing the heroine's attitudes to her father, husbands and lovers.

Strangers and Brothers C. P. (Lord) Snow's series of novels begun in 1940, some partly autobiographical, narrated by Lewis Eliot, treating in general the theme of conflict between conscience and ambition in the struggle for power in a CAMBRIDGE UNIVERSITY college, the world of scientific research, the civil service etc.; his *Corridors of Power* (1964) was a continuation of this theme in the political field.

Strangers' Galleries (Houses of Parliament) Galleries from which members of the public can listen to debates. Certain sections are reserved for 'distinguished strangers' (ambassadors etc.) and for those with special interest in a particular debate.

Strasbourgeoise (Cooking) With foie gras or sauerkraut.

Stratford Shakespearean Festival (1952) A world-famous festival of Shakespearean drama held from June to August each year at the Avon Theatre, Stratford, Ont.

Strathclyde University (1963) A technological university in Glasgow, originally the Glasgow Technical College, specializing in mechanical engineering and also having a business school.

Strathcona Cup (1903) A curling contest between Scotland and Canada.

Strathspey Cup A skiing competion held in the Cairngorms, Scotland, in April.

Stratofortress (1954) US BOEING B-52 8-jet strategic bomber, weight 175 tons, speed 650 m.p.h., combat radius 6250 miles; able to carry 4 hydrogen bombs (1·1 megatons) or 2 HOUND DOG missiles. The SAC was said to have about 450 of them in 1968. In the VIETNAMESE WAR they were used first from distant bases in Guam and the Philippines, later from Thailand.

Strawberry Hill The house at Twickenham, Surrey, rebuilt by Horace Walpole (1717-97) in a style generally held to herald the GOTHIC REVIVAL, and called at the time 'Gothick'.

Street, The (1) FLEET STREET, London, the world of newspapers and journalists. (2) WALL STREET.

Streetcar (1947) Common abbreviated title of Tennessee Williams's play of New Orleans, *A Streetcar Named Desire*. Blanche, Williams's usual faded Southern belle, is staying with her sister. Her brother-in-law Stanley, angry at her airs and graces, warns off a possible suitor. Blanche provokes Stanley to rape her, and is carried off to an asylum. (The French title is *Tramway*.)

Street Scene (1929) Elmer Rice's murder play set in a slum tenement, notable for its use of realistic sound effects. Kurt Weill and Rice made a musical version of it in 1947.

Street which is called Straight, The The covered (once colonnaded) street which runs east and west through Damascus, the scene of St Paul's conversion (*Acts* ix, 11).

Strength Through Joy A Nazi organization providing regimented leisure for German workers, including theaters, sport and, especially, foreign travel and cruises at cheap prices. (German, Kraft durch Freude.)

Strephon (1) A shepherd in Sir Philip Sidney's *Arcadia*. (2) Conventional name for any rustic swain. (3) Half-fairy, half-mortal son of IOLANTHE in the GILBERT AND SULLIVAN OPERA, who becomes a Member of Parliament.

Stresa Front (1935) A pact formed by Britain, France and Italy against a rearming Germany; it lasted 6 months. (Stresa, Italian Lake district, scene of the conference of Ramsay MacDonald, Flandin and Mussolini.)

Strife (1909) Galsworthy's play, giving a balanced presentation of both points of view in an industrial struggle between John Anthony ('No compromise') for the owners, and David Roberts ('No surrender'), the strike leader. Roberts's wife dies, both sides throw over their leaders and agree on the terms offered before the strike began.

Strike Command (1968) An RAF Command formed by combining the Fighter, Bomber and COASTAL COMMANDS.

Strine Used for 'Australian'; according to an Australian author the way the average Australian pronounces that word.

Strip, The Short name for SUNSET STRIP.

Stroganoff Used adjectivally of beef etc. sliced thin and cooked in a sauce of consommé, sour cream, mustard, onion and condiments. (Count Paul Stroganoff, 19th-century Russian diplomat and gourmet.)

Strongbow Nickname of Richard de Clare, Earl of Pembroke, one of the First Anglo-Norman adventurers to start the English conquest of Ireland in 1170. His tomb is supposed to be in Dublin.

Struwwelpeter (1847) Heinrich Hoffmann's illustrated book of cautionary verse for children, introducing such characters as Fidgety Phil (who would not keep still) and Little Johnny Head-in-air. It was written in German and translated into many languages. (German, 'shock-headed Peter'.)

Stuart Little (1945) A children's story about an adventurous little mouse, by E. B. White.

Stuart period (1603-1714) A blanket term in the decorative arts sometimes used to cover the JACOBEAN, RESTORATION, WILLIAM AND MARY and QUEEN ANNE periods.

Stuarts The dynasty that ruled Scotland 1371-1603 (Robert II-James VI), and England and Scotland 1603-1714 (James I-Queen Anne). (Originally Stewart or Steuart, a family founded by an 11th-century Breton immigrant who became Steward of Scotland to King David I; Robert II was son of Robert the Bruce's daughter; James VI and I was son of Mary Queen of Scots, James V's daughter, who adopted the spelling 'Stuart'.)

Stubbs Author's name used for his standard work, *The Constitutional History of England* (1874-78).

Student Nonviolent Coordinating Committee A US Negro movement, usually referred to as Snick or SNCC, founded in the 1960s by militant opponents of Martin Luther King's SOUTHERN CHRISTIAN LEADERSHIP CONFERENCE. Under Stokely Carmichael it aimed at BLACK POWER, and the word 'nonviolent' ceased to be appropriate.

Student Prince, The (1924) A famous light opera, music by Sigmund Romberg, libretto by Dorothy Donnelly. Among its highlights were the 'Drinking Song' and the waltz 'Deep in My Heart, Dear'.

Students for a Democratic Society See SDS.

Studley Royal An 18th-century house near Ripon, Yorkshire, with varied historical association.

Studs Lonigan trilogy, The (1932-35) James T. Farrell's exceptionally realistic story of the brief life of an Irish Catholic born in the Chicago slums about 1912. His potential ability and good qualities are overwhelmed from the start by his environment; he leads a life of aimless dissipation punctuated by spasmodic attempts to escape via physical-fitness classes, crude religion and right-wing politics.

Study in Scarlet, A (1887) Conan Doyle's first Sherlock HOLMES story.

Study of History, A (1935-61) Arnold Toynbee's 12-volume philosophical study of the pattern of rise, growth and fall of world civilizations. He believed that they rise always in, and spurred by, adverse conditions, and decay after creating a 'universal' religion. A 2-volume abridgment was later published.

Stukas (1937) German Junkers-87 dive-bombers, first tried out in the SPANISH CIVIL WAR and then used in the early stages of World War II. They dropped their bombs as they pulled out of an almost vertical dive, aiming at targets just ahead of advancing panzer units. Once the novelty had worn off, these tactics were easily mastered, with heavy loss to the Germans. (Abbreviation of German *Stutzkampfbomber*.)

Stupor Mundi Name given to the 13th-century Holy Roman Emperor Frederick II on account of his vast erudition combined with statesmanship and military competence. (Latin, 'wonder of the world'.)

Sturm und Drang (18th century) A German literary movement, of which the principal figures were Goethe and Schiller, in their early work, and which reacted against the rationalism and formalism of contemporary writers. (German, 'storm and stress', the title of a play which initiated the movement.)

Stylites Christians who practised a form of extreme asceticism started in the 5th century by the Syrian, Simeon Stylites, who spent some 40 years sitting on top of pillars; the practice continued till the 16th century. (From Greek for 'pillar'.)

Styx Russian beam-riding naval missile with a range of 20 miles; used by the Egyptians to sink an Israeli destroyer off Port Said in 1967.

Styx, Stygian Lake The hated river or lake which, in Greek legend, guarded the passage to the Underworld and over which CHARON ferried the dead.

SU A series of Soviet aircraft, including VTOL, swing-wing and (SU-9) supersonic strike fighter types. (For Pavel Sukhoi, designer.)

Sublime Porte (1) The Ottoman court at Constantinople. (2) Used as a synonym for the Turkish (Imperial) government. (French translation of Turkish for 'lordly gate'.)

Subtopia Name coined from 'suburban UTOPIA' for the fringe suburbs of large cities which have invaded the countryside, undistinguished and indistinguishable.

Süchow, Battle of (Nov. 1948) The decisive battle in which the Chinese Red Army defeated the KUOMINTANG forces; the Communist regime was established the following year. (City northwest of Shanghai in northwest Kiangsu province; also spelled Hsuchow.)

Sucker State Nickname of Illinois.

Sudeten crisis (1938) Hitler's claim to Czech SUDETENLAND on the grounds that the inhabitants were mainly German; contested by Czechoslovakia because it formed a natural frontier and provided skilled labor for Czech industry. The area was given to Hitler by the MUNICH agreement but restored after World War II to the Czechs, who expelled the German population.

Sudetenland A mountainous region formerly in Austria-Hungary and populated mainly by Germans. Strictly, it is the Sudeten range from the Oder to the Neisse on the border between Bohemia and Moravia (in Czechoslovakia) and Silesia (Poland); but in common usage incudes the Erz Gebirge (Ore Mountains) between Bohemia and SAXONY (East Germany). See SUDETEN CRISIS.

Sudra The lowest Hindu caste (except for the Untouchables), of peasants, artisans and laborers.

Suez crisis (29 Oct.-6 Nov. 1956) The situation which arose from Egyptian hostility to Israel; USA's consequent denial of finance for the ASWAN HIGH DAM; Nasser's nationalization of the Suez Canal as a substitute source of revenue, arousing British fears for freedom of passage through it; and Egyptian aid to Algerian rebels against France. Israel, Britain and France concerted attacks on Egypt which had to be called off within a week when Eisenhower and Dulles unexpectedly threatened financial retaliation.

Suez rebels Name given (1954) to Tory MPs who, headed by Capt. Waterhouse, defied their leaders by voting against the ratification of an agreement with Egypt for the withdrawal of British troops from the Suez Canal, 2 years before the SUEZ CRISIS.

Suffolk (sheep) A widely distributed breed of shortwool sheep, with black face, ears and legs; it produces good meat and a thick fleece.

Suffolk Punch A short-legged powerful farm horse, chestnut in color with flaxen mane and tail.

Sufism The MUSLIM form of GNOSTICISM; the Sufis were organized in orders of dervishes (fakirs), some of whom induced trancelike states by religious dances. (Arabic *suf*, 'wool', from the rough woolen garments worn.)

Sugar Bowl (1) Sports stadium at New Orleans, Louisiana. (2) The invitational BOWL GAME played in the Sugar Bowl usually with one team from the SOUTHEASTERN CONFERENCE.

Sugar State A later nickname for Louisiana earned by its postwar position as producer of almost all US-grown cane sugar.

Sulgrave Manor A small Elizabethan manor house near Banbury, Northamptonshire, built by George Washington's ancestor, a Mecca for American visitors.

Sullivan (James E.) Memorial Trophy (1930) An award made by the AMATEUR ATHLETIC UNION to the athlete who, by performance, example and influence as an amateur, has done most during the year to advance the cause of sportsmanship.

Sultan of Swat Another nickname for BABE RUTH. (Swat was also a principality, now absorbed in West Pakistan.)

Sumer The earlier name of Babylonia, which from about 3000 BC was a country of city-states (including UR OF THE CHALDEES), united only in religion.

Sumerians A non-Semitic race of unknown origin, possibly related to the aboriginal peoples of southern India, who settled in SUMER (southern MESOPOTAMIA) about 4000 BC. Deeply religious, they founded a civilization which, with their religion and cuneiform writing, was adopted by their successors, the Akkadians, Babylonians and Assyrians.

'Sumer is icumen in' The earliest known English lyric, dating to the mid-13th century; the second line is 'Lhude sing cuccu!', from which it gets its name 'Cuckoo Song'.

Sumitomo group A group of Japanese firms which has recently come to rival the MITSUI and MITSUBISHI GROUPS, with interests including banking, steel, chemicals, machinery, mining, electrical goods and insurance; the headquarters are in Osaka.

Summerhill A novel coeducational boarding school at Leiston, Suffolk, founded and run by A. S. Neill, a Scottish schoolmaster who began to propagate his views in the 1920s (*A Dominie's Log*, etc.). The children run the school, work when they feel like it and at what they choose. Staff stand by to help if asked.

Summit Conference See GENEVA SUMMIT CONFERENCE; PARIS SUMMIT CONFRENECE.

Summit project A US Army chemical warfare research project; see SPICE RACK PROJECT.

Sunday painter An amateur painter (only able to paint at weekends).

Sunderland (1937) A Short flying boat used in World War II; from it was developed the Empire class airliner which pioneered many overseas routes.

Sunderland ware (1740-1897) Earthenware made at several Sunderland (Durham) factories; notably the blotchy pink luster jugs decorated with transfer prints of the Wearmouth Bridge, opened 14 miles from Sunderland in 1796. Also noted for Sunderland lion ornaments and frog mugs.

SUNFED Initials standing for Special UN Fund for Economic Development, an organization mooted in 1952 to provide low-interest capital and free grants for major construction works in developing countries. The proposal was not approved, and the UNITED NATIONS SPECIAL FUND was instituted as a substitute.

Sunflower State Nickname of Kansas.

Sung dynasty (960-1279) The dynasty which ruled central China from Hangchow as capital, Genghis Khan having established Mongol rule in the north. It was an age of literary and artistic brilliance, famous for celadon ware and paintings of landscapes, animals, birds and flowers. The YÜAN DYNASTY followed.

Sunnites (Sunni) The orthodox MUSLIMS who accept Abu Bakr as having been rightfully chosen to succeed Muhammad as the first Caliph. (*Sunna*, book of sayings attributed to Muhammad, not recognized by the SHIITES.)

Suns The Phoenix Suns, NATIONAL BASKETBALL ASSOCIATION.

Sunset Strip A 1-mile section of Sunset Boulevard, Los Angeles, the psychedelic haunt of hippies, with blue movies, homosexual dance halls, topless waitresses and bottomless pop groups. It thus has claims to be the Sodom of some latter-day *Genesis*, where Lot's wife might be expected to turn into a pillar of rock candy.

Sunshine State Nickname of New Mexico, Florida and South Dakota.

Super Bowl (1967) The championship professional football game played between the conference champions in the NATIONAL FOOTBALL LEAGUE. Formerly played between the champions of the NFL and the AFL.

Superfortress The BOEING B-29, a US high-altitude, heavily armed giant bomber used (1944) in raids on Japan from bases in China, India and later the Marianas. It also made the first nonstop, flight-refuelled circumnavigation of the world (1949).

'Supermac' See VICKY.

Superman A concept developed by Nietzsche in THUS SPAKE ZARATHUSTRA. It is man at the utmost limits of his possible development, the objective towards which man should bend the whole of his will power, not shrinking from trampling on the weak if necessary, in the hope that in some future generation it will be achieved. The Nazis adapted this idea to fit their theory of German racial superiority.

'Superman' (1938) The hero of US comic strips and TV films, seemingly immortal; a shy bespectacled man who, when occasion arises, is transmogrified into a magnificent hero whose powers of flight and feats of strength (e.g. pushing planets back into their orbit) made HERCULES look very small beer—and his creator very rich.

Supersonics The Seattle Supersonics, NATIONAL BASKETBALL ASSOCIATION.

Super VC-10 (1965) An airliner developed from the VC-10 as a rival to the BOEING 707 on the transatlantic service.

Supreme Soviet (1936) The Parliament of the USSR, consisting of 2 Chambers (the Councils of Nationalities and of the Union) with equal powers; it replaced the Congress of Soviets. Although theoretically the highest organ of government, it meets for only a few days each year and then ratifies decisions already taken by its PRESIDIUM. It also elects the COUNCIL OF MINISTERS.

Surbiton (UK) A former municipal borough of Surrey, since 1965 part of the borough of KINGSTON UPON THAMES.

Surface, Joseph and Charles See SCHOOL FOR SCANDAL.

Surinam A state in South America, formerly called Netherlands Guiana.

Surrealism (1924) The artistic aspect of a general antibourgeois protest movement after World War I, a Freudian-inspired successor to DADAISM which aimed to lil erate the imagination from reason or aesthetic and moral considerations, using images from the artist's subconscious. Some (e.g. Dali, di Chirico) meticulously depicted incongruously juxtaposed objects in a highly evocative dreamworld; others (Miró, Ernst) created abstract forms or used inanimate *objets trouvés* (i.e. anything that took their fancy). The

movement gathered writers, film directors and others to its fold, usually briefly.

'Surrender of Breda' (1635) Velázquez' painting (in the PRADO, Madrid) depicting the Dutch surrendering the keys of Breda to the Spanish in 1625. Sometimes called 'The Lances'.

Surrey University (1967) Formerly Battersea CAT, moved to a new site near Guildford Cathedral.

Surtsey A new island created off the coast of Iceland by volcanic activity, 1963-65.

Surveyor US program of unmanned landings on the moon as a preliminary to APOLLO. Surveyor 1 made a soft landing (June 1966) and relayed pictures.

Survival of the Fittest A phrase first used by Herbert Spencer (see SPENCERIANISM) in regard to economic man. He opposed any state interference such as poor relief or free education, holding that it tended to perpetuate the survival of the unfit. Darwin used the phrase in connection with NATURAL SELECTION.

Susanna and the Elders (1st century BC) The story told in the Apocryphal book *The History of Susanna*, set in Babylon. Susanna repels the advances of 2 Jewish Elders who revenge themselves by accusing her of adultery. The prophet DANIEL interviews them separately, proves they are lying, and has them put to death. Hence the expression 'a Daniel come to judgment' used in Shakespeare's MERCHANT OF VENICE.

Sussex University (1961) A new foundation, at Stanmer, Brighton.

Sutter's fever (1848) The excitement generated by the discovery of gold at Sutter's Mill in the Sacramento valley 40 miles northeast of Sacramento, Calif., which precipitated the gold rush of the FORTY-NINERS.

Sutton London borough since 1965 consisting of the former boroughs of Sutton-Cheam and Beddington-Wallington and the urban district of Carshalton.

Sutton Hoo Site near Woodbridge, Suffolk, of a 7th-century AD SAXON royal ship burial, discovered in

1939. The varied treasures of silver and gold are in the British Museum.

Sutton Place An exclusive residential area of New York City resembling and just north of BEEKMAN PLACE.

Suvarov (Cooking) With foie gras, truffles and Madeira.

Suvla Bay Landing (1915) See DARDANELLES CAMPAIGN.

Svengali A character in George Du Maurier's novel *Trilby* (1894). A Hungarian musician and hypnotist, Svengali mesmerizes an artists' model, Trilby, into becoming a famous singer. When he dies the spell is broken, she loses her voice, and herself dies brokenhearted.

Sverdlovsk A city of the USSR, formerly EKATERINBURG.

Swahili (1) A BANTU people, originally of Zanzibar and the neighboring African coast. (2) Their language, which became the lingua franca of central Africa, taught in the schools of Kenya, TANZANIA and parts of the Congo. (Arabic, 'of the coasts'.)

Swallow National class of keelboat, once but no longer an Olympic class.

Swanee River Corruption of Suwannee River, which flows through Florida to the Gulf of Mexico; it is the river of Stephen Foster's 'Old Folks at Home' (1851) and many subsequent songs. (Suwannee is itself probably a Negro corruption of San Juanee, 'little St John'.)

Swanhild In Norse legend, the daughter of Sigurd (SIEGFRIED), wooed by a king who sends his son as his emissary. The son, falsely accused of seducing her, is sentenced to be hanged, and Swanhild, the innocent cause of the trouble, to be trampled to death by horses.

Swan Lake (1876) Tchaikovsky's ballet based on a German legend about a princess turned by a magician into a creature half swan, half woman. Siegfried falls in love with her but, cheated of happiness, they drown themselves in an enchanted lake.

Swann, Charles In Proust's REMEMBRANCE OF THINGS PAST, a man of Jewish blood accepted in high society, unlike his mistress (and later wife) ODETTE DE CRÉCY. He is the father of GILBERTE.

Swan of Avon, The Ben Jonson's name for Shakespeare, born at Stratford on Avon.

Swanscombe skull A fossil 150,000 years old, found in Thames gravels together with well-made flint tools; thicker than, but otherwise resembling, a modern human skull.

Swansea porcelain (1814-17) A porcelain factory which during its brief existence, like the NANTGARW firm with which it was connected, imitated the fine French wares. Billingsley worked at both factories.

Swarajist Party (1923-26) The moderate section of the Indian CONGRESS PARTY, led by C. R. Das and Motilal Nehru, which advocated Dominion status for India. (SANSKRIT *swaraj*, 'self-rule'.)

Swatantra (1959) A right-wing Indian political party, with strong influence in many parts of the country. It was founded by Rajagopalachari in his 80s after his break with the CONGRESS PARTY, and was dedicated to preserving the best of Indian traditionalism in the modern India created by Nehru. In 1967 it was the second largest party.

Swaythling Cup (1926) An international table tennis championship for teams of men.

Swedenborgianism (1788) The religion, founded in England, of those who accepted the claim of Emanuel Swedenborg (died 1772) of Sweden, made in his sixties after a distinguished career as scientist and philosopher, to be the prophet of the New Jerusalem that came into being after the Last Judgment, which he said had taken place in 1757.

Swedish Nightingale, The Jenny Lind, a Swedish coloratura soprano who became a popular idol in England when she sang Alice in Meyerbeer's ROBERT THE DEVIL (1847), and who then settled in England.

Sweeney A character appearing in several of T. S. Eliot's poems, representing modern man at his most earthy and unattractive level.

Sweeney Todd (1847) A lurid and highly popular melodrama concocted by Dibdin Pitt from a novelette about a 'demon barber' of FLEET STREET, London; there were other versions by various hands which were merged to form the definitive text of this hardy perennial.

'Sweet Adeline!' The BARBERSHOP classic, the tune composed by a Boston boy, Harry Armstrong, in 1896; with words by Richard Gerard Husch it was first published in 1903. The full title is 'You're the Flower of My Heart, Sweet Adeline!'. Jerome Kern composed the operetta *Sweet Adeline!* in 1929.

SWG Initials for (British) Standard Wire Gauge, a classification of the thickness of wire and rods; the highest numbers are the thinnest.

Swift and Company (1885) The biggest US meat-packing group, founded in Chicago by Gustavus Franklin Swift, who in 1877 had been the first to use refrigerator cars and later the first to make full use of animal byproducts; one of the 30 industrials that make up the DOW JONES Industrial Average.

Swingfire A British antitank weapon.

Swiss Admiral Nickname for a hotel doorman, referring to his uniform, which is often such as might have been designed for the admiral of a nonexistent navy.

Swissair The leading Swiss airline.

Swiss cheese US name for a hard cheese characterized by elastic texture, mild nutlike flavor and large holes that form during ripening, e.g. EMMENTALER, GRUYÈRE.

Swiss Family Robinson, The (1813) A children's story, on the lines of ROBINSON CRUSOE, about a clergyman and his family cast on a desert island; written by Prof. Wyss, a Swiss.

Swiss steak A slice of round steak into which flour is pounded, browned in fat and smothered in tomatoes, onions and other vegetables and seasonings.

Swiveller, Dick The eloquent clerk in *The* OLD CURIOSITY SHOP who marries the 'Marchioness', the overworked maid in his employer's household.

Swordfish A national one-design class of 15-foot dinghy, with molded plywood hull and metal mast.

Sword of Honor, The See SOVEREIGN'S PARADE, Sandhurst.

Sword of Honour, The (1952-61) Evelyn Waugh's trilogy of novels of World War II, consisting of: *Men at Arms*, *Officers and Gentlemen* and *Unconditional Surrender*.

Syanon Foundation An organization that tries to help drug addicts.

Sybaris An ancient Greek colony in southern Italy; the word 'sybarite' derives from legends of the luxury and self-indulgence of its people.

Sybil See TWO NATIONS.

Sydney Bulletin (1880) A leading Australian weekly, with general articles, short stories etc.

Sydney-Hobart race (1945) The chief Australian offshore yacht race, held annually.

Sykes-Picot agreement (1916) A secret Anglo-French agreement (published by Russia in 1918) demarcating spheres of influence on the breakup of the Turkish Empire. France was awarded Syria and Mosul, Britain northern Palestine, Transjordan and Iraq. The rest of Palestine was to be put under an international regime. (Sir Mark Sykes, Georges Picot.)

Syllabus errorum (1864) Pope Pius IX's encyclical condemning liberalism and nationalism; it greatly inflamed the anticlerical parties in France and Italy.

Sylphides, Les (1909) A one-act ballet first staged by Diaghilev's Ballets Russes. It is a purely romantic ballet without plot, to music written by Chopin.

Sylvaner A type of grape used in hocks etc.

Sylvia (1876) A ballet with music by Délibes, choreography by Louis Mérante and a story, taken from Tasso's *Aminta*, of how Sylvia, one of DIANA's huntresses, falls in love with a shepherd boy. EROS induces Diana to forgive her the crime of consorting with a mortal.

Symbolists A group of 19th-century French poets who, in reaction against the PARNASSIANS with whom they had earlier associated, aimed at individuality and freedom from Classical forms, and in particular made great use of esoteric symbols of their own devising, and of oblique suggestion in preference to direct statement. They exercised a wide influence on future generations not only of poets but of prose writers of the world. Led by Verlaine and Mallarmé, they acknowledged Gérard de Nerval as the source of their inspiration.

Symphonie fantastique (1830) Berlioz' romantic program music on 'episodes in the life of an artist'.

Symposium, The Plato's dialogue in which Socrates, Alcibiades, Aristophanes and others discuss the nature of love. (Greek, 'drinking together'.)

Syncom Name of a series of US synchronous communications satellites, i.e. of the type that appears 'stationary' as seen from the earth, permitting uninterrupted transmission. *Syncom 2* was the first to prove successful (1963).

Syndicalism (1907) A form of revolutionary Socialism which substitutes workers' for State ownership and control of industry, and advocates the abolition of the State. It achieved fame by violent 'direct action' strikes just before World War I, especially in France, but then faded into the background. See INDUSTRIAL WORKERS OF THE WORLD.

Synoptic problem, The The problem of the relationship of the Synoptic Gospels—*Matthew, Mark* and *Luke* —which, in contrast to *John*, give similar accounts of Christ's mission. The orthodox view is that *Mark* is the earliest, and the main source for the other 2 books. (From Greek for 'seeing together'.)

Syon House Historic Thames-side home at Brentford, Middlesex of the Dukes of Northumberland, with a fine Adam interior.

T

TAB The standard vaccine used in immunization against typhoid and paratyphoid.

Tabard, The The Southwark tavern from which Chaucer's Canterbury pilgrims set out. It was near LONDON BRIDGE in what is now the Borough High Street.

Tabernacles, Feast of the Jewish feast commemorating the wanderings of the Israelites in the desert, held (1970) in October. (*Tabernacle*, the portable tent they used as a sanctuary for the ARK OF THE COVENANT.)

Table Talk (1821-22) William Hazlitt's astringent essays on life and letters.

Tabs Name for undergraduates of CAMBRIDGE UNIVERSITY, short for Cantabs or Cantabrigians, the Latinized form of the name.

Tachisme See ABSTRACT EXPRESSIONISM.

Tacitean In the style of the Roman historian Tacitus (AD 55-117), famous for his incomparably terse and pregnant comments on character, such as *capax imperii, nisi imperasset*, '(he would have been taken for) an able ruler, had he not ruled' (of the Emperor Servius Galba).

Tacna-Arica dispute A dispute between Chile and Peru over possession of 2 provinces occupied by Chile after a war in 1880. In 1929 it was agreed that Chile should keep Arica and restore Tacna to Peru.

Tactical Electronic Warfare Support Arm (1968) A branch of the US Air Force formed to concentrate on ECM, using a number of old aircraft for the purpose.

Tadpole and Taper The twin political 'operators' of Disraeli's CONINGSBY and *Sybil*.

Taffrail The pen name of Capt. H. T. Dorling (born 1883), who served in the Royal Navy during both world wars, and wrote numerous books and stories about naval life.

Taft-Hartley Act (1947) Republican labor legislation canceling concessions gained under the NEW DEAL. It prohibited the closed shop and the use of union funds in national elections, and imposed long 'cooling-off' periods in trade disputes.

Tagalog The name of the Malayan language and people dominant in the Philippines. (From *taga*, 'native'; *ilog*, 'river'.)

Taipei The seat of government of Chiang Kai-shek in FORMOSA, and the capital of the island.

Taiping Rebellion (1851-64) A peasant revolt in China which aimed to establish a 'Heavenly Kingdom of Great Peace'; the rebels were able to dominate several provinces from their capital, Nanking, as the rest of the country was in chaos. The revolt was finally suppressed only with help from foreign officers, including General Gordon.

Taiwan Official name of FORMOSA.

Taj Mahal (1630-50) The white marble mausoleum, with pool and gardens, at Agra (UTTAR PRADESH) built by the MOGUL Shah Jahan to the memory of his favorite wife. (Corruption of his wife's title, Mumtaz Mahal, 'distinguished abode'.)

Tale of a Tub, The (1704) Swift's satire in which a man leaves a shirt each to his sons Peter (the Roman Catholic Church), Martin (Luther; the Anglicans) and Jack (John Calvin; extreme Protestants), on condition that they do not alter them. As time goes by, they all alter them, adding an ornament here, removing a button there. (Title based on sailors' custom of throwing an old tub to a whale – in this case Hobbes's LEVIATHAN – to divert him from attacking the ship.)

Tale of Two Cities (1859) Dickens's story of London and Paris during the FRENCH REVOLUTION; a French émigré returns to France to rescue a servant and is himself rescued by Sydney CARTON. The book gives an inaccurate picture of the revolution, based on Carlyle's account.

Tales of a Wayside Inn (1863) Longfellow's series of narrative poems on the lines of the CANTERBURY TALES, the first of them being *The Midnight Ride of* PAUL REVERE. Each of a party gathered in a NEW ENGLAND tavern tells a tale, with recent events sometimes transposed back to medieval settings.

Tales of Hoffmann (1881) Offenbach's opera inspired by stories written by E. T. A. Hoffmann (died 1822). Hoffmann, seated in a Nuremberg tavern, tells the story of his 3 love affairs and of how they were thwarted by his evil genius, who appears in various guises.

Tales of the Argonauts (1875) A story by Bret Harte, ARGONAUTS referring to the seekers of gold in California in '49.

Talisman, The (1825) Walter Scott's story of the Crusade led by Richard I, in which Saladin, in disguise, cures the ailing Richard with a talisman.

Tallin The capital of the Estonian SSR, formerly known by its Russian name, Revel.

Tallin system A Russian system for identifying and tracking hostile aircraft, being deployed on the northwest borders of the Soviet Union around TALLIN; at first mistakenly thought to be an ABM system.

Talmud The Jewish civil and religious law not contained in, though mainly derived from, the PENTATEUCH, and including the MISHNA. The Babylonian version carries more authority, and dates from the 5th-6th centuries AD; the shorter Jerusalem or Palestinian version was about a century earlier. (Hebrew, 'instruction'.)

Talos US ground-to-air 'point-defense' missile, designed to defend specific small targets; range 65 miles.

Tamburlaine, Tamerlane, Timur-i-Leng Mongol conqueror, descendant of Genghiz Khan, who from his capital at Samarkand conquered the Caucasus region, Persia and north India, and died while preparing to attack China. In Marlowe's play *Tamburlaine the Great* (1590) he is presented as corrupted by power and success. See BAJAZET. (The name means Timur the Lame.)

Tamerlane See TAMBURLAINE.

Tamiami Trail The Tampa-Miami highway in Florida.

Tamil The DRAVIDIAN LANGUAGE of southern Madras and northeast Ceylon.

Taming of the Shrew, The See KATHARINA.

Tammany Hall (1789) Originally a benevolent society, later an anti-British and then antiaristocratic political club which, from the early 19th century, developed into the official organization of the DEMOCRATIC PARTY in MANHATTAN and, through corruption and terror, came to dominate the Party system throughout New York State; synonymous with political graft and gangsterism. (Name of a 17th-century Delaware Indian chief.)

Tammuz The Babylonian vegetation god (derived from a SUMERIAN god), beloved by ISHTAR who brought him back from the Underworld each spring. He is the PHOENICIAN Adon, and the Greek ADONIS; compare also the PERSEPHONE myth.

'Tam o' Shanter' (1791) Robert Burns's poem of a drunk farmer who interrupts a witches' sabbath in the kirkyard of ALLOWAY and, pursued by CUTTY SARK to the Doon River, barely escapes with his life.

TAM-ratings Assessments of the numbers and composition of the audience for TV programs, obtained from meters attached to sample TV sets. (Initials of Television Audience Measurement, a service provided for advertisers and TV organizations, motion-picture companies etc. by NEILSEN in the US, and in Britain until 1968 by the ATTWOOD GROUP and then by AGB.)

Tanagra figures (350-250 BC) Terracotta statuettes found in thousands in ancient Greek graves, of exceptional charm even though their colors have flaked off. They depicted everyday scenes (e.g. a boy on a donkey, a dancing girl, 2 gossips). Similar figures were found in MAGNA GRAECIA and Asia Minor. (Tanagra, village in Boeotia where originally made.)

Tanaka Memorial (1927) A Japanese plan for world conquest, followed closely in subsequent aggression in China and in World War II; Japan denied its authenticity. (General Tanaka, prime minister, died 1929.)

Tancred (1) In Tasso's *Gerusalemme liberata*, a Crusader who unwittingly kills Clorinda, the Persian girl he loves; Rossini wrote an opera about him (1813). (2) A father in the DECAMERON who sends his daughter her murdered lover's heart; she commits suicide. (3) The 19th-century hero of Disraeli's novel of that name, who has a revelation in the Holy Land where he has gone on a 'new crusade'.

T & C Time and Charges, US equivalent of ADC.

T & G Common abbreviation for TGWU ('Transport and General').

Tanganyika A former British Trust Territory now, with Zanzibar, called Tanzania.

T'ang dynasty (AD 618-906) The most brilliant period of Chinese history and art. True porcelain was invented, and the tomb figures of animals (particularly horses) and people are famous. Naturalistic figure painting reached a high peak. The capital was Changan, former name of Sian (Shensi Province). The T'angs were succeeded after an interregnum by the SUNG DYNASTY.

Tanglewood The location of the Berkshire Festival (1934), a famous summer concert series given by the Boston Symphony Orchestra at Lenox, Mass. (Name of the estate donated for the purpose in 1937.)

Tanglewood Tales (1853) Children's stories, based on Greek myths, written by Nathaniel Hawthorne.

Tannenberg Site of 2 battles. (1) The defeat of the TEUTONIC KNIGHTS (1410) by the Poles and Lithuanians; (2) the overwhelming defeat (Aug.

1914) by Hindenburg of Russian armies which had invaded EAST PRUSSIA. (Village in Poland, formerly in East Prussia.)

Tanner, John The passionate rationalist to whom is attributed *The Revolutionist's Handbook* appended to Shaw's play MAN AND SUPERMAN. In the main body of the play he falls rather reluctantly into the arms of the charming Ann Whitefield but, since the 'Don Juan in Hell' scene in Act 3 is rarely staged, his exposition of Shaw's LIFE FORCE theme usually goes unheard.

Tannhäuser (1845) Wagner's opera giving his own version of a medieval legend about a fairyland (Venusberg) beneath a Thuringian mountain, where VENUS lures Tannhäuser, a German troubadour. He eventually breaks away from the spell of Venus and returns to find the loving Elizabeth still faithful to him. He unsuccessfully seeks the Pope's forgiveness, returns from Rome to find Elizabeth has died of despair, and himself dies.

Tannochbrae The fictitious Scottish town made famous in the BBC TV series, *Dr Finlay's Casebook*.

Tantalus In Greek mythology, a favorite of ZEUS who gets into trouble through stealing the gods' ambrosia for his friends, and serving up his son PELOPS as a dish for the gods. He is punished in Hades by having to stand in water which retreats when he tries to quench his thirst, and under a bough of fruit which moves away when he reaches for it. Hence to 'tantalize' and the 'tantalus', a stand for decanters, lockable so that the contents can be seen but not drunk.

Tanzania (1964) The independent East African state formed by the union of Tanganyika (a former British Trust Territory) and Zanzibar (a former British Protectorate).

Taoism (1) A Chinese mystical religion regarding which nothing is certain except the existence of its brief bible, *The Way of Life*, which preaches nonviolence and complete passivity in the face of evil. This is attributed to Lao-tse ('Old Philosopher'), who may never have existed, and it was possibly compiled about the 3rd century BC. (2) The unrelated and degenerate system of magic which usurped its name, gathering deities by the hundred from all quarters. (Chinese *tao*, 'way'.)

TAP Initials of the Portuguese name for Portuguese Airways.

Tapley, Mark The humble but indomitably cheerful companion who visits America with Martin in Dickens's MARTIN CHUZZLEWIT.

Tapline Abbreviated name of the Trans-Arabian Pipe Line Co. which, in association with ARAMCO, owns the oil pipeline from Saudi Arabia through Jordan and Syria to a Lebanon port.

Tara Hill A hill in Co. Meath, Ireland, the traditional capital of the FIR BOLG and their successors, where the FEIS OF TARA was held. Abandoned in the 6th century, only earthworks remain. See TARA'S HALLS.

Taranto raid (1940) The British Fleet Air Arm's attack on the Italian fleet in Taranto harbor, which inflicted severe damage by air torpedo.

Taras Bulba (1835) Gogol's novel of a 17th-century Cossack, Taras Bulba; he kills his son who, for the sake of a girl, has deserted to the Polish enemy. He and his other son are tortured to death by the Poles.

Tara's halls See TARA HILL. 'The harp that once through Tara's halls / The soul of music shed' are the opening lines of one of Thomas Moore's *Irish Melodies* (1807-35).

Tar Baby, The In UNCLE REMUS, a tar doll made by Brer Fox, to which Brer Rabbit gets himself stuck fast.

Tarbela dam See MANGLA DAM.

Targa Florio A road race for sports cars held in Sicily.

Tar Heel State Nickname of North Carolina. (Various fanciful derivations have been suggested.)

Tariff Commission, US (1916) A Federal agency that serves Congress as an advisory and fact-finding agency on commercial policy.

Tariff Reform A movement to end FREE TRADE and introduce protective tariffs for British industry, to meet in particular the growing threat of German competition; advocated by Joseph Chamberlain and his TARIFF REFORM LEAGUE, and linked with IMPERIAL PREFERENCE, it split the Conservatives and led to the Liberal landslide victory in the 1906 Election.

Tariff Reform League (1903) Founded to support Joseph Chamberlain's campaigns for TARIFF REFORM and IMPERIAL PREFERENCE.

Tarka the Otter (1927) The most popular of Henry Williamson's animal stories.

Tarot The fortune-teller's card pack, adapted by 14th-century Italians from the standard pack recently introduced from the East, with 22 added cards bearing symbols of virtues, vices, death etc.

Tarpeian rock A rock of ancient Rome on the CAPITOLINE Hill, from which traitors were cast to their death.

Tarquins, The The ETRUSCAN family that provided the 5th and 7th Kings of Rome (7th-6th centuries BC). The latter, Tarquinius Superbus, was expelled (510) and the Republic was founded. See LARS PORSENA; LUCRECE.

Tarr (1918) Percy Wyndham Lewis's novel of a cosmopolitan group of art students in Paris, led by an Englishman, Frederick Tarr.

Tarsus Birthplace of Saul (St Paul), 'a citizen of no mean city' (*Acts* xxi, 39), an ancient city of Cilicia (now in Turkey).

Tartar US ground-to-air 'point-defense' missile, designed to defend specific small targets; range 10 miles.

Tartare sauce Egg-mayonnaise flavored with mustard, capers etc.

Tartarin de Tarascon The typical Provençal braggart who tells of his astonishing exploits in 3 of Alphonse Daudet's books (1872-85).

Tartars (1) A Mongolian nomadic tribe, speaking a Turkish language, of obscure origin, probably from east Mongolia. The MANCHUS were a Tartar people. (2) Name applied by Europeans in the 13th century to all MONGOLS; they did not use the latter name until later. (3) MUSLIM inhabitants of the USSR, in the Tatar ASSR (capital, Kazan), Crimea (Krim Tartars) and southwest Siberia. They speak a Turkish language but have little Mongol blood in them. (Tartar is a long-established misspelling of Tatar.)

Tartarus A Greek name for the Underworld; in Homer, for the lowest depths of it, where the TITANS and other evildoers suffer eternal punishment.

Tartary European name used in the 14th century for a vast area of Central Asia and south Russia inhabited by 'TARTARS', i.e. MONGOLS.

Tartuffe The religious hypocrite of Molière's comedy (1664) of that name who is foiled in his attempts to swindle the credulous Orgon out of his money.

Tarzan The athletic scion of English nobility abandoned in infancy when his parents were killed in the African jungle, where he was brought up by apes. The hero of Edgar Rice Burroughs's *Tarzan of the Apes* (1914), he has since appeared in countless sequels, movies, comic strips and TV serials. Now a grandfather, he still goes on, though his creator died in 1950.

Tashkent Declaration (1966) A treaty renouncing the use of force in the Kashmir dispute between India and PAKISTAN, signed by the Russian premier Kosygin, who convened the meeting, President Ayub Khan and (just before his death) the Indian prime minister, Lal Bahadur Shastri. (Capital of Uzbek SSR.)

Tass (1925) Official Soviet Russian news agency. (Initials of Russian for Soviet Telegraph Agency.)

Tassili A plateau in the Sahara where Henri Lhote discovered (1956) thousands of NEOLITHIC rock paintings of people and animals.

Taste of Honey, A (1958) A play by Shelagh Delaney and the THEATRE WORKSHOP, about a young girl who is told by her mother to ruin her life in her own way, and does that; later made into a movie.

Tatars See TARTARS.

Tate, The (1897) Abbreviated name for the Tate Gallery, Millbank, London, an important collection of British art from the 16th century (including the Turner Bequest), and of 19th and 20th century foreign paintings, particularly Impressionists and Postimpressionists. (Sir Henry Tate, the sugar merchant, founder.)

Tatler, The (1709-11) A thrice-weekly periodical, consisting mainly of essays by Sir Richard Steele (under the name Isaac Bickerstaff), Addison and Swift. It was succeeded by *The* SPECTATOR.

Tattenham Corner A crucial corner of the Epsom racetrack (see EPSOM DOWNS), a sharp turn at the foot of a slope into the final straight.

Tattersall's (1) A London auction room for bloodstock, established near Hyde Park Corner (1766), and still functioning at Brompton nearby. (2) Tattersall's Committee, an unofficial body which supervises betting on horse races. (3) Tattersall's ring, the principal betting enclosure on a racetrack. (Richard Tattersall, stud-groom to the Duke of Kingston.)

Tatt's Common abbreviation for TATTERSALL'S.

Tau Beta Kappa (1885) A US fraternity or 'honor society' for those distinguished in the field of engineering.

Tauchnitz editions (1841) Cheap German paperback editions of English and American novels, once popular with continental travelers.

Taurus The Bull, 2nd of the constellations of the Zodiac, between ARIES and GEMINI; the sun enters it about April 21st. It contains the PLEIADES, HYADES, CRAB NEBULA and ALDEBARAN. Astrologers claim that those born under this sign may be unimaginative, slow, staunch.

Taylorian, The (1845) Abbreviated name of the Taylorian Institute, OXFORD UNIVERSITY, where modern languages are taught; it has an important library. (Endowed by Sir Robert Taylor, died 1788.)

Taylorism Scientific factory management, based on the works of F. W. Taylor (1856-1915), US engineer, who introduced the idea of time and motion study.

TCA Trans-Canada Airlines, now renamed AIR CANADA.

Teal Traina A New York fashion house.

Teamsters Union The International Brotherhood of Teamsters, a large union of truck drivers, renowned for its intransigence and corruption. The AFL/CIO expelled it in 1957, and in 1967 its leader, James Hoffa, was at last consigned to jail for trying to bribe a jury.

Teapot Dome scandal (1924) The discovery that the US Secretary of the Interior, Albert B. Fall, had leased to a private company government oilfields in the Teapot Dome reserve, Wyoming. He was convicted of receiving a large bribe and sent to prison.

Teazle, Lady In Sheridan's SCHOOL FOR SCANDAL, an attractive young girl from the country married to an old man, who finds her hiding behind a screen in Joseph Surface's rooms in circumstances not quite so compromising as they seem.

Tecumseh A SHAWNEE chief who, with his brother, the PROPHET, formed a confederacy of tribes in the northwest to oppose white expansion into the West. Despite support from the British in Canada, the Prophet was defeated at TIPPECANOE (1811) and Tecumseh was killed during the WAR OF 1812 at the Battle of the Thames (Moraviantown) near Chatham, Ontario (1813).

Teddy boys (1955) A nickname for the English working-class teen-agers who celebrated their newly gained economic emancipation by spending (collectively) vast sums on a caricature of Edwardian fashions, expensive hairstyles (with sideburns), and records of popular music. Other features of the new way of life were gang warfare, vandalism and sexual license; a sullen expression was also de rigueur. (Teddy for 'Edwardian'.)

Teddy Tail (1915) Hero of the first English strip-cartoon for adults, drawn by various artists and published in Northcliffe's *Daily Mail*.

Te Deum Opening words used as the name of a 4th-century hymn to the TRINITY attributed to St Ambrose. It is sung at church services and particularly at services of public thanksgiving. It has been set to music by Purcell, Handel, Haydn, Verdi, Bruckner and others. (Latin, *Te Deum laudamus*, 'we praise thee, O God'.)

Tedworth Drummer, The (1661) The first documented report of poltergeist phenomena. A vagrant drummer was arrested at Tedworth, Wiltshire, and his drum confiscated. Sounds of drumming, which could not be traced to any source, were intermittently heard over a long period in the house of the magistrate responsible.

Teheran Conference (Nov.-Dec. 1943) A meeting of Churchill, Roosevelt and Stalin immediately after the CAIRO CONFERENCE, at which Stalin agreed to coordinate a new Soviet offensive with OVERLORD.

Telemachus The son of ODYSSEUS, who grew up while his father was at Troy and helped him outwit the suitors on his return.

Telex A British Post Office service which hires out teleprinters to subscribers, enabling them to send printed messages over telephone lines to subscribers similarly equipped, at home or abroad.

Tell, William A legendary hero of 14th-century Switzerland. Forced by an Austrian tyrant to shoot through an apple placed on the head of his small son, he used a second arrow to kill his tormentor and then raised a rebellion. The story has no historical basis; it was used by Schiller in his play *Wilhelm Tell* (1804) and by Rossini in his opera (1829) of the same name.

Tell el 'Amarna See AMARNA. (*Tell*, 'mound'.)

Telstar 1 The first communications satellite to amplify the signals it relayed, launched from USA in 1962. Superseded by SYNCOM.

Telugu The DRAVIDIAN LANGUAGE spoken in ANDHRA PRADESH.

Tempest An international class of 2-man 22-ft, ½-ton keelboat designed by Ian Proctor, for which there is a world championship raced at Weymouth in August. The first English design to attain Olympic status.

Tempest, The (1611) Shakespeare's last play; see PROSPERO.

Templars (1) See KNIGHTS TEMPLARS. (2) Members of the Good Templars, a temperance society. (3) Lawyers and law students with chambers in the TEMPLE (London).

Temple, The (London) The site between FLEET STREET and the Thames originally occupied by the KNIGHTS TEMPLARS. Edward III gave it to the law students, for whom the INNER TEMPLE and Middle Temple were established.

Temple Bar (1673) Originally a CITY of London gateway, rebuilt by Wren to mark the City boundary at the junction of FLEET STREET and the Strand, close to the entrance to the TEMPLE. In 1878 it was moved to a private park at Cheshunt and replaced by a Victorian memorial.

Temple Church (1185) A church in the TEMPLE which incorporates the KNIGHTS TEMPLARS' 'round' church (a copy of the Church of the Holy Sepulcher at Jerusalem), now shared by the INNER TEMPLE and the Middle Temple. Badly damaged during World War II, it was restored in the 1950s.

Temps modernes, Les (1946) Sartre's existentialist magazine, the forum for his quarrel (1948) with Camus, who was quicker than Sartre to reject Communism.

Ten Commandments, The (1) Also called the Decalogue, of which there are differing versions in *Exodus* xx, 2-17 and *Deuteronomy* v, 6-21. They were given to Moses and the Israelites on Mount Sinai. See FIRST (etc.) COMMANDMENT. (2) The title of a spectacular movie (1923) by Cecil B. DeMille, which netted even more dollars than *Gone with the Wind*.

10 Downing Street The address of the British Prime Minister's official residence off WHITEHALL. See DOWNING STREET.

Tennant Trophy A skiing competition held at Glenshee, near Devil's Elbow, Scotland, in March.

Tennessee Valley Authority See TVA.

Ten Nights in a Barroom (1) A temperance novel (1854) by Timothy Shay Arthur, subtitled 'And What I Saw There'. (2) A melodrama (1858) by William W. Pratt, almost as popular as UNCLE TOM'S CABIN, and climaxed by little Mary's song at the barroom door: Father, dear Father, come home with me now.

1066 and All That (1931) A résumé of British history by R. J. Yeatman and W. C. Sellar, written as if by one of the less-gifted schoolboys. Kings and queens are tersely dismissed as 'good' or 'bad', their acts as 'Good things' or 'Bad things'. Genealogical trees of startling simplicity (and inaccuracy) and the richest of howlers combined to make the book a wonderful tonic during the Great DEPRESSION. A stage version was also very popular.

Tenth Commandment 'Thou shalt not covet thy neighbor's house . . .' (*Exodus* xx, 17). Split by Roman Catholics into 2 Commandments, the Ninth and Tenth.

Teocalli The AZTEC terraced pyramid with a flat top, on which a temple was built. (Literally, 'godhouse'.)

Terpsichore The Greek muse of dancing.

Terra Nova, HMS The ship in which Capt. Scott sailed on his last Antarctic expedition (1910).

Terrans Name used by science-fiction writers for the backward inhabitants of the speck in the universe commonly called the Earth. (Latin *terra*, 'earth'.)

Terrier US ground-to-air 'point-defense' missile, designed to defend specific small targets; range 10 miles.

Terror, Reign of (1793-94) The period of the FRENCH REVOLUTION during the regime of the COMMITTEE OF PUBLIC SAFETY from the overthrow of the GIRONDINS to the execution of Robespierre (THERMIDOR).

Terry A name associated with early American wooden clocks. Eli Terry opened his own shop in Plymouth, Conn., in 1793 and was the first to use standardized interchangeable parts.

Tertiary Period The earlier part of the CENOZOIC ERA, lasting from about 70 to 1 million years ago, divided

into the EOCENE, OLIGOCENE, MIOCENE
and PLIOCENE EPOCHS. During this
period modern types of mammals
and flowering plants gradually
evolved and, towards the end, the
AUSTRALOPITHECINES appeared. (Tertiary because the 2 earlier eras were
originally called Primary and Secondary.)

Terylene British trade name of a
synthetic polyester fiber made by ICI
at Wilton, Yorkshire; it has less elas-
ticity than nylon, but much greater
resistance to acids, creasing and to
deterioration in sunlight. Called
Dacron in USA.

Tess The ill-used heroine of Thomas
Hardy's *Tess of the d'Urbervilles*
(1891). Seduced by the squire's son
Alec, she marries the rector's son
Angel Clare who, finding that she is
'a maiden no more' (in the words of
the novel), deserts her. She returns
to the repentant Alec, where she is
found by the repentant Angel; she
kills Alec and is sentenced to death.
In the words of the pessimistic Hardy: The President of the Immortals
had ended his sport with Tess.

Test Act (1673) Enacted that all office holders must be members of the
Church of England and take oaths of
allegiance; passed by Parliament
after James, Duke of York (James II),
had declared himself a Roman Catholic.

Testament of Beauty (1929) A long
philosophical poem by Robert
Bridges written in loose alexan-
drines and idiosyncratic spelling, a
distillation of what he had learned
from life offered as guidance to a
despairing generation.

Testament of Friendship (1940)
Vera Brittain's biography of her
friend Winifred Holtby, the novelist.

Test-ban Treaty (1963) A treaty
banning nuclear tests in the atmosphere (but
not underground) of nuclear weap-
ons; signed by USA, Britain, USSR,
later joined by a hundred other
countries, but not by France.

Tetrazzini Name given to certain
elaborate dishes, e.g. Chicken Tetrazzini, Veal Tetrazzini, in honor of
the famous operatic soprano (1874-
1940).

Teufelsdröckh, Professor See SAR-
TOR RESARTUS.

Teutonic Knights (1190) A German
order founded at Acre to tend
wounded Crusaders. In the 13th-
14th centuries it campaigned against
the pagan Prussians and Lithuanians, and massacred the SLAVS. TAN-
NENBERG (1410) began its decline,
and it was dissolved by Napoleon,
but revived in Austria in 1840 as a
semireligious order which carries
out ambulance work.

Teutonic languages The Germanic
branch of the INDO-EUROPEAN LAN-
GUAGE group, of which the modern
representatives include German,
English, Dutch, and the Scandinavian languages. (From *Teutones*,
Latin name for the German tribes.)

TEV See TODAY'S ENGLISH VERSION.

Texaco (1926) An oil company
which operates throughout the
Americas and in Saudi Arabia etc.;
see BAHREIN PETROLEUM CO. One of
the 30 industrials that make up the
DOW JONES Industrial Average.

Tey, Josephine Pen name assumed
by Elizabeth Mackintosh when
writing detective stories, of which
the best was *The Franchise Affair*
(1948). She was also the Gordon
Daviot who wrote *Richard of Bordeaux*.

TGIF Thank God It's Friday! — a *cri
de coeur* alien perhaps only to STA-
KHANOVITES.

TGWU (1922) Initials of the British
Transport and General Workers
Union, the biggest British, or European, trade union, with a membership of bus drivers, quarrymen,
dock workers etc. Founded by Ernest
Bevin, and later associated with the
name of Frank Cousins, its headquarters are at TRANSPORT HOUSE,
Westminster.

Thailand Official name of Siam.

Thaïs (1) An Athenian courtesan,
mistress of Alexander the Great and
later wife to Ptolemy I, King of
Egypt; she is said to have persuaded
Alexander to destroy the Persian
capital, PERSEPOLIS, in 331 BC. (2) A
courtesan of 1st-century Alexandria
who became a nun and resisted seduction by her converter; the subject
of a novel by Anatole France (1890)
and an opera by Massenet (1894).

Thalia (1) The Greek muse of comedy and pastoral verse. (2) One of the GRACES.

Thames Cup (1868) An open event at HENLEY Regatta for eights not in the GRAND CHALLENGE CUP class.

Thames TV (1968) A commercial program-contracting company which provides weekday services for the London region (see LONDON WEEKEND TV). It was formed by Associated-Rediffusion and ABC-TV; the studios are at Teddington.

Thammuz See TAMMUZ.

'Thanatopsis' Perhaps the best poem by William Cullen Bryant, the poet of the Berkshire hills of western Massachusetts. Although written at the age of 16 (published 6 years later), it foreshadowed, in its rejection of PURITAN dogma, his conversion from Calvinism to Unitarianism, and also the recourse to Nature for solace, which became habitual with him. (Greek, 'a view of death'.)

Thanksgiving Day A national holiday on the fourth Thursday in November, commemorating the first harvest festival held by the PILGRIM FATHERS at New Plymouth in 1621. Turkey with cranberry sauce is the traditional dish on this day.

Thatcher Ferry Bridge (1962) A mile-long bridge over the Panama Canal near Balboa, 201 ft above water level.

Thaw murder case (1906) Harry Thaw, playboy son of a Pittsburgh millionaire, shot and killed the famous architect Stanford White at MADISON SQUARE GARDEN (which White had designed), allegedly to avenge the honor of his wife, the show girl Evelyn Nesbit. Thaw was found not guilty because insane, escaped, was given a similar verdict on a kidnapping charge (1917), released in 1924, and died 1947.

THC A synthetic form of hashish (Cannabis).

Theater of the Absurd, Cruelty, Fact See under those words.

Theatre Royal (London) The official name of the theaters better known as Drury Lane and the Haymarket.

Theatre Workshop A repertory theater started by Joan Littlewood in the East End of London during the 1950's, where plays such as FINGS AIN'T WOT THEY USED T'BE and *Sparrers Can't Sing* were built up by copious improvisation during rehearsals.

Thebes (Egypt) Ancient capital of Egypt during the MIDDLE KINGDOM, and a religious and cultural center under the NEW KINGDOM, situated at the bend of the Nile, on both sides of the river. The modern villages of KARNAK and LUXOR lie to the north and south of the site on the right bank, and the VALLEY OF THE KINGS on the left bank.

Thebes (Greece) The ancient capital of Boeotia; see OEDIPUS. (Named after the nymph Thebe; no connection with Egyptian Thebes.)

Theory of the Leisure Class, The (1899) A sociological study by the American left-wing economist, Thorstein Veblen, in which he popularized the term 'conspicuous consumption', a vice he attributed to the idle rich or leisure class, in the days before it became the vice also of the nonidle nonrich.

Theosophical Society (1875) Founded in New York by the Russian Mme Blavatsky, who claimed to be inspired by a White Brotherhood of adepts living in the Himalayas. It propagates a mixture of Hindu and Buddhist mysticism.

Thérèse Desqueyroux (1927) François Mauriac's novel of a woman who tires of her bourgeois husband, tries to murder him, and is acquitted at the subsequent trial.

Thermidor In the FRENCH REVOLUTION calendar, the month from July 19th to August 17th; 9 Thermidor (1794) is the date of Robespierre's assassination, marking the end of the Reign of TERROR and of the Revolution. In Communist jargon 'Thermidor' is consequently used of a victory of the bourgeoisie over revolutionaries. ('Hot month'.)

Thermopylae (480 BC) A narrow pass on the Greek coast opposite Euboea, where the King of Sparta, Leonidas, and 1000 SPARTANS and Thespians fought to the last man to delay the invading Persian host under Xerxes. Simonides wrote their epitaph: Go, tell the Spartans, thou who passest by, / That here obedient to their laws we lie.

Thersites In Homer's *Iliad* an ugly and scurrilous Greek with a gift for invective; Achilles killed him for jeering at him.

Theseus A major hero of Greek legend, the King of Athens who overcame the CENTAURS, slew Procrustes and the MINOTAUR, deserted ARIADNE, married first Hippolyta, the Queen of the AMAZONS against whom he was fighting, and after her death PHAEDRA. He appears in Chaucer and the MIDSUMMER NIGHT'S DREAM as Duke of Athens.

Thespian An actor or actress. (From *Thespis*, a Greek playwright or actor of the 6th century BC, of whom little is known.)

Thessalonica The Greek name of Salonika.

Thetis (1) In Greek legend, a NEREID, mother of ACHILLES. (2) Name of a British submarine that sank shortly before World War II.

Thieves' Kitchen, The FAGIN's nest of pickpockets in OLIVER TWIST.

Things Fall Apart (1958) A remarkable first novel by a Nigerian (IBO) writer, Chinua Achebe.

'Thinker, The' Rodin's sculpture; see 'LE PENSEUR'.

Thin Man, The (1934) Dashiell Hammett's last novel. Nick Charles, a retired detective, discovers that the thin man of the title, suspected of a murder, had himself been killed months before the crime was committed—by the real culprit. More notable for comedy than detective ingenuity, it gave birth to a series of extremely popular movies starring William Powell and Myrna Loy.

Thin Red Line, The (1) Nickname of the 93rd Foot (2nd Battalion The Argyll and Sutherland Highlanders), won at BALACLAVA. (2) Applied in general to British infantry in action.

Thira A Greek island in the Aegean where an American-Greek team found the remains of a large Minoan city, buried under volcanic ash about 1500 BC; it is regarded as possible evidence that the legend of ATLANTIS was based on memories of this disaster.

Third Coalition (1805-07) The final alliance against France, formed by Pitt and including Britain, Austria, Russia, and later Prussia. After the initial victory of TRAFALGAR it met with a series of defeats at ULM, AUSTERLITZ, JENA, Eylau and Friedland, and was ended by the Treaty of TILSIT. See NAPOLEONIC WARS.

Third Commandment 'Thou shalt not take the name of . . . God in vain' (*Exodus* XX, 7). To Roman Catholics this is the Second Commandment.

Third Estate (*Tiers État*) The Commons of the French STATES GENERAL. When Louis XVI insisted that the 3 Estates should have one vote each, so ensuring that the Commons would be outvoted, the latter broke away and formed the NATIONAL ASSEMBLY (June 1789).

Third Force (1945) General de Gaulle's conception of a European coalition, including West Germany, to form an economic and military unit big enough to compete with, stand up to and mediate between the 2 superpowers, USA and USSR. See also 'KEEP LEFT' GROUP.

Third International Alternative name of the COMINTERN.

Third Man, The (1950) Graham Greene's thriller set in postwar Vienna; made into a movie by Carol Reed with the popular Harry Lime theme tune played on a zither.

'Third of May, 1808, The' (1814) Goya's horrific picture of a firing squad, summing up the terror of the French occupation of Spain, which was also portrayed in his series of etchings entitled 'Disasters of War'. Now in the PRADO, Madrid.

Third Programme (1946) The original name of the BBC's third radio program, designed to appeal to a higher level of artistic and intellectual taste than the other programs. From 1957 its wavelength was shared with Network 3, which gave detailed coverage of major sporting events etc., and in 1970 the name was dropped.

Third Reading (Parliament) Generally, the final stage in the treatment of a bill in each House, which considers the bill as a whole and can make only minor amendments. If approved by both Houses, it becomes law on receiving the ROYAL ASSENT.

Third Reich (1933-45) Hitler's own name for the Nazi regime, which he said would last 1000 years. ('Third' because he regarded the HOLY ROMAN EMPIRE and the German Empire as the first 2 great periods of German dominance in Europe.)

Third Republic (1875-1940) The period of French history from the FRANCO-PRUSSIAN WAR to the capitulation of France and the institution of the VICHY GOVERNMENT; notorious in the 1920s and 1930s for the fratricidal strife of fractionalized chameleon parties under leaders all striving for office and most of them achieving it, if only for a few weeks.

Third World A term sometimes used of the Afro-Asian nations, now in disfavor as implying a unity of outlook and policy that does not exist.

'Thirteen Plots of May 13' (1958) The political turmoil in France which led, not without his connivance, to General de Gaulle's return to power.

13th Amendment (1865) The amendment to the US Constitution which abolished slavery throughout the Union.

38th Parallel (of latitude) The boundary between North and South Korea fixed in 1945 when they were occupied by Russian and US troops respectively; unaltered by the subsequent KOREAN WAR of 1950-53.

Thirty-Nine Articles (1571) A restatement of the Protestant doctrines of Cranmer's 42 Articles (1553), authorized by Elizabeth I, to which Anglican clergy are still obliged to subscribe.

Thirty-Nine Steps (1915) John Buchan's thriller in which Richard Hannay pursues German spies round Britain.

Thirty Years War (1618-48) A partly religious war between Protestants and Catholics which the HAPSBURGS used as a pretext for an unsuccessful attempt to gain control of the German states. Fought mainly by mercenaries, it devastated Germany which, however, retained its freedom. It started with a Bohemian Protestant revolt; Gustavus Adolphus of Sweden joined in on the Protestant side, as did France, which emerged the dominant European power. The Treaty of WESTPHALIA ended the war.

'This Land is Your Land' A patriotic folk song by Woody Guthrie.

Thomas Cup (1948) Men's international badminton championship. (Sir George Thomas.)

Thomas's (1213) Short title of St Thomas's Hospital, London, originally at SOUTHWARK, moved (1868) to the South Bank opposite the Houses of Parliament. (Named after St Thomas à Becket.)

Thomism The religious and philosophical doctrines of St Thomas Aquinas, since 1879 the official basis of Roman Catholic theology. Aquinas, striving to reconcile new learning with old belief, held that reason and faith could never conflict, since both derived from God and revealed him; and that there was no salvation outside the true Church. Thus, the unbaptized and those who died, unabsolved, in mortal sin were condemned to eternal torment. (Thomas of Aquino, a 13th-century DOMINICAN.)

Thor In Scandinavian mythology son of ODIN, god of thunder and war, after whom Thursday is named.

Thor US Air Force liquid-fuel IRBM, range 1500 miles, designed to carry a nuclear warhead; first delivered to the RAF in 1958.

Thorndyke, Dr A character created by R. Austin Freeman (1907); he is at once a leading criminal lawyer and a doctor of medicine who specializes in poisoning cases.

Thoroughbred The English racehorse, bred for speed by crossing domestic and Middle Eastern strains. The world's Thoroughbreds can, without exception, be traced through the male line to Matchem (1748), grandson of the Godolphin

Arabian, Herod (1758), great-grandson of the BYERLY TURK, or ECLIPSE (1764), great-grandson of the Darley Arabian. The average height is 16 hands. Compare STANDARDBRED.

Thoth The ancient Egyptian god of learning, wisdom and magic, represented in art as having the head of an ibis. Equivalent to the Greek Hermes. See HERMES TRISMEGISTUS.

Thousand and One Nights, The See ARABIAN NIGHTS.

Thousand Days, A (1965) An account of the presidency of J. F. Kennedy written by one of his aides, Prof. Arthur Schlesinger.

Thousand Island dressing Mayonnaise with various seasonings (e.g. chili sauce, green peppers, pickles, olives) and flavorings (orange, lemon).

Thousand Islands A group of over 1500 islands in the St Lawrence River at the outlet of Lake Ontario; some are Canadian, some in New York State, and several have summer resorts. Suspension bridges (one US, one Canadian) form a link across the river.

Thrale, Mrs See PIOZZI, HESTER.

Three Choirs Festival (1724) An English festival of sacred music held in September at Worcester, given by the choirs of Gloucester, Worcester and Hereford cathedrals.

Three-Cornered Hat, The (1919) Falla's ballet written for Diaghilev, with Massine as choreographer and Picasso as designer.

Three Kings, The Traditionally GASPAR, MELCHIOR and BALTHAZAR, who came to worship the infant Jesus. They are not mentioned in the New Testament, but are suggested by *Isaiah* lx, 3-6. See MAGI.

Three Musketeers, The (1844) Alexandre Dumas' popular novel, based on the semifictitious *Mémoires de M. d'Artagnan* by Courtilz de Sandras (1709), set in the 17th-century France of Cardinal Richelieu. The Musketeers, Athos, Porthos and Aramis, are members of Louis XIII's bodyguard, and are joined by the penniless Gascon, D'Artagnan. These characters reappear in various sequels.

Threepenny Opera (1928) Brecht's opera, with music by Kurt Weill, giving a modern sociological slant to Gay's BEGGAR'S OPERA. (German title, *Dreigroschenoper*.)

Three Plays for Puritans (1901) A volume of Bernard Shaw's plays, comprising *The Devil's Disciple, Caesar and Cleopatra* and *Captain Brassbound's Conversion*.

Three Rs, The A phrase for reading, writing and 'rithmetic, dating back to the early 19th century.

Three Sisters, The (1901) Chekhov's play of sisters in a provincial garrison town who hope officers of the regiment stationed there will rescue them from their drab lives and take them off to Moscow. Their schemes go awry, the regiment departs, and they are left still dreaming of Moscow.

Three Star (★★★) Cognac Trade term for standard quality brandy, probably 5 years old.

Three Weeks (1907) Elinor Glyn's Edwardian *succès de scandale*, memorable for its passionate heroine posturing about on leopard skins in a fantasy-*affaire* of the kind that the author seems to have acted out in real life with such an unlikely partner as Nathaniel Lord Curzon.

Thresher, USS An American nuclear-powered submarine which sank during her test trials in 1963, with the loss of 129 lives.

Throgmorton's plot (1584) One of several Roman Catholic plots against Elizabeth I. (Also spelled Throckmorton.)

Throgmorton Street The site of, and used for, the London Stock Exchange.

Thrones An order of angels; see CHERUBIM.

Through the Looking Glass (1872) (1) A sequel to ALICE IN WONDERLAND, in much the same vein; Alice climbs through a looking glass into a country set out like a chessboard, with walking, talking chessmen. (2) A suite for orchestra by Deems Taylor, in 5 'pictures'.

Thrums J. M. Barrie's imaginary town, representing his birthplace, Kirriemuir (Angus); the setting of his novel, *A Window in Thrums* (1889) and his novel and play, *The Little Minister* (1891).

Thunderbird   British Army's surface-to-air solid-fuel guided missile, made by BAC, and designed to be fired from a vehicle; range 28 miles.

Thunderbirds   The US Air Force precision flying team; compare BLUE ANGELS. (In American Indian folklore, the huge thunderbird could produce thunder and lightning.)

Thunderer, The   A nickname of the London *Times*.

Thundering Herd, The   Nickname of the largest stockbroking firm in the world, Merrill Lynch, Pierce, Fenner & Smith Inc. of New York.

Thunder over Mexico   (1932) One of 3 versions of Eisenstein's *Que viva Mexico!*, a vivid reconstruction of the Mexican Revolution, filmed in Mexico.

Thuringia   A former German province, capital WEIMAR, now in East Germany.

Thus Spake Zarathustra   (1892) The work in which Nietzsche developed his theory of SUPERMAN, using Zarathustra (ZOROASTER) as his mouthpiece.

Tia Maria   A Jamaican liqueur made of spirit distilled from sugarcane and flavored with Blue Mountain coffee.

Tichborne claimant   (1866) Arthur Orton, a Wapping butcher who claimed to be Roger Tichborne, heir to an ancient baronetcy, presumed drowned in a shipwreck. Although Lady Tichborne 'recognized' her son, he was unmasked after the longest trial in English history, and sentenced to 14 years.

Tichborne dole   A Lady Day ceremony at Alresford, Hampshire; in the 12th century Lady Tichborne as she lay dying made her skinflint husband promise to give to the poor all the farmland she could crawl round before a torch she carried burned out. She managed to get round no less than 23 acres, which still provide a dole of flour for the poor.

Ticker-Tape parade   A US specialty, in which streamers (including ticker tape) and confetti are thrown from upper stories over a passing parade for a celebrity.

Tien Shan observatory   A Chinese observatory in Sinkiang at a height of 6500 feet in the Tien Shan Mountains, where work began in 1958 on a 236-inch telescope, i.e. larger than that at MOUNT PALOMAR OBSERVATORY.

Tiergarten   The Berlin park made by Frederick the Great; it has been replanted with trees since the war.

Tietjens tetralogy   (1924-28) Ford Madox Ford's novels: *Some Do Not, No More Parades, A Man Could Stand Up* and *The Last Post*. They portray, impressionistically, the decline of the Edwardian upper classes, as exemplified by the hero, Christopher Tietjens. (Also known as *Parade's End*.)

Tiffany glass   A beautiful opalesque glass made by a process patented (c. 1880) by Louis Tiffany (1848-1933), son of the famous New York jeweler, and himself a painter, stained-glass artist and leader of the ART NOUVEAU movement in the US. Many vases were in the shape of flowers or plants; some pieces are marked 'Favrile', the name he invented for this type of glass.

Tiffany's   The fashionable New York jewelers.

Tiflis   The Russian name of Tbilisi (the Georgian name), capital of the Georgian SSR.

Tiger   (1941) A German infantry tank of World War II; 56 tons, 600 h.p., 25 m.p.h.

Tiger, The   A nickname of Georges Clemenceau, formidable French premier (1906-9, 1917-20).

Tiger at the Gates   (1955) Christopher Fry's translation of Jean Giraudoux' *La Guerre de Troie n'aura pas lieu* (1935). HECTOR persuades the Trojan leaders to avoid war with the Greeks, but the people, aroused by a lying rumor, precipitate one nevertheless.

Tigercat   A British missile, the land equivalent of the Navy's SEACAT.

Tiger Moth   See MOTH.

Tigers   The Detroit Tigers, AMERICAN (Baseball) LEAGUE, playing at the Tiger Stadium.

Tikopia A small Pacific island in the Solomons, known through intensive studies carried out there by the anthropologist Raymond Firth.

Tilbury Review (1588) The occasion when Queen Elizabeth addressed her troops on the approach of the Spanish Armada.

Till Eulenspiegel In German folklore, a practical joker who represents the despised peasant triumphing over the slick townsman; Richard Strauss used the legend in his tone poem, *Till Eulenspiegel's Merry Pranks* (1894). (German, literally 'owl-glass', 'mischief-maker'.)

Tillie and Gus (1933) A movie in which W. C. Fields plays Uncle Gus to a toddler then known as Baby LeRoy.

Tillings, Thomas A family of UK companies built up by Lionel Fraser; their activities include transport, vehicle distribution (Mercedes-Benz, VOLKSWAGEN, Stratstone), engineering, aerosols, glassware, textiles and clothing, insurance (Cornhill), publishing and printing (Heinemanns, Martin Secker & Warburg, Peter Davies), and building supplies.

Tilsit Old German name of Sovetsk, a town on the Niemen (Neman), formerly in EAST PRUSSIA, now in Lithuania, USSR.

Tilsit, Treaty of (1807) After Prussia's defeat at JENA, Napoleon met Tsar Alexander I on a raft at TILSIT and agreed to an alliance against Britain; PRUSSIA was divided up between a kingdom of WESTPHALIA under Jerome Bonaparte, a new duchy of Warsaw under the King of SAXONY, and Russia. See THIRD CO-ALITION.

Tilsit cheese An exceptionally foul-smelling cheese, highly prized by connoisseurs and still made at TILSIT (Sovetsk).

Time (1923) A weekly newsmagazine founded by Henry R. Luce and Briton Hadden; in 1936 its publishers launched *Life*, a weekly which specializes in high-quality and often sensational pictures. Time-Life and GENERAL ELECTRIC combined to form the General Learning Corporation. See also LIFE INTERNATIONAL.

Time and the Conways (1937) The first of J. B. Priestley's plays to show his preoccupation with theories of time (see SERIALISM). The Conway family experience a future event in the present.

Time Machine, The (1895) H. G. Wells's remarkable first novel, a science fiction tale of a man who was able to travel backward to the beginning of time and forward to an era when the sun is cooling down. He passes through an era when the Morlocks, descended from today's proletariat, live underground, herding aristocrats for meat.

Time of Your Life, The (1939) William Saroyan's play (for which he refused a PULITZER PRIZE) set in a San Francisco waterfront saloon where a rich idler, Joe, preaches sweetness and light to various eccentrics and layabouts menaced by Detective Blick of the Vice Squad (representing the forces of evil).

Times Square The New York theater and restaurant area adjoining BROAD-WAY at 42nd Street. (Named after the New York *Times*, which has now moved out of it.)

Timestyle A prose style personally imposed by Henry Luce on all his journals (TIME, *Life* etc.), but since his death ridiculed even by *Time*. The well-worn recipe may be exemplified by: At week's-end Skin-food Inc.'s balding, corpulent sacked-President Johnnie ('Wart-Hog') Smith wearily cracked. . . .

Timmins The site in east-central Ontario, Canada, of the Texas Gulf Sulphur Co.'s zinc-copper-silver mines, opened up in 1964.

Timon of Athens (1607) Shakespeare's play in which Timon discovers when he loses his riches that he has only fair-weather friends; he turns misanthrope and retires to a cave, with one faithful servant.

Timur See TAMBURLAINE.

Tin Drum, The (1959) A strange novel by a Danziger, Günter Grass. (German title, *Die Blechtrommel*.)

Tin Lizzie A contemporary nickname for the MODEL T Ford.

Tin-pan Alley Nickname for the district of New York where publishers of popular music congregated, originally in 14th Street, later in the TIMES SQUARE area; also applied to the composers of such music.

Tinsley Green A Sussex village near Crawley where on GOOD FRIDAY there is an international marbles contest for a silver cup; the village's association with the game goes back to 1600.

Tintagel Site of a castle on the north coast of Cornwall which figures in ARTHURIAN LEGEND as the home of King MARK; the ruins which can still be seen are of a later date. See CAMELOT. (Headland near Camelford.)

Tintern Abbey (1131) A CISTERCIAN abbey, now in ruins, on the Wye near Chepstow, Monmouthshire; the setting inspired Wordsworth's 'Lines Composed a Few Miles above Tintern Abbey' (1798), in which the poet communes with nature.

Tippecanoe, Battle of (1811) A battle near the confluence of the Tippecanoe and Wabash rivers in north Indiana in which General Harrison ('Old Tippecanoe'; see next entry), then governor of Indiana Territory, scored a nominal victory over the Shawnee chief, Tecumseh, who was receiving British aid from Canada, just before the WAR OF 1812.

'Tippecanoe and Tyler Too' A song and political slogan used during the 1840 campaign in which the Whig General William Henry Harrison (see last entry) and John Tyler were elected President and Vice-President of the US. The song had the refrain 'Van, Van is a used-up man', referring to President Martin Van Buren. The election was the first in which slogans, gimmickry, misrepresentation and ballyhoo reached the proportions which have since become standard.

'Tipperary' A music-hall song written and composed by 2 Birmingham men, which happened to become popular just before World War I, and was then adopted as the chief marching song of the British Expeditionary Force in France.

Tiresias In Greek legend, a blind seer of THEBES who plays a promi-

nent part in the OEDIPUS cycle of legends.

Tirol The Austrian Alpine province of which the capital is Innsbruck; it formerly included the ALTO ADIGE now in Italy.

Tiros Name of a series of US weather satellites which since 1960 have sent back continuous pictures of cloud cover. See NIMBUS; ESSA.

Titan (1959) US Air Force liquid-fuel ICBM, made by the Martin Co., which superseded the ATLAS. Titan I has a range of 8000 miles, Titan II more than 9000; both are designed to carry a 10-megaton warhead. Titan-C is a satellite-launching vehicle used in the first GEMINI launching.

Titania The name given by Shakespeare to the Queen of the Fairies in MIDSUMMER NIGHT'S DREAM; the wife of OBERON. By other writers she is called Queen Mab. Ovid gives Titania as a name of the goddess DIANA.

Titanic disaster (1912) The sinking of a White Star liner after striking an iceberg in the North Atlantic, with the loss of over 1500 lives.

Titans Giant children of URANUS and GE (sky and earth) who appear in a bloodthirsty series of early Greek legends. CRONUS led them in revolt against their father, and they in turn were vanquished by a new generation of gods led by ZEUS, who consigned them to TARTARUS.

Tithonus In Greek legend, a Trojan youth of great beauty with whom EOS, goddess of the dawn, fell in love. ZEUS conferred on him the gift of immortality but not of perpetual youth, and after a period of shriveled old age he turned into a cicada.

Titograd Modern name of the capital of Montenegro, Yugoslavia, formerly known as Podgorica.

Titoism The heresy, in Stalinist eyes, of believing that there are different roads to socialism (see POLYCENTRISM) and of acting on that belief. Tito, knowing that Yugoslavia's problems differed fundamentally from Russia's, refused to impose collectivization or to victimize the ku-

lak (rich peasant) class; in foreign affairs he took a neutral stand between the Soviet bloc and the West. For these crimes he was condemned by the COMINFORM (i.e. Stalin) in 1948 and, to the world's surprise, survived unscathed until normal relations were resumed in 1955.

Titus Andronicus (1594) A tragedy attributed to Shakespeare, a revenge play of the type of THE SPANISH TRAGEDY, full of corpses and atrocities. Titus is a Roman general.

Tiw, Tiu Scandinavian god of wisdom, after whom Tuesday is named.

Tizard mission A mission under Sir Henry Tizard sent to USA in September 1940 to communicate the findings of the MAUD COMMITTEE.

TKO (Boxing) Initials standing for 'technical knockout'.

TLC Initials standing for Tender Loving Care.

TM Initials used for Thames Measurement, a formula for rating yachts, still used by LLOYD'S but superseded for racing by the RORC RATING. It is based on waterline length and beam only. (Introduced by the Royal Thames Yacht Club.)

Toad of Toad Hall (1929) A. A. Milne's evergreen children's play based on Kenneth Grahame's WIND IN THE WILLOWS.

Tobacco Road (1932) Erskine Caldwell's novel of rural squalor in Georgia, which, like GOD'S LITTLE ACRE, sold in immense quantities, especially after it had been made into a successful play.

Tobit A book of the APOCRYPHA, telling the story of Tobit, a Jew in Nineveh during the BABYLONIAN CAPTIVITY, who sends his son Tobias to fetch 10 talents of silver he had deposited in Media. The angel RAPHAEL, in disguise, accompanies him, helps him get the money, cures Tobit's blindness, and then reveals himself.

Tobruk An important harbor in Cyrenaica in the North African campaign of 1941-42. Captured by Australians (Jan. 1941), it was left as an invested enclave from April-December (during which period the Australians were evacuated at their government's request); in June 1942 it was again surrounded and the garrison surrendered.

Toby (1) The dog in the Punch and Judy show. (2) See UNCLE TOBY. (3) A Toby jug that is generally used for ale and is shaped somewhat like a stout man with a cocked hat forming the brim; see next entry.

Toby Fillpot The person depicted in the standard Toby jug, said to be based on an 18th-century Yorkshireman, Harry Elwes, who once drank 2000 gallons of beer without taking food.

Toc-H (1915) A Christian voluntary organization which helps old and young, those in hospital, and refugees; it also forms social groups throughout the UK. (*Toc*, old army signalers' designation for letter T; for Talbot House, name of the first chapel and club founded by the Rev. 'Tubby' Clayton at Poperinghe, Belgium, in memory of Gilbert Talbot, killed in World War I.)

Today's English Version The latest American version of the Bible, prepared under the aegis of the AMERICAN BIBLE SOCIETY by Protestant scholars, but approved for Catholic use. It is distinctively American in tone.

Todd-AO (1955) A single-camera, single-projector, wide-screen cinema system designed to produce the effects of 3-projector Cinerama. (Michael Todd + American Optical Co.)

Todt Organization The German organization which conscripted labor for construction work, notably on the WEST WALL (1938) and the ATLANTIC WALL (1940). (Directed by an engineer named Todt.)

Tokaido Line (1963) The Tokyo-Osaka railroad which carries the blue-and-white 'bullet' expresses called HIKARI and KODAMA. It is an elevated line free of points, level crossings and sharp curves, permitting maximum speeds of 150 m.p.h.

Tokay, Imperial The fabulous Hungarian sweet wine, one of a family of Tokays, from the Austrian Emperor's own vineyards; much drunk in the best RURITANIAN circles.

Toklas, Alice B. The name borrowed by Gertrude Stein for her *Autobiography of Alice B. Toklas* (1933) about her life in Paris. In fact, it was her secretary's name.

Tokugawa Shogunate (1614-1868) The period during which Japan was ruled nominally by the Emperor at Kyoto, but actually by a military dictatorship in Tokyo of SHOGUNS of the Tokugawa family. The last Shogun resigned after failing to eject foreigners, and this led to the Imperial MEIJI RESTORATION.

Tokyo Rose Nickname of Mrs I. Toguri D'Aquino, sentenced (1949) in San Francisco to 10 years in prison for treason in broadcasting Japanese propaganda; paroled in 1956.

Told by an Idiot (1923) One of Rose Macaulay's early attacks on the illusions of mankind.

Tolkien Society of America Devoted to the study of the works of Professor J. R. R. Tolkien, author of The LORD OF THE RINGS.

Tolpuddle martyrs (1834) Six farm laborers who, ostensibly for administering an illegal oath but in effect for forming a trade union, were sentenced to 7 years transportation to Australia by an assize judge secure in the knowledge of the Whig government's antipathy to trade unionism. There was such a public outcry that the men were brought back 2 years later. (Tolpuddle, a Dorset village near Dorchester.)

Toltecs Early inhabitants of Mexico of whom little is known. In the 12th century AD some of them moved to Yucatan and merged with the MAYAN CIVILIZATION. Their legendary leader or god was QUETZALCOATL.

'Tom Bowling' Charles Dibdin's 18th-century sea-song in which Tom, 'the darling of our crew', represents the poet's brother: 'Faithful, below, he did his duty; / But now he's gone aloft'. (Name taken from that of the seafaring uncle of Smollett's RODERICK RANDOM.)

Tom Brown's Schooldays (1857) Thomas Hughes's novel of life at Rugby in the days when Thomas Arnold was its headmaster; there was a sequel, *Tom Brown at Oxford* (1861).

Tombs, The (1838) A prison in New York City, replaced in 1898.

Tom Collins A COLLINS made with OLD TOM GIN.

Tom, Dick and Harry Just anybody, the common herd; often used disparagingly.

Tom Jones (1749) Fielding's masterpiece, the long rambling story of the adventures of the likable rascal, Tom Jones, interspersed with the author's comments, addressed to the reader, on various social and moral issues. Also an outstanding comedy movie based on it. See Squire ALLWORTHY; BLIFIL.

Tomnoddy, My Lord A character in one of the INGOLDSBY LEGENDS.

Tom O'Bedlam Old name for a wandering beggar; many were, or pretended to be, mad (see BEDLAM); also called Abraham-men, after the name of a ward at Bedlam.

Tompion A name associated with the finest old English clocks and barometers. (Thomas Tompion, 1639-1715.)

Tom Sawyer (1876) Mark TWAIN'S novel about Tom, who runs away from his respectable Aunt Sally in Missouri and camps out on an island with his friend Huck Finn. They are presumed dead, and return in time to hear their praises sung at their funeral service. They have further adventures finding treasure buried by Injun Joe. The 2 friends reappear in HUCKLEBERRY FINN.

Tom Swift The inventive hero of a long series of exciting novels for boys written by Edward Stratemeyer (1862-1930), the creator of the ROVER BOYS.

Tom Thumb, General (1844) A midget, height 25 inches aged 4, 40 inches at death, exhibited in BARNUM & BAILEY SHOWS. He married, owned a yacht and bred racehorses. (Name taken from a 16th-century nursery story.)

Tom Tiddler's ground A place where money can be easily made. (From the children's game in which one side chants 'We're on Tom Tiddler's ground / Picking up gold and silver', and tries to keep the others out.)

Tom Tower Wren's clock tower at the entrance to Tom Quad, Christ Church (College) OXFORD UNIVERSITY. (Contains the bell, Great Tom.)

Tonga The Pacific kingdom of the FRIENDLY ISLANDS.

Tonkin, Tongking A former French protectorate, now part of North VIETNAM.

Tono-Bungay (1909) The best of H. G. Wells's novels, tells of George Ponderevo, son of the housekeeper of Bladesover (representing the house where the novelist's mother was lady's maid), apprenticed to his uncle Ponderevo, the village chemist who moves to London and makes a fortune out of a quack remedy he calls Tono-Bungay. The book depicts the passing of the old landed aristocracy, yielding place to brash get-rich-quick charlatans.

Tontons Macoutes Haitian secret police and personal bodyguard of PAPA DOC Duvalier; they have won an unenviable reputation for utter lawlessness. (From Tonton-Macoutes, 'Uncle Knapsack', the bogeyman of Haitian folklore.)

Tony Award The BROADWAY theater equivalent of the HOLLYWOOD OSCAR.

Toonerville Trolley A lumbering old trolley featured in Fontaine Fox's nostalgic daily comic page cartoon Toonerville Folks (1908), which gave a bird's-eye view of the goings-on of a gang of kids in a sleepy outer suburb.

Tophet (1) Mentioned in 2 Kings xxiii, 10 and Jeremiah xix, 6 as the place, near GEHENNA, where children were sacrificed to MOLOCH; later used as a refuse pit. (2) Hell. (Probably means 'fire place'; also spelled Topheth.)

Top of the Sixes A New York restaurant at the top of the tower of 666 FIFTH AVENUE, with spectacular views of the city.

Top of the Tower The revolving restaurant on top of the GPO Tower in London.

Top o' the Mark A restaurant on top of the Mark Hopkins Hotel, San Francisco, itself on top of NOB HILL.

Topsy The slave girl in UNCLE TOM'S CABIN who said she 'never was born . . . I 'spect I grow'd'.

Top Twenty A weekly 'chart' of the records of popular music that have sold best.

Torah (1) Jewish name for the PENTATEUCH; (2) the whole body of Jewish religious literature. (Hebrew, 'instruction'.)

Tordesillas, Treaty of (1494) An agreement to share newly discovered territories: Spain was to have those west of a line drawn from pole to pole 370 leagues west of the Cape Verde Islands, and Portugal those to the east (in effect, Brazil).

Tories Name given in the 1670s to the Court Party which supported Charles II and the ANGLICAN CHURCH against the Country Party (WHIGS), drawing its strength from country squires and clergy; the forerunner of the Conservative Party. Now used of right-wing Conservatives, or as a mildly hostile name for any Conservatives. (Originally the name of Irish outlaws who harried the English settlers.)

Torrey Canyon disaster (1967) The grounding of a US oil tanker off the Scillies, discharging vast quantities of oil to foul British and French coasts; she had to be destroyed by bombing.

Torricellian tube Early name for a mercury barometer. (In 1643 the Italian, Torricelli, demonstrated that changes in atmospheric pressure are shown by movements of a column of mercury in a tube closed at one end and inverted in a bowl of mercury; the space in the tube above this column, which contains mercury vapor, is called a Torricellian vacuum.)

Tory Democracy The new concept of British Conservatism introduced by Disraeli and propagated by Lord Randolph Churchill (see PRIMROSE LEAGUE), based on an appeal to the people to recognize that the interests of all classes of the nation are identical, and on government measures for the steady improvement of working-class conditions (see TWO NATIONS).

Tosca, La (1900) Puccini's opera, based on a French melodrama, in which the young painter Cavaradossi is sent to his death by the chief of police, Scarpia, who is murdered by the jealous singer Tosca, the young man's lover.

Tosti's 'Goodbye' (1881) A once extremely popular song composed by Sir F. P. Tosti, Italian-born composer who settled in England where he died in 1916.

To the Lighthouse (1927) Virginia Woolf's novel, a moving evocation of the changes wrought in a group of people by the passage of time. The lighthouse is the objective of a boating trip, postponed in the early section, but made many years later at the end of the book.

Tottenham (UK) A former municipal borough of MIDDLESEX, since 1965 part of the borough of HARINGEY.

Touchstone The cynical jester of the Duke's court in AS YOU LIKE IT.

Tour de France (1903) The major cycling race of the year in France, over a route of nearly 2800 miles of road (including mountainous stretches), taking over 3 weeks to complete.

Tournament of Roses See ROSE BOWL.

Touro Synagogue (1763) The oldest US synagogue, in Newport, R.I., designed by Peter Harrison in colonial style and now a historic site.

Tours, Battle of (732) The decisive battle in which the FRANKS under Charles Martel (grandfather of Charlemagne) finally checked the Arab conquest of Europe.

Tower Hamlets (1965) New inner London borough consisting of the former metropolitan boroughs of Bethnal Green, Poplar and Stepney, with headquarters at Cambridge Heath Road, E.2.

Tower of London (11th century) A Thames-side fortress which has been a royal palace, prison, mint, treasury, and observatory. It is now an armory and a museum containing the Crown jewels, garrisoned by the YEOMAN WARDERS.

Town Below, The (1944) English title of the first novel of the Canadian novelist Roger Lemelin, which won the Prix de la langue française; its French title is Au pied de la pente douce. It is an affectionate but realistic picture of the French-Canadian working class.

Toynbee Hall (1884) The Universities' Settlement in East London, a house of residence for men from OXFORD and CAMBRIDGE universities who want to do social work in the East End; the first of many such social settlements.

Toyota The largest of the Japanese automobile firms.

Toy Symphony (1788) A cheerful little symphony, formerly attributed to Haydn, but perhaps by Mozart's father.

Trabzon The modern Turkish name of Trebizond, a Black Sea port, formerly the ancient Greek colony of Trapezus.

Tractarians See OXFORD MOVEMENT. (So called from Newman's Tracts for the Times.)

Tractatus Logico-philosophicus (1922) The forbidding title of Wittgenstein's major treatise which inspired LOGICAL POSITIVISM. He held that the solution of philosophical problems was mainly a matter of accurate definition of the terms used, an aspect neglected in all previous philosophical systems.

Trader Horn (1927) The dryly humorous reminiscences of an illiterate English tramp, Aloysius Horn, as recorded by Mrs Lewis in South Africa. She read each chapter back to him and then appended his comments on it. Horn had been an ivory trader in West Africa in what he called 'the earlies', and tells of gorilla and elephant hunting, cannibalism and the local slave trade.

Trafalgar (21 Oct. 1805) Nelson's victory over a Franco-Spanish fleet which removed the danger of a French invasion of England; Nelson was fatally wounded. See THIRD COALITION. (Cape in southwest Spain, near Gibraltar.)

Trafalgar Square A London square laid out in 1829-41 to commemorate Nelson, whose statue stands atop a 184-ft column in the center, guarded by LANDSEER'S LIONS and surrounded by fountains. Facing it are the National Gallery, ST MARTIN-IN-THE-FIELDS, South Africa House, Canada House and the CAVELL MEMORIAL. It is a favorite venue for mob orators on Sundays, and for pigeons on weekdays.

Trail Blazers The Portland (Ore.) Trail Blazers, NATIONAL BASKETBALL ASSOCIATION.

Trail of Tears The trail over which the CHEROKEES and others of the FIVE CIVILIZED NATIONS were moved (1830-38) from the southeastern states across the Mississippi to the Indian Territory (Oklahoma), in circumstances of great hardship.

Train Bleu, Le An express train from Paris to Nice, all-sleeper and first-class only.

Traminer A type of grape used in hocks etc.

Tranby Croft scandal A case arising from an accusation of cheating at cards made at a country-house party in Yorkshire; King Edward VII (then Prince of Wales), who was a member of the party, had to give evidence in court.

Transbay Bridge (1936) A double-tiered bridge across the San Francisco Bay, joining Oakland to San Francisco in 2 main spans of 2310 ft each.

Trans-Canada Highway (1962) A 5000-mile all-season road from St John's, Newfoundland, to Victoria, British Columbia.

Transcendentalism (1840s) A mystical philosophical and literary movement associated particularly with the NEW ENGLAND writers Emerson and Thoreau. They disregarded dogma and relied on their own intuitions as the only guide to the comprehension of reality.

Transfiguration, The The scene described in Mark ix, 2-8, when Peter, James and John saw Jesus transfigured on a mountain with ELIJAH and Moses, and heard a voice coming out of a cloud, saying: 'This is my beloved Son: hear him'. The scene is portrayed by Raphael in a painting (1520) now in the VATICAN.

Transit Name given to US navigation satellites, first launched in 1961; they are orbiting radio beacons which permit very exact position-fixing by ships and submerged submarines.

Transjordan Older name of the kingdom of Jordan before it took over Palestine territory west of the Jordan.

Transkei (1963) The first BANTUSTAN, formed for the XHOSA. It has its own parliament (whites in the territory have no vote) and is given a large measure of self-government. Formerly in Cape Province, it lies southeast of LESOTHO.

Transport House (1928) The building in SMITH SQUARE, Westminster, shared as headquarters by the TGWU and the Labour Party.

Trans-Siberian Railroad (1904) At first a single-track line linking Chelyabinsk in the Urals via Omsk, Irkutsk, Chita and the CHINESE EASTERN RAILROAD to Vladivostok. In 1916 an all-Russian line was opened via Khabarovsk. The track was not doubled until the 1930s.

Transubstantiation The conversion of bread and wine at the Eucharist into the body and blood of Chirst; i.e. the doctrine of the REAL PRESENCE, first put forward in the 9th century and finally defined and accepted by the Roman Catholic Church at the COUNCIL OF TRENT.

Trappists (1664) An order of monks and nuns who revived the CISTERCIAN rule in a most rigorous form, including a vow of silence. They have monasteries in many parts of the world, including the US and Canada. (La Trappe, Normandy, France, where founded.)

Traquair One of the oldest inhabited houses in Scotland, at Innerleithen, near Peebles, associated with Scottish royalty since the 12th century.

Trastevere The region in Rome west of the Tiber, with narrow streets peopled by the most typically Roman of the populace—small shopkeepers, artisans etc. (Italian, 'across the Tiber'.)

Travellers' Club (1819) A London club in PALL MALL founded under the aegis of the first Duke of Wellington; members, under an outdated rule, must have traveled 500 miles from London. It is frequented by diplomats and Foreign Office officials, and is politically active.

Travels with a Donkey (1879) R. L. Stevenson's account of his travels in the Cévennes, the hills northwest of Avignon in France.

Traven, B. Pen name of the mysterious author of books sold by the million in Latin America and Russia. At his death in 1969 he was identified as Traven Torsvan, b rn in Scandinavia in 1890. His well-written novels (*The Death Ship*, published in Germany 1926) and short stories (*The Night Visitor*, published in England 1967) carry an anarchist message. Some of his work has been filmed, e.g. *The Treasure of the Sierra Madre* (John Huston, 1947).

Traviata, La (1853) Verdi's opera, based on La DAME AUX CAMÉLIAS, with the names of the characters changed (Marguerite becomes Violetta, Armand Alfredo). (Italian, 'the strayed woman'.)

Treasure Island (1883) The archetypal boy's story of buried treasure marked on an ancient map, written by R. L. Stevenson.

Treasure State Nickname of Montana.

Treasury bench In the House of Commons, the front bench on the SPEAKER'S right, where ministers sit.

Treaty Ports (1842-1947) The chief ports of China, some 40 in number, which came by treaty under the ownership or control of various Western powers, whose nationals enjoyed extraterritorial rights. This arrangement, a major irritation to the Chinese, was canceled from 1943 onwards.

Trebizond See TRABZON.

Treble Bob One of the principal methods of the change ringing of church bells.

Treblinka (1942-43) A Nazi extermination camp in Poland where some 800,000 Jews, mostly Polish, were killed in the gas chambers. In 1943 the Jews rose in revolt, burned down the camp and killed some of the staff. Some 600 escaped, but only 40 survived.

Tree of Knowledge, The The tree of the knowledge of good and evil whose fruit Jehovah told ADAM he must not eat (*Genesis* ii, 17). By eating it (*Genesis* iii, 6) Adam and Eve (i.e. mankind) lost their innocence, i.e. became able to distinguish right from wrong, and thus incurred moral responsibility. See The FALL; PROMETHEUS.

'Trees' (1913) A poem which brought fame to Joyce Kilmer and also to Oscar Rasbach when he made a popular song of it (1922). It begins 'I think that I shall never see/A poem lovely as a tree' and ends 'Poems are made by fools like me,/But only God can make a tree'.

Treetops Hotel A Kenya hotel literally built in a tree, from which visitors could watch wild game. It was destroyed by MAU MAU in 1954.

Trelawny of the 'Wells' (1898) Pinero's comedy of the actress, Rose Trelawny, who jilts an aristocrat to return to the stage, whither he follows her.

Trematodes See PLATYHELMINTHS.

Trent's Last Case (1912) A highly regarded detective story by E. C. Bentley in which Philip Trent, the artistic dilettante and amateur detective, solves the murder of an American millionaire.

Tre, Pol and Pen CORNISH name prefixes. Tre ('farm') is commoner in the east of the county, Pol ('pool') in the west, Pen ('peak') in the middle. There is an old saying: By Tre, Pol and Pen, / You shall know the Cornish men.

Trial, The (1925) Kafka's allegorical novel about 'Jozef K', arrested and tried on a charge that is never specified; it has been described as the PILGRIM'S PROGRESS of the subconscious, and represents a search for divine justice. (German title, *Das Prozess*.)

Trial by Jury (1875) A GILBERT AND

SULLIVAN (one-act) OPERA, in which Angelina sues Edwin for breach of promise before a susceptible judge who tries to solve a legal impasse by offering to marry plaintiff himself.

Trianon See GRAND TRIANON; PETIT TRIANON.

Trianon, Treaty of (1920) The postwar treaty with Hungary, which had to cede two-thirds of its territory, including Transylvania, Slovakia and Croatia, to neighboring states.

Triassic Period The earliest period of the MESOZOIC ERA, lasting from about 240 to 200 million years ago. Fossils of small warm-blooded mammals appear, together with dinosaurs, icthyosaurus and turtles. (Greek *trias*, 'triad', from a threefold subdivision of rocks of this period in Germany.)

Triborough Bridge (1936) (New York City) A system of bridges and viaducts spanning the East River, with 3 arms linking the boroughs of MANHATTAN, QUEENS and the BRONX.

Tricel (1954) A man-made fiber used particularly for pleated garments.

Trident (1964) A medium-range airliner developed by DE HAVILLAND and HAWKER SIDDELEY. Trident-3 has 3 rear-mounted engines and is the equivalent of the US BOEING 727. Trident-1 has twin engines.

Trident Code name for the Washington Conference (May 1943) of Churchill and Roosevelt, at which the former pressed for a landing in Italy. It was decided to step up the bombing of Germany and to open the SECOND FRONT in May 1944.

Triffids See DAY OF THE TRIFFIDS.

Trigorin See *The* SEA GULL.

Trilby Du Maurier's novel; see SVENGALI.

Trim, Corporal UNCLE TOBY's servant in TRISTRAM SHANDY, honest, ignorant but, unlike his master, voluble.

Trimalchio's Feast See SATYRICON.

Trinity, The God the Father, God the Son and God the HOLY GHOST. The dogma was laid down in the NICENE CREED that God is one but exists in 3 Persons, which are coeternal and coequal; the Son is begotten of the

Father, of one substance with the Father; the Holy Ghost 'proceeds' from Father and Son (from the Father only for the EASTERN ORTHODOX CHURCH; the word *filioque*, 'and from the Son', was added by the Council of Toledo in 589).

Trinity Sunday The Sunday after WHITSUNDAY.

Trinity term (UK) The legal term after EASTER, and at OXFORD UNIVERSITY the last term of the academic year (Easter term at CAMBRIDGE).

Tripartite Pact (Sept. 1940) The alliance which extended the ROME-BERLIN AXIS to include Japan; Germany and Japan were to unite to oppose any US interference with the development of their respective plans—the NEW ORDER IN EUROPE and the GREATER EAST ASIA CO-PROSPERITY SPHERE. The alliance was joined later by Hungary, Rumania, Bulgaria and others (called the Axis powers).

Triple Alliance (1882) Formed on Italy's accession, arranged by Bismarck, to the DUAL ALLIANCE (1879) of Austria-Hungary and Germany, which was directed against Russia and France. Italy broke away when World War I came (see LONDON, SECRET TREATY OF).

Triple Crown (1) The mythical award to the English, Scottish, Welsh or Irish international rugger team that in one season defeats all 3 of its opponents. (2) Also applied to a horse that wins the KENTUCKY DERBY, PREAKNESS and Belmont Stakes or (UK) the TWO THOUSAND GUINEAS, DERBY and ST LEGER.

Triple Entente An informal understanding (developing from the ENTENTE CORDIALE) between Britain, France and Russia, which took shape in 1907-08 in reaction to the TRIPLE ALLIANCE.

Tripolitan War (1911-12) A war waged by Italy against Turkey, forcing the latter to acknowledge the Italian conquest of LIBYA (Turkish Tripoli).

Tripos The final examination for an honors degree at CAMBRIDGE UNIVERSITY. (Variously explained.)

Trip to Jerusalem, The (1189) England's oldest pub, in an ancient cave, one of many hollowed out of the sandstone of Castle Rock, Nottingham.

Tristram In ARTHURIAN LEGEND, a nephew of King MARK of Cornwall who fell in love with his uncle's bride, ISEULT (Isolde), and was killed either by Mark or by his own wife. (Also spelled Tristam, Tristan.)

Tristram Shandy, Life and Opinions of (1759-67) A magnificently incoherent novel by Laurence Sterne, in which Tristram tries hard to tell the story of his life but does not get very far, being unable to resist any irrelevancy that may occur to him. See UNCLE TOBY; Corporal TRIM.

Tristan and Isolde (1865) Wagner's opera on the story of TRISTRAM and ISEULT.

Triton In Greek mythology, a sea-god, son of POSEIDON and AMPHITRITE; he is depicted in art as part man, part fish, and blowing his 'wreathed horn' (a conch, or shell) to soothe the oceans. 'Triton of (or among) the minnows', a phrase used by Shakespeare, signifies a person who appears great only because his followers or rivals are so insignificant.

Triton The US Navy's second nuclear-powered submarine.

Trobriand Islanders The inhabitants of islands off New Guinea, whose way of life is known to the world through the intensive studies of the Polish-born British anthropologist Malinowski.

Trocadero (1) A fortress at Cadiz captured by the French in 1823. (2) The name of the gardens in Paris now occupied by the Palais de Chaillot, across the Seine from the Eiffel Tower. (3) Name adopted by various hotels and restaurants.

Troika plan (1962) A plan put forward by Khrushchev for replacing the UN Secretary-General by a committee of 3. (Russian, a vehicle drawn by 3 horses abreast.)

Troilus and Cressida A troubadour's tale, with no classical basis, used by Boccaccio, Chaucer and Shakespeare among others; the Trojan hero Troilus falls in love with the faithless Cressida, whom PANDA-RUS persuades to yield to him; later she deserts Troilus for Diomede.

Trois Quartiers, Aux A large Paris department store near the LOUVRE.

Trojan Horse, The In Greek legend, the huge and hollow wooden horse, full of armed Greeks, which the Trojans, persuaded that it was an offering to the gods that might bring them luck, dragged into Troy. The Greeks emerged at night and took the city which had withstood a 10-year siege. Hence the expression 'I fear the Greeks even when they bring gifts' (*timeo Danaos et dona ferentes*).

Trojan War (12th century BC) The legendary siege of Troy by the Greeks under AGAMEMNON (see last entry). The end of the story is told in the ILIAD (partly) and the AENEID. The *casus belli* was HELEN OF TROY, but the legend probably had its origin in a struggle to control a main trade route between East and West; the strategic importance of Troy is evidenced by the remains of 9 successive cities built on the same site, near modern HISSARLIK at the entrance to the Dardanelles.

Trooping the Color (London) A ceremony performed by the Guards regiments (with the HOUSEHOLD CAVALRY in attendance) on or about the Sovereign's official birthday in June at HORSE GUARDS PARADE, WHITEHALL. (Particular instance of a traditional military ceremony.)

Tropic of Cancer (1934) Henry Miller's best-known work, banned in the US until 1961, a semiautobiographical account of his journey into the abyss of comprehensive degeneracy in the Paris of the early 1930s. He represents himself as emerging with a new understanding of life.

Trotskyism The advocacy of world Communist revolution instead of the 'SOCIALISM IN ONE COUNTRY' preached by Lenin and Stalin, which Trotsky regarded as a manifestation of undesirable Russian nationalism. (Leon Trotsky, opponent of Stalin, exiled 1924 and assassinated 1940.)

Trotwood, Betsey DAVID COPPERFIELD's aunt who had disowned him at birth because he was not a girl, but later champions his cause. Sharp-tongued but kindhearted, she also looks after Mr DICK.

Troubles, The (Jan. 1919-Aug. 1923) The period of civil war in southern Ireland, from the formation of the IRA to the capture by the IRISH FREE STATE forces of its leader, De Valera, and his imprisonment.

Trout Quintet, The Schubert's quintet for piano and strings, in which the fourth movement consists of variations on the tune of his song 'The Trout'.

Trovatore, Il (1853) Verdi's opera of violent passion, witchcraft and villainy among the Biscayan gypsies. (Italian, 'the troubadour'.)

Troy See TROJAN WAR.

Trucial States (Trucial Oman) Seven small independent sheikhdoms on the Persian Gulf; they are separate from the country of Muscat and Oman, which lies to the east and south. (Named from the truce made with Britian in 1820 which was combined with a promise to suppress piracy and the slave trade.)

Trud Soviet Russian newspaper for the workers, published by the central council of trade unions.

Truman Doctrine, The (1947) That whenever aggression, direct or indirect, threatened US security, action would be taken to stop it; pronounced when Congress authorized military aid to Greece and Turkey to counter and contain Communist activities.

Trusteeship Council (1946) The UN successor to the LEAGUE OF NATIONS MANDATES COMMISSION; it comprises member countries who administer trust territories and those members of the SECURITY COUNCIL who do not administer trust territories. Only New Guinea and Nauru (Australia) and Pacific Islands formerly mandated to Japan (USA) are still under trusteeship.

Tsaritsyn The city of USSR now known as Volgograd (and formerly as Stalingrad).

Tsarskoe Seloe One of the chief palaces of Imperial Russia, in PALLADIAN style, now a museum in the LEN-

INGRAD suburb of Pushkin. (Russian, 'Tsar's village'.)

Tschiffeley's Ride (1925-27) The journey of 13,350 miles from Buenos Aires to Washington, D.C., ridden by the Swiss-born Argentinian, A. F. Tschiffeley, using 2 horses only. His purpose was to demonstrate the stamina of a certain Argentinian breed. The journey took 2½ years.

T-shirt A casual cotton shirt for men, short-sleeved and collarless and often worn as an undershirt. (So called from its shape.)

TSR-2 A British nuclear bomber, the development of which was canceled in 1965 as too costly in favor of importing American F-111s. It was designed by Vickers Armstrong and GENERAL ELECTRIC for a speed of Mach 2 and a range of 1500 miles with a nuclear load.

Tsushima (May 1905) Scene of the crushing defeat inflicted by the Japanese Admiral Togo, in the straits between Japan and Korea, on the Russian fleet sent from the Baltic.

Tu Abbreviated name for a series of Russian aircraft, including the first Russian pure jet, Tu-104 (1956); the biggest Russian airliner, Tu-114 (1961), a sweptwing turboprop carrying up to 220 passengers; and Tu-144, due in service about the same time as CONCORDE, of which it is the slightly smaller equivalent, i.e. the first Russian supersonic airliner. (Abbreviated from the designer's name, Andrei Tupolev.)

Tuaregs The nomadic BERBER race of the Sahara, who wear veils as a protection from driving sand.

Tuatha Dé Danann In Irish legend, the successors to the FIR BOLG; they were driven into the hills by the 'Milesians' and returned as fairies. ('Tribes of Danu', the mother of the gods.)

Tube Alloys British wartime code name for atomic bomb research. See MAUD COMMITTEE; MANHATTAN PROJECT.

Tucker china Wares made by the first major producer of American porcelain, William Ellis Tucker of Philadelphia, Pa. (1826-32), and thereafter by his partner. Tucker's own products were typically decorated with sepia-painted scenes; his partner went in for SÈVRES-type enamel painting, with lavish gilt.

Tudeh Party (1946-49) In Persia, a Soviet-sponsored Communist separatist party which tried to establish a self-governing province of AZERBAIJAN, with its capital at Tabriz. The party was banned in 1949 after an attempt on the Shah's life. (Persian, 'the masses'.)

Tudor period (1485-1603) A period in the decorative arts typified by heavy oak furniture with bulbous legs, the elaborate 4-poster bed, linenfold paneling decorated with varied carved motifs, e.g. the Tudor rose.

Tudors The dynasty of English kings (1485-1603) begun by Henry VII (see BOSWORTH FIELD) and continued by Henry VIII, Edward VI, Mary and Elizabeth. (Henry VII was a grandson of Owen Tudor.)

Tuileries Paris gardens made in the 16th century and redesigned by the 17th-century landscape gardener Le Nôtre. They lie between the LOUVRE and the Place de la Concorde, and contain the JEU DE PAUME gallery of Impressionist paintings and the Orangerie (with a Claude Monet collection). (French *tuile*, 'tile'; the site was once a pottery clay pit.)

Tulane (1834) A university at New Orleans, La.

Tulip Mania (1630s) A wild outburst of speculation in tulip bulbs, which spread from Holland over Europe. Some varieties fetched $1200 apiece, and thousands of people went bankrupt when the market collapsed.

Tulliver aunts, The The strong- and narrow-minded Mrs Glegg and the self-centered hypochondriac Mrs Pullet who with Mrs Tulliver, Maggie's mother, form the trio of Dodson sisters in GEORGE ELIOT'S The MILL ON THE FLOSS. Poor Maggie was constantly reminded that 'no Dodson ever did' the things she did.

Tully An old-fashioned name for the Roman orator Cicero (Marcus Tullius), Cicero being merely a nickname ('warty').

Tunbridge ware A form of pictorial wood marquetry developed at Tunbridge Wells, Kent, from the 17th century, and particularly popular in the 19th century. Designs depicting old castles, landscapes etc. were made by assembling countless narrow strips of different woods, stained to varying shades by steeping in the local mineral waters. These were then sawn through lengthwise, producing many copies of the same design, which were then applied to boxes, trays etc.

Tupi-Guarani The AMERICAN INDIAN group of languages spoken over a wide area of Brazil and Paraguay.

Turandot (1926) Puccini's unfinished opera (completed by another hand). Turandot, Princess of China, will marry any suitor who can answer her 3 riddles; those who fail will be beheaded. An Unknown Prince solves them and then reveals himself as the son of Timur, King of Tartary. See LIU.

Turanian languages An old term for Asian languages which are neither SEMITIC or INDO-EUROPEAN, i.e. the URAL-ALTAIC LANGUAGES. (Turan, ancient name of the land east of Iran, Persia, beyond the OXUS.)

Turf Club (1868) A London club in Piccadilly where the social elite can keep in touch with racing results.

Turkish Blood A drink concocted of beer and red Burgundy.

Turksib (1931) Short title of the Turkestan-Siberian Railroad, which runs south from the Trans-Siberian Railroad at Novosibirsk to Alma-Ata and Tashkent.

Turl, The An Oxford street across which Jesus and Exeter colleges face one another.

Turn of the Screw, The (1898) Henry James's long short story about a governess whose 2 charges are under the influence of evil ghosts. It is the basis of a play and an opera, the latter by Benjamin Britten.

Turpin, Dick An 18th-century English highwayman who appears in several ballads and stories; see BLACK BESS. He was hanged for horse stealing.

Turveydrop A minor character in Dickens's BLEAK HOUSE, a dancing master, 'a very gentlemanly man', intensely selfish and vain.

Tuscany, The ranks of The ETRUSCAN army, the enemy; phrase from Macaulay's *Horatius* (see LARS PORSENA): And even the ranks of Tuscany / Could scarce forbear to cheer.

Tuscarora An Iroquoian race of North Carolina; they attacked the whites (1711-13) who had been kidnapping their children as slaves, and after defeat moved north to join the FIVE NATIONS. A few survive on the Canada-New York borders.

Tusitala The name given to R. L. Stevenson in Samoa. ('Teller of tales'.)

Tuskegee Institute (1881) A Negro coeducational college in eastern Alabama, founded by Booker T. Washington, Negro educationist.

Tutankhamen's Tomb (14th century BC) The first intact royal sepulcher of Ancient Egypt to be discovered, by Howard Carter (1922) in the VALLEY OF THE KINGS. Tutankhamen was AKHENATEN's successor.

Tutsi A Nilotic cattle people who once ruled BURUNDI and RWANDA in Central Africa. In 1964 the HUTU massacred the Tutsi of Rwanda, many of whom fled to the Kingdom of Burundi. Inexplicably, the feudal Tutsi were supported by the Chinese Communists. Also called Watutsi, Batutsi.

TVA (1933) Initials commonly used for the Tennessee Valley Authority, set up as a NEW DEAL measure in the backward, impoverished region along the Tennessee River, in Kentucky, Mississippi, Tennessee, Alabama, Georgia, North Carolina and Virginia. It constructed 21 dams for power generation, flood control and irrigation; taught antierosion and improved agricultural techniques; reforested the area; and stamped out malaria. This vast and successful venture was widely copied abroad, but at home was denounced as socialism and Federal interference in local affairs. Its latest major project is the 3 million kw nuclear plant at Browns Ferry, Ala.

Tver A Russian city of USSR, now renamed Kalinin.

TWA Trans World Airlines, the leading US rival to PAN AM.

Twain, Mark Pen name of Samuel Langhorne Clemens. (From the leadsman's call 'By the mark, twain', indicating a depth of 2 fathoms; used on Mississippi steamboats and elsewhere.)

Tweedledum and Tweedledee Names invented by an 18th-century poet for 2 people whose opinions or looks are alike; adopted by Lewis Carroll in THROUGH THE LOOKING GLASS for 2 pugnacious little fat men.

Tweed Ring, The A gang of TAMMANY HALL politicians under William M. (Boss) Tweed, whose malversations were first exposed in 1871; Tweed was convicted and died in jail, 1878. After gaining control of the NYC municipal treasury, they methodically milked it of perhaps as much as $200 million, using every trick known to fraudulent accounting.

Tweedsmuir, 1st Baron The novelist, John Buchan; Governor-General of Canada, 1935-40.

Twelfth Night January 6th, Christmas Day OLD STYLE, the feast of EPIPHANY, and once the culmination of Christmas festivities. (12 days after Christmas Day.)

Twelfth Night (1600) Shakespeare's comedy with a complicated plot centering around the confusion caused by the resemblance of twin brother and sister, the latter (VIOLA) disguised as a boy. The scene is ILLYRIA, and the minor characters include AGUECHEEK, BELCH, FESTE and MALVOLIO.

Twelfth of July 'The Glorious Twelfth', inaccurately celebrated as the anniversary of the Battle of the BOYNE, which took place on July 1st OLD STYLE (July 11th New Style); still an important date to ULSTER Protestants.

'Twelve Days of Christmas' An English 'cumulative' carol enumerating the gifts made to a lover on each day from Christmas to TWELFTH NIGHT: 'The first day of Christmas /

My true love sent to me/A partridge in a pear tree', followed by turtle-doves, French hens, colly birds, gold rings, geese, swans, maids, drummers, pipers, ladies and lords.

Twelve Pound Look, The (1913) J. M. Barrie's one-act comedy, like WHAT EVERY WOMAN KNOWS an attack on male egoism, personified in the pompous, ridiculous Harry Sims.

Twelve-tone music A system of atonal music introduced by Schoenberg which replaced the orthodox system of keys by a series ('tone-row') of 12 notes of the chromatic scale, all treated as equal importance, with no hierarchy of dominant notes or keynotes.

20th Amendment (1933) An amendment to the CONSTITUTION OF THE UNITED STATES providing that Congressional sessions should begin each January 3rd and that after national elections the President should be inaugurated on January 20th. See 'LAME DUCK' AMENDMENT.

20th Congress (USSR) The crucial meeting in February 1956 when Khrushchev denounced Stalin in his 'secret speech', and in a public speech announced a reversal of policy: peaceful coexistence; different paths to socialism; revolution without violence; abandonment of the doctrine of the inevitability of war with the West.

21st Amendment (1933) An amendment to the CONSTITUTION OF THE UNITED STATES repealing PROHIBITION.

'Twenty Questions' A radio version of the nursery game of 'animal, vegetable or mineral', immensely popular over a long period.

22nd Amendment (1951) An amendment to the CONSTITUTION OF THE UNITED STATES which limited tenure of the Presidency to 2 terms.

Twenty Thousand Leagues under the Sea (1869) Jules Verne's novel, written before submarines were invented, in which a party of scientists are captured by the mysterious Capt. Nemo and kept prisoners in his pirate submarine.

Twickenham A former municipal borough of MIDDLESEX, since 1965 part of the borough of RICHMOND UPON THAMES.

Twilight of the Gods See GÖTTER-DÄMMERUNG.

Twin Cities, The St Paul and Minneapolis, Minn., which face each other across the Mississippi.

Twins The Minnesota Twins, AMERICAN (Baseball) LEAGUE, playing at the Metropolitan Stadium. (See TWIN CITIES.)

'Twittering Machine, The' (1922) A watercolor and pen-and-ink drawing by Paul Klee, one of the best-known examples of his 'taking a line for a walk', in his own phrase. It is said to be a satirical skit on the machine age. (Museum of Modern Art, NYC.)

Two Cheers for Democracy (1952) E. M. Forster's sequel to ABINGER HARVEST.

Two Cultures The scientific and the classical and literary; C. P. (later Lord) Snow suggested (1959) that the conservative upper middle class, reared in the latter culture, underrated the vital importance to the nation of the former, which was lower middle class in origin.

Two-Eleven BAC 200-seat airliner being developed for BEA.

2,4-D A selective hormone weed killer for lawns.

Two Gentlemen of Verona (1595) Shakespeare's comedy about the changing loves and fortunes of Valentine and Proteus, 2 friends and rivals for the hand of the Duke of Milan's daughter.

Two Nations The rich and the poor in Britain at the time of the CHARTISTS; a phrase used as the secondary title of Disraeli's influential novel *Sybil* (1845), depicting the appalling condition of the working class.

Two Sicilies, Kingdom of the (1734-1860) The Spanish BOURBON kingdom of Naples (i.e. southern Italy) and Sicily.

Two Thousand Guineas A classic English flat race for 3-year-olds run over the ROWLEY MILE at the first Spring meeting, Newmarket.

2001: A Space Odyssey (1968) An unusual SF movie directed by Stanley Kubrick and scripted by the English astronomer-novelist Arthur C.

Clarke (who then published it in book form). It begins 3 million years ago when man-ape came under the influence of a magic programmed monolith which set him on his next stage of evolution, leaps to the near future when another mysterious monolith is uncovered on the moon, and goes on to a manned flight to Saturn (during which Hal, a computer, gets above itself and has to be disconnected) and into a world of poetic imagery and mystic speculation in strange contrast to the factual scientific style of earlier chapters.

Two Years Before the Mast (1840) Richard H. Dana's classic record of a sailor's life in the days of the sailing ship, to which he added in 1859 an account of a second voyage. Its revelations of the horrors of shipboard life, based on the author's personal experience, led to legislation to improve sailors' working conditions.

TW3 Abbreviation for TWTWTW, the initials of 'That Was the Week, That Was', the earliest of the BBC's late-night satirical TV programs of the 1960s, with David Frost as anchor man.

TWW Initials used for Television Wales and the West, the commercial company serving South Wales and the West; replaced in 1968 by HARLECH TV.

Tyburn Tree A triangular gallows near where the MARBLE ARCH now stands in London; until 1783 public executions took place there.

Tycho's star One of the 3 supernovae observed in the MILKY WAY, discovered in CASSIOPEIA by Tycho Brahe, the Danish astronomer, in 1751-52.

Tyler's Rebellion See PEASANTS' REVOLT.

Tyndale's Bible (1526-30) The first printed English Bible; William Tyndale's translation, into the plain Biblical English we know today, of the New Testament and some of the Old; the main source for subsequent English versions.

Tynwald The legislative assembly of the Isle of Man, consisting of the Lieutenant-Governor, the Legisla-

tive Council of 12 ex officio and nominated members, as an Upper House, together with the elected House of Keys. (Old Norse, 'field assembly'.)

Typee (1846) Herman Melville's novel about friends who desert their ship for a Polynesian island, where they are captured by the Typees. One escapes, the other is ensnared by the charms of a local girl but reluctantly decides to abandon this cannibal Paradise when a whaler puts in there.

Type 82 destroyers Provisional name for guided missile ships ordered by the Royal Navy in 1966, designed to use SEADART missiles and an Action Data Automation Weapon system fed by a new type of Anglo-Dutch 3-D radar.

Typhoid Mary Mary Mallon, a New York cook found in 1906 to be a healthy carrier of typhoid. Using false names, she persisted in continuing to cook for numerous households and institutions, but was eventually arrested and detained till her death 23 years later and 31 years after her identification as a carrier.

Typhoon (1903) Joseph Conrad's short novel, with a vivid description of a storm at sea, through which the unimaginative Capt. MacWhirr heroically brings his ship to safety.

Tyrian purple See PHOENICIANS.

Tyrol See TIROL.

Tyrone Guthrie Theatre The Minnesota Theatre Company's theater at Minneapolis, built to the specifications of Sir Tyrone Guthrie, who was its director (1962-65). The repertory season runs from June to December.

Tyrone rebellion (1597-1601) A rebellion in ULSTER led by Hugh O'-Neill, Earl of Tyrone. It was suppressed by Lord Mountjoy, the successor to the Earl of Essex (see ESSEX REBELLION). See ULSTER, PLANTATION OF.

Tzigane Hungarian gypsy; applied adjectivally to Hungarian gypsy music. See ATHINGANOI. (French form of the Hungarian name.)

U

U Burmese equivalent of 'Mr'.

U and non-U A class stratification of English people by speech habits, based on upper-class shibboleths, in a game popularized by Nancy Mitford (1955) from an idea suggested in a lecture by Professor Ross; thus e.g. 'lunch' is held to be non-U for 'luncheon'. (U = upper class.)

UAR Initials used for the UNITED ARAB REPUBLIC.

Ubangi-Shari A former French colony, now the Central African Republic.

Uber Cup (1956) Women's international Badminton championship.

U-boat German submarine. (For German *Unterseeboot*.)

Ubu Roi (1896) Alfred Jarry's burlesque of *Oedipus Rex*, in which a coarse and cowardly bourgeois makes himself King of Poland and, drunk with power, invades Russia, where he is soundly beaten.

'U' certificate Granted by the British Board of Film Censors to films suitable for Universal viewing, i.e. by unaccompanied children (see 'A' CERTIFICATE).

UDI Unilateral Declaration of Independence, made by the Smith regime in Rhodesia, 11 Nov. 1965.

Uffington White Horse See VALE OF THE WHITE HORSE.

Uffizi One of the 2 great art galleries in Florence (the other is the PITTI).

UFO Abbreviation for Unidentified Flying Object, the official name for a FLYING SAUCER or other phenomenon of that type.

Ugly American, The (1) A book (1958) by Eugene Burdick and William J. Lederer criticizing US policy in Southeast Asia. (2) Also adopted to personify the forces that spoil the countryside, destroy wildlife etc., e.g. indiscriminate use of pesticides, river pollution, increasing demands of road traffic, litter dropping etc.

'Ugly Duckling, The' An original fairy tale by Hans Christian Andersen about a cygnet hatched out by a duck. He is brought up to regard himself merely as an ugly duckling until one day he runs away and is adopted by swans who restore his self-respect. Andersen's moral is: it matters not to have been born in a duck yard if one has been hatched from a swan's egg.

UHF Initials used for Ultrahigh Frequency, the 300 to 3000 mc. bands used for TV and radar. They lie between the VHF and SHF (Superhigh) bands, the latter (3000 to 30,000 mc.) also used in radar.

Uhlans German cavalry (originally lancers) who played a prominent part in the early months of World War I. (Originally a Tartar word.)

Uhuru! The slogan used in the campaign for Kenya's independence. (Swahili, 'freedom'.)

Uitlander AFRIKAANS name for the British in the old Boer Republics of Transvaal and the Orange Free State. (Literally, 'outlander'.)

UK satellites A series of research satellites, part of the ARIEL program.

Ulan Bator Capital of the Mongolian People's Republic, formerly known as Urga.

Ulema These learned in MUSLIM law and theology; a term used in the Turkish Empire and revived (1931) when a league of Ulema was formed in Algeria as part of an Arab Muslim renaissance. (Arabic (plural) word, 'learned'.)

Ulm, Battle of (Oct. 1805) Napoleon marched 500 miles across Europe in 21 days and at Ulm overwhelmed Austria; he then occupied Vienna. See THIRD COALITION. (Danube port, now in Baden-Württemberg.)

Ulster (1) (Loosely) Northern Ireland. (2) The Celtic kingdom and former northern province of Ireland; now divided between the Six Counties forming Northern Ireland (Antrim, Armagh, Down, Fermanagh, Londonderry and Tyrone) and 3 counties in the Irish Republic (Cav-an, Donegal and Monaghan). The 9 counties together have a Catholic majority, but Protestant Antrim, Armagh, Londonderry and northern Down give the Six Counties a Protestant majority.

Ulster, Plantation of (1608-12) The colonization of ULSTER by Scottish Presbyterians and a few English after the TYRONE REBELLION had led to the forfeit of Ulster to the English Crown. See PLANTATIONS.

Ulster Covenant (Sept. 1912) The pledge to resist HOME RULE for Ireland signed at Belfast by the followers of Sir Edward Carson, and leading to the formation of the ULSTER VOLUNTEERS.

Ulster Volunteer Force A paramilitary force raised by Protestant extremists and quickly declared illegal (1966).

Ulster Volunteers (1912) Sir Edward Carson's 'private army' formed to resist HOME RULE.

Ultima Thule (1) The most northerly part of the world known to the Greeks and Romans. (2) A distant unknown land; the furthest limit attainable. (Latin *ultima*, 'farthest'; *Thule*, an island north of Britain, perhaps the Shetlands, Iceland or Norway.)

Ultramontanists Roman Catholics who believe in the absolute authority of the Pope even outside Italy. ('Beyond the mountains', i.e. the Alps.)

Ulysses The Latin name of ODYSSEUS.

Ulysses (1922) James Joyce's plotless account of one day in the lives of Leopold BLOOM, his wife Molly, and Stephen DEDALUS, in which stream-of-consciousness or interior monologue reveals their inmost thoughts in language replete with symbolism, allusion and portmanteau puns which demand a knowledge of several languages and all folklore to unravel.

'Ulysses deriding Polyphemus' (1829) One of J. M. W. Turner's masterpieces, now in the National Gallery, London. See POLYPHEMUS.

UN See UNITED NATIONS CHARTER.

Uncle Remus (1880) Joel Chandler Harris's book of American Negro folktales, as told by Uncle Remus to a white boy, with characters such as Brer Fox and Brer Rabbit.

Uncle Sam (1) The US government personified; (2) the US nation or people. (Possibly through the letters US stamped on kegs of meat for the army during the WAR OF 1812 being jokingly identified with Uncle Sam, i.e. Samuel Wilson, a meat packer.)

Uncle Toby The chief, though inarticulate, character in TRISTRAM SHANDY. An ex-officer, wounded in FLANDERS, who occupies himself by reconstructing Marlborough's campaigns in his garden, and, by dint of his complete guilelessness, eludes the advances of the buxom Widow Wadman. Tristram is his nephew.

Uncle Tom The chief character in UNCLE TOM'S CABIN, who is persecuted by Simon LEGREE and beaten to death. The term is used by US Negroes of a fellow Negro who is subservient to white Americans.

Uncle Tom Cobbleigh The best known of the various people who wanted to go to WIDDICOMBE FAIR; from the chorus 'Old Uncle Tom Cobbleigh and all'.

Uncle Tom's Cabin (1852) Harriet Beecher Stowe's novel about slavery in Louisiana and Kentucky, which greatly influenced opinion on the subject in the Northern states. See UNCLE TOM.

Uncle Wiggily A delightful rabbit in a series of children's bedtime stories first written for the Newark (N.J.) *Evening News* (1910) by Howard R. Garis, widely syndicated and then published in 35 books containing well over 1000 stories.

UNCTAD (1964) UN Conference on Trade and Development, held at Geneva. It showed that the dominant interest of the underdeveloped countries was in getting aid for economic development, and that political alignment with East or West was a matter of indifference to most of them.

UN Day See UNITED NATIONS DAY.

Underground Railroad A system of cooperation among antislavery people in the US before 1863 by which runaway slaves were secretly helped to escape to the north or to Canada.

Under Milk Wood (1954) Dylan

Thomas's radio play in which the inhabitants of the Welsh village of Llareggub, which lies under Milk Wood, muse aloud and betray their fears and desires and other inmost thoughts.

Undershaft, Andrew The father of MAJOR BARBARA in Shaw's play, an armaments tycoon with enlightened views. He observes that the world scraps obsolete machinery but not obsolete religion, morality or political constitutions. It is poverty, not sin, that breeds crime (a novel idea in those days).

Under the Greenwood Tree (1872) Hardy's rustic idyll of the love of a young couple whose path runs unusually smooth for a Hardy novel.

Under the Volcano (1947) Malcolm Lowry's Joyce-inspired novel of European expatriates in Mexico.

Undertones of War (1928) The poet Edmund Blunden's classic novel of World War I, giving a restrained presentation of the soldier's view of the war, in which he himself served.

Under Two Flags (1867) OUIDA's masterpiece of romantic fatuity. The hero is the Hon. Bertie Cecil, 1st Life Guards, who breakfasts exclusively off a glass of curaçao. Falsely accused of forgery, to save a woman's name he seeks anonymity in the ranks of the French Chasseurs in Algeria. After heroic deeds, this dedicated fall guy faces a firing squad but Cigarette, playmate of the regiment, clutching his reprieve shields him with her body and receives the fusillade intended for him. *Sunt lacrimae rerum!*

Under Western Eyes (1911) Joseph Conrad's novel about Russian revolutionaries in Geneva at the turn of the century.

Undine A water sprite who falls in love with a mortal in a German tale (1811) which was turned into an opera by E. T. A. Hoffmann (1816).

UNEF Initials used for UN Emergency Force, an international task force such as those which intervened in the SUEZ CRISIS and the Belgian Congo.

Unesco (1946) The UN Educational, Scientific and Cultural Organization, established to improve the quality of education, mass media and living standards; headquarters in Paris.

Unfinished Symphony, The (1822) Schubert's 8th Symphony of which he wrote the first 2 movements and part of the third. It is not known why he never finished it, and the manuscript was not discovered until 1865.

UN flag A blue flag with the globe (as seen from above the North Pole) surrounded by a wreath, all in white.

Ungulata An obsolescent term for the group of hoofed mammals, divided into the ARTIODACTYLA and the PERISSODACTYLA.

UNHCR See UNITED NATIONS HIGH COMMISSIONER FOR REFUGEES.

Unicef See UNITED NATIONS CHILDREN'S FUND. (Initials of original title: UN International Children's Emergency Fund.)

Uniform Time Act (1966) An Act which defined 8 standard time zones for the US and imposed (from 1967) uniform DAYLIGHT SAVING TIME on all states that did not contract out by specific legislation.

Unilever (1929) An Anglo-Dutch group, sixth largest in the world, with headquarters at London and Rotterdam, formed by merging Lever Bros (Sunlight, Pears, Lifebuoy, Lux soaps) and the Dutch Margarine Unie. Its largest, semiautonomous unit, the United Africa Co., has oilseed, timber, shipping, cement, beer and plastics interests in West Africa, mainly Nigeria and Ghana. Familiar brand names include Persil, Omo, Surf, Stork margarine, Gibbs's Pepsodent, Walls (ice cream and sausages), Mac-Fisheries, Birds Eye frozen foods, Atkinson's perfumes, Batchelor's peas; Thames Board Mills and British Oil and Cake Mills are other subsidiaries.

Union Carbide (1917) The second largest US chemicals group, with headquarters in New York; one of the 30 industrials that make up the DOW JONES Industrial Average.

Unionists In ULSTER an alternative name for Conservatives; after the Liberal split (1886) over Gladstone's Irish HOME RULE policy, Joseph

Chamberlain formed the Liberal Unionist Party, which joined (1895) a coalition government with the Conservative Party; this became the Conservative and Unionist Party. ('Union' here = union of all Ireland and Great Britain, i.e. opposition to Home Rule.)

Union Movement The British Union of Fascists in new guise, refounded by Sir Oswald Mosley in 1948; rather more than moribund.

Union of Democratic Control (Sept. 1914) A party formed by those, led by Ramsay MacDonald, E. D. Morel and Bertrand Russell, who opposed British entry into World War I; they advocated early peace negotiations, and open diplomacy to minimize the danger of stumbling into further world wars through secret diplomatic moves such as preceded the first.

Unitarians Christians who believe in the single personality of God and do not accept the TRINITY. The term covers various shades of belief, from a Jesus who had divine powers delegated to him to a Jesus who was merely a good man; Unitarians also reject original sin, atonement, eternal punishment and all creeds. Their Church originated in NEW ENGLAND.

Unitarian-Universalist Association (1961) A merger of the Universalist Church of America and the American Unitarian Association.

United One of the bigger US domestic airlines.

United Aircraft A large aircraft firm with headquarters at East Hartford, Conn.; it absorbed the firm started by Sikorsky, famous for his work on amphibians and helicopters, and the great Pratt & Whitney aero-engine concern. One of the 30 industrials that make up the DOW JONES Industrial Average.

United Arab Republic (Feb. 1958) Formed by Egypt and Syria; President Nasser retained the name for Egypt despite Syria's secession in 1961.

United Church of Christ (1957) A union of the General Council of the Congregational Christian Churches and the presbyterian Evangelical and Reformed Church.

United Empire Party A political party founded by Lord Beaverbrook and another Press Baron, Lord Rothermere, to get candidates into Parliament who would support EMPIRE FREE TRADE.

United Free Church of Scotland (1900) Formed by the Free Church of Scotland and the United Presbyterian Church; reunited with the Church of Scotland in 1929. See WEE FREES.

United Kingdom See ACTS OF UNION.

United Methodist Church (1) A merger (1968) of the METHODIST CHURCH (in the US) and the Evangelical United Brethren Church. (2) In Britain, formed 1907, rejoined the Methodist Church in 1932.

United Nations Building (1952) The headquarters of UN, in MANHATTAN, NYC, overlooking the East River.

United Nations Charter (June 1945) The agreement signed at San Francisco which set up the United Nations, with the chief aim of ensuring international peace.

United Nations Children's Fund or Unicef (1946) An organization set up to promote child health, nutrition and welfare programs.

United Nations Day October 24th, the day on which the UN came into existence in 1945.

United Nations High Commissioner for Refugees (UNHCR; 1951) Appointed to continue the work of the INTERNATIONAL REFUGEE ORGANIZATION, with headquarters at Geneva.

United Nations Pact (Declaration) Signed at Washington on 1 January 1942 by 26 Allied states (including Russia and China), by which they subscribed to the principles of the ATLANTIC CHARTER and promised not to make a separate peace with the Axis Powers. (The first official use of the phrase 'United Nations'.)

United Nations Relief and Rehabilitation Administration Better known as UNRRA.

United Nations Special Fund (1957) An organization which assists developing countries to finance major projects expected to produce early large-scale improvements in their economies.

United Provinces (India) Now renamed Uttar Pradesh.

United Steel (1918) A merger of UK family steel companies, making rails, diesel locomotives, coal derivatives and a wide range of other products; headquarters at Sheffield. See STEWART & LLOYDS.

United University Club (1821) A large London club in Suffolk Street, confined to members of OXFORD and CAMBRIDGE UNIVERSITIES, and frequented by senior civil servants.

Unités d'habitation Housing units designed by LE CORBUSIER, of which the most famous is the Cité radieuse at Marseilles (1952); virtually self-contained towns incorporating shopping streets, schools etc.

Universal Aunts An old-established London organization, designed primarily to render services to non-Londoners, by finding accommodation, doing their shopping, escorting their young daughters across London etc.

University Club (1865) A club with a large but limited membership of holders of university, college or (in special cases) honorary degrees, and graduates of military and naval academies.

University College, London (UCL; 1826) The largest unit of LONDON UNIVERSITY, to which are attached the SLADE SCHOOL, Bartlett School of Architecture and the UC Hospital medical school.

'Unknown Political Prisoner' (1953) Reg Butler's sculpture which won an international competition for a work on this theme.

Unknown Soldier, Tomb of the The tomb in the ARLINGTON NATIONAL CEMETERY where in 1921 the Unknown Soldier of World War I was buried, and in 1958 one unknown serviceman of World War II and one of the KOREAN WAR.

Unknown Warrior, Tomb of the (1920) The tomb of an unidentified soldier who was buried in Westminster Abbey as a representative of all who fell in World War I; there are similar memorials in other countries.

Unofficial Rose, The (1962) Iris Murdoch's novel about a circle of people who have reached the restless stage in their married lives; they have various schemes and ambitions but find in the end that they are largely creatures of circumstance or other people's interests, and that even if they attain an objective it disappoints expectation.

UNRRA (1943-49) UN Relief and Rehabilitation Administration. An organization to provide emergency, mainly US, aid to liberated territories of eastern Europe, China and, later, Austria, Italy etc.

UNRWA (1949) Initials of the UN Relief and Works Agency, established to resettle Arab refugees after the State of Israel had been formed.

Unter den Linden A mile-long street in East Berlin running from the BRANDENBURGER TOR past the Marx-Engels Platz (site of the Imperial Palace razed to the ground by the Russians) to the Alexander Platz. Once the center of Berlin life, with an avenue in the middle lined with lime trees until Hitler cut them down. (German, 'under the limes'.)

Untouchables Those in India who belong to none of the main castes; although 'Untouchability' was officially abolished in 1947, and their name altered to 'Scheduled Castes' or 'Depressed Classes', their very shadow, let alone their touch, is still regarded as polluting a high-caste Hindu.

UP (1907) Initials used for the United Press Associations, a SCRIPPS-HOWARD news agency; see UPI.

Upanishads (600 BC) The final stage of ancient Hindu literature, some 250 books of hymns and philosophical or mystical speculation, pantheistic in tenor, and a reaction from the earlier BRAHAMANAS. (SANSKRIT, 'sitting close to the instructor', i.e. 'esoteric'.)

Up-Biblum God (1663) The first translation of the Bible into an AMERICAN INDIAN LANGUAGE (an Algonquian dialect), made by John Eliot (see BAY PSALM BOOK) and printed at Cambridge, Massachusetts Bay Colony, a notable landmark in the history of American printing. It put into circulation the word 'mug-wump', used for the 'dukes' in *Genesis* xxxvi, 30. Also called the Indian Bible.

Up from Slavery (1901) The first of 2 autobiographies by Booker T. Washington (1856-1915), describing his progress from a Virginia slave hut to the TUSKEGEE INSTITUTE, and advocating industrial education rather than political agitation as a means of raising Negro status.

Up Front (1945) A collection of cartoons drawn by Bill Mauldin for the Mediterranean edition of STARS AND STRIPES; two unkempt and sardonic GIs, Willie and Joe, have no patriotic illusions as they slog their disenchanted way through the Italian campaign in World War II, as did Mauldin.

Up Helly A' A fire festival held in Lerwick, Shetland, Scotland, on the last Tuesday in January. Villagers in costume throw torches into a VIKING war galley. The custom dates back to the days of Norse rule (9th-15th centuries).

UPI (1958) Initials used for United Press International, a news-agency merger of the SCRIPPS-HOWARD UP and the Hearst INS (International News Service).

Upper Canada Village The restoration on the banks of the St Lawrence of a typical hamlet recalling the times and trials of the Loyalists who settled in Ontario from 1784. There are churches, houses and inns, together with the implements of village crafts, e.g. milling, cheese making, smithing, woodworking, in their original settings.

Up the Junction See CATHY COME HOME.

UPU Initials used for the Universal Postal Union, formed (1874) to foster cooperation between the nations' postal services. Nearly all countries are members; the headquarters are in Berne, Switzerland.

Ur- A prefix borrowed from German, meaning 'primitive', 'earliest', 'original', 'source of', as in 'Ur-HAMLET', a (lost) early version of Shakespeare's play.

Ural-Altaic languages A language family of northern Europe and Asia,

of which the FINNO-UGRIAN and ALTAIC LANGUAGES are divisions. (Named after the Ural and Altai mountain ranges.)

Uranus Chief of the earliest generation of Greek deities, god of the heavens, father of CRONUS who deposed him.

Urartu A powerful neighbor state to ASSYRIA in the 9th-7th centuries BC, centered on Lake Van and ruling over what is now Soviet ARMENIA and Persian AZERBAIJAN. Remarkable antiquities have been excavated there in recent years.

Urban League, National (1910) An interracial organization founded in New York to campaign for equal opportunities for Negroes in education, housing, welfare and employment.

Urdu The form of HINDUSTANI spoken by educated MUSLIMS in PAKISTAN and India, written from right to left in an Arabic-Persian script; the official language of West Pakistan. Although its grammar and everyday vocabulary closely resembles HINDI, it has borrowed much more from Persian, Turkish, English and, through religious sources, Arabic.

Uriah The Hittite husband of BATHSHEBA.

Urizen In William Blake's private mythology, the forces restricting man's full development, such as authority, repressive morality and dry rationalism; opposed by ORC, regenerated by LOS.

Urn Burial (1658) Sir Thomas Browne's essay which begins with a report on some Roman burial urns but grows into a general meditation on mortality and the vanity of human monuments; also known by its Greek name, *Hydriotaphia*.

Ur of the Chaldees A city of SUMER, and the birthplace of ABRAHAM (*Genesis* xi, 31); it was then at the head of the Persian Gulf, but the site is now more than 100 miles inland. Splendid treasures have been excavated there, including a famous gold statuette of a ram caught in a thicket, now in the British Museum.

Ursa Latin for 'bear'; hence *Ursa Major*, the GREAT BEAR; and *Ursa Minor*, the LITTLE BEAR.

US A tremendous onslaught on the VIETNAMESE WAR put on by the ROYAL SHAKESPEARE THEATRE CO. at the Aldwych, London. (US stands both for 'USA' and 'us'.)

USA (1938) A trilogy of novels by John Dos Passos, comprising The 42nd Parallel, 1919 and The Big Money, in which he gives a panoramic and cinematic survey of all facets of US life.

Uses of Literacy, The (1957) Richard Hoggart's honest, almost anthropological, analysis of the working class. Written by a highly educated member of that class from Leeds, Yorkshire, it deals despondently with the attitudes of workingmen to art, books, religion, domesticity etc.; he wonders whether the 'tamed helots of a machine-minding class' are 'exchanging their birthright for a mess of pinups'.

US News and World Report (1948) A weekly newsmagazine published in Washington, D.C.

USO (1941) The United Service Organizations, a private nonprofit agency which provides US forces with live entertainment, recreation and welfare services; the British equivalent is ENSA (Entertainments National Service Association).

Ussher's Notation (1654) The book responsible for the calculation that the world was created in 4004 BC, a date which used to appear as a marginal note to Genesis i; also adopted by FREEMASONS as the Annus Lucis (referring to Genesis i, 3, 'let there be light') from which they date official documents. (James Ussher, Archbishop of Armagh.)

US Steel (1901) Formed by J. P. Morgan by merging specialized firms, including Andrew Carnegie's, and now one of the largest US corporations, with interests that include mines, railroads, shipping, cement and many subsidiaries abroad. One of the 30 industrials that make up the DOW JONES Industrial Average.

Ute A group of Shoshonean Indians (see SHOSHONI) who gave their name to Utah and are also found in Colorado.

Uther Pendragon Father of King ARTHUR. (Pendragon, a Welsh title given to a paramount chief in times of crisis.)

Utilitarianism The view that actions are morally right if they are useful in promoting the greatest happiness of the greatest number; associated with J. S. Mill and Jeremy Bentham (18th–19th centuries).

Utopia The imaginary Pacific island described by St Thomas More (1516) in a witty satire, far ahead of its time, which contrasts England with a state ruled by philosophers, where there is religious toleration, no private property and a 6-hour day. (Greek, ou topos, representing 'Nowhere'—compare EREWHON—and eu topos, representing 'good place'.)

Utrecht, Peace of (1713) The treaty that ended the War of the SPANISH SUCCESSION. From France England gained Nova Scotia, Newfoundland and control of the St Lawrence (threatening French Canada); from Spain, Gibraltar and Minorca. Austria received the Spanish Netherlands (Belgium), Milan, Naples and Sardinia; the grandson of Louis XIV, Philip V, remained on the Spanish throne.

Uttar Pradesh, India Formerly the United Provinces.

U-2 aircraft A high-altitude photoreconnaissance plane used by the CIA (1956-60) to photograph Russia. It was exceptionally light in weight, had a range of 3000 miles, a speed of 500 m.p.h. and a ceiling of 90,000 ft. See next entry.

U-2 incident (1960) The shooting down by the Russians of an American U-2 reconnaissance aircraft over the Urals, which caused the cancellation of the PARIS SUMMIT CONFERENCE a few days later. The pilot Gary Powers (later released in exchange for a spy) confirmed that his plane was hit by a rocket at 65,000 ft. See last entry; ABEL SPY CASE.

U-235 The natural isotope of uranium used by Frisch and Peierls in the first demonstration of nuclear fission, at Birmingham, England.

Uxbridge (UK) A former municipal borough of MIDDLESEX, since 1965 part of the borough of HILLINGDON.

V

VA See VETERANS ADMINISTRATION.

VAD (1909) Initials used for the Voluntary Aid Detachments of men and women trained in first aid and nursing, formed by the British Red Cross Society and liable for war service with the forces.

Vail Cup A skiing contest held each February at Vail, in Colorado, the premier skiing state.

Vailima Letters (1895) The letters of R. L. Stevenson published the year after his death. (Vailima, the house in Samoa where he spent the last 6 years of his life.)

Vaisya The Hindu caste of farmers and traders. (SANSKRIT, 'peasant'.)

Valachi Papers, The (1969) Peter Maas's account of the revelations by Joe Valachi, a small-time mobster turned informer (1962) who poured forth invaluable information about COSA NOSTRA and MURDER INC. The book was published in England (1969) as The Canary That Sang.

Valentine (1940) A British infantry tank of World War I: 16 tons, 150 h.p., 16 m.p.h.

Valentine's Brook One of the major hazards of the GRAND NATIONAL.

Vale of the White Horse The valley which runs from near Swindon to Abingdon north of the Marlborough and Berkshire Downs, named after the white horse carved in the chalk hills near Uffington. See VWH.

Valhalla In Norse mythology, the hall in ODIN'S palace reserved for heroes selected by the VALKYRIES.

Valiant (1953) A British 4-jet V-BOMBER with swept-back wings, built by VICKERS to carry a nuclear load. It was withdrawn in 1965 on account of fatigue problems.

Valiant-for-Truth, Mr A character in Part II of PILGRIM'S PROGRESS whose last words are often quoted: My sword, I give to him that shall succeed me in my pilgrimage, and my courage and skill to him that can get it.

Valiant submarines British hunter-killer nuclear-powered Fleet submarines, with long endurance and immunity to detection, the Royal Navy's main striking force; the 6 already ordered may be joined by another 6 in the early 1970s. (Named after the Valiant, the first all-British nuclear submarine, commissioned in 1966; unlike the DREADNOUGHT, it has a Rolls-Royce reactor.)

Valjean See Les MISÉRABLES.

Valkyries Daughters of ODIN who charged into battles, selected those marked for death, and conducted them to VALHALLA. (Old Norse, 'choosers of the slain'.)

Valley Forge A village in southeast Pennsylvania, famous as the winter quarters of Washington in 1777-78 during the AMERICAN WAR OF INDE-PENDENCE, and now a State Park containing Washington's headquarters, a National Memorial Arch and other relics.

Valley of Ten Thousand Smokes A region in southwest Alaska created in 1912 by an exceptionally violent eruption of Mt Katmai, and not discovered for some years as the country was uninhabited. There are millions, rather than 10,000, vents ranging from the minute to 150-ft craters, emitting smoke or steam up to 1200°F. It is included in the Katmai National Monument (1918).

Valley of the Kings An area, once part of ancient THEBES, facing KAR-NAK and LUXOR across the Nile; the burial place of pharaohs of the 18th-20th Dynasties, the most famous being TUTANKHAMEN'S TOMB.

Valley of the Shadow of Death A place in PILGRIM'S PROGRESS full of Hobgoblins, Satyrs and Dragons of the Pit, through which Christian has to pass. (Phrase taken from Psalms xxiii.)

Vallombrosa A valley near Florence, familiar through Milton's lines in Paradise Lost: Thick as autumnal

leaves that strow the brooks / In Vallombrosa.

Valmouth The fictional English village where Ronald Firbank, in the
novel of that name (1918), gathers a
weird group of cranks and perverts.
The book was turned into a musical comedy by Sandy Wilson in
1958.

Valmy, Cannonade of (1792) The
occasion of the first appearance in
Europe of a disciplined national
democratic army, the French revolutionary army under Kellermann,
whose victory after a heavy artillery
duel over the best dynastic army
of Europe (the Prussians) caused
Goethe, who was present, to foretell
the advent of a new era in human
history. After their victory the
French occupied the AUSTRIAN NETH-
ERLANDS (Belgium). (Village between
Verdun and Paris.)

Valois, House of The CAPETIAN dynasty which ruled France 1328-
1589, and was succeeded by the
BOURBON dynasty in the person of
Henry IV of NAVARRE (who had married a Valois).

'Valse Triste' A famous Sibelius
waltz taken from his symphonic
poem *Kuolema*.

Vampire (1945) A DE HAVILLAND single-seater jet fighter with a speed of
550 m.p.h. It was replaced by the
VENOM.

Van Allen belts Belts of particles
emanating from the sun and trapped
by the earth's magnetic field; indications of their existence were first
given by the satellite EXPLORER 1.
Their altitude varies, the outer belt,
of electrons, being about 10,000
miles from the earth; the inner, of
protons, about 2000 miles up.

Vance, Philo The American amateur
detective who first appeared in *The
Benson Murder Case* (1926), created
in his own image by the learned art
lover who took the pen name of S. S.
Van Dine.

V & A Abbreviation in common use
for the Victoria and Albert Museum,
London.

Vandals An East German people allied to the WENDS, many of them

Arian Christians, who invaded Gaul
and Spain about AD 4000 and then
crossed to North Africa, where they
were vanquished by the Roman Beli-
sarius in 533. In 455 they sacked
Rome. Vandalism became a synonym for wanton destruction.

Vandenberg missile base US Air
Force base at Lompoc, north of Los
Angeles, used as a training ground
for IRBMS and ICBMS, and as a launching site for the Pacific Missile Range,
and for some satellites.

Vanderbilt (1872) A university at
Nashville, Tenn.

Vanderbilts American millionaire
family which made its fortune in
shipping lines and railroads; founded by Cornelius Vanderbilt, died
1877.

Van der Hum South African Cape
brandy with tangerine and a little
rum. (Afrikaans, 'What's-his-name'.)

Van Doos Corruption of Vingt-deux,
signifying the famous French-Canadian Royal Twenty-Second Regiment, with a distinguished record,
notably in the SOMME BATTLE (1916)
at Courcelette. Although the uniform
resembles that of British Guards
regiments, with red tunics and bear-
skins, orders are given in French.

Vanguard (1961) VICKERS turboprop
airliner, a larger version of the VIS-
COUNT, and similar to the BRITANNIA,
competition with which split the
market for both of them.

Vanguard (1958) US Navy's 3-stage
satellite-launching vehicle used to
launch the second US research satellite, *Vanguard 1*, during the IGY.

Vanitas In art, a still-life painting of
objects symbolic of man's mortality,
e.g. a skull, hourglass, guttering
candle.

Vanity Fair (1848) Thackeray's novel depicting the vanities and snob-
beries of London society in Hanoverian times, mainly through the
adventures of Becky SHARP.

Vanity Fair In PILGRIM'S PROGRESS a
perpetual fair at the town of Vanity,
where BEELZEBUB and his like sell
honors, preferments, kingdoms and
other vanities; when Christian and
Faithful refuse to buy anything they

are arrested, but escape.

Van Meegeren forgeries Remarkably skillful paintings in the style of various OLD MASTERS, the work of a Dutch artist, Hans van Meegeren, who made some $1½ million out of them; he was sent to prison in 1947 but died the same year. His motive was resentment at the critics' neglect of his own original work.

Varanasi, India Formerly BENARES.

Varden, Dolly The heroine of Dickens's BARNABY RUDGE, daughter of a locksmith. She wore a straw hat trimmed with ribbons, 'worn the merest trifle on one side – just enough to make it the wickedest and most provoking headdress that ever malicious milliner devised'. This started a fashion in hats which lasted for decades.

Varieties of Religious Experience (1902) The US philosopher William James's widely read study of the psychology of religion, from which he drew the pragmatic conclusion that any religion is true in so far as it provides emotional satisfaction. See PRAGMATISM.

VARIG The biggest of Brazil's many airlines.

Vasa, The A 17th-century Swedish man-of-war at Stockholm which sank in the harbor as soon as built and, found to be well preserved, was raised in 1964. She now lies in a dry dock, open to the public, and furnished with appropriate museum exhibits.

Vassall case (1962) (UK) The trial of John Vassall, sentenced to 18 years imprisonment for passing secret information to Russia; see RADCLIFFE TRIBUNAL.

Vassar (1861) One of the SEVEN SISTERS colleges, at Poughkeepsie, N.Y.

Vathek (1786)'FONTHILL' BECKFORD'S tale, a mixture of ARABIAN NIGHTS and GOTHIC NOVEL, in which a young Caliph sells his soul to the Devil and finds himself in the Hall of Eblis (see IBLIS).

Vatican, The (1) The Pope's palace on Vatican Hill, west of the Tiber adjoining St Peter's. (2) The Papal government; see next entry. (Latin, *Mons Vaticanus,* 'hill of the soothsayers'.)

Vatican City The independent Papal State (108 acres, 400 residents) established in Rome under the LATERAN TREATY. It includes the VATICAN, St Peter's and, outside Rome, CASTEL GANDOLFO. The Vatican Palace buildings include the SISTINE CHAPEL, 3 museums of antiquities and an impressive collection of OLD MASTERS in the Pinacoteca.

Vatican Council (1962-66) A council of some 3000 prelates from all over the world summoned to the Vatican by Pope John XXIII and continued under Paul VI. It condemned anti-Semitism, acknowledged that there were elements of truth in BUDDHISM, HINDUISM and ISLAM, declared that religious freedom was a fundamental human right, and dealt with various new problems of the modern world.

Vaudois See WALDENSIANS.

Vautrin A major character in Balzac's COMÉDIE HUMAINE, an ex-convict whose 'real' name was Jacques Collin. He turns up in several novels in the guise of a chief of police, a Spanish priest and philosopher etc. Like Valjean (Les MISÉRABLES), he is said to be based on Vidocq, a former chief gangster who became the first head of the Sûreté, in Napoleon's time.

Vauxhall Gardens (1660-1859) London pleasure gardens in Lambeth, where concerts and firework displays were held and balloon ascents were made; in later years they acquired an unsavory reputation. (Named after Fulkes, a medieval lord of the manor.)

Vauxhall 30/98 (1921) One of the great VINTAGE CARS.

V-bombers Name given to the British VALIANTS, VULCANS and VICTORS, built by different firms to different specifications but all able to carry a nuclear load at speeds normally just below Mach I. In 1969, when British POLARIS SUBMARINES became operative, they were diverted from their strategic role with NATO and elsewhere to a low-level tactical strike role and Britain ceased to be an independent nuclear air power.

VC Initials standing for VIETCONG.

VC-10 (1962) Britain's first big jet airliner, seating 150. A clear-wing design (i.e. with the 4 jets mounted in the rear fuselage) with a characteristic high tail plane, it was built by VICKERS and came into regular service in 1964. See SUPER VC-10.

VD Initials standing for Venereal Disease.

Vedanta The mystical system of philosophy based on the UPANISHADS and the older VEDAS. (SANSKRIT, 'end of the Veda'.)

Vedas (1500 BC) The oldest layer of Hindu religious writings, consisting of 4 main books (including the RIG-VEDA) of hymns, prayers and charms. The gods are represented as on the whole benevolent, and doctrines of asceticism and pessimism have not yet appeared. They are the works of the ARYAN conquerors of the Dravidian aborigines. (SANSKRIT, 'knowledge'.)

V-E Day May 8th, Victory in Europe Day, commemorating the formal ending of the war in Europe after the German surrender signed at Rheims on 7 May 1945.

Vega Brightest star in the northern sky, and 4th brightest of all stars; a white star in LYRA. (From Arabic name for the constellation Lyra.)

Vegas Short for Las Vegas, Nev.

Velvet Brueghel Nickname of Jan (1568-1625), son of PEASANT BRUEGHEL; so called because of his smoothly painted detailed studies of flowers and other still-life subjects.

Vendémiaire The first month of the FRENCH REVOLUTION calendar, from September 22nd to October 21st; 13 Vendémiaire (1795) is the date when Napoleon ended a Royalist insurrection in Paris with a 'whiff of grapeshot', one brief cannonade—the first step in his ascent to the throne as Emperor. See DIRECTORY. ('Vintage time'.)

Venerable Bede, The An English historian and scholar (died AD 735) who spent most of his life in a monastery at Jarrow, where he earned his posthumous title of 'Venerable' by writing commentaries on the Bible and a history of the English.

Venlo incident (Nov. 1939) The capture by a German counterespionage unit of 2 British officers in command of an MI-6 network operating in Europe; it led to the arrest of many other British agents. (Dutch town.)

Venom (1953) A DE HAVILLAND jet fighter with a speed of 640 m.p.h. It succeeded the VAMPIRE and was replaced by the HUNTER.

Venus Roman goddess equivalent to the Greek APHRODITE.

Venus Name given to Russian space probes directed at Venus. Venus 3 was the first man-made object to crash on a planet (1 March 1966). In October 1967 Venus 4 made a soft landing on Venus the day before the US MARINER 5 passed near the planet. Venus 5 and 6 also landed on the planet in 1969.

Venus and Adonis (1593) Shakespeare's first published work, a long poem in which ADONIS rejects VENUS's advances and is killed by a boar.

'Venus and Cupid' (1) A Velázquez painting in which CUPID holds up a mirror for the reclining Venus; now in the National Gallery, London. (2) A Titian painting now in the UFFIZI, Florence.

Venusberg See TANNHÄUSER.

'Venus de Milo' (2nd century BC) The best-known Greek sculpture, artist unknown, now in the LOUVRE. (French form of the name; Milo = Melos, the island where it was found in 1820.)

Vera (1967) Abbreviation for the Vera Institute of Justice, founded by a paper millionaire to improve New York's criminal justice system. In 1968 it launched the Manhattan Court Employment Project whereby minor offenders aged 17-45 are given a 3-month suspension of trial so that they can make a fresh start under the guidance of Vera counselors (themselves ex-convicts). If they seem likely to make good, the charge is dropped. (Named for founder's mother-in-law.)

Verdant Green, Adventures of Mr
(1857) A once popular novel about a
much put-upon undergraduate in his
first year at OXFORD UNIVERSITY, by
'Cuthbert Bede' (the Rev. E. Bradley).

Verdun (Feb.-June 1916) An exceptionally heavily fortified key point
on the Western Front, very nearly
taken by the Germans in a 5-month
siege of the French garrison, finally
abandoned.

Verdurins, The A nouveau riche
couple in Proust's REMEMBRANCE OF
THINGS PAST who occupy themselves
by launching artists at their innumerable soirées. After Verdurin's
death, his widow marries the Prince
de GUERMANTES.

Vereeniging Treaty (31 May 1902)
The treaty which ended the BOER
WAR.

Vernon, Dorothy See HADDON HALL.

Verrazano-Narrows Bridge (1964)
The world's longest single-span suspension bridge, connecting BROOK-
LYN and Staten Island; main span
4260 ft, side spans 1215 ft each.
(Named for the Florentine who
sailed into the Hudson River in
1524, long before Henry Hudson.)

Versailles, Palace of A palace built
by Louis XIV, and the permanent
home of Louis XV from 1738; Louis
XVI was the last king to live there.
Built to house 5000 people, with
huge gardens in which stand the
PETIT TRIANON and the GRAND TRI-
ANON, its most famous feature is the
Hall of Mirrors, where the 1919
treaty (see next entry) was signed.
(The town, built at the same time, is
13 miles southwest of Paris.)

Versailles Treaty (June 1919) The
treaty made with Germany after
World War I (there were separate
treaties for each ex-enemy country),
which like the others incorporated
the LEAGUE COVENANT. Germany lost
ALSACE-LORRAINE and other territory,
including all its colonies; military
occupation of the Rhineland and
payment of reparations were also
imposed.

Vesta The Roman goddess of the
hearth (the Greek Hestia); in her
temple in the Forum VESTAL VIRGINS

tended the sacred fire.

Vestal Virgins In Rome, patrician
priestesses of VESTA, selected at the
age of 6-10. They took a vow of 30
years' celibacy and were buried
alive if they broke it.

Veteran Car Run (1896) The London
to Brighton run held annually on a
Sunday in early November to commemorate the repeal of the regulation that a car had to be preceded by
a man with a red flag.

Veteran cars Cars of a date not later
than 1904.

Veteran Motor Car Club of America
(1938) A club for those interested in
VETERAN CARS, with headquarters in
Brookline, Mass.

Veterans Administration A US government agency that administers
benefits provided by law for veterans.

Veterans Day The day formerly
known as ARMISTICE DAY, and from
1971 kept as a legal holiday on the
fourth Monday in October.

Veterans of Foreign Wars US veteran organization founded before
World War I.

VFAX Provisional designation for
the US Navy's version of the FX, designed also to give tactical support
to ground forces.

VFW See VETERANS OF FOREIGN WARS.

VG Initials used for 'variable geometry', i.e. swing-wing or movable-
wing aircraft. The purpose of the
design is to combine fast flight with
short takeoff and landing.

VHF Initials used for Very High Frequency radio, which has short range
and consequent freedom from interference from neighboring stations.

Via Crucis See STATIONS OF THE
CROSS.

Via Dolorosa The route along which
Jesus had to carry his Cross to Calvary. (Latin, 'way of sorrow'.)

VIBGYOR Initials used as a mnemonic for the colors of the spectrum:
violet, indigo, blue, green, yellow,
orange, red; red having the longest
wavelength.

Viborg (1) A Danish town in Jutland.
(2) Swedish name for VYBORG.

Vicar and Moses A famous Staffordshire pottery group, perhaps made

by Aaron Wood (see WOOD FAMILY), representing a vicar asleep in his pulpit while his clerk reads the sermon.

Vicar of Bray The turncoat of a 17th-century song about a historical character who clung to his benefice by changing his creed 3 times under the last 3 Tudors. In the song he is transferred to 'good King Charles's golden days', and maintains: That whatsoever King shall reign, / I will be the Vicar of Bray, Sir! (Village near Maidenhead, Berkshire.)

Vicar of Christ A title of the Pope since the 12th century.

Vicar of Wakefield, The (1766) Oliver Goldsmith's story of the massive misfortunes that descend upon the gentle vicar, Dr Primrose, and his family; it appealed to the rapidly growing reading public of its time.

Vichy government The French government formed (June 1940) by Marshal Pétain on the fall of France, which made Vichy, in the unoccupied zone, its headquarters; it was forced into increasing collaboration with the Germans, who occupied northern (and from 1942 all) France. Laval and Darlan dominated the by then senile Pétain.

Vichy water (1) Bottled mineral water from the springs of Vichy, France, said to be good for gout, digestive troubles etc. (2) Soda water of similar composition.

Vickers Group (1862) The UK armaments and engineering group which has built all kinds of warships and liners; the Maxim gun; Spitfire, Wellington, Viscount and VC-10 aircraft; Valentine tanks. It has a 75% interest in the English Steel Corporation, and in recent years has branched out into office equipment (Roneo), chemical engineering, surgical instruments etc. See also BAC.

Vicksburg, Capitulation of (July 1863) The first major Confederate defeat in the Civil War, at the hands of Gen. Ulysses Grant. (Town on the Mississippi.)

Vicky The pseudonym of Victor Weisz (died 1966), a left-wing political cartoonist of Hungarian parentage who came to England in 1935.

From 1958 he became famous for his cartoons in the London Evening Standard, especially for his creation of 'Supermac' (Harold Macmillan in the guise of the strip cartoon character 'Superman').

Victor (1959) A British crescent-winged V-BOMBER built by Handley Page, designed to carry a nuclear load or BLUE STEEL at Mach 0.92 over a range of 2300 miles. Taken out of service in 1968.

Victoria Club A London bookmakers' club where periodical call-overs are held before the big races and furnish a guide to antepost betting prices.

Victoria Cross (1856) An award instituted by Queen Victoria which takes precedence over all other decorations (the equivalent of the US MEDAL OF HONOR). It is made to officers and men of the British armed forces for signal acts of valor or devotion to their country in the presence of the enemy.

Victoria Day (Canada) May 24th, a legal holiday; elsewhere called EMPIRE DAY, and then Commonwealth Day.

Victoria League A society to promote Commonwealth friendship by encouraging people in Britain to invite Commonwealth visitors to their homes; it also runs hostels for students.

Victoriana Furniture, silver, ceramics etc. of the age of Victoria (reigned 1837-1901), the earlier specimens of which are coming to be accepted as antiques as time moves on and the supply of real antiques begins to dry up; quaintness rather than artistic merit marks the later products.

Victoria Tower The tower of the Houses of Parliament, from which a flag flies when the House is in session. It houses the Norman-French originals of old Acts and also millions of ballot papers from the last General Election.

Victory (1915) Joseph Conrad's novel of exiles in the East Indies and of the mutual fidelity of Heyst and Lena, the girl he befriends. Their island home is invaded by thugs and she sacrifices her life to save his.

Victory, HMS (1765) Nelson's flagship, now lying in Portsmouth dockyard and open to the public. Officially she is the flagship of the Commander in Chief, Portsmouth, who occasionally gives a banquet in Nelson's dining cabin.

Victory garden A wartime vegetable garden (in the UK, 'allotment'), cultivated by noncombatant citizens for the temporary increase of domestic food production.

Vic-Wells The partnership of the OLD VIC and SADLER'S WELLS theatres.

Vielle Cure A golden liqueur made in the monastery of Cenon, near Bordeaux, from COGNAC, ARMAGNAC and aromatic herbs.

Vienna Award (1940) Hitler's decree that Rumania should restore half Transylvania to Hungary.

Vienna Declaration (1958) Made by the PUGWASH MOVEMENT, a warning, among other things, of the danger of radioactive fallout.

Vienna porcelain (1719-1864) The wares made at a factory which owed its early high reputation to having been the first to steal the secret MEISSEN recipe for hard-paste porcelain. The figures made in 1750-84 were of high quality; later work had little merit.

Vienna School (1920s) A philosophical school inspired by Ernst Mach which founded LOGICAL POSITIVISM. Wittgenstein (who went to Cambridge; see TRACTATUS LOGICO PHILOSOPHICUS) and Carnap (who went to USA) were among their number.

Vietcong (1958) The nationalist movement (including the NLF) in South VIETNAM which came under VIETMINH direction (1960) in opposing successive US-sponsored South Vietnamese governments by undeclared civil war which led to the VIETNAMESE WAR. ('Vietnamese Communists'.)

Vietminh (1941) Originally the resistance movement against Japanese occupation founded in ANNAM by Ho Chi Minh. After the war, in collaboration with Chiang Kai-shek's occupying forces, it gained control of North VIETNAM and strong support in the south (then under British

occupation); see VIETCONG. After DIEN BIEN PHU (1954), by then renamed the Fatherland Front, it installed the LAO DONG Communist government in North Vietnam. Despite the change of name, Vietminh is still used as a synonym for the regime in the north. ('League for the Independence of Vietnam'.)

Vietnam A country of Southeast Asia formed (1945) from the former French colonies of ANNAM, TONKIN and COCHIN CHINA, but divided at the 17th parallel of latitude between Communist North and non-Communist South Vietnam. (Chinese, 'farther south'.)

Vietnamese War (1964) The war between North Vietnam (see VIETMINH) and the US-sponsored government of South VIETNAM, and also the civil war against the VIETCONG who had gained control of much of the south. The US government was forced by events to step up its aid to the south from the supply of arms, military instruction and guidance, to full-scale military and especially air support against the Vietcong, which had been greatly assisted in its guerrilla tactics by terrain and by passive or active support from the local inhabitants. Later, massive air attacks on supply routes from the north, and on North Vietnam itself, became necessary.

Vieux Carré The old French Quarter in New Orleans, with narrow old streets, patios and exquisite wrought ironwork. Royal Street is famous for its shops, Bourbon Street for its honky-tonks. See also ANTOINE'S.

Vigilant A British antitank weapon, made by BAC.

Viipuri Finnish name for VYBORG (Viborg).

Vikings (8th-11th centuries) Scandinavian pirates who scoured the seas as far as the Mediterranean, Russia, Iceland and VINLAND, establishing colonies at Kiev, DUBLIN and the Isle of Man, among many others, and finally settling the DANELAW in England and Normandy in France; also called Norsemen or Normans. The typical Viking ship, with high prow and stern, was propelled by 20 oarsmen and a large square sail.

Vikings The Minnesota Vikings, NATIONAL FOOTBALL LEAGUE. Became member of the NATIONAL CONFERENCE, NATIONAL FOOTBALL LEAGUE in 1970.

Vilikins and his Dinah Characters of a COCKNEY mock-heroic ballad dating back at least to the early 19th century. (Vilikins for Wilkins.)

Villa Borghese The traditional name of a park in Rome and of a museum and art gallery in it. Officially it has been renamed the Villa Umberto I. (Former summer residence of the Borghese family.)

'Village Blacksmith, The' (1841) Longfellow's poem, among the best-known in the English language, beginning 'Under the spreading chestnut tree / The village smithy stands', and ending 'Something attempted, something done / Has earned a night's repose'.

Villa Mauresque Famous as Somerset Maugham's home for many years, at Cap Ferrat on the French Riviera.

Villa Umberto I See VILLA BORGHESE.

Ville radieuse See UNITÉS D'-HABITATION.

Villette (1853) Charlotte Brontë's largely autobiographical novel, in which Lucy Snowe goes to Villette (Brussels) as a schoolteacher and falls in love with Professor Paul (who is the Constantine Heger of Charlotte's own life).

Vilna, Vilno, Wilno Alternative spellings of Vilnius, capital of Lithuania.

VIM Initials standing for Vertical Improved Mail, a system of electronically controlled conveyors to speed delivery to and from each floor of lofty buildings.

Vimy The VICKERS biplane used in World War I, and by Alcock and Brown on the first nonstop transatlantic flight (1919).

Vimy Ridge The scene of heavy fighting on the Western Front during much of World War I. It was held by the French from September 1915 to May 1916, and recaptured by the Canadians in April 1917, with heavy loss of life. (Ridge 5 miles northeast of Arras.)

Vincennes porcelain (1738-51) The wares produced by the factory southeast of Paris which became world famous when it moved to SÈVRES.

Vinegar Joe Nickname of the American General Joseph Stilwell, who commanded Chiang Kai-shek's troops in Burma during World War II.

Vinland The part of North America discovered by the VIKINGS; usually identified with the island of Martha's Vineyard, Mass.

Vintage cars Cars made between 1919 and 1930.

Viola The heroine of Shakespeare's TWELFTH NIGHT; she disguises herself as a boy and becomes page to the Duke Orsino with whom she falls in love 'but let concealment, like a worm i' the bud. / Feed on her damask cheek' and 'sat like patience on a monument, / Smiling at grief'. The Duke falls in love with Olivia, the niece of Sir Toby BELCH and Olivia with the seeming page.

Violetta See TRAVIATA.

VIP Abbreviation for Very Important Person, which came into use in World War II to designate air passengers to be accorded special facilities and red-carpet treatment on arrival.

Virginia ham A flat lean hickory-smoked ham with dark red meat from a peanut-fed razorback hog such as is bred in the southeastern States.

Virginian, The (1902) The first 'Western', written by Owen Wister, about cowboys in Wyoming, complete with bad men, poker games and pistol duels.

Virginians, The (1857) Thackeray's sequel to HENRY ESMOND, about the twin nephews of Beatrix Esmond (now Baroness Bernstein), who fight on opposite sides in the AMERICAN WAR OF INDEPENDENCE. George Washington and Gen. Wolfe appear in the book.

Virginia reel US name for the Sir Roger de COVERLEY country dance,

which begins with 2 lines of partners facing each other.

Virgin Lands scheme (1954) In the
USSR, Khrushchev's ambitious
scheme which brought approximately a million new acres into cultivation, mainly under spring wheat,
in southwest Siberia and northern
Kazakhstan. It ran into DUST BOWL
trouble.

'Virgin of the Rocks' A famous
painting by Leonardo da Vinci, in
the National Gallery, London; another version is in the LOUVRE.

Virgin Queen, The A name for Elizabeth I of England who, at any rate,
never married.

Virgo The Virgin, 6th of the constellations of the Zodiac, between LEO
and LIBRA, representing a woman
holding an ear of corn, identified
with ISHTAR; the sun enters it about
August 21st. It contains a galaxy
cluster. Astrologers claim that those
born under this sign may be industrious, sensible and loyal.

Viscount (1953) The world's first
turboprop airliner, a 4-engined
medium-range product of the VICK-
ERS GROUP.

Vishnu One of the 2 main gods of
modern HINDUISM, and one of the
Trinity formed with SIVA and BRAH-
MA; a benevolent savior of mankind
who reappears on earth in successive incarnations, the eighth being
as KRISHNA, the ninth as BUDDHA.

Visigoths The Western GOTHS who
under Alaric sacked Rome (410),
and ruled Spain from Toledo until
the Moorish conquest (711).

Vision and Design (1920) Roger
Fry's collection of essays on the essential qualities and relations of
form in art.

VISTA Initials standing for Volunteers in Service to America, the
domestic equivalent of the PEACE
CORPS.

VistaVision (1954) A cinema system
using a frame (picture area) twice
the normal size to produce improved definition.

Vita Nuova, La (1291) Dante's
collection of poems linked by an
autobiographical prose account of

his love for BEATRICE. (Italian, 'new
life'.)

Vittoria, The The first ship to sail
round the world (1519-22); her crew
of 18 were the only survivors of an
expedition of 265 men in 5 ships
under Magellan, who was killed en
route in the Philippines.

V-J Day (USA), September 2nd, the
day the Japanese signed a formal
surrender (1945); (UK) August 15th,
the day Japanese surrender became
effective.

Vladimir One of the 2 tramps in
GODOT.

VMI (1839) The Virginia Military
Institute, Lexington, 'the WEST POINT
of the South', and the oldest state
military college. Students are organized as a cadet corps, wear uniforms and live in barracks; studies
include the arts and sciences, civil
and electrical engineering etc. In
the Civil War nearly all the cadets
served in the Confederate Army,
and today it numbers many generals and admirals among its alumni.

Vogue (1892) Condé Nast's glossy
women's magazine which in 1936
absorbed *Vanity Fair*; there is an allied British magazine (1916). Issued
20 times a year (in the US), it covers
fashion, house decoration, travel
and general topics, and publishes
short stories.

Voice of America A propaganda
organization run by the US Information Agency; it broadcasts in over 40
languages all over the world.

Voiceprint A pictorial representation of the human voice, the pattern
of which is as unique to each individual as are his fingerprints. Voice-
prints thus have potentialities in
identifying criminals. (Devised by
Lawrence Kersta at the Bell Telephone laboratories.)

Volapük (1880) An artificial language invented by an Austrian
priest; it was too complicated to
have the success of ESPERANTO, invented a few years later. ('English-
speech'.)

'Volga Boatmen, Song of the' A Russian folk song sung by the men who
towed barges along the Volga, with

the refrain: 'Yo, heave ho!' It was first popularized by the Russian bass singer Chaliapin.

Volgograd The current name of the city of Stalingrad, USSR.

Völkische Beobachter German daily newspaper which during the Nazi regime was Hitler's chosen mouthpiece. ('People's Observer'.)

Volkswagen The German automobile firm, the largest outside the US, in which the West German government holds 40% of the shares; headquarters at Wolfsburg, near Brunswick. It produced the ubiquitous 'BEETLE', a postwar development of Hitler's 'People's Car' (1938), and acquired (1969) control of NSU, its subsidiary Auto Union, and the NSU-Porsche sports car company.

Volpone (1605) Ben Jonson's satirical play on human greed and self-deluding folly. When a rich and childless Venetian, Volpone (the Fox), pretends to be dying, he is showered with gifts by those who hope to benefit under his will; when he pretends to be dead, he is blackmailed by his servant-accomplice. In the end the plot is revealed and all are punished.

Volstead Act (1919) The Act that defined 'intoxicating liquor', an essential preliminary to the enforcement of PROHIBITION.

Volsunga Saga The Icelandic saga from which the NIBELUNGENLIED is derived.

Voltaic Republic A West African state, formerly the French colony of Upper Volta.

Volta PPK James BOND's preferred automatic; it was used in real life by German plainclothes secret police. (PPK = *Polizei Pistol Kriminal*.)

Volta River project (1961) A hydroelectric and irrigation scheme in eastern GHANA, based on the damming of the River Volta at Akosambo 50 miles north of the new harbor of Tema. One of the chief purposes is to provide power for an aluminum smelter to process the bauxite in which the country is rich.

Voluntary Service Overseas A scheme under which young people volunteer for a year or so's service in developing countries, mostly in teaching posts. They are paid little more than their keep.

Volunteer State Nickname of Tennessee. (Furnished a large number of volunteers in the Civil War.)

V-1 The German flying bomb, first launched against London in June 1944 and later (Oct. 1944-Mar. 1945) against Antwerp, Brussels and Liège; the attacks ended when the launching sites were overrun in the Allied advance. The V-1 was a winged, pilotless plane with engines preset to cut out over the target. (V for *Vergeltung*, 'retaliation'.)

V-1000 A large VICKERS jet airliner which might have captured the market from the US BOEING and DOUGLAS firms in 1957, had it not been canceled in 1955, a decision sometimes quoted as a major disaster for the British aircraft industry.

Voortrekkers (1835-37) The 10,000 Boers who took part in the Great Trek away from British Liberal rule in Cape Colony, northeast to the Orange River Colony (Orange Free State) and later over the Vaal River to found the Transvaal Republic, then over the Drakensberg Mountains into Zululand and Natal.

Voronoff monkey-gland grafts A method of rejuvenating old men by the transplantation of apes' testes. Great claims were made, but the method is now discredited. (Serge Voronoff, Russian working in Paris; died 1951.)

Voroshilovgrad Now renamed Lugansk, see DONBAS.

Vortex, The (1924) Noël Coward's first big success, which shocked contemporary audiences by dwelling on drug addiction.

Voshkod Russian name for earth satellites manned by more than one person. *Voshkod 1* (1964) carried 3 men; *Voshkod 2* carried the first man to walk in space (1965).

Vostok Russian name for the first series of manned satellites. *Vostok 1*, launched 12 April 1961, carried the first man into space, Maj. Gagarin. Maj. Titov made 17 orbits in *Vostok 2*. *Vostok 3* and *4* made 48 orbits in company, the first double manned flight (1962). *Vostok 5* and *6* approached close to one another, one containing the first woman cosmonaut (1963).

Vougeot See CÔTE DE NUITS.

Voyage of the Beagle, The (1840) Darwin's journal of his trip (1831-36) to South America and Australia as naturalist aboard the survey ship *Beagle*. See DARWIN'S FINCHES.

Voyager US program to land an unmanned automated laboratory on Mars by 1975, to be dropped by an orbiting spacecraft and to relay back information, particularly on evidence of any life there; and a similar program for Venus. Both projects have been severely hampered by refusal to vote funds.

Vronski See ANNA KARENINA.

VSOP Initials standing for Very Superior Old Pale. They can be legally tacked on to the name of any brandy, good or bad, and thus have no meaning.

V/STOL Abbreviation for Vertical or Short Take Off and Landing, a term which includes aircraft needing a short runway and true VTOLS.

VT fuses Variable-time or proximity fuses, which cause shells to burst on coming within range of the target.

VTOL Abbreviation for Vertical Take Off and Landing, a term theoretically applicable to helicopters but reserved in practice for military aircraft needing no runway. They either have 2 sets of jets, one for vertical lift and the other for horizontal flight, or one movable set for both purposes. See FLYING BEDSTEAD; KESTREL; V/STOL.

V-2 The first guided missile, a liquid-fuel rocket developed at PEENEMÜNDE by von Braun, and first tested in 1942. V-2s were used against London (Sept. 1944-Mar. 1945), and from November 1944 against Antwerp. Each had a 1-ton warhead, and 4000 were fired. (V for *Vergeltung*, 'retaliation'.)

Vulcan Roman god equivalent to the Greek HEPHAESTUS.

Vulcan (1953) A British 4-jet V-BOMBER, the world's largest delta-wing bomber when it first appeared. It was built by Avro-Armstrong-Siddeley to carry a nuclear load or one Blue Star missile, at Mach 0.94 over a range of 2300 miles.

Vulgate Latin translation of the Bible made by St Jerome (end of 4th century), and still the basic text for the Roman Catholic Church.

VX A nerve chemical of which a minute droplet on the skin is sufficient to kill a man. In 1968, when it was being test-sprayed from an airplane, some drifted from the DUGWAY PROVING GROUND to Skull Valley, Utah, where it killed 6500 sheep.

W

WAAC See ATS.

WAAF Initials of the Women's Auxiliary Air Force; see WRAF.

Wac A member of the US Women's Army Corps established during World War II as successor to the Women's Army Auxiliary Corps.

'Wacht am Rhein, Die' (1840) A German patriotic song beginning: Es braust ein Ruf wie Donnerschall ('A shout rings out like a thunderclap').

Wade's roads The first hard-surfaced roads to be built in the Scottish Highlands, straight strategic roads built by Gen. Wade after the FIFTEEN; hence the old rhyme: Had you seen these roads before they were made, / You would lift up your hands and bless General Wade. ('Made' here means 'properly surfaced'.)

Waf Abbreviation for (one of the) Women in the Air Force, the women's component of the US Air Force formed after World War II, but not as a separate corps.

Wafd (1918) The Egyptian nationalist party. (Arabic, 'delegation'; so named because Zaghlul Pasha led a delegation to the British High Commissioner in Cairo demanding Egyptian representation at the PARIS PEACE CONFERENCE.)

Waffen-SS The more fanatical members of the SS, who fought with the German army in World War II as an independent so-called elite corps. ('Armed SS'.)

Wagner Act (1935) The Labor Relations Act which legalized collective bargaining and set up a NATIONAL LABOR RELATIONS BOARD, one of the NEW DEAL measures.

Wagon, The A name for the BIG DIPPER; see CHARLES'S WAIN.

Wagoner, The A name for AURIGA, and (less commonly) for BOÖTES.

Wagram (1809) Napoleon's costly victory over the Austrians. (Village near Vienna.)

Wahhabis Followers of the 18th-century MUSLIM puritan reformer Muhammad ibn-Abdul Wahhab, who advocated a very strict and ascetic form of the religion, and converted an ancestor of ibn-Saud, King of SAUDI ARABIA from 1932.

Waikiki Beach The LIDO of Hawaii, in Honolulu harbor.

Wailing Wall, The A wall in Jerusalem, traditionally part of SOLOMON'S TEMPLE, where Jews gather on Tish-ah-b'Ab (in August on the Gregorian calendar) to bewail the Temple's destruction. It adjoins a mosque, and MUSLIM-Jewish riots have been frequent there down the ages, and especially violent in 1929.

Waiting for Godot See GODOT.

Waiting for Lefty (1935) Clifford Odet's short play about a strike of US taxi drivers enraged by the murder of their leader, Lefty.

Walden (1854) Thoreau's description, subtitled 'Life in the Woods', of his experiment of living by himself in a cabin at Walden Pond on Emerson's estate at Concord, Mass. (1845-47). He occupied himself by tilling the soil and observing nature, but he was no hermit and continued to see his friends. See TRANSCENDENTALISM.

Waldensians (1170) An early Protestant sect which rejected papal authority; it survived persecution to join in the REFORMATION and still exists. The French name is Vaudois. (Founded by Peter Waldo of Lyons.)

Waldorf salad A salad of diced celery, apples, nuts etc., served with mayonnaise and sometimes with sliced bananas. (For the old Waldorf-Astoria Hotel, NYC.)

Wales, University of A federation of the colleges at Aberystwyth, Bangor, Cardiff and Swansea, together with a medical school and (the latest addition) the former Welsh CAT at Cathays Park, Cardiff.

Walker Art Gallery (1877) A collection, mainly of English paintings, at Liverpool.

Walker Cup (1922) Amateur golf contest between Britain and USA, held in alternate years, with 4 foursomes and 8 singles.

Walk of Fame The forecourt of GRAUMAN'S CHINESE THEATER, HOLLYWOOD, where the film stars' footprints are.

Wallace Collection (1900) An art collection, particularly of French furniture, pictures and porcelain, at Hertford House, Manchester Square, London. (Sir Richard Wallace, died 1890.)

Wallenstein (1799) Schiller's historical tragedy about the Austrian General Wallenstein who, after serving his country well in the THIRTY YEARS WAR, was murdered (1634) by his officers at the instigation of the Emperor, who had reason to suspect his loyalty.

Walloon Language or inhabitant of Belgium south of a line drawn approximately from Courtrai through Brussels to Liège. In contrast to the FLEMINGS, they are anticlerical, republican and culturally closer to the French than to Holland; relations between the 2 communities are bitter. The language is a dialect of French with Flemish borrowings.

Wall Street The chief financial center of USA, at the southern tip of MANHATTAN, NYC.

Wall Street crash (Oct. 1929) The sudden collapse of the New York Stock Exchange, caused by mass gambling in stocks pushed to excessive prices at a time when the economy was threatened by overproduction. The realization of this led to panic selling, the closing of banks and factories, mass unemployment, and an economic depression which spread to the rest of the world, especially Europe (see CREDITANSTALT).

Wall Street Journal (1889) The New York financial daily, published by DOW JONES & Co.

Walmer Castle The official residence at Walmer, Kent, of the Lord Warden of the CINQUE PORTS.

Walpole Society (1911) A society which encourages the study of the history of British art. (Named after Horace Walpole.)

Walpurgis Night The eve of May Day, when the witches made revel, especially (in German legend) on the BROCKEN, the setting of a famous scene in FAUST. (Feast day of St Walpurgis, an English abbess who introduced Christianity to the Germans in the 8th century.)

Walrus and the Carpenter, The Characters in a ballad recited by Tweedledee in THROUGH THE LOOKING GLASS, containing the lines: 'The time has come', the Walrus said, / 'To talk of many things: / Of shoes — and ships — and sealing-wax / Of cabbages and kings!'.

Walsingham Abbey An abbey between Wells and Fakenham, Norfolk, built on the site of the 11th-century Shrine of Our Lady of Walsingham, once visited by pilgrims from all Europe.

Walter Reed Army Medical Center An institution in Washington, D.C., comprising a hospital, dental center, institutes of research and pathology etc.; it also has a nuclear reactor to produce radioactive isotopes.

Waltham Forest (1965) A new London borough consisting of the former boroughs of Walthamstow, Chingford and Leyton; headquarters at Forest Road, E 17.

Walthamstow A former municipal borough of Essex, England, since 1965 part of the borough of WALTHAM FOREST.

Walton figures (1806-35) Staffordshire pottery figures which copied CHELSEA and DERBY groups for the cottage mantelpiece, complete with simplified bocages, made by John Walton of Burslem or his imitators. He also depicted biblical and rural themes. All were gaily painted in overglaze enamels, and sometimes marked with the title of the subject.

'Waltzing Matilda' Australian national song, written by Andrew Paterson (1864-1941), beginning: Once a jolly swagman camped by a billybong. (Waltz, 'carry'; Matilda, swag, hobo's roll.)

Walwal incident (Dec. 1934) A minor skirmish on the Italian Somaliland and Abyssinia border, used as a pretext for Mussolini's invasion.

Wampanoags American Indians

who occupied most of Massachusetts when the PILGRIM FATHERS landed, and after a long peace formed a confederation extending from Maine to Connecticut to resist the colonists in KING PHILIP'S WAR.

Wandering Jew, The A Jew of medieval legend who insulted Jesus on his way to the Crucifixion and was condemned to walk the earth until the Day of Judgment. Ahasuerus (=Xerxes) is one of the many names under which he appears. The best-known fictional treatments of this theme are *Melmoth the Wanderer* (1820) by C. R. Maturin, and *The Wandering Jew* (1845-47) by Eugène Sue.

Wandering Willie (1) The blind fiddler in Walter Scott's novel *Redgauntlet*, set in the period of the FORTY-FIVE. (2) The title of a poem by Robert Burns.

Wandervögel Hordes of hikers who used to roam the German countryside singing folk songs. Before World War I they were high-school boys and girls getting away from parents and teachers but otherwise conventional. Between the wars the prevailing spirit was quite different, leaning to socialism and sexual freedom. (German, 'birds of passage'.)

Wandsworth Inner London borough since 1965 consisting of the former metropolitan boroughs of Wandsworth and Battersea.

Wandsworth Prison Largest of British prisons; it takes only recidivists, mostly from south London where it is situated.

Wanstead and Woodford (UK) A former municipal borough of Essex, since 1965 part of the borough of REDBRIDGE.

Wantage   Research   Laboratory Headquarters of the UK ATOMIC ENERGY AUTHORITY's Research Group, with an Isotope School (1951) where new uses for isotopes are investigated. (Town in Berkshire.)

WAP WHITE AUSTRALIA POLICY.

Wapshot Chronicle, The (1957) John Cheever's humorous best seller satirizing American bureaucracy; *The Wapshot Scandal* (1964) is a sequel.

War and Peace (1869) One of Leo Tolstoy's 2 greatest novels. The vast canvas includes a study of the utter fortuitousness of war (Napoleon's defeat of Kutuzov at BORODINO in 1812); Pierre's capture by the French after his scruples had caused him to spare Napoleon's life at Moscow; his escape and marriage to the delightful Natasha; and his conversion by a peasant to the wisdom of a simple life (echoing a theme in ANNA KARENINA).

Warbeck Rebellion (1497) A Yorkist attempt to place Perkin Warbeck on the English throne. He was a native of Tournai masquerading as the younger of the PRINCES IN THE TOWER. With support from Burgundy, Scotland and Ireland, he landed in the southwest but deserted his forces at Taunton and was eventually executed.

Warburg Institute (1905) Originally a private research library founded at Hamburg, moved to London 1933 and since 1944 part of LONDON UNIVERSITY; devoted to the history of the classical tradition.

Ward, Artemus Pen name of the American humorist Charles Farrar Browne (1834-67), who wrote numerous sketches purporting to be the work of an illiterate traveling showman.

Ward Eight A cocktail of whiskey, lemon juice and grenadine, served in a tall glass with ice, soda and a garnish. (Probably named for the municipal division of Boston, Mass., where it originated.)

Warden, The (1855) One of Trollope's BARCHESTER NOVELS; the conscientious Rev. Septimus Harding accepts with great reluctance the well-paid sinecure post of warden of a hospital for 12 bedesmen, only to be hounded out of it by a press campaign.

Wardle, Mr The amiable host at DINGLEY DELL to the Pickwick Club in Dickens's novel. His daughters marry SNODGRASS and Trundle, and one elopes with Alfred JINGLE.

Wardour Street A street in Soho, London. (1) Formerly associated with fake antique furniture; hence

Wardour Street English, fake antique English of the 'quotha, methinks, anent, perchance' school. (2) Now associated with the cinema industry.

Ware, The Great Bed of An oak fourposter bed, nearly 11 ft square, thought to have been moved from Ware House to an inn in Ware, near Hertford, in the 16th century, and now in the Victoria and Albert Museum. It is mentioned in Shakespeare's TWELFTH NIGHT.

'Waring' (1842) Robert Browning's poem beginning: 'What's become of Waring / Since he gave us all the slip?' It refers to a friend of his who had emigrated to New Zealand.

War of 1812 A war between Britain and USA during the NAPOLEONIC WARS, arising from the Royal Navy's restrictions on the freedom of the seas which hurt American interests. US forces made unsuccessful attempts to invade Canada, but set fire to Toronto (1813); the British failed to take Baltimore (see STAR-SPANGLED BANNER) but burned Washington (1814). See GHENT, TREATY OF.

War of the Worlds, The (1898) H. G. Wells's story of the invasion of England by creatures from Mars (see MARTIAN INVASION SCARE); armed with a heat ray, they proved a formidable enemy until they were vanquished by our native diseases.

War on Want A London organization which seeks to educate the British public on the urgent need for a campaign against world poverty, and collects funds to use for this purpose in India and elsewhere.

Warren Commission (1964) The inquiry into the circumstances of President Kennedy's assassination, subsequently criticized for not examining more rigorously the unlikely suggestion that there was a conspiracy involving more than one assassin. (Earl Warren, Chief Justice of the Supreme Court.)

War Requiem (1962) Benjamin Britten's musical setting of a poem by Wilfred Owen, composed for the new Coventry Cathedral.

Warriors The San Francisco Warriors, NATIONAL BASKETBALL ASSOCIATION.

Warsaw Ghetto Rising (Apr.-June 1943) A pathetic revolt by the Jews against their German tormentors.

Warsaw Pact (1955) The Communist bloc's equivalent, and answer, to NATO.

Warsaw Rising (Aug.-Oct. 1944) An abortive attempt to seize Warsaw from the Germans, made by the Polish underground movement in the expectation of help from the approaching Russian armies, which was deliberately withheld as the revolt was led by non-Communists.

Wars of the Roses (1455-85) The civil war between the LANCASTRIANS and the YORKISTS, rival claimants to the throne descended from Edward III; ended by BOSWORTH FIELD. (Red and white roses were the badges respectively of Lancaster and York.)

Warspite, HMS The Royal Navy's third Fleet submarine, see VALIANT.

Warwick the Kingmaker Richard Neville, Earl of Warwick and Salisbury, who fought on both sides in the WARS OF THE ROSES, first putting the YORKIST Edward IV on the throne and then briefly restoring the LANCASTRIAN Henry VI.

Warwick University (1965) A new foundation, near Coventry.

Washington (1963) (UK) A NEW TOWN in Co. Durham, adjoining the existing town 5 miles from Gateshead, designed to take 70,000 inhabitants.

Washington and the Cherry Tree The story of the young George Washington's ruining his father's tree with a hatchet and owning up instantly with the words 'I can't tell a lie, Pa', which was first published 7 years after his death, but was publicized more widely, and in more decorous English, by Mark TWAIN ('Father, I cannot tell a lie'). There is no reason to believe it.

Washington Arch (1895) A memorial to Washington which dominates WASHINGTON SQUARE at the foot of FIFTH AVENUE, NYC; designed by Stanford White.

Washington Conference (1) A postwar meeting (1921-22) of the major powers which tried to ensure a lasting peace. It guaranteed Chinese independence, canceled the Anglo-Japanese alliance, and in general relieved tension arising from international rivalries in the Pacific area. Its chief success was the WASHINGTON NAVAL AGREEMENT. (2) For conferences during World War II, see ARCADIA and TRIDENT, their code names.

Washington Monument (1888) An obelisk in Washington, D.C., 555 ft high, with an elevator to the 500-ft level and 8 small lookouts.

Washington Naval Agreement (1922) The chief achievement of the WASHINGTON CONFERENCE (1921-22). It fixed a 10-year holiday from building capital ships, which were put on a 5:5:3 tonnage ratio as between Britain, USA and Japan, and limited in size. This and the agreement reached at the LONDON NAVAL CONFERENCE (1930) were denounced by Japan in 1934.

Washington pie A layer cake with jam or jelly filling. (For George Washington.)

Washington's Birthday February 22nd, a legal holiday except in Nevada, and in Hawaii known as Presidents' Day. From 1971 kept on the third Monday in February.

Washington Square (1) Once an exclusive residential district of New York City, at the southern end of FIFTH AVENUE on the edge of GREENWICH VILLAGE. (2) The title of a novel by Henry James, made into a play, The Heiress.

Washkansky case (1967) An attempt to save the life of Louis Washkansky (aged 55) in South Africa by transplanting into him the heart of a mortally injured girl. His death 18 days later was attributed to lung failure following double pneumonia, and not to heart failure. The case started a many-faceted controversy remarkable for the absence of dispassionate scientific assessment.

WASP Abbreviation for White ANGLO-SAXON Protestant.

Wasp of Twickenham, The The well-earned nickname of Alexander Pope who, during the latter half of his life, lived at TWICKENHAM (now part of GREATER LONDON).

Wasps, The (422 BC) Aristophanes' comedy, like The KNIGHTS an attack on CLEON, and on the Athenian weakness for litigation.

Wassermann test (1906) A blood test for syphilis, still in use.

Waste Land, The (1922) T. S. Eliot's first major poem, contrasting the sterility of modern civilization with the fertility of ancient beliefs. It is important for its complete break with poetic tradition, parallel with that of Joyce's ULYSSES. As with Joyce, his settings are taken from everyday life but his allusive comments of inspissated erudition demand from the reader a knowledge of several languages and of the books that have been important to the author, only partially supplied by enigmatic footnotes. It set a fashion by which many a modern poet is held incommunicado.

Watch, The Common abbreviation for The BLACK WATCH.

'Watch on the Rhine' See WACHT AM RHEIN.

Watch Tower Bible and Tract Society A name for JEHOVAH'S WITNESSES.

Water-babies, The (1863) Charles Kingsley's fairy tale of a chimney-sweep boy who falls in the river and is welcomed by the water-babies.

Waterford glass (1784-1851) Glass made by an English firm established in Waterford, Ireland, to evade tax. It is indistinguishable from Stourbridge and other English glass, although the myth that it has a distinctive blue tinge has been perpetuated by modern fakes purposely so colored.

Waterloo (18 June 1815) The final battle of the NAPOLEONIC WARS, in which Wellington held the French until Blücher arrived with his Prussians. After this defeat Napoleon abdicated and was sent to ST HELENA. (Village 8 miles south of Brussels.)

Watermen's Derby See DOGGETT'S COAT AND BADGE.

Water Music (1717) Handel's suite composed for a royal picnic on the

Thames, originally in 41 movements but now generally heard in Sir Hamilton Harty's version of 7 movements.

Water Rats, Grand Order of (1890) A British society, originally of music-hall artists, recruited by invitation, whose motto is Philanthropy, Conviviality and Social Intercourse. It holds a banquet with an impromptu, unorthodox cabaret on the last Sunday in November, before the pantomime season begins. The Order has collected vast sums for charity and helped to found the Variety Artists' Benevolent Fund. Its officers have titles such as King Rat, Scribe Rat. (Origin of name uncertain.)

Waterton Lakes National Park (1895) A small park in southwest Alberta, merged in 1932 with the GLACIER NATIONAL PARK in Montana.

Watkin's Glen An auto racing circuit in Finger Lakes Park, N.Y., where the US GRAND PRIX is held.

Watling Street A Roman road from London via St Albans to Wroxeter (near Shrewsbury); it was at one time the boundary between the ANGLO-SAXONS and the DANELAW.

Wats line Wide Area Telephone Service line, a system whereby customers pay a flat monthly fee for all calls placed within a selected wide area, instead of paying for each call.

Watson, Dr The slow-witted foil to Sherlock HOLMES, said to be a self-mocking portrait of his creator, Conan Doyle.

'Watson and the Shark' (1778) A painting by the self-taught Bostonian artist John Singleton Copley, who left America for good in 1774. On the Atlantic voyage, he met Brook Watson (a future Lord Mayor of London) who told him how a shark had taken his leg in Havana harbor. Copley painted a dramatic version of the incident, with Watson being saved from a school of sharks by a boatload of rescuers. (NATIONAL GALLERY OF ART, Washington.)

Watts A Negro ghetto in Los Angeles, the scene in August 1965 of a 6-day race riot marked by arson, looting and the death of 34 people. It was one of the worst of its kind in American history and shocked the whole nation.

Watt steam engine (1769) The engine developed by James Watt from the NEWCOMEN ENGINE by adding a separate condenser and an air pump. A few years later he joined Boulton at the Soho Ironworks, Birmingham, where his engine was further developed.

Watts Towers Several spires consisting of scrap steel rods and concrete and decorated with sea shells, broken bottles, bits of tile, and other odds and ends, erected by Sabatanio Rodia in his backyard over a period of 33 years. One tower is over 100 feet high. (WATTS, section of Los Angeles, Calif.)

Wave (1) A member of the Waves (Women Accepted for Volunteer Emergency Service), i.e. the Women's Reserve (which is not a separate corps) of the US Navy. (2) A woman serving in the US Navy.

Wavell's offensives The first (Dec. 1940-Feb. 1941) drove the Italians out of Egypt into LIBYA; the second (June 1941), known by the code name BATTLEAXE, failed, and Gen. Wavell was replaced by Gen. Auchinleck.

Waverley (1814) The first of Scott's WAVERLEY NOVELS, about a Capt. Waverley who fights for the YOUNG PRETENDER; it portrays the clash of the old feudal Highlands and the rising bourgeois Lowlands.

Waverley novels The novels of Sir Walter Scott, named after the first of them which was published anonymously, while subsequent books were described as being by 'the author of WAVERLEY'.

Waves, The (1931) Virginia Woolf's novel of the relationship of 6 sharply contrasted characters who were brought up together as children, as revealed through their inner thoughts. At the end, one of them sums up all their lives and sees that they fit together as if they had been one person.

Wayland the Smith English name of a figure in Scandinavian mythology.

The English Wayland was an invisible smith who lived in a cromlech near Lambourne, Berkshire; if you left a fee there he would shoe your horse for you while you slept.

Way of All Flesh, The   (1903) Samuel Butler's vitriolic novel reflecting his own revolt against his family and the Victorian Church.

Way of the World, The   (1700) William Congreve's comedy of Mirabell's efforts to marry the captivating Millamant, a play of scintillating if unfeeling wit.

Ways and Means, Committee of   A committee of the whole House of Commons which, on the basis of the Budget, gives detailed consideration to the means of raising the money voted by the Committee of Supply; its decisions are embodied in the Finance Act.

WCTU   Initials used for the Women's Christian Temperance Union, which dates back to 1874 (at Cleveland, O.) and later became international in scope.

We   (1) Lindbergh's account (1927) of his Atlantic flight in the SPIRIT OF ST LOUIS, written in collaboration with Fitzhugh Green. 'We' refers to pilot and plane. (2) English title of the Russian novelist Zamyatin's *My* (1924), a brilliant attack on totalitarianism in the guise of a 'UTOPIA' set in AD 2600, which led to his exile. It anticipated BRAVE NEW WORLD by 8 years and was written from first-hand experience of Bolshevist excesses.

Wealth of Nations, The   (1776) Adam Smith's *Inquiry into the Nature and Cause of the Wealth of Nations*, the first major analysis of economic theory; he emphasized self-interest and advocated free trade, which he was convinced would be adequately regulated by natural laws of universal application.

'Wearin' o' the Green, The'   (18th century) A self-pitying Irish street ballad: O Paddy dear, an' did ye hear the news that's goin' round? / The shamrock is by law forbid to grow on Irish ground! . . . / She's the most disthressful country that iver

yet was seen, / For they're hangin' men an' women for the wearin' o' the Green.

Weather Bureau, US   A component of the Environmental Science Services Administration; see ESSA.

Webster   (1828) The chief American dictionary, bought up by G. & C. Merriam Co. in 1844. In 1961 they published *Webster's Third New International Dictionary of the English Language* (more than 450,000 entries); also known as the Merriam-Webster unabridged, as the name Webster has been used by other firms. (First produced by Noah Webster.)

Wedgwood blue   A cold pale blue, slightly lighter than powder blue, used by WEDGWOOD as ground color for JASPER WARES.

Wedgwoods   (1759) A family firm of Staffordshire potters founded by Josiah Wedgwood at Burslem and moved to the Etruria factory in 1769. It produces JASPER WARE, black stoneware ('basaltes', from 1766), Queen's ware (a soberly decorated creamware) and, from 1878, bone china.

Wee Frees   Members of the Free Church of Scotland who refused to join the UNITED FREE CHURCH OF SCOTLAND in 1900.

Wehrmacht   The German armed forces. (German, 'defensive force'.)

Weimar   A German town which, when capital of the Duchy of Saxe-Weimar, was associated with Goethe, who lived there from 1775, holding a court post and directing the theater. Schiller also spent the last years of his life there, working with Goethe. (See next entry.)

Weimar Republic   (1919-33) The German Republic formed after the Kaiser's abdication, and suspended by Hitler. (Constitution formulated by the National Assembly sitting at Weimar, which at first was the new capital; now in East Germany, near Leipzig.)

Weir of Hermiston   (1896) R. L. Stevenson's last and unfinished novel, by many thought to contain his best writing. Archie Weir is banished by his father to live in the village of Hermiston, where he falls in love with a girl. The novel ends at this point, but the outline of the rest of the plot is known.

Welcome Wagon International A nonprofit welcoming service offered primarily to newcomers in the community to acquaint them with various organizations and activities within the area.

Welfare Administration (1963) A US agency of the Department of Health, Education and Welfare which administers aid to the aged, the young and the poor etc. Subsidiary departments include the Bureau of Family Services (which deals with the disabled, blind and aged), the Children's Bureau, the Office of Juvenile Delinquency and Youth Development, and a section for Cuban refugee problems.

Welfare State The system, introduced in Britain in 1948 and based on the National Insurance and NATIONAL HEALTH SERVICE Acts, whereby the social services of the country cease to be a form of poor relief. The main features are free medical services available to all, and the joint financing by employee and employer of insurance against old age, unemployment etc. (Phrase said to have been coined by William Temple, Archbishop of Canterbury.)

Welland Canal (1849) A canal in Canada that bypasses the falls and rapids of the Niagara River between Lakes Ontario and Erie. As redesigned in 1931, it is 28 miles long, has 8 locks and takes ships of 730 ft length and 75 ft beam.

Wellers, The In Dickens's novel, Sam Weller is Pickwick's loyal COCKNEY servant, full of wise saws and modern instances; his father, Tony, is a fat coachman with strong views on the place of women in a man's world.

Wellesley (1870) One of the SEVEN SISTERS colleges, at Wellesley, Mass.

Wellington A VICKERS twin-engined bomber used by the RAF in the early years of World War I. Nicknamed Wimpy, after J. Wellington WIMPY.

Wellington An ex-Admiralty sloop moored to the Thames Embankment, and serving as the floating Livery Hall of the Honourable Company of Master Mariners.

Wellington Museum See APSLEY HOUSE.

Well of Loneliness, The (1928) The first novel to deal sympathetically with the theme of lesbian relationships, written by (Margaret) Radclyffe Hall.

Wells, John Wellington The 'dealer in magic and spells' in Gilbert and Sullivan's The Sorcerer.

Wells Fargo (1850) A pioneer mail, courier and banking service in the developing West, which ran a stagecoach service between Sacramento (Calif.), Portland (Ore.) and Salt Lake City. Its founders also developed the AMERICAN EXPRESS CO. in the eastern states, and the 2 companies joined forces in 1925. (W. G. Fargo, died 1881, and Henry Wells, died 1878.)

Wellsian Resembling the world created by H. G. Wells in his novels of the future, from WAR OF THE WORLDS and The FIRST MEN IN THE MOON to The SHAPE OF THINGS TO COME.

'Well-tempered Clavier, The' The title of J. S. Bach's 48 preludes and fugues, written to demonstrate the advantages of 'equal temperament' (i.e. tuning the instrument so as to distribute inequalities of interval over all keys), then an innovation, now normal. See 48, THE.

Welsh Black A docile breed of longhorn dual-purpose cattle, bred in North Wales.

Welsh corgi A short-legged longbacked breed of dog with a foxy head. There are 2 varieties: (1) the Cardigan, with rounded ears, bowlegs and long tail; (2) the Pembroke, with pointed ears, straight legs and short tail. As Queen Elizabeth II's favorite breed, they have become very popular, despite their alleged bad temper.

Welsh Disestablishment A political issue in the years before World War I, since the disestablishment and disendowment of the Church in Wales, in deference to the great growth of Nonconformity there, was opposed by the House of Lords. An Act was passed in 1914 but because of the war remained inoperative until 1920.

Welsh dresser A heavy oak kitchen sideboard comprising a lower section of drawers and cupboards surmounted by open shelves for displaying plates and dishes; genuine old ones are prized antiques.

Welsh rabbit Melted and often seasoned cheese poured over toasted bread or crackers. (The variant 'rarebit' is an English genteelism.)

Welsh Wizard, The A nickname for David Lloyd George.

Welt, Die (1946) A Hamburg daily newspaper, originally started by the British occupation authorities. See SPRINGER EMPIRE.

Wembley (UK) A former municipal borough of MIDDLESEX, since 1965 part of the borough of BRENT.

Wenceslas The Good King Wenceslas of the carol was a 10th-century Duke of Bohemia converted to Christianity, who was assassinated by his brother for trying to convert his subjects.

Wends SLAVS of eastern Germany, once numerous and widespread, who now survive only in parts of SAXONY.

Wensleydale cheese Once a gourmet's delight, made in the North Riding of Yorkshire, England; the name, like that of double Gloucester, is now applied to cheeses which appear to lack character.

Wernher Collection A collection of OLD MASTERS, tapestries, FABERGÉ jewels and other *objets d'art*, on view at LUTON HOO.

Werther See SORROWS OF YOUNG WERTHER.

'We Shall Overcome' The civil rights movements song, heard wherever 2 or 3 protesters are gathered together.

Wesker trilogy (1958-60) The plays *Chicken Soup with Barley*, *Roots* and *I'm Talking about Jerusalem*, in which Arnold Wesker examines capitalism and socialism through the eyes of a London East End Jewish family.

Wesleyans See METHODISM.

Wessex (1) The kingdom of the West Saxons founded by Cerdic (Cedric) in the 6th century, which dominated all England from the time of Egbert and Alfred in the 9th century, but disappeared as a political unit under William I. It corresponded to Hampshire, Dorset, Wiltshire, Berkshire, Somerset and Devon. (2) The name given by Thomas Hardy to the setting of his Wessex novels, corresponding to Dorset and neighboring counties.

Westchester Cup (1886) An international polo match between Britain and USA.

Western, Squire In Fielding's novel, the semiliterate irascible father of Sophia, whom TOM JONES marries.

Western Empire, The See ROMAN EMPIRE.

Western European Union (1955) The name given to the BRUSSELS TREATY ORGANIZATION when it was expanded to include West Germany and Italy on their regaining full independent sovereign status. It continues to exist, overshadowed by NATO.

Western Reserve, The Land in northeast Ohio claimed by Connecticut (1786-1800) after it had relinquished all other claims to land in the West. (Under a royal charter of 1662 it had nominal rights to land from Naragansett Bay to the Pacific.)

Western Union (1851) The US telegraph company, originally of the western states, which merged with the American Telegraph Co. (controlling the east) and, forced out of the telephone business, concentrated on telegraph and cable communications, completing the first transcontinental line in 1861. Later it developed its own Telex system and in 1960 began work on a transcontinental microwave beam system.

West Germany See GERMAN FEDERAL REPUBLIC.

West Ham A former Essex county borough, since 1965 part of the London borough of NEWHAM.

West Indies Federation (1958-62) A group of British West Indies territories which broke up when Jamaica and Trinidad became Dominions. Most of the remainder agreed in 1962 to form a new federation (the

Eastern Caribbean Federation or 'Little Seven'), consisting of Barbados, the Leeward Islands and the Windward Islands, with a capital in Barbados.

Westinghouse Electric (1886) An electrical group that manufactures equipment for the generation, transmission and utilization of electricity, and initiated broadcasting in 1920 from its own radio station. One of the 30 industrials that make up the DOW JONES Industrial Average.

Westland Aircraft A group of UK firms including Saunders-Roe (see SR-N), the helicopter division of the Bristol Aeroplane Co., and Fairey Aviation. It is the largest manufacturer of helicopters in Europe. See BRITISH HOVERCRAFT CORPORATION.

Westminster, City of Inner London borough which in 1965 absorbed the former metropolitan boroughs of Paddington and St Marylebone.

Westminster, Palace of The official name of the Houses of Parliament, built on the site of the palace where the Kings of England lived from Edward I until Henry VIII moved to WHITEHALL Palace. The original building was burned down in 1834, only WESTMINSTER HALL surviving.

Westminster, Statute of (1931) The final definition of DOMINION STATUS.

Westminster Confession (1647) The declaration of CALVINIST beliefs accepted as the basis of PRESBYTERIANISM.

Westminster Gazette (1893) A distinguished Liberal evening, later morning, paper, absorbed by the (London) DAILY NEWS in 1928.

Westminster Hall The only surviving part of the old Palace of Westminster (see WESTMINSTER, PALACE OF); it was incorporated on the west side of the new Houses of Parliament. Built by William II and rebuilt by Richard II, it was used by early Parliaments, and until 1882 as the Courts of Justice.

Westminster Kennel Club (1877) The oldest US kennel club, in MADISON SQUARE GARDEN, NYC, founded primarily for owners of bird dogs; it now holds an annual show for all types.

Westphalia A former German duchy, capital Münster, incorporated in Prussia and now part of North Rhine-Westphalia.

Westphalia, Treaty of (1648) The treaty which ended the THIRTY YEARS WAR. France gained Alsace; Sweden POMERANIA; the United Netherlands and Switzerland were declared independent of the Empire; and the German states remained free from HAPSBURG rule. The Bohemian Protestants who started the war gained nothing.

West Point The US Military Academy at West Point, N.Y., on the Hudson River; the British equivalent is SANDHURST.

West Side Story (1957) Leonard Bernstein's extremely successful musical, devised and directed by Jerome Robbins who integrated fantastically energetic dances into a ROMEO AND JULIET plot set against a background of teen-age gang warfare in New York.

West Wall (or **Siegfried Line**) A line of German fortifications opposite the MAGINOT LINE and protecting the Rhineland; breached by the Allies in September 1944.

Westward Ho! (1855) Charles Kingsley's romance of gallant Elizabethan sea dogs, Spanish Dons and the INQUISITION.

West Wind, Ode to the (1820) Shelley's prayer to the wild West Wind, 'thou breath of Autumn's being', to scatter his 'dead thoughts over the universe / Like withered leaves to quicken a new birth'.

Wettin Name of a family going back to the 10th century, from which many European dynasties were descended. The Dukes of Saxe-Coburg-Gotha, and thus Albert, Prince Consort and his son, Edward VII, were Wettins. The name of the Royal family was changed to WINDSOR in 1917, although according to some authorities the correct name should be GUELPH or Wipper.

WEU See WESTERN EUROPEAN UNION.

Wexford, Massacre at (1649) See CROMWELLIAN SETTLEMENT.

WFTU (1945) Initials used for the World Federation of Trade Unions, founded by the union organizations of 54 countries, including USSR. In 1949 the CIO, the British Trades Union Congress and many others seceded to form the non-Communist ICFTU.

W. H., Mr The 'onlie begetter' to whom Shakespeare dedicated his *Sonnets*. His identity is an unsolved mystery, the strongest candidates being the Earl of Southampton (Henry Wriothesley) and the Earl of Pembroke (William Herbert).

What Every Woman Knows (1908) J. M. Barrie's play about the egoist John Shand, in which male pretensions to superiority are deflated.

'What hath God wrought!' The message which Samuel Morse in Washington, D.C., sent back to Alfred Vail in Baltimore, 24 May 1844, by telegraph. It was not the first telegraphed message, for others had been sent earlier in the month.

What Price Glory? (1924) A play by Maxwell Anderson and Laurence Stallings giving a realistic picture of World War I in all its brutality and squalor.

When We Were Very Young (1924) A collection of A. A. Milne's verse written for, and often about, his son CHRISTOPHER ROBIN; it includes the poems about young DUPREE and the king who plaintively asked for 'some butter for the Royal slice of bread'.

Which? See CONSUMERS' ASSOCIATION.

Whieldon ware (1) Varied types of Staffordshire earthenware made (1745-95) by Thomas Whieldon, who invented his own beautiful and distinctive brown, yellow, green and blue glazes and a tortoiseshell glaze, as well as using 2-colored clays under colored glazes. His work included TOBY jugs and charmingly naïve musicians, horsemen, women seated in chairs etc. (2) Similar wares made by others. See ASTBURY WARE.

Whiffenpoof song A YALE song adopted (1909) by the Whiffenpoof Society, an offshoot of the Yale Glee Club, with words freely adapted from Kipling's 'Gentlemen Rankers'

(see FROM HERE TO ETERNITY) and a tune probably composed by Guy Scull *c*. 1893; Rudy Vallee produced a revised version in 1936. (An imaginary creature mentioned in Victor Herbert's operetta *Little Nemo*, 1908.)

Whig Ascendancy The period (1714-60) from the accession of George I to that of Geroge III, during which the chief offices of state were given to the Whigs (e.g. Walpole, Pelham), who supported the Hanoverian succession. See JACOBITES.

Whig interpretation of history The view of English history as a steady progress, from the time of the Whig Revolution of 1688, and particularly in the period of Whig domination from 1714, towards Parliamentary democracy, religious toleration, social betterment, wealth, liberty and order. It was prominent in the works of Lord Macaulay, which reflected the general complacency of the Victorian era. Later historians paid greater attention to the horrors of the Industrial Revolution.

Whigs (1673) Originally the Country Party, formed by the Earl of Shaftesbury to exclude the Catholic James, Duke of York, from the succession. It opposed the Court (Tory) Party, stood for Parliamentary supremacy and religious toleration, drew its strength from NONCONFORMISTS and 'trade', and was the nucleus of the 19th-century Liberal Party. (Possibly from Scottish nickname for COVENANTERS, of unknown significance.)

Whip (1) A member of a legislative body chosen by his party primarily to secure attendance of party members at important sessions and to enforce party discipline. (2) A CHIEF WHIP or one of his assistants.

Whipsnade (1931) (UK) The zoo park of the Zoological Society, on Dunstable Downs, Bedfordshire, in which animals and birds enjoy the maximum possible freedom.

Whiskey Rebellion, The (1794) The first test of Federal strength, when impoverished mountain farmers of western Pennsylvania reacted violently to an excise tax on alcohol. Troops were called out and Washington rode to the scene with his Secretary of the Treasury, Alexander Hamilton. Republicans attacked the latter for high-handedness; he replied: I have long learned to hold popular opinion of no value.

Whisky Galore (1947) Compton Mackenzie's rampageous story of a cargo of whiskey washed ashore on one of the Western Isles of Scotland.

'Whistler's Mother' Popular name of the painting which Whistler titled 'Arrangement in Black and Grey — The ARTIST'S MOTHER'.

Whitaker (1868) Abbreviated title of *Whitaker's Almanac*, an English annual reference book containing 'an account of astronomical phenomena' together with a vast amount of information and statistics on every kind of subject, all excellently indexed. The centenary volume was published in 1968.

White Australia policy The policy of prohibiting the immigration of Asians, particularly Japanese and Chinese, into Australia. It is still in force though rarely acknowledged officially; known to Asians as the WAP.

'White Christmas' (1942) The ever-popular song, 'I'm Dreaming of a White Christmas' written by Irving Berlin for the movie *Holiday Inn*, and now an inescapable feature of the Christmas festival, being an easily sung nondenominational secular carol. In its original context it was in part an expression of homesick disillusion among troops then serving overseas. Heifetz made a violin solo of it.

White Dwarf The smallest type of stars, extremely dense and glowing feebly. They are formed when the helium nuclei in a RED GIANT fuse; the outer mantle is flung into space, leaving only the white-hot core, mainly of helium. White Dwarfs are common; they eventually evolve into supernovae.

White Friars See CARMELITES.

Whitehall (1) Originally a London palace built by Cardinal Wolsey, seized by Henry VIII. The only surviving part, the BANQUETING HALL, was added later. (2) The street running through this site, from TRAFALGAR SQUARE to the Houses of Parliament, lined with government departmental offices. (3) Hence, the British government; British bureaucracy.

Whitehall farce One of various farces staged at the Whitehall Theatre, London, by the actor-manager Brian Rix, notable for their bedrock humor. The most famous were the first two: *Reluctant Heroes* and *Dry Rot* (1950-58).

Whitehead, Cmdr. David Ogilvy's creation for a famous SCHWEPPE'S advertisement in USA; under the hypnotic gaze of this splendid specimen of high-ranking British naval officer, Americans first learned to drink tonic water with their gin, having previously only known it as quinine water.

White Highlands In Kenya, old name for the highlands around Nairobi, where settlement by white farmers began in 1902. Legends of the displacement of KIKUYU population are untrue; the area was almost uninhabited and belonged to the nomadic MASAI.

White Horse Inn An Austrian lakeside inn at St Wolfgang, made famous by a popular musical comedy of that name. (Translation of Austrian *Weisser Rössel*, literally 'white little horse'.)

White House, The (1799) The official residence and offices of the US president, at Washington. Hence used as a synonym for US presidential policy or office; the US executive.

White Knight In Lewis Carroll's THROUGH THE LOOKING GLASS the incompetent horseman and obsessional inventor who sang to Alice the inconsequent song about an 'aged aged man / A-sitting on a gate'.

White Lodge, The A house in Richmond Park, Surrey, built by George II; birthplace of the Duke of Windsor, it is now the home of the ROYAL BALLET SCHOOL.

White Man's Burden, The A name for the task of administering tropical countries in the days before imperialism became a dirty word;

it was the title of one of Kipling's poems.

White Man's Grave, The A name for West Africa, well earned in the 19th and early 20th centuries when the mortality among Europeans was extremely high.

Whiteoaks series, The (1927-60) A series of books by the Canadian novelist Mazo de la Roche chronicling the history of a Canadian family, and especially of the intrepid centenarian Adeline Whiteoak, from pioneer days to modern times. The first was *Jalna* (the name of their estate in southern Ontario), the last *Morning at Jalna* (published when she was 81).

White Queen, The A character in THROUGH THE LOOKING GLASS, a gentle, vague, stupid creature, a foil for the RED QUEEN. It was she who claimed that she could believe 'as many as 6 impossible things before breakfast', and who laid down the rule: Jam tomorrow, and jam yesterday—but never jam today.

White Rabbit The first character met by ALICE IN WONDERLAND; he reappears throughout the book, always in a pother.

White Russia English name of Byelorussia SSR.

White Russians (1) The people of Byelorussia or White Russia. (2) The anti-Bolshevists of the civil war period in Russia (1918-21).

White Sands A US Army missile range, in a desert valley of New Mexico, where the first American v-2 was tested (1946).

White's Club (1693) The oldest of London's clubs, in St James's Street, proudly aristocratic, philistine and Tory, with a name for late nights, gambling and eccentricity. It has no political importance.

White Slave Act See MANN ACT.

White Sox Chicago White Sox, AMERICAN (Baseball) LEAGUE, playing at Comiskey Park.

White Staves Name given to the ladies, dressed in white, who at BUCKINGHAM PALACE garden parties present guests to the Queen.

Whitmonday The Monday following WHITSUNDAY, until 1967 a bank holiday, which was then moved to the last Monday in May or the first in June, and called the Spring Holiday.

Whitney Museum of American Art (1930) A New York art gallery specializing in 20th-century American paintings, sculpture, prints etc., founded by Gertrude Vanderbilt Whitney and rehoused in 1966 in a building of strikingly original design.

Whitstable oysters The best English oysters, from Whitstable Bay, Kent.

Whitsunday The day appointed in the Christian Church to commemorate the descent of the HOLY SPIRIT on the Disciples, which occurred on the day of PENTECOST (*Acts* ii, 1-4). It falls on the seventh Sunday after Easter, between 10 May and 13 June.

Whittaker Chambers case See HISS CASE.

Whittle jet engine The world's first jet engine, designed in Britain by Sir Frank Whittle and tested in 1937. It was used in the first British jet plane, the Gloster E 28/39 of 1941 (see METEOR).

WHO (1948) Initials used for the World Health Organization, a UN international agency with headquarters at Geneva, which gives advice on and training in health administration, promotes international standardization in health matters, and coordinates measures against widespread diseases such as malaria.

Whodunit Colloquial term for a detective story.

Who's Afraid of Virginia Woolf? (1962) Edward Albee's melodrama set in a US university, where a history professor and the daughter of the college president whom he has married tear each other to shreds.

Who's Who (1849) An annual biographical dictionary, mainly of British subjects who have received honors or decorations, but also including distinguished foreigners.

Who's Who in America (1899) A biennial publication of short biographies of world notables, founded by Albert Nelson Marquis and now published by Marquis-Who's Who Inc. of Chicago.

Who Was Who A series of selected biographies from past editions of WHO'S WHO of people who have died since 1897, each volume covering a period of approximately 10 years.

Wicked Uncles, The Queen Victoria's uncles, the sons of George III, who included George IV, William IV, and the Dukes of Cumberland (later King of Hanover), Cambridge, York and Sussex.

Wickham, Mr A Jane Austen character; see BENNET FAMILY.

'Widdicombe Fair' An old Dartmoor ballad about a party who want to borrow Tom Pearse's grey mare to go to the fair; they are Bill Brewer, Jan Stewer, Peter Gurney, Peter Davey, Dan'l Whiddon, 'arry 'awk and UNCLE TOM COBBLEIGH. (A village on Dartmoor, now spelled Widecombe.)

Widener Collection One of the major collections in the NATIONAL GALLERY OF ART (Washington), donated by Jos. E. Widener and including Rembrandts, Van Dycks, Vermeers, sculptures and works of decorative art.

Widmerpool See MUSIC OF TIME.

Widowers' Houses (1892) Bernard Shaw's first play, dealing with the iniquities of slum landlordism.

Widow Twankey A stock pantomime character, played by a man. (Obsolete slang for 'gin'; from Chinese Tun-ki, a kind of green tea.)

Widow Wadman See UNCLE TOBY.

'Wiegenlied' The German for 'Cradle Song', the title of various songs by Brahms, Schubert, Mozart etc.

Wiener Schnitzel A veal cutlet dipped in egg and crumbs and fried in deep fat; the Austrian name for the French escalope de veau. ('Vienna cutlet'.)

Wife of Bath A rumbustious and much married pilgrim in Chaucer's CANTERBURY TALES, who favors obedience and generosity in husbands. See next entry.

Wife of Bath's Tale, The In the CANTERBURY TALES, the story of one of King ARTHUR's knights who, to save his life, has to find out what women love most. The answer (sovereignty over their husbands) is revealed to him, on condition he marries her, by an old witch who then turns into a beautiful girl.

Wigan Pier Allusions to this became a standard music-hall joke (Wigan itself being regarded as a joke, and being far from the sea); the phrase was adopted by George Orwell in his ROAD TO WIGAN PIER(1937), essays on social problems.

Wightman Cup The Anglo-US women's international lawn-tennis team competition.

Wild Bill Donovan See OSS.

Wild Bill Hickok US marshal who after an adventurous career, the theme of many westerns, was killed at Deadwood, South Dakota, in 1876. (See DEADWOOD DICK.)

Wild Duck, The (1884) Ibsen's play on the theme that for some people only self-deception makes life bearable.

Wilde (Oscar) case (1895) The trial for homosexual offenses of the writer Oscar Wilde; he was found guilty and given a 2-year sentence. He had himself precipitated the case by bringing a libel action against the 8th Marquess of Queensberry whose son, Lord Alfred Douglas, was the *casus belli*.

Wilderness Road The road linking Virginia and Lexington, Ky., over the CUMBERLAND GAP, following an old Indian trail (the Warriors' Path) widened by Daniel Boone in 1775. Used by wagon traffic from 1795, it opened up the Ohio Valley and Kentucky's BLUEGRASS.

Wilhelmstrasse Once used as a synonym for the German Foreign Office, which was situated in the Berlin street of that name.

Willard A name associated with early Massachusetts clocks made by 4 brothers and their sons at Grafton (from c. 1765), Roxbury, Boston and Lexington. Simon, the most famous, patented the banjo clock (1802) at Roxbury; Aaron produced the Massachusetts shelf clock.

Willesden (UK) A former municipal borough of MIDDLESEX, since 1965 part of the borough of BRENT.

William and Mary College (1693) Ancient foundation at Williamsburg, Va.

William and Mary period (1689-1702) A transitional period in the decorative arts from that of the RESTORATION to that of Queen Anne. The characteristic innovation was the curved stretcher for tables and chairs, an idea brought from Holland by DUTCH WILLIAM's cabinet-makers. The tallboy came into vogue.

William of Orange William III of England, Prince of Orange, James II's nephew and son-in-law, invited by WHIGS and some TORIES to England at the GLORIOUS REVOLUTION.

Williamsburg, Colonial A restoration of 18th-century buildings and living conditions in historical areas of Williamsburg, Va., between Yorktown and Jamestown, which was founded as a palisaded outpost in 1663 and became capital of Virginia from 1699. In area over 3000 acres, it includes a reproduction of the old Capitol, the governor's palace, Raleigh Tavern and some 500 Colonial buildings, with craft shops, gardens etc. Restoration began in 1926, financed by John D. Rockefeller Jr.

William the Silent Sobriquet of the Prince of Orange who was the Dutch nationalist leader against Spanish rule in the 16th century; so called because he knew when to keep his own counsel.

Willing's Press Guide An annual index and handbook of the world's newspapers and periodicals, started nearly a century ago.

Williwaw A name local to Alaska for a squally cold wind which blows down the mountains into the deep valleys in the fall.

Willow Pattern (1780) A traditional English design on blue and white china invented by Thomas Turner of CAUGHLEY. The story of the mandarin chasing his daughter and her lover was invented to account for the design, of which there are many versions. Approximately, the fewer people on the bridge the earlier the china; the number of apples on the tree also helps in assigning date and maker.

Willy One of the pen names of CO-LETTE's first husband, Henri Gauthier-Villars, music critic and journalist. Colette for a time wrote under the name of Colette Willy.

Wilmington, Long Man of An ancient figure of a man 230 ft high, with a staff in each hand, cut in the chalk downs of Windover Hill above the Sussex village of Wilmington, near Eastbourne. He may represent the war god Woden (ODIN).

Wilson cloud chamber (1912) Apparatus invented by C. T. R. Wilson which, through being saturated with water vapor, makes visible the tracks of ionizing radiations, e.g. alpha, beta, gamma and X rays.

Wilton carpets Generic term for a type which differs from AXMINSTER CARPETS by having most of the pile yarn woven into the backing, which is smoother. There are no multicolored Wiltons.

Wilton House The 17th-century home at Wilton, near Salisbury, of the Earl of Pembroke, particularly famous for the perfect proportions of Inigo Jones's 'double-cube' room.

Wimbledon (UK) A former municipal borough of Surrey, since 1965 part of the borough of MERTON.

Wimbledon (1877) Short name of the amateur lawn tennis world championships (men's and women's singles, doubles and mixed doubles), played at the end of June at the ALL ENGLAND LAWN TENNIS AND CROQUET CLUB, Wimbledon Park, London. They were thrown open to professionals in 1968.

Wimbledon Cup A rifle-shooting competition for individuals, held at Bisley in July; the range is 600 yd.

Wimpy Trade name for a beef hamburger with 'secret' spices added, sold in bread baked to a special recipe at 'Wimpy Bars'; invented in Chicago. The firm of J. Lyons have a monopoly of its sales everywhere outside the USA. (From POPEYE's companion, J. Wellington Wimpy, rarely seen without a half-eaten hamburger.)

Wimsey, Lord Peter The benevolent amateur detective created by Dorothy Sayers, who first appeared in *Whose Body?* (1923).

Winchester rifle (1866) US magazine rifle; the .44 model (1873) is famous as a sporting rifle. (O. F. Winchester, Manufacturer.)

Wind Cave National Park (1903) A park in the Black Hills of southwestern South Dakota; the limestone cave is so called because the wind blows into it when the barometer falls, and out when it rises. The internal formations are unique, having a honeycomb pattern, tipped with white crystals. The park also contains buffalo herds, elk etc.

Wind in the Willows, The (1908) Kenneth Grahame's children's story of Mole, Water Rat and Mr Toad, which contains the immortal phrase: there is *nothing* . . . half so much worth doing as simply messing about in boats. TOAD OF TOAD HALL, the voluble, self-centered road hog, though urged by Badger to mend his ways, finishes in jail.

Windmill, The The London vaudeville theater which became famous during World War II for its proud slogan 'We Never Closed', having kept going throughout the air raids, giving its almost nonstop (6 performances a day) production of the *Revudeville* show.

Windmill Hill people NEOLITHIC AGE farmers of southern England (2500–1800 BC). (Named after an ancient campsite near AVEBURY, Wiltshire.)

Windscale Site of the UK ATOMIC ENERGY AUTHORITY's experimental AGR reactor, which began feeding the National Grid in 1963. (Coastal site near Ravenglass, Cumberland.)

Windsor, House of The official designation of the Royal Family since 1917. In 1960 the Queen decided that certain of her descendants should bear the family name of Mountbatten-Windsor. See WETTIN; GUELPH.

Windsor Castle A royal castle, where the Sovereign still frequently resides, which towers over the Thames-side town of Windsor and is connected by the Long Walk (a 3-mile avenue) to the extensive Windsor Great Park to the south. An earth and palisade fortress was built there by William the Conqueror and the first stone building, the Round Tower, added in the 12th century. Much of the castle and park is open to the public, including the State Apartments and ST GEORGE'S CHAPEL. The park, traversed by a main road, includes the beautiful Saville Gardens and Virginia Water.

Windsor chair A traditional English style of plain wooden chair, with a back consisting mainly of straight rods, and with straight legs slanting outwards.

Windsor Greys The Royal horses used in ceremonial processions, formerly kept at Windsor, now at the BUCKINGHAM PALACE mews. The original Hanoverian breed was dispersed during World War I and later replaced from various sources; they do not, therefore, represent any specific breed.

Windsor Herald An officer of the COLLEGE OF ARMS.

Windy City, The A nickname for Chicago, earned by its exposed position on the southwest shore of Lake Michigan.

Winesburg, Ohio (1919) Sherwood Anderson's 23 sketches of people in a small Midwest town, reduced to psychological chaos by sexual frustration and the shackles of convention. Empathy is the chief characteristic, conveyed in poetic but simple language.

Winfrith Site of the UK Atomic Energy Research Establishment, where a reactor has been tested as part of the international DRAGON PROJECT. A high-temperature steam-generating heavy-water reactor (SGHWR) has been developed to produce power at a more competitive price than the AGR reactor. It began to feed the National Grid in 1968. (A heath north of Lulworth Cove, Dorset.)

'Winged Victory of Samothrace' (200 BC) A sculpture in the form of a ship's figurehead, commemorating a victory of the people of Rhodes; the original is now in the LOUVRE.

Wingless Victory See NIKE APTEROS.

Winkle, Nathaniel In Dickens's PICKWICK PAPERS, a great sportsman, according to all accounts (which happened to be false), and the son of a Birmingham wharfinger.

Winnie Nickname of Winston Churchill.

Winnie The OSCAR of the fashion industry, in the form of a bronze statuette.

Winnie-the-Pooh (1926) A. A. Milne's story for children of all ages about the teddy bear Pooh and his friends Piglet (whose ancestor was Trespassers W), Wol the Owl, and EEYORE.

Winslow Boy, The (1946) Terence Rattigan's play, based on the historical Archer-Shee case, about a naval cadet falsely charged with theft and his father's struggle against Admiralty indifference to clear his name.

Winston The chestnut police horse ridden for many years by the Queen at the TROOPING OF THE COLOR; he was killed in an accident in 1957.

Winter Garden A famous old theater in New York City.

Winter Palace (1762) The tsars' baroque palace at LENINGRAD, now a major art gallery and museum.

Winterreise (1827) The second of Schubert's song cycles; 24 songs with words by Wilhelm Müller on the theme of a journey that revives memories of an unhappy love affair. (German, 'winter journey'.)

Winterset (1935) One of Maxwell Anderson's most successful plays, a verse drama based on the SACCO AND VANZETTI case. Gangsters frame an Italian-born radical who is executed for a murder they committed; his son is diverted from taking revenge through falling in love with the sister of a repentant member of the gang; lest their guilt be revealed, the gangsters murder both.

Winter's Tale, The (1611) Shakespeare's play about King Leontes of Sicily who is morbidly suspicious of his faithful wife Hermione, and puts her in prison; see also AUTOLYCUS; PERDITA AND FLORIZEL.

Winterthur Museum The Henry Francis DU PONT Museum at Winterthur near Wilmington, Del.; it has 100 American period rooms from the 17th to the early 19th centuries.

Winter War, The (1939-40) A name for the Russian campaign against Finland.

Wipers See YPRES.

Wisdom of Jesus Alternative name of ECCLESIASTICUS.

Wisdom of Solomon A book of the APOCRYPHA traditionally attributed to SOLOMON but probably compiled in Alexandria about the 1st century BC. The first part exhorts orthodox Jews to remain true to their religion and discusses wisdom in human affairs. The second part is a fanciful history of the Jews.

Wise forgeries Forgeries of rare Victorian first editions, by T. J. Wise, an outstanding and respected authority on books; discovered a few years before he died in 1937.

Wise Men of the East See MAGI.

Wisley Gardens Showplace of the Royal Horticultural Society, near Ripley, Surrey.

Witan (Witenagemot) The council which advised ANGLO-SAXON kings. (Old English, 'meeting of wise men'.)

Witt Collection The COURTAULD INSTITUTE OF ART's unique collection of photographs of all noteworthy paintings and other works of art; there is also a library of reference books on art.

Wittelsbachs The dynasty which ruled Bavaria from 1180 to 1918, when King Ludwig III abdicated.

Witwatersrand The full name of the Rand, the Transvaal goldfields. (AFRIKAANS 'white waters ridge'.)

Wizard of Oz, The A character in Frank Baum's classic fairy tale *The Wonderful Wizard of Oz* (1900), its many sequels, a musical extravaganza (1903), silent (1925) and Technicolor musical movies (1939), the latter with a song hit, 'Over the Rainbow', added, and in countless versions continued by other hands after Baum's death. Oz is a happy land to which Dorothy and her dog Toto are whirled by a cyclone from her drab Kansas home; there she encounters the Wizard, a talking Scarecrow,

Cowardly Lion, Tin Woodman and many others.

WLA See WOMEN'S LAND ARMY.

WMO (1950) Initials used for the World Meteorological Organization, a UN international agency with headquarters at Geneva.

Wobbly Nickname for a member of the INDUSTRIAL WORKERS OF THE WORLD.

Woburn Abbey The Georgian home of the Dukes of Bedford near Bletchley, Bedfordshire, with 14 richly decorated State Apartments, and a park containing bison and deer. Equipped with unprecedented facilities for mass feeding and entertainment, including an antiques market, it is an easy winner of the STATELY HOMES Stakes.

Woburn Abbey (1962) A very showy floribunda rose with semidouble orange flowers and vigorous growth.

Woden English form of ODIN.

Wolfe, Nero The detective of Rex Stout's novels, who first appeared in *Fer-de-lance* (1934). A fat epicure and orchid-grower, he is the only armchair sleuth in fiction, leaving all the necessary errands to his assistant, Archie GOODWIN.

Wolfenden report (1957) (UK) The report of a committee on homosexual offences and prostitution. (Sir John Wolfenden, former headmaster of Shrewsbury, chairman.)

Wolfe-Noel Cup A squash rackets contest between British and US women's teams.

Wolf Rock (1870) A UK lighthouse and rock halfway between Land's End and the Scilly Isles.

Wolf's Lair Fanciful name given to Hitler's wartime headquarters in EAST PRUSSIA.

Wolfson empire See GUS.

Wolverine State Nickname of Michigan.

'Woman in White' An early Picasso, copies of which sold in immense numbers in the USA.

Woman in White, The (1860) A mystery story by Wilkie Collins, in which the villain, Count Fosco, attempts to substitute a bogus heiress for the Woman in White, who is in a lunatic asylum.

Woman's Relief Corps, National (1883) An auxiliary of the GAR, with headquarters in Springfield, Ill.

Woman Who Did, The (1895) Grant Allen's novel about a woman who preached and practiced the doctrine that marriage is incompatible with the emancipation of women. Although a serious novel, the title inevitably became a catchphrase for what in those days was called a 'fallen woman'.

Women in Love (1920) D. H. Lawrence's novel in which he analyzes the unexpressed instinctive feelings that mold human relationships. See BRANGWEN, GUDRUN; BRANGWEN, URSULA.

Women's Clubs, General Federation of (1890) A national and international organization to promote interest in education, philanthropy, public welfare, moral values and the arts. The headquarters are in Washington, D. C.

Women's Land Army (1917) A UK corps of Land Girls formed to release agricultural workers for military service in World War I; it was reformed in 1939.

Women's Social and Political Union (1903) The original suffragette organization formed by Mrs Emmeline Pankhurst.

Wonder State Nickname of Arkansas.

Woodbine Willie Nickname of a famous padre of World War I, the Rev. Studdart Kennedy. (Name of a cheap cigarette popular with the troops.)

Wood family (potters) The Burslem (Staffordshire, England) family of Ralph Wood (1715-72) who worked in the ASTBURY-Whieldon tradition and may have made the first TOBY jug; his brother and modeler, Aaron (1717-85), to whom is attributed the VICAR AND MOSES group; his son Ralph II (1748-95), who used a wider range of colors in the PRATTWARE style; and his nephew Enoch (1760-1840) who introduced bright enamel colors and made accurate portrait busts, e.g. of Wesley.

Wood Green (UK) A former municipal borough of MIDDLESEX, since

1965 part of the borough of HARIN-GEY.

Woodhenge   The archeological site near STONEHENGE where traces of 6 concentric circles of timber posts were discovered by aerial photography. They date back to the late NEOLITHIC AGE.

Woodhouse, Mr   See EMMA.

Woods of Bath, The   John Wood the Elder (1705-54), the chief architect of the Upper Town, Bath; and his son John (1728-81) who completed his father's work and designed the Royal Crescent at Bath.

Woodstock   (1826) Walter Scott's novel of the ENGLISH CIVIL WAR, in which Oliver Cromwell and the fugitive Charles II figure prominently. Woodstock was a royal lodge (later to be replaced by Blenheim Palace) looked after by a fiery Cavalier, Sir Henry Lee, to whose daughter Lee's ROUNDHEAD nephew and Charles II both pay court.

Wookey Hole   A series of caves near Wells, Somerset, England, with multicolored stalactites, where remains of PALEOLITHIC man have been found.

Woolsack, The   (1) A large square cushion stuffed with wool on which LORD CHANCELLORS have sat since Edward III's time, originally as heads of the Court of CHANCERY, now as SPEAKERS of the House of Lords. (2) Used as a synonym for 'Lord Chancellorship'. (Introduced when the wool trade was of prime importance to England.)

Woolwich   A former London metropolitan borough, since 1965 divided between the boroughs of GREENWICH and NEWHAM.

Woolwich Royal Arsenal   The UK government arsenal developed on the south bank of the Thames near London from an early Tudor Powder House, supplemented by a foundry in 1716. The WOOLWICH ROYAL MILITARY ACADEMY was built inside its walls. By 1966, when it was closed down, the Arsenal covered 1200 acres.

Woolwich Royal Military Academy   (1741) Until 1946 the training college for future officers of the Royal Artillery, Royal Engineers and Royal Signals; now moved to and merged with SANDHURST.

Woolworths   (1879) A vast international group of chain stores, which started in Utica, N.Y., as a '5-cent store' (i.e. all articles were sold at that price), later a 5 and 10 cent store. Branches were established in England after World War I as 3d and 6d stores, and the organization has continued to expand in various countries ever since. One of the 30 industrials that make up the DOW JONES Industrial Average.

Woolworth weapons   Name given to nuclear weapons within the financial capacity of smaller nations; the probability that these might be developed became a cause for alarm from 1960 onwards.

Woomera   (1946) The British rocket range in South Australia, 100 miles northwest of Port Augusta, where the first British atomic missile was exploded in 1953.

Wooster, The Hon. Bertie   The amiable nitwit of innumerable P. G. Wodehouse stories who has constantly to be rescued from disaster by his valet JEEVES.

Worcester, Battle of   (1651) An engagement in which Cromwell almost annihilated the forces of Charles, Prince of Wales, who escaped to France, thus ending the final phase of the ENGLISH CIVIL WAR.

Worcester Pearmain   A fine-flavored red dessert apple, ripening in September. (Possibly from Latin *Parmanus* 'of Parma'.)

Worcester porcelain   (1751) The wares produced by a factory at Worcester which frequently changed its name; see (in chronological order) DR WALL PERIOD; ROYAL WORCESTER PORCELAIN CO.; FLIGHT & BARR; CHAMBERLAIN WORCESTER.

Worcestershire sauce   A proprietary bottled piquant sauce made from a secret recipe 'obtained from a Worcestershire gentleman' in 1845. The original manufacturers were Lea & Perrins at Worcester, England, now bought up by Armour of Chicago. It is said to contain vinegar, soya and many spices.

Work in Progress Provisional name given by James Joyce to FINNEGANS WAKE during the 17 years he spent writing it.

Work points See MILTON WORK POINT COUNT.

World Almanac, The (1868) A reference book published annually (except for one brief break) by various newspaper groups, and containing '1 million useful facts', mainly about the US.

World Bank (1946) The International Bank for Reconstruction and Development, set up after BRETTON WOODS to provide long-term loans for reconstruction in war-devastated countries, and for the exploitation of natural resources and the provision of public utilities in developing countries; half the capital was supplied by USA and Britain.

World Council of Churches (1948) A body representing the ecumenical movement towards cooperation between the Churches; ANGLICAN, Protestant and ORTHODOX CHURCHES are members, but not the Catholics.

World Cup (1930) A solid gold cup (formerly the JULES RIMET TROPHY, which was permanently awarded to Brazil after their third championship) presented to the national team winning the soccer championship of the world, held every 4 years under the auspices of FIFA.

World Day of Prayer The first Friday in Lent, observed by ecumenical Christians around the world as a day of worship and prayer for missions.

World Disarmament Conference (1932-34) A Geneva meeting of 60 nations (including USA and Soviet Russia – not members of the LEAGUE OF NATIONS) defeated in its ambitions by French demands for prior guarantees of security (against Germany) in the form of an international army; Hitler's advent to power and Germany's withdrawal from the League; and Russian insistence on complete world disarmament combined with a rejection of its international supervision. The complete failure of the conference led to a massive increase in world armaments.

World Food Council The executive body of the FAO.

World Health Organization See WHO.

Worldly-Wiseman, Mr A character in PILGRIM'S PROGRESS who tries to persuade Christian to give up his pilgrimage for ease and plenty.

World Refugee Year (1959-60) A year in which a concerted international effort was made to solve outstanding problems regarding refugees.

World Series (1903) A best-of-seven-games competition played each autumn between the winning teams of the 2 major baseball leagues (the National and American) to determine the professional champions of USA.

World Trade Center The PORT OF NEW YORK AUTHORITY's project, authorized in 1966, to bring the export-import business community together in a block of buildings covering some 5 acres of downtown New York, dominated by the 2 tallest buildings in the world.

Worms, Diet of (1521) The Imperial assembly before which Luther was haled and outlawed by the Emperor Charles V after he had refused to recant.

Wormwood Scrubs A prison for first offenders only, in West London.

Worth, Patience A spirit who, as it is claimed, from 1913 dictated to Mrs Curran (born in the Midwest), mainly through a ouija board, about 3 million words of fiction, poetry, proverbs and prayers, some in 17th-century English dialect. These works displayed a knowledge of history quite outside Mrs Curran's range. Patience said she was a 17th-century Dorset farm girl who migrated to America and was murdered by Indians. The case was exhaustively investigated, without any logical explanation emerging.

Wotan German form of ODIN.

Wozzeck (1912) Alban Berg's opera based on a grim 19th-century play about a half-witted army private who murdered his wife.

WPA Initials used for the Works Progress (later 'Projects') Administration (1935-43), a NEW DEAL agency which created jobs for the unemployed by constructing roads, bridges, buildings etc.; it also ran schemes to employ writers, artists and actors.

WRAC See ATS.

WRAF (1918) The Women's Royal Air Force; disbanded after World War I and re-formed as the WAAF (Women's Auxiliary Air Force) from units of the ATS. It retained this name from 1939 to 1948, then reverting to its original title and becoming a permanent unit.

'Wreck of the Hesperus, The' (1841) Longfellow's ballad, based on a contemporary event, beginning with perhaps the most widely known lines of English poetry: It was the schooner Hesperus, / That sailed the wintry sea; / And the skipper had taken his little daughter, / To bear him company.

'Wreck of the Old 97, The' A modern hillbilly classic about a wreck near Danville, Va., in 1903, recorded in 1924. The author of the words is unknown (although there have been many claimants); the tune is that of 'The Ship that Never Returned' by Henry C. Work (1832-84).

Wren Colloquial name for a member of the WRNS (Women's Royal Naval Service) formed in 1917, re-formed in 1939, and now a permanent unit.

Wrigley Field The home of the Chicago CUBS; as there are no lights there are no night games.

WRNS See WREN.

Wrong-way Corrigan Douglas Gorce Corrigan, who flew the Atlantic (1938) without a permit; he said he intended to fly the other way. This held the world record for lame excuses until 1969 when an elderly lady who drove 10 miles down the wrong side of England's premier motorway told the police that she sensed something was wrong, as all the traffic seemed to be going the other way.

WRVS (1938) The Women's Royal Voluntary Service (until 1966 the Women's Voluntary Services) formed for ARP (Air Raid Precautions) duties. In peacetime it performs a wide range of social services, e.g. MEALS-ON-WHEELS, helping in flood disasters etc.

Wurlitzer organ The cinema organ, an electronic contraption which produces a rich variety of sounds not unlike music, although its chief glory is when it sinks into the bowels of the auditorium, bathed in colored light.

Wuthering Heights (1847) Emily Brontë's grim masterpiece recounting the disruption of the EARNSHAW FAMILY by HEATHCLIFF. (Wuthering, Yorkshire dialect for 'stormy'.)

WVS See WRVS.

Wyandotte A medium-sized American breed of dual-purpose domestic fowl. (Named after an American Indian tribe.)

Wyatt's rebellion (1554) An uprising in Kent led by Sir Thomas Wyatt in protest at Queen Mary's alliance with Spain. It led to the execution of Lady Jane Grey (who was not implicated) and the imprisonment of the future Queen Elizabeth in the Tower.

Wyclif's Bible The fruit of Wyclif's demand (see LOLLARDS) that the Bible should be available to Englishmen in their own language; the first complete English translation, in 2 versions, neither printed, made at the turn of the 14th century.

'Wyndham Sisters, The' (1900) John Sargent's famous painting of 3 decorative young women in white, draping themselves on a sofa against a green drawing-room background. (Metropolitan Museum of Art, NYC)

'Wynken, Blynken and Nod' A 'Dutch lullaby' by Eugene Field (1850-95), later set to music. It begins: Wynken, Blynken and Nod one night / Sailed off in a wooden shoe — / Sailed on a river of crystal light / Into a sea of dew.

Wynne (Greville) case (1963) The Moscow trial of the English businessman who acted as courier in the PENKOVSKY SPY CASE. He was given an 8-year sentence, but exchanged for Gordon LONSDALE in 1965.

X

X The film rating signifying 'persons under 17 not admitted', under the Motion Picture Code of Self-Regulation; this age limit may vary in certain areas.

X, Les (France) Students and alumni of the École Polytechnique (1794) founded as a school for military engineering, science and mathematics. It now has enormous prestige, providing technical officers for the army, navy and air force as well as the elite of the higher civil servants. In OLD BOY NET-manship Les X yield to no man. (Colloquialism for 'mathematicians'.)

Xanadu The place where Coleridge's KUBLA KHAN 'did . . . a stately pleasure-dome decree' and where 'ALPH, the sacred river, ran'. *The Road to Xanadu* (1927) by J. L. Lowes is a thorough and fascinating piece of detective work on the sources of the names and allusions in this poem and in *The Rime of the* ANCIENT MARINER.

Xanthippe A bad-tempered wife. (Name of Socrates' wife.)

'X' certificate (1951) Granted by the British Board of Film Censors to films banned to children under 18.

Xerox Proprietary name of an improved system for photocopying documents of all kinds, now in general use. (From Greek word for 'dry'.)

Xhosa The most numerous BANTU race of South Africa, found particularly in TRANSKEI.

XJ6 A range of 2.8 and 4.2 liter Jaguar sedans introduced in 1968.

X-1 etc. rocket planes See BELL X-1, 2 ETC.

Y

Y, The   The ultimate abbreviation for YMCA.

Yahoos   The bestial creatures in human form whom the HOUYHNHNMS keep in subjection, in GULLIVER'S TRAVELS; they represent Swift's conception of mankind at its worst.

Yak   A series of Soviet military and civil aircraft, including the supersonic Yak-28 of the 1960s. (For Yakovlev, the designer.)

Yale   (1701) The second oldest US university, at New Haven, Conn.

Yale Bowl   (1914) YALE University's sports stadium.

Yale-Harvard Regatta   (1852) The first US intercollegiate athletic contest, a 4-mile race for 8-oared shells on the Thames at New London, Conn., in June, with the prestige of the other duel on the other Thames (see BOAT RACE).

Yalta Conference   (Feb. 1945) The meeting at which Roosevelt, Churchill, and Stalin discussed postwar problems, the setting up of UN and the entry of Russia into the war against Japan. (Crimean holiday resort.)

Yalu River   The river forming the boundary between Korea and China, prominent in the RUSSO-JAPANESE and KOREAN WARS.

Yank   (1942-45) The chief GI weekly magazine of World War II, first published in New York, eventually reaching a circulation of 2½ million in 22 editions for different fronts.

Yankee   A term originally applied by the New York Dutch to the New Englanders. In the South, it is a term of abuse for a Northerner. (Possibly from Dutch *Janke*, 'Johnny', but many other derivations have been suggested.)

Yankee (bet)   A complex bet on 4 selections, comprising 6 doubles, 4 trebles and an accumulator.

Yankee Clipper   The name of the APOLLO 12 Command Module.

Yankee Doodle   A tune of unknown origin, the words to which were possibly added by a British soldier just before the AMERICAN WAR OF INDEPENDENCE and adopted by their American opponents. (YANKEE + doodle = ? tootle, i.e. a tune for the flute or fife.)

Yankees   The New York Yankees, AMERICAN (Baseball) LEAGUE, playing at the YANKEE STADIUM.

Yankee Stadium   Baseball stadium in the BRONX, NYC, home of the New York Yankees. It is also used for football games and other events.

Yarborough   A hand at bridge with no card higher than a 9. (Earl of Yarborough, who laid 1000-1 against its occurring, about half the mathematical odds.)

Yard, The   (1) HARVARD YARD. (2) Abbreviation for SCOTLAND YARD.

Yarrow, The   A river in Selkirkshire, Scotland, which has inspired many poems, notably some by Wordsworth and Walter Scott.

Yasnaya Polyana   The Tolstoy family estate south of Moscow, where Count Tolstoy, the novelist, was born and lived until shortly before his death. The house is now a Tolstoy museum.

Yassiada trial   (1960-61) The trial of the Turkish premier, Menderes (who was executed), and of some 400 of his supporters, held on Yassiada island.

YD   The Yankee (26th) Division, originally composed of NATIONAL GUARD troops from the NEW ENGLAND (Yankee) States.

Yearling, The   (1938) The most successful of Marjorie Kinnan Rawlings's novels, describing an incident on a backwoods farm in north Florida. A father orders his young son to shoot his pet fawn, which is eating the corn; this minor tragedy in the boy's life helps to bring him to maturity.

Yellow Book, The   (1894-97) An illustrated quarterly made famous by the contributions of Aubrey Beardsley, Max Beerbohm and others.

Yellowhammer State A nickname for Alabama, after its state bird.

Yellow Jack Old name for yellow fever.

Yellow Kid, The (1895) The first comic-strip cartoon, printed in color, an early experiment in color printing, in a New York newspaper, from which the Yellow Press gets its name.

Yellow Peril, The The threat that overpopulation in China and Japan would imperil the Western world; a phrase used by the German Kaiser at the turn of the century, and revived after the publication of The RISING TIDE OF COLOR.

Yellowplush Correspondence, The (1838) Thackeray's book of sketches purporting to have been written by a London footman, Mr C. J. Yellowplush. It has dated in the way that 19th-century *Punch* jokes about flunkeys have, and no longer amuses.

Yellow Press (1895) The cheap sensational newspapers. (See YELLOW KID.)

Yellow River The Hwang Ho, China.

Yellowstone National Park (1872) The first of the world's national parks, in northwest Wyoming and adjacent areas of Montana and Idaho, on a volcanic plateau averaging 8000 ft and almost encircled by mountains. It contains the Yellowstone River canyon, spectacular falls, more geysers than the rest of the world together, and one of the finest wildlife sanctuaries, with moose, grizzlies etc.

Yellow Transparent A variety of apple.

Yeomen of the Guard (1485) The BEEFEATERS proper, who together with the GENTLEMEN AT ARMS form the Queen's dismounted bodyguard. One of their duties is to search the vaults under the Houses of Parliament before the STATE OPENING — an echo of the GUNPOWDER PLOT. They wear the same uniform as the YEOMEN WARDERS plus a crossbelt. Their Captain is the Assistant CHIEF WHIP in the House of Lords.

Yeomen Warders The guards of the TOWER OF LONDON; see BEEFEATERS.

Yerkes Observatory (1897) The University of Chicago's observatory at Williams Bay, Wis., with the world's largest (48-inch) refractory telescope.

Yeshiva University (1886) The oldest Jewish university in the USA, in New York City.

Yeti See ABOMINABLE SNOWMAN.

Yezhovshchina Russian name for the period of the particularly barbarous purges presided over by N. I. Yezhov as head of the NKVD (1936-38).

Yggdrasil, Igdrasil In Scandinavian myth the tree of the world, an ash with roots in the underworld which rises up to heaven and embraces the universe.

YHA (1930) (UK) Initials used for the Youth Hostels Association, a self-governing organization to provide hostels for young hikers (also available to the not so young). Simple accommodation and fare at minimum prices are provided in return for cooperation in such minor tasks as washing up. At some hostels there is provision for joint study of natural history.

Yiddish The language of Jews in Europe and America, compounded of medieval German, Hebrew, Polish, Russian and other languages, and written in the Hebrew alphabet. (From German *jüdisch*, 'Jewish'.)

YMCA Signifies Young Men's Christian Association.

YMHA Signifies Young Men's Hebrew Association.

Yoga (300 BC) Name given to various forms of Hindu mystic practice which aim at union with God through asceticism, meditation and a complicated series of difficult breathing exercises and postures (such as the 'lotus position' often depicted in Hindu art). (SANSKRIT, 'union'.)

Yogi A practitioner of YOGA.

Yoho National Park (1886) A Canadian park on the western slopes of the Rockies in British Columbia, on the Alberta border; it adjoins the Banff and Kootenay parks and is famous for its game sanctuary, mountain climbing and scenery. (Cree word meaning 'astonishment'.)

Yoknapatawpha County The setting of most of William Faulkner's novels, an imaginary county of the state of Mississippi.

Yom Haatzmaut A recently introduced Jewish festival, held in May, celebrating the establishment of the modern state of Israel.

Yom Kippur The Jewish fast day, the Day of Atonement, observed eight days after ROSH HASHANAH (*Leviticus* xvi).

Yorick (1) In Shakespeare's play, the murdered king's jester, whose skull HAMLET apostrophizes in a famous speech beginning 'Alas! poor Yorick' in the graveyard scene. (2) A parson in Sterne's TRISTRAM SHANDY, who claims descent from (1). (3) The name under which Sterne wrote his SENTIMENTAL JOURNEY.

York Herald An officer of the COLLEGE OF ARMS.

Yorkists Descendants of Edmund, Duke of York: Edward IV and V, Richard III (1461-85). See WARS OF THE ROSES.

York round In archery, a match in which 6 dozen arrows are shot at distances from 60 to 100 yards.

Yorktown, Siege of (1781) The last major event of the AMERICAN WAR OF INDEPENDENCE; Lord Cornwallis, finding himself cut off by the Americans on land and blockaded by the French fleet, surrendered to Washington. (Town in southeast Virginia.)

Yoruba A semi-BANTU race of Western Nigeria.

Yosemite National Park (1890) A park in east-central California with mountainous country of unusual beauty, the Yosemite and other impressive gorges, many high waterfalls and 3 groves of giant sequoias.

You Never Can Tell (1897) G. B. Shaw's comedy of a wife who unwittingly invites her ex-husband to lunch while staying at a Torbay hotel with her daughter, who has fallen in love with a local dentist. The hotel's headwaiter, William, sagely smooths out various difficulties that arise, the title being one of his favorite aphorisms.

Young England (1840s) A group of young Tory critics of Peel, led by Disraeli, which had for its testament his novels CONINGSBY and SYBIL and the doctrines of TORY DEMOCRACY.

Young England (1934) A serious patriotic play which seized the imagination of London's younger generation, who turned up night after night to chant the 'strong' lines just before the cast could get to them, so that the entertainment was transferred from the stage to the audience, greatly prolonging the run of what had been turned into a boisterous farce.

Young Farmers' Clubs (1932) (UK) Rural clubs for people of both sexes aged 10-25, which aim to produce 'good farmers, good countrymen and good citizens'. Amateur dramatics, sport, training in public speaking and home crafts are among their many activities.

Younghusband Mission (1904) A British mission which went to Lhasa and signed a treaty with the DALAI LAMA, as a measure against a supposed Russian threat to India. (Sir Francis Younghusband.)

Young Jolyon The nonconforming Forsyte of A MODERN COMEDY, who married Irene, divorced wife of Soames Forsyte.

Young Plan (1929) A scheme for German payments of reparations which superseded the DAWES PLAN and was equally unsuccessful.

Young Pretender Charles Edward Stuart, 'Bonnie Prince Charlie', son of the OLD PRETENDER; died 1788. See FORTY-FIVE.

Young Turks (1) A militant nationalist movement which forced the Sultan Abdul-Hamid to restore the 1876 Constitution in 1908 and deposed him in 1909; (2) hence applied to the militantly radical or reformist group of a political party.

Young Visiters, The (1919) A story written by Daisy Ashford at the age of 9; the hero is Mr SALTEENA.

Young Woodley (1928) Van Druten's play of a schoolboy who falls in love with his housemaster's wife; it was banned for a time, such was the climate of opinion a generation ago.

Youth Fellowship The organized youth group of a Protestant Christian Church or denomination.

Ypres The name of 3 long, bloody and inconclusive battles (including PASSCHENDAELE) of World War I fought around the Belgian town of Ypres, south of Ostend, in 1914, 1915 and 1917.

Ypres, 1st Earl of Field Marshal Sir John French, Commander-in-Chief of the British Expeditionary Force until Haig took over in 1915; made a peer in 1921.

Ysolde, Yseult Alternative spellings of ISEULT.

Yüan dynasty (1279-1368) The dynasty established by Kublai Khan, the first Mongol Emperor of China; it lasted until the MING DYNASTY restored Chinese rule. In art, this period saw the first blue-and-white and copper-red underglaze porcelain; the painting of landscapes in ink was developed. The capital, Peking, was visited by Marco Polo.

Yugoslavia (1929) Name given to the state which from its establishment in 1918 had been called the Triune Kingdom of the Serbs, Croats and Slovenes; it was first used when King Alexander established a military dictatorship. (Meaning 'country of the southern Slavs.')

Yukon standard time The civil time of the 135th meridian, 4 hours slower than EASTERN STANDARD TIME; observed in northwest Yukon.

Yuma A race and linguistic family of Indians of the desert regions in the Lower Colorado region, chiefly noted for their fierce tribal feuds.

Yvetot, Le Roi d' (1). A French expression for a good easy-going king. (From a town in Normandy, the lord of which was given the honorary title of king.) (2) Title of a French anti-Napoleonic song (1813) beginning: Il était un roi d'Yvetot / Peu connu dans l'histoire.

YW A further abbreviation for YWCA.

YWCA Signifies Young Women's Christian Association.

YWHA Signifies Young Women's Hebrew Association.

YY Pen name of Robert Lynd, British essayist (1879-1949).

Z

Zabern incident (1913) The climax of numerous German saber-rattling incidents in Alsace, which created great scandal in France and led to rioting. (Garrison town near Strasbourg, now known by its French name, Saverne.)

Zadig The virtuous young Babylonian philosopher, in Voltaire's novel of that name (1748), who learns from his own successive disasters that evil is a necessary concomitant of good.

Zadok the Priest (1) The priest appointed by King SOLOMON in place of the last of the house of Eli (I Kings ii, 35); he was regarded as the ancestor of the SADDUCEES. (2) Title of Handel's Coronation Anthem.

Zaibatsu The large industrial combine in Japan, dissolved by the Allies after World War II, but reformed in 1952.

Zambia An African republic, before 1964 known as Northern Rhodesia.

Zarathustra A spelling of ZOROASTER used by Nietzsche in THUS SPAKE ZARATHUSTRA.

Zauner, Café An Austrian patisserie shop at Bad Ischl, made famous through its patronage by the Emperor Franz Josef.

Zebu Humped Indian cattle, gray or black, used in India for working and for milk.

Zeeman effect (1896) The difference in light emitted by atoms when they pass through a magnetic field; its discovery made it possible to plot the direction of the magnetic field of the Sun and in interstellar space.

Zen A peculiarly Japanese form of BUDDHISM, which inspired the SAMURAI to do whatever seemed good to them ('acting on intuition'). By destroying the habit of rational thought it seeks to produce sudden intuitive flashes of enlightenment. The more serious-minded BEATNIKS of California suddenly took it up and for a time it became fashionable

in such circles, but it was unassimilable by Western minds, which can see no point in asking asinine questions to which there are no answers.

Zend-Avesta The ZOROASTRIAN and PARSI scriptures (*avesta*) with interpretations (*zend*). The earliest manuscript is 13th century, but the scriptures are attributed to Zoroaster (6th century BC). (Zend was at first incorrectly assumed to be the name of the language—which is allied to Old Persian—in which the *Avesta* were written.)

Zenith The town where BABBITT lived.

Zenocrate Wife of TAMBURLAINE.

Zeta (1958) The (UK) ATOMIC ENERGY AUTHORITY's fusion (thermonuclear) reactor at CULHAM LABORATORY which it was hoped might produce power from the sea; owing to misinterpretation of initial data it was thought that it had achieved the first step towards controlled thermonuclear power, but this belief proved unfounded. The reactor is still however used in plasma physics research.

Zeus The chief Greek god, son of CRONUS. He spent much of his time hiding his amours from his formidable sister-wife HERA by consummating them in a series of extraordinary disguises, e.g. a shower of gold or a swan. He was quick to hurl thunderbolts at those who displeased him. Superficially, he might thus seem a cowardly bully, unworthy of high office, but these legends have, of course, deeper significance. His Roman counterpart is Jupiter.

Zeus (1963) US antiballistic missile rocket for interception at heights of about 60 miles; see NIKE-ZEUS.

Ziegfeld Follies A series of lavishly spectacular revues staged in New York by Florenz Ziegfeld in most years from 1907 to the year before his death in 1932. It was the proving ground for countless songwriters, comedians and others who later became famous on stage and screen, and particularly remembered for its glamorous chorus; see ANNA HELD GIRLS.

Zimbabwe (1) Ruins of extensive dry-stone buildings in southeast Rhodesia, east of Bulawayo, probably built in the 17th-18th centuries, although some timber found there has been carbon-dated back to the 6th century. There were fragments of MING and other oriental pottery, presumably brought by Arab traders, but the buildings themselves are now thought to be the work of an African tribe. (2) African nationalist name for Rhodesia. ('Stone houses', in the language of the Shona of Mashonaland.)

Zimri (1) The captain of chariots of I *Kings* xvi, 9-20, who usurped the throne of ISRAEL and, when himself overthrown, committed suicide. (2) Dryden's name in ABSALOM AND ACHITOPHEL for George Villiers, 2nd Duke of Buckingham.

Zinjanthropus (Nutcracker Man) At first taken to be the earliest specimen of AUSTRALOPITHECINE, found in OLDUVAI GORGE in 1959; now generally classified as Paranthropus, a form of ape which branched off quite early from the main AUSTRALO-PITHECINE line leading to modern man, and became extinct.

Zinoviev letter (1924) A letter supposed to have been addressed by the COMINTERN secretary, Zinoviev, to the British Communist Party, advocating red revolution. Forged in Germany, it was published in the London *Daily Mail* by some Conservatives a few days before the Conservative electoral victory which deposed the first Labour government. There was a loud Labour outcry at the time over these tactics, but it is now thought to have had very little impact on the phlegmatic electorate.

Zion (1) The hill in Jerusalem on which SOLOMON'S TEMPLE stood. (2) Hence a synonym for Jerusalem, ISRAEL or Christianity.

Zionism (1896) A movement for the establishment of a Jewish state in

Palestine (then Turkish). In those days the lunatic fringe saw 'World Zionists', as Senator McCarthy saw 'pinkos', lurking in every corridor of power. See ZION; PROTOCOLS OF ZION.

Zion National Park (1919) A park in the heart of southwest Utah, containing desert country with the magnificent Zion Canyon, up to 2500 ft deep with multicolored precipitous sides; the floor of the canyon is 4000 ft above sea level.

ZIP code A 5-digit code added to postal addresses; the first 3 give the State and place of delivery, the last 2 the post office or postal zone. (For Zone Improvement Plan.)

Zollverein German for Customs Union, applied specifically to that formed in 1834 by most of the German states (except Austria) under Prussian leadership.

Zond Name of a series of Russian space-probes. *Zond 1* and *2* passed close to Venus and Mars respectively in 1965, but radio contact was lost. *Zond 3* photographed the far side of the moon and then passed into orbit round the sun, as planned. *Zond 5* (1968) orbited the moon and splashed down successfully in the Indian Ocean after a 7-day flight.

Zonta International (1919) An association of service clubs for professional and business women, the first of which was formed in Chicago; its aim is to promote world peace and fellowship. (Sioux word, 'to be trusted'.)

Zoroaster (6th century BC) The traditional founder of ZOROASTRIANISM. (Greek form of Persian Zarathustra.)

Zoroastrianism An ancient Persian religion, traditionally founded by ZOROASTER, based on the conflict between AHURA MAZDA and AHRIMAN. See THUS SPAKE ZARATHUSTRA; ZEND-AVESTA.

Zuider Zee See IJSSELMEER.

Zuleika Dobson (1911) A satirical fantasy by Max Beerbohm about the lovely Zuleika, an ex-conjuror of outstanding inability, with whom all the men of OXFORD UNIVERSITY fall desperately in love, to the point of mass-suicide. So she leaves for fresh woods and pastures new—by train to Cambridge.

Zulu   A numerous BANTU race of South Africa, chiefly found in north-east Natal.

Zuñi   A small community of PUEBLO INDIANS in New Mexico; see SEVEN CITIES OF CIBOLA.

Zurich, Faceless Gnomes of   A phrase attributed to George Brown when Minister of Economic Affairs in 1964, referring to the anonymous but powerful international bankers of Switzerland.

Zurich agreements   (1959) The agreements reached by Britain, Greece and Turkey, under which the British colony of Cyprus became an independent republic.